W9-AMI-225

ENGAGE THE ENEMY MORE CLOSELY

by the same author

THE DESERT GENERALS
THE SWORDBEARERS: Studies in Supreme Command in the First World War
BRITAIN AND HER ARMY, 1509–1970
THE COLLAPSE OF BRITISH POWER
MARLBOROUGH
BONAPARTE
THE GREAT WAR
THE AUDIT OF WAR: The Illusion and Reality of Britain as a Great Nation

ENGAGE THE ENEMY MORE CLOSELY

The Royal Navy in the Second World War

Correlli Barnett

W· W· Norton & Company
New York London

First American Edition, 1991

Photoset by Rowland Phototypesetting Ltd,
England

Manufactured by The Haddon Craftsmen.
Printed in the United States of America.

Library of Congress Cataloging-in-Publication Data

Barnett, Correlli
Engage the enemy more closely : the Royal Navy in the Second World War / Correlli Barnett.—1st American ed.
p. cm.
Includes bibliographical references and index.
1. World War, 1939–1945—Naval operations, British. 2. Great Britain. Royal Navy—History—World War, 1939–1945. I. Title.
940.54′5941—dc20 90–46009

D770.1B28

ISBN 0–393–02918–2

W. W. Norton & Company, Inc.
500 Fifth Avenue, New York, N.Y. 10110
W. W. Norton & Company, Ltd.
10 Coptic Street, London WC1A 1PU

1 2 3 4 5 6 7 8 9 0

In memory of
my kinsman Bernard Miller
and
my friend and colleague Stephen Roskill

And in gratitude to them and to all others
who in 1939–1945 kept the sea that is
the wall of England

Contents

Part III THE LONG VOYAGE HOME

Part IV VICTORY

APPENDIXES

List of Photographs

List of Maps

Author's Acknowledgments

Yet again I must first of all thank my wife Ruth for accurately typing a fair copy of a much edited and added-to working script, for pointing out lapses in clarity or style, and for so ably fulfilling the roles of one-woman general staff and commissariat.

Secondly I wish to express my deep gratitude to Admiral of the Fleet The Lord Lewin, KG, GCB, LVO, DSC, for reading the entire typescript and making numerous criticisms and suggestions, and thereby saving me from many errors of fact or interpretation. I wish similarly to thank Commander Michael Wilson, RN, and Mr Dan Van Der Vat for their painstaking scrutiny of the typescript and their comments and suggestions; Brigadier Shelford Bidwell, OBE, for his kindness in commenting on the draft chapter on the Italian campaign; and Commander Sir Godfrey Style, CBE, DSC, RN, for his advice and help. The errors of fact or historical judgment that remain are entirely the responsibility of the author.

I wish to express my gratitude to my publishers, Mr Ion Trewin and Mr John Bright-Holmes, for all their support and good counsel; to Mrs Stephanie Darnill for her meticulous editing and compilation of the index; to Mr Alec Spark for drawing the charts and maps; and to Miss Katherine Bright-Holmes for finding the pictures, mainly from the Imperial War Museum (Mr Paul Kemp) and the Hulton Picture Library. To my present and past colleagues in the Churchill Archives Centre (Miss Elizabeth Bennett, Mr Victor Brown, Miss Lesley James, Mrs Sheila Clare, Mrs Marilyn Collins, Mrs Caroline Gill and Mrs Margaret Williams), I give my special thanks for all their help in various ways during my research in the naval collections held in the Centre. For access to these collections, I wish to thank the Master, Fellows and Scholars of Churchill College in the University of Cambridge.

I would like to express my indebtedness to the Deputy Keeper of Public Records, Mr Duncan Chalmers, and his Search Room staff at the Public Record Office, Kew, for their unfailing helpfulness and courtesy; to Commander David Brown, RN and his staff at the Naval Historical Branch; and to Air Commodore Henry Probert, MBE, Group-Captain T. C. Flanagan, RAF, and the staff at the Air Historical Branch for their valuable and freely given assistance, as well as to Miss Mary Kendall, Librarian of Churchill College, and the staffs of the Library of the Royal United Services Institute for Defence Studies, the London Library, and the Library of the University of East Anglia. I would also like to give my thanks to Mrs Joan Revel-Walker and to Mr and Mrs Alan Eden-Green who also helped.

The author wishes to pay tribute to his late colleague Captain Stephen Roskill's monumental official history *The War at Sea*, which remains after a quarter of a century unrivalled in its closely detailed coverage of all British naval operations. The author has also enjoyed the good fortune to be able to draw on the abundance of unpublished material in the Roskill Papers and other important naval collections in the Churchill Archives Centre. The author wishes to pay tribute likewise to the work of the late Rear-Admiral R. M. Bellairs and subsequent Heads of the Naval Historical Branch and their research teams in compiling the Naval Staff Narratives and Battle Summaries (now in the Public Record Office) from original logs, signals and reports of proceedings. These accounts have constituted an indispensable source for all later historians of the war at sea, including the present author. The author also wishes to express a particular debt to Professor Sir Harry Hinsley and his co-authors, E. E. Thomas, C. F. G. Ransom and R. C. Knight, for their magnificent study *British Intelligence in the Second World War*, which has placed every aspect of the war in a new light, and to pay tribute to the late Dr C. B. A. Behrens for her study of *Merchant Shipping and the Demands of War*, an invaluable and enlightening source in regard to the logistics of British seapower and Britain's oceanic economy.

The author is indebted to the following for permission to quote from private papers in their copyright: Mrs Philip Doyne-Ditmas for the letters of her father Commander Robert Bower, RN; Mrs Jane Smith for the letters and papers of her father Mr Hugh Clausen; the Earl of Cork and Orrery for the letters of his father Admiral of the Fleet The Earl of Cork and Orrery; Mr William Crutchley for the letters of his father Admiral Sir Victor Crutchley; Lady Cunninghame-Graham for the letters and papers of her husband Admiral Sir Angus Cunninghame-Graham; Mrs Sophie Forgan for the letters of her father Admiral Sir William Davis: the Rt Hon. The Lord Denning, PC, LLD for the unpublished memoirs of his brother Admiral Sir Norman Denning; Mr David Edwards for the letters and diaries of his father Admiral Sir Ralph Edwards; Vice-Admiral Sir John Hayes, KCB, OBE, for his own letters; Professor Richard Keynes, FRS, for his own letters and papers; Admiral of the Fleet Lord Lewin for his own wartime midshipman's log; Admiral Sir Julian Oswald, GCB, ADC for the letters and papers of his father Captain G. H. Oswald, RN; Captain George Pound for the letters of his father Admiral of the Fleet Sir Dudley Pound; Major-General Charles Ramsay, CB, for the letters, diaries and papers of his father Admiral Sir Bertram Ramsay; Mr Nicholas Roskill for the papers of his father Captain S. W. Roskill, RN; Commander John Somerville, RN, for the letters of his father Admiral of the Fleet Sir James Somerville; Commander Sir Godfrey Style, CBE, DSC, RN, for his own letters; Mrs Peter Thellusson for the letters of her father, Admiral of the Fleet Sir Philip Vian.

The author has made the most exhaustive efforts to trace all copyright owners of unpublished material quoted in this book, including taking advertisements in national newspapers, but in several cases without success. To these copyright owners he expresses his apologies, and his hopes that they will get in touch with him through his publishers, so that proper acknowledgment may be made in future editions.

The author is also indebted to the following publishers for permission to quote from copyright works in their control: B. T. Batsford Ltd for *The Battle of Matapan* by S. W. C. Pack; Book Club Associates for *Winston S. Churchill* by Martin Gilbert; Cassell plc for *The Second World War* by Winston Churchill; Faber and Faber Ltd for *The Nine Days of Dunkirk* by David Divine; HMSO for *Victory in the West* by L. F. Ellis and *Grand Strategy* by Michael Howard; Hodder and Stoughton Ltd for *The Right of the Line* by John Terraine; Hutchinson and Co. for *Sailor's Odyssey* by Admiral of the Fleet Lord Cunningham; and Lionel Leventhal Ltd for *Memoirs: Ten Years and Twenty Days* by Admiral Karl Dönitz.

Extracts from Crown Copyright material are reproduced with the permission of the Controller of Her Majesty's Stationery Office to whom I and my publishers would like to express our gratitude for being allowed to draw on the information in certain of the maps in Captain S. W. Roskill's *The War at Sea* as well as to quote from its text and reproduce certain illustrations.

Author's Preface

This book is first and foremost the story of the ships' companies of the Royal Navy in their service from the first day to the last of a six-year war. It is a study of how duty, discipline, comradeship and a quenchless sense of humour prevailed over extremes of fatigue and hardship, and triumphed over fear even among the worst of hazards. It describes how these qualities, allied to superb seamanship and a Nelsonian readiness always to engage the enemy more closely, brought the Royal Navy through the most dangerous crisis in its history and rewarded it with victory.

The heart of the narrative consists therefore in the Royal Navy's operations in all their varied nature and in waters from the Arctic to the Indian Ocean and the Pacific – fleet actions; desperate rescues of defeated expeditionary forces; unequal battles against enemy air attack; prolonged struggle with the U-boat for Britain's very survival; work of the little ships such as minesweepers; exploits of British submarines; and finally amphibious landings of ever greater scale and complexity, culminating in the invasion of Normandy on 6 June 1944. Into this account is woven that parallel struggle between British and enemy cryptographers for the priceless ability to read the other side's mind and purpose.

Operations then – the unceasing and ubiquitous demands of the sea service from the outset of the conflict – provide the keynote of the Royal Navy's war. It makes a striking contrast with the Royal Air Force's dominant theme of the gradual development of the bomber offensive against German cities, or the British Army's theme of expansion after early disasters into a mass citizen force. The contrast goes further. By 1943, when Royal Air Force Bomber Command and the British Army entered their period of largest-scale fighting and severest casualties, the Royal Navy had already fought its most desperate battles and suffered the majority of its wartime losses in ships heavier than a corvette, including all five of those capital ships and all five of those fleet aircraft carriers that were sunk.

Yet this is not a history of naval operations and their conduct in the narrow traditional sense. It ranges from the policies of Cabinets and Allied summit conferences to the design of warships, their armaments and other equipment; from portraits of political and service leaders to industrial resources; from national wealth to naval training; from grand strategy to inter-service and inter-Allied cooperation – and rivalry. It examines such questions as the dispute between the Admiralty and the Air Ministry over the use of airpower at the time when the Battle of the Atlantic was in its most crucial stage. It reassesses Britain's 'blue water' strategy in the Mediterranean and Middle East, and traces how the Americans were also drawn into it despite their own preference for a 'Continental' strategy of reopening a Western Front in France. The book also probes deeper, into the very nature of twentieth-century British seapower. For the purpose throughout is to place the war fought by the Royal Navy in the context of all those decisions (pre-war as well as wartime) and all those factors which determined where and when the ships' companies must fight, for what object, with what kind of ships and aircraft, and against what odds.

May 1990

CORRELLI BARNETT
East Carleton, Norfolk

Churchill College
Cambridge

NOTE FOR THE READER. For the sake of clarity the narrative concentrates in due sequence on one campaign or theatre or main topic at a time, rather than advances chronologically across the board. Given, however, that the same ships fought in more than one sea area, the reader should be warned that it sometimes happens that a ship sunk in one chapter turns up afloat in a later chapter.

'Engage the Enemy More Closely'

Nelson's last signal at the battle of Trafalgar,
flying in HMS Victory *until shot away*

PROLOGUE 1918

'The German Ensign Will Be Hauled Down At Sunset'

At 7.30pm on 15 November 1918 – thick fog and pitch dark – an officer in the gold sleeve rings and stars and the prim wing collar of a rear-admiral of the Imperial German Navy came aboard the battleship HMS *Queen Elizabeth*, the flagship of the Grand Fleet moored in the Firth of Forth; his mission to negotiate the ending of the most recent of all the last two centuries' challenges to British mastery of the sea. As Rear-Admiral Meurer and his staff stepped out of the night on to the holystoned deck, they found brilliant electric lights glaring upon them – the first intimidating device in the deliberately dramatic stage-management of the occasion by Admiral Sir David Beatty, the Commander-in-Chief, Grand Fleet.

Two British naval officers wearing swords now conducted Meurer and his colleagues between lines of Royal Marines with fixed bayonets to the companion ladder that led down to Beatty's great dining cabin. Here Beatty himself, sitting beneath an old portrait of Viscount Nelson, Vice-Admiral of the Blue, victor of the Nile and Trafalgar, greeted Meurer with the question: 'Who are you?' Only when Meurer had identified himself and produced his credentials as plenipotentiary for the German Navy did Beatty invite him to be seated.

The scene in the great cabin was set with all the ceremony of formal surrender. Beatty – handsome, arrogant, an actor-manager's visage – flanked by his senior colleagues sat on one side of the baize-draped table, and the tense, pallid Meurer and his staff of four on the other. Behind the German delegation, on chairs set back against the bulkhead, sat the two British escorting officers, with hands on the pommels of their sheathed swords. Beatty handed Meurer a document bearing in two columns the conditions to be imposed and the operational orders to be obeyed. Meurer asked for, and was granted, permission to consult his high command, whereupon he was conducted back through the Royal Marines and the blinding lights to embark for the twelve-mile journey back to his own ship, the *Königsberg*, through the midst of the most powerful concentration of seapower in history. Next day he returned, again in dense fog, to sign the documents proffered him, his attempted cavils brushed aside, himself visibly on the point of collapse.

On 21 November 1918, a clear day, there followed the climax of Beatty's studied drama. Early in the forenoon he took the entire Grand Fleet to sea, thirteen squadrons deployed in two great columns: 33 battleships (five of them from the United States Navy), nine battlecruisers, 27 cruisers and flotillas of destroyers. At about 8.30am the German High Seas Fleet was seen ahead, approaching in a single column headed by the cruiser HMS *Cardiff*. At the appointed rendezvous 40 miles west of May Island *Cardiff* led the enemy ships between the two columns of the Grand Fleet on the opposite course. When the two fleets were abeam Beatty made the prearranged flag signal 'ML',[1] and the Grand Fleet turned 180 degrees to take station on both sides of the High Seas Fleet; guards escorting a prisoner. As the two fleets steamed in three columns for the Firth of Forth at 12 knots, the British crews for the first time could observe at close quarters the great German vessels which had hitherto only been glimpsed as distant North Sea silhouettes or reeks of funnel smoke along misty horizons. In the van was the battleship *Friedrich der Grosse*, flying the flag of Rear-Admiral von Reuter (commanding the High Seas Fleet), followed by eight more battleships; in the centre, the battlecruisers that had fought so skilfully at Jutland, *Seydlitz*, *Derfflinger*, *von der Tann*, *Moltke*, and the newer *Hindenburg*; in the rear, seven light cruisers and 49 destroyers.

In contrast to the immaculate ships of the Grand Fleet, the German vessels made a depressing spectacle of failure and despair – gone the bright brasswork and shining grey paint of pre-war Kiel regattas, and instead tarnish and rust. On the neglected decks unkempt sailors casually leaned against the rails: the sullen face of the régime of revolutionary sailors' councils that had ruled the ships since that mutiny of the High Seas Fleet on 3 November which had precipitated the final collapse of Imperial Germany and the ending of the Great War.

At 11am Beatty made a signal to Rear-Admiral von Reuter: 'The German Flag will be hauled down at sunset today, Thursday, and will not be hoisted again without permission.'[2] That evening, with both fleets at anchor in the Firth of Forth and as British buglers sounded the call of 'Sunset' across waters reflecting the last of the wan November sun, the Imperial German ensign was obediently hauled down. Here was the perfectly contrived conclusion to the Royal Navy's day of triumph; the quiet fall of the curtain on Beatty's entire stage-management from the moment of Meurer's first visit to the *Queen Elizabeth*. But the stage-management had a purpose beyond ceremony and celebration. It was intended to proclaim the triumphant victor taking the abject surrender of a beaten enemy fleet – exactly because Beatty himself well knew that such was not the truth.

The High Seas Fleet had not surrendered to the British or even to the Allies as a whole; it was being interned as part of the general armistice which suspended hostilities on 11 November 1918. And Beatty and his Grand Fleet had been merely appointed the agent for the Allies in executing the internment, which would have taken place in neutral ports if a neutral country could have been found willing to take the German ships. Nor had the High Seas Fleet ever been beaten by the Grand Fleet. Instead it came to the Forth as a prize of the national defeat of Imperial Germany brought about by the victories of the Allied armies over the German Army on the Western Front from July 1918 onwards; victories which were in turn the fruits of the grim battles of attrition in France and Flanders in 1916–17, if partly also of the Allied naval blockade. This was no aftermath of Trafalgar, then. Neither Meurer nor von Reuter was a Villeneuve giving up his sword on the quarterdeck of the *Victory*. When Beatty had learned that the High Seas Fleet had mutinied rather than go to sea again, so denying him his last chance of destroying it in battle, he wrote to his mistress: 'The Fleet, my Fleet, is brokenhearted, but are still wonderful, the most wonderful thing in Creation and although it would appear that they can never achieve their hearts' desire, they preserve a cheerfulness which is extraordinary.'[3] Fearing that 'we are not going to win in the [Allied War] Council all that our great Silent Victory entitles us to,'[4] Beatty had urged that Britain should insist on the German High Seas Fleet surrendering to him as Commander-in-Chief, Grand Fleet, the capitulation to be signed on the quarterdeck of his flagship. But in the face of opposition from Allied delegates, surrender to the Royal Navy was emasculated into internment by a neutral power, later to internment by the Allies as a whole. It was entirely appropriate therefore that Admiral of the Fleet Sir Rosslyn Wemyss, the First Sea Lord, should write to Beatty conveying his sympathy with the Grand Fleet over the 'incompleteness' of the victory.[5]

Yet this incompleteness, so successfully masked by Beatty's stage-management of the German internment, went much deeper than a failure to destroy the enemy fleet in Nelsonian style in battle. Despite all the seamanship, courage and endurance of the ships' companies, the Royal Navy's record during the Great War as a whole was tarnished by doubts about the professional abilities of its officer corps; about its staff work and doctrine; about the technology of its ships, weapons and equipment. More deeply still, the course of the war had put in question the very strategic and economic basis of the worldwide oceanic trading empire which British seapower had grown up to protect.

From 1904, when the fast expanding Imperial German Navy was first perceived by the Admiralty as the major threat Britain now had to face, British naval policy had been obsessed with outbuilding the Germans in 'Dreadnought' battleships (with all-big-gun main armaments) and battlecruisers, so that in a war Britain could bring overwhelming strength to bear in the expected decisive battle for naval mastery with the German High Seas Fleet in the North Sea. When the Great War broke out in 1914, Britain had won this building race, with the Royal Navy outnumbering its opponent by 24 modern battleships to sixteen, and with four more under construction, as compared to Germany's three; in battlecruisers it outnumbered the Imperial German Navy by nine ships to five.[6] Not surprisingly, therefore, the High Seas Fleet showed no eagerness to encounter such odds in open battle, preferring diversionary sorties in the hope of catching and destroying a detached portion of the Grand Fleet. Although after the outbreak of war British seapower quickly swept the world's seas clear of German shipping, and in a matter of months caught and sank Admiral Graf von Spee's squadron of cruisers in the southern oceans, the Grand Fleet itself had remained an impotent spectator during the decisive land campaigns of 1914 on the Western and Eastern Fronts that shaped the future anatomy of the conflict. It was proof of the limitations of seapower in a struggle against a great continental state.

Not until 31 May 1916 had the Royal Navy been offered the chance of realising its dream of a steam-driven Trafalgar in which British seamanship and British broadsides would annihilate the upstart High Seas Fleet. For the plan of the German Commander-in-Chief, Admiral Reinhard Scheer, to entice part of the Grand Fleet into a trap went wrong and instead Admiral Sir John Jellicoe, the British C-in-C, brought him to battle at Jutland with 28 battleships to sixteen and nine battlecruisers to five. Yet the results of the encounter proved so discreditable to the Royal Navy that dispute over who or what was responsible for the failure to destroy Scheer was to smoulder on for decades. The Battle of Jutland put the entire British naval system to proof and failed it.

In the first place the tally of losses told heavily in German favour. The High Seas Fleet sank 111,980 tons of British warships and inflicted casualties of 6,945. The Grand Fleet sank only 62,233 tons of German ships (including a badly damaged battlecruiser later sunk by the Germans themselves) and inflicted casualties of 2,921.[7] In the preliminary action between Admiral Beatty's Battle Cruiser Fleet of six battlecruisers and four fast and powerful Queen Elizabeth class battleships and the five battlecruisers of Admiral Hipper's Scouting Group One, Beatty had lost two battlecruisers blown up; Hipper none. Whereas Hipper's ships scored 52 hits, Beatty's scored only 32.[8] In the main encounter of the fleets later that day, another British battlecruiser (*Invincible*) was also blown up and sank instantly. Although the German battlecruisers took the most appalling cumulative punishment in the course of the battlecruiser action and then in the fleet battle (*Lützow* sustained 22 heavy shell hits), none sank in action. No wonder Beatty observed to his flag captain as he saw the *Queen Mary* explode and vanish under a pall of smoke: 'Chatfield, there seems to be something wrong with our bloody ships today.'[9]

The blatantly adverse balance of material and human loss at Jutland led to exhaustive investigations and discussions by the Admiralty, and has been the subject of detailed researches by distinguished naval historians ever since.[10] The cumulative results of these investigations show that in every particular British naval technology was inferior to German.

Because of the mistaken belief that speed and gunpower were more important than protection, British battlecruisers were much more lightly armoured than the Germans': *Queen Mary*, for example, displaced 27,000 tons as against the 24,000 of *Seydlitz*, yet carried only 3,900 tons of armour compared to the German ship's 5,200 tons. A 6- to 9-inch armoured belt amidships on British battlecruisers (depending on the 'vintage') compared with a 9¾- to 13-inch belt on

German.[11] The British battlecruisers were particularly vulnerable to plunging fire striking the upper side of the hull or the deck, and it is believed that all three sunk at Jutland succumbed to closely grouped salvoes of this kind; the effect probably being made the more instantly catastrophic in at least one instance by a flash down into a magazine from a cordite fire in a turret. Firing tests after the war against the armour plate of the German battleship *Baden* suggested that German plate was in any case superior in resistant quality to British.[12]

Such German superiority in quality of armour only served to accentuate the consequences of another British technological shortcoming – in the armour-piercing shell and its burster. British steel (made by the ordinary open-hearth process) was inferior to German (made in electric crucibles) and tended to break up on first striking armour plate. Moreover, the British burster, amatol, was more unstable than TNT, the German burster, and tended to explode prematurely on impact. British guns and shells, taken together, possessed poorer ballistic qualities than the German, because the steel from which British guns were manufactured and the method of fabrication were both inferior to German. Even before the war it had been Admiral Jellicoe's opinion, as Controller of the Navy, that German guns, though lighter and smaller in calibre than their British equivalents, performed better in all respects.[13]

Yet British inferiority in armour, guns and ammunition does not supply the whole explanation of why the balance sheet of losses so favoured the High Seas Fleet. The High Seas Fleet had shot more accurately too, partly because of its own superb stereoscopic rangefinders, but mostly because the British Admiralty before the war had refused to adopt a revolutionary fire control system designed by Arthur Pollen, a brilliant young inventor. His 'Argo Clock' produced constantly updated ranges and bearings of the enemy, and automatically corrected them for the changes in both its own and the target ships' courses and speeds during the flight of the shell; in other words, it was a mechanical analogue computer.[14] It had been eventually rejected by the Admiralty in 1908 without a final trial, in favour of a more elementary system designed by a naval officer in imitation of Pollen's invention; an example of the 'Not Invented Here' syndrome which says much about the closed institutional mind of the Navy 'Establishment' in this era.[15] Had all British capital ships been equipped with Pollen's 'Argo Clock' at Jutland, so ensuring swift target acquisition and accurate ranging throughout all the alterations of course made by the two fleets, the outcome of the intermittent salvoes amid the mists might after all have been that destruction of the High Seas Fleet by sheer weight of numbers for which the Royal Navy pined.

Yet defective technology, reflecting the scientific and technical backwardness of British industry, was not the only ingredient in the British failure to annihilate at Jutland. During Britain's post-Trafalgar mastery of the oceans in the tranquil decades of the Victorian peace, the Royal Navy's whole system of command and control, its doctrines and its style of leadership, had become the reverse of Nelsonian. Efficiency came to mean precisely executed but unrealistic evolutions – the naval equivalent of parade-ground drill: it came to mean ships as bright as a Life Guard's breastplate, even if gunnery practice, so dirtying to the decks, had thereby to suffer. The ten years of breakneck modernisation and reorganisation begun after 1904 by the ruthless Admiral Sir John Fisher as First Sea Lord did much to jerk the Royal Navy from a kind of exclusive yacht club into a modern fighting service: manoeuvres became more realistic; the range at which gunnery was practical lengthened from 2,000 yards in the 1890s to 14,000 yards just before the Great War.

Yet the reforms were too short-lived to be more than superficial. In 1914 the Royal Navy still remained wedded to a discipline more rigid and authoritarian than that of the Prussian army; its concept of command and leadership was still based on the principle of blind obedience to orders and unquestioned deference to the wisdom of superiors. As a result, initiative was extinguished in favour of all-pervasive centralisation of decision. This reached its apogee in the Grand Fleet at Jutland, when Jellicoe tried to control the whole fleet from the flagship *Iron Duke*; and momentary opportunities to engage the High Seas Fleet as it sought an escape route home were missed because those British ships or squadrons which actually sighted the enemy shrank from acting without orders. Such extreme centralisation naturally entailed a dense traffic of signals from a flagship: in the case of Jellicoe's *Iron Duke* at Jutland, one flag signal every 1.7 minutes during the daylight action; in the case of Beatty's *Lion* one every 2.4 minutes.[16]

The same authoritarian belief that all thinking and all decision should be vested in one man at the top had also led to the Royal Navy's stubborn opposition to the creation of a general staff (that Prussian innovation for the collective management of modern war which every European army had adopted long before the Great War) and to the accompanying neglect of proper staff training and higher professional education. Not until 1912 had the Naval War Staff been set up (and even then with less power and responsibility than its military equivalent, the Imperial General Staff), together with an embryo Staff College. The Navy still remained essentially true to the tradition of the God-given authority of 'salt-horse' admirals who had learned their trade by successively driving ships, squadrons and fleets – self-educated 'practical' men. The Admiralty therefore entered the Great War without any comprehensive and pondered strategy for waging it, relying instead on such obvious expedients as blockading Germany (in the event damaging to the German war economy) or seeking to bring the High Seas Fleet to battle, or such wild notions as landing an expeditionary force on Germany's Baltic coast.

The want of a well-run-in staff system at the Admiralty, and the trained and experienced staff minds to work it properly, was tragically displayed during the Jutland battle, when the Operations Division, in its contempt for the work of the Intelligence staff of 'Room 40', either passed on to Jellicoe misleadingly incomplete versions of signals intelligence obtained by Room 40's decrypting of German radio traffic or failed to pass vital decrypted signals on at all. In particular this denied Jellicoe exact information about the High Seas Fleet's escape course for home on the night after the battle.[17] The lack of fruitful cooperation between the Operations Division and Room 40 was the more lamentable in that Room 40's performance under Admiral 'Blinker' Hall in intercepting and decyphering German radio traffic rendered it one of the outstandingly brilliant facets of the wartime Royal Navy.[18]

Because the Admiralty had no corporate brain capable of thorough intellectual analysis of strategic and operational problems, Britain very nearly lost the war altogether in the first half of 1917. Germany's sink-at-sight U-boat campaign against Allied and also neutral shipping (in designated war zones) caused such colossal and rising losses of merchant ships as to threaten Britain with imminent starvation and the stoppage of her war industries. In the event it was not the High Seas Fleet and its great battleships, on which the Royal Navy's anxious eyes had been so long focused, that proved to be the mortal danger to Britain, but some 100 frail submersible craft manned by only 5,000 German sailors. By April 1917, a month when nearly 900,000 tons of merchant shipping were lost, this tiny fraction of the German war effort had brought the world's greatest seapower within sight of total national catastrophe, for the Admiralty had absolutely no idea how to defeat the U-boat, since its own cherished expedient of patrolled sea lanes for merchant ships was so evidently a failure. Jellicoe, now First Sea Lord, warned the War Cabinet: 'It is impossible for us to go on with the war if losses like this continue.'[19] In the amateurism of its staff work, the Admiralty even made the elementary howler of wildly exaggerating the number of ships arriving and leaving British ports each week by counting in small coastal craft and cross-Channel ferries as well as ocean-going trade,[20] so proving to its own satisfaction that it would be impossible to convoy such a volume of traffic.

Only after prolonged argument, pressure from Cabinet ministers, and urging by Beatty (now C-in-C, Grand Fleet) did the Admiralty reluctantly and belatedly adopt the convoy system in May 1917.[21] This marked a return to the well-proven expedient of the age of sail against French (and in 1812–14, American) surface raiders. By July sinkings had dropped back to 500,000 tons; by September to 350,000 tons – figures which spelt failure for Germany. In defeating the U-boat the Royal Navy made its greatest contribution to the Allied victory in the Great War, for by so doing it enabled Britain herself to survive as an arsenal, a base and a source of armies; it made the Atlantic safe for the passage to France of hundreds of thousands of American troops month by month in 1918.

Thanks to the convoy system the U-boat's targets were no longer scattered abundantly along the sea lanes, but gathered into relatively few groups of up to fifty ships. As a result the U-boat found the horizons emptied of shipping; she might cruise for days without sighting a victim. When she did encounter a convoy, her limited underwater speed only enabled her to attack one or two vessels before the convoy drew out of range. And to launch an attack on a convoy invited immediate and deadly counter-attack by the convoy escorts. For in 1917–18 the Royal Navy quickly became the world's leader in anti-submarine warfare tactics and equipment, thanks to close cooperation with university scientists mobilised into the war effort and to new technologies developed in British industry; all a happy contrast to the record of the Grand Fleet. While lurking submerged the U-boat faced detection by hydrophone listening gear and destruction by depth-charges lobbed from the sterns of warships in convoy escorts or hunting groups.

Yet there was a revolutionary new dimension to this twentieth-century version of the old struggle between convoys and raiders – airpower. Flying boats and non-rigid 'dirigibles' or airships (really powered sausage balloons) ranged over the North Sea from bases as far spread as the Shetlands and Dunkirk, searching for U-boats as they cruised on the surface to and from their hunting zones.[22]

The Royal Navy had already taken to the air before the outbreak of war, when powered heavier-than-air flight was still less than a decade old. In December 1911 Lieutenant Sampson successfully flew off the forecastle of HMS *Africa*, the first of several such experiments. In May 1912 the Naval Wing of the Royal Flying Corps was formed; in 1914 it became the Royal Naval Air Service. From a strength of 93 aircraft and 727 personnel on 4 August 1914, the Navy's air component was to grow to nearly 3,000 aircraft and 55,000 personnel by April 1918.[23] The Great War was a time of groping towards the true future of maritime airpower; it witnessed prolonged debate over the proper roles and the most suitable kinds of flying machines; tension between a sceptical and obstructive old guard at the top of the Navy and a youthful generation of flying enthusiasts backed by a few far-sighted admirals, among whom Sir David Beatty was the most eminent and influential.[24]

At first it was believed that the rigid airship, as spectacularly developed by Count Zeppelin for the German Navy, would provide the ideal instrument of air cooperation with the fleet; a steady platform with long endurance for distant reconnaissance. By 1917–18, however, the emphasis had shifted to shipborne heavier-than-air aircraft, partly because of British technical backwardness in airship construction; partly because of the rapid progress made in fixed-wing aviation at sea during three years of war. In 1914 the Admiralty had converted three cross-Channel steamers into seaplane carriers, the seaplanes taking off by means of discardable wheeled trolleys and, on return, landing on the sea by means of their floats next to the carrier for recovery by crane. On Christmas Day, 1914, occurred the first seaborne airstrike in history, when seven aircraft from these carriers attempted unsuccessfully to bomb Zeppelin sheds at Cuxhaven.[25]

However, by the end of 1916 the Admiralty had become convinced that aircraft with wheeled undercarriages, as used on land, were superior to seaplanes for fleet work: faster, easier to handle on shipboard. On 2 August 1917 Squadron-Commander E. H. Dunning made history by being the first man to land an aircraft on a ship under way when he put his Sopwith 'Pup' down on HMS *Furious* in Scapa Flow. *Furious* herself marked an intermediate stage in the development of the true aircraft carrier. Originally a battlecruiser, her forward main turret had been replaced by a flying-off deck. In 1918 the after turret was replaced in turn by a landing deck, but her two flight decks still remained separated by the conventional placing of masts, bridge and funnel amidships on the centre line. Although the first true aircraft carrier with a full-length flight deck, HMS *Argus*, was launched in December 1917, she was still undergoing flying trials when the war ended.[26]

Nevertheless, the Grand Fleet by this time was carrying over

100 aircraft in its conventional warships for reconnaissance and interception, flying them off turntable launch platforms mounted on gun turrets, as recommended in February 1917 by the Grand Fleet Aircraft Committee (one of Beatty's initiatives). These aircraft eclipsed Germany's earlier air superiority over the North Sea with the Zeppelin, now demonstrated to be slow, unwieldy and very vulnerable.

As early as 1912 pioneering minds had looked to torpedo-carrying aircraft as a means of sinking warships at far longer ranges than even the biggest gun. There followed in July 1914, at Calshot, a naval air station on Southampton Water, the first successful attempt to drop a torpedo into the sea from an aircraft. The cause was vigorously promoted by Captain Murray Sueter, Director of the Air Department of the Admiralty in 1914–15 and Superintendent of Aircraft Construction in 1915–16, an outstanding personality among the band of young, radically-minded naval officers who gravitated to the exciting new field of aviation. In spring of 1915 he won Admiralty permission for an experimental strike against Turkish shipping in the Dardanelles, and on 14 and 17 August that year three seaplanes from the seaplane carrier *Ben-My-Chree* succeeded in torpedoing and sinking three Turkish steamers at anchor. As the commander of the *Ben-My-Chree*, C. L'E. Malone, reported to Sueter, the operation had to be regarded as 'the forerunner of a line of development which will tend to revolutionize warfare'.[27] And in 1917 Sir David Beatty, as C-in-C, Grand Fleet, urged that a major attack on the High Seas Fleet in harbour by 121 aircraft from eight carriers (to be improvised from merchant ships) should be put in preparation.[28] Unfortunately various problems, most notably immense delays in delivery of the aircraft by the manufacturers, meant that the intended air strike could not be launched before the war ended.

In contrast, then, to the sclerotic conservatism prevailing in the traditional 'big-gun' Navy, the Royal Naval Air Service was alive with new ideas and creative enthusiasm, placing the Royal Navy ahead of all others in development of airpower at sea. Yet even before the Great War came to an end this British leadership in naval aviation had been touched with blight; its future already placed in doubt.

For on 1 April 1918 a third armed service had been inaugurated in Britain, in the shape of the Royal Air Force. This radical innovation had been recommended by a Cabinet Committee on Air Organisation and Home Defence against Air Raids (chaired by Field-Marshal Smuts) which had been set up in 1917 as a consequence of the light damage but vast alarm caused in the London area by raids in June and July of that year by German Gotha heavy bombers. Against all the other operational evidence of the war that airpower was simply an extra dimension to land and sea warfare respectively, the Smuts Committee fatefully argued that

> an air fleet can conduct extensive operations far from, and independently of, both army and navy . . . the day may not be far off when aerial operations with their devastation of enemy lands and destruction of industrial and populous centres on a vast scale may become the principal operations of war, to which the older forms of military and naval operations may become secondary and subordinate.[29]

Thus out of panic reaction to a few small German air raids on London was born that fallacious concept of the independent nature of airpower and of its future capability to win wars on its own which was to exert the most profound consequences on British grand strategy and defence policy in the 1920s and 1930s and later during the Second World War.

It followed from this new belief in the independence and unity of airpower that, as the Smuts Committee recommended, and the Cabinet approved, an Air Ministry should be created 'to control and administer all matters in connection with aerial warfare of all kinds whatsoever . . .'[30]

And so, on All Fools' Day, 1918, the Royal Naval Air Service (along with the Royal Flying Corps) disappeared, its assets and personnel being vested in the new Royal Air Force. Henceforth the future of Britain's maritime airpower lay primarily in the hands of a service and a ministry holding the doctrinaire belief that an air force's main task lay in the strategic bombing of enemy cities, and that all else was secondary, if not actually wasteful diversion. Before two months had elapsed the First Lord of the Admiralty, Sir Eric Geddes, was already complaining that 'our fears as to the desirability of the transfer are being confirmed as time goes on. The use of aircraft with the Navy is not developing as it should . . . we do not feel that our particular and rather specialised side of the problem is receiving the attention that it should.'[31] Yet the new organisation was not merely causing short-term difficulties; it was also setting in train grievous long-term consequences in regard to the Royal Navy's own appreciation of the potential of maritime airpower. For almost all the Navy's bright air-minded officers opted to transfer from general naval service to the new Royal Air Force; men such as Arthur Longmore, Frederick Bowhill, Christopher Courtney, who would make outstanding air marshals before and during the Second World War. This loss impoverished the Navy of talent of which it would one day stand in dire need;

it served also immeasurably to weaken the voice of aviation within the Navy between the world wars, so allowing the 'big-gun and battleship' school to dominate the Navy's doctrine and development.

The Royal Navy therefore emerged from the Great War with an ambiguous, even contradictory, record. In the kind of sea warfare for which it had almost exclusively prepared – the clash of battlefleets – it had disappointed itself and the nation. At unforeseen and novel forms of sea warfare – against the U-boat and in the air – it had shown remarkable powers of innovation and operational effectiveness, even though this could hardly be said of the Admiralty Board itself. In any case the Royal Navy in 1918 was confirmed and strengthened in its historic position as the world's greatest instrument of seapower, with 61 battleships (including old pre-Dreadnought types) to defeated Germany's 40, France's 40, the United States' 39, and Japan's 13; 120 cruisers to Germany's 35, the US's 35, France's 29 and Japan's 26; 443 destroyers to Germany's 200, the US's 131, France's 91 and Japan's 67.[32]

And yet, and yet, even this colossal naval preponderance had not been enough by itself to guarantee the security of the British Empire, that global scatter under the Union Flag of colonies and dominions, of protectorates and bases, of islands and continents and portions of continents. To meet the German challenge after 1904 Admiral of the Fleet Sir John Fisher, as First Sea Lord, had thinned out Britain's distant fleets and squadrons – in the Far East and Pacific, even the Mediterranean – in order to concentrate in home waters. During the Great War it was the French Navy which had been largely responsible for securing the Mediterranean, that key to the imperial route to India via the Suez Canal, while the Imperial Japanese Navy (thanks to the Anglo-Japanese Alliance of 1902) had been responsible for the Far East and Pacific, even escorting Australian and New Zealand troop convoys to the European theatre.

The various countries of the British Empire themselves were quite incapable of their own defence. The white dominions – Canada, South Africa, Australia and New Zealand – possessed only small citizen armies with which to protect vast territories; and only tiny navies, the largest, the Royal Australian Navy, numbered one battle-cruiser, four light cruisers and three destroyers. India had no navy to defend her long coastlines; and even during the war had swallowed a garrison of 15,000 British soldiers. Far from being the massive buttress of British power the British people believed it to be, the Empire was in reality appallingly vulnerable and dependent on Britain.

This was a truth obscured by the particular pattern of the Great

War. It was a European war; the Mother Country, not the dominions or India or the colonies, had lain under attack. The Empire had therefore been free to send its forces overseas to Britain's succour in her fight with Germany. But if, through a future shift in the world strategic balance, this lucky pattern of the Great War was not repeated, and the Empire and its vital sea routes – in the Far East and Pacific; in the Mediterranean – came under direct threat at the same time as Britain, then the Empire (and especially Australia and New Zealand, 10,000 miles away from the Mother Country) would represent not a limited source of strength to Britain, but an immense source of weakness and, above all, an insoluble strategic problem for the Admiralty. As the Australian Prime Minister, Billy Hughes, was to tell the 1921 Imperial Conference:

> Look at the map and ask yourselves what would have happened to that great splash of red down from India through Australia to New Zealand, but for the Anglo-Japanese Treaty. How much of these great rich territories and portions of our Empire would have escaped had Japan been neutral? How much if she had been our enemy? It is certain the naval power of the Empire could not have saved India and Australia and still been strong enough to hold Germany bottled up in the narrow seas . . .[33]

If the Great War, with all its pride and propaganda about the Empire's contribution to victory, had concealed from the British that the Empire was a potential drain on British strength, a cause of strategic overstretch, it had all too brutally demonstrated the United Kingdom's own vulnerability as an island and commercial power dependent for survival on ships steaming to and from the ports of the globe; a vulnerability especially as compared with continental economies with safe internal land communications such as the United States and Germany. After all, even with only a single major naval foe to cope with, and powerful allies at sea, the Royal Navy had only narrowly averted national starvation and the collapse of British war industry at the hands of the U-boat. In the high Victorian era of Free Trade and unchallenged British naval mastery, the pattern of island Britain at the centre of an oceanic world economy had seemed the very secret of Britain's industrial and commercial success. Now in a different world it rendered Britain's existence more precarious than that of any other great power.

Yet in the aftermath of victory and the beginning of a new era (as men hoped and believed) of peace and prosperity, such gloomy analyses were far from British minds. On 21 June 1919 even the physical relics of the German naval challenge vanished when the High

Seas Fleet was defiantly scuttled by its own crews in its last place of internment in Scapa Flow. A week later the hapless German delegation to the Paris Peace Conference signed the Treaty of Versailles in the Hall of Mirrors in the Palace of Versailles; a treaty which limited the future German Navy to six obsolete small battleships, six light cruisers and twelve destroyers; limited new armoured ships built as replacements for the old battleships to 10,000 tons displacement; forbade submarines and naval aircraft altogether; provided for the demolition of all naval installations and defences within fifty miles of the German coast and for the destruction of the fortifications of the island of Heligoland, outer barbican of the German North Sea bases. Here, then, was the total elimination of the latest challenge to British naval mastery. The Royal Navy, overwhelmingly the greatest in the world, now cruised on seas shared only with the fleets of friendly powers; and Britain and her Empire had never seemed more safe.

Yet only two decades later this naval mastery had vanished, and instead the Royal Navy was facing the prospect of the hardest fight of its history. In June 1939, exactly twenty years to the month after the signing of the Versailles Treaty, the Chiefs of Staff spelt out the predicament in which the Navy had come to be placed:

> We are now faced with the situation in which we may be involved in a war against Japan . . . and with the probability that Germany and Italy will also be ranged against us. The question, therefore, at issue is whether, in existing circumstances, our defence forces are strong enough to safeguard our territory, trade and vital interests against these three Powers simultaneously . . .[34]

The Royal Navy, wrote the Chiefs of Staff, had only eleven capital ships ready for sea. Yet a fleet sufficient to meet the Imperial Japanese Navy alone would have to number eight capital ships: 'i.e., one less than the Japanese'. But in order to secure the European theatre, including the United Kingdom and its sea communications – 'the decisive theatre', in the judgment of the Chiefs of Staff – 'we must therefore retain at least six capital ships in Home Waters and the Atlantic. In addition, three capital ships are required to retain control of the Eastern Mediterranean . . .' The conclusion was plain: 'Having regard to the strengths of the German and Italian Fleets, it is clear that the despatch of eight capital ships would endanger our position in Europe to an extent which . . . would be quite unjustifiable.' Therefore only two capital ships could be sent to the Far East in the event of a Japanese attack – six short of the minimum needed.[35]

Here, then, were the mathematics of potential catastrophe; the outcome of a prolonged double process of reduction in the fighting power of the Royal Navy and of multiplication of Britain's likely enemies, old and new. And indeed the root causes of all the Navy's coming tribulations and enduring strategic dilemmas during the Second World War, of its worst disasters and most tragic losses, are to be found in the twenty years of national illusion, neglect and belated awakening that had gone before.

PART I

BRITANNIA LETS THE TRIDENT SLIP

1

Dreams of Peace and the Shrinking Navy, 1918–1931

Even by the time the Versailles Treaty was signed on 28 June 1919 new anxieties, new dilemmas, had begun to confront the Admiralty and the British Cabinet; and at the root of them all lay the enduring conundrum of how a small island nation could find the resources to protect an Empire scattered across the face of the oceans and incapable of defending itself.

In 1914 the British national debt had stood at £650 millions; by 1919 it had swollen to £7,435 millions. Here was one obvious measure of the lasting drain on the nation's wealth caused by the Great War. In addition, Great Britain had accumulated debts to the United States of £1,365 millions.[1] With the urgent need to restore the economy to its pre-war prosperity, and to recover export markets lost while British industry was mobilised to produce munitions, it was little surprise that Lloyd George's coalition government looked in 1919 for huge cuts in government expenditure, and especially in the service estimates. At Treasury behest, the service departments were told to plan future expenditure on the basis that Britain would not be engaged in a major war for ten years; the beginnings of what became known as 'the ten-year rule'. Whereas expenditure on the Navy in 1918–19 had been £344 millions, in 1919–20 it fell to £154 millions, and by 1920–21 to £76 millions.[2] Worse was to come. In 1921 the post-war economic boom collapsed, and the heavy industries which had formed the foundation of British pre-eminence as 'the Workshop of the

World' – steel, shipbuilding, cotton, coal – lay in deep slump, their export markets lost to new competitors often with more modern plant and more up-to-date methods.

Nor was this to be merely a temporary recession, as was hoped at the time; it was to persist right through the 1920s when the rest of the industrialised world was enjoying unexampled prosperity. Moreover, the war and the new political and economic world patterns that were its consequences destroyed Britain's old position as the centre (especially the financial centre) of a global web of trade and payments; and in particular New York and the dollar began to rival London and the pound sterling. In the eighteenth and nineteenth centuries, British seapower and Britain as a trading nation had risen together to world supremacy: the Royal Navy had protected the trade and helped in the conquest of markets, while in turn the trade and the markets paid for the Navy. Now the opposite, downward spiral had begun.

In the wake of the 1921 slump the government appointed a Committee on National Expenditure under Sir Eric Geddes, which recommended ruthless cuts in government spending ('the Geddes Axe'), including the armed forces. It wanted the Navy estimates for 1922 to be reduced by a quarter, from £81 millions to £60 millions; a reduction to be bitterly fought by the Admiralty, but with only partial success.[3]

Yet at this very same period of straitened national resources and sharpening financial stringency the Admiralty was having to face the prospect of a new naval building challenge on a vast scale, this time from the United States, for Anglophobes on the US Navy Board were determined to destroy British naval supremacy. In autumn 1919 the Admiralty warned the Cabinet that if Great Britain failed to build new heavy ships and America completed her 1916 building programme (six battleships and six battlecruisers), then by 1923 'we shall have passed to the position of being the second naval power'.[4] Even the Japanese would by then have four new battleships and four new battlecruisers, all more powerful than Britain's latest ship, the battlecruiser *Hood*, completed in 1920. But how could war-weakened Britain hope to outbuild the richest and most powerful industrial country in the world?

This was not the only dilemma, however, to impale the Cabinet and the Admiralty at this period. The Anglo-Japanese Treaty was due to expire in 1922. Should it be renewed or not? To renew it would alienate the United States, already antagonistic towards Japanese expansionist ambitions in China and the Far East; and this would hardly help Britain to reach an accommodation with the American government on naval limitation that would spare her the choice between a ruinous naval race and accepting that the Royal Navy must now take second place to the United States Navy. But not to renew the treaty would offend the Japanese, on whose goodwill and naval cooperation the security of the British Empire east of Suez had depended during the Great War; and whose potential (let alone actual) hostility would immensely add to Britain's intractable problems of imperial defence.

The British government was in the event rescued from both dilemmas by an American invitation to participate in an international conference in Washington in 1922 to settle outstanding problems in the Far East and Pacific, and to reach agreement on limitation of naval armaments. But the result of the Washington Conference was to weaken British naval strength while increasing the potential dangers to the British Empire. For the hapless British delegation accepted American proposals for a 5:5:3 ratio in capital ships as between the United States Navy, the Royal Navy and the Imperial Japanese Navy, with a total tonnage of 500,000 each for America and Britain and 300,000 for Japan. Even Beatty, the First Sea Lord, had by now accepted that Britain's historic naval supremacy was finished, and that parity with the United States was the best that could be hoped for. The Washington Treaty also limited the size of battleships to 35,000 tons as compared with the 48,000-ton battlecruisers then on the Admiralty's drawing-board. The two new battleships permitted to Britain under the Treaty, designed in 1922 and completed in 1927, HMSs *Nelson* and *Rodney*, proved ugly and cumbersome beasts, handling badly and unable to fire their 16-inch guns (all forward of the tower) abaft the beam because of the blast effects on the control tower.

Moreover, the United States proposed a 'ten-year holiday' in naval building (that is, with few exceptions no new building of capital ships whatsoever). Beatty fiercely resisted this, arguing (rightly, as was to be proved in the event) that such a total cessation of new construction would lead to the decay and disappearance of the specialised dockyard and technological resources needed to build battleships and their heavy armaments. He strove – in vain – for a slow but steady replacement programme instead; and warned that as British ships were already older than American, the end of the 'ten-year holiday' would find the Royal Navy inferior in fighting power to the United States Navy. He was overridden by the politicians leading the British delegation – Balfour, the Foreign Secretary, and Lord Lee of Fareham (an Americanophile), the First Lord of the Admiralty – in their eagerness for a settlement that would avert the costs of a naval building race.

Henceforward, therefore, British naval policy was to be governed not by changing strategic need, but by the 5:5:3 ratio. And the 5:5:3 ratio was purely arbitrary, taking no account of the fact that while America was a continental state with few overseas possessions and relatively little dependence on foreign trade, and Japan was a regional Pacific power, Great Britain had a global Empire and an enormous and vital seaborne trade to protect. So it was that only four years after the German High Seas Fleet steamed into internment under British guns, and as a result of a diplomatic defeat in the face of a far stronger American bargaining position, Britain had had to yield up her maritime supremacy and also accept a future navy of a size totally unrelated to her strategic commitments.

All this was potentially the more dangerous because of another treaty signed in Washington, a vague and woolly Four-Power Pacific Treaty between Britain, the United States, France and Japan which replaced the old Japanese alliance. From this time on, Japan was to figure in all British strategic discussions as the principal naval menace Britain had to meet. As Beatty told the 1926 Imperial Conference, whereas before 1914 the strategic centre of gravity had been in Europe, now it had shifted to the Far East.[5]

Nevertheless the Washington Conference was acclaimed at the time as a major first step towards the goal of universal disarmament. Such disarmament, along with the new League of Nations (founded in 1919) and its machinery for peacefully settling disputes between nations and curbing aggressors, would ensure that there would be no more war – or so believed the romantic internationalists, such as Lord Robert Cecil, Clifford Allen and Gilbert Murray, who now dominated British opinion. All three political parties in Britain during the 1920s were committed to faith in disarmament and in the League of Nations as the keys to the security of the British Empire.[6] This faith all too conveniently justified the cuts in defence expenditure pursued by both Conservative and Labour governments in the 1920s in order to limit the burden of taxation on Britain's lagging economy. Back in 1918, when the concept of a league of nations was originally under study in Whitehall, the Admiralty had warned that a covenant obliging Britain to take action other than for self-protection actually *increased* British strategic responsibilities, and might require a *larger* navy.[7] Such a commonsensical view was far remote from the minds of politicians and public opinion in the decade of peace propaganda that culminated in the Kellogg Pact of 1928, by which the signatory nations renounced war as an instrument of policy.

Indeed, British Cabinets even chose to neglect the naval defence of the British Empire itself against the one evident potential threat – that of Japan. As the Conservative Chancellor of the Exchequer, Winston Churchill (the pre-war battleship-building First Lord of the Admiralty, but now a Gladstonian economiser who successfully urged that the 'ten-year rule' be made permanent), told his Prime Minister, Stanley Baldwin, in 1926, there was not 'the slightest chance' of war with Japan in their lifetime.[8] The barometer of British naval policy in the 1920s with regard to Japan was provided by the rate of progress on the Singapore naval base, because without a fully equipped and defended base in the Far East Britain would be unable to dispatch her battlefleet from home waters and the Mediterranean, and would therefore be powerless to protect her interests and territories, or even exert any decisive political leverage in Far Eastern affairs. In 1922 Beatty, as First Sea Lord, had wanted the base to be fully operational by 1925, but Baldwin's incoming Conservative government decided on the grounds of financial stringency to proceed only slowly with the construction work. In 1924 Ramsay MacDonald's minority Labour government cancelled work on the base, putting its faith instead in the League, disarmament and a new international spirit of conciliation. In November 1924 Baldwin's returning government decided to restart work on the base in principle but not in fact, instead appointing a sub-committee of the Committee of Imperial Defence (CID) to report on the whole question. This sub-committee recommended postponing work on the main defences until 1926. In that year further modest instalments of construction were authorised. In 1928 the Chiefs of Staff, after further study, recommended more delays in the construction of the defences, partly because of shortage of money, partly because of unresolved technical and tactical uncertainties. Even the first stages of the defensive shore batteries were not now to be completed until 1933. In December 1928 the Conservative Cabinet agreed to a Committee of Imperial Defence recommendation that no work on shore batteries at Singapore should be carried out in 1929–30, during which time the technical and tactical questions relating to the base's defence were to be studied yet again. The base was now not to be fully completed until 1935 at the earliest – ten years later than Beatty had wanted. In 1929 the new Labour government stopped all further work yet again, in defiance of a warning by the naval staff that without Singapore the British Empire in the East and Pacific was defenceless. It did so partly because the Treasury wanted to save money, partly because a new naval disarmament conference was pending, and as the Cabinet Fighting Services Committee recorded, '. . . we consider that to continue the entire Singapore scheme in complete disregard of the possibilities of the Conference would be indefensible . . .'[9]

This naval conference, held in London in 1930, completed the demolition work on British seapower begun at Washington in 1922 and continued piecemeal by Conservative and Labour Chancellors of the Exchequer thereafter. By the London Naval Treaty the Labour government agreed to cut the number of cruisers from 70 to 50, even though in 1929 the then First Sea Lord, Admiral of the Fleet Sir Charles Madden, had warned that 50 was 'a starvation number' when measured against the needs of an oceanic Empire and a homeland utterly dependent on seaborne supplies.[10] In any event, Britain's actual cruiser strength had by this time dropped to 54, with only four under construction, as against the 114 at the outbreak of the Great War, a total which had proved operationally insufficient in the event. Of the fifteen capital ships permitted under the Washington Treaty, seven were unmodernised veterans of the Great War, five had been sent to the dockyards between 1924 and the 1930s for superficial modernisation (new anti-torpedo bulges; modified funnel and bridge structures), one (*Hood*) dated from 1920 and was already obsolescent (especially with regard to armour protection), and only two vessels (the battleships *Nelson* and *Rodney*) could be said to be truly up-to-date, even if of a flawed compromise design, both being completed in 1927.[11]

Thus the opening of the 1930s found the Royal Navy technologically obsolescent as well as truncated by treaty – no longer a war-hardened fighting service, but once again a kind of fashionable yacht club more apt for elegant displays of ship-handling and royal tours of the Empire than for battle; its old Victorian vices of social and technical snobbery, stiff hierarchy and spit-and-polish once more in the ascendant. The Royal Naval Colleges at Osborne and Dartmouth continued to instil unthinking obedience to superiors, while the élite gunnery school, HMS *Excellent*, avoided all painful analysis of the lessons of the Great War in favour of uncritical loyalty to tradition and a belief in parade-ground smartness.[12]

Worse, the Royal Navy now lagged behind where in 1918 it led the world – in carrier-borne airpower. This was not a question of the numbers of carriers themselves, for in 1932 Britain possessed six (including *Courageous* and *Glorious*, 22,000 tons, completed in 1928 and 1930, and based on the hulls and machinery of light battlecruisers completed in 1917) to Japan's three and America's three. The British inferiority lay in aircraft, with a total of only 150 obsolete aircraft of limited performance (and mostly gunnery spotters)[13] to the US Navy's over 400 aircraft, including 90 embarked in each of its big new 33,000-ton carriers *Lexington* and *Saratoga*. Moreover, both the American and Japanese Navies had developed far more advanced carrier-borne aircraft (torpedo-carriers and dive-bombers), together with heavy armour-piercing bombs.[14] Though all major navies still continued to rate the battleship as the arbiter of seapower and the core of the fleet, the US and Japanese Navies had by now developed a semi-independent role for the carriers as a long-distance strike force, whereas in the Royal Navy the carriers were still seen very much as an adjunct to the battlefleet, with their primary roles reconnaissance, air defence (though the strike role was not excluded), and spotting the fall of shot for ships' guns (the last especially the role of aircraft embarked in battleships and cruisers). In sum, naval aviation enjoyed nothing like the relative importance within the Navy in Britain that it did in Japan and America.

Part of the problem lay with the uncertainty as to whether the aircraft of the period really could sink free-moving battleships in war, as opposed to peacetime trials such as the famous occasion in 1921 when US Army Air Corps bombers under the redoubtable General 'Billy' Mitchell sank the interned German battleship *Ostfriesland*, a defenceless hulk at anchor. In all the major navies the proponents of airpower and the believers in the battleship fiercely debated the question right through the 1920s. In Britain it was studied by two heavyweight Whitehall committees, the Post War Questions Committee (set up in 1919; reporting in 1920)[15] and the Bonar Law Committee (set up in 1921 to consider the whole question of future battleship construction).[16] The evidence to both committees consisted more of emotional assertions by 'big-gun' admirals and airpower fanatics like Air Chief Marshal Sir Hugh ('Boom') Trenchard, the Chief of the Air Staff, than of numerate operational analysis. Although these committees pronounced in favour of a continued future for the battleship, the argument, feeding on further inconclusive trial bombings, smouldered on into the 1930s without being resolved – as indeed it did in the American and Japanese Navies too. But in Britain the debate was complicated and embittered by the circumstance that the protagonists were two rival departments of state, the Admiralty and the Air Ministry. What should have been purely technical and tactical questions became rallying cries in a fierce Whitehall power battle as to which department and which armed service should control carrier-borne aviation.

For the decision in 1918 to transfer the naval air service to the new Royal Air Force did not go unchallenged. Throughout the 1920s the Admiralty and the Air Ministry pulled and tugged at each other over the key question of how the responsibilities for the Fleet Air Arm should be shared between them. The matter was pondered at length by yet more high-powered government committees.[17] In the end it took an intervention by the Prime Minister himself, Stanley Baldwin, in 1926 to impose the final fuzzy compromise settlement that was to endure until 1937, though this by no means put a stop to the skirmishing between Admiralty and Air Ministry. Baldwin ruled that the RAF was to continue to be responsible for 'raising, training and maintaining' the Fleet Air Arm (as it was called after 1924), while the Admiralty was to exercise operational and disciplinary control over it at sea. The Fleet Air Arm's pilots were to be drawn from the Navy and Air Force in the ratio of 70:30.[18]

Thus the entire development of carrier aviation in Britain – ships, aircraft, weaponry, strategic role and tactics – came to depend on collaboration between two mutually suspicious departments of state, each jealously pursuing its own group interest and each with very different priorities, in contrast to the US and Japan, where carrier aviation was the exclusive responsibility of the Navy. To make matters worse, the Admiralty had abolished the wartime Air Division of the naval staff under a flag officer, and relegated air questions to a minor section under a captain. Not even within the Navy itself, therefore, did carrier aviation enjoy strong advocacy from an officer of authority, such as the US Navy enjoyed in Rear Admiral William A. Moffett, Chief of the Navy Department's Bureau of Aeronautics from 1921 to 1933.

Yet if the Royal Navy was technologically backward, its paint was fresh and its brasswork bright. When the pale grey vessels of the Mediterranean Fleet were joined by the dark grey of the Atlantic Fleet in some anchorage in the sun such as Gibraltar or Pollensa (Majorca) or Grand Harbour, Malta, for the annual fleet manoeuvres, the spectacle was magnificent enough for British seapower at its Victorian apogee. And this very reversion from the wartime Grand Fleet to the two main fleets of the Victorian era in itself lends emphasis to the neo-Victorian character of the Navy in the late 1920s and early 1930s, a character manifested by the routine and pleasures of peacetime naval life; the 'Upstairs-Downstairs' social divide between upper-middle-class deck officers and the rest, be they engineer officers, petty officers or lower deck, which showed little change from the 1880s. A letter from Admiral Sir William Fisher, C-in-C, Mediterranean Fleet, written on board his flagship HMS *Queen Elizabeth* in the Greek port of Navarino in 1932 catches the atmosphere perfectly:

> Nevil and I had a very memorable early morning partridge shoot in Cyprus – starting at dark and catching the dawn – chill – and then hot sun . . . Athens was a scream. Ciss and Ros going great guns and having arrived in *Briony* three days before I got there in *Queen Elizabeth*, they were in the big Athens society whirl when we met. Dinners, dances, night clubs, etc. Athens is thoroughly demoralised anyhow when the Fleet is there . . .[19]

On the China Station, it would be tennis and duck shooting and the fleet regatta; sundowners and supper on the veranda of the club; and even the lower deck would have their Chinese servants.[20] The Navy's ports of call as it 'showed the flag' round the world might have been chosen from a luxury travel brochure – Villefranche on the Côte d'Azur, Hawaii, Samoa, Bermuda – all of them calling for cocktail parties under broad awnings spread above white decks as the Royal Marine band played the latest popular hits; and for return visits ashore for balls and picnics. The duties of His Majesty's ships in this era of an apparently Victorian peace restored and of imperial power apparently perpetuated could include such heavy tasks as transporting colonial governors in full dress and befeathered cocked hats from island to island in the West Indies, with salutes of fifteen or seventeen guns being ceremonially discharged at every landfall.[21]

The actual fitness of the Royal Navy for the sterner purposes of defending British dominions and colonies, British trade and British interests, and providing essential leverage behind British foreign policy (let alone fulfilling Britain's limitless obligations under the Covenant of the League of Nations) was bleakly described in April 1931 by the then First Sea Lord, Admiral of the Fleet Sir Frederick Field, in a memorandum to the government committee preparing for the forthcoming League of Nations disarmament conference. While other countries had increased their naval spending in recent years, wrote Field, the British Commonwealth 'has accepted a naval strength which, in certain circumstances, is definitely below that required to keep our sea communications open in the event of our being drawn into a war. In defensive material, in the modernisation of ships . . . we are below the standard of the other powers . . .'[22] Field went on to spell out British weaknesses item by item, the worst of them being printed in his report in heavy black type:

> The number of our capital ships is now so reduced that should the protection of our interests render it necessary to move our fleet to the East, insufficient vessels of this type would be left in Home Waters to ensure the security of our trade and territory in the event of any dispute arising with a European power.[23]

Field once again stated the naval staff's conviction that 50 cruisers was 'definitely insufficient'. In destroyers too the Navy was dangerously weak. In 1918 Britain had possessed 433, all of which had been needed in the Great War. The permitted figure under the 1930s London Naval Treaty was some 120. Moreover, Field pointed out, 55 of these would be obsolete by 1936. The Fleet Air Arm numbered only 159 shipborne and land-based aircraft, as compared with Japan's 115 shipborne and 296 land-based. Under current plans the Fleet Air Arm would still only number 225 aircraft by 1937. There were no adequately defended ports in the entire Commonwealth.

Field capped his dismal survey by making clear that the Royal Navy had not only declined in its *relative* strength, but 'owing to the operation of the "Ten-year decision" and the clamant need for economy, our *absolute strength* also has . . . been so diminished as to render the fleet incapable, in the event of war, of efficiently affording protection to our trade.'[24]

Barely twelve years had passed since that day when Beatty and the Grand Fleet had escorted the German High Seas Fleet into internment, and British seapower had stood at its apogee. And it was to be only four months after Admiral Field wrote his anatomy of British naval weakness that, on 18 September 1931, the Japanese Army began to occupy the Chinese province of Manchuria, in clear breach of the League of Nations Covenant and in brutal challenge to the faith of idealistic internationalists and disarmers that the League of Nations could ensure the peace of the world. The Japanese action marked the opening of a new era in world affairs wherein the harsh realities of aggression and military force would dispel the illusion of the 1920s that great powers like Britain could find security on the cheap by disarming and putting their faith in the League. But the damage to the Royal Navy had already been done. To repair it would not be so simple. It would take time and money – if there proved to be enough of either.

2

The Triple Threat and Belated Rearmament, 1932–1939

As the Chiefs of Staff remarked in their 1931 Annual Review of imperial defence, the Manchurian crisis had come 'out of a clear sky'.[1] Since under the League of Nations Covenant Britain was obliged in the last resort to join in military action to curb aggression and restore the status quo, she was suddenly confronted with the possibility of armed conflict with Japan – ten years earlier than allowed for under the current 'ten-year rule'. In January 1932 the possibility came nearer when Japanese and Chinese forces clashed round the International Settlement of Shanghai, so directly menacing British investments and trading interests in China. The Chiefs of Staff therefore made 'prompt enquiry as to our own readiness to face sudden aggression by Japan', and concluded that the position was 'as bad as it could be':[2]

> In a word, we possess only light naval forces in the Far East; the fuel supplies required for the passage of the Main Fleet to the East and for its mobility on arrival are in jeopardy; and the bases at Singapore and Hong Kong, essential to the maintenance of a fleet of capital ships on arrival in the Far East, are not in a defensible condition. The whole of our territory in the Far East, as well as the coastline of India and the Dominions and our vast trade and shipping, lies open to attack.[3]

Given this state of disarmament, it is hardly surprising that in the end Britain limited her actions over the Japanese occupation of

Manchuria to voting in support of a toothless League of Nations statement in February 1933 calling for the restoration of Chinese sovereignty in the province. But when Japan simply walked out of the League, so dealing a shattering blow to its mystique, Britain began to pay the long-term price for having sided diplomatically against Japan. Henceforward she had to treat Japan as a live and ever-present menace to the British Empire in the East and Pacific rather than as a sleeping one. That was strategic problem enough – especially for the Royal Navy. But on 30 January 1933 Adolf Hitler became Chancellor of the German Reich, with a stated political programme of destroying the 1919 Versailles peace settlement, especially its restrictions on the strength of the German armed forces. In October 1933 the Foreign Office warned the British government that Germany 'was once more manifestly a public menace; the spirit of that country is worse than at any time since 1914'.[4]

The consequence was, as the Chiefs of Staff pointed out in their Annual Review for 1933, that Britain now had to face threats at both ends of the British imperial 'dumb-bell': 'The Far East . . . remains a potential danger zone, and its importance from the point of view of Imperial Defence has in no way diminished. But, during the last year . . . a second danger zone has appeared in Europe itself.'[5] The Chiefs therefore again confronted the reluctant politicians with stern realities: '. . . we should like to put on record our opinion that Germany is not only starting to rearm, but that she will continue this process until within a few years hence she will have to be reckoned as a formidable military power.'[6]

However, the Chiefs of Staff could at least take comfort from the good relations existing with France and Italy, powers whose fleets and air forces in the Mediterranean lay athwart the principal line of communication between the United Kingdom and the other end of the imperial 'dumb-bell', in India, the Far East and Pacific; and especially since, in the Chiefs of Staff's words, 'our defensive arrangements in the Mediterranean are in many respects obsolete'.[7]

By the spring of 1935, when Hitler openly reintroduced conscription and announced the existence of the Luftwaffe (both major breaches of the Versailles Treaty, soon to be followed by another, the rebuilding of the U-boat arm) the twin threat to the opposite ends of the British Empire had become brutally plain; the dilemma for British strategy – above all, naval strategy – deeply disquieting. For in May 1935 Hitler generously announced that he would accept a limit for the German Navy of 35 per cent of the Royal Navy. At the resulting Anglo-German negotiations in London in June the German delegation revealed what this limit meant – six new battleships, 44,000 tons of aircraft carriers, eighteen cruisers, 37,500 tons of destroyers and 17,500 tons of submarines to be built by 1942.[8] But such was the Admiralty's anxiety in the face of the Japanese menace that it reckoned any limitation on the future German Navy to be better than none; and it advised the Cabinet to close with the German *diktat* without delay, lest it should be increased. In the face of German rush tactics and blackmail Britain therefore threw away the provisions of the Versailles Treaty which prohibited the rebirth of the German naval challenge[9] – accepted that in the future the Royal Navy might again have to face German heavy ships in the North Sea and Atlantic, and the lurking U-boat, but this time on top of the Japanese naval threat in eastern waters.

As the Defence Requirements Committee (set up by the Cabinet in 1933 to consider all aspects of imperial defence and rearmament) wrote in its third report in November 1935:

> We cannot over-emphasise the difficulties of conducting naval warfare against highly efficient enemies in two theatres so widely separated . . . it would be suicidal folly to blind our eyes to the possibility of a simultaneous or practically simultaneous threat on both fronts; and if we do not possess forces sufficient to provide a deterrent this double emergency is the more likely to occur. If there is a danger from Japan at all, it reaches its maximum from the point of view of probability and extent when we are preoccupied in Europe. Unless we can provide a sufficient defence for that emergency, Australia, New Zealand, India, Burma, the rich colonies East of Suez and a vast trade will be at their mercy, and the Eastern half of the British Empire might well be doomed.[10]

No wonder the Chiefs of Staff in their Annual Review in April that same year had anxiously reminded the Foreign Office: 'That should we be called upon to fight Germany and Japan simultaneously without allies is a state of affairs to the prevention of which our diplomacy would naturally be directed.'[11]

But instead British diplomacy now proceeded to raise up a *third* potential enemy, and, moreover, an enemy exactly endangering that main imperial line of maritime communication through the Mediterranean. The enemy was Fascist Italy, which, in the course of 1935, first threatened to invade Abyssinia and then, in October, finally did so. Although Britain herself had no imperial interest at stake at all in this quarrel, she chose to align herself against Italy in the League of Nations in accordance with the League Covenant and in the cause of 'collective security', largely because of the pressure of British public opinion as influenced by vociferous idealists such as the League of

Nations Union. The strategic consequences of Britain's quixotry were aptly summed up by the First Sea Lord, Admiral of the Fleet Sir Ernle Chatfield:

> It is a disaster that our statesmen have got us into this quarrel with Italy who ought to be our best friend because her position in the Mediterranean is a dominant one . . . the miserable business of collective security has run away with all our traditional interests and policies, with the result that we now have to be prepared to fight any nation in the world at any time.[12]

As the Abyssinian crisis worsened, the British Cabinet found itself caught in the scissors between the demands of British public opinion that Britain should lead the League of Nations in 'stopping' Italian aggression, and the strategic reality of British naval and military weakness. It was indeed a grim irony that the very peace propagandists who in the 1920s had successfully urged unilateral disarmament on British governments were now in 1935 no less fervently urging that Britain take strong action (such as oil sanctions) against Italy, even at the risk of war. Yet the Chiefs of Staff had warned the Cabinet in the early days of the crisis that a naval war with Italy was bound to lead to losses of British ships, so that 'the British fleet, already weak, will be still further reduced. There is bound to be a danger, therefore, that the results of a war with Italy would be to leave the British fleet temporarily weakened to such an extent as to be unable to fulfil its world-wide responsibilities.'[13]

Even the prolongation of the Abyssinian crisis without war proved enough to swallow up Britain's available striking power at sea. In February 1936 the First Lord of the Admiralty warned the Cabinet that 'the position of the Fleet in the Mediterranean was becoming intolerable. Seven months ago we brought it up to war strength without mobilisation. The result was that the leave of large numbers of personnel was long overdue and many ships ought to be recommissioned.' He added: 'If a capital ship were withdrawn and paid off it would mean we should have only seven capital ships in commission . . . we could not afford to overlook Japan.'[14] By May that year the Navy was indeed left with only seven capital ships in service out of a paper total of fifteen, which, as the First Sea Lord remarked to a Cabinet Committee studying the problem, 'was quite inadequate for any other purpose than the present contingency'.[15]

The flight of the Emperor of Abyssinia to London on 2 May 1936 and the complete occupation of his country by the Italians mercifully put an end to the British Cabinet's immediate dilemmas over the

Mediterranean. Nevertheless, Britain's half-hearted chivalry on behalf of Abyssinia at the League of Nations left behind another grim long-term strategic legacy; and again above all for the Royal Navy. For, as the Chiefs of Staff pointed out in their Annual Review for 1937, 'we must face the fact that, whether Italy is friendly or the reverse, the days are past when we could count automatically on a friendly and submissive Italy. For henceforward we will have to look to a rival . . .'[16]

Thus it had come to pass that Britain had raised up a *third* potential threat on top of those from Germany and Japan; and from a naval power lying astride the main British imperial lifeline through the Mediterranean. Could British diplomacy remove any of these menaces and so find escape from an otherwise insoluble strategic dilemma? Although Neville Chamberlain, as Chancellor of the Exchequer in the National Government in 1934, had urged on his colleagues the importance of making a deal with Japan at China's expense in order to restore the old Anglo-Japanese entente, the Cabinet would not stomach the idea, partly because of its own scruples, partly because it feared the scruples of public and parliamentary opinion. Chamberlain's later attempts as Prime Minister in 1937–39 to rid Britain of the German menace by offering Hitler a free hand in Central and Eastern Europe in return for a new European 'peace' settlement proved a humiliating catastrophe. His equally naïve efforts to ingratiate himself with the Italian dictator Mussolini were mercilessly snubbed.

As a result, therefore, in 1939 the British Empire in its worldwide spread still had to face the triple threat. Moreover, Britain had been unable to make a countervailing alliance against Japan with America which could have enlisted the United States Navy in the defence of Australia and New Zealand. Tentative exchanges with Washington in 1937, when Japan had embarked on a full-scale invasion of China proper (and had actually sunk an American gunboat on the Yangtse by air attack), and low-level naval staff conversations early in 1938 had failed to produce any firm Anglo-American commitment for naval cooperation in the Far East and Pacific. In 1939 the United States still remained sunk in deep isolationism; no comfort for the beleaguered British Empire there.[17] In the case of France, the British Cabinet (supported by the Chiefs of Staff, who were only too conscious of the weakness of the British Army and the obsolescence of its equipment) had dourly refused until the spring of 1939 to contemplate a formal alliance for fear of being drawn into a ground war on the continent of Europe. Chamberlain and his colleagues only recanted in January–February 1939 because a rumour that Germany was about to invade the Netherlands panicked them into at least recognising the somewhat obvious fact that the Low Countries and France were vital to Britain's own security, and more so than ever in the age of the bomber.

The gruesome plight into which British illusions and diplomatic folly had delivered Britain and her unfortunate armed forces by 1939 was eloquently summed up by the Chiefs of Staff in a memorandum that April:

> We are considering a situation in which we, allied to France, would be engaged in war with Germany and Italy simultaneously and when Japan would also be a potential enemy . . . The British Empire and France would thus be threatened at home, in the Mediterranean and in the Far East at the same time, and it would be hard to choose a worse geographical combination of enemies.[18]

The strategic problem thus presented to Britain was the more desperately intractable because the various parts of the British Empire made such small contributions to their own defence and to the common imperial defence. In 1935 the New Zealand squadron of the Royal Navy possessed only two cruisers, while the Royal Australian Navy numbered an active fleet of no more than three cruisers, three destroyers, two sloops and a survey ship. The Royal Canadian Navy, designed for coast defence, comprised four destroyers in 1935 and six in 1939.[19] Even by 1939 no common imperial strategic plans existed; no common commands, staffs or headquarters. The truth was that as a peacetime naval and military alliance the British Empire did not exist, except for representative dominion ships and military contingents taking part in the Spithead Reviews and the London processions held to celebrate George V's Silver Jubilee in 1935 and George VI's Coronation in 1937.

From the Imperial Conference of 1921 to that of 1937 British governments under the urging of service departments (especially the Admiralty) had sought to evolve a collective imperial defence policy with agreed contingency plans and joint staff structures, so that dominion forces could be slotted into place under British leadership in time of war. In particular, the British government sought some formula by which the dominion navies could become pieces in an imperial naval mosaic arranged by the Admiralty. The British attempts utterly failed, even at the 1937 Imperial Conference, held in the shadow of the now evident triple threat; torpedoed again and again by the Afrikaner-dominated government of South Africa and by Canada under the premiership of Mackenzie King, a man jealous of Canadian independence and resentful of Britain's traditional dominance. In every imperial conference South Africa and Canada successfully blocked any proposal, any form of words, which suggested that the British Empire constituted or should constitute a collective strategic entity.[20] Even a conference of Britain and the 'loyal' dominions of Australia and New Zealand on defence in the Pacific, held in Wellington at the invitation of New Zealand in April 1939, resulted in no joint regional command or staff structure, no common strategy, although New Zealand agreed to man a third cruiser in the New Zealand squadron and Australia to increase her cruisers from three to five, while both dominions agreed to closer cooperation with the Royal Navy.[21]

The minuscule size of these dominion navies, even when thus expanded, underlines how overwhelmingly the responsibility for defending the Empire in its global sprawl continued to rest on Britain, a European offshore island state now directly menaced by the German prong of the triple threat. The Admiralty in particular stood committed by the oft-repeated but increasingly hollow promise to Australia and New Zealand to despatch the British main fleet to Singapore in the event of Japanese aggression – 'this heavy commitment', as Admiral of the Fleet Lord Chatfield (now Minister for the Coordination of Defence) described it in spring 1939.[22] Thus the security of the United Kingdom and the Empire alike came to depend on the timeliness, speed and scale of Britain's own rearmament.

Already in 1932, with the crisis following the Japanese occupation of Manchuria and with German democracy all too evidently dying under the impact of the world slump and political extremism, had come the deepening swell and falling glass that warned of approaching storm after the international sunshine of the 1920s. Nevertheless, and despite the urgent warnings of the Chiefs of Staff, the National Government under MacDonald and Baldwin had refused to sanction any rearmament, but instead merely abolished the 'ten-year rule'. In November 1933, with Japan and Nazi Germany (as it had now become) both out of the League of Nations and Germany out of the world disarmament conference (and known to be secretly rearming), the Cabinet appointed the Defence Requirements Sub-Committee of the Committee of Imperial Defence to study the whole field of grand strategy and defence policy. It reported in March 1934, taking Nazi Germany as the paramount threat and estimating that Britain had five years in which to make good her defences.

In July that year the Cabinet sanctioned a modest five-year programme of remedying the accumulated deficiencies in the *peacetime* strengths of the armed forces, including major refits and modernising of some of the Navy's now obsolete capital ships, *Malaya*, *Warspite* and *Renown*. In 1935, in the face of the worsening international turbulence and the stiffening winds of crisis – Abyssinia; the German announcement of conscription and the existence of the Luftwaffe – the Cabinet approved an enlarged programme for the RAF, but nothing extra for the Navy or the Army. Not until February 1936 and after many more months of deliberation and report did the Cabinet finally heed the storm warnings and opt for large-scale rearmament – true expansion of the armed forces, including, at long last, a major warship building programme. It was just one month before the first squall blew of the tempest to come: the German Army's reoccupation of the demilitarised zone of the Rhineland in defiant breach of the Versailles Treaty.

Thus the British Cabinet had only decided to make a start at restoring the combat power of the Royal Navy *four years* after the Chiefs of Staff and the Admiralty had given their measured warnings in the shadow of the Manchurian crisis. Now, under the new programme, ships were to be laid down in 1936–37 for commissioning in 1940–41. The time lost was thus irrecoverable. What then accounted for this dangerous delay in beginning to repair British seapower? There was a cluster of inter-related reasons. In 1932–34 the National Government under Ramsay MacDonald and Stanley Baldwin was reluctant to load the slump-hit British economy with a costly rearmament programme, especially since the government continued to delude itself with naïve hopes that something might yet be salvaged from the now moribund World Disarmament Conference. Moreover the Cabinet was all too conscious of the prevailing pacifistic tenor of public opinion, which, fearful of another war combining the horrors of the 1914–18 Western Front with the terrors of the destruction of British cities by the bomber, still reposed its faith in disarmament and the League of Nations. Inside and outside Parliament the Labour and Liberal opposition parties bitterly denounced even the modest programmes for making good deficiencies in peacetime defences announced by the government in 1934–35.

Not until November 1935 did the government feel able to go to the country in a general election with defence (allegedly in support of the League and 'collective security') as a major theme in its manifesto – and only after its crushing victory in that election did it feel able to embark on the large-scale rearmament programme announced in February 1936. Even then the programme was denounced as 'warmongering' and 'the road to war' by the Labour and Liberal parties.[23]

In the case of the Royal Navy, moreover, there was an added reason for the delay – the building 'holiday' for capital ships under the Washington Treaty, as extended by the London Naval Treaty of 1930, did not expire until the end of 1936.

It was one thing to decide on the rearmament programme, including new ships for the shrunken and obsolescent Navy; quite another to carry it out by the general target date of 1940. Britain's sagging economy and increasingly fragile balance-of-payments set financial limits on how much could be done and how quickly, while material bounds were set by what the Defence Policy and Requirements Committee called 'the limited output of our existing industrial resources'.[24] This combination of financial and technological weakness impelled the Cabinet more than once between 1935 and 1938 to reject proposals for a 'New Standard Navy' big enough to secure European waters and the Atlantic while at the same time deterring or fending off a Japanese attack in the Far East – twenty battleships, fifteen aircraft carriers, 100 cruisers, 198 destroyers, 82 submarines.[25] Instead the rearmament programme aimed at a Navy of fifteen capital ships, eight aircraft carriers, 70 cruisers, 144 destroyers and 55 submarines by 1940 – in fact, a fleet not greatly larger than that of 1936 except in cruisers, but composed of new or modernised ships rather than the worn-out and obsolete.[26]

For the government had had to accept that Britain's economic resources were simply not big enough to meet the naval demands imposed on her by the existence of the British Empire and by the triple threat to it; certainly not on top of the cost of the RAF's expansion, to which the Cabinet in its fear of the bomber gave overriding priority. The resulting strategic conundrum had to be left to the Admiralty to solve as best it could.

Even the agreed building programme, calling for five new battleships and four carriers to be laid down in 1937–39, plus five cruisers every year, ran into severe enough production difficulties. Just as Beatty had unavailingly warned at the Washington Conference in 1922, the battleship building 'holiday' had in the event caused the decay of the specialised plant needed to manufacture heavy guns and their mountings. The firm of Beardmores, before 1914 one of the two main British suppliers, presented in 1937 the problem, according to Lord Weir (the government's Chief Industrial Adviser), of 'raising what might be termed a scrap-heap to an efficient unit'.[27] The British steel industry could not supply enough armour plate for the new cruisers and carriers, and so orders for 15,000 tons had to be placed in Czechoslovakia.[28] In spring 1938 the decision had to be taken to buy

40mm anti-aircraft guns from the Swedish firm of Bofors, because the equivalent Vickers design had proved useless. It was not even possible to produce the Bofors gun under licence in Britain because, in Lord Weir's words, of the 'limited and inexperienced capacity' in the United Kingdom for manufacturing automatic guns and their mountings.[29] Indeed, wherever precision engineering was required, the Admiralty encountered especially grim production problems. For instance, British contractors found it difficult to manufacture intricate fuze mechanisms to the fine accuracy needed for reliable operation.[30] Delivery of radio and Asdic* equipment became worryingly late. But the Admiralty's special anxiety lay in the field of gunnery fire control systems, without which a warship's ability to acquire and destroy targets is crippled. In late 1937 the Admiralty was reporting in tones of despair that the country 'has been scoured to find firms willing to undertake the task, but without success'.[31] As a result, wrote the Admiralty, new cruisers would be delivered in 1937 without their high-angle fire control systems, which were essential against aircraft (see below, p. 47).[32]

The design, development and delivery of new and battle-worthy carrier aircraft were likewise bottlenecked by the backwardness and incompetence of the manufacturers. The Royal Air Force too suffered from this same problem in the late 1930s: the Spitfire, for instance, was over a year late in reaching the squadrons.[33] But the two principal aircraft firms allotted to supplying the Fleet Air Arm, Blackburns and Faireys, were inefficient even by the standards then generally prevailing in the industry. As late as November 1937 Blackburns could not promise that deliveries of the new Skua fighter/dive-bomber (specification issued 1934) would reach sixteen per month before December 1938, and even so the Air Ministry reported that the Director of Aircraft Production 'has no confidence in this programme, and is unable to forecast deliveries at present'.[34] In 1938 further production hold-ups and technical problems with the Skua confronted the Navy with the prospect of sending its carrier pilots to war in Nimrods and Ospreys, slow and obsolete biplanes. A stop-gap ordered off the drawing board from Faireys, the Fulmar, proved an equal disaster in production and performance.[35] By the time both were in service in the first half of 1940, they were already obsolescent by Japanese or American standards.[36] And Faireys made no less of a muddle of the design, development and production of the Fleet Air Arm's designated replacement for its sturdy but out-of-date biplane

* Today called 'sonar': the term generally employed in this book.

torpedo/reconnaissance aircraft, the Swordfish. The new Albacore was ordered in May 1937, but did not enter carrier service until 1941, when it too was already obsolescent.[37]

Yet these problems over new carrier aircraft partly derived from the pernicious transfer in 1918 (confirmed in 1926) of responsibility for aircraft procurement for the Fleet Air Arm from the Admiralty to the Air Ministry. In the closed mind of the Air Ministry and Air Staff in the 1930s the strategic bomber came first and foremost in order of priority, with the land fighter (for United Kingdom air defence) a grudging second, and maritime aviation (whether carrier or shore-based) relegated to the leftovers in terms of administrative drive and industrial resources.[38]

In 1936, with a major expansion of the Fleet Air Arm at last in the offing, the Admiralty therefore called for a fresh government examination of the 1918 compromise dividing responsibility for the Fleet Air Arm between the Navy and the Air Force. There ensued another bitter Whitehall battle, this time between the current Chief of the Air Staff, Air Chief Marshal Sir Edward Ellington (an immovable Trenchardite in his conviction that the heavy bomber supplied the answer to every problem of modern war), and the First Sea Lord, Admiral of the Fleet Sir Ernle Chatfield, together with their 'front men', the Secretary of State for Air (Lord Swinton) and the First Lord of the Admiralty (Sir Bolton Eyres-Monsell). A parallel campaign was fought out in the letter columns of *The Times* by such veterans as Admiral of the Fleet Sir Roger Keyes, Trenchard himself, Marshal of the Royal Air Force Sir John Salmond and Admiral Richmond, the naval historian and commentator.

The battle ran on into 1937, with two major enquiries and reports by the new Minister for the Coordination of Defence, Sir Thomas Inskip.[39] In his second report, in July 1937, Inskip pronounced that 'when so much that concerns the air units depends upon the Naval element in the ship and the Fleet, the Admiralty should be responsible for selecting and training the personnel, and generally for the organisation of the Fleet Air Arm'.[40] Nevertheless, Inskip disallowed the Admiralty's demand for a return of all shore-based maritime airpower (such as flying boats) as well, which remained under Royal Air Force control, and subject to persistent neglect, with unfortunate consequences during the Second World War. The Cabinet approved Inskip's recommendations on 29 July 1937. So after nearly twenty years of fumbling and neglect the Navy was at least handed back responsibility for its own carrier aviation. The Admiralty forthwith proceeded to restore the Great War post of 'Fifth Sea Lord and Chief of the Naval Air Services' and the Air Division of the Naval Staff in order to discharge that responsibility; and appointed Admiral the Hon. Alexander Ramsay, a former Rear-Admiral, Aircraft Carriers, as the new Fifth Sea Lord.

Nonetheless, the reorganisation brought in its train many detailed problems concerning transfers of personnel from the RAF, recruitment, a shortage of technical and middle-rank officers, and the transfer of necessary Fleet Air Arm shore bases,[41] just at the time of an all-too-belated attempt vastly to expand naval aviation. Here was yet another factor in the backwardness of the Royal Navy's carrier arm and its concept of carrier warfare in the late 1930s compared with the American and Japanese Navies.

Those navies, while also still regarding the battleship as the key to command of the sea, had long been practising long-range air strikes by fast carrier task groups. In an exercise in 1929 by the United States Navy over 260 aircraft took part in a 'battle' between two fleets for control of the Panama Canal. Manoeuvres in the Pacific in 1932 with three fast carriers demonstrated that airpower would in the future dominate the attack and defence of convoys, and that the first phase of a clash of fleets would take the form of an attempt by the rival carrier forces to destroy each other – exactly as was to happen in the battles of the Coral Sea and Midway in 1942.[42] In the Imperial Japanese Navy, Admiral Isoruku Yamamoto, who in 1935 was appointed Chief of the Navy's Air Division and who in earlier posts had done much to build up the Japanese carrier arm, himself ardently believed that the future at sea belonged to the carriers and their torpedo and dive-bombers; and in 1941, as C-in-C of the Combined Japanese Fleet, he was to plan the strike on Pearl Harbor.[43]

The design of American and Japanese aircraft carriers reflected this positive belief in airpower. Lightly armoured – the American ships had unarmoured decks – and with the flight deck and hangar deck built as a superstructure above the hull, they were indeed aircraft *carriers*, their overriding purpose to carry and fly the maximum number of aircraft. The USS *Lexington* and *Saratoga* embarked 90 aircraft each on their 30,000 tons; the three-ship Yorktown class (commissioned 1938–39) up to 80 aircraft on 19,000 tons displacement. The Japanese *Kaga* and *Akagi* (completed 1928) embarked 60 aircraft each on displacements of 30,000 tons; the *Soryu* and *Hiryu* (completed 1938) 63 each on 16,000 and 18,500 tons displacement. It was the American and Japanese philosophy that preservation of the carriers themselves from air attack was the job of their fighter aircraft, although the Americans had also developed advanced techniques of damage control, such as contra-flooding after a torpedo hit to maintain the ship on even keel.

The Royal Navy, however, despite occasional air strike exercises, continued to see the principal roles of the carrier as air defence of the fleet and distant reconnaissance. It placed much more emphasis on the carrier as a *ship* able to preserve itself from attack by means of a well armoured hull and flight deck. In the new Illustrious class (23,000 tons displacement; four ships laid down from 1936 onwards) as in the *Ark Royal* (23,000 tons; laid down 1935; commissioned 1938), the hull was carried up to the flight deck, making an integral boxlike structure of immense strength. The side armour was 4½ inches thick; the deck armour 3 inches thick. It was indeed British doctrine in the 1930s that the carrier's defence under close air attack should be to stow all aircraft below and turn the ship into a shut-up armoured shelter. Yet a severe penalty in striking power had to be paid for the weight of the armour – the Illustrious class had only a single hangar and could embark only 36 aircraft, less than half the complement of the equivalent American Yorktowns, and significantly fewer than the 63 aircraft in the smaller Japanese *Hiryu* and *Soryu*, or the 72 in the *Ark Royal*.[44]

The design of Britain's new battleships presented a much more important problem (as it seemed to the Admiralty) and at the same time a more complicated one. So many factors had to be balanced one against another in order to produce an optimum fighting 'package'. In the first place, the 35,000-ton displacement limit under the Washington Treaty was not due to expire until the end of 1936; and in the meantime there seemed at least a chance that it would be prolonged afterwards by voluntary option on the part of the principal naval powers, according to the terms of the second London Naval Treaty, signed in March 1936, along with a limit of main armaments to 14-inch calibre. Government concern for economy also impelled the Admiralty towards a choice of the 35,000-ton battleship as the smallest and therefore the cheapest practicable size. Moreover, given the new need for powerful but weight-consuming anti-aircraft armaments, the Admiralty decided that the 14-inch gun was technically the heaviest main armament that could be comfortably installed on 35,000 tons.

In April–May 1936 the resulting design for the future King George V class was finally agreed – twelve 14-inch guns in three novel quadruple turrets (later modified to ten guns in two quadruple turrets and one twin), a dual-purpose (surface and anti-aircraft) secondary armament of sixteen 5.25-inch guns, plus some 80 assorted rapid-fire light anti-aircraft guns; a speed of 27½ knots. In particular – the lessons of Jutland here – the new ships were given immensely strong armour protection, the weight being concentrated over vital areas: up to 15 inches on the sides and 6 inches on the deck. The 'KGVs' were in fact better armoured than either their German or American contemporaries in design, even though these well exceeded the 35,000-ton limit. The stolid rectangular lines of the British ships belied their fighting effectiveness, just as the beautiful shapes of the *Bismarck* and the American Iowas with their clipper bows gave an impression of immense power that was belied by their thinner armour and, in the case of *Bismarck*, an outdated concept of distributing armour protection. Moreover, the 'KGVs' represented a far better investment than the two Japanese 64,000-ton 18-inch gun monsters, *Yamato* and *Mushashi*, which for all their unexampled weight of armour, proved, like British, German and American battleships, to be all too sinkable by air attack.[45]

The first ship of the new class, *King George V* herself, was laid down in January 1937, but not commissioned until October 1940, and the second, *Prince of Wales*, laid down at the same time as the *KGV*, was not completed until March 1941.[46] While they were under construction, the Royal Navy therefore had to look to the modernising of Great War veterans to provide it with capital ships sufficiently up-to-date in armaments, fire-control, armour and machinery to be fit for war in the age of the bomb and torpedo. In 1936 the battleship *Malaya* emerged from a three-year refit; next year *Warspite* completed a four-year reconstruction that included new engines and boilers as well as extra armour, a new bridge structure, new anti-aircraft armament and a modification to her 15-inch guns to give a maximum elevation of 30 degrees and a range of 32,000 yards. Nevertheless she still retained her obsolete 6-inch guns in battery, not turrets. In 1937 similar programmes of reconstruction were put in hand with the *Queen Elizabeth* and *Valiant*, both of whom had their 6-inch batteries replaced by twenty 4.5-inch dual-purpose guns in twin turrets. In the event these reconstructions were not completed before war broke out in September 1939. In 1936–39 the battlecruiser *Renown* too was virtually rebuilt from the hull upwards, but not her sister ship the *Repulse*, nor the *Hood*, at 41,200 tons displacement Britain's largest warship. *Hood*'s reconstruction, planned to start in 1939, was abandoned because of the outbreak of war:[47] as a consequence her impressive size and beauty of line served to disguise the reality of an obsolete and vulnerable ship.

With cruisers and destroyers too the legacy of international naval limitation – even though it had never amounted to a building 'holiday' as with capital ships – added grievously to the Royal Navy's problems in designing and building new vessels in the mid-1930s. By the 1930 London Naval Treaty the Labour government had accepted the 'starvation number' of 50 cruisers within an overall tonnage limit of 328,200 tons. Because of the unique scale and vulnerability of Britain's seaborne trade, the Admiralty had elected in the early 1930s to plan for the maximum number of new cruisers possible within the total permitted tons displacement even though this had meant going for 6-inch gun ships of only 7,250 tons displacement (the Leander class, launched 1931–34), or even 5,220 tons (the Arethusa class, launched 1934–36), as against the proportionately fewer 8-inch or 6-inch gun 10,000-ton cruisers being built by Japan and the United States or later by Germany. When in 1935 the Admiralty came to select cruiser designs for the new rearmament programme, it again had to strike a difficult balance within restricted funds and shipyard resources between ships powerful enough to meet enemy heavy cruisers in battle and yet numerous enough to protect British trade and also work with the main fleets. It found its compromise solution in the design of the Towns class of 6-inch gun heavy cruisers (9,100 tons displacement; later ships 9,400 tons; and of which HMS *Belfast*, commissioned in August 1939 and now moored as a museum ship in the Pool of London, is the last survivor). The first 'Town', HMS *Southampton*, was completed in 1937. There followed in the 1938 estimates the Colonies class design of heavy cruiser (8,000 tons and twelve 6-inch guns), a development of the 'Towns' design. All were still building when war broke out. Though all lighter than their foreign equivalents, these new cruiser designs were to prove stout fighting ships alike in the freezing gales of the Arctic, the huge seaways of the Atlantic and the blue, brilliant, bomber infested Mediterranean. The rearmament period light cruiser design, the Dido class (5,450 tons; later ships 5,770 tons), was supposed to carry ten 5.25-inch guns in twin turrets, but because of the demands of the new battleships and aircraft carriers for these turrets, two 'Didos' had to make do with eight 4.5-inch guns.[48]

With the design of destroyers the Admiralty faced a similar hard choice between sheer numbers and the fighting power of the individual vessel, for here too the 1930 London Naval Treaty had imposed a limit: of 150,000 tons overall. In the early 1930s the Admiralty had – as with cruisers – opted for the maximum number possible, even though this meant vessels of around 1,500 tons displacement compared with the destroyers of 2,500 tons – virtually light cruisers – favoured by the French and German navies. But in the case of destroyers the Admiralty added to its own problem by conceiving the primary role of this type of vessel in Jutland terms as 'massed attacks [on enemy fleets] by day and attacks against screened fleets by night', coupled with defence of British fleets against submarines by providing a sonar screen.[49] Up to 1936, therefore, a British destroyer's main armament lay in torpedo tubes rather than guns. However, by this time the Japanese Fubuki class destroyers were carrying six 5-inch guns in twin turrets, while Germany was about to build destroyers with five 5.9-inch guns – almost the calibre of the main batteries in cruisers. Between 1934 and 1936 the Admiralty therefore evolved a new generation of bigger destroyer which mounted eight 4.7-inch guns in twin turrets, as well as a short-range anti-aircraft armament, on a 1,850 tons displacement (the London Treaty limit) at the price of reducing the number of torpedo tubes.[50]

The first ships of the new generation, the Tribal class, were launched from June 1937 onwards, but problems with the delivery of gun mountings meant that in 1938 completed vessels had to be sent on sea trials while still devoid of guns.[51] Unfortunately the Admiralty's continued fixation with future Jutlands led it to give overriding priority in the new designs (within the limits of space and weight) to low-angle fire against surface targets (such as enemy destroyers) over high-angle fire against aircraft, especially dive-bombers; and the Tribals' 4.7-inch guns had a maximum elevation of only 40 degrees. This mistaken choice in otherwise admirably sturdy ships was to be tragically punished by the Luftwaffe off Greece and Crete in 1941.

But Jutland – that is, a future Jutland fought against the Japanese fleet in Far Eastern waters – befogged the Royal Navy's thinking over the entire horizon of maritime warfare in the years before the Second World War, and not just with regard to the design of destroyers or the relative importance of battleships and carriers. The role of the British submarine service, for its part, was seen merely as ancillary to the operations of the battlefleet: reconnaissance, attacks on enemy warships; defence of fleet bases such as Singapore against approaching hostile squadrons. Construction of new submarines therefore took a low priority in the Navy's rearmament programme after 1936, and the number of orders up to 1939 (eighteen to 1937, fourteen in 1938–39) only equalled boats either already over age or due to be over age by 1939.[52] But far more dangerous was the Admiralty's parallel neglect of the potential threat to Britain's own survival posed by *enemy* submarines. The neglect – or rather, minimising – of this was truly remarkable in view of the dreadful experience of 1917, when the U-boat had brought the United Kingdom within a few weeks of famine and industrial standstill. Despite that grimly effective demonstration of the true role of the submarine, the Admiralty in the 1920s and 1930s chose to believe that technical progress in the performance of sonar (echo-sounding gear for detecting submerged U-boats) would 'greatly lessen the effectiveness of the submarine as a weapon against shipping'.[53] Since Germany was in any case forbidden U-boats under the Versailles Treaty (a restriction only formally lifted in 1935 by the Anglo-German Naval Agreement) the Admiralty was convinced in the early 1930s that British commerce had much more to fear from German surface raiders such as the Deutschland class of 10,000-ton 11-inch gun 'pocket battleships'.

The Admiralty's faith in improved sonar, coupled with the priority given anyway to types of ship for service with the battlefleet, also misled it into neglecting the construction of anti-submarine escort vessels. In 1934 it reckoned that some 100 such ships would be needed for all purposes, whereas in 1918 the Navy had been deploying 300 in protection of convoys alone.[54] Only in 1937, with the rearmament programme now gathering momentum and all Britain's great departments of state urgently studying solutions to the practical problems of future war, did the question of securing Britain's essential imports (guesstimated to amount in wartime to 47 million tons a year)[55] come to be seriously examined afresh. A Shipping Defence Advisory Committee was set up under the Committee of Imperial Defence (CID) in February 1937, composed of representatives of the Admiralty, the Board of Trade, Lloyds and the Shipping Federation, to produce recommendations across the whole field of trade defence. It soon accepted that once again Britain would have to resort to the convoy system. But the Admiralty – and despite its belief that improved sonar had greatly lessened the menace posed by the U-boat – had to admit that in the opening stages of a war 'the naval forces are hardly adequate to provide fully effective numbers for escorting our convoys'.[56] In an attempt to remedy this want, the Shipping Defence Advisory Committee sponsored such emergency measures in 1937–39 as putting 6-inch guns into strengthened fast liners (later commissioned under the White Ensign as 'Armed Merchant Cruisers'). It mooted the idea of equipping as many merchant vessels as possible with rapid-fire light anti-aircraft guns (foreign again: this time the Swiss 20mm Oerlikon; a British design again proving unsatisfactory).[57] The idea was not to be realised in full until the middle years of the war.

It must therefore be accounted the Admiralty's most serious failure of judgment in the years between the world wars that, with eyes focused on the battlefleet, it ducked until too late the enormous operational and quantitative problems of once again having to set up a complete convoy system and defend this against the U-boat. Indeed, as late as 1939 some admirals still hankered after the 'offensive' tactic, discredited in 1917, of the 'hunting group' roaming the seas after U-boats.

Yet at the root of this failure, as of other misreadings of the true naval lessons of the Great War – to say nothing of want of vision with regard to the potential of carrier striking power – lay a single common factor: the want of organised, scientifically conducted operational research. No such department was set up by the Admiralty until 1942. In the case of the long-running argument about the warship's future chances against air attack, for example, it was not until 1935 that an anti-aircraft department was created at HMS *Excellent*, the Navy's gunnery school; not until 1938–39 that numerical calculation and objective analysis took the place of dogmatic assertion by rival enthusiasts, thanks to the reports of the ABE Committee ('Assessors on Bomb versus Battleship Experiments' Committee; renamed in March 1938 the 'Sub-Committee on Bombing and A-A Gunfire Experiments'). The second interim report of the committee in 1938 specifically indicted the lack of facilities for research and development in the field of anti-aircraft fire control.[58] Its third report in January 1939 estimated that two hits would be scored by aircraft on every carrier and one on every cruiser for each bomber shot down by the ships' gunfire, and that destroyers were 'virtually defenceless against air attack':[59] hardly welcome mathematics to the admirals (see below, pp. 47–8).

This was not the only example of the uneven coverage and quality of Admiralty research between the wars. Despite the founding of the Admiralty Research Laboratory in 1920, 'salt-horse' sailors continued to be suspicious of intruders such as scientists into their traditional craft 'mystery'. There was, for instance, no research department concerned with the structure and design of ships, including a structures laboratory, despite repeated urging by successive Directors of Naval Construction since 1918. Not until June 1943 was the Naval Construction Research Establishment created.[60]

Broadly it could be said that while those technical shortcomings revealed by battle experience during the Great War had been cured by 1939, the problems arising out of new developments, especially air power, had not. The modernised capital ships and the new ones under construction by 1939 certainly enjoyed much better armour protection, better underwater subdivision and much reduced vulnerability of magazines to flash cordite fires than ships at Jutland. Thanks to prolonged study leading to the adoption of new detonators and bursters, British heavy shells no longer suffered from a tendency to break up on impact or detonate prematurely; instead it was to be German shell technology that would be found wanting in the Second World War. With regard to fire control of main armaments against surface targets, most of the Royal Navy's ships had been equipped by 1939 with calculators virtually identical to Pollen's 'Argo Clock'.[61] But it was another story with the fire control of anti-aircraft guns, where the Navy committed just the same kind of blunder before 1939 as it had before 1914 in regard to fire control against ships: it opted for an inferior system, and in this case founded on fallacious principles.

In the words of Captain Stephen Roskill, the distinguished naval historian, gunnery specialist and in 1939 a member of the naval staff,

> The truth was that as long ago as the late 1920s the Admiralty had gone for the wrong sort of control system – one in which the enemy aircraft movements were in effect guessed instead of being actually *measured* and the measured results used to provide the required control data. This latter, called a 'tachymetric system', was the proper answer . . .[62]

In Roskill's judgment the culprits were the Naval Ordnance Department and its specialist officers 'not properly trained in scientific design and armament engineering', and unwilling to seek outside expert advice. The Admiralty's decision may also have been influenced by pressure from British engineering firms, which were incapable of designing and manufacturing such sophisticated precision equipment as the tachymetric system, and could hardly cope with the cruder equipment finally adopted (see above, p. 38).[63] In 1937 the inefficiency of the chosen system (HACS = High Angle Control System), now very belatedly getting into quantity production, was alarmingly displayed in a trial during which a Queen Bee radio-controlled target aircraft circled the Home Fleet for two and a half hours unscathed by the fleet's fire.[64] By this time it was too late to switch to a true tachymetric system – not least because Britain could not make it. In 1938 the Admiralty's Director of Scientific Research, C.S. Wright, described HACS as 'a menace to the service'.[65] Unlike the German and United States Navies, which had adopted tachymetric anti-aircraft fire control systems, the Royal Navy was to enter the Second World War firing at enemy aircraft with the hopeful wildness of aim of a tyro shot trying to bring down fast flying grouse. The Mediterranean Fleet in particular was to be cruelly handicapped in its prolonged battles in 1940–42 with the Regia Aeronautica and the Luftwaffe by the shortcomings of

HACS – colossal expenditure of ammunition without commensurate protection of the fleet or destruction of enemy aircraft. HMSs *Prince of Wales* and *Repulse* were similarly to suffer under Japanese air attack off Malaya in December 1941.

It was no compensation that in 1939 experimental air-warning radar had been fitted to two ships (the battleship *Rodney* and the cruiser *Sheffield*) and that in August that year the anti-aircraft cruiser *Curlew* was fitted with the prototype of all the wartime Royal Navy's air-warning sets. By this time, in any case, the German Navy was beginning to equip with the Seetakt gunnery-ranging radar, and the United States Navy with the XAF air-warning and gunnery radar.[66] These pioneer developments in three navies marked the beginning of the radar revolution that was to transform every aspect of sea warfare during the wartime years.

As serious – perhaps more serious – was the Admiralty's neglect between the wars of Intelligence, in both its operational and technical aspects. The superb radio intercept and cypher breaking organisation built up by 'Blinker' Hall in Room 40 which had read the vital German signals during the Jutland action was quickly run down after the Great War, and in 1922 responsibility for cypher Intelligence was transferred from the Admiralty to civilian control. Even in the 1930s, and despite urging by Captain Lord Louis Mountbatten, little technical research was conducted into cryptoanalytical technology. Although the Admiralty conducted trials with encyphering machines (the prototypes of the wartime German 'Enigma' and the RAF 'Typex'), the work was dropped. As a result of such neglect, the Admiralty even by the outbreak of the Second World War could not read either the German or Japanese naval cyphers. On the other hand B-Dienst of the German Navy's Intelligence Division had penetrated the Royal Navy's own cyphers, and during the Abyssinian crisis in 1935–36 had been able to monitor all the movements of the Mediterranean Fleet.[67] Operational Intelligence too grew sleepy between the wars: there was no accurate evaluation of the future U-boat threat; no recognition of the potential danger of U-boat surface attacks at night (a tactic already practised before the end of the Great War), and against which the Royal Navy's vaunted sonar would be useless.

Not until the mid-1930s did the Naval Intelligence Division of the Naval Staff experience a revival and swift expansion under Vice-Admiral Sir William James's encouragement as Deputy Chief of Naval Staff. In 1936 – the year when in Intelligence, as in so many things, Britain finally resolved to prepare itself for war – the Joint Intelligence Committee was founded, through which the three services and the

Foreign Office pooled resources and results in order to provide the Chiefs of Staff Committee with the Intelligence necessary as a basis for strategic policy making and decision. In June 1937 Lieutenant-Commander Norman Denning was tasked with designing a wartime Operational Intelligence Centre (OIC), and in November that year the Centre was formally set up and staffed with signals experts. From this beginning was to grow the collective brain and nerve centre of the whole war at sea. Under Rear-Admiral J. A. J. Troup, the Director of Naval Intelligence from 1936 to 1939, High Frequency Direction Finding (HF/DF) stations were constructed in the north of the British Isles in order to monitor German Navy signals traffic and ship movements; and a teleprinter net was installed to link the OIC to naval headquarters and stations, coastal watchers and RAF Coastal Command.[68]

Coastal Command was itself yet another product of the year of 1936, the UK-based Royal Air Force then being reorganised into the three great Commands – Coastal, Fighter and Bomber – with which it was to wage the Second World War. Between that year and the outbreak of the conflict in 1939 Coastal Command, under its first three Air Officers Commanding-in-Chief, Air Marshal Sir Arthur Longmore (in 1936: naval flyer in the Great War), Air Marshal Sir Philip Joubert de la Ferté (1936–37) and Air Marshal Sir Frederick Bowhill (1937–41: another former naval flyer), began to reforge the links between the shore-based component of maritime air power and the Navy which had rusted away since 1918. Nevertheless, for all the good will displayed by its chiefs towards the Navy, their keenness for close cooperation, Coastal Command from its birth was to be the poor relation within an air force entranced by a dream of strategic bombing; and it was to remain in 1939 weak in numbers, obsolescent in aircraft and with its principal role the passive one of reconnaissance.[69] In particular, the question of air cover for convoys (and air attack on U-boats) was little considered – not least because the Admiralty, in its sublimely complacent playing down of airpower, remained persuaded that the anti-aircraft fire of the escorts would by itself ensure the protection of convoys from enemy aircraft, and that the improved sonar would enable the Navy to hunt down U-boats without much need for help from the RAF.

Taken all in all, therefore, the Royal Navy's responses to the technical and operational puzzles involved in refurbishing British seapower in the late 1930s suggest a narrow professionalism of outlook too much influenced by loyalty to tradition and too little blessed with innovative imagination. And indeed the Navy's topmost leadership on the eve of the Second World War failed to measure up to the standards of Nelson or Barham or Beatty in broad strategic wisdom, sharpness of intellect or sheer personality. The shortcoming did not lie in the fleet commands. Admiral Sir Andrew Cunningham, appointed C-in-C, Mediterranean Fleet, in June 1939 – salty, vigorous, blunt-speaking – was the embodiment of the Royal Navy's best tradition of fighting sailors that extended back through Hawke, the victor of Quiberon Bay in 1759, to Blake, the Commonwealth's formidable 'general at sea' and the scourge of the Dutch. Admiral Sir Charles Forbes, the C-in-C, Home Fleet, shared Cunningham's characteristic of unshakability. A subordinate judged him to have had 'a fine brain and a tremendously powerful character'.[70] Nevertheless, and unlike Cunningham, he lacked, according to the same witness, 'that panache of which one would have liked to see more in a great commander-in-chief. I had, for example, at the request of many captains, to *force* him to visit ships and their people. When he got there and spoke – shortly and to the point – to ships' companies, he impressed as a rock of ages type of character.'[71]

The problem lay with the Navy's chief himself, the First Sea Lord after June 1939, Admiral of the Fleet Sir Dudley Pound. Pound was only appointed at that time because sickness, premature death and early retirements had thinned the field of choice. In 1935, Rear-Admiral B.H. Ramsay, an exceptionally able officer, resigned as Chief of Staff of the Home Fleet because the Commander-in-Chief, Admiral Sir Roger Backhouse, set aside the modern staff system in favour of tightly personal command by himself, down to dealing in detail with all incoming fleet signals and business. Ramsay was later to return to active service, and command the Dunkirk evacuation in 1940 and the Allied naval forces in the D-Day Landings in 1944. In 1936 the then second-in-command of the Mediterranean Fleet and a potential First Sea Lord, Admiral Sir Geoffrey Blake, suffered an accident and had to be invalided. In 1937 Admiral Sir William Fisher, a sailor of imposing presence who had brought the Mediterranean Fleet to a high state of efficiency during the Abyssinian crisis, and another among potential First Sea Lords, died suddenly at the age of 62 – 'a very great blow', as Admiral of the Fleet Sir Ernle Chatfield put it.[72] Chatfield himself, whose professional stature, experience and sagacity were unrivalled, became Minister for the Coordination of Defence in January 1939, and so was lost to the Navy. His successor as First Sea Lord was Backhouse, the arch centraliser; a man who as well as hating a staff system avoided larger questions of naval strategy and policy in favour of close interest in technical detail. One colleague judged him 'too weak; too fearful of accepting responsibility'.[73] But Backhouse in any case resigned in June 1939 because of ill health, and died of a cerebral tumour in July. From a now scant field Admiral Sir Dudley Pound, the C-in-C, Mediterranean Fleet, was duly appointed Backhouse's successor.

Pound was to hold the key post of First Sea Lord until his own death in 1943. The Royal Navy was therefore to be directed for the first three years of the Second World War by a stop-gap appointee who had never been earmarked for promotion to so exalted a strategic role. Chatfield had in fact once specifically told Pound that he was *not* going to be First Sea Lord.[74] In 1936 Admiral Sir John Kelly, the C-in-C, Portsmouth, had told Chatfield in a letter that 'D.P. would not be a success in my opinion. In the first place, he suffers from being not quite a gentleman: a disastrous lacuna in a First Sea Lord. He is too pig-headed; too unwilling to recognise that there may be another side of the question.'[75] For Pound was a hard-working plodder of limited intellectual range and interests; another arch centraliser in the Victorian/Edwardian naval mould; a 'good plain cook' devoid of personal charisma. His Flag Captain when he was C-in-C, Mediterranean Fleet, judged him many years later as 'certainly not a genius and I question whether he was even a great man. He had a slow but good brain and got to the top by sheer hard work . . .'[76] Another witness who was at that same period on the staff of the Navy's Tactical School wrote of Pound:

> We used to get all his exercise papers and I remember that the Orders for an exercise contained detailed plans for practically every unit during [the] whole exercise, this of course meant that the enemy were told what to do! 'Initiative' was obviously considered a dirty word.[77]

Did Pound immerse himself in detailed executive driving of his fleet because he felt himself out of his depth and inferior in larger questions of naval strategy? Another former subordinate, Admiral Sir Gerald Dickens, records of him as Commander of the Second Battle Cruiser Squadron in 1929–31:

> When I joined *Repulse*, fresh from the I.D.C. [Imperial Defence College], he said 'How do I study strategy?' I laughed – thinking he was getting at me – and said, 'Too late now, Sir.' He looked rather surprised, but showed no sign of annoyance. The fact was that – at least that was my impression – he had never given much time to reading and the teachings of history, which explains much about his composition . . .[78]

Pound's lack of wide strategic grasp and his habit of directing in detail were the more a potential handicap in war because the Admiralty, unlike the War Office or Air Ministry, was an operational headquarters; it exercised supreme command over the Royal Navy in all seas and oceans. Whereas the Chiefs of the Imperial General Staff and the Air Staff could only issue broad strategic directives to Command or theatre commanders-in-chief, the First Sea Lord (and Chief of Naval Staff) could, if he so wished, personally control the day-to-day dispositions of fleets, task forces, squadrons and convoys, even individual ships. And Pound was by no means a fit man in 1939, being disabled by an arthritic hip which gave him great pain and denied him sleep. 'When I saw him just after the war started,' writes an eyewitness, 'he hobbled into the ops-room at Coastal Command, & I noticed with horror that he had become a worn-out old man. His hair was snow-white and wispy, his face seamed and ashen, & there was a noticeable distortion of one eye . . .'[79]

At the beginning of 1936 it had been planned to complete the British rearmament programme in the course of 1940. That was the year when the first of the Royal Navy's new battleships and aircraft carriers would, it was hoped, be commissioned. But in September 1938 the Munich crisis put Britain's rearmament and Britain's armed forces to the test of imminent danger of war, and, unsurprisingly, found them wanting. The aftermath of the crisis therefore witnessed searching inquests in Whitehall into the state of progress in rearmament; the drafting of urgent measures to speed up the re-equipment of the services – and especially expand production of fighter aircraft for the defence of British cities against the dreaded bomber. There was anguished consideration of how the cost of such accelerated rearmament (and particularly the RAF programme) could be squared with Britain's rapidly worsening balance-of-payments problem.[80]

The Admiralty, for its part, reported in October 1938 to the new Cabinet Committee on Defence Programmes and Acceleration that there were not enough escorts for all duties, and that it therefore wished to order a new type of vessel costing half as much as a destroyer. These vessels, later called 'corvettes', were to become the indispensable workhorses of the Battle of the Atlantic. The Admiralty also reported that there existed 'extremely serious deficiencies' in the Fleet Air Arm; that there was a shortage of skilled ratings; and that more armour plate would have to be ordered from Europe.[81] Britain's limited technological resources were still acting as a powerful brake on rearmament. The Minister for the Coordination of Defence reminded the Defence Programmes and Acceleration Committee that 'the real bottlenecks consist of certain highly specialised products, e.g., fire control gear, gun-mountings, predictors and the like . . .'[82]

As 1938 turned to 1939 the sense of urgency, of time running out, sharpened. It was now known in London that Hitler had conceived a total contempt for his dupe at Munich, Neville Chamberlain; a contempt all too likely to dissolve any remaining diplomatic caution. Moreover, France, deprived of her militarily strong Czechoslovakian ally by the Munich surrender and now alone face to face with the German Army, was bringing heavy pressure on Britain to promise to fight alongside France if she were attacked, and in particular commit a British Expeditionary Force to the French Army's support. Such a policy of 'continental commitment' had always been anathema to Chamberlain. It took the panic rumour in January 1939 that Hitler was about to invade the Netherlands to induce Chamberlain and his Cabinet to reverse this strategic isolationism, and undertake to send an expeditionary force to France in the event of war. But this belated switch in grand strategy meant that the Royal Navy would now have the extra task of protecting the British Expeditionary Force's line of communication across the Channel; it meant that Britain became more deeply committed to resisting the German prong of the triple threat; even more strategically stretched and divided in purpose. For while the Navy still thought primarily in terms of fleet battles (and that could only mean the Japanese), the British Army now looked to a renewed Western Front, and the Royal Air Force to the air defence of the United Kingdom against the German bombers and its own bomber offensive against German cities.

Henceforward through the passing months of 1939 the sense of the imminent approach of war grew ever keener – the background and the spur to the Admiralty's own last-minute efforts to bring Britain's available naval strength up to combat readiness. On 15 March German troops occupied the rump of Czechoslovakia, so finally shattering Chamberlain's policy of appeasement. Panicked by rumours of a further German coup, this time against Romania, Chamberlain now issued 'guarantees' to Romania and Poland. In the Polish case Chamberlain committed Britain to going to war if ever Poland believed her independence to be threatened, so forfeiting Britain's freedom of military decision in regard to Germany. In April Fascist Italy invaded and occupied Albania, an alarming reminder of the Italian prong of the triple threat.

That same month Britain and France held high-level staff meetings in London in order to concert their operational war plans and evolve a common grand strategy. In May Italy and Germany signed the 'Pact of Steel', a formal military alliance. In June Japanese troops violated the British concession area at Tientsin in China, subjecting British citizens to brutal indignities; a sudden flare-up in the Japanese menace at the worst possible time, which evoked anxious recognition by the Admiralty and the Cabinet that Britain could not hope to find a fleet for the Far East as well as guard against the German and Italian Navies in the European threatre. And in August Hitler began fomenting a new crisis, this time over the League of Nations Free City of Danzig (today Gdansk) and the so-called Polish Corridor between West and East Prussia (taken from Germany by the 1919 peace settlement), certain that Chamberlain would give way again, just as he had at Munich.

Meanwhile the Admiralty had been month by month hastening on its final preparation for war. Early in 1939 it sought to overcome a shortage of junior executive officers by forming a list of some 3,000 supplementary reserves with nautical experience (such as amateur yachtsmen). These, together with the peacetime Volunteer Reserves and later the 'Hostilities Only' officers formed 'the Wavy Navy' (so called from the undulating gold rings on their sleeves), who were to serve with such professionalism during the Second World War, even rising to command their own ships or submarines. The regular long-service establishment of the Navy was enlarged from 119,000 to 178,000.[83] In the spring the Admiralty brought the Operational Intelligence Centre (OIC), with its interlinked Surface Ship Plot and Submarine Tracking Room, to a state of war readiness.[84] An operational handbook for 'Defensively Equipped Merchant Ships', together with instructions on signalling, was issued to the Merchant Navy. Measures were finalised for introducing war-risks insurance (as in the Great War) and for placing the entire British merchant fleet under Admiralty control. That March new *Fleet Tactical Instructions* and *Fighting Instructions* were also issued, both documents still laying emphasis on the manoeuvring of battlefleets of up to a dozen capital ships.[85] The *Fighting Instructions* struck a note of true Jutland-style rigidity: 'Prior to deployment, the Admiral will control the movements of the battle fleet as a whole. He will dispose the guides of divisions on a line of bearing at right angles to the bearing of the enemy battle fleet . . .'

But no equivalent instructions had been drafted for convoy operations; a notable omission. On 26 May 15,000 reservists were called up in order to bring the Reserve Fleet (composed of older warships) to a state of readiness by 15 June.[86] In June a special section of the Trade Division of the naval staff was created to carry out the task of installing defensive armaments in all the 5,500 vessels (3,000 of them ocean-going) of the Merchant Navy.[87] That same month a commander from the Plans Division was sent to Washington for talks with Admiral Leahy, the American Chief of Naval Operations, and his Director of Plans about possible cooperation in the Far East and Pacific. As was the case with the earlier talks in 1938, no firm commitments resulted. Nevertheless the meetings marked a further modest step from the Anglo-American naval rivalry of the 1920s towards the close and cordial alliance of the 1940s.

In August, as the crisis over Danzig and the Polish Corridor erupted, the Admiralty set in motion the last detailed arrangements for bringing the Navy to full war readiness. Between 15 and 21 August joint Navy and RAF exercises were held to test Coastal Command's operational plans, and when they ended most of the RAF squadrons moved to their war stations. Almost immediately Coastal Command began flying reconnaissance patrols to monitor German warship, submarine and merchant ship movements. On 26 August the Admiralty assumed control of all British merchant shipping. On the last day of August, with the Polish crisis now at exploding point and the German Army massed and poised along the Polish frontier, all the ships of the Home Fleet reached their war stations.

That same day Admiral Sir Charles Forbes, flying his flag in HMS *Nelson*, sailed from Scapa Flow with the Home Fleet (four capital ships, one carrier, two cruisers and ten destroyers: a small fraction of the fleet Sir John Jellicoe had commanded in 1914) in order to patrol the waters between the Shetland Isles and Norway – Germany's only maritime access to the world. On 1 September 1939, as the panzer divisions squealed and clattered their way into Poland and the howling Stukas dive-bombed all who moved on Polish roads, be they soldiers or old women or young children, the Admiralty sent warning telegrams to the Navy naming Germany and Italy as potential enemies, and ordered the general mobilisation of naval reserves.

At 1117 on 3 September, seventeen minutes after the British ultimatum to Germany to withdraw her troops from Poland had expired without reply from the German government, the Admiralty despatched a 'Special Telegram' marked MOST IMMEDIATE to all His Majesty's ships:

'TOTAL GERMANY repetition TOTAL GERMANY.'[88]

The Royal Navy was once more at war – in such fighting strength and against such potential odds as had been bequeathed by the policies of successive British governments over the previous twenty years.

3

'Winston Is Back'

At 1800 hours in the evening of England's first day of the Second World War, Winston Churchill entered the red-brick Georgian Admiralty building in Whitehall to take up once again the post of First Lord of the Admiralty which he had occupied with such dynamic impact from 1911 to 1915. In anticipation of Churchill's early arrival, the Admiralty had already signalled the Navy: 'Winston is back.' The Prime Minister, Neville Chamberlain, had offered Churchill his old post and invited him to join the War Cabinet only a few hours after Chamberlain's own toneless radio announcement to the British people that Britain was at war with Germany. Now, with the ultimate failure of his stubborn effort to avert war by placating Hitler, Chamberlain sought to lend a semblance of fighting spirit to his Cabinet by asking the arch critic of his policy of appeasement to accept office under him.

For Churchill himself his return held a curious Rip-van-Winkle-like quality:

> So it was that I came again to the room I had quitted in pain and sorrow almost exactly a quarter of a century before, when Lord Fisher's resignation [as First Sea Lord] had led to my removal from my post as First Lord and ruined irretrievably, as it proved, the important conception of forcing the Dardanelles. A few feet behind me, as I sat in my old chair, was the wooden map-case I had had fixed in 1911, and inside it still remained the chart of the North Sea on which each day, in order to focus attention on the supreme objective, I made the Naval Intelligence Branch record the movements and disposition of the German High Seas Fleet. Since 1911 more than a quarter of a century had passed, and still mortal peril threatened us at the hands of the same nation . . .[1]

Later that evening he presided over his first meeting of the Admiralty Board, sitting in the familiar high-backed dark leather and mahogany First Lord's chair at the head of the broad table, a portrait of Nelson watching him from the opposite wall of the floridly carved eighteenth-century room. Here in this same room, his predecessor Lord Barham and his colleagues, bewigged beneath the coffered ceiling, had plotted the strategy that defeated the landlubber Bonaparte's naval combinations in 1804–5 and led to the annihilating victory of Trafalgar and that long British naval mastery which, since 1918, the internationalists, disarmers and economisers (including Churchill himself when Chancellor of the Exchequer) had whittled away. For Churchill, with his sense of history as a continuing drama, to sit again in that chair in that room marked a deeply emotional moment – as was evident to the admirals looking along the table at their new chief. The then Third Sea Lord wrote later:

> To a few words of welcome from the First Sea Lord he replied by saying what a privilege and honour it was to be again in that chair, that there were many difficulties ahead but together we would overcome them. He surveyed critically each one of us in turn and then, adding that he would see us all personally later on, he adjourned the meeting. 'Gentlemen,' he said, 'to your tasks and duties.'[2]

Presently the First Sea Lord, Admiral of the Fleet Sir Dudley Pound, came to see Churchill in his room. At this first meeting each eyed the other, according to Churchill, 'amicably if doubtfully'.[3] And wary might Pound well be, for Churchill's previous tenure of the Admiralty had bequeathed a memory of a restlessly interfering First Lord who liked to order in detail the deployment of fleets and the manoeuvres of ships and squadrons; who was prone to urge irresistibly on his colleagues grand but unsound strategic visions, such as the calamitous attempt in 1914 to hold Antwerp against the German Army by means of a hastily thrown together Royal Navy landing force, or the later and even more calamitous attempt in 1915 to force the Dardanelles Straits and reach Constantinople, capital of Germany's ally Turkey, firstly by means of sending battleships up the narrow and mine-infested channel between hills bristling with shore batteries, and then by means of an improvised expeditionary force lacking proper landing ships and craft. But on Churchill's part there was also reason for wariness at this first official encounter with Pound, for his previous First Sea Lord in 1914–15, Admiral of the Fleet Lord Fisher, had fought him over the conduct of the Dardanelles campaign with a cumulative violence and bitterness that passed the bounds of the pathological. The quarrel had culminated in Fisher's furiously abrupt resignation in May 1915, which precipitated the fall of Asquith's Liberal government, and Churchill's own traumatic loss of office.

However, the admiral who now limped in on a stick to see him was no Fisher, no near genius blazing with energy and self-will and driven by visions of a technological revolution in sea warfare. Pound's big-nosed features were homely, rugged, undistinguished; those of a countryman in from the plough or the forge – or a sailor from a windjammer home from the sea. The voice was deep, enhancing the impression of ruggedness; the manner slow and steady. And appearance did not mislead, for this was a man whom his contemporaries judged a plodding second-rater, with a mind untroubled by large strategic visions. A simple man and solidly middle-class, he did not belong to that brilliant, even flashy, political-cum-social world which was Churchill's milieu – as it had also been Fisher's and Beatty's. One colleague, for example, noted Pound's 'simplicity of soul and desire for affection'[4]; another that while Pound enjoyed 'an orderly and logical mind' he was 'not perhaps a man of great imagination or insight',[5] while a third was to recollect: 'Old Pound, splendid chap as he was, did not engender confidence. We felt rightly or wrongly he never had any very abiding convictions as to the proper and correct strategical deployment and use of naval forces.'[6]

Nevertheless, he was, according to the same colleague, 'the personification of loyalty';[7] and loyalty to the extent of dog-like devotion was what from that day forth Dudley Pound, the plain and simple sailor, gave to Winston Churchill the heroic leader. Here then was exactly the naval instrument for which Churchill would have wished: a Berthier to his Napoleon. For straight away Churchill laid his own grasp on the tiller of British seapower – no mere political head presiding over a service department, but a supreme naval commander running the entire complex of strategy and operations through Pound as his executive Chief of Staff or even sometimes directly. That first night of war Churchill, elated at his release from the impotence of his 'wilderness years' as a mere back-bencher, worked on into the small hours; next morning he issued the first of a never-ending torrent of urgent enquiries and instructions, each of them embodying his restless will to action. These missives were to be nicknamed 'the first lord's prayers', because so many began with the formula 'Pray inform me . . .' or 'Pray why has . . . not been done?' He had indeed much the same sharpening effect on the Admiralty, the naval staff and the Navy at large as a new and ruthlessly exacting captain on a ship's company.

'From the very first day,' remembered the then Deputy Director of the Trade Division of the naval staff, 'even I in my subordinate situation became aware of this presence and I amongst others began to receive little notes signed W.S.C. from the private office demanding weekly reports of progress direct to him . . . It was like a stone thrown into a pond, the ripples got out in all directions, galvanising people at all levels to "press on" – and they did.'[8]

Mercifully the worst strategic horrors imagined in pre-war Admiralty and Chiefs of Staff appreciations had so far failed to come about. Japan remained neutral, her army not only deeply embroiled in the war with China but also having suffered a stinging defeat in Mongolia in June 1939 at the hands of a Soviet army under General Georgi Zhukov. A war of conquest against the European empires in the Pacific and South-East Asia was at present far from the Japanese government's mind. To the British naval staff the Imperial Japanese Navy therefore remained a potential menace rather than an immediate threat likely at any moment to demand the deployment of the British main fleet in the Far East. Italy, the central prong of the triple threat, likewise remained neutral, Mussolini's 'Pact of Steel' with Hitler turning out for the time being to resemble a pact of well boiled spaghetti. For Italy was once again waiting to rush to the aid of the victor, as a French diplomat had put it in 1915 when Italy belatedly entered the Great War on the side of the Allies. But if Italy ever went to war the British and French fleets in the Mediterranean together should have no difficulty in dealing with her navy. The Italian Navy was at present outnumbered by two battleships to three British and five French, and seven 8-inch gun cruisers to three British and six French. Only in 6-inch gun cruisers and destroyers did the Italians enjoy a modest superiority in surface ships, of eleven cruisers to three British and four French, and 61 destroyers to a combined Allied total of 57. In submarines the Italians' superiority was greater – 105 to 65.[9]

And the German Navy, the one active enemy at sea, remained in 1939 far short of the formidable threat it had constituted in 1914, or *would* have constituted if the war had begun in 1944, the date to which, at Hitler's behest, the German naval construction programme had been geared. Admiral Erich Raeder, Commander-in-Chief of the German Navy, had been aiming in his 'Z Plan' eventually to create a fleet of thirteen fast battleships, 33 cruisers, four aircraft carriers, some 250 U-boats and a swarm of big destroyers – all of them modern ships to the best specifications German technology could contrive.

Raeder intended that the surface ships should not operate as a single body like the Imperial High Seas Fleet, the strategic failure of which in the Great War was now plain, but in the form of task forces ranging the Atlantic to destroy the shipping that alone made it possible for Britain to wage war. A Royal Navy so much smaller in all classes of vessels than in 1914 and with a relatively small proportion of new or modernised battleships (even when current building plans had been completed) would have been hard put indeed to cope with such an offensive even if Italy and Japan had remained neutral.

Fortunately Hitler's diplomatic miscalculations over Poland plunged the German Navy into a war for which it was relatively even less ready at the time than the Royal Navy. Its heavy ships numbered only the two fast battleships *Scharnhorst* and *Gneisenau* (31,800 tons displacement; nine 11-inch guns; 32 knots); the three 'pocket' battleships (*Panzerschiff*): *Deutschland* (renamed *Lützow* in November 1939), *Admiral Graf Spee* and *Admiral Scheer* (all 12,100 tons displacement; six 11-inch guns; 26 knots); and two ancient battleships, the *Schlesien* and *Schleswig-Holstein*, obsolete even before the Great War. Otherwise it consisted of five cruisers (including the 8-inch gun heavy cruiser *Admiral Hipper*), seventeen destroyers and 56 U-boats, of which but 35 were immediately operational, and only 21 suitable for service in the Atlantic.[10] Captain Karl Dönitz, in 1939 the *Führer der U-boote*, bitterly condemned the neglect of U-boat construction in 1937–39 in favour of surface ships. 'Seldom indeed,' he was to write in his *Memoirs*, 'has any branch of the armed forces of a country gone to war so poorly equipped. It could, in fact, do no more than subject the enemy to a few odd pin-pricks. And pin-pricks are no means with which to try and force a great empire and one of the foremost maritime powers in the world to sue for peace.'[11] And yet even in that first autumn of the war the Royal Navy was to discover how deep and painful a local wound could be inflicted by such a 'pin-prick'.

German maritime aviation in September 1939 was in little better state than the U-boat arm. No aircraft carrier having yet been completed, all aircraft except for a few reconnaissance aircraft catapulted from battleships were land-based: 120 of them at North Sea bases and 108 at Baltic ones. The majority were the slow Heinkel 115 twin-engined general purpose/torpedo-bomber floatplane (186 mph; range 1,740 miles). In addition the Luftwaffe had earmarked six *Gruppen* of Heinkel 111 bombers for mine-laying and attacks on shipping.[12] The German Navy therefore offered no such formidable and concentrated air threat to surface warships as did the Imperial Japanese Navy's superbly practised and equipped carrier arm.

On a mere count of ships and aircraft, therefore, the Royal Navy at the outbreak of war appeared to enjoy an overwhelming superiority over its single current enemy, and this was so even after allowing for such imperial diversions as deploying a fleet of three battleships, a carrier and six cruisers in the Mediterranean to watch the Italians, and a carrier (the old *Eagle*) and four cruisers on the China Station. The Home Fleet at Scapa Flow in the Orkneys alone comprised five battleships (*Nelson*, *Rodney*, *Royal Oak*, *Royal Sovereign* and *Ramillies*); two battlecruisers (*Hood* and *Repulse*); two carriers (*Ark Royal* and *Furious*); fifteen cruisers and an anti-aircraft cruiser; seven destroyers; and twenty-one submarines. The Humber Force numbered two cruisers and nine destroyers; the Channel Force two battleships (*Resolution* and *Revenge*), two carriers (*Courageous* and *Hermes*), two cruisers and an anti-aircraft cruiser and five destroyers. In addition there were eighteen destroyers based on Plymouth, ten on Portsmouth, nine on Dover, six on Portland and eight on Rosyth and Milford Haven. All this amounted to an apparently formidable total with which to hold the ring in the North Sea, block the exits to the Atlantic, and defend home waters. Moreover North Atlantic Command and South Atlantic Command added another ten cruisers (eight of them in the South Atlantic) and thirteen destroyers to the forces available to defend the trade routes.[13] Further distant still were stationed four cruisers (including His Majesty's Australian Ship *Perth*) on the American and West Indies Station, and three more cruisers on the East Indies Station. And the dominions also made their modest contribution to the Empire's global naval strength: four cruisers in the Royal Australian Navy (apart from *Perth*) and five destroyers; two cruisers in the New Zealand Division of the Royal Navy; six destroyers in the Royal Canadian Navy.[14] The French Navy too, even though its main effort lay in the Mediterranean, contributed powerful extra support in the North Atlantic in the shape of its '*Force de Raid*' of two modern fast battleships (*Dunkerque* and the *Strasbourg*), a carrier, three cruisers and ten destroyers (one of them a 2,500 tonner).[15]

Yet when the comparative modernity of British and German ships is taken into consideration, and with it comparative speeds and fighting strength, the British margin of superiority becomes much more slender. Of Admiral Sir Charles Forbes's heavy ships in the Home Fleet (the very core of British seapower), only two, *Hood* and *Renown*, were both fast enough and powerful enough to catch and fight the *Scharnhorst* and the *Gneisenau*, or even the three 'pocket battleships'. *Nelson* and *Rodney* with their 16-inch guns (though dating from 1927, the Royal Navy's most modern capital ships) could not steam faster

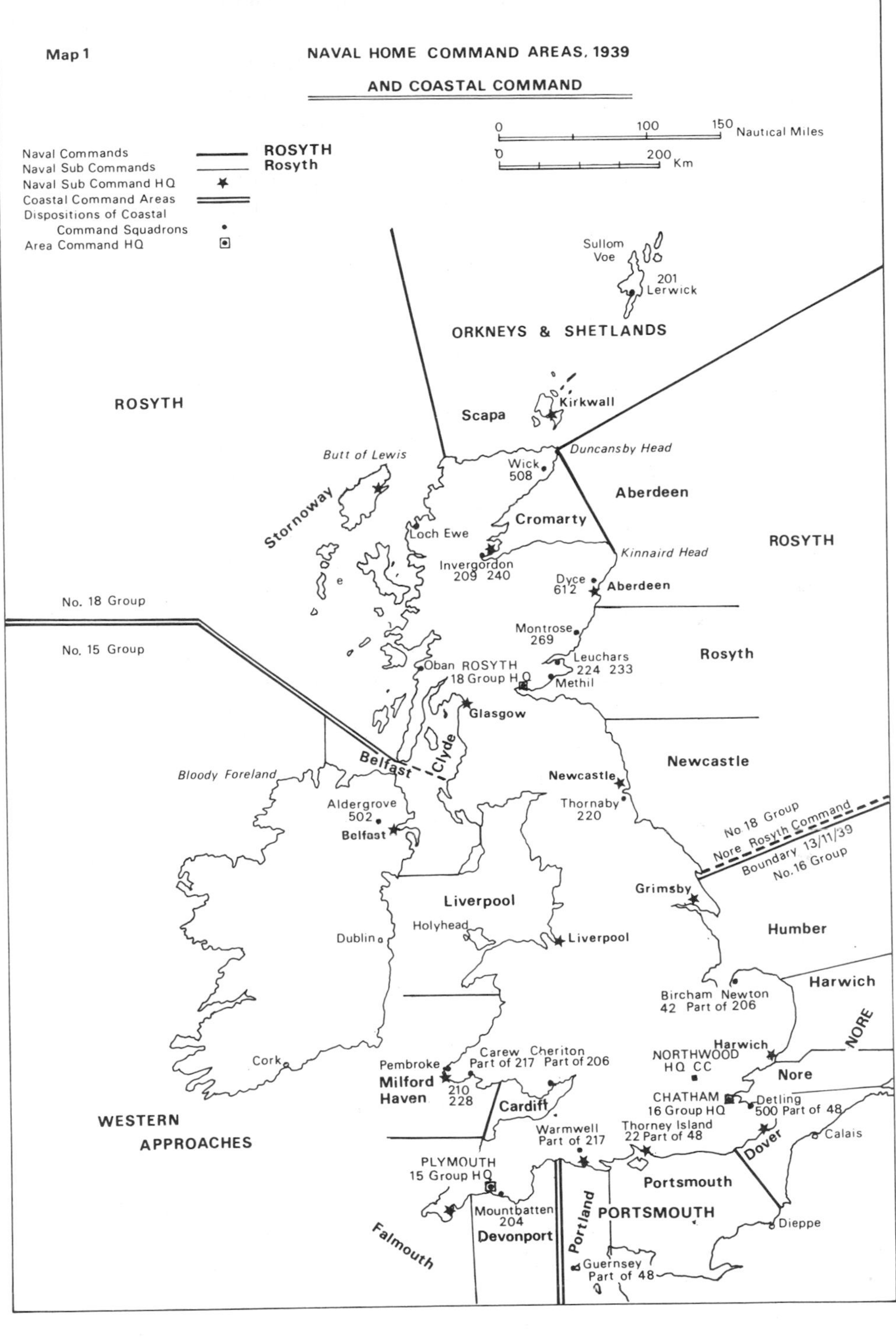

Map 1
NAVAL HOME COMMAND AREAS, 1939
AND COASTAL COMMAND
0
100
150
Nautical Miles
0
200
Km
Naval Commands
Naval Sub Commands
Naval Sub Command HQ
Coastal Command Areas
Dispositions of Coastal Command Squadrons
Area Command HQ
ROSYTH
Rosyth
Sullom Voe
201
Lerwick
ORKNEYS & SHETLANDS
ROSYTH
Scapa
Kirkwall
Duncansby Head
Butt of Lewis
Wick
508
Aberdeen
Stornoway
Cromarty
Loch Ewe
Kinnaird Head
ROSYTH
Invergordon
209 240
Dyce
612
Aberdeen
No. 18 Group
No. 15 Group
Montrose
269
Leuchars
224 233
Rosyth
Oban ROSYTH
18 Group HQ
Methil
Glasgow
Belfast
Clyde
Newcastle
Bloody Foreland
Newcastle
Thornaby
220
Aldergrove
502
Belfast
No 18 Group
Nore Rosyth Command
Boundary 13/11/39
No.16 Group
Liverpool
Grimsby
Holyhead
Dublin
Liverpool
Humber
Harwich
Bircham Newton
42 Part of 206
NORE
Harwich
Cork
Carew Cheriton
Part of 217 Part of 206
NORTHWOOD
HQ CC
Pembroke
Milford Haven
210
228
Nore
CHATHAM
16 Group HQ
Detling
500 Part of 48
Cardiff
WESTERN APPROACHES
Warmwell
Part of 217
Thorney Island
22 Part of 48
Calais
Dover
PLYMOUTH
15 Group HQ
Portsmouth
Mountbatten
204
Devonport
Portland
PORTSMOUTH
Dieppe
Falmouth
Guernsey
Part of 48

than 23 knots, as against the German battleships' 32 knots. The remaining British 'R' class battleships were unmodernised and vulnerable veterans of the Great War, incapable of making more than 21 knots. And, of course, the *Hood*, though fast as well as being the biggest warship in the world, was herself a virtually unaltered floating museum of 1920 naval technology. In cruisers, those workhorses of patrolling and trade protection, the Royal Navy was desperately weak, given the vast sweeps of water to be covered – and given too that the enemy could pick his own time and place to launch a sortie. As a consequence the Navy was soon to find itself compelled to supplement the cruisers on its patrol line covering the exits from the North Sea to the Atlantic with 'armed merchant cruisers', bulky, unarmoured and vulnerable liners newly equipped with 6-inch guns. Destroyers for fleet and convoy work, humble escort vessels such as sloops and corvettes, were likewise desperately scarce, minesweepers too; and these shortages would continue until the first of twenty new Hunt class escorts were delivered in the second half of 1940, and fourteen new minesweepers (ten of them the improved Bangor class) from the end of 1940 onwards.[16]

In maritime aviation Britain was still ill-prepared either to defend its own battle squadrons and merchant shipping against enemy air and U-boat attack, or to counter-attack the German Navy on or beneath the surface. Of the 60 Fleet Air Arm aircraft embarked in the Home Fleet's sole modern carrier *Ark Royal*, 42 were obsolete though rugged and versatile Swordfish biplanes, fifteen the disappointing and already obsolete Skua, and three of the equally disappointing Roc. The Channel Force carriers *Courageous* and *Hermes* embarked together another 45 Swordfish. The Mediterranean Fleet's carrier *Glorious* was in little better case, with twelve Sea Gladiator biplane fighters (a type already obsolete as a land fighter) and 24 Swordfish, plus a further twelve Swordfish based ashore at Dekeila in Egypt. On the China Station the *Eagle*'s complement, at eighteen Swordfish, was a mere gesture towards maritime airpower.[17] Nor could Royal Air Force Coastal Command make up for the Fleet Air Arm's deficiencies, for in September 1939 its aircraft too were few and out-of-date. Its workhorse was still the Avro Anson, with a range of only 510 miles, endurance of four and a half hours, a cruising speed of 114 knots and a tiny bomb load of two 100-pounders. As early as November 1937 the Air Staff had wanted a replacement but here again the aircraft industry let the armed services down, for neither the Bristol Beaufort nor the Blackburn Botha torpedo-bombers were to reach the squadrons before 1940; and the Botha was to prove in the event another complete operational failure.[18] Because of these production delays, 250 Lockheed B14s (named by the RAF the 'Hudson') had therefore to be ordered from America, but by the outbreak of war only one squadron had been equipped with them. The Hudson enjoyed almost double the Anson's range, five times the bombload, and could fly faster and for longer. In the meantime two Coastal Command squadrons were still flying the 1928 Vickers Vildebeest! The position with regard to flying boats for long-distance sea surveillance was even worse: the new Saro Lerwick had proved another of the British aircraft industry's fiascoes, and only two squadrons had so far been equipped with the Short Sunderland, one of its successes.[19] Here Britain had again to resort to American technology, and order the Consolidated PBY-5 flying boat (to be known to the RAF as the 'Catalina'), in service with the United States Navy since 1936; however deliveries to Britain were not expected until 1941.[20]

It was therefore an ironic enough comment on these weaknesses in maritime aviation and on the related obsession of the RAF with the idea of a bomber offensive against enemy cities that the very first British air operations in the Second World War took the form of Bomber Command attacks on the German naval bases at Wilhelmshaven and Brunsbüttel. Fifteen Blenheims set out for Wilhelmshaven on 4 September; ten of them found the target through thick cloud, but only one hit an enemy vessel, the pocket battleship *Admiral Scheer*, the bombs bouncing harmlessly off the armoured deck into the water. The only actual damage to the enemy was caused by a Blenheim crashing on to the fo'c'sle of the training cruiser *Emden*. Of fourteen Wellingtons despatched to Brunsbüttel the majority turned back or failed to locate their objectives due to bad weather, the only damage inflicted here being to the sides of the dock.[21] A squadron of British warships in the North Sea at the last moment averted an attack on them by a section of three Wellingtons by belatedly making the Royal Navy's recognition signal for the day. The operations of 4 September cost the RAF seven out of 29 aircraft.[22] All in all, as John Terraine points out in *The Right of the Line*, it proved a sharp first lesson for the RAF in the harsh school of war in terms of all-weather navigation and target acquisition.[23]

Yet for the Royal Navy too the opening phase of the conflict – in fact, the whole period of Churchill's tenure of the Admiralty – was to prove a time of painful learning; but in the Navy's case, often of relearning old lessons forgotten or disdained since the Great War. For Churchill himself it was to be a time also for reinventing old strategic follies in new guises, but with no happier results than in 1914–15.

The first of the lessons had not been slow in coming. At 2100 on 3 September 1939 the outward-bound liner *Athenia*, 13,581 tons, was torpedoed and sunk some 250 miles north-west of Ireland by the U-30, with the loss of 112 lives, including 28 American. It was this event that next day prompted Churchill's first 'prayer' in office, demanding from the Director of Naval Intelligence 'a statement of the German U-boat forces, actual and prospective, for the next few months . . .'[24] The news of the sinking evoked in the public memory the torpedoing of the Cunard liner *Lusitania* by a U-boat in 1915, also with the loss of American lives; and the British press treated the incident as a timely reminder of unchanged German frightfulness. In fact, the commander of the U-30, Lieutenant F.J. Lemp, had breached Hitler's strict orders to wage submarine warfare according to the Hague Convention in order not to embitter Britain and France against the peace moves he meant to make once Poland was crushed. Only by stages did Hitler relax restrictions on U-boat operations until by mid-November 1939 all ships, including liners, could be attacked without warning if 'clearly identified as hostile', while neutral shipping was warned not to enter a designated war zone eastwards of Longitude 20° West, that of Iceland.[25]

By this time, however, the reintroduction of the convoy system had robbed the U-boat of such prey as the *Athenia*, ships sailing singly out of peacetime into war. The very first convoy, of eight ships, actually left Gibraltar for Cape Town on the day before Britain declared war. From 6 September shipping along the East Coast between the Thames and the Firth of Forth was organised into convoy. Next day outward bound ocean convoys began, sailing on alternate days from Southend and Liverpool. They were escorted only as far as Longitude 12° West, just west of Ireland, and two days after losing their escort the convoys dispersed into individual sailings. Southward bound ships from both these alternate convoys were re-formed off the Scilly Islands into new convoys for Gibraltar, escorts from which picked them up west of the Straits of Gibraltar. The first homeward-bound convoy sailed from Freetown, Sierra Leone, on 14 September; next day there followed the first from Kingston, Jamaica. On 16 September convoy HXF1 steamed away from Halifax, Nova Scotia; the first of all the long procession of Halifax convoys that were to sustain the British war effort in the next five and a half years with North American weapons, aircraft, machine tools and food despite all the hazards of tempest,

U-boat, surface raider and marauding German aircraft. Convoys between Bergen in Norway and Methil in the Firth of Forth began to operate in the first week of November 1939, a week or so before the U-boats were finally freed to sink at sight.[26]

The routines of the escorts' war established themselves. At Defence (Cruising) Stations men could go below to eat and sleep in closed-up mess decks crammed with bodies, kit and hammocks; the bulkheads running with condensation, the air thick with human exhalations. At Action Stations at guns and depth-charge launchers on decks often swept with spray or during long watches on equally open bridges, cold and tiredness were kept at bay with snatched meals ('Action Messing') of the ubiquitous Navy pea soup and corned beef 'wedgies' (or 'sarnies': sandwiches), or mugs of 'kye' (or 'ky' or 'ki'), the thick cocoa drink made from crumbled slabs of unsweetened chocolate mixed with condensed milk – the high spot of a night watch. Down below, engine-room and boiler-room staffs sweated in their deafening, oil-stinking ovens; sonar operators sat in their cubby-holes, earphones clamped to head, intent to catch the echo rebounding from the hull of a U-boat submerged in ambush.

Yet the operational lesson apparently taught by the opening phase of the struggle with the U-boat was misleading, for it seemed to confirm the complacent pre-war Admiralty appreciation that the convoy system plus improved sonar had neutralised the menace, even though it was known that the enemy at present had only a few boats at sea. In September, a month when many ships were still sailing independently, the Allies lost 41 ships (153,879 tons). In October the total fell to 27 ships (134,807 tons); in November 21 ships (51,589 tons); in December it rose modestly to 25 ships (80,881 tons). These were totals far short of the horrific 881,000 tons lost in April 1917 alone; and in any case only twelve of the 114 ships lost had been sunk in convoy.[27] And meanwhile German shipping had been once again swept from the seas by British seapower. Of the individual vessels which tried to sneak home to Germany after the outbreak of war no fewer than seventeen were intercepted by the Royal Navy between 7 September 1939 and 4 January 1940.[28] This renewed ring of blockade was completed by the establishment of contraband control over neutral shipping. The Navy's Northern Patrol, watching the seas between south of the Faeroes to Iceland, intercepted and sent into port for search (mostly Kirkwall, the main contraband control base) over 300 neutral ships in the first four months of the war.[29]

Blockade rated as a major factor in the Allied grand strategy for eventually bringing down Nazi Germany, for economic warfare experts in Whitehall believed that the German economy was already stretched to the limit, and therefore vulnerable either to shortages of key raw materials or to strategic bombing of vital industrial plants. Yet the economists miscalculated; Germany was still operating an almost peacetime economy, with immense potential for industrial mobilisation. Moreover, the Russo-German Pact of August 1939 gave Germany general access to Soviet oil, coal and wheat; and Hitler's pre-war development of 'Autarky' (economic self-sufficiency) had successfully put German technological genius to work on inventing substitutes for such imported raw materials as rubber. In the Second World War Germany was not to be the economic prisoner shut up by blockade in Central Europe and progressively starved which she had been during much of the Great War. In fact, contrary to the prevailing assumption among Whitehall planners in 1939, Germany was far better placed economically to last out a long war than Britain herself, despite Britain's vaunted access by sea to the resources of the world. For by the outbreak of the war Britain was, as the Treasury warned, already within a year or so of running out of foreign exchange with which to buy those resources.[30]

Whatever might be the hopes for the eventual slow strangulation of Germany by blockade, it was all too immediately apparent that British seapower could do nothing to succour Poland in her brief, lone and desperate fight against the German armies converging deep and fast into her heartland. From the first day of the war Admiral Sir Charles Forbes took the Home Fleet on repeated offensive 'sweeps' across the North Sea, but netted nothing; vain gestures with silent guns in the mists and rain. Here to be learned afresh was an old lesson that dated back through the Great War and the conflict with Bonaparte to the struggle against Philip II's Spain under Elizabeth I – that seapower alone is impotent in relation to the outcome of a decisive land campaign on the continent of Europe.

It was exactly this galling impotence – together with the apparently only passive defence against the U-boat offered by escorted convoys – which stirred Churchill's restlessly aggressive mind to look for means by which the Royal Navy could directly strike at Germany and her armed forces. Only two days after his return to the Admiralty, he was urging the formation of 'Units of Search', consisting of one cruiser and one aircraft carrier, to seek and find surface raiders such as pocket battleships. He also favoured hunting groups to range the seas after U-boats, his views here chiming with a strong school in the Admiralty itself which included Pound. But during the very next week following Churchill's memorandum to the First Sea Lord advocating 'Units of

Search', the enemy wrote his own lethal comments on this 'offensive' concept. The Admiralty had temporarily detached the Home Fleet carrier *Ark Royal* and the Channel Force carrier *Courageous* with small destroyer escorts as two hunting groups against U-boats in the Western Approaches. On 14 September the *Ark Royal* was attacked by the U-39 west of the Hebrides, but fortunately the torpedoes exploded prematurely – at this period German magnetic pistols for detonating torpedoes were unreliable; a failure in German technology – and the *Ark*'s escorting destroyers promptly sank the U-boat. Although the encounter thus ended well, the Royal Navy came very close to losing its single modern carrier.

But only three days later the U-29 (Lieutenant-Commander Schuhart) sighted the *Courageous* (Captain W. T. Mackaig-Jones) in the Bristol Channel escorted by only two destroyers, two others having been sent to the aid of an attacked merchant ship. Thanks to 'Horchdienst' ('listening service') intercepts of British radio traffic and B-Dienst's ability to read the Admiralty cypher, the U-boat command was well aware that *Courageous* was cruising in this sea area. At 1950 (British time) Schuhart fired three torpedoes at the huge bulk of the 22,500-ton carrier at a range of less than 3,000 yards. Two of them struck home, and within fifteen minutes *Courageous* sank with the loss of 518 lives, including her captain. In that single brief encounter and in the course of a relatively minor mission Britain had lost one-sixth of her strength in large carriers; a grievous and needless waste of assets.[31] This marked the abrupt end of the Navy's employment of fleet carriers as submarine hunters. The sinking reminded Churchill himself, with his ever-present memories of the previous war, of the day almost exactly 25 years ago when the U-9 sank three old British cruisers in quick succession off the Dutch coast, and demonstrated for the first time the submarine's true potential as a free-ranging predator.[32]

On 26 September *Ark Royal* again came perilously near destruction – this time at the hands of the Luftwaffe; a new lesson for the Royal Navy to learn, if it were willing to do so. The *Ark Royal* was at the time serving as part of a task force including capital ships, sent to the Heligoland Bight to cover the escape on the surface of a damaged British submarine, *Spearfish*. It was a bright morning, beginning with a sunrise like, wrote an eyewitness, 'a luxurious fan spread from horizon to horizon'.[33] Since *Ark Royal* had no radar, warning of imminent air attack depended on lookouts with binoculars. At 1100 shadowing aircraft were seen low on the horizon. By this time *Ark Royal*'s Swordfish aircraft were already on distant patrol. Skua fighters were flown, and one shot down a Dornier flying boat; so far, so good. But then began the first air attack in history on a fleet at sea, striking suddenly out of high clouds. As the *Ark Royal*'s anti-aircraft guns opened fire, and the great ship heeled as she steamed at full speed under full starboard helm, a Heinkel 111 bomber dived on her from 5,000 feet, releasing a 1,000-kilo bomb at 1,500 feet. The bomb exploded in the water only twenty feet from the port bow.

'It was so close,' wrote the *Ark Royal*'s gunnery officer, Lieutenant-Commander T. V. Briggs, 'that the whole ship reared up and heeled several degrees to starboard. We thought we had been hit.'[34] So did the German pilot; and German propaganda broadcasts, claiming that the *Ark* had been sunk, mockingly asked the Admiralty: 'Where is the *Ark Royal*?' Wrote Briggs later, 'This was a superb and bravely executed attack against fierce A.A. fire.' It was followed by low level attacks against the fleet, although only HMS *Hood* received any damage at all: '. . . one could see through binoculars that a great flake of armour had been knocked off her side plating, where a bomb had hit it and it glanced off into the sea'.[35] But the Admiralty only drew from this novel experience the lulling lesson that the danger of air attack on a fleet had been much exaggerated.[36]

Only a month after the U-29 torpedoed the *Courageous*, another of Dönitz's U-boats gave a fresh and even more sensational demonstration of the Royal Navy's continued vulnerability to underwater attack, sonar notwithstanding, and also taught again another of the old lessons unlearned by government and Navy after the Great War: in this case, the importance of secure fleet bases. In the small hours of 14 October 1939 – a clear but moonless night sky brightly flared by the northern lights – the U-47 (Lieutenant-Commander Prien) slid on the surface into the Home Fleet main base of Scapa Flow via Kirk Sound, the eastern gap between the Orkneys mainland and the island of Lamb Holm. Riding the top of high water, Prien successfully crept through the very narrow channel between the sunken blockships across the Sound and the mainland; an operation to prickle the neck, not least when the U-boat's hull scraped the bottom and ran her bows into the cable of a blockship. Once through into the wide waters of the Flow Prien sighted (as he thought) two battleships alongside the north shore: in fact, the battleship *Royal Oak* (27,500 tons) and the old seaplane carrier *Pegasus*. At 0058 on 15 October he fired three torpedoes at the *Royal Oak*; only one hit home and that was so far up in the bows as to cause little damage. On board *Royal Oak* the Captain (Captain W. G. Benn, RN) and some of his officers who went forward to investigate concluded that it must have been some minor internal explosion.

Meanwhile Prien, with exemplary coolness of nerve, turned away to reload, then attacked again at 0116. This time all three torpedoes struck, and the *Royal Oak*, one of Britain's only eleven operational capital ships, capsized thirteen minutes later with the loss of 833 members of her company including Rear-Admiral H. E. C. Blagrove (commanding Second Battle Squadron). While British vessels frantically depth-charged the Flow behind him, Prien took U-47 out of the narrow passage past the blockships against a 10-knot current. The whole operation had been carefully planned by Dönitz, the *Führer der U-boote*, on the basis of a complete set of aerial photographs of the British base taken by the Luftwaffe, which had revealed the gap past the blockships exploited by Prien.[37]

When Churchill was brought the news of the sinking, recalled an eyewitness, 'tears sprang to his eyes and he muttered, "Poor fellows, trapped in those black depths." '[38] Yet he had other reasons for strong emotion over the loss of the *Royal Oak*. For only a month earlier, and within a fortnight of taking office, he had travelled to Scapa Flow to visit the Home Fleet and confer with Admiral Forbes. Here he had learned at first hand that, just as at the beginning of the Great War in 1914, Scapa Flow (Britain's main fleet base in conflicts with Germany) was so deficient in defences as to render it unsafe for the fleet to use it as a haven; truly an old lesson now to be painfully relearned. All the elaborate boom and net defences against submarines, all the shore defences and batteries erected during the Great War had been demolished in the years of 'peace' and economy that followed; and never restored. The anti-submarine defences at the outbreak of the Second World War consisted only of a single line of nets across the main entrance of Hoxa, Switha and Hoy, while the eastern entrances (including the one used by U-47) were only partially blocked by what remained of the 1914–18 blockships and a few extra recently placed hulks. Of three more blockships despatched since the war began to close these eastern channels, two had been sunk en route, and a third arrived the day after the *Royal Oak* was lost.

Nor was Scapa better defended against the new threat of bomber attack, for it was equipped with one temporary radar station, only eight obsolete 4.5-inch anti-aircraft guns, and altogether lacked short-range anti-aircraft batteries. A letter from Forbes to the Admiralty on 5 September had explained just why Scapa was so ill-prepared. In the first place – and this was, of course, Chamberlain and the final gasps of appeasement – the government had instructed even in 1939 that nothing must be done which would indicate to the British public and press or Germany that the Royal Navy was preparing for war against Germany. Secondly, there was a lack of local labour to carry out various works, while outside labour could not easily be brought in because of shortage of accommodation. And finally there were the hiatuses caused by deaths of the Controller of the Navy (Vice-Admiral Sir R. G. H. Henderson), in May 1939 and the then First Sea Lord (Backhouse) in July.[39] As a result of Scapa's vulnerability Admiral Forbes was compelled to rotate his fleet between Loch Ewe, the Clyde and Rosyth when not at sea hunting German warships (as he in fact was when the U-47 sank the *Royal Oak*).

Three days after the *Royal Oak* went down it was the Luftwaffe's turn with two squadrons of Junkers 88 twin-engined bombers to test the defences of the Home Fleet's main base, but they found the Flow empty now except for the Great War veteran battleship *Iron Duke* (once Jellicoe's flagship), now used as a base ship and floating coastal defence battery. The German bombers damaged her so badly below the water line with a near miss as to compel beaching her in shallow water. One Junkers was shot down by anti-aircraft fire. The base's fighter defence, obsolete Fleet Air Arm aircraft, was too slow to intercept the 280 mph Ju 88s. This raid came the day after attacks in similar strength on warships in the Firth of Forth, slightly damaging the cruiser *Southampton* (mercifully a bomb passed through her without exploding) and a destroyer. The Forth lay within the air cover provided by the modern aircraft of Fighter Command, which shot down two of the Junkers. The Luftwaffe's raids on British naval bases had therefore so far proved hardly more successful than Bomber Command's on German.

Nonetheless, as Churchill now wrote to Pound, the Home Fleet had been 'driven out of Scapa through pre-war neglect of its defences against air and U-boat attack'.[40] So began fresh and urgent discussions to resolve the problem of this outcast fleet. On 31 October Churchill, Pound and the Deputy Chief of the Air Staff (Air Vice-Marshal R. E. C. Peirse) visited Forbes in his flagship, then moored in the Clyde. All agreed that Loch Ewe, being even more undefended than Scapa though some 130 miles more distant from German bases, exposed the Fleet to great danger. The Admiralty opinion favoured basing the Fleet in the Clyde but Forbes strongly urged that this was too remote (200 miles south of Loch Ewe) to enable him to intercept German sorties into the Atlantic via the Iceland–Faeroes gap. Rosyth was ruled out because the narrow single channel through the Firth of Forth would facilitate enemy air or U-boat attack. Forbes finally convinced Churchill that Scapa Flow was still strategically the right place for the Fleet's base, and that its defences should therefore be put in order as an utmost priority. The conference thereupon agreed to do the work that ought to have been done in peacetime: extra booms, nets and blockships for the eastern channel into the Flow, minefields, electric indicator loops on the seabed to detect the passage of hostile vessels, more patrol craft, coastal defence batteries to cover every approach, 88 heavy and 40 light anti-aircraft guns, searchlights, balloon barrages, an extra radar station. Two squadrons of modern monoplane fighters would be stationed in the North of Scotland to provide air cover, with a further four squadrons available to meet heavy attack. But all the new base installations would take four to five months to complete. In the meantime the Home Fleet would have to continue resorting to its temporary and hazardous anchorages on the west coast of Scotland, hundreds of miles further distant than Scapa from the key strategic areas of the Norwegian and North Seas.[41]

Now a further tragic instalment in sailors' lives was about to be paid for pre-war political folly and neglect – in this case, the Labour government's insistence in 1930 on accepting the 'starvation number' of 50 cruisers in the London Naval Treaty negotiations, despite the pleas of the then First Sea Lord, Admiral of the Fleet Sir Frederick Field; a number only increased to 58 (including eight dominion ships) by the outbreak of war. At 1551 on 23 November 1939 – rain showers but otherwise good visibility; wind north-north-west, Force 5, sea rising – the armed merchant cruiser *Rawalpindi* (16,700 tons; Captain E. C. Kennedy, RN) on the Northern Patrol between the Faeroes and Iceland sighted a German fast battleship (classed by the Royal Navy as a 'battlecruiser') four miles to westwards; and reported the sighting to Admiral Forbes, C-in-C, Home Fleet, in the Clyde. Shortly afterwards Kennedy signalled that the enemy ship was actually a pocket battleship, the *Deutschland*. In fact his first identification had been the correct one: for he had seen the *Scharnhorst*, which was steaming on a course 300° in company with her sister ship *Gneisenau* on their first joint sortie of the war.

Kennedy, with four elderly 6-inch guns mounted in his high-sided, unarmoured and highly vulnerable vessel, was therefore confronting a combined broadside of eighteen radar-directed 11-inch guns. Even the odds which Kennedy believed he was facing were heavy enough – six 11-inch and eight 5.9-inch guns mounted in a well armoured warship. It was now to fall to Kennedy to be the first commander of a King's ship in the Second World War to demonstrate instinctive obedience to the spirit of Nelson's final flag signal at Trafalgar: 'Engage the enemy more closely!'

Gneisenau and *Scharnhorst* had sailed from Wilhelmshaven on 21 November, Vice-Admiral Wilhelm Marschall (Flag Officer in Command) flying his flag in the *Gneisenau*. His operation order laid down the purpose of the sortie:

> In accordance with the directive of the C-in-C Navy on the threatening of the N. Atlantic shipping routes and the consequent diversion and concentration of the enemy forces attainable by it, I intend to break through into the area Iceland–Faeroes. From this position to advance towards the suspected enemy patrol lines, to feint a break-through with the battleships into the N. Atlantic by steering a westerly course, and finally by sheering off to the North and by use of the long nights, to make home waters again at high speed.[42]

Neither German ship glimpsed any British aircraft during their run northwards to the Norwegian coast and then north-westwards into the Iceland–Faeroes gap on 21–23 November; an indication of Coastal Command's poverty of resources for long-range sea surveillance. It was the *Scharnhorst*, on *Gneisenau*'s starboard beam, which at 1507 (British time) on 23 November spotted the *Rawalpindi* to starboard, reporting accordingly to the flagship. After an exchange of VHF radio signals between the two German ships, the *Scharnhorst*, on Vice-Admiral Marschall's command, changed course from 300° to 000° and increased speed from 18 to 24 knots in order to investigate the strange merchant ship; 'a large ship,' according to *Scharnhorst*'s radio report, 'two masts, one funnel.' At 1532, at a range of 21,000 yards, 'after ascertaining from the foretop that this was a vessel of considerable size and considering it possible from her constant alteration of course that she was an auxiliary cruiser', recorded Captain Kurt Hoffman later in *Scharnhorst*'s log, 'I ordered "Action Stations!"' A minute later, as his ship's company tumbled to Action Stations to the blare of klaxons, Hoffman signalled Marschall: 'Large merchant vessel. Course approximately 180°. Vessel turning away. I am closing her.' At 1535, course 060°, position 63°48′N, 11°40′W, *Scharnhorst* signalled *Rawalpindi*: 'To British merchant cruiser – Heave to. Do not use radio. Where from and where bound?' Then in English: 'What ship? Do not use your wireless.' The *Rawalpindi* replied that she had understood, but instead of compliantly heaving to, she altered course further to the south-east and increased speed. At 1539 *Scharnhorst*'s main batteries reported ready for action. *Rawalpindi* now bore 055°, range about 17,000 yards and shortening. By 1555, with the November dusk already beginning to dim the light, the range was down to under 9,000 yards. Seven minutes later, as *Rawalpindi*'s crew began dumping smoke floats overboard, Captain Hoffman ordered a warning shot to be fired across her bows. One minute later, as more smoke floats were dropped, and it being 'now beyond a doubt that the vessel was a merchant cruiser', he immediately gave orders to open fire.

At 1604 *Scharnhorst*'s radar-directed guns fired their first salvo at a range of about 8,250 yards, the 11-inch shells soon smashing through the *Rawalpindi*'s thin plating and setting her ablaze. At 1607 the British ship returned the fire, probably inflicting at this time the one hit suffered by *Scharnhorst*, a 6-inch shell on the quarter deck which failed to penetrate the armour. While *Scharnhorst*'s guns pounded the *Rawalpindi*'s unarmoured bulk, the British ship's salvoes were falling some 100 yards astern of her enemy. At 1610 Kennedy and his crew enjoyed a brief respite because the *Rawalpindi* was momentarily screened by smoke, mist and shell splashes, but next minute the *Gneisenau* joined in too. By now the *Rawalpindi* was burning fiercely amidships. Yet her guns were still in action, their fall of shot now some 400 yards on *Scharnhorst*'s port side. At 1614 hours *Scharnhorst* turned away to starboard because of false reports of approaching torpedo tracks. At 1617 the German ships ceased fire. The action had lasted barely ten minutes.

The November afternoon had now thickened into deep dusk under a bright moon, so that the flames from the doomed *Rawalpindi* were the more luridly visible from the German ships. At 1630 there was an explosion on board. Fifteen minutes later the German ships began looking for and picking up survivors in boats. Between 1715 and 1735, as the *Rawalpindi* was riven by further explosions, came her repeated last signal: 'Please send boats.' She remained afloat until 1920, when after two more explosions the flames that had marked her position were engulfed by darkness. Kennedy and 270 members of his ship's company perished; 38 survived, 27 of those being picked up by their adversaries.

In the meantime there had occurred a further encounter in the dusk and rain squalls. At 1814 hours, *Gneisenau* sighted a strange vessel some six and a half miles distant, and Vice-Admiral Marschall ordered his ships to cease picking up survivors and steer to the eastward at high speed. Very soon *Scharnhorst*'s after range-finder and her foretop also reported what appeared to be a large warship astern showing no lights. The ship was in fact HMS *Newcastle*, which had almost simultaneously sighted the German ships. The *Newcastle*, nearest cruiser to the *Rawalpindi* in the Northern Patrol line, had steamed at utmost speed to her support as soon as she heard her initial signals that she was in the presence of the enemy. At 1815, according to her log, HMS *Newcastle* (9,500 tons; Captain J. Figgins) 'sighted darkened ship Brg [bearing] 070° 13000ˣ [yards]'.[43] Two minutes later she 'sighted 2nd darkened ship to Starbd of first'. Henceforward Admiral Forbes and the Admiralty knew that they had to deal with two German battleships. At 1822, with the enemy apparently closing, Captain Figgins turned the *Newcastle* away and reduced to 15 knots. At 1824 when visibility had dropped to two cables (about 400 yards) in rain squalls, the *Newcastle*, lacking radar like most British ships at this time, lost touch with the enemy. At 1833 Figgins adopted a course and speed 'as requisite to regain contact'. Twenty minutes later the *Rawalpindi* was sighted bearing 140° 'heavily on fire'. At 1859 the *Newcastle*'s log noted: 'Light reported brg 290° . . . increased speed to 25 to investigate . . .' But the light was not confirmed, and at 1917 the *Newcastle* altered back towards the *Rawalpindi* – just about the time the merchant cruiser finally sank. The German battleships, for their part, did not seek to attack and sink the unidentified British warship, being dissuaded – too easily? – by the poor visibility and the need to put about in order to engage. They slipped away at high speed behind a smoke screen and trailing curtains of rain. The German tactical retreat proved the prelude to strategic retirement. Vice-Admiral Marschall, knowing from Horchdienst radio intercepts that his presence had been reported by the *Rawalpindi* and that all available British forces would be hunting for him, now abandoned his plan of feinting into the North Atlantic, and instead began to follow a tortuous route home – no question here of 'Engage the enemy more closely', nor of the bold enterprise of such earlier corsairs against the Royal Navy as the Frenchman the Bailli de Suffren or the American John Paul Jones.

Nonetheless, Marschall had by now achieved one of the major objectives of his sortie, namely, 'the consequent diversion and concentration of the enemy forces'. For British seapower was like a tightly stretched web: pressure at one point pulled it and weakened it elsewhere. On receipt of *Rawalpindi*'s report of a pocket battleship in the Iceland–Faeroes gap Admiral Forbes ordered the Home Fleet, then in the Clyde, to raise steam as quickly as possible, while the Admiralty began to redeploy all Britain's naval strength in the North Atlantic and home waters in order to hunt down what was suspected to be the *Deutschland*. But these very counter-measures in turn show up item by item how scanty the Royal Navy's available resources, how inadequate its preparedness for war, were in relation to its commitments, even in the face of so limited a threat as the existing German Navy; and, in the present case, so limited an apparent threat as Marschall's sortie.

It was because of the defenceless state of Scapa that Forbes was temporarily based in the Clyde, which in turn meant that he required an extra 24 hours' steaming to reach the sea area for intercepting an enemy retirement. In any case, his own strength had been reduced by detachments and the loss of the *Royal Oak* to two battleships (*Nelson* and *Rodney*), the cruiser *Devonshire* and seven destroyers. He had no carrier with him, for the battleship *Warspite* was away escorting a Halifax-bound convoy, while the battlecruiser *Repulse* and the carrier *Furious* were already at Halifax, Nova Scotia, ready to cover a homeward-bound convoy; the *Hood* was in Plymouth. This dispersal of striking power to cover the Atlantic routes in the face of another threat (see below, pp. 78–80) had been inevitable in view of the Royal Navy's overall shortage of capital ships, carriers and cruisers.

Now the Admiralty sought in haste to reconcentrate its scattered strength in order to meet the German sortie (known from *Newcastle*'s reports to consist of two heavy ships). The *Warspite*, *Repulse* and *Furious*, together with cruisers at present spread out on patrol or escort duties, were all ordered to converge on a blocking position in the Denmark Strait, gateway to the Atlantic, while the *Hood* and the French battleship *Dunkerque* were also ordered to the same area from the south. But all this was exactly what Vice-Admiral Marschall and his C-in-C, Admiral Raeder, had hoped for; and what they now knew from Horchdienst intercepts and B-Dienst decrypts of Admiralty encyphered signals that they had successfully brought about.

Admiral Forbes's own hopes of getting between the supposed *Deutschland* and the other unidentified German warship sighted by *Newcastle* and their home base were to be spoilt by further British deficiencies. The Naval Intelligence Division, not having broken the German naval cyphers, could offer no such guidance to Forbes about Marschall's movements as German Intelligence was providing to Marschall about Forbes's. Having no carrier with him, Forbes could not carry out his own air search, while Coastal Command failed to locate the enemy amid the North Sea mists and cloud. On the contrary, it was German flying boats which reported the position of some of Forbes's ships, so helping Marschall to choose the best timing and courses for his evasive manoeuvres on the successful run home. Even the original departure of the *Scharnhorst* and *Gneisenau* from Wilhelmshaven without detection had been made the easier because Coastal Command lacked the appropriate aircraft and equipment to carry out regular reconnaissance or aerial photography of the German fleet bases.[44]

As it was, Forbes could only sweep the sea from a midway position between the Faeroes and Norway like a blind man waving a stick, while Marschall danced round him, making adroit use of the cover provided by bad weather and poor visibility to slip through the British cruiser screen and back to Wilhelmshaven, reached on 27 November.

But this was not the sum of Forbes's woes. Firstly, the *Rodney* had developed serious rudder defects and had to be sent back to port. Then, on 4 December, when Forbes, returning from his fruitless hunt for Marschall, took his fleet into Loch Ewe on a brief visit in order to refuel his destroyers, the hull of his flagship *Nelson* was severely damaged by a magnetic mine laid in the Loch by a U-boat. The *Nelson* was thus another important casualty of the Navy's lack of a secure base; and another triumph for the German Horchdienst or 'Y' Intelligence and cryptoanalysis, which had revealed the Home Fleet's supposedly top secret occasional use of Loch Ewe. *Nelson* was not to return to active service until August 1940. The total of fifteen capital ships allowed Britain under the Washington Treaty had now shrunk to nine actually available for sea: here was taught again the old lesson about the inevitability in war of attrition of numbers by enemy action, mechanical wear and tear, and the need for major refits. Moreover, the *Hood*, herself badly overdue for a refit, could only steam 25 knots – not fast enough to catch a German pocket battleship (26 knots) let alone a German battleship (32 knots). Not until the end of the year was Admiral Forbes (by then flying his flag in the *Warspite*) again to command a balanced fleet, *Rodney*, *Repulse* and the carrier *Furious* all having rejoined him.

Even as Forbes was returning to port at the beginning of December after his failure to intercept the *Scharnhorst* and *Gneisenau*, another hunt was already up for a German raider – this time far off in the South Atlantic.

On 21 and 23 August 1939, during the final diplomatic crisis over Danzig that led to the outbreak of war, the pocket battleships *Admiral Graf Spee* and *Deutschland* had sailed from Germany for their intended zones of operation – the *Graf Spee* in the South Atlantic and the *Deutschland* in the North Atlantic. Their simple strategic purpose was to strain British seapower to the uttermost by offering a constant but elusive threat to merchant shipping routes, as the German Naval Staff operation order of 4 August 1939 spelt out:

> Enemy naval forces, even if inferior in strength, are only to be attacked if this should be necessary to achieve the main objective. Frequent changes in the operational area will provoke uncertainty and delays in the sailing of enemy shipping, even if no material success is achieved. The temporary appearance of German warships in remote areas will add to the enemy's confusion.[45]

The two pocket battleships were only permitted by Hitler to commence operations on 26 September, after the failure of his 'peace' initiative in the wake of the crushing of Poland. On 1 October the Admiralty's suspicions that at least one raider was at large were confirmed when the crew of the merchant ship SS *Clement*, sunk by the *Graf Spee* off Pernambuco on 30 September (and her first victim), reached South America after being picked up by another vessel. Then on 21 October 1939 the crew of a sunk Norwegian ship, landing in the Orkneys after being rescued from their boats, reported that their ship had been destroyed by the *Deutschland* on 14 October some 400 miles to the east of Newfoundland. This alerted the Admiralty that two powerful raiders were at large in the Atlantic.

Its response to the sinking of the *Clement* was prompt and on the largest scale possible within straitened overall resources – just as the German naval staff had intended. From 5 October onwards and in collaboration with the French Navy no fewer than eight powerful hunting groups (in all comprising three aircraft carriers, three battleships and fifteen cruisers) were formed to deal with two German ships. Force F (the cruisers *Berwick* and *York*) covered the North American and the West Indies Station; Force G (the cruisers *Exeter* and *Cumberland*; joined later by the *Ajax* and *Achilles*) the eastern coast of South America; Force H (the cruisers *Sussex* and *Shropshire*) the Cape of Good Hope; Force I (the cruisers *Cornwall* and *Dorsetshire*, and the carrier *Eagle*) off Ceylon; Force K (*Ark Royal* and *Renown*) the area Pernambuco–Freetown; Force L (the battleship *Dunkerque*, the carrier *Béarn* and three 6-inch gun French cruisers) was based on Brest; Force M (two 8-inch gun French cruisers) on Dakar in French West Africa; and Force N (the battleship *Strasbourg* and the British carrier *Hermes*) the West Indies. As soon as the *Deutschland*'s presence at sea became known on 21 October, the cruisers of Force F were reallotted to escort work with Halifax convoys. To form these hunting groups ships had to be drained away from the Home Fleet (*Ark Royal* and *Renown*; hence Forbes's weakness a month later when chasing *Scharnhorst* and *Gneisenau*); the Channel (*Hermes*); the Mediterranean (*Sussex* and *Shropshire*); and China (*Cornwall*, *Dorsetshire* and *Eagle*).[46]

On top of all this, the Admiralty allotted three extra battleships (*Warspite*, *Resolution* and *Revenge*) and two extra cruisers (*Emerald* and *Enterprise*) to the escort of North Atlantic convoys; and moved the battleship *Malaya* and the carrier *Glorious* through the Suez Canal to the Indian Ocean.

It was a mark of Admiral of the Fleet Sir Dudley Pound's limited powers of strategic comprehension that he should have been puzzled as to the German objective in bringing about this dispersal of Allied naval strength; surely, he asked, the enemy should have desired to induce its concentration in the home waters where it would be exposed to attack by his powerful air force?[47] Churchill rather agreed: how, he asked in a memorandum to the First Sea Lord, Deputy Chief of Naval Staff and the Controller on 23 October 1939, could the enemy have 'foreseen the extent to which we should react on the rumour of the *Scheer* [in fact, the *Graf Spee*] in South Atlantic? It all seems quite purposeless; yet the Germans are not the people to do things without reason . . .'[48]

The scale of the Allied counter-measures against the two pocket battleships also offered a tribute to the innovative technical skill of the ships' designers. Although the ships were much more heavily armoured than a large cruiser, their main battery of six 11-inch guns in two triple turrets, together with a secondary armament of eight 5.9-inch guns, outgunned even big 8-inch gun cruisers, let alone Britain's light 6-inch gun cruisers. Their 54,000 brake horsepower diesel engines gave them full power at instant readiness, unlike orthodox steam-turbine ships, which required many hours to raise steam from cold, and even took time to work up from cruising speed to maximum speed. Diesel propulsion also gave the pocket battleship a radius of action of 10,000 miles at cruising speed, even without refuelling from their attendant supply ships – more than twice that of a steam-turbine-propelled heavy ship. A catapult seaplane and search radar enabled the pocket battleship to scan the seas for victims or enemy warships. On the basis of comparative specifications, therefore, Allied cruisers, though they could outsteam the pocket battleships' 26 knots, were too weak in main armament to fight them, while Britain's old battleships, at speeds of 21 to 23 knots, were too slow to catch them. Only the battlecruisers *Renown* and *Repulse* (*Hood* being in need of a refit) and the modern French battleships *Dunkerque* and *Strasbourg* (specifically built to deal with the German vessels) were both fast enough and sufficiently heavily gunned and armoured.

The *Deutschland* (Captain Paul Wenneker) in the North Atlantic strictly obeyed the German naval staff's order during the course of her two and a half month's cruise, sinking only two merchant ships and capturing (but later releasing at a Norwegian port) another, the American SS *City of Flint* – just enough to advertise her presence, keep the Admiralty sweating for the safety of its convoys, impose maximum strain on the Royal Navy in those waters, and especially weaken the Home Fleet. In the middle of November the *Deutschland* (soon to be renamed the *Lützow*, because it would hardly do if 'Germany' were ever to be sunk) slipped back home via the Denmark Straits between Greenland and Iceland. The *Admiral Graf Spee* (Captain Hans Langsdorff), however, continued to pose an ubiquitous threat to British merchant shipping, true to the tradition established in 1914 in the same southern oceans by the admiral after whom she was named. Once again Churchill, with his memories as First Lord in the Great War, was struck by the sense of history and a strategic dilemma repeating themselves:

> The disproportion between the strength of the enemy and the countermeasures forced upon us was vexatious. It recalled to me the anxious weeks before the action at Coronel and later at the Falklands in December 1914, when we had to be prepared at seven or eight different points, in the Pacific and South Atlantic, for the arrival of Admiral von Spee with the earlier edition of the *Scharnhorst* and *Gneisenau*. A quarter of a century had passed, but the puzzle remained the same.[49]

The puzzle was that of locating a tiny sliver of metal on a vast surface of water; a sliver always in secret, unpredictable motion. Sea-borne or land-based air search could do little to help, given Britain's exiguous air resources and mostly obsolete and short-ranged aircraft. Instead Forces G, H and K, under the operational command of the Commander-in-Chief, South Atlantic (Admiral G. H. d'Oyly Lyon), lurched blindly about the ocean, guided only by such radio reports as some of *Graf Spee*'s victims were able to transmit before being silenced. Captain Langsdorff, for his part, struck at points as unexpectedly far apart as he could contrive. After sinking the *Clement* off Pernambuco (Brazil) on 30 September, he steered eastwards for the still mostly unconvoyed shipping route off Africa between the Cape of Good Hope and Europe, sinking four ships between 5 and 10 October; then doubled back into the central wastes of the South Atlantic to destroy another merchant ship, the SS *Trevannion*, on 22 October, before ceasing operations and lying quiet for a period in order further to confuse the Royal Navy. Luck had, however, been with him, for the cruiser *Cumberland* had failed to pass on to Admiral Lyon a radio report from the *Graf Spee*'s victim of 5 October, the SS

Newton Beech, relayed on by another merchant ship, that she had been stopped by a pocket battleship. The *Cumberland*, observing radio silence, had wrongly assumed that the report would anyway have been passed to the British naval base at Freetown, Sierra Leone, which in fact it had not. Then again, on 9 October aircraft from the *Ark Royal* (on passage to Freetown) sighted a stopped merchant ship near the Cape Verde Islands – in fact, the *Altmark*, the *Graf Spee*'s supply ship. However, the *Altmark* successfully bluffed that she was the American SS *Delmar*. Vice-Admiral Wells (Vice-Admiral, Aircraft Carriers) in the *Ark Royal*, having no destroyers with him (another result of the Navy's shortage of ships), decided not to close with the alleged 'SS *Delmar*' in order to verify her identity.

After sinking the SS *Trevannion* on 22 October, Langsdorff had taken the *Graf Spee* eastwards round the Cape of Good Hope into the Indian Ocean, turning up off Mozambique on 15 November to sink a small tanker and next day stop a Dutch ship. He thereupon doubled back westwards into the central wastes of the South Atlantic; then eastwards again to attack the Cape-to-Europe shipping route once more, sinking the SS *Doric Star* on 2 December and the SS *Tairoa* the day after. Now he doubled back yet again, this time due west, sinking another ship in mid-Atlantic on 7 December. All this time Lyon's hunting groups had been clutching for Langsdorff and missing – Forces H and K south of the Cape of Good Hope, Forces M and N patrolling from Dakar; Force G spread between the Falklands, the River Plate and Rio de Janeiro.

Then at long last had come hard and relatively up-to-date intelligence, when a distress signal was received from the *Doric Star* in the middle of the South Atlantic on 2 December. Admiral Lyon immediately redeployed his hunting groups: Force H to protect the Cape shipping route in the area of St Helena; Force K to sweep north-westwards to 28° South, 15° West before steering for Freetown. But these sweeps, too, missed the *Graf Spee*, by now steaming clear to the westward. For all the technology of twentieth-century war, the Admiralty and British admirals at sea were just as much groping and guessing with regard to the *Graf Spee* as their predecessors of the age of sail in 1804–5 seeking Admiral Villeneuve's fleet after its escape from Toulon, when even Nelson guessed wrong and searched the eastern Mediterranean while Villeneuve was in fact heading for the West Indies.[50]

And it was successful guesswork, or professional intuition, of the traditional kind which now enabled Commodore Henry Harwood,

ɔove) 'All the ceremony of formal surrender.' miral Sir David Beatty, Commander-in-Chief of Grand Fleet, receives a German delegation in his ;ship HMS *Queen Elizabeth,* to negotiate the ɛrnment of the Imperial German High Seas Fleet, 15 vember 1918. Painting by Sir John Lavery. (IWM)

(Below) 'Her impressive size and beauty of line served to disguise the reality of an obsolete and vulnerable ship' – the battlecruiser HMS *Hood* (41,200 tons displacement), which was sunk by the *Bismarck* on 24 May 1941. (IWM)

(*Above*) British battleships in line ahead in peacetime – 'Before the Second World War . . . a future Jutland against the Japanese fleet in Far Eastern waters befogged the Royal Navy's thinking.' (IWM) *(Below, left)* Admiral Sir Charles Forbes – 'a sea officer of faultless manners and a deep sense of loyalty' – Commander-in-Chief, Home Fleet, 1938–40. (IWM) *(Below, right)* Admiral of the Fleet Sir Dudley Pound, First Sea Lord and Chief of Naval Staff, 1939–43. 'He ran the Navy as if he were the executive officer of a ship, endlessly prying into and arranging matters of detail.' (IWM)

'o fewer than eight powerful hunting groups were rmed to deal with two German ships. . . .' The Pocket attleship *Admiral Graf Spee (right),* six 11-inch guns, ided, with her sister ship *Deutschland,* Allied shipping September–December 1939. The *Graf Spee* was uttled off Montevideo on 17 December 1939 after eing attacked by the cruisers *Exeter, Ajax,* and *Achilles.* Hulton) *(Below)* 'Churchill laid his own grasp on the ler of British seapower' as First Lord of the Admiralty, 939–40, Prime Minister and Minister of Defence, 940–45. Here he is being cheered by the ship's company HMS *Exeter* in February 1940 when they returned to ymouth from the *Graf Spee* battle. (Hulton)

(Left) 'Nothing could have been more Nelsonian.' The German-occupied Norwegia port of Narvik after the attack, on 10 April 1940, by British destroyers under Captain Warburton-Lee, RN, later awarded the Victor Cross. (IWM) *(Below)* The harbour at Dunkir – 'that horrific landfall' – showing the moles from which the majority of the 338,000 Allied soldiers rescued during 'Operation Dynamo' were lifted. (IWM)

commanding Force G (flying his broad pendant in HMS *Ajax*; Captain C. H. L. Woodhouse), at last to solve the puzzle. Although the *Doric Star* had been sunk some 3,000 miles to the east of Harwood's present position off the estuary of the River Plate, Harwood reckoned that the enemy might now choose to attack the abundant merchant shipping clustering round the Plate and Rio de Janeiro – as Harwood had always believed he would do sooner or later. Harwood, calculating that the *Graf Spee* could reach Rio by 12 December and the area of the River Plate a day later, concentrated Force G accordingly. He ordered HMS *Exeter* (8,390 tons; six 8-inch guns; Captain F. S. Bell) up from Port Stanley in the Falklands, whence she had gone for repairs, to join *Ajax* (7,030 tons; eight 6-inch guns) and her sister ship the New Zealand manned *Achilles* (Captain W. E. Parry) at a rendezvous some 150 miles off the entrance to the River Plate by 0700 on 12 December.

With his squadron united, Harwood then steamed towards the position 32°S, 47°W, 'chosen from my Shipping Plot', wrote Harwood in his despatch, 'as being at that time the most congested part of the diverted shipping routes, i.e., the point where I estimated that a raider could do most damage to British shipping'.[51] Harwood – a well-jowled face beneath the uniform cap; tropical white jacket tight on a big-framed body verging on the portly – might have stepped from a Reynolds portrait of an eighteenth-century British sea officer; he certainly exemplified the fighting and tactical instincts of the best of them. At 1200 on 12 December 1939 he signalled his captains as to how he meant to fight the *Graf Spee* if and when they encountered her: 'My policy with three cruisers in company versus one pocket battleship, Attack at once by day or night. By day act as two units, 1st Division (AJAX and ACHILLES) and EXETER diverged to permit flank marking. First Division will concentrate gunfire. By night ships will normally remain in company in open order.'[52]

By thus attacking the *Graf Spee* from two sides Harwood hoped to divide the German fire, so giving his lighter ships the best chance of overcoming the longer range and heavier broadside of the *Graf Spee*'s six 11-inch guns.

At 0614 next day, 13 December 1939, with the squadron steering 14 knots on a course 060°, position 34° 34′S, 49° 17′W, the *Ajax* spotted a hazy line of smoke to the north-west, and Harwood ordered the *Exeter* to close and investigate. At 1616 the *Exeter* reported by signal lamp: 'I think it is a pocket battleship'; and almost simultaneously made the flag signal: 'Enemy in sight.'[53] Even as the alarm rattlers and bugles were sounding in the British ships for Action Stations, with many sailors tumbling straight out of their hammocks, the *Admiral Graf Spee* fired her first salvo.

Captain Langsdorff had chosen to head for the abundant prey off the River Plate even though on 4 December the German naval staff had given him – thanks again to 'Y' intercepts and decrypts of British signals – a broadly accurate picture of British dispositions in the South Atlantic, including information that *Ajax*, *Achilles*, *Exeter* and *Cumberland* (the latter in fact at the Falklands for repairs) were covering the South American coast. When *Graf Spee*'s search radar revealed the presence of ships to the south-west at about 0500 on 13 December, Langsdorff had altered course to investigate them – and so unwittingly helped Harwood to spring the trap tight shut. The *Graf Spee*'s reconnaissance aircraft being unserviceable, it was her lookouts which sighted the masts of the British squadron in the brilliance of a southern sunrise, at first reporting that it consisted of the *Exeter* and two destroyers. This information tempted Langsdorff to close on them in order to destroy so weak a force. Too late he realised that he was committed to battle with three cruisers. Now, using the immediate acceleration of his diesels, he steered for his enemy at 24 knots, hoping to engage before the steam-driven British ships could work up from cruising speed to full power.

It was a fine, clear sunny day, with a moderate south-easterly breeze and a slight sea. As the action opened, *Graf Spee* – a squatly piled silhouette dominated by the tall control tower typical of German naval architecture – was steering south-east, with the *Ajax* and *Achilles* steaming north-east to cross her bows and work round to her port beam, and the *Exeter* breaking away from her consorts north-westwards to engage the enemy to starboard; the British cruisers, in contrast to the *Graf Spee*, almost yacht-like in their low, racy lines. From the *Exeter*'s fore- and main-mastheads, yardarm and gaff streamed four Battle Ensigns, while the *Achilles* proudly flew the New Zealand flag from her mainmast. It was still to be flying after her White Ensign had been shot away.

From her very first salvo at a range of 19,000 yards, which threw up gouts of water round the *Exeter*, the *Graf Spee*'s gunnery (its ranging aided by the ship's radar) lived up to the exemplary standards of quick and sustained accuracy set by Hipper's battlecruisers at Jutland in 1916 and Vice-Admiral Graf Spee's own ships in the South Atlantic in 1914. With both her triple 11-inch turrets concentrating on the *Exeter*, her third salvo straddled the British ship, scoring one hit which wrecked the *Exeter*'s Walrus aircraft just when it was about to be catapulted as a gunnery spotter. At 0624, after the *Exeter* had fired eight 8-inch gun salvoes in return, the *Graf Spee* landed a direct hit on the *Exeter*'s 'B' turret, putting it out of action, a hail of shell splinters sweeping the bridge and wrecking the wheelhouse communications. Captain Woodhouse had thereafter to con the ship from the after steering position, and even then for a time only by a chain of messengers passing instructions. Nevertheless still steering to engage the enemy more closely, *Exeter* twice fired torpedoes but without success. Although the *Exeter* had been hitting the *Graf Spee* again and again, her 8-inch shells had neither disabled the German ship nor her main turrets. The *Ajax* and *Achilles*, closing the range from 19,000 yards to 13,000 and steaming at 28 knots to get across the *Graf Spee*'s bows, were also firing fast and accurately, but their 6-inch guns were even less able to inflict immediately critical damage. They themselves were coming under heavy fire from the German ship's secondary armament of 5.9-inch guns.

At about 0636, with the *Ajax* and *Achilles* now almost ahead of the *Graf Spee*, Langsdorff hauled round from an easterly course to the north-west and laid smoke. Now on a roughly parallel course to the *Exeter* instead of opposite, the *Graf Spee* continued to smash at Harwood's most powerful ship with relentless accuracy, until by 0650 the British cruiser was taking water forward, listing heavily to starboard, and reduced to only one of her four turrets. Telephone and radio communications alike were knocked out; fires were burning fiercely below decks; and yet still the *Exeter* steamed at full speed, still her remaining turret kept firing. Forty minutes later, however, water thrown up by a near miss by an 11-inch shell came flooding through a shell hole in the side and short-circuited the electricity supply to her remaining turret. Captain Bell was forced to break off the action and turn away to the south, his main anxiety now to keep his ship afloat.

This was Langsdorff's opportunity to follow and finish off the helpless *Exeter*. Instead he allowed himself to be distracted by the combined fire of the *Ajax* and *Achilles*, ordered by Harwood at 0710 'to close the range as rapidly as possible' in order to take the pressure off the *Exeter*.[54] At 0720 both ships 'turned to starboard to bring all guns to bear. Our shooting appeared to be very effective, and a fire was observed amidships in GRAF SPEE.'[55] Langsdorff, himself a torpedo specialist, took his heavy ship westwards with rapidly jinking alterations of course and smoke screens in order to avoid British torpedo attacks and throw off the British gun-layers. At 0725 the *Graf Spee* put the *Ajax*'s two after turrets out of action with a direct 11-inch shell hit, while at the same time her secondary armament of 5.9-inch guns scored two hits on the *Ajax*'s bridge. All this time the British cruisers were firing fast and accurately, although their 6-inch shells still could only inflict superficial damage to the *Graf Spee*'s structure and equipment. By 0738, with the range down to 8,000 yards, Langsdorff was on the verge of finally crushing his remaining opponents; and Harwood was having to accept that his bid to defeat a pocket battleship with three cruisers had for the moment failed. As he wrote in his despatch:

> At this time I received a report that AJAX had only 20 per cent of ammunition left and had only three guns in action, as one of the hoists had failed in 'B' turret and 'X' and 'Y' turrets were both out of action.
>
> GRAF SPEE's shooting was still very accurate and she did not appear to have suffered much damage.
>
> I therefore decided to break off the day action and try and close in again after dark. Accordingly at 0740 AJAX and ACHILLES turned away to the east under cover of smoke.[56]

One of the *Graf Spee*'s last salvoes brought down the *Ajax*'s main topmast: it fell, said an eyewitness, in true Trafalgar-like style.

This was again a time for Langsdorff to 'engage the enemy more closely', with every chance of destroying Harwood's two light cruisers. But, just as earlier when the *Exeter* had seemed at his mercy, he failed to do so, continuing to steer away westwards, instead of going about in order to attack. Even when Harwood turned his ships again to follow the *Graf Spee* at a range of 19,000 yards, *Achilles* on her starboard quarter, and *Ajax* on her port, Langsdorff kept to his course westwards, content to fire the occasional salvo to warn his British shadowers to keep their distance. To fail successively in this way to finish off the crippled *Exeter* and now two heavily outgunned light cruisers, one of them damaged, displays a fatal want of judgment on Langsdorff's part, or perhaps of professional nerve, although his personal courage is not in doubt. More inglorious still, he had decided – without consultation with his senior officers – to seek refuge in the neutral Uruguayan port of Montevideo on the north side of the estuary of the River Plate, slipping in without a pilot in the dark towards midnight.

Why did Langsdorff take these un-Nelsonian decisions, so much in contrast with Harwood's resolute attack with inferior forces? According to his own battle report to Berlin signalled from Montevideo on 15 December:

> After EXETER has moved off, light cruisers move off to a great distance and remain to the NE and SE. To break out to open sea and shake off these two cruisers is obviously impossible.
>
> Inspection of direct damage reveals that all galleys except for the Admiral's galley have been badly damaged. Water entering flour store endangers bread supply while a direct hit on the forecastle makes ship unseaworthy for North Atlantic in winter. One shell pierced armour belt while the armoured deck is torn in one place. Damage in after part of the ship . . . As ship cannot be made seaworthy for breakthrough to the homeland with means on board, decided to go into the River Plate at risk of being shut in there.[57]

It was a tribute to the shooting of the lighter British ships that they had succeeded in inflicting this amount of damage – damage sufficient to destroy Langsdorff's will to fight, if not immediately to disable his ship. However a more personal factor may have contributed to Langsdorff's loss of will, according to later testimony by several of his officers. Already over-strained by more than two months of lone operations under constant threat of detection and destruction by the Royal Navy, Langsdorff had suffered two flesh wounds and had also been knocked temporarily unconscious during the action with Harwood. Did he abandon an encounter more than half won and make for Montevideo because his powers of decision and judgment had been enfeebled by shock?[58] What is certainly true is that Harwood had embarked on the action having expected it and having decided how he meant to fight it, whereas Langsdorff stumbled into it, and thereafter played it by ear: decisions made in haste amid the racket of battle, the fall of shot, the temporary obscuring of the bright day by his own and enemy smoke screens; amid the need to order frequent changes of course to dodge British shell fire and torpedoes. Yet it is hard not to think that Langsdorff's and Harwood's contrasting fighting decisions were instinctively guided by their national maritime heritages. Behind Harwood stood four centuries of victory in close quarters attack; behind Langsdorff a naval tradition barely forty years old, and, with brief and rare exceptions, one of raiding and evading and ultimately of defeat.

Far off in London the First Lord of the Admiralty had excitedly watched every move in the hunt for the *Graf Spee* from his map room in the red-brick Admiralty building overlooking the gravel sweep of Horse Guards parade; a spectator on a distant touchline eager to tell his team how to win. On the basis of radio reports via America at six hours' delay, wrote an eyewitness:

> . . . Winston was most anxious to send telegrams to Harwood about the dispositions of the three cruisers off the River Plate, and various other instructions. Pound insisted that Harwood should be allowed to deploy his ships as the situation demanded, and that information from the Admiralty should be confined to the reinforcements being sent, oil tankers, repair facilities, etc . . .[59]

Now it was time for the crews of the *Graf Spee* in the Plate and for Harwood's ships still at sea to tackle the grim aftermath of battle: to try to patch up men and metal alike torn and ripped or scorched by fire; to wrap the dead in canvas for burial. It was time too for the opposing commanders to decide on the future courses of action. Harwood, for his part, knew that for the next twenty-four hours he would have to meet a sortie by the *Graf Spee* with only *Achilles* and the damaged *Ajax*. The crippled *Exeter* was limping away to the Falklands for emergency repairs; her replacement, the *Cumberland* (ordered up from Port Stanley by Harwood at 0946 on 13 December) would not arrive before the evening of the 14th. The Admiralty had signalled the *Ark Royal*, *Renown* and the cruiser *Neptune* to fuel at Rio and then to steam at once for the Plate. Yet this overwhelming strength could not be in place until noon on 19 December. The conclusion was plain. 'I requested His Britannic Majesty's Minister, Montevideo,' wrote Harwood in his despatch, 'to use every possible means of delaying GRAF SPEE's sailing, in order to gain time for reinforcements to reach me . . .'[60]

For Langsdorff, suddenly removed from the anonymity of the ocean spaces and placed under the glare of world publicity, his damaged ship offshore the object of the curiosity of the crowds of Montevideo citizens, the dilemma was very different. No powerful warships were ever coming to his rescue; safe return of the *Graf Spee* depended on himself and his ship's company, and the seaworthiness and battleworthiness of his ship. Partly on the advice of his engineers, partly in order to give time for U-boats at least to reach the area, Langsdorff asked the German ambassador to obtain permission from Uruguay for the *Graf Spee* to remain in Montevideo for fourteen days – later 30 days – in order to effect essential repairs. Thus both the British and German commanders and their countries' ambassadors were seeking the same objective – to delay the *Graf Spee*'s sailing. In the event the Uruguayan government gave Langsdorff 72 hours only.

In order to dissuade Langsdorff from making an early sortie, the British government now released false information that the *Ark Royal* and *Renown* had already left Rio and were approaching the Plate. This 'disinformation' was apparently confirmed when two officers in the *Graf Spee* separately reported that they had 'seen' a carrier and a battlecruiser in the estuary. Writhing mentally in the trap of his own making, Langsdorff decided that to seek battle would lead to the certain loss of his ship and the pointless sacrifice of his crew. In Berlin Grand Admiral Raeder, the C-in-C of the German Navy, and Hitler both agreed that it was out of the question to accept internment of the *Graf Spee* by Uruguay. An attempt to seek sanctuary in the Argentinian capital and port of Buenos Aires was ruled out. This left only one alternative, discussed by Langsdorff with his officers: to scuttle the ship outside Uruguayan territorial waters. Raeder and Hitler left the final decision to Langsdorff.[61]

At 1815 on 17 December 1939, the *Graf Spee*, with a skeleton crew, weighed anchor and moved slowly away into the estuary. At 1936 her white, black and red swastika ensign was hauled down. Twenty minutes later the *Graf Spee*'s structure was shattered by a series of carefully placed explosions, and, reeking flame and smoke, she settled on a sandbank. HMSs *Ark Royal* and *Renown* were still 1,000 miles distant. Three days later Langsdorff, wrapping himself in the Imperial German ensign, shot himself in the temple, because, as he wrote in a final letter, 'I alone bear the responsibility for scuttling the Panzerschiff ADMIRAL GRAF SPEE. I am happy to pay with my life to prevent any possible reflection on the honour of the flag.'[62] In the fate of the ship and her captain there was, therefore, more than a hint of Germanic *Götterdämmerung*; an echo of the hauling down of the Imperial ensign in the High Seas Fleet in November 1918 and the scuttling of that fleet in 1919; an echo too of the final destruction of Admiral Graf Spee himself and his ships at the Battle of the Falklands in 1914.

In the Admiralty there was justified jubilation. After two and a half months of fruitless steaming and the loss of two great ships, the Royal Navy had been rewarded with a triumph in traditional style; to be celebrated in due time by march pasts and civic receptions when Harwood's ships returned to England and New Zealand early in the New Year. The task forces mobilised from the Navy's already stretched resources to deal with *Graf Spee* and *Lützow* could be redeployed now that the first major threat to British sea communications of the war had been overcome.

But already German technology had been posing a fresh threat – the magnetic mine – and compelling the Royal Navy to relearn another forgotten lesson.

After the outbreak of war both the Royal and the German Navies began to lay barrages of orthodox contact mines as in the Great War. The principal German minefield ran some 80 miles north from the Friesian Islands to the latitude of Jutland in order to protect the North Sea naval bases from a direct British approach, while the Admiralty attempted to protect Britain's east coast shipping by declaring a mined area between the Tyne and Humber, later extended to the whole east coast between the Pentland Firth and Essex. But in fact no mines were laid until 1940. The old Dover barrage of 1914–18, barring the Straits of Dover to U-boats attempting the direct passage from their bases to the Atlantic, was re-created during the first month of war – two successive barriers of shallow and deep-laid mines, comprising nearly 7,000 in all, with a double system of electric indicator loops on the seabed between them to reveal the passage of U-boats. After three U-boats were destroyed in the new Dover barrage in October, Dönitz abandoned the attempt to use this direct route, and his captains now had to make the long passage round the north of Scotland to their hunting areas, so drastically reducing their operational range.

From the first week of the war, however, Germany embarked on a campaign of offensive minelaying – ambushes beneath the sea off Britain's own ports, coasts and naval bases. Most of these were of orthodox contact mines, of which the German Navy had over 20,000 in stock. One such minelaying operation, off the Tyne, by five destroyers covered by the cruisers *Leipzig*, *Nürnberg* and *Köln*, on 12–13 December gave the British submarine service the opportunity for its biggest success so far in the war. The *Salmon* (Lieutenant-Commander E. O. B. Bickford), which had already sunk the U-36 with torpedoes, attacked the German squadron on its homeward voyage in the Heligoland Bight at dawn on the 14th, damaging *Nürnberg* and *Leipzig* so severely that they were out of action until May and December 1940 respectively – a serious reduction in Germany's slender strength in cruisers during what was to be a decisive campaigning year at sea. Nonetheless, the German minelaying campaign in British waters, quite apart from causing vast disruption to coastal traffic, was to lead to the loss of 79 merchant ships, totalling 262,697 tons, in the first four months of the war.

As early as 16 September the damaging of the SS *City of Paris* by an underwater explosion confirmed Admiralty fears that the enemy was also using magnetic mines – that is, mines laid on the seabed and exploded by the influence of a ship's magnetic field on the mine's electro-magnetic detonating mechanism. In the shallow waters of the Continental Shelf round the British Isles, such seabed explosions could seriously damage or sink a ship. It was such a mine laid five weeks earlier by a U-boat which on 4 December had put the battleship HMS *Nelson* out of action for nearly a year. On 21 November the back of the new 10,000-ton cruiser *Belfast* was broken in the Firth of Forth by another one, compelling her virtual reconstruction later in the dockyard. In December Captain Lord Louis Mountbatten's ship, the destroyer *Kelly*, had her stern blown off.

By now the Luftwaffe had joined in, dropping magnetic mines by night into such vital and constricted sea areas as the Thames Estuary. For the Admiralty the problem lay not in the quantity of magnetic mines to be swept – in fact only 470 were laid in the first three months of the war, while Germany's total stock on the outbreak of war came to more than 1,500 – but in that at present no technical means existed either to neutralise ships' magnetic fields, or to sweep magnetic mines. The disruption to British shipping was therefore out of all proportion to the number of mines. In November only two out of three deep-water channels in and out of the Port of London through the Thames Estuary remained open, and it was feared for a time that Britain's largest port might be closed altogether. In November the problem came before the War Cabinet itself, which considered it so serious as perhaps to constitute Hitler's vaunted 'secret weapon'.[63]

Yet the magnetic mine was no novelty. The Royal Navy itself had laid an early type off Zeebrugge and the mouth of the River Scheldt in 1918; and had its own design ready for production in 1939, a pilot order being given in July. As the First Sea Lord wrote on 24 October 1939 to Admiral Sir Andrew Cunningham, the C-in-C, Mediterranean Fleet: 'It is really the limit that after knowing about magnetic mines since the last war, no practical method of dealing with them had been evolved.'[64] Meanwhile the Germans themselves had conducted trials with a magnetic sweeping device as early as summer 1938, although it was not fitted operationally until October 1939.[65] In fact the Admiralty had carried out some research in the 1930s, but it had yielded no practicable results: another consequence of the rivalries and overlaps between the various research establishments.[66] Now emergency development of counter-measures was confided to the Electro-Magnetic Group at the Admiralty Research Laboratory. Its work was vitally assisted when on 25 November a complete unexploded magnetic mine was recovered intact from the mudflats off Shoeburyness and taken apart by Lieutenant-Commander J. G. D. Ouvry with exemplary skill and courage, so revealing its precise electro-magnetic principles.

The Admiralty Research Laboratory found the eventual answer to the magnetic mine in installing 'de-gaussing' coils (named after the nineteenth-century German mathematician, K. F. Gauss, an outstanding scientist in the field of electro-magnetism) round the hulls of ships in order to render them magnetically neutral. But the conversion of more than 3,000 vessels in the Royal Navy and the Merchant Marine imposed colossal demands on the cable manufacturers and the shipyards, and the work could only proceed slowly. For the moment, as the German naval staff gleefully recognised at the end of October 1939, the Royal Navy was unable to sweep these mines. By January 1940, the Germans embarked with high hopes on mass production of mines, with a target of 48,000 contact mines and 21,500 magnetic by March 1942[67] – by which time the British would have completed their de-gaussing programme.

The truth was that with regard to the magnetic mine the German naval staff had committed the classic military blunder of prematurely introducing a potentially decisive weapon at a time when only small quantities were as yet available. As 1939 turned to 1940 it was not British counter-measures that led to the waning of the threat, therefore, but exhaustion of the small German stocks of this kind of mine.[68]

The first three months of the war at sea had thus resembled the initial circling of two wrestlers – their tentative attempts to get a hold – before they close in a grapple for victory with all powers stretched to the limit. The German Navy, however, had succeeded in causing disruption to British seaborne trade and stretching the Royal Navy's resources out of all proportion to the relatively few submarines, surface warships and mines which it had so far employed. Understandably Churchill chafed at this opening phase of the war at sea, and especially at the almost wholly defensive nature of the Royal Navy's operations as it reacted to the enemy's various 'pin-pricks'. He itched to use British seapower as a grand strategic instrument that would pluck the initiative in the war at sea as a whole out of Hitler's hands. As he wrote to Pound on 5 December 1939:

> An absolute defensive is for weaker forces. If we go on indefinitely like this we shall simply be worried & worn down, while making huge demands upon the national resources . . . I cd never be responsible for a naval strategy wh excluded the offensive principle, & relegated us to keeping open the lines of communication. Presently, you will see the U-boats in the outer seas. What then?[69]

It had been only three days after his return to office that he first mentioned to the First Sea Lord a visionary concept for a seaborne offensive against Germany. On 12 September he had embodied the concept in a five-page memorandum for the benefit of his naval advisers. Soon he was to dub his scheme 'Operation Catherine' – not because it represented the First Lord's own brain spinning on its axis throwing out sparks, but after Catherine the Great, Empress of Russia.

Churchill's plan envisaged a self-supporting task force of two or three old 'R' class battleships, a carrier, five cruisers, two destroyer flotillas, some submarines, supported by supply ships and 'turtle-backed blistered tankers' (against both air and submarine attack) carrying three months' supply of oil. The battleships would also each be rendered invulnerable to air and submarine attack by means of 2,000 tons of extra armour plate and anti-torpedo blistering, at the sacrifice of two out of four of their 15-inch gun turrets. A dozen specially converted vessels would serve as 'mine-bumpers' to precede the task force as it steamed at some 15 knots (the maximum speed of the old battleships after conversion) through the Skagerrak, Kattegat and the narrow 'Sound' between Denmark and Sweden into the Baltic. Having established British command of the Baltic, the task force would cut Germany off from her vital Swedish iron-ore supplies and other imports. Even more important, it would, in Churchill's reckoning, very likely induce the neutral Scandinavian states to enter the war on the Allied side, so providing the task force with a Swedish base. It could even persuade Soviet Russia, now linked to Nazi Germany by the 1939 Treaty of Friendship, to fight in the Allied cause. All in all, Churchill believed 'Operation Catherine' to be 'the supreme naval offensive open to the Royal Navy'.[70]

'Operation Catherine' belongs not to the world of real war but rather to that of imaginative war fiction, taking as it did little heed of tedious nuts-and-bolts, whether strategic or matériel, such as (for example) the difficulty of obtaining the necessary armour plate out of the restricted capacity of the British steel industry at a time when Britain was proposing to embark on mass tank production for the Army on top of the existing programme of warship construction. It came into the same category of Churchillian cigar-butt strategy as his 1915 brainwave of capturing the Friesian island of Borkum, or even the Dardanelles expedition itself: glibly attractive when arrowed broadly on a map of Europe, but a nonsense in terms of the technical means and military forces available, of the enemy's potential reaction, and of all the wider political and strategic probabilities.

In particular, it meant robbing Admiral Sir Charles Forbes, C-in-C, Home Fleet, of three of his precious battleships, so it was no wonder that he was largely kept in the dark about 'Catherine'. When the First

Sea Lord, Sir Dudley Pound, wrote to Forbes in his own hand on 15 September he only mentioned that

> the First Lord may say something to you about the scheme which is called by a name beginning with the letter 'C'. For this scheme has the idea of fitting some of the 'R' class with deck protection and extra bulges. I think there is a very good deal to be said for the scheme when the situation is sufficiently cleared for us to be able to put two or three of the 'R' class into dockyard hands for something like nine months . . .[71]

Here then was the first occasion when Pound, as professional head of the Navy, had to deal with one of Churchill's grandiose strategic inventions; and he now adopted what was to be in his invariable policy in the coming years of not openly challenging Churchill's views but, instead, under cover of an apparent willingness, patiently bringing up all the nuts-and-bolts problems in the course of a deliberately protracted study. As he confided to Forbes in this same letter:

> . . . until we are quite certain that neither Italy or [sic] Japan will join Germany, I feel it would be quite wrong to reduce the strength of our battlefleet by that number. Please do not raise this question, but if the First Lord mentions it it would be helpful if you took this line. I am just as keen on what is termed the 'Naval Offensive' as he is, but I do not feel that we are justified in risking our whole sea supremacy on what must, after all, be something of a gamble.[72]

And on 20 January 1940, after 'Catherine' had been finally put in abeyance, he explained his tactics more openly to Forbes: 'My feelings also were largely influenced against throwing cold water on any offensive operation so long as it appeared feasible. Hard facts and the attitude of Russia have brought the powers that be round to my way of thinking . . .'[73]

In pursuance of this policy of attrition Pound had therefore written encouragingly to Churchill on 19 September 1939 that there can be 'little doubt that if we could maintain control of the Baltic for a considerable period it would greatly enhance our prestige'.[74] But then came the cavils aimed at starting the rivets of Churchill's project and inducing it eventually to founder. It could only succeed if Russia did not join Germany's side, and if Britain was sure of 'the *active* co-operation of Sweden for the supply of oil and the use of a base and her repair facilities'. Moreover, the Baltic task force '*must* be such that we can with our Allies at that time win the war without it, in spite of any probable combination against us'[75] – in other words, even if the Royal and French Navies had to fight Italy and Japan as well as Germany. In laying down these preconditions Pound – or the Plans Division of the naval staff – had exposed the fundamental unrealism of 'Catherine'. For none of those preconditions could be met. In the first place, it is hard to comprehend how Churchill could hope that Sweden would abandon her profitable neutrality because of the entry of a British task force into the Baltic, or that Russia would wish to invite a German attack. The task force itself would lock up a considerable portion of British seapower, which, as the events of the next two months were to demonstrate, was hard pressed enough to deal with four German battleships, a handful of U-boats, and some 1,000 magnetic mines; let alone find a 'main fleet' to fight Japan as well if need be. The task force's line of communication through the Sound, Skagerrak and Kattegat and thence back across the North Sea would lie on the immediate flank of the German Navy based at Kiel and Wilhelmshaven, to say nothing of the Luftwaffe operating at relatively short range, while a pounce by the German Army through virtually unarmed Denmark and the establishment of heavy shore batteries on the Sound would effectively cut the task force off in the Baltic.

Nonetheless, although Churchill acknowledged in reply to Pound's first note on the topic that at present his decision 'is only for exploration; & no question of *action* arises,' he added: 'But the search for a naval offensive must be incessant.'[76] So studies for 'Catherine' were to go on, involving more and more staff time and resources. Indeed, Churchill secured the appointment of Admiral of the Fleet the Earl of Cork and Orrery, a fiery 65-year-old veteran on the half-pay list, to head a planning staff. Cork's first appreciation on 26 September proposed assembling the task force in the second week of January 1940, giving it a month of training and rehearsal, and then steaming off for the Baltic on 15 February – absurdly optimistic timings in view of the industrial and dockyard work needed for converting the ships into armoured turtles. In any event, Cork upped Churchill's original estimate of numbers by two carriers and nine cruisers.[77] Come November and the 'R' class battleships had had to be diverted to protecting North Atlantic convoys against the German surface raiders; and on the 22nd of the month Churchill postponed the operation until 30 April 1940. Perhaps most potentially serious of all Churchill's euphoric miscalculations related to the question of air attack on the task force by the Luftwaffe, for he believed as strongly as any 'gun and battleship' sailor that the fleet's own anti-aircraft fire would be enough to protect it against aircraft; the false lesson learned from the Luftwaffe's near-miss of the *Ark Royal*. As he wrote to President

Roosevelt on 16 October: 'We have not been at all impressed with the accuracy of the German air bombing of our warships. They seem to have no effective bomb sights.'[78]

With the cunning of an old badger (which he so closely resembled), Sir Dudley Pound gradually wore Churchill down over the months by his strategy of apparent willingness coupled with the protracted identification of operational difficulties. By the end of the year Pound felt able to voice open opposition to 'Catherine'. On 31 December he wrote to Churchill: ' "Catherine" is a great gamble, even if there were adequate fighter protection for the Fleet, and if Russia were on our side and we had the use of Russian bases. As neither of these conditions will be present, I consider that the sending of a Fleet of surface ships into the Baltic is courting disaster.'[79] On 10 January 1940 Pound submitted a further memorandum which relentlessly listed all the hazards, foreseeing that the fleet would be 'battered and mauled' by air attack, mines and U-boats on its way into the Baltic, where, having no secure base of its own, it would have to resort to an ill-protected Swedish anchorage where it would be exposed to further air and U-boat attack. Then there were the far-reaching strategic risks: 'The loss of such a large proportion of our Fleet would be the surest inducement to either Italy or Japan to come in against us.' Pound therefore urged 'most strongly' that all special preparations for 'Catherine' should be dropped.

Right up to this point Churchill had been arguing back tenaciously in defence of 'Catherine'; now, partly because Lord Cork reported that small progress had been made in the necessary ship conversion work so far, he 'reluctantly' agreed that 'Catherine' was off for 1940, although a small staff should continue to study it. The single casualty of 'Catherine' was Captain V. H. Danckwerts, Naval Staff Director of Plans, sacked almost certainly because of his trenchant criticisms of the scheme (reflected in Pound's memoranda); the first, but by no means the last, officer in all three services to be hounded out of his post during the war for opposing Churchill's will.[80]

Thus Pound's devious strategy of wearing Churchill down by protracted indirect resistance had proved ultimately successful – but at what cost in waste of time and staff resources? In any event, Churchill had had another naval stratagem in view since September, and one no less guaranteed in his estimation than such earlier dead certs as the forcing of the Dardanelles and the capture of Borkum (to say nothing of 'Operation Catherine') to cripple a great continental power.

4

'A Very Hazardous Affair': Norway, 1939–1940

Mined round Gällivare in northern Sweden, the iron ore upon which depended Germany's great steel industry, the basic sinew of her power, was shipped for most of the year from the port of Luleå down through the Baltic. However during the winter months when Luleå was closed by ice the ore was railed westwards to the ice-free Norwegian port of Narvik, and thence taken by ship down the length of the Norwegian coast. During the Great War this winter traffic had sought refuge from the Royal Navy by making use of the Innereled or 'Inner Leads' – the narrow stretch of Norwegian territorial water lying between Norway's outer string of islands and the mainland – until in 1918 Allied pressure induced the Norwegians to lay mines therein.

On 19 September 1939, having already discussed the matter (along with 'Operation Catherine'), with his naval advisers, the First Lord of the Admiralty proposed to the Cabinet that detailed plans should be put in hand for the Royal Navy to mine Norwegian territorial waters if Norway should prove unwilling to do it again herself; and on the 23rd he followed up with a powerful written broadside: 'It must be understood', he wrote, 'that an adequate supply of Swedish iron ore is vital to Germany and the interception or prevention of these Narvik supplies during the winter months, i.e., from October to the end of April, will greatly reduce her power of resistance.'[1] One of the aims of 'Operation Catherine' was of course to block the shipment of the ore direct from Sweden to Germany from May to September via the Baltic.

Henceforward, till the beginning of April 1940, Churchill was tirelessly to urge 'by every means and on all occasions'[2] his case for naval action to close Norwegian waters to German iron-ore supplies and German warships. Chamberlain and his Cabinet, however, proved deeply reluctant to contemplate violating Norway's neutrality, both out of moral scruple and out of fear of the political consequences in terms of world opinion. On 14 December, armed with fresh evidence of shipments of ore via the 'Leads' and also of recent violations of the neutrality of Norwegian waters by German warships, Churchill proposed that four or five destroyers shall be sent forthwith into 'the more lonely parts' of Norwegian waters 'for the purpose of arresting all ships carrying ore to Germany'.[3]

He followed this up two days later with another of his broadside memoranda, in which he argued to his Cabinet colleagues that the stopping of this traffic would rank 'as a major operation of war', and that no other expedient 'for many months to come' would give so good a chance of 'abridging the waste and destruction of the conflict, or perhaps preventing the vast slaughters which will attend the grapple of the main armies'.[4] He further claimed that if Germany's supplies of ore could be cut off from all sources until the end of 1940, 'a blow will have been struck at her war-making capacity equal to a first-class victory in the field or from the air, and without any serious sacrifice of life'; it could even prove 'immediately decisive'. He was not at all bothered at the thought that the Germans might respond by intervening with 'brute force' in Norway and Sweden, because in his judgment there was no reason why, with Britain's command of the seas, British and French troops should not 'meet the German invaders' on Scandinavian soil. 'At any rate,' he proclaimed with his usual assurance, 'we can take and hold whatever islands or suitable points on the Norwegian coast we choose. Our northern blockade of Germany would then become absolute.'[5]

By this time, however, Churchill's purely naval scheme had been overshadowed by a far more grandiose project – nothing less than the commitment of an Anglo-French expeditionary force to northern Scandinavia.

On 30 November Soviet Russia had invaded Finland. Soon her lumbering armies were halted or routed in the winter snows by a brave and brilliantly conducted Finnish defence. In the democracies sympathy and admiration welled up for the gallant Finns, another small nation defending its independence against tyranny; volunteers sprang forward to go and fight with the Finnish Army; the despatch of (all too scarce) arms and equipment was set in hand. In such a climate of opinion larger possibilities seemed to open up. Churchill himself expressed them to the War Cabinet on 11 December: 'It would be to our advantage if the trend of events in Scandinavia brought it about that Norway and Sweden were forced into war with Russia. We would then be able to gain a foothold in Scandinavia with the object of helping them, but without having to go to the extent of ourselves declaring war on Russia.'[6] This foothold would permit Britain to use Norwegian ports in the North Sea and Swedish ports in the Baltic against Germany.

On 19 December while the British War Cabinet was still chewing over how best to play the Finland card, the Allied Supreme War Council in Paris recommended that an expeditionary force of 3,000–4,000 men land at Narvik and proceed to seize the Swedish orefields round Gällivare. Norway's and Sweden's consent to this invasion was to be obtained – naïve hope – on the score that the Allies were joining them in support of Finland and in their own defence against Soviet attack.[7] Next day at the British Cabinet's Military Coordination Committee Churchill enthusiastically supported this ambitious proposal[8] – as he was to continue to do at all the anxious Cabinet discussions on it during the rest of December and on into the New Year.

On 31 December the Chiefs of Staff (COS) submitted a 22-page blessing: the opportunity 'is a great one, and we see no prospect of an equal chance being afforded us elsewhere'.[9] The possibility of obtaining decisive results, wrote the COS, rendered the operational risks acceptable. If the Germans sought to forestall the Allied intervention, then a scratch force would have to be put ashore at Narvik with the task of picketing the railway to the Swedish orefields and destroying the port facilities at Luleå; this force to be later strengthened by 'an adequately equipped and properly prepared expedition'.

In another report of 5 January 1940, the COS pondered the consequences of the Germans establishing themselves in southern Norway, and drew the conclusions that the Allies could not stop the enemy landing at Oslo and Kristiansand by surprise, nor reaching Stavanger if he employed airborne troops rather than seaborne, but that they could hope themselves to occupy Bergen and Trondheim before him since a German seaborne attack on these ports was 'extremely improbable' and an airborne landing 'scarcely less so'.[10] Narvik was not mentioned at all, being quite out of the question as a German objective. The COS recommended that from the moment the Allies finally decided to stop the iron-ore traffic a contingency force of troops and transports should be held ready 'for instant despatch' to seize Stavanger, Bergen and Trondheim. They warned that in any case the Allies could not be ready to land at Narvik to protect the railway to Gällivare until the end of March. Thus the proposal to mine the 'Leads' and the larger project of an expeditionary force to Norway and Sweden alike assumed that German action would be tightly constrained by British command of the sea. Indeed at this time neither Churchill nor Chamberlain believed that a German invasion of Norway was likely.[11]

When the War Cabinet debated Scandinavian strategy on 2 and 3 January 1940, the Chief of the Imperial General Staff (CIGS) warned them that an expedition against the inhabitants' wishes would be a 'very hazardous affair', and he noted that 'we had no ski-troops immediately available' – a point of some importance in regard to terrain snowbound until summer.[12] Prompted by his military advisers, the Secretary of State for War, Oliver Stanley, pronounced against landing troops at Stavanger, Bergen and Trondheim: 'History provided many examples of campaigns which had begun by the despatch of minor detachments, and which had ended by swallowing up large armies.' But the First Lord of the Admiralty insisted that the Allies should be ready to send battalions 'at any rate' to Stavanger and Bergen. 'There was no reason,' he went on, 'why this small diversion should develop into a large commitment, unless we wished it to.'

Now began three months of havering on the part of the War Cabinet as to what to do and when to do it. Fierce opposition by Norway and Sweden to diplomatic soundings about a possible Allied intervention induced the Cabinet on 12 January to postpone both the First Lord's minelaying plan and the larger land project, while asking the COS to report on the operational problems of capturing the Gällivare orefields in the face of Norwegian and Swedish opposition.[13] In their report on 28 January[14] the COS proposed landing five Allied divisions at Trondheim and Namsos in central Norway, and two brigades at Narvik with the job of marching up the railway to Gällivare. It would also be necessary to deny the Germans Bergen and Stavanger. Up to 40 destroyers (about a quarter of Britain's total operational strength) would be needed for close escort work, as well as a mass of merchant shipping, while it would become the Home Fleet's principal task to protect the convoys. The COS calculated the necessary air cover as one fighter squadron for Narvik; two fighter, two bomber squadrons and one army cooperation squadron operating over southern Sweden, plus an advanced base for four heavy bomber squadrons operating from the United Kingdom – around 160–180 aircraft in all.

The tally of naval, air and land forces required ought to have damned the whole idea of intervention in Scandinavia for good, given the Allies' overall scarcity of well-equipped troops and modern aircraft. But all three Chiefs of Staff – even the Chief of Air Staff, Air Chief Marshal Sir Cyril Newall – dangerously underestimated the decisive nature of the threat posed by the Luftwaffe, although in an earlier section of their report of 28 January, they did acknowledge that the air forces which the Allies could make available 'would be unlikely to satisfy' the Norwegian and Swedish governments (as an inducement to abandon their neutrality) in the face of the 'overwhelming scale of air attack' which the Germans could apply.[15] Moreover the COS grossly underestimated the possible speed and northward reach of the German moves into Norway. Then again, they failed to point out to the politicians, as they ought to have done, the military and naval realities underlying the whole project of a major campaign in Scandinavia: the strain on the Royal Navy and British merchant shipping of sustaining indefinitely an 800-mile-long supply route across the North Sea; the fact that the available land forces mostly consisted of ill-trained and grossly under-equipped Territorial divisions quite unfit to meet the Wehrmacht in battle; and the strategic danger of diverting large Allied resources to Scandinavia when a massive German invasion of France and the Low Countries was expected any month.[16] Churchill may therefore be forgiven for his own consistent neglect of the realities of comparative combat strength and efficiency in his enthusiasm for a 'supreme strategy to carry the war into a theatre where we can bring superior forces to bear, and where a decision can be obtained which rules all other theatres . . .'[17]

Racked by debate and torn by doubt, Chamberlain's Cabinet alternately tottered towards, and then away from, a final decision; with Churchill urging that his project for mining the 'Leads' should go ahead without delay, rather than wait until it was eventually decided to land expeditionary forces in Norway. On 7 February the Cabinet instructed the COS to begin tri-service preparations for such expeditionary forces. On 17 February there came by way of an interlude to the Whitehall discussions a *Boy's Own Paper* adventure when, on Churchill's instructions, the destroyer HMS *Cossack* (Captain P. L. Vian, RN) sent a boarding party with revolvers and drawn cutlasses aboard the *Graf Spee*'s old supply ship *Altmark* as she lay in Jössingfjord in Norwegian territorial waters. The *Altmark* was on her way home with captured British merchant seamen locked below decks, undetected by the Norwegians who 'searched' the vessel at Bergen. With the boarding party's shout of 'The Navy's here!' resounding in the ears of a delighted British public, Churchill tried to persuade the Cabinet that here was the perfect excuse and timing for launching his minelaying operation. But the Cabinet would only authorise him to 'make all preparations', so that if it were subsequently decided to lay a minefield in Norwegian territorial waters, 'there would be no delay in carrying out the operation'.[18]

Now it was March; and on the 12th the War Cabinet finally reached a decision to land a force at Narvik first of all, with follow-up landings later at Trondheim as soon as Narvik was taken, and possibly also Stavanger and Bergen.[19] They also appointed Major-General P. J. Mackesy to command the Narvik land force and Admiral Sir Edward ('Teddy') Evans, a sixty-year-old Great War destroyer hero, to command the naval side. On the very next day the Finns, having been at last overwhelmed by Russian weight of numbers, made peace with the Soviet Union, so destroying the Allies' essential pretext for military intervention in Scandinavia. What now to do? Churchill, true to his pugnacious instincts, urged that the Narvik landing should still go ahead. But on 14 March the Cabinet decided to cancel the operation, and stand down and 'disperse the expeditionary forces prepared for the Scandinavian expedition'.[20] So ended dismally the months of argument for and against Churchill's minelaying proposal and that grander project of maritime strategy of opening up a major theatre of war in Norway and Sweden.

Within a fortnight the enemy began to make his own impact on this scene of procrastination and futility. For from 26 March onwards came hardening evidence that Germany might herself be about to mount some kind of Scandinavian operation. But what?

As early as 10 October 1939 Grand Admiral Raeder had proposed to Hitler that it would be advantageous to secure U-boat bases along the Norwegian coast. When he raised the question again in December, a pro-Nazi Norwegian politician, Vidkun Quisling, was also proposing to Hitler that a coup d'état should be carried out with German help which would bring Norway within Germany's strategic perimeter. Hitler expressed the view that, while he would prefer the Scandinavian states to remain neutral, he could not allow them to be used by the Allies as a means of strangling Germany. He therefore ordered planning to begin for two alternatives: one, a coup d'état by Quisling assisted by minor German forces; and two, a full-scale invasion and occupation. Detailed planning by a special working group of the OKW (Oberkommando der Wehrmacht) began on 27 January. The British boarding of the *Altmark* on 17 February 1940 clinched growing

German suspicions based on Sigint ('signals intelligence') that the Allies might be intending to land in Scandinavia on the pretext of aiding the Finns. On 21 February Hitler placed General von Falkenhorst in command of the project, reporting directly to himself. The strategic aim was to give cover to the right wing of the German Army on the continent of Europe, to provide wider scope to the German Navy, and to secure the iron-ore route.

Falkenhorst was allotted six divisions – all that could be spared in view of the pending great offensive on the Western Front; and, except for one mountain division, troops recently recruited and, by German standards, not highly trained. Falkenhorst had at his disposal an inter-service planning staff. On 1 March Hitler issued the directive for 'Fall Weserübung' ('Operation Weser Exercise'); three days later, with mounting apprehension lest the British soon intervene, Falkenhorst issued orders that preparations should be so advanced by 10 March that 'Weserübung' could be launched at four days' notice. On 26 March Raeder was arguing that despite the Finnish surrender Britain was bound sooner or later to seek to control Norwegian coastal traffic, perhaps even invade Norway. He therefore urged that Germany should strike before the nights grew too short, that was, before 15 April; whereupon Hitler fixed the date for 'Weserübung' for 7 April, about the time of the new moon. On 2 April he postponed the operation to the 9th because of continuing winter ice in the Baltic.

Except for a few training vessels and for ships in the dockyard, the entire German Navy was committed to ferrying, and covering, no fewer than six separate groups of landing forces which were to seize Norwegian ports from the capital, Oslo, in the south all the way to Narvik in the far north – and in the face of British seapower. Artillery, equipment and supplies for the landing force were to be embarked separately in transports disguised as merchant ships, which (being slower than the warships) would sail earlier in order to arrive on time. The Luftwaffe was to provide 500 Junkers transport aircraft for the rapid forward deployment of troops (including parachute troops), 290 bombers, 40 divebombers, 100 fighters, 40 long-range reconnaissance aircraft, and 30 coastal patrol aircraft. For the Luftwaffe, as well as the German Navy and Army, 'Weserübung' required meticulous planning for the forward movement of essential ordnance, airfield equipment and installations. All in all, this complex combined air, land and sea operation over distances of up to 1,000 miles and improvised in less than two months, displays German staff work and inter-service cooperation in their brief springtime of high professional achievement.[21] Success depended on speed, single-minded boldness of execution and, above all, surprise. As Raeder reported to Hitler on 9 March:

> The operation is in itself contrary to all principles in the theory of naval warfare. According to this theory, it could be carried out by us only if we had naval supremacy. We do not have this; on the contrary, we are carrying out the operation in the face of a vastly superior British Fleet. In spite of this, the C-in-C Navy believes that, provided surprise is complete, our troops can and will successfully be transported to Norway. On many occasions in the history of war those very operations have been successful which went against all the principles of warfare, provided they were carried out by surprise.[22]

On 3 April the tankers and merchant ships of the supply echelons slipped out of North German ports towards their Norwegian destinations. At 0300 on 7 April – a new moon; a dark night – the task forces with the furthest distances to go – Groups 1 and 2 destined for Narvik and Trondheim, with their troops crammed into fourteen destroyers – were led out of Schillig Roads by the battleship *Gneisenau* (wearing the flag of Vice-Admiral Günther Lütjens) in company with the *Scharnhorst* and the heavy cruiser *Admiral Hipper*. Lütjens was aware that in the course of his more than 800-mile voyage he would be exposed to the threat of an overwhelming potential concentration of Allied seapower: up to seven battleships, one or two aircraft carriers, fourteen cruisers, six destroyer flotillas. He could only put his trust in secrecy and surprise, and in the cover provided by the bad weather and poor visibility predicted by the meteorologists. The bad weather soon materialised – by the evening of 7 April Lütjens's squadron was pitching and rolling in a Force 7, and still rising, south-westerly gale, with green seas sweeping the destroyers from stem to stern so that it was difficult to keep them on course at the designated squadron speed of 26 knots; and with the miserable soldiers who were packed into their narrow spaces being violently seasick.[23] Nonetheless, 35 aircraft of Bomber Command found Lütjens's task force and bombed it, hitting nothing. Next day, 8 April, the remaining task forces put to sea for the nearer destinations of Bergen, Egersund, Kristiansand and Oslo. Except for troops for the overland invasion of Denmark, the parachute units for the seizing of Norwegian airfields and the Luftwaffe's aircraft, the 'Weserübung' forces were now irrevocably committed to the gamble.

As early as December 1939 the first whispers hinting at a possible German move against Scandinavia had been picked up by the British

Secret Intelligence Service (SIS) – reports of the assembly of expeditionary forces, of combined operations exercises in the Baltic and of the conversion of merchant ships to carry warlike stores.[24] Similar reports in January 1940 were confirmed in February when the British military attaché in Stockholm passed back to Whitehall a warning by his Romanian colleague that Germany was preparing to occupy southern Norway and the Swedish orefields. On 11 March the Foreign Office was told by a secret German source that an operation was being planned against Denmark and Norway. From 26 March to 6 April came a series of circumstantial reports via the British embassy in Stockholm pointing at imminent German action – concentration and loading of ships in Baltic and North Sea ports and the massing of troops and aircraft; reports from the Swedish general staff and the American ambassador in Copenhagen pointing at a German attack on Norway (including Narvik) and Denmark on 8 April. On the night of 6–7 April Bomber Command aircraft sighted much activity in certain German ports, while a photo-reconnaissance of Kiel by Coastal Command revealed similar sinister bustle. A heavy increase was noted in German radio traffic. On 7 April took place the unsuccessful attack by Bomber Command on Lütjens's task force, reported by the aircrews as consisting of one battleship, two cruisers and a destroyer escort.

Yet Whitehall failed to collate all this cumulative but disparate data into a clear picture of German intentions – a failure in Intelligence akin to that of the Americans before the Japanese strike on Pearl Harbor in December 1941, although the British in 1940 lacked the clinching evidence of intercepted enemy cypher traffic.[25] Here lay a crucial factor in the disastrous course of the coming campaign in Norway. It occurred firstly because the Intelligence services had not yet recovered from pre-war neglect and disorganisation. Each branch tended to work in its own compartment without an effective agency to coordinate their efforts and results. The Admiralty's own Intelligence services were particularly fragmented. While NID 1, as the geographical branch of the Naval Intelligence Department covering Germany, processed the various SIS and embassy reports about German plans, the Operational Intelligence Centre (OIC) did not receive the same comprehensive spread of material. To make matters worse, NID 1 and OIC were anyway in a state of mutual distrust so often characteristic of departments in a bureaucracy, while NID 17, the Director of Naval Intelligence's executive branch which was supposed to coordinate their work, failed to do so. In these lapses in liaison can be heard an echo of similar Admiralty failures during the Battle of Jutland.

There was a second reason why Whitehall failed to read German intentions. It fell into the classic error of believing or disbelieving Intelligence reports according to whether or not they fitted in with its own *idées fixes*. Thus Military Intelligence, identifying six German divisions in North-West Germany, could not believe that a major campaign was in train because it reckoned that 20 or 30 divisions would be needed for an invasion of Scandinavia. When the NID received the report via the American ambassador in Copenhagen that the Germans were going to seize Narvik on 8 April, it simply refused to credit it, at first thinking that 'Narvik' must be a misprint for 'Larvik', a port in southern Norway. Foreign Office officials for their part thought such reports amounted to no more than 'the usual [German] threats'.[26] Even when on 7 April Bomber Command found the powerful German task force steering north-west towards Norway, the DNI (Director of Naval Intelligence) himself in passing the information on to Forbes at Scapa added: '. . . all these reports are of doubtful value and may well only be a further move in the war of nerves.'[27] As late as 8 April a Military Intelligence appreciation, although acknowledging that Germany could carry out 'limited operations' against the Norwegian coast, saw such action to be 'by no means likely' and of not much advantage to the Germans; it saw no profit at all for Germany in occupying Denmark. In the words of Professor Sir Harry Hinsley, the official historian of British Intelligence in the Second World War:

> It was a conclusion which reflected the outlook of the whole of Whitehall at this time when, in the absence of the incontestable intelligence from Sigint and from regular photographic reconnaissance, there was also no adequate machinery, within the departments or between them, for confronting prevailing opinions and lazy assumptions with rigorous and authoritative assessments of the massive but miscellaneous information about the enemy that was nevertheless available.[28]

In this needless fog of uncertainty the Allies took the final decisions over their own action in Norway. On 28 March the Supreme War Council finally agreed to mine Norwegian waters ('Operation Wilfred') on 5 April.[29] What with the rumours of impending German moves of some kind and the likelihood of a German reaction to the mining, the question now arose again of possible Allied military action in Norway. This caused the Secretary of State for War, Oliver Stanley, to remind the Cabinet on 29 March that as a result of its decision a fortnight earlier to disband the expeditionary force, it was now 'out of the question' to send the two divisions originally intended, while only a brigade remained available to go to Narvik and another small force to Stavanger.[30] The Chiefs of Staff therefore began to ponder afresh the contingency of landing Allied troops at Bergen and Trondheim 'in sufficient force to secure them as bridgeheads for possible extended operations' – which meant of course 'at least the possibility that it might be necessary' to reassemble the troops and transports dispersed since 14 March.[31] There were now only four days left before the 'Weserübung' supply echelons were due to sail; eight days before the German task groups for Narvik and Bergen would steam out of Schillig Roads; only eleven days before all the 'Weserübung' forces would strike home with ruthless energy.

On 3 April occurred an unconnected event which would nevertheless exercise its own fateful influence over the campaign in Norway. Winston Churchill succeeded Admiral of the Fleet Lord Chatfield as the regular Chairman of the Cabinet's Military Coordination Committee – its executive organ for deciding strategy and overseeing operations. (Chatfield had resigned as Minister for the Coordination of Defence, and was not replaced.) On the eve of 'Weserübung', therefore, Churchill added to his existing authority over maritime operations as First Lord the chairmanship of the committee which would (subject to ultimate Cabinet approval) run the Norwegian campaign.

On 5 April the Cabinet postponed the execution of 'Wilfred' to the 8th, but the minelaying task force sailed nevertheless on 5 April. 'Wilfred' consisted of three separate minelaying operations: Force WB (two destroyers) was to simulate the laying of mines off Bud (62° 54′ North, 6° 55′ East); Force WS, consisting of the minelayer HMS *Teviot Bank* (5,087 tons) and four destroyers was to lay mines off Stadlandet (62° North, 5° East); and Force WAV, with four minelaying destroyers and four escort destroyers, was to mine off Hovden in Vestfjord in the approaches to Narvik (67° 24′ North, 14° 36′ East).[32] On hearing a report that all four Norwegian coastal defence ships were in the Narvik area, Admiral Forbes ordered Vice-Admiral W. J. Whitworth (Flag Officer, Battle Cruiser Squadron) to sea with HMS *Renown* and screening destroyers *Greyhound*, *Glowworm*, *Hyperion* and *Hero* in order to protect the minelayers from Norwegian interference.

No landing forces were despatched at this time, but a contingency plan had finally been drawn up whereby Stavanger, Bergen, Trondheim and Narvik were all to be seized as soon as it became clear that the Germans were taking the offensive in retaliation for the British minelaying. The troops (amounting to eight battalions in all) were ready to move by 7 April: those for Stavanger and Bergen in the cruisers *Devonshire*, *Berwick*, *York* and *Glasgow* at Rosyth, and those for Trondheim and Narvik in transports in the Clyde, under the escort of the cruiser *Aurora* (flying the flag of Admiral Sir Edward Evans) and six destroyers. Since none of these forces was to sail until clear evidence had been received of a German attack, the initiative and the advantage of time, those priceless and usually irrecoverable assets in war, were thus tamely handed to the enemy. Moreover, Churchill and Pound omitted to order Forbes and the main body of the Home Fleet out of Scapa to a covering position in the central North Sea ready to intervene in whatever events might be provoked by 'Wilfred'.[33]

On 6 April, in the face of the mounting evidence that the Germans were going to launch a major operation on the 8th, the Deputy Director of Operations (Home) on the Naval Staff, Captain Ralph Edwards, sought to persuade Pound and Churchill to delay 'Wilfred' for twenty-four hours – but in vain. Next day, a Sunday, when the First Sea Lord was away fishing at Romsey, Edwards renewed his urgings in favour of postponement, this time to Churchill and the Deputy Chief of Naval Staff, Rear-Admiral T. S. V. Phillips. Neither would agree; and Churchill, for his part, could not bear to see yet another postponement of 'Wilfred' at this last moment after so many earlier setbacks. As Edwards noted at the time: 'I am sure we ought to cancel Operation Wilfred. Winston however is obsessed with the idea of forcing enemy ships out of the fjords into the open waters and I fear we shall be compelled to continue.'[34]

But there was another reason why Churchill, Pound and Phillips all discounted the likelihood of an imminent large-scale German invasion of Norway. They interpreted the air sighting of Lütjens's task force by Bomber Command as revealing a fresh attempt by the German battlecruisers to break out into the Atlantic via the Iceland–Faeroes gap and attack British shipping routes.[35] When Pound returned to the Admiralty about 2000 on 7 April, he 'went' for Edwards, in Edwards's own words, 'for – as he put it – trying to lead the naval staff away from the main objective which was the defence of the Atlantic convoy routes. He would not listen to my arguments that all the evidence tended to suggest that Norway was to be the victim.'[36]

In any case, the sailing of the Home Fleet from Scapa was delayed some four hours that day because of an inexcusable Admiralty failure promptly to pass on to Forbes, the C-in-C, the report from the Bomber Command force that at 1325 it had attacked Lütjens's squadron steering north-west off the entrance to the Skagerrak. Not until 1727 did Forbes order his Fleet to raise steam, and not until 2015 had the whole Fleet cleared the Flow.[37]

Now followed two further errors of judgment. In the first place,

Forbes left his one available carrier, *Furious*, in the Clyde because of apprehension lest she suffer the fate of *Courageous*, even instructing her to release some 120 seamen to the destroyers to serve as possible boarding parties. It was not until 1630 on 8 April that the Admiralty intervened to order the *Furious* to join the Fleet; not until 0400 on 9 April that she embarked aircraft, though no fighters. Once at sea she steamed at 28 knots in order to catch up.[38]

Admiral Sir Charles Forbes himself was the human equivalent of the eighteenth-century 74-gun ship-of-the-line – a solid, reliable, and rugged performer in all situations and all weathers; a sea officer of faultless manners and a deep sense of loyalty both to superiors and subordinates. His Flag Lieutenant, Godfrey Style, was to recall how Forbes, physically of small stature, 'stood on his own bridge, always calm, always the same and ALWAYS correctly dressed, without mufflers or other fancy gear . . . never more than his British Warm [a short, close-fitting navy-blue overcoat] . . .'[39] Now this 'foursquare'[40] sailor, flying his flag in HMS *Rodney*, was leading the Home Fleet into the first, and one of the most important, of the maritime campaigns of the Second World War. However, foursquare traditionalist that he was, and in common with most admirals of his generation, Forbes did not yet appreciate the crucial importance of seaborne airpower; hence his decision to leave the *Furious* behind. Now came his second error of judgment. He led the Home Fleet at high speed on a north-easterly course which would take it well outside the tracks of the German task forces heading towards central and southern Norway. This error also sprang from traditionalism of outlook – for Forbes too shared the preoccupation with the majestic clash of heavy ships. His mind, like Churchill's and Pound's, was focused on the German battleships and their supposed sortie towards the Atlantic via the Iceland–Faeroes gap, and on the importance of intercepting them and bringing them to action: this it was that determined his choice of a north-easterly course. But the German naval command was in fact successfully selling its opponent a dummy, for at around 2000 hours on 8 April Lütjens, having left Group 2 west of Trondheim and escorted Group 1 to the vicinity of Narvik, sheered off with *Gneisenau* and *Scharnhorst* to the north, intending later to turn west, so simulating an attempt to break out into the Atlantic.

All that therefore stood in the direct track of the German invasion forces were submarines, the destroyers of 'Wilfred's' minelaying groups and Vice-Admiral Whitworth with HMS *Renown* and her escorting destroyers. These now proceeded to redeem as best they might the strategic misjudgments of the C-in-C and the Admiralty.

At 0815 on 8 April the destroyer *Glowworm* (which had become detached from Whitworth's screen during the night when searching for a man overboard) encountered the German destroyers of Group 2 (the Trondheim group) in a Force 8 gale, and despite the heavy odds immediately steered to engage. At 0950 the heavy cruiser *Admiral Hipper*, sent back by Lütjens, found *Glowworm* in close action with the German destroyer *Bernd von Arnim*. At 0957 *Hipper* opened fire with her 8-inch guns at 9,000 yards, hitting *Glowworm*'s bridge with her first salvo. The *Glowworm* replied with torpedoes and a smoke screen. As *Hipper* in pursuit emerged from the smoke, she saw *Glowworm* at close range on the starboard bow, and *Hipper*'s captain (Captain Heye) decided to ram the smaller British vessel. However, the *Hipper* answered her helm so slowly that the *Glowworm* succeeded in ramming the German cruiser first, ripping off some 150 feet of *Hipper*'s side plating before passing astern with her own bow broken off, a heavy list, and sinking. At 1000 *Glowworm* blew up and disappeared. The *Hipper* rescued one officer and 37 of her ship's company, although her captain, Lieutenant-Commander G. B. Roope, was lost when he fell back into the gale-swept sea while being hoisted aboard. For his unhesitating engagement of more powerful warships in superior numbers even to the point of ramming, Roope was to be posthumously awarded the Victoria Cross.[41]

On intercepting the *Glowworm*'s 'enemy' reports, Forbes redeployed his forces: the battlecruiser *Repulse*, the cruiser *Penelope* and four destroyers were detached to *Glowworm*'s aid while Whitworth in *Renown* was ordered to cut off the enemy if heading for Vestfjord. At this point the Admiralty (really Churchill and Pound, as inseparable in naval command as Rodgers and Hammerstein in music) made the first of its disastrous direct interventions in the campaign, by ordering all the destroyers of Force WAV (the Vestfjord minelaying group) to join Whitworth, which thus left Vestfjord and the approach to Narvik without direct cover.

By now even the Admiralty had accepted that yesterday's Intelligence about a German invasion of Norway might be true. Confirmation had come when the Polish submarine *Orzel* sank the enemy troopship *Rio de Janeiro* off Kristiansand early on 8 April. Although the Admiralty informed Forbes that an invasion operation was taking place, the Commander-in-Chief continued to steer north-east rather than east to intercept it. At 1430 on the 8th a flying boat flown off by Forbes to search ahead of him reported a battleship, two cruisers and two destroyers in 64° 12′ North, 6° 25′ East steering west – in fact, *Hipper* and four destroyers marking time (hence the meaningless westerly course) before attacking Trondheim according to schedule on the morrow. Forbes therefore altered course by stages to north-west in order to intercept what he believed might be the enemy's main body.[42] By this time Forbes too had run into the same rising gale which had been tossing Lütjens's ships about, and it compelled him to reduce speed for the sake of his destroyers. The C-in-C now appreciated that there could be one enemy battleship north of him en route for Narvik, and other strong forces down south in the Skagerrak or Kattegat. He therefore ordered the battlecruiser *Repulse*, the cruiser *Penelope* and some destroyers to reinforce Whitworth to the northwards while he himself turned south with the battleships *Rodney* and *Valiant*, the cruiser *Sheffield* and a destroyer screen.

In the event it was Whitworth with the *Renown* who encountered the *Gneisenau* and *Scharnhorst* and their destroyer escort at 0337 on 9 April (D-Day of 'Weserübung') some 50 miles off Vestfjord as the German ships were steering north on their diversionary course. It was now blowing a full gale, with mountainous seas and sudden curtains of snow or rain. At 0405 the *Renown* opened fire with her 15-inch guns at a range of about 15,000 yards. Twelve minutes later she knocked out the *Gneisenau*'s main gunnery control system, which persuaded the enemy to run for it. In the stern chase now ensuing, Whitworth hit the *Gneisenau* twice again at 0434 and knocked out a forward turret. However the weather itself was on the side of the German ships as Whitworth was later to recall:

> The chief feature of this running action was a heavy head sea, which forced *Renown* to slow down in order to fight her fore turrets. The Germans on the other hand could disregard the damaging effects of heavy water coming over their forecastles and continue to fight their after turrets whilst steaming at high speed.
>
> It is noteworthy that the Germans always jinked when they saw our salvoes fired, thus throwing us out for line.[43]

Although at times Whitworth drove *Renown* up to 29 knots, the two German ships had disappeared from view amid the squalls by 0660. Nevertheless, a British force had once again asserted the moral supremacy born of centuries in attacking without hesitation a more powerful enemy force. Yet the fact that Whitworth had been compelled to fight with one lightly armoured and elderly battlecruiser against two modern battleships was a mark of the Admiralty's failure (and, initially, Forbes's too) to read German strategic intentions correctly and concentrate Britain's naval resources in the key sea area.

Now followed the calamitous penalty for all the failures of

Intelligence and the resulting mistaken deployment of the Fleet. On 9 April, while Whitworth was fighting the *Gneisenau* and *Scharnhorst*, all the 'Weserübung' task groups enjoyed a clear run to their objectives except for valiant resistance by Norwegian coastal defence vessels and shore batteries. Despite losing the new heavy cruiser *Blücher* to the guns and torpedoes of Norwegian forts in Oslofjord, Group 5 successfully landed an infantry division round Oslo while parachute and airlanding troops seized the airfield. Group 4, led by the cruiser *Karlsruhe* and helped by heavy bombing by the Luftwaffe, were in possession of Kristiansand and Arendal by mid-afternoon. Group 3, with part of 69th Infantry Division embarked in the cruisers *Köln* and *Königsberg*, took Bergen despite damage to the *Königsberg* by shore batteries – to the vast relief of the Group Commander, Vice-Admiral Schmundt, who had considered that his force was the most likely of all to be intercepted by the British fleet. Stavanger, the other objective of Group 3, succumbed to air assault. After heavy preliminary bombing, parachute troops took the nearby airfield, so permitting two infantry battalions to land in Ju 52 transports. The infantry then took the city, some eight miles away, from the landward side.

At Trondheim, Group 2 began creeping in through the tortuous fjord at 0300 led by the *Hipper*. Unscathed by the fire of shore batteries (later captured by landing parties) the *Hipper* and a destroyer anchored off the city, whereupon two companies of the 138th Mountain Regiment landed at the quay from motor boats and marched up the street to take surrender of the local Norwegian commander at his headquarters. Furthest north of all, at Narvik, Group 1, its soldiers embarked in nine destroyers, seasick, cold and tired after the gales, crept into Ofotfjord in the dawn amid snow showers. Two destroyers were detached to land troops on both sides of the narrowest neck of the fjord to seize shore batteries; a third landed troops on Baroy Island, which commanded the southern seaward entrance to the fjord. The remaining six destroyers moved up the fjord, sinking the feeble Norwegian coast defence vessels *Eidsvoll* and *Norge* on the way. By 0800 Narvik and its surroundings were in German hands; the operation was complete which Churchill and the naval staff had always taken to be utterly out of the question.

Meanwhile German army units moving overland, coupled with seaborne landing forces, had occupied the whole of Denmark, a virtually unarmed country, by the time many of its inhabitants awoke that Sunday morning – an event which hardly confirmed the argument of the pre-war British disarmament movement that defencelessness would ensure immunity from aggression.

'Weserübung' had thus far proved an audacious gamble brilliantly executed; a success thanks to the crystal-clear overall aim and the resolute, energetic tactical offensives by Groups 1 to 6. In Norway the Germans had won the priceless advantage of possession of the ground – certainly possession of the essential keys to the ground, such as major ports and airfields. It remained for them to pour in the remainder of their six divisions and advance inland up the valleys against weak Norwegian forces to complete their occupation. The German success also meant that from this moment onwards the Allies could only react belatedly and piecemeal, whether by sea, land or air – like a boxer already sent staggering by his opponent's first sudden punch. To this disarray were now to be added confusions and contradictions in the directing of Allied counter-measures; and most of all in the Admiralty itself.

After news had come in of the German attacks on Norwegian ports, Admiral Forbes (now reinforced by nine more British and French cruisers and thirteen destroyers but still critically lacking a carrier) proposed to attack the German task force at Bergen. The Admiralty, however, wanted him to attack Trondheim and watch Narvik as well. At 1130 Forbes therefore detached Admiral Layton with four cruisers (*Manchester*, *Southampton*, *Glasgow* and *Sheffield*) and seven destroyers to destroy the one German cruiser believed to lie at Bergen. However, Layton had some 80 miles to go. In such circumstances cruisers were a poor substitute for a strike by carrier aircraft. In the early afternoon and before he could arrive, RAF reconnaissance aircraft reported that there were in fact two enemy cruisers in Bergen (the *Köln* and *Königsberg*) plus the old training cruiser *Bremse*. Nevertheless, Forbes still wished Layton to press home his attack. But now came another of the Admiralty's interferences – an order cancelling the operation, apparently in the mistaken belief that the shore batteries were now operational in German hands. Here was the first great muffed opportunity in a scramble of a campaign, for Layton would have caught not only the three German cruisers but also the rest of Group 3's ships, and at a time when in fact German army units had not yet restored Bergen's batteries to readiness.[44] Instead Layton and his cruisers, together with those of Admiral Edward-Collins, swept the Norwegian coast as far south as Utsire in order to interrupt supplies and reinforcements for the German garrisons at Stavanger and Bergen. They met nothing.

Meanwhile Forbes with the main body of the Home Fleet, now including the carrier HMS *Furious*, having steamed south as far as

59° 44′ North, 2° 57′ East (off the Norwegian coast roughly midway between Bergen and Stavanger), turned again to the north. In the afternoon of 9 April, under a cleared sky, he encountered for the first time what was to prove the decisive factor in the Norwegian campaign whether at sea or on land, when Luftwaffe bombers swung down to attack his fleet. Although only the destroyer *Gurkha* was sunk and minor damage inflicted to other ships (including the flagship) the fleet's anti-aircraft fire had failed to prevent the enemy pressing home his attacks – even despite some ships expending up to 40 per cent of their stocks of ammunition. The C-in-C quickly drew the appropriate lesson: henceforward even with a carrier present the Home Fleet would not operate within the zone controlled by German land-based air power; that was, the whole sea area from Bergen (inclusive) southwards.[45]

At Narvik more British confusions of orders and intentions on 9–10 April were to result in an episode of heart-stirring but needless courage and sacrifice. In conformity with instructions received directly from the Admiralty in the late forenoon of 9 April Captain Warburton-Lee (commanding the 2nd Destroyer Flotilla in Whitworth's squadron) led five destroyers – *Hardy*, his own ship; *Hotspur* (Commander H. F. H. Layman); *Havoc* (Lieutenant-Commander R. E. Courage); *Hunter* (Lieutenant-Commander L. de Villiers); *Hostile* (Commander J. P. Wright) – up Ofotfjord in order to sink or capture enemy ships and transport in Narvik, and, at his discretion, put a landing party ashore to recapture the town. Enquiry of a Norwegian pilot station at the entrance to the fjord revealed to him that he faced six big German destroyers (in fact it was ten). When Warburton-Lee reported this to Whitworth and Forbes, adding the words 'Intend attacking at dawn high water', Whitworth (who had now been joined by a second battlecruiser, *Repulse*) considered reinforcing him with the battlecruiser *Renown*, even though it would mean some delay. He decided not to, partly because the Admiralty had bypassed him to deal directly with Warburton-Lee. As Whitworth wrote later: 'I have always regretted that I did not intervene, and order Warburton-Lee to postpone his attack until *Renown* could join him. Now that I know that the Admiralty had no special intelligence not available to myself, this regret is all the more poignant.'[46]

The Admiralty (this meant Churchill in a high state of executive excitement in the map room, as an eyewitness noted)[47] signalled Warburton-Lee at 2200 on 9 April (over the signature of the First Sea Lord, although the language is unmistakably Churchillian): 'You alone [author's note: what about Forbes or Whitworth?] can judge

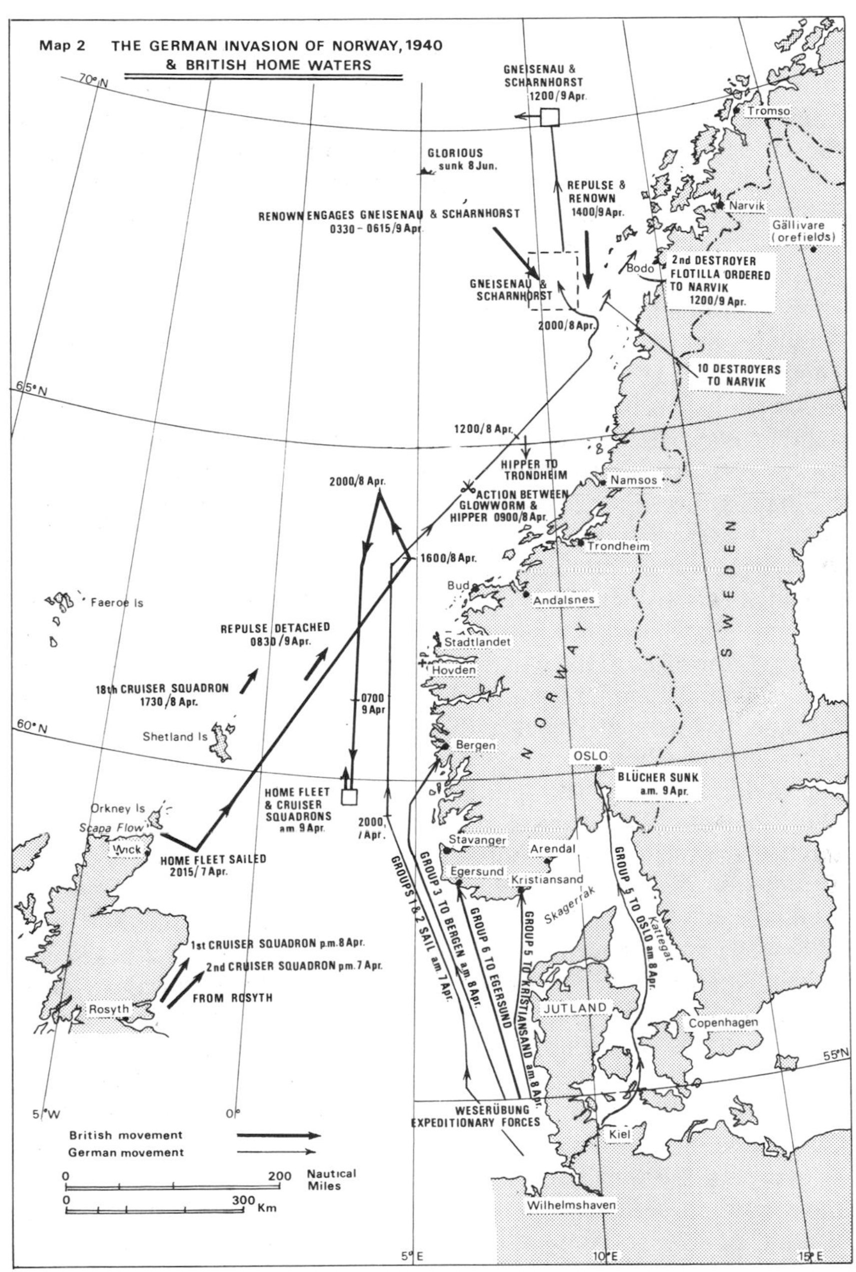
Map 2 THE GERMAN INVASION OF NORWAY, 1940
& BRITISH HOME WATERS
GNEISENAU & SCHARNHORST 1200/9 Apr.
Tromso
GLORIOUS sunk 8 Jun.
REPULSE & RENOWN 1400/9 Apr.
RENOWN ENGAGES GNEISENAU & SCHARNHORST 0330 - 0615/9 Apr.
Narvik
Gällivare (orefields)
GNEISENAU & SCHARNHORST
Bodo
2nd DESTROYER FLOTILLA ORDERED TO NARVIK 1200/9 Apr.
2000/8 Apr.
10 DESTROYERS TO NARVIK
65°N
70°N
1200/8 Apr.
HIPPER TO TRONDHEIM
2000/8 Apr.
ACTION BETWEEN GLOWWORM & HIPPER 0900/8 Apr.
Namsos
Trondheim
1600/8 Apr.
Bud
Andalsnes
Faeroe Is
REPULSE DETACHED 0830/9 Apr.
Stadtlandet
Hovden
18th CRUISER SQUADRON 1730/8 Apr.
0700 9 Apr
NORWAY
SWEDEN
60°N
Shetland Is
Bergen
OSLO
BLÜCHER SUNK a.m. 9 Apr.
HOME FLEET & CRUISER SQUADRONS am 9 Apr.
Orkney Is
Scapa Flow
Wick
HOME FLEET SAILED 2015/7 Apr.
2000, / Apr.
Stavanger
Arendal
Egersund
Kristiansand
Skagerrak
Kattegat
GROUPS 1 & 2 SAIL a.m. 7 Apr.
GROUP 3 TO BERGEN a.m. 8 Apr.
GROUP 6 TO EGERSUND
GROUP 5 TO KRISTIANSAND a.m. 8 Apr.
GROUP 5 TO OSLO a.m. 8 Apr.
1st CRUISER SQUADRON p.m. 8 Apr.
2nd CRUISER SQUADRON p.m. 7 Apr.
FROM ROSYTH
Rosyth
JUTLAND
Copenhagen
55°N
5°W
0°
WESERÜBUNG EXPEDITIONARY FORCES
Kiel
British movement
German movement
0 200 Nautical Miles
0 300 Km
Wilhelmshaven
5°E
10°E
15°E

whether, in these circumstances, attack should be made. We shall support whatever decision you make.'[48]

At dawn on 10 April Warburton-Lee's five destroyers began to steam up Ofotfjord in its jaggedly winding channel beneath high cliffs crowned with snowfields. Constant sweeping veils of snow concealed the British ships until they arrived off Narvik itself, when the sky cleared to reveal the new moon in the paling sky. Warburton-Lee had achieved complete surprise: in a short and ferocious action his ships sank two German destroyers (including that of the enemy commodore) by torpedo and badly damaged three more by gunfire, as well as sinking several merchant ships in a second attack.[49]

But now the British flotilla found itself in a trap, for three more big enemy destroyers emerged from a side fjord beyond Narvik harbour to engage him as he retired seawards, while two others appeared from another concealed inlet ahead of him, barring his escape. Another savage encounter in the narrow waters ensued, the British destroyers pitting four (five in the case of *Hardy*) 4.7-inch guns each against the enemy's five 5.9-inch. Soon the *Hardy* was hit in the bridge (killing Warburton-Lee and most of those with him) and engine rooms. Blazing furiously, she was beached. Astern of her, *Hunter* was also hit and set ablaze. As she lost way *Hotspur* ran into her, for *Hotspur*'s steering controls had been damaged by another German hit. Nonetheless *Hotspur*'s captain, now conning her from the after steering position, managed to get clear again and head for the open sea while *Hunter* sank. To cover the *Hotspur*'s escape, the *Havoc* and *Hostile* closely engaged the enemy, who did not press his own attacks home, partly because of acute shortage of fuel. On their way back down Ofotfjord the British destroyers encountered and set ablaze the German ammunition ship *Rauenfels*, the flames leaping high against a backdrop of snow-capped rock. Soon the *Rauenfels* blew up and sank.

Nothing could have been more Nelsonian than Warburton-Lee's resolute attack on a superior enemy force, for which he was awarded a posthumous Victoria Cross. His ships had sunk two big German destroyers for the loss of two smaller British; had badly damaged five more for the disabling of the *Hotspur*; had sunk some six enemy supply ships, including the *Rauenfels* with its essential munitions for the German troops ashore at Narvik. It all made glorious copy for British newspapers and weekly magazines. But if only the Admiralty had left the conduct of operations to Whitworth, and Whitworth had reinforced Warburton-Lee with one of his two battlecruisers, the entire German force could have been sunk without loss.

Apart from Warburton-Lee's attack at Narvik, the only effectively destructive response by the Royal Navy to 'Weserübung' during the first hectic two days when the German operation was at its most precarious and vulnerable took the form of attacks by the Fleet Air Arm and the submarine service, those junior branches of a 'big-gun' navy. Early on 10 April fifteen Skua fighter/dive-bombers from 600 and 603 squadrons from Hatston in the Orkneys – led by Captain R. T. Partridge, RN, and Lieutenant-Commander W. P. Lucy, RN, and flying at the limits of their range – bombed and sank the cruiser *Königsberg* in Bergen harbour; the first time in the history of war that a major warship had been sunk by air attack. This success contrasted with the failure of twelve Wellingtons and twelve Hampdens of Bomber Command to inflict any significant damage during an attack on Bergen the previous evening. Meanwhile British submarines in the Skagerrak were exploiting the movement of major German warships back to home ports immediately after the landings in Norway in order to evade attack by the Home Fleet. On the night of 9 April the submarine *Truant* torpedoed the cruiser *Karlsruhe* and damaged her so severely that the Germans themselves had to sink her three hours afterwards. Twenty-four hours later the submarine *Spearfish* torpedoed the pocket battleship *Lützow*, blowing off her propellers and badly damaging her stern. Towed into Kiel, she was not to be recommissioned until 1941. Other submarines, including the Polish *Orzel*, sank several merchant ships and tankers too during the early days of the campaign.[50]

Back in Whitehall, in tranquil panelled rooms far removed from heaving seas, driving snow and screaming dive-bombers – the contrast was to supply a leit-motif of the coming campaign – Britain's collective leadership strove to keep up with the rush of events. At Cabinet in the early forenoon on 9 April after the first sensational news of 'Weserübung' had come in (but not yet of the unimagined German capture of Narvik) the CIGS, General Sir Edmund Ironside, and Churchill strongly advocated that Narvik should be occupied by a British force, together with combined operations to prevent the Germans from consolidating their positions at Trondheim and Bergen.[51] There was just one snag. The very day before Churchill and Pound had ordered the disembarkation of the troops being held on board cruisers at Rosyth in the Clyde to meet the contingency of a German intervention in Norway in response to 'Wilfred'; and had despatched the cruisers without the troops to join the Home Fleet. At the same time the cruiser escort for the troopships in the Clyde was also ordered to sea, thus stranding the troopships. Britain therefore now had no ready expeditionary force whatsoever with which to intervene immediately in Norway against the German invaders. Churchill's and Pound's disastrous decision stemmed from their stubborn belief on 7 April that the reported movements of major units of the German Navy presaged an enemy attempt to break out into the Atlantic and attack British convoys; a belief which had blinded them to all the cumulative Intelligence pointing towards an invasion of Norway.

Now, in the forenoon of 9 April, the War Cabinet could only lamely instruct the Chiefs of Staff to 'set on foot preparations for military expeditions to recapture Trondheim and Bergen and to occupy Narvik';[52] just a little late. Indeed, by the time the Cabinet met again at noon that day the news had come in that the Germans had already seized Narvik anyway. From this moment forward, therefore, the Norwegian campaign was a lost cause, for the initial errors and consequent loss of time, fatal in themselves, were inevitably to lead to half-cock operations hastily mounted with scratch forces.

5

A Churchillian Disaster: Norway, 1940

On 12 April Admiral Whitworth took the battleship *Warspite* (allotted to him by the C-in-C, Home Fleet) and nine destroyers up the Ofotfjord to Narvik, while aircraft from the *Furious* bombed the harbour ahead of him; and proceeded relentlessly to hunt down and sink the remaining German destroyers in the remotest recesses of the fjords. It was the operation that he would have carried out two days earlier with *Renown* but for the Admiralty's interference vis-à-vis Warburton-Lee. Whitworth now considered the possibility of putting ashore a landing party to retake Narvik, but decided that such a party would not be strong enough to turn out a garrison of 2,000 German soldiers.

At this point Churchill in his impatience would not wait until a military force could be reassembled for this task, but wanted the Navy to do the job on its own – the same mistake he had made over forcing the Dardanelles in 1915. As Whitworth was steaming back down Ofotfjord towards the sea he received an Admiralty signal urging him to occupy Narvik forthwith 'in order to secure an unopposed landing later'.[1] Whitworth replied that this should be the function of a military force from the United Kingdom, which he judged could take Narvik 'by direct assault without fear of meeting serious opposition on landing'.[2] He was right – the garrison had lost its ammunition supply in the *Rauenfels* and its motor transport in another sunk vessel, and Hitler even thought of ordering it to withdraw. Yet Whitworth could actually have had a military force with him at that moment, if only Churchill and Pound had not stranded it in the United Kingdom by their instructions on 7 April, in which case Narvik would have quickly fallen. As it was, it did not succumb until 28 May.

On the day of Whitworth's attack, a hastily reconstituted military force under the command of Major-General Mackesy sailed from the Clyde for the Narvik area under a strong naval escort commanded by Admiral of the Fleet the Earl of Cork and Orrery (replacing Evans). Lord Cork was a fiery old Great War veteran on the retired list, and typical of Churchill's penchant for illustrious reputations won long ago. Mackesy's command consisted of the 24th Guards Brigade, which had been piled into merchant ships without artillery, engineers or transport,[3] unequipped for and incapable of either making an assault landing or advancing inland. Mackesy was instructed by the CIGS to secure a foothold near Narvik whence could be launched a major operation to eject the Germans from the town once he had been reinforced. The operation, codenamed 'Rupert' (a Churchillian invention from Prince Rupert of the Rhine), was ambitiously intended, according to the Military Coordination Committee, to secure Narvik as a base 'from which to reach out to the Gällivare orefields'.[4]

Already half-cocked as a very conception, 'Rupert' was now further compromised by command arrangements which repeated, and even improved on, all the confusions of British joint maritime operations from that of Lord Howard of Effingham and the Earl of Essex against Cadiz in 1596 to the Dardanelles itself. No supreme commander was appointed; Mackesy and Cork were supposed jointly to frame operations. True to a hallowed tradition, they quarrelled instead. Mackesy received instructions from the CIGS; Cork from the First Sea Lord and (more and more as time went on) the First Lord. Cork's command was quite separate from that of Forbes, the C-in-C, Home Fleet, who had to support him and protect his 800-mile-long lines of communication. Moreover, although Forbes's was the senior post, old Lord Cork as an Admiral of the Fleet was senior to Forbes. Thus their relations too were not always to be smooth.

To confusion of command was now added confusion over campaign priorities, which altered almost day by day, not least because the mind of the First Lord of the Admiralty and Chairman of the Military Coordination Committee was puffed this way and that by the shifting breezes of opportunity. Although on 10 April the Cabinet at Churchill's urging had chosen Narvik as the Allied objective, it authorised the COS the very next day to study a possible second operation (dubbed 'Maurice' by Churchill after the seventeenth-century Prince of Nassau) against Trondheim too, Churchill being then all in favour. But at a War Cabinet on 12 April he opted instead for concentrating all resources on Narvik – as the CIGS himself urged.[5] Optimistic as ever, Churchill claimed that plans for this 'were well advanced', and 'the landing could be made within a few days ... We could be reasonably sure of success at this point, and a success would show that we should be able ultimately to clear the Germans out of all the ports in which they obtained a foothold.'[6] On 13 April, despite his renewed plea that nothing 'must be allowed to deflect us from making the capture of this place [Narvik] as certain as possible', the Cabinet decided that Trondheim too should be recaptured. Next day however Churchill, intoxicated by the news of Whitworth's devastation of the German destroyers at Narvik, changed his mind again. He now believed that an Allied occupation of the town 'would not be seriously opposed', and he told the Cabinet that the naval staff thought that 'it might be possible' to land directly at Trondheim as well. He further reported that small scratch forces of seamen and marines were going to be landed at Namsos (a port north of Trondheim) and Alesund later that same day and next morning[7] – the very kind of 'ineffectual operations along the Norwegian coast' against which he had just been warning the Cabinet only the day before.[8] He now reckoned that a landing to retake Trondheim 'did not appear to involve unjustifiable risks'.[9]

That afternoon the Military Coordination Committee under his leadership decided to divert the 146th (Territorial) Infantry Brigade from 'Rupert' to 'Maurice', even though the Committee noted that its training 'was not yet advanced', so tending 'to increase the risk of the operation'.[10] Worse, the Brigade's stores and ordnance were not 'tactically loaded' in the ships for immediate use on landing, a fact neglected by Churchill and his luckless committee as they framed strategy off the map.[11] By this time Churchill had come to consider Trondheim 'an even greater prize than Narvik'.[12] He had in fact now stumbled on a strategic truth, for, as the German command itself well recognised, the Trondheim area, the gateway to Norway's long narrow waist, was the key to control of the whole country to the northwards, including Narvik.

So it was that when the Allies finally became committed to major land operations in Norway a week after 'Weserübung', they split their hastily improvised and ill-equipped forces between two strategic objectives 400 miles apart instead of concentrating them on one chosen aim. For the Royal Navy the task of putting ashore, and thereafter protecting and sustaining, these two far separate expeditionary forces was to strain its resources in ships and the endurance of the ships' companies to the uttermost.

Norway in 1940 serves as the precursor for such later maritime campaigns as the Allied landings in French North Africa in November 1942 ('Operation Torch'), the D-Day invasion of Normandy in 1944, and the entire United States offensive against Japan in the Pacific from 1942 to 1945, for here for the first time were seen fleet carriers, battleships, cruiser forces and destroyer escorts working together to cover and support major expeditionary forces ashore. But those later maritime operations were to be thoroughly planned and prepared beforehand. Their combined task forces were to be organised and rehearsed for their roles in good time. They were to enjoy unified command chains and specially equipped combined headquarters ships. They were to include fleet trains of oilers and supply ships to maintain the fleet on station without the need to rotate warships back to a distant shore base whenever fuel or ammunition ran low. None of these favourable factors existed in 1940. Instead, Admiral Forbes and the Home Fleet had been launched precipitately into a campaign for which they (and the British Army too) were in no sense prepared, and in which they were to be called upon to cope at short notice with the vagaries of Whitehall map warfare.

But the central operational problem for Forbes lay in the Luftwaffe operating at short range from Norwegian airfields. At its peak strength in early May the Luftwaffe numbered 710 aircraft, of which 360 were bombers, 50 dive-bombers, 50 modern single-engined monoplane fighters and some 60 long-range reconnaissance types.[13] On 13 April the Air Ministry withdrew the only two bomber squadrons serving with RAF Coastal Command back to Bomber Command, so leaving Coastal Command with virtually no striking force.[14] Bomber Command itself regarded air attack on German forces in Norway as a deviation from the pure Trenchardite doctrine of the strategic air offensive against enemy industries and cities. Although this offensive had yet to begin, lest it should unleash a much more powerful Luftwaffe attack on Britain, Bomber Command was jealously conserving its strength for the great day. Between 7 April and 10 May the Command flew fewer than 800 individual sorties against targets in Norway, compared with over 600 sorties in a fortnight flown by just two squadrons of Fighter Command from forward airstrips near Narvik.[15]

Apart from these Fighter Command squadrons, which in any case did not operate until the second half of May in time for the final offensive against Narvik, and a short-lived attempt to base a few RAF Gladiator biplane fighters on a frozen lake at Lesjaskog in central Norway late in April (an experiment abruptly ended when German bombers broke up the ice), the task of air defence of the Allied expeditionary forces and their bases as well as of the Fleet itself fell entirely on the aircraft and the anti-aircraft guns of the Royal Navy. However, even when the Home Fleet's only carrier *Furious* had been reinforced by the *Glorious* and the recently commissioned *Ark Royal* from the Mediterranean Fleet (making half of the Navy's strength in fleet carriers), their 120 assorted Skuas and Swordfish could be no match for the Luftwaffe either in performance or numbers.

It may be guessed, therefore, what were Forbes's sentiments on 17 April when, as the two allied expeditionary forces were beginning their separate campaigns, he received Churchill's assurance that all that had happened 'makes me sure that Hitler has made a grave strategic blunder in giving us the right, as we have always had the power, to take what we like on the Norwegian coast'.[16] Forbes can hardly have shared Churchill's evident relish in the same letter at the prospect of 'an increasingly vigorous campaign being fought along the Norwegian coast during the summer, and I trust we shall be able to beat them out of all their lodgements and establish ourselves in their place right down to Bergen'.[17] For Churchill in the Admiralty map room, playing at moving ships and soldiers around like an absorbed Victorian child on the nursery floor, had not even begun to learn the new lesson so sharply taught to Forbes by the Luftwaffe off the Norwegian coast on 9 April – any more than he had learned the old lesson of the Dardanelles about the dangers of improvising large-scale combined operations.

On 15 April, nearly a week after the launch of 'Weserübung', the Allied attempt to eject the Germans from Norway began when Convoy NP1 – three liners carrying the 24th Guards Brigade, and escorted by the battleship *Valiant* and nine destroyers – disembarked 'Rupertforce' at the little port of Harstad in Andfjord, the northern approach to Narvik. This cluster of brightly painted wooden houses at the edge of icy water was the designated base for operations against the German garrison holding Narvik and its environs. For the first time Admiral Lord Cork, the naval commander, and Major-General Mackesy, the land force commander, met each other (having sailed in separate ships). Cork wanted to attack Narvik without delay. Mackesy did not, because snow to a depth of four feet covered the entire region; because the Guards Brigade had no field or anti-aircraft artillery whatsoever (and of course no skis, snowshoes or Arctic warfare training); and because a direct assault would involve landing from open boats *à la* Gallipoli on beaches swept by German fire. Mackesy's caution displeased Churchill, who thereupon persuaded in turn the Chiefs of Staff, the Military Coordination Committee and the Cabinet to send Mackesy a prodding signal which he had drafted. It began:

> Your proposals involve damaging deadlock at Narvik and the neutralisation of one of our best brigades [sic]. We cannot send you the Chasseurs Alpins. HMS WARSPITE will be needed elsewhere in two or three days. Full consideration should therefore be given by you to an assault upon Narvik by WARSPITE and the destroyers. The capture of the port and town would be an important success. Send us your appreciation and act at once if you consider right. Matter most urgent.[18]

Churchill also sent a 'Personal and Private' signal to Cork, so thus bypassing the First Sea Lord, the naval staff and the C-in-C, Home Fleet inviting him to sneak on his military colleague Mackesy, and so poaching on the War Office's responsibilities: 'Should you consider that situation is being mishandled, it is your duty to report either to me personally or to the Admiralty about it, and what you would do yourself.'[19] But Cork reported that he felt bound to yield to the unanimous opinion of his military colleagues that an immediate assault was not a feasible operation of war.

On 20 April, Churchill persuaded the Cabinet to appoint Cork over Mackesy as commander of all the Narvik forces. It was the first concrete manifestation in the present war of his impatience with military realism. 'It seems to me,' he told Cork in another direct personal signal just after midnight on 21 April, 'that you can feel your way and yet strike hard. Please keep us informed as much as possible. Ask for what you want. Remember Luleå [the Swedish Baltic port] is open in about a month. Count on unflinching support of your friends at the Admiralty.'[20] For Churchill was still dreaming of a swift overland march from Narvik into neutral Sweden and the Gällivare orefields, Narvik having again for him taken over from Trondheim the role of 'greater prize'.[21] But his chosen fire-eater, Lord Cork, proved no better able than Mackesy to walk over waist-high snow. On 24 April Cork took the *Warspite*, three cruisers and eight destroyers up Ofotfjord with the aim of bombarding the German garrison into surrender. After blasting away in vain for three hours against targets invisible under heavy fresh snow cover, Cork retired disconsolate. No quick success then – instead a protracted siege, during which the Allied forces in the Narvik environs were to be eventually built up to

30,000 men, including a Polish brigade, the French *Chasseurs Alpins* and a demi-brigade of the Foreign Legion, together with some artillery and tanks.

Each fresh landing or further overland advance to close the ring on the German garrison was to depend on the close support of the guns and carrier aircraft of the Royal Navy. But it was also to fall to those guns and aircraft to protect the Allied forces and their bases from the Luftwaffe, especially the main base at Harstad. The carrier *Furious* (whose aircraft had bombed ahead of Whitworth's squadron at Narvik on 12 April) remained under Cork's command as his only source of air power until 26 April when, with her speed reduced to 20 knots by two near misses by German bombs that jarred her turbines and with only six serviceable aircraft left, she returned to the Clyde for repairs. Cork was then reduced to a squadron of slow Walrus biplane amphibians until the carrier *Ark Royal* arrived on 6 May after service off central Norway. In the judgment of Admiral Forbes, the C-in-C, Home Fleet, at this time: 'The main threat to the whole area is the enemy air power, and this is so real that it is scarcely an exaggeration to say that the Allied forces are maintaining their position by bluff.'[22] He went on to list over a dozen warships or merchant ships sunk, beached or damaged by German air attack. He noted that 'HARSTAD is the main base in the Narvik area for personnel and stores, the town is built of wood and every house is crammed to the roof. The A/A protection ashore consists of four 3.7″ guns, and the fire fighting appliances are nil.' Then there was the U-boat threat as well: 'Harstad, which is the main anchorage for transports, etc, is entirely open to submarine attack . . .' It was indeed beyond Forbes's resources in escort vessels, especially destroyers (yet another enfeebling legacy of the disarmament years), to provide screens for Allied shipping in the Narvik region from both bombers and U-boats, not least because of, in Forbes's own words, 'the vast extent of water to be covered'.[23]

Yet it was the two Allied expeditions to central Norway – while they lasted – that stretched and strained Forbes's fleet even more severely still, for here the Luftwaffe was operating in much more formidable strength, while the Allied ground operations themselves proved even more catastrophically half-cocked than those round Narvik – and even more prone to interference by the eager scanner of maps and charts back in Whitehall.

On 15 April small landing parties of seamen and marines went ashore at Namsos and Andalsnes, to the north and south of Trondheim – ordered there by Churchill and his colleagues with the purpose of distracting German attention from the proposed direct Allied seaborne assault on Trondheim ('Operation Hammer'). The party at Namsos reported next day that the little port possessed no unloading facilities and that its hinterland lay under deep snow. The decision was nevertheless taken in Whitehall to land 'Mauriceforce' (146th Infantry Brigade) in order both to strengthen the hoped-for diversion from the Trondheim attack, and also to support Norwegian units inland. Under cover of darkness on 16 and 17 April Mauriceforce disembarked at Namsos amid dire confusion stemming from the fact that the ships' crews and the troops lacked the equipment and the training for such a disembarkation, especially at night in a port without unloading facilities. Next day, lacking artillery, motor transport, tanks and air cover, and having left many stores in the ships, the unfortunate Territorials of 146th Brigade were taken by train to join Norwegian troops nearer towards Trondheim.[24]

The troops for Andalsnes, 'Sickleforce', 148th Infantry Brigade (also Territorials) had to transfer at sea from their transport, the liner *Orion*, to the cruisers *Galatea* and *Arethusa* and the anti-aircraft cruisers *Carlisle* and *Curacoa* for the landing because of the danger of air attack. The original loading of supplies into the *Orion* had been muddled enough; now their further transfer to the cruisers, together with the disembarkation and unloading at Namsos, again by totally inexperienced soldiers and sailors, led cumulatively to chaos. An eyewitness wrote of the conditions of stores in the *Orion* when the time came to offload:

> At the bottom of the hold was a vast pyramid of stores of every description, with men of a number of units climbing over it like flies looking for anything with their own unit's markings. The impression was that as any load came to the cranes, it was lifted, lowered and released over the pyramid.[25]

Hardly had these unfortunate forces got ashore at Namsos and Andalsnes when their roles were abruptly changed in Whitehall from the secondary one of diversion to the primary one of capturing Trondheim. For the proposal for a direct seaborne assault on the port ('Hammer') had been reluctantly abandoned by Churchill and his Cabinet colleagues in the face of professional opposition.

When the proposal (which was to be carried out by the main body of the Home Fleet) had been first put to Admiral Forbes on 14 April, he had replied that enemy bombing 'would start almost immediately' and that 'to carry out an opposed landing . . . under continuous air attack was not feasible'.[26] But Churchill, failing to comprehend the danger posed by the Luftwaffe, sought to argue Forbes down in a signal sent at 0121 on the 15th which ended: 'Pray consider this important project further.'[27] As a sweetener, Churchill promised that the attack 'could not take place for seven days devoted to careful preparation'.[28] On the following day he also told the Military Co-ordination Committee that 'Time was necessary to plan what was a hazardous and, if successful, would be a brilliant operation'.[29] Yet only two days later, when he sent an emissary (Rear-Admiral L. E. Holland) to see Forbes in his flagship in Scapa with details of the plan and a personal letter urging its merits, the date for 'Hammer' was named as 22 April; four days' notice for an operation not yet even finally decided on.[30]

Forbes had in fact earlier consented to carry out 'Hammer' provided the troops were transported in cruisers rather than vulnerable liners. But now he was aghast at the prospect of mounting a complex combined tri-service operation against a formidable enemy with hardly more notice than would be suitable for arranging a family trip round the bay. However, fortunately for him and his fleet, the Chiefs of Staff (COS) unanimously decided on 19 April that to take an armada into the confined waters of Trondheimfjord (an almost landlocked salt-water lake) would incur too great a risk from German air attack, both to the ships and to the landing forces during their run-in.[31] It is also possible that they drew a lesson from the experience the day before of the cruiser HMS *Suffolk*, which had been given the task of closing Stavanger airfield by bombardment as a preliminary to 'Hammer' (which the bombardment in fact failed to do). In the course of her withdrawal, the *Suffolk* had to endure seven hours of continuous Luftwaffe attack before Fleet Air Arm Skuas from Hatston arrived to protect her; and finally arrived back in Scapa so badly damaged that her quarter deck was awash.

The COS having put down 'Hammer', the First Sea Lord, Admiral Pound, had then played the cunning badger again by suggesting that Trondheim should instead be taken by Mauriceforce and Sickleforce in a pincer movement overland from north and south, whereupon Churchill gave way, accepted this proposal and sold it to the Cabinet. Pound's plan was, however, a military nonsense, because such hopelessly raw formations as 146th and 148th Brigades (initially lacking such basics as artillery) even when reinforced by regular British and French units, were to prove quite incapable of holding their own advanced positions against the German Army and the Luftwaffe, let alone push on towards Trondheim. Did Pound really believe his plan could succeed – or did he urge it as a device to get his own service out of 'Hammer'?

In the event only a week elapsed before the Trondheim 'pincers' had both been outfought in the field and thrown into retreat. Meanwhile the Royal Navy and the ships of the French Navy had been ferrying supplies and reinforcements to these doomed enterprises through the hazards of bomber and U-boat. On 18 April Admiral Edward-Collins with the cruisers *Galatea* and *Arethusa*, the anti-aircraft cruisers *Carlisle* and *Curacoa*, and two destroyers brought in 1,000 soldiers to Andalsnes and the port of Molde, further down Ramsdalfjord towards the sea. When Edward-Collins sailed for home in the small hours of the 19th he left the two anti-aircraft cruisers behind to serve as the only protection of Mauriceforce's bases against the Luftwaffe, no land-based anti-aircraft guns being available owing to the belated rearmament of the British Army. Next day the Luftwaffe began to launch continual daylight raids on Andalsnes, which restricted port operations to the brief and shrinking hours of the northern spring nights. On 24 April, by which time the two anti-aircraft cruisers – themselves prime German targets – had fired off most of their ammunition, *Curacoa* was hit and badly damaged. For the crews of *Curacoa* and *Carlisle*, as for the crews of other anti-aircraft ships which rotated to Norwegian ports that month, the daylight hours tested professional concentration and steadiness of nerve to the limit, as bombs constantly punched up pillars of white water from the fjords, and the 4-inch anti-aircraft guns and 2-pounder pom-poms crashed and drum-rolled, and the ships heeled under helm in violent evasive manoeuvres. Here for the first time was experienced that ordeal by prolonged air attack which would later become commonplace for Allied sailors in the Mediterranean and the Pacific.

The Navy's run of supplies and troops to Sickleforce and Mauriceforce went on. On 22 April the cruiser *Arethusa* brought into Andalsnes a few light anti-aircraft guns and the RAF advance party which was to organise the air-strip on the frozen lake at Lesjaskog. Next day Admiral Edward-Collins was back with another 2,000 soldiers for Sickleforce, carried in the cruisers *Galatea*, *Sheffield* and *Glasgow* and six destroyers. Two days later it was the turn of Vice-Admiral Sir Geoffrey Layton with the cruisers *Birmingham*, *Manchester* and *York*, together with three destroyers, to deliver the last reinforcements for the unfortunate Sickleforce – 1,600 soldiers and 300 tons of stores. On each occasion the task force unloaded and sailed again as quickly as possible in order to minimise the period of exposure to air attack while helplessly secured alongside.

North of Trondheim, at Namsos, the Navy's operations in support of Mauriceforce proved shorter lived. On 19 April the anti-aircraft cruiser *Cairo* led in four French transports carrying the *Chasseurs Alpins* and escorted by the cruiser *Emile Bertin* and French destroyers. The Luftwaffe found them; the bombing began and the *Emile Bertin* was damaged by a bomb. On 22 April more French reinforcements arrived at Namsos, but by now the port was suffering such continual heavy bombing that, although the troops themselves were disembarked, their storeships could not be unloaded. Henceforth further French reinforcements were to be diverted to the Narvik area, even though some stores and guns were still landed at Namsos on 27–28 April.

Just as at Narvik, the Royal Navy's carriers did what they could to provide air cover to the expeditionary forces and their bases in the face of the huge numerical and qualitative superiority of the enemy's land-based air force. HMS *Glorious* and *Ark Royal* joined the Home Fleet from the Mediterranean Fleet on 23 April, and sailed for central Norway next day under the command of Vice-Admiral L. V. Wells (Flag Officer, Aircraft Carriers), with eighteen RAF Gladiator fighters intended to operate from the frozen surface of Lake Lesjaskog. They were escorted by the cruiser *Berwick*, the anti-aircraft cruiser *Curlew* and six destroyers. Late that day the Gladiators were successfully flown off to their frozen lake, where in three brief days of action they made another contribution to the Norwegian campaign's catalogue of courage and hapless improvisation, shooting down six German aircraft for no loss of their own in the air, but having ten of their aircraft destroyed on the ground while being rearmed and refuelled. This process proved calamitously slow because the scratch groundcrew lacked adequate refuelling and starter-battery recharging equipment and because there was only one armourer for the squadron's 72 Browning machine-guns. On 27 April fuel for the surviving Gladiators (now based on another airstrip) ran out, whereupon the aircraft were destroyed and the personnel re-embarked.[32] Henceforward the task of providing air cover for the central Norway forces reverted entirely to the Fleet Air Arm. It had already been doing its best: from 24 to 26 April a few Skua fighters were maintained over Namsos and Andalsnes, while on 25 April 34 Skuas from *Glorious* and *Ark Royal* bombed Trondheim, followed by a second strike on the 28th by eighteen Skuas from *Ark Royal*. Neither attack caused serious damage. On the previous day Vice-Admiral Wells had had to detach *Glorious* to return to the United Kingdom in order to refuel; she did not rejoin him until 1 May – another demonstration of the operational cost to the Navy of depending for resupply on United Kingdom bases.[33]

After the decisive repulse of the pincer movements on Trondheim, the prospect of evacuation from Central Norway was gloomily debated in Whitehall from 23 April onwards. Churchill at first peddled the idea of reviving 'Hammer', only to have it knocked on the head on 26 April by the COS as a 'somewhat hazardous operation'; the COS also pointed out that Britain could not find the anti-aircraft guns to protect Trondheim even if it could be captured. Thereafter Churchill veered between supporting evacuation in order to concentrate on Narvik (his first choice), and wishing to delay evacuation as long as possible. Finally he suggested that Mauriceforce and Sickleforce should be dispersed into small parties to carry on a guerrilla campaign. This idea, fanciful even for him, was overridden by Chamberlain on the advice of the CIGS; and so on the evening of 27 April, in the wake of an Allied Supreme War Council meeting, the Military Coordination Committee came to the decision that the evacuations from central Norway should begin in three days' time.[34]

Now began the Royal Navy's worst ordeals in the Norwegian campaign. For the first time in the present war it would fall to its ships to rescue a defeated expeditionary force from a foreign shore and then bring it sadly home in the teeth of ferocious air attack.

In a prelude to the main evacuations the cruiser *Glasgow* went into the little port of Molde on 29 April under cover of darkness to pick up King Haakon VII of Norway, Crown Prince Olaf, and the Norwegian gold reserve. It was a scene of lurid drama: the town blazing furiously, the British cruiser going alongside the quay with her hoses pumping water on the fires; the King and his suite welcomed aboard from a tug (they could not reach the quay because of the fires) to the squeal of the bosun's pipe; dark, flame-flickering water opening between the ship's side and King Haakon's homeland as the *Glasgow* made for the open sea.[35]

Next night, 30 April, the cruisers *Galatea*, *Arethusa*, *Sheffield* and *Southampton* with a transport and six destroyers picked up 2,200 Allied soldiers from Molde and Andalsnes; on 1 May it was the *Manchester* and *Birmingham*, the anti-aircraft cruisers *Calcutta* and *Curlew*, together with five destroyers that brought off another 1,500 men from Andalsnes. It fell to HMS *Calcutta* and the sloop HMS *Auckland* to wait behind for the rearguard of Sickleforce. This was expected to number some 200 men, but in fact more than 700 soldiers assembled on the quayside. With calm professionalism the Navy got them all aboard within a quarter of an hour; battle-weary and bomb-shaken men thankful to be relatively safe and sheltered at last. Although the

Luftwaffe had bombed Andalsnes during the daylight hours each day of the evacuation and on 30 April and 1 May even at night, it had failed to prevent the Royal Navy from completing its mission of rescue, or to sink or damage a single ship.

Responsibility for the evacuation of the survivors of Mauriceforce from Namsos fell to Admiral J. D. H. Cunningham, who had left Scapa on 29 April with the cruisers *Devonshire* and *York*, the French cruiser *Montcalm*, five destroyers and three French transports, later to be strengthened by four more destroyers which had sailed in advance. On the night of 1 May (intended to be the first of two nights for the evacuation) the masts of Cunningham's force stood clear above what should have been a concealing bank of fog – perfect aiming marks for the Luftwaffe – while Namsos itself lay in clear moonlight and already rocking to German bombs. Cunningham therefore decided to postpone the evacuation for 24 hours and complete it in a single night, judging that 'to attempt to spread evacuation over two would be courting disaster'.[36] The Commander of Mauriceforce, Major-General Sir Adrian Carton de Wiart, VC, believed that to take off some 5,700 men in one brief night was impossible. But, as he was to acknowledge, he 'learned in a few hours that the Navy do not know the word'.[37] While Cunningham with the *Devonshire*, *Montcalm* and four destroyers remained in support outside the fjord, Captain P. L. Vian in the destroyer *Afridi* led in the remaining warships and the three French transports. Two of these latter went alongside the quay directly to embark troops, while the third and the cruiser *York* took on troops ferried out by destroyers and small craft. HMS *Afridi*, with Mauriceforce's rearguard on board, was the last ship to leave, her melancholy final task to destroy by gunfire the rearguard's belatedly provided motor transport on the quayside.

But the Luftwaffe did not let go so easily. At 0845 that forenoon, when offshore fog had lifted, it began a relentless onslaught on Cunningham's ships that lasted until 1530 and the task force was 200 miles out to sea. According to Admiral (then Captain) Vian writing in 1960:

> When the air attacks began, it was soon evident that the Junkers 88, which we knew by now so well, had been reinforced that morning by the Stuka dive-bomber, which we knew not at all. Up to that time they appear to have been used almost exclusively against troop formations ashore, or against guardships stationed at the ports. Almost at once a Stuka scored a hit on the *Bison*.[38]

As the *Afridi* went to pick up survivors from the *Bison* (a French destroyer) she too was hit and sunk.[39] Nevertheless the Stukas and the Junkers 88s failed to destroy any of the cruisers and transports laden with soldiers; and on 5 and 6 May Cunningham's task force steamed safely into Scapa Flow.

So in bravery and futility ended the ill-considered, ill-founded and absurdly optimistic Allied expedition to central Norway. It now remained to resolve the situation at Narvik.

The evacuations from central Norway at least brought immense relief to the Home Fleet, hitherto stretched between supporting three Allied bridgeheads hundreds of miles apart, as well as continuing its normal role of guarding against a breakout into the Atlantic by German heavy ships. In particular Admiral Forbes was now able to move his carriers north to cover in rotation the successive Allied local landings nearer and nearer to Narvik and also to protect Allied bridgeheads and bases. *Ark Royal*, which joined Admiral Lord Cork on 6 May, remained until 20 May, when HMS *Furious* ferried in some RAF Gladiators to operate from airstrips painfully constructed at Bardufoss and Bodo, and returned again to the Clyde. On 28 May the carrier *Glorious* reached Narvik waters with a squadron of RAF Hurricane 8-gun fighters, which, flying from Bardufoss, provided invaluable air cover for the final Allied offensive. Both these latter precious ships made the voyage from the United Kingdom without destroyer escort, so weak now was Forbes in this essential class of ship.[40] The siege of Narvik alone therefore sucked in, by rotation, three out of the Navy's six fleet carriers, as well as the anti-aircraft cruisers *Cairo* and *Curlew* (the latter sunk on 26 May), those substitutes for the land-based anti-aircraft batteries of which the Allied expeditionary force was so short.

It fell to the sturdy workhorses of the campaign, the cruisers and destroyers, to provide close fire support to each Allied landing or advance during the closing of the ring round the German garrison. On 7 May, in the eerie half-light of a northern summer midnight, the cruisers *Effingham* and *Aurora* and five destroyers led by the battleship *Resolution* covered a successful landing at the head of Herjangsfjord, north of Narvik, by French troops in four infantry assault craft and the single motor landing craft available. On the night of 27 May, the eve of the final successful assault on Narvik, the broadsides of cruisers *Cairo*, *Coventry* and *Southampton*, together with five destroyers, opened the way for another landing south of the town by French and Norwegian troops.[41]

However, just at this period when Admiral Forbes was enabled to concentrate his scarce resources on Narvik waters, new distractions from outside the Norwegian theatre of war served to drain ships from his command. For in the wake of the weakening of the Mediterranean Fleet in April by the transfer of the battleship *Warspite* and the carriers *Glorious* and *Ark Royal* to the Home Fleet, the long dormant Italian factor in the triple strategic threat to the British Empire had shown disquieting signs of reawakening. There were fears of Italian aggression in the Balkans; worse, that Mussolini might now choose to enter the war on Germany's side. So back to the Mediterranean went *Warspite* on 24 April, followed in the middle of May by the anti-aircraft cruiser *Carlisle*, seventeen destroyers and two sloops.[42] Nearer home there was continued apprehension that the expected grand German offensive against France and the Low Countries might soon be launched; and on 7 May the Admiralty transferred *Galatea* and *Arethusa* from the Home Fleet to Sheerness in the Thames Estuary, and eight destroyers to Harwich, on the Essex coast opposite Holland.

On 10 May apprehension became fact when 137 German divisions began to roll across the western frontiers of the *Reich*. Within five days Holland had capitulated and the French front on the Meuse had been smashed. Each further day brought the panzer divisions closer and closer to the Channel coast; the danger swiftly grew that the Allied Northern Army Group (including the British Expeditionary Force) might be cut off from the main body of the French Army and forced back to the North Sea coast of Flanders. This looming crisis drained away still more of Forbes's strength – three destroyers to the Humber on 18 May, the cruisers *Manchester* and *Sheffield* to the same destination on 26 May.[43] As a result Forbes was left with no available escorts for his precious carriers or other heavy ships: hence the appallingly risky lone voyages of *Glorious* and *Furious* to Narvik on 20 and 28 May.

By this time the German offensive in the West had brutally thrust home the strategic truth which ought to have been obvious to Churchill and his colleagues from the very birth of the idea of an Allied intervention in Scandinavia back in the winter – that, given Allied (especially British) military weakness and shortage of equipment, any forces sent to Scandinavia must be an enfeebling diversion from the crucial theatre of France and the Low Countries. Churchill was now no longer First Lord of the Admiralty but Prime Minister and Minister of Defence – by a neat coincidence of history appointed in Chamberlain's place on the first day of the German offensive, 10 May; and by an equally neat historical irony, as a result of a political crisis in which Chamberlain had been blamed for the fiascoes in Norway. In

Churchill's place as First Lord of the Admiralty was appointed the Labour and Co-operative Member of Parliament, A. V. Alexander, a Somerset countryman and a sound administrator, who, unlike his predecessor, was to enflame neither the Cabinet, nor the Admirals. So on 20 May, as the German spearheads approached Arras and the awful prospect loomed of having to evacuate the BEF from France, Churchill is found signalling Lord Cork to complain about the continued stagnation around Narvik and point out that the Narvik expedition 'is eating up large quantities of shipping and other essential supplies. More destroyers will be needed in the South very soon . . .'[44] By the 23rd he had concluded that the Narvik forces must be withdrawn; Britain was going to need them for her own defence.[45] In the meantime Cork had planned the final assault on Narvik for 28 May. It was now decided in London that its capture and the final defeat of the German garrison should merely serve the purpose of covering the evacuation of the Allied forces. This was to be completed by 8 June.

On 31 May there began therefore the dismal and hazardous process of winding up the campaign which Churchill had hoped would last all summer and culminate in the occupation of the Gällivare orefields. Under cover of darkness the advanced base of Bodo, with its airstrip, was evacuated. The town itself had now been reduced by the Luftwaffe to smouldering embers. The first convoy carrying stores, guns and tanks had already left the main Allied base area at Harstad. A second convoy carrying equipment sailed on 7 June. For Admiral Lord Cork, however, the greater problem lay in safely getting away the 24,500 Allied soldiers in and around Narvik in the face of German air power, even though the carriers *Ark Royal* and *Glorious* joined him on 2 June, their aircraft supplementing the RAF Hurricanes and Gladiators of 46 and 263 Squadrons, which operated with formidable effect from the airstrip at Bardufoss until the last moment.

In order to minimise the danger to his convoys from bombers, Cork established a rendezvous for the fifteen troopships (two of which were not needed in the event) some 180 miles off shore, and brought in the ships two at a time to Harstad, where they were loaded with soldiers and stores ferried from Narvik by destroyers. In the small hours of 7 June the first homeward convoy of 15,000 soldiers in six liners and the veteran (partly disarmed) cruiser *Vindictive* left the assembly area at sea for home. In the early forenoon of 9 June followed the second troop convoy (four liners, three small merchant vessels; 10,000 men). This convoy was later joined by the cruiser *Southampton*, which at 0900 the previous day had embarked Admiral Lord Cork, Lieutenant-General Sir Claude Auchinleck (who had replaced the luckless Mackesy as commander of the land forces), the French General Béthouart, and the rearguard.[46]

Yet all unknown to Cork his complex and protracted evacuation and his ill-protected troopships on the high seas were exposed to appalling danger. For the *Scharnhorst* and *Gneisenau*, escorted by the heavy cruiser *Hipper* and three destroyers, were off the Norwegian coast looking for just such an opportunity. Vice-Admiral Marschall, flying his flag in the *Gneisenau*, had left Kiel on 4 June with orders to attack the Allied base at Harstad. Three days later he refuelled his ships at sea 500 miles west of Tromso in northern Norway, and then turned to a course just west of south. By now he knew from the customary invaluable decrypts of British cypher radio traffic that the Allies were evacuating Narvik, and that their convoys were in the process of steaming across the North Sea for home. In the early forenoon of 8 June he spread his ships out like the fingers of a hand grasping for a victim.

Yet it was not until more than twenty-four hours later that Admiral Forbes left Scapa for Norwegian waters with the battleship *Rodney* (flag) and the battlecruiser *Renown*. No prior concentration of the Home Fleet in the north-central North Sea to cover the evacuations and convoys had been ordered, either by the Admiralty or Forbes himself, even though Cork had asked for such cover, and even though Forbes had requested to be informed of convoy movements. This initial failure to concentrate powerful forces at sea apparently stemmed from complacency induced by the failure of German warships or U-boats to interrupt Allied lines of communication during the campaign itself.[47] However, it also stemmed from yet another failure in the Admiralty's gathering of Intelligence, its evaluation and operational application. The relatively new techniques of Wireless Traffic Analysis (that is, monitoring the pattern and density of enemy radio traffic, and drawing inferences therefrom) had suggested for the previous fortnight that some kind of German naval offensive in the North Sea was pending. On 29 May and again on 7 June the Naval Section of the Government Code and Cypher School (GC and CS) at Bletchley Park repeated these indications to the Admiralty Operational Intelligence Centre (OIC). But OIC, in its scepticism about the value of such untested techniques, failed to pass the warnings on to the Home Fleet. Moreover, in a very proper concern for secrecy about the Allied evacuation movements, only a few senior staff in OIC, and no one at GC and CS at Bletchley, were informed that they were to take place; not even Coastal Command was informed, which accounts for its failure to carry out air searches of the sea areas through which the convoys had to pass.[48]

There now ensued an error of judgment curiously similar to that which had originally given the 'Weserübung' forces a clear run to their destinations on 7–8 April, and springing from the same British obsession with a German breakout on to the Atlantic convoy routes. On receipt on 5 June of a false sighting north-east of the Faeroes by a British 'Q' ship (a reconnaissance vessel disguised as a merchantman) of German heavy ships heading towards Iceland, Forbes ordered Admiral Whitworth to sea with the *Rodney* and *Renown*, two cruisers and five destroyers with the task of intercepting these supposed raiders. To meet and defend Cork's homeward-bound convoys, Forbes only despatched the battleship *Valiant*.[49] In these faulty dispositions of the Home Fleet lies one reason why Marschall with the *Scharnhorst* and *Gneisenau* now came to inflict the last and most grievous single wound of the Norway campaign on the Royal Navy.

In the small hours of 8 June eight Hurricane and ten Gladiator fighters of 46 and 263 Squadrons, RAF, from Bardufoss successfully landed on HMS *Glorious* – the first time such modern land-based aircraft and their pilots had ever carried out such a delicate evolution, and of course without benefit of arrester hooks to engage the carrier's arrester wires. *Glorious* then set a lone course for home, escorted only by the destroyers *Acasta* and *Ardent*. It has never been established for certain why Lord Cork permitted this risky procedure rather than keep her in company with the rest of his task force. What *is* known is that the captain of the *Glorious*, Guy D'Oyly Hughes, was a throwback to the worst kind of arrogant, authoritarian and choleric Edwardian naval officer. In the words of one former Fleet Air Arm subordinate, '. . . D-H was a very vain man and would not admit his ignorance on air matters and tried to enforce his views by bullying and bluster . . .'[50] D'Oyly Hughes was a submarine specialist with only ten months' prior experience in a carrier. His dangerously unrealistic orders for air operations earlier in the Norway campaign had brought him into violent collision with his Naval Commander (Air), Captain J. B. Heath, RN. When Heath protested against these orders Hughes gave way to ungovernable rage, later putting Heath ashore at Scapa to await a court martial on the charge of cowardice in the face of the enemy. It is therefore possible that Hughes, in an unbalanced desire to pursue the charge against Heath, persuaded Lord Cork to let him take *Glorious* on ahead.[51]

In the afternoon of 9 June *Glorious* was steaming homewards at a modest 17 knots with steam in only twelve of her eighteen boilers.

Not one of her aircraft was armed and at instant readiness on the flight deck, and no air search or air cover was being flown, although some aircraft in the hangar deck (congested with the Gladiators and Hurricanes) were at ten minutes' notice. It was a clear day, with maximum visibility, but nevertheless no lookout had been posted in the crow's nest. The wind was north-west, Force 2 to 3.[52] At 1600 (British summer time) the German battlecruisers sighted the funnel smoke of this flightless and sitting steel duck. At 1630 *Scharnhorst*'s 11-inch guns opened fire at 28,000 yards, the shells plunging down steeply with the usual Germanic accuracy on to the lightly armoured carrier. Serious damage to *Glorious*'s hangar deck was soon followed by more hits abaft the engine room which started uncontrollable fires.

Now once again, British destroyers sacrificed themselves in an attempt to save a situation in the face of great odds. The *Acasta* (Commander C. E. Glasford) and *Ardent* (Lieutenant-Commander J. F. Barker) laid a smoke screen temporarily to shield the *Glorious* from enemy range-finders and steamed at utmost speed to engage their 32,000-ton opponents with torpedoes. At about 1728 *Ardent*, having fired all her torpedoes, succumbed to the German battleships' crushing weight of fire and capsized. Some twelve minutes later *Glorious* herself, by now a blazing hulk with a heavy list to starboard, also capsized and sank. This did not deter *Acasta* from making a final run at the enemy, her 4.7-inch guns firing vainly at thickly armoured targets, a last salvo of torpedoes tracking for the German ships' more vulnerable hulls below the waterline. One torpedo struck home abreast of *Scharnhorst*'s after main turret, knocking out two of her three engine rooms and reducing her speed to 20 knots. But at 1808 *Acasta*, riven by huge internal explosions and with flames and smoke pouring from most of her length, was also reduced to a sinking condition. Only 45 men out of the 1,474 in the ships' companies of the *Glorious*, *Acasta* and *Ardent* were later rescued. All the gallant RAF pilots of 46 and 263 Squadrons went down with the carrier; a tragic loss and a needless waste of men of high skill, too few of which did Britain possess.[53] Thus had the Royal Navy lost one-sixth of its global strength in fleet carriers – and just as needlessly as HMS *Courageous* in September 1939. But at least Vice-Admiral Marschall and his battleships had missed the greater prize of Lord Cork's convoys packed with troops. When, after taking the damaged *Scharnhorst* into Trondheim, Marschall made a fresh sortie with *Gneisenau* and *Hipper* on 10 June, he was far too late to intercept them.

Neither Admiral Forbes in Scapa Flow nor the Admiralty had received *Glorious*'s 'enemy' report (in any case cut short by German fire), while *Acasta* and *Ardent*, in the thick of a desperate encounter, had sent none. Forbes was first alerted in the forenoon of the next day, 8 June, that the German battleships were in the area of the British convoy routes home by a report from HMS *Valiant*, which had just been informed by the hospital ship *Atlantis* that she had been stopped the day before by *Gneisenau* and *Scharnhorst* (when the troopship *Orama*, in company with her, was sunk by the *Hipper*). *Valiant*'s report was confirmed in the afternoon of 9 June in dismaying fashion by the German radio announcement of the *Glorious*'s sinking. Only now, therefore, did Forbes put to sea in the *Rodney* and with *Renown* (which had returned from the vain sortie towards Iceland), ordering the *Repulse* (still off Iceland) to join him as quickly as possible.

There then followed the last blunder of the campaign. On 11 June air search from the *Ark Royal* (which had now joined Forbes) revealed that the two German battleships and the *Hipper* lay in Trondheim harbour. It was therefore decided to launch an air strike – but with Skua dive-bombers rather than Swordfish torpedo-carriers. However, the 500-pound bomb carried by the Skua, though effective against the deck armour of a cruiser like the *Königsberg* (sunk at Bergen on 10 April), could not penetrate a battleship's deck armour. To sink or seriously damage such a ship required a torpedo. But Pound, Forbes and Rear-Admiral Phillips (Deputy Chief of Naval Staff), all traditionalists with no first-hand aviation experience, failed to understand this; and Pound in particular entertained a prejudice against the Swordfish, a much more versatile and effective weapons platform than its antique appearance suggested. Throughout the campaign there had been repeated mishandlings of naval aviation, partly owing to a refusal to seek or heed the specialist advice of the airmen in the Naval Staff's Naval Air Division – these officers having too few gold rings on their sleeves to warrant their being consulted by admirals.[54] Before the raid on Trondheim, however, the airmen on the naval staff at least were able to persuade their superiors to give Forbes latitude to use Swordfish aircraft if he wished. Forbes did not so wish. On 12 June 1940 fifteen Skuas attacked the German ships in Trondheim; one bomb hit the *Scharnhorst*'s deck but failed even to explode; eight Skuas failed to return to the *Ark Royal*.[55]

The Norwegian campaign cost the Royal Navy an aircraft carrier, two cruisers, seven destroyers, one sloop and four submarines. The German Navy suffered absolutely and relatively far worse: three cruisers, ten destroyers and six U-boats sunk; three battleships, two cruisers and several smaller vessels damaged (including two of the battleships badly damaged).[56] But this favourable balance could not disguise the fact that Britain, a great naval power, had suffered a strategic defeat in a major maritime campaign at the hands of a continental land power with a small navy – in considerable part because of flaws in the British command and control system and the errors of judgment and the vacillating purpose of the Navy's political and professional leadership. The campaign demonstrates how many old operational and strategic lessons had still to be learned afresh; how many new lessons had yet to be digested. In particular it reveals how under-equipped and backward in thinking were the Royal Navy and Royal Air Force Coastal Command in regard to the air dimension, and how poor was the apparatus for gathering and disseminating operational Intelligence compared with the enemy's. On 15 June 1940 Admiral Sir Charles Forbes (who of course could not know that the enemy was able to read much of the Royal Navy's encyphered radio traffic) reported to the Admiralty that the loss of *Glorious* owing to

> the quite unexpected appearance of enemy forces . . . shows that it is absolutely essential that our scheme of air reconnaissance should be overhauled . . . The enemy reconnoitres Scapa daily if they consider it necessary. Our reconnaissances of the enemy's main bases are few and far between . . . It is most galling that the enemy should know just where our ships . . . always are, whereas we generally learn where his major forces are when they sink one or more of our ships.[57]

But by the time Forbes wrote this report the disasters in Norway had been eclipsed by catastrophe on the grandest scale in France and the Low Countries, the consequences of which were already transforming the shape of the war, and presenting the Royal Navy with the grimmest challenge of its history.

6

'Operation Dynamo': the Dunkirk Evacuation

Like a warship lying off a city that was being engulfed by volcanic lava, British seapower could be no more than the impotent spectator of the catastrophe which overwhelmed the Allied armies in the West after 10 May 1940. While Dutch resistance was being crushed in just five days by savage Luftwaffe attack, by German airborne forces landing deep behind the inundations of 'Fortress Holland' and by a panzer division thrusting overland by means of key bridges seized by surprise, the Royal Navy could only lay a minefield off the Dutch coast, and despatch a cruiser squadron (the 2nd: Admiral Edward-Collins) and some destroyers to protect the minelayers, bring away the Dutch gold reserve, rescue Queen Wilhelmina and the Dutch Crown Princess, and attempt to demolish the port installations at Ijmuiden, The Hook and Flushing (so far as the local authorities would consent). To the south, while the German Army Group 'A' drove across the Belgian plain towards Brussels and Antwerp, frontally attacking the Allied Northern Army Group including the British Expeditionary Force (BEF), the Royal Navy's contribution consisted of sending demolition parties into the port of Antwerp, and successfully bringing back to England 26 merchant ships, 50 tugs and some 600 barges and dredgers.[1] And while the seven panzer divisions of Army Group 'B' smashed the French front on the Meuse and scythed westwards to the Channel coast, reaching it on 22 May and completely cutting off the Allied Northern Army Group from the main body of the French Army, the Admiralty could do no more than make arrangements for switching the BEF's supply route from Le Havre to Boulogne, Calais and Dunkirk. It was all a fresh demonstration of the impotence of maritime supremacy to affect the issue of a decisive campaign on land, and of the slow and uncertain effect of blockade on the ability of a continental state like Germany to wage war on the grand scale.

Even after the German panzer thrust reached the sea west of Abbeville and swung northwards in the direction of the Channel ports, so threatening to cut the Allied Northern Army Group off from the coast, Churchill and the French high command alike had continued to cherish the fantasy that a combined Allied counter-stroke from north and south of the panzer corridor could yet save the battle. But Field-Marshal Lord Gort, the C-in-C, BEF, a practical, severely realistic fighting soldier who had already measured at first hand the chaos and demoralisation of the French command system and the exhaustion of offensive power in the Northern Army Group, finally decided in the evening of 25 May that the BEF must fall back immediately on the Channel ports. Four hours later Churchill came independently to the same conclusion.

At 1900 on 26 May, therefore, the Admiralty made a signal to Vice-Admiral B. H. Ramsay (Flag Officer Commanding Dover) that 'Operation Dynamo' was to commence 'with the greatest vigour'.[2] The Admiralty hoped that this operation might at best succeed in rescuing a total of 45,000 Allied soldiers (a small fraction only of the Northern Army Group) over two days, after which evacuation would probably be ended by enemy action.

The headquarters of the Vice-Admiral, Dover, were located deep down in the chalk behind the famous 'white cliffs', in galleries and little chambers excavated by French prisoners during the Napoleonic Wars – the last time that England had faced a formidable enemy across the narrow seas. The main gallery ended in a windowed embrasure in the cliff face overlooking the harbour and the Channel; where a cannon had once pointed towards the French, Ramsay had his own office. The narrow iron balcony beyond served Ramsay as the stern walk of a ship-of-the-line; a place of momentary refuge in sun and breeze, yet in plain hearing of the unceasing guns and bombs across the Channel. Deepest inside the chalk was a large conference chamber which, during the Great War, had housed an electrical power plant and was therefore known as the 'Dynamo Room'. Since the daunting task of rescuing as many men as possible from the stricken

Northern Army Group had been assigned to the Vice-Admiral, Dover, and his headquarters, and since the Dynamo Room was to serve as the nerve centre of the operation, 'Dynamo' seemed a natural choice for the operation's codename. But in retrospect it sums up perfectly the whole character and spirit of the enterprise.

The Vice-Admiral, Dover, himself, Bertram Ramsay, as a former member of the directing staffs of the Naval Staff College and the Imperial Defence College, exemplified the younger generation of highly professional sailor. Ramsay, son of an ancient Highland family long resident in the Lowlands, combined austere personal integrity, high professionalism and a personal warmth which won the enthusiastic loyalty of his subordinates. His resignation from the Navy in 1935 as a consequence of his clash when Chief of Staff, Home Fleet, with Admiral Sir Roger Backhouse, the then C-in-C and one of the old school of 'do-it-all-yourself' admirals, had in the event caused only a temporary check in his career. While on the retired list he had been asked to report on the condition of Dover as a defended operational base. The report led to a £750,000 programme of re-equipment and to the earmarking of Ramsay himself for the command at Dover in the event of war. In September 1939 Dover Command was duly set up under him as Flag Officer, although he remained on the retired list. At first Ramsay was subordinate to the C-in-C, Nore, but soon he was reporting direct to the Admiralty. Here then was an admiral with the character to bear the weight of responsibility for a desperate and dangerous venture, and the training and mental calibre to lead what would grow in the course of 'Dynamo' into the largest staff of any admiral ashore or afloat, and tri-service at that.

The dynamo had first begun to turn a week before the Admiralty's executive signal on 26 May. A joint services conference was held at the War Office in London on 19 May to discuss the temporary (as it was then hoped) supply of the BEF through Boulogne, Calais and Dunkirk. But the meeting also considered 'the hazardous evacuation of very large Forces'; a contingency nonetheless still thought to be 'unlikely'. It was decided to delegate control of these operations to the Vice-Admiral, Dover, and to place all available shipping at his disposal. So swift was the advance of the panzer divisions and the consequent worsening of the plight of the Allied forces to the north of the German breakthrough that in the next two days, 20 and 21 May, further meetings were held, this time at Dover, to tackle the question of large-scale evacuation. It was confirmed that all sea movements would be placed under Ramsay's control, and that Army,

Ministry of Shipping and RAF liaison officers should be attached to his staff. As Ramsay confided to his wife in a letter on 21 May, '... things are getting even more hectic, & more & more tasks & responsibilities are being thrown on to me. The situation is really grave and I just fail to visualise what it will be in 4 or 5 days time ...'[3]

In fact Ramsay's ships were already in the thick of the battle at Boulogne and Calais, where the French garrisons had been hastily strengthened by troops transported from England, for it was crucial to prevent for as long as possible the panzer divisions driving on up the coast to Dunkirk and so finally cutting off the BEF from rescue. The sieges of Boulogne on 22–25 May and Calais on 22–26 May set in miniature the pattern to come at Dunkirk – the Army (the Guards and Royal Artillery in Boulogne; the Queen Victoria's Rifles, the Rifle Brigade and the Royal Tank Regiment in Calais) holding fast against colossal odds until the moment came for evacuation by cross-Channel ferry steamers escorted by the Navy's destroyers; the ports themselves smashed into ruins and lying under palls of smoke; navigation in congested channels and basins amid wrecks and mines under a hail of bombs and shells demanding superb ship-handling. In the case of Calais there was to be in fact no final evacuation of the garrison, for such was the need to win maximum time for the BEF to fall back on Dunkirk that the riflemen were ordered to fight on to the end. The cost to the Royal Navy and the French Navy of these preliminary operations was high. By the time Boulogne fell Ramsay was left with only two undamaged destroyers. When on 24 May, having received fresh reinforcements, he despatched the destroyers *Grafton*, *Greyhound* and the Polish *Burza* to join the *Vimiera* and *Wessex* off Calais in bombarding German troops on shore, the Luftwaffe promptly sank the *Wessex* and damaged the *Burza* and *Vimiera*.

A letter from Ramsay to his wife on 23 May gives an insight into the strain already being imposed on him and his staff by this mere prelude to the main operation to come:

> Things are so desperately serious ... I have now been entrusted with 'What is to happen'. No bed for any of us last night and probably not for many nights. I'm so sleepy I can hardly keep my eyes open, and we are all the same ...
>
> We've been on the telephone to everyone from the P.M. downwards, and the situation only becomes more & more difficult from hour to hour ...[4]

And he added, thinking of Boulogne and Calais:

> It's hateful having to order ships to do things and go places where one knows they are going to get bombed to blazes and to send troops into what I know to be an inferno . . .

Yet Ramsay and his staff were also having to grapple at the same time with the much vaster problems of organising in breakneck haste the mass evacuation of the BEF and French troops from Dunkirk.

> Days and nights are all one & we are dealing with a situation as complex as it is unsavoury . . . [he wrote to his wife on 25 May]. It's been my lot to operate the naval part of this & any thing more difficult and unpleasing I've never been faced with. At this very moment, we are racked with anxiety about the situation in Calais . . . We are also working in several dimensions as well at the same time and the offices are a veritable beehive of naval & military officers.[5]

By 26 May the BEF had succeeded in falling back into the Dunkirk perimeter despite the efforts of troops from two German army groups, closing in from north and south, to trap them or overwhelm them. How the BEF so succeeded belongs to the history of the land campaign: suffice to say that, while the stout defence of Boulogne and Calais helped, as did the decision by Hitler and his generals to hold back the panzer divisions for employment in the next phase of the Battle of France (against the main body of the French Army covering Paris), it was above all due to the BEF's own fighting qualities and to the imperturbable leadership and sure tactical dispositions of its C-in-C, Lord Gort.

By 29 May the remains of the French 1st Army too had poured back into the congested beach-head. Behind the protection of the devoted British and French rearguard manning the defensive perimeter some 400,000 Allied soldiers, exhausted after more than a fortnight of marching and fighting, were now spread across the wide beaches and the grassy dunes that stretched on both sides of Dunkirk, or crowded into the shattered town. The Allied army sprawled against the barrier of the sea like a great wounded beast finally cornered by the hunters; and the whole world was watching, waiting to witness its expected death throes. Yet beyond the wide sands bright under the summer holiday sunshine, between shore and horizon, the soldiers could see that the Navy was there and that they were not forsaken.

The key to 'Dynamo's' prospects of success lay in lifting capacity. But this obvious truth embraces huge problems not easy to solve under the hounding pressure of time and the enemy's air and land attack.

In the first place lifting capacity depended on the available resources of ships and craft which the Admiralty and the Ministry of Shipping could mobilise for Ramsay's use out of Britain's already tightly stretched Navy and Merchant Marine. This mobilisation began a week before 'Dynamo's' commencement; it gathered momentum during the operation as one desperate day followed another. Every strand of England's great maritime heritage came to be represented in the flotilla plying between the bomb-rocked and bullet-raked beaches, the burning port and the safety of home. The Admiralty managed to put 39 destroyers including the Polish *Blyskawica* at Ramsay's disposal – one fifth of the Navy's remaining total after the losses in Norway and off Calais and Boulogne. Given all the continuing demands of Atlantic convoy escort, the still continuing Narvik operation, the Mediterranean Fleet and the Far East, and the evident future requirements of Britain's own defence against invasion, this marked a courageous acceptance of great risk; and there was to be a moment when the Admiralty would have its second thoughts. Also under the White Ensign sailed the anti-aircraft cruiser *Calcutta*, 38 minesweepers, 61 minesweeping craft, 18 anti-submarine trawlers, a sloop, two gunboats hardly fit for the open sea, six corvettes and 76 miscellaneous small craft, including motor boats, flare-burning drifters, yachts and a pinnace.

The major contribution of the Merchant Marine lay in 36 personnel carriers – pre-war passenger ferries (four of them French) from the cross-Channel and Irish sea routes – some of the crews of which had already endured their full ration of fear and exhaustion in the hazardous crossings to Calais and Boulogne. But also under the Red Ensign served seven hospital carriers (also pre-war ferries), three stores ships; tugs and trawlers and dredgers; even London Fire Brigade fire-floats; fishing boats (some of them still under sail); cockle boats that had never ventured beyond the shallow waters and mud banks of the Thames Estuary. And then there were the other 'little ships' that were to pass into the Dunkirk legend – the frail yachts and small craft belonging to peacetime weekenders and holidaymakers who loved 'messing about in boats'; either seagoing vessels from the little anchorages round England's southern coasts, or river craft which had never before seen the open sea. To bring together this swarm of small craft was the triumph of the Admiralty Small Boat Pool; to organise and equip it that of the Navy base organisation at Ramsgate, which issued 1,000 charts (600 of them with routes to Dunkirk already laid off) and 500 sets of routing instructions; and which carried out all the necessary mechanical and electrical repairs, in some cases on very ancient engines indeed.[6]

Yet the sea heritages of the Low Countries and France too made their important contributions. From the Netherlands came 43 'schuyts', translated in Royal Navy English as 'skoots': handy, robust motor vessels which with the Navy personnel aboard proved among the most versatile of all the vessels employed in 'Dynamo'. Belgium supplied five modern tugs, again robust all-purpose craft apt for operating in confined waters; and many trawlers as well. The French Navy deployed nineteen destroyers or torpedo boats. And all three countries furnished their own 'little ships' and the courage of their crews – launches, barges, drifters, eel boats. A total of over 900 ships and craft of all types and sizes and speeds thus passed under the control of the Vice-Admiral, Dover, and 848 of them saw service in 'Dynamo'. To organise and operate them all as a coherent whole therefore constituted an outstanding feat of staff work on the part of Ramsay and his headquarters.

The second decisive factor in determining how many soldiers could be brought home lay in the means and methods for getting them from shore to ship. The very gently shelving sandy beaches and shoaling waters of the coast on both sides of Dunkirk meant that only small craft could get in close enough to take on soldiers, and even then the soldiers would have to wade far into the sea to meet them. In Dunkirk itself the vast inner docks had been rendered totally unusable by German bombing. This left as a possible embarkation point the outer basin, embraced by two narrow latticework wooden moles of relatively light construction stretching about a mile seawards: the West Mole from the oil terminal and the East Mole from the town itself, neither designed for the berthing of ships like ferries and destroyers. With the West Mole apparently inaccessible through the burning oil terminal, and the East Mole reckoned to be unsuitable for the berthing of large vessels, it therefore seemed that 'Dynamo' could be decisively choked at the very points of embarkation.

But in any case there was a third determinant of carrying capacity – the length and duration of transit between England and Dunkirk. The shorter the route, the more voyages a vessel could make in a given timespan. Two routes were plotted at the outset of 'Dynamo': Route 'Z' direct from Dover to the French coast off Calais and then along the coastline to Dunkirk (at 39 sea miles, the shorter), and Route 'Y' round the north of the Goodwin Sands and due eastwards to a point well to the east of Dunkirk, and then abruptly south-south-west to approach the beaches and the port via the 'North Channel' (87 sea miles). However, as early as 27 May the advance of the German Army beyond Gravelines brought the final section of Route

'Z' under heavy artillery fire, so rendering it dangerous to use. Ramsay was forced to switch his effort to Route 'Y', which doubled the distance and halved the potential load capacity. Then again, this whole sea area crowded with shipping would have to be protected as best it could be against attacks by German surface ships or U-boats.

Yet another major factor determining 'Dynamo's' degree of success was supplied by the Luftwaffe. The German Navy, gutted by its losses off Norway, and the German Army were very content to leave it to the Luftwaffe to seal the fate of the Allied Northern Army Group by breaking up any attempt at evacuation. The Luftwaffe was to do its formidable best, as the losses to Ramsay's ships and the horrific experiences of his ships' companies would testify.

And still there remained the imponderable factors; above all, the weather. Even a moderately choppy sea of the kind so frequent in the Straits of Dover would bar many of the small craft, and certainly river boats, from sailing at all. Moreover, the breaking waves of such a sea would render embarkation from the beaches impossible. A full Channel gale, by no means unusual even in summer, would wreck the entire operation. But virtually throughout the course of 'Dynamo' the sea was to remain calm under a warm sun, the run of good weather marred only by occasional fog, and on 31 May by the short but unpleasant waves rolled on to the beaches by a north-easterly breeze, temporarily halting the process of picking up soldiers from the shallows. As Ramsay thankfully noted in his despatch:

> The operation was favoured by extremely good weather. It was found, however, that any northerly wind caused a surf, which greatly reduced the rate of lifting from the beaches. It must be fully realised that a wind of any strength in the northern section between South West and North East would have made evacuation impossible. At no time did this happen.[7]

If there were a true 'miracle of Dunkirk', it surely lay in this blessing of generally fine weather.

And the last of all the factors governing success, a factor again incalculable in advance: how long could the ships' companies keep going without sleep; keep on returning to the bombs, the shells, the machine-gun bullets and the vengeful scream of the diving Stukas?

No wonder that at the start of 'Dynamo' the target of the operation was limited to 45,000 men to be lifted probably only over two days, out of possibly ten times that number in the Allied armies falling back on Dunkirk. In fact on the first full day of the operation, 27 May, no more than 7,669 soldiers were brought back to England, a highly unpropitious beginning. To find solutions to an operational problem so complex and so vast in scale might have defied months of study and preparation, but Ramsay and his staff in Dover, and the Navy and Army personnel across in Dunkirk itself, could only improvise from day to day and hour to hour. If oil and coal fuelled the ships, then adrenalin fuelled those who sailed in them and those who directed them.

On that first full day of 'Dynamo' Captain W. G. Tennant, RN, sailed for Dunkirk in HMS *Wolfhound* with a beach party of twelve officers and 150 ratings to organise the embarkation arrangements on the spot as Senior Naval Officer ashore. The Luftwaffe introduced him to the operational realities by dive-bombing *Wolfhound* every half hour during the voyage out. Tennant found the situation in Dunkirk so grim that he signalled Ramsay that even a second night's evacuation was problematical. But that night, as the flames were roaring out of burning warehouses, Tennant took a desperate chance which succeeded in transforming the prospects for 'Dynamo': he signalled a ship to berth alongside the East Mole. The experiment succeeded. Henceforward the narrow planking of the East Mole and the skill of the captains who laid their ships alongside its relatively fragile latticework would provide the means of escape for thousands upon thousands of Allied soldiers. This was only the first, though the most momentous, of Tennant's contributions, for as Senior Naval Officer in Dunkirk he was tirelessly to tackle a myriad day-to-day local problems in the port and along the beaches. Then, on 29 May, the 'frontline' organisation for directing the evacuation was completed by the appointment of Rear-Admiral W. F. Wake-Walker as 'Rear-Admiral, Dover' (with two retired rear-admirals to help him) to control all movements at sea off the French and Belgian coasts.

To relieve the strain on Ramsay himself, responsible for organising and directing the entire operation and deploying all its resources, the First Sea Lord despatched Vice-Admiral Sir James Somerville as a volunteer for the role (though not the title) of second-in-command. Ramsay expressed his appreciation of this in a letter to his wife written at 0100 on 27 May: 'James Somerville is here helping me & I couldn't wish for anyone better . . .'[8] In the same letter he gave an inkling of his own state of mind as 'Dynamo' got under way:

> I have on at the moment (it's 1 a.m.) one of the most difficult and hazardous operations ever conceived and unless le bon Dieu is very kind there will be certain to be many tragedies attached to it. I hardly dare to think about it & what the day is going to bring with it . . . How I would love to cast

> off the mantle of responsibility which is mine & become just peaceful & retired once again . . . Poor Morgan [Captain L. V. Morgan, his Chief of Staff] is terribly strained & badly needs a rest. Flags [Flag Lieutenant] looks like a ghost . . . All my staff are completely worn out & yet I see no prospect at all of any let up . . . As for my ships they have not a moment's rest unless they are damaged badly.

On 28 May, thanks to Tennant's successful experiment the night before with the East Mole, Ramsay shifted the balance of his resources from the slow and laborious work of lifting from the beaches towards embarkation direct from the outer harbour and its moles with larger vessels, mostly destroyers. Although crammed with machinery and weapons and not at all designed as personnel carriers, the destroyers were to pack in 900 men and more at a time during 'Dynamo'; their upper decks so covered with a bee-swarm of khaki that the guns could not be fought and the ships heeled alarmingly under helm while avoiding air attack because of the top-heaviness. That day of 28 May no fewer than 17,804 men were brought home to England – for Ramsay an encouraging result. This was also the day when the Dutch 'skoots' began an invaluable shuttle service from Ramsgate and Margate. However, on the other side of the ledger, one of the big personnel carriers, *The Queen of the Channel*, had been sunk, and several others hit.

For operations in the coming night and day Ramsay allotted seven personnel carriers, three hospital ships and two destroyers to the task of embarking from the East Mole; some twenty destroyers, nineteen minesweepers (some of them paddle-steamers), seventeen drifters, and upwards of twenty skoots and a medley of smaller craft to lifting from the beaches. This effort succeeded in bringing back 47,310 soldiers, nearly three times the previous 24 hours' total; 33,558 of them from the harbour and 13,752 from the beaches. Yet the cost to Ramsay's command had been desperately high. The destroyers *Montrose* and *Mackay* were damaged by collision and grounding, victims of the appalling navigational conditions, while the *Wakefield* and *Grafton* had been torpedoed and sunk in the night by a German E-boat and the U-62. During the day the Luftwaffe bombed and sank the destroyer *Grenade* and damaged the destroyers *Gallant*, *Greyhound*, *Intrepid* and *Saladin* and the French *Jaguar* as well as the sloop *Bideford*. Luftwaffe bombs also sank the personnel carriers *Mona's Queen*, *Normannia*, *Lorina* and *Fenella*, and damaged the *Canterbury*. The tally of Luftwaffe kills that day was completed by the merchant ship *Clan Macalister*, the boarding vessel *King Orry*, and the special service vessel

Crested Eagle, as well as many smaller craft. The *Grenade*, *Jaguar*, *Fenella*, *Crested Eagle* and *Canterbury* had all been caught by the same attack coming out of the late afternoon sunshine while they were alongside the East Mole embarking troops.

These losses caused Ramsay worry enough. But later that day the First Sea Lord and Chief of Naval Staff, Sir Dudley Pound, added to his anxieties by withdrawing all the big modern destroyers in an overriding concern to preserve the Navy's scarce resources in this type of ship for such tasks as escorting Atlantic convoys, on which Britain's long-term survival depended. Ramsay was left with only fifteen destroyers, some of them dating from the Great War, and capable of lifting no more than 17,000 men in 24 hours. Pound persisted in taking this decision despite Ramsay's strenuous efforts to dissuade him. It was not the only occasion during 'Dynamo' when Ramsay felt that the Admiralty did not properly support him or understand the operational realities – as for example, when it later resisted his requests that his exhausted ships' companies should be relieved by fresh ships and crews. In a letter of 7 June to his wife, when it was all over, he listed among the main sources of personal strain during the operation 'the continuous struggle with the Admiralty to make theory see the necessity of giving [way] to what is practicable'.[9]

On 30 May, Ramsay and his staff calculated that this withdrawal of destroyers would reduce his total daily lift to 43,000 soldiers, when a lift of 55,000 was needed. Early that afternoon he therefore embarked on another hard-fought action by telephone with Pound, this time successfully. In the delicate phrasing of Ramsay's despatch: 'Verbal representations being made to the C.N.S., authority was received for the return to the Dover Command of the modern destroyers released the night before.'

Ramsay had now brought a new route into operation for daylight hours, Route 'X', midway between Route 'Y' and the abandoned Route 'Z'. At 55 sea miles it meant a considerable saving over Route 'Y''s 87 sea miles; it was also better protected against surface attack by sandbanks and nearby British minefields. It took the Germans three days to discover the adoption of the new route – a welcome respite.

The day of 30 May saw 'Dynamo' bring home 53,823 soldiers. By now the shore-and-ship organisation under Rear-Admiral Wake-Walker and Captain Tennant was working as smoothly as could be hoped in such desperate circumstances. The apparent scene of sprawling confusion along the wide foreshore under the bombs and shells concealed a pattern of ordered movement by the vast regatta of

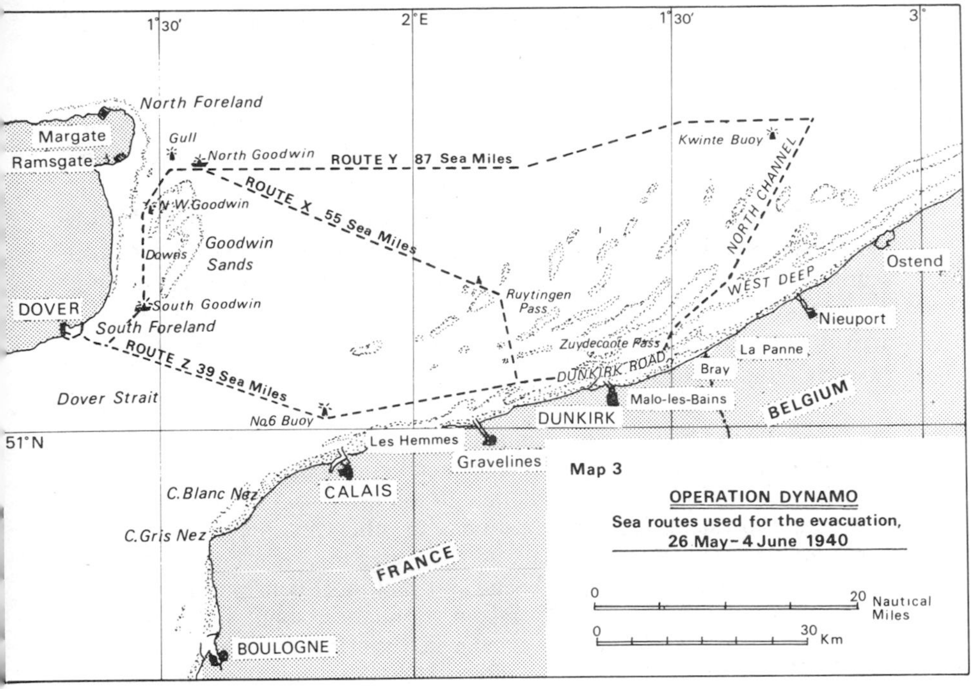

Map 3

OPERATION DYNAMO

Sea routes used for the evacuation, 26 May–4 June 1940

1°30′ 2°E 1°30′ 3° 51°N

North Foreland
Margate
Ramsgate
Gull
North Goodwin
ROUTE Y 87 Sea Miles
Kwinte Buoy
NORTH CHANNEL
ROUTE X 55 Sea Miles
N.W. Goodwin
Downs
Goodwin Sands
South Goodwin
DOVER
South Foreland
ROUTE Z 39 Sea Miles
Dover Strait
No.6 Buoy
Ruytingen Pass
Zuydecoote Pass
DUNKIRK ROAD
WEST DEEP
Ostend
Nieuport
La Panne
Bray
Malo-les-Bains
DUNKIRK
BELGIUM
Les Hemmes
Gravelines
CALAIS
C. Blanc Nez
C. Gris Nez
FRANCE
BOULOGNE

0 20 Nautical Miles
0 30 Km

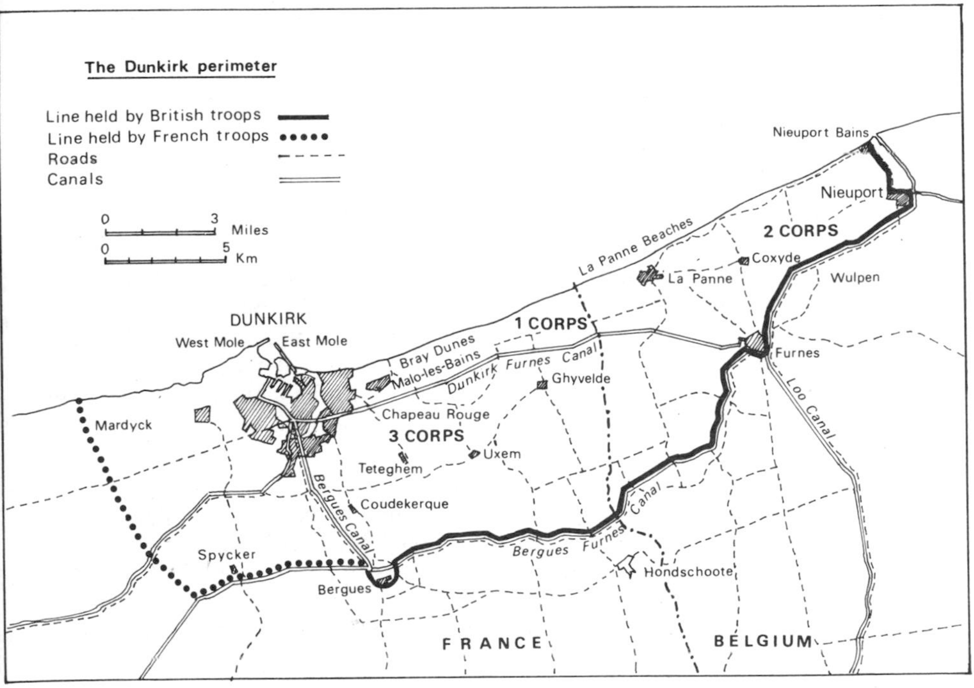

The Dunkirk perimeter

Line held by British troops
Line held by French troops
Roads
Canals

0 3 Miles
0 5 Km

Nieuport Bains
Nieuport
2 CORPS
La Panne Beaches
Coxyde
La Panne
Wulpen
DUNKIRK
1 CORPS
West Mole
East Mole
Bray Dunes
Malo-les-Bains
Dunkirk Furnes Canal
Ghyvelde
Furnes
Loo Canal
Mardyck
Chapeau Rouge
3 CORPS
Uxem
Teteghem
Bergues Canal
Coudekerque
Canal
Bergues Furnes
Spycker
Hondschoote
Bergues
FRANCE
BELGIUM

assorted smaller craft, which succeeded in lifting as many as 29,512 soldiers in the course of the day – the largest number ever lifted from the beaches and the highest proportion of the total lift in any one day of 'Dynamo'. The eyewitness accounts of the masters of the extraordinary mixture of small vessels and craft operating to and from the beaches record with English understatement the courage and seamanship which alone enabled 'Operation Dynamo' to succeed. The coxswain of the Ramsgate lifeboat, H. Knight, describes how on arrival off the beaches late on 30 May when the freshening north-easterly wind was causing a surf, they

> . . . found naval ratings who manned wherries were not skilled at handling small boats under such conditions; members of the lifeboat crew took their boats and places, and although an intensely dark night managed by shouting to establish communication with officer in charge of troops on beach; arranged for men to take to the water in batches of eight which was the capacity of the small boats, and each boat conveyed them to the lifeboat, thence to the waiting craft in attendance; about 800 were safely transported on Thursday night and when the last three boatloads were being taken from the water, the officer called, 'I cannot see who you are; are you a naval party?' He was answered, 'No, Sir, we are members of the crew of the Ramsgate lifeboat' . . .[10]

The owner of the *Constant Nymph*, a river motor boat from Isleworth on the Thames, Dr Smith, appealed to the Commodore at Sheerness (who was fuelling and victualling motor boats) to be signed on for Dunkirk. By 1800 on the 30th the *Constant Nymph* was chugging out of Sheerness basin with a crew of two young naval ratings. Dr Smith narrates:

> We arrived at Dunkirk about dusk and turned along the beach eastwards for a few miles . . . At first we could find no life on the beach, but after a short time were hailed by Frenchmen and for a little while found Frenchmen only, and made one or two full journeys back to the ship [the Dutch skoot *Jutland*] with them. The procedure was to tow the whaler and cutter to the beach and swing them round and cast off tow in about 3 feet 6 inches (my draught being 2 feet 6 inches). The cutter then dropped her grapnel and went in as close to as she dared without grounding the whaler, and the troops waded out to board them. As soon as the two boats were full they called for the motor-boat and pulled up on the cutter's grapnel; I would come past and take the cutter's tow rope in passing and swing out towards the ship which had to lie about three-quarters of a mile to a mile out.
>
> While the whaler and cutter were loading I patrolled parallel with the

> beach . . . my job was to pick up any swimmers or waders and any odd craft which had put out from the shore.[11]

Another Thames motor boat, the *Bonny Heather*, reached Dunkirk as part of a little convoy of motor boats towing ship's lifeboats. She made seven complete round trips between Ramsgate and Dunkirk, each time crammed with 60 men and upwards – as well as working between the beaches and the ships offshore. The skipper of the smack *Seasalter* from Burnham-on-Crouch, L. W. Salmons, describes how after a day's oyster-dredging he and his crew volunteered for Dunkirk and set off in another little convoy:

> It was 6 p.m. when we spotted the coast and picked up Dunkirk lighthouse right ahead. We could still hear aircraft above. Then the fog lifted altogether and the A.A. guns let loose at the planes, one of which spotted us, dived low, and machine-gunned us, but missed. He was so low I could see the crosses, the under-carriage stowed away, and the dirty oil marks.
>
> The soldiers were coming off the beach clinging to bits of wood and wreckage and anything that would float. As we got close enough we began to pick them up and with this we went to and fro bringing off as many as it would dare hold . . . When we had got a load we would take them off to one of the ships lying off in deep water.[12]

On the following day yet another of these innumerable little convoys, this time of six cutter-rigged cockle boats from the Thames Estuary, was attacked on its way over by some 40 German bombers, but succeeded in evading the bombs by abrupt changes of course. The cockle boats then began to ferry soldiers from the outer end of the East Mole to the skoot *Tilly*. As A. J. Dench, skipper of the cockle boat *Letitia*, describes:

> On going in for the third time, a shell burst between the last boat of them, and us, we turned back, to go out, but the [Navy] signaller that we had on board, and had only been 'out' for about six weeks, and never before been under fire, said, 'We've got to go in again' so we went in . . .[13]

And thus it was for the little ships day after day, the essential first link in Ramsay's chain of rescue that led from the Dunkirk perimeter across the sea to England. The tribute later paid by the captain of the destroyer HMS *Icarus* in a letter to the crew of the Margate lifeboat *Lord Southborough* may serve for them all:

> On behalf of every officer and man on this ship I should like to express to you our unbounded admiration of the magnificent behaviour of the

> crew of the lifeboat *Lord Southborough* during the recent evacuation from Dunkirk. The manner in which, with no thought of rest, they brought off load after load of soldiers under continuous shelling, bombing and aerial machine-gun fire will be an inspiration to us all as long as we live. We are proud to be fellow countrymen of such men.[14]

Meanwhile at an inter-service conference at Ramsay's headquarters in the forenoon of 30 May, it had been agreed to continue the evacuation 'with the utmost vigour' in order to reduce the BEF to a rearguard of 4,000 men by the early hours of 1 June. This meant that Ramsay had to commit his very last reserve of small craft, known as the 'special tow'. 'The Tempo still increases,' he wrote to his wife during a brief lunch break on the 30th, 'and everyone is getting cooked to a turn. It simply can't last much longer at this pace, and what happens when we have to stop doesn't bear thinking about. It is inevitable that thousands and thousands will never be able to get off.' And he went on:

> I had quite a good sleep last night as I got to bed at 2 o'clock & got up at 7.15, the best I've had for days . . . Many fellows in my office never get to bed at all, but just lie down & doze off for an hour or so . . . There is thick fog just now which is disaster from the point of view of transport but a relief for Dunkirk and the ships at sea from bombing. But every moment is precious and I'm afraid on balance we may be badly down . . .[15]

In the forenoon of 31 May came grim tidings from Dunkirk, when Wake-Walker reported that evacuation from the beaches was being severely impeded by surf and Tennant signalled that enemy bombing and artillery fire were rendering evacuation from the moles appallingly dangerous. With ten personnel carriers and three hospital ships already despatched to Dunkirk during the night, none of which had yet returned, Ramsay decided to halt further sailings of this kind of vessel for the time being. But in the afternoon the surf abated; at dusk the 'special tow' arrived from Ramsgate in a five-mile stream of small vessels (including ruggedly beautiful Thames sailing barges); and, despite the bombing and shelling, the personnel carriers and hospital ships already at Dunkirk, along with destroyers and other ships, continued to lift from the moles. By midnight 68,014 soldiers had been embarked – 22,942 from the beaches and 45,072 from the harbour – the zenith of 'Dynamo's' daily achievement.

Next day, however, 1 June – fine, calm and sunny – marked in turn the climax of the Luftwaffe's effort to prevent the quarry from finally slipping away. The skipper of the barge *Royalty* lying off the beaches,

H. Miller, recorded the opening of this onslaught by two air fleets with a phrase that would have been familiar enough to Nelson or Hawke or Drake, and which unconsciously but very properly placed 'Dynamo' in the grand context of England's maritime past: 'We were setting our topsail . . .' he wrote, 'when a large number of German planes appeared overhead and immediately started bombing and machine-gunning us.'[16] The long bright day ahead was to prove the most devastating of all to the destroyers and the personnel carriers. The Luftwaffe first struck at 0720, when RAF fighter cover had temporarily returned to base. Until the next RAF patrol reached the scene at 0900 the German bombers had only to contend with the anti-aircraft fire of the warships – and these were now desperately short of ammunition. The Stukas howled down in relays from 10,000 feet through the shrapnel bursts at ships jinking as they best could in narrow, congested and wreck-strewn waters. The destroyer *Keith*, flying the flag of Rear-Admiral Wake-Walker, was the first casualty: seriously damaged in the first two waves of attack, she finally sank when bombs from the third wave hit her under the bridge. The master of the tug *Cervia* was an eyewitness of the first attack:

> A British destroyer outside of us began to fire at the enemy planes and bombs began to fall near her as she steamed about. At full speed with her helm hard to port nine bombs fell in a line in the water, along her starboard side, and they exploded under water, heeling the destroyer over on her beam ends, but she was righted again . . .[17]

When the *Keith* sank at last, Admiral Wake-Walker and his staff transferred to a motor torpedo boat, only to be dive-bombed yet again, though fortunately not hit. This was only the beginning: before 0900 a second destroyer, the *Basilisk*, had been lost; another, *Ivanhoe*, reduced to a wreck under tow; and four more damaged; the fleet minesweeper *Skipjack*, loaded with troops, had also been sunk. In the high sun of midday the Luftwaffe was back again in force. The French destroyer *Foudroyant*, caught in a narrow channel some four miles off the East Mole and unable to manoeuvre, was 'submerged', in the words of a French account, 'in a cloud of Stukas', and sunk.[18] HMS *Havant* was the next, but mercifully the last, to go. The day had proved as disastrous to the Royal Navy's destroyer strength as a fleet action. Yet the surviving destroyers kept at it. *Codrington*, *Sabre*, *Windsor*, *Whitshed* and *Winchelsea* brought away thousands more soldiers that day.

The big personnel carriers – the pre-war ferries which had carried holiday-makers on their way to Paris and the Côte-d'Azur, or the quieter pleasures of Ireland or the Isle of Man – also fell victim to the Luftwaffe's supreme effort to halt the evacuation. Some of these ships had been offering themselves as prime targets ever since the beginning of operations off Boulogne and Calais some ten days previously, and in Admiral Ramsay's judgment, 'the captains and crews . . . were feeling the strain when Operation Dynamo started'.[19] The unremitting nature of their task is well illustrated by the *Royal Sovereign*'s record on 30 May. At 0530 she completed embarking a full load of soldiers. At 1135 she was back in Margate disembarking. At 1300 she was steaming for Dunkirk once again. At 1820 she was at anchor taking on another load.[20] A schedule such as this is easily stated. What it meant to carry it out is vividly evoked by an account by Captain Hill, master of the hospital ship *Isle of Guernsey*, of his experiences on 30 May. The ship crept into Dunkirk harbour in the small hours to find the night sky and the whole devastated area lit up by fires. While the *Isle of Guernsey* was embarking 490 wounded men, she was 'shaken every few minutes by the explosion of bombs falling on the quay and in the water'. On the way home:

> Just outside we found the sea full of men swimming and shouting for help, presumably a transport had just been sunk. As two destroyers were standing by picking these men up, we threaded our way carefully through them and proceeded towards Dover. It would have been fatal for us to attempt to stop and try to save any of these men, as we made such a wonderful target for the aircraft hovering overhead with the flames of the burning port showing all our white paintwork up.[21]

The first personnel carrier to be sunk on the black day of 1 June was the *Prague*, which arrived at Dunkirk while the Luftwaffe was launching its opening attack. Having successfully embarked 3,000 French soldiers and set course for the English coast, the *Prague* was bombarded off Gravelines by German land-based artillery and then dive-bombed, although not directly hit on either occasion. However, the force of the explosions repercussing through the water inflicted serious structural damage and put one engine room out of action. Slowly sinking, the *Prague* made the best speed she could while the destroyer *Shikari*, the paddle minesweeper *Queen of Thanet* and the corvette *Shearwater* worked desperately to take off her load. This they largely succeeded in accomplishing before she finally beached herself.

Next to be lost was the coal-burning *Scotia*. On her way to Dunkirk she had been warned by a destroyer with gallows humour that it was 'Windy off No. 6 buoy'. So it proved: on her way home with 2,000

French soldiers the *Scotia* was attacked off No. 6 buoy by twelve German aircraft in three waves of four. Hit abaft the engine room, on the poop deck and by a bomb that went down the after funnel, the *Scotia* began to sink by the stern. The destroyer HMS *Esk* came to the rescue: her captain, Commander Couch, RN, manoeuvring his ship with consummate seamanship close up to one side and then the other of the sinking *Scotia*, succeeded in saving all but 300 of those aboard her despite continuing air attack. Nor was the *Prague* the last personnel carrier to be lost that day: in the early afternoon the paddle minesweeper *Brighton Queen*, with 700 French and Moroccan troops embarked, was hit by Stukas and sank.

And still, with very few exceptions, the remaining personnel ships sailed on between Dunkirk and England through the sunshine as if the dive-bombers could drop nothing more dangerous than could seagulls – the *Maid of Orleans* (she made six trips during 'Dynamo' and earned special praise from Ramsay), the *Royal Daffodil* (seven trips), the *Royal Sovereign* (six trips) and *King George V* (five trips: the three latter vessels also being mentioned in Ramsay's despatch), together with the minesweeper (ex-passenger ship) *Medway Queen* and the hospital ship *St Helier*. For all the Luftwaffe's day of fury on 1 June, in which it had sunk 31 vessels of various types, 64,429 Allied soldiers had been brought away from Dunkirk by midnight.

But where was the RAF during that day, and all the other days of 'Dynamo'? For the soldiers and sailors under the lash of the Luftwaffe, air cover meant the reassuring spectacle of British aircraft constantly overhead, or visibly bombing the besieging German Army. They were not afforded this spectacle; instead the sky seemed every day filled with the Luftwaffe; and their resentment grew. As Ramsay put it in his despatch:

> Rightly or wrongly, full air protection was expected, but instead, for hours on end the ships offshore were subjected to a murderous hail of bombs and machine-bullets . . .
>
> The system of co-operation between the Naval and R.A.F. Commands does not permit of direct contact with the R.A.F. operational units allocated for duty with the Naval Command. For this reason much time appears to be lost . . . Delays and lags occur, resulting often in the R.A.F. effort being brought to bear either in the wrong place or at the wrong time, or with inadequate force.[22]

There was substance in this criticism. Except for the ill-equipped Coastal Command and a handful of slow 'Army cooperation' aircraft (mostly artillery spotters), the RAF's pre-war development had concentrated on the close-range air defence of the United Kingdom and on pursuit of the Trenchardite dream of a strategic bomber offensive against the German economy. Close tactical support of the Army and Navy, at which the Luftwaffe was so proficient, had yet to come, forced on the RAF by the realities of war. Thus it was that during the nine days of Dunkirk Coastal Command flew 171 reconnaissance sorties, Bomber Command 651 (mostly at night against German rear areas), and Fighter Command 2,739.[23] The RAF shot down 132 German aircraft for the loss of 145 of its own, including 99 fighters.[24] Yet Fighter Command faced a hard problem: it dare not commit the full strength of the UK's own air defence for fear of the future; the 200 fighters of No. 11 Group actually committed were heavily outnumbered by the 300 bombers and the 550 fighters available to the Luftwaffe. To rotate continuous patrols over Dunkirk meant inferiority of numbers and defeat in detail; to despatch forces strong enough effectively to meet the Luftwaffe in combat meant gaps in cover of the kind which the Luftwaffe exploited so effectively in the early forenoon of 1 June. The dilemma was insoluble; the soldiers' and sailors' mistrust of the airmen unappeasable.

And the Luftwaffe certainly achieved one major success on 1 June. It compelled the Royal Navy to modify the scope of the evacuation, with consequent effect on lifting capacity. At 1800 Ramsay received a signal from Dunkirk: 'Things are getting very hot for ships; over 100 bombers on ships since 0530, many casualties. Have directed that no ships sail during daylight. Evacuation by transports therefore ceases at 0300. If perimeter holds will complete evacuation tomorrow, Sunday night, including most French . . .'[25] Ramsay therefore ordered all ships to withdraw before daylight on 2 June, as he signalled the Admiralty. The Admiralty itself, alarmed by the heavy losses, had in any case signalled Ramsay (the messages crossed) directing him to suspend the evacuation from 0700 on 2 June until the following night at 1730.

By this time only some 3,000 to 4,000 men of the BEF remained in the shrunken perimeter, plus an unknown number of French soldiers – perhaps 25,000, perhaps as many as 40,000. Ramsay therefore planned the coming night's operation for a lift of 25,000. From 1700 on 2 June onwards the rescue fleet began once again to set course for Dunkirk – thirteen personnel carriers, two store ships, eleven destroyers, one special service vessel, nine drifters, six skoots, two armed yachts, a gunboat, and finally the civilian motor boats crewed by volunteers and naval personnel[26] – and by midnight it had brought the 2 June total of soldiers rescued to 26,256. Half an hour before midnight, the *St Helier* had slipped her moorings and made for England with the last of the British Expeditionary Force aboard; and Captain Tennant had made the historic signal to Dover Command: 'B.E.F. evacuated'.

However, there still remained the French, including the rearguard manning the perimeter defence. It was unthinkable to abandon them, and yet Ramsay's sailors – Royal Navy and Merchant Marine alike – were reaching the point of total exhaustion where they simply would be unable to go on. In a few cases civilian masters were refusing to take their ships to sea again, some succumbing to strain sooner than others. On 28 May the master of the *Canterbury*, the large personnel carrier, had only sailed for a third trip to Dunkirk after receiving a direct order and with a naval officer and some ratings aboard 'to augment and stiffen the crew'.[27] On the 29th, and after one round trip, the captain of the *St Seiriol* had refused to sail. The ship finally put to sea after the captain had been put under open arrest and an RN party put aboard, but was hit and damaged on her way home; it proved to be her last trip.[28] In the evening of the terrible day of 1 June the *Tynwald* at Folkestone, having completed three trips in 'Dynamo', also refused to sail; and a naval guard (at which the crew shouted abuse) was posted alongside her at her berth. She sailed 24 hours later with a relief crew and a Royal Navy party, though with her chief officer serving as Master and five others of her own ship's company. She eventually completed five trips.[29]

On 2 June two other ships, the *Malines* and the *Ben-My-Chree*, also refused to sail again. On receiving a written enquiry as to whether he was willing to sail, the master of the *Ben-My-Chree* replied by letter: 'I beg to state that after our experience at Dunkirk yesterday, my answer is "NO".'[30] An armed naval guard was posted on the gangways and abreast of the ship. Then, in a distant ripple from the nerve-rasping violence of Dunkirk into this quiet English harbour, the bayonets of Royal Navy bluejackets were levelled at British merchant seamen. According to Admiral Ramsay's despatch:

> As the ship berthed the crew were demonstrating and shouting that they were going to leave the ship, and on the brow being run out, they attempted to do so with their kits. Leading Stoker Booth ordered his men to come on guard and advanced up the brow with fixed bayonets. The crew returned on board at once, where they remained until the relief crew arrived.[31]

The captain and crew then left the vessel, although here too the chief officer remained as acting skipper, as well as four other members of the crew. On sailing at 1905 on 2 June the *Ben-My-Chree* was damaged in a collision and could not complete the trip. *The Manxman*, having completed three trips out of an assignment of five, likewise refused to sail on that day, and her crew as well had to be replaced, while the *Malines*, which had refused to sail the day before, now left Dover without instructions for the quieter port of Southampton.[32]

For Ramsay the exhaustion of his ships' companies, even those of the Royal Navy, had now become the crucial factor bearing on his ability to prolong 'Dynamo' further. He wrote in his despatch with regard to 3 June:

> No assurance could be obtained that this coming night would terminate the operation and considerable anxiety was felt regarding the effect of the gradual exhaustion of the officers and men of the ships taking part in Dynamo. This exhaustion was particularly marked in the Destroyer force the remnants of which had been executing a series of round trips without intermission for several days under navigational conditions of extreme difficulty and in the face of unparalleled air attack.

And so:

> The Vice-Admiral accordingly represented to the Admiralty that the continuance of the demands made by the evacuation would subject a number of officers and men to a test which might be beyond the limits of human endurance, and requesting that fresh forces should be used if evacuation had to be continued after the coming night, with the acceptance of any consequent delay.[33]

Nonetheless Ramsay had already issued his orders for another night's operation – all his destroyers and nine out of ten personnel ships were to go, as well as the usual mixture of supporting vessels. In the evening he was informed by the British Naval Liaison Officer at the French naval HQ that some 30,000 French soldiers remained at Dunkirk, and that – welcome news this – the French Admiralty had agreed that 'evacuation should be terminated that night if possible'.[34]

And so for the last time ships under the White Ensign and vessels and craft under the Red Duster made that horrific landfall. 'We arrived off Dunkirk breakwater at 11.57 p.m.,' wrote Captain Clarke of the personnel carrier *Princess Maud*. 'We entered the pier-heads, and looked for a berth. The narrow fairway was crammed to capacity . . . Wrecks dotted the harbour here and there. The only light was that of shells bursting, and the occasional glare of fires . . .'[35]

At about 0150 on 4 June the *Princess Maud*, loaded – overloaded –

with French soldiers, cast off and sailed. At 0255 the *Royal Sovereign* followed her – the last of the passenger ships to leave, and herself having completed six trips and lifted a total of 6,858 soldiers in the course of 'Dynamo', one-tenth of all those rescued by the personnel carriers.[36] There were other records set that last night – the paddle minesweeper *Medway Queen* completed her seventh trip; the old destroyer *Sabre* completed her tenth, having brought home a total of 5,000 men. Meanwhile the French Navy had been mounting its own supreme last effort to get its comrades of the Army away, with no fewer than 63 vessels of all kinds working in and around Dunkirk. Together the Allied ships succeeded in lifting a further 26,175 soldiers in the 24 hours to midnight, 4 June. But the process of evacuation had actually ceased in the small hours of that day as one by one the British and French vessels slipped their moorings and departed.

The very last ship of all to leave was HMS *Shikari*, one of the Navy's oldest destroyers (launched 1919). At 0340, in the bleak dawn light and to the rattle of German machine-guns nearby, she moved away from the East Mole with her decks packed with French soldiers, leaving astern the wrecked port and town and the pall of dark smoke that towered above it, and the French rearguard which was still staunchly holding off the German besiegers.

At 1423 on 4 June the Admiralty made a signal formally closing down 'Operation Dynamo'. Instead of the 45,000 soldiers it was originally hoped might be rescued, a total of 338,226 had been brought out – 308,888 of them in British vessels. If personnel evacuated in the week before 'Dynamo' itself are included, the grand total rises to 366,162. But the losses to the Royal Navy and the Merchant Marine were equivalent to those of a major sea battle. Of 38 destroyers, six had been sunk, fourteen damaged by bombs and twelve by collision; and at the end of 'Dynamo' the Royal Navy's total strength in destroyers not in the dockyards had dropped to only 74. Of 46 personnel carriers (including hospital carriers and stores ships) nine were sunk and eleven damaged (eight of them so badly as to force their withdrawal from service).[37]

Next day Ramsay, in a letter written to his wife – 'now all is done and the task is behind' – summed it up: 'The relief is stupendous. The results are beyond belief.' And then, expressing himself with a candour unqualified with false modesty, as a man properly may to his wife, he went on:

> The success is mostly due to the first class direction and management of the show, equally with glorious courage, skill & endurance of the personnel

of all the ships. The one without the other would have been ineffective. We can always count on the glorious deeds but less often on good direction and management. This may sound as self-praise but is nevertheless the plain truth. You know me well enough to know that I count little for myself & think solely of the wider aspect of the object to be gained. My staff were so well chosen & so efficient that they worked like a perfect machine . . .[38]

But perhaps the last word on 'Operation Dynamo' and what it meant to the trapped Allied army is best left to a soldier. A British officer wrote of the moment when he was hoisted from the sea off the beaches on 28 May:

From the instant I landed on my head in the lifeboat a great burden of responsibility seemed to fall from my shoulders. A curious sense of freedom took possession of me. All the accumulated strain of the last few hours, of the last day or so, vanished. I felt that my job was over. Anything else that remained to be done was the Navy's business. I was in their hands, and had nothing more to worry about . . .[39]

In reporting the final result of 'Dynamo' to the House of Commons Winston Churchill, the Prime Minister, rightly warned: 'We must be very careful not to assign to this deliverance the attributes of victory. Wars are not won by evacuations . . .'[40] Nevertheless 'Dynamo's' success may in hindsight be judged one of the deciding factors of the Second World War. Churchill himself eloquently pictured to the Commons the scale of the catastrophe that had been averted by Ramsay and his ships and sailors: 'The whole root and core and brain of the British Army, on which and around which we were to build, and are to build, the great British Armies in the later years of the war, seemed about to perish upon the field or to be led into ignominious and starving captivity.'[41] But there was more to it even than preserving the cadre of future armies; there was the question of the British nation's will to fight on alone should their French ally soon sue for an armistice (a contingency for which the British government and Chiefs of Staff were already preparing). 'Dynamo', its heroism, efficiency and success, morally drew the sting from the German triumph in the West; it gladdened and uplifted British hearts in the face of calamities about to unfold.

In the short term, however, the evacuation consummated the destruction of the Allied Northern Army Group. On 5 June the German Army attacked southwards against the remaining portion of the French Army – 140 divisions against 49 French and one British (51st Highland). Within five days the French front had been broken up and the panzer spearheads began a pursuit that was swiftly to take them to the Swiss frontier and the Atlantic coast, and induce the French government to ask for an armistice. For the Royal Navy this fresh enemy victory once again meant the hasty mounting of desperate evacuations. At St Valéry-en-Caux on 10 June fog baulked the attempt to rescue the trapped 51st Highland Division: only 2,137 British and 1,184 French soldiers were brought off the beaches beneath the tall cliffs, and next day some 6,000 men of the Highland Division surrendered. However, 11,059 soldiers were successfully lifted from Le Havre between 10 and 13 June.[42]

This proved merely the preliminary to the final evacuation from France of all British personnel (including two divisions sent to Brittany at the end of May) through the ports of Cherbourg, St Malo, Brest, La Pallice and St Nazaire from 16 to 25 June, the same day that the armistice terms between France and Germany came into effect. Here were acted out yet again the familiar scenes of hazardous navigation by vessels of all shapes and sizes under punishing air attack. At St Nazaire on 17 June the liner *Lancastria*, packed with 5,800 soldiers, was hit and set on fire, sinking within fifteen minutes with the loss of some 3,000 lives. This was the worst of the losses during these post-Dunkirk evacuations, which succeeded in bringing back to England a total of 144,171 British, 18,246 French, 24,352 Polish, 4,939 Czech and 163 Belgian troops.[43] From 19 to 22 June the Royal Navy also had to carry out the melancholy task of evacuating 22,656 people of military age, women and children from British territory soon to be abandoned to the enemy – the Channel Isles. Once seapower had protected the islands against Bonaparte; it could not preserve them against Hitler in the face of the Luftwaffe a brief flight away on French airfields.

Now in every European port from the Arctic ocean to the Spanish frontier flew the red, white and black swastika flag of Nazi Germany, and the entire grand-strategic shape of the war had been transformed.

The Western Front, that centre of gravity of the Great War where Britain had deployed an army of 56 divisions, and where the German Army had been ultimately gutted and defeated – the theatre re-created in September 1939 and where the Allies had hoped eventually to repeat their victory of 1918 – was no more. The French Army, which had borne the brunt of the fighting on the Western Front in 1914–16 while Britain was creating her mass Army, and which fielded 94 divisions in May 1940, had been struck out of the strategic balance sheet, leaving Britain with a handful of ill-equipped divisions to face a German Army with an order of battle of some 160 divisions. The Luftwaffe was no longer distant on German bases, but just across the Channel and the North Sea: an enormous enhancement in its operational effectiveness against the United Kingdom, especially in potential tonnage of bombs deliverable. The German Navy's U-boats and their covering aircraft would now enjoy direct access from occupied France via the Bay of Biscay to Britain's vital Atlantic shipping routes instead of the long circuitous route round the north of the British Isles: a vast increase in their operational effectiveness as well.

At the same time the powerful French Navy, the cooperation of which had up till now enabled the Royal Navy's global sums to come out in the black, had vanished from the war, condemned by the armistice terms to immobilisation in French ports. And to make this loss even harder to cope with, Fascist Italy had declared war on 10 June, so that the Royal Navy now confronted alone the new threat posed by the modern Italian battlefleet in the Mediterranean – four battleships (plus two nearing commission), nineteen cruisers, 52 fleet destroyers and 115 submarines[44] – to say nothing of the Italian Air Force operating over the Central Mediterranean from nearby shore bases. In the face of this threat, the main imperial lifeline and trade route through the Mediterranean had been abandoned even before the Italian declaration of war, on 16 May, so lengthening the voyage from the United Kingdom to Suez from 3,000 to 13,000 miles, and to Bombay from 6,000 to 11,000 miles.

Yet this desperate scene of strategic isolation only marked the logical denouement of – and perhaps retribution for – British foreign and defence policy from 1919 to 1939: the steadfast refusal to stand with France vis-à-vis Germany either diplomatically or militarily; the priority given in the rearmament programme to the air defence of the United Kingdom over the expansion of the Army in readiness for a Continental campaign; and indeed the refusal to accept any kind of 'Continental commitment' until as late as spring 1939, so resulting in Britain's merely minor military contribution to the great battle in the West in May and June 1940. The entire thrust of British pre-war policy had been to turn the back on the Continent of Europe, leave France to cope as best she might with the German Army, and meanwhile prepare for a quite separate struggle between Germany and Britain in the air over the United Kingdom. Now that this situation had actually come about, it no longer seemed quite such a good idea.

Moreover the irruption of Italy into the war, just at the moment when France was collapsing, marked the final pay-off for Britain's opposition at the League of Nations in 1935–36 to Italy's conquest of Abyssinia. So in June 1940 Britain without an ally found herself at war with two out of the three powers which had offered the pre-war 'triple threat' to the worldwide British Empire, while the third, Japan, could not be neglected, especially in view of the fall of France and the consequent vulnerability of French Indo-China, and indeed Britain's own evidently desperate plight. That month Japan demanded that Britain close the 'Burma Road' between her colony of Burma and Nationalist Chinese territory, over which Western supplies flowed to aid the Nationalists in their war against the Japanese invader; and Britain complied. That month too the British government had to inform Australia and New Zealand that it was now 'most improbable' that Britain could send a large enough fleet to Singapore to defend them against the Japanese, since the Royal Navy was fully committed to fighting Germany and Italy; the two dominions must therefore look to the United States for succour. Thus history was at last calling the bluff that was the British Empire.

The loss of Europe entailed other heavy consequences, particularly for British seapower. Before that loss something like twenty per cent of Britain's imports had come from near sources like Europe itself, the Western Mediterranean and North Africa; by 1941 the proportion was to drop to four per cent, while the proportion of imports from North America over the precarious 3,000-mile Atlantic sea lanes had risen from 36 per cent to 54 per cent.[45] This switch from short or medium-distance sea routes to long ones demanded a much larger commitment of shipping (and therefore of escorts too) because of the increase in 'round-voyage time' – up from an average of 99 days before the fall of France to 122 days afterwards.[46]

Deprived of a Western Front, Britain was reduced to her traditional 'blue water' strategy of using maritime power to sustain land campaigns in far-off peripheral theatres wherever she saw a chance of engaging a portion of the enemy's armies. From June 1940 onwards this meant the Italians in their African colonies of Libya, Ethiopia and Somaliland. But to maintain large modern mechanised armies and also air forces in the backward countries of the Middle East and Africa necessitated the creation of huge base facilities, virtually satellite war economies, on the spot; and especially in Egypt, the central British Middle-East base area. All the necessary equipment and supplies to establish these facilities would have to be shipped out by the 13,000-mile route round the Cape of Good Hope and the Red Sea at a further enormous expense in shipping. Similarly the build-up of the armies themselves – manpower, tanks, trucks and guns, and the continuing flow of reinforcements and replenishment – would depend on ships plying the same circuitous route. The ports too in these backward regions, in particular Alexandria, Port Said, and Suez (the main terminal points for Middle East supply and trooping), were ill-equipped and inefficient and so further wasteful of shipping resources because of slowness of turn-round. By autumn 1941 the supply and reinforcement of the British imperial military effort in the Middle East was to be swallowing up over four million tons of merchant shipping.[47]

It should not be imagined, therefore, that, because Britain was willy-nilly reduced to campaigning in the Middle East and Africa as a result of the disappearance of the Western Front, this offered (thanks to seapower) a uniquely advantageous way of making war, as some historians would have us believe. It did not: on the contrary no form of warfare could have been less cost-effective in terms of military strength in the field measured against resources invested – including, most important of all, resources of merchant shipping and also escorts, of which Britain was now so critically short. 'Blue water' strategy was to impose a terrible and sometimes near breaking strain on a Royal Navy rendered by pre-war disarmament and wartime loss too small for its global commitments.

At a deeper level still, the very foundations of Britain's world power as a maritime nation were about to collapse. That power had rested since the eighteenth century on the wealth produced by seaborne trade under the protection of the Royal Navy; wealth which had enabled Britain to wage successful war against Napoleon Bonaparte and Kaiser Wilhelm II. But by the summer of 1940 this was no longer the case. Overseas earnings (after the conversion of export industries to munitions production) were nothing like enough to support the war effort of a great power with a world empire to protect and equip; and particularly since Britain was making huge dollar purchases of machine-tools, steel, aircraft and weapons from the United States as a result of the weakness of her own industrial base. In August 1940 the Chancellor of the Exchequer, Sir John Simon, warned the Cabinet in a memorandum that the total cost of purchases from the US in the next twelve months would amount to $3,300 million, while Britain's resources in foreign exchange and dollar securities came to only £490 million. Britain would therefore exhaust her gold and dollar reserves by December 1940.[48] In a word, she would be bankrupt; incapable either of waging a war or sustaining her national life out of her own resources.

Quite apart, then, from the immediate danger of invasion, Britain after the fall of France found herself in a predicament unique in her history, largely the result of the follies and illusions of governments and people in the inter-war years – a war without an ally against two great powers and potentially three; an ill-defended and immensely vulnerable Empire; an inadequate industrial machine; insufficient national wealth; and armed forces still too weak to meet the immense strategic burdens now falling upon them. And of the three armed forces, it was upon the Royal Navy that the greatest burden and the greatest strain was to fall, for its role was all-pervasive and its service in the face of the enemy unceasing.

PART II

STORM FORCE

7

The Wall of England

At 0631 on 3 July 1940, with the sea calm and the Mediterranean sun climbing already warm through a haze, the ships of Force H streamed paravanes as a precaution against possible mines guarding their objective. At 0830 the hands were closed to Action Stations, but the 15-inch guns of the battlecruiser *Hood* (flying the flag of Vice-Admiral Sir James Somerville, commanding Force H) and the battleships *Resolution* and *Valiant* were kept trained fore and aft – a sign of Somerville's continuing hope that they would not have to be fired that day in the fulfilment of his task. Steaming in company with the three heavy ships were the carrier *Ark Royal*, the cruisers *Arethusa* and *Enterprise* and a screening force of eleven destroyers. At 0910 the task force arrived off its destination, the port of Oran and the nearby naval base of Mers-el-Kebir in Algeria, then constitutionally part of metropolitan France. At anchor within Mers-el-Kebir lay the most powerful single squadron of the French Navy, including the modern fast battleships *Dunkerque* and *Strasbourg* and the older battleships *Bretagne* and *Provence*.

Despite the prevailing haze, 'the upper works of the French heavy ships were clearly visible over the breakwater,' wrote Somerville in his report on the day's events, 'although only the actual tops and masts could be seen from a position northwest of the fort [guarding the entrance to the base]'.[1] These were the ships, manned by French sailors so recently the comrades in arms of the Royal Navy, which Somerville knew that he might be forced to sink within a few hours. It all depended on the outcome of negotiations about to be conducted on his behalf by his French-speaking emissary, Captain C. S. Holland, with Admiral Gensoul, flag officer commanding the French battle squadron. By prior agreement with the French authorities, Holland had already gone in ahead in the destroyer HMS *Foxhound* to rendezvous with Gensoul's flag lieutenant outside Mers-el-Kebir's defensive boom.[2] Now Somerville himself could only steam slowly up and down outside Mers-el-Kebir and Oran while he waited through an interminable furnace-hot day for Holland to signal back reports on the progress of negotiations; a time of impotence and uncertainty, that worst of combinations.

It did not relieve Somerville's anxiety or his anguished conscience in the face of the possibility of having to slaughter French sailors that he had received a signal the night before from the First Sea Lord telling him that the War Cabinet 'will be impatiently awaiting news of "Catapult". I hope therefore you will be able to send short messages at intervals such as "Emissary has made contact", "French ships in harbour", etc.'[3] This signal (the language of which strongly suggests the Prime Minister's authorship) encouragingly ended: 'You are charged with one of the most disagreeable and difficult tasks that a British Admiral has ever been faced with, but we have complete confidence in you and rely on you to carry it out relentlessly.'

As early as 25–27 May, when 'Dynamo' was just getting under way, the War Cabinet (of five members, as against a peacetime Cabinet's twenty) and the Chiefs of Staff had already begun to ponder the implications of a final French collapse and capitulation. On 7 June, two days after the Germans struck at the remaining portion of the French Army on the Somme and the Aisne, Admiral of the Fleet Sir Dudley Pound held a meeting with senior colleagues in his room at the Admiralty to discuss the future of the French Fleet if France should conclude an armistice with Germany. His own view, vigorously repeated, was that: '. . . as long as the French Fleet was above water it would be impossible to stop the Germans putting pressure on the French, thus re-acting on whoever had control of the French Fleet. He was sure that the only solution was to sink the French Fleet.'[4]

When on 22 June the British leadership received news of the draft Franco-German armistice terms, it was dismayed to learn that Article 8 demanded that all French warships be collected in specified French ports, demobilised and 'disarmed under German or Italian control', while French ships at present beyond French territorial waters were to be recalled to France. However, as Pound reported to the War Cabinet that evening at Chequers, Admiral Darlan, Commander-in-Chief of the French Navy, had ordered his admirals 'not to accept orders from a foreign government' and to 'fight to the finish' if threatened.[5] It was Pound's opinion that Darlan was taking 'all possible steps' to prevent his fleet being used against Britain.

In the coming days Britain was to receive repeated assurances from the French that their fleet would be scuttled rather than be allowed to fall into Axis hands. But in view of the German record for well prepared surprise take-overs, and, more broadly, the evident haplessness of Marshal Pétain's new government in the face of Axis power, could Britain rely on such assurances? The Prime Minister thought not. In his words to the Cabinet on 22 June: 'In a matter so vital to the safety of the whole British Empire, we could not rely on the word of Admiral Darlan . . .'[6]

In the evening of 24 June, while the War Cabinet was again in session, news came in that the French had finally signed the armistice, which came into effect immediately. Of all the host of dangerous problems unleashed by the lapse of Britain's principal ally into uneasy neutrality, none was more urgent than this one of the French Fleet; and Churchill confronted it with the ruthless decision of a Cromwell or a Nelson, telling his colleagues that they must act 'solely in accordance with the dictates of our own safety'.[7] The Cabinet therefore decided to despatch an ultimatum to Pétain's government demanding that it scuttle the ships at Oran (the most formidable French squadron of all) 'within a time to be specified' or Britain would 'take action by force against them'.[8] It also discussed the operational problems of sinking the French ships, which Pound advised could only be successfully done 'in a surprise attack carried out at dawn and without any form of prior notification'. Yet even now, with Churchill and his colleagues piloting the British people through their worst storm for centuries, the Cabinet found it 'hard to make' a decision to order 'the destruction of people who only 48 hours before had been Allies . . .'[9]

Intelligence sources, including Sigint, returned no sure guidance – only the disturbing possibility that the Germans were signalling instructions to the French Navy in Darlan's name.[10]

On 27 June the news that Pétain had appointed Darlan Minister of Marine, so rendering him a willing political colleague in a collaborationist government instead of the professional head of the Navy, impelled the War Cabinet to make final decisions, for the active deployment of the French Navy in the service of either Britain or the Axis could sway the whole balance of the war at sea, and in particular transform the prospects for a German invasion of England.

At present, French warships were dispersed in harbours hundreds of miles, even a thousand miles, apart, so lessening the danger of a sudden complete seizure by the Axis, but equally presenting the Royal Navy with a multiple rather than a single operational problem. In British ports were the old battleships *Courbet* and *Paris*; the big destroyers *Léopard* and *Le Triomphant*, and the smaller *Mistral* and *Ouragan*; seven submarines (including the *Surcouf*, at 3,250 tons the largest submarine in the world); six torpedo boats and some minesweepers. At Mers-el-Kebir were known to lie the battleships *Dunkerque*, *Strasbourg*, *Bretagne* and *Provence*, a seaplane carrier and six large destroyers; and nearby in Oran seven more destroyers and four submarines. At Casablanca in French Morocco and Dakar in French West Africa lay respectively the new battleships (not yet completed and armed) *Jean Bart* and *Richelieu* (the latter in Pound's estimate the most powerful ship afloat). In Alexandria harbour, under the guns of the British Mediterranean Fleet, lay Admiral Godfroy's squadron of one old battleship (*Lorraine*), three 8-inch gun cruisers and one light cruiser.[11]

The War Cabinet's first overt action was to forbid French warships now in British ports and at Alexandria to put to sea – in Godfroy's case, under pain of being bombarded if he sought to do so. It also decided that the seizure or destruction of the French battle squadron at Mers-el-Kebir – 'Operation Catapult' – would take place on 3 July, the earliest date according to Pound that a superior British force could reach the scene.[12] Next day a conference attended by the Commanders-in-Chief, Western Approaches and Portsmouth, and chaired by the First Sea Lord resolved that the simultaneous seizure of French warships in British ports (codenamed 'Grasp') 'would be best accomplished by very large British forces being sent on board the ships in the middle of the night to take the ship's company by surprise'.[13] At Portsmouth in the small hours of 3 July the tactic proved bloodlessly successful; at Plymouth, however, two British officers, a rating and a French rating were killed or mortally wounded in a fracas on board the submarine *Surcouf*. While 'Grasp' had certainly delivered the French ships in British ports into the hands of the Royal Navy, the timing and mode of its execution, along with the death of the French rating, appeared to the French (and not least to Admiral Gensoul in Mers-el-Kebir, when the news reached him in the forenoon of 3 July) to display Albion at its most '*perfide*'.

At Alexandria Admiral Sir Andrew Cunningham, the Commander-in-Chief, Mediterranean Fleet, robustly signalled the Admiralty that he was 'most strongly opposed to [the government's] proposal for forcible seizure of ships in Alexandria', adding that 'he could not see what benefit is to be derived from it'.[14] He expressed himself equally opposed to the use of force at Oran, contending that such actions would alienate the French throughout the French Empire. In reply the Admiralty told him that he could offer Godfroy the alternatives of demilitarisation in Alexandria harbour or being sunk. By the late hours of 4 July, and despite the repercussions from events at Oran on the 3rd, Cunningham had succeeded by patient, personal, courteous and understanding diplomacy in reaching an agreement with Godfroy by which the French admiral demilitarised and immobilised his ships by surrendering the breech-blocks of the guns, discharging fuel oil, and reduced manning to skeleton crews. Cunningham was not helped by Pound's (and Churchill's) prodding signal halfway through the negotiations instructing him to tell Godfroy to reduce his crews 'at once', nor encouraged by its nagging conclusion: 'Do not (Repeat) NOT fail.'[15]

But at least London allowed Cunningham extra time to negotiate, while he also enjoyed the decisive advantage of having Godfroy's squadron already under his guns in Alexandria harbour. It was otherwise with Somerville and Admiral Gensoul at Oran, for Gensoul's powerful battle squadron supplied the main focus of the Cabinet's anxieties over the French Navy. Somerville was accorded little time in which to achieve his mission and little latitude in negotiation, being instead whipped along by Churchill's and Pound's urge to impose a quick, even if violent, solution. Somerville's command, Force H, the 'detached squadron' (in the Admiralty's phrase) formed to fill the vacuum in the Western Mediterranean and the waters off Africa created by the defection of the French Navy, was not even activated until just five days before the date set for 'Catapult'. Only on 30 June, three days beforehand, did the Naval Staff signal the War Cabinet's instructions to Somerville. He was to offer Admiral Gensoul four options with a six-hour time limit for acceptance:

1. Put to sea and join forces with the British;
2. Sail to a French West Indian port, there to demilitarise his ships;
3. Sail with reduced crews to any British port;
4. Scuttle all his ships within six hours of the offer of the British ultimatum.[16]

Failing Gensoul's acceptance of one of these choices, Somerville was ordered 'to endeavour to destroy ships at Mers-el-Kebir but particularly *Dunkerque* and *Strasbourg*', using 'all means at your disposal'.[17] Somerville was further ordered to destroy the warships in the port of Oran itself 'if this will not entail any considerable loss of civilian life'. One way or another, 'Catapult' was to be completed by the end of 3 July.

In the evening of 30 June Somerville held a meeting in his flagship HMS *Hood*, then moored with the rest of Force H at Gibraltar, in order to hammer out how best to sink Gensoul's ships if this after all had to be done. Present were Admiral Sir Dudley North, Flag Officer, North Atlantic (headquarters at Gibraltar), Vice-Admiral Wells (Flag Officer, Aircraft Carriers, flying his flag in *Ark Royal*, part of Force H) and Captain C. S. Holland, a strongly Francophile officer who had until recently been naval attaché in Paris and who was highly knowledgeable about the French Navy and its leaders. Wells, for his part, ruled out an attack by torpedo aircraft as being 'difficult and unproductive' unless anti-aircraft fire could be silenced first. Torpedo attack by destroyers was also ruled out because of net defences round the French heavy ships and the restricted space in the basin. It was finally decided, according to Somerville's later report on 'Catapult', that in the case of Mers-el-Kebir

> a round or two should be fired to show that we were in earnest, and if this failed to bring acceptance of our terms, a limited period of gunfire and/or bombing should be used to cause evacuation of ships, final sinking being effected by torpedo-bomber attack or demolition, according to circumstances.
>
> It was thought that to complete destruction by gunfire would require a great deal of ammunition and cause very great loss of life.
>
> In the case of Oran, it was agreed that gunfire would cause very severe civilian casualties and it was hoped that the action taken at Mers-el-Kebir would induce the French to scuttle their ships at Oran.[18]

This evident operational lukewarmness towards a violent solution merely reflected a deeper personal repugnance. As Somerville records: 'After the conclusion of this meeting, Admiral North, Vice-Admiral Wells and Captain Holland all expressed themselves as strongly opposed to the use of force. They considered that there was little fear of the French allowing their ships to fall into German hands.'[19] Moreover, the view held by Somerville 'and which was shared by others present . . .' was that it was 'highly improbable that the French would use force to resist our demands'. Next day Somerville signalled his doubts to the Admiralty about the use of force, putting forward an alternative suggestion of giving Gensoul advance warning of British action. But Churchill and Pound proved implacable; back came the signal:

> It is most undesirable that you should have to deal with French Fleet at sea and consequently about twelve hours' warning, as suggested in your 0812 of 1st July, is not repetition not acceptable. Hence, you should arrive in the vicinity of Oran with your force at whatever time you select, and send your emissary ashore, subsequently taking such action as you consider fit with your force before time limit expires.[20]

On 2–3 July, around midnight and after (their favourite time for drafting important operational signals: hence their naval staff nickname of 'the Midnight Follies') Churchill and Pound drew up the final text of the ultimatum which Somerville was to present to Gensoul. For all the florid language about Britain being committed to restoring 'the greatness and territory of France', the four options remained as drafted on 30 June. They did not include demilitarisation of French ships on the spot, as offered to Godfroy, nor did they permit of any postponement beyond 3 July in the execution of 'Catapult', nor any extension of the six-hour time limit of the ultimatum.

In this haste may be detected a characteristic Churchillian impatience for ruthless action, especially in the present case against the French who had in his view so shamefully dropped out of the war, together with an understandable wish to impress world (and especially American) opinion in the most dramatic possible fashion with Britain's resolve to fight on. Nor should be forgotten the sheer pressure on the Prime Minister of grappling with calamity on the grand scale. When in the forenoon of 3 July ('Catapult' day) Pound in fact drafted a signal to Somerville permitting him to offer Gensoul demilitarisation of his ships where they were, the War Cabinet turned down his draft on the score that 'this would look like weakening'.[21]

At 0135 on 3 July, as the great ships of Force H were steaming for Oran under shroud of night, the final signal from the Admiralty before the loosing of 'Catapult' reached Somerville: it reminded him that it was 'very important' that the operation be completed during daylight that day. But, thanks to the wonder and the curse of modern radio communications, Somerville was to hear from London again and again during the long, hot hours to come, while he himself waited anxiously for news from Captain Holland in Mers-el-Kebir.

At 0810 Holland was met outside the boom by Gensoul's barge bearing his flag lieutenant, 'an old friend of mine', recorded Holland.[22] Now came the first setback: Gensoul refused to see Holland personally, so making it impossible for Holland to open a friendly preliminary softening-up discussion before presenting the War Cabinet's written ultimatum. Instead the flag lieutenant took the ultimatum to Gensoul, delivering it to him in his flagship *Dunkerque* at 0935. 'At this point,' according to Holland, 'it was observed that the battleships were furling awnings and raising steam.'

Some two and a half hours now passed while Holland in *Foxhound*, Somerville in *Hood* and the War Cabinet in London all waited for Gensoul's response. At around noon Somerville signalled London that he was giving the French admiral until 1500 (later extended to 1530) to reply to the British terms. At 1232 London signalled Somerville that if he thought the French were preparing to leave harbour he 'should inform them that if they moved, he would open fire'.[23] This crossed a signal from Somerville: 'Am awaiting reply to letter before opening fire.'[24] At 1236 he signalled to Holland asking whether he reckoned there was now any alternative to bombarding the French ships. But Holland recommended that the French should be asked for a final reply before fire was opened, his appreciation of the French character being that 'an initial refusal will often come round to an acquiescence'. Holland himself 'felt most strongly that the use of force, even as a last resource, was fatal to our object'. He therefore used 'every endeavour to bring about a peaceful solution' even at the cost of delaying the carrying out of the War Cabinet's orders.[25]

At around 1500 Gensoul at last consented to meet Holland in person on board *Dunkerque*, which encouraged Somerville to postpone action yet again: as he signalled to London, 'I think they are weakening.' At 1615 Holland was piped over the side of the French flagship and ushered into Gensoul's cabin, where he found the Admiral 'clearly extremely indignant and angry at the course of events'.[26] As they talked, it seemed gradually to dawn on Gensoul that the British might actually use force. But in any event he was playing for time; British Intelligence decrypts in London of French cypher traffic that afternoon revealed that the French Admiralty had signalled him that all other French naval forces in the Mediterranean had been ordered to his support and that he was 'to answer fire with fire'.[27] Passing this intercept on to Somerville at 1614, London added: 'Settle this matter quickly, or you may have reinforcements to deal with.' But Somerville was still awaiting further news from Holland or his return. Meanwhile in *Dunkerque* Holland convinced himself that 'we had won through and he [Gensoul] would accept one or other of the proposals'. What he could not know, and what the Admiralty omitted to pass on to Somerville, was that the decrypt of the French Admiralty signal to Gensoul revealed that Gensoul had misrepresented the British terms to his superiors as consisting only of two alternatives – join the British fleet or scuttle – rather than the actual four (see above, p. 175). At 1715, just about the time when Gensoul was finally rejecting the ultimatum, a signal reached him from Somerville stating that unless he accepted by 1730 Force H would sink his ships.

When the crestfallen Holland left the *Dunkerque* after a 'friendly' leavetaking he noted that the French battleships were in 'an advanced state of readiness for sea', with control positions manned, range-finders trained on Force H, and tugs at their sterns. But although Action Stations was being sounded, there was little bustle among the crews, many of whom remained on the upper decks. As Holland passed on his way back to *Foxhound* the officer of the watch in the *Bretagne* saluted smartly. It seemed as if the French could not really believe that they were about to be victims of British broadsides.

At 1755 (*Foxhound* having got clear after laying magnetic mines across the harbour entrance) *Hood*, steaming at the head of Somerville's line at 17 knots, opened fire at 17,500 yards, quickly followed by *Resolution* and *Valiant*. So at long last, and for the first time in the Second World War, there was taking place that collision of battle squadrons on which the Admiralty's mind had been so focused in the peacetime years. Yet by a sad irony the British line was not engaging the Japanese Fleet, as the Admiralty had always imagined, nor even the German or Italian capital ships, but the Royal Navy's old eighteenth-century enemy and twentieth-century ally.

Owing to the continuing haze and the smoke pouring from French ships raising steam, the upper works of *Hood*'s target, a ship of the Dunkerque class lying northernmost of the battleships anchored abeam bows to the mole, 'were indistinct and difficult to range on; in consequence the nearby lighthouse of MERS-EL-KEBIR was used for ranging'.[28] The other two British capital ships were also using the lighthouse as an aiming mark, content to make, as *Resolution*'s report put it, 'a general shoot into the area of the anchorage'.[29] The same haze and smoke made it difficult for Somerville's ships to observe the fall of shot, but a Swordfish from *Ark Royal* saw from a height of 7,000 feet the first salvo burst in a line across the *Commandante Teste* (the seaplane carrier), the *Bretagne* and the quarter deck of the *Strasbourg*. 'The second salvo,' according to the report of the Swordfish crew, 'hit the *Bretagne* which blew up immediately and enveloped the harbour in smoke.'[30] From the *Valiant* the death of the *Bretagne* at 1758 (hit in the after magazines) appeared as 'a thick, slowly rising mushroom of smoke . . . behind the breakwater reaching to a great height'.[31] When the smoke cleared, the Swordfish crew could no longer see the *Bretagne*, but observed a fire aft on the *Commandante Teste*, while the

Dunkerque appeared to have grounded bows on shore opposite to her berth, after hitting a mine. It was learned later that the *Provence* too had beached (see pp. 171, 174).

The French ships, caught in confined waters with fields of fire partly masked by their neighbours, replied as best they could, their shells throwing up – to the curious interest of the unscathed British – pink and green water splashes. The dye in the nose-cones of the shells served to identify each ship's fall of shot. At 1804 Somerville ordered a cease-fire to give the French crews an opportunity to leave their vessels. By now more than 1,250 French sailors lay dead under the water or beneath the reeking smoke, most of them in the *Bretagne*. In the British heavy ships the cease-fire was welcome enough; so sulphurously hot was the evening that in HMS *Resolution* the temperature in the magazines and shell-handling rooms rose to 96°F, and the crews began to suffer from contaminated air as well as the heat.[32]

At 1812 the Swordfish sighted five destroyers followed by the *Strasbourg* leave the harbour and head along the coast, the report being received in *Hood* at 1820. However, Somerville did not, in his own admission, 'attach sufficient weight to this report' – partly because he had been so certain that the French would leave their ships once the British bombardment opened, and partly because of earlier but false reports of French movements towards the open sea.[33] Only after a confirming report at 1830 did he steer to the east in pursuit. At 1838 he altered course to 080° and at 1902 increased speed to 25 knots (the best that *Hood* could manage) in an effort to bring the *Strasbourg* to action, but then ceased fire and turned away to avoid a torpedo attack by the French destroyer escort. Somerville was to acknowledge that his general dispositions for 'Catapult' 'did not make sufficient provision for dealing with any French ships that might attempt to leave harbour . . .'

Now it was the turn of six Swordfish from HMS *Ark Royal* to try to stop the *Strasbourg*, crossing ahead of her and attacking from the landward side with the French ship (which was making enormous quantities of black smoke) silhouetted against the afterglow. At 2055 the Swordfish came in at a height of twenty feet with 300 yard intervals between them, torpedoes dropping from beneath their fixed undercarriages into a calm sea. But although the crews believed they might have scored two or three hits, the *Strasbourg* got clear away under cover of darkness (Somerville deciding against a night action) to reach safe haven in Toulon.

Three days later the *Ark Royal*'s aircraft attempted to finish off the *Dunkerque* in Mers-el-Kebir, flying from 7,000 feet down the path of the rising sun after its rays had lit up the ship. The crews reported that five out of six torpedoes had struck home and one had failed to explode.

On 8 July, far off in Dakar in West Africa, the battleship *Richelieu* was attacked by a force composed of the small carrier *Hermes* and the cruisers *Dorsetshire* and *Australia* under Captain R. F. J. Onslow, RN. In the small hours a motor boat penetrated the harbour defences and dropped depth-charges under her stern: they failed to detonate. Three hours later torpedo-bombers obtained one hit which distorted a propeller shaft and flooded three compartments – enough to give the French a year's repair work to render her fully seaworthy, although the ship could still have put to sea in an emergency.

So in blood and destruction, to the accompaniment of anguish beneath the White Ensign and abiding hostility beneath the Tricolor, Britain had largely eliminated the French Navy as a factor in the strategic balance of the war. But even as one alliance at sea was foundering in bitterness, Britain was seeking to construct another to replace it. And, by an irony, the most important lever in her diplomacy lay in the disposition of the British Fleet, should Britain follow France into defeat and surrender.

On 11 September 1939 President Roosevelt had written to Churchill to suggest that he keep in touch personally by diplomatic bag 'with anything you want me to know about'.[34] In expressing gladness at seeing Churchill back in his old job of First Lord of the Admiralty, Roosevelt reminded him that during the Great War the two of them had occupied similar posts, Roosevelt then being Assistant Secretary of the Navy. This letter marked the beginning of what was to swell into a copious and ever more intimate exchange between Roosevelt and 'Former Naval Person', as Churchill dubbed himself after becoming Prime Minister. But from September 1939 until Churchill's appointment to this office the correspondence had remained scanty and intermittent, just as Britain's general relations with America while Chamberlain remained head of government were characterised by a mutual distance and even suspicion.[35]

Yet Roosevelt himself wished to help the Allies as far as American opinion in Congress and at large made possible while at the same time keeping America out of the war. In October 1939 a Western hemisphere Neutrality Zone was proclaimed, a maritime extension of the Monroe Doctrine, warning belligerent ships to keep out of a sea area 300 miles wide drawn round the Americas, with the exception of Canada and European colonies. Roosevelt hoped that this zone, patrolled by the US Navy, would deter German warships and so enable the Royal Navy to conserve escort ships for service elsewhere, but in fact it brought little operational relief.[36] In November a revised Neutrality Act ended the American embargo on supplying arms to the belligerents in favour of trade equally with them all on a cash and carry basis, which in fact heavily favoured France and Britain because of their command of the sea lanes to America. So began to swell an immense tide of Allied orders for arms of every kind, including aircraft, which steadily helped to lift American industry out of the Depression. After the fall of France Britain took over French orders as well, pinning faith in America's willingness to continue deliveries even when the money ran out. Thus Britain's expiring wealth laid the foundation for America's colossal wartime technological expansion.

It was the collapse of France and with her the disappearance of that key piece of strategic furniture, the Western Front, which altered everything for Roosevelt as it had for Churchill. No longer could America enjoy the profitable security of being the 'arsenal of democracy' while Britain and France waged and won the actual war against Nazi Germany. Indeed, it was possible – and some Americans, like Joseph Kennedy, the ambassador in London, deemed it highly likely – that Britain herself would soon succumb to Germany's overwhelming might. This would leave the United States without a foreign shield between herself and a Europe dominated by Germany, and at a time when she also had to watch Japanese ambitions in the Pacific. In particular, the British Fleet could well pass under Axis control if Britain had to make peace, for the Fleet would constitute Britain's only bargaining counter in seeking to soften German terms. In that eventuality the United States Navy would be hard put to defend both the Atlantic and the Pacific.

To keep the British going was therefore perceived by Roosevelt as an American interest, providing it could be done without compromising the US's neutrality or affronting isolationist opinion. But were the British able and willing to keep going? In May and June 1940 Roosevelt himself expressed some doubts, although they were partly dispelled by Churchill's ruthless solution of the problem of the French Navy.

Churchill for his part recognised all too clearly that, in the words of the Chiefs of Staff, Britain's long-term chance of survival absolutely depended on American willingness 'to give us full economic and financial support, *without which we do not think we could continue the war with any chance of success*'.[37] For the next eighteen months he was to strive with consummate persistence and skill to draw America step by step into the war. Moreover, from the 1930s to the end of his life he was inspired by a romantic vision of a world free and at peace under the guardianship of the English-speaking peoples; and as an Englishman half-American by birth he saw a 'special relationship' between Britain and America as fundamental to the realisation of his vision.

Nevertheless the vision did not blind him to the present realities of power and necessity. He bargained as toughly as a man could from the weakness of an imperial power past its zenith, its financial and strategic foundations crumbling, with the new imperial power which, in all its young strength and with no enemies at its throat, was supplanting the old. Over relations with the United States as in the other grand issues bearing on Britain's survival in the desperate summer of 1940, Churchill was at his best: far-sightedness rooted in faith and resolution; driving will to win tempered by understanding and patience; grasp of the fundamental strategic simplicities born of long ministerial experience and a high sense of history.

The first test case for his American policy was provided by the Royal Navy's desperate need for escort ships. The new class of vessel specially designed for convoy work, the Hunt class of 900–1,000 ton destroyers, were not due to be commissioned until 1941, yet the attrition of war had reduced the Navy's strength in fleet and escort destroyers from the already insufficient number of 202 at the outbreak of war to a mere 74 out of the dockyards by June 1940 – far too few to guard the vital Atlantic convoys, provide screens for Britain's main fleets and also to supply the Navy's principal instrument for striking at a German invasion armada. On 15 May, in his first letter to Roosevelt as Prime Minister and 'Former Naval Person', Churchill therefore asked for 'the loan of forty or fifty of your older destroyers to bridge the gap between what we have now and the large new construction we put in hand at the beginning of the war'.[38]

Roosevelt, however, turned down the request, preferring to wait upon events. Stalemated negotiations dragged on into August.[39] The Americans sought to elicit from the British a firm promise that the British Fleet would be transferred to North American bases in the event of Britain having to sue for peace, while Churchill endeavoured to twang American nerves with hints that in such a circumstance his successor as Prime Minister might have to surrender the Fleet in order to obtain better terms from Germany: the implication being that it was in America's interest to lend Britain's present leadership all possible support in order to avert such a dire happening. In late August, a further modest step towards Anglo-American naval understanding was made when Admiral Robert L. Ghormley led a three-man delegation to London to hold staff talks; the Americans listening, the British expounding. Ghormley himself thereafter stayed on in London as 'Special Naval Observer' in close, but still one-way, liaison with the Admiralty. In the later months of 1940 he was to urge Washington to permit full mutual discussions of common strategic problems, but in vain. Nonetheless, he did succeed in establishing a cordial personal relationship with the British naval staff; the modest beginning of what eventually was to become the closest cooperation in history between two national navies.

On 2 September 1940 a deal was at last struck over Churchill's request for the transfer of American destroyers. Britain obtained fifty 'moth-balled' Great War American vessels, while in a *quid pro quo* Britain granted the United States 99-year leases of land on eight British possessions in the Caribbean and western Atlantic on which to establish naval and air bases, and also undertook to make a public declaration that the Royal Navy would not be scuttled or surrendered if the waters around the British Isles became untenable. It was a highly unequal exchange which illustrated the weakness of Britain's position and America's determination to exploit it (as Churchill himself well recognised). Nevertheless the British government could comfort itself that the 'destroyers-for-bases' deal marked for the first time an open official American commitment to Britain's cause, as distinct from mere commercial sales of arms; a significant step along the path towards direct American involvement in the war. And there was an uncovenanted advantage, in that American bases in this key strategic region necessarily meant the deployment of American armed force, so serving in the future to lighten Britain's own global burdens a little.

Yet these dearly bought destroyers did not in the event bring swift relief to the Royal Navy. Quite apart from requiring radical alterations to their armament and the fitting of modern sonar, they proved to be in such poor shape mechanically that months of work were needed to fit them for sea service. According to Rear-Admiral Stuart Bonham-Carter, writing from the dockyard at Halifax, Nova Scotia, to the Assistant Chief of Naval Staff (Foreign) in October 1940, the destroyers appeared at first sight 'to be in a fairly good shape but, after taking them over, one could see they may have to have a lot done to them before becoming really efficient', and he explained that in particular they had developed engine-room defects which could only have been found out in advance by complete stripping down.[40] Only nine of these ancient four-funnel destroyers were in service by the end of the year and only 30 by May 1941.

Shortage of escort ships of all kinds, but especially destroyers, therefore supplies the leitmotiv of the Royal Navy's operations in home waters and the Atlantic throughout the second half of 1940 and on into 1941. For in escorts lay the key to the Navy's two most urgent problems – that of defeating a German attempt to invade England, and that of guarding the convoys which carried home the steel and machine tools and weapons, the foodstuffs and the fuel oil, without which British resistance to Nazi power would in any case swiftly wither.

Kepe then the sea that is the wall of England:
And then is England kept by Goddes hande.

So adjured Bishop Adam de Moleyns in 1436. Time and again since then great enemies had mustered their power beyond that 'wall', determined to surmount it and subdue the islanders to their will. In 1588, when the Royal Navy was still small and young, the Spain of Philip II, then the world's greatest seapower, had posed the most dangerous threat of them all, seeking with the Armada to land a great army on the English shore, only to be thwarted by England's fledgling navy. In 1803–5 (the intervening centuries being studded with invasion scares that had come to nothing in the face of wind, tide and the Royal Navy) it was the turn of Bonaparte, the self-styled 'Napoleon, Emperor of the French', to puzzle how to pass his Grande Armée over the English Channel, which he regarded as 'a ditch which will be leaped whenever one has the boldness to try'.[41] The First Lord of the Admiralty of the time, Admiral Lord Barham, had assured his anxious Cabinet colleagues: 'I do not say the French cannot come; I only say they cannot come by sea.' So, in the zenith of the Royal Navy's size and fighting efficiency, it proved.

From the 1840s onwards, however, the coming of the steamship had posed a new kind of threat to 'England's wall'. No longer would an invader be dependent on the vagaries of wind, but be able to steam across the Channel at will, choosing his own moment to slip past the Royal Navy's guard and land an army by surprise. So was born the fear of the 'bolt from the blue' invasion: in the Victorian era, invasion by the French, the traditional enemy; and after 1900 by the Germans. Yet the Admiralty remained confident that in the face of British seapower Germany with her much smaller High Seas Fleet would be unable to do more than sneak small landing forces through to the British coast. In the event, during the Great War, Germany mounted no invasion attempt of any kind although the British government held back troops from the Western Front just in case.

Now it was the summer of 1940, and Hitler's victorious army stood along the cliffs and dunes where Philip II's *tercios* and Bonaparte's Grande Armée had waited in vain for safe passage to England. To the islanders themselves, as they erected pill-boxes and tank-traps and strung barbed wire along the beaches and between the ice-cream kiosks of seaside resorts, it was therefore a situation rendered familiar enough by their history – bracing rather than frightening. Who could really imagine that soldiers in coal-scuttle helmets and field grey would be seen marching through the gentle and hitherto inviolate landscapes of Sussex and Kent, or Norfolk and Suffolk? This was the kind of thing that only happened to other nations.

For Britain's political and military leadership too – and for none more than Churchill, with his vivid sense of the English story – 1588 and 1803–5 lived again in 1940; but in their case it conferred no comfortable feeling of immunity. Not only was the British Army after Dunkirk virtually unarmed (there was only enough equipment for two divisions in the whole United Kingdom) but this time there existed an altogether new dimension to the threat of invasion – airpower.

On 25 May, even before the lesson of Norway had been driven home by the Luftwaffe over Dunkirk, the Chiefs of Staff reported to the Cabinet that the Royal Navy's ability to defeat an invasion force while at sea depended on its power to operate in the face of heavy air attacks. They went on to state that the Royal Navy could not count on operating surface forces in strength in the southern part of the North Sea and the English Channel at all – the very seas that the Germans must be expected to try to cross.[42] After studying this report Churchill posed the Chiefs of Staff the direct question: 'Can the Navy and the Air Force hold out reasonable hopes of preventing serious invasion . . . ?' The Chiefs of Staff replied that for as long as the Royal Air Force remained 'in being', then the Navy and the Air Force between them 'should be able to prevent Germany carrying out a serious sea-borne invasion of this country'.[43] But if Germany obtained air superiority, then the Navy could hold up an invasion 'for a time', but not 'for an indefinite period'. Once a large-scale invasion began, Britain's land defences would not be strong enough to prevent the German Army establishing a firm beach-head, nor from then successfully exploiting inland. Therefore, they concluded, 'the crux of the matter is air superiority'.

Thus the decisive role, the task of delivering a victory that would save the island from the invader, which in 1588 and 1803–5 had belonged to the Royal Navy, now in 1940 fell to the Royal Air Force.[44] Yet it would still fall, as in Nelson's and Barham's day, to the Royal

Navy, whether operating beneath the cover of British air superiority or, if need be, without it, to make plans to destroy the enemy's invasion flotilla once it set course for England. The Admiralty and the naval staff addressed themselves to this traditional problem in a novel guise.

As in 1803–5 the enemy controlled the entire Continental coast opposite England from Denmark to Finisterre; an invasion force might venture across the North Sea from the Low Countries or the North German and Danish ports to East Anglia, or it could follow the Bonapartian plan of a short passage across the Straits of Dover. But unlike in 1803–5 – or 1914–18, for that matter – the enemy in 1940 possessed only a negligible surface fleet, for the German Navy, even at the outbreak of war a fraction of the size of the old Imperial High Seas Fleet, had been drastically written down in the Norwegian campaign. British Intelligence reckoned that its operational strength in the summer of 1940 comprised the two fast battleships *Scharnhorst* and *Gneisenau* (in fact both damaged and unfit for sea), two old, slow and weak pre-Great War battleships, two heavy and at least two – possibly four – light cruisers (in fact only two cruisers in all were fit for sea), between seven and ten destroyers, 40 to 50 U-boats (whereas in July only 28 were actually operational), a similar number of torpedo boats and some twenty or so lighter craft.[45] As the German naval leadership bleakly recognised, this was a pitifully inadequate force with which to cover a vast invasion flotilla of transports and barges against the Royal Navy. No wonder Grand Admiral Raeder demanded as an essential prerequisite for an invasion that Germany enjoy absolute control of the air over the Channel.[46]

It was at the end of May, while 'Dynamo' was in full spate, that the Admiralty sent a directive to all home Commanders-in-Chief outlining its anti-invasion strategy: one little altered in the course of the summer and autumn, and which broadly followed the precepts laid down by the Admiralty in 1803–5, and, for that matter, by Lord Howard of Effingham, Raleigh, Drake and Hawkins in the 1580s. Believing that the enemy would choose the shortest crossing and be prepared to accept 'catastrophic losses' in order to land an army in England, the Admiralty stressed the importance of 'attack before departure' (shades of Drake's successful raid on the Spanish Armada in Cadiz in 1587), which therefore demanded 'early indication of assembly by our intelligence and reconnaissance'.[47] When the assembly of an invasion fleet had been detected by these means, it was to be bombed, mined and shelled in its anchorages. If it nevertheless proved impossible to destroy the invasion fleet before it put to sea, then it would be attacked 'at the point of arrival' (shades of the English fireships after the

Armada's arrival at Gravelines in 1588). Since the exact point of landing could not be known in advance, the Admiralty judged that 'our forces must be disposed to cover the area Wash to Newhaven as a whole'.

The directive then turned to a third eventuality – 'the happy possibility that our reconnaissance might enable us to intercept the expedition on passage'. It reckoned that to destroy the expedition at sea would demand four destroyer flotillas (36 ships at full strength), their firepower being further strengthened by cruisers. These flotillas were to be based in the Humber, Harwich, Sheerness and Portsmouth or Dover, where they would be well placed to attack the expedition on arrival no matter what the point of landfall. The Admiralty proposed in addition that 'the maximum number ... of destroyers, escort vessels, corvettes, etc, as can be spared from escort duties should be allotted to the area'. On top of all this, small craft were to be 'collected immediately for watching close inshore and hampering the enemy's operations'. The Admiralty thought that the transit of the invasion fleet might be accompanied by a diversionary sortie of the two German fast battleships in northern waters, perhaps also by a foray into the southern North Sea by the two old battleships *Schlesien* and *Schleswig-Holstein* and up to five cruisers, and it therefore appreciated that the Royal Navy would have to hold ready sufficient heavy ships and cruisers to deal with these threats.

Comprehensive though these plans were, they committed virtually half of Britain's remaining destroyer strength to a defensive screen widely spread round England's south-eastern shores, so inevitably denuding Western Approaches Command (responsible for the Atlantic convoys) and the Home Fleet. By the end of July there were 32 destroyers and five corvettes in the Nore Command alone. What was more, six cruisers were also removed from the Home Fleet, already weak enough in this class of ship, and similarly dispersed to south-eastern naval bases. This provoked Admiral Forbes tartly to request the Admiralty to inform him which Home Fleet cruisers could still be considered as coming under his command. Nor was this all: as early as 17 May the Admiralty (and this really meant Pound) had suggested to Forbes that the Home Fleet's battleships too should come south to Plymouth.[48] At the other end of the scale, anti-submarine trawlers were taken away from escort duty and sent to join the new 'Auxiliary Patrol' of some 1,000 armed trawlers and drifters, of which about a third were always on patrol watching for an invasion fleet.

Admiral Forbes himself vigorously opposed this draining of strength away from his fleet and from the task of protecting merchant shipping, for he believed that no invasion attempt was possible until and unless Fighter Command was decisively beaten by the Luftwaffe. He judged that there would then be time enough to redeploy the Home Fleet for a last battle to prevent a successful invasion. In May he successfully resisted a proposal that he should bring his fleet down to Plymouth; in July he likewise opposed a suggestion that he should detach two of his battleships to Liverpool. He did, however, agree that if there were signs that the enemy was preparing to invade across the North Sea, he would transfer the Fleet from Scapa southwards to Rosyth. The dispute was finally resolved on 20 July when an Admiralty directive laid down that British heavy ships should not move into the southern North Sea unless German capital ships were being used to cover an invasion force, in which event 'our own heavy ships are to engage them at the earliest opportunity'.[49]

Needless to say, the Commanders-in-Chief whose commands covered the possible invasion coasts (Portsmouth, Dover, The Nore) took a very different view; they wanted to have and to hold all the destroyers and cruisers that the Admiralty was good enough to send them. In the words of Admiral Sir Reginald Plunket Ernle-Erle-Drax, C-in-C, The Nore (the command stretching from the Dover Strait to Flamborough Head on the east coast), 'to destroy an invading force we need gunfire and plenty of it'.[50]

But the key to this whole argument over the Royal Navy's correct deployment lay in the degree of advanced warning of invasion that might be expected. As experience during 'Dynamo' had shown, reinforcements could reach Dover from Rosyth within 24 hours. Even ships escorting convoys in the Western Approaches were within a few days' recall. Was the Admiralty really justified in reckoning on such short notice of an invasion attempt that it was right to keep so many of the Navy's precious destroyers and cruisers week after week along England's south-eastern shores? The answer to this question lies in the Intelligence data available to the Admiralty at the time.[51]

Although the Government Code and Cypher School at Bletchley Park had begun to break the Luftwaffe Enigma-machine cypher regularly during the Norwegian and French campaigns (yielding by inference useful information about the operational plans of the German Army and Navy as well), it was still to be months before the German Navy Enigma could be similarly read reliably and in quantity. After the French campaign even the Luftwaffe Enigma traffic slackened off because of increased use of landlines. However, in late June and early July, it did yield references to the forward deployment of aircraft and other preparations indicating a major offensive effort by the Luftwaffe; references also to the installation of long-range artillery to command the Straits of Dover. In London the Joint Intelligence Committee (JIC) was alarmed enough by these decrypts to give mid-July as the date from which onwards 'a full-scale invasion' might be expected. In fact the decrypts related to the Luftwaffe's coming attempt to smash the Royal Air Force as the essential preliminary to an invasion; and the opening phase of this air battle, in the form of fighter sweeps over the Channel and southern England, actually began on 10 July. Yet the JIC might surely have guessed that the Enigma decrypts pointed towards a Luftwaffe offensive rather than an invasion, for photo-reconnaissance showed that no assemblage of barges and other sea transport had yet taken place in Channel and North Sea ports. Moreover, it was unrealistic to credit even German staff work with the ability to organise a massive tri-service operation like an invasion within less than a month of the ending of the strenuous French campaign.

Unfortunately, Military Intelligence (MI) made its own contribution to this scare by arguing that an invasion might take such unorthodox forms as tanks ferried in motor boats to a wide frontage of coast, rather than the traditional pattern of a fleet of transports and barges carrying an expeditionary force together with all its stores and equipment, and escorted by warships. The Naval Intelligence Department (NID), for its part, regarded MI's concept as fanciful, not least because there was no evidence that the necessary pool of motor boats existed. But unfortunately the naval staff itself (this again really means Pound, abetted by the VCNS, Rear-Admiral T. S. V. Phillips) believed in this figment of MI's imagination – hence the haemorrhage of ships away from the Home Fleet and the Western Approaches to picket the invasion coasts.

As Pound explained to the Prime Minister early in July, possibly with the success of 'Weserübung' in mind, '. . . we cannot therefore assume that special craft will not have been provided, or that past military rules as to what is practicable and what is impracticable will be allowed to govern the action taken'. He encouragingly added that the Germans might get as many as 100,000 men ashore with little or no warning by making a number of separate attacks and feints at widely dispersed points in a carefully chosen combination of calm weather and low visibility, from ports as far apart as Biscay and Norway. This could be achieved by means of hundreds of fast motor boats previously assembled but undetected by reconnaissance in French and Dutch ports, and expeditions using larger vessels and tank-landing craft assembled beyond the range of reconnaissance in Biscay and the Baltic.[52] Thus, by an irony, the First Sea Lord accepted the possibility of that 'bolt from the blue' which his predecessors before the Great War had so derided. It must be said that Pound's picture of German strategy, for which no supporting evidence existed at that time or later in the year, was more worthy of the author of *The Riddle of the Sands* than the professional head of the Royal Navy. Churchill himself in commenting on Pound's memorandum found it 'very difficult to visualise' an invasion by means of swarms of small motor boats.

It was after the middle of August that Sigint started to pick up reliable evidence that German preparations for an invasion were indeed now in progress, although neither then nor later was any reference to an exact date or place of invasion ever detected. From the beginning of September photo-reconnaissance provided confirmatory proof of the assemblage of barges and other craft in Ostend, Dunkirk and Calais. This evidence hardened day by day until on 7 September the Photographic Reconnaissance Unit (PRU) warned that a well-organised and large-scale movement of barges to forward Channel bases was taking place; it noted that moon and tide on the south-east coast of England would be favourable to an invasion attempt between 8 and 10 September (dates also currently coming up in reports from diplomatic and Special Intelligence Service sources). The JIC therefore advised the Chiefs of Staff that an invasion might be attempted at any time, and at 2007 on 7 September 1940 GHQ, Home Forces, issued the codeword 'Cromwell', the signal to bring all the home defence forces to a state of readiness.

In fact Hitler had directed at the end of July that all preparations for 'Sealion' (British Sigint only picked up this codename for the invasion on 21 September) must be completed by the middle of September, but, as with his earlier contingency plans for risky forward moves, such as against Czechoslovakia in 1938 and Poland in 1939, he left himself free to choose at the last moment whether to launch his forces or not. By 7 September, when GHQ, Home Forces, signalled 'Cromwell', he had still not made up his mind, for although there were signs that Fighter Command might be beginning to weaken, the outcome of the attrition battle waged by the Luftwaffe against Fighter Command since 8 August ('Adler Tag') still lay in doubt.

Thus the invasion scare of early July, causing the premature and prolonged deployment of so many of the Navy's stretched resources round the south-eastern coasts, was not really warranted by the available and broadly accurate Intelligence data on the progress of

German preparations. In the light of that data, mid-August was the very earliest when all those cruisers and destroyers needed to be drawn away from the Home Fleet and the Western Approaches, although Forbes was probably correct in judging that that decision could even wait until the air battle was lost and won.

The Admiralty was now to prove no less tardy in perceiving that the invasion threat had passed – again despite cumulative and reliable data from Intelligence sources. On 14 September Hitler postponed for the third time his decision to order the ten-day count-down period for 'Sealion', which meant that the operation could not now be launched until 27 September, that being the last day of favourable moon and tide before 8 October. On 15 September Fighter Command crushingly defeated the Luftwaffe's climactic mass attack in the Battle of Britain. Two days later Hitler postponed the count-down for 'Sealion' yet again, this time also ordering some of the invasion barges to be dispersed. Even by 15 September British analysis of the volume of German naval radio traffic was already suggesting that invasion preparations had begun to wane, while on 20 September photo-reconnaissance confirmed this with proof that five destroyers and a torpedo boat had been withdrawn from Cherbourg and that assemblies of barges were beginning to thin out. At the end of September the PRU reported that the number of barges in the main invasion ports from Flushing to Boulogne had fallen by nearly a third within less than a fortnight.

Puzzlingly, however, Sigint and SIS sources also yielded clues at this time suggesting that 'Sealion' was still alive and preparing to pounce.[53] Once again Forbes, that commonsensical sailor, got it right, judging as early as 15 September that Fighter Command's successes 'had removed the threat of invasion completely'; he therefore pressed a reluctant and obstinate Admiralty to redeploy ships back to the Home Fleet and the Atlantic. On 28 September he sent a powerful letter to the Admiralty in which he summed up the strategic view he had held throughout the invasion summer, and urged that

> . . . the Army, assisted by the Air Force, should carry out its immemorial role of holding up the first flight of an invading force and that the Navy should be freed to carry out its proper function – offensively against the enemy and in defence of our trade – and not be tied down to provide passive defence to our country, which had now become a fortress.[54]

On 31 October at a meeting of the War Cabinet Defence Committee the Prime Minister directly asked Admiral Forbes whether he believed that an invasion was still possible. Echoing Barham in 1804 Forbes robustly answered that 'while we are predominant at sea and until Germany has defeated our fighter forces invasion by sea is not a practical operation of war'.[55]

Nearly three weeks earlier Hitler had himself come to the same conclusion, putting off 'Sealion' on 12 October until spring 1941; in fact for good. Like Bonaparte he was turning his back on the stubborn islanders behind their 'ditch' and preparing to march his army off eastwards to attack a more accessible Continental victim. So Britain would survive to serve as the catalyst for ever greater American involvement in the war and eventually as the base for an Anglo-American grand-strategic counter-offensive against Hitler's Europe. The Royal Navy's mastery of the Narrow Seas, protected this time by the Royal Air Force's hard-won victory in the Battle of Britain, had once again preserved the cause of freedom, once again decided the course of history.

Now winter was coming on with its short days and bad weather. At the 31 October meeting of the War Cabinet Defence Committee Forbes advised his colleagues that this rendered an invasion even less possible. By this time, in the light of fresh and clinching evidence from Enigma decrypts and other sources, others in high places were ready to agree with him. The Defence Committee concluded that an invasion had become 'relatively remote' and that it was now 'essential to reduce to a minimum' the light naval forces allotted to anti-invasion duties, and redeploy them to protect British trade routes.[56] For meanwhile the U-boats had been enjoying what their crews dubbed 'the happy time', prowling seas largely emptied of British men of war and preying virtually unscathed on defenceless merchant shipping.

On 23 June, immediately after the Franco-German armistice, Karl Dönitz, now a Rear-Admiral and C-in-C, U-boats, had arrived on the French Atlantic coast to carry out a tour of inspection of ports as suitable U-boat bases. On 7 July the U-30 became the first U-boat returning from an Atlantic voyage to replenish with fuel and torpedoes at Lorient, and by 2 August the dockyard there was ready to undertake U-boat repairs. From then on U-boats no longer returned to German bases for replenishment and shore leave, but only to French Biscay ports. On 29 August Dönitz transferred his headquarters from near Wilhelmshaven to Paris in an interim move while a new command centre with elaborate signals links was installed at Kerneval near Lorient.[57] The dockyard at Lorient proved in the event to be more efficient than Germany's own overworked yards in servicing and repairing U-boats, so that whereas in September 1939 to July 1940 the proportion of boats on offensive sorties to the total number of operational boats was 1 to 2.35, in the period July 1940 to July 1941 the proportion improved by almost a quarter to 1 to 1.85.[58] This was by no means the only factor in raising the operational productivity of the U-boats. As Dönitz wrote later:

> Before July 1940 the U-boats had to make a voyage of 450 miles through the North Sea and round the north of Great Britain to reach the Atlantic. Now they were saving something like a week on each patrol and were thus able to stay considerably longer in the actual area of operations. This fact, in turn, added to the total number of U-boats actively engaged against the enemy.[59]

In directing his U-boats to rich hunting areas Dönitz enjoyed the colossal advantage up to August 1940 that the German Navy's B-Dienst could read up to 50 per cent of the Royal Navy's signals, though not the cyphers used by Cs-in-C and flag officers. Even after the cyphers were changed in August B-Dienst found Merchant Navy radio traffic almost as rewarding. On the other hand, and fortunately for the desperately pressed Royal Navy, Dönitz still suffered from crippling handicaps which prevented him from unleashing what at that period might easily have proved a war-winning offensive. Owing to the mistaken earlier priority given to surface ships in the German Navy's construction programme and the current need to allot more boats to training he was still very short of operational U-boats, able only to keep a maximum of eight or nine at sea at any one time. Moreover, German torpedoes had proved a technological disaster. Inaccurate depth-setting caused them to run too deep, while they were also highly prone to failing to detonate because of the faulty design of the magnetic pistol (supposed to fire in response to a ship's magnetic field).[60] In June 1940 the U-boat arm was even compelled to revert to primitive 1914–18 contact pistols while a new and effective magnetic pistol was developed.

Yet after weighing handicaps against advantages Dönitz, the most formidably intelligent, resourceful and relentless opponent that the Royal Navy had had to fight since the Dutchmen de Ruyter and van Tromp in the seventeenth century, decided to launch a major U-boat offensive – in fact, the first phase of what in March 1941 Winston Churchill was to dub 'the Battle of the Atlantic'. Dönitz's opening offensive proved, he wrote in his memoirs after the war, 'particularly successful', and mostly because of the shortage of British escort ships in the Atlantic, as he himself acknowledged: 'The U-boats encountered a large number of vessels sailing independently while convoys were weakly escorted . . .'[61]

It was the heyday of the individual hunt for victims by U-boat aces such as Kretschmer and Prien, heroes to the German public. In June 1940 they sank 58 ships of 284,113 tons; in July, 38 ships of 195,825 tons.[62] Even though in July the Admiralty responded to the establishment of U-boat bases on the Biscay coast by switching the main British convoy route from the south to the north of Ireland, the enemy soon discovered the new routing, and in August (the month when Hitler declared a total blockade of Britain, even neutral ships now being liable to be attacked on sight) sank 56 ships of 267,618 tons, plus another fifteen of 53,283 tons by Luftwaffe long-range bombers now based on French Atlantic coast airfields as well as on Norwegian.[63]

For the British government and naval staff these were worrying enough figures, far outstripping the rate of output of new merchant tonnage by British shipyards. Yet in September Dönitz introduced a new and much more sophisticated system of U-boat warfare – attack on a convoy by a 'wolf pack' of several boats, coordinated by U-boat Command by radio and employing the tactic already well tried at the end of the Great War whereby the boats ran in on their targets at night on the surface, and so outwitted the British under-water sound detection gear.

In order to concentrate a 'wolf pack' Dönitz needed advance warning of a convoy's location and course, either from B-Dienst intercepts or from a Luftwaffe aircraft, or a U-boat on patrol. Once a U-boat had reported the presence of a convoy, it would remain with it as a radio 'marker' on which the 'wolf pack' could home before deploying ahead of the convoy and astride its course. Whether Dönitz received the necessary advanced warning therefore partly depended on luck. In September luck – in the shapes of a chance encounter of a convoy by a U-boat and a revealing B-Dienst intercept – favoured Dönitz, enabling his 'wolf packs' to make a brilliant début. On the 10th of the month four U-boats attacked a homeward-bound convoy from North America in a Force 8 gale and sank five ships.[64] On the 21st–22nd five boats ambushed a convoy of fifteen ships, sinking eleven and damaging a twelfth. These successes helped to lift the September total of sinkings to 59 ships of 295,335 tons, with another fifteen of 56,328 tons falling victim to the Luftwaffe.[65] Next month saw the 'wolf packs' sink 38 ships belonging to three different convoys on three consecutive nights. The deadly pattern of the Battle of the Atlantic had now been established – not only for those in war rooms responsible for its strategic conduct, but also for those in the front line at sea, as the war diary of Lieutenant-Commander Kretschmer of the U-99 for the night of 18–19 October 1940 starkly recorded:

> 2330. Now attacking right wing of the last line [of the convoy] but one. Bow shot at a large freighter. The vessel zig-zagged, with the result that the torpedo passed in front of her and hit instead her even bigger neighbour after a run of 1,740 yards. The ship, about 7,000 tons, was hit below the foremast and sank quickly by the bows with, I presume, two holds flooded.
>
> 2358. Bow shot at large freighter approx 6,000 tons. Range 750 yards. Hit below foremast. The explosion of the torpedo was immediately followed by a high sheet of flame and an explosion which ripped the ship open as far as the bridge and left a cloud of smoke 600 feet high. Ship's forepart apparently shattered. Ship still burning fiercely, with green flames.[66]

In this month the U-boats alone sank a record total of 63 ships of 352,407 tons including, on the 26th, the 42,348-ton Canadian Pacific ship *Empress of Britain*, the only one of the great British liners to be lost during the war.[67]

This was a total so worrying as to bring about the War Cabinet Defence Committee's decision on the 31st to transfer the maximum number of escorts from anti-invasion duties back to trade protection. Fortunately, however, ferocious and continual Atlantic storms brought some relief in November and December by hampering U-boat operations, and the tonnage of ships lost in these two months dropped to 146,613 tons and 212,590 tons.[68] But while the U-boats were struggling against gales and raging seas, the German surface raiders were enjoying their own 'happy time'.

Since the spring the enemy had despatched six long-range armed merchant raiders, much more strongly built and gunned than British 'armed merchant cruisers', to roam the South Atlantic and the Indian Ocean (and even the Pacific, where some of them were replenished by the Japanese) in search of lone and helpless victims. By the end of the year the six ships – *Atlantis*, *Orion*, *Widder*, *Thor*, *Pinguin* and *Komet* – had destroyed 54 ships totalling 366,644 tons.[69] For the Admiralty the problem here lay not only in the extra loss of shipping in itself but also, as with the *Graf Spee* and the *Admiral Scheer* in 1939, in the immense disruption and uncertainty caused by the raiders' far-spread exploits, to counter which demanded the deployment of a disproportionate (and ill-spared) number of British warships.

But this was not all. On 5 November the Admiralty received the chilling report by radio from a homeward-bound Halifax convoy

(HX84) of 37 ships that it was being attacked by the *Admiral Scheer* – the first the Admiralty knew that the pocket battleship had broken out into the North Atlantic via the Denmark Straits without being detected by aircraft of Coastal Command or by surface patrols. The convoy's only escort was the 14,000-ton armed merchant cruiser *Jervis Bay* (Captain E. S. F. Fegen, RN), another of those weakly armed and vulnerable ex-liners with which the Royal Navy had had to make up the shortfall in heavy ships and cruisers bequeathed by the disarmament policies of the 1920s and early 1930s. Nevertheless Fegen, like Kennedy of the *Rawalpindi* the previous year, unhesitatingly steamed to engage the enemy, 6-inch guns against 11-inch, thin plating against thick armour, while signalling his convoy to disperse. Within twenty minutes the *Jervis Bay*, a shattered hulk with her bridge aflame, had capsized, taking Captain Fegen down with her. Yet Fegen's self-sacrifice (for which he was awarded a posthumous Victoria Cross) had won enough time for all but five ships of the convoy to escape. That night, in an episode later celebrated in a feature film, the crew of the tanker *San Demetrio*, having taken to the boats when the *Admiral Scheer* set her on fire, later reboarded her and put the fires out, bringing her eventually safely home to England.

But disruption rather than tonnage was the *Admiral Scheer*'s aim, and this she had achieved. In vain hope of catching her if she were on a short raid or on her way back to port Admiral Forbes deployed the battlecruisers *Hood* and *Repulse*, three cruisers and six destroyers from Scapa across the approaches to the French Atlantic ports of Brest and Lorient, while he himself took *Nelson* and *Rodney* to cover the Iceland–Faeroes gap. At this point, however, Pound intervened directly in the C-in-C's dispositions, despatching part of the battlecruiser force to the point where the *Scheer* had last been sighted, and allotting the *Rodney* to the task of escorting homeward-bound convoys.[70] Yet all this was groping in the blind, for the *Scheer* had vanished far into the South Atlantic, to reappear at widely different points, snapping her jaws on unwary merchant ships, and so keeping the naval staff's nerves freshly rasped.

On 24 November the Admiralty ordered the formation of three hunting groups to track down the pocket battleship and the disguised merchant raiders – Force K, consisting of the recently commissioned new aircraft carrier *Formidable* and the cruisers *Norfolk* and *Berwick*, to be based on Freetown; the small carrier *Hermes* and a cruiser on St Helena; and the cruisers *Cumberland* and *Newcastle* to reinforce the South American Division. Yet this too was groping in the blind, for so few ships could not effectively trawl such a vast area of sea. Then, in December, to add to the Admiralty's problems and cause yet further British redeployment, the cruiser *Admiral Hipper* also escaped into the Atlantic and attacked a convoy. Fortunately her voyage proved a brief one since she lacked the endurance of a pocket battleship, and on 27 December she returned to Brest, the first large German warship or merchant raider to use a French base. On the same day the *Scharnhorst* and *Gneisenau*, now repaired at last, themselves set course for the Atlantic but – even more fortunately for the Admiralty – both ships returned to port after the *Gneisenau* had been damaged by seas off the Norwegian coast.

But the *Admiral Scheer* and the six disguised merchant raiders (the latter heavily armed, adept at adopting the identity of some innocent vessel, and soon to be augmented by others) would remain at sea for many months yet – the effective and highly economical means whereby Grand Admiral Raeder could keep tweaking and straining the tightly stretched net of British seapower, while his C-in-C, U-boats, got on with the main battle of attrition against Britain's shipping capacity.

In combating the U-boat the Royal Navy and Royal Air Force Coastal Command suffered the disadvantage of having to respond defensively to the initiative which Dönitz had so boldly seized. Yet they were just as starved of resources as Dönitz and perhaps even more crippled by defective or unsuitable equipment. And whereas Dönitz had begun to implement a thoroughly pondered strategy with proven tactical systems, the Royal Navy and Coastal Command were still feeling their way from pre-war false doctrine towards effective anti-U-boat tactics and an integrated air/sea command.

For the ill effects of the 1918 separation of the air and surface dimensions of seapower between two services had only been partially remedied by the 1937 compromise by which the Royal Navy got back control of carrier aviation while the Royal Air Force retained responsibility for the land-based maritime air operations. It helped that the primary role of such operations was freshly defined as 'trade protection, reconnaissance and cooperation with the Royal Navy'.[71] But like all compromises its success depended on the spirit in which it was worked. Fortunately Air Chief Marshal Sir Frederick Bowhill, Air Officer Commanding-in-Chief, Coastal Command, from 1937 onwards, was no Trenchardite airpower fanatic, but a former naval officer who had volunteered for the Royal Naval Air Service in 1913, commanded a seaplane carrier in the Great War, and had undertaken a permanent commission in the new Royal Air Force in 1919. Under his leadership, and thanks to his deep-rooted understanding of sea warfare, Coastal Command faithfully interpreted its task as serving the operational needs of the Navy, especially in regard to protection of trade. By 1940 close cooperation already existed between Coastal Command headquarters and the Admiralty's Submarine Tracking Room, while the techniques of combined operations between aircraft sweeping ahead on a convoy and the surface escorts were beginning to evolve in the hard school of experience.

It was therefore by no means helpful when in November 1940 Lord Beaverbrook, the Minister of Aircraft Production, proposed a typical press-baron's short-cut answer to the question of integrated air-sea warfare: nothing less than a return to the pre-1918 situation, with Coastal Command handed over to the Navy. It would be hard to imagine a more ill-timed and disruptive proposal, or one more likely to reawaken maximum ill-feeling between the Air Force and the Navy. So once again, but now in the midst of war, Whitehall pondered this stale and poisonous issue. Nevertheless, in the face of the organisational complications of carving up the Royal Air Force and of the Admiralty's own tribute to 'the already excellent cooperation which exists between Coastal Command and the Navy', the Cabinet Defence Committee (advised by Churchill that it would be disastrous at that stage of the war 'to tear a large fragment from the Royal Air Force')[72] agreed on 4 December not to disturb the existing good relationship between the services.

A joint report in March 1941 closed the matter by reaffirming 'the predominance of the naval element in the existing operational partnership for the protection of sea-borne trade'. In effect this meant that the Admiralty exercised overall direction of the employment of Coastal Command, even though actual command of air operations remained vested in the Coastal Command hierarchy and the AOC-in-C. On 7 February 1941 a fully integrated joint headquarters for the Navy's Western Approaches Command (formerly at Plymouth) and Coastal Command's No. 15 Group had been opened in Derby House, Liverpool, to conduct the Battle of the Atlantic. The new headquarters, with its operations room and telephone, radio and teleprinter links, was Britain's answer to Dönitz's command centre at Kerneval; its location in the north-west of the country resulting from the switch of the main Atlantic convoy route from the south to the north of Ireland in response to Dönitz's offensive from Biscay ports.

Coastal Command was thus willing enough to help the Navy combat the U-boat; its weakness in 1939–41 lay in sheer shortage of aircraft and adequate equipment, which paralleled the Navy's own dearth of escort vessels. The Command particularly lacked modern long-range aircraft suitable for air-search and attack far over the Atlantic. The Saro Lerwick flying-boat, intended to replace the Short Sunderland, had proved by the spring of 1940 to be yet another of the aircraft industry's turkeys, its handling characteristics so bad as to render it unfit for operational service. The Sunderland therefore had to be put back into production, at the cost of several months of worryingly slow deliveries. Meanwhile Coastal Command was forced to keep flying its antique biplane flying-boats, the Saro London and the Short Stranraer. The bulk of the Command's land-based aircraft still consisted of ten squadrons of Avro Ansons, an adaptation of a civilian airliner: reliable enough (hence the nickname 'Faithful Annie'), but armed with only two .303 machine-guns, able to carry no more than four 100-pound bombs and with a range of only 660 miles. The Command's sole resources in up-to-date land-based aircraft consisted of a single squadron of Lockheed Hudsons.

This paucity of long-range aircraft meant that even after the establishment of air bases in Iceland (occupied by British and Canadian troops in May 1940) Bowhill's efforts to extend British air cover further over the convoy routes were frustratingly cramped. Meanwhile the Luftwaffe's four-engined Focke-Wulf Kondor reconnaissance bombers could sweep the Atlantic as far out as to the westward of Iceland, thanks to their range of over 2,000 miles, and could sink a merchant ship with just one of their four 550-pound bombs.

By contrast even a direct hit by the 100-pound bomb carried by most Coastal Command aircraft could not even harm a U-boat, while even the heavier Coastal Command standard bombs, of 250 pounds and 500 pounds, could only damage a U-boat's pressure hull if they exploded no further distant than six and eight feet respectively. That Coastal Command was equipped with these squibs was the fault of the pre-war Admiralty which had specified them in the face of experience in the Great War that bombs of at least 500 pounds were required to kill a U-boat.[73] What was more, in 1939–40 Coastal Command aircraft lacked an efficient bombsight, forcing crews to attack from such low levels as to risk destruction by the explosion of their own bombs (as indeed happened to several aircraft in 1939).[74]

In any case, for Coastal Command to attack U-boats it first had to find them. But it had been trained and equipped instead to search for enemy battle squadrons and surface raiders – the result of the pre-war Admiralty's obsession with heavy ships and also its smug conviction that sonar provided such a complete answer to the U-boat that there would be little role for aircraft in anti-submarine warfare. To locate battleships or cruisers by visual sighting from a patrolling altitude was one thing; to spot a U-boat's slim and almost awash hull and tiny conning-tower in a waste of moving water was quite another, even in clear daylight, let alone in murky weather or darkness. Yet when Coastal Command began to redirect its operations towards the submarine, it found itself blinkered by want of modern electronic search aids. Neither its own aircraft nor ships of the Royal Navy were equipped with direction-finding apparatus for fixing the position of U-boats by their radio signals, a particularly regrettable lack in view of the copious radio traffic generated by Dönitz's centralised deployment of wolf packs. By late 1940 only a dozen Coastal Command aircraft had been so far equipped with the first airborne search radar, the heavy and unreliable ASV (Air-to-Surface Vessel) Mark I, which demanded that the aircrew fly at a height of only 200 feet if the radar operator were to distinguish a U-boat from the 'clutter' of the sea's moving surface; a height that gave a maximum search range of only three and a half miles.[75] In spring 1940, 4,000 improved Mark II sets designed for mass production were ordered, but such were the technological shortcomings of the British radio and precision engineering industries that by October 1940 only 45 sets had reached the squadrons. In any case, even when radar enabled an aircraft to locate a U-boat down to within half a mile, Coastal Command had as yet no flare or other illuminant capable of lighting up the target for the final sighting and attack, for the pre-war design of flares had proved next to useless for the purpose.

All these deficiencies in aircraft and equipment would be gradually – far too gradually – made good in the course of 1941–43, but meanwhile Coastal Command remained a sea bird weak on the wing, short of sight and blunt of beak.

By the end of 1940 the year's total of shipping losses had mounted to 3,991,641 tons, of which the U-boat alone had accounted for 2,186,158.[76] And of this horrific total no fewer than 3,599,242 tons had been sunk in the Atlantic and home waters.[77] No wonder Churchill told Roosevelt in a year's-end letter surveying the state of the war that, though the danger of invasion had receded, an 'equally deadly danger' lay in 'the steady and increasing diminution of our shipping tonnage':

> . . . The decision for 1941 lies upon the seas. Unless we can establish our ability to feed this Island, to import the munitions of all kinds which we need, unless we can move our armies to the various theatres where Hitler and his confederate Mussolini must be met, and maintain them there, and do all this with the assurance of being able to carry it on till the spirit of

> the Continental Dictators is broken, we may fall by the way, and the time needed by the United States to complete her defence preparations may not be forthcoming.[78]

To the Royal Navy, then, had fallen the fundamental role in Britain's war. Yet Churchill recognised that keeping the seas open (and above all the Atlantic) was in itself a purely defensive function, forced on the Royal Navy by the onslaught of the enemy. So even amid the perils and calamities of 1940 he pined as strongly as ever to use seapower offensively in order to hurt the enemy in his turn. While the evacuation from Dunkirk was still running its course he had urged on the Chiefs of Staff the importance of not allowing 'the completely defensive habit of mind . . . to ruin all our initiative'.[79] 'We ought,' he went on, 'to organise raiding forces and keep the Germans guessing at what points along the hundreds of miles of coast under their control we should strike them next. Plans should be made for transporting and landing tanks and for the raising of 5,000 parachute troops.' In June a new Directorate of Combined Operations was created, first under Lieutenant-General A. G. B. Bourne, Royal Marines, and then from 17 July Admiral of the Fleet Lord Keyes, one of Churchill's favourite veteran heroes from the Great War. From this humble beginning in the midst of defeat was to grow the expertise, the operational doctrine and the specialised equipment which eventually made possible the D-Day landings in 1944.

But in the summer of 1940 Churchill's mind was already vaulting towards 'specially trained troops of the hunter class who can lead a reign of terror' up and down the coasts of Europe, at first by what he called a 'butcher and bolt policy', but later, he hoped, by the surprise capture of places like Calais and Boulogne.[80] His aggressive spirit in a desperate situation was admirable, but these projects boded a repetition of the futile 'descents' on the French coast so beloved of Pitt the Elder in the Seven Years' War and Pitt the Younger in the French Revolutionary War. Worse, his two particular pet projects in late 1940 for seaborne expeditions display him relapsing from grandeur of vision as a national leader into his old failing of stubborn refusal to take note of operational realities.

In the case of 'Operation Workshop' (originally conceived by Keyes at the end of October), a project for the capture of the Italian island of Pantellaria, about 150 miles north-west of Malta, the Chiefs of Staff were unenthusiastic (to say the least). Admiral Sir Andrew Cunningham, the C-in-C, Mediterranean (backed by the First Sea Lord) was forcefully opposed to it, on the grounds that Pantellaria was of little strategic value and that 'Operation Workshop' would lay a needless extra burden on the Mediterranean Fleet. Nevertheless, the Prime Minister kept plugging it week after week, even asking the Chiefs of Staff in January 1941 to consider the project yet again. It was not until April that 'Workshop' was formally abandoned. But despite the time-wasting staff study and argument, 'Workshop' at least never got as far as sucking in scarce troops, shipping and warships. It was otherwise with 'Menace', the operation to occupy the naval base of Dakar in French West Africa, which in terms of basic political and military misjudgment, hasty improvisation and humiliating failure, was to be a replay of the landings in Norway.

The concept originated at the beginning of July 1940 with enticing promise of much strategic reward for a minimal and risk-free British military investment. Nine days before his expulsion by the French the British Consul-General in Dakar averred to London that many of the local civil and military leaders were so keen to continue the war at Britain's side that an early appearance by the Royal Navy would lead to a bloodless coup d'état. His report served to confirm earlier optimistic reports via the Colonial Office by British liaison officers still in French West Africa. On 5 July Churchill minuted that the Consul-General's suggestion 'appears to be of the utmost importance'.[81] General Ismay thereupon banged back a sober military appreciation of the strength of Dakar's defences (including the battleship *Richelieu*), indicating that caution was called for.

This exchange established the pattern, familiar enough, of the developments which now ensued: demands for action as soon as possible from an enthusiastic Churchill; operational difficulties fully spelt out by the unhappy military, who nonetheless complied with the Premier's wishes. Indeed, at the beginning Churchill even bypassed the Chiefs of Staff machinery altogether in favour of consultation with an informal clique of advisers in touch with de Gaulle,[82] who together cooked up the first operational plan, code-named 'Scipio', in which de Gaulle's Free French forces were to play the active role. On 4 August the COS gave their reluctant support to 'Scipio' on the clear understanding that the British role was to be limited to providing equipment and the naval escort. Within three days – for this time Churchill was, as the record shows, truly bulldozing the project through – it had become accepted that British troops too would be involved. Impatient with the COS's caution, Churchill instructed them: 'Let a plan be prepared forthwith . . .'[83] The resulting plan called for an assault landing on Dakar by more than five battalions of Royal Marines, the date being then set for 8 September. On 13 August

Churchill successfully sold 'Menace' (as it was now retitled) to the War Cabinet.

Detailed preparations against the clock now began, the professionals asking in vain for a month's postponement in order to remedy all kinds of shortcomings and properly to organise and rehearse a tricky combined operation; Churchill chafing at every delay. The force commanders, Vice-Admiral J. H. D. Cunningham and Major-General N. M. S. Irwin, both able and forceful professionals, and their staffs fully shared the COS's (and Joint Planning Staff's) pessimism, leaving London for Dakar with the belief that 'unless received with open arms we were in for a defeat, ships' guns being no match for shore guns'.[84] The First Sea Lord and the Board of Admiralty, for their part, regarded 'Menace' as an unacceptable diversion of over-stretched naval resources, but did not choose to push their objections to the point of threatening resignation.[85] Intelligence about the French defences, about the attitudes of the local French authorities, even about the nature of the beaches at Dakar, was vague, misleading or nonexistent.[86] During the voyage to Dakar Cunningham and Irwin discovered to their chagrin that the War Office had failed to make available to them a copy it possessed of the complete up-to-date French defence scheme for West Africa. They now learned that these defences were in all respects very much stronger than they had planned for.[87] By contrast, gross security leaks in London by the careless Free French had turned the 'Menace' expedition into something of a coming public event.

The expedition finally arrived off Dakar at about 0500 on 23 September 1940, a morning of thick fog. It consisted of the carrier *Ark Royal*, the battleships *Barham* and *Resolution*, the cruisers *Devonshire*, *Australia* and *Cumberland*, nine destroyers, together with two troopships carrying 4,270 British soldiers, as well as Free French troopships and 2,400 soldiers.[88]

In execution 'Menace' provided a perfect illustration of Murphy's Law that everything which can go wrong, will. De Gaulle's emissaries were received with gunfire rather than rapture by the local French authorities, compelling the 'Menace' commanders after all to resort to force in obedience to their directive. But while a hundred 15-inch shells from the British battleships inflicted no damage on Dakar's shore batteries, the French counter-bombardment by those same batteries and by the battleship *Richelieu* damaged the *Cumberland* and lightly damaged two destroyers.[89] An ill-coordinated landing attempt by the Free French on Rufisque beach on the opposite side of the bay to Dakar harbour dismally failed. It had not been a good first day.

At 2105 the joint commanders received the signal from the Prime Minister: 'Having begun we must go on to the end. Stop at nothing.'[90] In the following forenoon the British squadron therefore resumed the process of emptying its magazines, again without result, while aircraft from *Ark Royal* launched dive-bombing and torpedo attacks on the *Richelieu*, but missed her. Eight British aircraft were lost. The French vigorously returned the British fire, straddling *Resolution* and hitting *Barham*.

That evening de Gaulle, ever a realist, advised the British commanders that '*l'affaire de Dakar est terminée*'. But after he returned to his cabin Cunningham and Irwin decided to have one more try on the morrow, signalling this intention to London at 0147 on the 25th. Already, at 0005, Churchill had sent one of his back-seat driver's signals, long and peevish, to the force commanders, demanding 'full and clear' reports on all that was going on, questioning why the bombardment had not inflicted 'grave damage', and asking why they did not 'force a landing' on Rufisque beach.[91] In the brilliant sunshine of the forenoon of the 25th the British squadron tried again to crush the French shore defences and ships by bombardment. The *Richelieu* and the *Barham* hit each other without inflicting serious damage. The *Resolution* was torpedoed by the sole remaining French submarine at Dakar, the *Beveziers*, which hit her amidships while she was under full helm, flooding her port boiler room and causing a 12½ degree list to port. *Resolution* was compelled to withdraw at 12 knots behind a smoke screen laid by destroyers. The crippling of *Resolution* settled the matter, not only for Cunningham and Irwin, but even for Churchill in London: '. . . Unless something has happened which we do not know which makes you wish to attempt landing in force, you should forthwith break off . . .'[92]

'Operation Menace' had cost the Royal Navy one battleship put out of action for a full year and one cruiser for six months (*Fiji*; torpedoed by a U-boat on the outward voyage), and nineteen aircraft destroyed.[93] The cost in terms of Britain's prestige, especially in regard to American opinion, was dear enough. The American military attaché in London, General Raymond E. Lee, all too accurately regarded 'Menace' as 'probably another of Churchill's military inspirations, like Antwerp', writing that it 'appears to have been as great a mistake as the attempt upon Norway'.[94] Yet, as similar exercises with similar results in the years to come were to demonstrate, 'Menace' even when coming on top of Norway, had taught the Premier nothing; his enthusiasm for quickly cobbled up combined operations still remained quenchless.

But in any case by the time 'Menace' took place he had already lighted upon the theatre of war where on the grandest scale seapower could take the offensive in conjunction with the British Army and so seize back the initiative from the enemy. It was that classic scene of the past triumphs of British 'blue water' strategy forever associated with Nelson's immortal memory: the Mediterranean and its shores.

8

'Blue Water Strategy': The Mediterranean, 1940

In 1937, confronting the problem of the triple German–Italian–Japanese threat to the British Empire and the worst possible case of simultaneous wars against all three powers, the Chiefs of Staff had been quite certain that conflict with Italy in the Mediterranean and the Middle East came third in order of strategic priority. In their view the United Kingdom and Singapore constituted 'the keystones' of British world strategy.[1] Any reinforcement of Egypt weakened Britain in the face of Germany, while lack of strength in the Mediterranean would not be nearly so serious as the surrender of British seapower in the Far East. The COS therefore pronounced: 'This situation demands recognition of the principle that no anxieties and risks connected with our interests in the Mediterranean can be allowed to interfere with the despatch of a fleet to the Far East.'[2] Since to pass convoys through the Mediterranean to the Suez Canal (the traditional imperial lifeline) in the face of the hostility of the Italian Navy would entail major fleet operations, the COS judged that the consequence of war with Italy must be the diversion of this lifeline to the Cape route – thus, although the COS did not say so, vitiating the whole traditional purpose of the sprawling British involvement in Egypt and the Middle East built up since the early nineteenth century.

However, by 1939 the order of strategic priority had begun to shift and blur. In April British and French staffs pondered the prospects of a long war against Germany and Italy. Although this must begin with an initial defensive while the Allies gradually mobilised their resources, the two staffs saw the hope of taking the offensive against Italy even in this opening phase – in their words, 'holding' Germany and 'dealing decisively' with Italy.[3] Moreover, Chamberlain's efforts in the spring and summer of 1939 to build up a Balkan diplomatic front against German and Italian expansion in any case necessitated the maintenance of a show of naval strength in the Mediterranean.[4] And yet on the other hand the Chiefs of Staff were still reckoning in June 1939 that 'if Japan joined our enemies, a British Fleet would have to be despatched to the Far East, and only very reduced British light naval forces would remain in the Mediterranean. In consequence the control of sea communications in the East Mediterranean would pass to Italy . . .'[5]

In the event, during the first nine months of the war when both Italy and Japan happily remained neutral, the demands of operations against the German Navy alone in home waters, the Atlantic and Indian Ocean proved sufficient to drain away the fighting power of the Mediterranean Fleet – all three of its battleships (including *Warspite*, the flagship), the single aircraft carrier (*Glorious*), the 1st Cruiser Squadron, the depot and repair ships, many destroyers. By December 1939 the Mediterranean Fleet had been reduced to four small cruisers, one Australian flotilla leader, four Australian destroyers and two submarines.[6]

When from March 1940 onwards signs accumulated that Mussolini might after all be girding himself to enter the war on Germany's side, Britain began steadily to reconstitute her Mediterranean Fleet and reinforce her air and land forces in Egypt – partly as a deterrent, partly as a precaution. On 27 March the Admiralty despatched the submarine depot ship *Medway* and the repair ship *Resource* to Alexandria, and ordered ten submarines from the Far East to the Mediterranean; on 3 May the battleships *Royal Sovereign* and *Malaya* reached Alexandria after release from North Atlantic convoy duties; and on 14 May the C-in-C, Mediterranean, Admiral Sir Andrew Cunningham, was able to hoist his flag again in the battleship *Warspite* on her return from operations off Narvik. Later in the month the battleship *Ramillies* and the aircraft carrier *Eagle* joined the Fleet from the Indian Ocean. As May turned to June cruisers too sailed in from the far distant stations: the *Orion* from the American and West Indies, *Neptune* from the South Atlantic, *Gloucester* from the East Indies, HMAS *Sydney* from Australia, and *Liverpool* from the China Station.[7] In addition there had been placed under Cunningham's command the French squadron under Vice-Admiral Godfroy consisting of the battleship *Lorraine*, four cruisers and three destroyers.

Meanwhile the Allies had been debating their strategy for the Mediterranean theatre should Italy enter the war. It had to be broadly defensive, with the principal objectives of securing French and British controlled territories along the North African and Levant shores from Italian invasion, and keeping open essential Mediterranean communications. Nevertheless the French command also invoked splendid visions of attacks on the Italian Dodecanese Islands in the Aegean, the occupation of Crete, even an expedition to Salonika, just as in the Great War, in order to open up a Balkan Front. But in any case both Allies concurred in seeing the Mediterranean in the event of Italian belligerence as a major theatre of war rather than a side show – a theatre in which the key factor must lie in seapower.

On 10 June, as the German Army swept the wreckage of the French Army past Paris in final rout, Mussolini duly declared war; on 22 June, the signing of the Franco-German armistice confronted Churchill and his strategic advisers in London and the three British service Commanders-in-Chief in the Middle East with the collapse of all previous assumptions and strategies with regard to a conflict with Italy. Now two out of the three threats to the British Empire had become actual instead of potential; worse, Britain had to contend with them both without an ally, and while still remaining alert to the third and as yet still quiescent threat, Japan.

Given this catastrophically altered situation, should Britain attempt to go on alone with the strategy of trying to damage Italy in the Mediterranean and Middle East (and in her empire in East Africa) while holding fast against Germany? Or should she revert to her pre-war global order of strategic priority, and evacuate the Mediterranean, perhaps even Egypt, in order to concentrate her available strength on the German war (indeed, her own survival) and at the same time provide forces in hand to defend her empire in the Far East and Pacific against Japan if need be? For the Royal Navy, appallingly overstretched as it already was, and with the vital Atlantic sea lanes already in jeopardy, the dilemma was particularly acute.

The First Sea Lord and Chief of Naval Staff, Admiral of the Fleet Sir Dudley Pound, and his Deputy Chief of Naval Staff, Rear-Admiral T. S. V. Phillips, were convinced that 'Atlantic trade must be our first consideration', as Pound put it to Cunningham on 16 June,[8] six days before the Franco-German armistice came into effect. On 17 June Pound therefore circulated a draft memorandum by the Director of Plans to the Chiefs of Staff formally recommending 'the withdrawal of the Eastern Mediterranean Fleet to Gibraltar as soon as it is apparent that French control of the Western Mediterranean is about to be lost to us'.[9] The draft, which enjoyed Pound's blessing, argued that the reasons given by the COS as recently as 27 May for keeping the Fleet in the eastern Mediterranean – to maintain economic pressure on the Axis, to secure Egypt and act as a stabilising influence on Turkey and other countries of the region – were all now invalidated. It was apparent that Turkey 'has little or no intention of honouring her obligations [under a Treaty of Mutual Assistance signed by her, France and Britain in 1939]; that Egypt is also equally dilatory and that the setbacks which the allied cause has suffered during the last few weeks have so shaken the confidence of the smaller nations in our ability to achieve victory that the presence of a British Fleet in the Eastern Mediterranean can do little to influence the political situation'. Moreover, the purposes of blockade could be fulfilled merely by blocking the Suez Canal.

The Director of Plans went on to urge strongly that from the point of view of 'purely naval strategy the position of the Mediterranean Fleet at Alexandria is unsound for the following reasons':

(a) It does not lie between the Italian Fleet and our vital Atlantic trade routes.
(b) With France out of the war, an increasingly heavy scale of Italian and German air attack can be brought to bear on the Fleet both at sea and in harbour.
(c) Alexandria lacks adequate repair facilities; our Fleet will be a wasting asset and will not be available to reinforce our forces in the vital areas at home and in the Atlantic.

The Chiefs of Staff referred this hottest of strategic potatoes to the Joint Planning Sub-Committee for urgent report.[10] By an irony it was the naval member of this committee, Captain C. S. Daniel, who had in his other capacity as Admiralty Director of Plans drafted the memorandum for Pound, albeit reluctantly.[11] Now he concurred with his fellow members of the Joint Planning Sub-Committee in submitting a report which effectively torpedoed Pound and Phillips.[12]

This report conceded that the German occupation of French Atlantic ports (and possibly of Spanish too) would heavily increase the scale of attack on Britain's Atlantic trade; that extra battleships for escorting Atlantic convoys could only come from the Mediterranean Fleet; and that there was 'from the purely naval point of view in relation to the war at sea as a whole . . . a strong case for withdrawing our Fleet from the Eastern Mediterranean at once . . .' But it pointed out that there were highly important military, economic and political factors to be weighed also. The British army in Egypt was designed to defeat the Italians in the Western Desert; it was not strong enough to defend the coast from Mersa Matruh to Haifa against seaborne landings. The withdrawal of the Fleet 'would be interpreted throughout the Middle East as a sign of weakness. It would probably involve, almost at once, an internal security problem in Iraq . . .' It would leave Turkey more open to German pressure. Moreover, 'a military withdrawal from the Middle East (which might ultimately be forced on us if the Fleet were withdrawn for a long period) would lose us our position in South East Europe, in Palestine and Transjordan and throughout the Middle East. It would complicate our position in India and would increase the temptation to which Japan was subject to attack our Far Eastern possessions . . .' Then again, the effect of a withdrawal on South Africa, Australia, New Zealand and India 'might be discouraging'. And the loss of control over Egypt and Iraq would mean that the blockade of the Axis would be 'seriously prejudiced'. Since the Joint Planners did not consider that 'the withdrawal of the Fleet is, at present, a vital necessity from the naval point of view', they came to the conclusion that the political, economic and military reasons for keeping the Fleet in the eastern Mediterranean outweighed the purely naval arguments for pulling it out.[13]

It will be seen that whereas for the Admiralty Britain's own survival as a European island in a death grapple with Germany constituted the supreme question, the Joint Planners were overwhelmingly concerned with Britain's traditional world-wide imperial position and obligations.

The Joint Planners' report was naturally not at all to Pound's liking, and after 'a full discussion' on 18 June,[14] the COS instructed the Joint Planners to give it further consideration, especially in regard to the future of the French Fleet, the implications of Spain turning hostile, and the oil position in the Middle East; in particular the security of the Haifa and Syrian pipeline terminals. In the meantime Cunningham had replied personally to Pound's signal of 16 June advocating withdrawal of his Fleet to Gibraltar in characteristically forthright terms:

> that although I considered it feasible to move the faster portion of the fleet westward from Alexandria through the Mediterranean and the rest through the Suez Canal, the effects of this withdrawal would mean such a landslide in territory and prestige that I earnestly hoped such a decision would never have to be taken. As already pointed out, the Commander-in-Chief, Middle East [General Sir Archibald Wavell] considered Egypt would

> become untenable soon after the departure of the fleet. Added to that Malta, Cyprus and Palestine could no longer be held, while the Moslem world would regard it as surrender . . . I was fully aware of the paramount importance of our Atlantic trade and home defence, but . . . I felt that with our present forces we should be able to safeguard these in addition to maintaining the Eastern Mediterranean. The Italian battle fleet had so far shown no signs of activity, and from all the indications available to me it did not seem that they were yet considering serious fighting. I was of the opinion that the battleships we had were sufficient to contain the Italian heavy ships with something in hand, and that the route to Malta could be opened when required.[15]

The Prime Minister, for his part, would have none of Pound's and Phillips's doubts. For him it went without saying that the present British position in the Mediterranean and Middle East must be maintained and strengthened; after all, here remained the only land fronts where British armies could meet the enemy in battle. In his view the theatre presented splendid opportunities for taking the offensive by land and sea against Italy just as soon as her expected invasion of Egypt had been defeated; it offered the hope of early victories to encourage an embattled British nation. It could eventually serve as the base for grander strategic combinations against the Axis powers. After all, the Mediterranean had for centuries offered inspiration to British 'blue water' strategists seeking to exploit sea-power as an alternative to a Continental commitment. Here Nelson's fleet had enabled British armies to inflict their first defeats on Bonaparte's troops – in Palestine in 1799, Egypt in 1801 and southern Italy in 1806. Here Churchill himself as First Lord of the Admiralty in the Great War had pursued his vision of beating Germany via the back door of the Dardanelles by means of Allied seapower; and it was here too that Lloyd George had wanted to use seapower to establish fighting fronts in the Balkans and Anatolia; here at Salonika where the Allies had in fact established such a front in 1916–18, yet another scene of Great War stalemate.

On 23 June, in his capacity of Minister of Defence, Churchill formally vetoed the proposal to withdraw the Fleet from the eastern Mediterranean; and on 3 July the Chiefs of Staff drafted a memorandum (later endorsed by Churchill and the Defence Committee and despatched to Cs-in-C and British representatives abroad) confirming the intention to hold the Middle East, and especially Iraq, Palestine, Aden, Egypt and Sudan, and stating: 'It is intended to retain the fleet in the Eastern Mediterranean as long as possible.'[16]

In this way a fundamental, even if in the circumstances probably inevitable, grand-strategic choice came to be made – bearing out Lord Kitchener's dictum in 1915: 'We cannot make war as we ought; we can only make it as we can.'[17] The decision reversed the pre-war order of global priorities, and opened the way for the Mediterranean and Middle East to become the main focus of the British Empire's war-making for nearly four years, thereby sucking in an ever-swelling military and logistic investment. By this grand-strategic choice Britain committed herself to fighting Italy in defence of an imperial lifeline which in any case she could no longer use; a war in direct defence of no economically or sentimentally important part of the British Empire; a war unrelated to the United Kingdom's own direct strategic interests as an island 22 miles off the north-western coast of a European continent occupied by Nazi Germany, and dependent for life itself on the North Atlantic sea lanes. Thus it was that Britain, unable in her present impotence to slug it out with Hitler, found herself reduced to trying to kick his dog Mussolini – the inglorious dénouement of British 'total strategy' pursued during the two decades since the victorious days of 1918 when Field-Marshal Haig with an army of more than 50 divisions on the decisive front of the Great War had played the major part in driving Imperial Germany to sue for an armistice.

A month after the commitment to the Mediterranean and Middle East had been made Churchill spelt out the implications for the Far East and Pacific in letters to the Prime Ministers of Australia and New Zealand. In the first phase of an Anglo-Japanese war, he wrote:

> . . . we should of course defend Singapore, which if attacked – which is unlikely – ought to stand a long siege. We should also be able to base on Ceylon a battle-cruiser and a fast aircraft-carrier, which, with all the Australian and New Zealand cruisers and destroyers, which would return to you, would act as a very powerful deterrent upon the hostile raiding cruisers.
>
> We are about to reinforce with more first-class units the Eastern Mediterranean Fleet. This fleet could of course at any time be sent through the Canal into the Indian Ocean, or to relieve Singapore. We do not want to do this, even if Japan declares war, until it is found to be vital to your safety. Such a transference would entail the complete loss of the Middle East, and all prospect of beating Italy in the Mediterranean would be gone . . .[18]

For the British Empire in the Far East and Pacific, for the Royal Navy wherever its ships floated, but above all for the Mediterranean

Fleet, it now only remained to live with the consequences of Churchill's choice of grand-strategic priority.

In the thick heat of evening on 7 July 1940, the Mediterranean Fleet slipped its moorings in Alexandria harbour, slid past Vice-Admiral Godfroy's disarmed French ships, and headed for the open sea. Its purpose was to sweep into the central Mediterranean in order to cover the passage of two convoys from Malta back to Alexandria, taking it into waters which for Mussolini must be a most sensitive area of his proclaimed '*Mare Nostrum*'. Cunningham, flying his flag in the battleship HMS *Warspite*, had with him the battleships *Malaya* and *Royal Sovereign*, the aircraft carrier *Eagle*, the 6-inch gun cruisers *Orion*, *Neptune*, *Sydney* (Australian), *Gloucester* and *Liverpool*, and seventeen destroyers. A little after 0800 on 8 July – an ultramarine sea a-glitter in bright sunshine, the customary Mediterranean escort of plunging dolphins and leaping flying-fish – Cunningham received a report from a British submarine, HMS *Phoenix*, that at 0515 she had sighted two Italian battleships and four destroyers some 200 miles to the eastwards of Malta, and steering south. Cunningham guessed that these ships were escorting a convoy from Italy to Tripolitania; he therefore instructed the Vice-Admiral, Malta, to despatch flying-boats to shadow them, and himself steered to the north-westwards at 20 knots.

All too soon the new nature of sea warfare declared itself – first the Italian reconnaissance aircraft glinting high up in the blue; then, within around an hour, the bombers, flying at around 12,000 feet, and soon after that, the erupting foam of bomb explosions round the British men of war. Through the day bombers from Dodecanese airfields came and went; but mercifully only hit the cruiser *Gloucester*. As Cunningham reported to Pound in a private letter on his return to base, 'GLOUCESTER took a bomb on her compass platform. Such bad luck! Killed everyone on the bridge and some below it. She can steer from for'ard but has to control her fire from aft. The fore director circuits were just mashed up.'[19]

At 1510 a Malta flying-boat also reported seeing two enemy battleships steering southwards, now in a position about a hundred miles north-west of Benghazi, in Cyrenaica, and accompanied by six cruisers and seven destroyers – almost certainly covering an important convoy. Cunningham swung his fleet on to a course towards the Italian fleet base at Taranto, in the toe of Italy, in order to get between the enemy and his base. At dawn on the following day, 9 July, the *Eagle* flew off three reconnaissance aircraft. During the forenoon these aircraft and the Malta flying-boats confirmed that an enemy fleet of at least two battleships, twelve cruisers and many destroyers was at sea some 50 miles off Cape Spartivento (the 'toenail', as it might be said, of Italy), and some 90 miles to the westward of the British Fleet. Although Cunningham had with him only four 6-inch gun cruisers, including the damaged *Gloucester*, and was handicapped by the slow speed of his unmodernised Great War battleship *Royal Sovereign*, he steered to engage.

Towards 1500 – a north-easterly breeze, a Mediterranean summer sky lightly stippled with high cloud, visibility ten to fifteen miles – the *Orion* and *Neptune*, scouting ahead of the battleships, sighted Italian cruisers and destroyers. At 1508 the *Neptune* (Captain Rory O'Connor, RN) became the first British warship in the Mediterranean since Nelson's time to make the signal: 'Enemy battle fleet in sight.' At 1513 a column of four 8-inch gun enemy cruisers opened fire on the 7th Cruiser Squadron (Vice-Admiral J. C. Tovey). Soon *Warspite*'s 15-inch guns were firing at a range of 26,000 yards in support of Tovey's hard-pressed ships. At 1530 the Italian cruisers turned away behind a smoke screen. At 1553 *Warspite* opened fire on the leading Italian battleship. Shortly afterwards both Italian heavy ships were in action, their salvoes straddling the British flagship at extreme range. But Cunningham enjoyed the satisfaction of watching 'the great splashes of our 15-inch salvoes straddling the target', and then, at 1600, of seeing 'the great orange-coloured flash of a heavy explosion at the base of the enemy flagship's funnels. It was followed by an upheaval of smoke, and I knew she had been hit at the prodigious range of thirteen miles.'[20]

Following the precedent of so many enemy admirals down the centuries in the face of the Royal Navy's broadsides, the Italian flag officer, Admiral Riccardi, now sought refuge in escape, retiring behind a smoke screen that drifted in a dense pall across the western horizon. A spotting aircraft from *Warspite* reported that the Italian fleet was making for the Straits of Messina at high speed and in great confusion, their disarray heightened by being bombed by mistake by their own shore-based aircraft. Cunningham attempted to work round behind the enemy smoke screen, but by the time his destroyers got clear, the Italian fleet had disappeared. For the next two and three-quarter hours the Italian Air Force (Regia Aeronautica) carried out mass attacks on Cunningham's fleet, concentrating on the flagship with her distinctive slab-sided bridge structure and the carrier *Eagle*. Each were bombed five times, but without damage.

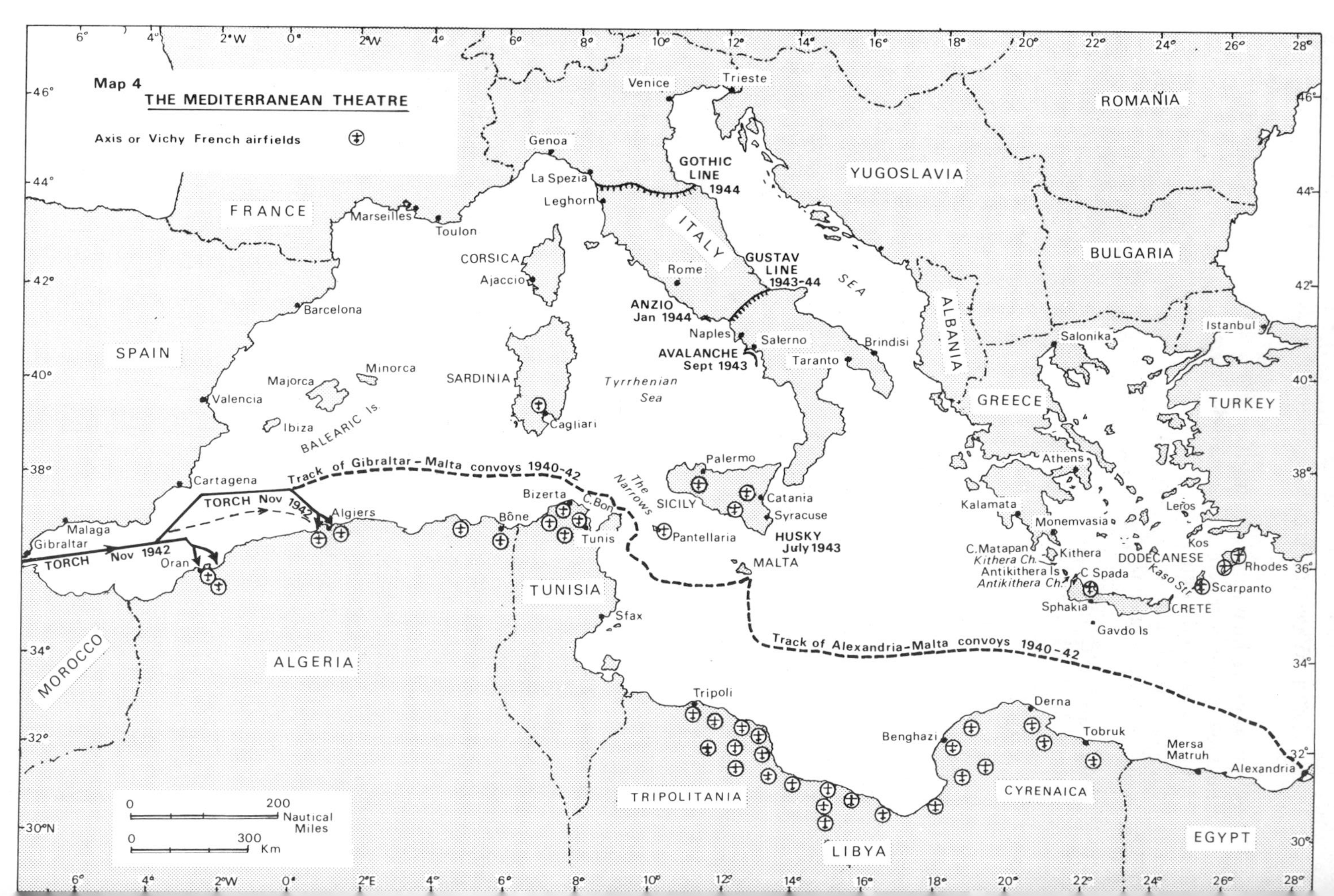
Map 4
THE MEDITERRANEAN THEATRE
Axis or Vichy French airfields
FRANCE
SPAIN
MOROCCO
ALGERIA
TUNISIA
TRIPOLITANIA
LIBYA
CYRENAICA
EGYPT
ITALY
YUGOSLAVIA
ROMANIA
BULGARIA
ALBANIA
GREECE
TURKEY
CORSICA
SARDINIA
SICILY
MALTA
CRETE
DODECANESE
BALEARIC Is
Gibraltar
Malaga
Cartagena
Valencia
Barcelona
Majorca
Minorca
Ibiza
Marseilles
Toulon
Genoa
La Spezia
Leghorn
Venice
Trieste
Ajaccio
Cagliari
Rome
Naples
Salerno
Taranto
Brindisi
Palermo
Catania
Syracuse
Pantellaria
Oran
Algiers
Bône
Bizerta
C.Bon
Tunis
Sfax
Tripoli
Benghazi
Derna
Tobruk
Mersa Matruh
Alexandria
Salonika
Istanbul
Athens
Kalamata
Monemvasia
C.Matapan
Kithera Ch.
Kithera
Antikithera Is
Antikithera Ch.
C Spada
Sphakia
Gavdo Is
Kaso Str
Scarpanto
Rhodes
Kos
Leros
GOTHIC LINE 1944
GUSTAV LINE 1943-44
ANZIO Jan 1944
AVALANCHE Sept 1943
HUSKY July 1943
TORCH Nov 1942
TORCH Nov 1942
Track of Gibraltar-Malta convoys 1940-42
Track of Alexandria-Malta convoys 1940-42
The Narrows
Tyrrhenian Sea
SEA
0 200 Nautical Miles
0 300 Km
6° 4° 2°W 0° 2°E 4° 6° 8° 10° 12° 14° 16° 18° 20° 22° 24° 26° 28°
46° 44° 42° 40° 38° 34° 32° 30°N

> It was most frightening [Cunningham wrote later]. At times a ship would completely disappear behind the great splashes, to emerge as though from a thick, dark wood of enormous fir trees. I was seriously alarmed for the old ships *Royal Sovereign* and *Eagle*, which were not well protected. A clutch of those eggs hitting either must have sent her to the bottom.[21]

Small and old though Cunningham's only carrier, HMS *Eagle* (Captain A. R. M. Bridge, RN) was, with only seventeen Swordfish and two Gladiators aboard, it gave a convincing demonstration of the potential of seaborne airpower in fleet operations by launching invaluable air searches and by hitting a cruiser and sinking a destroyer. Cunningham reported to the First Sea Lord in a personal letter on 3 August 1940:

> EAGLE's work has been above all praise. The greatest credit naturally goes to Bridge, the Captain . . . Quiet, imperturbable and thorough, he has carried out his flying programmes to the minute whether bombs were falling thick about him or not.
>
> To me EAGLE's survival unhit is nothing short of a miracle as she has been a special object of attack.
>
> [Commander] Keighley Peach is in charge of flying, but when we got a brace of Sea Gladiators, he volunteered to go up himself and, although shot through the leg the first day, brought down two Italian planes the second. Not bad for a man of 38 years old.[22]

In the evening of 9 July Cunningham steamed to within 25 miles of the Calabrian coast before abandoning the chase and making for the waters south of Malta in order to fulfil the original purpose of the sortie, that of covering the movement of two convoys, one fast and one slow, from Malta to Alexandria. In one of these were travelling the C-in-C's own wife and two daughters. During the return voyage from 9 to 12 July Cunningham took his ships far to the southward of the enemy air bases in the Dodecanese, only to run into relentless attack instead from bombers based in the Italian colony of Libya. At one moment on 12 July 24 heavy bombs fell along the port side of *Warspite* simultaneously, and another twelve on her starboard bow, all of them mercifully just out of line. Cunningham records that on the same day he saw the *Sydney* 'completely disappear in a line of towering pillars of spray as high as church steeples. When she emerged I signalled: "Are you all right?" to which came the rather dubious reply from that stout-hearted Australian, Captain J. A. Collins, "I hope so."'[23] In Cunningham's words in his letter to Pound, 'Literally we have had to fight our way back to Alexandria against air attack.'[24]

To Cunningham the sortie to Calabria and back had therefore

offered a grimly sobering tutorial on the impact of land-based air power on naval operations, and on the technological shortcomings of his own fleet, the legacy of the years of faith in disarmament as a means of imperial defence. Of his four battleships only the flagship *Warspite* had been modernised in terms of armament, propulsion and armoured protection. In his private letter to the First Sea Lord summing up the lessons of the action, he drew attention to what he called a 'serious thing': 'Their [the enemy's] battleships and 8-inch cruisers straddled us comfortably at 26,000 yards and more and I don't think any ship but WARSPITE crossed the target. Neither MALAYA nor ROYAL SOVEREIGN ever got into range, the latter's full speed being 18 knots!'[25] This was 6 knots slower than *Warspite*'s maximum of 24 knots – a speed itself 3 knots slower than Italy's reconstructed older battleships and hopelessly outstripped by the 30 knots maximum of Italy's two new ships, *Vittorio Veneto* and *Littorio*, now coming into service. Moreover, the *Royal Sovereign*, the least modernised of Cunningham's battleships, was also particularly vulnerable to bombing because of insufficient deck armour. Wrote Cunningham in his letter to Pound:

> My heart was in my mouth lest ROYAL SOVEREIGN should be hit, as if she had taken one of the nests of bombs that were dropping about, I think she'd have gone to the bottom or, at any rate, as we were only 25 miles from the Calabrian coast we should have had to sink her. In fact I don't think it is a bit of good taking these unprotected old battleships up the coast unless we are fully prepared to lose one.
>
> Don't think I am discouraged. I am not a bit, but with our facilities at Alexandria also within bombing range, the damaged ship is a nightmare, especially one 900 miles away from her base.[26]

When it came to cruisers, the pre-war Admiralty's decision to spread its ration of tonnage under the 1930 London Naval Treaty over more 6-inch gun cruisers rather than fewer and bigger 8-inch ships now put Cunningham at a further disadvantage. As he explained to the First Sea Lord:

> Tovey was also up against six to seven 8-inch cruisers and about four to five 6-inch cruisers and, of course could make no headway [to get within range] as they [the Italians] obscured themselves in smoke at about 22,000 yards. I know I said I could do without 8-inch cruisers, but I would dearly like the YORK and EXETER [32 knot ships of around 8,400 tons armed with six 8-inch guns].[27]

These cruisers so wished for by Cunningham dated from 1928–

29; three further vessels of the same class had, however, been cancelled in 1930 by MacDonald's Labour government.[28]

And the little aircraft carrier *Eagle* (first commissioned in 1923), despite all her enterprise off Calabria, could not provide the effective air cover and strike force of which Cunningham stood in such urgent need. 'We want some fighters badly,' he told Pound. 'At the moment EAGLE carries two Gladiators on her upper deck – Fleet Air Arm spares – and one of them brought down a bomber two days ago, but died in doing it.'[29]

Cunningham concluded this letter to Pound by summing up his weaknesses and his needs in terms which demonstrated that the action off Calabria had indeed taught him sobering lessons:

> (i) With my force as at present constituted I do not say that I cannot go and command the Central Mediterranean, but there is considerable risk of losing an old battleship and, unless the object to be attained is worth losing a battleship, I do not feel we should approach, or even engage the enemy fleet under, their coast in daylight.
>
> (ii) I feel I must have some fighters in a good and, if possible, armoured carrier for the protection of the fleet.
>
> (iii) I must have at least one more capital ship and a cruiser or two, which can reply to the enemy's fire at his own range.[30]

Nevertheless, though he did not say so, even these additions to his strength – should he be accorded them – would not redress his sheer inferiority of numbers in all classes of vessel except battleships. In round terms he was at present outnumbered by the Italian Navy by seven heavy cruisers to none, by twelve light cruisers to nine, by 59 fleet destroyers to 25, and by 98 submarines to 24.[31]

And yet Cunningham enjoyed some advantages. The first of them – the ability to read the high-grade Italian naval cyphers – proved alas shortlived. These had been broken as far back as 1937.[32] Thanks to the British ability to read signals sent in the general Italian Navy codebook, no fewer than ten Italian submarines were located and sunk or captured between 10 June and 5 July 1940 – a major blow to the morale of the Italian submarine arm, helping to account for its poor subsequent achievement despite its numbers.[33] On 29 June the Royal Navy recovered the new naval codebook for the Italian equivalent of the 'Enigma' machine (less complex than the German, with four rotors and no plug board) from the submarine *Uebi Scebeli* west of Crete. This ability to read the enemy's high-grade cyphers, coupled with monitoring of his radio traffic by direction-finding stations and low-grade Sigint, had enabled Cunningham clearly to recognise the Italian plan for the action off Calabria for what it was: a trap in which the British fleet was supposed to be destroyed by submarine and bombing attack, but one into which the British admiral deliberately walked 'with his eyes open'.[34] In Cunningham's own words: 'We intercepted most of the Italian Admiral's signals as we had the decode on board from one of the sunk submarines and most interesting they were.'[35]

Unfortunately this priceless source of Intelligence dried up from July 1940 onwards. On 5 July the Italians introduced a new cypher for submarines, and on 17 July new cypher tables for their surface navy, and on 1 October new tables for their top secret naval cyphers. Moreover they also changed their low-grade codes and cyphers, making even these more difficult to break. Never again, except for a brief period in 1941, were the British able to read Italian signals traffic; henceforward the Mediterranean Fleet, like the Home Fleet in 1939–40, had to sweep the seas virtually blind,[36] guided only by low-grade Sigint's radio traffic analysis, which was 'at best inadequate and on occasions led to false conclusions'.[37] This frustrating blindness was worsened by the severe shortage of photo-reconnaissance aircraft in the Mediterranean theatre.[38]

The collapse of British Intelligence with regard to the Italian Navy enabled the enemy to pass 690,000 tons of shipping in fast convoys to Libya between June and December 1940 with only two per cent loss,[39] while between June and October the Mediterranean Fleet itself made no fewer than sixteen sweeps in search of the enemy but only sighted his ships three times.[40]

Another factor lay behind these figures: Italy's own Intelligence services and aerial reconnaissance enabled her naval high command to keep continual tabs on British fleet movements, and in this way time and route their own convoys and fleet sorties accordingly.[41] 'Our principal trouble,' wrote Cunningham to Pound on 3 August 1940, 'is that we cannot move without our movements being known. There is no doubt that the Italians have now got a very efficient reconnaissance going. They send planes over Alexandria every day and no force in the last three weeks has been at sea without being discovered and bombed, in some cases very heavily.'[42]

However, although the superlative Intelligence Cunningham had enjoyed at the time of the action off Calabria had proved so brief an asset, others of his advantages endured throughout the Mediterranean war. The first lay in the professional efficiency and fighting spirit of his Fleet, hastily reassembled though it had been. In contrast to the *arriviste* Italian Navy, with its scant history of battle (even if it could look back to the naval traditions of Italian city states like Genoa and Venice) and its tendency to spend too much time in port rather than at sea, the Mediterranean Fleet embodied a tradition of seamanship and victory in close-quarters attack that went back through its triumphs under Nelson, its greatest ever commander, through the sea fights against the royal French Navy in the wars of the eighteenth century, to the Commonwealth's 'General at Sea', Blake, in his 1654 cruise against the Barbary pirates. The Royal Navy had asserted its moral domination in that first major encounter off Calabria, when Cunningham's ships, for all their technical inferiority, steamed straight for an enemy, who, in the C-in-C's words, 'as soon as WARSPITE hit him in the ribs at 26,000 yards . . . screamed for a smoke screen, ordered 25 knots and turned 90 degrees away'.[43] On 19 July, the Australian cruiser *Sydney* repeated the lesson by attacking two Italian cruisers north of Crete and reducing one of them, the *Bartolomeo Colleoni*, to a hulk dead in the water, later sunk by British destroyers.

Cunningham's second greatest asset – and certainly his Fleet's *greatest* asset – lay in his own qualities of leadership. During the Napoleonic Wars old Lord St Vincent had pronounced that the Mediterranean command required 'an officer of splendour';[44] and in 1940 this is exactly what it had.

Cunningham had been appointed in May 1939 in succession to Sir Dudley Pound on the latter's elevation to First Sea Lord. The voyage out from Marseille to Alexandria in the cruiser *Penelope* had come as a welcome liberation from his job as Deputy Chief of the Naval Staff to the centralising Backhouse.

> I felt great joy at being at sea again steaming at high speed in perfect weather to what I have always considered as the finest appointment the Royal Navy has to offer [he remembered later]. I probably knew the Mediterranean as well as any naval officer of my generation. Of my forty-one years' sea-going service since leaving the *Britannia*, I had spent about ten-and-a-half years there in different ships, a goodish slice of a lifetime.[45]

In the forenoon of 5 June 1939 he had hoisted his flag (the St George's Cross of England) in HMS *Warspite*, and all the responsibilities of a great fleet with a war in the offing had now become his; the top of the ladder he had started to climb in 1893 when he first donned the uniform of the Royal Navy as a cadet in the training ship *Britannia*.

Cunningham was 56 years old. A stern visage ruddy from the sun and salt-laden winds; a grim mouth and a jawline like a battleship's bow; a searching stare – all expressed a formidable authority. Yet it was a visage saved from arrogance or pomp by a hint of humour and kindliness about the eyes. Cunningham stood some 5 feet 10 inches: a spare and muscular body tense with a Nelsonian impatience for action; an impatience often manifested to his wary staff by a tigerish pacing of the deck. Cunningham's impact on the Fleet after Pound's somewhat reserved personality and bureaucratic methods had been drastic and immediate. When his staff presented him with elaborate Pound-style draft orders for a six-day exercise, he wrote across the draft in red ink: 'Too long, too complicated. Cut.' The staff obediently reduced the orders to fifteen pages, a fraction of their original bulk. This time Cunningham wrote in the margin: 'I agree with the second sentence of paragraph 29, and little else.' When the staff looked up the paragraph, they found that the sentence in question read: 'The Fleet will be manoeuvred by the Commander-in-Chief.' And it was – without any written orders at all, and entirely by visual signals.[46]

For Cunningham, like Nelson, was a superb handler of ships and squadrons. Lord Mountbatten later recorded his impression (when a captain) of Cunningham as Rear-Admiral, Destroyers, in the Mediterranean in 1934 personally manoeuvring 36 ships: 'In spite of his rather red and watery eyes he always saw everything first, long before the officer of the watch, the look out, or the Yeoman of Signals. No move escaped his eagle-eye. It was the greatest one-man performance I have seen on the bridge of a ship . . .'[47]

Yet this tactical skill in controlling many vessels did not mean a rigid and remote Jutland-style central direction of the Fleet in action. Cunningham wrote later:

> The time for central direction is in previous exact and detailed tactical training, so that every commander will know, should he be in doubt, exactly how the Commander-in-Chief is thinking. Nelson's instructions – drafted eleven days before Trafalgar – 'in case signals cannot be seen, or clearly understood, no captain can do very wrong if he places his ship alongside that of an enemy' is a nice case of a simple direction covering all eventualities.[48]

Nelson's restless urge to lay his ships alongside the enemy and destroy him utterly spoke straight to Cunningham's own temperament. A colleague recalled that 'A.B.C's most conspicuous quality was his intense spirit of attack – or the offensive, if you prefer it – which he brought to bear on whatever he undertook. He could be, and often was, the most biting driver; but never without acute perception that the thing could be done the way he wanted it, and, what is more, would be done.'[49]

An amendment made by Cunningham to the draft Mediterranean Fleet Tactical Instructions breathes this ruthless spirit of aggression. As drafted by the staff, one paragraph prescribed (because the Italians were laying mines from their coast out to the 200 fathom line): 'If the enemy Fleet is damaged and retires, the British Fleet is to pursue relentlessly until the 200 fathom line is reached.' The C-in-C scrawled a correction in the margin: '. . . until the enemy is sunk. Damn the 200 fathom line! Where the enemy battle fleet can go, we can follow.'[50] Here was an echo down two centuries of Hawke chasing Conflans into Quiberon Bay in 1759 despite a following gale and a lee shore.

Cunningham believed that moral dominance over the enemy was fundamental to success. Soon after the Calabria action, when ships' companies were tired and boilers were due for cleaning, a report came in that a very old and feeble Italian torpedo boat was on passage from Taranto to Tobruk in Libya. Cunningham ordered: 'Send out a division of destroyers and sink her.' When his staff protested on the grounds that the destroyers should be cleaning boilers and that anyway the torpedo boat presented no threat, Cunningham replied: 'We must never let the enemy think that it is safe to go to sea; we must make him think that he is only safe when in harbour. Contrariwise, our Fleet must feel that it is natural for them to be at sea. Go on, send the destroyers and sink the poor inoffensive bugger!'[51]

Cunningham, Scots by descent, came of the middle class, a son of the Professor of Anatomy at the Royal College of Surgeons in Dublin, a dedicated professional through and through. Long service in destroyers rather than battleships, the more usual and fashionable avenue to flag rank, had fostered and formed his special qualities as a leader. As he himself wrote in 1930 when he was actually commanding the new battleship HMS *Rodney*:

> Big ship time is said to be necessary to us all. I have never found it so. What I do know is that any captain will tell you that the best officers to be found in big ships have come from submarines or destroyers. It is my experience here. I would far rather be first lieutenant of a destroyer than about tenth down the list in a battleship.
>
> I have always maintained there is more real discipline in destroyers than big ships, and of course we are always in so much more touch with our men. The skipper of a destroyer gets soaked to the skin on the bridge just the same as any sailor, but his opposite number [in a battleship] walks dry-skinned from his luxurious cabin where he has been sitting aloof from all goings on, to an equally luxurious bridge.[52]

Years later men were vividly to remember the young Cunningham in his early destroyer commands – 'the red-faced Lieutenant-Commander on the *Scorpion*'s bridge', with 'markedly penetrating blue eyes',[53] is the recollection of Captain Francis Flynn. His reputation as a martinet given to terrifying explosions of anger and luridly Anglo-Saxon language whenever disappointed in his expectation of faultless performance became a legend in the Navy. And yet there was another side to him, as his Gunnery Officer in the *Rodney* remembered: 'Behind all his ferocity there was the kindest heart imaginable. I think it was these two "opposites", laced with an almost boyish sense of humour, that captivated and bound us to him.'[54]

Cunningham was no C-in-C to do his own staff work, an aspect of his profession which bored him vastly; rather he was happy to delegate the detailed working out of operational plans and administrative arrangements, in particular to his extremely able and hard-working Chief of Staff, Rear-Admiral A. U. Willis, slight, sharp-nosed, quick-minded. It was a relationship between executive commander and senior staff officer not unlike that customary in the old German Army of the Great War.

As early as 1922, when Cunningham was commanding a destroyer flotilla, he had formulated for himself three principles of conduct, expressed in phrases which he would often repeat for the benefit of those about him, and which stuck in the mind of at least one of them down the years: 'Duty is the first business of a sea officer'; 'N.D.B.G.Z. (No difficulty baffles great zeal)', and 'Intelligent anticipation must be your watchword.'[55] As Commander-in-Chief, Mediterranean, in 1940, Cunningham, despite his unstinting fulfilment of the first of his maxims, was to find the other two tested to the edge of destruction.

The strategic patterns of the long struggle had been revealed in that first sortie to the Calabrian coast; patterns determined above all by the shape of the Mediterranean itself in relation to Italian territory and British bases. The Mediterranean is well over 2,000 miles long from Gibraltar in the west to Palestine and Syria in the east, but only 500–600 miles across at its widest points, from Algeria (French) to the Riviera coast of France and Italy in its western basin, and from the Libyan coast to Corfu in its eastern basin. The two basins are separated by the so-called 'Sicilian Narrows', less than 100 miles across, between Sicily and Tunisia. Italy's north–south sea routes to the Libyan ports of Tripoli, Benghazi and Tobruk were consequently short, easily covered by land-based aircraft as well as by the Italian battlefleet, and distant from the Royal Navy's main fleet base at

Alexandria by at least two days' steaming. The British line of communication through the Mediterranean, however, followed virtually the inland sea's entire length, from Gibraltar (base of Admiral Somerville's Force H) to Alexandria and Suez; and the central third of the distance lay between Libya to the southwards and Sicily and southern Italy to the northwards – well within close range of Italian air and fleet bases, and running through the particularly dangerous Sicilian Narrows, mined out to the 200 fathom line. This was why the Mediterranean had had to be abandoned as a route for normal merchant shipping by way of precaution even before Italy entered the war; this was why Pound reckoned that to pass vital military supplies right through would entail major fleet actions.

Thus from the very beginning of the campaign neither side enjoyed 'command of the sea' as formulated in the writings of naval theorists like Mahan and Corbett. Instead the Mediterranean was a disputed zone where each side sought to fulfil certain tasks – above all, the running through of essential convoys – and at the same time prevent the enemy from doing likewise. The key to the whole strategic pattern lay in the island fortress of Malta, lying some 60 miles south of Sicily and under the British flag since 1800. It supplied a refuge and refuelling point for warships or merchant ships midway between Gibraltar and Alexandria, and a staging post for the Royal Air Force aircraft in transit; it could serve as the base for submarine and light surface forces striking at Italian convoys plying to and from Libya; a base too for invaluable air searches and photo-reconnaissance. For all these reasons Malta was to remain the focus of Britain's strategy in the Mediterranean for the next three years; sometimes a great asset, sometimes a supreme problem.

As the longtime base of the Mediterranean Fleet Malta ought to have been by the summer of 1940 fully fortified and equipped with all necessary ship repair facilities, and with a powerful anti-aircraft defence and fighter cover. Thanks to the ravages of pre-war policy it was none of these things. At the outbreak of war with Italy only 34 heavy and eight light anti-aircraft guns had been installed out of an approved scale of 112 and 60 respectively. There was only one radar set, and only three fighter aircraft, obsolete biplane Gloster Gladiators nicknamed 'Faith', 'Hope' and 'Charity'.[56] Here, in Malta's vulnerability, lay therefore one of the worst and most unceasing of the anxieties crowding in on Cunningham. To run convoys in and out of Malta in order to build up its defences, reinforce it with fresh aircraft so that it could survive ever fiercer air attack, and keep it supplied with essential food, fuel, ammunition and other materials, would demand hazardous large-scale operations by both the Mediterranean Fleet and Force H – a major commitment of naval resources.

Yet whereas Cunningham for his part could concentrate his attention and his ships on the struggle within the Mediterranean, his opposite number at Gibraltar, Vice-Admiral Sir James Somerville (Flag Officer, Force H), could be, and sometimes was, called to operate far outside that sea as well as inside. Nonetheless, his principal roles were to bar the Straits of Gibraltar to enemy or Vichy-French ships seeking to enter or leave the Mediterranean; to escort eastbound convoys to Malta or to rendezvous with Cunningham's Fleet; and conduct offensive sorties in the western basin of the Mediterranean against the Italian Navy or shore targets.

Small of stature and with open, boyish features which belied his 58 years, Somerville was renowned in the Navy for his salty – some thought coarse – sense of humour and racy speech larded with foul language. Such ebullience manifested his derisive dislike of stuffiness and pompous consciousness of rank; it enabled him to achieve an easy rapport with younger officers and the lower deck. Himself quick-thinking and impatient, he was easily irritated by minds that moved more slowly and deliberately than his. However, the bouncy bonhomie consorted with a high professionalism and technical awareness; Somerville was a very modern admiral. As the Royal Navy's Director of Signals before the war he had energetically pushed on development of the Type 271 anti-submarine search radar (see below, p. 256–7), which was to prove one of the most valuable items of equipment in the Battle of the Atlantic. Now as flag officer of a force including an aircraft carrier, he insisted on flying with his aircrews in order the better to understand their tasks and problems. Although Somerville was by instinct as much of a fighting admiral as Andrew Cunningham, he tempered pugilism with a cool operational judgment. This made him less willing to gamble than Cunningham, as had become clear during that first joint operation in July 1940 to bring the convoys back from Malta to Alexandria which resulted in the action off Calabria.

Before the operation Cunningham had urged Somerville to launch carrier air strikes on Italian ships in Naples, Trapani, Palermo or Messina, but this proposal in Somerville's estimation came into the category of what he called 'wild adventures'. He had agreed instead to attack Cagliari in Sardinia, a nearer objective, but met such ferocious bombing south of Minorca on the way out that he decided to turn back to Gibraltar, on the grounds that the *Ark Royal*, one of the Royal Navy's at present only two modern carriers, was too precious to risk for the sake of a mere diversion.[57] As Somerville expressed it in a letter to his wife: 'Anyhow I'm quite convinced that what I did was right though the Admiralty have maintained a frigid silence on the subject.'[58] Writing again three days later, he told her that he detected 'a certain critical note that I didn't adventure enough the other day. Well it seems to me just a matter of balancing up what is worth while and what is not, and before we throw a party they must give me some idea of how much they want to spend . . .'[59] But Somerville was correct about the 'critical note': by his aborting of the mission the Admiralty and even more Churchill himself were confirmed in their impression at the time of the Oran operation on 3 July – five days before the Calabrian sortie – that the Flag Officer, Force H, lacked the right pugilistic instincts. Yet the ships' companies of Force H itself did not share such doubts. According to a private letter from a newly retired admiral to the First Sea Lord in December 1940, when Somerville was under severe criticism (see below, p. 242):

> . . . James Somerville has instilled in his command a wonderful sense of trust in himself and admiration for his leadership – if only one analyses all that he has been asked to do, he has done it really well . . .
>
> . . . taking it by and large, he has done damned well and has got a jolly good team working under him who have every confidence in him. I remember so well when he was RA (D) [Rear Admiral, Destroyers] how all the Destroyer Flotillas thought the world of him and he pushed them devilish hard.[60]

In the event, however, the differing professional temperaments and diverging responsibilities of the two British 'doorkeepers' (as Cunningham dubbed them) at the opposite ends of the Mediterranean did not affect their mutual respect or close and cordial working relationship; not least because even Cunningham's Drake-like raiding instincts had been somewhat cooled by the waterspouts raised by Italian bombs round his ships on his voyage home to Alexandria from Calabria. From July 1940 until March 1941 (when Britain was to send an expeditionary force to Greece) the central theme of the sea war in the Mediterranean was to be supplied by the closely coordinated joint operations by the Mediterranean Fleet and Force H to cover the 2,000 mile-long passage of vital convoys and naval reinforcements in the teeth of constant air attack and possible ambush by the Italian Fleet, a theme not however unmarred by Churchillian interventions.

On 1 August 1940, twelve Hurricane 8-gun monoplane fighters successfully landed at Malta from the ancient small carrier HMS *Argus* to reinforce the island's exiguous air defence. Yet to carry out this operation, codenamed 'Hurry', had involved almost the whole strength of the Mediterranean Fleet and Force H together. While Somerville with *Argus*, the battlecruiser *Hood*, the battleships *Valiant* and *Resolution*, two cruisers and ten destroyers sailed eastwards from Gibraltar to the flying-off position, Cunningham sought to divert the Italian Fleet and Air Force from moving to meet Force H in the western Mediterranean by a sortie from Alexandria to a position west of Crete with the carrier *Eagle* and the battleships *Malaya* and *Warspite* (flag). Cunningham also arranged for cruisers and destroyers already carrying out a sweep in the Aegean to make a well-timed feint westwards through the Kithera Channel; and for other ships to simulate an imminent attack on the island of Kastellorizo in the Dodecanese.

In the event the battleships and the *Eagle* had to return prematurely to Alexandria because of mechanical trouble with the *Malaya*. Yet this only served to heighten Italian uncertainty as to Cunningham's true intentions, so inducing the enemy to remain tucked up in harbour. In the meantime Somerville had been selling his own dummy to the enemy by detaching the *Ark Royal* (escorted by the *Hood*) to launch an air strike on Cagliari. In the early daylight of 2 August the force of eight Swordfish aircraft destroyed hangars and aircraft, started fires and laid mines inside the outer harbour. By 0445 that same morning the *Argus* reached her position for launching the Hurricanes, which, to a roar of Rolls-Royce Merlins across a quiet sea, took off for Malta. By 4 August Somerville's ships had safely returned to Gibraltar.

On 30 August was launched the next Mediterranean 'milk run' – 'Operation Hats' – this time with the object of passing major fleet reinforcements along the full length of the Mediterranean to Cunningham. For the First Sea Lord had taken due note of Cunningham's statement of his weaknesses and needs in his letter of 13 July, and had embarked on a general redeployment and strengthening of the British naval resources in the Mediterranean. Force H had been ordered back to England after 'Hurry' as part of this process; when Somerville returned to Gibraltar on 28 August, his command freshly consisted of the modernised battlecruiser *Renown*, the unmodernised battleship *Resolution*, the carrier *Ark Royal*, the cruiser HMS *Sheffield* and seven destroyers. Of these ships only the *Sheffield* was equipped with radar.[61] Cunningham himself was to be reinforced by the new armoured carrier *Illustrious*, the modernised battleship *Valiant*, and the anti-aircraft cruisers *Coventry* and *Calcutta*. *Illustrious*, *Valiant* and *Coventry* were all equipped with radar.

At 0845 on 30 August Somerville (flying his flag in *Renown*) put to sea from Gibraltar with the largest British fleet seen in the Mediterranean since the placid days of peacetime – the whole of Force H (except for *Resolution*; too slow), all the ships due to reinforce Cunningham, and seventeen destroyers of the 8th and 13th Destroyer Flotillas. Soon the great, gaunt Rock dwindled astern as Somerville shaped a course to eastwards at a speed of 15½ knots, zig-zagging as a precaution against submarines. The broad plan for 'Hats' was that Force H should accompany Cunningham's reinforcements as far as a position south-east of Sardinia before turning back to Gibraltar, whereupon the reinforcements would steam on alone through the Sicilian Narrows to a rendezvous with the Mediterranean Fleet.

Except for the destruction of two Italian reconnaissance floatplanes by Skuas from the *Ark Royal*, the day of 31 August passed quietly for Somerville's command. At 1400 clocks were advanced two hours to synchronise with the Zone 3 time kept by the Mediterranean Fleet. At 2150, when Somerville's command had reached 39° 30′N, 4° 01′E, the destroyers *Velox* and *Wishart* were detached to carry out 'Operation Squawk', another of the Royal Navy's carefully designed feints. When the two destroyers were north of the Balearic Islands and still steering to the north-east they were to make a series of radio signals during the night in order to mislead the Italians into thinking that Somerville's entire fleet was heading north-east for the Gulf of Genoa. The transmissions were also to serve the second purpose of covering the low-power signals from the *Ark Royal* during flying operations in the next phase of 'Hats', the launching of another strike on Cagliari. At 2200, under cover of dark, Somerville's force altered course without signal from north-east to south-east. At 0325 on 1 September, at a distance of 115 miles from Cagliari, the fleet altered course in order to fly off the strike force: nine Swordfish each armed with four 250lb general-purpose bombs and eight 25lb incendiary bombs. The aircraft formed up over flame floats dropped ten miles away from the fleet, and flew in to Cagliari through clear, starlit skies. At 0600 the Swordfish dropped their bombs on the airfield installations 300 feet below, lit up by drifting parachute flares. As the aircrews swung back towards the carrier they could see fires sparking and glowing behind them. By 0800 all the Swordfish had safely landed back on the carrier.

Somerville now altered course to the south-westwards with the object of deceiving the Italians into believing that the main objective of the British sortie from Gibraltar had been to attack Cagliari, and that the fleet was now returning to harbour. However, as Somerville wrote in his report later, 'As the Force was apparently not being shadowed at this time, it is probable that this ruse failed.'[62] At 1030 he changed course again to 080°. From this time onwards he maintained two fighter patrols of six aircraft each over the fleet, for he was now heading into the zone of maximum danger from the Italian Air Force. Yet the day passed without incident except for a tragic mistake whereby Fulmar fighters from *Illustrious* hit a British Hudson patrol aircraft.[63]

At 2200 on 1 September, in position 38° 06′N, 10° 51′E, roughly midway between the south-eastern tip of Sardinia and the western tip of Sicily, the reinforcements for Cunningham (designated 'Force F') parted company in the dark without signal and set course to the south-eastwards.

His principal task accomplished, Somerville now turned north and then west, increasing speed to 24 knots. In the dark small hours of 2 September the *Ark Royal*'s aircraft again attacked Cagliari – without loss but also without success because haze and low cloud obscured the target. At 0800 Somerville increased speed to 26 knots and headed westwards, reaching Gibraltar in the forenoon next day without having been attacked by Italian aircraft – much to his surprise, since he had been in effective range of the enemy's air bases for at least 48 hours, and also much to his regret, since he had prepared a welcome in the form of standing fighter patrols and a closely concentrated AA-gun defence which he had hoped would 'deliver a blow to the Italian Air Force which might have a telling and lasting effect'.[64]

In the meantime Cunningham had left Alexandria early in the forenoon of 30 August with *Warspite* (flag), *Malaya*, *Eagle*, *Orion*, *Sydney* and nine destroyers, his mean line of advance 310° at 16 knots.[65] At 1430 the Fleet was sighted and shadowed by an Italian Cant Z 510 aircraft, which was later shot down. Between 1650 and 1800, however, another shadower was heard high above. At noon next day the battlefleet rendezvoused with Tovey's 3rd Cruiser Squadron (*Kent*, *Gloucester* and *Liverpool*) south-west of Cape Matapan, on the southern coast of Greece. Cunningham had dovetailed into his movements during 'Hats' the passing of two stores ships and a tanker to Malta escorted by four destroyers, this convoy having sailed earlier. During the afternoon of 30 August Italian aircraft attacked the three merchant ships, badly damaging the steering gear of the stores ship *Cornwall* and starting a fire. Nonetheless her master, Captain F. C. Pretty, kept his station by steering with his engines. At 1600 Cunningham altered the Fleet's mean line of advance to 180° 'with the object of giving the impression that the Fleet had merely been covering an Aegean convoy, and was now returning to Alexandria . . .'

Thirteen minutes later there came a report from HMS *Eagle*'s search aircraft that the enemy battlefleet – two battleships, seven cruisers and some destroyers – lay 180 miles distant on a 210° bearing from the *Warspite* in her present position of 36° 01′N, 21° 08′E.

Cunningham now faced the dilemma of whether or not to steer to engage. It would be easy for the enemy to evade during the dark hours thanks to superior speed, while sending light forces to attack the Malta convoy. Cunningham therefore decided, in the words of his report, that 'he must return to protect the convoy during the night, ready to engage the enemy if he came on and hoping that daylight would bring a chance of action'. But next day a Royal Air Force flying-boat from Malta sighted the enemy warships at the entrance of the Gulf of Taranto heading for home, a disappointment to Cunningham, who had been looking forward to banging them about again. No Italian aircraft were seen that day, possibly because of Royal Air Force attacks on Libyan airfields or because of the destruction of the shadower the day before, while the Fleet steamed on westwards towards its rendezvous with its reinforcement ships. At 0800 on 2 September the mean line of advance was altered to 320° (position 35° 25′N, 13° 48′E), and an hour later the lookouts sighted the distinctive piled silhouette of the battleship *Valiant* and, even more welcome, the slab shape of *Illustrious* approaching after a safe passage through the Sicilian Narrows.

Now it was time to carry out the next task in this carefully welded multiple operation. While the Fleet cruised all day about 35 miles south of Malta, *Valiant*, *Coventry* and *Calcutta* put into Grand Harbour in order to land army and air force personnel and stores, including such desperately needed items as eight 3.7-inch anti-aircraft guns, predictors, height finders, replacement anti-aircraft gun barrels, 100 Bren light machine-guns and 10,000 rounds of Bofors ammunition.[66] This was the second attempt that day by these ships to enter harbour, the first being aborted because of German air attack. Midshipman Terry Lewin in the *Valiant* recorded in his journal: 'We proceeded up the Grand Harbour to the cheers of civilians and the garrison. Perhaps they realised that we brought a mail, or, more important, valuable additions to their AA defence' – to which somewhat dismissive remark his 'snottie nurse' (LieutenantCommander Michael Penton) added the marginal comment: 'I think it was a *tremendous* moral fillip. No battleship had been there for months, & the small island must have felt very lonely and in the front line.' The unloading was stopped twice by air raids.

> Soon after seven o'clock [noted Midshipman Lewin], when there were still a few more stores to come inboard, we sent all visitors ashore and let go our wires. We were cheered by even bigger crowds than welcomed us. Both on our way in and out of harbour we paraded Guard and band, a touch which must have impressed the Maltese considerably. They saw us at sea, being bombed and firing at aircraft; half an hour later we were entering harbour with band playing.[67]

At 1645 Cunningham had detached the 1st Battle Squadron (Rear-Admiral H. D. Pridham-Wippell: *Malaya*, *Eagle*, *Coventry* and eight destroyers), together with the 3rd Cruiser Squadron, to steam on ahead eastwards ready for the next phase of 'Hats'. At 1945 the Commander-in-Chief turned to the eastward himself in order to pick up *Valiant* and head for Crete. However, because the *Valiant*'s departure had been delayed until 1900 by the Stuka attacks on Grand Harbour, problems occurred in making the rendezvous, and radio silence had to be temporarily breached. The *Valiant* finally joined Cunningham at 2200.

Cunningham now commanded a technologically transformed fleet. Instead of relying for warning of enemy approach on the sharp eyes of lookouts peering through sun-dazzle or haze or cloud or darkness – just like Nelson or Jellicoe – he could depend on his radar operators watching their dim screens in darkened offices to detect hostile aircraft at a distance of up to 50 miles or more. For the first time too he had a big modern armoured carrier, which, coupled with the *Eagle* in a carrier squadron under the command of Rear-Admiral A. L. St G. Lyster (the new Flag Officer, Aircraft Carriers, Mediterranean), at last gave his Fleet adequate protection against Italian air attack and also a powerful air strike force. That first day she joined, the *Illustrious* demonstrated her value in sight of the entire Fleet when her Fulmar fighters, in Cunningham's words, 'quickly tumbled' two Italian shadowing aircraft into the sea

> to loud cheers of the ships' companies, who had had just about as much as they could stand of being bombed without retaliation. The tremendous effect of this incident upon everyone in the fleet, and upon the Commander-in-Chief as much as anyone, was indescribable. From that moment, whenever an armoured carrier was in company, we had command of the air over the fleet. By that I do not mean that bombing ceased. Far from it. But we felt that we now had a weapon which enabled us to give back as good as we were getting.[68]

Cunningham intended that even the homeward voyage to Alexandria with his augmented fleet should pay a further operational dividend, as he had informed the First Sea Lord in a personal letter written on 19 August:

> Returning from Malta it is my intention to pass the whole force, convoy as well [a south-bound Aegean convoy; another example of splicing a subsidiary task into the main operation] . . . north of Crete and hit Rhodes a crack with the aircraft from the two carriers. The Rhodes aircraft have been very annoying to us and I propose to give them another dose as well and probably a bombardment very soon after return.[69]

The two carriers had been ordered to fly off every available Swordfish armed as dive-bombers except an anti-submarine patrol of four. The *Illustrious* was also ordered to fly two flights of six Fulmar fighters each to act as fighter cover over the two targets, the airfields at Maritza and Callato. In *Illustrious* the launching of the strike began at 0345, when she was in a position 35° 38′N, 26° 07′E, with the wind direction 340°, speed 18 knots; the heavy old biplanes lumbering into a moonless sky clear except for a little haze between 1,000 and 8,000 feet. Unfortunately the ninth aircraft to take off caught a wing on the island bridge structure, blocking the deck and preventing the last three aircraft from taking off – including the leader of the strike force. The attack had been carefully timed for the most favourable light over the target: just enough to see, but not enough easily to be seen.

Illustrious's aircraft began peeling off in their dive-bombing runs at around 0600, forty minutes before sunrise. As they climbed away from Callato airfield they could see explosions and fires. Meanwhile the *Eagle*'s aircraft at Maritza had hit a main hangar, whence came a series of small explosions, suggesting that ammunition had been detonated, and had also blown up and set on fire a petrol dump. It all made a good début for the Mediterranean Fleet's new carrier squadron. HMAS *Sydney* did her part too in disheartening the Italian Air Force by bombarding Scarpanto airfield, her escort destroyers sinking two torpedo boats for good measure. Next day Cunningham's fleet sailed into Alexandria – and fulfilled the final task of 'Hats' by delivering 250 tons of stores for the Army and Air Force, including 28 anti-tank guns.

For all its risks, 'Hats' had proved a totally successful experiment – not least because of the supine performance of the Italian Navy and Air Force. The Premier made haste to send a personal message of congratulation to Cunningham, but nevertheless coupled praise with a nagging remark about the importance of continuing to strike at the Italians during the winter.[70] He was not pleased with Cunningham's reply which reminded him that successful operations in the central

Mediterranean depended on ample reconnaissance by long-range Royal Air Force aircraft (of which there was still a great lack) and pointed out that his Fleet lacked enough destroyers adequately to screen it against submarines.[71] And Churchill grumpily minuted to Pound on 6 September that the success of 'Hats' showed that it would have been

> quite easy to have transported the armoured brigade through the Malta channel, and that it would now be in Egypt, instead of more than three weeks away . . . [see below] I am not impressed by the fact that Admiral Cunningham reiterates his views. Naturally they all stand together like doctors in a case which has gone wrong. The fact remains that an exaggerated fear of Italian aircraft has been allowed to hamper operations.[72]

By the second week of August 1940 the War Cabinet and Chiefs of Staff had decided to send out an armoured brigade to strengthen General Sir Archibald Wavell's undermanned and overstretched Middle East Command. The brigade's equipment would comprise much of the first fruits of British war production – 150 light, cruiser and infantry tanks, 48 anti-tank guns and 250 anti-tank rifles, 20 Bofors light anti-aircraft guns, 48 25-pounder field guns, 50,000 anti-tank mines, spare parts and radio kit.[73] Since the outcome of the Battle of Britain still lay in doubt, with German invasion preparations in full spate, this decision to send a precious armoured brigade and its weaponry out of the kingdom to Egypt must in retrospect stand as one of the greatest gambles of the Second World War. It arose in its turn from that earlier grand-strategic choice, made almost by default, to develop the Mediterranean and Middle East into a major offensive theatre of war.

Churchill himself had urged that part of the armoured brigade – and in particular the heavily armoured 'I' tanks, essential for attacking Italian defensive positions in the Western Desert – should be despatched by the direct route through the Mediterranean in four transport ships under the protection of 'Operation Hats'. Having foregone the tanks for the defence of England, he wished to see them in the field in the Middle East with the least delay, rather than uselessly packed in transports taking the long route to Egypt via the Cape and the Red Sea. However, he met with united opposition from his professional advisers. On 11 August Cunningham (who would have to bear direct operational responsibility for the safety of these ships within the Mediterranean) had signalled that the practicability of passing them through as part of 'Hats' could only be decided by actual trial and error: the tank transports might arrive unscathed, or they might be a total loss. What was certain was that their presence (with a speed of only 16 knots) must dangerously lengthen the time which Force H and his own Fleet would be exposed to Italian bombing. Nevertheless, if the urgency to get the tanks to Egypt was so great as to justify the risks both to the transports and to the Fleet, he would undertake the operation subject to certain conditions.[74]

Next day the Cabinet Defence Committee, chaired by the Prime Minister, had thrashed the matter out. The First Sea Lord warned his colleagues that the presence of 'relatively slow M.T. ships accompanying the Fleet through the Mediterranean would restrict liberty of movement and reduce its effective speed, thereby increasing its vulnerability to attack by aircraft, submarines, motor torpedo-boats and destroyers'.[75] Moreover, the Italians

> were bound to become aware of the passage of M.T. ships along the North African coast and they could not fail to deduce their destination. They would thus have at least two days' warning to prepare concentrations of aircraft, submarines and small surface craft to attack the convoy in the narrow part of the Central Mediterranean. In these circumstances [went on the First Sea Lord], the chances of the convoy getting through were remote and it was quite possible that the M.T. ships would be lost and that the warships would sustain damage. The Commander-in-Chief, Mediterranean Fleet, was of the same opinion.

At the head of the table in the bleak Cabinet War Room deep down in the bunker next to the Admiralty building, the Prime Minister listened to this exposition with thunderous impatience. When Pound finished, Churchill hastened to assert:

> . . . in the light of recent experience of convoys passing between Malta and Egypt, the Admiralty appeared to take an unduly pessimistic view of the risks involved. In his opinion it should be possible to pass a convoy of three fast ships through to Egypt without great difficulty. The presence of these ships with the Fleet should act as 'bait' and should draw down upon them concentrations of Italian Naval Units, thereby affording the declared opportunity to inflict serious damage upon the Italian Navy.

But he added: 'Nevertheless he felt bound to accept the opinion of the Naval Staff although he was not in agreement with it.'

General Sir Archibald Wavell, the C-in-C, Middle East (who had flown to London in order to confer), had supported the First Sea Lord's view:

> . . . as much as he would like the reinforcements to reach Egypt at the earliest possible date, the risks of losing them in passage through the Mediterranean, and the fact that if this equipment were lost much of it could not be replaced for several months, would not in his opinion justify the gain in time.

So the decision came to be taken – finally confirmed four days before 'Hats' began – to send the armour via the Cape route. In retrospect it is hard not to think that the success of all the complicated manoeuvres and feints during the operation might well have been compromised by the shackling presence of the transport ships and their precious cargoes – as Pound and Cunningham had feared before the event.

The movement of this armoured brigade constituted only one element in the huge investment in shipping resources during the second half of 1940 needed in order to build up the British Empire's land and air forces in the Middle East. From August to December no fewer than 76,000 men were shipped from the United Kingdom, and nearly 50,000 from India, Australia and New Zealand, together with vast tonnages of equipment and supplies, from railway engines to engineering plant.[76] To escort this endless procession of convoys laid another heavy task on the Royal Navy, and especially in the Red Sea, where the route was potentially dominated by enemy ships and aircraft based on the Italian colony of Eritrea. Fortunately they showed no more enterprise than their confrères in the Mediterranean, relapsing into quiescence after their first and only surface attack on a convoy of 20–21 October was beaten off with the loss of one out of four destroyers by the British escort.[77] Yet the Red Sea climate itself was hostile enough to the crews of escort ships constantly steaming with over-driven engines, for temperatures rose to 100°F in the living spaces and an unbelievable 170° in the engine rooms. On the other side of Africa too, many more merchant ships with Navy escorts were ferrying crated aircraft from Britain to Takoradi on the Gold Coast, there to be reassembled and flown across the continent to strengthen the Royal Air Force in Egypt. On all this unsung service of the Royal Navy in the waters from the Atlantic to the Gulf of Suez and the Indian Ocean utterly depended Churchill's Mediterranean strategy.

For Cunningham and Somerville personally there was an added strain – the Premier's enthusiasms for operational fantasies born of a gut-urge to smash at the enemy; his ruthless meddling in operational matters whenever impatience drove him to anger. In the case of Somerville and even more his colleague Admiral Sir Dudley North, the Flag

Officer, North Atlantic (headquarters, Gibraltar), the farcical expedition to Dakar in September 1940 ('Operation Menace'; see above, pp. 203–5) saw both types of strain coincide. On 6 September, two days after Force H returned to harbour following 'Hats', Somerville, as instructed, despatched HMS *Ark Royal*, the battleships *Barham* and *Resolution* and nine destroyers south to Freetown, ready to act as the naval support to 'Menace'. This left him at Gibraltar with no more than the battlecruiser *Renown* and six destroyers in order to fulfil his primary mission of commanding the Straits of Gibraltar, and guarding against an Italian Fleet sortie in the western Mediterranean. In the small hours of 11 September he received a report that six warships burning navigation lights had been sighted in the Mediterranean some 70 miles east of Gibraltar and steaming westwards at high speed – confirming earlier reports from the Consul-General in Tangier that Vichy French ships might soon proceed out of the Mediterranean.

Somerville at once ordered *Renown* to one hour's readiness for full speed. Receiving no orders from the Admiralty to move against these technically neutral vessels, Somerville ordered *Renown* to revert to two hours' notice for steam. Not until the early afternoon did he receive Admiralty instructions to go to sea and make contact with the French force. Since this entailed recalling destroyers at present out hunting a submarine or on patrol and then refuelling them, it was clear to him that if the French were intending to head south to Casablanca, he was already too late to intercept them. At 1546 came further instructions from the Admiralty: there was no objection to the French force going to Casablanca, but they could not be permitted to go on to Dakar. At 1600 Somerville cleared Gibraltar with *Renown* and four destroyers, steering to the south-westward at 24 knots. Shortly afterwards he received a report that the French ships had entered Casablanca at 1610. Next day Somerville searched for the French ships between Casablanca and Dakar, signalling a sighting to the Admiralty (though without response from it in terms of further orders). In the forenoon of 14 September the Admiralty ordered him to return to Gibraltar.[78] In fact the French squadron, having left Dakar, was heading for Libreville in Gabon, far to the south of Dakar.

In London there was deep anger at the failure to intercept the French squadron during its passage of the Straits of Gibraltar; and the Prime Minister's fury (especially after the humiliating failure of 'Menace' a fortnight later) meant that a scapegoat had to be found. The First Sea Lord was of the same mind – selecting not Somerville, the Flag Officer, Force H, but Admiral Sir Dudley North, the Flag Officer, North Atlantic Station, who – though the division of responsibility had never clearly been defined by the Admiralty – was certainly not Somerville's superior since the Admiralty issued orders direct to Somerville.

On 15 October North was accused of failure 'in an emergency to take all prudent precautions without waiting for Admiralty instructions' – i.e. by ordering Force H to sea – and relieved of his command. Yet Force H at the time when Somerville first ordered it to one hour's readiness for full speed could have only consisted of *Renown* and one available destroyer – as the *Admiral Graf Spee*'s fate suggests, not necessarily a match for three modern French 8,200-ton cruisers each with nine 6-inch guns and four torpedo tubes, and three 'super-destroyers' each displacing some 2,600 tons and mounting five 5.5-inch guns and nine torpedo tubes; and all of them faster than the *Renown* and the small British destroyers.[79] The charge against North was thus baseless on two counts: first, it did not accord with the operational facts, including the Admiralty's own sloth in issuing instructions, and secondly, because it was for Somerville rather than North to decide that Force H should go to sea. In any event North had on his own initiative ordered an air search which soon revealed that the French were heading south and not, as London most feared, north and back to France.

The true villain of 'the Dudley North affair' lay in Churchill's diversion of most of Somerville's strength to support the Dakar operation, coupled with Pound's failure to issue clear directives on operational policy towards the French Navy and on the command relationship between Force H and the North Atlantic Station.[80]

At the end of November 1940 it was Somerville's turn to be struck by a squall of the Prime Minister's and the First Sea Lord's impatient wrath, when a Board of Enquiry was set up by the Admiralty to investigate his conduct in another Mediterranean convoy operation even before he had returned to Gibraltar from the operation.

The purpose of this 'Operation Collar' (these sartorial codenames were Cunningham's invention) was to pass ships both ways between Gibraltar, Malta and Alexandria. Cunningham was relinquishing the old slow battleship *Ramillies*, together with the high-freeboard cruiser *Berwick* (9,750 tons, eight 8-inch guns; launched 1926)[81] and the 6-inch gun cruiser *Newcastle*, for service in the Atlantic against German raiders, while at the same time passing a convoy of four merchant ships from Alexandria to Malta. From Gibraltar eastbound were to sail three merchant ships (two for Malta, one for Alexandria), together with the cruisers *Manchester* and *Southampton* (9,100 and 9,400 tons respectively, each with twelve 6-inch guns),[82] four minesweeping corvettes and destroyers as reinforcements for Cunningham's fleet. Once again the safe transit of these groups of ships between the cover provided by Force H on one side of the Sicilian Narrows and the Mediterranean Fleet on the other demanded carefully planned intricate movements. Cunningham's part in these was accomplished without event when the four merchant ships, together with the three warships he was relinquishing, safely reached Malta early on 27 November. Later in the forenoon the *Ramillies*, *Newcastle*, *Berwick* and five destroyers left Malta, joined up with the anti-aircraft cruiser *Coventry* (so together forming Force D), and steamed north-westwards in company to the rendezvous with Somerville.

For Somerville, however, 'Operation Collar' proved not so smooth. When 'Collar' was still being planned, he had voiced anxiety lest the Italian Fleet should take advantage of its central position in the Mediterranean (in strategic terms, the classic advantage of 'interior lines') to concentrate its available strength (which he estimated at three battleships, five to seven 8-inch gun cruisers and several 6-inch gun cruisers) against Force H, consisting only of *Renown*, *Ark Royal* and *Sheffield*.[83] It disturbed him that the efficiency of *Ark Royal*'s torpedo strike force was 'low' owing to lack of practice and a high percentage of inexperienced air crews. He had therefore requested that he be reinforced for the coming operation by the battleship *Royal Sovereign*. However, in Somerville's own words, 'The Commander-in-Chief, Mediterranean, was frankly sceptical and considered I was unduly pessimistic. In his opinion, the probability of an Italian concentration in the Western Mediterranean was more remote now than at any time since Opcration HATS [some three months earlier].'[84] In the event, the *Royal Sovereign* did not accompany Force H because repairs on her could not be completed in time. Somerville was also anxious about the combat effectiveness of the two cruisers he was escorting outwards as reinforcements to Cunningham and the other two he was later bringing back to Gibraltar. On the outward voyage *Manchester* and *Southampton* would each be packed with 700 Royal Air Force and Army personnel, so impairing their fighting efficiency, while the corvettes could only manage 14 knots. On the return voyage the *Berwick* would only be capable of 27 knots instead of 32 because of turbine troubles, while *Newcastle*'s boilers were defective and unreliable.

On 27 November 1940, midway between Cape Spartivento in Sardinia and the Tunisian coast, on a calm sea under a blue sky so clear that visibility was 30 miles at a height of 10,000 feet, all Somerville's apprehensions were fully borne out. While still shepherding his convoy eastwards and with the rendezvous with Force D still to be made, air search reports came in that a powerful Italian force of battleships and cruisers was approaching from the north. On the basis of these reports Somerville estimated the enemy to consist of one Littorio class and one Cavour class battleship, plus a group of three 8-inch gun cruisers and possibly a third group consisting of more cruisers. He guessed correctly, for in fact Admiral Angelo Campioni, the Italian C-in-C, on learning that Force D had left Gibraltar, had ordered a concentration at sea of the battleships *Vittorio Veneto* and *Giulio Cesare*, seven 8-inch gun cruisers and sixteen destroyers.

Somerville's first concern now was to link up with Force D, which was successfully accomplished before noon. He then spread his augmented cruiser strength of five ships in a screen with *Ramillies*, *Renown* and destroyers astern of them (all steering due north) to the northward of the convoy on its eastbound course. A strike by torpedo aircraft from *Ark Royal* on the Italian battleships failed to achieve a hit, owing largely to lack of training of the crews, and so the outcome of the encounter turned on the surface ships. This by now had begun with a brisk exchange of fire between the British and Italian cruisers, further enlivened by some 15-inch salvoes from *Renown* (and even two from *Ramillies*). The Italian cruisers swung to a course east-north-east in order to draw the British on to their heavy ships, which were sighted at 1300. As 15-inch shells begun to plunge among them, the British cruisers sought in their turn to draw the Italians on to the *Renown* and the *Ramillies*. However, the Italian Fleet once again flinched from engaging the enemy more closely, instead continuing on its previous course. At 1318, with the enemy out of range, the action died away.

Now Somerville confronted an urgent and tricky decision – whether to pursue the enemy, or fall back to cover his convoy and *Ark Royal*. He judged that it was not possible for *Renown*, a battlecruiser, to take on two Italian battleships, one of them a powerful new ship, while the old *Ramillies* was so slow (20.7 knots) that by the time Force H caught up with the Italians she would have still been some 30 to 40 miles away. In any case, the *Renown* had developed a hot bearing on one propeller shaft, reducing her own speed to 27½ knots at 1207 hours. Of Somerville's cruisers, two were packed with RAF and Army personnel and two more were mechanically defective. Above all, he had to consider the convoy of merchant ships with their vital supplies and the corvettes which he must pass through the Sicilian Narrows – with a cramping speed of only 14 to 15 knots.[85] Somerville therefore decided to break off the pursuit of the Italian battlefleet. As he wrote in his report to the Admiralty: '. . . I was not prepared to hazard the achievement of my main objective, the safe passage of the convoy, unless there was substantial assurance that I could inflict material damage on the enemy by the destruction of one or more of his battleships.' This was a decision very similar to that taken by Cunningham during the first phase of 'Hats' (see above, p. 231). And despite Italian air attack, that main objective of passing the convoy safely through was successfully accomplished. By 30 November all the complex transit arrangements in 'Operation Collar' had been completed, with Force H home in Gibraltar with *Ramillies*, *Newcastle* and *Berwick*, and the Mediterranean Fleet back in Alexandria with *Manchester* and *Southampton*; the merchant ships safe in Malta and Alexandria; and the minesweeping corvettes anchored in Suda Bay, Crete.

It therefore came as a bitter surprise to Somerville to learn on his arrival at Gibraltar that the Admiralty, without even waiting for his report on 'Collar', had ordered a Board of Enquiry into his decision to discontinue the chase of the Italian Fleet.

This Board of Enquiry was a further manifestation of Churchill's deep and unceasing urge to see the enemy's nose bleed, and of the facile belief which he shared with Pound and the VCNS, Phillips, that the primary objective of naval strategy must always be to seek out and destroy the enemy's battlefleet – what might be called 'the Jutland syndrome'. It may also be (for there are parallels in Churchill's treatment of soldiers as well as sailors) that he had by now come to see Somerville, like North, as having 'not got the root of the matter in him'.[86] He had been vexed by Somerville's agonised reluctance to sink the French ships at Oran while a chance remained of a peaceful solution; by Somerville's clear support for North over the passage of the French cruisers through the Straits of Gibraltar. And, earlier, in that same November as 'Operation Collar', a major task to be carried out by Force H within another complex trans-Mediterranean convoy operation – 'Coat' – had gone sadly wrong.

The task here was to fly twelve Hurricane monoplane fighters from the elderly small carrier *Argus* (launched 1917) to Malta as desperately needed reinforcements for the island's air defence. Somerville had gone to sea on 15 November an anxious admiral, reckoning that Force H was 'quite inadequate numerically to deal with a potential Italian concentration'. On 16 November, the day before the Hurricanes were due to be flown off, he was writing: 'I've got the blasted old *Argus* like a millstone round my neck. In this weather [a blow from the west with 'a nasty sea'] I much doubt if we can make good more than 12 knots when we turn back tomorrow . . .'[87] Keen therefore not to go further eastwards into the orbit of Italian air and surface forces than need be, especially in view of reports from Malta that an Italian battle squadron was concentrating south of Naples, he asked the professional advice of the airmen in *Argus* as to the furthest west position it would be safe to fly off the Hurricanes.

On the basis of this advice the Hurricanes were launched before dawn on 17 November 1940 when the *Argus* lay some 400 sea miles from Malta, each of the two flights being led by a Fleet Air Arm Skua. Only four Hurricanes and one Skua made safe landing – with their petrol tanks virtually dry. All the rest ran out of petrol over the sea and were lost. A Board of Enquiry subsequently attributed the loss to errors of navigation and a failure of the pilots to keep to the most economical cruising speed, the distance being well within the endurance of the aircraft.[88] Nonetheless, Somerville reproached himself on the day after the loss of the aircraft: 'I feel now that in spite of the risk of meeting superior Italian surface forces it would have been better if I had proceeded 40 miles further east . . .'[89]

Now it was the beginning of December, and Somerville was facing the Board of Enquiry into his failure to pursue the enemy fleet during 'Collar'. However, this Board did not prove a tame instrument of Prime Ministerial wrath. Its President, Admiral of the Fleet the Earl of Cork and Orrery, himself wrote to Somerville: 'I hope you do not feel I have not sympathised with you in the position in which you have been placed after your successful action last week. I do so very much.'[90] Cork asked him not to judge the Admiralty too harshly because (in his words) of the people inside and outside it (meaning, according to Somerville, Churchill and the VCNS, Phillips) who, impatient to get results and ignorant of the facts, 'will always raise their voices'. In Cork's opinion, a Board of Enquiry in fact offered the best way of disposing of their criticisms – and so it proved, for the findings of the Board completely upheld Somerville's decisions. The Commander-in-Chief, Mediterranean Fleet, for his part wrote to Pound in answer to a letter from the First Sea Lord:

> You ask me if I was surprised at the Board of Enquiry on Force H's action south of Sardinia. You will wish me to speak out quite frankly and say that I was very sorry for the decision, more specially as the Board was set up even before Force H had returned to harbour.
>
> The action was an unsatisfactory one. When one is burdened with a convoy one's hands are always tied to a certain extent. Of course the Fleet

> Air Arm got no hits, although they claimed to have done so, and it is obvious that all the enemy ships had the legs of Force H.[91]

According to his memoirs Cunningham thought it

> intolerable that a Flag Officer, doing his utmost in difficult circumstances, should be continuously under the threat of finding a Board of Enquiry waiting for him on his return to harbour if his actions failed to commend themselves to those at home who knew little or nothing of the real facts of the case. Such pre-judgement is not the best way to get loyal service.[92]

From 16 to 24 December Cunningham successfully carried out the last major Mediterranean transit operation of 1940; another series of interlocking movements involving convoys both ways between Malta and Alexandria, and of other convoys in the Aegean, coupled with air strikes and bombardments of Italian bases in the Dodecanese and elsewhere *en passant*. But it had been intended that before the end of the year yet a further convoy (codenamed 'Excess'), composed of five merchant ships loaded with ammunition, crated Hurricanes for Malta and other urgently needed stores, would be escorted through from Gibraltar to the eastern Mediterranean. However, at the news that the German heavy cruiser *Hipper* was at large in the Atlantic (see above, p. 198), Force H was ordered into that ocean to hunt her down. Despite an exchange of fire between the *Hipper* and the *Berwick* in appalling weather, Force H's mission proved unsuccessful; worse, *Renown* was so damaged by heavy seas as to require repairs in Gibraltar dockyard. In consequence, the passage of the 'Excess' convoy had to be postponed until 6 January 1941 – a delay that was to entail unforeseen and calamitous penalties (see below, pp. 319–21).

By this time, however, tremendous events had transformed the whole pattern of the war in the Mediterranean and Middle East. On 28 October the Italian Army in Albania (occupied by Italy since spring 1939) invaded Greece – a stroke made by Mussolini behind Hitler's back, much to the Führer's pique. Next day the Royal Navy began to establish an advanced base at Suda Bay, Crete, while Air Chief Marshal Sir Arthur Longmore, the Air Officer Commanding-in-Chief, Middle East, despatched a mixed squadron of Blenheim fighters and bombers to Athens. By 8 November the Greeks had inflicted a humiliating defeat on the invaders; by the end of November they had thrown the Italians well back into Albania, where the front was to remain largely stabilised throughout the winter. And on 11 November, while the Greeks were so spectacularly thrashing the

Italian Army, it was the turn of Cunningham's fleet to thrash the Italian Navy – and without any of his battleships firing a shot.

When Rear-Admiral Lyster arrived in *Illustrious* at the beginning of September to take command of the carrier squadron, he raised at his first interview with Cunningham the question of launching an air strike on the Italian battlefleet while it lay at anchor in Taranto harbour. Cunningham was enthusiastic; indeed he had already mentioned such an idea in letters to the First Sea Lord, who, battleship-minded as he was, conceived of the operation, in Cunningham's words, as 'the last dying kick of the Mediterranean carrier before being sent to the bottom'. However, wrote Cunningham in his memoirs, 'to Admiral Lyster and myself the project seemed to involve no unusual danger'.[93] The idea had first been mooted during the Abyssinian crisis in 1935–36, when Admiral Sir William Fisher had been Commander-in-Chief of the Mediterranean Fleet. In 1938 it was revived when Lyster was Captain of the carrier *Glorious*, only to be squashed by the new C-in-C, the Jutland-minded Dudley Pound. Now Lyster's moment had come after all.

By mid-October plans for 'Operation Judgment' were well advanced, and the C-in-C hoped to celebrate Trafalgar Day (21 October) by repeating by novel means Nelson's annihilation of an enemy fleet, but a fire in *Illustrious*'s hangar forced a postponement to 11 November, the next suitable moon period. There followed another setback because of problems with *Eagle*'s aviation fuel system, so making it necessary to employ one carrier instead of two, even though five of *Eagle*'s Swordfish, together with experienced night-flying aircrews, were embarked in *Illustrious*. 'Operation Judgment' was spliced into yet another complex pattern of convoys and transit operations to be conducted jointly with Force H (and preceding 'Coat' and 'Collar'). By dawn on 11 November Cunningham (flying his flag in *Warspite*) with the battleships *Barham*, *Ramillies*, *Valiant* and *Malaya*, the carrier *Illustrious*, two cruisers and thirteen destroyers was steaming north-eastward away from the Malta sea area towards the position from which would be flown the first air strike in history ever to be launched on a battlefleet within a defended naval base.

Illustrious (laid down in 1937, launched in April 1939) was the first of the Royal Navy's new fleet carriers to come into service. Displacing 23,000 tons, with deck armour 2½ to 3 inches thick, and side armour of up to 4½ inches, sixteen dual purpose 4.5-inch guns in twin turrets, six 8-barrelled pom-poms, and equipped with radar, she could steam 31 knots and carry a maximum of 36 aircraft.[94] The arrival of this formidable ship in the Mediterranean had alone made the planned strike possible. A second essential factor lay in the recent re-equipment of Royal Air Force No. 431 Flight on Malta with American Glenn Martin Maryland aircraft (range 1,210 miles; ceiling 26,000 feet; speed 278 mph), able to maintain a photo-reconnaissance watch on Taranto. These aircraft provided the planners of the strike with pictures showing in comprehensive detail the layout of Taranto's defences, including anti-torpedo nets and balloon barrages. The latest photographs, flown to *Illustrious* in the afternoon of 11 November, showed five battleships at anchor in the outer harbour, while a Royal Air Force Sunderland flying-boat reported that a sixth heavy ship was joining them. The well practised aircrews therefore knew the exact positions of their targets.[95]

At 1900 Cunningham detached *Illustrious* (flying the flag of Rear-Admiral Lyster) and her screen of four cruisers and four destroyers to steam to her flying-off position about 170 miles south-east of Taranto, making the signal to Lyster: 'Good luck then to your lads in their enterprise. Their success may well have a most important bearing on the course of the war in the Mediterranean.'[96]

For all ships' companies in the Fleet there was now nothing more to do but endure the tension of waiting for news of success or disaster. On Cunningham, Lyster and their staffs bore the added strain of knowing just how strong were the defences which the Swordfish must penetrate. And for the Swordfish aircrews themselves the waiting period in the *Illustrious* before take-off – supper, a last briefing, the climb into the open cockpits of the old biplanes, the flight deck of the carrier stretching ahead in the cold gleam of the moon – was a time when the bravest might feel the mouth go dry and the palms grow damp.

At 2040 the twelve aircraft of the first wave of the strike force (drawn from Nos. 813, 815 and 824 Squadrons of the Fleet Air Arm, and led by Lieutenant-Commander K. Williamson, RN) roared away down the deck one by one and lumbered up and away. At 2057 they took up formation and headed for Taranto. By 2100 the second wave of only nine aircraft (three had force-landed in the sea during earlier flights) (from Nos. 813, 815, 819 and 824 Squadrons, led by Lieutenant-Commander J. W. Haley, RN) was waiting ranked for take-off; at 2130 they were airborne, all except for an unlucky one which suffered damage to the fabric covering of a wing in a collision while taxiing, and returned to the hangar deck for repairs. But by 2200 it too was setting its own lonely course for Taranto, for its crew was determined not to be left behind. While the pilot, Lieutenant

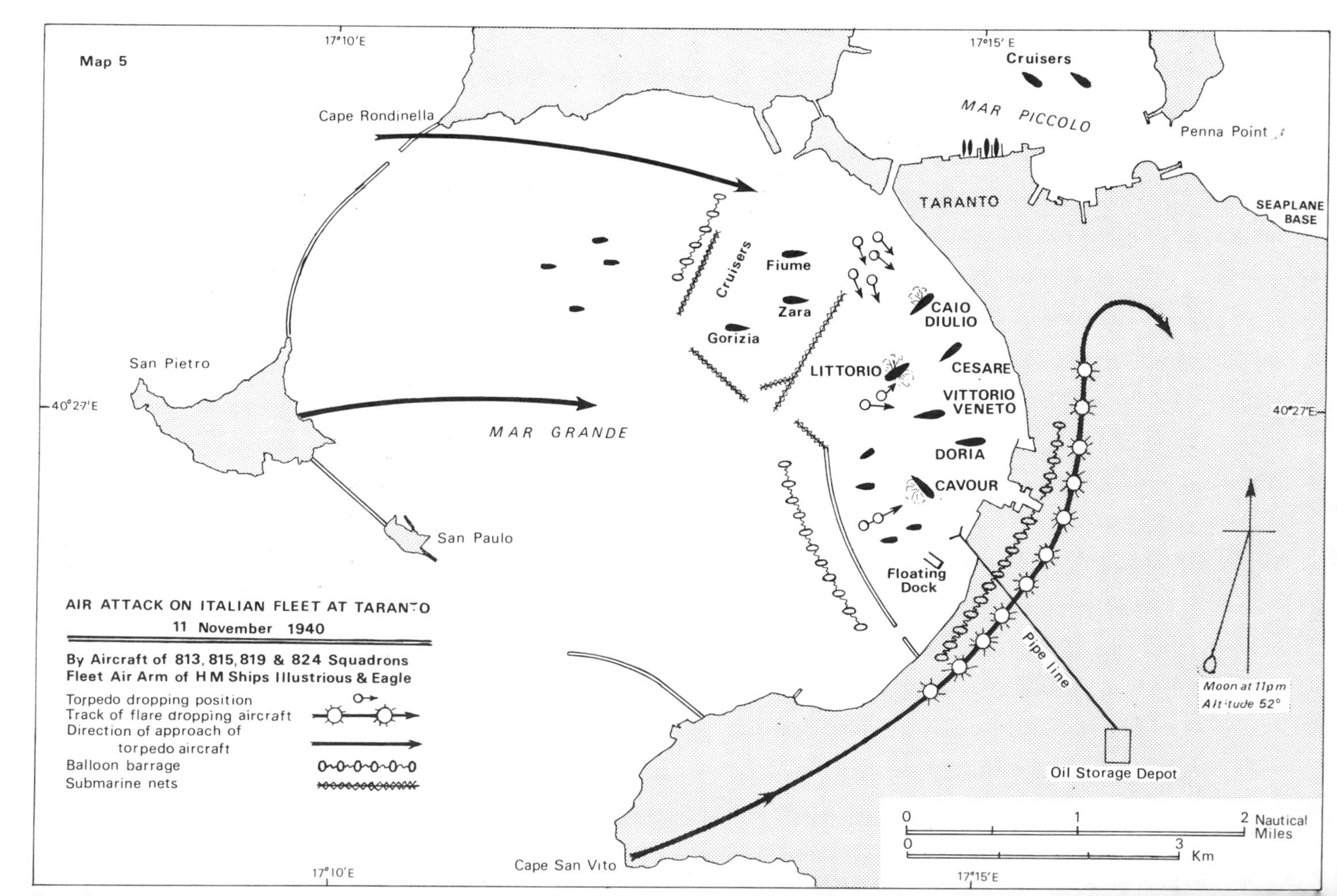
Map 5
17°10′E
17°15′E
Cruisers
MAR PICCOLO
Penna Point
Cape Rondinella
TARANTO
SEAPLANE BASE
Cruisers
Fiume
Zara
Gorizia
CAIO DUILIO
CESARE
LITTORIO
VITTORIO VENETO
DORIA
CAVOUR
San Pietro
40°27′E
MAR GRANDE
San Paulo
Floating Dock
Pipe line
Moon at 11pm
Altitude 52°
Oil Storage Depot
AIR ATTACK ON ITALIAN FLEET AT TARANTO
11 November 1940
By Aircraft of 813, 815, 819 & 824 Squadrons
Fleet Air Arm of H M Ships Illustrious & Eagle
Torpedo dropping position
Track of flare dropping aircraft
Direction of approach of torpedo aircraft
Balloon barrage
Submarine nets
0 1 2 Nautical Miles
0 3 Km
Cape San Vito
17°10′E
17°15′E

E. W. Clifford, had been urging the repair crews to do their utmost, his observer, Lieutenant G. R. M. Going, was up on the *Illustrious*'s bridge successfully persuading the captain, Denis Boyd, to allow them to go.

For the aircrew members, each solitary in his open cockpit, the flight meant time to think and think again about what lay ahead; cruising at about 130 mph at 8,000 feet through 8/10ths thin cloud under a three-quarters moon, it also meant 'the sort of cold', recorded Lieutenant Maund, 'that fills you until all else is drowned save perhaps fear and loneliness . . .'[97] Only eight aircraft made the first strike, four having got separated in cloud. It was just before 2300 that the flare-dropper broke away from the formation to make its preparatory run over Taranto, while the main force of torpedo-bombers swung westward in order to position themselves for the attack.

The climactic moment in the career of the Swordfish aircraft had now arrived. Quaintly old-fashioned though the Swordfish was, with its open cockpits and its big, ungainly biplane structure, it enjoyed the affection and the respect of its crews because of its sturdiness and capacity to take punishment, and its stability as a weapons platform. The 690 HP Bristol Pegasus IIIM3 radial engine gave it a maximum speed of 154 mph, with a service ceiling of 10,700 feet and a range of just over 1,000 miles. It could carry either one 18-inch torpedo or one 1,500 pound mine hung between its fixed undercarriage, or 1,500 pounds of bombs beneath the fuselage and wings. It was virtually defenceless, having only a single .303-inch Vickers machine-gun firing forward through the propeller hub, and a Vickers or Lewis gun mounted in the observer's cockpit. Its drawback for such an attack as 'Judgment' lay in its slow speed during the long descent and run-in to drop torpedoes, exposing it to the full storm of anti-aircraft fire.[98]

The aerial photographs had shown that the six Italian battleships and three cruisers, together with some destroyers, were moored on the shoreward side of Taranto's outer harbour, the 'Mar Grande', partly protected on the surface by a breakwater, partly by anti-torpedo nets, while three balloon barrages to the west, south and east of the ships offered partial protection against air attack. Inland from the 'Mar Grande', through a narrow entrance, lay the inner harbour or 'Mar Piccolo', where two more cruisers and four destroyers were moored. Powerful shore-based anti-aircraft batteries supplemented the warships' own anti-aircraft armaments. Taranto was no soft target. But 'Judgment' had been meticulously planned and rehearsed.

First, the flare-dropping Swordfish laid a line of twelve flares along the side of the 'Mar Grande' lying to the south-east of the anchored

Italian battleships and then went on to bomb the base's oil-storage depot. While the single dive-bomber simultaneously attacked the 'Mar Piccolo', the five torpedo-bombers now dived out of the west down from 8,000 feet towards the cluster of Italian battleships gauntly lit up by the line of parachute flares beyond them, and steered through the gap between the westernmost balloon barrage and the shore. At a height of 30 feet the Swordfish homed in on their targets through a multi-coloured storm of anti-aircraft fire, 'red, white and green onions streaming past the cockpits', and nostrils filling with the acrid powder smell of incendiary bullets.[99] Once the Mark XII torpedoes had been dropped into the water at ranges of 400 to 1500 yards and were thrusting their warheads of 388 pounds of high-explosive forward at 25 knots, at a depth setting of 34 feet, the Swordfish jinked (not their best trick) through the gunfire and over the battleships' masts into the inner harbour and then away.

As the second wave of Swordfish approached Taranto they could see flames and the huge firework display of anti-aircraft fire from 60 miles away. One observer wrote: 'I gazed down upon a twinkling mass of orange-red lights which I knew was a solid curtain of bursting shell through which we had to fly. It looked absolutely terrifying.'[100] Once again flare-dropping aircraft illuminated the target from the east while the torpedo-bombers (five in number this time) came in from the west; once again the Swordfish pilots pressed home their attacks at a height of 30 feet but this time to within 500 to 800 yards of the enemy. When this wave too had done its work and was turning for home, Lieutenants Clifford and Going arrived to finish off the night's events by dive-bombing cruisers and destroyers in the 'Mar Piccolo'. They landed back on *Illustrious* half an hour after the second wave, at around 0330 on 12 November. Only two Swordfish had failed to return; an incredibly small loss in view of the hazards – and of the achievement.

For next day photo-reconnaissance revealed the scale of the disaster which had overtaken the Italian battlefleet. One battleship, the *Conte di Cavour*, lay beached with almost all her decks under water, and two others were evidently badly damaged, with the *Italia* (as the *Littorio* had been renamed) well down by the head. In fact, the *Cavour* had suffered such serious damage from a torpedo exploding in the water beneath her keel that, though she was later raised, she never went to sea again. The *Italia* had been struck by no fewer than three torpedoes, and was to remain in the dockyard for four months, while the *Caio Diulio*, another victim of a torpedo exploding beneath her keel, was to be out of action for six months.[101] By way of bonus, the heavy cruiser *Trento*, some destroyers and the oil storage depot sustained bomb hits. And during the night Pridham-Wippell and the cruisers *Orion*, *Sydney*, *Ajax* and the destroyers *Nubian* and *Mohawk* had raided into the Straits of Otranto and sunk all four ships of an Italian convoy. Mussolini's cup of joy was thus filled to the brim.

When *Illustrious* and her escorts rejoined the main body of the fleet that forenoon of 12 November, Cunningham signalled: 'Manoeuvre well executed.' Coming from Cunningham this was praise verging on hyperbole.

It must be left to Cunningham himself to sum up the success of 'Operation Judgment':

> Taranto, and the night of November 11th–12th, 1940, should be remembered for ever as having shown once and for all that in the Fleet Air Arm the Navy has its most devastating weapon. In a total flying time of about six and a half hours – carrier to carrier – twenty aircraft had inflicted more damage upon the Italian fleet than was inflicted upon the German High Seas Fleet in the daylight action at the Battle of Jutland.[102]

Taranto indeed marked the dethronement of the battleship as the arbiter of seapower after four centuries, and the opening of a new era of naval warfare – although diehard 'big-gun' sailors were still to blind themselves to this truth. Its immediate effect was to swing the maritime balance in the Mediterranean decisively towards the Royal Navy, and to complete the discouragement of the Italian Navy and its leaders. On 12 November every warship in Taranto capable of going to sea steamed away to safer harbours on the west coast of Italy, so leaving Cunningham master of the eastern Mediterranean and of the Aegean, where British convoys now constantly plied between Egypt and Greece. It was only a fortnight after 'Judgment', during 'Operation Collar', that the menace of attack by aircraft from the *Ark Royal* was enough to dissuade Admiral Campioni from pressing home an attack on Somerville's outweighted Force H, and encourage the Italian C-in-C to make off home instead.

Yet Taranto and the Greek Army's successes did not complete the tally of Allied triumphs in the Mediterranean theatre during the final months of 1940. On 9 December the long-cherished central purpose of Churchill's 'blue water' strategy – a major offensive by the British Army – was fulfilled at last. For on this day troops, tanks, guns, ammunition and equipment which the Merchant Marine and Royal Navy had borne to the Middle East during long months of arduous service at sea were launched into battle against the Italians in the Western Desert.

In September the Italian 10th Army in Libya had lumbered into

Egypt as far as Sidi Barrani, there to entrench itself in a chain of fortified camps. Now the 13th Corps, under the command of Lieutenant-General Sir Richard O'Connor and composed of British and Indian troops, attacked these positions from the rear and in three days consummated a staggering victory, smashing three enemy army corps and taking 38,000 prisoners (including four generals), 73 tanks and 237 guns.[103] Within a week O'Connor had expelled the Italians from Egypt and invaded Libya, laying siege to the fortress of Bardia. And the Royal Navy too was there, ferrying supplies and water to the advancing army; bombarding Italian troops in retreat along the coast road. This was the work of the new Inshore Squadron, under the command of Rear-Admiral H. B. Rawlings (Flag Officer, 1st Battle Squadron), consisting of the 1916-vintage monitor *Terror*, with two 15-inch guns and three 1915-vintage river gunboats, *Ladybird*, *Aphis* and *Gnat*, each with two 6-inch guns. From time to time the Royal Australian Navy joined in too with its destroyers *Vampire*, *Vendetta* and *Waterhen* under the command of Captain H. M. L. Waller, RAN, of HMAS *Stuart*.

On 3 January 1941 General O'Connor launched the 6th Australian Division, spearheaded by heavily armoured 'I' tanks, against Bardia's defences; by the 5th Bardia was in his hands, along with 40,000 prisoners, 128 tanks and 400 guns, and 13th Corps was already driving westwards to cut off the fortress of Tobruk, its next objective.

O'Connor's truly sensational victories sparkled against the darkest setting of the war, lifting the hearts of the British and their Allies and friends at the end of a year of disaster. They vindicated the belief of the British Chiefs of Staff in April 1939 that early successes could be won against Italy while the Allies were still girding their strength for a grand offensive against Germany – vindicated too Churchill's gamble in despatching precious tanks and personnel to the Middle East when Britain itself lay under threat of invasion.

With the triumphs of the Greek Army over the invaders of its homeland, the Royal Navy's strike at Taranto (equivalent in effect to a decisive victory in a great sea fight), and now this epic advance against heavy numerical odds by O'Connor's British Empire forces, fortune filled the sails of the Allied cause in the Mediterranean theatre and wafted it on waves of hope into 1941.

9

'Grey Water Strategy': The Atlantic, 1941

While 'blue water strategy' in the Mediterranean might at best gain some famous local victories on the periphery of the war with Nazi Germany, it could neither win that war for Britain, nor even lose it for her. Rather, Britain's fate depended – now that the danger of a German invasion of England had apparently passed – on 'grey water strategy' alone: that is, on the conduct of the month-in, month-out battle of attrition in the Atlantic wastes.

Just as with the earlier struggle with the U-boat during the Great War and the simultaneous war-deciding land battles of attrition on the Western Front, the success or failure of Britain's 'grey water strategy' was measured by a grim accountancy of comparative losses: the ratio of merchant ships sunk to U-boats destroyed or captured; the relative numbers of trained Allied merchant seamen and German submariners blown up, drowned or maimed set against the numbers of fresh volunteers coming forward to replace them; the total tonnage of shipping lost measured against the output of Britain's shipyards, and of U-boats sunk against Germany's new production; the tonnage of merchant shipping held up at any one time in British ports unloading and reloading, or immobilised in yards awaiting repair; the 'productivity' of U-boats in terms of ships sunk per U-boat per sortie.

To the opposing admirals and their staff these statistics were the equivalent of profit-and-loss accounts or monthly cash-flow figures to the directors of hard-pressed rival businesses. They were scanned with equal trepidation and hope by Grand Admiral Raeder, the head of the German Navy, in Berlin, and Admiral of the Fleet Sir Dudley Pound, the First Sea Lord, in London; by Rear-Admiral Karl Dönitz in his U-boat Command bunker at Kerneval near Lorient and Admiral Sir Martin Dunbar-Nasmith, C-in-C, Western Approaches, in Plymouth and, from 7 February 1941, in Liverpool. The statistics were no less a matter of central concern to Winston Churchill, all too anxiously aware as he was that they charted Britain's very ability to carry on the war; and on 6 March 1941 he issued a directive proclaiming that what he called 'the Battle of the Atlantic' had begun, with an enemy attempt 'to strangle our food supplies and our connection with the United States'.[1]

Yet all this cold accountancy represented an appalling human experience, as the seamen of both sides sought to survive each other's violence and the ferocity of the ocean itself – heavy-laden merchant ships labouring slowly through the huge Atlantic seas, their crews always conscious that at any moment a torpedo could consign them suddenly to those seas in frail boat or raft; the escorts plunging and rolling, their bridges swept by spray and green water, their ships' companies cold, wet and exhausted, eyes and nerves strained by unremitting watch for shadowing Focke-Wulf Kondors, for the U-boat's squat conning tower amid the seaway; the crews of hunted U-boats closed up in their cramped metal capsules, listening grey-faced and silent to the thunder of depth-charges, to the drumming of their hunters' propellers overhead.

Courage, then, hardiness, and a sheer will to endure constituted the essential dynamic of the Battle of the Atlantic. But the key to the struggle between opposing sailors at sea, and to the 'grey water strategy' conducted by opposing admirals in their war rooms, alike lay in technology; in the contest between Allied and German 'boffins' in their research centres to invent new devices to find and destroy the enemy; in the competition between British and German industry to transform as quickly as possible the scientists' inventions into effective equipment in the hands of sailors and airmen. But in fact, of course, these three levels of the Battle of the Atlantic – tactical, strategic and technological – were always closely intermeshed, one reacting upon another. At the beginning of 1941 both sides were still learning through hard experience, still in a relatively early stage of evolving their techniques of attack and defence; still indeed building up their numerical strength.

For Dönitz this build-up of strength had long taken top priority, for in the U-boat itself, especially the Type VIIC, he already possessed a rugged and well-tried weapons system effectively linked to his command centre by radio. Of 753 tons displacement on the surface and 857 tons submerged, the Type VIIC enjoyed a range of 6,500 miles at 12 knots. Her 2,800 bhp diesel-electric engines gave a maximum surface speed of 17.2 knots (faster than many British escorts), while her 750 shp electric motors gave a maximum underwater speed of 8 knots, though only for a brief time before the batteries were exhausted. She was armed with one 88-mm gun, one 20-mm flak gun, and five 21-inch torpedo tubes.[2]

The U-boat's one partial weakness for the time being lay in the torpedo itself, for the unreliability of the new magnetic pistol had compelled the German Navy to revert to the Great War type contact pistol detonated by a direct hit on an enemy vessel. Such a direct hit was less destructive than the explosion beneath a ship's bottom (so breaking its back) made possible by the magnetic pistol, which (when it worked properly, as did the British version, the Duplex, at Taranto) was activated by the target vessel's magnetic field. The German Navy had also encountered difficulties with the depth setting of its torpedoes (see above, p. 194). Not until 1942 would Dönitz's Torpedo Inspectorate solve these problems, which in the meantime both reduced the effectiveness of U-boats and increased torpedo expenditure (thus sometimes leaving U-boats with no more remaining aboard with which to attack subsequent targets).

By April 1941 Dönitz's total strength in boats had for the first time passed the 100 mark, one-third of them operational, the remainder refitting, working up efficiency in the Baltic, or training relays of new crews. Of the operational boats, about twenty were at sea in April 1941; by June the figure had risen to 32.[3] Yet this was still only a tenth of the figure which Dönitz had calculated before the war would be necessary in order to achieve a decisive victory by 'wolf-pack' tactics. For U-boats came low in the scale of Nazi Germany's priorities, especially when it came to rationing out steel; a crass error of grand-strategic judgment on the part of its leadership. Moreover, Admiral Raeder still remained faithful to his concept of deploying powerful surface raiding forces against British sea communications; he cherished bright hopes of his two new 52,600-ton battleships *Bismarck* (already operational) and *Tirpitz* (still working up); and yet more heavy cruisers and an aircraft carrier were on the stocks. This programme had consumed, and was still consuming, enormous industrial resources.

Hitler himself, a Central European landlubber, took little interest in the maritime war; his mind was filled with his forthcoming project to conquer Soviet Russia, 'Operation Barbarossa' (eventually launched on 22 July 1941). Reichsmarschall Hermann Göring, for his part, regarded airpower and the Luftwaffe as his personal barony, not to be shared with anyone. It was only in January 1941, seven months after the German occupation of the French Atlantic coast, that Hitler ordered Göring to place KG [*Kampfgeschwader*] 40, a bomber group composed of Focke-Wulf Kondors and based on Bordeaux, under Dönitz's operational control, in order to remedy to some extent the lamentably poor cooperation between Navy and Luftwaffe. Even so, KG 40 was only able to fly about two Kondors a day, and, with the focus of the battle in the Atlantic shifting to northern waters, their range now proved insufficient despite such expedients as extra fuel tanks and flying the aircraft on to Norway at the end of a sortie. What was more, the Condor crews proved inexpert in accurately reporting the position and course of convoys when they did find them, so misleading rather than guiding the U-boats as they groped on the surface for a victim. Only nearer home, on the routes of the Freetown –Gibraltar–England convoys, were the Kondors to prove a really effective help to the U-boats.[4]

Although in Dönitz's eyes the U-boat arm in 1941 was neglected, under-strength and ill-supported by the Luftwaffe, it nevertheless appeared to the British Prime Minister and the Admiralty as a lethally effective threat, especially in view of the Royal Navy's own inadequate resources. On 22 December 1940 the C-in-C, Western Approaches, Admiral Dunbar-Nasmith, wrote to the First Sea Lord on the whole topic of 'Protection of Trade in the Western Approaches', analysing the reasons, in his words, 'why the Convoy system, which achieved almost complete success in 1914–18, and again in the first half of 1940, is now failing to obtain similar results'.[5] There was the obvious factor of the installation of U-boat and Luftwaffe bases on the French Atlantic coast, which had compelled Britain to abandon the Channel and the South-Western Approaches as a convoy route and shift all convoys to the North-Western Approaches. But this factor only served to emphasise existing shortages of escort ships and weaknesses in technology. Wrote Dunbar-Nasmith: 'Our escorts have been too limited in number and ill-equipped to withstand the enemy's new method of attacking on the surface at night, particularly when the convoy is straggling and the visibility poor.'[6] Moreover: 'The majority of the officers and men of newly-commissioned ships have had no previous experience of A/S warfare, and shortage of escorts has prevented their getting the training desirable.'

The effects of this basic shortage, went on Dunbar-Nasmith, were worsened by the wear and tear caused by operating in northern waters where the winter gales were stronger; 'the greater proportion [of escorts] are out of action undergoing damage repairs'.[7] That same ferocious environment likewise curtailed the performance of the instrument of anti-submarine warfare in which the Admiralty before the war had placed its unreserved faith – sonar, or as the Royal Navy termed it at the time, Asdic. For, in Dunbar-Nasmith's words, 'The rougher weather experienced also makes the operation of the Asdic equipment less efficient.'

'*Less* efficient' was, to say the least, an understatement. The truth about Asdic is more bluntly spelt out in the Naval Staff History study, *Defeat of the Enemy Attack on Shipping 1939–1945*. In the first place, its maximum range was only 1,500 yards. Secondly:

> Neither bearing nor ranges could be read accurately. For bearings there was a possible error of a few degrees – for ranges a possible error of 25 yards. It was also rarely possible to discriminate between submarine and non-submarine targets. The depth of a submerged U-boat could not be ascertained and it was not possible to detect a surfaced one. In addition very considerable skill and experience was required by the operators. The efficiency of the set rapidly fell off at speeds above 20 knots, in rough weather, and in waters with steep temperature gradients.[8]

In fact, to sum it up:

> The result of the surface U-boat attack was that the Asdic was practically useless. In the vicinity of a convoy even its hydrophones, which hitherto had often been relied upon at night or in thick weather, became more generally a source of confusion.[9]

The escorts were therefore forced back on the ability of the human eye to spot a U-boat's low silhouette in all weathers and conditions of light.

But Asdic/sonar did not constitute the Royal Navy's only technical handicap in the face of the U-boat. The escort vessels themselves (fleet destroyers aside) lacked the cruising range for trans-Atlantic work, and were mostly incapable of catching a U-boat even when one was sighted; the latest types now coming out of the shipyards still being slower than a U-boat on the surface[10] – more legacies of wrong-headed pre-war decisions. While the twenty 907-ton Type I Hunt class escort destroyers of the 1938 programme (launched between December 1939 and September 1940), were certainly fast enough at 26 knots, they proved 'unsatisfactory' for ocean service, and were to be mostly employed in home waters. The 137 Flower class sloops (925 tons; later reclassed as corvettes), which had been ordered before the war for coastal work and which only came into service during 1940–41 were found as early as the end of 1940 to be 'almost useless as ocean escorts in winter owing to their excessive rolling and lack of manoeuvrability'.[11] Nonetheless, so desperately short of escort vessels was the Royal Navy that this class of ship was to supply the workhorse of the Battle of the Atlantic for years to come. Their design had to be extensively modified in order to render later ships more habitable for the overcrowded crews and give them greater firepower and endurance, but the improved versions were not to see service until 1943. Since the 'Flowers' could only make a maximum speed of 15 knots (though their designed speed was 16½), they were too slow to catch up a U-boat on the surface.

It brought some relief in the early months of 1941 that the old four-stack United States destroyers were at last being commissioned after modernisation. But in the meantime the main burden of protecting convoys fell on the Royal Navy's scarce resources of older fleet destroyers, supplemented by some sonar-equipped fleet minesweepers, enabling an average provision of two escorts per convoy of up to 40 to 50 merchant ships.

Unfortunately the principal anti-submarine weapon, the depth-charge, was technically little better than that used in the Great War, with a lethal radius of some seven yards only. The system for launching the charges – release into water from stern chutes and projection outward on both beams from throwers in a pattern of five – required that the ship had first to overrun the U-boat, so for technical reasons forcing a loss of sonar contact at close range during and immediately after the attack.[12] Although thrown-ahead depth-charges had been developed in the Great War, it was not until January 1942 that a new version dubbed the 'Hedgehog' – a multi-spigot mortar firing 24 contact-fuzed 65-pound projectiles forward some 230 yards in an elliptical pattern – came into service.

All these shortcomings in vessels and equipment essentially stemmed from the pre-war Admiralty's complacent neglect of the entire problem of convoy protection and anti-submarine warfare. But already British science was working on a new means of locating the surfaced U-boat in all conditions of weather and light. By February 1941 the Admiralty Signal School had developed an experimental centrimetric radar set, which, installed on a land-based tower, proved capable of following a submarine up to a range of 7½ nautical miles. The Captain of the Signal School on his own initiative ordered components for 150 of these sets (called 'Type 271'), as well as the hand-building in the laboratories of 24 copies of the prototype. By April 1941 sea trials in the new corvette *Orchis* demonstrated that the set could pick up a surfaced submarine at 4,000 to 5,000 yards and the periscope of a submerged submarine at 1,100 to 1,500 yards. By July 1941 25 corvettes had been fitted with Type 271 radars, and by the end of the year 100 sets had been manufactured and 50 ships equipped.[13]

High Frequency Direction Finders (HF/DF) for locating a U-boat by its radio transmissions offered yet another means of detection. As early as July 1940 it had been recognised that HF/DF mounted in the convoy escort could reveal the presence and bearing of a U-boat, but, owing to production delays and the need to gain experience in operating the kit, it was not until a year later that the first set came into use at sea.[14] High Frequency Direction Finders were also urgently needed for another purpose – to enable the Royal Navy to locate *British* ships in the vast spaces of the Atlantic. On 12 March 1941 Admiral Sir Percy Noble, who had just replaced Dunbar-Nasmith as C-in-C, Western Approaches on 17 February, wrote to the First Sea Lord: 'Under present conditions many hours are wasted both in the air and on the sea – tugs trying to find derelects [sic], escorts trying to meet convoys, valuable independently routed ships giving anxiety as to their position . . .'[15]

But in any event neither HF/DF nor centrimetric radar could be of much use against surface attacks by U-boats at night (their preferred tactic) because of the lack of an effective means of illuminating a U-boat once detected for the kill. Not until autumn 1941 did 'Snowflake', a brilliant new pyrotechnic illuminant, replace the virtually useless existing star-shell.

And Royal Air Force Coastal Command too in 1941 was still striving to overcome the technical and numerical weaknesses bequeathed by past neglect, to equip itself with new types of aircraft, instruments and weapons, and to evolve new techniques of searching for U-boats and destroying them. Its old workhorses, the land-based Avro Anson and the Short Sunderland flying-boat, were being steadily supplemented by the American Lockheed Hudson and the Consolidated Catalina flying-boat. The Catalina, though lightly armed and heavy to handle, had an endurance of nearly 3,000 miles. Some squadrons of Vickers Wellington and obsolete Armstrong Whitworth Whitley bombers were transferred from Bomber Command to Coastal Command; and the robust Wellington became one of the Command's most reliable performers. The new Bristol Beaufort twin-engined torpedo-bomber was also joining the squadrons in replacement of the ancient Vildebeest.

But despite the establishment of air bases in Iceland (see below, p. 263) in order to extend air search and convoy protection as far out into the Atlantic as possible, there still remained an 'air gap' beyond the effective operational outward range (that is, allowing two hours on station) of Wellingtons (400 miles) and even Catalinas (400 to 600 miles); a gap which, as the AOC-in-C, Coastal Command, Sir Frederick Bowhill, 'stressed again and again',[16] could only be filled by very long range aircraft. In June 1941 a squadron was therefore formed of the untried Consolidated B-24 Liberator four-engine bomber, which after modification could provide protection to convoys at up to 750 miles from base. The squadron, based in Iceland and Northern Ireland, became operational in September. But its value was short-lived: by October its original strength of twenty had dwindled to only ten because of wastage and transfers to Ferry Command. By the beginning of 1942 the AOC-in-C, Coastal Command, was having to face the unwelcome fact that his single Liberator squadron 'was being allowed to die and that there was no agreed future policy for the building up of any long-range force . . .'[17]

In any event Coastal Command's means of finding and killing U-boats remained feeble enough. Although radar had been fitted experimentally in some aircraft since early 1940, development experienced 'many teething troubles',[18] and it was only in January 1941 that the first reliable ASV (Air-to-Surface-Vessel) radar began to be installed. Coastal Command's aircraft still lacked an effective bombsight (as well as heavy enough bombs), and they had to make do with adapted naval depth-charges, the depth-setting of which had to be fixed before take-off. This meant that if the charge was set to go off deep against a diving submarine, it would be useless against a submarine still on the surface. So Coastal Command would have to make shift as best it could while a shallower depth-charge pistol and a low-level sight were being developed.

Moreover, the Command, like the Royal Navy, possessed no effective means of illuminating a submarine at night. Not until 1943 was a slow-dropping flare to come into service. On 4 May 1941 a successful trial was held of the 'Leigh Light', an airborne searchlight proposed by Squadron-Leader H. de V. Leigh, a Great War pilot now on personnel duties at Coastal Command HQ. With the AOC-in-C's backing, Leigh had succeeded in installing a 24-inch naval searchlight in the under-turret of a Wellington equipped with ASV radar. In the trial against a British submarine, the Wellington's crew (including

Leigh in order to operate his light) first located the target by radar; after which, according to a Navy observer of the test:

> The aircraft was not heard by the submarine until it [the submarine] had been illuminated, and was able to attack down the beam for 27 seconds before being pulled out at 500 feet. This effort was most impressive, and there seems no doubt that, given an efficient aircraft crew and good team work, this weapon would be invaluable in attacking U-boats on the surface at night and in low visibility.[19]

But the Leigh Light was not to be in operational use for another year, the victim of initial opposition by the new AOC-in-C, Coastal Command, Air Marshal Sir Philip Joubert de la Ferté (who replaced Bowhill in June 1941), and of the usual problems of 'technology transfer' from the experimental stage to general installation.

All these weaknesses in equipment, when coupled with the shortage of aircraft for adequate training in ASV radar operation and marksmanship, limited the effectiveness of new tactics adopted in June 1941 whereby the Command's aircraft (now painted in white camouflage) were to approach a U-boat unseen through clouds thanks to ASV radar and attack U-boats by surprise, hoping to hit them during the 25-second interval between the time the U-boat's watch spotted the aircraft and the U-boat's complete disappearance into the depths.

Thus in the air and at sea the prospects for the Battle of the Atlantic in 1941 might be said to have turned on a balance between British and German deficiencies. Yet in command and control organisation the British had forged well ahead, especially with regard to cooperation between ships and aircraft. On 15 February 1941 Coastal Command was placed under the operational control of the Admiralty, though not under its direct command. Naval Cs-in-C in the various naval command areas would now state their operational requirements to their Coastal Command Group opposite numbers, who would then issue orders to the squadrons.[20] The closest links henceforth were to exist between Coastal Command Headquarters and the Admiralty's Submarine Tracking Room in London, while the new C-in-C, Western Approaches, Admiral Sir Percy Noble, and Air Vice-Marshal J. M. Robb, commanding No. 15 Group. Coastal Command (covering the North-Western Approaches), shared a new joint headquarters safe beneath a thick concrete roof in Derby House, Liverpool. Across one wall of the operations room was displayed the current Operational Plot of the state of the Battle of the Atlantic, based on information fed in by teleprinter from the Operational Intelligence Centre in the Admiralty 'Citadel' in

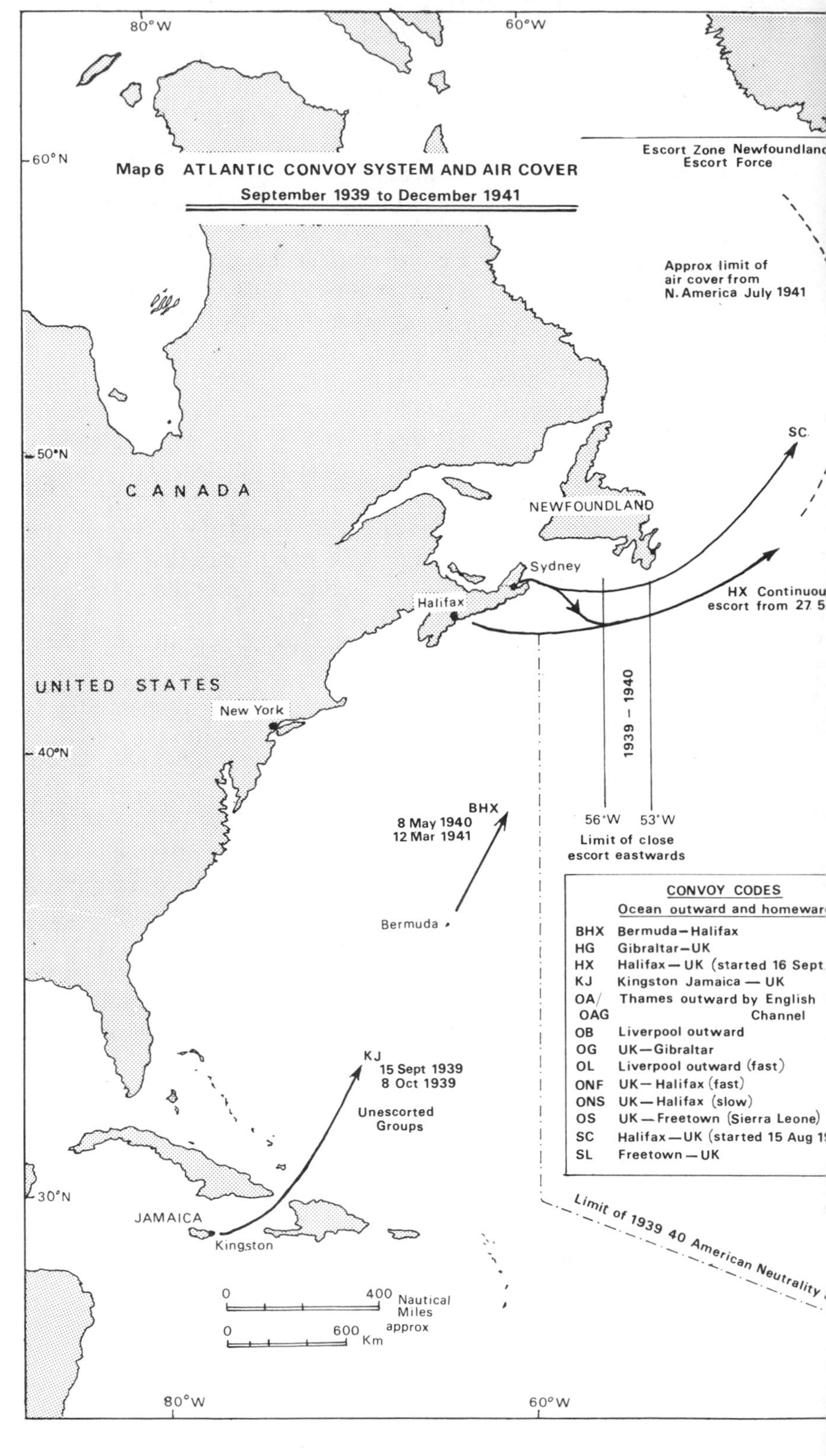

Map 6 ATLANTIC CONVOY SYSTEM AND AIR COVER
September 1939 to December 1941
80°W
60°W
60°N
50°N
40°N
30°N
Escort Zone Newfoundland
Escort Force
Approx limit of
air cover from
N. America July 1941
CANADA
NEWFOUNDLAND
SC
Sydney
Halifax
HX Continuous
escort from 27.5
UNITED STATES
New York
1939 – 1940
56°W
53°W
Limit of close
escort eastwards
BHX
8 May 1940
12 Mar 1941
Bermuda
CONVOY CODES
Ocean outward and homeward
BHX Bermuda–Halifax
HG Gibraltar–UK
HX Halifax–UK (started 16 Sept
KJ Kingston Jamaica – UK
OA/OAG Thames outward by English Channel
OB Liverpool outward
OG UK–Gibraltar
OL Liverpool outward (fast)
ONF UK–Halifax (fast)
ONS UK–Halifax (slow)
OS UK–Freetown (Sierra Leone)
SC Halifax–UK (started 15 Aug 1
SL Freetown–UK
KJ
15 Sept 1939
8 Oct 1939
Unescorted
Groups
JAMAICA
Kingston
Limit of 1939 40 American Neutrality
0
400
Nautical
Miles
0
600
approx
Km

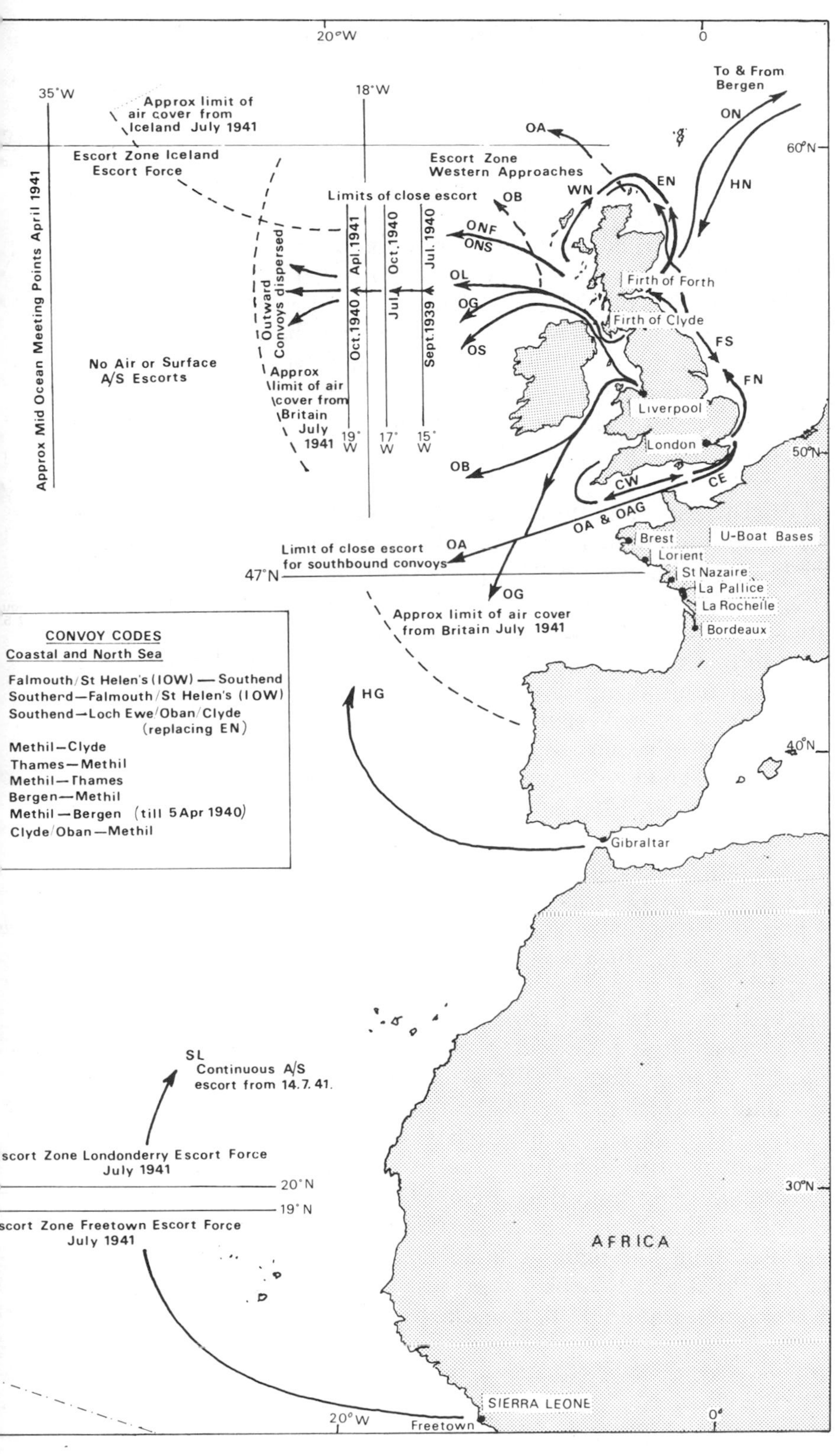

20°W
0
To & From
Bergen
35°W
Approx limit of
air cover from
Iceland July 1941
18°W
ON
OA
60°N
Escort Zone Iceland
Escort Force
Escort Zone
Western Approaches
EN
HN
WN
Approx Mid Ocean Meeting Points April 1941
Limits of close escort
OB
ONF
ONS
Outward
Convoys dispersed
Apl.1941
Oct.1940
Jul.1940
Firth of Forth
OL
OG
OS
Oct.1940
Jul.
Sept.1939
Firth of Clyde
FS
No Air or Surface
A/S Escorts
Approx
limit of air
cover from
Britain
July
1941
FN
Liverpool
19° W
17° W
15° W
London
50°N
OB
CW
CE
OA & OAG
Brest
U-Boat Bases
Limit of close escort
for southbound convoys
OA
Lorient
47°N
St Nazaire
La Pallice
OG
La Rochelle
Approx limit of air cover
from Britain July 1941
Bordeaux
CONVOY CODES
Coastal and North Sea
Falmouth/St Helen's (IOW) — Southend
Southerd—Falmouth/St Helen's (IOW)
Southend→Loch Ewe/Oban/Clyde
(replacing EN)
Methil—Clyde
Thames—Methil
Methil—Thames
Bergen—Methil
Methil—Bergen (till 5 Apr 1940)
Clyde/Oban—Methil
HG
40°N
Gibraltar
SL
Continuous A/S
escort from 14.7.41.
scort Zone Londonderry Escort Force
July 1941
20°N
19°N
30°N
scort Zone Freetown Escort Force
July 1941
AFRICA
SIERRA LEONE
20°W
Freetown
0°

London. This highly sophisticated modern headquarters, with its large joint staffs, compared with Dönitz's 'corner shop' at Kerneval in a bunker so cramped it was nicknamed 'the Sardine Tin', and staffed by just six young U-boat officers plus the lieutenant-colonel commanding the Luftwaffe's KG 40.[21] Moreover, the British side of the battle was being overseen by no less than a War Cabinet Committee – the Battle of the Atlantic Committee – presided over by Churchill himself, comprising the chiefs of the naval and air staffs and eminent scientific advisers, while Dönitz enjoyed no such concerted backing from the top; indeed little backing at all. And the course of the year was to bring forth another British advantage, one sensed by Dönitz in the very operational pattern of the struggle, yet remaining for him a mystery the secret of which he could not plumb.

The balance sheet for the month of January 1941 favoured the British, for, thanks to winter weather and evasive routing of convoys, sinkings by U-boats dropped to 21 ships of 126,782 tons, many of them stragglers or caught in mid-ocean before convoys had formed up or after they had dispersed. Although the Luftwaffe's Kondors accounted for a further twenty ships of 78,517 tons, the combined total came to not much more than half that of the previous October.[22]

But the February statistics swung heavily back in the German favour, with 39 ships totalling 196,784 tons falling victim to the U-boat, and another 27 totalling 89,305 tons to the Kondor. Sinkings by surface raiders brought the grand total to more than 100 ships and 400,000 tons for the first time since October 1940. Ten ships of 52,875 tons fell victim alone to the first successful cooperation between KG 40 and the U-boats, when on 22 February a Kondor accurately reported the position of convoy OB288 to U-73, so leading to a relentless assault by a wolf pack of seven boats without the loss of a single U-boat or aircraft. Nevertheless, the enemy still found half of his sinkings in hapless stragglers. The dismaying February figures were enough to spur Churchill into issuing his 'Battle of the Atlantic' directive and setting up the War Cabinet Battle of the Atlantic Committee, which met for the first time on 19 March.

By an irony the month of March was regarded as disastrous by both sides – by the British because total losses reached over half a million tons for the first time since June 1940, and by Dönitz because no fewer than five of his U-boats were sunk by convoy escorts, a fifth of his operational strength. It stung Dönitz the more that two of his 'aces', Prien and Schepke, were lost with their boats, and a third, Kretschmer, captured. This marked the final close of the era of the individual aces in the North Atlantic; henceforward Dönitz switched almost entirely to wolf packs. It was therefore in April 1941 that the true Battle of the Atlantic, the conflict of wolf pack versus the convoy system, really began.[23]

The fact was brutally signalled at the beginning of the month by an attack by seven U-boats on convoy SC26 in longitude 28°W before the anti-submarine escort had joined and when its only protection lay in the armed merchant cruiser HMS *Worcestershire* (not equipped to fight U-boats). Six ships were sunk and the *Worcestershire* herself damaged. But on the 5th, the destroyer *Wolverine* and the sloop *Scarborough* of the newly joined escort sank the U-76, whereupon the enemy gave up his attack.

Dönitz's evident strategy of pushing his U-boats further out into mid-Atlantic in search of soft targets beyond the cover of surface escorts and air patrols in turn provoked further British counter-measures. That month No. 15 Group, Coastal Command, established bases for Sunderlands of 204 Squadron and Hudsons of 269 Squadron in Iceland, while the Royal Navy opened an advanced fuelling base for escort vessels at Hvalfjord, north of Reykjavik. By mid-April convoys could be covered as far as 30°W, and by the end of the month as far as 35°W. At the same time they were re-routed nearer Iceland in order to maximise the escorts' endurance on station, while the escort forces themselves were strengthened by some sonar-equipped fleet minesweepers. Thus Iceland (first occupied by British forces in May 1940) had now fully assumed its role as the key to the struggle by the King's ships and aircraft to keep open the North Atlantic lifeline. A familiar landfall for the rest of the war to the weary men on bridge or in cockpit, it was the very embodiment of the harshness of that struggle. Captain S. W. Roskill, RN, the British official naval historian, remarks on 'its bleak and precipitous coastline, the deep inlets which formed its harbours, the poor holding ground which gave ships constant anxiety and, in particular, . . . the violence of its sudden, blinding and shifting storms'.[24]

> The treachery of the Icelandic climate during the long winter months, the inhospitality of its harbours and the virtual certainty that little rest or relaxation would be possible in them soon aroused the British sailor's intense dislike of the place. To come in from fighting the enemy and the elements only to find that the fury of the latter had followed him with intensified malevolence awoke all his wide capacity for sardonic humour.[25]

The rerouting of convoys nearer to Iceland led to the uncovenanted benefit of compelling the U-boats to make longer voyages to their hunting grounds, so reducing their productive time on station. Moreover, the long spring days in this northerly latitude cramped their operational effectiveness, because it became too hazardous for them to shadow a convoy on the surface in daylight within range of British air patrols, while the night hours did not afford enough time for them to catch up and strike. In the same period Coastal Command introduced a new tactical system which rendered the role of the shadowing U-boat in daylight even more hazardous. Instead of aircraft giving only close protection to a convoy from stations on either bow as hitherto, they deployed round the convoy at considerable distances or swept well ahead of it. This surveillance and defence in depth forced attacking U-boats to submerge on approach to a convoy, so crippling their mobility, for their maximum economical speed when running on their batteries was barely five knots, and even often preventing them from developing their attacks at all.[26]

Yet Western Approaches Command, for its part, still lacked enough escort ships, especially destroyers, for which there were other urgent demands. In answer to a plea from Sir Percy Noble, the C-in-C, Western Approaches, the First Sea Lord explained on 16 April:

> The fact that I had a whip round to try and produce some more craft for the North-Western Approaches will prove that I am as keen as you are on building up your forces as much as possible.
>
> I have had to send Mountb's [sic] party [of destroyers] to the Mediterranean, and C-in-C, Home Fleet, had to replace them and you, I regret, must fill up C-in-C. We cannot have our capital ships risked for want of escorts.[27]

Towards the end of April submerged U-boats attacking in daylight sank four ships in convoy HX121 south of Iceland in 60°W, despite its escort. Nevertheless the corvette *Gladiolus* found one of the U-boats, the U-65, on the surface and destroyed her. It was encouraging too that in the entire month only ten ships had been sunk by U-boats while in convoy and only four of those in escorted convoys. It was the stragglers and the independent sailings that were still providing Dönitz's boats with their main stock in trade, bringing the total U-boat sinkings for April to 43 ships of 249,375 tons.

In May the accountancy of destruction swung strongly in Germany's favour, with the U-boats sinking 58 ships of 325,492 tons – half of them unescorted vessels in the Freetown area, whither the crafty Dönitz had deployed six boats in search of just such easy prey. Yet even on the trans-Atlantic route the U-boat gained two major successes. At the beginning of the month the outward bound convoy

OB318 lost five ships as against one U-boat destroyed by its anti-submarine escort. A fortnight later the homeward-bound convoy HX126 from Halifax, Nova Scotia, with only an ocean escort (i.e., to protect it against an enemy surface ship raider), was ambushed by a pack of nine U-boats south of Greenland in about 40°W, in that mid-Atlantic gap still covered neither by air patrols nor by anti-submarine escorts. Nine ships were lost, four of them after the convoy had been scattered. It was enough to induce the Admiralty, in collaboration with the Royal Canadian Navy, finally to inaugurate end-to-end surface escorts.

For that month a British-Canadian conference met to review the whole question of the air and sea defence of North Atlantic shipping. It agreed that, thanks to the arrival in service of the long-range Catalina, air cover would now be provided as far out as 700 miles from the British Isles, 400 miles from Iceland and 500 miles from Newfoundland. These arcs would, however, still leave an air gap of some 300 miles which could only be closed by very long range aircraft such as the Liberator. It was in this air gap that during the next two years Britain would come to within an ace of losing the Second World War. The conference also decided to base a powerful force of escorts at St John's, Newfoundland, and in the course of June this force reached a total of 30 destroyers, nine sloops and 24 Canadian-built Flower class corvettes. On 27 May 1941 the first convoy to enjoy the protection of an anti-submarine escort throughout its trans-Atlantic voyage, HX129, sailed from Halifax.

This inauguration of end-to-end escorts had only been made possible because at long last the shipyards of Canada and Great Britain had built enough escort vessels, supplemented by the old four-stack American destroyers and a recent transfer of ten ocean-going US coastguard cutters to the British flag. The Royal Navy's strength in destroyers and escort destroyers had now risen to 248 (of which 50 were undergoing refits), 99 corvettes and 348 assorted trawlers, sloops, coastguard cutters and anti-submarine yachts,[28] a figure which permitted the average number of escorts per convoy to be increased to five. Yet even with another 157 destroyers and 99 corvettes building (55 of them in Canada), the Admiralty still reckoned that it lacked sufficient ships adequately to protect the trade routes in the future against the enemy's own ever-increasing numbers of U-boats and also find a surplus to allow for the formation of hunting groups to destroy wolf packs once detected.

Despite the new British counter-measures the June figures again seemed to favour the U-boats, which sank sixty-one ships totalling

310,143 tons. When the Joint Planning Staff in London surveyed the cumulative overall shipping balance sheet that same month, they therefore found the arithmetic deeply discouraging. Britain and her Allies (those European states like Norway and the Netherlands which had lost their territories but retained their merchant fleets) had begun the year 1941 with shipping resources between 1.5 and 2.5 million tons smaller than at the outbreak of war. During the three months of March, April and May 1941 they had lost a total of 1,728,649 tons from all forms of enemy action and natural causes (817,887 tons from the U-boat alone): the equivalent of an annual loss of nearly 7 million tons. Moreover, well over a million tons of damaged shipping currently lay immobilised in repair yards, the victims of delays owing to antique shipyard equipment and equally antique management and trade-union practices; the equivalent of several million tons out of service annually.

Already British imports of dry cargo (including absolutely vital American technology as well as food) were running at only some 73 per cent of estimated tonnage requirements, while imports of oil were running at a tenth below. At the current rate of imports, therefore, a deficit of nearly 7 million tons of raw materials and semi-manufactured goods and two million tons of food would have accumulated by the end of 1941. Oil stocks, already dangerously low, would be down by another 318,000 tons. Certainly Britain could live for a time by running down stocks, but what then? At current rates of merchant shipping loss, calculated the Joint Planners, Britain was likely to be down another 5 million tons of shipping at the very least by the end of the year – yet the combined annual output of all the yards of the Commonwealth for dry-cargo ships came to barely 1 million tons. Britain would be fortunate if she could buy or charter as much as another half a million tons by way of supplement.

The Joint Planners therefore drew the almost despairing conclusion that 'it is only from a reduction in the rate of loss that a real margin of safety can be acquired'.[29] It was all too reminiscent of Jellicoe's doom-laden pronouncement to the Cabinet as First Sea Lord at the height of the 1917 U-boat campaign: 'It is impossible for us to go on with the war if losses like this continue.'[30]

Yet the June balance sheet was deceptive. Only thirteen ships out of the 61 lost had been sunk in convoy, while to destroy them had cost Dönitz three U-boats – two of them when an onslaught by ten boats on a single convoy off Greenland, the homeward bound HX133, was crushingly defeated by a swift and sudden British concentration of a powerful hunting group of two destroyers, ten corvettes and a sloop. And this tactical success proved to be merely the prelude to a startling shift in the strategic balance in July and August, when total U-boat sinkings dropped away to 22 ships of 94,209 tons and 23 of 80,310 tons respectively, less than a third of previous monthly totals.

The cause of these successes lay in the most astonishing, most closely guarded secret of the maritime conflict with Nazi Germany during the Second World War; one so precious that even the official naval historian writing in the 1950s was unable to refer to it. Yet it alone supplies the key to understanding the evolving pattern of the Battle of the Atlantic during the second half of 1941. For by mid-summer the Government Code and Cypher School (GC and CS) at Bletchley Park, near Buckingham (codename 'Ultra'), had broken the German Navy's 'Home Waters' Enigma, and was thus able to read Dönitz's top secret radio traffic at only short delay.

It had taken more than a year of patient analysis, of well planned captures and sheer luck – starting with luck. In April 1940 the Royal Navy had captured the German patrol boat VP2623 off Norway and retrieved Enigma settings that enabled GC and CS to read retrospectively the naval Enigma for six days, so providing important insights into the German Navy's wireless and cypher organisation.[31] GC and CS then established that the German Navy's Enigma machine now selected from a total of eight wheels instead of the five on the Luftwaffe machine – far more difficult to break – and that the Navy employed two keys, 'Home Waters' and 'Foreign', for both U-boats and surface ships, the 'Foreign' key being reserved for operations in distant waters. Over 95 per cent of all Enigma traffic was encyphered in the 'Home' key, which proved so formidably complex that GC and CS only succeeded in breaking it sufficiently to read another five days' traffic relating to April and May 1940, and then only by February 1941. It was evident that no progress could be made without important captures of code material, or, better still, a naval Enigma machine.

Naval Intelligence Division, and GC and CS, therefore decided to profit from the forthcoming Commando raid on the Lofoten Islands on 4 March 1941 by organising a special effort to seize such material – and successfully turned it up in the captured armed trawler *Krebs*. Thanks to this the Bletchley Park cryptographers managed to break the whole of the Enigma traffic for April at up to ten days' delay, and much of the May traffic at only three to seven days' delay. Moreover, the traffic read for February and April had revealed that the Germans kept one weather ship on station north of Iceland and another in mid-Atlantic, both carrying Enigma machines. On 7 May the Royal Navy captured the *München*, so enabling GC and CS to read the June Enigma traffic almost currently; and on 28 June, a date chosen because it fell just before the next month's Enigma settings came into force, the *Lauenburg* was likewise cut out, making it possible for the July traffic to be read also without delay.

Meanwhile had occurred another remarkable stroke of luck. On 9 May the captain of the destroyer *Bulldog* thought better of ramming and sinking the U-110, caught on the surface during an assault on the convoy OB318, and sent a boarding party to capture her instead. And aboard her was treasure indeed: an Enigma machine complete with a signal ready set for transmission, together with the special settings for 'officer-only' signals and the codebook for transmitting the short-range sighting reports ('*Kurzsignale*') used by U-boats shadowing a convoy in order to call in a wolf pack.

The Bletchley Park analysts' final assault on the crumbling cryptographic fortress of the naval Enigma was further helped by flank attacks via lesser hand-codes and cyphers, in particular a dockyards hand cypher ('*Werft*') and a meteorological cypher. Some of the traffic in these was found to be also transmitted in the Enigma, so offering valuable extra clues to the cryptographers as day by day they bent their brains and their electro-mechanical 'Bombes' to reading current Enigma traffic. By the beginning of August 1941 GC and CS had achieved complete mastery over the Enigma 'Home Waters' settings; a mastery which it was to retain until the end of the war, with a customary delay of only a few hours and a maximum of seventy-two.

Already in May the still tardy readings of the naval Enigma had permitted the Intelligence Centre (OIC) Operational to read every signal passed within Dönitz's U-boat Command and to construct a complete and constantly updated picture of Dönitz's dispositions, strategy and tactics. Then at last in June GC and CS could read Enigma fast enough to enable the Admiralty to anticipate German tactical operations. Thus it knew that convoy HX133 had been sighted by the enemy on 23 June; it knew that a wolf pack of ten boats was closing to attack it; and this was why it was able to order the escorts of two outward-bound convoys to leave their charges and reinforce HX133's own escort force to the combined total of two destroyers, ten corvettes and a sloop which in a running battle between 24 and 29 June sank the two U-boats for the loss of only five ships in the convoy.

Now came the larger strategic rewards of Bletchley Park's triumph. Since the winter of 1940–41 Western Approaches Command had resorted to the evasive routing of convoys away from suspected U-boat hunting areas, but this had been very much a matter of professional hunches and guesswork. With the new ability to read Dönitz's current operational plans as if British admirals and their staffs were present beside him at his chart table in Kerneval, evasive routing of convoys became a precision exercise. Even in June the Admiralty succeeded in routing convoys so that the baffled U-boats made no sightings at all in the North Atlantic until encountering HX133. In July they patrolled in vain for three whole weeks, succeeding only once in the month in locating and attacking a convoy, OG69 – in any case not a trans-Atlantic convoy, but one proceeding through the eastern Atlantic on the run between Britain and Africa. In August, and despite a temporary slowing down in the speed of Enigma decrypts, the Admiralty was again able to steer all but one convoy clear of Dönitz's gropings for a target. When Dönitz shifted his boats to the trans-Atlantic routes (after attacking another convoy on the Britain–Africa route) they searched the wide ocean in vain for ten days.

Frustrated and perplexed, he transferred his effort to waters between Northern Ireland and Iceland, whereupon his unfortunate captains found themselves under a ferocious air and surface attack mounted by a forewarned British command. One U-boat was sunk and another, U-570, captured. The U-570, the first to surrender to an aircraft of Coastal Command, was unlucky enough to surface south of Iceland immediately beneath a Hudson of 269 Squadron on convoy patrol. The Hudson promptly depth-charged the U-boat and damaged it before it could submerge, and then persuaded the captain by machine-gun fire to raise the white flag. Later a Catalina relieved the Hudson in keeping watch on the surrendered boat until a trawler arrived to tow it back to Iceland. This capture too proved a bonus for the Bletchley Park cryptographers.

For Dönitz the dismal course of July and August meant failure in the fundamental requirement of U-boat warfare – in the location of targets, never easy at the best of times with so few U-boats and so much ocean. He could not understand why no matter how he redeployed his boats they still found themselves searching empty horizons. In his own words in his memoirs:

> Time and again there occurred between one convoy battle and another a long hiatus during which the U-boats swept the seas fruitlessly in a vain attempt to find the enemy. These 'dead' periods naturally caused the U-boat sinking potential to fall. Time and again U-boat Command re-examined the whole problem in an effort to try and find some way of improving this unsatisfactory state of affairs. It was obvious that the main cause was the dearth of U-boats and the lack of 'eyes' with which to search the vast Atlantic expanses. But was it not possible that there might be other reasons to account for our meagre success in locating shipping? Was

there any chance, for example, that the enemy had some means of locating U-boat dispositions and of routing his shipping clear of them?[32]

For, as he wrote at the time, 'coincidence alone it cannot be . . .'[33] He ruled out spies as the source of British information, while German cryptographic specialists were absolutely certain that Enigma was impregnable. That left High Frequency Direction Finding (HF/DF), as the most likely culprit; but unfortunately for Dönitz not the true one.

Nonetheless the fall in sinkings by the U-boats in July and August was not solely accounted for by the Admiralty's operational use of Enigma decrypts: the enhanced air and surface protection over the North Atlantic, including end-to-end escorts, provided another helpful factor; and so too did important operational changes in the Admiralty's whole convoy system. For from 18 June, five months after Admiral Sir Percy Noble had first made the suggestion, the Admiralty raised the minimum speed limit for independent sailings (those gifts to the prowling U-boat) from 13 to 15 knots, so leading to a sharp reduction in such sailings, and hence a fall in sinkings thereof from 120 ships in the three months April to June to only 25 ships in July–September.

But in September the U-boats found targets more easily again, launching mass attacks on four convoys, two of them slow homeward-bound convoys (SC42 and 44) caught south of Greenland, outside the range of Coastal Command's Whitleys and Wellingtons, and two others homeward-bound from Freetown and Gibraltar (SL87 and HG73). Convoy SC42 originally consisted of no fewer than 64 ships and was creeping across the ocean at perhaps 6 to 7 knots escorted by one Canadian destroyer and three corvettes; the whole sprawling armada reeking smoke that must have been visible, as the convoy commodore noted, 30 miles away. During the night hours of 9–10 September under a U-boat's moon a savage battle ensued with a pack of eight U-boats (no fewer than seventeen had been called in). As many as four of them were sighted on the surface running down the columns in the middle of the convoy, one of which was chased by HMCS *Skeena*. Eleven ships went down; seven more in the darkness of 10–11 September. Even though two Canadian corvettes, which had been directed by the Admiralty to the rescue, sank the U-501, and a fresh escort group from Iceland of five warships which reached the convoy at noon on the 11th sank another, the U-207, it was a thick sea mist and not the escorts which prevented the enemy from renewing his attacks the next night as well. The unfortunate SC42 had contributed half the total of 36 ships lost in these four convoys.

Of the two homeward bound convoys from Gibraltar and Freetown, HG73 was spotted by a Condor off Cape St Vincent, and shadowed for five days. On this occasion cooperation between KG 40 and U-boat Command proved all too successful: a wolf pack closed on the convoy and sank nine out of its 25 merchantmen despite a very strong escort of ten ships. There were particular reasons for the U-boats' success against HG73, reasons which also embodied an old lesson, for, as Admiral Noble reported to the Admiralty on 5 October, although the escort was strong in numbers it 'suffered from a lack of training as a team, having only recently been formed to meet the call for all-through escort to and from Gibraltar . . .' Noble suggested that it would be desirable to introduce carefully selected junior Royal Navy commanding officers into corvette groups. He urged too that there was a 'vital need' to ensure the 'minimum dislocation of groups' and provide reasonable time for training between trips, 'since MAINTENANCE and TRAINING are the two hinge pins of success. The escort group of HG73 is an example of what we may expect if these rules are not strictly adhered to.'[34]

Dönitz's better success in September owed itself partially to the increased number of operational U-boats which the shipyards and the crew training courses had placed in his hands – now rising towards 80, as against 30 in April. Yet in fact this shift in the balance of the visible struggle out on the high seas was mainly a reflection of a further shift in the balance of the secret electronic war of Sigint, this time towards U-boat Command. For Dönitz, suspecting that HF/DF fixes were enabling the British to locate his U-boats and follow their movements, had been cutting down as far as possible on the volume of U-boat/U-boat-Command radio (and hence Enigma) traffic. Likewise suspecting that there might be internal leaks within U-boat Command itself, he had since mid-June been introducing various coding devices to disguise the position of U-boats on the standard U-boat grid by means of 'relating positions at sea to fixed points of reference – Franz, Oscar, Herbert, etc – arbitrarily chosen and changed at short intervals'.[35] On 11 September Dönitz superseded such measures (which had only temporarily slowed the work of the Bletchley Park cryptographers) because he had found, in Professor Hinsley's words, 'that the fixed reference-point system was too cumbersome, and the source of miscalculations by U-boats'. In the new system 'the digraphs of the naval grid squares were separately encyphered before the texts of their messages were encyphered on the Enigma machine'.[36] Although the Operational Intelligence Centre

(OIC) and GC and CS were eventually to defeat this new system to a large extent, it meant that for some weeks, in Professor Hinsley's words, 'the identification of the positions given in the instructions to the U-boats was a protracted process involving some guesswork'.[37]

But in October U-boat successes fell away again, to 32 ships of 156,554 tons; a quarter less than in September.[38] For by now GC and CS were providing the Admiralty's Operational Intelligence Centre at only 26 hours' delay with a complete picture of U-boat deployment and Dönitz's tactical instructions, enabling the Admiralty to reroute no fewer than fifteen convoys during the month. Once again Dönitz's patrol lines swept the seas in vain search for mysteriously elusive convoys, only succeeding in attacking one North Atlantic convoy (SC48) and one on the Africa–Gibraltar–England route. Moreover, the improvement in Coastal Command's air cover was also making its impact, for the U-boats sank no vessels within 400 miles of a Coastal Command base and only twelve in the range 400 to 600 miles occasionally patrolled by Catalinas.[39] There was a further factor: in September Dönitz had been ordered by Hitler and Raeder to divert six U-boats into the Mediterranean to aid the Italian Navy, so weakening his October effort in the Atlantic.

However, October 1941 is notable in the history of the Battle of the Atlantic for another reason – on 17 October the United States destroyer USS *Kearney* was torpedoed and damaged by a U-boat during a night battle against a wolf pack south of Iceland while escorting a Britain-bound convoy (SC48) of 50 ships; and on 31 October the destroyer USS *Reuben James* was sunk by another U-boat while escorting the Britain-bound convoy HX156. She was the first American warship to go down in the Battle of the Atlantic. These two events explosively drove home to the world the month-old fact that the United States of America, though still technically neutral, had joined in the battle on Britain's side.

Ever since the summer of 1940 Churchill had continued to seek by patient, well-tuned diplomacy to draw the United States, through the medium of President Roosevelt, into the fight against Nazi Germany, judging this to offer Britain's only long-term hope of survival and victory. Roosevelt himself, a crafty politician sensitive to strong isolationist opinion in Congress and the American public at large, had moved cautiously; more cautiously than the desperately pressed British wanted. Again and again he promised more than he later performed.[40] But for evident strategic reasons, the security of the Atlantic was of direct concern to the American government. On 1 March 1941 the United States Navy created the Support Force Atlantic Fleet, composed of three squadrons of destroyers and four squadrons of Catalinas and Martin Mariners, to be based on new and exclusively American bases constructed in Northern Ireland (Londonderry) and Scotland. The making of joint arrangements between an American team, led by Admiral Ghormley, and the Admiralty for setting up and operating the new bases signified another step along the road to complete comradeship-in-arms, even though Ghormley emphasised the importance politically of keeping US and British forces distinct both in organisation and tasks.[41]

In April 1941 Roosevelt extended the zone covered by the Western Hemisphere Neutrality Patrol eastwards to 26°W, which included most of Greenland where the United States had just acquired the right to establish bases. Within this zone American warships would report the position of sighted U-boats to the Admiralty but not attack them themselves. Next month Roosevelt transferred a carrier and four destroyers from the Pacific to the Atlantic via the Panama Canal, soon followed by three battleships, four cruisers and fourteen destroyers. He proposed to the British government that American forces should assume the defence of Iceland in place of British forces, although it was not until 7 July that this was carried out. That month also American forces took over the Canadian harbour at Argentia, Newfoundland, and began to develop it into a major naval base which was operational in August, when it served as the rendezvous for the first summit conference between Churchill (who had crossed the Atlantic in the new battleship HMS *Prince of Wales*) and Roosevelt (embarked in the cruiser USS *Augusta*).

At this conference Roosevelt agreed to implement the at present shelved American 'Western Hemisphere Defence Plan Number 4', by which United States warships would assume responsibility for escorting North Atlantic convoys west of 26°. Churchill in reporting this to the Cabinet described the decision as this 'unparalleled gesture of friendship by a neutral power'[42] and hoped that the measure would be implemented by the end of the month. 'The President's orders to these escorts,' he told his colleagues, 'were to attack any U-boat which showed itself, even if it were 200 or 300 miles away from the convoy. Admiral Stark [the US Chief of Naval Operations] intended to carry out this order literally, and any commander who sank a U-boat would have his action approved. Everything was to be done to force an "incident".'[43] But in the event it was German action which gave Roosevelt the political pretext finally to carry out his promise.

On 4 September the destroyer USS *Greer* was attacked by the U-boat which it had been tracking, and counter-attacked it with depth-charges. That same day Roosevelt exploited this incident in one of his famous radio 'fireside chats' to the nation as an opportunity and a justification for announcing that henceforth the US Navy would protect all merchant ships 'of any flag' within American defensive waters.[44] Although Roosevelt did not say so on the radio, 'American defensive waters' were now extended to 10°W, little more than 400 miles from the west coast of Scotland. On 16 September, and for the first time, a British convoy (the homeward bound HX150 of 50 ships) sailed under United States Navy escort.

In conformity with the newly agreed division of responsibility in the North Atlantic, the US ships took over from the Royal Canadian Navy at the 'Western Ocean Meeting Points' 150 miles south of Argentia and handed on the convoy to the Royal Navy at the 'Mid-Ocean Meeting Points' south of Iceland in about 58°N, 22°W.[45] By now too United States Navy Catalinas and the United States Army Air Corps B-29s based on Argentia were working closely with the Royal Canadian Air Force over the Western Atlantic, while other Catalinas had been stationed in Iceland to work with Coastal Command.

For the Royal Navy this final commitment of the United States Navy to the Battle of the Atlantic signified an immense lightening of the burden. As Captain Roskill, the British official naval historian, writes, what it meant 'to the Admiralty, to the Flag Officers, to the captains and crews of the ships and aircraft who had for so long fought this vital and unending struggle alone, may not be easily realised by posterity'.[46] Yet the glory and the achievement of that successful lone struggle belonged to the little but growing Royal Canadian Navy and Royal Canadian Air Force as well as to the Royal Navy and the Royal Air Force. And Canada's great port of Halifax had served – as it would continue to serve – as the rendezvous and departure point for the convoys which in constant progression bore the North American supplies across the ocean to Britain, without which she could neither wage war nor even live. Canada had been, and would remain, the essential western buttress of Britain's Atlantic bridge.

Now it was November 1941 and for two months Dönitz had been fighting three navies instead of two. His patrol lines of U-boats proved even less lucky in trawling targets than in October, no matter how he altered their search tactics, thanks to GC and CS's now complete ability to read the 'Home Waters' Enigma key at short delay. On 22 November Dönitz ordered all his Atlantic boats to concentrate in the waters off Gibraltar, thereby acknowledging the decisive defeat of his first major wolf-pack offensive in the Battle of the Atlantic. In the whole of November his boats sank only thirteen ships of 62,196 tons.

(Above) 'The stolid rectangular lines . . . belied their fighting effectiveness' – HMS *King George V*, name ship of the new class of battleships laid down during pre-war rearmament: 36,570 tons displacement (44,000 tons full load), ten 14-inch guns. (IWM)

(Top left) Admiral Sir Max Horton *(left)*, Commander-in-Chief, Western Approaches 1942–45 – 'He matched Dönitz in ruthless will to win.' Admiral Sir John Tovey *(right)*, Commander-in-Chief, Home Fleet, 1940–43 – 'a hardened steel integrity'. (Crown copyright) *(Top, right)* A. V. Alexander, First Lord of the Admiralty 1940–45, Labour MP for Hillsborough. He gave no trouble either to the Prime Minister or to the First Sea Lord. (IWM) *(Below)* 'The vast armada of escort carriers . . . that would traverse the oceans in coming years derived from *Audacity*.' HMS *Audacity* (5,500 tons), carrying six Grumman Martlet fighters; commissioned September 1941, sunk December 1941. (IWM)

bove) 'Stout fighting ships alike in the freezing gales the Arctic, the huge seaways of the Atlantic, and the ıe, brilliant, bomber-infested Mediterranean' – HMS *effield,* a 'Town' class cruiser laid down during the e-war rearmament period, 9,100 tons displacement, elve 6-inch guns; here escorting convoy KMF 1 to the orch' landings in North Africa, November 1942. (IWM)

(Below) 'A new generation of bigger destroyers which mounted eight 4.7-inch guns in twin turrets . . . on a 1,850 tons displacement' – HMS *Ashanti* of the 'Tribal' class launched from 1937 onwards. The *Ashanti* served with distinction escorting convoys in the Arctic (she is pictured in Hvalfjord, Iceland, in 1942) and the Mediterranean. (IWM)

'The new class of vessel specially designed for convoy work, the Hunt class of 900–1,000-ton destroyers, were not due to be commissioned until 1941.' HMS *Ledbury (above)* on completion in early 1942. (IWM) *(Below)* 'Almost useless as ocean escorts in winter owing to their excessive rolling and lack of manoeuvrability' – HMS *Bluebell*, a 'Flower' class corvette (925 tons). Despite their shortcomings the Flowers were the workhorses of the Battle of the Atlantic. (IWM)

(*bove*) 'An entirely novel
eapons system for destroying the
'rpitz' – X-craft midget submarine
0 tons; 51 feet long; 6½ knots on
e surface and 5 knots submerged;
ew of three volunteers). On 22
eptember 1943 three X-craft put
e battleship *Tirpitz* out of action
r six months. (Crown) (*Inset*)
'heir experiences might have
ome from a boy's adventure story.'
ieutenant B. C. G. Place, RN,
ommander of the X7, was awarded
e VC for his part in crippling the
'irpitz in its Norwegian anchorage.
IWM) (*Right*) 'The same game of
unt and be hunted as in the Battle
f the Atlantic, but with the roles
eversed.' Lieutenant-Commander
1. D. Wanklyn, VC, and crew of
IMS *Upholder,* one of the British
ıbmarines preying on Axis
hipping in the Mediterranean in
940–43. (IWM)

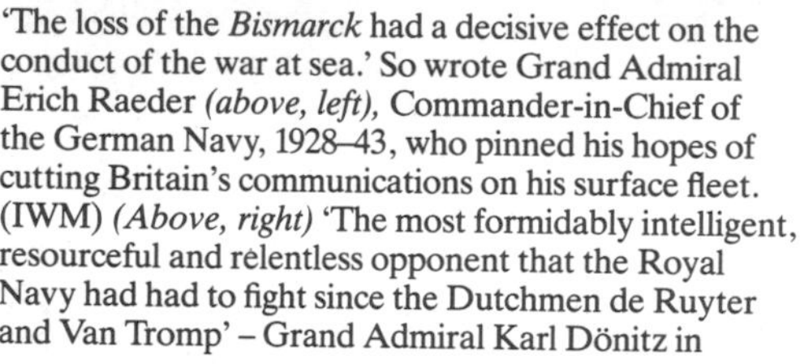

'The loss of the *Bismarck* had a decisive effect on the conduct of the war at sea.' So wrote Grand Admiral Erich Raeder *(above, left),* Commander-in-Chief of the German Navy, 1928–43, who pinned his hopes of cutting Britain's communications on his surface fleet. (IWM) *(Above, right)* 'The most formidably intelligent, resourceful and relentless opponent that the Royal Navy had had to fight since the Dutchmen de Ruyter and Van Tromp' – Grand Admiral Karl Dönitz in command of the U-boat arm, 1936–43; C-in-C of the German Navy 1943–45. On the left is Albert Speer, Reichsminister for Armaments, who kept U-boat construction rising despite Allied bombing. (IWM) *(Below)* 'Oceanic submersible Volkswagens, rugged and reliable.' A 750-ton Type VII U-boat, with a range on the surface of 10,000 miles and 130 miles submerged. It carried five torpedo tubes and twelve torpedoes. (IWM)

The *Scharnhorst (above)* was brought to three hours' notice for steam.' The German fast battleship, sister ship to the *Gneisenau (below),* carried nine 11-inch guns on 31,800 tons displacement. These formidable surface raiders shared a dramatic dash up-channel from Brest to the German ports in February 1942. *Scharnhorst* was sunk by the Home Fleet off Norway's North Cape on 26 December 1943. (IWM)

'*Bismarck*'s vast hull carried formidable weapons systems.' At 52,600 tons full load, a speed of 30.8 knots and eight 15-inch guns, she was one-fifth heavier, three knots faster, and more heavily gunned than the King George V class, but less well armoured. (IWM) (*Inset*) Vice-Admiral Günther Lütjens, commander of her

In December, when his strength in the Atlantic had been reduced to a mere 27 boats by further diversions to the Mediterranean at Hitler's insistence, sinkings in all waters stood at 26 ships of 124,070 tons – barely more than half the tonnage of December 1940, and achieved at the cost of ten U-boats.[47]

The Royal Navy had also been experimenting successfully with ingenious new means of defending convoys against the Focke-Wulf Condors of KG 40. In December 1940 the first fighter catapult ship, HMS *Pegasus*, converted from a Great War seaplane carrier, had gone to sea with a convoy. She carried three Fulmar fighters. In April 1941 she was followed by three more 'Fighter Catapult Ships' (as they were now designated), *Springbank*, *Maplin* and *Ariguani*, each converted from a merchantman to carry one fighter. A fourth conversion, the *Patria*, was sunk before she could embark her aircraft. By July all the fighter catapult ships were deployed on the Gibraltar convoy route, favourite hunting territory for the Kondors, and on 3 August a Kondor crew was astonished to be attacked and shot down 400 miles out to sea from the Iberian coast by a fighter whose proper habitat lay in the sky over England. The Hurricane (piloted by Lieutenant R. W. H. Everett, RNVR) had in fact been catapulted from the *Maplin*.

A start had also been made in April in fitting catapults to fifty merchantmen to be known as 'Catapult Aircraft Merchantmen' ('CAM ships'), and they began to go into service in the early summer. Unlike the fighter catapult ships, the CAM ships remained merchantmen plying under the Red Ensign, their crews merchant seamen except for the pilot (seconded from Royal Air Force Fighter Command) and for the maintenance staff of their single Hurricane. The pilots flying from both kinds of catapult ship had to be exceptionally brave men because there was no means of recovering them at the end of a sortie except by fishing them from the sea after they had parachuted from their aircraft or landed in the water – which was fortunately achieved in the case of Lieutenant Everett. Sadly the *Springbank* was sunk in September during the U-boat onslaught on convoy HG73, while in the following month the *Ariguani* was badly damaged.

In September was commissioned HMS *Audacity*, the prototype of the light escort aircraft carrier. It marked one of the most significant developments in the history of maritime airpower. The *Audacity* (5,527 tons; 15 knots)[48] had been converted from a German prize, the merchant ship *Hannover*, by installing a simple flight deck above the hull; she carried six American Grumman Martlet fighters (maximum speed at 19,400 feet, 318 mph).[49] Employed on the Gibraltar route, she provided, in Dönitz's rueful words, 'a continuous air umbrella'[50] which deprived the Kondors of their ability to shadow British convoys for the benefit of U-boats or themselves bomb hapless strays. A Martlet from *Audacity* (Commander D. W. McKendrick, RN) bagged her first Condor during a major convoy battle on 20–21 September. In December *Audacity*'s aircraft played a key role in the defeat of a mass U-boat attack on convoy HG76 by driving off the shadowing Kondors (downing two of them), attacking surfaced U-boats and reporting back their positions. It was thanks to the combined efforts of *Audacity*'s aircraft and the surface escorts that four U-boats were destroyed for the loss of only two merchant ships; a notable tactical victory. But she herself succumbed to a torpedo on the night of 19 December, when against the advice of the convoy escort commander, Commander F. J. Walker, RN, she was steaming outside the convoy's defensive screen.

Nevertheless *Audacity* had proved the point – the escort carrier offered the real answer to the marauding Kondor. More than that, it vindicated the War Cabinet Battle of the Atlantic Committee's far-sighted judgment in May 1941 in being 'deeply impressed' with the anti-U-boat potential of the escort carrier, and in looking ahead to the day when *Audacity* (having defeated the Kondor) would carry Torpedo-Spotter-Reconnaissance aircraft in order 'to provide a convoy with its own anti-submarine air patrols'.[51] In the event this development fell not to *Audacity*, but to her successors, of which five were on order in 1941 from British yards, and seven more in American yards under Lend-Lease, all bigger than *Audacity* and, unlike her, equipped with hangars. The vast armada of escort carriers, the majority of them American-built, that would traverse the oceans in coming years derived from *Audacity*. She and the other 1941 experiments in the air defence of convoys brilliantly demonstrated that the creative imagination which had inspired the Royal Navy to pioneer the aircraft carrier itself during the Great War was still in successful flight.

When the final balance sheet for 1941 in the Battle of the Atlantic came to be struck, it showed that 496 ships totalling 2,421,700 tons had been sunk by all forms of German attack – U-boat, surface raider and bomber. The total for all theatres came to 4,328,558 tons – awful enough, but far short of the Joint Planners' fear back in June that 7 million tons could well be lost by the end of the year.[52] Britain's jugular vein had been temporarily squeezed, not severed. Yet for all the endurance and professional skill of the crews of His Majesty's ships and aircraft and of the Merchant Marine on the high seas, the decisive instrument of the deliverance lay in the teams of civilians in the quiet huts of Bletchley Park who had broken Dönitz's Enigma cypher. To them for the time being belonged the place of honour on 'the right of the line'.[53]

For Dönitz himself, meditating the failure of his 1941 campaign, the only certain figure was that he had lost 35 U-boats in the course of the year. No wonder that, in his own words, 1941 came to an end 'in an atmosphere of worry and anxiety for U-boat Command'.[54]

In the meantime Grand Admiral Raeder, his Commander-in-Chief, had made his climactic effort to fulfil his own long-cherished strategy of breaking down Britain's sea communications by means of powerful raiding forces of surface warships. In contrast to the endless grinding attrition between U-boat and convoy, this had been an episode imbued with all the elements of an ancient Nordic saga – perilous questings through ice-girded and mist-shrouded seas; bloody combat and heroic death; the strivings of men and the workings of fate.

10

'The Bismarck *Must Be Sunk At All Costs'*

Towards noon (German time) on 18 May 1941 the battleship *Bismarck* (Captain Ernst Lindemann), flying the flag of Vice-Admiral Günther Lütjens, cast off from her moorings alongside the wharf of the Baltic naval base of Gotenhafen and moved slowly away into the roadstead. As the 150,000 horsepower Brown-Boveri turbines hummed deep down in the ship, the band on the quarterdeck played 'Muss i denn', the traditional German military song of departure on a campaign; the one sung by Ludendorff's soldiers 23 years earlier as they marched up to the line for the great 1918 March offensive on the Western Front. For an astute observer on shore here was a clue that this time *Bismarck* was sailing on more than another training exercise. During the next eight hours *Bismarck* lay at anchor out in the roadstead completing the loading of supplies and fuel. Unfortunately the rupturing of an oil fuelling pipe prevented her tanks being topped to capacity. At 0200 on 19 May, she weighed anchor and steamed westwards for the Kattegat and the North Sea, rendezvousing in the forenoon with the heavy cruiser *Prinz Eugen* (Captain Helmuth Brinkmann; 14,800 tons displacement, eight 8-inch guns) and an escort of three destroyers.

'Operation Rheinübung' ('Rhine Exercise') was under way.

Grand Admiral Raeder had been maturing the strategic concept underlying 'Rheinübung' since the Atlantic raids undertaken by the battleships *Scharnhorst* and *Gneisenau* and the cruiser *Hipper* at the end of 1940 (see above, pp. 73–6). In January 1941 he had sent the two battleships to sea on another joint foray under Lütjens's command. Baulked by British counter-moves from breaking through into the Atlantic by the direct route between Iceland and the Shetlands, Lütjens had skilfully doubled back, rounded the north of Iceland and reached the Atlantic sea routes via the Denmark Strait. His first encounter was with Convoy HX106, escorted by the unmodernised old battleship *Ramillies*. True to his instructions to avoid embroilment with British heavy ships, Lütjens fled as soon as *Ramillies*'s funnel was seen to emit dark smoke, suggesting that she was working up to full speed in order to engage. In the scornful words of a German naval historian: 'The ancient *Ramillies* had only to let off a few angry puffs of smoke and both German battleships despite their modern fire-control and the proven effectiveness of their guns, even at long range – sought safety in escape.'[1]

From then on Lütjens's ships had ranged as far south as Sierra Leone and as far west and north as waters near Halifax, and they, along with the pocket battleship *Scheer* in the Indian Ocean and the *Hipper* on the Azores route, sank or captured 48 ships totalling nearly 270,000 tons by the end of March, when they all returned to port – *Scharnhorst*, *Gneisenau* and *Hipper* to Brest; *Scheer* to Kiel. And, just as in the previous year, the disruption to British sea communications, the strain on the Royal Navy of searching for the elusive raiders and at the same time striving to protect the trade routes from attack, had been out of all proportion to the size of force employed. At this period too no fewer than six German merchant raiders were hunting as far afield as the Antarctic, East Africa and the waters between South America and South Africa, so adding enormously to the strain and disruption. All these prolonged and distant cruises of warships were made possible by the advanced posting of supply ships and oiltankers in various sea areas, at a period when the Royal Navy, lacking fleet trains, remained leashed to fixed naval bases; a heavy handicap.

Raeder now believed therefore that in the near future he could 'strike the British supply system a mortal blow'.[2] For the new battleship *Bismarck* was already nearly worked up, while her sister ship *Tirpitz* had joined her in the Gulf of Danzig in April for her own working-up. What might not be achieved by a raiding task force composed of these two ships (the most powerful in the world except for the two Japanese *Yamatos*) and the proven veterans *Scharnhorst* and *Gneisenau*? Wrote Raeder in a directive on 2 April 1941: 'As soon as the two battleships of the Bismarck class are ready for deployment, we will be able to seek engagement with the forces escorting enemy convoys and, when they have been eliminated, destroy the convoy itself.'[3]

However, he was not prepared to wait for *Tirpitz* to finish working up: 'As of now, we cannot follow this course [of deploying both new battleships], but it will soon be possible, as an intermediate step, for us to use the battleship *Bismarck* to distract the hostile escorting forces, in order to enable the other units engaged to operate against the convoy itself.'[4] Unfortunately the *Scharnhorst* and *Gneisenau* were at present in the dockyard in Brest undergoing refits – in *Scharnhorst*'s case, a major overhaul of her engines which meant that she would not be ready for sea until June. All this much reduced the scope of Raeder's plans:

> At the earliest possible date, which it is hoped will be during the new-moon period of April, the *Bismarck* and the *Prinz Eugen*, led by the Fleet Commander, are to be deployed as commerce-raiders in the Atlantic. The *Gneisenau* will also be sent into the Atlantic, but that will depend on when her repairs have been completed.[5]

At this point Royal Air Force Coastal Command intervened. On 6 April at first light a Beaufort torpedo aircraft of No. 22 Squadron, commanded by Flying Officer K. Campbell, skimming the sea below masthead level and just clearing the mole, pressed home an attack on the *Gneisenau* in the inner harbour of Brest to loose a torpedo at a range of only 500 yards. The Beaufort crashed into the ground after being riddled with concentrated anti-aircraft fire, killing the heroic Campbell and his crew of three. But even before they died, their torpedo had wrecked *Gneisenau*'s stern. Six days later, when she had been moved into dry dock Bomber Command, in one of its interventions in the naval war, hit her with four bombs. Raeder's grand design had now shrunk to the *Bismarck* and *Prinz Eugen*.

It was Lütjens's opinion, as the force commander designate, expressed to Raeder at a briefing in Berlin on 26 April, that there was 'a powerful case for waiting until at least the *Scharnhorst* has been repaired – if not until the crew of the *Tirpitz* have finished their training'.[6] Raeder disagreed: the approach of short summer nights, the danger that America might enter the war in the future, the need to keep the momentum going in the Atlantic battle, the need to divert British naval strength from the Mediterranean, all these factors argued in his view for action without delay. Convinced or otherwise, Lütjens acquiesced obediently. Hitler himself, when briefed on 5 May aboard the *Bismarck*, did not prohibit the operation even though he had his doubts, especially with regard to the danger of air attack.

Lütjens's operational brief from OKM (*Oberkommando der Kriegsmarine*) was true to the ambiguous pattern of earlier German raiding, and the very reverse of the deep instinct of the Royal Navy to 'engage the enemy more closely' whenever possible: 'Once again the primary objective is the destruction of the enemy's carrying capacity. Enemy warships will be engaged only in furtherance of this objective, and provided such engagements *can take place without excessive risk*.'[7] Lütjens finally went to sea in *Bismarck* in a mood of sombre duty, even fatalistic acceptance of death to come.[8]

For he was far from the British model of extrovert admiral exemplified by such men as Andrew Cunningham and James Somerville; rather he was a man as tightly buttoned up as his uniform jacket. His taciturn and aloof manner, severe visage relieved only by full, strongly carved lips, and intense, even troubled, gaze, all suggested a deeply serious professional; one anxious – perhaps over-anxious – not to fail in his duty. The Captain of the *Bismarck*, Ernst Lindemann, cool, competent and devoted though he was, might rather have been taken for a chief engineer or accountant in a German industrial cartel than for a fighting sailor, with sharp, pale eyes in a sharp face, grimly zealous, and his straight, oiled hair brushed flat to a narrow, big-eared head. Thus, although Lütjens's and Lindemann's mission rendered them latter-day pirates or corsairs, neither man was blessed with the adventuring temperament or the personal magic of a Francis Drake, a Bailli de Suffren or a John Paul Jones – or, for that matter, one of Dönitz's young U-boat aces.

Like every member of his ships' companies, Lütjens was very conscious that *Bismarck* and *Prinz Eugen* were about to brave the power and wrath of what was still one of the world's two greatest seapowers; aware that their first success would draw a swarm of battleships, aircraft carriers and cruisers into a hunt for them. But Lütjens and Lindemann and all their sailors put their faith in the *Bismarck* herself, as formidable a fighting ship as German technology could contrive, and, at 52,600 tons full load, a fifth heavier than the Royal Navy's new battleships *King George V* and *Prince of Wales*. From clipper bow to cruiser stern *Bismarck* was 823½ feet long; the rakish sweep of her superstructure up to her fighting top and cowled funnel the very expression of speed and power. Her beam of 118 feet compared with the 103 feet of the King George Vs and the 108 feet of the new American Iowa class battleships. A main armoured belt 12.6 inches thick, and horizontal deck armour 4½ inches thick protected her magazines and machinery, along with an internal 'bulge' of oil and water storage compartments on beams against torpedoes. *Bismarck*'s 150,000 horsepower turbines driving three shafts (uprated from an original 138,000 horsepower) gave her a maximum speed of 30.8 knots, as against *King George V*'s 27.5 knots; her range (providing that her oil tanks had been filled to the brim) was 8,000 miles at a cruising speed of 19 knots. A novel feature of her design lay in her twin rudders, but when a training exercise postulated that the rudders had been jammed by damage, it had been found to be very difficult to keep the ship on course by steering with the propellers.

Bismarck's vast hull carried formidable weapons systems. Her main battery of eight 15-inch guns in twin turrets (protected by armour up to 14 inches thick) compared with *King George V*'s ten 14-inch guns. She inherited from her Great War predecessors the proven excellence of Zeiss stereoscopic range-finders. These were mounted in revolving cupolas above the three armoured fire-control stations – forward of the bridge, in the foretop above the bridge, and aft. Attached to these cupolas were the mattress-like latticework aerials of the radar sets which could supply accurate ranges in pitch dark or foul weather. Ranges and bearings (the latter provided by the directors: periscope-like optical devices protruding through the top of the fire-control stations) were fed into a computing system comparable to the British fire-control clock, which then locked the 15-inch guns on target. Following the system employed with such success by Hipper's battle-cruisers at Jutland and since adopted by the Royal Navy too, *Bismarck*'s gunners were practised at opening fire with a 'bracketing group' of salvoes, three in the air at the same time separated by fixed range, usually 400 yards. As a gunnery officer in the ship wrote later of such training practices, 'we usually succeeded in boxing or straddling the target on the first fall of shot'[9]; the result of accurate ranging thanks to superb range-finders.

As well as her main battery, *Bismarck* was equipped with a secondary (anti-destroyer) armament of twelve 5.9-inch guns in twin turrets, a heavy anti-aircraft battery of sixteen 4.1-inch guns in twin turrets, plus sixteen 37mm anti-aircraft guns (also in twin turrets), plus again thirty-six 20mm light anti-aircraft guns.[10] Some experts have argued that *Bismarck* was old-fashioned in having both a 5.9-inch secondary armament against surface targets and a 4.1-inch heavy anti-aircraft battery, instead of a weight-saving dual-purpose secondary armament like the sixteen 5.25-inch guns carried by the King George Vs. Yet in action *Bismarck* was to use her 5.9s against aircraft as well as her 4.1s. Moreover, her anti-aircraft armament enjoyed no fewer than six separate director controls, so giving flexibility in acquiring targets.

Experts have equally argued that the designers of *Bismarck* had followed an outmoded Great War pattern of widely distributing the armour over the hull instead of the more modern 'all or nothing' technique practised by British and American designers, whereby the given weight of armour was concentrated over the vital spaces, leaving the rest of the hull unprotected (which in the case of the King George Vs, gave a maximum thickness of armour in the main belt of 15 inches to *Bismarck*'s 12.6, and 6-inch horizontal deck armour over the magazine to the German ship's 4½ inches.[11] But needless to say, no such cavils troubled the minds of Lütjens, Lindemann and the ship's company as they steamed westwards through the Baltic from Gotenhafen on 19 May 1941 in hopeful expectation of a successful foray.

Next day, shimmeringly bright, found the squadron passing through the Great Belt between Denmark and Sweden; the destroyers in the van, then the huge *Bismarck* with Lütjens's flag of a black Maltese cross on a white ground at her peak and *Prinz Eugen* (named after Prince Eugène, Marlborough's devoted Austrian comrade during the War of the Spanish Succession) following astern. On the starboard beam in clear sight lay the Swedish coast, and around the great grey ships a bright green sea bobbed with busy fishing boats. By now the ship's company of the *Bismarck* (2,200 strong, counting extra Luftwaffe personnel to operate her three aircraft) knew their mission, for Captain Lindemann had told them over the tannoy the previous day that they were setting forth on a three-month cruise in the Atlantic to devastate British convoys. He ended his address with the traditional German hunter's toast: 'Good hunting and a good bag!'[12]

At 1300 another warship appeared to starboard and for a time steamed on a parallel course: it was the Swedish cruiser *Gotland*. Lütjens therefore signalled Group North (the German naval command responsible for all operations north of the English Channel): 'At 1300 the aircraft-carrying cruiser *Gotland* passed in clear view, therefore anticipate formation will be reported.' But the C-in-C Group North, General-Admiral Rolf Carls, complacently replied: 'Because of the strictly neutral conduct of Sweden, I do not think the danger of being compromised by the Swedish warship is any greater than from the already present systematic enemy surveillance of the entrance to the Baltic.'[13]

In fact, a member of the Swedish naval staff passed the information the same day to his friend the Norwegian military attaché in Stockholm, who passed it straight to the British naval attaché, who reported it to the Admiralty at 2100 (British time) that night. The report tied in ominously with information previously derived from decrypts of the Luftwaffe Enigma that Condors had been carrying out unusually intense reconnaissance of the ice edge between Jan Mayen Island and Greenland.[14] These decrypts had already spurred the C-in-C, Home Fleet, Admiral Sir John Tovey, to instruct ships patrolling the Denmark Strait to heighten their vigilance, and in particular to order the cruiser HMS *Suffolk* specially to watch the waters along the ice edge. Now the Admiralty asked that Coastal Command photo-reconnaissance Spitfires based at Wick in northern Scotland should reconnoitre the Norwegian coast in order to locate the German squadron. Just two hours after *Bismarck* and *Prinz Eugen* anchored in Bergen fjord at 1100 hours on 21 May (British time, which will be henceforth used throughout the account of the pursuit of the *Bismarck*), one of the Spitfires, piloted by Flying Officer Suckling, was high overhead with its camera busy. At 1828 the Admiralty Operational Intelligence Centre alerted all naval commands to the discovery recorded on the returned Spitfire's film, adding: 'It is evident that these ships intend to carry out a raid on trade routes.'[15]

In Scapa Flow Admiral Sir John Tovey brought the flagship *King George V* (Captain W. R. Patterson) and the 2nd Cruiser Squadron (Rear-Admiral A. T. Curteis: *Galatea*, *Aurora*, *Kenya* and *Neptune*) to short notice for steam. He instructed Rear-Admiral W. F. Wake-Walker, commanding 1st Cruiser Squadron (*Norfolk* and *Suffolk*) to continue watching the Denmark Strait, and Vice-Admiral L. E. Holland (commanding the Battle Cruiser Force, and flying his flag in the 42,000-ton battlecruiser *Hood*) to sail with *Hood*, the battleship *Prince of Wales* and the destroyers *Electra*, *Anthony*, *Echo*, *Achates* and *Antelope* in order to cover *Norfolk* and *Suffolk*. At 0050 on 22 May *Hood* led the Battle Cruiser Force out past the Hoxa boom and set course for Denmark Strait. Tovey also ordered the cruisers *Manchester* and *Birmingham*, at present on patrol between Iceland and the Faeroes, to refuel at Skalfjord in Iceland and resume their watch. The battlecruiser *Repulse* and the new fleet carrier *Victorious* had been due to sail on 22 May as escort to the Middle East troop convoy; now the Admiralty placed them instead at the disposal of the C-in-C, Home Fleet.

While all this bustle of orders and sailings and redeployments was in train, Lütjens was oiling *Prinz Eugen* in Bergen from the tanker *Wollin*, but surprisingly failing to oil *Bismarck* herself which had sailed from Gotenhafen with tanks not completely full, and which had burnt about a ninth of her full-load capacity in the course of the voyage to Norway. It is true that Lütjens knew that there was an oiler, the

Weissenburg, waiting for him in the Arctic a day or so away; nevertheless it seems strangely neglectful not to take every opportunity to top up *Bismarck*'s tanks during so hazardous a venture. In any event, Lütjens's decision to call in at Bergen at all, overturning his previous decision to head straight for the Arctic and the *Weissenburg*, can be questioned,[16] for it lost him a day and also exposed him to possible detection by the frequent British air surveillance of the Norwegian coastline – which in the event is what happened, as Lütjens himself was well aware, the photo-reconnaissance Spitfire having been belatedly spotted by the German ships. Perhaps he had taken too much assurance from a Luftwaffe photo-reconnaissance report the previous day that three heavy ships (*King George V*, *Prince of Wales* and *Hood*) and a carrier (*Victorious*) were at that time all still at anchor in Scapa Flow.

At 1945 on the 21st Lütjens put to sea again and set a course due north at 24 knots, detaching the destroyers to Trondheim in the small hours of the 22nd. By 2100 that day *Bismarck* and *Prinz Eugen* were in 68°N, 3°W, in the same latitude as the Denmark Strait north of Iceland, and steaming westwards towards it. In choosing this circuitous course, he had ignored the advice of Group North to steer directly for the Atlantic between Iceland and the Faeroes; he had also decided not to go further north still in order to refuel from the *Weissenburg*. Like his predecessor Admiral Scheer on his way to Jutland in May 1916, Lütjens had no idea that strong British forces were already at sea to intercept him (in Lütjens's case, the *Hood* and *Prince of Wales*), although he did know from signals from Group North (drawing on German Intelligence sources) that his departure from Gotenhafen and passage of the Kattegat had been detected and that the British had ordered air searches for him. That very evening Group North had even confirmed to him from further Luftwaffe photo-reconnaissance that the main body of the Home Fleet still remained in Scapa Flow.

For Tovey and the Admiralty the time since the Spitfire photo-reconnaissance aircraft had radioed at 1300 on 21 May that *Bismarck* and *Prinz Eugen* were in Bergen fjord had passed in anxious and baffled waiting for news as to whether or not they had subsequently put to sea again. An attempt to find and bomb the German ships in Bergen fjord on that afternoon miscarried in dense fog. Daylight on the 22nd brought even worse weather, with cloud over the North Sea down to 200 feet. Up in the Denmark Strait the cloud was unbroken down to 300 feet, with curtains of rain closing visibility to less than half a mile, so that reconnaissance aircraft could see nothing. However, the commanding officer at the Fleet Air Arm station at Hatston in the

Orkneys, Captain H. L. S. J. Fancourt, decided on his own initiative to send a Glenn Martin Maryland twin-engined reconnaissance aircraft to look for the *Bismarck* and *Prinz Eugen* along the Norwegian coastline.

The Maryland was piloted by Lieutenant (A) N. N. Goddard, RNVR, and crewed as usual by Lieutenants Armstrong and Milne. Lieutenant G. A. ('Hank') Rotherham (then flying a desk as second-in-command of the station) volunteered to fill the vacant job of Observer. The aircraft crossed the North Sea flying either beneath the clouds at heights down to 50 feet or above the clouds at 3,000 feet. Over the Norwegian coast the sky cleared, allowing Goddard to descend to 1,000 feet and begin his search. In Rotherham's words:

> We ran up inside the fjords to the anchorage [at Bergen], but it was bare. After we had circled to look into all of the possible holes and corners to be sure we hadn't overlooked anything I directed Noel over Bergen Harbour to see if she had moved there. This was too much for the Germans and they opened up with everything they had. We shot across the harbour and out to sea losing height as we went . . .[17]

In confirming that 'Bergen was clear' they supplied the key piece of information which the C-in-C, Home Fleet, needed; and Tovey later showed his appreciation by writing in his despatch: 'This skilful and determined reconnaissance is deserving of the highest praise, as is the initiative of Captain Fancourt in ordering it.'[18] Rotherham's report reached Tovey in his flagship at 2000 that evening of the 22nd. It then fell to Tovey, studying the charts with his staff, to guess the enemy's present course and deploy the Home Fleet accordingly.

It was the first of all the consequence-laden choices that would fall to him in the coming week as the admiral bearing the greatest single responsibility for catching and destroying Lütjens before he could disappear into the wide Atlantic. Tovey – small, lean-featured, straight of nose and mouth, eyes blue beneath hooded lids; a tough face sometimes set in resolute purpose, sometimes sparkling with humour – was well-equipped by character, experience and judgment to bear that responsibility. Like Cunningham, he had been formed by early service in destroyers, commanding HMS *Onslow* in the thick of the Battle of Jutland. Although just as deeply serious a man as his opponent Lütjens, indeed a devout Christian who prayed night and morning, he enjoyed good living and good company. He was liked for his warm and outgoing personality and respected for his forthright leadership. In 1940 Cunningham, a difficult man to please, had appointed Tovey to command all the Mediterranean Fleet's cruisers and destroyers, and later recorded his appreciation of Tovey's 'advice, outspoken criticism, loyal support, cheerful optimism and imperturbability . . .'[19]

At the core of his character lay a hardened steel integrity which forbade him to compromise with what he believed to be wrong. An admiral wrote of him when he was captain of the *Rodney*: 'Captain Tovey shares one characteristic with me. In myself I would call it tenacity of purpose. In Tovey I can only call it sheer bloody obstinacy.'[20] Tovey had demonstrated at his first meeting with the Prime Minister on appointment as C-in-C in December 1940 that his professional integrity was proof even against Churchill. As he confided in a letter to Cunningham, 'You know the PM much better than I do, and you will understand how I loved him almost at first sight, but he made some such astounding statements about naval warfare . . . [that] I still don't know if he was wanting to find out if I was prepared to applaud everything he said or whether he really believes half of what he says.'[21] But in regard to conduct of the pursuit of the *Bismarck*, Tovey was to discover that Churchill could indeed 'really believe' at least one truly astounding Prime Ministerial naval directive.

Although it was always possible that *Bismarck* and *Prinz Eugen* might be making for a port in northern Norway or even steaming to strike British bases in Iceland, Tovey was convinced that their objective must be the obvious one of the Atlantic convoy routes. Yet he had no means of judging whether the enemy ships would pass north or south of Iceland. He therefore signalled the cruiser *Suffolk* to rejoin the *Norfolk* in watching the Denmark Strait and the ice edge off Iceland, and the cruiser *Arethusa* to join *Manchester* and *Birmingham* in forming a patrol line between Iceland and the Faeroes. He requested Coastal Command to supplement these patrols by flying air searches over the Denmark Strait (180 miles across), the Iceland–Faeroes gap (255 miles wide), the Faeroes to the Shetlands (165 miles across) and also the Norwegian coast. He ordered Vice-Admiral Holland with the *Hood* (Captain R. Kerr, RN) and *Prince of Wales* (Captain J. C. Leach, RN) to cover the cruisers in the Denmark Strait north of 62°N, while he himself with the remainder of the Home Fleet would cover the passages south of 62°N.

At 2245 on 22 May 1941, an hour and a half after Lütjens, far to the north, had turned his ships westwards for the Denmark Strait, Tovey in his flagship *King George V* led the carrier *Victorious*, the cruisers *Galatea*, *Aurora*, *Kenya*, *Hermione* and the destroyers *Intrepid*, *Inglefield*, *Punjabi*, *Lance*, *Active* and *Windsor* out of Scapa Flow and headed due west.

The *Victorious* (23,000 tons displacement; 31 knots) had only just been commissioned, for, being a product of belated British rearmament, she was not even launched until eleven days after the outbreak of war. Moreover, when the Admiralty placed her at Tovey's disposal, she had been about to leave for the Middle East crammed with crated Hurricanes, and her available striking force consisted of only nine Swordfish and six Fulmars, while her aircrews lacked training and experience. Tovey's flagship *King George V* (36,750 tons displacement; 44,000 tons full load) was the first British battleship to be commissioned since the 1920s 'naval holiday', having been laid down in January 1937 at the very start of the rearmament programme and completed in December 1940. She had served as a flagship of the Home Fleet for only a month. Compared to the crew of the *Bismarck*, which had been training intensively in the Baltic since August 1940, her ship's company was still relatively raw. Furthermore, her two quadruple 14-inch turrets were of a novel design not yet tried and tested in action. The battlecruiser *Repulse* (27,333 tons displacement; six 15-inch guns), which joined the Fleet from the Clyde off the Butt of Lewis in the forenoon of 23 May, dated from 1916. Despite some strengthening of her weak armour protection in 1919–20 and new anti-aircraft batteries in the late 1930s, she remained essentially unmodernised.

It was hardly an overwhelming force, therefore, that Admiral Tovey was taking to sea to meet the *Bismarck*, either in numbers or in fighting power. Nor was the Battle Cruiser Force under Vice-Admiral Holland, now well on its way to the Denmark Strait, in better case. The battlecruiser *Hood* had been designed before the Battle of Jutland, although her armour protection was improved somewhat as a consequence of that battle. She had been due for radical reconstruction when the Second World War broke out and compelled it to be postponed. Despite her size and majestic appearance, therefore, she still suffered from fundamental weaknesses in armour similar to those of the three battlecruisers lost at Jutland – in particular, main deck armour over the magazines only three inches thick. The *Prince of Wales* (sister ship to *King George V*) had only been completed in March 1941 and still had Vickers's technicians aboard to sort out various teething troubles, especially with her 14-inch turrets.

For Tovey himself, steaming westwards through appalling weather, 23 May was a day of waiting and waiting for news of the vanished enemy. None of the intended air searches could be flown because of cloud and rain, under cover of which Lütjens's ships might have already succeeded in slipping through the Royal Navy's still wide open net. Then at 2032, when the flagship was some 230 miles northwest of the Butt of Lewis in about 60° 20′N, 12° 30′W, came a signal from the *Norfolk* (Captain A. J. L. Phillips, RN). The *Bismarck* had been sighted in the Denmark Strait.

It was in fact Wake-Walker's other ship the *Suffolk* (Captain R. M. Ellis, RN) which saw her first at 1922 as the long Arctic evening began to draw in. Above the ice edge along the Greenland coast and out across the water for some ten miles the weather was clear and bright, while the remainder of the Strait as far as Iceland seventy miles away was shrouded in dense mist. Down that corridor of bright weather (so avoiding the British minefields stretching eastwards to the north cape of Iceland) between the ice edge shining blue-white and the Greenland glaciers on their starboard beam and the abrupt wall of fog lying to port Lütjens's ships had been steaming south-westwards at 27 knots since they left the welcome cover of rain, snow and cloud astern during the afternoon. It was *Suffolk*'s starboard after lookout, Able-Seaman Newall, who spotted the *Bismarck*'s great piled shape seven miles away bearing 020° (about 55 miles north-west of Iceland's North Cape) and then *Prinz Eugen* too.

For the first time during the pursuit of the *Bismarck* the alarm bells clanged through a British warship and the crew rushed and clambered pell-mell to Action Stations, as *Suffolk* radioed her 'enemy report', turned 90° to port and headed at utmost speed for the shelter of the wall of fog. One hour later the *Norfolk*, closing to make contact with the enemy, sighted the *Bismarck* only six miles off, and for the first time *Bismarck*'s great guns boomed out in anger. The *Norfolk*, unscathed, turned away and sent her 'enemy report' at 2032. This reached the Admiralty at 2103, before *Suffolk*'s report had come through, and was immediately broadcast to all ships.

Admiral Tovey now knew that the enemy lay some 600 miles away from his flagship to the north-west; a long haul. He turned the Battle Fleet to 280° and increased speed to 27 knots. Back in London, in the spacious War Room created by knocking together several small offices, the First Sea Lord, the VCNS, (Rear-Admiral T. S. V. Phillips), and the naval staff anxiously studied the operational wall chart of the war at sea in the light of *Norfolk*'s report. No fewer than eleven convoys were at present out in the North Atlantic, six homeward bound and five outward. The most important of these was the convoy of five troopships bound for the Middle East which had left the Clyde the day before escorted by the cruisers *Exeter* and *Cairo* and five destroyers – potentially just a quick breakfast for the *Bismarck*. The

Admiralty therefore made a signal at 0050 on the 24th to Admiral Somerville (Flag Officer, Force H) at Gibraltar to rendezvous with the convoy in 47° 20′N, 26° 05′W. By 0200 Force H (which Somerville had brought to two hours' notice for steam as soon as he received *Norfolk*'s enemy report) was clear of Gibraltar harbour and steaming west at 25 knots: the battlecruiser *Renown* (flag), the carrier *Ark Royal*, the cruiser *Sheffield*, and the destroyers *Faulkner*, *Forester*, *Foresight*, *Foxhound*, *Fury* and *Hesperus*. Lütjens however had been told by Group North that Force H was safely far up the Mediterranean.

In the Denmark Strait on the night of 23–24 May – a spring Arctic night of twilight – the weather had turned foul, with squalls of rain or snow. Yet *Norfolk* and *Suffolk* hung on to the enemy as he steamed at 27 to 28 knots south-westwards, sometimes sighting him looming through the murk, only to lose him again in a squall except as glowing blips on *Suffolk*'s radar screen (*Norfolk* had no radar). As Tovey wrote in his despatch: 'With great skill in very difficult conditions, the cruisers shadowed the enemy as they followed him to the south in a momentous and persistent chase.'[22] When twilight lightened into day on the 24th, the *Bismarck* could be seen about twelve miles to the south. At 0325 she seemed to turn to starboard, so *Suffolk* turned likewise to keep her distance. As she swung it exposed the aircraft on her catapult to the half gale of wind, which caught and crumpled it. At 0445 *Norfolk* intercepted a report from *Icarus*, one of the Battle Cruiser Force's destroyer escort, giving her position: it was only a short distance astern of *Norfolk*. For the first time Rear-Admiral Wake-Walker knew that his two cruisers were no longer alone in the presence of the powerful German ships, but that Vice-Admiral Holland was close at hand with *Hood* and *Prince of Wales*; and half an hour later *Norfolk*'s lookout spotted their smoke on the port bow.

When at 2054 the previous evening Holland had received *Suffolk*'s first report that she had sighted *Bismarck* (placing her about 300 miles away, bearing 5°), he had thereupon turned to 295° and increased speed to 27 knots in order to cut the German squadron off. At 2318 he ordered his six destroyers to form a screen ahead. At midnight came a further report that the enemy was 120 miles distant, bearing 020°, and steering approximately 200°. Eight minutes later Holland reduced the Battle Cruiser Force's speed to 25 knots and altered course to due north to complete the interception. It was a night of moderate swell, the wind Force 4 to 5 from the north. Holland expected that he might make contact with the enemy at any time after 0140 on the 24th; and at 0015 the two British heavy ships hoisted their big battle ensigns and began their final preparations for battle: the transformation of wardrooms into emergency hospitals; the donning of anti-flash white hoods and gloves to protect against burns, and of clean socks and underwear in 'a ritual the British Navy has always observed before battle to prevent wounds from infection'.[23]

Throughout the ships, in hot oil-smelling engine rooms, in the shell-handling rooms and magazines closed tight shut by anti-flash doors, in the cramped 15-inch and 14-inch turrets under their carapaces of steel, in transmitting (fire-control) rooms and high up on the bridge, the small hours were a time of dry-mouthed tension – not least when Wake-Walker's cruisers lost the enemy in a snow storm and the flow of their situation reports dried up. At 0031 Holland signalled the *Prince of Wales* that 'if the enemy was not in sight by 0210 he would probably alter course to 180° until cruisers regained touch and that he intended both ships to engage *Bismarck*, leaving *Prinz Eugen* to *Norfolk* and *Suffolk*'. However, it seems that this signal was not repeated to the cruisers.

Although the *Prince of Wales*'s Walrus biplane amphibian had been readied to take off on a reconnaissance, the weather had so worsened that it was defuelled and stored. Holland now saw little chance of engaging before full daylight and wished to give his crews a chance to rest, so at 0103 he altered away from the enemy to 200°. A mixture of relief and anticlimax swept the ships.[24] At 0247 *Suffolk* regained contact with the enemy and began to report his bearings. At 0353 Vice-Admiral Holland increased speed to 28 knots. At 0400 the *Bismarck* was estimated to lie only twenty miles to the north-west. By 0430, the eager eyes of the lookouts could see up to twelve miles across the now rough and rising sea. The order was given to refuel *Prince of Wales*'s Walrus, but the operation was held up because of water in the petrol, and the action was to begin and the Walrus itself to be damaged and jettisoned overboard before it could be flown off. *Hood* was now steaming at 28 knots on a course of 240°. At 0510 Holland ordered his force to the first degree of readiness; men began again to wind themselves up for battle. Twenty-five minutes later the *Bismarck*'s silhouette was seen on the horizon; she lay seventeen miles distant to the north-west, bearing 335°. Ahead of her could be seen the *Prinz Eugen*, a smaller but very similar silhouette.

For Vice-Admiral Holland the moment had now come to decide his mode of attack, knowing as he did that the *Hood* was vulnerable to German plunging fire smashing through her 1½–3-inch thick unhardened horizontal deck armour, and knowing too that, on the other hand, the *Prince of Wales* was so brand new that neither the ship nor her crew was nearly well enough worked up for so formidable a task as fighting the massive *Bismarck*. Holland himself, a gunnery expert, was both able and ambitious; one officer who knew him well described him as 'that very clever coolheaded Lancelot Holland'.[25] It is clear from his actions that Holland had no doubt that he must immediately engage the *Bismarck* rather than simply support Wake-Walker in shadowing her until Tovey could come up with the Home Fleet – just as Beatty had had no doubt at Jutland that he must immediately engage Hipper's battlecruisers rather than draw them on to Jellicoe and the Grand Fleet.

The parallel does not stop there: Holland like Beatty enjoyed superiority of numbers in heavy ships, but inferiority in actual fighting effectiveness (in Beatty's case, in terms of his battlecruisers). Holland's deployment too was curiously comparable to Beatty's in 1916. Beatty had attacked at high speed and with his ships on a line of bearing that placed the enemy well before the beam, where the midships and after turrets of the British battlecruisers could hardly bear at the moment when both sides opened fire;[26] Holland's final deployment similarly placed *Bismarck* and *Prinz Eugen* too fine on the starboard bow for his ships' after turrets to bear.[27] Beatty in 1916 had placed his lightly armoured battlecruisers in the van, his squadron of powerful Queen Elizabeth battleships in the rear; Holland in 1941 placed the vulnerable old *Hood* ahead of the strongly armoured new *Prince of Wales*. And, finally, Beatty in 1916 had exercised tight tactical control over his Fleet from his flagship; Holland in 1941 did likewise, manoeuvring his two ships together as a single unit in accordance with the centralising 1939 Fighting Instructions drawn up by Pound, rather than permit Captain Leach in *Prince of Wales* to manoeuvre independently and perhaps confuse the enemy by a different line of approach. Why this impetuous and ill-conceived deployment? As that fellow sailor who knew Holland well wrote years later: 'I just can't understand the tactics of the *Hood* action. It's so unlike that very clear coolheaded Lancelot Holland.'[28]

So it was that, at 0537 on 24 May, Holland turned the *Hood* and *Prince of Wales* together by blue pendant 40° to starboard towards the enemy, and four minutes later stationed *Prince of Wales* 080° from *Hood*. At 0549 he altered course to 300° by another blue pendant turn, and designated the left-hand German ship (in fact, the *Prinz Eugen*) as the target by the signal G.S.B. 337L1. The mistake was corrected by the signal G.O.B.1 ('Shift object one right') just before fire was opened. Interestingly enough, there had been comparable confusions over initial targeting in Beatty's force at Jutland. The British ships were now encountering a heavy head sea, which swept green water over the *Prince of Wales*'s low forecastle (a weakness in the design) and spray over her fore turrets – and over *Hood* likewise, a notoriously 'wet' ship. By 0552 the range was down to about 25,000 yards and *Hood*'s 15-inch guns crashed out their first salvo. *Bismarck*, with the British ships well placed on her beam, replied with the same devastatingly immediate accuracy as Hipper's battlecruisers at Jutland (which also had their enemies well placed on the beam) and straddled *Hood* with her second or third salvo, igniting anti-aircraft rockets on deck. According to the Naval Staff Battle Summary, 'A fire broke out in the *Hood* near the port after 4-in gun which quickly spread till the whole midship part seemed to be in flames, burning with a pink glow shrouded in dense smoke.'[29]

The *Prince of Wales* opened fire at 0553 (with only six out of her ten 14-inch guns bearing), her first salvo an 'over' and only her sixth a straddle; not a good performance. But she was contending with heavy handicaps. The large 42-foot main range-finder at the back of 'A' turret and the 35-foot 'Duplex' (two-in-one) range-finder at the back of 'B' turret were both blinded by continuous streams of spray and water as the ship steamed at high speed into the strong wind and rough seas (*Hood*'s main range-finders were similarly mounted down on the turrets). This left only the 15-foot range-finders on the director control tower clear of spray and able to operate, but in terms of accuracy the range was extreme for such small range-finders. Moreover both of *Prince of Wales*'s radars (Type 284 set and Air Warning) had been kept switched off until 'Enemy in sight' as a precaution against detection by the enemy, and so they too could give no range. According to Lieutenant C. G. A. Murphy, RN, then in charge of the main armament transmitting station:

> When 'enemy in sight' was passed to the T.S. I was most anxious for a range of any description, but none was forthcoming from *any* source. The 42 foot R/F in A was largely underwater, the other in Y was not bearing, so I felt entirely dependent on radar. When nothing showed on the dials I ordered the operator to contact the 284 Radar Office by telephone and so far as I can remember from the growing tenseness he was told that Radar was jammed . . . [in fact, by the ship's high-powered radio signalling 'enemy report' to the Admiralty]. At no time during the action did I see a Radar range . . .[30]

The *Prince of Wales* therefore opened fire on the basis of a guesstimate calculated from one range obtained by the 15-foot range-finder on the director control tower.[31]

By now *Prinz Eugen* had joined in with her 8-inch guns, but *Norfolk* and *Suffolk* (also 8-inch gun ships) were too far astern to take part in the action. At 0555 Holland again manoeuvred *Hood* and *Prince of Wales* together by blue pendant, this time two points to port, a change of course which opened *Prince of Wales*'s 'A' arcs. At 0600 *Hood* hoisted a second 'two blue' pendant for another turn two points to port in order to bring the after turrets of both ships fully to bear. The signal fluttered down the halyard, the British ships began to come round, and *Bismarck* fired her fifth salvo. At least one shell, possibly more, plunged down on *Hood*, smashed through her thin deck armour and penetrated deep into her after magazine. *Hood*, for so long the very symbol of British seapower, was now rent in two by 'a huge explosion rising apparently between the after funnel and the main mast. The fore part began to sink separately, bows up, whilst the after part remained shrouded in a pall of smoke. Three or four minutes later, the *Hood* had vanished between the waves, leaving a vast cloud of smoke drifting away to leeward.'[32] She sank in 63° 20′N, 31° 50′W, taking with her Admiral Holland, her captain, Captain Ralph Kerr, RN, and more than 1,400 of her ship's company. There were only three survivors. It was an uncannily exact repetition of the last moments of the three battlecruisers lost at Jutland.

As the *Prince of Wales* violently altered course in order to avoid the wreckage the *Bismarck* swung her guns on to her. At a range now of only 18,000 yards *Bismarck*'s 5.9s were in action as well as her eight 15-inch; and within a very short time she had hit *Prince of Wales* with four heavy shells and three smaller. At 0602 a 15-inch shell (which did not explode) wrecked *Prince of Wales*' bridge, killing or wounding most of those present; at the same time another heavy shell holed her hull aft and let in 400 tons of water. At 0613 with the range down to 14,500 yards Captain Leach turned her away to 160° behind a smoke screen. As she swung, the after quadruple 14-inch turret (with a total revolving weight of about 1,500 tons) jammed on its ring; an untimely 'teething trouble' with a novel design in action for the first time. Despite the efforts of the members of the crew and Vickers's technicians to free the turret, its four guns were not all operational again until 0825.[33]

During the action – which, incredibly, had only lasted some twenty minutes – *Prince of Wales* had fired eighteen salvoes from her main armament and five from her secondary. And the *Bismarck* had not gone unscathed: one 14-inch shell passed right through her hull forward, causing her to ship 2,000 tons of water and forcing her to reduce speed, and also springing an oil leak which left a slick astern and further depleted her fuel reserves, while a second hit damaged a generator room and an engine room.

In the light of the destruction of the *Hood* both sides had now to consider their future courses of action. In the German ships there was tremendous elation; no wonder. But there was also a keen expectation that *Bismarck* would now close on *Prince of Wales* and finish her off too. Lütjens, however, with his tightly buttoned sense of obedience, would not budge from Raeder's instructions to avoid needless embroilment with the Royal Navy; especially when it might lead to further damage to *Bismarck* that could deliver him to whatever forces might already be gathering beyond the horizons to net him. In any case the damage done to *Bismarck* by *Prince of Wales*'s hits weighed heavily on him. The hit in the bows had not only led to the leak of fuel oil and the tell-tale slick far astern, but had also put oil pumps and pipeline valves out of action, so depriving the engines of 1,000 tons of oil in the forward tanks. Having neglected to fill up either from the *Wollin* or the *Weissenburg*, Lütjens now had to watch his fuel state with all the anxiety of a motorist in the midst of the Sahara. Moreover, the need to counter-flood aft in order to restore the ship's trim after the serious flooding forward through the shell-hole, coupled with the knocking out of one engine room by *Prince of Wales*'s midship hit below the armour belt, had reduced *Bismarck*'s speed to 28 knots. Lütjens therefore came to the conclusion that he must abort his mission and make for a convenient dockyard for repairs. At 0900 that morning he signalled home that he was going to take the *Bismarck* to the French Atlantic port of St Nazaire, and meanwhile detach *Prinz Eugen* for commerce raiding.[34]

For the Royal Navy the problems were more complicated. It was the Fleet radio officer, Commander Jacobs, who personally told Admiral Tovey, C-in-C Home Fleet, the news of the *Hood*'s destruction, his voice strident with the shock of it. 'All right, Jacobs,' Tovey calmly replied. 'There's no need to shout.'[35] Tovey's flagship, *King George V*, still lay 360 miles east of the scene. After discussion with his Chief of Staff, Commodore E. J. P. Brind, and his operations officer, Commander Robertson, in the plotting room next to the admiral's bridge, Tovey decided to steer just south of west. This would well place him to intercept Lütjens if the German admiral sought to double back to Germany north or south of Iceland, and equally to intercept him if he continued southwards. But he could not hope to join Wake-Walker and bring Lütjens to action until 0700 on 25 May at the earliest; a long time during which much might happen.

Upon Rear-Admiral Wake-Walker's own shoulders had suddenly

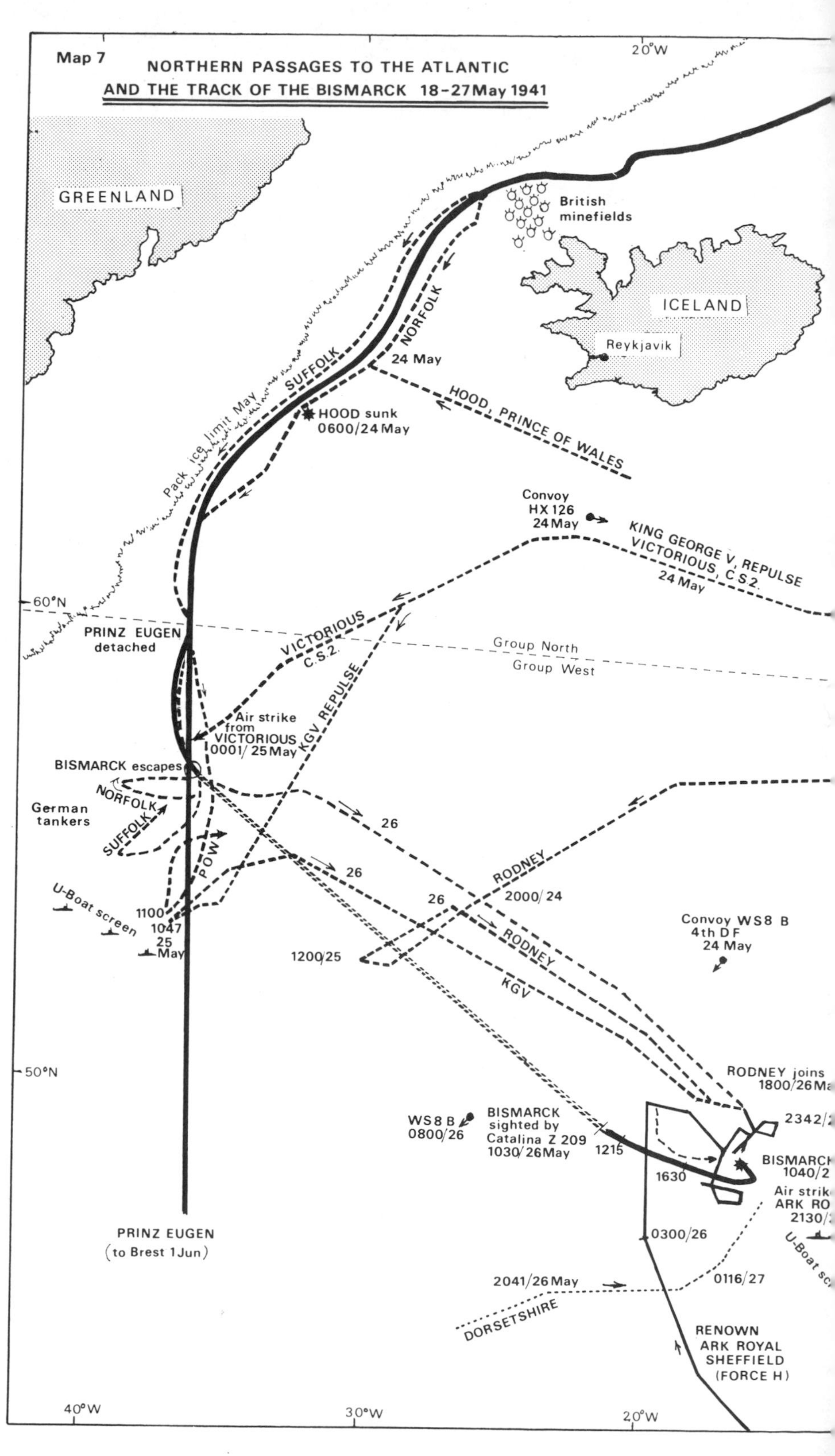

Map 7
NORTHERN PASSAGES TO THE ATLANTIC
AND THE TRACK OF THE BISMARCK 18–27 May 1941
20°W
GREENLAND
British minefields
ICELAND
Reykjavik
NORFOLK
24 May
SUFFOLK
Pack ice limit May
HOOD sunk 0600/24 May
HOOD, PRINCE OF WALES
Convoy HX 126 24 May
KING GEORGE V, REPULSE VICTORIOUS, C.S.2. 24 May
60°N
PRINZ EUGEN detached
VICTORIOUS C.S.2.
Group North
Group West
Air strike from VICTORIOUS 0001/25 May
KGV REPULSE
BISMARCK escapes
NORFOLK
German tankers
SUFFOLK
POW
26
26
RODNEY
2000/24
26
U-Boat screen
1100
1047
25 May
1200/25
RODNEY
KGV
Convoy WS8 B 4th DF 24 May
50°N
RODNEY joins 1800/26Ma
2342/
WS8 B 0800/26
BISMARCK sighted by Catalina Z 209 1030/26May
1215
1630
BISMARCK 1040/2
Air strik ARK RO 2130/
0300/26
U-Boat sc
2041/26 May
0116/27
DORSETSHIRE
RENOWN
ARK ROYAL
SHEFFIELD
(FORCE H)
PRINZ EUGEN (to Brest 1 Jun)
40°W
30°W
20°W

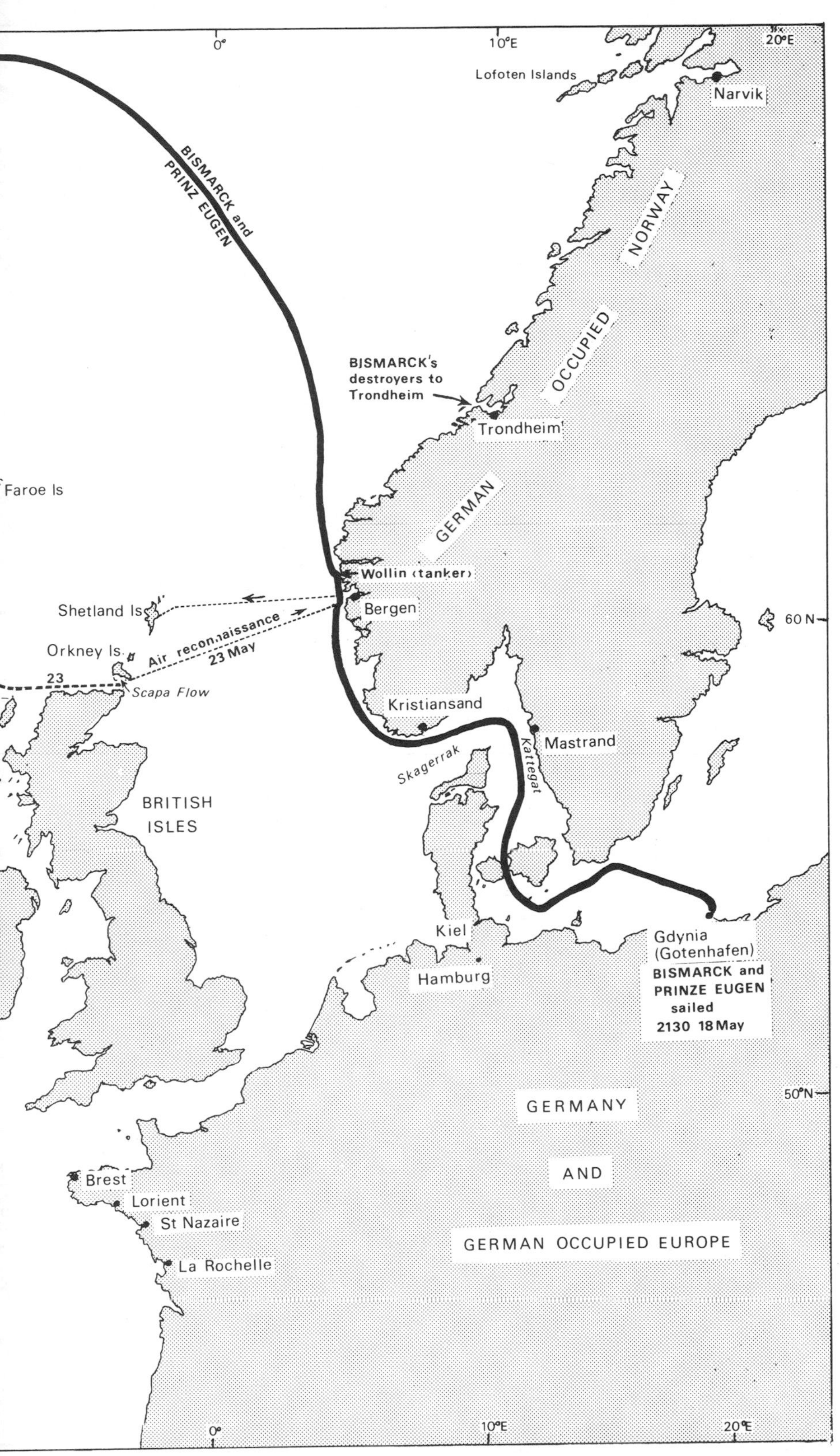
0°
10°E
20°E
Lofoten Islands
Narvik
BISMARCK and PRINZ EUGEN
NORWAY
OCCUPIED
GERMAN
BISMARCK's destroyers to Trondheim
Trondheim
Faroe Is
Wollin (tanker)
Shetland Is
Bergen
60 N
Orkney Is.
Air reconnaissance 23 May
23
Scapa Flow
Kristiansand
Mastrand
Skagerrak
Kattegat
BRITISH ISLES
Kiel
Gdynia (Gotenhafen)
Hamburg
BISMARCK and PRINZE EUGEN sailed 2130 18 May
50°N
GERMANY
AND
GERMAN OCCUPIED EUROPE
Brest
Lorient
St Nazaire
La Rochelle

fallen the command of the *Prince of Wales* as well as his two cruisers, together with the enormous responsibility of coping with the *Bismarck* until the Royal Navy's slowly gathering forces could concentrate and destroy her. Wake-Walker had been the offshore commander of the Dunkirk evacuation, a testing enough assignment which he had fulfilled with calm efficiency. Tall and burly, he balanced a sober professionalism with hobbies such as sketching and hunting for rare wild flowers.[36] He and Tovey were personal friends; a useful bond of trust and understanding amid the present hazards and uncertainties. He now faced a choice: he could renew the action with the *Bismarck*, or, in the words of the Naval Staff Battle Summary, 'make it his business to ensure that the enemy should be intercepted and brought to action by the Commander-in-Chief'.[37] Wake-Walker's dominant worry lay in the fighting state of the *Prince of Wales*:

> I had seen her [he wrote in his report later] forced out of action after 10 minutes' engagement, at the end of which her salvoes were falling short and had a very large spread indeed. As a result of the action she was short of one gun and her bridge was wrecked. She was a brand-new ship, with new turrets in which mechanical breakdowns had occurred and were to be expected, apart from the damage, and she had had a bare minimum for working up. I had been unable to observe any hits for certain on the *Bismarck* and her [*Bismarck*'s] shooting had given striking proof of its efficiency. To put it in a nutshell, I did not and do not consider that in her then state of efficiency the *Prince of Wales* was a match for the *Bismarck*. This, however, was by no means the deciding factor . . .[38]

For Wake-Walker appreciated that the object was the destruction of the *Bismarck* and he knew the C-in-C was on his way: 'I had two broad alternatives, one to ensure that she was intercepted by the Commander-in-Chief, the other to attempt her destruction with my own force.' He reckoned that the second course could only lead to greater damage being inflicted on *Prince of Wales* than on *Bismarck*, after which the cruisers, at the range at which they would have to engage, 'would be exposed to the fire of the *Bismarck* and *Prinz Eugen* hitting their large and unprotected machinery spaces and water line . . .'[39] He therefore decided that his proper task was to shadow the *Bismarck*, employing the *Prince of Wales* as support on which *Norfolk* and *Suffolk* could fall back if they were attacked. 'The decision was not an easy one . . .'[40] It was, however, one which the C-in-C endorsed in his own despatch: 'I had complete confidence in Rear-Admiral Wake-Walker's judgment.'[41]

But in the Admiralty War Room the Prime Minister (who had now become a more or less permanent fixture there because of his anxious fascination with the hunt for the *Bismarck*) and the First Sea Lord, in the aftermath of the unimaginable loss of the *Hood*, were deeply angered at Wake-Walker's decision. Abetted and encouraged by the VCNS, Phillips, that combative little terrier, they despatched that afternoon a prodding signal to Wake-Walker of the familiar kind, asking him what his intentions were about the *Prince of Wales* re-engaging the *Bismarck*. Wake-Walker replied that he did not think *Prince of Wales* should re-engage until other heavy ships had made contact or failed to do so. He added that he doubted if she had the speed to force an action in any case.[42]

This answer far from satisfied the angry and impatient men in London; rather it excited the kind of vindictive bullying, especially on Pound's part, that had inspired the Board of Enquiry into Somerville's decision not to pursue the Italian Fleet during 'Operation Collar' in November 1940. Immediately after Admiral Tovey's return to Scapa Flow at the end of the hunt for the *Bismarck*, Pound was to telephone him to say (according to Tovey's later account) that

> . . . he wished Wake-Walker and Jack Leach brought to trial by court-martial for not re-engaging the *Bismarck*. I explained that the action taken by both these officers was exactly what I wished, the last thing I wanted was for the *Bismarck* to be pushed further to the West and away from my own force. He stated he still wished them to be brought to trial. I replied nothing would persuade me to do so. He informed me the Admiralty would order a trial. I replied that if they did I would act as Prisoner's Friend, if necessary resigning my command to do so. I heard no more about it.[43]

When the *Hood* sank, the *Norfolk* was lying about fifteen miles to the north-west, and coming up at 28 knots. Wake-Walker therefore ordered the *Prince of Wales* to follow at her best speed, so that *Norfolk* could retire on her if attacked. At 0757 the *Suffolk* reported, accurately, that the *Bismarck* had reduced speed and appeared to be damaged. A little later a Sunderland from Iceland confirmed that she was leaving a large oil slick astern. All that day *Norfolk* and *Suffolk* hung on to *Bismarck* and *Prinz Eugen*, keeping up a constant flow of enemy reports, but always on the alert lest *Bismarck* should go about and seek to attack them. Coastal Command too was keeping watch on the German ships, and at 1535 a Catalina in sight of *Norfolk* was able to report that *Suffolk* lay 26 miles distant, with *Bismarck* fifteen miles ahead and *Prinz Eugen* ahead of her.

In the afternoon a cold mist shrouded quarry and pursuer; *Suffolk* temporarily lost radar contact; and Wake-Walker, his trained professional instinct a-prickle, ordered *Norfolk* to turn 360° to port, a complete circle which lengthened her distance from *Bismarck*'s last observed position by some three miles. In fact *Bismarck* had indeed just swung to port across *Norfolk*'s bows in the mist, and but for his timely manoeuvre Wake-Walker would have encountered the German battleship at the deadly range of a mile or so.[44] At 1841 the shifting mist opened to reveal *Bismarck* about eight miles distant; her 15-inch guns crashed out, and the two British cruisers and *Prince of Wales* fired back; then the mists closed again. Once more all depended on *Suffolk*'s radar.

In the Admiralty War Room, 24 May was spent in redeploying every available unit of British seapower in order to hem in the *Bismarck* whichever course she took. Five hours before *Hood* was blown up the Admiralty had already ordered the cruisers *Manchester*, *Birmingham* and *Arethusa* to patrol north of Langanaes (the north-easterly point of Iceland) in case the German Admiral tried to double back to base via the Denmark Strait. At 1022 the battleship *Rodney* (33,950 tons displacement, nine 16-inch guns), at present escorting the liner *Britannic* with four destroyers westwards, was ordered to leave the *Britannic* and steer south-westwards on a course to intercept *Bismarck*, then some 550 miles to the north-west. Unfortunately the veteran *Rodney*, in dire need of a refit, could barely make 21 knots. The even more aged *Ramillies*, escorting convoy HX127 from Halifax, Nova Scotia, and lying some 900 miles south of the *Bismarck*, was ordered to abandon her convoy and steam northwards in order to station herself to the west of the enemy. The equally aged *Revenge* in the port of Halifax and the cruiser *Edinburgh* patrolling in the Atlantic were both ordered to close in as well. By 1800 that evening four battleships, two battlecruisers, twelve cruisers, two aircraft carriers and a swarm of destroyers were already on the move. The credit belongs to Rear-Admiral T. S. V. ('Tom') Phillips, the VCNS, who, in the words of an eyewitness, 'was right on the ball the whole time, and who took a decisive part in the coordination of all the British forces'.[45]

The First Sea Lord's own attention was – perhaps fortunately – almost entirely engrossed by the Prime Minister,[46] for in Tovey's judgment Pound was 'neither a great tactician or [sic] strategist [although] he firmly believed he was . . .'[47]

During the day Tovey himself in HMS *King George V* (110,000 horsepower steam turbines; speed 27½ knots) became more and more concerned that the *Bismarck* might outrun his attempt at interception unless she could be slowed down. Yet Tovey's only means of slowing her lay in the carrier *Victorious* (Captain H. C. Bovell) and her nine Swordfish torpedo aircraft (825 Squadron, Fleet Air Arm), and six Fulmar fighters (802 Squadron), whose pilots were desperately new to the job. Nevertheless, at 1440 he ordered Rear-Admiral Curteis (Flag Officer, 2nd Cruiser Squadron) to take *Victorious* and the cruisers *Aurora*, *Kenya* and *Hermione* to a flying-off position 100 miles east of the *Bismarck*.

As Tovey made the signal 'Good Luck', Curteis set off at 28 knots, course 280°, guided throughout by reports from *Norfolk* and *Suffolk*. However, it later became clear to Curteis from these reports that there was no hope of *Victorious* getting within 100 miles of the target before 2300 that night. He therefore decided to fly off his strike an hour earlier at a distance of 120 miles. At 2208 with the wind blowing fresh from the north-west *Victorious* turned to 330° and slowed to 15 knots in order to launch her aircraft. It was not going to be an easy first mission for the green aircrews. According to the Naval Staff Battle Summary: 'The weather was as bad as it could be. The flying deck presented a chilly prospect of dark foaming seas, rain and scudding cloud in a leaden sky, the heavily loaded planes gathered way very slowly. They were off at 2210/24 and disappeared into cloud and rain squalls.'[48]

The squadrons (led by Lieutenant-Commander (A) Eugene Esmonde) located Wake-Walker's shadowing ships by air-to-surface radar, whereupon *Norfolk* directed them on to the enemy. Just before midnight – in those latitudes, the time of sunset – Esmonde brought his lumbering biplanes down and in towards *Bismarck*, the main attack coming in on her port side, and a diversion by one aircraft on her starboard side, each aircraft carrying one 18-inch torpedo with Duplex pistol set to 31 feet. As the Swordfish rode steadily towards the *Bismarck* the length of her massive superstructure erupted in a continuous blaze of gun-flashes as every calibre of gun, from the 20mm Oerlikons up to the main armament, was brought into action. Nevertheless the Swordfish held on to drop their torpedoes.

It now fell to *Bismarck*'s captain to try with great skill to comb the torpedo tracks, the huge ship heeling at each turn, while all the Swordfish climbed away unscathed – possibly because the battleship's violent changes of course made it hard for the anti-aircraft batteries to hold their targets. A shadowing Fulmar saw one great column of smoke erupt from the *Bismarck*'s starboard side, followed by a reduction in her speed. When all the aircraft returned to *Victorious* darkness was falling and the carrier's homing beacon had failed. Esmonde's inexperienced crews had to make safe landings by means of radar and the improvised light of a signal projector. Two of the Fulmars ditched, but the crews were rescued. However, despite the aircrews' bravery, the single torpedo to hit *Bismarck* ran shallow instead of at 31 feet, and only exploded harmlessly against the battleship's armoured belt, killing one warrant officer; the ship's first fatal casualty.

In the mists of late afternoon, and under cover of *Bismarck*'s brief exchange of fire with Wake-Walker's ships, *Prinz Eugen* and the German flagship had parted company according to Lütjens's plan. As he steamed on alone in the small hours of 25 May, Lütjens knew (from a signal by Group West based in Brest) that Force H with its carrier was now in the eastern Atlantic; he knew too from the Swordfish attack that there was also a carrier some 100 miles distant from him. His greatest worry therefore lay in the uncanny ability of the shadowing British cruisers' radar to detect his every change of course. If he were to escape the powerful forces that must be closing towards him, he must find a means of dodging that unwavering electronic eye.

In the case of Tovey and the Admiralty it was exactly that constant tag by *Suffolk* on *Bismarck*'s position, course and speed which made it possible for them to deploy and direct the hunt, even though the relative speeds of hunters and hunted still rendered ultimate interception a matter of the narrowest margin.

Then, at 0306 on 25 May, *Suffolk* lost the *Bismarck*, and at once the British command was groping in the blind. According to Admiral Tovey, writing later in his despatch:

> The loss of touch, when it came, was caused primarily by over-confidence. The RDF [radar] had been used so skilfully that it engendered a false sense of security . . . The *Suffolk* was shadowing from the extreme range of her instrument, losing touch on those parts of her [anti-submarine] zig-zag which took her furthest from the enemy. The enemy altered sharply to starboard while the *Suffolk* was moving to port and by the time she got back had gone.[49]

This is a little unfair: if there was carelessness, it sprang from sheer tiredness rather than over-confidence. In any case, Lütjens and Lindemann had turned away more than 90° to the westward with the very intention of shaking off their shadowers. They now proceeded to take *Bismarck* in a complete clockwise circle, crossing their own track an hour later some 30 miles astern of Wake-Walker's ships and setting course 130° for Brest and safety. However, Wake-Walker himself wrongly guessed that the enemy had steered a westerly course, searching in vain in that direction for several wasted hours.

The day of 25 May therefore passed for the British in frantic but unsuccessful searches by sea and air for a vanished enemy; in competing guesses as to which course he might be steering; and positively misleading snippets of Intelligence. Catalinas from Iceland swept the seas all day but sighted only friendly ships. Bletchley Park could not directly help the search because it was currently taking some three to seven days to decrypt the naval Enigma signals – nothing like quick enough for a fast-moving chase where hours counted.[50] In the Admiralty War Room that day bafflement bred a mounting tension – not least because of the Premier's powerful presence and personal involvement. For so much was at stake, with the balance of attrition in the Battle of the Atlantic currently swinging towards Dönitz's U-boats, the need to avenge the *Hood*'s tragic but humiliating loss and restore the prestige of the Royal Navy in British and world opinion. Churchill himself was at first convinced that Lütjens was doubling back towards the Denmark Strait and Germany: it took much to persuade him otherwise.[51]

Tovey, for his part, continued for several hours to steer south-westwards, whereas unbeknown to him the *Bismarck* had crossed his wake about 100 miles astern at approximately 0800, steering south-east.

The only clue came from rough HF/DF fixes on *Bismarck*'s copious radio traffic with the German naval high command. For Lütjens apparently saw no reason to observe strict radio silence because he wrongly believed that he was still being closely tagged by *Norfolk* and *Suffolk*. Unfortunately misunderstandings between the Admiralty and Tovey's staff over the plotting of these HF/DF fixes misled the C-in-C into believing that *Bismarck* was indeed, as Churchill reckoned, heading for the Denmark Strait, and at 1047 Tovey reversed course and headed north-westwards at 27 knots. At noon the *Rodney* (280 miles distant from the flagship to the south-east) and *Ramillies* in mid-Atlantic conformed to this movement. Except for Force H coming up from the south-east and still 1,300 miles away, all the British forces now lay far astern of the *Bismarck* and steering 90° away from her.

As further HF/DF fixes came in during the forenoon, opinion began to harden in the Admiralty War Room that the *Bismarck* was steering for a French Bay of Biscay port.[52] As early as 1023 the Admiralty signalled Somerville (Force H) and Wake-Walker to proceed on this assumption – which Wake-Walker was already doing. At 1158 it signalled *Rodney* in similar terms. But then at 1428 it instructed *Rodney* to proceed instead on the assumption that the enemy was steering for the Iceland–Faeroes gap (a Churchillian intervention?); false guidance that was only rescinded at 1805. In the meantime, and by no means enlightened by these contradictory Admiralty signals, Tovey had continued to steer north-east, his mind nevertheless more and more uneasy as to whether this was the right course. At 1810, now convinced that *Bismarck* must be making for a French port, he turned south-east. Shortly afterwards the Admiralty confirmed to him from an Ultra decrypt of a Luftwaffe Enigma signal (to the Luftwaffe Chief of Staff, then in Athens) that such was the case.

Thanks to his almost eight-hour-long diversion in the wrong direction, Tovey now lay 150 miles astern of *Bismarck*: a colossal handicap in a race to catch her before she reached the French coast. His fleet was now desperately short of fuel after four days' hard steaming, and, lacking fleet oilers, he had to detach the battlecruiser *Repulse* to Newfoundland to refuel, the *Prince of Wales* and the cruiser *Hermione* to Iceland. He was also forced to slow his remaining cruisers to 20 knots in order to conserve oil; HMS *Victorious* and the invaluable *Suffolk* likewise. All his screening destroyers had had to leave him too. At 2238 that night Tovey signalled the Admiralty that even the flagship might have to reduce speed because of shortage of fuel.

For Force H, coming up from the south-east, it had been a day of struggle against heavy seas, wind, rain and mist. At 0900 Somerville detached three destroyers back to Gibraltar to refuel in accordance with an Admiralty signal that Force H 'might be required for extended operations . . .'[53] At 1100, when Force H was in 41° 30′N, 17° 06′W, Somerville received the Admiralty signal to proceed on the assumption 'that the enemy had turned towards Brest at 0300'.[54] Somerville therefore altered course to 360°, speed 24 knots, the north-westerly wind and sea both rising. At 1215 he altered again to 345° in order to reach a position early next day to fly air searches from the *Ark Royal* over a wide spread of the Bay of Biscay. Still the weather grew rougher and rougher, forcing him to slow to 21 knots at 2340, to 19 at 0020 on the 26th and down to 17 at 0112. Because he had heard nothing from the Admiralty concerning the whereabouts of *Scharnhorst* and *Gneisenau* since a report at 1515 on 23 May that they were still in Brest, Somerville felt 'some anxiety' on their score, 'as I could not entirely discount the possibility that one or both battlecruisers might have put to sea to support *Bismarck*'.[55] At 0300 on 26 May he altered to 000° in order to reach a flying-off position further to the east, for he reckoned that *Bismarck*, with the benefit of a following wind, would have made a better speed of advance than Force H.

But the problem for Somerville, as for Tovey, as for the Admiralty, remained that no one knew exactly where *Bismarck* was. The first, the essential, task for 26 May must be to find her.

In the *Bismarck* herself on 25 May what should have been a day of cautious hope about the prospects of reaching Brest was turned by an incredible act of poor leadership on Lütjens's part into a day when the morale of the ship's company sagged towards a sense of hopelessness. Addressing the ship's company on the tannoy Lütjens began by congratulating them on sinking the *Hood*, but then remarked – according to eyewitnesses later – that 'the enemy will try to concentrate his forces and bring them into action against us'.[56] He confirmed to them that *Bismarck* was now on its way to a French port, and went on: 'On our way there, the enemy will gather and give us battle. The German people are with you, and we will fight until our gun barrels glow red-hot and the last shell has left the barrels. For us seamen, the question now is victory or death.'[57]

The impact of this piece of libretto for a maritime *Götterdämmerung* on a ship's company of young and impressionable conscripts, many of whom had never been on the high seas before, was immediate and catastrophic. In the words of one officer, 'the high morale that permeated the ship was irretrievably lost'.[58] A petty officer recalled: 'The Fleet Commander's words had a devastating effect on us. They were taken to mean that we were sentenced to death, whereas we had been already reckoning when we would arrive in France.'[59] The tone of Lütjens's address is all too consistent with his introspective and intense temperament, not to say the fatalistic mood in which he had gone to sea. Nevertheless as an engineer lieutenant-commander put it later, 'Whether the Fleet Commander simply made a bad choice of words or whether the crew sensed his innermost fears must remain an open question.'[60] Captain Lindemann did his best to put things right by a brief and positive tannoy address of his own and by talking to members of the crew on his rounds. But although it helped a little, morale in *Bismarck* had been fatally damaged. The ship's officers and petty officers began to be seen wearing unfastened up lifejackets, a sight unlikely to raise the crew's spirits. Moreover, it is hard not to think that this lowering of morale must have had its effect on the ship's actual fighting effectiveness.

Dawn on 26 May found Force H in the latitude of Brest with half a gale blowing from the north-west. Still bothered that *Gneisenau* and *Scharnhorst* might be at sea, Somerville flew an air search to the west and north at 0716 before looking for *Bismarck* herself. At 0835, when *Ark Royal* was in 48° 26′N, 10° 13′W, ten Swordfish took off on that urgent quest. The wind was now blowing Force 7 from 320°, 'sea rough, sky overcast, visibility 10 to 12 miles', according to Somerville's report.[61] Because of the weather the Fulmars could not be employed to give greater range of search. It proved a tricky enough operation even for the robust old Swordfish, as Somerville described: 'ARK ROYAL's round down [after end of the flight deck] was rising and falling 56 feet at times, as measured by sextant. The handling of the aircraft on the flight deck was always difficult and several slid bodily across the deck which was wet with spray.'[62]

One by one the Swordfish staggered off the plunging deck into the wind; one by one an hour later they made a hazardous return landing after having seen nothing but wind-whipped sea. Could Coastal Command do better?

When late on the 25th the Admiralty liaison officer with Coastal Command, Captain Charles Meynell, took the Admiralty operation staff's proposals for the morrow's air searches to Air Marshal Sir Frederick Bowhill, the AOC-in-C, Coastal Command, Bowhill, that one-time sailor, rightly guessed (as Pound and Phillips had not) that Lütjens would not steer straight for Brest, but take a diversionary course south before bearing east. He therefore urged that there should be an extra patrol flown to cover a more southerly area than provided for in the Admiralty's existing plans.[63]

It was therefore entirely thanks to Bowhill that at 1030 on the 26th a Catalina of 15 Group, Coastal Command, from Iceland (piloted by Flying Officer Dennis Briggs, and with a neutral American 'Special Observer', Ensign Leonard Smith, USN, as co-pilot), sighted the *Bismarck* through a gap in the cloud, placing her in 49° 30′N, 21° 55′W – some 690 miles 96° from Brest. With *Bismarck* putting up a storm of fire that peppered the Catalina with shrapnel holes, Briggs and Smith found close shadowing a hazardous business, and at 1125 they lost her again. But at almost the same time two Swordfish from *Ark Royal* fitted with long-range tanks sent earlier at Somerville's order and guided by the Catalina's report also found the *Bismarck*, placing her some 25 miles further to the west than had the Catalina's crew. At noon *Ark Royal* flew off long-range shadowers, and these, regularly relieved during the day, were to send back a constant flow of precise reports until they were recalled at 2230.

Admiral Tovey himself in *King George V* received the Catalina's report at 1043. Pleased though he was that at last the *Bismarck* had been found again, he could not take comfort from the report. At *Bismarck*'s estimated speed of 21 knots, she could reach safe haven in Brest on 27 May and be under cover of powerful land-based airpower long before that. Since *King George V* lay some 130 miles to the north of her, it was highly unlikely that *Bismarck* could now be intercepted unless she was somehow slowed down. Moreover, while *Bismarck* could run home at full speed to the point of empty tanks, all the British ships had to make a long voyage home in the face of possible air and U-boat attack; and Tovey was already confronting the possibility that he might have to call off his chase for want of fuel. For the time being, however, he kept going at 26 knots, altering to 130° at 1155.

All now depended on *Ark Royal*'s Swordfish, especially since Somerville had been instructed by the Admiralty that his battlecruiser, *Renown*, 'was not to become heavily engaged with BISMARCK unless the latter was already heavily engaged with either KING GEORGE V or RODNEY'.[64] At 1315 Somerville detached the radar-equipped *Sheffield* to close and shadow the *Bismarck*, then some 40 miles south-west of his flagship. By an omission with 'serious consequences' the visual signal was not repeated to the *Ark Royal*. At 1450 fifteen Swordfish set off to attack the *Bismarck*, one of them, however, making an emergency return soon after. Owing to the foul weather a planned diversion by the Fulmars had to be abandoned. Over the target area the visibility was appalling, but one aircraft succeeded in locating a single lone ship with its air-to-surface radar. Unfortunately the ship was the *Sheffield* – which, owing to the failure to repeat to *Ark Royal* the signal detaching her, *Ark Royal*'s strike force did not know was now shadowing *Bismarck*; and at 1550 the Swordfish launched eleven torpedoes at the unlucky cruiser. Fortunately the Duplex magnetic pistols malfunctioned, two torpedoes exploding as they hit the water, three more as they crossed *Sheffield*'s wake, while the cruiser successfully evaded the rest by combing her tracks. At 1720 the strike force landed back on *Ark Royal* – and the *Bismarck* was still steaming on unscathed for Brest.

In the Admiralty War Room, anxiety and frustration fuelled the itch to intervene in both Pound and Churchill. Wrote an eyewitness: 'The staff were against sending the cautionary signal to James Somerville about not getting engaged with BISMARCK, but the First Sea Lord was insistent.'[65] The Premier himself, true to his form in both world wars, really wanted to mastermind the chase:

> As events moved towards their climax the Prime Minister took a closer interest and hardly ever left the War Room. The First Sea Lord supported by the First Lord [A. V. Alexander] did wonders in restraining him from sending impulsive signals of instructions to Tovey and others engaged in these operations . . .[66]

Just as soon as the first strike force returned to *Ark Royal* at 1720, another, this time of sixteen aircraft, was put in preparation as fast as possible. At 1747 the *Sheffield* reported that she had sighted the *Bismarck* in about 48° 30′N, 17° 20′W, and was taking station about ten miles astern of her. At 1915 the second strike force (in the event, fifteen aircraft strong) roared one by one down *Ark Royal*'s flight deck and away. This time great care was taken to avoid errors or failures. The torpedoes were armed with contact pistols instead of Duplex, and set to run at 22 feet. The strike force was ordered to home on *Sheffield* first by direction-finding signals, and the cruiser was then to redirect them on to the *Bismarck*.

At 2035 the strike force reached the *Sheffield*, which informed them by signal lamp that *Bismarck* bore 110°, distant twelve miles. At 2040 the Swordfish flew on towards their target in six sub-flights in line astern.

At just this moment Somerville in *Renown* received a signal from the Commander-in-Chief in *King George V* giving his position, course and speed at 1800 as 49° 48′N, 17° 33′W, 100°, 22 knots. Shortage of fuel was now causing Tovey 'grave anxiety'.[67] By noon the flagship was down to 32 per cent of capacity, while *Rodney* (which joined him at 1806) had reported that she would have to turn back to refuel by 0800 next day. At 1705 Tovey had reduced his speed to 22 knots in order to conserve fuel, which meant that it was quite impossible for him to make up the ninety miles that still separated him from the *Bismarck*. He therefore informed Somerville that 'unless the enemy's speed was reduced he would have to return in KING GEORGE V at midnight to refuel, leaving RODNEY to continue the chase'.[68] The only hope left for Tovey was *Ark Royal* and her aircraft. Then at 1830 he received a stark report from Somerville on the results of the first air strike (that on *Sheffield*): 'Estimate no hits.'[69] To Tovey and his staff this seemed to mark the end: gloom settled on the flagship. Then came a fresh signal from Somerville that *Ark Royal* had launched another strike. Hope revived; and with it the anguish of waiting.

As the fifteen Swordfish neared the *Bismarck* they ran into thick cloud banking up from 700 feet to between 6,000 and 10,000 feet and became split up. Each sub-flight took its own course through the cloud and then down under its base, there to find the *Bismarck*'s great dark-grey shape beneath greeting them 'with intense and accurate fire from the first moment of sighting until out of range'.[70] The Swordfish buzzed round the stern and towards both beams of the battleship like a swarm of hornets, all but one of them making their final runs undeterred by the storm of anti-aircraft fire. Thirteen torpedoes were dropped, and two hits (possibly three) were observed – one certain hit on the port side amidships, and the second on the starboard side well aft. At 2125 the last Swordfish climbed away to return to *Ark Royal*. The attack had lasted just half an hour, but it was one of the most decisive half hours in the history of naval warfare. For the aft torpedo hit had reduced the proud and powerful *Bismarck* to a helpless cripple.

The hit was in fact so luckily placed as truly to represent the workings of fate. For of the *Bismarck*'s 823 feet of length, the torpedo had happened to strike the one-fortieth which was the great ship's weakest and yet most vital part (apart from the actual screws and rudders) – the steering rooms where powerful electric motors operated the huge twin rudders. Moreover, at the speed *Bismarck* was steaming the torpedo would have passed harmlessly astern if it had been dropped only seconds later than it was. The effect of the hit was to jam *Bismarck*'s rudders in their existing position – which, since she had been at that moment taking violent evasive action, was 'port 12°'. *Ark Royal*'s shadowing aircraft high above observed the amazing consequences as *Bismarck* helplessly made two complete circles to port.

In the stricken ship damage-control parties and divers worked desperately to try to free the rudders, but the steering motor rooms were flooded up to the main deck, and incoming surges of sea water as the ship pitched made their work impossible. The best that could be achieved was to centre one of the two rudders; the other remained fixed immovably in its 'port 12°' position. Meanwhile Captain Lindemann tried every method of steering by the engines and propellers – but, just as on the Baltic exercise months before, it proved impossible to keep *Bismarck* on course by this means. Desperate measures such as blowing away the rudders, or taking a U-boat in tow as a steering drag, were put forward and discarded. Nothing could prevent the *Bismarck* from turning her head into the wind.

And here fate seemed to be at work again, for the wind was blowing strongly from the north-west – the direction of the pursuing Home Fleet. Moreover, in order to prevent *Bismarck* from wallowing and yawing helplessly she had to be kept under way. And so all through the night of 26–27 May 1941, she steamed at 7 to 8 knots towards her hunters, delivering herself to the kill.

But she could still fight. When, as the sun was setting on the 26th, Admiral Vian (4th Destroyer Flotilla) in HMS *Cossack*, with the Polish destroyer *Piorun* and the *Maori*, *Zulu* and *Sikh* arrived on the scene to shadow *Bismarck*, the German battleship swiftly straddled them. Vian had been ordered by the Admiralty at 0200 that day to leave the convoy he was escorting and join the C-in-C, who was now without a destroyer screen. On hearing the Catalina's sighting report, Vian on his own initiative altered to the south-east in order to close the *Bismarck*. All through the night Vian launched torpedo attacks, being determined, as he wrote to Tovey afterwards, firstly, 'to deliver to you at all costs the enemy, at the time you wished. Secondly to try to sink or stop the enemy with torpedoes in the night if I thought the attack should not involve the destroyers in heavy losses.'[71] Vian's 'Tribals', being mainly gun ships, had only four torpedo tubes instead of the usual eight, and no re-loads. Each destroyer could therefore only launch one attack with all four torpedoes fired at once to give a spread.

It proved a night of gallant but vain enterprise ('a model of its kind' according to Tovey's despatch) on the part of the British destroyers, and on the part of the *Bismarck* a night of radar-directed gunfire which although straddling Vian's ships again and again, failed to hit or sink any of them; a night lurid with gunflashes and star-shell. In the *Bismarck* members of the crew were now haplessly falling asleep at their stations in total exhaustion.

> When, after midnight [wrote one of her gunnery officers], it was announced that work on the rudders had ceased, hope evaporated. The older men took the news as a sentence of death for ship and crew. Everyone had to find his own way of dealing with the inevitable. Some fell into a mood of total indifference, in which nothing more could have any effect on them.[72]

Admiral Tovey learned of the crippling torpedo hit on *Bismarck* by a report from *Sheffield* at 2136 on the 26th that the enemy was steering 340° and then four minutes later 000°, from which it was plain that her steering was damaged. Buoyed up by fresh hope the C-in-C turned at once to the south, hoping to make contact with the *Bismarck* from the east in the failing light. At 2208 came a confirming report from Force H that *Bismarck* had been hit. By now the light was thickening, *King George* V was yawing and pitching horribly in the following wind and steep seaway, rain squalls were obscuring vision. Knowing that the crippled *Bismarck* was heading north towards him at about 10 knots, Tovey therefore decided to haul off to the east and north, and work round ahead of the German ship to attack her from the west at dawn. Later, however, Vian's night-time reports about the continuing accuracy of the enemy's fire persuaded the C-in-C to wait for full daylight before engaging from the west 'with the full advantages of wind, sea and light'.[73] Before midnight he signalled these intentions to Somerville, instructing him that *Renown* and *Ark Royal* were to keep not less than twenty miles to the southward of *Bismarck*.[74] Then, in his sea-cabin behind the flagship's bridge, he drafted a message to the ship's company:

> To K.G.V.
> The sinking of the *Bismarck* may have an effect on the war as a whole out of all proportion to the loss to the enemy of one battleship. May God be with you and grant you victory.[75]

In the *Rodney*, as in the flagship, the announcement that they were going to engage the *Bismarck* at dawn was greeted with cheers throughout the ship.

Daylight on 27 May brought a heavy, sullen grey sky, a rising sea, and a tearing wind from the north-west. Tovey, back in his sea-cabin after a night of work, prayed, in his own words, 'for guidance and help', for although he had no doubt that the *Bismarck* would be sunk, he feared she might inflict heavy damage and casualties on his own ships. As he prayed his anxieties dissolved into calm. It was, he said, 'as if all responsibility had been taken from me, and I knew everything would be all right'.[76] At 0708 he signalled the *Rodney* (Captain F. H. G. Dalrymple-Hamilton, RN) to keep station six cables or more from *King George V*, and (unlike Holland with regard to Leach) gave Dalrymple-Hamilton freedom of action to adjust his own bearings as he wished. At 0737 Tovey altered to 080°, *Rodney* taking station 010° from the flagship. At 0820 the flagship's lookout sighted *Norfolk* on the port bow; the cruiser signalled: 'Enemy, 130°, 16 miles.' So at long last for Tovey the denouement had arrived. In *King George V* the order was given: 'On tin hats!' Three minutes later the squat, piled shape of *Bismarck* emerged from a rain squall on the starboard bow: 'Enemy in sight.'[77]

Because of the north-westerly gale Tovey had concluded that wind and sea made it most undesirable to attack from windward. He had therefore decided to approach the *Bismarck* on a north-westerly bearing, and then, providing the enemy continued to steer northwards, deploy to the south on an opposite course at a range of some 15,000 yards. When *Bismarck* was sighted she bore 118°, distant 25,000 yards. The two British battleships were then steering 118°, eight cables apart – in other words they were steering directly towards their victim in line abreast. At 0847 *Rodney* opened fire; *King George V* a minute later.

In the *Bismarck* the mood of officers and crew could not have made a more bitter contrast with that prevailing in Tovey's ships. Lütjens remained as ever buttoned into himself, with no heartening words to utter on the eve of action; rather an air of fatalistic melancholy. Lindemann too had capitulated to indifference and despair. His former adjutant, now a gunnery officer, found even him that morning wearing an open lifejacket:

> I had to look twice to believe it . . . he seemed strangely detached from his surroundings. He saw me coming but did not return my salute, which I held as I looked at him intently in the hope that he would say something in return. He did not say a word. He did not even glance at me. I was greatly disturbed and puzzled . . .[78]

From the very top, therefore, had seeped down the dejection that permeated the whole ship's company and seemed to rot a fighting efficiency in any case impaired by desperate tiredness; evidence perhaps of the shallowness of the young German Navy's tradition compared with that of the Royal Navy, and a consequent moral brittleness in its leadership.

The *Bismarck* opened fire at 0850 after turning as best she could to open her 'A' arcs; the salvo fell short. Her third straddled the *Rodney*, the nearest shell raising a huge column of water only twenty yards from her. She continued to straddle with succeeding salvoes, but scored not a single hit. Her constant yawing as she laboured along at 10 knots made it hard for her transmitting rooms (fire-control centres) to keep her guns accurately on target, while her inability to manoeuvre meant that she herself offered the British battleships an easy aiming mark. Moreover she was outgunned by eight 15-inch guns to nine 16-inch and ten 14-inch. It was little wonder that the speed and accuracy of her fire gradually fell away.

At 0854 the cruiser *Norfolk* joined in from the east at a range of ten miles with her 8-inch guns. At just this moment *Rodney* fired her third salvo and landed one 16-inch shell on *Bismarck*'s forecastle and another on her superstructure amidships. At 0859 the *King George V* altered to the south to bring the *Bismarck* on the beam; the *Rodney*, two and a half miles astern, followed suit although manoeuvring independently of the flagship. Clouds of cordite smoke reeking towards the enemy made spotting difficult, and the British ships had to resort to radar range-finding. Now the *Bismarck* shifted her fire to the *King George V* – again no hits.

At 0902 a 16-inch shell from the *Rodney* smashed down on to the *Bismarck*'s upper deck forward and reduced her fore turrets to a shambles of riven metal, the gun muzzles of turret 'Anton' drooping down towards the sea; those of turret 'Bruno' cocked uselessly into the air in the wrong direction. Yet somehow guns in one or other of these turrets were brought into action again later. According to an American observer in *Rodney*, Lieutenant-Commander J. M. Wellings, USN: '*Bismarck* continued to fire regularly until between 0902 and 0908 when her firing became irregular and intermittent . . . only one salvo was observed from the forward turrets after this period. This salvo was fired at 0927 . . .'[79] At 0904 the cruiser *Dorsetshire* (Captain B. Martin, RN; brought in from convoy escort duty) joined the action. In *King George V* the range remained steady at 12,000 yards between 0910 and 0915. At 0916, with *Bismarck*'s bearing drawing rapidly aft, Captain Dalrymple-Hamilton turned *Rodney* 16 points to port in order to head her off; the flagship followed suit soon after. Both ships, now steaming north in the same direction as *Bismarck*, reopened fire to starboard – *Rodney* at a range of only 8,600 yards; *King George V* at 12,000. About this time Tovey remarked to Captain Patterson, the captain of the *King George V*: 'Get closer, get closer, I can't see any hits!'[80] *Bismarck* now shifted her fire back to *Rodney*, but by now only one turret (aft) remained in action; more near misses, but still no hits. By now the German ship was ablaze amidships, her internal spaces reeking with fumes and littered with the maimed and the dead, her fire-control instruments shot away – listing to port but still crawling through the water.

At 0931 she fired her last salvo. Between 0925 and 1015 the two British battleships poured in salvoes from main and secondary armaments at ranges down to 2,900 yards, finally reducing *Bismarck* to a wreck pouring out great clouds of greenish yellow smoke lit by flame. Yet still she floated, her magazines and machinery spaces intact; a tribute to Germany's skill in building stout ships. *Rodney* had fired 380 rounds of 16-inch shell and 718 rounds of 6-inch; *King George V* had fired 339 rounds of 14-inch and 660 rounds of 5.25-inch; *Norfolk* and *Dorsetshire* 781 rounds of 8-inch – a combined total of 2,878 rounds.[81] This huge total of rounds fired, many of them at virtually point-blank range, suggests a certain lack of accuracy in British gunnery. Certainly *King George V* found ranging difficult because of cordite, smoke and water spouts concealing the target, as well as because of a breakdown in her radar. She also suffered from mechanical failures in her 14-inch turrets, just like *Prince of Wales* three days earlier, which reduced her firepower by 80 per cent for seven minutes and 40 per cent for twenty-three.[82]

At 1025, in answer to an enquiry from Somerville, Tovey signalled that *Bismarck* 'was still afloat'; three minutes later he added that 'he could not get her to sink by gunfire'; and shortly after that again that 'he had been forced to abandon the action on account of fuel'.[83] So after all Tovey had to leave it to the cruisers to finish *Bismarck* off with torpedoes. Anticipating this order, *Dorsetshire* fired two torpedoes into her starboard side and one into her port. *Bismarck*, now with a heavy list to port, began to settle slowly by the stern. About this time, according to one German witness, a scuttling party opened her sea-cocks and activated time-fused charges in the cooling water intakes. At 1036, with her flag still flying, she rolled over and disappeared in 48° 10′N, 16° 12′W, taking with her Lütjens, Lindemann and all but 110 members of her company of 2,200.

As Admiral Tovey generously acknowledged: 'She put up a most gallant fight against impossible odds, worthy of the old days of the Imperial German Navy.'[84]

In language with a true Nelsonian ring, Admiral Tovey wrote in his despatch:

> Although it was no more than I expected, the co-operation, skill and understanding displayed by all forces during this prolonged chase gave me the utmost satisfaction. Flag and Commanding Officers of detached units invariably took the action I would have wished, before or without receiving instructions from me. The conduct of all officers and men of the Fleet which I have the honour to command was in accordance with the tradition of the service.[85]

Yet it was his own style of command, so different from the centralising rigidity of Jutland as re-embodied in the 1939 Fighting Instructions, which had fostered this spirit of initiative. Tovey went on with characteristic generosity of spirit to say: 'Force H was handled with conspicuous skill throughout the operation by Vice-Admiral Sir James F. Somerville, KCB, DSO and contributed a vital share in its successful conclusion.' And, whether or not Tovey knew by this time how hard the naval staff had striven in the Admiralty War Room to keep the Prime Minister and the First Sea Lord off his back, he had praise for the Admiralty too: 'The accuracy of the enemy information supplied by the Admiralty and the speed with which it was passed were remarkable and the balance struck between information and instructions passed to forces out of visual touch with me, was ideal.'[86]

But privately he was angered by one notable exception to this ideal balance. At 1137 that forenoon of 27 May 1941 when he was steaming for home having accomplished his task, the First Sea Lord made him a signal that had in fact been drafted by Churchill and sent at his behest. It read:

> We cannot visualise situation from your signals. *Bismarck* must be sunk at all costs, and if to do this it is necessary for *King George V* to remain on the scene then she must do so even if subsequently means towing *King George V*.[87]

Few will disagree with Tovey's later verdict that this was 'the stupidest and most ill-considered signal ever made'.[88]

After the killing of the shark came the hunting of piranhas – the powerfully armed raiders disguised as innocent merchantmen and the supply ships on which they depended.[89] Thanks to the picture of the deployment of the supply ships built up through Ultra decrypts of the 'Home Waters' naval Enigma, seven of these were disposed of by 21 June 1941, and another seven (including the weather ship *Lauenburg*) sunk or captured between 21 June and 11 July. But the raiders themselves when far off in the South Atlantic or beyond used the 'Distant Waters' Enigma cypher, which GC and CS never penetrated to the end of the war.[90] Nevertheless on 8 May HMS *Cornwall*, alerted by a victim's radio call, sank the raider *Pinguin* in the Indian Ocean.

On 19 December the raider *Kormoran* was caught off Western Australia by HMAS *Sydney* which incautiously approached to within 2,000 yards to identify her. On being challenged to give a secret identifying call sign, the *Kormoran* opened fire first, hitting the *Sydney* under the bridge and torpedoing her. There followed for some two hours a furious action in which the *Kormoran* was badly damaged and set ablaze, to be later scuttled by her crew. The *Sydney* herself had her two forward turrets put out of action, and when the exchange of fire ceased with the fall of night she steamed slowly away blazing furiously, later to blow up and sink with all hands; a sorry and possibly needless end for a ship which had served with such distinction in the Mediterranean in 1940.

But three days later HMS *Devonshire* avenged her by sinking the raider *Atlantis* off the Cape of Good Hope. She found the *Atlantis* thanks to GC and CS decyphering a 'Home Waters' Enigma signal instructing U-boats to rendezvous with the *Atlantis* in order to refuel from her. The remaining four raiders at large in 1941 made safe return to Germany between August and December.

Although the disguised raiders were to sneak back to the high seas in 1942, the German warships were never to return. For in hunting down and destroying the *Bismarck* the Royal Navy had sunk not just a single battleship, however formidable; it had sunk Grand Admiral

Raeder's entire strategy, so long pursued, of breaking down Britain's Atlantic communications by means of a surface fleet. When the *Prinz Eugen* returned to Brest on 1 June 1941 with engine trouble, it marked the end of all operations in the Atlantic by German battleships, pocket battleships and cruisers, even though the mere threat was to preoccupy the Admiralty and tie down British heavy ships until 1944. The death of the *Bismarck* destroyed Hitler's always lukewarm support for Raeder's strategy; it vindicated Dönitz's argument since long before the war that surface forces consumed enormous resources of material and manpower that could be far more cost-effectively employed in expanding the U-boat fleet. As Raeder was ruefully to acknowledge: 'The loss of the *Bismarck* had a decisive effect on the conduct of the war at sea.'[91]

However, by the time the Royal Navy had won this, its first strategic victory in the Second World War, Churchill's 'blue water' strategy in the Mediterranean had collapsed in catastrophe; and it had been the Mediterranean Fleet which, even more than the British and Dominion armies, had paid the gruesome price.

11

Greek Prelude: The Battle of Matapan

The year had begun so well. On 5 January 1941 General O'Connor's Western Desert Force completed the capture of the Italian fortress of Bardia, just across the Egyptian frontier into Libya, together with 400 guns, 138 tanks, and over 700 trucks, inflicting losses of over 40,000 men killed, wounded and prisoners. On 21 January it was the turn of the fortress port of Tobruk. After a brief Hurricane bombardment, heavily armoured 'I' tanks followed by infantry of the 6th Australian Division smashed through the defensive perimeter into the heart of the fortress. This time the bag amounted to 25,000 prisoners, 208 guns, 23 medium tanks and over 200 trucks.

Now came the bold, brilliant climax of O'Connor's campaign: an advance by his worn-out armour across abominable desert tracks to cut off the remainder of the Italian 10th Army as it retreated from Benghazi along the coast road to Tripolitania. On 6 February O'Connor closed his trap at Beda Fomm, south of Benghazi, with just half an hour to spare. All that day the desperate Italians strove to break through and escape – and failed. By the evening O'Connor had consummated that rarest of military achievements, a victory of total annihilation. In the course of his ten-week campaign he had advanced 500 miles, destroyed an army of ten divisions, taken 130,000 prisoners, 400 tanks, 1,290 guns and two major fortresses, all for the cost of 476 British Empire troops killed, 1,225 wounded and 43 missing.[1] Thanks to O'Connor's leadership and to the skill and spirit of his British,

Indian and Australian soldiers, Winston Churchill's Mediterranean 'blue water' strategy had thus been for the moment crowned with an unimagined triumph; the reward for all the effort invested in building up the Middle East forces and their base installations, all the Royal Navy's months of hazardous service along the sea lanes that led from Britain and the Empire to Alexandria and Suez.

And the Royal Navy itself had directly played an important part in the Desert offensive. On 3 January 1941 *Warspite*, *Barham* and *Valiant* bombarded Bardia. The ancient Great War monitor, *HMS Terror* (two 15-inch guns) and the three gunboats *Ladybird*, *Aphis* and *Gnat* of the Inshore Squadron (Captain H. Hickling, RN) had also bombarded the defences of Bardia and Tobruk as well; and hammered the retreating Italians as they straggled westwards on the coast road. Still more important, the flow of seaborne supplies which alone had kept O'Connor's little army in the field and able to advance depended solely upon the Navy. As Cunningham wrote to the First Sea Lord on 18 January, three days before the fall of Tobruk:

> Our commitments in support of the Army in the Western Desert grow daily and with the fall of Tobruk expected in a day or two, they will reach, I hope, a peak. Everything is going by sea including, since a few days ago, practically all the personnel. The strain on our destroyers and small auxiliary craft is tremendous and also it is very difficult to find the right type of shipping for the job. Small coastal carriers are what are required but there just aren't any.[2]

With O'Connor's final destruction of the Italian 10th Army at Beda Fomm on 6 February 1941, Tripolitania (the western province of Libya) lay open to a further British advance, for only a few demoralised, disorganised and ill-equipped Italian troops remained to defend it. O'Connor therefore planned to make an immediate advance as far as Syrte, and then, on 20 February, launch an armoured striking force along the coast road to Tripoli while the Royal Navy landed an infantry brigade from the sea. But by now it was known in London and Cairo that a new, much more formidable, foe lay just over the strategic horizon in the Mediterranean theatre – drawn in by the very brilliance of O'Connor's victories in the Desert, by the Greek Army's valiant success in throwing the Italian invader back into Albania, and by the Royal Navy's domination of the Mediterranean waters despite the Italian Navy and Air Force. For Hitler had decided to come to the rescue of his humiliated friend Mussolini.

The German forward build-up in the Balkans and Mediterranean had been steadily plotted by GC and CS at Bletchley Park through decrypts of the Luftwaffe Enigma and also the German railway administration Enigma, as correlated with other sources of Intelligence.[3] By the end of December 1940 the British knew that Germany was deploying for a major offensive in the Balkans, the tide of troops and aircraft lapping down through compliant Hungary and Romania, with the ultimate objective in all likelihood being Greece. By 9 January 1941 the Defence Committee in London had become – wrongly – convinced from the latest decrypts that the German offensive could be launched as early as 20 January. By late January further decrypts led the Director of Military Intelligence to believe that the Germans had now deployed 23 divisions in Romania, while the British embassy in Bucharest reported that the Germans would march into Bulgaria on 17 February. Military Intelligence therefore now calculated that the Germans could be on the Greek frontier with five divisions by 12 March and reach Athens with ten divisions from mid-April onwards. Here then was a colossal new weight poised to drop into the delicate balance of British 'blue water' strategy in the Mediterranean and Middle East theatre, and especially General Wavell's finely calculated deployment of his scanty land forces, already stretched from the Western Desert to East Africa.

Yet it was Cunningham's Fleet rather than Wavell's land forces which first took the shock of the German advent in the Mediterranean theatre. By 15 December 1940 Air Intelligence (AI) and GC and CS had accumulated evidence from the Luftwaffe Enigma and other sources that the Luftwaffe's 'Fliegerkorps X' (including a squadron specialising in attacks on shipping) was being moved south to Italian bases. By the first week of January 1941 it was known that the Luftwaffe had set up bases in Sicily, whence it could command the passage between the western and eastern basins of the Mediterranean, through the Sicilian Narrows and the skies over Malta only some 60 miles away. London and Cairo also took note of an Italian broadcast on 2 January welcoming the Luftwaffe to the Mediterranean war. By 10 January the strength of 'Fliegerkorps X' in Sicily had actually risen to 96 bombers and 25 twin-engined fighters.[4]

But regrettably the available Intelligence about 'Fliegerkorps X's' arrival and its estimated strength (put at 80 aircraft) were not passed to either the Mediterranean Fleet or Force H, although whether this omission is to be blamed on the Air Ministry or the Admiralty cannot now be established.[5] The omission was the more regrettable because, from 6–7 January, the Mediterranean Fleet and Force H were at sea engaged in yet another complicated trans-Mediterranean operation, covering the passage of the convoy (codenamed 'Excess') postponed from December 1940. Apart from one hour's warning from a radio intercept by the 'Y' officer ('Y' = interception of enemy radio traffic) in HMS *Warspite*, the Fleet's first intimation that the Luftwaffe had arrived over the Mediterranean in force took the form of Stukas screaming down on it in relays shortly after noon on 10 January.

Four days earlier the four merchant ships to be convoyed – one bound for Malta with 4,000 tons of ammunition, 3,000 tons of seed potatoes and a deck cargo of twelve crated Hurricanes; the three others bound for Piraeus with urgent supplies for Greece – had sailed from Gibraltar escorted by destroyers and a new radar-equipped cruiser *Bonaventure* (5,450 tons displacement; ten dual-purpose 5.25-inch guns; eight 2-pounder anti-aircraft guns; eight 0.5-inch machine guns).[6] Early next morning Admiral Somerville followed with the main body of Force H: HMS *Renown* (flag), the battleship *Malaya*, *Ark Royal*, *Sheffield* and six destroyers. Meantime Admiral Cunningham had despatched Rear-Admiral E. de F. Renouf from Alexandria to Malta with the cruisers *Gloucester* (flag) and *Southampton* and two destroyers with 500 soldiers and airmen aboard. On 7 January Cunningham followed with the main body of the Mediterranean Fleet – *Warspite* (flag), the battleship *Valiant*, the carrier *Illustrious* and seven destroyers. At first all went well. In the evening of the 9th Somerville safely handed over his convoy off Bizerta to Renouf after Italian high-level bombers had scored the usual alarming near-misses, but no hits; he then turned back for Gibraltar; an uneventful home voyage. Cunningham's light forces meanwhile successfully covered the movements of two merchant ships westwards to Malta and two small convoys eastwards from Malta, the C-in-C himself steering to a rendezvous with the 'Excess' convoy. At dawn on 10 January, to the west of Malta, he received a report from *Bonaventure* that she had sighted two enemy destroyers; and almost at the same time gun flashes could be seen ahead. Cunningham increased to full speed ahead, and reached *Bonaventure* to find her and the destroyer *Hereward* firing into a blazing Italian destroyer, which soon blew up. The united fleet now turned to follow the convoy eastwards.

However, almost at once the destroyer *Gallant* in the Fleet's screen had its bow blown clean away by a mine; the first bad news. While she was being towed into Malta under escort, two Italian torpedo bombers came in low to attack the *Valiant*, but both torpedoes passed astern. The four Fulmar fighters patrolling high above the Fleet dived down to chase the Italians away. Almost immediately radar picked up a large formation of enemy aircraft approaching from the north, and the *Illustrious* turned into the wind to fly off more fighters. Too late: before these aircraft or the original four Fulmars could regain sufficient height 43 Junkers Ju 87 Stuka divebombers were over the Fleet and diving to the attack.[7]

The Mediterranean Fleet had grown accustomed enough to attacks by Italian bombers from heights of up to 10,000 feet, even though its ships' companies found it cumulatively wearing to be near-missed again and again. The margin of bomb-aiming error from this height with so small and elusive a target as a ship violently altering course was such as to make very long odds against direct hits as opposed to near-misses. But a Stuka attack was altogether different, as Cunningham and his fleet quickly discovered:

> We opened up with every AA gun we had [wrote Cunningham] as one by one the Stukas peeled off into their dives, concentrating the whole venom of their attack upon the *Illustrious*. At times she became almost completely hidden in a forest of great bomb splashes. One was too interested in this new form of dive-bombing attack really to be frightened, and there was no doubt we were watching complete experts. Formed roughly in a large circle over the fleet they peeled off one by one when reaching the attacking position. We could not but admire the skill and precision of it all. The attacks were pressed home to point-blank range, and as they pulled out of their dives some of them were seen to fly along the flight-deck of the *Illustrious* below the level of her funnel.[8]

At this range there could be no mistake. 'I saw her [the *Illustrious*] hit early on just before the bridge,' wrote Cunningham later, 'and in all, in something like ten minutes, she was hit by six 1,000-lb bombs, to leave the line badly on fire, her steering gear crippled, her lifts out of action, and with heavy casualties.'[9] Just like the *Bismarck*, the wounded *Illustrious* turned helplessly in circles until, after three hours, she was able to steer by her main engines. As she struggled towards the shelter of Malta harbour escorted by the Fleet, the bombers came back four more times – the Stukas twice, and Heinkel 111 medium bombers twice – hitting her with another 1,000-lb bomb. At 2100 she finally limped into the Grand Harbour, her survival being, as Cunningham wrote to the First Sea Lord, 'a fine advertisement for British shipbuilding'.[10] Nonetheless, she had been so severely damaged as to require long months in a main dockyard – if she could be safely got away from Malta.

The Mediterranean Fleet had suffered its most serious setback in the war so far. 'We had plenty to think about,' was how Cunningham drily summed it up:

> In a few minutes the whole situation had changed. At one blow the fleet had been deprived of its fighter aircraft, and its command of the Mediterranean was threatened by a weapon far more efficient and dangerous than any against which we had fought before. The efforts of the Regia Aeronautica were almost as nothing compared with those of these deadly Stukas of the Luftwaffe.[11]

Now, more than ever, the Mediterranean Fleet was to suffer from the pre-war Admiralty's decision to adopt the inferior and inaccurate High Angle Control System (HACS) instead of tachymetric fire-control. The harsh lesson taught by the knocking out of the *Illustrious* was repeated at 1500 next day when Admiral Renouf, with the cruisers *Gloucester* and *Southampton* (neither fitted with radar), was jumped by twelve Stukas attacking out of the sun. *Gloucester* was hit in the director tower by a bomb which then penetrated five decks. Although it mercifully failed to explode, it nevertheless inflicted severe local damage and killed nine members of the crew. The *Southampton*, however, was hit by two or three bombs which started raging fires that could not be quenched. Shortly after 1900 she had to be abandoned and sunk by torpedo.

With the Fleet back in Alexandria, Cunningham's immediate anxiety lay in the need to get *Illustrious* away from Malta, where she was being subjected to constant further German air attack, which inflicted yet further damage, and more casualties than she had suffered in the earlier attacks at sea. The dockyard staff worked frenziedly under fire to make her sufficiently seaworthy to make a dash for Alexandria, and on the night of 23 January she slipped away and set course at 24 knots. At noon on 25 January *Illustrious* steamed into Alexandria to roaring cheers from the ships' companies of the Fleet.

Already, on 12 January, the Admiralty had decided to send Cunningham the new carrier *Formidable* (then in the South Atlantic) as a replacement. But it would be well into March before she could arrive via the Cape of Good Hope and the Suez Canal. But then came a further complication: from late January onwards the Canal itself was recurrently blocked by wrecks caused by mines dropped from the air, often of the acoustic type to which there was no available technical answer. This closure of the Canal impeded the exchange of *Illustrious* and *Formidable* as well as the routine traffic of warships and merchant vessels between the Red Sea and the eastern Mediterranean. For the Royal Air Force the new need to strengthen the air defence of the Canal against the minelayers meant yet a further stretching of scarce resources already pulled as far apart as Greece, Malta, Libya and East

Africa. And for the Army it meant a recurrent throttling of its supply line from the outside world to the Mediterranean and Middle East theatre's main arrival ports, Alexandria and Port Said.

At the other end of the Mediterranean, however, Admiral Somerville and Force H had provided welcome compensation for Cunningham's setback at the hands of 'Fliegerkorps X'. On 6 February 1941 Somerville sailed from Gibraltar with the *Renown* (flag; Captain R. R. McGrigor), *Malaya* (Captain A. F. E. Palliser), *Ark Royal* (Captain C. S. 'Hooky' Holland), *Sheffield* (Captain C. A. A. Larcom) and ten destroyers with the aim of bombarding Genoa, Italy's largest port (where it was believed one of the battleships damaged at Taranto was being repaired), and of launching air strikes against La Spezia and Leghorn.[12] The operation entailed an outward voyage of 700 miles, the final leg lying in the enemy's own home waters and within easy range of his land-based aircraft. Somerville's best protection lay in the very boldness, not to say cheek, of the enterprise. For the Italians never expected a British task force to flaunt the White Ensign in the Gulf of Genoa itself, and they had taken no measures to prevent such an incursion.

Between 0600 and 0707 on 9 February spotting aircraft were catapulted from *Renown*, *Malaya* and *Sheffield*. Landfall was made off Portofino at 0649, the shoreline shrouded in mist, the mountains behind silhouetted against the sky. At 0710 *Renown*'s spotter reported that no battleships were present in Genoa; an error, for *Diulio* lay in the dry dock, unrecognised.

> The scene off Genoa was almost dramatic in its contrasts. It was a calm Sunday morning, the foreshore hidden from view in the haze, above which the mountains stood out, turning from grey to rose in the rising sun; there was nothing to break the peace and silence. Suddenly at 0714 the *Renown* opened fire.[13]

At a range of ten to fourteen miles 15-inch and 6-inch salvoes smashed on to industrial targets and the dry docks, while HMS *Renown*'s secondary armament fired on the waterfront itself. At 0745 the British ships ceased fire and turned away to the south, leaving astern the gratifying sight of flames, explosions and billowing smoke on the Genoa shoreline that indicated (correctly) that much destruction had been inflicted, although the battleship *Diulio* in dry dock was not hit. However the *Ark Royal*'s air strike against an oil refinery at Leghorn caused only slight damage, although others of her aircraft successfully laid mines in both entrances to the La Spezia naval base.

Somerville safely reached Gibraltar on 11 February, the Italians having missed their chance of intercepting him partly because of poor visibility which hampered air reconnaissance, but even more because of poor liaison between their naval and air commands.

Somerville's raid was celebrated by the British press as a Drake-like singeing of Mussolini's chin-stubble; and for the same reasons it caused lively dismay in Italy. Yet such a hit-and-run raid, however successful, could not alter the fact that the début of 'Fliegerkorps X' in Sicily had transformed the naval prospects in the central Mediterranean. Churchill's long-cherished project of capturing the Italian island of Pantellaria in the Sicilian Narrows ('Workshop') had to be postponed again for a month on 18 January and finally cancelled two days later.[14] Cunningham wrote to the First Sea Lord that he was 'indeed thankful that WORKSHOP was not being carried out. I don't think there is much doubt we should have lost both the Glen ships [fast troop carriers] and anything else lying off the island.'[15] The Prime Minister himself had drawn the opposite conclusion from the crippling of *Illustrious* on 11 January and the loss of *Southampton*. Regretting 'bitterly'[16] that he had been persuaded [in December 1940] to postpone 'Workshop', he minuted for the Chiefs of Staff on 13 January that it was 'necessary now that "Workshop" should be reviewed . . . I should be glad if revised and perfected plans would be ready by today week . . .'[17] It was only at the Defence Committee meeting on 20 January that he at last gave way to the united opposition of the Chiefs of Staff and accepted 'Workshop's' abandonment.[18]

Yet 'Workshop' was not the only gleaming strategic trinket to catch Churchill's eye at this period in spite of the pervasive British weakness in the Mediterranean theatre and the ominous German build-up. At the same Defence Committee on 20 January he told his colleagues that he wanted a plan studied 'to capture Sardinia', a project involving 40,000 troops and all the requisite transports and powerful escorting naval forces.[19] Yet another plan – 'Mandibles' – was afoot for invading the Italian Dodecanese islands and seizing the main island of Rhodes, in this case a plan actually enjoying the support of the three service Cs-in-C in the Mediterranean. In February 1941 two separate preliminary attempts were made to land forces on the outlying islands of Kaso and Kastellorizo. Both attempts failed, partly because of tactical and command errors on the British side, partly because of unexpectedly vigorous Italian counter-action;[20] two more examples to add to the long historical tally of botched British combined operations.

It was the very flexibility of seapower that made it possible for Churchill to espouse such schemes as 'Workshop' and 'Mandibles' –

a flexibility no less seductive to him than to his predecessor Pitt the Younger in plotting similar 'descents' here and there along the coasts of Bonapartian Europe. Yet it was Greece which, in the early months of 1941, presented the Prime Minister and his colleagues with the overriding choice in Mediterranean 'blue water' strategy. For Ultra decrypts and other Intelligence made it more and more plain that she was almost certain to fall victim soon to a German 'blitzkrieg'.

Should a large (in British terms) expeditionary force be transported to Greece by the Royal Navy in order to fight alongside the Greek Army against the invading Germans? Such an expeditionary force could of course only be found from the veteran troops and the tanks of O'Connor's Western Desert Force. Or should the Royal Air Force squadrons (some 80 serviceable aircraft[21]) already in Greece remain the limit of British aid? These questions aroused the same kind of argument in the Cabinet Defence Committee as that over intervention in Scandinavia in 1939–40. On the one hand there was a debt of honour to do all that lay in Britain's power to save a brave ally; and coupled with that, the political need (especially vis-à-vis the United States) not to be seen callously to abandon the Greeks. On the other hand there was the cold accountancy of available divisions, tanks, guns, aircraft and stocks of ammunition on each side; and so far as German figures were concerned, accountancy largely derived from decrypts of Enigma traffic.

By 10 January accumulating evidence from the Secret Intelligence Service (SIS) and diplomatic sources as well as from Ultra had convinced the War Cabinet Defence Committee (see above, p. 319) that Germany would invade Greece as early as 20 January. A sense of urgency now impelled the Committee to instruct the Chief of Air Staff to signal Air Marshal Sir Arthur Longmore, the AOC-in-C, Middle East, that he was to fly to Athens to offer immediate help to the Greeks. Since O'Connor was at that time preparing his onslaught on Tobruk, Wavell, on behalf of all three Middle East Cs-in-C, replied to the CIGS, Dill, that the signal to Longmore

> fills us with dismay. Our appreciation here is that German concentration is move in a war of nerves with the object of helping Italy by upsetting Greek nerves, inducing us to disperse our forces in Middle East and to stop our advance in Libya. Nothing (*repeat* nothing) we can do from here is likely to be in time to stop German advance if really intended, it will lead to most dangerous dispersion of force and is playing the enemy's game . . . I am desperately anxious lest we play enemy's game and expose ourselves to defeat in detail.[22]

But the Prime Minister implacably replied through the Chiefs of Staff that the evidence showed the enemy was not bluffing:

> Destruction of Greece would eclipse victories you have gained in Libya and might affect decisively Turkish attitude, especially if we had shown ourselves callous of fate of allies. You must therefore conform your plans to larger interests at stake. We expect and require prompt and active compliance with our decisions for which we bear full responsibility.[23]

Mercifully, however, the Greek government at this time declined the British offer of an expeditionary force, while Intelligence sources had now come to suggest that it would after all take the Germans some two months to deploy against Greece. O'Connor was thus granted a reprieve – fruitfully employed by him in completing the destruction of the Italian 10th Army and clearing Cyrenaica.

Three days after O'Connor's climactic victory at Beda Fomm Wavell signalled London: 'The extent of Italian defeat at Benghazi [sic] seems to me to make it possible that TRIPOLI might yield to small force if despatched without delay.'[24] This was certainly O'Connor's appreciation (see above, p. 318). If successful such an advance would end the war in North Africa, so permanently securing Egypt and the Suez Canal from land attack; it would provide the Royal Air Force with air bases from which to cover the central Mediterranean. Indeed, the fundamental military principle of 'the maintenance of the aim' suggested that O'Connor's victory should be exploited to the uttermost. Nevertheless, Churchill successfully swayed a meeting of the Defence Committee on 10 February in favour of his own view that O'Connor should be halted for the sake of aiding Greece. According to the minutes the Prime Minister

> . . . did not think that it was necessarily impossible for the Greeks and ourselves to hold the Germans, who would be advancing down the Struma valley. The Greeks might be able to disengage a few Divisions in time, and if we could support them with air and mechanised forces, we might delay them long enough to encourage the Turks, and possibly the Yugoslavs, to join in the battle.[25]

The Committee agreed that Britain should send aid to the Greeks if asked, and 'that no serious operation should be undertaken beyond Benghazi [sic] which should be held as a secure flank for Egypt'; that therefore 'we should shift the largest possible force from Egypt to the European Continent, to assist the Greeks against a probable attack through Bulgaria'.[26]

The record makes clear that, just as in the case of Norway, Churchill urged this fateful strategic choice in defiance of the military accountancy. On 11 February, in a further Defence Committee discussion on the question, General Sir John Dill, the CIGS, pointed out that it would be difficult for Wavell to find four divisions for Greece in the immediate future, because – except for the 'green' 2nd Armoured Division (still forming) – all his troops were engaged in operations. To this Churchill retorted: 'We would have to intervene with at least 4 divisions, rising to 6 or 10 in the summer. Out of the great mass of men accumulating in the Middle East, great efforts must be made to produce more mobile formations.'[27]

Yet such a massive build-up and continuing campaign thereafter would require a proportionate logistical effort, especially in terms of ammunition, not only for the British Empire troops but also for the Greek Army, and at a time when such resources were desperately scarce in the Middle East theatre. As the Chiefs of Staff pointed out in a paper on 10 February, Britain could only supply a proportion of the Greek Army's ammunition requirements, while 'the artillery weapon situation is still more difficult', not least because the Greeks needed 350 (mule) pack artillery equipments, which Britain did not even manufacture.[28]

Nevertheless such key considerations never came under discussion in the Defence Committee when the crucial decision was being reached to stop O'Connor in his tracks.

On 11 February Wavell was instructed:

> You should therefore make yourself secure at Benghazi and concentrate all available forces in the Delta in preparation for a movement to Europe . . . Our first thoughts must be for our ally Greece, which is actually fighting so well. If Greece is trampled down or forced to make a separate peace with Italy, yielding also Air and naval strategic points against us to Germany, effect on Turkey will be very bad. But if Greece with British aid can hold up for some months German advance, chances of Turkish intervention will be favoured. Therefore it would seem that we should try to get in a position to offer the Greeks the transfer to Greece of the fighting portion of the Army which has hitherto defended Egypt [i.e. O'Connor's Western Desert Force] and make every plan for sending and reinforcing it to the limit with men and material.[29]

The burden, risk and likely cost to the Royal Navy in the Mediterranean in particular of the proposed grand exercise in 'blue water strategy' could not have been more plainly spelt out than it was in a joint telegram by the three Commanders-in-Chief in the

Mediterranean and Middle East theatre, Wavell, Cunningham and Longmore, about the weakness of their resources in terms of existing or projected tasks.

> From the naval point of view the new policy creates a heavy commitment in safeguarding the line of supply through Aegean, and will entail establishing bases in Greek Islands and in Turkey . . . We are already completely extended in so far as our present resources are concerned in covering the long lines of sea communication on Libyan coasts and in dealing with protection of Libya in addition to our own Mediterranean bases. Admiralty are meeting our requirements in cruisers and light craft for this purpose . . . but this programme does not complete until May. If the Balkan situation develops meanwhile, the present acute shortage in light craft escorts, local defence units and personnel for shore bases will become critical unless our resources continue to be built up as rapidly as possible . . .[30]

The telegram went on to note the shortages of anti-aircraft guns and aircraft, and tellingly to express the three Commanders-in-Chiefs' general misgivings:

> Finally we feel there may be a tendency at home to over-estimate our actual resources in Middle East when assessing our ability to meet the varying commitments.[31]

On the same day Admiral Cunningham signalled to the Admiralty:

> If the Germans operate air force from Bulgaria, as appears to be their obvious intention, shipping in North Aegean will be gravely threatened by bombing and in ports such as Salonika and their approaches by aircraft minelaying . . . obviously it will be a task of considerable magnitude to provide and organise this protection [of convoys by fighters] from Greece, which has few developed landing grounds and where scale of air attack will be high. We shall do our best to get convoys through, but we must be prepared for casualties to ships and troops.
>
> The magnetic and acoustic mine threat is, however, more serious because it is not possible with existing resources to keep clear yet more areas such as Salonika, its approach and island harbours . . .[32]

But Churchill brushed aside such considerations – just as he did the heavily adverse military odds on land as calculated at this time from the latest Ultra Intelligence and other sources. According to these calculations German strength in Romania now stood at 23 divisions, while five German divisions could be on the Greek frontier by 12 March and ten divisions in Athens between mid-April and mid-May. The most that Britain could send to Greece, as Churchill was aware, was three infantry divisions and one armoured brigade; and only exiguous air cover could be provided for them against the Luftwaffe. Indeed the Premier actually opted for the Greek adventure in the face of apparent odds far more adverse than in reality, for German strength in Romania then stood at nine divisions, not 23. O'Connor's excellent if fleeting chance of taking Tripoli, so preempting a German intervention in Africa, had therefore been sacrificed to what was in all military respects another unrealistic gamble. Churchill chose Greece over Tripoli primarily for political reasons, if not simply moral ones, telling the Defence Committee on 10 February that it would be 'wrong to abandon the Greeks, who were putting up a magnificent fight, and who were prepared to fight the Germans, so that we could later help Turkey, who was shirking her responsibilities . . .'[33] He added that 'we could not blame the Greeks if they bowed to the superior force of the Germans if we refused them help'.

On 12 February the Foreign Secretary, Anthony Eden, and the Chief of Imperial General Staff, General Sir John Dill, were despatched to the Middle East to concert plans with the three Cs-in-C and the Greek government, and seek to drum up active support from Turkey and Yugoslavia – the old Great War fantasy again of a Balkan coalition, for which Eden was to find no takers either in Ankara or Belgrade. On the same day Major-General Erwin Rommel arrived in Tripoli in advance of the German field force that he was to command. During the following week Churchill too late began to have second thoughts about the Greek adventure, and on 20 February he signalled Eden in Cairo: 'Do not consider yourselves obligated to a Greek enterprise if in your hearts you feel it will only be another Norwegian fiasco. If no good plan can be made please say so. But of course you know how valuable success would be.'[34]

Unaccountably Wavell now expressed the opinion that there was a fair military chance of stopping the Germans in Greece; Dill somewhat wanly concurred; and Eden signalled home on 24 February that all three of them advised the government to despatch the 'maximum' British military and air support at 'the earliest possible moment'.[35] In London, the Director of Military Intelligence, drawing on the latest clues from Enigma – which indicated that the German attack was going to be on a formidable scale – gloomily noted that 'we must be prepared to face the loss of all forces sent to Greece'.[36] A memorandum by the Chiefs of Staff on 24 February, drawing up a balance sheet of resourccs and prospects, also vented the deepest misgivings.

'We are undertaking a commitment,' they wrote, 'of which we cannot foresee the extent.'[37] It noted again 'the acute shortage of artillery and equipment for the Greeks', as well as the risk to Egypt from an enemy counter-stroke in the desert. As for the Royal Navy, on which this fresh adventure in 'blue water' strategy totally depended, the Chiefs of Staff noted that there 'would be a considerable air menace to our lines of communication to Greece, and the reduction of the Dodecanese becomes urgent. It must be repeated that, if the war spreads to the Far East, the position of our forces in Greece will be precarious if we withdrew important units of the Mediterranean Fleet to go eastward . . .' Their advice to the government hardly amounted to enthusiastic endorsement of the adventure:

> It goes without saying that the expedition must be a gamble, but our representatives on the spot, after conference with the Greeks, and full examination of the Greek plan, evidently think there is a reasonable prospect of holding up a German advance. We feel we must accept their opinion.[38]

That day the Cabinet debated the telegrams from Eden and Dill, together with the Chiefs of Staff report. Despite his belated second thoughts about the risks and costs, Churchill said 'he was himself in favour of going to the rescue of Greece, one of the results of which might be to bring in Turkey and Yugoslavia, and to force the Germans to bring more troops from Germany. The reaction of the United States would also be favourable . . .' Despite this dream of a Balkan coalition, the Prime Minister did acknowledge on the other hand, that 'the difficulties of maintaining an army on land must not be under-rated, for it would have to be supplied by ships going round the Cape of Good Hope'.[39]

Others too expressed concern about the problem of seaborne supply. The Australian Prime Minister, Robert Menzies, who was present (Australian forces forming so large a part of the expeditionary force), asked: 'Could our shipping maintain the strain of the operation?' The Minister of Aircraft Production, Lord Beaverbrook, likewise thought that 'the effect of the enterprise on our shipping resources should be closely examined'.[40] Nevertheless, the Cabinet decided to approve the despatch of forces to Greece, and in a further meeting next day the Prime Minister remarked that he 'felt no doubt' that the decision was right despite the shipping problem.[41] The Cabinet took note that German troops had been encountered for the first time in the Western Desert clash at El Agheila, on the border between Tripolitania and Cyrenaica.

On 4 March 'Operation Lustre' – the transport of the British Commonwealth expeditionary force to Greece – duly began. As the first ships were about to sail, Admiral Cunningham signalled the Admiralty that he wished to make it clear that a big risk was being taken, principally because of the weakness of the convoys and the ports of disembarkation against air attack. Apart from a run to Malta with one convoy after *Formidable* had arrived, he went on, the moves to Greece would absorb the whole energies of the Fleet for the next two months at least. Meanwhile the Cyrenaican supply line to the Desert Army would go almost unprotected, and the proposed landings in the Dodecanese would have to be postponed.[42]

This same day Dill in Athens learned from the Greek Commander-in-Chief, General Papagos, that no preparatory work had been done as promised on the defensive position to be occupied by the British expeditionary force along the River Aliakmon, and that only much smaller Greek forces than promised could now be redeployed alongside the British. Meanwhile in a Chiefs-of-Staff meeting in London the Minister of Shipping said he was 'very concerned' about the number of ships to be held in the Middle East for 'Lustre', evoking the retort from the Prime Minister (and Minister of Defence) that extra shipping must be found from the 2,200,000 tons at present 'lying idle under repair' [in the United Kingdom].[43] The Chiefs of Staff noted that Dill's disquieting news, coupled with the likely timing and weight of the German onslaught, meant that the hazards of the enterprise had been greatly increased.[44]

Next day, 5 March, the First Sea Lord, as spokesman for the Chiefs-of-Staff, told the Defence Committee that the three Middle East Cs-in-C had been asked for an appreciation of the time it would take the Germans to reach the Aliakmon line, also for a report on the Suez Canal situation (i.e., the effects of aerial mining of the Canal on the vital line of communication to the Mediterranean and Greece) and 'a report on the probable ammunition situation during the proposed campaign. [The ammunition aspect had tended to disappear into the background] . . .'[45] The First Sea Lord added that until answers were received to these queries, the Chiefs-of-Staff were not in a position to revise their previous views.

But it was far too late to ask these questions, and no answers in fact were ever received. However, on 8 March the British military mission in Athens reported that the Greek Army's artillery ammunition in the present war against the Italians would only last until mid-April

– just about the time the German invasion could be expected.[46]

By now even Churchill, in the face of all this rising doubt, had become fully seized by a belated realism; and on this same day, with the agreement of the Defence Committee, he signalled Eden in Athens to express their heavy misgivings concerning the Greek C-in-C's failure to implement his promises, with regard to the state of the Greek Army, and with regard to the political complications in respect of the Dominions of Australia and New Zealand over risking their divisions in Greece. All this, he told Eden in a telegram:

> . . . makes it difficult for Cabinet to believe that we now have any power to avert fate of Greece unless Turkey and/or Yugoslavia come in, which seems most improbable. We have done our best to promote Balkan combination against Germany. We must be careful not to urge Greece against her better judgement into a hopeless resistance alone when we have only handfuls of troops which can reach the scene in time . . .[47]

It must be said that all these were considerations which were equally valid on 10 February, when the Prime Minister persuaded his colleagues to take the original and now irrevocable decision to halt O'Connor in favour of the Greek adventure. Moreover, in a remarkable volte-face, Churchill had by now changed his entire view of the strategic and political value of going to Greece anyway, telling Eden in the same telegram that 'loss of Greece and Balkans by no means a major catastrophe for us provided Turkey remains honest neutral . . .'; and he alluded to the possibility of instead resuming 'Mandibles' (the Dodecanese operation) or, of all things, an advance on Tripoli.[48]

However, Eden replied next day that the three theatre Cs-in-C remained of the opinion that 'Lustre' should continue. On 7 March the War Cabinet argued long and hard for the last time about the Greek enterprise, but finally 'confirmed the decision to give military assistance to Greece, and agreed that all arrangements to this end should proceed'.[49]

Just four days later Cunningham was writing to the First Sea Lord: 'I hope it will turn out that our policy of helping Greece is the right one. To me it is absolutely right [on grounds of politics or honour?] but I much doubt if our resources, particularly naval and air, are equal to the strain.'[50] Cunningham was especially worried about the weakness of the Royal Air Force in the theatre, now that air power had become the key to operations on sea and land:

> There seems to me some bad misunderstanding about the state of our Air Force out here. I feel the Chiefs of Staff are badly misinformed about the

> number of fighter squadrons available. Longmore is absolutely stretched to the limit and we seem to have far fewer than is supposed at home. We are getting sat on by the Germans in Cyrenaica, the figures there are over 200 German and Italian fighters against 30 of our own. It seems to me that if the fighter situation is not taken in hand drastically and speedily we are heading straight for trouble – not only in Greece but if the Germans advance in Libya we have no air forces to stop them and actually very little else either.[51]

Throughout March 1941 warships plied between Alexandria and Port Said and the Greek port of Piraeus, taking the soldiers of the New Zealand Division, 6th Australian Division and 1st Armoured Brigade (the élite of Wavell's forces) from the palm trees, the ancient stinks and clamorous humanity of Egypt to the thyme-scented rocks tumbling down the northern slopes of Mount Olympus where they were to meet the expected German invasion. On disembarkation at Piraeus the troops were counted off by the German military attaché (Germany and Greece not of course yet being at war). Until after 24 March the movement of the merchant ships which transported the guns, tanks, trucks, ammunition and other supplies could be protected against attack by the Italian Fleet only by Vice-Admiral Pridham-Wippell's Light Forces (or Force B), consisting of the cruisers *Orion* (flag), *Ajax*, HMAS *Perth* and *Gloucester*, and four destroyers – because Cunningham himself with the battlefleet had been busy running the second supply convoy of the year into Malta by the customary feat of operational juggling. Two days after he returned to Alexandria came the bad news that his ill-protected forward base at Suda Bay, Crete, had been daringly attacked by six aquaplaning Italian motor boats loaded with explosives, and HMS *York* (his only 8-inch gun cruiser) so badly damaged that she had to be beached: a novel turn in the remorseless grind of attrition.

Early in the forenoon of that same day Cunningham received from the Admiralty various Ultra decrypts of Luftwaffe and Italian Navy Enigma signals which the Admiralty believed must point to a major enemy operation soon in the Aegean or eastern Mediterranean.[52] On 25 March a Luftwaffe signal had ordered all twin-engined fighters in Libya to fly to Palermo for 'special operations', and an Italian Navy signal had stated that the 25th was D – 3 for an operation involving Rhodes Command. On 26 March further signals revealed that air reconnaissance and air attacks on Allied airfields in the Aegean were to precede and accompany a certain operation; also that information had been requested about British convoys plying between Egypt and

Greece. Yet these somewhat mysterious clues could not even guide the C-in-C as to whether the impending attack on his convoys was going to be launched by air or surface forces. It was therefore in the usual sea-mist of uncertainty that Cunningham issued his first orders that evening in what was to be the climactic battle of his career as C-in-C of a fleet. He stopped a south-bound convoy from sailing from Piraeus, ordered a north-bound convoy to reverse course (under cover of darkness), and signalled Pridham-Wippell (already in the Aegean) to be south-west of Gavdo Island (south of Crete) at daylight on the 28th.

At 1230 next day came hard news at last, when a Royal Air Force flying-boat based in Crete reported three Italian cruisers and a destroyer 75 miles east of Sicily and steering towards Crete. Cunningham thereupon decided to put to sea with the battlefleet after nightfall. He intended that in the meantime the fleet lying at anchor in harbour should present a misleading picture of inactivity to the enemy air reconnaissance – which it successfully did, for at 1900 an Italian aircraft reported home that the British Fleet was still at Alexandria. In a personal deception plan to hoodwink the Japanese consul in Alexandria, a keen golfer suspected of spying for his Axis friends (and, in Cunningham's words, 'with a southern aspect of such elephantine proportions when he bent over to putt that the irreverent Chief of Staff had nicknamed him "the blunt end of the Axis"'),[53] Cunningham went ashore that afternoon to play golf, conspicuously carrying a suitcase as if he meant to spend the night ashore. He returned to his flagship after dark, and at 1900 the Fleet slipped its moorings and headed westwards course 300°, 20 knots: the *Warspite* (Captain D. B. Fisher; flag), *Barham* (flag of Rear-Admiral 1st Battle Squadron, Rear-Admiral H. B. Rawlings; Captain G. C. Cooke), *Valiant* (Captain C. E. Morgan), the carrier *Formidable* (Captain A. W. La T. Bisset) and the destroyers *Jervis*, *Janus*, *Nubian*, *Mohawk*, *Stuart*, *Greyhound*, *Griffin*, *Hotspur* and *Havock*.[54] By a mischance the flagship passed too close to a mudbank on the way out of harbour, so filling her condensers with mud and reducing her speed to 20 knots.

At dawn on 28 March an air search by four Albacores and a Swordfish was flown from *Formidable*. At 0722 one of them reported sighting four cruisers and four destroyers in 34° 22′N, 24° 47′E, steering 230°; twenty minutes later a second aircraft reported four cruisers and six destroyers in 34° 05′N, 24° 26′E. Since these fixes roughly corresponded with Pridham-Wippell's expected position, it was first believed that the aircraft had sighted him rather than the enemy. All doubt was, however, dispelled when at 0827 the C-in-C received a signal from Pridham-Wippell's flagship *Orion* (sent 0802) that she had sighted three enemy cruisers bearing north, distant eighteen miles, course eastward. Yet even now Cunningham could not be sure whether or not any enemy battleships might be present, because in the past British lookouts had taken battleships to be cruisers. He could only increase speed to 22 knots, the best that *Warspite* and *Barham* could manage, and alter course to 310° to support Pridham-Wippell.

In fact Admiral Iachino had sailed from Naples at 2100 on 26 March with the modern battleship *Vittorio Veneto* (flag; 41,377 tons displacement; nine 15-inch guns; 30 knots) and four destroyers, later to be joined from other Italian bases by the six 10,000-ton 8-inch gun cruisers *Trieste*, *Trento*, *Bolzano*, *Zara*, *Fiume* and *Pola*, the two 6-inch gun cruisers *Abruzzi* and *Garibaldi* and nine destroyers. This formidable striking force's task, undertaken in response to pressing German requests, was to attack the convoys carrying the British expeditionary force to Greece. At dawn on 28 March Iachino's fleet was deployed in three separate groups, course 130°: *Vittorio Veneto* and four escorting destroyers on the starboard station, with a group of three cruisers (*Trieste*, *Trento* and *Bolzano*) and three destroyers some ten miles on the flagship's port bow, and the third group (the remaining five cruisers and six destroyers) some twenty miles further still to port. At 0643 the flagship's spotter aircraft sighted four cruisers and four destroyers steering south-east at 18 knots only 50 miles distant – in fact, Pridham-Wippell's Force B. Judging that the presence of this cruiser squadron must signify that a convoy was near, Iachino increased to 30 knots in happy anticipation of a fruitful forenoon of destruction. At almost the same moment that the *Orion* sighted an Italian cruiser (in fact, *Trieste*) the *Trieste* herself sighted the British cruisers.

With four 6-inch gun ships Pridham-Wippell was confronting three 8-inch gun cruisers. As he wrote in his report of proceedings later: 'Knowing that vessels of that class could outrange my squadron and that, having a superior speed, they could choose the range, I decided to try to draw them towards our own battlefleet and carrier.' He therefore swung his ships to 140° and increased to 28 knots. At 0812 the Italian ships opened fire at a range of thirteen miles; at 0829, with the range down to twelve miles, *Gloucester* fired back, but her salvoes fell short. The Italian ships ceased fire and altered to the westward, Pridham-Wippell conforming in order to keep touch. But although he could not know it, he now stood in real danger of being cornered between the *Trieste* group and Iachino's other cruiser group, to say nothing of *Vittorio Veneto* herself. At 1058, when the *Orion*'s guncrews were sitting out on the turrets in the morning sunshine, an officer on the bridge paused in munching a sandwich to remark to Pridham-Wippell's Staff Officer (Operations): 'What's that battleship over there? I thought ours were miles away.'[55] Almost immediately the first of *Vittorio Veneto*'s salvoes whistled down round the British cruisers.

Back in the *Warspite*, Cunningham and his staff read the intercepts of Pridham-Wippell's next signals to his ships with a surge of excitement:

'Make smoke by all available means.'

'Turn together to 180°.'

'Proceed at your utmost speed.'

To Cunningham, the old destroyer commander, the import of these signals was immediately plain enough – Pridham-Wippell had sighted the enemy battlefleet. The *Warspite* was, however, still some 80 miles away from the scene; her maximum speed still down from 24 knots to 22 knots, which was in any case the very best the unmodernised old *Barham* could manage. So once again Cunningham had to endure the teeth-grinding frustration of trying with old, slow heavy ships to bring to action a modern enemy battlefleet several knots faster. It was a time for the 'caged tiger act' as his staff colloquially called it:

> He would pace the one side of the Admiral's bridge, always the side nearest the enemy; the speed of advance of the battleship was never fast enough for him and every second was grudged when a turn from the main line of advance was required for operating aircraft . . . we adjusted our actions accordingly.[56]

Cunningham was particularly annoyed by the reduction in *Warspite*'s speed. Aware that the Fleet Engineer Officer, Engineer Captain B. H. H. Williams, was on board, he sent for him, and, in his own laconic words, 'told him to do something about it'.[57] The flagship's speed duly rose. Cunningham's anxiety was the greater because the previous night the cruiser *Gloucester* in Force B had reported that engine trouble had cut her speed to 24 knots, which could imperil Pridham-Wippell's escape from danger. But as Cunningham put it in his memoirs, 'the sight of an enemy battleship had somehow increased the *Gloucester*'s speed to 30 knots'.[58]

The C-in-C, pacing his bridge, knew that 'something had to be done',[59] and quickly, to save Pridham-Wippell from destruction. That 'something' could only be a carrier air-strike. Cunningham had intended to delay such a strike until the Italian fleet was close enough for his battleships to come up and finish off any crippled vessels. Now he felt he had no alternative but to send in HMS *Formidable*'s torpedo aircraft (already airborne) straight away. At 1127 Lieutenant-Commander Gerald Saunt, commanding officer of 826 Squadron, led the strike force of six Albacores in two sub-flights in an attack on *Vittorio Veneto*'s starboard side. All six torpedoes missed: two ahead, four astern. Nevertheless, the attack sufficed to induce Iachino to break off his pursuit of Pridham-Wippell's Force B and turn for home (course 300°) at 25 knots, such was now Italian fear of British carrier aircraft.

With Force B safely taking station ahead of his heavy ships, Cunningham now faced the familiar problem of how to catch an Italian battlefleet legging it home much faster than his own best speed. 'It was a bitter anti-climax,' wrote the fleet gunnery officer, 'and no prudent staff officer approached the "caged tiger" without good cause . . .'[60] As it had been in past actions in the Mediterranean and as it was to be again with the *Bismarck* in two months' time, the one hope lay in the Fleet Air Arm, that pre-war naval orphan. But HMS *Formidable* (23,000 tons displacement; 32 knots; launched less than three weeks before the war broke out) had only 27 serviceable aircraft on board, of which thirteen were Fulmar fighters. Her total strike force amounted to ten of the new Fairey Albacore torpedo-bombers (maximum speed at 4,000 feet 161 mph; cruising speed 126 mph; range 820 miles)[61] and four Swordfish – a derisory strength compared with the mass carrier air groups now training for war in Japanese and American carriers, and quite insufficient to swamp the powerful anti-aircraft defence of a modern fleet. In the event the second strike force flown from the *Formidable* at Cunningham's orders only consisted of three Albacores and two Swordfish of 829 Squadron escorted by three Fulmars of 803 Squadron. While these were searching for the *Vittoria Veneto*, Royal Air Force Blenheim medium bombers from Crete bombed Iachino's ships from high altitude, causing alarm but no damage; the first time the Royal Air Force cooperated with the Navy in attacking an enemy fleet at sea in the Mediterranean.

For Cunningham the early afternoon of 28 March was still 'caged tiger' time, as *Warspite*, *Barham*, *Valiant* and *Formidable* steamed on across a flat calm sea, white bow waves cutting through purple-blue silk; black, grey and white dazzle paint, White Ensigns and the C-in-C's St George's flag of England at *Warspite*'s mainmast brilliant in the afternoon sunshine against a cobalt sky. Then, at 1510, one of *Formidable*'s aircraft reported the *Vittorio Veneto* as lying about sixty-five miles ahead, in 34° 50′N, 22° 10′E, and still steering westward. At 1519 Lieutenant-Commander J. Dalyell-Stead took his three Albacores down out of the sun and in towards the battleship's bows, while the two escorting Fulmar fighters machine-gunned her bridge and superstructure in order to distract the AA batteries. Admiral Iachino later recorded his admiration for the crew of the leading aircraft (Dalyell-Stead; his observer, Lieutenant Cooke; and air gunner, Petty-Officer Blenkhorn) as he watched them approach to within 1,000 yards of his flagship before dropping their torpedo, even though they were by now flying through a hurricane of anti-aircraft fire. Badly hit, they crashed into the sea off the starboard bow. Wrote Iachino: 'And so died a brave pilot without the satisfaction of knowing that his attack had been successful.'[62]

And successful it was. As the torpedo track bubbled through the water towards *Vittorio Veneto*, the great ship swung to starboard to comb the track. Too late: the torpedo struck her aft about sixteen feet below the waterline and just above the port outer screw, making her stagger as if hit by an enormous fist. At 1530, with thousands of tons of water flooding in through the hole, the engines stopped, and the Italian flagship began to settle by the stern. It was almost an exact preview of the lucky hit on the *Bismarck* eight weeks later; a demonstration that in the most powerful of battleships there was a point which was both vital and inherently unprotectable. Although Dalyell-Stead (who was awarded the posthumous DSO) had scored the only hit even though others were claimed by his comrades, it was enough. At 1558 a shadowing aircraft reported: 'Enemy has made a large decrease in speed.'[63]

Nevertheless frantic work by damage-control parties enabled *Vittorio Veneto* within an hour to make 15 knots. Since she was still 60 miles ahead of the British fleet, this meant that Cunningham could not overhaul her before dusk. At 1644 he therefore ordered Pridham-Wippell to go ahead with Force B at full speed to regain surface touch with the enemy, the destroyers *Nubian* and *Mowhawk* to act as a visual signal link between him and Pridham-Wippell.

Cunningham now needed, in his own words, 'to signal some plan for the night which was coming on', despite a situation which was still very confused for '. . . we continued to receive reports showing another enemy force containing battleships to the north-west of the *Vittorio Veneto*. These reports, as we discovered later, were incorrect. The force referred to consisted entirely of cruisers [in fact, *Zara*, *Fiume*, *Pola*, *Abruzzi* and *Garibaldi*] . . .'[64] What Cunningham urgently wanted was hard information, and at 1745 the flagship catapulted its reconnaissance aircraft with the C-in-C's own observer, Lieutenant-Commander A. S. Bolt, on board. By 1830 Cunningham was receiving from him an exemplary series of accurate reports describing how the Italian fleet had now been concentrated into a mass round the *Vittorio Veneto*, with a column of destroyers on one side of her and of cruisers on the other, with a destroyer screen ahead; course about 300°, speed 12 knots, distant from the *Warspite* some 50 miles, bearing 292°. Cunningham therefore ordered *Formidable* to launch a third air strike.

Composed of six Albacores and two Swordfish of 826 and 828 Squadrons, plus two Swordfish of 815 Squadron based in Crete, and led once again by Lieutenant-Commander Saunt, it went in just as the Mediterranean dusk was fast turning to dark. According to Saunt's observer in the leading Albacore, Lieutenant H. F. E. Hopkins:

> When we eventually went into the attack from the dark side with the Italians silhouetted against the last glow of light in the west, we found that we had been spotted at long range and were met with an impassable barrage of fire. We were forced to withdraw, and split up and come in again individually from different angles. The barrage of fire put up by the Italians was immensely spectacular but not very effective. A good deal of hose-piping [wild firing] went on which resulted in a number of their ships hitting each other but little damage to our aircraft.[65]

Although the strike force claimed hits, Cunningham could not be sure of this. Pridham-Wippell had now made contact with the enemy, who lay nine miles to the north-west. Cunningham faced a challenge alike to his professional judgment and to his personal mettle as a leader of a fleet.

> Now came the difficult moment of deciding what to do [he wrote in his memoirs]. I was fairly well convinced that having got so far it would be foolish not to make every effort to complete the *Vittorio Veneto*'s destruction. At the same time it appeared to us that the Italian admiral must have been fully aware of our position. He had numerous cruisers and destroyers in company, and any British Admiral in his position would not have hesitated to use every destroyer he had, backed up by all his cruisers fitted with torpedo tubes, for attacks on the pursuing fleet. Some of my staff argued that it would be unwise to charge blindly after the retreating enemy with our three heavy ships, and the *Formidable* also on our hands, to run the risk of ships being crippled, and to find ourselves within easy range of the enemy dive-bombers at daylight.[66]

As Cunningham delicately put it in his memoirs, 'I paid respectful attention to this opinion, and as the discussion happened to coincide with my time for dinner I told them I would have my evening meal and would see how I felt later.'[67] But his staff recalled the scene in rather different terms. According to the fleet gunnery officer:

> The well-known steely blue look was in A.B.C.'s eye, and the staff had no doubt that there was going to be a party . . . I think that A.B.C. had probably made up his mind by about 8 p.m. to send the light forces into the attack and to follow up with the battlefleet, but he nevertheless, on this occasion, went through the formality of asking the opinion of certain staff officers. Neither the staff officer operations nor the master of the fleet liked the idea much, and said so in their very different ways. The fleet gunnery officer said he was keen to let the guns off, but the battleships hadn't had a night practice for months and there might well be a pot mess with star-shells and searchlights if we got into confused night action. A.B.C. took one look at his supposed helpers and said 'You're a pack of yellow-livered skunks. I'll go and have my supper now and see after supper if my morale isn't higher than yours.'[68]

When the C-in-C returned to the bridge after his supper, his morale was higher than theirs. At 2037 he made the executive signal to the 14th and 2nd Destroyer Flotillas:

> Destroyer flotillas attack enemy battlefleet with torpedoes. Estimated bearing and distance of centre of enemy battlefleet from Admiral 286° 33 miles at 2030.
>
> Enemy course and speed 295° 13 knots.[69]

In fact the Italian fleet actually lay 57 miles ahead of *Warspite*, and steaming at 19 knots – with the result that when late that evening Captain P. J. Mack, commanding the destroyers, believed that he was crossing ahead of the *Vittorio Veneto*, the battleship had already passed well clear of his intended trap and lay some 30 miles to the northward. It was by no means the only confusion and lost opportunity during a night which would fully bear out Clausewitz's dictum that 'War is the province of uncertainty'.

Less than half an hour after Mack's destroyers began to hunt ahead at 28 knots, course 300°, like a pack of eager hounds, the C-in-C received a report from Pridham-Wippell: 'One unknown ship 240° five m, apparently stopped. My position 35° 20′N, 21° 6′E.'[70] This ship had been picked up by the radars in *Ajax* and *Orion*. Pridham-Wippell, thinking that the stopped ship could be the Italian battleship herself, decided to leave her to the C-in-C to deal with while he pressed on after the enemy's main body at 20 knots. This speed was ample to catch up a foe making according to the most recent reports only 13 knots. In fact, however, *Vittorio Veneto* had just worked up to

19 knots. On receipt of Pridham-Wippell's report Cunningham altered course to 280° in order to investigate, his three heavy ships and the carrier in single line ahead at 3 cables (about 600 yards) apart. At 2203 the *Valiant*'s radar (the flagship was not so equipped) located a stopped ship eight to nine miles distant, bearing 244°. According to *Valiant*'s signal, which reached the C-in-C seven minutes later, the strange vessel was more than 600 feet long. 'Our hopes ran high,' wrote Cunningham in his memoirs. 'This might be the *Vittorio Veneto*. The course of the battlefleet was altered 40 degrees to port together. We were already at action stations with our main armament ready. Our guns were trained on the correct bearing.'[71]

The contrast could not have been greater between Cunningham's present eagerness for battle and the night action at Jutland in 1916, when the Grand Fleet refused to become embroiled with the High Seas Fleet and steamed on in a stately line ahead. For Cunningham was benefiting from the lessons which the Royal Navy had assimilated from Jutland and the consequent immense progress in equipment and fleet training for night fighting before the Second World War. Yet Cunningham added to the recipe his own special spice as a leader. In the words of the fleet gunnery officer, Commander Geoffrey Barnard, 'A.B.C. turned the battlefleet together to investigate, handling the fleet from this moment until midnight in the same way as he would have handled a division of destroyers.'[72] The Admiralty Fighting Instructions ordained that whenever enemy destroyers might be present at night, a battlefleet should turn away to avoid the danger of torpedo attack. On the *Warspite*'s bridge, as the distance between the fleet and the stopped ship (which might well be escorted by destroyers) narrowed, Cunningham's staff therefore advised him to make the signal 'Blue Four' – a turn away. But Cunningham replied: 'If that's the enemy, we will turn towards and find out what sort they are and how soon we sink them. FOUR BLUE': i.e., a turn towards.[73] As an eyewitness commented: 'It thus occurred for the first time in a night encounter either in peace or war a battlefleet turned towards an unknown force of enemy ships.'[74]

The fleet steamed on under a moonless, clouded sky in quarter line. At 2220 the *Valiant*'s radar reported the stopped ship bearing 191°, distant four and a half miles – on the fleet's port bow. Only three minutes later, however, the destroyer *Stuart* to the starboard of the fleet sighted fine on her *starboard* bow two large ships with a smaller one ahead and three smaller ones astern. Even before the *Stuart*'s alarm report reached the flagship, the C-in-C and his new Chief of Staff, Commander John Edelsten, had seen these ships for themselves through their binoculars. According to Cunningham, the Chief of Staff, scanning the horizon to starboard, 'calmly reported that he saw two large cruisers with a smaller one ahead of them crossing the bows of the battlefleet from starboard to port. I looked through my glasses and there they were . . .'[75] An ex-submariner on his staff, Commander Power, an expert on ship recognition, pronounced the larger ships to be two Zara class 8-inch gun cruisers. By radio the C-in-C now signalled his fleet to turn back into line ahead for the final approach to the enemy. Cunningham and his staff had by this time gone aloft to the small captain's bridge where he could enjoy a better all-round view of the action to come.

> I shall never forget the next few minutes [he wrote a decade later]. In dead silence, a silence that could almost be felt, one heard only the voices of the gun control personnel putting the guns on to the new target. One heard the orders repeated in the director tower behind and above the bridge. Looking forward, one saw the turrets swing and steady when the 15-inch guns pointed at the enemy cruisers. Never in my whole life have I experienced a more thrilling moment than when I heard a calm voice from the director tower – 'Director layer sees the target'; sure sign that the guns were ready and that his finger was itching on the trigger. The enemy was at a range of no more than 3,800 yards – point-blank.[76]

How had these Italian cruisers and destroyers come to be wandering so far from the main body of the Italian fleet and across the bows of the British fleet? They had been ordered back by Iachino under the command of Vice-Admiral Cattaneo to the aid of the stopped ship – which was in fact the cruiser *Pola*, crippled by a torpedo from one of *Formidable*'s aircraft during the third, dusk, British air-strike. Iachino had issued this order because he had no idea at all that the enemy battlefleet lay anywhere near the scene, and believed that his only danger lay in the British aircraft carrier and its escort.

Iachino was later to complain sourly about lack of aerial reconnaissance and fighter cover afforded him during his sortie by the Regia Aeronautica and the Luftwaffe; about the generally poor cooperation between land-based airpower and his fleet. Nonetheless, around 0900 on 28 March he had received a report from the Italian island of Rhodes in the Dodecanese that at 0745 a reconnaissance aircraft had sighted a carrier, two battleships, nine cruisers and fourteen destroyers 'in sector 3836/0 course 165° 20 knots'.[77] But since Iachino himself had been in this position at that time, he radioed back to Rhodes to accuse it of committing a crass mistake. Information as late as 2000 that evening indicated to him that Cunningham's fleet was certainly at sea, but still some ninety miles astern of him. He therefore believed that Cattaneo would run no risk. In Iachino's words, 'It never occurred to me that we were within a relatively short distance of the entire British force. I thought the British cruisers had decided to turn back leaving only two destroyers to deal with us.'[78]

Now Cattaneo and his ships' companies were about to pay a terrible price for their C-in-C's misjudgment. Moreover, since no Italian warships were equipped with radar, a grievous disadvantage at night, Cattaneo could have no advance warning of the approach of the British battlefleet; nor could he know that thanks to radar Cunningham was exactly tracking him far beyond the range of the human eye in the dark.

For Cunningham himself this was the supreme moment of his career, coming forty-four years after he first joined HMS *Britannia* as a cadet of fourteen.

> It must have been the Fleet Gunnery Officer, Commander Geoffrey Barnard, who gave the final order to open fire [he was to remember]. One heard the 'ting-ting-ting' of the firing gongs. Then came the great orange flash and the violent shudder as the six big guns bearing were fired simultaneously. At the very same instant the destroyer *Greyhound*, on the [destroyer] screen, switched her searchlight on to one of the enemy cruisers, showing her momentarily up as a silvery-blue shape in the darkness. Our searchlights shone out with the first salvo, and provided full illumination for what was a ghastly sight. Full in the beam I saw our six great projectiles flying through the air. Five out of the six hit a few feet below the level of the cruiser's upper deck and burst with splashes of brilliant flame. The Italians were quite unprepared. Their guns were trained fore and aft. They were helplessly shattered before they could put up any resistance. In the midst of all this there was one milder diversion. Captain Douglas Fisher, the captain of the *Warspite*, was a gunnery officer of note. When he saw the first salvo hit he was heard to say in a voice of wondering surprise: 'Good Lord! We've hit her!'[79]

Broadside after broadside from all three British battleships smashed into the enemy cruisers – HMS *Valiant* fired five in just over three minutes, a rate faithful to the tradition of Nelson's Mediterranean Fleet at Trafalgar, and which astonished and delighted Cunningham. The *Fiume* was quickly engulfed in vivid orange flame; she sank three-quarters of an hour later. The *Zara* too, hit in the forward 8-inch turret, the bridge and the engine room, was soon ablaze and listing heavily, the belching flames fearsomely illuminating the billows of smoke rising from her into the night sky. Abandoned by her crew, she was eventually sunk at 0240 on 29 March by torpedoes from the destroyer *Jervis*.

The attack by Cunningham's fleet lasted no more than four and a half minutes, for the approach of three Italian destroyers (one of which was seen to fire torpedoes) on the port bow compelled Cunningham to turn the fleet 90° together to starboard to avoid them. But the battleships had already done their work. There now followed a chaotic mêlée between British and Italian destroyers in darkness blindingly lit by gunflashes and explosions. In the early stages of this confusion the destroyer *Havock* was straddled in error by a salvo from the *Warspite* (fortunately without damage), and the *Formidable* (which had hauled out of the line before the action) was nearly fired on by the flagship's secondary armament. Thereafter the C-in-C took the heavy ships eastwards clear of the scene. In the course of the night's mêlée the Italian destroyers *Alfieri* and *Carducci* were both sunk. But it was not until 0403 on the 29th that the cruiser *Pola*, the catalyst that brought about the whole battle, was sunk by torpedoes from the destroyers *Nubian* and *Jervis* after her surviving crew had been taken off.

So ended the Battle of Cape Matapan. It had cost the Italian Navy three heavy cruisers, two destroyers and the lives of 2,400 officers and seamen, Vice-Admiral Cattaneo among them.

The *Vittorio Veneto* nevertheless continued to make good her escape home to Taranto. This was partly because Captain Mack, commanding the British destroyer flotilla pursuing her, had turned across her track believing *he* was ahead of *her* when in fact *she* was by now well ahead of *him*. However, a somewhat ambiguous order by Cunningham also contributed to the *Vittorio Veneto*'s escape. At around 2300 on the 28th he ordered all ships not engaged in sinking the enemy to withdraw to the north-eastwards, which caused Pridham-Wippell to abandon his efforts to find the Italian flagship.[80] Cunningham had only intended to give the destroyers a free hand to attack any large ship they might suddenly encounter in the dark, and also to make it easier for the Fleet to reconcentrate on the morrow.

Next morning the Fleet steamed for home through the sad wrack left behind by its victory, floating on a calm, sun-bright sea filmy with oil – boats, rafts, bits of debris, corpses. In the afternoon, as Cunningham made for Alexandria, came the avenging air attacks, but these were largely broken up by *Formidable*'s fighters, although several heavy bombs fell perilously close to the carrier. In the early evening of 30 March 1941 the Mediterranean Fleet safely and triumphantly moored in Alexandria, having won the Royal Navy's greatest victory in a fleet encounter since Trafalgar; and, as it was to prove, the last in all its long history.

The Battle of Cape Matapan completed the destruction of the Italian battlefleet's will to take the offensive. And it was partly thanks to this that the British expeditionary force to Greece was not forced at the end of a disastrous campaign to capitulate with its back to the sea.

12

Catastrophe in the Mediterranean, 1941

On 27 March 1941 the pro-German government of Yugoslavia was overthrown in a coup d'état and replaced by a new leadership; an event which impelled Hitler now to regard Yugoslavia as his enemy, and to recast his offensive strategy in the Balkans to include her conquest. It was this unforeseen event – one quite unconnected with the British commitment of an expeditionary force to Greece – and the consequent need to deploy fresh German forces which led to the postponement of Hitler's attack on the Soviet Union by a month, with possibly decisive effects on its success.

At the very last moment, therefore, fortune had vouchsafed Churchill two-thirds at least of his dream of a Balkan coalition, only Turkey among his hoped-for Allies remaining both neutral and excluded from Hitler's aggressive plans. Yet the strategic outcome swiftly proved what a military fantasy it had been to expect peasant armies, however numerous, to prevail against the Luftwaffe and the panzer divisions. On 6 April the German forces struck into both Greece and Yugoslavia. Within two days they had smashed through the Yugoslav front in southern Serbia and began to swing south through the Monastir gap, so deeply turning the left flank of the Greek and British defence along the Aliakmon position. Meanwhile the German 12th Army was thrusting from Bulgaria directly into Greece with ten divisions supported by some 800 aircraft. Five of these divisions, including three panzer, were soon advancing against the British Commonwealth expeditionary force (two infantry divisions and a single armoured brigade), while the Luftwaffe, undeterred by a ten times weaker Royal Air Force, bombed and machine-gunned at will just as in Norway. As the official history of the war in the Mediterranean and Middle East tersely sums up: 'The British campaign on the mainland of Greece was from start to finish a withdrawal.'[1] In the coming days the power and weight of the German offensive, the disintegration of the Greek Army (already exhausted by its heroic winter campaign against the Italians in Albania), and the capitulation of Yugoslavia on 17 April, all served fully to bear out the deep misgivings about an expeditionary force's operational chances that had been voiced earlier in London and Cairo by the realists (including Wavell himself initially). On 21 April, with the British forces now back on the Thermopylae position covering Athens and the Greek Army of the Epirus (on the Albanian front) cut off and about to surrender, the decision was taken to evacuate. And so it again fell to the Royal Navy to save what it could of a British army at the end of a foredoomed campaign.

On the day the decision was reached, Cunningham and the main body of his fleet (three battleships, the *Formidable*, two cruisers and a destroyer screen) were actually at sea returning to base after an extraordinarily hazardous but successful 900-mile voyage to bombard Tripoli, the main Axis port in Libya (see below, p. 366). Not until 23 April was Cunningham back in Alexandria. The evacuation had been originally set for 28 April, but such was the speed of the German advance and the unfolding peril to the British expeditionary force that 'Operation Demon' (codename for the evacuation) had to be brought forward to the 24th, the very next day after Cunningham's return to harbour.

'Demon' proved a combined replay of the evacuations from Norway and Dunkirk, but even more hazardous. Just as in Norway soldiers wordless with fatigue, dazed by unceasing air attack, trudged the last sour kilometres of retreat along mountain roads and down to the sea, kept going by the hope that when they reached the coast the Navy would be there. Just as in Norway (but unlike at Dunkirk) the evacuation would have to be conducted far from British bases, without fighter cover and within easy range of German shore-based airpower. Moreover in contrast to both Norway and Dunkirk there were few available harbours with jetties or wharves capable of taking vessels as big as destroyers or passenger ships, for the main port of Piraeus itself had been totally wrecked on 6–7 April in a Luftwaffe raid which devastatingly blew up an ammunition ship. So soldiers would have to be mostly lifted from the beaches – picked up, as from the sands of

Dunkirk – by small craft and ferried out to the waiting ships off shore for the voyage to safety. And there was always the possibility that these operations, hazardous as they must be in the face of German airpower, might be further imperilled by the intervention of the Italian battlefleet.

Seven beaches were selected for the embarkation, spread all the way round the deeply indented southern coasts of Greece from Raphina and Porto Raphti on the south-eastern shore of Attica to Megara between Athens and Corinth, and Nauplia, Tolon and Monemvasia at the head of the Gulf of Nauplia in the Peloponessus.[2]

To coordinate the movements of troops down to the beaches with the arrival of the nightly lifts by the Navy demanded fast and flexible planning, the closest liaison with the military command on shore; not easy when ship-to-shore communication came to depend on unreliable field radios. Rear-Admiral H. T. Baillie-Grohman was sent to Greece to work with General Sir Henry Maitland Wilson (commanding the British Commonwealth forces) and take control of inshore operations. It was Baillie-Grohman's first task to requisition and crew local Greek fishing caiques, motor boats and other small craft. To help him and also to provide beach parties he was given the entire ship's company of the bomb-damaged cruiser *York* lying at Suda Bay, Crete. Vice-Admiral Pridham-Wippell was placed in overall command of the evacuation (Ramsay's job in 'Dynamo'), with his headquarters at Suda Bay. He had at his disposal four cruisers (*Orion*, his flagship; *Ajax*, *Phoebe* and HMAS *Perth*); the three anti-aircraft cruisers *Calcutta*, *Coventry* and *Carlisle*; some twenty destroyers; three sloops; HMS *Glenearn* and HMS *Gleneagle* ('Infantry Assault Ships' adapted from merchant vessels, carrying landing craft instead of boats); nineteen middle-sized troopships; and an assortment of small craft, including the forerunners of the tank landing craft.

On 24 April, starting day for 'Demon', Cunningham made the signal:

> The object is to embark men, if possible, with arms; but no material must be allowed to take precedence to men. Troopships with men embarked to sail direct to Alexandria, except 'Glen' ships which must unload at Suda Bay and do a second embarkation. Destroyers to take their troops to Crete, where they will be transferred later.[3]

The pattern of Namsos, Andalsnes and Dunkirk quickly re-established itself. Between the avenging enemy and the embarkation stood a resolute rearguard, this time of New Zealand, Australian and British troops, still able and willing to throw the Germans back in local counter-strokes. Under cover of night the troops for embarkation left the areas just inland where they had discharged the miserable task of wrecking their heavy equipment, and filed down to the beaches and the waiting naval beach parties. Then began the slow, frustratingly slow, work of ferrying them out to the waiting ships while the short hours of darkness hastened by. It was a scene of apparent confusion, but actual efficiency and discipline, as dog-tired beach parties coped with sudden changes of plan caused by local problems and the availability of ships. And then for the soldiers the long dusty march under the Luftwaffe's bombs and machine-gun fire was over; exchanged for the relative security of a King's ship and the comfort of strong Navy cocoa. But with daylight and the voyage back to Crete or, 400 miles longer, to Alexandria came the Luftwaffe.

On 25 April the troopship *Ulster Prince* and the transport *Pennland* both succumbed to German bombs; on 26 April the *Glenearn* was bombed and disabled on her way to Nauplia and had to be towed back to Suda Bay. On the 27th the Dutch transport *Slamat* was caught in daylight by dive-bombers with a full load of troops on her way back to Crete and set on fire. She had gallantly but ill-advisedly hung on at Nauplia an hour longer than ordered rather than leave some troops behind. As the *Slamat* sank, the destroyers *Diamond* (Lieutenant-Commander P. A. Cartwright) and *Wryneck* (Commander R. H. D. Dean) were themselves dive-bombed while picking up survivors. Early that afternoon the bombers were back to finish them off, and this time sank both ships so swiftly that only one officer, forty-one ratings and eight soldiers were saved. This same afternoon the merchant ship *Costa Rica* too was sunk, although almost all her crew and soldiers were rescued. In all the Luftwaffe sank 26 Allied ships during the evacuation, including five hospital ships.

By the 28th most of the remaining troops (except those now cut off by the enemy) lay at Monemvasia, Kalamata and on Kithera Island. Pridham-Wippell therefore ordered a cruiser and four destroyers to Monemvasia, three sloops to Kithera, and HMAS *Perth* and a force of destroyers to Kalamata. All went well on Kithera and at Monemvasia, where at 0300 on the 29th Major-General Freyberg (commanding the New Zealand Division) and Baillie-Grohman embarked in HMS *Ajax* after the last of the soldiers had been lifted. At Kalamata, however, some 7,000 soldiers were eventually left behind and forced to surrender. The destroyer HMS *Hero*, sent ahead of the force led by *Perth*, arrived off the port at 2045 to observe and hear heavy fighting going on. A signal was flashed from the shore: 'Boche in harbour.' Passing this report on to the *Perth* the captain of the *Hero* sent his first lieutenant ashore to investigate in person the true state of affairs. At 2100 the first lieutenant reported back that it was still possible to lift troops from the beach. However, owing to radio trouble this information was not received in the *Perth* until 2211: too late, because at 2129 the Captain of the *Perth* had ordered his force to withdraw. Having himself seen the tracer on shore and heard the sounds of heavy fire, and on the basis of the earlier report that the enemy had occupied the harbour, he had decided that too few soldiers could be lifted to justify the risk to his ships. In Cunningham's retrospective judgment, this was 'a most unfortunate decision'.[4] Nonetheless the *Hero*, together with the newly arrived destroyers *Kandahar*, *Kingston*, and *Kimberley*, succeeded in lifting 324 soldiers from the beach by means of their whalers. Even this effort did not mark the end of 'Demon': over the next two nights the *Hero*, *Kimberley* and *Isis* brought off another 235 soldiers.

In all the Royal and Merchant Navies rescued 50,732 soldiers (including some Greeks and Yugoslavs), of which only 14,000 were lifted from wharves or jetties, as against the 58,364 British Commonwealth troops originally transported there in the 'Lustre' convoys. Like Dunkirk, this seemed a miraculous deliverance. It owed itself partly to the Luftwaffe's failure to bomb at night; partly to the cowed Italian Fleet's supine neglect of a singular opportunity to intervene against lightly protected convoys at a time when Cunningham had had to keep his battleships in Alexandria for want of enough destroyers both to screen them and also take part in the evacuation.

Yet the main credit for the success of 'Demon' – as of 'Dynamo' – belongs to the professionalism, resourcefulness and resolve of British sailors, from Baillie-Grohman on a foreign and unfamiliar coast struggling to organise and schedule the embarkations amid all the shifting confusions of a lost campaign, to Pridham-Wippell in Crete, beset by lack of news, grappling with poor communications and redeploying his scant resources in ships at the briefest notice, and to all the ships' companies whose fortitude and zeal had made it possible for merchant ships each to lift up to 3,500 soldiers a night, cruisers up to 2,500 and destroyers to jam-pack themselves with more than 800 each.[5]

Nevertheless, thankful though this deliverance was, it could not compensate for the complete and calamitous failure in which the Greek adventure had ended; a failure that had cost the British Commonwealth forces 12,000 killed, wounded and missing, 209 aircraft, 8,000 trucks and all the expeditionary force's ill-spared tanks and artillery, plus a mass of stores of every kind.[6]

Now, with the Germans and Italians occupying all of mainland Greece and the Greek islands, plus the Dodecanese, it was evident that Crete must be a likely Axis objective; and the Ultra decrypts of Luftwaffe Enigma signals confirmed this from 26 April onwards.[7] Should the British make a major military investment in the defence of the island, at a time when the resources of Middle East Command were already worryingly stretched in meeting existing or potential crises from the Western Desert to Syria and Iraq? What were the chances of a successful defence? How strategically important was Crete? These questions were now answered or ignored in London in familiar style. The Prime Minister signalled Wavell on 28 April that Crete 'must be stubbornly defended', although he told the War Cabinet the same evening that he was 'somewhat doubtful of our ability to hold Crete against a prolonged attack'.[8] His doubts were justified. General Sir Henry Maitland Wilson reported to Wavell on 27 April on the operational chances in the light of the extreme weakness of the Royal Air Force on Crete (six Hurricanes and seventeen various obsolete aircraft); the awkward configuration of the island (160 miles long and 40 miles across at the widest point, with only a single and very bad main lateral road); the presence of a semi-circle of nearby enemy air bases from Greece to the Dodecanese; and the fact that Crete had not a single large port, while such harbours as could take even a small cargo vessel all lay on the exposed northern coast. It was Wilson's judgment that 'unless all three services are prepared to face the strain of maintaining adequate forces up to strength, the holding of the island is a dangerous commitment, and a decision on the matter must be taken at once'.[9] As the official history points out, in view of the irremediable weakness of the Royal Air Force on Crete, 'this was tantamount to saying that he did not think the island could be successfully defended'.[10]

But Wavell could only confirm the instructions he had received from London that Crete must be fought for. This decision remained unchanged despite later indications from Ultra that the scale of the German onslaught, especially in airborne forces, was going to be colossal; indications that roused serious doubts in the garrison commander himself, General Freyberg, as to whether he could hope to hold off such an onslaught with the forces at his disposal.[11] Moreover little attention was paid in London to the long-term strategic implications of holding Crete indefinitely after a German attack was defeated (as was hoped), especially in regard to the strain on, and the attrition of, warships and merchant shipping in waters utterly dominated by enemy airpower.

On 20 May, after five days of ferocious air attack on the British defences at Maleme and Heraklion, the enemy launched 'Operation Merkur' ('Mercury') – 13,000 parachute and glider troops of 'Fliegerdivision 7' in over 500 transport aircraft and 72 gliders; a tactical air force of 228 bombers, 205 dive-bombers, 233 fighters and 50 reconnaissance aircraft.[12] The second echelon consisted of 9,000 mountain troops to be flown in by transport aircraft as soon as Maleme airfield had been captured. Only heavy loads such as a panzer battalion, artillery and ammunition supplies were to be sent later by sea. British interpretations of the latest Ultra Intelligence, though exaggerating all the German figures, indicated clearly enough that the main weight of the attack would indeed come from the airborne rather than the seaborne forces.[13] Freyberg however believed that if the Royal Navy could prevent the passage of seaborne forces (which he in any case doubted because of German air superiority), his forces could defeat the parachute and glider troops alone.

He was not alone in this traditionalist view that the main threat lay from the sea. In the words of the unpublished Naval Staff History of the campaign, 'Airborne invasion was known to be impending, but it appeared almost inconceivable that airborne invasion alone could succeed against forewarned [through Ultra] troops'; hence a seaborne invasion was seen as essential. It followed from this belief that 'destruction of the reinforcing troop convoys would eventually win the day'.[14] In other words, as the British command saw it, the key role in the coming battle to hold what Churchill described as an outpost of Egypt[15] was to fall to the Mediterranean Fleet.

It was not a role which Cunningham could contemplate with much joy. In his own words:

> . . . the main difficulty, of course, was that Alexandria was some 440 miles from the scene of action, while it was impossible to use Suda Bay because of the continuous air attacks. It was hardly to be expected that the Italian fleet would remain passive while an attack upon Crete was in progress, so this made it necessary for us to provide battleship cover off the western end of the island.[16]

But Cunningham's greatest anxiety lay in his virtually total lack of air cover. On Crete itself at Maleme were three Royal Air Force Hurricanes, three Fleet Air Arm Gladiators and three Fulmars, aircraft and crews being alike worn out after weeks of fighting against overwhelming odds in Greece; all were put out of action during the preliminary German air strikes. The carrier *Formidable* was likewise suffering from wear and tear following recent hazardous operations (see below, p. 366), and was reduced to only four serviceable aircraft; she did not joint the Fleet off Crete until 25 May, five days after the German offensive began.[17]

In brief, Cunningham knew he had to pit his ships against a vast number of aircraft operating within close range of their airfields. 'The obvious policy,' he wrote, 'was not to commit our forces to the northward of Crete during daylight unless enemy forces were known to be at sea . . .'[18] He divided his fleet into four forces: Force A, with two battleships and five destroyers, was to provide general support from a position to the west of Crete, while Forces B, C and D (each composed of the two cruisers plus destroyers) were to carry out nightly sweeps in the Aegean on the northern sea approaches to the island. He held back two battleships, the *Formidable*, four cruisers and sixteen destroyers in Alexandria as a reserve. With these four widely dispersed task forces to coordinate, Cunningham reluctantly decided that for the first time he must exercise command from on shore, where he could also keep in close touch with his fellow Commanders-in-Chief.

The start of 'Operation Merkur' on 20 May announced itself to the British Empire defenders of Crete when the sky filled with hundreds of Junkers 52 transport aircraft. From these peeled away stick after stick of parachute troops, soon followed by troop-carrying gliders. That evening in the dusk, while New Zealand troops and 'Fliegerdivision 7' were fighting a brutal close-range battle for control of Maleme airfield, Cunningham's task forces steamed through the Kaso and Antikithera channels to patrol north of the island. But that night they only encountered six Italian torpedo boats (duly shot up). Meanwhile three destroyers bombarded Scarpanto airfield in the Dodecanese. The following forenoon, however, gave the first taste of what was to come, for Forces A, D and C were all heavily bombed. Force C in particular was attacked continuously from 0950 to 1350, and at 1249 the destroyer *Juno*, hit by a bomb, sank in two minutes.

During the night-time sweeps on 21–22 May the Fleet had its revenge, for at 2330 on the 21st Force D (Rear-Admiral I. G. Glennie: the cruisers *Dido*, *Orion* and *Ajax*, and the destroyers *Janus*, *Hereward*, *Kimberley* and *Hasty*) massacred an enemy convoy on passage to Crete. In two and a half hours at least twelve caiques, two or three steamers, a steam yacht and one of the escorting torpedo boats were located in the dark by radar and sunk, leaving some 4,000 German soldiers to drown. By this time Glennie's flagship, the *Dido*, had fired off some 70 per cent of her anti-aircraft ammunition, and the *Orion* and *Ajax* 62 and 58 per cent of theirs. Rather than comply with Cunningham's instruction to join Force C in a daylight northward hunt for further convoys, Glennie therefore retired southwards. The Luftwaffe's retribution fell instead on Force C (Rear-Admiral E. L. S. King; the cruisers *Naiad* and HMAS *Perth*, the anti-aircraft cruisers *Calcutta* and *Carlisle*, and the destroyers *Kandahar*, *Kingston* and *Nubian*). While King's task force was itself successfully smashing up another enemy convoy south of the island of Milo, German bombers relentlessly pounded down on his ships despite all the high explosive that the ships' anti-aircraft batteries could pump into their path.

Having lost the *Juno* only the previous day, being like Glennie low in anti-aircraft ammunition, Admiral King now decided to steer no further to the northward in pursuit of the remainder of the convoy, but instead alter westwards for the Kithera channel exit from the Aegean. It was Cunningham's very typical personal judgment later that King had failed to engage the enemy closely enough: 'It is probable that the safest place was amongst the enemy convoy, and retirement could not better the most unpleasant position in which he found himself.' Also, the destruction of that large convoy would have justified severe losses. While acknowledging that it was easy to criticise from a distance and also that King found himself in 'a cruel situation', Cunningham nevertheless held that 'if the enemy is in sight on the sea, air attacks or other considerations must be disregarded and the risks accepted.'[19] In any event King's initial attacks induced the convoy to turn back; no German troops got through.

As Force C retired it was bombed without cease for three and a half hours. The *Naiad* was badly damaged, with two turrets out of action, several compartments flooded, and her speed cut to 16 knots. The *Carlisle* too was hit, and her captain, Captain T. C. Hampton, killed. At 1321 King was all too relieved to see the battleships of Force A coming up from the westward.

Rear-Admiral H. B. Rawlings (Flag Officer, Force A), flying his flag in the battleship *Warspite*, and with the battleship *Valiant* and the cruisers *Gloucester* and *Fiji* in company, had earlier been joined by Glennie's Force D. The combined squadron was patrolling some 20 to 30 miles west of the Kithera channel when Rawlings learned that the *Naiad* had been seriously damaged and her speed reduced, so placing King's Force C in peril. He therefore decided to risk entering the Aegean in daylight and steered to King's support at 23 knots. At 1332, just as Rawlings and King joined company, three Messerschmitt ME 109 fighter-bombers roared out of low cloud to attack the *Warspite* down the fore and aft line in what a connoisseur eyewitness described as 'a beautiful attack to watch'.[20] One bomb struck home, wrecking the starboard 4-inch and 6-inch batteries and damaging the No. 3

boiler room fan intakes. *Warspite* emitted a cloud of dense smoke and her speed dropped away for a time.

The combined force (commanded by King as the senior officer present) now steered west to clear the Aegean – still under fierce air attack. The first victim was the unsupported destroyer *Greyhound*, whereupon King ordered the cruisers *Gloucester* (Captain H. A. Rowley) and *Fiji* (Captain P. R. B. W. William-Powlett) and the destroyers *Kandahar* and *Kingston* to her assistance – despite the hard lesson learned in the Mediterranean never to detach ships, but always move a force as a whole. The cruisers arrived to find the *Greyhound* sunk (she had been hit twice and went down in two minutes). While they were rescuing survivors the Luftwaffe struck at them too. At 1550 the *Gloucester* took several bomb hits and was brought to a stop badly on fire and with her upper deck a shambles of torn and mangled metal. Reluctantly the captain of the *Fiji* decided that he could not remain with her, but dropped boats and rafts for her crew. The body of the captain of the doomed *Gloucester*, Captain H. A. Rowley, was washed up four weeks later on the coast of Egypt at Mersa Matruh.[21]

Now it was *Fiji*'s turn, and for three and a quarter hours German aircraft relentlessly sought to sink her. Finally,

> after surviving some 20 bombing attacks . . . she fell victim to a single ME 109. The machine flew out of the clouds in a shallow dive and dropped its bombs very close to the port side, amidships. The ship took up a heavy list, but was able to steam at 17 knots until half an hour later when another single machine dropped three bombs which hit above 'A' boiler room; the list increased and at 2015 she rolled right over.[22]

She sank some 50 miles south-west of Gavdo Island.

The destroyers *Kandahar* and *Kingston* lowered boats and rafts for the survivors, but could not stay because of the acute danger from further air attack. Nevertheless they returned under cover of night and picked up 523 of the *Fiji*'s company: exhausted men who had lost their 'home', and who, after being adrift on a dark sea, found themselves saved after all. The two destroyers had already endured twenty-two air attacks between 1445 and 1920. At 2245 the destroyers set course to rejoin Rear-Admiral King south of Crete.

Meanwhile the *Valiant* had been hit aft at 1645 by two bombs dropped from high level, though without serious damage.

During the night the destroyers *Decoy* and *Hero* embarked the King of Greece and his suite, the British ambassador and other important personages at Agriarumeli on the southern coast of Crete – a melancholy echo of similar liftings of dispossessed monarchs by the Royal Navy in 1940.

For Cunningham in Alexandria that evening and night the strain of command was all the greater because he could no longer lead his fleet into battle, but only wait for news to reach him over a signal net that was suffering from serious lags:

> In my office ashore close to the war room where the positions of all our ships were plotted hour by hour on the large-scale chart, I came to dread every ring on the telephone, every knock on the door, and the arrival of every fresh signal. In something less than twelve hours of fighting against the unhampered Luftwaffe we had lost so much, two cruisers and a destroyer sunk, with two battleships and two cruisers damaged. Most of the ships were woefully short of ammunition, and I very well knew the anxiety and physical strain under which their devoted officers and men were working.[23]

Cunningham could only signal to all his ships: 'Stick it out. Navy must not let Army down. No enemy forces must reach Crete by Sea.'[24] It might be said that this signal was as redundant as Nelson's signals at Trafalgar ordering his fleet to engage the enemy more closely and that 'England expects . . .' The Navy did not let the Army down, and no German troops did reach Crete by sea. But to achieve this was taking what may without undue melodrama be termed the 'death ride' of the Mediterranean Fleet.

When at 2230 on 22 May Cunningham received a 'Most Immediate' signal from King reporting the loss of *Gloucester* and *Fiji* and the grim state of ammunition stocks, a 'calligraphic error' in the signal (either phonetic or in the handwriting of the draft) made it appear that the battleships were 'empty' of their pom-pom ammunition, when in fact the typed version of the signal next morning confirmed that they had 'plenty'.[25] Misled by this garbled signal, Cunningham at 0408 on the 23rd ordered Force A back to Alexandria. This – in particular – deprived the destroyers *Kelly* (Captain Lord Louis Mountbatten commanding 1st Destroyer Flotilla), *Kashmir* (Commander Henry King), and *Kipling* (Commander A. St Clair Ford) of support on their passage back to Alexandria after patrolling to the north of Canea and Maleme during the night.

At 0755 on 23 May, when the flotilla lay in 34° 50′N, 24° 05′E, some thirteen miles to the south of Gavdo Island, 24 Stukas howled down on them out of the morning sky. The *Kashmir* was hit and sunk in just two minutes. The *Kelly* was struck by a large bomb while steaming 30 knots on full starboard helm, and still had considerable way on as she capsized to port. In an episode that was later to form part of the Mountbatten legend, the *Kelly* floated upside down for half an hour before she finally sank, leaving her survivors bobbing in the water round her captain under German machine-gun fire. The *Kipling* picked up 279 men from the water, including – as the world was to be reminded – Mountbatten himself, and made course for Alexandria. Between 0820 and 1300 she was attacked by no fewer than 40 aircraft, dropping 83 bombs, but emerged miraculously unscathed. She had to be met by HMS *Protector* fifty miles from Alexandria and towed in because she was now completely out of fuel. After the event Cunningham could not make up his mind whether the two destroyers might have been saved by the presence of Force A, or whether the Luftwaffe would have overwhelmed its defences and sunk yet more ships.[26]

On this day came another of the Admiralty's direct interferences with operations at sea. Because of the scale and lethal effectiveness of German airpower in the waters south of Crete as well as north of it, Cunningham (after consultation with Wavell) had at 1130 ordered the troopship *Glenroy*, then on the way to the island with reinforcements, to turn back to Alexandria. At about 1600, 'to my amazement', according to Cunningham:

> the Admiralty sent a direct message to the *Glenroy* ordering her to turn north again, and about an hour later sent me a signal urging that her reinforcements be landed if it could be done that night. Of course, it was much too late, so I ordered the *Glenroy* back to Alexandria, and informed the Admiralty that if she had proceeded north she would have arrived at daylight, the worst possible time for air attacks . . . The less said about this unjustifiable interference by those ignorant of the situation the better.[27]

On the night of the 23–24 May the destroyers *Jaguar* (Lieutenant-Commander J. F. Hine, Senior Officer) and *Defender* landed stores and ammunition at Suda and took off some 'useless military mouths'. By daylight on the 24th these two destroyers on their way back to Alexandria and the minelayer *Abdiel* on passage in the reverse direction with more supplies to be landed the following night were for the time being the only warships left at sea, for Cunningham had been compelled to withdraw all the rest in order to refuel and restock with ammunition. At this point came signals from the Admiralty saying that it was vital to stop seaborne expeditions reaching Crete in the next day or two, even at the cost of serious losses to the Fleet, coupled with a signal from the Chiefs of Staff asking for Cunningham's appreciation of the naval situation. To the Admiralty Cunningham pointed out that Crete lay 400 miles from the Fleet's base and that his ships were at present out of fuel and shells. To the Chiefs of Staff he signalled that 'the scale of air attack now makes it no longer possible to operate in the Aegean or in the vicinity of Crete by day. The Navy cannot guarantee to prevent seaborne landings without suffering losses which, added to those already sustained, could very seriously prejudice our command of the Eastern Mediterranean.'[28] But the Chiefs of Staff replied that 'the Fleet and the Royal Air Force were to accept whatever risk was entailed in preventing enemy reinforcements reaching Crete. If enemy convoys were reported north of Crete, the Fleet would have to operate in that area by day, although considerable losses might be expected . . .'[29]

Hardly surprisingly, Cunningham, in his words, 'found this message singularly unhelpful. It failed lamentably to appreciate the realities of the situation.'[30] Tight-lipped, he signalled back on 26 May:

> It is not the fear of sustaining losses but the need to avoid losses which will cripple the fleet without any commensurate advantage which is the determining factor in operating in the Aegean. As far as I know, the enemy has so far had little if any success in reinforcing Crete by sea . . . The experience of three days in which two cruisers and four destroyers have been sunk, and one battleship, two cruisers and four destroyers severely damaged shows what losses are likely to be. Sea control in the Eastern Mediterranean could not be retained after another such experience.[31]

In any case by this time the Fleet was at sea again. Flying his flag in the *Queen Elizabeth* Pridham-Wippell had taken the 1st Battle Squadron (*Barham*, the carrier *Formidable* and eight destroyers) on a strike against the airfield of Scarpanto. At 0330 on 26 May, when 100 miles south-south-west of the objective, *Formidable* flew off a strike force of four Albacores and five Fulmars which took the enemy completely by surprise and damaged aircraft ranged on the ground. As usual the following forenoon brought the Luftwaffe's retribution, in the course of which *Formidable*'s remaining eight serviceable aircraft made twenty-four flights, and in twenty combats shot down two enemy aircraft for certain, plus two probables, for the loss of one Fulmar. But there was still an awful long way to go to Alexandria. At 1320 when Force A was some 150 miles south-west of Kaso Island, it was attacked by twenty dive-bombers, this time coming from the direction of North Africa: another accurate attack pressed home through a dense pattern of shell-bursts. HMS *Formidable* was hit twice, blowing out her starboard side between Numbers 17 and 24 bulkheads, and putting out of action the 'X' turret and her cable and accelerator gear.

The destroyer *Nubian* (Commander R. W. Ravenhill) was struck right aft, blowing off her stern. Nevertheless she was still able to steam at 24 knots, and reached Alexandria that night escorted by HMS *Jackal*. Force A made course eastward until nightfall, when *Formidable* parted company for Alexandria with a destroyer escort.

Meanwhile the *Glenroy*, escorted by the anti-aircraft cruiser *Coventry*, and the destroyers *Stuart* and *Jaguar* had been making for Crete in order to land more reinforcements and fuel. At 1820 Stukas set ablaze the petrol cans stacked on the *Glenroy*'s decks; a grim moment with eight hundred soldiers aboard. In order to bring the wind aft to prevent the fire spreading, the *Glenroy* had to turn south, away from Crete. So much time and distance were therefore lost in putting the fire out before she could resume her course for Crete that it had become impossible to land her troops before daylight, and Cunningham therefore once again recalled her. Nevertheless, the minelayer *Abdiel* and the destroyers *Hero* and *Nizam* put troops and supplies ashore at Suda on the night of 26–27 May; the last reinforcements to be landed.

At 0859 next forenoon Pridham-Wippell with Force A (*Queen Elizabeth*, *Barham* and six destroyers) was steering northwest for Kaso Island in order to cover their withdrawal when he was jumped by fifteen twin-engined Junkers 88 divebombers and Heinkel 111 medium bombers attacking out of the morning sun. The *Barham* was struck by a bomb on 'Y' turret and had two anti-torpedo bulges flooded by near misses. A fire took two hours to extinguish. At 1230 Cunningham ordered Pridham-Wippell to turn back for Alexandria; he reached harbour at 1900.[32]

By this time the land battle for Crete had been won in any case by General Kurt Student's 'Fliegerdivision 7' backed by the close support of the Luftwaffe.[33] British preparations to defend the island had been belated and hasty; the defence was desperately short of anti-aircraft artillery as well as lacking mobility; above all, it was crippled by a virtually total want of air cover. Moreover, the garrison commander, General Freyberg, had failed to appreciate that the struggle for the island turned on the local battle for control of Maleme airfield. He shared with the rest of the British chain of command right up to the Chiefs of Staff in London a continued fixation that the real key to the struggle lay in German seaborne troop convoys following up the airborne assault. Partly because of less than quick and energetic reaction on the part of the British commanders on the spot, the Germans were able to seize Maleme and use it from 22 May onwards to fly in a constant stream of Junkers 52 transports ferrying troops of the 5th and 6th Mountain Divisions. This build-up proved decisive in overcoming a tenacious but too passive a defence. By 26 May the solidly established German invaders were launching a major offensive eastwards against the British 'stop' position, breaking through it and encircling Freyberg's force reserve. On the 27th Wavell signalled London that, in view of the collapse of the front, he had ordered Crete to be evacuated as quickly as possible; the Chiefs of Staff replied at once giving their own authorisation.

So ended for the Royal Navy the first phase of the Crete campaign, in which despite grievous loss and damage it had prevented the enemy from passing a single vessel through to the island. Cunningham knew well what it had cost his sailors in physical and mental exhaustion; how much of their store of courage had been expended in enduring for day after day the constant menace and actual terror of air attack. 'I have never felt prouder [he wrote in his despatch] of the Mediterranean Fleet than at the close of these particular operations, except perhaps at the fashion in which it faced up to the even greater strain which was so soon to be imposed on it.'[34]

For yet again – and this time within less than a month – it was to be the Navy's task to bring away a beaten British Imperial Army from a foreign shore in defiance of swarming bombers. Already Cunningham had lost in Cretan waters two cruisers and four destroyers, while two battleships, his only carrier, a cruiser and a destroyer had been put out of action.[35] Now he had to rescue as many as he could of the 22,000 soldiers of 'Creforce', the majority of them from the narrow beach and tiny harbour of Sphakia on Crete's rugged southern coast; the remainder from Heraklion on the northern coast, which, although it possessed a small harbour with a jetty, was dangerously exposed to air attack, lying as it did only 90 miles from Scarpanto airfield. Once more the Commander-in-Chief turned his worn-out and often damaged ships and his weary crews towards the enemy.

On 28–29 May, the first night of the evacuation, Force C (Captain S. H. T. Arliss) with the destroyers *Napier*, *Nizam*, *Kelvin* and *Kandahar*, safely lifted 700 soldiers from Sphakia and landed rations for the 15,000 men gathering on shore after a desperate march over mountain passes. But Force B at Heraklion, commanded by Admiral Rawlings (flying his flag in the cruiser *Orion*), with the cruisers *Ajax* and *Dido*, and the destroyers *Decoy*, *Jackal*, *Imperial*, *Hotspur*, *Kimberley* and *Hereward*, suffered calamitously. On the outward voyage from Alexandria a near miss damaged the *Ajax*, and it was decided to return her to harbour. It is possible that the damage report to the captain was exaggerated and that therefore *Ajax*'s return may not have been necessary.[36] Force B reached Heraklion at 2330, whereupon the destroyers entered the harbour to begin ferrying troops out to the cruisers. By 0245 this operation had been successfully completed, and a quarter of an hour later *Kimberley* and *Imperial* embarked the rearguard. At 0320 Rawlings's squadron steamed for Alexandria at 29 knots with all 4,000 men of the Heraklion garrison aboard. But at 0345 *Imperial*'s rudder jammed, nearly causing her to collide with the cruisers. Rawlings ordered *Hotspur* to take off *Imperial*'s load and sink her. To enable *Hotspur* to carry out this order and then rejoin him Rawlings reduced his squadron's speed to 15 knots; and just after daylight *Hotspur* with 900 men aboard caught the squadron up.

However, Force B was now some one and a half hours behind schedule, and the sun was already rising when Rawlings turned south for the Kaso Strait, the eastern passage round Crete for Alexandria. 'There on watch like birds of ill omen silhouetted against the early dawn, hung four JU 88s.'[37] Although Cunningham had arranged with Air Marshal Longmore for the Royal Air Force to fly fighters over Force B from 0630 onwards, the fighters never found the task force. From 0600 to 1500 Rawlings's unprotected ships were to be subjected to continuous and all too successful bombing. The first casualty came at 0625 when the *Hereward* (Lieutenant W. J. Munn, RN) was hit by a bomb, lost speed and had to leave her place in the destroyer screen. Since his squadron was still exposed in the middle of the Kaso Strait, Rawlings concluded that he dare not imperil it by delaying to aid the *Hereward*; a harsh and difficult decision. Force B last saw the *Hereward* making for the coast of Crete some five miles off with her guns still firing. She sank on the way.

Then at 0645 the *Decoy*'s engines were damaged by a near miss, forcing Rawlings to reduce the squadron's speed to 25 knots. At 0730 his own flagship was likewise slowed by a near miss, bringing the speed of advance down to 21 knots. At 0815 *Dido* had her 'B' turret put out of action by a bomb; threequarters of an hour later it was the turn of *Orion*'s 'A' turret. At 1045, with Rawlings's task force now some 100 miles south of Kaso, eleven Stukas screamed down on *Orion*. One bomb went through the bridge, put the conning tower out of action, and burst in the densely crowded stokers' mess deck, killing 260 men and wounding 280, mostly evacuated soldiers; an appalling scene of butchery in confined space. Clearing these decks of bodies offered one of the most unpleasant experiences of the campaign to sailors already at the limits of fatigue: an experience shared by working parties sent from other ships. Three of the *Orion*'s engineer officers were also killed, while the ship herself was grievously mauled –

communications between the bridge and the engine room destroyed; steering gear out of action; three boiler rooms damaged; oil contaminated with salt water. Henceforth the speed of Rawlings's force oscillated between 12 and 25 knots, with an average of 21 knots.

Thankfully this had been the last Stuka attack. But at 1300, 1330 and 1500 there came more bombing from high altitude. As the Naval Staff History recounts: 'The first and only friendly fighters seen were two naval Fulmars of the Fleet Air Arm. They were due at noon and were there on the stroke of the hour.'[38] Royal Air Force fighters in the course of their vain attempts to find Rawlings did nevertheless succeed in shooting down two Ju 88s for the loss of one Hurricane.

At 2000 on 29 May Rawlings brought Force B into Alexandria harbour, his flagship down to only 10 tons of fuel and only two rounds of 6-inch high-explosive ammunition. The scene was observed by the Commander-in-Chief with keen dismay:

> I shall never forget the sight of those ships coming up harbour, the guns of their fore-turrets awry, one or two broken off and pointing forlornly skyward, their upper decks crowded with troops, and the marks of their ordeal only too plainly visible. I went on board at once and found Rawlings cheerful but exhausted. The ship was a terrible sight and the mess deck a ghastly shambles.[39]

This had been only the beginning: Cunningham knew that the Navy's major effort to lift troops from Sphakia was yet to come, and it was to Sphakia that nearly threequarters of Freyberg's army had retreated. He therefore found himself, in the laconic words of the Naval Staff History, 'in a most unpleasant predicament'.[40] He was particularly worried about the fast transport ship *Glengyle*, which was already at sea and due to pick up 3,000 soldiers on the night of 29–30 May. It was a day of anxious consultation with his Army colleagues and with the Admiralty in order to establish whether he was justified, in his words, 'in accepting the anticipated scale of loss and damage to his already weakened Fleet'.[41] He assured the Admiralty that he was 'ready and willing to continue the evacuation as long as a ship remained to do so, realising that it was against all tradition to leave troops deliberately in enemy hands'.[42] And so the evacuation went on – for three more nights.

By 0320 on 30 May Force D (Rear-Admiral King, flying his flag in the *Phoebe*), with HMAS *Perth*, the anti-aircraft cruisers *Coventry* and *Calcutta*, the transport *Glengyle* and the destroyers *Jervis*, *Janus* and *Hasty*, had embarked 6,000 soldiers from Sphakia. Three Luftwaffe attacks the following forenoon succeeded only in putting one of *Perth*'s boiler rooms out of action, and with – for once – two or three Royal Air Force fighters overhead, Force D reached Alexandria unscathed. Meanwhile Force C (Captain Arliss) with the destroyers *Napier*, *Nizam*, *Kelvin* and *Kandahar* had left Alexandria for Sphakia at 0915 to carry out a further lift of troops. Unfortunately *Kandahar* had to return to harbour because of a mechanical defect. Then, at 1530, three Ju 88s attacked from astern, their dive unseen by lookouts. A near-miss so damaged *Kelvin* that her speed was cut to 20 knots, forcing her to return to port. The two surviving ships reached Sphakia at 0030 on the 31st, and in two and a half hours each took aboard 700 soldiers. On the homeward voyage twelve Ju 88s did their best to sink them, but succeeded only in slowing them by near misses.

Now Cunningham confronted yet another dilemma. He had been asked by Freyberg to make one last lift of 3,000 men from Sphakia on the night of 31 May–1 June, yet the capacity of all his remaining available ships amounted to only 2,000. Worse, Captain Arliss signalled on his way back to Alexandria that there were in fact as many as 6,500 waiting to be lifted. Cunningham therefore ordered Vice-Admiral King (he had been promoted on 30 May), who had sailed at 0600 on the 31st with the *Phoebe* (flag), the fast minelayer *Abdiel* and the destroyers *Kimberley*, *Hotspur* and *Jackal*, to increase his lift to 2,500. Later still Cunningham made a fresh signal telling him simply to fill his ships to the limit. At 0300 on 1 June King's squadron finally left Sphakia with nearly 4,000 soldiers crammed aboard.

There followed the final calamity. Cunningham had despatched the anti-aircraft cruisers *Coventry* and *Calcutta* to rendezvous with King in order to provide extra protection against the Luftwaffe on the homeward voyage. A hundred miles from Alexandria the two ships were attacked by two Ju 88s diving out of the sun. The first bomber narrowly missed *Coventry* but the second hit *Calcutta* with two bombs, and she sank in a few minutes. The *Coventry* succeeded in picking up 23 officers and 232 ratings before returning to Alexandria.

The Royal Navy had rescued from Crete as many as 16,500 soldiers out of a total garrison of 22,000. Yet the cost of firstly defending Crete against seaborne invasion and then mounting this rescue operation equalled that of a great fleet battle. Cunningham had deployed a total strength of four battleships, one carrier, eleven cruisers, a minelayer and 32 destroyers. Out of this total one battleship (*Warspite*) had been so damaged as to require 22 weeks' repair work and another (*Barham*) six weeks', while the carrier *Formidable* would require twenty weeks' repair work. As well as three cruisers sunk, five had been so damaged as to need from two-and-a-half to eleven weeks' repair; and in addition to six destroyers sunk, another seven had been so damaged as to require one to sixteen weeks in the dockyard.[43]

So, with the complete destruction as a fighting force of a second British expeditionary force on Greek soil and the effective halving of the operational strength of the Mediterranean Fleet, came to an end at last the Greek adventure and the concomitant fantasy of a Balkan front. On 30 May Cunningham unburdened himself to the First Sea Lord in a personal letter. 'There is no hiding the fact,' he wrote, 'that in our battle with the German Air Force we have been badly battered. I always thought we might get a surprise if they really turned their attention to the fleet. No A/A fire will deal with the simultaneous attacks of 10–20 aircraft.'[44] After referring to his 'very heavy losses', Cunningham went on:

> I would not mind if we had inflicted corresponding damage on the enemy but I fear we have achieved little beyond preventing a seaborne landing in Crete and the evacuation of some of the Army there. I feel very heavy hearted about it all.
>
> I suppose we shall learn our lesson in time that the navy and army cannot make up for lack of air forces. Three squadrons of long range fighters and a few heavy bombing squadrons would have saved Crete for us.

But it was not only loss of or damage to ships that disturbed Cunningham. 'I have been rather anxious about the state of mind of the sailors after 7 days' constant bombing,' he told the First Sea Lord. '. . . AJAX out of the last 60 days has spent less than 10 nights in harbour I believe. DIDO has had one in the last 21 days, and so on. The destroyers are the same – just very tired.' And with regard to the morale of his ships' companies, he proceeded tactfully to give Pound a lesson in the art of leadership: 'I had hoped that, realising the work they were doing and what they were up against, the fleet might have received a message of encouragement from the Board which I feel would have done a lot of good.' He concluded his letter by saying that if the government wished to relieve him (as it had just relieved Longmore), he would not 'feel in any way annoyed, more especially as it may be that the happenings of the last few days may have shaken the faith of the personnel of the fleet in my handling of affairs'. But Pound and the Board of Admiralty, even Churchill, retained full confidence in him.

This was perhaps surprising, because only a month beforehand Cunningham had again bluntly opposed another of the Prime Minister's operational bright ideas – an idea brought forth by the disaster which had by then overtaken the British land forces in the Western Desert as the consequence of the original decision in January 1941 to halt O'Connor in full cry of victory and despatch the best of his troops and armour to Greece.

On 31 March Major-General Erwin Rommel launched his first offensive in Libya, some six weeks earlier than either the British Middle East Command or his own high command believed feasible. Punched about by Rommel in a hurry, Neame, the inexperienced British general who had replaced O'Connor, and his raw formations (an Australian brigade group and the 2nd Armoured Division) were swiftly routed. On 6 April both Neame and O'Connor (sent up by Wavell to 'advise' Neame) were captured. On 28 April Rommel reached the Egyptian frontier. All that remained of O'Connor's conquests was the isolated fortress of Tobruk, which Wavell had ordered to be held in order to hinder a German advance to the Nile.

Suddenly the Western Desert was promoted again by the Prime Minister from a merely secondary importance to a matter of supreme concern. On the day that Rommel reached the Egyptian frontier Churchill issued a War Cabinet directive stating that the loss of Egypt and the Middle East 'would be a disaster of the first magnitude', and that 'not only must Egypt be defended, but the Germans have to be beaten and thrown out of Cyrenaica'.[45] Thus began an immense effort, enormously costly in military and logistical resources (especially shipping), to repeat O'Connor's victory from scratch and re-create the discarded opportunity of clearing Italian North Africa altogether. And every stage of the process was to make its exigent demands on the Mediterranean Fleet.

The first such demand was made even while Rommel was still hounding Neame's raw troops out of Cyrenaica. Churchill believed that the key to halting Rommel in his rush towards Egypt lay in blocking the port of Tripoli, thus – so Churchill judged – starving him of supplies sent by sea from Italy. On 15 April 1941 the Admiralty (or, rather, Pound, tamely acquiescing again in the Premier's desires) signalled the C-in-C, Mediterranean, that the battleship *Barham* and a 'C' class cruiser were to be sacrificed as blockships.[46] Cunningham, horrified at the thought of losing two of his precious ships (especially the battleship) in so questionable a venture, signalled back: 'Such a price is only justified if . . . success of operation is reasonably assured and if . . . result will be efficacious. I do not consider either condition will be fulfilled.'[47] He went on: 'Even if we are successful we shall have lost a first-class fighting unit. Rather than send in HMS *Barham* . . . . I would prefer attack with whole Battle Fleet and accept risk.'

It was Cunningham's opinion that what he later called 'this extraordinary message' had been 'apparently dictated by someone who appeared to know little of Tripoli or to have any true realization of our circumstances in the Mediterranean'.[48] For 'Operation Lustre' (see above, pp. 331–3) was then in full swing: there was Malta to think of; and any sortie to Tripoli would require a round trip of some 1,800 miles in the face of the Luftwaffe. Nevertheless the Admiralty passed on to Cunningham next day by way of reply the text of a Prime Ministerial directive dated 14 April:

> Every convoy which gets through must be regarded as a serious naval failure. The reputation of the Royal Navy is engaged in stopping this traffic.
>
> The effectual blocking of Tripoli would be well worth a battleship upon the active list.[49]

There followed more sharp exchanges between Cunningham and London in which Pound warned Cunningham that the failure of the Navy to concentrate on the prevention of convoys reaching Libya 'will be considered as having let side down'.[50] Finally, however, Cunningham's unswerving opposition to sacrificing the *Barham* carried the day. Instead, at 0700 on 18 April he sailed from Alexandria for Tripoli (flying his flag in the *Warspite*), with the *Barham*, *Formidable* (all three ships to be badly damaged off Crete a month later), the *Valiant*, *Phoebe*, *Calcutta* and screening destroyers. 'My personal fears,' wrote Cunningham many years later, 'ranged from the complete loss of a ship in a minefield to heavy damage to them all through dive-bombing.'[51] It proved a brilliantly planned and executed raid. Approaching Tripoli under cover of night, the four bombarding ships – *Warspite*, *Barham*, *Valiant* and the cruiser *Gloucester* (which had now joined) – rounded a light shown by the submarine *Truant* as a navigation mark four miles off the harbour entrance, and for three-quarters of an hour blasted the harbour installations and the shipping within. Then, 'in an anti-climax as pleasing as it was unexpected', the fleet steamed back to Alexandria without incurring the vengeance of the enemy air forces.

Yet only two enemy merchant ships and a destroyer had been sunk.[52] Cunningham signalled the Admiralty: '. . . in spite of our immunity on this occasion, I do not consider in general that the results to be expected justified hazarding the whole Mediterranean Battle

Fleet in mineable waters and exposed to potentially heavy air attacks at such a distance from its base.'[53] The argument muttered on, with Admiralty and Prime Minister favouring Cunningham with various suggestions as to how best to stop the Axis convoy traffic, including the stationing of a battleship at Malta. 'I was beginning to get seriously annoyed,' wrote Cunningham. 'This constant advice, not to say interference, in how to run our own business from those who seemed to be unaware of the real facts of our situation did not help us at all. They were a mere source of worry.'[54]

To Cunningham the key to the problem – indeed the key to the entire problem of maritime control in the Mediterranean – lay in air power and the British want of it. 'We urgently needed long-range fighters to give air cover to our convoys in every area; sufficient short-range fighters to give us control of our bases in Malta, Alexandria, Suda Bay and Tobruk; and adequate reconnaissance aircraft to give us the same information of the enemy's movements at sea as the enemy possessed of ours.'[55] And he added: 'Why the authorities at home apparently could not see the danger of our situation in the Mediterranean without adequate air support passed my comprehension. However, within about a month the bitter lesson was to be learnt, in Crete.'[56]

For the Royal Navy in the Mediterranean as for the British Commonwealth Army in the Middle East, the War Cabinet's renewed enthusiasm for achieving a decisive victory in North Africa meant having to do all over again what it did in 1940, and in the Navy's case with shrunken, not expanded, resources. It would be called upon to struggle with the enemy battlefleet and air forces for the use of the central Mediterranean as a convoy route, undertake the hazardous task of supplying Malta, and provide direct support for the Army along the coast of Libya. Even before the Greek adventure had come to an end, the pattern had begun to repeat itself. Just as the key to O'Connor's Desert offensive in 1940 had lain in the 'I' tanks shipped to Suez round the Cape, so hopes of a new offensive in 1941 depended on a consignment of nearly 300 cruiser tanks, the first batch to come off the assembly lines of Britain's belatedly expanded production. Whereas in 1940 the Admiralty and the C-in-C, Mediterranean, had successfully opposed the Prime Minister's wish to send the 'I' tanks by the direct route through the Mediterranean, in 1941 Churchill, itching to attack Rommel at the least delay, prevailed in his desire to despatch the 'Tiger' convoy (bearing the 295 'Tiger cubs', as the cruiser tanks were dubbed, plus 53 crated Hurricanes) by this route. 'Operation Tiger' entailed another complicated series of interlocking movements by the whole of the Mediterranean Fleet and Force H, whereby the five fast ships carrying the tanks could be passed from escort to escort like a game of pass-the-parcel all the way from Gibraltar to Alexandria. As usual, other operations were slotted in: a fast and a slow convoy to Malta from Alexandria; bombardments of Benghazi during the Fleet's outward and homeward voyage; the passing of the battleship *Queen Elizabeth* and the cruisers *Naiad* and *Fiji* to Cunningham as welcome reinforcements.

'Operation Tiger' began on 6 May, just after the Mediterranean Fleet had evacuated the expeditionary force from Greece and three weeks before its coming 'death ride' off Crete. Thanks above all to unseasonably bad weather in the Mediterranean – cloud, rain and fog – which largely shielded the operation from enemy air reconnaissance and attack, 'Tiger' was successfully completed by 12 May,[57] when both Force H and the battlefleet safely anchored in their base ports. Only one of the five transports, the *Empire Song*, was lost, with 57 tanks and 10 crated aircraft, and this owing to a mine in the Sicilian Narrows. Nevertheless Cunningham was well aware of how lucky he and Somerville had been.

> Unfortunately [he writes in his memoirs] the apparent ease with which a convoy was brought from end to end of the Mediterranean caused many false conclusions to be drawn at home, and I think made some people think we were exaggerating the dangers and difficulties of running convoys and operations of any sort in the face of the vigorous action of the Luftwaffe. Before long the dismal truth was painfully to be brought home to them.[58]

In the event the strategic impact of the 'Tiger cubs' on the Desert War went off at half-cock because they were used in a premature and abortive offensive in June 1941 ('Battleaxe') undertaken by Wavell at the Prime Minister's urging before the Army could be thoroughly trained and prepared. Ninety-nine tanks were lost in action.

Now began five months of preparation on a vast scale for a fresh offensive. Already in 1941, between January and July, no fewer than 239,000 soldiers and over a million tons of vehicles, fuel and stores had arrived by sea to be unloaded in Egypt. Yet the object of this colossal and ever-increasing effort was to defeat a German expeditionary force of just two under-strength panzer divisions and a trucked infantry division; hardly a hundredth part of the army of the one power, Germany, which threatened the United Kingdom's own survival – barely a fiftieth of the army with which Hitler invaded Soviet Russia in 'Operation Barbarossa' on 22 June 1941. Did the swelling British military investment in the Middle East represent the rational pursuit of strategy or a growing obsession?

For the Royal Navy these months of military preparation brought no comparable respite or recuperation of strength; rather, continual service, a remorseless attrition, with the nourishing of Malta and Tobruk preoccupying Cunningham and Somerville above all else. Between April and June Force H made as many as five sorties towards Malta in order to fly off air reinforcements either from the *Ark Royal* alone or together with either *Furious* or *Victorious*. Of the 189 Hurricanes which reached the island from these carriers about half flew on to Egypt at the end of July to swell the Desert Air Force. It was between the second and third of these sorties that Force H had been summoned from the Mediterranean to join the hunt for the *Bismarck* – an illustration alike of the flexibility of seapower and of how hard the task forces of the Royal Navy were being worked.

In July and August followed two more sorties by Force H, this time to run convoys of troops and stores into Malta in the continuing effort to transform the island from a beleaguered fortress into a base for offensive operations by sea and air. For 'Operation Substance' on 20–28 July Somerville was reinforced with the battleship *Nelson* and the cruisers *Edinburgh*, *Manchester* and *Arethusa* from the Home Fleet. Despite all his careful preplanning and attempts at diversion, he was attacked on the outward voyage by high-level and torpedo bombers. The *Manchester*'s speed was slowed by a torpedo hit, compelling her to return to Gibraltar, while the destroyer *Fearless* was so badly damaged that she had to be sunk. 'Operation Style', on 31 July–4 August, was carried out by Force X (the cruisers *Hermione* [Captain G. N. Oliver], and *Arethusa*, the fast minelayer *Manxman* and two destroyers) without loss, however, and 130 tons of stores and 1,750 soldiers and Royal Air Force maintenance personnel landed in Malta.

Thanks to these 'milk runs' by the Royal Navy, the combatant strength of the garrison had now risen to 22,000, and its defences now comprised 112 heavy and 118 light anti-aircraft guns, plus 104 guns of various calibres suitable for the field. Stocks of military stores stood at eight months' supply. Whereas in January 1941 there had been only one fighter squadron on the island, there were fifteen Hurricane Is and 60 Hurricane IIIs at the beginning of August.[59] The neglect of the years of peace had at last been repaired.

On the orders of the Chiefs of Staff, Somerville ran yet another convoy to Malta in late September, this time ferrying 50,000 tons of fuel and food in eight merchant ships. 'Operation Halberd' demonstrates the scale of the naval resources required by the effort to keep Malta going. The escort all the way to Malta was provided by Force X (Rear-Admiral H. M. Burrough, flying his flag in the cruiser *Kenya*), and composed of five cruisers and nine destroyers. Somerville with Force H, reinforced from the Home Fleet to a strength of three battleships (*Nelson*, flying his flag, *Prince of Wales* and *Rodney*), the carrier *Ark Royal* and a further nine destroyers, covered the convoy against the Italian battlefleet and the enemy air forces. Further air cover was supplied by 22 Beaufighters and five Blenheims from Malta. This was not all: the Mediterranean Fleet also put to sea in order to create a diversion in the eastern Mediterranean, while submarines were posted in advance as pickets off Italian naval bases. Nonetheless, 'Halberd' did not go without loss, for *Nelson* was severely damaged by a torpedo from an Italian aircraft and her speed cut to 15 knots, and one of the merchant ships, the *Imperial Star*, had to be sunk after she too had been hit by a torpedo.

Such commitment and risk could only be justified if Malta proved a profitable investment as a base from which the flow of Axis supplies to Libya could be interrupted. Until the arrival on Trafalgar Day 1941 of Force K, commanded by Captain W. G. Agnew (of the *Aurora*), composed of two cruisers from the Home Fleet (*Aurora* and *Penelope*) and two destroyers (*Lance* and *Lively*) released from Force H, no surface ships were based on Malta. Until then the task of attacking Italian convoys had fallen to the Royal Navy's submarines and the Royal Air Force. From June to October (inclusive) the Royal Air Force sank 24 ships totalling 101,894 tons and His Majesty's submarines fourteen ships of 74,694 tons.[60] In the clear ultramarine waters of the Mediterranean was played out between submarines and escorts the same game of hunt and be hunted as in the Battle of the Atlantic, but with the roles reversed – British submariners enacting those scenes of peering into periscopes or silently listening to the thunder of enemy depth-charges rendered so familiar to cinema audiences by war films featuring German U-boat crews. On 18 September 1941 HMS *Upholder* (Lieutenant-Commander M. D. Wanklyn, later awarded the VC) bagged the biggest single prizes of all this onslaught on Italian shipping, when she sank the 19,500 ton liners *Neptunia* and *Oceania*, two out of the three ships in a fast convoy to Tripoli.

Although British submarines and aircraft were inflicting cumulative losses greater than new construction in Italian yards, two-thirds of the cargoes despatched to Libya were still getting through.[61] It took the cruisers and destroyers of Force K to bring the fraction of cargoes reaching Libya in November down to under 40 per cent of those despatched. On 9 November Force K sank or set on fire every one out of seven ships intercepted off Cape Spartivento. On 21 November the Italians aborted an attempt to run two separate convoys through from Naples under strong escort after the submarine *Utmost* had torpedoed the cruiser *Trieste* and a Swordfish of 830 Squadron, Fleet Air Arm, had performed a similar service for the cruiser *Duca della Abruzzi*, forcing both to limp back to Messina. On 24 November it was Force K's turn again, when HMS *Penelope* sank two German ships loaded with bombs, fuel and trucks. And on 30 November Force K, together with Force B (Rear-Admiral H. B. Rawlings) with the cruisers *Ajax* (flag), and *Neptune* and two destroyers, sank an auxiliary cruiser and a tanker, and blew up an escorting destroyer. Royal Air Force Blenheims also sank one merchant ship and damaged two others. Only one enemy ship in this convoy made it to Tripoli.

The decision back in April to hold the fortress of Tobruk, isolated far behind Rommel's forward troops on the Egyptian frontier, had laid on the Mediterranean Fleet the burden of another dangerous and continuing 'milk run'. During the 242 days of the siege, the Navy shipped into Tobruk 72 tanks, 92 guns, 34,000 tons of stores and 34,113 fresh troops. It shipped out 32,667 troops, plus 7,516 wounded and 7,097 prisoners – all this along an enemy coastline and within a few miles of his airfields.[62]

This very large turnover of troops is accounted for by the replacement of the 6th Australian Division in September and October by the 70th (British) Division, in compliance with the demand made by the government of Britain's Commonwealth ally, Australia; a needless extra burden on the hard-pressed Inshore Squadron and a burden to which Cunningham himself had been 'much opposed'.[63] For the ships' companies the Tobruk run meant navigating accurately at night through minefields, negotiating the harbour boom and finding a berth in a harbour littered with wrecks, also in the dark, and then completing the process of unloading and loading within an hour. When the siege finally ended in December 1941 the Royal Navy had lost twenty-five vessels sunk and nine seriously damaged; the Merchant Marine five ships sunk and four seriously damaged. Two hospital ships had also been attacked and badly damaged.[64] No wonder, then, that after the war Cunningham was to say that if Tobruk 'was rightly described as "a running sore" to the enemy, it was something equally painful for the Royal Navy.'[65]

Nevertheless, the worst attrition of all in 1941 was yet to come – worse even than the battle against the Luftwaffe off Crete, for it destroyed the very core of the Royal Navy's striking power in the Mediterranean.

On 13 November 1941, Force H, fearing U-boat attack, was zig-zagging across a smooth sea under low cloud on the last thirty miles of its return voyage to Gibraltar from yet another sortie to fly aircraft into Malta. Visibility was good except during occasional rain squalls. At 1540, when Somerville altered to 290° on the next leg of the zig-zag, speed 18 knots, the carrier *Ark Royal* (Captain L. E. H. Maund) altered to 286°, speed 22 knots, in order to leave her station to fly off aircraft. A minute later, in position 36° 03′N, 4° 40′W, she was shaken by an explosion under her bottom between keel and starboard side – whether a contact or non-contact explosion was never established[66] – caused by a torpedo from the U-81 (Lieutenant Friedrich Guggenberger), one of eighteen U-boats recently transferred from the Atlantic. According to the subsequent technical report on the loss of the ship, 'The ship whipped violently, aircraft loaded with torpedoes bouncing off the Flight Deck and spreading their under-carriages before settling again.'[67]

The *Ark Royal* immediately listed 10° to starboard and 'S' boiler room began to flood. Soon almost all power was lost. By 1602 the list had reached 18° and over the tannoy, which had been temporarily restored to life, came the orders: 'Hands to station for abandon ship', and 'Everyone over the port side.' From deep down in the machinery spaces men came clattering up ladders to the open air, not knowing how many more minutes the ship might last. But in fact there followed some fourteen hours of struggle to save the *Ark Royal*. Around 1700 all steam was lost, which killed the pumps and other auxiliary machinery, including the turbo-generators which supplied electric power. At 2055 she was taken in tow at 2 knots by the tug *Thames*. Between 1815 and 2215 devoted work by repair parties succeeded in gradually restoring steam to the port boiler room and with it, electric power. But then came further trouble – owing to the increasing list sea water spilled over into the elbow of the port boiler room funnel uptake, so blocking the escape of fumes. 'As a result,' recorded the technical report, 'boiler castings became red-hot and fires broke out.'[68]

As the flames spread the boiler room had to be abandoned, so losing all steam and hence all power in the ship for good. The *Ark Royal* was now just 22,000 tons of metal dead in the water. By 0215 on 14 November her list had reached 17°; by 0400 when Captain Maund gave a final order to abandon ship, a terrifying 27°. At 0430, with the list at 35°, the last man scrambled down the port side to be rescued by attendant destroyers. At 0613, when the list had reached 45°, the *Ark Royal* capsized and sank.

The Court of Enquiry attributed her loss partly to shortcomings in the damage-control measures taken after she was hit: 'It is considered that if, when steam finally failed, the port engine room and boiler room had been flooded to upright the ship there would have still been ample buoyancy for the ship to reach harbour.'[69] But the court acknowledged that the need for drastic counter-flooding might not have been appreciated because the book issued to the ship illustrating flooded compartments gave no examples of lists greater than 8°. The court also acknowledged the problems caused by steeply sloping decks slippery with oil, and the breakdown of the ship's communication systems for want of power: '. . . all messages had to be passed by messenger or human chain which slowed down all action . . .'[70]

Nevertheless *Ark Royal* owed her demise primarily to flaws in her own design, which had never been rectified in the dockyard because she had been in almost continuous service at sea. She was the Royal Navy's first modern fleet carrier, designed in 1935 and built as part of the initial and modest rearmament programme aimed at remedying the accumulated deficiencies caused by the defence cuts of the 1920s and early 1930s. Her designers had routed the boiler room uptakes beneath the lower hangar deck; and this, according to the technical report, 'proved a vulnerable feature at the end, as the flooding of the port boiler room finally occurred when the angle of the heel was about 19°. This restricted the passage available for funnel gases and a fire resulted.'[71] The uptakes had been routed in this way because it was impossible to route them further up in the ship, that is, through the lower hangar deck itself, because this would have restricted the number of aircraft carried. Since *Ark Royal* was not protected by an armoured flight deck (unlike later carriers of the Illustrious class), it would have been ideally desirable to armour the funnel uptakes themselves. But, as the technical report remarked, this 'would have involved substantial additional weight of armour, which could not be accepted, as the ship's displacement was limited to 22,000 tons in anticipation of the Geneva Convention [a hoped-for but aborted fresh international agreement on the limitation of armaments] . . .' As a result, some risk of flooding via the unarmoured uptakes had to be accepted.[72]

The final misfortune proved to be, in the words of the enquiry report, that this was 'the first known case' when a single torpedo blew a hole in a ship's bottom 'so large as the reported size, 130 feet long', leading to an immediate list 'much greater than anticipated'.[73] Once all steam was lost, so too was power for every piece of equipment in the ship, including the electricity supply and hence telecommunications. This was because of another basic weakness in her design, for all the auxiliary machinery in the ship was powered solely by steam from the boiler rooms, even the electricity supply by means of turbo-generators; there were no stand-by sources of power at all. Moreover, the electrical problem was worsened in the event because the main switchboard was located low enough in the ship to be itself affected by flooding even while there was still steam power available. Later aircraft carriers suffered from none of these shortcomings. The final technical flaw lay in that when portable pumps were put aboard from another ship, their plugs and sockets were not compatible with those in the *Ark Royal*.

The *Ark Royal*'s fate after such brave service (including the decisive strike on the *Bismarck*) thus exemplifies two recurring strands in the twentieth-century history of British seapower – weaknesses in the design and technology of major warships, and the pernicious influence of the inter-war pursuit of naval limitation agreements.

On 18 November, four days after the loss of HMS *Ark Royal* and nearly a year after O'Connor began his offensive at Sidi Barrani, the new 8th Army, over 100,000 strong, with nearly 700 assorted tanks, launched 'Operation Crusader'; the end product of all the resources in shipping and escorts invested in the supply and reinforcement of the Middle East theatre since the disasters in Greece and Crete; the end product too of the Royal Navy's repeated Mediterranean convoy operations and its months of unrelenting service off the Libyan coast in support of Tobruk. And while the armies collided in confused tank battles in the Cyrenaican desert, the Royal Navy once again did its part, running more supplies into Tobruk (at the cost of the fast merchant ship *Glenroy*, veteran of the Crete evacuation, torpedoed, beached, but eventually towed back to Alexandria; and the Australian sloop *Parramatta*), and bombarding the German defences at Halfaya Pass and Bardia.

On 23 November, however, a crisis in the land battle (the 8th Army had failed to relieve Tobruk, while its tank losses were apparently so high that the army commander wished to break off the offensive) evoked a signal from the Prime Minister to Cunningham that it was vitally important to stop enemy ships transporting supplies, above all of fuel, through to Benghazi: 'I shall be glad to hear through the Admiralty what action you propose to take . . .'[74] There ensued a brief but sharp exchange between the Commander-in-Chief, Mediterranean, on the one hand and the First Sea Lord and the War Premier on the other, in which the C-in-C again sought to educate the desk men in London about the operational risks and realities – not least the Fleet's current acute shortage of fuel, and 'the difficulty of intercepting a convoy by a force based 550 miles from the scene of operations and under constant enemy observation'.[75]

In the early hours of 24 November, however, Cunningham received intelligence that two enemy convoys were actually at sea heading for Benghazi. He therefore ordered the cruisers of Forces K and B to intercept them while he himself took the battlefleet (*Queen Elizabeth*, flying his flag, *Barham* and *Valiant*) to sea in order to cover the operation in case Italian heavy ships intervened. Next day, at about 1630, with the battlefleet on patrol between Crete and Cyrenaica, Cunningham was having tea in his bridge cabin when he 'suddenly heard and half-felt the door give three distinct rattles and [I] thought we had opened fire with our anti-aircraft guns'.[76]

> I went quickly up the one ladder to the bridge, and then I saw the *Barham*, immediately astern of us, stopped and listing heavily to port. The thuds I had heard were three torpedoes striking her. She had been torpedoed by a U-boat. The poor ship rolled nearly over on to her beam ends, and we saw men massing on her upturned side. A minute or two later there came the dull rumble of a terrific explosion as one of her main magazines blew up. The ship became so completely hidden in a great cloud of yellowish-black smoke, which went wreathing and eddying high up into the sky. When it cleared away the *Barham* had disappeared. There was nothing but a bubbling, oily-looking patch on the calm surface of the sea, dotted with wreckage and the heads of swimmers. It was ghastly to look at, a horrible and awe-inspiring spectacle when one realized what it meant.[77]

Although Vice-Admiral Pridham-Wippell and some 450 others were rescued, 55 officers and 806 men, including the ship's captain, Captain G. C. Cooke, died with the ship.

Barham had fallen victim to the U-331 (Lieutenant Hans-Dietrich Baron von Tiesenhausen), another of the U-boats transferred from the Atlantic by the German naval command in response to British devastation of Mediterranean convoys. The Royal Navy in the Mediterranean had already paid dearly for the respite thus accorded the Admiralty in the Battle of the Atlantic (see above, pp. 274–5).

In the final month of 1941 came yet more salvoes of disaster. On 14 December the cruiser *Galatea* sank almost immediately off Alexandria after being struck by two torpedoes from a U-boat. Four days later a force of three cruisers (*Neptune*, *Aurora* and *Penelope*) and four destroyers (*Kandahar*, *Lance*, *Lively* and *Havock*) which had sailed from Malta to intercept a convoy off Tripoli ran into a minefield in heavy seas and blustering wind. The *Neptune* sank after hitting four mines, with only a single survivor, while *Aurora* was badly damaged and *Penelope* lightly damaged; the destroyer *Kandahar* also sank after her stern had been blown off. Force K, which had done such execution since its arrival at Malta in October, was now reduced to one cruiser, *Penelope*. Then, on 19 December, the remaining battleships of the Mediterranean Fleet succumbed in Alexandria harbour itself to the smallest and cheapest of conceivable weapons systems – explosive charges fixed to the ships' bottoms by two-men Italian Navy teams in diving suits riding astride 'human torpedoes'. Cunningham, standing on the quarter deck of his flagship, the *Queen Elizabeth*, himself witnessed the culminating catastrophe of 1941. Just before 0600:

> . . . there was a violent explosion under the stern of the tanker *Sagona*, lying close to the *Queen Elizabeth* with the *Jervis* [destroyer] alongside. Both the tanker and the destroyer were badly damaged, the *Sagona* badly holed aft with her rudder and screws damaged. The *Jervis*'s injuries were to keep her in dock for a month.
>
> About twenty minutes later I saw another heavy explosion under the *Valiant*'s foreturret, and four minutes after that, when I was right aft in the *Queen Elizabeth* by the ensign staff, I felt a dull thud and was tossed about five feet into the air by the whip of the ship and was lucky not to come down sprawling. I saw a great cloud of black smoke shoot up the funnel and immediately in front of it, and knew at once that the ship was badly damaged. The *Valiant* was already down by the bows. The *Queen Elizabeth* took a heavy list to starboard.[78]

Thanks to this final attack by six brave and bold Italian sailors the Mediterranean Fleet entirely ceased to exist. Cunningham's remaining strength consisted of just three light cruisers (*Naiad*, *Dido* and *Euryalus*) and a handful of destroyers. At the far end of the Mediterranean Somerville's Force H had been reduced by losses, damage, and Admiralty withdrawal of ships for service elsewhere to one old battleship (*Malaya*), the obsolete carrier *Argus* and one cruiser, the *Hermione*. In the course of 1941 the pursuit of an opportunistic 'blue water' strategy in the Mediterranean had cost the Royal Navy a total of one battleship sunk and four badly damaged, one carrier sunk and two damaged, seven cruisers sunk and ten damaged, sixteen destroyers sunk and twelve damaged, one monitor sunk, and five submarines sunk and three damaged.[79]

Yet at the year's end the positive results of 'blue water' strategy had hardly justified this catastrophic loss, let alone paid a dividend on the huge investment of British resources in the Mediterranean and Middle East. By this time the 8th Army's offensive in Libya – the spearpoint of 'blue water' strategy once the evacuation of Crete had closed the Greek adventure – had certainly forced Rommel into retreat, marking the first victory of British Commonwealth forces over German troops in the Second World War. The 8th Army had taken 36,000 prisoners and reduced Rommel's tank strength to only thirty. This was a welcome enough success just when the Red Army was fighting titanic battles in front of Moscow and Leningrad against the main strength of the Wehrmacht. Yet the 8th Army's own striking power had been so worn down that there could be no immediate prospect of pushing on towards Tripoli. At the beginning of 1942 the Desert campaign came to rest exactly where O'Connor had been halted at London's orders a year before, at El Agheila, on the border between Cyrenaica and Tripolitania.

Nor could Cunningham and Somerville hope for replacement of their lost or damaged ships (the latter often condemned to many weeks of repair in dockyards as far afield as North America). For in that same devastating final month of 1941 the third of the triple threats to the British Empire in its worldwide sprawl – the threat that had been smouldering ever since Britain had chosen to affront Japan in the Manchurian crisis ten years earlier; really ever since Britain failed to renew the Anglo-Japanese alliance twenty years earlier – at last exploded. On 7 December Britain found herself at war with three great powers simultaneously – the pre-war Chiefs of Staffs' ultimate nightmare. The moment of bankruptcy for British 'total strategy' since the end of the Great War had arrived.

13

The Sinking of HMS Prince of Wales *and* Repulse

On 12 August 1941 the Chiefs of Staff met to consider a telegram about future United States negotiating policy towards Japan which the Foreign Secretary had just received from the Prime Minister at the summit conference then being held with President Roosevelt aboard HMS *Prince of Wales* and the USS *Augusta*, in Placentia Bay, Newfoundland. Such was the gulf between Japan's expansionist ambitions in China and South-East Asia and America's tough conditions for a general settlement that, as Churchill reported, the negotiations 'show little chance of succeeding'.[1] In fact, in Churchill's words, the 'President's idea is . . . to procure a moratorium of say 30 days in which we may improve our position in Singapore area and the Japanese who have to stand still . . . President considers a month gained will be valuable.'[2]

For the Chiefs of Staff, for the First Sea Lord above all, the arrival of this telegram signified that the defence of the British Empire in South-East Asia and the Pacific had ceased to be an anxiety nagging continually at the back of the mind while war was being waged against Germany and Italy with all available resources, and had become instead an urgent problem demanding answer – if such could be found. The Chiefs of Staff forthwith instructed the Joint Planners to report on 'what steps could be taken in the immediate future to improve our position in the Far East'.[3]

At the 1923 Imperial Conference, held a year after Britain had allowed the Anglo-Japanese alliance to lapse and instead signed the Washington Treaties drastically limiting the size of the Royal Navy, that shrewd Boer Jan Smuts, Prime Minister of South Africa, had doubted whether the proposed new naval base at Singapore would offer any protection to Australia and New Zealand unless Britain could send the battlefleet – and believed that Japan was unlikely to attack unless she had support in Europe. If this were so, Smuts asked, would it be feasible to divide the Royal Navy, now Britain no longer enjoyed the old huge superiority? Leo Amery, then First Lord of the Admiralty, and himself a believer in the greatness of the British Empire, had admitted in reply: 'Of course it is perfectly feasible that, if there were a European combination against us at the same moment as war was declared against us by Japan, we should be in a position of extraordinary difficulty.'[4]

From the Manchurian crisis of 1931–32 onwards the possible advent of this 'position of extraordinary difficulty' had haunted the imaginations of British policy-makers and strategists, especially at times of diplomatic crisis in Europe, and more especially still if Japan had concurrently perpetrated local acts of aggression or insult against the British presence in China. Between the summers of 1940 and 1941 the advent had grown more and more probable rather than merely possible, and in circumstances far grimmer than had been foreseen even by the most pessimistic before the war. For in the immediate aftermath of France's collapse, Marshal Pétain's government had haplessly granted Japan the right to station armed forces in the northern part of the French colony of Indo-China; and a year later, on 24 July 1941, the Japanese proceeded to occupy the whole of the colony, giving their navy a magnificent forward base in the natural harbour of Camranh Bay and their air force fields in southern Indo-China from which to dominate Siam and the South China Sea. The Royal Navy's fleet base at Singapore was no longer protected by over three thousand miles of distance from Japanese strike forces based in the home islands, but instead had become an outpost exposed to attack at relatively close range.

And by now Britain herself was not only fighting for life itself against Nazi Germany (owing to the collapse of the Western Front in May 1940 and the loss of France as an ally), but also massively committed to conducting Churchill's 'blue water' strategy in the Mediterranean and Middle East, in complete reversal of pre-war strategic priorities whereby the Mediterranean was if necessary to be abandoned in order to concentrate a great battlefleet to send to

Singapore. By August 1941, what with the twin demands of 'grey water' strategy in the Atlantic and 'blue water' in the Mediterranean already severely over-stretching the Royal Navy's resources in every kind of ship, Leo Amery's 'position of extraordinary difficulty' had already come about even without an actual Japanese attack.

The problem of over-stretch was the worse because new construction of ships since 1939 had barely kept pace with the losses sustained in two years of war, let alone enabled the Royal Navy to expand in proportion to its constantly increasing commitments. In July 1941 the First Sea Lord, in a memorandum opposing yet further allotment of industrial capacity to the aggrandisement of Bomber Command at the expense of naval construction, noted that the total strength of the Navy in ships of sizes down to sloops was now 369, as against 366 on the outbreak of war; and pointed out that in the Great War 'numbers of ships . . . had increased by some 40 per cent at the end of the first two years'.[5]

Several factors account for this failure to increase the size of the Royal Navy. In the first place, such new construction as was authorised had been delayed by the backwardness of British shipyards and the sloth and restricted practices of their workforces.[6] According to the First Sea Lord in July 1941, of the new ships expected in January 1941 to be completed by 30 June, 81,000 tons (including three cruisers, twelve destroyers and three submarines) had not yet been delivered.[7]

But secondly and more importantly, Britain was more painfully caught than ever between the scissors of her strategic obligations as the Mother Country of an Empire on the one hand, and, on the other, her own inadequate financial and industrial base which made it impossible to afford or even to build and equip the size of Navy needed to fulfil those obligations. In January and February 1940 the First Sea Lord and the naval staff had fought an unavailing battle with the War Cabinet for a major new building programme of four battleships as well as two 15-inch battlecruisers.[8] So highly did Pound and his VCNS, Rear-Admiral T. S. V. Phillips, still rate the battleship that they were even prepared to sacrifice new construction of carriers and cruisers for the sake of their proposed programme, although also, to be fair, for the sake of the largest possible expansion of the anti-U-boat and anti-mine flotillas.[9] Pound's pleas for new battleships were to no avail; the pressure on Britain's inadequate shipbuilding industry to construct new merchant ships as well as escorts was such that in March 1940 the War Cabinet decided that all long-term programmes must be abandoned.

Nevertheless in September 1940 the First Sea Lord and Phillips sought to revive the battleship programme. Pound believed that work on the *Howe* (last of the 14-inch King George V class), and on the *Lion* and *Temeraire* (16-inch gun ships of a new class already laid down) should all proceed; and that two more ships of this class, *Thunderer* and *Conqueror*, should be laid down as soon as possible. He also argued that a further ship, the *Vanguard*, making use of the 15-inch guns and turrets installed in the *Courageous* and *Glorious* before their 1920s conversion from battlecruisers to aircraft carriers, should also be built. He reckoned that all these battleships were needed to match the expected combined strength in heavy ships in 1945 of Germany, Italy and Japan. Although he thought it 'desirable' to order another fleet carrier, he told the Controller of the Navy he would not do so at the expense of a battleship. The Controller in reply had to point out to this simple sailor an industrial fact of life: the demands for armour plate of such a programme would necessitate the immediate stoppage of production of tank armour.[10]

Undaunted, the Admiralty continued to push for the resumption of a major long-term construction programme. At the beginning of 1941 their modified shopping list comprised the two 16-inch battleships *Lion* and *Temeraire*, two fleet carriers, ten cruisers and forty to fifty destroyers.[11] In view of the limited capacity for making armour plate and the continued pressure on shipyards exerted by the desperate need to build new merchant ships and escorts and repair damaged ones, the Admiralty's latest shopping list proved merely more wishful thinking. On 26 March 1941 the Prime Minister, wearing his other personality of sober and realistic judgment (it was the month when he proclaimed 'the Battle of the Atlantic'), issued an instruction that no naval vessel was to be undertaken that could not be completed by the end of 1942. The pre-war hope of a 'Two-Power Standard' fleet or even just an 'enhanced One-Power Standard' fleet (see p. 37, above) had thus finally foundered on the rock of Britain's 'less than One-Power Standard' industrial resources.

The Admiralty's problem was rendered even more acute in the latter months of 1941 because nearly a third of the Navy's ships lay immobilised in the dockyards either having battle and storm damage repaired or being refitted and modernised. In the quarter July to October 1941 the number of vessels of corvette size and above in the dockyards for major work stood at no fewer than 132 (seventeen of them in American yards).[12] The inordinate time taken by British yards to complete the work served to aggravate this drain on fighting strength at sea, and at the same time justifiably enrage the Premier.

Thus it was that, at 1 August 1941, the Royal Navy had only ten capital ships in service, though four more were due to leave the dockyards during that month and the first week of September. The *King George V*, *Prince of Wales* and *Malaya* were with the Home Fleet; *Barham*, *Valiant* and *Warspite* with the Mediterranean Fleet; *Nelson* and *Renown* with Force H, and the two unmodernised Great War battleships *Ramillies* and *Revenge* with the North Atlantic Escort Force.[13]

How then was the Admiralty to find a fleet for Singapore, as had been repeatedly promised (though with waning conviction) to Australia and New Zealand before and since the outbreak of war with Germany and Italy? It went far deeper than a mere question of naval strategy and deployment. As Sir Samuel Hoare, the then First Lord of the Admiralty, had remarked to the 1937 Imperial Conference, 'the very existence of the British Commonwealth as now constituted' rested on the ability of Britain to send a battlefleet to Singapore.[14] But this in turn posed an even more profound question about Britain's very own existence as the centre of this oceanic empire, the immediate practical implications of which were so starkly confronting her leaders in the summer and autumn of 1941. For in retrospect it can be seen that it was an illusion for the British to believe that the Commonwealth and the Empire made Britain a great world power. Rather the strategic and economic balance sheet in 1941 demonstrates that the Commonwealth and Empire (with the notable exception of Canada and perhaps South Africa) were not an asset, but a net drain on Britain's strength; a predicament. For the imperial pink splashed across the map of the world in British atlases did not represent strength, as the British romantically believed, but one of the most outstanding examples of strategic overstretch in history.

In the first place Britain, an island in the northern seas, would not already have become entangled in a war in the Mediterranean and Middle East if it had not been for the British naval and military presence developed in this theatre during the previous century and a half in order to protect the imperial route to India, the Far East, Australia and New Zealand. Yet the contributions thus far made to Britain's war with Germany (and Italy) by Australia, New Zealand and India – some five divisions and six cruisers – were too small to balance the enormous British commitment of military and material resources to the Middle East and the deployment in the Mediterranean of about a third of the Royal Navy's strength. Nor did it make up for the British troops stationed in India and further British garrisons in Burma and Malaya.

In any event, the approach of war with Japan was to draw Dominion ships and divisions back from the Mediterranean and Middle East to the defence of their own countries. The military and naval contributions of the Empire lying east of Suez to Britain's own struggle in Europe therefore did not even begin to compensate for the British obligation to wage an extra war against Japan in the Empire's defence by land and above all by sea; a huge potential burden on a nation of only 45 millions, and one impossible for the Royal Navy to bear.

Nor, in the second place, did the Empire and Commonwealth east of Suez constitute an economic asset of such value to Britain as in itself to warrant preserving at the cost of an extra maritime war. India, poverty-stricken and backward, devoid of key raw materials, actually drew on British shipping resources in order to fill her essential needs for imports. Australia and New Zealand, which had been among Britain's major peacetime sources of meat and dairy produce, had now dwindled to minor importance in this regard because it was uneconomic in shipping capacity to haul such supplies over the 12,000 miles from these dominions rather than over the much shorter Atlantic routes from North and South America. Burma and Borneo, for their part, were relatively minor producers of oil. Even Malaya, the most single valuable territory in the British Empire and a prolific earner of dollars, producing a third of the world's rubber and well over half the world's tin, was hardly worth a war with a great power on top of an existing war. And the civilian trade and supply of the whole Indian Ocean area (the core of the traditional British imperial structure) from Australasia to East Africa, from India and South-East Asia to Egypt, were swallowing by the second half of 1941 over 331,000 tons of shipping in continuous employment – enough to bring an additional 800,000 tons of desperately needed imports to Britain across the North Atlantic.[15]

But of course British policy towards the Empire and Commonwealth east of Suez was not, could not be, shaped by such cost-benefit analysis. There was the question of Britain's imperial pride and prestige, while in the case of Australia and New Zealand in particular Britain's 'alliance' with them derived from kinship, from common history and culture, and from loyalty to a common Crown, not from the logic of strategic and economic advantage. These, the dominions closest to Britain in race and sentiment, happened to be the furthest away in distance – settled in that halcyon epoch of the early nineteenth century when the Royal Navy's supremacy had turned the oceans of the world into a British pond, and when Japan had been a feudal society locked up in self-imposed isolation. The haphazard workings of history and the accidents of geography had thus bequeathed a strategic absurdity: an alliance between two vulnerable and dependent small nations in the Pacific and a protecting power in Europe already stretched to the limit in the struggle for its own survival. But ties of blood, strong feelings of family loyalty and obligation, made it unthinkable, certainly unthought, for Britain's leadership to do other than seek by all means possible to preserve Australia and New Zealand from attack.

Given Britain's own peril the most desirable means must lie in deft diplomacy aimed at averting a conflict.[16] Yet British diplomacy in the Far East had lacked essential leverage ever since the lapsing of the Anglo-Japanese Treaty in 1922, for by failing to renew the treaty Britain lost Japan as an ally but failed to gain America instead, despite periodic efforts so to do, as at the beginning of 1937 (see above, pp. 33, 55). Stanley Baldwin had warned in 1932 that Britain would 'get nothing out of Washington but words, big words, but only words';[17] and that was indeed all Britain did get from America in regard to the Japanese menace right up to, and including, 1941. Thus lacking the support of an ally in the East, Britain could only look to her own strength to back her diplomacy. Unfortunately that had been lacking too. Whereas up to the mid-1930s Britain had had available a battlefleet for deployment in eastern waters but no naval base to which to send it, after the mid-1930s – and above all in 1941 – she had the naval base, but no available fleet. It had taken remarkable conduct of grand strategy and high policy on the part of successive British Cabinets to achieve this neat but paralysing sequence.

How then could a weightless diplomacy preserve the British Empire in the East from Japanese ambition? In the 1930s Neville Chamberlain (when Chancellor of the Exchequer) and the Chiefs of Staff had advocated 'strategic appeasement' – neutralising the Japanese prong of the triple threat by means of a deal with Japan over spheres of influence in China. However, the scruples of Cabinet and public opinion alike had ruled out such a cynical exercise in *realpolitik*. After the outbreak of war with Germany, and especially in the wake of France's collapse and the addition of Italy to Britain's foes, there was renewed advocacy of strategic appeasement on the part of Sir Robert Craigie, the ambassador in Tokyo, and the Chiefs of Staff, deeply worried as the latter were about Britain's global plight. In July 1940 the Chiefs of Staff advised the Cabinet that in present circumstances British policy should aim at avoiding a clash with Japan, and not merely that: 'A general settlement, including economic concessions to Japan, should be concluded as soon as possible. Failing this settlement, our general policy must be to play for time, cede nothing till we must, and build up our defences as soon as we can.'[18]

But it was illusion to believe that Britain any longer retained even the prestige needed to promote some general settlement of Far Eastern problems. Instead of 'strategic appeasement', therefore, Britain found herself in 1940 haplessly descending into 'tactical appeasement' – a sheer giving way in the face of Japanese menaces and demands, a process which even Churchill then saw as unavoidable. Already, on 10 July (the Battle of Britain was just opening; German preparations for 'Operation Sealion' just beginning) Britain had had to agree to a Japanese demand to close the Burma Road (the route by which trucks carried American supplies into China in support of Chiang Kai Shek), although only for three months. At the end of July Britain further agreed to withdraw her garrison from Shanghai and her gunboats from the River Yangtse. Yet though such diplomatic retreats might buy time they could not buy long-term Japanese non-belligerency, for in Britain's pitiful state of weakness, Japan might simply take what she wanted by armed force whenever she wished. Appeasement out of fear and weakness was as unlikely to achieve permanent results in the Far East as it had been in Europe.

That left one other expedient, pursued in vain during the 1930s, but in Britain's desperation worth another try – that of enlisting the strength of the United States to shield the British Empire in the Far East and Pacific, just as that strength was already being enlisted in the cause of Britain's own survival. In regard to Japan, however, British policy-makers saw American strength as serving in the first place as a deterrent. Sadly for the British, however, Washington proved less interested in preserving the British Empire in the East than it did in preserving Britain herself as a convenient bulwark between Nazi Germany and the United States. Indeed, from President Roosevelt downward there was instinctive suspicion of British 'imperialism'. Moreover, the axis of American naval strategy in the Pacific lay westwards from the west coast of America through the advanced fleet base of Pearl Harbor, Hawaii, to the Philippines, now an internally self-governing Commonwealth, though America retained control over foreign affairs and defence. For the Americans the British concept (now vitiated by weakness) of a naval war against Japan in the China Sea and based on Singapore was irrelevant, peripheral.

Thus while Britain and the United States shared the broad objective of averting further Japanese expansion, their interests had little in common beyond that. It is hardly surprising that British efforts in 1940–41, either at the level of government – including Churchill himself toadying valiantly to Roosevelt – or at the level of staff talks, to induce the Americans to rescue Britain from her imperial predicament in the East came to little. In the summer of 1940 the United States declined either to threaten the Japanese with a full economic embargo, as the British wished, or make a *démarche* in regard to a general settlement of Far Eastern problems. This American inaction had led directly to the British diplomatic surrenders over the Burma Road and the garrison and gunboats in China.

In late January 1941, after cordial enough meetings and exchanges of secret information between representatives of the British and United States naval staffs, formal staff conversations were held in Washington at which the British delegation pressed again the key importance (as they saw it) of Singapore, and urged that America should base there as strong a detachment of her Pacific Fleet (including battleships) as possible. An American battlefleet to Singapore! It was a solution to the imperial dilemma that would have astonished and dismayed Beatty and Amery. It marked a tacit acknowledgment that after two decades Britain's imperial bluff had at last been called by events; and that she had reached the point of bankruptcy in terms of world maritime power. But the proposal was to no avail: the Americans declined to bail the British out. The final record of the staff conversations found a polite formula to express the deep divisions of view between the Royal and the United States Navies over Far Eastern strategy: 'It was agreed that for Great Britain it was fundamental that Singapore be held; for the United States it was fundamental that the Pacific Fleet be held intact.'[19]

When in February 1941 there occurred a brief scare that Japan was about to strike (taken more seriously in London than in Washington) Churchill sought once again to wring some kind of public guarantee out of Roosevelt that the United States would go to war if the British Empire in the East were attacked. 'I think I ought to let you know,' he wrote, 'that the weight of the Japanese Navy, if thrown against us, would confront us with situations beyond our naval resources.' He proceeded to attempt to tweak the President's nerves by pointing at the 'awful enfeeblement' of the British war effort which would be caused by Japanese belligerence, and told him: 'Everything that you can do to inspire the Japanese with the fear of a double war may avert the danger.'[20] But Roosevelt proved quite unwilling to make any such public declaration as would saddle the United States with a *de facto* alliance with Britain in the Far East.

So the British continued to squirm in their imperial dilemma, the more so because Robert Menzies, the Prime Minister of Australia, pressed Britain to state exactly what she meant to do in fulfilment of her obligations as Mother Country to defend Australia in the event of Japanese aggression. When in March 1941 Menzies called in on Cunningham in Egypt en route for London, the C-in-C, Mediterranean, was astonished to find that the Australian Prime Minister was 'still obsessed with the idea that we should send 3 or 4 battleships to Singapore!'[21] The Chiefs of Staff bluntly informed Menzies in April that in view of Britain's existing commitments, of the potential dangers in the European theatre, and of the Royal Navy's available strength in capital ships, it would 'be misleading to attempt to lay down possible strength in the Far East in advance and propose a movement timetable. It is vital to avoid being weak everywhere. All we can say is that we should send a battle-cruiser and an aircraft carrier to the Indian Ocean. Our ability to do more must be judged entirely on the situation at the time.'[22]

At a British, Dutch, Australian and American staff conference in Singapore that same month (the second such, with the Americans this time present as participants rather than observers; a tiny advance) the American delegation still refused to agree to any joint contingency arrangements that might imply a political commitment to go to war if the Japanese violated other than American territory.

The most Admiral Harold Stark, the Chief of Naval Operations in Washington, was willing to do was to relieve the pressure on the Royal Navy in the Atlantic by transferring three battleships, an aircraft carrier, four cruisers and nineteen destroyers from the Pacific to the Atlantic, thus freeing British ships for service elsewhere. In June 1941, however, the devastation of the Mediterranean Fleet off Greece and Crete prompted Stark to ask the British Chiefs of Staff whether the Royal Navy could still find a task force for the Far East, and even suggested transferring a further three American battleships from the Pacific to the Atlantic. The Chiefs of Staff replied that until repairs to the *Prince of Wales* (damaged in the *Bismarck* chase) and refits of *Rodney*, *Renown* and *Royal Sovereign* were completed in August, it would only be possible to send two 'R' class battleships from the Atlantic to the Far East after their relief by US battleships. They added that the Royal Navy was equally strapped for cruisers. It was their advice to Stark, therefore, not to transfer more battleships from the Pacific: 'We consequently feel that at the present time the need for a deterrent against Japan is greater than it was and that it outweighs the extra effect on Germany that would be produced by [such] a move . . .'[23] So nine battleships, three aircraft carriers, twenty-one cruisers and sixty-seven destroyers remained at Pearl Harbor, while

Singapore remained a base without a fleet and without prospect of one.

By now not only the Chiefs of Staff but also the Cabinet and the Prime Minister had come to the conclusion that deterrence rather than appeasement offered the better means of preventing further Japanese expansion; a major turnabout in attitude. That deterrence, in the British view, should take the form of a clear warning to Japan from the United States, backed by the presence of the American battlefleet at Pearl Harbor, that she would respond to any Japanese aggression against British or Dutch interests in South-East Asia. The Japanese occupation of the whole of French Indo-China in July 1941 seemed to push American policy the way the British wished, for Roosevelt thereupon froze all Japanese assets in America and proclaimed a harsh economic embargo, including – the most damaging of all – oil. Though not consulted beforehand, the British and Dutch governments made haste to follow suit.

At the Atlantic Conference next month Churchill employed all his skill at persuasion, all his force of personality, to persuade Roosevelt to cap this embargo with a powerful declaration that – in the words of the British draft handed to him – 'any further encroachment by Japan in the South-West Pacific would produce a situation in which the United States Government would be compelled to take counter-measures even though these might lead to a war between the United States and Japan'.[24] Churchill, over-optimistic once again, informed his Cabinet colleagues that Roosevelt had promised him 'on more than one occasion' to use this British formula, and that he, Churchill, was 'confident that the President would not tone it down'.[25]

But Roosevelt proved as ever long on cloudy promises and short on delivery. The note actually handed to the Japanese ambassador in Washington on 17 August 1941 stated that if Japan took any further steps towards the military domination of neighbouring countries the United States 'would be compelled to take immediately any and all steps which it may deem necessary towards safeguarding the legitimate rights and interest of the United States'.[26] Far from being the deterrent declaration covering British and Dutch territories and interests, as Churchill intended, it expressly disclaimed any such American concern and involvement.

Britain now had the worst of both worlds – committed to a joint economic embargo of Japan severe enough to provoke rather than postpone Japanese aggression, yet without the protection of a United States deterrent warning to Japan and without any assurance whatever that the United States would come to Britain's aid in the event of a

Japanese attack on British interests only. It has to be asked whether British policy vis-à-vis Japan and the United States in the summer of 1941 was not ill-judged in pushing for a firm diplomatic stand against Japan, even in falling in so tamely with the American embargo, given Britain's own naval weakness and America's unwillingness to commit herself to the obligations of an alliance. It is a policy that only makes sense in the light of Churchill's and Eden's overriding objective, worth in their view all the incidental risks and setbacks, 'to get the Americans into the war';[27] and what better means than a collision in the Far East between Japan and America?

While the US Secretary of State, Cordell Hull, and the Japanese ambassador in Washington, Nomura, still talked on month by month, with the British government reduced to a poorly briefed bystander, Britain could only look to her own armed forces to deter the Japanese from directly attacking the British Empire in the Far East and Pacific, or to defend that Empire if deterrence failed. With the ultimate inability of British statesmanship to find a political and diplomatic answer to Britain's imperial conundrum, the problem became a purely strategic one, to be tackled by the Chiefs of Staff, especially the First Sea Lord, and, of course, also Churchill, wearing his other hat as Minister of Defence.

Singapore was not, had never been designed to be, a fortress capable of resisting a siege *en règle* by an expeditionary force, but instead to be a naval base for the replenishing of a battlefleet and for carrying out all but the most major repairs to damaged ships: a complex of oil storage tanks, workshops, heavy handling equipment, and a dry dock capable of taking a battleship. In any case, no location could have been more unsuitable than Singapore island and Singapore city for a fortress to be defended against close-range attack, if necessary street by street, house by house; for a fortress the garrison of which must be sustained by a resolute civilian population of high morale. For Singapore was a swarming polyglot city of Malays, Indians and Chinese, all totally unconcerned about the fate of the British Empire, and a handful of imperial rulers in white ducks or khaki drill whose minds (with rare exceptions) were ossified by the arrogance of race and empire and the hierarchical snobberies of colonial society, and those energies had been unsprung by long service in damp heat, by a social round lubricated by an excess of gin-slings and stingahs (whiskies and soda), and by pampering at the hands of multitudes of native servants.

The planners of the naval base in the 1920s and early 1930s had taken it as a premise that the only danger to it lay in a long-distance strike by a Japanese fleet before the British battlefleet could arrive from home waters and the Mediterranean. To guard against this danger, coastal defence batteries had been installed on both sides of the eastern entrance of the Johore Strait (running between Singapore island and the southern tip of Malaya) so as to command the approach to the naval base, which was situated on the northern tip of Singapore island barely a mile across the strait from the Malayan province of Johore – three batteries each of two 6-inch guns, one battery of three 9.2-inch and one of three 15-inch. On the southern tip of the island near the city of Singapore four more batteries each of 6-inch guns and one of three 9.2-inch defended the seaward approach to, and the entrances of, Keppel Harbour. Another battery of two 6-inch guns was sited on the western point of the island to command the western entrance to Johore Strait, the entrance furthest away from a Japanese fleet's direct line of approach.[28] These batteries, being intended for use against enemy warships, were mostly stocked with armour-piercing shell, and quite unsuitable for the bombardment of troops in the field.

In May 1937, however, a report by the Chiefs of Staff had challenged the basic premise that the main danger to the Singapore base lay in Japanese attack by sea. It was possible, the Chiefs of Staff argued, and in character for the Japanese to prepare a secret expedition before war was declared. The Japanese might aim to establish air forces to operate from shore bases 'and to land army forces in the Malayan Peninsula to advance on Singapore. The Japanese may hope by the combined effect of attrition, air and land attack to force our garrison to surrender before our fleet can arrive to relieve it.'[29]

The Chiefs of Staff remarked that while the east coast of Malaya was difficult country, the west coast enjoyed good communications, although the rubber and coconut plantations offered poor visibility. They reckoned that the Japanese would need up to two divisions for the invasion of Malaya; and wrote that they could not rule out the possibility of the Japanese landing in Siamese territory at Chumpon and Singora, then moving by road to seize the airfields at Victoria Point and Alor Star. Or the Japanese might land at Penang, giving them an overland advance of some four hundred miles to Singapore. Despite the risks of such an invasion, wrote the Chiefs, 'we cannot exclude the possibility that the Japanese may attempt operations of this character . . . If they overcame the difficulties of effecting a landing in Malaya and prevented our reinforcements reaching Singapore, they might consider they had a reasonable chance of capturing the base within two months.'[30] The COS then summarised the form Japanese operations might take: convoys to Malaya, an advance through Malaya, leading to 'close investment of Singapore Island, and command of the naval base by artillery fire';[31] and they repeated that this process might be accomplished within two months of the outbreak of war.

This COS paper of 1937 constitutes a very remarkable work of accurate prophecy; its existence demolishes the post-1942 legend (largely fostered by Churchill) that no one had ever thought in terms of a Japanese attack on Singapore by the back door overland. From 1937 onwards British plans to defend the base consequently rested on the need to prevent the Japanese landing in, and advancing through, Malaya. They also rested on an understanding that the key to achieving this now lay in air power; and that therefore the land defence of Malaya must be sited far enough north to cover the airfields at Alor Star and Victoria Point. In July 1940, in one among several reassessments of the problem between 1937 and December 1941, the Chiefs of Staff reiterated that it was no longer sufficient to concentrate on the defence of Singapore alone, and that the whole of Malaya must be held; that this depended on airpower, which in turn would mean that the land forces in Malaya would have to be greatly increased in order to defend the airfields.[32]

It has to be said that despite such papers put before him as Minister of Defence and discussed in Cabinet, Churchill himself refused to accept that Singapore was incapable of surviving attack if Malaya was lost; and he believed to the last that Singapore was in itself a 'fortress'. In September 1940, for instance, having affirmed his faith that the Japanese danger to Singapore was anyway remote, he proceeded directly to contradict the Chiefs of Staff's judgment that all Malaya must be held. He urged that the defence of Singapore could be entrusted to a strong local garrison and the 'general potentialities of seapower'. The defence of the whole of Malaya, he proclaimed, 'cannot be entertained'.[33] Even as late as a week after the Japanese had actually landed in northern Malaya in December 1941, Churchill was minuting to Ismay for the Chiefs of Staff: 'Beware lest troops required for the ultimate defence Singapore Island and fortress are not used or cut off in Malay peninsula. Nothing compares in importance with the fortress.'[34]

Since Churchill had been Chancellor of the Exchequer in Baldwin's Cabinet between 1924 and 1929 when plans for the Singapore naval base and its shore batteries were being discussed and evolved, and since he had specifically studied, and replied to, the Chiefs of Staff's wartime views on the necessity of a landward defence of Singapore sited in northern Malaya covering the essential British airfields, it is astonishing to read in his war memoirs that 'it had never entered my head that no circle of detached forts of a permanent character protected the rear of the famous fortress. I cannot understand how it was I did not know this. But none of the officers on the spot and none of my professional advisers at home seem to have realised this awful need . . .'[35]

From this inexplicable delusion or *idée fixe* that Singapore was a fortress rather than merely a naval base with shore batteries against sea attack were to follow grievous consequences and tragic loss. Yet the idea that Singapore island should have been girdled with Maginot Line-like forts was anyway preposterous, because the naval base itself, lying on the northernmost tip of the island, would have been in the front line, under close-range artillery fire from the Japanese besiegers across the Johore Strait, and therefore unusable; and without use of the naval base Singapore lost all strategic importance, worth no greater military investment than Hong Kong with its six battalions.

The problem for the Chiefs of Staff, for the recently appointed Commander-in-Chief, Far East, Air Chief Marshal Sir Robert Brooke-Popham, the General Officer Commanding Malaya, Lieutenant-General A. E. Percival, and the Air Officer Commanding Far East, Air Vice-Marshal C. W. H. Pulford, in August 1941 lay in that while they were charged with fulfilling the broad plan drawn up by the Chiefs of Staff and approved by the Cabinet (with the Prime Minister in the chair) a year earlier by which Singapore was to be defended by land/air forces in northern Malaya, nothing like enough troops and aircraft had been provided. Even by the outbreak of war in December 1941, the army remained a third smaller than Percival reckoned in August to be necessary, as well as wholly without tanks, while the total of first-line aircraft in Malaya amounted to only 180, as against the target figure of 336 modern aircraft considered by the Chiefs of Staff to be the minimum required. Moreover the aircraft were in fact obsolescent or obsolete: American Brewster Buffalo day fighters, old and worn-out Blenheim I night fighters, Vildebeest torpedo-bombers.[36] These weaknesses resulted from the priority necessarily given to the defence of the United Kingdom itself and the other priority which the War Cabinet had chosen to give to the Mediterranean and Middle East since 1940.

The defence plan for Malaya and Singapore, though based on a correct reading of Japanese strategy, was thus hopelessly flawed in practice by want of resources. Yet the purpose of the whole exercise, to secure the naval base, had in any case been rendered pointless because there was no British fleet available to send there; and no likelihood of there being available in the foreseeable future one large enough or composed of modern enough ships to confront the Japanese fleet in battle.

It fell to the First Sea Lord and naval staff that August to decide what the Royal Navy could do in lieu of such a large and modern battlefleet; what strategy it should adopt in place of its pre-war vision of a new and better Jutland in the China Sea. On the day following receipt of the Prime Minister's warning telegram from the Atlantic Conference, the Joint Planners (on the advice of the Naval Staff) recommended despatching to the East by mid-September one battleship (either *Barham* or *Valiant* from the Mediterranean) and that by the end of the year four of the old unmodernised 'R' class battleships should follow. It was not proposed to send at the present time any cruisers or fleet destroyers, for the latter could not be spared from either the Atlantic or Mediterranean until the US Navy had deployed additional patrols in the Atlantic. The Joint Planners also recommended sending if possible one aircraft carrier (probably the old *Eagle*) with the battleships.[37]

A week later a meeting chaired by the First Sea Lord on his return from Placentia Bay concluded that

> should the U.S.A. provide a sufficiently strong striking force of modern battleships capable of engaging TIRPITZ [*Bismarck*'s sister ship] and be prepared to allow one of these ships to replace one of our own KING GEORGE V class if damaged, then it would be possible to send one of the KING GEORGE V Class to the Far East or Indian Ocean in addition to NELSON, RODNEY, 4 'R' Class and RENOWN.[38]

In the meantime, with *Tirpitz* to watch, Pound did not believe that any of the Royal Navy's only three modern battleships (the *King George V*, *Prince of Wales* and *Duke of York*) could be spared from the Atlantic. To give Pound due credit, his assessment of the Far Eastern problem throughout was founded on commonsensical acceptance that the lack of an available battleworthy fleet meant that the Singapore base, along with the entire strategy that had been its *raison d'être*, was now a write-off. In an appreciation written back in August 1940 he had stated: 'There is no object in sending a Fleet to Singapore unless it is strong enough to fight the Japanese Fleet. Singapore is inferior to Trincomalee as a base from which to protect our trade in the Indian Ocean.'[39] Now in August 1941 he proposed assembling a homogeneous fleet of old, slow, heavy ships capable of protecting that Indian Ocean trade, and based on Trincomalee, nearly 2,000 miles west of Singapore. But in any case even this defensive fleet could not be fully assembled before March 1942.

Churchill's diagnosis of the problem was, however, entirely different. In the first place he judged that, given a show of joint deterrence by America and Britain, Japan was very unlikely to attack at all. As late as 20 October 1941 he was averring to the COS Committee that 'he did not believe that the Japanese would go to war with the United States and ourselves'.[40] Therefore he believed that British naval strategy in the Far East should be based on the concept of deterrence. This deterrence should take the form of a British '*Bismarck*' or '*Tirpitz*' offering an elusive menace to Japanese offensive plans, and in the event of conflict tying down a disproportionate number of Japanese capital ships. On 25 August Churchill put forward his proposal to Pound in a personal minute:

> Such a force should consist of the smallest number of our best ships. We have only to remember all the preoccupations which are caused us by the *Tirpitz* – the only capital ship left to Germany against our 15 or 16 [sic] battleships and battlecruisers – to see what an effect would be produced upon the Japanese Admiralty by the presence of a small but very powerful force in Eastern waters . . .
>
> The most economical disposition would be to send DUKE OF YORK . . . to the East. She could be joined by REPULSE or RENOWN and one aircraft carrier of high speed. This powerful force might show itself in the triangle Aden–Singapore–Simonstown. It would exert a paralysing effect on Japanese naval action.[41]

But thus to snatch an analogy between the effect of *Tirpitz* on the Royal Navy and the potential effect of a King George V and an old battlecruiser on the Japanese Navy was to repeat the same mental pattern that led him to believe that Singapore was a 'fortress' – the pattern of reacting emotionally to verbal symbols rather than coldly appraising the realities. In the first instance, the *King George V* (at some 38,000 tons displacement, 44,000 tons full load, and ten 14-inch guns) was smaller and less well armed than Japan's newest battleship, the 70,000-ton, 18-inch gun *Yamato*, whereas *Tirpitz* (like *Bismarck* in its time) exceeded even the most modern British capital ships in her combination of speed, size and gunpower. Secondly, Japanese naval aviation, shore and carrier based, was far more numerous than the meagre air resources successfully employed by the British to cripple the *Bismarck*. Thirdly, unlike *Bismarck* and *Tirpitz*, none of the three King George Vs had yet had time to work up to full operational efficiency, although Churchill proposed that the *Duke of York*, if sent to the East, could work up during 'her long safe voyage'.[42] Fourthly, whereas German battleships once into the Atlantic could refuel from previously posted oilers, the British ships the Premier wished to despatch to the East would be tied to fixed bases for refuelling, given the British lack of fleet oilers. And finally German battleships were free to roam on the offensive wherever they chose, while British heavy ships in Far Eastern waters could hardly avoid being drawn into action in defence of British trade or territories – especially Malaya and Singapore.

On receipt of this minute, the First Sea Lord made haste to begin one of his devious delaying actions, minuting in his own hand to the Director, Tactical and Staff Division of the Naval Staff: 'Please let me have detailed reasons based on experience of K.G.V. and P. of W. why it would not be sound for a new ship of this class to be sent abroad before she has had a thorough working up.'[43] A brief duly supplied by the DTD enabled Pound to write to Churchill on the 28th: 'I fully appreciate the attractiveness of sending one of the KING GEORGE V class to the Indian Ocean when fully worked up, but after considering this most carefully I cannot recommend it for the reasons given in this memorandum'; and he went on in well-chosen detail about the need for time to work up the crew and the complex modern machinery and electronic gear.[44]

These proved only the ranging shots in a protracted battle. The very next day Churchill replied in a long memorandum instructing the First Sea Lord on various naval matters:

> It is surely a faulty disposition to create in the Indian Ocean a fleet considerable in numbers, costly in manpower and maintenance, but consisting entirely of slow obsolescent and unmodernised ships which can neither fight a fleet action with the main Japanese force nor act as a deterrent upon his modern fast heavy ships, if used singly or in pairs as raiders. Such dispositions might be forced upon us by circumstances; but they are inherently unsound in themselves.[45]

He did not want to employ the 'R' class battleships on convoy work in the Indian Ocean, because if so 'it would be necessary to have one or two fast heavy units which would prevent the enemy from detaching individual heavy raiders without fear of punishment' – a point which ignored the experience of 'R' class battleships on convoy work in the Atlantic, where they had succeeded in warning off German heavy ships. The Premier further proceeded:

> No doubt the Australian Government would be pleased to count the

> number of old battleships in their neighbourhood, but we must not play down to uninstructed thought. On the contrary, we should inculcate the true principles of naval strategy, one of which is certainly to use a small number of the best fast ships to cope with a superior force.
>
> The potency of the dispositions I ventured to suggest in my minute M.819-1 [of 25 August] is illustrated by the Admiralty's own extraordinary concern about *Tirpitz*. *Tirpitz* is doing to us exactly what a K.G.V. in the Indian Ocean would do to the Japanese Navy. It exercises a vague, general fear and menaces all points at once. It appears, disappears, causing immediate reactions and perturbations on the other side.[46]

He concluded this exposition by referring to Japanese hesitation about going to war against the United States, the USSR and Great Britain: 'Nothing would increase her hesitation more than the appearance of the force I mentioned in my minute M.819-1, and above all of a K.G.V. This might indeed be a decisive deterrent.'[47]

However, the Premier more than somewhat undermined his own argument by also remarking that the fact that the Admiralty considered that three K.G.Vs must be used to contain *Tirpitz* 'is a serious reflection upon the design of our latest ships, which through being undergunned and weakened by hangars in the middle of their citadels, are evidently judged unfit to fight their opposite number in a single ship action'; and by noting, with reference to the Admiralty's apprehensions about the *Tirpitz*, 'the proved power of Aircraft Carriers to slow down a ship like *Tirpitz* if she were loose'.[48]

There the matter rested for six weeks, while the Americans and Japanese negotiated on in Washington. But on 2 October the Americans handed the Japanese a note stating that a hoped-for meeting between the Japanese Prime Minister, Prince Konoye, and President Roosevelt could not take place unless Japan first accepted the basic American principles for a settlement. Since these included Japan's withdrawal from her conquests in China, this effectively torpedoed any real hope in Tokyo that a deal might be done. On 7 October the supposedly moderate Konoye resigned, to be replaced by General Tojo, a soldier still on the active list, and a notorious expansionist. On 16 October, even before Tojo's appointment had been announced, Eden was minuting Churchill that Konoye's fall was 'an ominous sign'; that the next government would be 'once more under the influence of extreme elements'; that the current Soviet defeats at German hands 'must inevitably be having their effect upon the Japanese appetite'.[49] Although Eden acknowledged that there was nothing yet to show 'in which direction Japan will jump, if any,' he averred that 'it is no doubt true that the stronger the joint front that the ABCD [America, Britain, China and the Dutch] powers can show, the greater the deterrent to Japanese action'.[50] And he went on: 'In this connection you will recall that we discussed some little time ago the possibility of capital ship reinforcements to the Far East. The matter has now become urgent, and I should be glad if it could be discussed at the Defence Committee meeting tomorrow afternoon.'[51]

It was thanks to this initiative of Eden that British naval strategy with regard to the Far East now entered its final crisis. Next day at the Defence Committee Churchill repeated his opinions that the Admiralty's proposal to send a fleet composed of half a dozen old battleships was unsound because they would be 'neither strong enough to engage the weight of the Japanese Navy, nor yet fast enough to avoid action except in circumstances of their own choosing'; and that the example of the *Tirpitz* showed that the presence of one modern capital ship in Far Eastern waters 'could be calculated to have a similar effect on the Japanese naval authorities, and thereby on Japanese foreign policy':[52]

> The *Repulse* had already reached the Indian Ocean. No time should now be lost in sending the *Prince of Wales* to join up with her at Singapore. We could afford to accept some risk of the *Tirpitz* breaking out into the Atlantic in the knowledge that we ought by air action from aircraft carriers to be able to slow her up to become a prey for the heavy metal of our capital ships.[53]

Rear-Admiral Phillips, the Vice Chief of Naval Staff, who had attended the meeting in the place of the First Sea Lord (absent on leave), reported to Pound later that the Premier 'at once raised the old question of sending out the PRINCE OF WALES and gave the Defence Committee all the arguments that he had used before. He was also scathing in his comments on the Admiralty attitude to this matter.'[54] In the absence of the First Sea Lord, it fell to the First Lord, A. V. Alexander, to point out that whereas the *Tirpitz* 'was a threat to our trade convoys in the Atlantic, our dispositions in the Far East would be governed more by the need to protect our own trade routes than to raid Japanese shipping'.[55]

Nevertheless Eden urged that

> From the point of view of deterring Japan from entering the war, the despatch of 1 modern ship, such as the *Prince of Wales*, to the Far East would have far greater effect politically than the presence in those waters of a number of the last war's battleships. If the *Prince of Wales* were to call

at Cape Town on her way to the Far East, news of her movements would quickly reach Japan and the deterrent effect would begin from that date.[56]

By an irony Eden, the man whose suave persuasion had played a key role in finally getting Britain committed to the Greek adventure, was now playing a similar role over the despatch of the *Prince of Wales* to the East, for his assurance about the deterrent effect on Japanese policy that would be exerted by her sailing thither provided just the influential backing Churchill needed to sway his colleagues. As the VCNS reported to Pound:

> The First Lord and I defended the position as well as we could, but the Prime Minister led other members of the Defence Committee to the conclusion that it was desirable to send the PRINCE OF WALES to join the REPULSE and go to Singapore as soon as possible. The Admiralty expressed their dissent.[57]

A final decision was however left until 20 October, after the First Sea Lord returned from leave. The matter was first discussed that day by the COS Committee with Churchill (as Minister of Defence) in the chair. The First Sea Lord made the Admiralty's case as fully and strongly as he could, repeating the reasons against taking any of the King George Vs away from the Atlantic, and then turning to the problem of the Pacific:

> . . . the deterrent which would prevent the Japanese from moving southwards would not be the presence of 1 fast battleship. They could easily afford to put 4 modern ships with any big convoys destined for an attack in Southern waters. What would deter them, however, would be the presence at Singapore of a force (such as the *Nelson*, the *Rodney* and the R-class battleships) of such strength that to overcome it they would have to detach the greater part of their fleet and thus uncover Japan . . .[58]

When Churchill intervened at this point to say that he had understood that the 'R' class battleships would be used in the Indian Ocean for convoy escort duties, Sir Dudley Pound answered that 'this would be so until it became necessary to concentrate in the Far East. The aim had always been to constitute a battle fleet with this as a nucleus.'[59]

Pound's problem as always was that the Royal Navy was just too small to meet its commitments. On 1 October 1941 its total of capital ships available for sea had stood at only nine: four with the Home Fleet (*King George V*, *Prince of Wales*, *Malaya* and *Repulse*, although *Prince of Wales* was at that time at Gibraltar and *Repulse* on detachment in the South Atlantic); three with the Mediterranean Fleet (*Queen*

Elizabeth, *Barham* and *Valiant*); *Resolution* in the West Indies and *Revenge* in the Indian Ocean. For *Nelson* had been badly damaged in the Mediterranean by a torpedo on 27 September (see above, p. 370), while repairs to the *Royal Sovereign* (earmarked for the Indian Ocean) were not due for completion before 15 October and to the *Duke of York* (Home Fleet) and *Ramillies* (also earmarked for the Indian Ocean) not until the 23rd, the refit of the *Renown* not until the 30th, and major repairs to the *Warspite* in the USA not until 15 December.[60]

Confronted with such weakness, Pound was throughout thinking as best he could of likely real operational contingencies and requirements in the Far East. As a handwritten note to Alexander (maddeningly undated but certainly of early October) makes clear, he even still had at the back of his mind that it might be necessary to withdraw the Mediterranean Fleet and send it to the Far East[61] (see above, pp. 209–12). In contrast the Prime Minister's mind was dwelling on symbols and gestures, because he believed, in his own words at the time, that the Naval Intelligence Department 'are very much inclined to exaggerate Japanese strength and efficiency';[62] because, as he told the COS meeting on 20 October, 'he did not foresee an attack in force on Malaya' and because he did not believe the Japanese would go to war with the United States and ourselves.[63] Such comfortable illusions made it possible to repose faith in the deterrent value of a symbolic battleship and the gesture of sending it to the East; and in this Churchill was again backed by Eden, who repeated to the Chiefs of Staff the assurance he had made four days earlier to the Defence Committee, but in even more certain language: 'From the political point of view there was no doubt as to the value of our sending, at the present time, a really modern ship.'[64] To be fair to Churchill and Eden, their view was supported by the C-in-C, Far East, Air Chief Marshal Sir Robert Brooke-Popham, who had cabled on 1 October to stress 'the propaganda value of even one or two battleships at Singapore', to which the COS had replied on 3 October after consultation with the Foreign Office, of all people, on a strategic mission. 'We are in general agreement.'[65]

The Prime Minister now proceeded to tell the Chiefs of Staff meeting that he 'would like to see the *Prince of Wales* sent and the situation reviewed when the *Nelson* had been repaired'.[66] The First Sea Lord, isolated and outgunned, thereupon lowered the flag in surrender:

> . . . he fully realised the value of a report from Cape Town of the arrival there of the Prince of Wales. He suggested that she should be sailed

forthwith to that destination, a decision as to her onward journey being taken in the light of the situation when she arrived at Cape Town.[67]

This was agreed by the Committee. Their decision was ratified later that day, 20 October, by the Defence Committee, on the grounds that the political need to send the ship to Singapore (the destination given in the minutes) was so urgent 'as to outweigh objections hitherto advanced by the Admiralty on strategical grounds'.[68] It was to no avail, therefore, that the C-in-C, Home Fleet, Admiral Sir John Tovey, signalled the First Sea Lord that evening:

> I wish to urge as strongly as I can that despatch of PRINCE OF WALES to Far East should not take place.
>
> Passage of Atlantic convoys is vital to our existence and their stoppage would rapidly result in our losing the war. There is no comparable interest in the Far East.
>
> [The *King George V* being the only remaining battleship capable of bringing *Tirpitz* to action] . . . Damage or minor defect to KING GEORGE V would leave *Tirpitz* virtually unopposed.
>
> . . . I am convinced this proposal involves a risk which cannot be justified under any circumstance even if Japan enters the war.[69]

For Churchill and Eden had finally had their way. On 25 October HMS *Prince of Wales* (Captain J. C. Leach), wearing the flag of (Acting) Admiral Sir Tom Phillips, Commander-in-Chief, Eastern Fleet, and escorted only by the destroyers *Electra* and *Express*, slipped her moorings in the Clyde, and, as the Royal Marine band played her away, put to sea.

For all Churchill's and Eden's confident assertions about the Japanese leadership's mental processes and intentions, the truth is that neither the British nor the American governments and their professional advisers, nor their ambassadors in Tokyo, enjoyed solid, precise intelligence about Japan's plans or their timing. This was despite the success of American cryptographers ('Magic') in breaking the Japanese diplomatic 'Purple' cypher (equivalent of the German 'Enigma' machine), so enabling them to read the traffic between Tokyo and the Japanese ambassador in Washington.[70] The revealing material thus yielded by 'Magic', together with important clues from other sources, such as radio traffic analysis, went partly to waste because Washington as yet possessed no coordinated machinery for gathering Intelligence, collating it and presenting it to the decision-makers, such as Britain had created since 1939. Some 'Purple' intercepts were never even decrypted; others simply yellowed in the pigeon-holes of the decrypters.[71] The historian of American Intelligence before the Pearl Harbor attack sums up what 'Magic' and other sources had revealed about Japanese plans:

> It is clear enough that Japan was preparing for an all-out war with England and America, but it is nowhere clear whether she intended to make the first move by attacking either power directly, or whether she was preparing to meet a sudden blow from England or America . . . in response to further Japanese moves to the south . . . [although 'Magic' signals were 'not unambiguous' on these questions] . . . they indicated quite clearly a level of tension where an accident on either side could open a full-scale war.[72]

The British in particular, last in the line to receive gleanings from 'Magic' and then by no means all of them, could only guess, grope and argue about Japanese intentions and plans – the Joint Intelligence Committee, the Foreign Office and Sir Robert Craigie, the ambassador in Tokyo, the Foreign Secretary and the Prime Minister themselves.[73]

In point of fact the Japanese leadership had decided at an imperial conference on 2 July 1941 that Japan would expand southwards (the Imperial Japanese Navy's preferred strategy) by occupying the European empires in South-East Asia, rather than northwards against Soviet Russia from the conquered territory in China, in direct fulfilment of the alliance with Germany under the Tripartite Pact (the Army's preference). This southward expansion was nevertheless to be accomplished if possible without incurring American hostility. Thanks to 'Magic' the Americans learned the gist of this decision, soon to bear fruit in the occupation of French Indo-China. In consequence of the American (and British and Dutch) freezing of Japanese assets as a result of this occupation, oil supplies to the Japanese effectively dried up as from 26 July, which meant that the Japanese Navy's oil stocks would last no more than eighteen months and the Army's no more than a year. If Japan were ever to go to war, she must therefore do so as soon as preparations could be completed, and certainly not later than December 1941, before the monsoon broke in South-East Asia.[74]

At another imperial conference on 6 September it was decided that preparations for war must be completed by early October. If the negotiations in Washington had failed by then to achieve an acceptable settlement, Japan would take the decision whether or not to go to war. On 1–2 November, after General Tojo had replaced Prince Konoye, the Japanese leadership gave the diplomats an extension until the end of November to bring off an agreement, after which date, in the event of failure, war with the United States would automatically follow.

Meanwhile the Japanese armed forces had completed their studies of alternative strategic plans of conquest by mid-August, and had drawn up detailed operational plans and timetables for the chosen strategy by the end of September. These called for the destruction of the United States Fleet at Pearl Harbor by a surprise carrier strike without declaration of war, followed by the occupation of Hong Kong, the Philippines, Malaya and Burma, and the Dutch East Indies. The conquest of Malaya was to be completed within a hundred days of the outbreak of war. This war plan was finally approved on 5 November 1941. Two days later all Japanese forces were warned that the approximate date for the opening of hostilities would be 8 December (East Longitude Time). Landings in southern Siam (at Singora) and northern Malaya were timed for the small hours of the 8th (local time).[75]

Clearly the arrival in mid-November of one modern British battleship could have no effect either on the now predetermined course of Japan's national policy or on her war plans. Churchill's and Eden's shot in the dark could do nothing but waste the ammunition.

Mystery surrounds the reasons for choosing Sir Tom Phillips, hitherto VCNS, and without sea-going experience in the present war, to command the so-called Eastern Fleet, really only a squadron, and for the destination finally given him, because no documentation survives.[76] It is clear, however, that Phillips was Pound's enthusiastic personal choice; his protégé indeed. In a private letter of 25 February 1943, Pound wrote: 'As you know, he was extremely junior for the appointment of Commander-in-Chief, Eastern Fleet, and I daresay I have been criticised for sending him there. However, I have never for a moment regretted it as he was fitted for high command . . .'[77] Since the outbreak of war in 1939 Phillips – short, stocky, dynamic, full of terrier-like aggression – had acted as the third member with Pound and Churchill in the triumvirate of back-seat drivers continually prodding flag officers at sea to show more fight and enterprise; and the First Sea Lord had found him personally and professionally the most congenial of subordinates. As Pound expressed it in a letter to Lady Phillips in January 1943:

> He had such a wonderful combination of brilliance, soundness of judgment and drive, and he was head and shoulders above his contemporaries . . .

> If fate had decided to take him from us I am glad that we had been able to show what trust and confidence we placed in him by making him C-in-C, Eastern Fleet, with a double step in rank – which I think is unique in the service.[78]

The Prime Minister (who had also found Phillips's eagerness for offensive action congenial, although they had clashed over the Greek adventure) happily agreed to the proposed appointment.[79] Now, after more than two years spent navigating a desk, Phillips was commanding a 'fleet' thus far consisting of one battleship and two destroyers, with Cape Town as his immediate destination. This given destination accorded with the Defence Committee's endorsement on 20 October of the First Sea Lord's suggestion that the *Prince of Wales* should be sent there in the first instance, when a further decision could be taken as to whether or not she should go on to Singapore – almost certainly a tactic on the part of that wily old badger Pound to delay a final commitment to sending her to the Far East until and unless it could no longer be avoided. Nevertheless, the very next day the Assistant Chief of Naval Staff (Foreign) informed all naval authorities on behalf of the Admiralty: '*Prince of Wales*, wearing the flag of Admiral Sir Tom Phillips, C-in-C, Eastern Fleet, and escorted by *Electra* and *Express* will leave UK shortly for Singapore.'[80]

No intervening order has been found in the records to explain this discrepancy in the stated destinations. It may simply be that since the entire debate about British strategy in the Far East had revolved round Singapore, it was taken for granted by the naval staff and by Phillips himself that this was to be his ultimate destination unless the mission was specifically aborted at Cape Town.[81] To thicken the mystery, however, the Prime Minister in a note to the First Sea Lord on 1 November made use of the phrases 'If it is decided that *Prince of Wales* should go on to Singapore . . .' and 'assuming we go on eastward', while Pound in reply next day wrote: 'It is my intention to review the situation generally just before *Prince of Wales* reaches the Cape.'[82]

Was Churchill merely being unusually tactful in his phrasing in view of the First Sea Lord's past opposition to the whole idea? Did Pound himself really believe that he still enjoyed any choice? On 6 November, while *Prince of Wales* was still steaming south towards Cape Town on a sunny voyage complete with the traditional larkings of a 'crossing-the-line' ceremony, Phillips signalled the Admiralty about his future movements after reaching the Cape. He suggested that he should remain there from 17 to 24 November for maximum publicity, but that if 'early arrival at Singapore be more important than publicity, this time could be reduced to 48 hours at some inconvenience to engine room and store departments . . .'[83] He added: 'If earliest arrival at Singapore is desired, HMS *Prince of Wales* could arrive there 12 days after leaving the Cape, destroyers being left behind when clear of the Cape area . . . If destroyers remain in company throughout, HMS *Prince of Wales* could arrive Singapore 19 days after leaving Cape.' That Phillips by now – if not earlier – took it as read that Singapore was his destination is clinched by his proposal in this same signal that *Repulse* should arrive there in company with the flagship.[84]

Two days later he confirmed his proposal that only the battlecruiser *Repulse*, and not the old 'R' class battleship *Revenge*, should go to Singapore as well as *Prince of Wales*, on the score that a force of two capital ships 'should cause the Japanese concern but should be regarded by her more as a raiding force than as attempt to form a line of battle against her', whereas the addition of one 'R' class ship 'might give the impression that we are trying to form a line of battle, but could only spare 3 ships, thus encouraging Japan'. He thought it best for *Revenge* to remain in the Indian Ocean until joined by *Royal Sovereign* and *Ramillies*, when all three could come on to Singapore in January 1942.[85]

On 11 November the Joint Intelligence Committee took note of the recent American Sigint disclosure that Japan had fixed 25 November as the deadline for a successful outcome of the Washington talks. It appeared, therefore, that her final decision for peace or war was only a fortnight away. In the light of this Intelligence the Admiralty on this same day, 11 November, signalled to the Simonstown naval base at the Cape that the urgency of arrival at Singapore 'necessitates stay of *Prince of Wales* being as short as possible over 48 hours . . .'[86] and to Phillips: 'As it has been necessary for political reasons to announce the strengthening of our forces in the Eastern area, it is considered undesirable for capital ships to arrive at Singapore without destroyer screen . . .' and that therefore *Prince of Wales* and *Repulse* were to proceed to Singapore as soon as practicable after arrival of the destroyers in Ceylon.[87]

By the time Phillips reached Cape Town on 16 November (the day after the Japanese Southern Army had ordered its formations to make final preparations for the attack on Malaya), it had been therefore settled that he was to take only two capital ships and a meagre destroyer screen on to Singapore; an unbalanced force and therefore an unsound strategic decision. It had been intended to give him the aircraft carrier *Indomitable*, the only such ship available (*Ark Royal* had been sunk on 14 November, squeezing the Navy's resources in carriers still further, see pp. 372–4), but – mercifully for her and her crew – she had run aground off Jamaica. Nor were there any cruisers available after the Mediterranean Fleet's fearsome losses. The unfortunate Phillips and his ships' companies were now finally committed to a naval nonsense in pursuance of a futile political gesture.

For the ships' companies of *Prince of Wales* and her escorting destroyers themselves the two-day stay at Cape Town afforded the opportunity for a run ashore in a city hardly touched by war. 'We were given a wonderful reception,' remembered one officer in *Prince of Wales*. 'Officers were entertained privately, functions arranged for the men and an orgy of shopping indulged in.'[88] No record has been found to indicate that Phillips's future movements were in fact reconsidered in London during this stay. On 18 November *Prince of Wales* set course eastward for Colombo, escorted for part of the voyage by a squadron of huge albatrosses which 'came within yards to glide uncannily along beside the quarter deck, with no visible life except the blink of a yellow eye as they returned our stares'.[89]

On arrival at Colombo on 28 November Phillips flew ahead to Singapore to confer with service chiefs there. HMS *Prince of Wales* then rendezvoused south of Ceylon with the *Repulse* and her two escorting destroyers (which had already arrived at Trincomalee) for the final run to Singapore. About noon on 2 December the island appeared as a smudge on the port bow. Two great ships steamed past Singapore city's straggling waterfront, round the island to the eastern entrance of the Johore Strait lying between the powerful coastal batteries in their steel casemates, and up the strait, no wider than a river, between the swampy, jungly shorelines of Johore and Singapore island. In the thick, damp heat, the *Prince of Wales* secured alongside in the naval dockyard, while the *Repulse* came to a buoy nearby; and a reception party of service and civilian grandees processed up the brow of the flagship to welcome this 'fleet' that after two decades of talk had at last arrived at Singapore.

By this time it had become clear in London that the despatch of the *Prince of Wales* and *Repulse* was not after all acting as an effective political deterrent to Japan, and that, as the First Sea Lord had feared all along, the ships now faced real operational dangers. On 1 December 1941 (it was the day the Japanese forces were told that the decision for war had been taken) the First Sea Lord personally signalled Phillips:

> You and I are in agreement that C-in-C, E.F., should normally be afloat. It is possible, however, that during the present period of uncertainty whilst

> conferences are in progress you might consider it desirable to send *Prince of Wales* and/or *Repulse* away from Singapore in order that the uncertainty of their whereabouts would discomfort the Japs.
>
> Under these circumstances you might find it necessary to hoist your flag on shore temporarily.[90]

Two days later (and one day after the Japanese had confirmed the date of their attack for 8 December, East Longitude Time), came another worried personal signal from the First Sea Lord, this time conveying Intelligence that Japanese submarines were heading south from Saigon, probably to watch Singapore. He required Phillips to consider two alternatives: one, ask Admiral Hart (the C-in-C of the US Asiatic Fleet at Manila) to send eight US destroyers to Singapore on a visit so that they would be available 'if the balloon goes up'; and, two, 'To get *Prince of Wales* and/or *Repulse* away from Singapore to the Eastward'.[91]

The same day Phillips replied to Pound's first signal, explaining why the First Sea Lord's suggestions could not be immediately acted upon:

> It has been necessary to put in hand retubing of distiller of HMS *Prince of Wales* today 3rd December. Work should be completed in 7 days and distiller at maximum 72 hours notice during work. Ship capable of proceeding for 48 hours on reserve feed tanks.
>
> I intend to send HMS *Repulse*, HMAS *Vampire* and HMS *Tenedos* on short visit to Port Darwin leaving Singapore Friday 5 December.[92]

While this work was carried out, the *Prince of Wales* was dry-docked so that her bottom could be scraped free of barnacles. These were hardly the best conditions for bringing the ship's company to a peak of fighting efficiency. 'The immediate effect,' recollected one officer, 'sitting as we were in a reflecting cauldron of baking concrete, was of terrific, damp, enervating heat.'[93] The heat was especially sapping on men entirely unacclimatised to it. While the *Repulse* and her escort of destroyers steamed towards Darwin, over 2,000 miles distant, and the ship's company of the *Prince of Wales* stewed in sweat-soaked cotton rig, Phillips himself flew to Manila to confer with Admiral Hart. Hart consented to move one destroyer division to Singapore on the outbreak of a war, but otherwise the two Cs-in-C did not go beyond agreeing such general principles as that the British battlefleet based on Singapore should act as a striking force against Japanese movements in the China Sea, the Dutch East Indies or through the Malay barrier; that the joint British–Dutch–American cruiser force (USS *Houston* and

Marblehead, HMS *Cornwall*, HNLMS *Java*) should be based on the Dutch East Indies, eastern Borneo and Darwin to cover convoys in that region; and that HMAS *Australia* or *Canberra*, and HMAS *Perth* and HMNZS *Leander* should protect trade in Australasian waters.[94] Details of such cooperation were to be worked out by the two staffs.

But the most astonishing decision taken by the two admirals, in view of the history of the Singapore base and the strategic purpose it had always been supposed to fulfil, was (as Phillips reported to the First Sea Lord) that Singapore was unsuitable as a main base for future offensive operations; that Manila was the only possible alternative; and that measures were in hand to enable the British Eastern Fleet (once fully assembled) to move there by 1 April 1942.[95]

On 3 December – far, far too late to be of any help to British policy or strategy – Britain had at last obtained from the United States (by word of the President) an assurance that America would furnish armed support if British or Dutch possessions in the Far East came under attack.[96]

On 6 December two large convoys escorted by Japanese warships were sighted by a RAF Hudson from Khota Baru in northern Malaya on a westerly course off the southern tip of Indo-China, prompting the Admiralty to request the C-in-C, Eastern Fleet, to report what action would be possible if it became apparent that these convoys were heading for Siam, Malaya, Borneo or the Dutch East Indies. Phillips replied that if the relative strength of the enemy force permitted, he would attempt to attack it by night or day; if the British squadron were inferior in strength, he would attempt a raid, and the air forces would attack with bombs and torpedoes in conjunction with the surface forces.[97]

The *Repulse* was now hastily recalled, arriving back at Singapore at 1600 on 7 December (local time) to find the naval base abuzz with rumour of Japanese convoys and the C-in-C's visit to Manila. An electricity of expectancy enlivened the ships' companies that evening as they sweated below or stood about on deck in the stillness of the evening. Lights still shone out across the water, despite a supposed 'brown out' to reduce their brilliance. It hardly mattered: the island was illuminated almost to the light of day by the vast white disc of a tropical moon.

In the small hours the alarm rattles sounded and over the tannoy came the bugle call of 'Repel Aircraft'. In both heavy ships, men piled out of bunks and hammocks, grabbed tin hats and gas masks and swarmed to their Action Stations. At around 0400 on 8 December (local time), searchlights picked up seventeen aircraft flying towards the base at about 10,000 feet after having bombed Singapore and its airfields; and the Eastern Fleet fired its first salvoes in anger – from the 5.25-inch high-angle secondary armament of the *Prince of Wales* in her dry dock down to Bofors guns, the tracer of which drooped away well below the unscathed Japanese formation as it swung eastwards and disappeared. A member of a 2-pounder pom-pom crew in the *Repulse* was to record: 'It was not an impressive display of fire control discipline and a terrible waste of ammunition.'[98] Later the ship's commander broadcast over the tannoy that the aircraft had indeed been Japanese, that a Japanese carrier force had struck at the US Fleet in Pearl Harbor, that the Japanese Army was at this moment landing in northern Malaya, and that, together with the United States, Britain was at war with Japan.[99]

In the gun room of the *Prince of Wales* that forenoon, recorded another eyewitness, breakfast 'was a sombre meal'.[100] For the buck which had been fumbled, dodged or passed by the politicians for twenty years had finally stopped there with Admiral Sir Tom Phillips and his two capital ships and his four destroyers.

At 0800 on 8 December (local time) Admiral Phillips officially took over command of all HM ships in the Far East from Vice-Admiral Sir Geoffrey Layton, C-in-C, China. Layton's four 'D' class cruisers (4,850 tons displacement; launched towards the end of the Great War) were at sea on trade protection duties, and in any case unfit to serve with a battle squadron. At 1230 Phillips – having already visited RAF headquarters to discuss air support with Air Marshal Pulford – held a conference in the flagship about future operations. Present were his Chief of Staff, Rear-Admiral A. F. E. Palliser, tall and lanky in contrast to his C-in-C, 'the little Napoleon' as some dubbed Phillips; the Captain of the Fleet, Captain L. H. Bell; the commanding officers of *Prince of Wales* (Captain J. C. Leach) and *Repulse* (Captain W. G. Tennant); and staff officers. They confronted a gruesome dilemma, for the assumptions underlying the despatch of their ships to Singapore had now been blown away by the Japanese, who *had* ventured to attack America and Britain together, who *had* already mounted a major invasion of Malaya. Moreover, the other, implicit, assumption that if the worst came to the worst Britain could count on the powerful US Fleet in the Pacific had also been blown away, for the Japanese strike on Pearl Harbor had sunk four battleships, badly damaged two others, and inflicted some damage on two more. Although by sheer good fortune the two US carriers currently stationed at Pearl Harbor had been at sea and so escaped, the balance of seapower had banged down heavily in Japan's favour, and the rich lands of European empire in the East now lay open to Japanese expeditionary forces.

Since it would now be pointless to vanish among the islands exercising vague menaces, as originally proposed by Churchill, Phillips's obvious objective must be the Japanese transports pouring troops ashore at Singora (in Siam) and Khota Baru, where already the British defence was crumbling and the airfield in danger. Everyone in the cabin of the *Prince of Wales* that forenoon was well aware that in northern Malaya and its airfields lay the essential key to the survival of Singapore itself. What were Phillips's chances of pouncing on these transports and destroying them? The Japanese naval forces were estimated at one modernised old battleship (probably the *Kongo*), seven cruisers (three of them 8-inch gun) and twenty destroyers. In fact the forces in the Gulf of Siam itself numbered eight cruisers (five 8-inch, two 5.5-inch), fourteen destroyers and twelve submarines, while in support off Indo-China lay two battleships, two more 8-inch cruisers and ten destroyers.[101] Thus though Phillips had no cruisers and was outnumbered five to one in destroyers (even on British estimates), he could at least assume, though wrongly, that *Prince of Wales* and *Repulse* could comfortably outmatch a *Kongo*.

The real puzzle for Phillips and his captains and staff that morning lay in Japanese air power, about the strength and efficiency of which little was known. According to the Naval Staff History 'reports on the capability of Japanese air personnel had for a number of years been consistently adverse, and may have tended to discount the possibility of their delivering a heavy scale of attack at long range'.[102] Sir Dudley Pound himself acknowledged after the event: 'I think we all underestimated the efficiency of the Japanese air forces, and certainly did not realise the long ranges at which they could operate.'[103] In the Mediterranean and British home waters no torpedo or dive-bombing attacks had been made on ships at a range greater than 200 miles from shore airfields; and it was over 300 miles to Singora and Khota Baru from the fields in southern Indo-China. It is known (though no detailed account of the C-in-C's conference survives) that Phillips expressed anxiety about going to sea without enough destroyers to screen his heavy ships and when there was considerable doubt as to whether the RAF would be able to provide the fighter cover he had asked for. Nevertheless he decided that he must carry out a sortie against the Japanese transports in view of the desperate need to defeat the landings in southern Siam and northern Malaya. Calculating that, given fighter support and surprise, his two heavy ships would have a good chance of 'smashing the Japanese forces' at Singora and Khota Baru, Phillips told his captains that he proposed to attack those forces shortly after dawn on 10 December.[104]

The Commander-in-Chief's plan, according to Captain Bell, Captain of the Fleet, was

> to detach the destroyers, which he considered very vulnerable to air attack, at midnight on 9th/10th December, and make a high speed descent on Singora with the heavy ships, relying on surprise and the speed of the battleships' attack to avoid damage. He calculated that the Japanese aircraft would not be carrying anti-ship bombs and torpedoes, and his force would only have to deal with hastily organised bombers from Indo-China during its retirement.[105]

Thus was the decision taken that 'Force Z' (as Phillips's present nucleus of an Eastern Fleet was designated) would seek out and engage the enemy. Yet the Japanese air forces in southern Indo-China actually numbered 99 bombers, 39 fighters and six reconnaissance aircraft; the bombers' crews highly trained in the attack of ships.[106] Taking these aircraft and the numerically powerful Japanese surface and submarine forces together, 'it will be seen,' comments the Naval Staff History, 'that Admiral Phillips's chance of carrying out his raid without being brought to action by very superior forces was slender in the extreme'.[107]

At 1735 on 8 December (local time) *Repulse* 'slipped from her buoy, "pointed ship" and slowly gathered way saluting the flagship as we passed her,' recalled one of her officers. 'The thunderous vibration of the ship's propellers while turning slowed to a more rhythmic beat as we steamed down the channel to the sea, following astern of the destroyers *Vampire* and *Tenedos*. The two other destroyers of our screen, *Electra* and *Express*, were already at sea, waiting for us outside the boom. *The Prince of Wales* followed astern of us.'[108] At 1830 Force Z passed the boom and the flagship took station ahead of *Repulse*. The two ships' lack of practice of working in company soon revealed itself in difficulties in keeping station: 'The tropical night closed in quickly and the weather began to deteriorate with heavy rain squalls, which made station-keeping difficult. The faint stern light of the flagship was just visible above the pale scut of her wake, and the broad zig-zag which the force was carrying out did not make things easier.'[109]

Admiral Phillips had chosen to steer to his objective by a wide evasive detour – at first east-north-east until he cleared the Anamba Islands, and then at 0400 on 9 December altering to the north, zig-zagging at 17 knots. He had now briefed his ships' companies as to the purpose of the sortie in a long explanatory signal. He hoped, he told them, 'to surprise the enemy shortly after sunrise tomorrow Wednesday':

> We may have the luck to try our metal against the old Japanese battlecruiser *Kongo* or against some Japanese cruisers and destroyers . . . We are sure to get some useful practice with the HA [high-angle anti-aircraft] armament. Whatever we meet I want to finish quickly and so get well to the eastward before the Japanese can mass too formidable a scale of attack against us, so shoot to sink![110]

Yet by this time, as Force Z ran north through a grey day of rain squalls and mist patches, Phillips knew that he would enjoy no fighter cover during his strike, and also that he faced a formidable air threat. For just before he sailed he had been told that it was doubtful whether after all the Royal Air Force could fly fighters over the Singora area on 10 December. This grim news had been confirmed by a signal received at 0125 on the 9th from his Chief of Staff (ashore at Singapore): 'Fighter protection on Wednesday 10th will not, repeat not, be possible.' Palliser added: 'Japanese have large bomber forces based Southern Indo-China and possibly also in Thailand.'[111] Khota Baru airfield had already been evacuated and the British grip on other northern airfields was slipping. In actual fact, Air Marshal Pulford was evacuating his few surviving aircraft from all the northern air bases. Nevertheless, despite Palliser's signal Phillips decided that he would still carry out his intended operation on the morrow – provided he was not spotted by Japanese aircraft that day.

Why did Phillips not call off the sortie at this point? It must be guessed that he still failed to appreciate the mortal danger posed by Japanese aircraft, even though as Vice Chief of the Naval Staff for more than two years of war he could hardly have failed to be aware of the impact of airpower on surface naval operations. Yet, unlike other admirals who might have been appointed C-in-C, Eastern Fleet, instead of him, he had never personally experienced air attack on a task force at sea. Moreover, he retained his passionate pre-war belief in the battleship and the firepower of its modern anti-aircraft armament, writing in a typically pugnacious memorandum in August 1940 in favour of a large battleship construction programme:

> The fact that the capital ship is the foundation of our naval strength has always been known to the Admiralty but as a result of the experience of the past year even those misguided persons who thought of the capital

> ship as dead have come to their senses and realise that without it all other forces, naval military and air, would be of no avail to us.[112]

That Phillips did not fully comprehend the peril incurred by warships while making deep sorties without fighter cover in the teeth of enemy air power is demonstrated by Admiralty signals (in which he as VCNS certainly had a hand) prodding flag officers off Norway in 1940 and in the Mediterranean in 1940–41 (especially with regard to operations off Crete) to take greater risks. Was he even aware of the shortcomings of the High Angle Control System (HACS) and the resulting inaccuracy of British ships' anti-aircraft fire? But in any case it was profoundly contrary to his own fiery, aggressive temperament to break off an operation once begun. He had been, after all, a moving spirit (with Pound and Churchill) in setting up the Court of Enquiry into Somerville's decision not to continue pursuing the Italian Fleet off Cape Spartivento in November 1940[113] (see above, p. 241). Phillips was therefore hardly likely to emulate that prudence in others which he had perceived as faint-hearted want of enterprise.

Force Z steamed on, the rain clouds and mists providing welcome cover from prying aircraft, even though at 0620 a lookout in the Australian destroyer *Vampire* thought he had spotted one for a few seconds. At 1532 Phillips received a cautionary signal from his Chief of Staff in Singapore:

> . . . Enemy apparently continuing landing in Khota Baru areas which should be fruitful as well as Singora . . . On the other hand enemy bombers on South Indo-China aerodromes are in force and undisturbed. They could attack you five hours after sighting and much depends on whether you have been seen today.[114]

It was in fact a Japanese submarine – the easternmost of a line of six picketing the southern approaches to the landing areas – that first sighted Force Z at 1340, and reported its course and speed, so enabling the Japanese C-in-C, Vice-Admiral Kondo, to order a concentration of two battleships, six heavy cruisers and numerous destroyers to intercept the British squadron. At Saigon the Japanese 22nd Air Flotilla swapped the bombs already loaded for a raid on Singapore for torpedoes and armour-piercing bombs, and took off to find the impudent British; fortunately for Phillips, on this occasion without success. Between 1700 and 1830 the protective rain clouds over Force Z gave way to a clear sky; and at 1740 lookouts in the flagship sighted three Japanese reconnaissance aircraft (in fact flown from Japanese cruisers), which, albatrosses presaging tragedy, shadowed Force Z until dusk.

Phillips now recognised that he had lost all chance of attacking the Japanese transports by surprise, and that he himself stood in danger of violent air attack within a few hours. At 2015, under cover of night, he therefore turned south for Singapore, some 500 miles distant via the east of the Anamba Islands. The morale effect on the ships' companies of this decision resembled that produced on the *Bismarck*'s crew by Lütjens's failure to pursue and finish off *Prince of Wales* after sinking the *Hood*. According to an officer in the *Repulse*, 'The ship's company did not react at all well and were very cast down as the news filtered round, but the routine and duties of the night watches took over as we steamed south at twenty knots.'[115]

Unbeknown to Phillips he was sighted again at 0210 on 10 December by another patrolling Japanese submarine. After firing five torpedoes without a hit, she reported back Force Z's position, speed and now southerly course. As a result of this report twelve aircraft took off from Saigon while it was still dark with the task of picking up and shadowing the British ships. Just before dawn there followed no fewer than 85 twin-engined Mitsubishi G3M Naval Type 96 strike aircraft (maximum range 2,722 miles at a cruising speed of 173 mph),[116] of which 34 were high-level bombers and the remainder torpedo-carriers.

At 0035 on 10 December Phillips received a report from his Chief of Staff in Singapore that the Japanese were making a fresh landing at Kuantan, deep behind the British defence in northern Malaya, and lying more than 150 miles south of Khota Baru and a similar distance south-south-west of Force Z's present position. Phillips now had to take another hard decision. Should he hold on to the south in order to make good his escape as best he might? Or should he make a distant diversion westwards in order to attack this reported new Japanese convoy? He reasoned that it lay some 400 miles distant from Japanese airfields and that the enemy would not expect Force Z to be so far south by daylight. 'On these grounds,' writes the Naval Staff History, 'the Admiral deemed surprise probable and the risk justifiable and at 0052 10th December altered course accordingly, increasing speed to 25 knots.'[117]

Phillips aimed to be off Kuantan by 0800. But at 0645, shortly after sunrise, while he was still steering westwards, the *Repulse* signalled that she had sighted an unidentified aircraft, almost certainly hostile. Nevertheless Phillips continued to hold his course for Kuantan in his riskiest gamble so far. He did so without asking for fighter cover from the airfields in southern Johore and Singapore Island, of which he was now in range, although there was no point in maintaining radio silence now that he had been spotted. Even his patron, the First Sea Lord, was to find this omission inexplicable, writing privately to Cunningham in January 1942:

> I hold most strongly that he was absolutely right to do as he did up to a certain moment, and that was when he was sighted at 6.45 in the morning by an aircraft which was presumably an enemy one. I see no reason why he should not have asked for fighter cover, but he may well have been influenced by the fact he was 400 miles from the established enemy aerodromes . . . and that all he could ask for was a standing patrol and what they could have sent him would really have been little good.[118]

Yet in Phillips's place Somerville or Cunningham would have been only too glad to see even a few friendly fighters, and would have made every effort to ensure that the Royal Air Force sent them. Was the omission another sign of Phillips's lack of personal experience of air attack at sea and a consequent under-rating of the air threat, especially from the scorned Japanese?

One eye-witness contends that a 'brain as crystal clear as Phillips's' would not make such a mistake as to neglect the need for fighter support; but that instead Phillips believed that his Chief of Staff, Palliser, was bound to appreciate that Force Z had gone to Kuantan in consequence of the signal about the Japanese landing there, and that Palliser would therefore arrange for air cover on his behalf. Phillips himself would in consequence see no need to break radio silence.[119] But Palliser, lacking the gift of second sight, had no idea that Phillips had taken Force Z to Kuantan, or even that he had abandoned his original sortie.[120]

It turned out that the report about the Japanese landings at Kuantan was wholly false; for a Walrus seaplane catapulted from *Prince of Wales* found nothing untoward, and the destroyer *Electra*, sent ahead by the C-in-C to reconnoitre the little port, reported 'complete peace'. Now Phillips was presented with the last of his choices – whether to get away to the southwards at utmost speed before time finally ran out, or to delay in order to investigate with his two capital ships a small steamer towing a string of barges which had been observed at extreme visibility at 0700 during the run-in. Phillips chose to steer east and then north after this unidentified but in any case negligible assemblage, apparently reluctant to the last to give up his sortie as having been in vain.

Shortly after 1000 came a report from the destroyer *Tenedos* (which had been detached earlier to return to Singapore) that it was being bombed by Japanese aircraft 150 miles to the south of Force Z. The barges were now forgotten as Phillips altered to the south-west and increased to 25 knots. At 1020 a shadowing aircraft was spotted from the *Prince of Wales*, and Force Z assumed the first degree of anti-aircraft readiness: tin hats, anti-flash hoods, guns manned. The sun was now shining hot and bright out of a clear sky. Almost immediately *Repulse*'s radar picked up an aircraft bearing 220°. At 1100 Phillips altered course to 135° by blue pendant signal, bringing the two heavy ships into starboard quarter line. A few minutes later nine enemy aircraft (Japanese accounts say eight) were seen approaching on the starboard bow at a height of 10,000 feet – 'small silver aircraft flying towards us in a tight line-abreast formation'.[121] Neither now nor at any time during the action did Phillips order a smoke screen. At 1113 Force Z opened fire. The Japanese aircraft flew steadily on through the winking explosions and puff-balls of smoke and down *Repulse*'s fore-and-aft line to straddle her at 1122 with an accurate stick of bombs – one near miss to starboard, seven very close to port, and a hit on the port hangar which went through and burst on the armour beneath the marines' deck, causing a fire (soon put out) on the catapult deck.[122]

This proved merely the overture. At 1142 a group of nine torpedo-bombers in close formation came in high from the port bow, used a patch of cloud on the port beam as cover in which to execute a series of turns together; and then gradually descended towards their target, stringing out into 'a loose, staggered line ahead', before launching their attack in waves of two or three in line abreast.[123] It was, the victims quickly learned, the standard tactical pattern for Japanese torpedo-bomber pilots. They executed the attack as if they simply had not noticed the fire being blasted up at them by 66 anti-aircraft guns of 4-inch calibre and upwards (including *Prince of Wales*'s sixteen 5.25-inch) and 74 2-pounder pom-poms.[124] Captain Bell, the Captain of the Fleet, later remarked that the attack was 'very well executed and the enemy in no way perturbed by our gunfire'.[125] As the Japanese aircraft made their final run-in, *Repulse*, swinging to starboard, escaped damage, but *Prince of Wales*, swinging to port, was hit aft at 1144 on the port side abreast of 'P3' and 'P4' turrets and probably by another torpedo simultaneously abaft 'Y' (main armament) turret. These were 24-inch torpedoes with warheads of 1,210-pound, as against the 18-inch torpedoes with 300-pound warheads used by the Fleet Air Arm in their strikes against *Bismarck* and Italian battleships. The results of the first two hits on *Prince of Wales*, and particularly the one aft, proved devastating, as was finally confirmed by a Royal Navy diving team which examined the wreck of the ship in 1966.[126] This torpedo blew a hole twelve feet in circumference in the hull, smashed the 'A' bracket holding the outer port propeller shaft, and bent the shaft itself. The distorted shaft revolving at full power caused thunderous vibration throughout the ship. Worse, it thrashed open watertight bulkheads and shattered fuel and oil pipes along its length. The way was clear for water pouring in through the hole blown by the torpedo in the after end of the shaft passage to reach the vitals of the ship, rendering nought all her carefully designed anti-torpedo protection. 'B' engine room, 'Y' boiler room, the port diesel generator room and the 'Y' turret action machinery room all swiftly filled with sea water.

With some 2,400 tons of water aboard, *Prince of Wales* listed 13° to port and settled by the stern until, by 1220, the port side of the quarter deck was awash despite counter-flooding. With both port propeller shafts out of action and her steering gear crippled – very similar to the damage inflicted by the Fleet Air Arm on *Bismarck* and *Vittorio Veneto* – the *Prince of Wales* now helplessly turned in a circle at 15 knots.

This was not all. The shock of the explosion and the swift inrush of water largely knocked out her electric power supply. Five out of eight dynamos quickly succumbed, four of them those supplying the after part of the ship. The damage-control parties then failed to switch power from the remaining three dynamos to the after part by means of the ring-main breakers; a failure never explained. Instead *Prince of Wales*'s damage-control parties repeated the error of the *Ark Royal*'s by devoting their energies to running emergency lines to individual points – in this case, to the forward 5.25-inch turrets. The after 5.25-inch twin turrets, having lost power, could only be slowly operated by hand. Fan-ventilation and telephone communication in the after part of the ship were similarly dead. In the dim light of emergency lamps men sweated to the point of collapse in the remaining engine and boiler rooms as temperatures climbed to 150°F. But, far more serious still, nine out of the ship's eighteen pumps had died with loss of electric power, all of them in the stricken after part of the ship. The mass of water continuing to flood through the hole made by the torpedo could not be pumped out.

At 1210, with the ship's steering motors dead, Captain Leach had hoisted 'not under control' black balls. The pride of modern British warship design and construction had been reduced by one attack by enemy aircraft to a cripple. It was the later opinion of at least one distinguished sailor that weaknesses in her design rendered her 'not

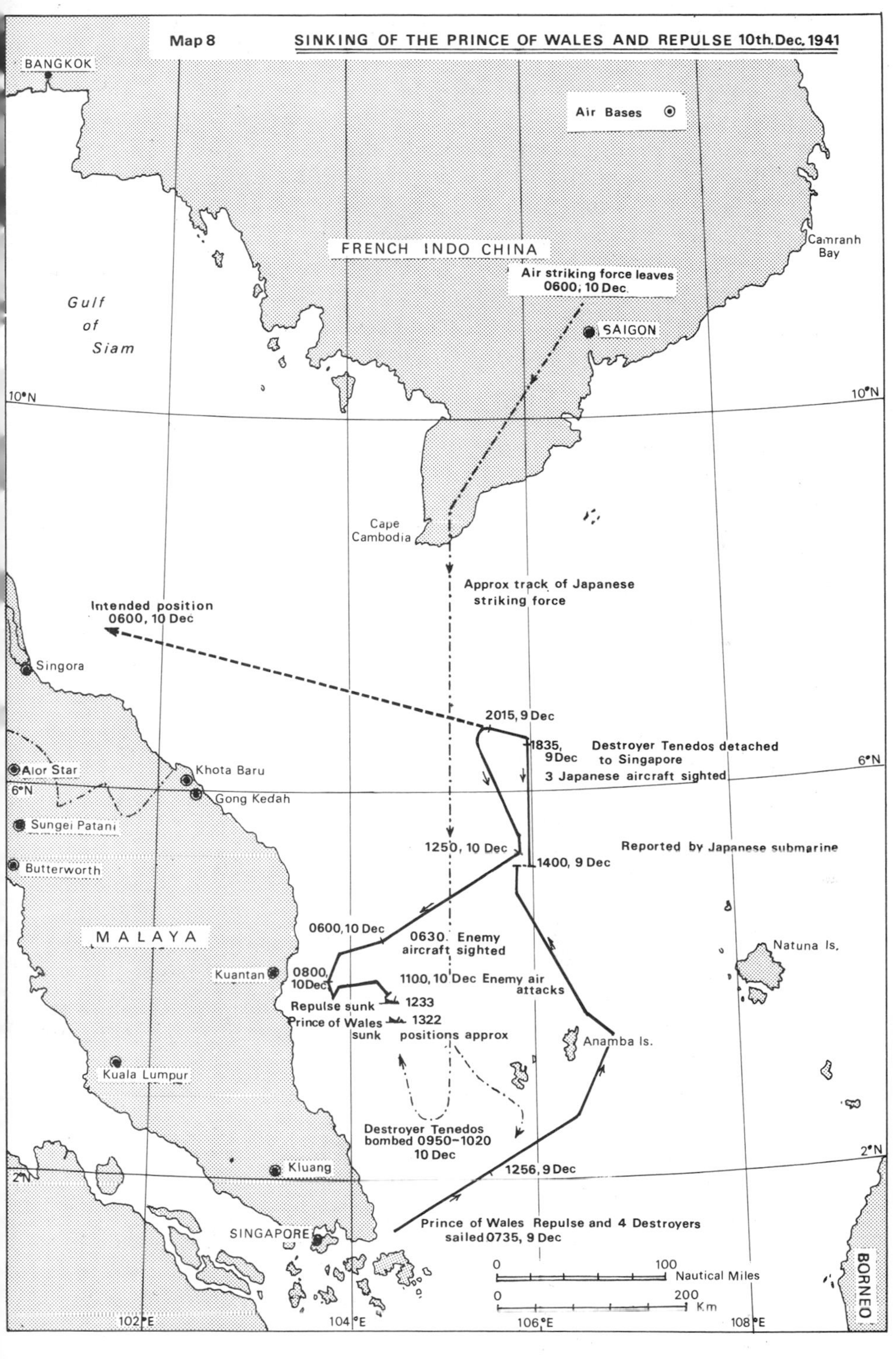
Map 8
SINKING OF THE PRINCE OF WALES AND REPULSE 10th.Dec.1941
BANGKOK
Air Bases
FRENCH INDO CHINA
Camranh Bay
Air striking force leaves 0600, 10 Dec.
Gulf of Siam
SAIGON
10°N
10°N
Cape Cambodia
Approx track of Japanese striking force
Intended position 0600, 10 Dec
Singora
2015, 9 Dec
1835, 9 Dec
Destroyer Tenedos detached to Singapore
3 Japanese aircraft sighted
6°N
Alor Star
Khota Baru
6°N
Gong Kedah
Sungei Patani
1250, 10 Dec
Reported by Japanese submarine
1400, 9 Dec
Butterworth
0600, 10 Dec
0630. Enemy aircraft sighted
MALAYA
Natuna Is.
Kuantan
0800, 10 Dec
1100, 10 Dec Enemy air attacks
Repulse sunk
1233
Prince of Wales sunk
1322
positions approx
Anamba Is.
Kuala Lumpur
Destroyer Tenedos bombed 0950–1020 10 Dec
2°N
Kluang
2°N
1256, 9 Dec
Prince of Wales Repulse and 4 Destroyers sailed 0735, 9 Dec
SINGAPORE
0
100
Nautical Miles
0
200
Km
BORNEO
102°E
104°E
106°E
108°E

as good structurally as some people thought'.[127] Certainly a later enquiry under Lord Justice Bucknill into the ship's loss found weaknesses in the layout of her electrical system, which failed to comply with principles laid down by the Controller of the Navy in 1938; and as a consequence other King George Vs were to undergo major improvements in this regard. The routing of ventilation shafts and cable ducts was also criticised (shades of *Ark Royal*). The enquiry recommended that the vulnerable stern part of the ship should be isolated by an extra, and strengthened, bulkhead. So far as her damage-control parties are concerned, there can be little doubt that they, like the rest of the ship's company, were not at the peak of efficiency simply because there had never been time to work up properly since she was commissioned.

Meanwhile Captain Tennant of the *Repulse* had sent an emergency radio signal to Singapore at 1150 that Force Z was being attacked; the only signal ever received on shore to indicate that air support was urgently needed. Six minutes after this Tennant succeeded in combing all the tracks of nine torpedoes launched by a further group of Mitsubishis, and two minutes later again *Repulse* was missed by high-level bombers while under helm at speed. Tennant now brought the *Repulse* closer to the flagship to ask if he could assist her; there was no reply. Soon it was *Repulse*'s turn again. A group of nine torpedo-bombers were spotted low on the horizon on the starboard bow. When three miles distant they split up into two sub-flights for the final run-in. The right-hand flight approached from starboard and dropped their torpedoes at a range of 2,500 yards just as the old battlecruiser began to swing to comb them. The other flight made a dummy run at the *Prince of Wales*, lying abaft the *Repulse*'s port beam, but then banked in a tight turn back to attack the *Repulse* from the port side. One torpedo struck home amidships 'with a great jarring shudder, as though a giant hand had shaken the ship', recalled one officer.[128] Yet *Repulse* still steamed at 25 knots; still her 4-inch guns and eight-barrelled pom-poms strove to put a cage of high explosive round the wounded ship.

At the same time *Prince of Wales*, incapable of manoeuvre, was attacked from starboard and hit twice forward of the breakwater and just before the bridge. Two minutes later, at 1226, she took two more torpedoes, this time aft near the 'Y' turret and abreast of 'B' turret. The consequent flooding had the effect of reducing her list to port to 3°, but the starboard outer propeller shaft was stopped, and the flagship's speed fell away to only 8 knots.

The attackers now concentrated their effort on the *Repulse*, attacking from all directions so that it was impossible for Captain Tennant to comb every track. One of the ship's officers has described what followed:

> Again the sky was blackened with shell-bursts from our fire, but the aircraft came on relentlessly to drop their torpedoes, the tracks of which could be seen heading straight for us. With the ship already committed to a swing to starboard to meet the attack from that side, the torpedoes were unavoidable and we were hit three times with only seconds separating the explosions. The first exploded near the Gunroom, the second abreast the mainmast, which shook and swayed, the heavy steel wire shrouds whipping violently. The ship seemed to stagger in her stride and I knew instinctively that this was the end, that *Repulse* was doomed.[129]

In fact she had been hit by four torpedoes, not three. Listing heavily to port *Repulse* turned 90° to starboard, which brought her fine on the *Prince of Wales*'s quarter and on a parallel course. Over the tannoy (which was fortunately still working) Captain Tennant now ordered everyone on deck:

> The decision for a commanding officer to make [he wrote later], to cease all work in the ship below, is an exceedingly difficult one, but knowing the ship's construction I felt very sure that she would not survive four torpedoes, and this was borne out, for she only remained afloat six or seven minutes after I gave the order for everyone to come on deck . . .[130]

Inexorably *Repulse* rolled to port as men scrambled up her ever more sloping decks and tilting ladders to reach the ship's side beyond the starboard rails. One survivor was to remember

> the strange sensation of walking down the ship's side just abreast of the bridge. As I reached the bilge keel the ship was still moving through the water, the ship's side was horizontal and I was standing upright . . . hundreds of men were now standing on the ship's side and bilge keel; some already sliding down the round bottom before making a last jump . . . I took my cap and shoes off and looked at the numerous heads of those who, forward of me, had already jumped, and were floating past as the ship was still moving ahead at about five knots, even though on her beam ends. It was now or never and I took a deep breath and jumped . . .[131]

Captain Tennant himself was to recollect looking over the starboard wing of the bridge when the *Repulse* had reached a 30° list and seeing the commander and two or three hundred men collecting on the starboard side of the ship:

I never saw the slightest sign of panic or ill discipline. I told them from the bridge how well they had fought the ship, and wished them good luck. The ship hung for at least a minute and a half to two minutes with a list of about 60° or 70° to port and then rolled over at 1233.[132]

The C-in-C ordered the destroyers *Electra* and *Vampire* to pick up the survivors, who numbered 42 out of 66 officers (including Tennant himself) and 754 out of 1,240 ratings. The task was accomplished without interference from Japanese aircraft, which had more important prey to kill.

The *Prince of Wales* was now steaming north at 8 knots. Soon after *Repulse* went down nine high-level bombers flew over the flagship from port to starboard, turned, and ten minutes later attacked from ahead and down the centre line as usual. From the compass platform the ship's torpedo officer watched the attack come in: 'Some guns in the forward group still going. Again steady formation of nine – waited for bombs to arrive – Captain said to Admiral "now", and we all laid flat – pattern hit ship aft.'[133] Luckily only one bomb struck home and that only caused superficial damage.

This was the last attack. But in any case *Prince of Wales* was dying minute by minute. At 1250 she signalled Singapore naval base: 'EMERGENCY. Send all available tugs . . .'[134] Eleven minutes later she repeated it. But she was beyond the succour of far-off tugs. The destroyer *Express* came alongside her starboard quarter and began to take off the wounded; the Carley floats (rafts) were launched and the gripes (bands holding the boats in place) were cast off the boom boats. By 1310 she was settling fast and listing heavily to port, a fact which impressed itself on one survivor when he 'suddenly saw that the sea was lapping at the support of the lowest pom-pom mounting. The sea near the base of the funnel! It struck me in a flash that not only was the ship heeled over but also very low in the water and the end probably a matter of minutes . . .'[135] Captain Leach now gave the order to don lifejackets and abandon ship. At 1320 *Prince of Wales* began to heel steeply, watched by appalled survivors on board the *Express*:

The great battleship continued to roll slowly away; as her upperworks dwindled and then vanished, the grey paint on her hull changed to brown as the dividing black line of her boot-topping rose out of the water, and the men at the guard rails began to climb over and slide down this treacherous slope.[136]

As they slid they had good cause to be grateful that the ship had

had her bottom scraped at Singapore, for otherwise their flesh would have been torn and ripped by a mass of barnacles.

At 1320 HMS *Prince of Wales*, flagship of Force Z and the Eastern Fleet, capsized and sank in 3° 33.6′N, 104° 28.7′E (the exact position was established when the wreck was located by HMS *Defender* in 1954), taking Admiral Sir Tom Phillips and Captain Leach with her. Ninety out of 110 officers and 1,195 out of 1,502 ratings were rescued.

To destroy Force Z had cost the Japanese only eight aircraft – another cruel demonstration of the ineffectiveness of the capital ships' anti-aircraft fire[137] and in particular of the technical shortcomings of the fire-control system adopted by the Admiralty before the war (see above, p. 47).

The *Prince of Wales* had succumbed to four, possibly six, 24-inch torpedoes with 1,210-pound warheads, and one bomb; the *Repulse* to five torpedoes and one bomb.[138] By comparison, the *Bismarck* finally sank after being hit by three 18-inch aircraft torpedoes with 300-pound warheads and five, possibly as many as twelve, 21-inch torpedoes with 600 pound warheads, together with innumerable 14-inch and 16-inch shells.[139]

As HMS *Prince of Wales* went down, eleven Royal Air Force Brewster Buffalo fighters arrived on the scene, prompting a distant group of Japanese bombers to jettison their bombs and make for home. The Buffaloes had been kept on standby at Sembawang airfield on Singapore Island to give air protection to Force Z. Tennant's emergency signal had reached the Air Operations Room at 1219, and the Buffaloes were in the air only seven minutes later. It has to be asked again: why did not the C-in-C himself ask for fighter protection – and in good time? Now the Buffaloes patrolled overhead while the survivors of both ships were being picked out of the water or from Carley floats and boats.

So all the debates about Far Eastern strategy and the dilemmas of imperial defence in Cabinet, Imperial Conference and Chiefs of Staff Committee, all the international naval conferences and naval limitation treaties, all the diplomacy in Tokyo and Washington, ended with sailors swimming for their lives in a tepid, sunlit sea 8,000 miles from England and, in the case of the survivors of the *Repulse*, giving while they did so three cheers for their captain and their lost ship.[140]

In the week following the destruction of Force Z the British defence of northern Malaya collapsed, with the consequent final loss of the airfields already abandoned by the Royal Air Force. The foundations of British strategy for securing Singapore had been swept away. The campaign now degenerated into a retreat interrupted by transient attempts at a stand by ill-equipped, under-trained and often ill-led British Imperial troops; stands in which they were swiftly outmanoeuvred and outfought by the advancing Japanese. The scenario so graphically portrayed by the Chiefs of Staff in their 1937 memorandum, of a Japanese march on Singapore overland down the west coast of Malaya, was coming true day by day. But in any case there was now no longer any point in trying to hang on to Singapore, a naval base without hope of a fleet, other than the political one of prestige. The cool strategic brain of a Moltke or a Wellington would have recognised this and begun to evacuate British civilians and military 'useless mouths' in good time, and even to thin down the fighting troops to a rearguard – not least because Burma, the eastern gate to India, was clearly the next British objective on Japan's programme of conquest, where all available forces now needed to be concentrated.

The First Sea Lord, to give credit to his common sense, warned the First Lord in a hand-written exchange of notes on 21 January 1942 (by which time the Japanese were nearing Singapore via Johore): 'If we pour reinforcements into Singapore and these reinforcements only affect the length of time Singapore can hold by a week or two we shall have squandered our reinforcements to no purpose and left Burmah [sic] very weak.'[141] For the Prime Minister, however, Singapore remained 'a famous fortress' to be defended to the last. At the turn of the year he had been instrumental in persuading the Chiefs of Staff, the Defence Committee and the Cabinet to divert major military formations into Singapore[142] – two brigades of the 17th Indian Division (previously earmarked for the defence of India) and the 18th (British) Infantry Division, then at sea en route for India. Soft and unfit for battle after a two-month voyage packed in troopships, the 18th Division arrived just in time to surrender with the rest of the garrison of the indefensible island on 15 February 1942, after the Japanese had occupied the now empty naval base and captured the water supplies on which the teeming city of Singapore depended.

Had Malaya and Singapore been evacuated in time like Greece and Crete, Britain would still have sustained – as in those cases – a disastrous defeat. As it was, by insisting that Singapore be reinforced and defended to the uttermost, Churchill inflated defeat into a highly dramatised catastrophe; a catastrophe which inflicted a mortal blow on British imperial prestige.

Now it was the turn of the Dutch East Indies and the British colony of Burma. Sir Dudley Pound had warned the First Lord in his note on 21 January the Royal Navy could do nothing to protect Burma against a Japanese seaborne expedition: 'We have not, and shall not have in the near future, sufficient naval strength in the Indian Ocean to dispute the passage of their convoys.'[143] In the event, the Japanese invaded Burma overland from Siam, and repeated their Malayan pattern of success against the British Commonwealth army defending the colony; an army weaker than need be because the formations that might have reinforced it had marched instead into Japanese prison camps in Singapore.

In the case of the Dutch East Indies the Western Allies (as they had now become by grace of Japanese aggression rather than their own will and foresight) belatedly set up a joint command (ABDA: American–British–Dutch–Australian) under a Supreme Commander, General Sir Archibald Wavell, now the British C-in-C in India. Once again the unfortunate Wavell had been handed immense responsibilities coupled with scant resources; and at this time expected to save a disintegrating situation by ad-hockery even more desperate than in the Middle East and Mediterranean in 1940–41.

The climactic moment for the naval side of this ad-hockery occurred on 27–28 February 1942, when the Dutch Admiral K. W. F. Doorman (flying his flag in the cruiser *De Ruyter*) led out the Allied 'Combined Striking Force' from Sourabaya to attack a Japanese invasion force heading for eastern Java. Doorman's command consisted of two 8-inch cruisers (HMS *Exeter* and the USS *Houston*), three 6-inch (HMAS *Perth*, HNLMS *De Ruyter* and *Java*), and the nine destroyers (HMS *Electra*, *Encounter* and *Jupiter*, HNLMS *Witte de With* and *Kortenaar*, and the USS *John D. Edwards*, *Alden*, *Ford* and *Paul Jones*). The ships lacked common signal codes and had never trained or exercised together. True to each of their naval traditions, they fought with skill and bravery as individual ships, but as a squadron were beaten by their numerically well matched but homogeneous Japanese enemy, Admiral Takagi's force of two 8-inch cruisers, two 5.5-inch cruisers and fourteen destroyers. The *Exeter* (veteran of the River Plate battle) proved the first casualty, hauling out of the line after a hit in the boiler room that brought her speed down to 15 knots. Next to go were the Dutch destroyer *Kortenaar*, torpedoed, and HMS *Electra*, repeatedly hit during an attempt by the British destroyers to attack the Japanese squadron with torpedoes. When Admiral Doorman sought to resume his attack on the Japanese convoy after dark, HMS *Jupiter* blew up, probably on a Dutch mine; and then, in a night encounter with the Japanese cruisers *Nachi* and *Haguro*, both the *De Ruyter* and the *Java* were torpedoed and sunk, Admiral Doorman going down with his flagship.

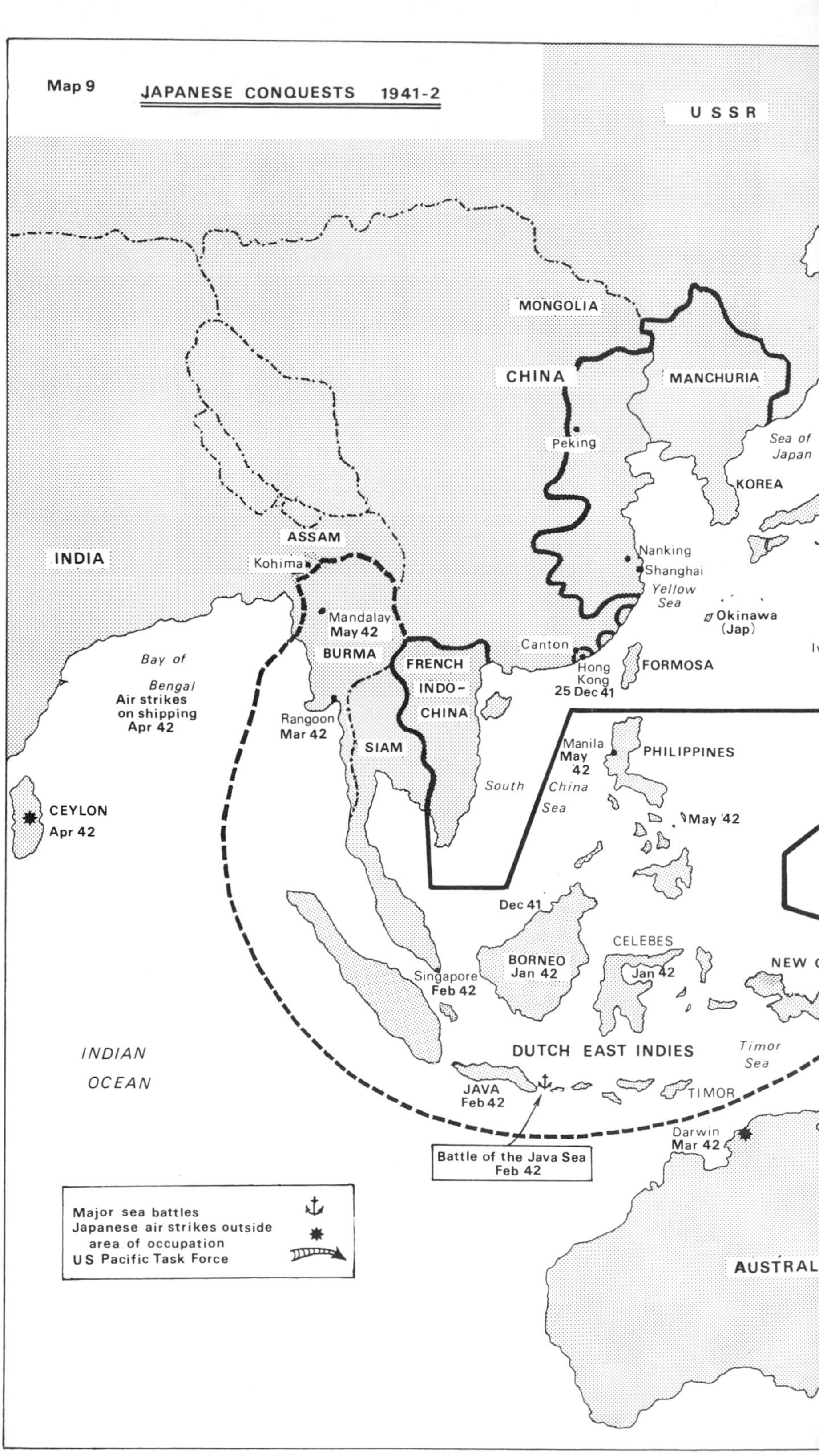
Map 9
JAPANESE CONQUESTS 1941-2
USSR
MONGOLIA
CHINA
MANCHURIA
Peking
Sea of Japan
KOREA
ASSAM
INDIA
Kohima
Nanking
Shanghai
Yellow Sea
Okinawa (Jap)
Mandalay May 42
BURMA
Canton
FRENCH INDO-CHINA
Hong Kong 25 Dec 41
FORMOSA
Bay of Bengal
Air strikes on shipping Apr 42
Rangoon Mar 42
SIAM
Manila May 42
PHILIPPINES
South China Sea
CEYLON Apr 42
May '42
Dec 41
CELEBES
BORNEO Jan 42
Jan 42
Singapore Feb 42
DUTCH EAST INDIES
Timor Sea
INDIAN OCEAN
JAVA Feb 42
TIMOR
Darwin Mar 42
Battle of the Java Sea Feb 42
Major sea battles
Japanese air strikes outside area of occupation
US Pacific Task Force
AUSTRALI

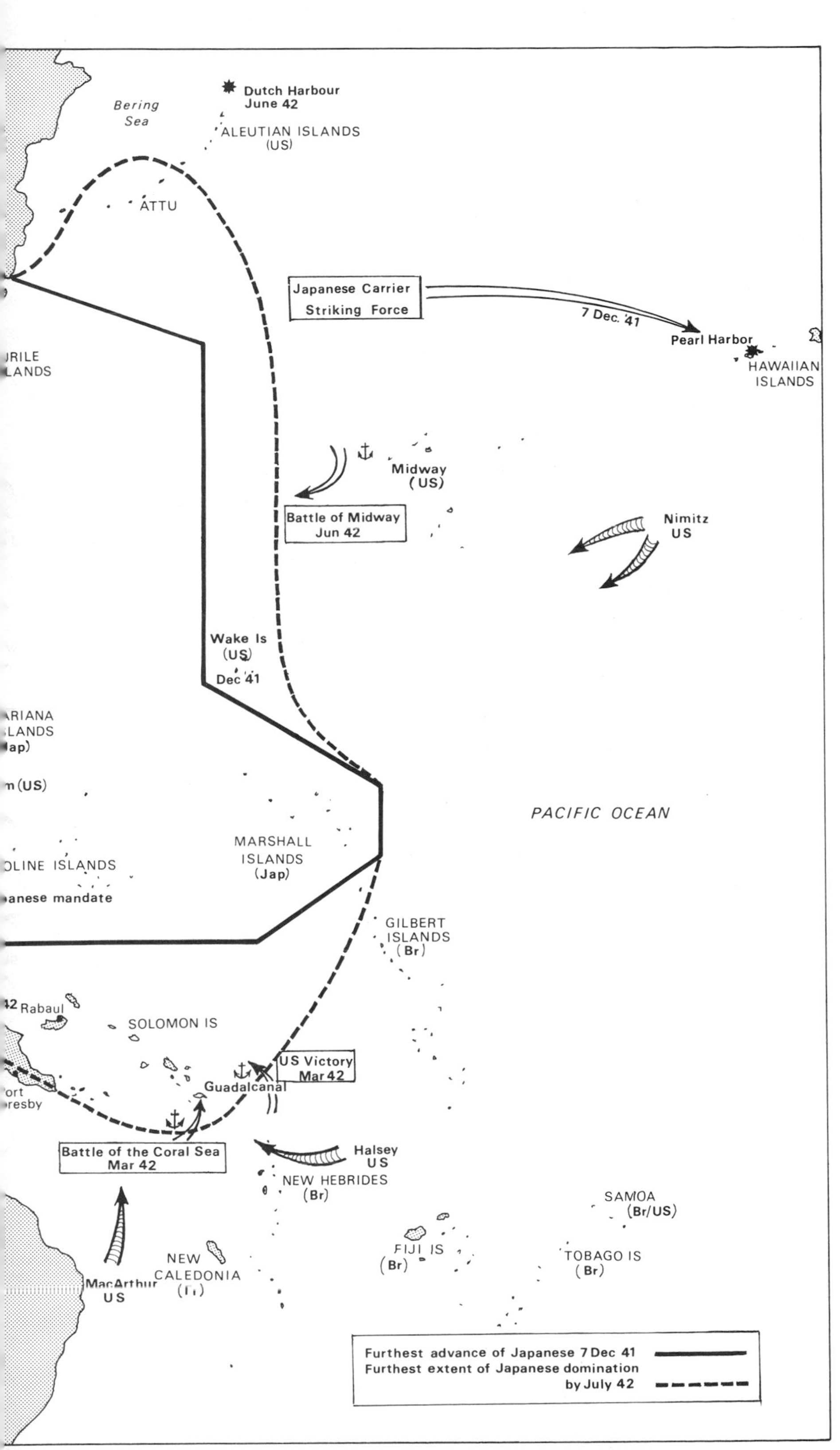
Dutch Harbour
June 42
Bering Sea
ALEUTIAN ISLANDS
(US)
ATTU
Japanese Carrier
Striking Force
7 Dec. '41
Pearl Harbor
HAWAIIAN ISLANDS
Midway
(US)
Battle of Midway
Jun 42
Nimitz
US
Wake Is
(US)
Dec '41
PACIFIC OCEAN
MARSHALL ISLANDS
(Jap)
GILBERT ISLANDS
(Br)
Rabaul
SOLOMON IS
US Victory
Mar 42
Guadalcanal
Battle of the Coral Sea
Mar 42
Halsey
US
NEW HEBRIDES
(Br)
SAMOA
(Br/US)
FIJI IS
(Br)
TOBAGO IS
(Br)
NEW CALEDONIA
MacArthur
US
Furthest advance of Japanese 7 Dec 41
Furthest extent of Japanese domination by July 42

The USS *Houston* and HMAS *Perth* now returned to Sourabaya to refuel, then set course for the Sunda Strait and safety. On their way in the dark they ran into the Japanese 'Western Invasion Force' in the act of disembarking, and for a brief happy time shot up the transports, sinking two. They were then engaged by Admiral Kurita's squadron of three cruisers and thirteen destroyers, fighting on under a glaring tropical full moon until reduced by gunfire and torpedoes to sinking wrecks. Next it was *Exeter*'s turn, intercepted in the forenoon of 1 March by four heavy cruisers and three destroyers. Her big battle ensign flying bravely from her mainmast, she fought it out for an hour and a half before a torpedo finally put her under. Both her escorting destroyers *Encounter* and *Pope* were also sunk.[144] With the Battle of the Java Sea there came to an end – not ingloriously – three centuries of English and Dutch seapower in Far Eastern waters.

As the Japanese swept on to conquer the Dutch East Indies while simultaneously advancing southwards through the island chains of the south-west Pacific, the Dominions of Australia and New Zealand could only look to America and the United States Navy to protect them, now that the imperial connection with Britain had proved to be – as they had more and more suspected – strategically worthless, despite the premium they had paid in the form of troops and ships in the Middle East and Mediterranean and an Australian division in Malaya. Yet for Britain and the Royal Navy, on their side, the passing of these dominions into American protection meant relief at long last from what Admiral of the Fleet Lord Chatfield had so justly characterised in 1939 as 'this heavy commitment'.[145]

It was not, of course, the only uncovenanted service done to Britain by Japanese aggression besides the terrible loss and humiliation. There was another, of supreme value. For the strike on Pearl Harbor had succeeded where all Churchill's tireless cajoling of Roosevelt had failed – in getting America into the Second World War. The United States Navy, only temporarily disabled at Pearl Harbor (as the Japanese C-in-C, Admiral Yamamoto, well recognised) and backed by America's enormous industrial strength, was at last fully in the fight alongside the Royal Navy.

'The accession of the United States makes amends for all,' Churchill had signalled to Eden on 12 December 1941, 'and with time and patience will give certain victory.'[146]

PART III

THE LONG VOYAGE HOME

14

'If We Lose the War at Sea, We Lose the War'

From the outbreak of war in 1939 to the end of April 1942 (when Japan largely attained her planned perimeter of conquest and incidentally sank an additional two British cruisers and a carrier in the Indian Ocean: see below, pp. 863–4) the Royal Navy had lost five capital ships, equal to a third of its original strength; from then on to the end of the war with Japan in August 1945, none. In fleet aircraft carriers the figures were four sunk by the end of April 1942, but only one during the rest of the war; in cruisers sixteen and twelve; in destroyers 78 and 55; and in submarines 44 and 30. Only in corvettes (the new type of escort vessel coming into service from mid-1940 onwards) and fleet minesweepers were the Royal Navy's losses heavier from the beginning of May 1942 till August 1945 than from the outbreak of war to the end of April 1942.[1]

These stark figures demonstrate a truth easily forgotten – that, with one outstanding exception, the worst of the Royal Navy's war was over before either the British Army or the Royal Air Force had got their acts together and begun to undertake operations on a grand scale.

In the case of the Royal Air Force, its single major contribution to the war, even if an historic one, so far lay in Fighter Command's victory in the Battle of Britain. Despite the personal courage of its pilots and the willingness of at least two of its leaders, Air Chief Marshals Sir Frederick Bowhill (AOC-in-C, Coastal Command, until June 1941) and Sir Arthur Longmore (AOC-in-C, Middle East, until

May 1941), to participate fully in the Army's and Royal Navy's battles, the Royal Air Force had made a feeble showing in Norway, France, Greece and Crete, and not much better over the Atlantic and the central Mediterranean. It had lacked the right kind of aircraft and, just as important, the right kind of training and doctrine for effective cooperation with the other armed services. Even by spring 1942 it remained incapable of doing for the British Army what the Luftwaffe had done for the German Army, or of doing to the enemy warships what the shore-based naval Japanese air forces had done to Force Z. This is hardly surprising in view of the air staff's long-held doctrinaire belief that the overriding priority for an air force lay in the bomber offensive aimed at destroying the enemy's industrial machine and civilian morale; and the War Cabinet's understandable decision in 1940 that in Bomber Command lay Britain's only hope of defeating Germany.

To enable the necessary mass heavy bomber force to be built up in the United Kingdom all other demands on British airpower, from the Battle of the Atlantic to the Navy's and the Army's need for support in their operations in the Middle East and Far East, had been placed a poor second. Yet it was not until May 1942 that Bomber Command launched its first effective attack on a German city, the 1,000-bomber raid on Cologne. This was laid on by the new AOC-in-C, Bomber Command, Air Marshal Sir Arthur Harris, as a public relations stunt to convince doubters that the bomber, if given absolute priority of resources, could win the war. Up till then the Royal Air Force had been learning painfully by experience, firstly, that it was impossible to fulfil its pre-war intention of bombing by daylight because of the rate of loss of aircraft, and secondly, after it had turned to night bombing in 1940, that its crews, lacking electronic navigation systems like the German X-Gerät and seeking their targets only by means of astronavigation, could not even find a German city, let alone a petrol-from-coal plant or a power station. While the Royal Navy was fighting its hard-run battles in the Atlantic and the Mediterranean through 1940 and 1941, Bomber Command, the air staff's 'war winner', was largely ploughing up German fields. Only by the beginning of 1943, with new navigational aids in quantity and new operational techniques such as the Pathfinder Force, would the great bomber offensive at last really get under way, and the Royal Air Force too enter upon its time of close engagement with the enemy and of dreadful attrition.[2]

For the British Army the period 1939 to spring 1942 had been one of hectic belated expansion from a small peacetime professional force, really an imperial gendarmerie, to a mass army based on conscription and intended ultimately for continental war; a process hindered by bottlenecks in the design, development and production of equipment, especially tanks.[3] Meanwhile it had fallen to the unlucky regulars, the Territorials and the first wave of conscripts to fight unavailingly in all the disastrous campaigns of 1940–42, from Norway to Malaya. Even the British (and Commonwealth) Army's two victories, both in North Africa – Western Desert Force's over the Italians and the new 8th Army's over Rommel in November and December 1941 in the first British set-piece offensive of the war against German troops – were no more than small-scale colonial campaigns when measured in the scale of German operations in the West in 1940 and in Russia after 22 June 1941, or British operations on the Western Front in the Great War. Not until 1944 would Britain field mass land forces in a decisive campaign against a main body of the German Army.[4]

Thus in spring 1942 the great battles of the British Army and the Royal Air Force were still to come. In contrast, the Royal Navy had been engaged at full stretch in continuous operations in all the ubiquity and variety of the sea service since the very first day of the conflict. Seapower had supplied the essential, all-pervasive element in an island nation's waging of war and indeed the sustaining of its own national life. The Navy, even more than the Army, had borne the brunt of Churchill's desperate opportunist efforts during the years of defeat to hit the enemy somewhere, somehow, and so seize back the initiative which the enemy was wielding with such assurance; his efforts to keep the war aflame so that America would believe that Britain's cause was worth backing. And for want of an air force properly designed, trained and equipped for maritime operations the Navy's ships had had to be sacrificed in unequal battles against enemy airpower – in the Far East as well as the Mediterranean.

Even for the hard-pressed soldiers there had been pauses between campaigns; periods of rest and of preparation for the next battle. But the endless round of convoys in home waters, in the Atlantic, and in the Mediterranean; the extra burden of Arctic convoys to Russia from 1941 (see below chapter 23); the repeated evacuations of vanquished expeditionary forces; the fleet battles; the bombardments of enemy bases; the support of the Army's operations ashore in Norway, Crete and North Africa; the anxious hunts for German raiders; the ambushing of Italian convoys between Sicily and North Africa by cruiser and submarine; the humdrum but vital work of laying and sweeping mines; all these had denied the Royal Navy such respites.

The theme, then, of the Royal Navy's war up to the spring of 1942, if it can be called a theme, consisted in coping valiantly, cheerfully and unceasingly in all weathers with every kind of task and challenge, often more than one at a time. But henceforward the tumult of the storm was gradually to abate. Never again – with one grand exception – were the King's ships to be required to engage the enemy so closely, so continuously and so widely against such odds. For one thing, now that America had become an ally there was no longer quite the same pressure on the Prime Minister to hazard the British armed forces on hasty opportunist strokes; instead time could be taken to forge a sound long-term Anglo-American grand strategy, time also thoroughly to prepare in adequate strength joint offensive operations in pursuance of that strategy.

For another thing, the openings for Churchillian interventions had been virtually (but, as events were to show, not entirely) exhausted by the very success of German and Japanese conquest – for where now did there remain fresh Norways or Greeces or Singapores to tempt the gambler?

Above all, the fact that the Stars and Stripes now flew alongside the White Ensign was step by step – but by no means at once – to lift from the Admiralty the near-breaking strain of 1939–41 when a 'One-Power Standard' navy had had to cope alone with the triple threat. By a decision at the Washington Conference in December 1941 the Royal Navy's responsibilities were limited to the eastern half of the North and South Atlantic, the Arctic convoy routes to Russia, the Mediterranean and the Indian Ocean. The western half of the Atlantic and the entire Pacific and Far East (including Australia and New Zealand) became the responsibility of the United States Navy, to which, therefore, now fell the task of fighting the Japanese main fleets. This was not all: American warships would eventually be made available to fill the gaps in the Royal Navy's line of battle in European waters; they would participate in strength in future Allied landings in the course of the conflict with Germany and Italy.

The global war now to be jointly waged by Britain and America would, like Britain's earlier single-handed fight, be absolutely dependent on sea communications. Although America might be a continental power in scale and geographical location she was really an island writ large, a super-Britain, in the context of fighting Japan and Germany, for her armies could only engage those of her distant enemies by grace of command of the sea. In the case of Japan, herself an island seapower whose newly acquired empire also depended on maritime communications, America would be fighting a like animal, two sharks manoeuvring for the kill in clear Pacific waters. But in the case of

Nazi Germany America faced the same problem as Britain before her, that of a seapower seeking to take the offensive against a land power. Germany could not be crippled by a maritime blockade as in the Great War because her conquests had given her overland access to all the food and raw materials she needed. Leaving aside the dream entertained by British and American airmen of victory by bombing, this meant that sooner or later the German Army in the West would have to be engaged in battle and defeated.

So to engage it would entail landings on an enemy coast: it would entail expeditionary forces despatched by sea. Yet the size of assault forces that could be put ashore would be determined by the available number and capacity of landing ships and landing craft; a cramping handicap compared with the abundant road and rail links at the disposal of a continental power deploying for an offensive on an existing land front or for an invasion across a frontier. Moreover, the overall size of the whole expeditionary force – follow-up formations as well as initial assault forces – was itself determined by the available lift of troops and supply ships across the Atlantic. Here again was a throttling disadvantage compared with a continental enemy who could freely redeploy armies on the largest scale, thanks to the carrying capacity of Europe's dense transport network.

These handicaps became quickly and dismayingly apparent in discussions between the British and American Chiefs of Staff during the Washington Conference in December 1941. For the consensus was that the maximum force that could be transported across the Atlantic in 1942 by the available shipping lift would be about fifteen divisions; hopelessly inadequate even in conjunction with British divisions in the United Kingdom to take on a defending army of the size that Germany could easily deploy at will in the West. Even in 1943 the shipping lift was only likely to permit a build-up to 40 to 50 divisions; still not enough to enable the Allies to bludgeon their way from the English Channel to Berlin in the face of the likely opposition.[5]

Thus Allied global strategy and plans for theatre operations alike were dominated from the first by the question of shipping capacity and landing-craft lift, and the consequent difficult choices and hard bargains that had to be made over priorities. 'Shipping,' wrote Churchill afterwards of this time, 'was at once the stranglehold and sole foundation of our war strategy.'[6]

At the Washington Conference Roosevelt and Churchill and their assembled Chiefs of Staff and civil servants attacked with a will the problems of framing a common grand strategy and mobilising their joint resources to provide maximum shipping capacity. The circumstances and the atmosphere were very different from the Placentia meeting only four months earlier. No longer was America an arm's-length friend prudently clinging to a formal neutrality, but, with her isolationism raped by Japanese torpedoes and her neutrality sunk in the muddy eddies of Pearl Harbor, a fully-fledged ally. The conference was held during the fleeting moment when Britain's naval and military power, now nearing its apogee of expansion, broadly matched that of the United States, which had as yet hardly begun to muster its overwhelmingly greater resources, and when the British could speak with the authority of hard-earned expertise to Americans new to the game. In forging and carrying out a common grand strategy the new allies enjoyed an advantage denied to the British and French in both world wars – they spoke almost the same language, and to some extent shared a common political heritage. Perhaps most important of all, they could enjoy the same jokes. These were the lubricants that from the start enabled the formal machinery of the alliance to function, even if a few individual senior officers on both sides were to supply the occasional grit.

The British Chiefs of Staff and the Prime Minister came to the conference comprehensively prepared; the American Joint Chiefs and the President, their minds busy with the aftermath of the catastrophe at Pearl Harbor, not so. The statement of global strategy eventually agreed by the conference, 'WW1', was an amended version of a draft tabled by the British Chiefs of Staff. It confirmed the fundamental choice that had been first agreed at staff talks in February 1941 and later reaffirmed at the Atlantic Conference in August that Germany must be beaten first: '. . . notwithstanding the entry of Japan into the war, our view remains that Germany is the prime enemy and her defeat is the key to victory'.[7] The memorandum looked ahead – very much in outline – to a return of the Allied armies to the Continent of Europe in 1943 'across the Mediterranean, from Turkey into the Balkans, or by landings in Western Europe', such operations being only 'the prelude to the final assault on Germany itself'.[8] To avoid controversy the exact nature of this assault was left for the moment undefined.

Though 'WW1' was broadly enough drafted, one thing was quite clear – its implementation utterly depended on the Allies being able to retain control of the Atlantic and having enough shipping to ferry great American armies across to Britain. On this control depended too the specific Allied operation for 1942 successfully sold to the Americans by the Prime Minister in Washington – an invasion of French North Africa, in conjunction with an offensive through Tripolitania by the 8th Army. Even this invasion (codenamed 'Gymnast') would need, so calculated the Allied staffs, the transit by sea of at least six divisions, half of them American, half British.

Yet despite the conference decision that Germany must be beaten first, the demands for shipping made by the Japanese war, a war of vast ocean distances, asserted themselves from the very beginning. The conference had to accept a proposal by General Marshall, US Army Chief of Staff, to reduce the first lift of American troops to Iceland and Northern Ireland by two-thirds in order to release ships to form a January troop convoy to the Pacific theatre.[9] This kind of seepage of shipping (and later of landing craft) from the German war to the Japanese war was to recur again and again.

To carry out the Allied grand strategy that had now been agreed between the President and the Prime Minister (acting as the 'main board' of the alliance) called for a joint 'executive board'. This machinery too the Washington Conference successfully created, in the form of the 'Combined Chiefs of Staff Committee' (composed of the chiefs of staff of each armed service of both countries). The Combined Chiefs were charged with providing the political leaders with professional advice on all strategic questions during the periodic summit conferences. In between conferences they were to act as a standing body to oversee the execution of agreed Allied strategy; they were to issue directives to theatre commanders in the name of both governments. Such a degree of integration of high command authority had never before been achieved between allies – or even between Britain and the Dominions.

In spite of the transient balance of strength between Britain and the United States in December 1941, it was plain that the centre of gravity of Allied power (especially industrial) must henceforward lie in the United States; and that the permanent location of the Combined Chiefs of Staff machine must therefore be in Washington. In consequence Britain set up in Washington an outstation of her own Chiefs of Staff Committee – the British Joint Staff Mission. Its members would sit with the American Joint Chiefs of Staff as the Combined Chiefs of Staff Committee for the transaction of regular business, except at summit conferences or other occasions when the British Chiefs would be participating in person.

The British Joint Staff Mission was to be headed by Field-Marshal Sir John Dill, until 25 December 1941 the Chief of the Imperial General Staff, a man with exactly the qualities of high professional ability, personal integrity and tact needed to create a fruitful working relationship with the leaders of the American fighting services. As the personal representative of Churchill in his capacity of Minister of Defence Dill also enjoyed direct access to President Roosevelt. The senior naval member of the Joint Staff Mission, Admiral Sir Charles Little, brought the authority of a former Second Sea Lord to the task of deputising for the First Sea Lord in discussions with the US Chief of Naval Operations (Admiral Harold E. Stark until March 1942, then Admiral Ernest J. King).

The Washington Conference proved, however, unable to agree to a civil equivalent of the Joint Chiefs; that is, a joint supply board with responsibility for planning and deploying economic resources, from raw materials and munitions to shipping. Instead it settled for two committees, one in Washington and the other in London, both to advise on the allotment of all munitions resources, which were now 'deemed to be in a common pool'.[10] The conference did, though, set up in Washington a Combined Raw Materials Board and – of key importance to a maritime alliance – a Combined Shipping Adjustment Board. On the new board sat Sir Arthur Salter, Head of the British Merchant Shipping Mission, a distinguished public servant whose experience of shipping problems in wartime stretched back to 1917, and Admiral E. S. Land of the US Maritime Commission. The new Board was directed 'to adjust and concert in one harmonious policy' the work of the Ministry of War Transport and the US Maritime Commission in maximising shipping resources, also now deemed to be pooled.[11]

A depressing balance sheet of needs and resources presented itself to these new Allied bodies responsible for conducting a joint maritime global war. In the first place the Royal Navy possessed not a single modern (or modernised) capital ship in the eastern Mediterranean or Indian Ocean. One Great War veteran, HMS *Malaya*, was with Force H at Gibraltar. The brand new battleship *Duke of York*, not yet worked up, was serving in December and January as transport for the Prime Minister to and from the Washington Conference. Admiral Tovey's Home Fleet amounted to the battleships *King George V* and *Rodney*, the battlecruiser *Renown*, ten cruisers and some eighteen destroyers; a slender enough force with which to guard against possible breakouts into the Atlantic by *Scharnhorst*, *Gneisenau* and the heavy cruiser *Prinz Eugen* from Brest or by the powerful *Tirpitz*, the pocket battleship *Scheer* and the heavy cruiser *Hipper* from the Baltic; and at the same time protect Arctic convoys from sorties by the latter ships.[12]

Of the Royal Navy's five serviceable fleet carriers, one, the new *Victorious*, was with the Home Fleet, another, the elderly *Eagle*, with Force H, and the remaining three, the large modern *Indomitable* and

Formidable, and the small old *Hermes* (the first carrier in the world to be built from the keel upward, but soon to be sunk by the Japanese) were with the reconstituted Eastern Fleet and its four unmodernised 'R' class battleships based on Ceylon. Cruisers and destroyers too were scarce after their slaughter in the Mediterranean, as the First Sea Lord explained in a letter to Cunningham at the end of 1941: 'There is nothing I should like better than to send you a present of twenty or thirty destroyers and a dozen cruisers . . . You know, however, how desperately hard-pressed we are in every direction, and this will account for the smallness of our presents.'[13] And in every theatre shore-based maritime air forces remained weak and ill-equipped.[14]

After Pearl Harbor the serviceable strength of the United States Navy in battleships amounted to only three, all hitherto with the Atlantic Fleet but now transferred to the Pacific Fleet. With these ships and four fleet carriers (one of these too being transferred from the Atlantic), the Americans had to confront Japan's eleven battleships and six fleet carriers; gruesome odds.

But it was in the humble escort vessel in the Atlantic, one of the essential keys to mastering the U-boat, that the Royal Navy and the US Navy suffered from the most worrying shortages. In March 1942 the two navies calculated that they were 710 short of their operational requirements (242 British and 468 American).[15]

Only the shipyards of Britain and America could put an end to this prevailing dearth of warships of almost every kind. The US Navy Department had already embarked on a vast building programme which by summer 1945 would have completed ten battleships, eighteen fleet carriers, nine light carriers and 110 escort carriers, 45 cruisers, 358 destroyers, and 504 escorts.[16] At the end of 1941 American yards were building 300 frigates alone, of which it was hoped that 200 would be delivered by the end of 1943. On the other hand the Admiralty found itself once again baulked by Britain's limited and outdated shipbuilding capability. On the day that Pound received news of the sinking of *Prince of Wales* and *Repulse* he wrote to the Prime Minister to plead that 'in the situation created by the loss of three capital ships [i.e. including *Barham*] in a fortnight, it is important to make every effort possible to speed up the completion of the *Anson* and *Howe* [of the King George V class] and grant them 1(a) priority'.[17] Churchill consented to this, but only one further battleship was to be started by Great Britain during the war, the *Vanguard*, and she did not come into service until 1946. Only two fleet carriers, *Indefatigable* and *Implacable* (laid down in February and November 1939), were building in January 1942, and although in the middle of that year the Admiralty drew up an ambitious programme of thirteen to twenty new vessels of this class, only one, *Audacious*, was actually laid down during the war, and even she was not completed until the year after it was over.[18] In retrospect it is remarkable that Britain did not order and complete a single fleet carrier, the new arbiter of seapower, within the compass of the Second World War, for both *Implacable* and *Indefatigable* had been ordered in 1938. For the new class of escort carrier for convoy work Britain looked almost entirely to American production.[19] Of the other new class, that of light fleet carrier, four were ordered from British yards in spring 1942 and twelve more by the end of the year, but only six of them were to come into service before the end of the German war.[20]

Britain's naval shipbuilding resources, already partly diverted to ship repair work, had been pre-empted by the essential production of escort vessels. Even so, cramped shipyard layouts, antiquated methods and obstructive trade unions[21] ensured that targets here were not met. Naval tonnage of all kinds completed in 1941 came to less than four-fifths of the expected total, while only 38 destroyers had been produced by April 1942 as against the 61 forecast in July 1941.[22]

However, the balance sheet for Allied merchant shipping at the beginning of 1942 looked much more cheerful than for warships. In the first place total sinkings in the second six months of 1941 had dropped to 1,323,276 tons, less than half those of the first six months, and December sinkings in the North Atlantic from all causes were down to a mere 50,582 tons[23] – the result of the current British ability to read U-boat cyphers and so route convoys clear of wolf-pack ambushes (see above, Chapter 9). Dry-cargo ship losses in the second half of 1941 equalled an annual rate of about 2.6 million deadweight tons, which compared with projected building programmes for 1942 of 1.5 million tons in Britain and Canada and about 7 million in the United States, of which a large share was to be allotted to Britain under Lend-Lease. If – and events were soon to make their sour comment on that 'if' – losses continued through 1942 at the same rate as in the latter part of 1941, Britain would actually see an increase in available dry-cargo tonnage of about 3 million.[24] No wonder Sir Arthur Salter could comfortably assert in December 1941: 'The shipping problem as it had been posed nine months before had been solved.'[25]

Yet paradoxically the entry of the United States into the war threw a shadow over this enticing prospect, for now her own needs for shipping were to compete with Britain's. How much of those 7 million tons of new construction would she be able and willing to spare for her ally? Moreover the patterns of the two countries' requirements differed greatly. For while the United States might be a super-island in the context of conducting a maritime war, and therefore needed an immense number of ships in order to deploy her armed forces to theatres overseas and then to nourish their campaigns, she was not an oceanic *economy* like Britain, but a self-contained continental economy with consequently small economic need for merchant tonnage. By contrast Britain needed shipping first and foremost to sustain her own national life and her war production with vital imports – as well as sustain the dependent economies of the Indian Ocean area. Thus British (really Eastern Hemisphere) *economic* requirements were to compete with American (largely Western Hemisphere; the Pacific) *military* requirements. If British demands for American ships were to be fully met, it would have to be at the expense of the American armed forces and their ability to wage war.[26]

There existed a further mismatch between the shipping and shipbuilding patterns of the two allies. The Americans were already getting into the swing of turning out 'Liberty' ships almost like Ford cars – well-laid-out modern yards with the latest equipment assembling prefabricated sections on the flow-line principle. In consequence their production of dry-cargo ships was to exceed their losses. But British yards, with their essentially Edwardian layouts and technology, were building far fewer than Britain was losing.[27] Nevertheless, even America's net gain of construction over loss was still not enough to meet the expanding needs of her own armed forces, let alone bail out the British. Here then were conundrums enough for the Joint Shipping Adjustment Board to solve.

Nevertheless, after much patient negotiation in Washington, a working balance was achieved between these clashing needs. As it turned out, Britain was to enjoy the use of even more American tonnage in 1942 than in 1941, equal to up to a ten per cent addition to the British merchant fleet.[28] The drawback lay in that the British could never know if and when the Americans might call some of this shipping back to meet their own military needs, so leaving Britain with a shortfall she could not possibly fill from her own resources. Yet Britain offered a trade-off for American merchant ships. America's deployment of even larger forces overseas demanded troopships, and since America in peacetime had not been a leading passenger carrier, she lacked enough suitable vessels. So most of the 27,000 American troops who crossed the Atlantic to Britain in the first quarter of 1942, plus 16,500 of those who crossed the Pacific to the Far Eastern fronts, did so in ships flying the Red Ensign;[29] and this was merely the beginning of this British service.

But all this intricate, patient Anglo-American budgeting of shipping resources could be reduced to nonsense by another factor, incalculable, unpredictable – Admiral Dönitz's U-boats and Grand Admiral Raeder's surface ships.

Dönitz knew, Sir Dudley Pound knew, Churchill knew, that in the Atlantic Britain could still lose the war despite her new alliance with the United States. In the First Sea Lord's own words in March 1942, 'If we lose the war at sea, we lose the war.'[30] As his plain sailor's mind had grasped early on and never let go thereafter, the Atlantic constituted the one decisive front for Britain, in comparison to which all else – whether 'blue water' strategy in the Mediterranean, the Army's battles in the Western Desert, the Royal Air Force's vision of a bomber offensive, or that other war in defence of Empire in the Far East – was secondary and dependent. In this centrality of the Battle of the Atlantic lay, then, the true leitmotiv of the war for the Royal Navy, even if so far overlaid by all the other episodes and encounters and dramatic losses of the conflict at sea.

Up till the moment of America's entry into the war, the Battle of the Atlantic had constituted a purely defensive campaign fought to keep open Britain's lifeline. All the resources and all the effort devoted to the battle had done nothing to inflict damage in turn on Nazi Germany's capacity to wage war, since she was a continental state whose strength resided in a great army and whose economy did not depend on sea communications. The Atlantic struggle thus serves to demonstrate the comparative disadvantage suffered by Britain by virtue of being an island state and an oceanic economy.

But the advent of America as a belligerent totally transformed the strategic significance of the Atlantic. Instead of being a *voie sacrée* maintaining the garrison of a beleaguered fortress, it became the potential route – if it could be kept open – by which great American armies could be deployed in the United Kingdom alongside the British Army for the eventual invasion of Hitler's Europe. On the Atlantic struggle now turned, therefore, not just Britain's continued survival, but also ultimate victory by the Western Allies over Germany. And this is why the Atlantic constituted the one theatre where the worst of the Royal Navy's war was still to come.

At the end of 1941 the U-boat arm had suffered, in Dönitz's own words, 'a heavy defeat', forcing him to withdraw boats from the Atlantic crossings to the sea area of Gibraltar. Though Dönitz's careful investigation of possible security leaks within his command failed to discover the fact, it was the ability of Bletchley Park to read his Enigma signals traffic that had been primarily responsible for his current setback. No wonder the year went out, as Dönitz wrote, 'in an atmosphere of worry and anxiety for U-boat Command'.[31] But paradoxically the entry of the United States into the conflict (Hitler had declared war on her on 11 December, four days after Pearl Harbor) was swiftly to revive Dönitz's fortunes, for a luxuriant, unconvoyed and hitherto inviolate traffic lay open to attack right along the east coast of the United States and down into the Caribbean.

At the beginning of 1942 Dönitz commanded a total of ninety-one operational U-boats. Twenty-three of them were now in the Mediterranean, another six posted west of Gibraltar, and four off Norway. Of the remaining fifty-eight, over half lay in the dockyards under repair. This left Dönitz with only twenty-two boats in the Atlantic out of which ten or twelve were usually in transit to and from their operational cruises.[32] It is a remarkable comment on Germany's pre-war and wartime failures to appreciate the value of the U-boat as a weapon against Britain that after two and a half years of conflict Dönitz could only deploy some ten or twelve U-boats at a time in his main offensive against Allied shipping.

Dönitz himself now urged OKM (*Oberkommando der Kriegsmarine*) to release U-boats from the Mediterranean and the Gibraltar area in order to deploy the maximum strength for the massacre of the unprotected shipping in American waters in the necessarily brief period before the United States Navy established a convoy system. At first OKM refused, and Dönitz had to launch his new offensive with only five U-boats. On 2 January 1942, at his further and urgent persuasion, OKM relented and released to him seven large long-distance boats hitherto earmarked for the Mediterranean.[33] On 13 January the first U-boats arrived off the American coast to find an almost unbelievable scene of coastal towns ablaze with lights, lighthouses and lightships sweeping their helpful guiding beams, ships with undimmed navigation lights steaming along the normal peacetime routes. So began what the U-boat arm called the second 'happy time' (the first being the autumn of 1940, the opening of the first wolf-pack offensive against British convoys).

Since this second 'happy time' belongs to the history of the United States Navy rather than the Royal Navy, it only needs to be said here that the Americans had remembered nothing from the lessons of the Great War and learned nothing from the experiences of the British in the present war. They had made no preparations for quickly setting up a convoy system. Instead they believed in the old fallacy of the 'offensive' hunting group trawling the oceans for U-boats, and even in the other old fallacy of the patrolled 'safe' shipping lane along which unconvoyed vessels sailed independently but predictably, to the jubilation of U-boat commanders. For the U-boat commanders a 'happy time' it certainly was: in the first fortnight of the campaign they sank thirteen ships totalling 100,000 tons in American and Caribbean waters, often ships bound to or from Britain. In February this figure was exceeded by sinkings within the American Eastern Sea Frontier Command alone. In March the U-boats put down twenty-eight ships of 159,340 tons in the Eastern Sea Frontier and another fifteen of 92,321 tons in the Gulf and Caribbean Commands.[34] What was even worse was that oil tankers, on the cargoes of which the conduct of modern war so utterly depended, made up 57 per cent of that lost tonnage.[35]

For the Royal Navy these U-boat successes proved especially galling. Admiral Sir Percy Noble, C-in-C, Western Approaches Command, wrote to the First Sea Lord on 8 March 1942: 'Western Approaches Command find itself in the position to-day of escorting convoys safely over to the American eastern seaboard, and then having the disappointment of finding that many of the ships thus escorted are easy prey to the U-boats which have placed themselves down the American seaboard and in the Caribbean.'[36] The Admiralty did their best to help the Americans, transferring to them ten corvettes and twenty-four anti-submarine trawlers, and by training their new American crews in the techniques of anti-submarine warfare. These were services for which on 9 May Admiral Stark (now head of the US Naval Mission in London in succession to Ghormley) warmly thanked Pound, in particular paying tribute to 'the outstanding work done by the training schools'.[37]

The British also did their best to overcome American reluctance to convoy. On 19 March the First Sea Lord told the new Chief of Naval Operations and Commander-in-Chief of the United States Fleet (COMINCH), Admiral King, that 'he regarded the introduction of convoy as a matter of urgency',[38] while Churchill personally signalled Roosevelt to express his 'deep concern'.[39] The obstinate King argued that 'inadequately escorted convoys were worse than none', which, as the British official naval historian points out, was 'the exact opposite to all that our experience had taught'.[40] On 19 June General Marshall, the US Chief of Staff, wrote to Admiral King to say that losses off the American Atlantic seaboard and in the Caribbean 'now threaten our entire war effort . . .'; in fact, he went on, '. . . I am fearful that another month or two of this will so cripple our means of transport that we will be unable to bring sufficient men and planes to bear against the enemy in critical theatres to exercise a determining influence on the war'.[41]

But by this time the lessons taught perhaps more effectively by Dönitz than by Pound had sunk in, and the US Navy had come to accept that what President Wilson back in the Great War had likened to 'chasing hornets all over the farm'[42] was useless. King was able to reply to Marshall on 21 June detailing all the emergency measures that had now been taken, including a coastwise escort system since 15 May, although he acknowledged that heavy losses were still occurring outside that zone. Wrote the now belatedly enlightened King:

> But if all shipping can be brought under escort and air cover our losses will be reduced to an acceptable figure. I might say in this connection that escort is not just *one* way of handling the submarine menace; it is the *only* way that gives any promise of success. The so-called patrol and hunting operations have time and again proved futile . . .[43]

The 'happy time' along America's eastern seaboard was over, as Dönitz had to admit.[44] But it still continued in the Caribbean, where in May and June 1942 his U-boats sank 148 ships totalling 752,009 tons.[45] From the end of June, however, the convoy system was introduced in the Caribbean too, with the result that, in Dönitz's words, 'it became obvious that the main effort in the U-boat war would have to be switched back to wolf-pack attacks on convoys [in the North Atlantic]'.[46]

So the relief afforded to the Royal Navy in the Atlantic by the concentration of U-boat strength on the 'happy time' off America was now coming to an end. Moreover, Dönitz was to renew his offensive against Britain's lifeline with a colossal double advantage – for whereas since the beginning of February 1942 GC and CS at Bletchley Park had lost the ability to pinpoint U-boat deployments, the German B-Dienst had been able since December 1941 to read both the main Royal Navy cypher and also the cypher for Anglo–US–Canadian signals traffic in the Atlantic.[47]

It was therefore fortunate for the Admiralty as it faced Dönitz's renewed campaign in summer 1942 that, back in February, Hitler himself had removed one of its major anxieties from the Atlantic scene: the constant threat posed from their French base at Brest by those formidable surface raiders, the fast battleships *Scharnhorst* and

Gneisenau. For at a conference with his admirals on 12 January he had directed that the two ships plus the heavy cruiser *Prinz Eugen* should return to Germany. Sadly, however, the circumstances of their homeward voyage in February cast the bleakest light on the state of British airpower over the sea and of cooperation between the Royal Navy and the Royal Air Force in the third year of the war.

The *Scharnhorst* and *Gneisenau* had put into Brest on 22 March 1941 after an Atlantic foray but, except for one short voyage by *Scharnhorst* to La Pallice in July of that year, had thereafter remained in Brest for almost eleven months, a constant worry to the Admiralty. There they had been bombed again and again, starting with an attack by Fleet Air Arm torpedo bombers on the *Gneisenau* the very day she reached Brest which inflicted widespread damage. On the night of 10 April 1941 Bomber Command had reluctantly lent a hand, and hit her in dock with three bombs, one of them heavy, which along with near-misses on the dockside further mauled her.[48] On 1 June 1941 the *Prinz Eugen* had joined the two battleships after her short-lived sortie with the *Bismarck*. A month later it was her turn to be visited by Bomber Command, when a bomb went through her port side forward, down through the armoured deck, and exploded below to destroy the switch room, amplifier and compass compartments and gunnery transmitting station. On 24 July, while *Scharnhorst* was in La Pallice during her brief excursion, fifteen bombers scored five hits on her, causing damage to a turret, engine room machinery and fuel tanks, together with flooding of compartments, the starboard propeller shaft tunnel and dynamo room. Next day she limped back to Brest, there to remain until February 1942 except for one day at sea on gunnery exercises.

Grand Admiral Raeder perceived these ships as exercising the traditional menace of 'the fleet in being', and indeed the repeated attempts by British aircraft to destroy them offers proof of how real that menace was to the British leadership. Hitler, however, had become obsessed with the belief that Norway stood in danger of Allied seaborne invasion. After protracted arguments with his Naval Staff, Hitler provisionally decided late in 1941 that the three ships must be transferred to a Norwegian base. At the conference on 12 January 1942 he confirmed this decision, but not only on the grounds of the defence of Norway, as the record of the meeting makes clear:

> He compared the situation of the Brest group with that of a patient having cancer, who was doomed unless he submitted to an operation. An operation on the other hand, even though it might have to be a drastic one, would

offer at least some hope that the patient's life might be saved. The passage of the German ships through the Channel would be such an operation and had therefore to be attempted.[49]

Thanks to 729 photo-reconnaissance missions flown over Brest between 28 March 1941 and 12 February 1942 (costing nine Spitfires)[50] and to the watch kept by local agents of the Special Intelligence Service, the British authorities were well aware that the German ships had been damaged, but they could not exactly establish their state of fitness for operations.[51] Then in December 1941 and January 1942 Ultra decrypts of Enigma signals revealed that the gun crews of all three ships had been sent to the Baltic for firing practices in the *Scheer* and *Hipper*. As early as 24 December the Admiralty was warning Coastal, Bomber and Fighter Commands that the ships might break out of Brest at any time. By the beginning of February all Intelligence sources confirmed that the three ships were putting to sea every night for steaming trials. On 3 February the Admiralty appreciated: 'most probable course of action of enemy ships now at Brest will be to break eastwards up the Channel and so to their home ports'.[52]

Both the Admiralty and the Royal Air Force began to put into operation contingency plans matured over a whole year for dealing with a German dash up the Channel and through the Straits of Dover. Air squadrons were placed at indefinite short notice, while the C-in-C, Nore (Vice-Admiral Sir George H. D'O. Lyon), was requested to reinforce Dover Command with six destroyers and up to six motor torpedo boats. The Admiralty also placed the minelayer *Manxman* under Dover's orders.[53] The Naval Staff History rightly comments that the striking power of these naval forces 'was not great'.[54] At the request of the Vice-Admiral, Dover (still Bertram Ramsay), six Swordfish of 825 Squadron, Fleet Air Arm, at Manston in Kent were placed at his disposal. Air and sea cooperation in the Dover Command area was to be coordinated by Ramsay and the AOC, No. 11 Group, Royal Air Force (who actually shared a joint headquarters with the C-in-C, Nore).

It was not easy for Ramsay to guess the German plan and frame his own preparations accordingly. He could not expect his 'slender forces'[55] to remain on standby indefinitely, and therefore must determine as best he could the likely time of German arrival in the Straits of Dover.[56] He could not depend on air reconnaissance at night to tell him of enemy whereabouts, but he could hope for sufficient warning by daylight if the weather were fair. Since it would take the

German ships some fourteen hours to pass up Channel and through the Straits and the southern North Sea, it seemed certain to Ramsay that the enemy would time their arrival in the Dover Strait during darkness within two hours of high water, making use also of the maximum hours of darkness for their passage up Channel. He could expect that shore-based radar would give first warning of the enemy's presence when the German ships were south-west of Cap Gris Nez – about one hour's steaming from the Straits. He therefore decided that his sea and air forces must be brought to immediate notice every night for a period straddling high water at Dover. However, he appreciated on 11 February that for the next three days the times of high water were 'unsuitable in that it requires a daylight passage of the Channel or a daylight passage of the Strait'.[57]

Ramsay's plan was to launch combined attacks by Swordfish and motor torpedo boats in the Straits, in order to cripple the enemy while he was within range of British shore batteries and radar; and later to launch a destroyer attack beyond the Strait to the eastward where the destroyers would have freedom of manoeuvre unconstrained by British minefields or enemy shore batteries. Meanwhile aircraft of Bomber and Coastal Commands under fighter cover were to bomb the enemy as heavily as possible. If the enemy chose to pass the Straits by night in moonlight he was to be attacked by the six Swordfish operating as a squadron, but if during a dark period, by them singly, directed on to the target by the Royal Air Force Controller at Swingate; the target itself being lit by flares dropped by Hurricanes.

These British contingency plans were flawed by one basic miscalculation. For the German naval command did not intend the three ships to approach and run through the Straits of Dover under cover of night, but in full daylight. They reckoned that it was more important to conceal the ships' departure from Brest than their passage through the Straits, on the grounds that the Home Fleet at Scapa, if promptly alerted to the squadron's sailing, would have time to intercept it off Terschelling.

The German plan was as bold and the German arrangements were as comprehensive and effective as those of 'Operation Weserübung' back in April 1940. With the fate of the *Prince of Wales* and *Repulse* much in their minds, the Germans well appreciated the risk the *Scharnhorst* and *Gneisenau* would take in steaming for about eleven daylight hours within never more than 200 miles of London and mostly within a very short flying time of British airbases. The Luftwaffe's Third Air Fleet (Field-Marshal Hugo Sperrle) in northern France was therefore to maintain a continuous patrol of sixteen fighters over the ships during the hours of daylight, with further reserves on standby to intervene if needed. Diversionary raids were to be launched on Portsmouth and on British ships just as the operation began. Three E-boat (fast torpedo boat or '*S-boot*') flotillas and three torpedo boat ('*T-boot*') flotillas were to rendezvous with the heavy ships off Cap Gris Nez and screen them during the most dangerous passage. The ships were to sail from Brest at 1930 (BST: British Summer Time – one hour ahead of Greenwich Mean Time) on 11 February, four days before the new moon, and pass the Straits of Dover at 25 knots at about 1130 the next forenoon.

At 2245 on 11 February 1942 the *Scharnhorst* (flying the flag of Admiral O. Ciliax), *Gneisenau*, *Prinz Eugen* and six destroyers cleared the Brest net barrage at 17 knots. At 2343 Ciliax increased to 27 knots on reaching the open sea. Astern of him Bomber Command was ferociously bombing the now empty berths in Brest. Neither Enigma nor other Intelligence sources had revealed to the British the actual time and date of the German departure, or that it had taken place.[58]

Nevertheless Coastal Command had that evening mounted its regular patrol over the Western English Channel of two Hudsons equipped with airborne radar, which might have been expected to pick up the German squadron. Unfortunately the radar set of the first Hudson, which was searching the Brest area itself, broke down owing to mechanical failure. Although the crew reported this at 2113 before returning to base, no relief aircraft was despatched. The radar of the second Hudson, cruising later that evening between Ushant and the Ile de Bréhat, also broke down.[59] Regrettably no one made sure that the news of these breakdowns was passed to Vice-Admiral, Dover.

Owing, then, to a double failure of British technology, Ciliax's squadron steamed eastwards through the night entirely undetected. A dawn air search by two Spitfires as far west as Fécamp missed it too. At 0700 on 12 February the air and sea forces at the disposal of Vice-Admiral, Dover, having been at fifteen minutes' alert from 0400, reverted to four hours' readiness. Meanwhile thick snow on Norfolk airfields had prevented the planned southward transfer of fourteen Fleet Air Arm Beaufort torpedo-bombers from the Scottish station of Leuchars. The German squadron steamed on unscathed for the Dover Straits at 27 knots, the big ships' clipper bows cleaving through a slight to moderate sea, the wind astern, Force 4, the visibility some three to five miles, Messerschmitt 109s circling protectively overhead. By 1000 the British command was reckoning that, as the Naval Staff History puts it, 'the prospect of an enemy break-through had become unlikely'.[60]

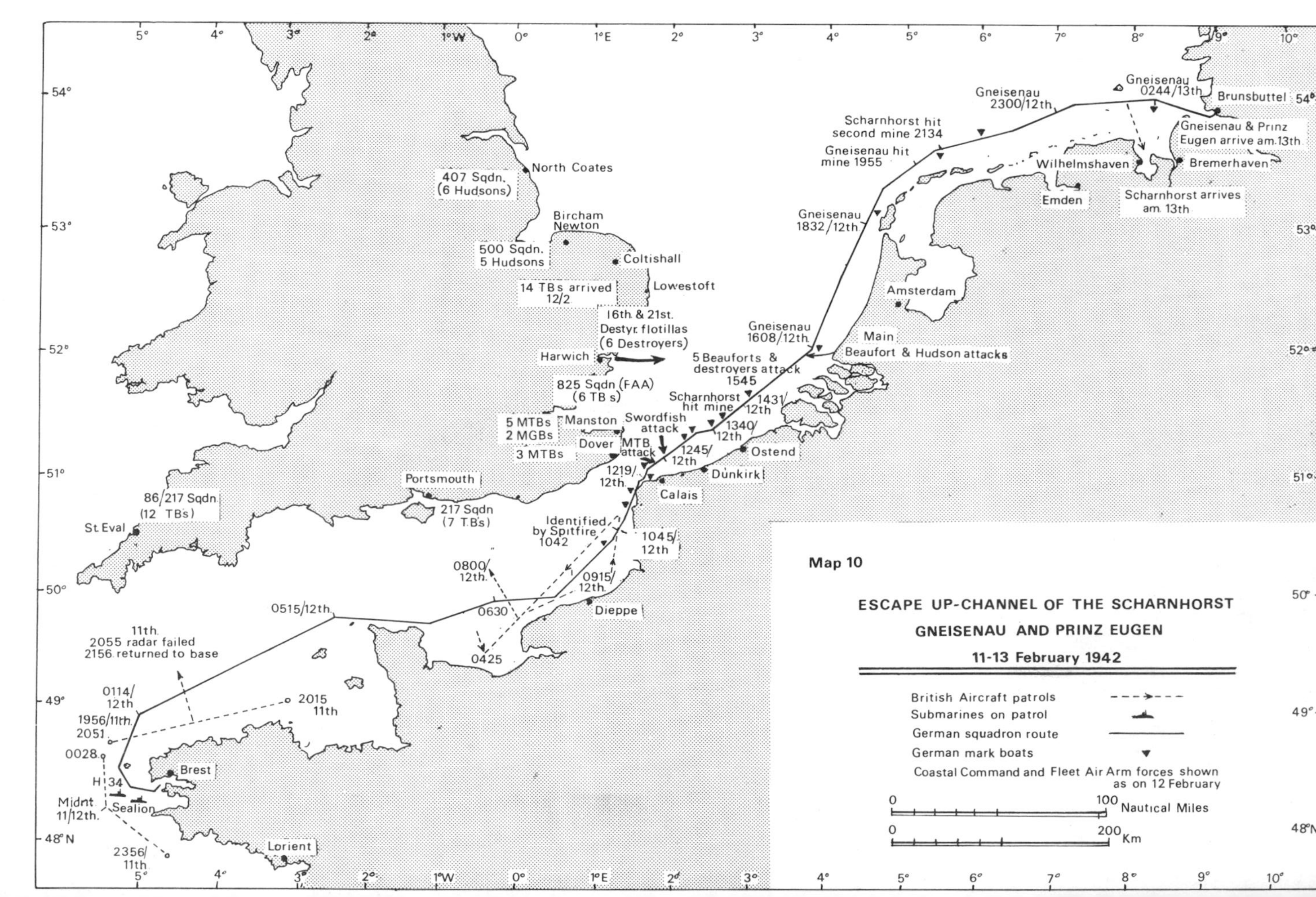

Map 10
ESCAPE UP-CHANNEL OF THE SCHARNHORST
GNEISENAU AND PRINZ EUGEN
11-13 February 1942
British Aircraft patrols
Submarines on patrol
German squadron route
German mark boats
Coastal Command and Fleet Air Arm forces shown as on 12 February
0 100 Nautical Miles
0 200 Km
North Coates
407 Sqdn. (6 Hudsons)
Bircham Newton
500 Sqdn. 5 Hudsons
Coltishall
Lowestoft
14 TBs arrived 12/2
16th & 21st. Destyr. flotillas (6 Destroyers)
Harwich
825 Sqdn (FAA) (6 TB s)
5 MTBs 2 MGBs
Manston
Dover
3 MTBs
Swordfish attack
MTB attack
Portsmouth
217 Sqdn (7 T.B's)
86/217 Sqdn (12 TB's)
St Eval
Gneisenau 0244/13th
Brunsbuttel
Gneisenau 2300/12th
Scharnhorst hit second mine 2134
Gneisenau hit mine 1955
Gneisenau & Prinz Eugen arrive am.13th
Wilhelmshaven
Bremerhaven
Emden
Scharnhorst arrives am. 13th
Gneisenau 1832/12th
Amsterdam
Gneisenau 1608/12th
Main Beaufort & Hudson attacks
5 Beauforts & destroyers attack 1545
Scharnhorst hit mine
1431/ 12th
1340/ 12th
1245/ 12th
Ostend
Dunkirk
1219/ 12th
Calais
Identified by Spitfire 1042
1045/ 12th
0800/ 12th
0915/ 12th
0630
Dieppe
0515/12th
0425
11th 2055 radar failed 2156 returned to base
0114/ 12th
2015 11th
1956/11th
2051
0028
Brest
H 34
Midnt. 11/12th.
Sealion
2356/ 11th
Lorient

Then, at 1045, shore-based radar picked up a group of shipping 27 miles south-west of Cap Gris Nez, whereupon reconnaissance aircraft from No. 16 Group, Coastal Command, and No. 11 Group, Fighter Command, were alerted for take-off. The Swordfish crews of 825 Squadron Fleet Air Arm at Manston in Kent were brought to immediate readiness and the aircraft loaded with torpedoes set to run deep; the Beaufort torpedo-bombers of No. 16 Group, Coastal Command, likewise. At 1050 reconnaissance aircraft of Fighter Command's No. 11 Group reported sighting a cluster of 25 to 30 vessels, but made no mention of the presence of the German heavy ships or the *Prinz Eugen*. At long last at 1105 Group Captain F. V. Beamish of No. 11 Group positively identified them, reporting the fact on landing four minutes later.

But it now took nineteen minutes for this desperately urgent information to pass up through No. 11 Group to Fighter Command headquarters, across to the Admiralty and then back down to Ramsay's headquarters in Dover. And by the time that Beamish sighted the enemy ships, they were already only six miles west of Boulogne, and no more than an hour's steaming from the Dover narrows. For Ramsay and the rest of the British sea and air commands the enemy's sudden appearance came, writes the Naval Staff History with some understatement, 'as an unpleasant surprise'.[61] The British response now necessarily took the form of a scramble against time to implement the long-agreed contingency plans. At 1145 Ramsay made the first of eight emergency signals alerting the British forces to the fact that the German ships were now passing Boulogne at about 20 knots, and giving updates on their progress.[62]

At 1156 Ciliax rounded Cap Gris Nez and began to enter the Straits proper, ordering his destroyers to lay a smoke screen between him and the English coast. At 1210 British shore batteries along the famous white cliffs opened fire at maximum range. At 1245 they ceased fire, having discharged 33 rounds without scoring a hit. By now Ciliax was clear of the narrow neck between Dover and Calais.

Between 1230 and 1245 Ramsay launched simultaneous attacks with his five motor torpedo boats and the six Fleet Air Arm Swordfish. The MTB attack (led by Lieutenant-Commander E. N. Pumphrey, RN) proved another poor advertisement for British technology, this time with regard to the design and manufacture of fast motor boats, for the engines in two of them broke down, while according to Admiral Ramsay later, their best speed as well as their armaments were outclassed by those of the German E-boats.[63] For all the determination of their crews, the attempt to press home the attack to killing range was thwarted by the E-boat screen and by a well-directed fire from the German destroyers.[64] It did not help that there also occurred torpedo misfires.

The six Swordfish proved no more effective. It had been arranged that they should be protected by five squadrons of Fighter Command. At 1220 Wing-Commander J. Constable-Roberts, Air Staff Officer at Ramsay's headquarters, despatched the Swordfish because the German ships had increased to 27 knots. He was counting on the assurances of No. 11 Group, Fighter Command, that, as arranged, full fighter cover and anti-flak aircraft would be rendezvousing by now over Manston. But No. 11 Group only 'believed' that this was the case: it had in fact no accurate plot or information about the location of its aircraft, which in the event failed to turn up over Manston at 1125 as agreed.[65] At 1228 Lieutenant-Commander E. Esmonde, RN, commanding the six Swordfish of 825 Squadron, decided to fly on to attack the German ships even though only one squadron of ten Spitfires had joined him. He did so because he judged that the opportunity to attack the enemy in the Straits was so fleeting that he dare not hang about for the missing fighters. As Ramsay was to write in his report, the lack of the planned fighter cover was 'a major tragedy'.[66]

The first sub-flight of Swordfish was led by Esmonde himself, the second by Lieutenant J. C. Thompson, RN. Ten minutes out to sea from Dover they were jumped by a mass of Messerschmitt 109s and Focke-Wulf 190s which got through the outnumbered Spitfire screen and succeeded in damaging every aircraft in Esmonde's sub-flight and probably some of Thompson's as well. Undaunted, Esmonde led his squadron in towards the German squadron at around 50 feet in steady level flight, heading through the smoke and over the destroyer and E-boat screen into the winking flashes of the heavy ships' anti-aircraft fire. By this time the lower port wing of Esmonde's own Swordfish had been almost completely shot away, and yet the sturdy old biplane still flew. Some 3,000 yards from the German ships Esmonde was finally shot down by the storm of anti-aircraft fire; it is not known whether he succeeded in dropping his torpedo. He was awarded a posthumous Victoria Cross. Despite grave damage, the second Swordfish dropped its load at 3,000 yards, then crashed into the sea. Its crew were rescued by British MTBs. The third aircraft got in as close as 2,000 yards, even though the pilot (Sub-Lieutenant Rose, RN) had been badly wounded in the back, before it too crashed into the sea; the crew also to be rescued by the friendly MTBs. The second sub-flight was last seen steering a steady course for the enemy;

not one of its three aircraft survived. No British torpedo struck home.[67]

This futile attack with its tragic loss of brave men offers a bitter tactical contrast with the Japanese attacks on the *Prince of Wales* and *Repulse*. In the first place the obsolete Swordfish with their top speed of 154 mph could not compare with the twin-engined Mitsubishi G3M Navy Type 96s, with their top speed of 232 mph.[68] The belatedness of pre-war rearmament coupled with the Admiralty's and Air Ministry's peacetime neglect of maritime strike aircraft had sent Esmonde and his crews into battle against a powerful enemy squadron and swarms of enemy fighters in aircraft so slow as to render them perfect practice targets for the enemy. But Esmonde's own tactical leadership has been questioned too. Why did he elect to make a long and level approach at 50 feet when he well knew how vulnerable his sluggish aircraft were, so giving the German fighter pilots and anti-aircraft gunners an absolutely predictable aiming mark? Why did he not instead dive to the attack only at the last moment, then level out to launch torpedoes, as other Fleet Air Arm leaders had successfully done against Italian ships and he himself against the *Bismarck*? Why did he not stalk his enemy through the cloud cover, jinking and weaving as he came, like the Japanese aircraft off Kuantan? To one Fleet Air Arm veteran, Commander G. A. Rotherham, the explanation may well be that Esmonde 'believed that he was on a one-way mission. A devout Catholic, he went to confession before leaving . . .'[69]

Now it was the turn of the Royal Air Force to have a shot at sinking or crippling the German ships as they steamed up the Belgian and Dutch coasts. From 1445 to 1700, no fewer than 242 aircraft of Bomber Command took to the air in the attempt. Of this vast air fleet only 39 aircraft actually managed to locate and attack the enemy through the cloud, scoring no hits and inflicting no harm. Bomber Command lost fifteen bombers shot down and twenty damaged. Between 1540 and 1710, 28 Beaufort twin-engined torpedo bombers (the first modern British aircraft of their type, only in service since 1940: maximum speed 265 mph), together with Beaufighters and Hudsons, joined in, dropping thirteen torpedoes but making no hits. Three Beauforts were lost.

This was by no means the sum total of British airpower put up that day: Fighter Command flew 398 aircraft, of which seventeen were lost. To the destroyers of the Nore Command, operating out of Harwich to launch their own attacks on the German ships that afternoon, it seemed as if the skies above were crammed with aircraft of every shape and size – ME 109s and the occasional Beaufort at low level; Hampden and Dornier bombers and ME 110 twin-engined fighter-bombers higher up; and higher still a few four-engined Halifax heavy bombers. Also observed by the destroyer crews as taking part in this circus were Junkers 88s, Heinkel 111s, Spitfires, Wellingtons, Whirlwind fighters and Manchester twin-engined heavy bombers.[70]

While all this aerial uproar was in progress, Admiral Ciliax suffered a heart-jerking setback from another cause altogether. At 1431 his flagship struck a mine off the estuary of the River Scheldt, cutting all electric power and stopping her engines. Nevertheless her damage-control parties and engineering staff restored her to full serviceability within half an hour.[71] It was as well, because at 1517 Captain C. T. M. Pizey, RN, commanding the five destroyers from Harwich (one, HMS *Walpole*, had had to return to port with main bearing trouble), detected Ciliax's squadron by radar and steered to attack. It was now blowing hard with a heavy swell from the west, visibility about four miles, which aided the destroyers in making their approach.

At 1542 the German battleships came into sight, and Captain Pizey swung his destroyers by divisions for the final run-in. It proved yet another maritime 'charge of the Light Brigade'. The first division – *Campbell*, *Vivacious* and *Worcester* – came under accurate fire from the battleships' 11-inch main armaments, tall shell splashes straddling them again and again. Meanwhile the destroyers themselves were blazing away with their 2-pounder anti-aircraft guns at attacking German aircraft. The first division launched torpedoes at about 2,400 yards; none hit. The second division following astern – *Mackay* and *Whitshed* – launched torpedoes at 4,000 and 3,000 yards: no hits either. Meanwhile *Worcester* had been badly damaged by German fire, although she was eventually able to crawl back to Harwich.

Again unscathed, Admiral Ciliax steamed on. Pizey's gallant but vain attack offers another sour comment on the legacy of past national neglect. All his ships were of Great War design, and were completely outclassed in size (four of them some 1,000 tons displacement; two of them 1,500 tons) and armament (four with four 4-inch guns; two with five 4.7-inch) by their modern opponents, two 'Z' class destroyers of 3,600 tons and four 5.9-inch guns, and four others of 2,400 tons and five 5-inch guns.[72] Moreover, the worn-out British ships could now only steam at a maximum of 25–30 knots as against the modern German ships' designed speed of 38 knots.[73] Their normal role indeed was that of escorting coastal convoys. That they should have been called upon to try to sink the *Scharnhorst* and *Gneisenau* behind a powerful destroyer and E-boat screen was a consequence of a combination of factors: the grossly insufficient strength in destroyers with which the Royal Navy had entered the war; the loss of 107 in action since; the delays in new construction; and the necessary apportioning of scarce modern large destroyers to fleet work or ocean escort duty.

After 1700 on 12 February 1942 Admiral Ciliax steamed tranquilly north-north-east up the Dutch coast between Maas and the Texel, the crucial and most perilous part of his voyage now successfully accomplished, his ships once again under the cover of darkness. However, by an irony it was during this last lap to German ports that later that evening he sustained his worst setback, for the *Gneisenau* hit a mine off Vlieland at 1955 and the *Scharnhorst* (which had become separated) another mine in the same area at 2134; both mines having been dropped earlier by Bomber Command in its only useful contribution to the day. The *Gneisenau* suffered only minor damage and was able to steam on at 25 knots in company with *Prinz Eugen*, reaching the mouth of the Elbe at 0700 on 13 February. But the *Scharnhorst*, her engines stopped, was helplessly drifting. It was not until 2223 that her repair parties got two out of her three engines working again, and she began to limp at 12 knots towards Wilhelmshaven and safety with 1,000 tons of water sloshing about below and her turret training gear out of action.

That Bomber Command during the night of 26–27 February hit *Gneisenau* in dock at Kiel with a heavy bomb which burned her out to a useless hulk did nothing to assuage British anger and disquiet at the failure of the Royal Navy and Royal Air Force to prevent the passage of the German ships through the Channel. The cheek of it! *The Times* compared the successful Ciliax to the failed Duke of Medina Sidonia in 1588, and reckoned that this was the most mortifying affront to the pride of British seapower in home waters since the Dutch came up the Medway in 1666.[74] The government appointed a Board of Enquiry under Mr Justice Bucknill whose findings were not published until 1946;[75] and the Air Ministry requested the AOCs-in-C of its three Commands to examine the question of coordination of joint operations and make appropriate recommendations. The Bucknill Enquiry found – how could it find otherwise? – that liaison arrangements between the Royal Air Force and the Royal Navy and within each service had simply not been up to mounting a successful joint air and sea offensive operation. It noted that the training of Bomber Command, being concentrated on area bombing of German cities by night, was 'not designed for effective attack on fast-moving warships by day'.[76]

In point of fact this want of training for operations over the sea also made it even harder for Bomber Command crews to find ships in the first place and then tell friend from foe than for Coastal Command or Fleet Air Arm crews. The Harwich Force had endured some nasty moments thanks to Bomber Command during that afternoon of 12 February, and hence had good reason to be grateful for the bombers' lack of accuracy. But, to be fair, Coastal Command Beauforts also aimed a torpedo or two at the Harwich destroyers, while Fighter Command Spitfires for their part failed to locate the German squadron early in daylight on the 12th, and later, having sighted a group of ships off Cap Gris Nez, failed to identify the presence of the two battleships.

The truth is that this episode, taken as a whole, serves as an indictment of the entire British development of airpower in relation to maritime war since the founding of the Royal Air Force as an independent arm in 1918 at the expense of the old Royal Naval Air Service. On the one hand there was the under-strength and under-equipped (especially in modern strike aircraft) Coastal Command and Fleet Air Arm. On the other there was the ever-increasing force of medium and heavy bombers which, together with a powerful home fighter force, the Air Staff cherished as the foundation of its historic claim that 'airpower' was an independent entity necessarily to be wielded by central control, and capable of being switched at will from strategic bombing to operations over the sea. Yet in fact, as the passage of *Scharnhorst* and *Gneisenau* demonstrated, the belief in the all-purpose versatility of such an independent air force was fallacious, because maritime operations (and for that matter the tactical support of armies) demanded rigorous specialised training and carefully worked out tactics and integrated inter-service command and control systems.

The contrast between the sprawling organisational confusion and feeble efforts of British air operations only a few miles from the British home base itself against the two German battleships and the lethal attack on *Prince of Wales* and *Repulse* by the highly trained and specialised Japanese shore-based Naval Air Force at a range of 400 miles from advanced airfields themselves thousands of miles from Japan could not have been more glaring. How might the day of 12 February 1942 have gone if the old Royal Naval Air Service had not been abolished in 1918?

But the air staff's fallacy that airpower was an independent entity fulfilling itself through the heavy bomber had long been also exercising a just as baneful but much more dangerous effect on the Atlantic war of attrition against the U-boat. In consequence one of the two dominant themes of the Atlantic war during 1942 lay in what the First Sea Lord laconically dubbed at the time 'The Battle of the Air' – a prolonged bombardment and counter-bombardment of heavy memoranda between the Admiralty and the Air Ministry, fierce duels of debate in committee, and Jove-like – or perhaps Solomon-like – interventions by the Prime Minister.

In December 1941 total merchant shipping losses in the North *and* South Atlantic stood at a mere 56,957 tons. In July 1942, after the U-boats' 'happy time' off America and in the Caribbean had been brought to an end by convoy and Dönitz had resumed his old offensive against the main trans-Atlantic shipping route, they rose to a dreadful 513,937 tons.[77] In August the figure rose even higher to 543,920 tons, confirming that the July total was no freak; confirming too that Dönitz could now achieve devastating results even without benefit of a 'happy time'. It marked an astounding and unlooked for reversal of the position at the turn of the year when Dönitz was confessing to gloom and defeat, and the Allies were congratulating themselves that the U-boat had been largely mastered. The reversal had stemmed not from a major change in the balance of strength, armament or fighting tactics at sea, but from a victory and a defeat in the secret competition between the code-breakers of Bletchley Park and the B-Dienst for the priceless ability to read the other side's naval cyphers; the second dominant theme of the Atlantic struggle in 1942.[78]

In September 1941 B-Dienst had begun to read the main Royal Navy cypher (Naval Cypher No. 2) with an ease and speed it had not enjoyed since August 1940. In December 1941 it also began to read a special cypher (Naval Cypher No. 3) which the Admiralty had provided the previous summer for joint Allied communications in the Atlantic. Finally, in February 1942 B-Dienst completed a full reconstruction of Cypher No. 3, in which was sent most Allied signals relating to Atlantic convoy traffic. Henceforward until June 1943 and with only two short interruptions, B-Dienst was to provide Dönitz's U-boat Command with as much as 80 per cent of Allied signals about convoy movements, sometimes giving ten or twenty hours' notice of forthcoming route changes.[79] It was as if a ghostly enemy admiral were present in the Operations Room of Western Approaches Command monitoring the Allies' most secret decisions.

At almost the same moment German counter-measures made to disappear from the bunker of U-boat Command an equivalent spectral British admiral who, thanks to Ultra decrypts of the German naval

Enigma, had bent over the chart table with Dönitz during much of 1941. Although Dönitz and his experts never came to suspect that the Enigma itself had been broken, they had embarked in November 1941 on ever more elaborate coding of operational instructions to U-boats before they were even encyphered on Enigma. As the official historian of British Intelligence in the Second World War, Professor Sir Harry Hinsley, describes:

> The new system was one by which the Christian name, surname and address of an imaginary person indicated the table that was in use at any one time for encoding the large square digraphs of the [standard North Atlantic] grid. By informing the U-boats that a new address was in force, the U-boat Command could bring a new set of digraph equivalents into use at once at frequent intervals; and since it did frequently change addresses, the problem of decoding the positions given in the Enigma signal was to resist systematisation and to require continuous ad hoc research until a copy of the address book was captured from U-505 in June 1944.[80]

This made it hard enough for Bletchley Park. But then, and far worse, on 1 February 1942 U-boat Command began to make use of a fourth wheel on their Enigma machines, so immensely multiplying the complexity of the electro-mechanical encyphering; and all at once Ultra went blind. On 9 February the Tracking Room in the Admiralty Operational Intelligence Centre in its first weekly U-boat situation report since the addition of the fourth Enigma wheel acknowledged that 'since the end of January no Special Information has been available about any U-boats other than those controlled by Admiral Norway'. It went on to add: 'Inevitably the picture of Atlantic dispositions is by now out of focus and little can be said with any confidence in estimating the present and future movement of the U-boats.'[81]

Although British Intelligence had by now accumulated a vast amount of knowledge about how U-boats and U-boat Command operated, and could still draw on other sources of information such as the Secret Intelligence Service or the unaltered German Home Waters Enigma (for U-boat movements in the Bay of Biscay or off Norway), it still remained true that from now on it would be impossible for Bletchley Park and the Operational Intelligence Centre to make accurate and up-to-date plots of U-boat deployments or anticipate their tactical movements in the Atlantic. This meant that no longer could convoys be steered clear of ambushing wolf packs. It was the more worrying for the Admiralty that this crippling setback occurred just as U-boat numbers began to rise steeply, from a daily average of 22 at sea in the Atlantic in January 1942 to 86 in August.[82]

Because Ultra had been blinded, airpower assumed an even greater, indeed decisive, importance in the Battle of the Atlantic – in the flying of protective patrols over convoys, in searching for and destroying U-boats in concert with escort ships; above all, in the form of Very Long Range (VLR) aircraft to cover the present mid-Atlantic air gap where around a third of all convoy losses occurred. And it was exactly the Admiralty's urgent need for a greater Royal Air Force effort against the U-boat, and especially for the deployment of more VLR aircraft, that fuelled the 1942 'Battle of the Air'.

15

'The Battle of the Air', 1942

There was, of course, no novelty in an anguished plea for more aircraft over the sea. Not only the Admiralty itself but also Air Marshal Sir Frederick Bowhill, AOC-in-C, Coastal Command, until May 1941, had constantly pressed the Air Ministry since the beginning of the war to divert more resources to the maritime war. Bowhill's successor, Air Marshal Sir Philip Joubert de la Ferté, a man whose distinguished appearance and brilliant personality (not untinged with arrogance) matched the splendour of his surname, had sent two powerful letters on 4 July 1941 to the Chief of Air Staff and on 5 September to the Air Ministry calling for Bomber Command to smash up the U-boat bases on the French Atlantic coast while they were still being built. He was crushingly snubbed by the Air Ministry, whose highest body, the Air Council, wrote to the Chief of Air Staff:

> It considered that the AOC-in-C, Coastal Command, in common with the Admiralty, had overlooked the long-term indirect contribution which the bomber offensive had made and was still making to our security at sea by attacks, not only on the main German ports, but on the German industrial effort as a whole . . . The Air Ministry had accepted that the bomber force should support the naval strategy more directly when the Battle of the Atlantic was in its earlier and critical stage but there seemed no justification whatever for a return to this defensive strategy now when conditions at sea had so much improved and we were beginning to develop fully the air offensive to which we must look for winning as opposed to not losing the war.[1]

So the Todt Organisation had been left in tranquillity to complete the giant U-boat pens under their bomb-proof carapaces of reinforced concrete from which Dönitz's crews were to mount their 1942 offensive. Meanwhile all new deliveries of long-range aircraft were going to Bomber Command (to which in autumn 1941 Churchill had even suggested transferring some Coastal Command aircraft), and Coastal Command entered 1942 with only an average of 156 aircraft of all kinds available for service on any day out of a total strength of 505; a proportion that bore witness to a poor maintenance organisation, it has to be said. The Air Staff had actually even come to believe that too much of Bomber Command's effort was already being diverted from German cities to such fringe activities as attacking the *Scharnhorst* and *Gneisenau* in Brest. They itched to concentrate all their bombers on the task of, as they believed, winning the war. On 9 February 1942 (two days before these ships sailed from Brest) their case was put forward by the Secretary of State for Air, Sir Archibald Sinclair, in a memorandum entitled 'Bombing Policy'.[2] Here was the opening salvo in what the First Sea Lord would drily call 'the Battle of the Air'.

The airmen's fire was quickly returned by the First Sea Lord, who pronounced himself all in favour of the bomber offensive 'provided certain limited naval requirements are met'. He proceeded to put in orders for six and a half squadrons of Wellingtons (to be transferred from Bomber Command to Coastal Command) and for 81 American-built Flying Fortresses or Liberators to cover the mid-Atlantic air gap.[3] Since U-boats were now being built at a rate of twenty a month, the Admiralty wanted an air offensive to be mounted in the whole Bay of Biscay area by day and night, coupled with more patrols over the North Atlantic. In this regard the Admiralty noted that aircraft fitted with ASV (anti-submarine radar) and shallow-setting depth-charges with a powerful new explosive, Torpex, were at last available.

Joubert, by the nature of his job a 'navy-blue' airman, sided with the Admiralty, telling the Air Ministry on 19 February:

> . . . the prospect of Coastal Command being able to work at reasonable efficiency appeared to be becoming more and more remote. The promise of centrimetric ASV fitted Liberators had come to nothing, the one Liberator squadron was being allowed to die out and there had been a continuous change of policy with regard to this long-range aircraft.[4]

Joubert was even so blasphemous as to challenge his superiors on the fundamentals of Air Staff theology ('Theos' being the heavy bomber):

> While fully aware of the importance of the sustained bomber offensive, it

> appeared to him that, if England was to survive this year, in which we were already losing shipping at a rate considerably in excess of American and British building output, some part of bomber offensive would have to be sacrificed and a long-range type such as the Lancaster diverted to the immediate threat on our Sea Communications.[5]

The Chief of Air Staff, Air Chief Marshal Sir Charles Portal, answered to the effect that the Americans would be cross if their Liberator aircraft were diverted from bombing, while he, Portal, was strongly opposed to transferring Lancasters as they were the only aircraft that could carry 8,000 lbs of bombs to Berlin.[6]

On 5 March the First Sea Lord, after much indignant internal discussion and memoranda within the Admiralty, slammed before the Cabinet Defence Committee a statement of 'Air Requirements for the Successful Prosecution of the War at Sea'. This statement, like Joubert's, went to the heart of the matter:

> If we lose the war at sea we lose the war.
>
> We lose the war at sea when we can no longer maintain those communications which are essential to us . . .[7]

The First Sea Lord went on to explain that this could happen either by 'reduction of our Merchant ship tonnage generally to such an extent that it can no longer bring us the minimum of essential supplies', or 'reduction of our Tanker tonnage to a degree which will seriously immobilise our armed forces'. In the face of the U-boat, therefore, 'we must provide the necessary shore-based aircraft for the adequate protection of our convoys and shipping'.[8] This time Pound widened the Admiralty's claims from a mere request for more airpower over the sea to a demand for control of such airpower in all theatres of war: 'If we are not to conduct the war at sea at a disadvantage we must have naval operational control of all aircraft employed on sea operations, on lines similar to those now in force with the Coastal Command in Home waters.'[9]

Moreover, he also wanted the Royal Navy to be 'intimately associated with the training in sea operations of personnel of Coastal Command aircraft'.[10] To this statement was appended another shopping list of the Admiralty's global requirements for shore-based air support, amounting to a total of 1,940 aircraft, of which 900 were needed in home waters and the Atlantic, as against Coastal Command's present strength of 519.[11]

Now it was the Air Staff's turn, through the Secretary of State for Air, to lobby the Defence Committee. In their memorandum,

'Requirements in Long-Range General Reconnaissance Aircraft'[12] they argued that

> ... our experience clearly proved that Long-Range General-Reconnaissance duties can only be usefully undertaken by aircraft fitted with A.S.V. The installation of this equipment is a lengthy process and no squadrons of Bomber Command could be modified and put into service for some months. By this time the planned expansion of Coastal Command in Long-Range G/R aircraft will already have made good the present weakness. The transfer of bomber squadrons from Bomber Command without the necessary modification would be a dispersion of our bomber resources in an attempt to contribute defensively to the control of sea communications over immense areas of ocean where the targets are uncertain, fleeting and difficult to hit ...

With tactical adroitness the memorandum did acknowledge: 'Nevertheless it is clearly encumbent on us in the Air Ministry to do our utmost to meet Admiralty requirement as expeditiously as possible ...'

Even so, and although the Air Staff had to admit that there would be no substantial improvement in Coastal Command's resources until the second half of the year, and that up to June the Command 'will be seriously under-strength in Long-Range reconnaissance aircraft',[13] it refused to transfer four Wellington squadrons from Bomber Command. In its view they were better employed over Germany. Though Coastal Command was to receive some radar-fitted flying boats, they too would only come into service between May and December. So all that the Air Staff would offer at present was a loan of one Whitley squadron (to be equipped with ASV) from Bomber Command. For the Air Staff's faith in the bomber offensive as a strategic cure-all remained unshaken:

> It remains the opinion of the Air Staff that squadrons of Bomber Command could best contribute to the weakening of the U-boat offensive by offensive action against the principal industrial areas of Germany within our range, including the main naval industries and dockyards. To divert them to an uneconomical defensive role would be unsound at any time. It would be doubly so now when we are about to launch a bombing offensive of which we have high expectations and which will enable us to deliver a heavy and concentrated blow against Germany when German morale is low and when the Russians are in great need of our assistance.[14]

The protagonists clashed in person when these papers were debated by the War Cabinet Defence Committee on 18 March,[15] Portal and

Pound arguing the toss over such matters as whether or not the Wellington had sufficient range to patrol the outer Bay of Biscay area. Portal then came to the heart of the matter – as the Air Staff perceived it:

> If the Admiralty demands were met, it would mean a considerable reduction in the strength of Bomber Command. The question was whether the war effort would be best assisted, and the maximum help to Russia given, by maintaining the maximum offensive against Germany or by diverting resources to defensive patrolling over the sea.[16]

When Portal offered the loan of two Whitley squadrons, Pound observed that two squadrons would be 'of little value';[17] he wanted a large area of the sea covered by patrols, otherwise the plan 'would fall to the ground'. After Portal had glumly remarked that this would involve 'a very great air effort', the Prime Minister intervened to say that he did not see how we could expect to patrol large areas by day and night. The only upshot of the meeting was that the Chief of Air Staff and the First Sea Lord were asked to make further proposals.[18]

By now the Army, in the person of the Chief of the Imperial General Staff, Sir Alan Brooke (who replaced Dill on Christmas Day 1941), had joined in the battle, for the Army was no less angry and anxious than the Navy about what it saw as the often ineffective and grudging air support provided by the Royal Air Force. In fact the Army and the Royal Navy were now essentially proposing that the Royal Air Force be reorganised so as to provide air forces in every theatre dedicated to land and sea operations and under military and naval control.[19] As the Chief of Air Staff bitterly pointed out in a paper on 1 April these proposals meant 'in substance if not in name the division of the Air Force into three separate services':[20] in other words, a return to the pre-1918 position.

The Chief of Air Staff now defended the present organisation of the Royal Air Force on the same grounds that the airmen of 1918 had justified its original creation – the theoretical indivisibility of airpower:

> With the help of the United States of America we are well placed to subject the Axis powers to the full rigour of an overwhelming air superiority which will be decisive in the struggle ahead. To achieve this the Royal Air Force must be held together. If we now split it up we shall at best delay victory; at worst it may elude our grasp.[21]

And again:

> The first principle of air warfare is to concentrate the maximum air

> strength on whatever task may be of decisive importance at the time . . . Only a flexible force, under commanders whose profession is air warfare, can offer the full assistance required [by the Army and Navy] . . .[22]

The Chief of Air Staff left little doubt as to what he personally thought constituted airpower's decisively important task, arguing that the Army's and Navy's demands for aircraft would 'automatically extinguish any hope of development of that Bomber offensive which has been postulated by the British and American Chiefs of Staff as one of the essential measures for winning the war as opposed merely to not losing it'.[23]

These exchanges marked only the beginning of the 'Battle of the Air', in which for the rest of 1942 each side's case was again and again re-spliced for further use. The First Sea Lord's files for 1942 bulge with elaborately detailed draft answers to specific points either made by the air staff or thought likely to be made by it.[24] But at the core of it all lay a simple strategic equation. Britain, an island seapower of relatively small population, had not been able to engage the German Army in the West in battle since the collapse of the Western Front in 1940. She had therefore clutched at the promise of victory through the destruction of the German industrial economy by bombing. In 1942 Bomber Command believed itself at last ready and equipped to achieve this. In reverse, Germany, a continental land power, had always lacked the means directly to attack and conquer Britain, as evidenced by the abandonment of 'Operation Sealion' in 1940. She had therefore also resorted to an attempt to bring about the collapse of her enemy's economy – in her case by means of the U-boat. Thus in 1942 Germany and Britain were each pursuing the same basic strategy against one another. The difference lay in the effectiveness of the means the two opponents were employing.

By the beginning of 1942 Dönitz's handful of operational U-boats had already inflicted enormous cumulative loss on British shipping and for a period in mid-1941 caused the British government to wonder if Britain could indeed survive (see above, Chapter 9). In 1942 his boats, still only a fraction of the German war effort even though their total number was now gradually rising towards 400, were sinking an average of 450,000 tons of shipping a month in the North Atlantic, including more oil tankers than were being built. To the British government it seemed increasingly evident that, as things stood, Dönitz was well on his way to achieving decisive victory in the Atlantic and with it the collapse of the British economy. As Churchill wrote on 24 October: 'There preys upon us as the greatest danger to the

United Nations [as the Allied countries were now collectively called], and particularly to our Island, the U-boat attack.'[25]

No such comparable peril to the German war economy was resulting from Bomber Command's efforts in 1942, even though Bomber Command and the colossal industries that supported it were engrossing a major slice of British national resources. Unkind critics pointed this out at the time – even casting doubt as to whether Bomber Command at its future point of greatest expansion could actually bring about the promised collapse of the German industrial machine. True, Lord Cherwell (the Prime Minister's personal scientific adviser, and a man whose wartime record shows him to have been more often wrong than right) was convinced that German industry would stop if the roofs were removed from workers' dwellings.[26] But in a report in April 1942 Sir Henry Tizard, a far more able scientist, demolished Cherwell's fallacious mathematical calculations and concluded that 'a policy of bombing German towns wholesale in order to destroy dwellings cannot have a decisive effect by the middle of 1943, even if all the heavy bombers and the great majority of Wellingtons produced are used primarily for this purpose'.[27]

His conclusion was endorsed by Mr Justice Singleton, appointed by the War Cabinet on 16 April 1942 to answer the question: 'What results are we likely to achieve from continuing our air attacks on Germany at the greatest possible strength during the next 6, 12 and 18 months respectively?'[28] The Judge pronounced on 20 May after pondering the evidence: 'I do not think it [the bomber offensive] ought to be regarded *as of itself* sufficient to win the war or to produce decisive results; the area is too vast for the effort we can put forth . . .'[29] In particular, he did not think that 'great results can be hoped for within six months from "air attacks on Germany at the greatest possible strength . . ." '[30] In fact post-war calculations by the British Bombing Survey Unit using German data estimated that in 1942 bombing reduced German war production by only 0.5 per cent.[31]

There was another aspect to this enormous discrepancy between the effectiveness of U-boat Command's attack on the British war economy in 1942 and Bomber Command's attack on the German war economy. On the information then available to Whitehall there was no likelihood whatsoever that Bomber Command could bring down Germany before U-boat Command brought down Britain. Thus, long before Bomber Command could mount its ultimate full-scale offensive its bombers would be, on present showing, grounded on their airfields because the U-boats in the Atlantic would have cut off their petrol supply.

None of these considerations, not even the last, were to weigh with the air staff, let alone with the new AOC-in-C of Bomber Command, Air Marshal Sir Arthur Harris, for these were men of faith, true to the gospel according to Trenchard. Naturally the reverse was true of the Admiralty, watching with something near to horror the monthly statistics (the accuracy and implications of which no one could question) of shipping losses in the Atlantic. Despite the April decision of the Chiefs of Staff that eight Liberator aircraft and four squadrons of Wellingtons and Whitleys must be lent to Coastal Command, the tonnage of merchant ships sunk in the Atlantic in May reached a staggering 585,431 tons.[32] No wonder a fresh statement of the Admiralty's case drafted on 10 May conveys a sense of near desperation:

> What the Admiralty press for now with all urgency is that:
> (a) The increased number of aircraft of the right type necessary to safeguard our vital sea communications should be provided.
> (b) The organisations of Bomber Command should be such that our bomber squadrons are capable of locating and attacking targets at sea with success.

And the First Sea Lord added a final paragraph to the draft in his own hand in pencil:

> (c) All types of aircraft which may be required to operate over the sea should receive such training as will enable them to do this with success.[33]

On 2 June Pound consulted his commanders-in-chief at the Admiralty. Afterwards Sir John Tovey, C-in-C, Home Fleet, recorded in a letter to the First Sea Lord the forthright views he had expressed at that meeting:

> . . . the whole strategy of the war was governed by sea communications . . . disasters had resulted and would result from our failure to protect our communications and interrupt those of the enemy. As the war progressed air co-operation had become increasingly necessary, till now the Navy could no longer carry out its much increased task without adequate air support; that support had not been forthcoming. The aircraft at the disposal of Coastal Command and of the corresponding squadrons abroad were quite inadequate to meet their commitments.[34]

Requisite air cooperation at sea meant, wrote Tovey, reducing some other air activity, and the only possible candidate lay in 'the force employed in bombing the cities of Europe':

> This force had for long enjoyed absolute priority in the design and supply of aircraft and crews and was at this time carrying out its first 1,000 bomber raids on the Ruhr. Whatever the results of the bombing of cities might be, and this was a subject of keen controversy, it could not of itself win the war, whereas the failure of our sea communications would assuredly lose it.[35]

Tovey therefore wanted Bomber Command's efforts scaled down 'enough to allow the Navy and the Army the support without which they could not play their part'. And he acidly commented: 'It was difficult to believe that the population of Cologne would notice much difference between a raid of 1,000 bombers and one by 750 . . .'[36]

Tovey concluded by reminding the First Sea Lord that he had informed the Lords Commissioners of the Admiralty that

> . . . in my opinion the situation at sea was now so grave that the time had come for a stand to be made, even if this led to Their Lordships taking the extreme step of resignation. I was supported in my contentions by Admiral of the Fleet Sir Charles Forbes and Admiral Sir Andrew Cunningham . . .[37]

Although Their Lordships were not attracted to this suggestion, it nevertheless offers proof of how deep feelings were now running in the Navy on the question of maritime airpower. Thus fortified, Pound handed a note to his fellow Chiefs of Staff at a meeting on 16 June bluntly stating that 'the present threat to our sea lines of communication, on the security of which our existence and ultimate victory depended, called for an immediate increase in the strength of the land-based air forces working with the Navy . . .'[38]

But Portal, with sublime intellectual arrogance, wrote that he was not convinced that 'the peril at sea was as great as the First Sea Lord argued'.[39] He comfortably assumed that the figures 'show that sinkings should be overtaken by new construction later this year'. Hence before a decision was taken to increase land-based air forces supporting the Navy 'our shipping position should be examined to ascertain whether our position was sufficiently serious to warrant further reduction of our bomber offensive'.[40] As it was, he found the First Sea Lord's request for more aircraft 'wholly unacceptable',[41] because in his view there was not yet sufficient evidence that the peril at sea justified what he called 'severe curtailment' of the air offensive against Germany.

He lamented that Bomber Command's operational strength had shrunk from 1,000 aircraft to 750 since the beginning of 1942 while Coastal Command's had risen from 482 to 568. It was, grumbled Portal, 'a depressing thought that after nearly three years of war so great a proportion of our effort should still be used in a defensive role (sic)'.[42]

In the absence of the Prime Minister and the CIGS in America, the Chiefs of Staff Committee chewed over the conflicting arguments again on 24 June – the month when shipping losses in the Atlantic alone reached 649,832 tons, and in all seas a truly horrifying 834,196 tons.[43] However, the Chiefs could only decide that the First Sea Lord and the Chief of Air Staff should each nominate an officer to draw up joint recommendations to the Committee on 'general policy for the employment of the air forces'.[44] These officers (Rear-Admiral E. J. P. Brind and Air Vice-Marshal J. C. Slessor, Assistant Chiefs of Naval and Air Staffs) duly reported on 2 July,[45] recommending that 54 long-range aircraft were needed for home waters, the Bay zones, the Western Approaches and for support of the Home Fleet, plus a further 72 long-range general-reconnaissance aircraft. They also recommended that two Lancaster squadrons (36 aircraft) should be transferred temporarily from Bomber Command to Coastal Command, in return for the medium bomber squadrons at present on loan.[46]

Here was essentially an endorsement of the Admiralty's case. Unsurprisingly therefore the Chief of Air Staff rejected the report out of hand. He wrote that the suggested transfer of Lancasters would only achieve results against U-boats 'at the expense of three months' work in Bomber Command'[47] where, by bombing German ports and laying mines, they would damage enemy shipping and U-boats:

> I am convinced that greater value to the war effort as a whole would be obtained from these two squadrons if they remain in Bomber Command than if they are lent to Coastal Command. I am so strongly convinced of this that I regard the loss of these two squadrons to Bomber Command as unacceptable.[48]

Instead he suggested employing Bomber Command aircraft to supplement the efforts of Coastal Command by flying thirty sorties of Whitleys and twenty sorties by Lancasters over the sea each week. The Brind–Slessor report thus died the death.

On 18 July, however, the Chiefs of Staff in reporting to the War

Cabinet on the 'Provision of Aircraft for the War at Sea' seemed after all to accept the Admiralty's case:

> . . . we have taken into account that the Navy is stretched to the limit and that shipping losses are dangerously high. These losses not only menace the import situation of the United Kingdom but absorb a high proportion of the productive capacity of the United Nations; they most seriously restrict our ability to nourish and reinforce our forces overseas, and also hamper dangerously our future strategy . . .[49]

The Chiefs therefore agreed that Bomber Command aircraft should be used to supplement Coastal Command until that Command's strength in Liberators and Flying Fortresses had been built up to 54. Whitley training aircraft from Bomber Command would be committed to long-range anti-submarine patrols, along with some Lancasters (though still under the operational command of the AOC-in-C, Bomber Command), although the latter loan was to be less at the expense of the bomber offensive than of the far more useful activity of mine-laying at sea. Yet the Chiefs of Staff acknowledged that the number of aircraft available from Bomber Command for anti-submarine operations each week would fluctuate according to training requirements and the need to pull them back whenever 'very large-scale raids' were mounted on Germany. The Royal Navy was thus placed at the mercy of Air Marshal Sir Arthur Harris's conception of weekly operational priorities. In any event the crews of the Whitley training unit (nine aircraft) were not to prove very adept at the specialised task of U-boat hunting. All this was well short of satisfying the Navy's needs.

'The Battle of the Air' was, however, far from over. The Premier decided that the compromise proposals, though to be put in hand at once, should be discussed by the Cabinet along with a paper 'Air Against the Sea'[50] submitted by S. M. Bruce, the accredited Representative of the Australian government, who sat on occasion as a member of the British War Cabinet. At the meeting on 12 August (with Clement Attlee, the Deputy Prime Minister, in the chair, Churchill being on his way to Cairo) Bruce observed that he 'was disturbed to find that we were working on the basis of providing the minimum for the task of securing our vital communications . . .'[51] He criticised the current Chiefs of Staff proposals as failing to subordinate the bomber offensive to the needs of the war at sea. But the meeting only resulted in a request to the Air Ministry for more facts and figures. All now depended on the Prime Minister descending from the clouds (quite literally, on his return from Cairo by air) to give judgment.

By this time Churchill had been got at by Air Marshal Sir Arthur Harris in a personal letter of 17 June 1942 which improperly bypassed the official chain of command. Harris was blessed with a stubborn will, high executive ability and outstanding powers of leadership. But he was so afflicted by mental tunnel vision that in regard to the wider scene of grand strategy it is fair to apply to him the epithet 'stupid'. His letter to Churchill was entirely characteristic, the pen dripping with the adrenalin of the 1,000-bomber raid on Cologne on 30 May. He assured the Prime Minister that the proper use of airpower would bring victory 'speedy and complete', and warned him against allowing that airpower to become 'inextricably implicated as a subsidiary weapon in the prosecution of vastly protracted and avoidable land and sea campaigns':[52]

> . . . The success of the 1,000 Plan has proved beyond doubt in the minds of all but wilful men that we can even today dispose of a weight of attack which no country on which it is brought to bear could survive. We can bring it to bear on the vital part of Germany. It requires only the decision to concentrate it for its proper use.[53]

In Harris's thoughtful analysis Coastal Command was 'merely an obstacle to victory'.[54]

Churchill himself no longer felt quite the same enthusiasm for the heavy bomber as he had in 1940–41 when Britain stood alone and the bomber provided the only hope of ever striking directly against Germany. But although he did not now buy Harris's views in all their extravagance, he did feel a natural affinity with the pugilism innate in them and the man behind them. On 21 July, in a survey of grand strategy,[55] Churchill tolled a bell for the Admiralty's hopes:

> . . . it would be a mistake to cast aside our original thought . . . that the severe, ruthless bombing of Germany on an ever-increasing scale will not only cripple her war effort, including U-boat and aircraft production, but will also create conditions intolerable to the mass of the German population.
>
> It is at this point that we must observe with sorrow and alarm the woeful shrinkage of our plans for bomber expansion.[56]

He firmly placed the bomber offensive as 'second only to the largest military operations which can be conducted on the Continent' as a means of breaking the German will. He therefore called for renewed intense efforts by the Allies 'to develop during the winter and onwards ever-growing, more accurate and ever more far-ranging bomber attacks on Germany . . .'[57]

Not that he ignored the Battle of the Atlantic, so long a principal care of his. If the first main fact in the war situation lay in the 'immense power' of the German war machine, he wrote, the second lay in 'seaborne tonnage. We can only get through this year by running down our stocks heavily'; on no account must stocks be so run down as to imperil 1943. Furthermore Churchill perfectly well understood the direct relationship between the Battle of the Atlantic and the bomber offensive, acutely noting that '. . . it might be true to say that the issue of the war depends on whether Hitler's U-boat attack on Allied tonnage or the increase and application of Allied air-power reach their full fruition first'.[58]

Yet despite the clear evidence that the U-boat attack was at present well ahead in this race for full fruition, Churchill still allowed 'the Battle of the Air' to drag on without a final decision, even permitting the circulation to the War Cabinet of fundamentalist tracts by Harris and old Trenchard, the still living Messiah of strategic bombing.[59] On 17 September, however, he minuted the Secretary of State for Air on the necessity of raising Bomber Command from its present 32 operating squadrons to 50 by the end of the year – two of these to come from Coastal Command.[60]

Four days later the AOC-in-C, Coastal Command, wrote to the First Sea Lord almost despairingly about the state of the anti-submarine war.[61] U-boats now completed came to 335; those in operation to 205. Twenty-two new boats were being turned out every month, but the rate of destruction 'is not better at the moment than 6/7 a month'. Joubert pointed out that 'unless some radical change in the rate of destruction takes place we are faced with an ever increasing fleet of U-boats at sea', while on the other side of the ledger:

(i) We are losing Tankers faster than we are building them.
(ii) We are losing merchant ships at the approximate rate of building, but the immense quantities of material and valuable lives lost in the sinkings are irreplaceable.
(iii) We are unable to conduct the offensives necessary for victory at the time, and on the scale, which are desirable.
(iv) The standard of living of the people of the Allied Nations is much reduced by inability to ship required raw materials and consumption goods.[62]

The 'Battle of the Air' mounted towards another climax. On 5 October the First Sea Lord submitted to the Defence Committee the weightiest naval salvo of all, entitled 'The Needs of the Navy'.[63] He set out to prove that in all respects (and not merely in regard to airpower over the sea) the Royal Navy was playing Cinderella to the Royal Air Force's privileged ugly sister. Indeed, 'The Needs of the Navy' provides a gruesome summary of the general state of British seapower three years after the outbreak of war and two decades after the Washington Treaty. Resorting to heavy black type by way of emphasis, the First Sea Lord read the lesson:

> Since the war began, we have been struggling to build up our war production potential in men, machines and material, but daily ships are sunk with finished weapons aboard, thus losing the work of weeks, and possibly months of hundreds of workmen. The sum of such losses may cost us in equipment far more than a heavy defeat in battle . . .
>
> . . . we have lost a large measure of control over our sea communications. This has already had, and is having a far-reaching effect not only on the maintenance of the United Kingdom but on our ability to take the offensive . . . in fact, we have reached the point at which we are unable to carry out concurrently those operations which the present state of the war so urgently demands.

The Royal Navy had 'much less than half' the number of fleet aircraft carriers required to achieve 'the proper balance' of Britain's main naval forces, while 'another year will elapse before the proportion of obsolescent aircraft in the aircraft carriers of the Fleet is reduced to a reasonable figure'. At present, the First Sea Lord went on, the Fleet Air Arm's aircraft were almost wholly out of date: 141 Swordfish, 66 Fulmar fighters, 112 Albacores, 42 Sea Hurricanes. Of modern types, no Barracuda torpedo-bombers had yet been delivered (production delays yet again), and no Fireflies, although 54 Seafires (an adapted Spitfire) were in service.

Turning from carriers to the humble but essential escort ships, the First Sea Lord pointed out that the number available equalled only 40 per cent of those needed, 'while the minimum target figures of shore-based aircraft agreed with the Air Ministry for operations over the sea will only be met to the extent of 75 per cent by 1st November 1942'. More than that, the present Royal Air Force programme for meeting the minimum needs of the war at sea 'will not be fulfilled until the latter half of 1943'.

The Royal Navy was also, argued Pound, Cinderella in terms of manpower and industrial resources. Its personnel numbered 500,000 as of June 1942 compared with the Army's 2,428,000 and the Royal Air Force's 833,000. The industrial labour force producing for the Navy numbered 717,000 compared with 1,245,000 in the Ministry of Aircraft Production (out of the latter total, just nine per cent were producing for the Fleet Air Arm).

'The facts outlined above,' wrote the First Sea Lord, 'lead to the inevitable conclusion that the foundation upon which the whole structure of our strategy rests is in danger.'[64] He therefore urged that industrial resources be switched to the Navy, especially in regard to the production of new aircraft, and in particular that the minimum air requirements of the war at sea as agreed by the War Cabinet back in August should be met, especially in long-range aircraft and replacement of existing types with those with longer range. And he made one final, fundamental demand – that air operations over the sea should enjoy 'priority second only to the needs of the fighter defence of the United Kingdom'.[65]

Within the Admiralty, as the Naval Staff waited for the Defence Committee to give its decision on 'The Needs of the Navy', a profound gloom prevailed. The Assistant Chief of Naval Staff (Home), Rear-Admiral Brind, wrote to the First Sea Lord on 18 October that, quite apart from the forthcoming need to provide maritime air cover for convoys in transit to the invasion of French North Africa ('Operation Torch'; see below, pp. 555–6), the Battle of the Atlantic 'continues to go against us, and we have the gap between Newfoundland and Iceland in which our convoys are at the mercy of the U-boat. At the moment the main weight of the air escort work is being carried by 17 Liberators . . .'[66] He feared that the air staff's claim of priority for the bomber meant that 'we can expect no help from Bomber Command either in the offensive against submarines, the attack on blockade breakers or even in effective attack against warships . . .' Far from accepting any reduction in Coastal Command, the ACNS (H) went on, 'it is essential that our maritime aircraft should be strongly reinforced . . .'[67]

On 24 October 1942 Churchill, in his capacity as Minister of Defence, handed down in a paper entitled 'Policy for the Conduct of the War' a fresh judgment on the rival claims of the bomber offensive and the mortal struggle against the U-boat. It was not a judgment to comfort the Royal Navy; nor one which in retrospect enhances Churchill's stature as grand strategist clear-cut in decision:

> There preys upon us as the greatest danger to the United Nations, and particularly to our Island, the U-boat attack. The Navy call for greater

> assistance from the air. I am proposing to my colleagues that we try for the present to obtain this extra assistance mainly from the United States, and that we encroach as little as possible upon our Bomber effort against Germany, which is of peculiar importance during these winter months. I have, on the contrary, asked for an increase in the Bomber effort, rising to 50 squadrons by the end of the year. Thereafter our bombing power will increase through the maturing of production. It may be that early in 1943 we shall have to damp down the Bomber offensive against Germany in order to meet the stress and peril of the U-boat war. I hope and trust not, but by then it will be possible at any rate to peg our Bomber offensive at a higher level than at present. The issue is not one of principle, but of emphasis. At present, in spite of U-boat losses, the Bomber offensive should have first place in our effort.[68]

On 30 October the Chiefs of Staff followed this up with a report on 'Anglo-American Strategy'[69] which while acknowledging the vital importance of sea communications laid the greater weight on Allied attrition of German resources and willpower. They reckoned that thanks to better accuracy and bigger bombloads strategic bombing as a means of such attrition 'is susceptible of the greatest development and holds out the most promising prospects'. They looked forward to the 'progressive destruction and dislocation of the enemy's war industrial and economic system, and undermining of his morale to a point where his capacity for armed resistance is fatally weakened . . .' The Chiefs therefore recommended that within the broad Allied strategy for eventually invading Europe the Allied bomber force 'should be expanded as rapidly as possible to a target figure of 4,000 –6,000 heavy bombers . . . by April 1944'.

This appeared to mark the Air Ministry's and the air staff's final victory over the Admiralty in the 'Battle of the Air', with all that that implied for the U-boat war. But at this point Portal committed a tactical error by putting in to the Chiefs of Staff Committee (allegedly in response to a COS request) a report[70] which spelled out in speculative statistical detail just how between 4,000 and 6,000 British and American heavy bombers could in 1944 'shatter the industrial and economic structure of Germany to a point where an Anglo-American force of reasonable strength could enter the Continent from the West'. The contribution of 58 towns to the German war effort, equalling a third of German industry, would, he asserted, be 'eliminated'. Averred the Chief of Air Staff: 'Germany is in no condition to withstand an onslaught of this character . . .'

These complacent assertions could only invite attack. This the First Sea Lord proceeded to deliver with a fearsome weight of argumentative fire. He pointed out that the present import requirements for aviation fuel (4½ million tons for all theatres, including 1¼ million tons into the United Kingdom alone) demanded the help of 154 American tankers.[71] But the bomber programme as outlined by Portal would require the import of another 5 million tons in 1944 into the United Kingdom over and above the present 1¼ million. Yet, reckoned the First Sea Lord, it was 'virtually certain' that United States tanker building could not cope with such a load unless it was 'immensely increased'. (It should be remembered here that tanker losses so far in 1942 had been huge, and that oil stocks of all kinds in the United Kingdom now stood at a worryingly low level.[72]) Pound went on to remind his colleagues of the demand for shipping space that would also be made by the requisite imports of bombs, spares, personnel and all kinds of equipment.

He therefore urged (just as he had in the spring) that the whole complex issue be referred to objective scientific and technical analysis, especially in regard to the effects of such a build-up of the bomber force on the rest of the Allied war effort. Peevishly the Chief of Air Staff rejected this suggestion, on the grounds that Lord Cherwell's opinion should be good enough.

Nonetheless the 'Battle of the Air' was in flux again after all, with the apparent unanimity of the Chiefs of Staff's decision on 30 October in favour of priority to the bomber being now revealed as a sham. On 18 November the First Sea Lord put the Royal Navy's case yet again, this time to the new Cabinet Anti-U-boat Committee.[73] He went equipped with a succinct five-page brief;[74] and he made as his central theme the need for Very Long Range aircraft to protect the North Atlantic convoys:

> We must be able to send aircraft to any threatened Transatlantic convoys. Until, and even after, Auxiliary Carriers are with all convoys we need very long range aircraft to bridge the gap between the areas which can be protected by existing aircraft.
>
> Very early action is therefore required to provide these 'very long range aircraft'. It has been estimated that at least 40 (with the necessary backing) are required, divided between Newfoundland, Iceland and Northern Ireland.[75]

He therefore proposed:

(a) As an emergency and temporary measure comb out all resources of the United Nations for Liberator I [range 2,400 miles] and Liberator II [a bomber version, range 1,800 miles]. It is understood that the latter can be converted back into Liberator I. These aircraft would not meet full requirements, but would go far towards giving the extra protection while more permanent provision is being prepared.

(b) Convert the necessary number of the most suitable bomber type into 'very long range G.R. aircraft' with an operational range of 2,500 miles with 2,000 lbs depth charge load.[76]

Pound said that the exact number of VLR aircraft could not be estimated at that stage. 'When details of the aircraft are known it can be estimated how many will be required to cover all the threatened convoys, but it is clear that the number will be small by comparison with the total production of this kind of aircraft . . .'[77] Forty VLR aircraft together with Liberator IIIs (range 1,680 miles) for 86 Squadron, Coastal Command, would enable the force available to cover North Atlantic convoys and the Bay of Biscay area to rise from the present three squadrons of Liberator IIIs to four squadrons, plus three VLR Squadrons.[78] A further squadron of LR aircraft would be wanted to escort convoys in the South-Western Approaches. Pound emphasised that 'economy in numbers of aircraft is achieved by re-equipping existing Coastal Command Squadrons with longer range aircraft. A re-equipment of Squadrons is required rather than an increase.'[79]

The First Sea Lord's brief summarises with heavy emphasis what the entire 'Battle of the Air' had been about – the switching of just 40 suitable VLR aircraft from Bomber Command to Coastal Command:

> The key to the whole problem at the moment is to get at least 40 long range aircraft to re-equip selected squadrons now in Coastal Command . . . Added to this we must provide 10cm. A.S.V. for the Bay.[80]

Pound made this ultimate plea at a time when, in the words of the Assistant Chief of Naval Staff (Trade), 'our shipping position has never been tighter'.[81] In October 1942 637,833 tons of shipping had been lost in all seas and from all kinds of enemy action; of that total over 400,000 in the North and South Atlantic.[82] Since the Whitehall 'Battle of the Air' had begun in February 1942, over 4.4 million tons had been sunk in the North Atlantic alone.[83] These were the statistics of impending catastrophe.

At the meeting of the Cabinet Anti-U-boat Committee on 18 November the Chief of Air Staff at last went some way to conceding the Admiralty's case.[84] He offered to transfer 30 Halifax heavy bombers to Coastal Command to strengthen the offensive against

U-boats in transit in the outer zone of the Bay of Biscay, and to replace in December and January the Wellingtons at present patrolling the inner zone with two squadrons of more modern aircraft fitted with the Leigh Light and the new 10cm radar (see pp. 479–80, 580–2).

Yet these final concessions on the part of the Air Staff proved in the event an empty triumph for the Admiralty. For one thing, the first of the squadrons equipped with the new 10cm radar was not to come fully into service until March 1943;[85] for another, the crucial problem of the mid-Atlantic air gap remained without a solution, because at the beginning of 1943 there were still to be fewer than twenty VLR aircraft in service with Coastal Command.[86]

And meanwhile Admiral Dönitz was continuing to torpedo his way towards final victory. Over the full twelve months of 1942 his U-boats had sunk 6,266,215 tons of Allied shipping; more than 80 per cent of the Allies' total loss from all forms of enemy action of 7,790,697 tons.[87] In January 1943 imports into Britain were less than half the figure for January 1941 and nearly 42 per cent down on the figure for January 1942. In the three months November 1942 to January 1943 nearly half of Britain's consumption of raw materials – the stuff of war production – had had to come from stocks.[88] At the present rate those stocks would soon be exhausted. Then what?

At issue, then, in 'the Battle of the Air' had been nothing less than Britain's very survival. This renders it the most important single British strategic debate of the war. It is, moreover, the one case where Britain's survival was imperilled not so much by enemy action in itself as by blind folly within Britain's own leadership.

The impact of that folly on the course of the struggle out in the Atlantic was sharpened by errors in operational policy and by the shortcomings of British technology. In 1942 both Admiral Pound and Air Marshal Joubert chose to pursue an aerial version of the naval fallacy of the 'offensive' or hunting strategy against the U-boat, concentrating some two-thirds of Coastal Command's patrol effort on an attempt to find and destroy U-boats in transit across the inner and outer Bay of Biscay zones. But the so-called 'Bay offensive' proved no more than an inconvenience to Dönitz's captains. Out of 265 U-boat crossings of the Bay during the first five months of 1942 only 24 were sighted by Coastal Command, even though the boats often ran on the surface in broad daylight; and not one was sunk.[89]

In June the Leigh Light (see above, pp. 258–9), enabling an aircraft to illuminate a U-boat brilliantly at night for the final kill, at last came into service – more than a year after it had been successfully tested.

For this long delay Joubert himself was partly to blame, for when Assistant Chief of Air Staff (Radio) at the Air Ministry in 1941 he had backed the Leigh Light's rival, the Turbinlite; and then, on being appointed AOC-in-C, Coastal Command, he had returned Squadron Leader Leigh to his normal duties while development of the Turbinlite proceeded. After two months, however, Joubert realised (as he himself handsomely admitted) that he had been wrong, and that the Leigh Light was better suited to the job than the Turbinlite.[90] It was not until mid-August 1941 that Leigh resumed his development work; not until the autumn that the Air Ministry could be persuaded to approve the experimental fitting of the Leigh Light to six Wellingtons. When Joubert asked the Ministry to increase the order for Leigh Lights to 36 sets, the Whitehall desk pilots refused on the ground that the results of trials and operational experience with the first six aircraft must be awaited before a larger order was placed. In December 1941 satisfactory trials encouraged Joubert again to ask the Ministry to order 30 Leigh Lights and allocate the same number of Wellingtons to take them. The Ministry would only agree to twenty on top of the original order for six, stubbornly arguing that the equipment of further aircraft must await operational experience.

The first of the initial six operational Leigh Light Wellingtons did not reach crew training until early January 1942, though ordered in the previous autumn. Joubert had to inform the Air Ministry that as a result of this infuriating delay operational experience against U-boats was unlikely in the near future. According to the Air Historical Branch Narrative, *The Royal Air Force in the Maritime War*,[91] he pointed out to the Air Ministry that 'unless it was possible to allocate twenty Wellingtons forthwith, the continuity of fitment work would be broken and months elapse before the 20 sets of equipment on order could be installed and the completed aircraft delivered'. On 28 February 1942 the Ministry at last ordered the expansion of the existing Leigh Light flight into a squadron of twenty Wellingtons, and asked the Ministry of Aircraft Production to allocate the aircraft as they came out of the factories.[92]

Unfortunately Vickers, the manufacturers of the Wellington, were, according to a secret wartime expert report, an outstanding example of the 'British Disease', with 'no system of line production throughout the whole organisation'.[93] Thanks to this shambles of mismanagement and appalling productivity the Wellingtons to be fitted with Leigh Lights did not become available as quickly as hoped, and despite all Joubert's proddings only five of them were in service by May 1942.[94] Thus it was that failure in the aircraft factory conspired with inertia and obstruction inside the Air Ministry to deny Coastal Command and the Royal Navy the Leigh Light aircraft they so urgently wanted. Even at the beginning of June 1942 the Air Ministry is found resisting Joubert's proposal that other types of aircraft should be fitted with Leigh Lights; it did so for the standard reason that more operational experience was needed first.[95]

In July 1942 a Leigh Light Wellington killed a German U-boat (U-502) in the Bay for the first time, its ASV II radar having first located the boat running on the surface in the pitch dark – for the German officer of the watch on his conning tower a sudden brilliant stab of light, a roar of engines overhead and then the lethal thunder of high explosive. But Dönitz quickly countered the Leigh Light offensive by instructing his captains to travel submerged at night and on the surface by day. Although a Leigh Light Wellington sank another U-boat in August, the Bay offensive continued to prove disappointing in terms of results in proportion to effort.

It is therefore somewhat surprising to find Joubert in September freshly advocating that the Bay should serve as the main focus for the Royal Air Force's and even the Royal Navy's counter-measures against the U-boat. He considered that the alternative of concentrating joint anti-submarine efforts on the open Atlantic was 'a policy to be avoided at all costs':[96]

> Scientific analysis of the situation shows that if the Allied Nations concentrate their effort at the decisive points, which are the transit areas employed by the U-boats and their bases and building yards, the prospect of victory is many times greater than if an attempt is made to protect our shipping in all possible U-boat operational areas. In the Atlantic alone there is an area of 10,000 × 500 sq. miles in which the U-boats can operate. The transit areas are only a fraction of this space. It seems, therefore, to be commonsense to concentrate our available A/S forces in the transit areas and on the bases and building yards.[97]

It was all specious enough, but wholly mistaken. In the first place, Bomber Command's attempts to damage Dönitz's Atlantic coast bases came to nought against their 26-feet-thick concrete roofs, while according to the official historians of the bomber offensive the effect of the numerous attacks carried out in 1942 by Bomber Command on the ports where U-boats were built was 'negligible'[98] – as indeed was accurately monitored at the time by the Ministry of Economic Warfare.[99] Secondly, it was not aircraft over the Bay area that most worried Dönitz, but aircraft over his intended victims in the open Atlantic. On 3 September he noted in the U-boat Command's war diary that two days earlier an air escort had appeared over a convoy 800 miles out from England and 400 miles from Iceland:

> By systematically forcing the boats under water [he wrote] it made them lose contact at evening twilight, thus spoiling the best prospects for attack of all boats in the first four moonless hours of the night . . . The convoy operation had to be broken off in the morning of 2.9 as it no longer seemed possible for boats to haul ahead in the face of the expected heavy enemy air activity . . .[100]

Dönitz went on to remark that U-boat Command 'sees with extreme anxiety' the time when such air escorts 'would spread to all parts of the Atlantic', so signifying 'an unendurable reduction in prospects for success'.[101]

Ironically enough, just about the time when Joubert was urging that all efforts should be concentrated on the Bay of Biscay, Dönitz was equipping his boats with an electronic device called 'Metox' which could give warning of existing British radar transmissions so that a U-boat could dive out of harm's way. By nullifying at a stroke the effectiveness of radar-directed night attack by Leigh Light Wellingtons Metox marked the defeat for the time being of Coastal Command's Bay offensive.[102] Nonetheless Joubert still persisted with his favoured strategy. From June 1942 to January 1943 an average of 3,500 patrol hours were flown over the Bay zones each month, at a total loss of some 100 aircraft – for a bag of only seven U-boats sunk and five damaged. Meanwhile just a third of that flying time employed in escorting and supporting convoys in the North-East Atlantic had not only prevented many U-boat attacks but also had destroyed seventeen U-boats and badly damaged over twenty.[103]

The answer to Metox lay in the new 10cm radar (ASV III), its wavelength too short for Metox to pick up. Moreover, this super-accurate narrow-beam new radar could pinpoint a U-boat through all the 'clutter' of the sea's moving surface. It was indeed the complete answer to Coastal Command's problems of detection and attack. Unfortunately throughout 1942 ASV III was to be found not in aircraft but in factories in various stages of delayed assembly.

Ten cm radar required a new kind of thermionic valve, the cavity magnetron, to produce the requisite power. The magnetron had been invented by two brilliant British scientists, Dr J. T. Randall and Mr H. A. H. Boot, early in 1940, and a production prototype had been ready by the summer of that year. It was at this point that the problems began, because the British electrical industry simply lacked the technical and managerial capability to put such advanced technology as the magnetron into large-scale production and it had to be handed over to the Americans to manufacture. In any case, British production of the complete ASV III equipments was seriously held up because of shortcomings in the supply of precision-engineering components and in final assembly.[104] This was why two years after the production prototype not a single ASV III had yet seen service in a Coastal Command aircraft. Indeed such was the reigning confusion and delay in all fields of British radar and radio production in mid-1942 that the Cabinet appointed a senior judge, Lord Justice Du Parcq, to investigate the entire question and make recommendations (see below, pp. 580–2).[105]

There was a further complication. The magnetron also formed the key component in Bomber Command's new target-finding device H2S, technically very similar to ASV III. This led to keen competition between the two Commands for the dribble of hand-built production impatiently awaited in the closing months of 1942. When in November it was decided that forty H2S sets should be converted into ASV IIIs for installation in Liberators and Wellingtons, it therefore marked one of the Admiralty's and Coastal Command's more notable successes in 'the Battle of the Air'.[106] But such were the production bottlenecks that it was not to be until February–March 1943 that the first squadron equipped with ASV III actually came into service.

It was some compensation that, from mid-1942 onwards, Coastal Command aircraft began to be equipped with depth-charges filled with a powerful new explosive, Torpex, and fitted with shallow-setting pistols effective against U-boats on the surface or just diving,[107] which largely accounts for the rising number of U-boats actually destroyed in the Atlantic in the second half of the year.

The Royal Navy also was still greatly hampered during 1942 by want of the right ships and equipment for anti-submarine warfare. Its mainstay for escorting convoys remained the Flower class corvettes, of which 56 had been ordered in the summer of 1939. They rolled like barrels in a seaway and their designed speed was only 16½ knots as against the big U-boats' 18½ knots on the surface. In practice, the four-cylinder triple-expansion engines (an obsolete design adopted because it happened to be available and within the capabilities of the British marine engineering industry, as the large-scale manufacture of diesels was not) could normally manage only 14 to 15 knots.[108] The new River class frigates were still being awaited three years after the war broke out; the British shipbuilding industry lacked enough of the long building slips needed for their construction.[109] Most of the escorts in service were therefore too few and too slow to hunt detected

U-boats to death, and with a margin of only 3 to 4 knots over a 'fast' convoy's speed any prolonged diversion could easily mean losing the convoy. Escorts of all kinds were also too few to permit thorough tactical training as units.

Only in September 1942 did the Royal Navy form its first escort group with the specific task of hunting down U-boats once detected near a convoy. With ten escorts and an oiler it began work on 22 September with the slow outward-bound convoy ONS12, and although it too never operated as a tactical group it did succeed in driving two shadowing U-boats beneath the surface.[110] The demand for escort ships made by the forthcoming invasion of French North Africa in November prevented any more such escort groups being formed in the Eastern Atlantic, although a 'Western Support Force' of three destroyers based on St John's, Newfoundland, was set up to provide extra protection to convoys in the lethal mid-Atlantic air gap.[111]

It did not help that escorts, including destroyers, could run short of fuel and be compelled to leave their convoys early in order to make for port. This problem again owed itself at least partly to obsolescent British marine technology, for the Royal Navy's destroyers (even the latest) were equipped with boilers of lower steam pressure (at 300 pounds per square inch) than American destroyers (at 600 pounds per square inch) and less efficient turbines, so leading to wasteful fuel consumption and consequently shorter endurance. Whereas the Americans drew on the competitive resources of their 'land' boiler and turbine companies (i.e., those who supplied plant for such as power stations), the British shipbuilding industry relied entirely on a too cosy coterie of specialised marine engine and boiler manufacturers whose designs were essentially of 1918 vintage.[112] However, from June 1942 the practice was at last introduced of refuelling escorts from accompanying tankers.[113]

Although the escort carrier had been recognised back in 1941 as an essential tool of convoy protection, only four were in service by late 1942 and those were earmarked either for 'Torch' or for convoys to North Russia.[114] By the end of 1942 shore-based medium-range aircraft (Wellingtons, Whitleys, Sunderlands and Catalinas) could cover the Atlantic as far out as 200 miles east of Newfoundland, 500 miles south of Iceland and 600 miles west of the British Isles.[115] In the absence of escort carriers the remaining gap in mid-Atlantic could only be covered by VLR Liberator Mk I aircraft, the sticking point in 'the Battle of the Air'; and often the number of such aircraft actually available for operations in late 1942 fell to around six. The combined consequences of the grievous shortage of VLR aircraft and the complete lack of escort carriers is spelt out by the Official Naval History:

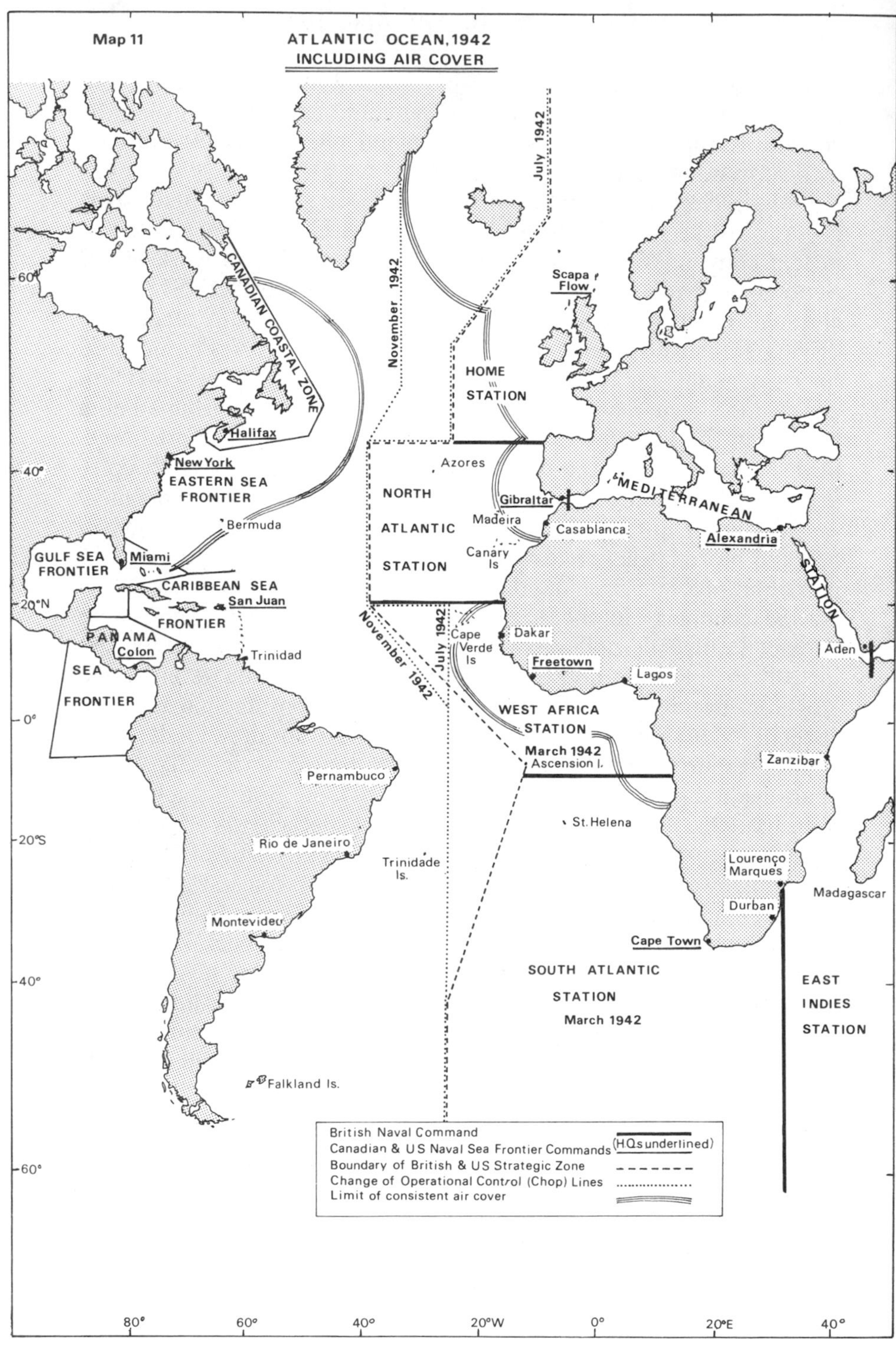
Map 11
ATLANTIC OCEAN, 1942
INCLUDING AIR COVER
CANADIAN COASTAL ZONE
November 1942
July 1942
Scapa Flow
HOME STATION
Halifax
New York
EASTERN SEA FRONTIER
Azores
NORTH ATLANTIC STATION
Gibraltar
MEDITERRANEAN
Madeira
Casablanca
Alexandria
Bermuda
Canary Is
GULF SEA FRONTIER
Miami
CARIBBEAN SEA
San Juan
FRONTIER
PANAMA
Colon
SEA
FRONTIER
Trinidad
November 1942
July 1942
Cape Verde Is
Dakar
Freetown
Lagos
Aden
STATION
WEST AFRICA STATION
March 1942
Ascension I.
Zanzibar
Pernambuco
St. Helena
Rio de Janeiro
Trinidade Is.
Lourenço Marques
Madagascar
Durban
Montevideo
Cape Town
SOUTH ATLANTIC STATION
March 1942
EAST INDIES STATION
Falkland Is.
British Naval Command
Canadian & US Naval Sea Frontier Commands
(HQs underlined)
Boundary of British & US Strategic Zone
Change of Operational Control (Chop) Lines
Limit of consistent air cover
60°
40°
20°N
0°
20°S
40°
60°
80°
60°
40°
20°W
0°
20°E
40°

> Meanwhile, in mid-Atlantic, between latitude 35°N and 65°N and longitude 10°W and 50°W, ship after ship went down for lack of air cover for convoys: August, 29 ships of 156,049 tons; September, 18 ships of 108,768 tons; October, 24 ships of 172,173 tons; November, 27 ships of 166,809 tons; December, 24 ships of 127,844 tons.[116]

Utter and early disaster was alone staved off by the five Liberator Is of 120 Squadron, Coastal Command, based in Iceland, although appalling weather in December helped by greatly reducing U-boat operations. In October (first fruits of 'the Battle of the Air') one squadron of twelve Liberator Mark IIIAC was formed in England; next month a US Liberator Mark IIIA squadron was allotted to Coastal Command for operations over the Atlantic. But these measures brought no instant relief because it was to take months to convert the bombers into fully equipped VLR anti-submarine aircraft.[117]

Thus the protracted nature of the 'Battle of the Air' and the belatedness of the decision to provide Coastal Command with VLR aircraft at the expense (small) of Bomber Command caused the entire British anti-submarine effort to remain lopsided, with too much of the burden falling to the Royal Navy's escort ships. As the ACNS (H) wrote to the First Sea Lord on 20 December 1942:

> Experience shows quite clearly that surface escorts alone without air co-operation cannot give sufficient security to convoys unless in overwhelming strength; it is also clear that an air escort unaided by surface vessels is not sufficient. The most effective and economical use of our resources requires a careful balance in the combined use of surface and air escorts.[118]

Meanwhile it was the crews of the escort ships and the merchant marine who were paying the price for this lack of balance. And what that price amounted to in the iron coinage of hardship, danger and demands on human courage is epitomised by the homeward voyage in October of just one out of the 180-odd convoys which crossed the Atlantic that year, Convoy SC104.

On 10 October 1942 Escort Unit B6 of the Liverpool Escort Force rendezvoused with Convoy SC104 at 1300 in 47° 57′N, 51° 35′W, relieving Task Unit 24.18.3 of the Western Local Escort which thereupon returned to St John's. Escort Unit B6 consisted of the destroyers *Fame* (launched 1934; 1,350 tons displacement; 35½ knots; two 4.7-inch guns; four Oerlikon guns; a 'Hedgehog' anti-submarine mortar) and *Viscount* (launched 1917; 1,120 tons; 25 knots; two 4-inch guns)[119] and four Flower class corvettes (all launched mid-1941; 925 tons displacement; one 4-inch gun; one 2-pounder anti-aircraft gun).[120] Their names, evoking the gentle charms of an English country garden – His Majesty's ships *Acanthus*, *Eglantine*, and *Montbretia*, and His Norwegian Majesty's ship *Potentilla* – contrasted poignantly with the harshness of their task in war. The Senior Officer commanding B6 was Commander R. Heathcote, RN, captain of the *Fame*. Now the thirty-six merchant ships of SC104, deployed in several columns, lay in his care: his responsibility to shepherd them safely to England and home.

For two deceptive days the convoy steamed eastwards with the sweep of sea bounded by its horizon empty but for itself. The first warning that peril was beginning to encircle it came at 1624 on 12 October, when HF/DF (High-Frequency direction finding) picked up the bearing of a U-boat's radio transmission on the convoy's starboard bow. After Heathcote had ordered *Montbretia* to investigate this, a further bearing indicated that there was another U-boat prowling to port – and that the first U-boat too had moved over to port, possibly to get to windward of the convoy.[121] As dusk thickened over the grey waters B6 adopted Night Stations: *Viscount* on the starboard quarter of the convoy; *Montbretia* ahead of the starboard column; *Eglantine* to starboard of the convoy's front; *Fame* on the starboard quarter; *Potentilla* on the port bow; and *Acanthus* ahead of the port column. Heathcote had already arranged with the convoy commodore to make various evasive alterations of course during the night.

In wheelhouses and chart rooms and on open bridges in a bitter wind nerves began to tighten in the knowledge that at least two U-boats lurked behind the blank face of the sea like crocodiles awaiting their chance of meat.

> Although it promised to be a dark night, owing to negligible moon and heavy clouds [wrote Heathcote in his report], bright Northern Lights kept the visibility of the convoy up to at least four miles, except during the short snow showers, and the alterations of course evidently did not pass unnoticed.

Twenty minutes before midnight three D/F bearings fixed a U-boat four and a half miles astern of the middle of the convoy. The destroyer *Fame*, on going to investigate, made radar contact at about 4,000 yards, and closed for the kill. At this point the radar broke down because of the heavy pounding of the ship. *Fame* had other problems too: 'Speed was reduced to 12 knots to reduce spray on the bridge, which made an efficient lookout impossible and the search continued for half an hour on this bearing.' She saw nothing and resumed her station at 0115 on 13 October. Shortly afterwards another HF/DF fix placed a U-boat four miles outside *Eglantine*, but she too found nothing. A night of stealthy menace ended with a false alarm at 0411. The weather was now all too favourable to the stalking U-boats: 'Conditions for R.D.F. [radar] and asdics [sonar] were very bad owing to the steep and rising sea, while spray and occasional snow showers hampered visibility.' Heathcote ordered *Viscount* ahead of the convoy, and *Acanthus* to its starboard quarter.

At 0450 SC104 took its first casualty, the Norwegian merchantman *Fagersten*, stopped and sinking astern of Column Ten. No rockets had been seen, no signals of distress received. HMS *Fame* searched for her attacker without success. At 0508 an explosion was followed by rockets arcing in the night sky, whereupon Heathcote ordered 'Operation Raspberry', a standard tactical drill for depth-charging in a pattern over the area of U-boat attack. At 0515 'Snowflake', an illuminant, was fired: a ghastly light over a desolate sea. Nothing was seen. More than an hour later Heathcote learned that three ships had been sunk and that no one had yet gone to the rescue of the crews. He ordered *Potentilla* to search for survivors at daylight and return to the convoy at dusk.

The daylight hours of 13 October brought more bearings and some sightings of U-boats; but each time the U-boat dived before an escort ship could close her. Convoy SC104 was now battling against that other Atlantic enemy – the weather. When at 0922 the convoy altered to 045° in order to regain the convoy route after evasive changes of course, the commodore reported that several of the merchantmen could not steer this course because of the heavy seas. Heathcote had to alter back to 075° as the only alternative to heaving to.

By the afternoon it had become clear from HF/DF bearings that the convoy was being shadowed by one U-boat on each quarter, with indications that a third and possibly a fourth U-boat were also around. Heathcote therefore despatched *Eglantine* to the rear to work under *Viscount*'s orders. In the evening he faced a fresh worry: although he had ordered his ships to be back in station by 2100, *Viscount* and *Eglantine* had been delayed in a hunt for a U-boat seen on the surface, while *Potentilla* was still searching for survivors who might yet be floating on the icy wind-whipped rollers and could not be back in station until 0400. This left him with only *Montbretia* on the convoy's starboard bow, *Acanthus* on the port beam and *Fame* zig-zagging across the stern.

It was the more worrying that his ships' radars and sonars were confused by the echoes of wave crests and noisy turbulence of rough seas. By around midnight two more ships, *Empire Mersey* and *Southern Empress*, had been picked off by U-boats. By this time the *Viscount* and a U-boat had had a brief but violent encounter in the darkness and atrocious weather. At 2043 *Viscount* spotted a U-boat surfacing ahead only 800 yards distant. She increased to full speed, her helm hard to port. The U-boat captain swung hard to starboard and managed to clear *Viscount*'s bow by about three hundred yards. Although *Viscount* now opened fire, her 'B' gun could only get off five rounds before the gunlayer and trainer were blinded by spray. As *Viscount*'s captain later reported:

> VISCOUNT continued her turn under full rudder and went in to ram, but heavy water coming over the bridge obscured the submarine which altered course to port and dived. A last glimpse of the conning tower, as it disappeared, was seen from VISCOUNT's bridge [about 30 yards on the port beam] . . .

With sonar rendered useless by the motion of the ship, *Viscount* had no alternative but to return to her station with the convoy.

The small hours of 14 October saw more blind gropings in the dark for elusive U-boats seen for an instant before diving; more vain chases; more ships going down as the columns steamed slowly on. In one chase by *Viscount*, 'the submarine was going down-wind and almost down-swell and was extremely difficult to keep in sight owing to the height of the swell, while the top of an occasional wave gave a very good imitation of a submarine, the white crest representing the wake'. At daylight Heathcote found that fifteen ships were now missing from his convoy, though fortunately nine of them later rejoined. It was enough, however, to have lost six vessels in two days with half an ocean still to cross. Heathcote later confessed that on this morning his own feelings 'amounted almost to despair, but these feelings did not appear to be shared by other officers and men in FAME'.

During daylight on 14 October many HF/DF fixes as well as sightings confirmed that the four U-boats were clinging persistently to SC104's flanks and rear despite all Escort Unit B6's efforts to drive them away. In the evening the favourable visibility which had helped the U-boats in stalking their prey grew mercifully worse. Commander Heathcote prearranged more evasive changes of course for the night hours with the convoy commodore, and stationed his escorts closer to the convoy than laid down in Admiralty tactical instructions. During the night of 15–16 October Heathcote's ships made no fewer than six radar contacts and succeeded in driving off all would-be attackers. And HMS *Viscount* did much more than merely drive off a U-boat after her radar picked it up 6,200 yards off the port bow at 2331. At 2342, with the range down to 2,000 yards, 'revolutions for 26 knots were ordered,' wrote her captain, Lieutenant-Commander Waterhouse in his report, 'and course set to ram.' At 2344 *Viscount*'s lookouts sighted the U-boat through the darkness fine on the port bow completely surfaced. Simultaneously the U-boat must have spotted *Viscount* because her diesels immediately thrust her to high speed while she 'snaked in line', starting with a swing to port:

> VISCOUNT followed her swing to port but failed to catch her as she swung back to starboard. The U-boat Captain then 'committed suicide' by swinging back to port right across the bows of VISCOUNT who was turning under full starboard rudder. VISCOUNT struck the U-boat on her port side, about 20 feet abaft the conning tower . . . The stem hit her fairly, then lifted and crashed down on top of her, pinning her for about 15 seconds before she dragged clear to port with her back broken . . .

She passed slowly down *Viscount*'s port side as *Viscount* drew ahead; an opportunity for the British destroyer to give her broadsides from every calibre of gun. *Viscount* finished the job by placing a heavy depth-charge set to 140 feet alongside the U-boat (U-619) as she sank stern first at 2347.

But *Viscount* herself had suffered serious damage in her bows, letting in much water. Even though Commander Waterhouse had her load shifted (including fuel oil) aft in order to raise her buckled bow plates above the waterline, this proved only partially successful, and he was ordered by Captain (D), Liverpool, to make for home independently. *Viscount* reached Lough Foyle safely at 2130 on 18 October.

After the *Viscount* parted company Commander Heathcote, as Senior Officer, Escort Unit B6, found himself with just his own destroyer, *Fame*, with the requisite speed and weaponry effectively to hunt and kill his remaining pursuers. Mercifully, however, the small hours of 16 October passed quietly; the day dawned fairly calm, with gratifyingly low visibility. *Potentilla* was able to transfer to the SS *Souderoy* nearly 100 survivors who for up to two days had been packed into her cramped spaces. At sunrise came a welcome sight – a Liberator flying overhead. It reported that a U-boat had dived some five miles astern of the convoy. Heathcote now sought to shake off the enemy altogether under cover of the poor visibility by an alteration to 130° at 1220 – but to no avail, because at 1407, *Fame*, two miles ahead of Column Four of the convoy, got a clear sonar signal of a U-boat 2,000 yards distant. Heathcote increased to 15 knots and at 1413 dropped a ten depth-charge pattern set to 50 and 140 feet over the U-boat's likely position. With visibility now up to a mile, Heathcote was just preparing to use *Fame*'s 'Hedgehog' to launch more depth-charges forward over the bows when . . .

> a large bubble was seen followed by the bow of a submarine breaking surface at a very steep angle. Speed was increased to 18 knots and fire opened with every weapon which would bear. By the time FAME reached the position of the submarine she was on even keel and stopped. Engines were stopped before the bow hit a glancing blow. The submarine scraped down the starboard side. A 5-charge pattern was dropped when the submarine was abreast of the stern while FAME made another circle to come up to attempt to board. The convoy were now steaming past on either side, most of them firing everything they had got. The submarine crew were now abandoning ship . . .

As the submarine settled slowly on even keel, Lieutenant P. M. Jones boarded her from *Fame*'s whaler and retrieved her documents. He scrambled back into the whaler just one minute before the U-boat sank.

Nothing could have been more true to the spirit of Nelson and his captains at Trafalgar than *Viscount*'s and *Fame*'s actions in ramming the enemy, laying themselves alongside him, and then sinking him by sheer weight of fire. But *Fame*, like *Viscount*, paid dearly for her success – ripped right along her waterline by the tin-opener of the U-boat's thick plating and hydroplanes. Her stem was twisted and her after magazine was flooded. The pumps were only just able to hold the water level steady until collision mats could be put in place. Commander Heathcote therefore stopped her and listed her to port while rags, wedges, pieces of wood, items of stores – anything that would serve – were stuffed into the rip. Heathcote himself was now overtaken by a kind of a hangover of second thoughts after the violence of the action, for he was already regretting that he had rammed the U-boat, both because of the damage to his own ship and also because he had forfeited the chance of salvaging the enemy.

'At the time, however,' he wrote in his report, 'I was faced with an apparently little damaged submarine in low visibility in the middle of a large convoy.' It is little wonder, then, that Heathcote, in his own words, 'wished to make very certain of this submarine, which proved to be U-253'. Nevertheless, he too now had to part company and make for port: 'Though loath to leave the convoy, I felt it would be foolish with a potentially dangerous leak in the engine-room to delay my arrival in Harbour . . .' At 1815 on 16 October he ordered Lieutenant-Commander C. A. Monsen, RNorN, to take command of the escort. *Fame* herself reached Liverpool safely on 19 October.

Now Commander Monsen was left with just the four 'Flowers' to guard 28 surviving ships. That same evening he demonstrated that the Viking spirit was just as much alive in Norwegian seamen as the Nelson spirit in British. When at 2140 his radar operator detected a submarine, Monsen ordered full speed. To the thunderous vibration of her reciprocating engines *Potentilla* closed on the enemy until the U-boat was sighted dead ahead 400 yards off, and steering straight for the corvette.

> We were now doing 16 knots [wrote Monsen in his report] and the submarine probably more. As a ramming ahead just would make a mess of it with more than 30 knots [combined] speed, ship was given a kick to starboard and then hard a-port. The submarine passed down our port side with a terrific speed, distance between ships less than 30 yards . . .

Potentilla opened fire with her 4-inch gun, her Oerlikons and 2-pounder pom-pom, scoring several hits. 'Helm was given hard-a-port in order to ram. By now the submarine started to dive and we passed over her swirl as she disappeared dropping the last three charges of the pattern . . .' Although further depth-charges brought up an oil slick, the U-boat had in fact escaped. Nevertheless she was the last U-boat to trouble the convoy despite unexplained bursts of fire from the convoy and the occasional false alarm on 17 October, a day blessed with thick, concealing fog; two days later Convoy SC104 and its war-sustaining cargoes made safe landfall in the Mersey. Time now for the sailor home from sea briefly to enjoy the warmth of a family welcome; the love of a lonely, anxious and for the moment thankfully relieved wife or girlfriend. For all too soon the sea service, with all its hardships and hazards, would call him back again.

It was rare for convoys in 1942 to come through with relatively light losses like SC104 and its hard-fighting escort. Later that October SC107 had fifteen ships totalling 88,000 tons sunk before an air escort arrived. Off Madeira SL125 lost thirteen ships in a seven-day battle without a single U-boat being sunk in compensation.[122] These were the kind of massacres which brought the count of merchant shipping lost in 1942 to the U-boat up to its horrifying total of 1,160 ships and 6,266,215 tons.[123]

Yet at least the fast liners – the Cunarders *Queen Elizabeth* (83,675 tons), *Queen Mary* (81,235 tons), *Aquitania* (44,786 tons), the French ship *Ile de France* (43,450 tons) and the Dutch *Nieuw Amsterdam* (36,287 tons) – succeeded in repeatedly plying the Atlantic literally stuffed with American troops (*Queen Elizabeth* was carrying 15,000 per trip) without falling victim to U-boats. Too fast at around 28 knots for surface escorts to keep up, they had to make the mid-ocean crossing entirely unprotected except by their own speed, some 10 knots more than the fastest U-boat on the surface. Despite all Dönitz's successes, 'Operation Bolero', the accelerating movement of American forces to the British Isles, succeeded to the limits of the capacity of the ships available. In the first quarter of the year 13,698 US service personnel arrived in the United Kingdom; in the second 42,314; in the third, 131,850; in the last, 63,000.[124]

So even though Britain's own survival lay in increasing jeopardy as the months of 1942 passed, the Allied leadership could nonetheless argue hopefully about where best to launch these American forces alongside the British in the first joint Allied expedition of the German war. To Churchill and the British Chiefs of Staff, though not to the Americans, the choice always seemed obvious: the Mediterranean. Yet an ultimate decision in favour of that theatre depended on the fate during 1942 of Britain's existing 'blue water' strategy there – a fate for long much in doubt.

16

The Verdun of Maritime War: Malta, 1942

Throughout much of 1942 the island of Malta served less as a British strategic asset than as a hostage to the enemy. In the face of Axis air superiority the remaining surface warships based there had to be withdrawn to Alexandria in April; soon afterwards even the submarines had to follow, because enemy bombing was so ferocious that they had been compelled to remain submerged in harbour throughout the daylight hours. They were not to return to Malta until August. With the dying away of attacks from Malta against enemy convoys plying between Italy and North Africa, Axis losses of merchant ships on this route dropped to less than one per cent in April.[1] For the foreseeable future Malta had thus ceased to function as an offensive base. Instead it was now the Verdun of maritime war. For just like Verdun and the French leadership in 1916 – or, for that matter, the besieged German Army at Stalingrad and Hitler in 1942–43 – Malta had become for the British leadership a matter of prestige and pride, a symbol of heroic resistance. This was proclaimed by the award of the George Cross to the islanders by King George VI on 16 April 1942. And like Verdun and Stalingrad the 'George Cross Island' triggered powerful emotions which dictated that it must be held no matter what the cost in resources, risk, losses, and distortion of the balance of strategy as a whole. In the case of the British leadership and the people of Malta there existed a special bond of loyalty and obligation. In Churchill's words when writing to the First Sea Lord in June to call for a fresh effort 'on the grand scale' to succour the island: 'We are absolutely bound to save Malta in one way or another'; and he asked Sir Dudley Pound to assure Field-Marshal Gort, the Governor, that 'the Navy will never abandon Malta'.[2] There was no need for such an assurance: Admiral Cunningham himself was resolved that 'we must take great risks to keep Malta supplied'.[3] As he comments in his memoirs: 'Incidentally, I am unaware if anyone had suggested abandoning the island. Certainly the Navy had not.'[4]

Yet to fulfil this commitment to Malta demanded attempt after attempt 'on the grand scale' to fight supplies and reinforcements of aircraft through to the island in the face of overwhelming Axis air superiority. Of the sixty supply ships despatched in 1942, only thirty arrived; twenty were sunk and ten had to turn back. These perilous voyages cost the Royal Navy one fleet aircraft carrier, two cruisers, one anti-aircraft cruiser and nine destroyers sunk and many other warships badly damaged.[5]

However, it was not just in regard to the Royal Navy that Malta in 1942 served as a hostage to the enemy, but also in regard to the Army's conduct of the land campaign in North Africa. For in the airfields in the northerly bulge of Cyrenaica lay the key to control of the central Mediterranean convoy routes. In British hands these airfields ensured fighter cover far to the westward over the route from Alexandria to Malta, while at the same time permitting the Royal Air Force to attack Rommel's supply ships en route between Italy and Libya. In German and Italian hands these airfields ensured the reverse – virtual free passage of stores vessels and tankers to Rommel; virtual closing of the route to Malta from the eastwards. As a consequence British military planning in 1942, and especially the timing of Desert offensives, could not be determined solely by military considerations such as the prevailing balance of land forces in numbers of troops or quality and quantity of weapons, or comparative states of training. Instead GHQ, Middle East's freedom of strategic choice was cramped by the imperative need to take or hold the Cyrenaican airfields for the sake of Malta.

In the spring months of 1942 in particular, after Rommel had forced the 8th Army back from the El Agheila defile to Gazala and recaptured these airfields, Churchill and the Chiefs of Staff were to nag away at the C-in-C, Middle East, General Sir Claude Auchinleck, to launch an offensive at minimum delay. In the words of a COS telegram to him at the beginning of March:

> The dominant factor in the Mediterranean and Middle East situation at

> the present time is Malta . . . If we do not succeed in running a substantial convoy into Malta by May, the position there will be critical . . . A convoy can only be run [from the east] if we can use the landing grounds in Western Cyrenaica. Hence the recapture of these is vital to your whole situation.[6]

Despite Auchinleck's reluctance to commit his ill-trained and heterogeneous army with its inferior tanks to a premature offensive – and despite the Middle East Defence Committee's argument that, since Malta in its present impotence could little affect enemy supplies, its fall would not necessarily be fatal to the security of Egypt – the War Cabinet decided that the island was of such supreme importance that a battle must be fought in the Desert to save it. Auchinleck was therefore directed against his better judgment that the latest acceptable date for an offensive would be one timed to help the passage of the proposed June dark-period (little or no moon) convoy from Alexandria to Malta.[7]

When in the event Rommel pre-empted this offensive with one of his own on 26 May, Malta even played an indirect role in the crushing defeat and rout of the 8th Army that followed. For the need to protect huge dumps established just behind the 8th Army's front at Gazala for the planned British offensive, and therefore vulnerable to enemy armoured columns, shackled the British command's freedom of manoeuvre, compelling it to fight a forward battle rather than a defence in depth.

The influence of Malta on land strategy manifested itself once again in August 1942, after Auchinleck had halted Rommel and thrown him on to the defensive in the First Battle of Alamein during the previous month. For when Churchill began to press Auchinleck and thereafter his successor, General Sir Harold Alexander, to launch a fresh Desert offensive not later than September, Malta bulked large in his argument, on the familiar score that the Cyrenaican airfields must be seized back in order to provide air cover for a convoy from Alexandria that it was hoped to run in November in order to relieve the island's now desperate straits. Nevertheless Alexander – really Montgomery, the new 8th Army commander – successfully insisted that the army could not be adequately trained and equipped for an offensive until mid-October.

Even so, it was the plight of the island – along with the Prime Minister's own political need for a striking British victory[8] – which rendered it a matter of absolute necessity rather than mere choice to launch the offensive at Alamein against strong German defences at all. For it can be argued that, on purely military grounds, there would have been advantage in leaving Rommel where he was, withering on the vine of an inadequate line of communications up to 1,500 miles long, until the Anglo-American landings in French North Africa ('Torch') at the beginning of November far in his rear and threatening his main base of Tripoli eventually forced him to retreat. The costly attrition battle of Second Alamein might thus have been avoided, and Rommel might instead have been attacked in the open field in the course of a difficult retreat. But the need to have the Cyrenaican airfields in British hands by mid-November in order to cover the Malta convoy which had now been scheduled to sail in the second half of that month utterly precluded such a Wellingtonian waiting game.[9]

It is an irony that the British came close to being relieved of their liability of Malta by the Axis powers themselves, albeit the relief would have been at the cost of a moral shock as devastating as the Japanese capture of Singapore which finally resolved that particular strategic problem after twenty years. In the early months of 1942 long discussions took place within the German and Italian high commands (also involving Hitler and Mussolini) about the relative priority between an airborne operation to capture Malta, 'Operation Herkules', and an offensive by Rommel against the 8th Army in the Gazala Line. Eventually, on 4 May, Hitler issued a directive postponing 'Operation Herkules' until mid-July or even mid-August, when Rommel should have completed his Desert victory. In any case Hitler was less than enthusiastic about 'Herkules', shrewdly foreseeing 'a perpetual blood-letting' in the process of holding Malta and supplying it once taken.[10] At the end of June, after Rommel had routed the 8th Army in the Gazala battles, 'Herkules' was in fact dropped in favour of a supreme effort to conquer Egypt. The defeat of this effort in the First Battle of Alamein finally killed off 'Operation Herkules'.

So Malta remained a British problem, above all for the Royal Navy and the Merchant Marine; the epitome of the entire cost-ineffective 'blue water' strategy in the Mediterranean and Middle East by which Britain, to paraphrase Lord Kitchener, continued to make war as she must rather than as she ought.

For Admiral Cunningham, with his flagship *Queen Elizabeth* lying very low in the water in Alexandria harbour (although with decks sufficiently above the surface of the water to permit the morning ceremony of 'Colours' to be performed), the opening of 1942 marked the nadir of his command of the Mediterranean Fleet. He no longer possessed a single aircraft carrier or serviceable battleship in the face of an Italian battlefleet numbering four or five modern or modernised heavy ships and backed by very strong shore-based air forces. This weakness prompted him to protest forcefully in a letter of 9 January 1942 against the First Sea Lord's intention to deny him reinforcements of heavy ships in order to build up the Eastern Fleet.[11] In the first place, so he argued, 'the defeat of Japan will not necessarily win the war while the defeat of Germany will mean the defeat of Japan'. Secondly, shore-based bombers in the current state of Royal Air Force efficiency over the sea could not provide a substitute for battleships against enemy heavy ships.[12] 'Battleships,' wrote Cunningham, 'can only be replaced by air forces trained in sea operations consisting of adequate reconnaissance and striking forces operating under my close control . . .'[13]

This was a clear reference to the Mediterranean theatre's own 'Battle of the Air' in 1941, in which Cunningham and the new AOC-in-C, Middle East, Air Marshal Sir Arthur Tedder, had disputed about the need for a Mediterranean 'Coastal Command' consisting of squadrons specially trained for maritime warfare and under the operational control of the Royal Navy. As a compromise No. 201 Group, RAF, had been reorganised and renamed in October 1941 as No. 201 (Naval Cooperation) Group, with its primary function defined as 'the conduct of operations at sea and cooperation with the Mediterranean Fleet as required by the C-in-C, Mediterranean'. But this had far from satisfied Cunningham's wish for a shore-based naval air striking force as numerous and as effective against enemy ships as the Luftwaffe's Mediterranean Fliegerkorps or the Japanese naval air force which had so recently sunk *Prince of Wales* and *Repulse*.[14] Indeed, so he wrote to the Vice Chief of Naval Staff in the same letter of 9 January 1942, 'I fear from their last two convoy operations [attacked by the Royal Air Force without success] the enemy have learnt the utter futility of our air forces over the sea . . .'[15]

Within the next two weeks Cunningham made two successful attempts to run essential fuel oil into Malta and bring out empty merchant vessels, at a cost of one destroyer (*Gurkha**) torpedoed by a U-boat and one merchantman sunk after being set on fire by a Ju 88; and he fairly acknowledged the efficiency of the Royal Air Force's Naval Cooperation Group in flying reconnaissances and fighter cover from Malta and from airfields in the Cyrenaican bulge during the

* The second *Gurkha*, formerly the *Larne*, renamed in honour of the regiments. The first *Gurkha* had been sunk off Norway in 1940.

operations. But by the beginning of February the 8th Army had lost the latter airfields to Rommel's winter counter-stroke. On 7 February Cunningham sent a personal message to the First Sea Lord 'setting out the situation at Malta in all its grim bleakness. I pointed out in so many words the serious effect upon the island caused by our recent reverse in Libya . . .' In particular, in Cunningham's words, 'we were thus faced with a period during which the passage of convoys to Malta from the east could only be carried out at very great hazard, as there was a long stretch over which no air cover could be provided. At the same time he could provide no surface force to act as a deterrent to Italian heavy ships.'[16] On the other hand, however, Malta's general supplies could last no longer than the beginning of June, and its stock of aviation spirit no longer than the beginning of August. Cunningham therefore reckoned that he must run in a convoy before the Axis air forces could be reorganised on the captured airfields and while the enemy was still preoccupied with land operations in Libya.

And so in the afternoon of 12 February the first of the major Malta convoys of 1942 sailed from Alexandria – the fast (15 knot) big merchant ships *Clan Chattan*, *Clan Campbell* and *Rowallan Castle*, escorted by the anti-aircraft cruiser *Carlisle* and seven of the new Hunt class escort destroyers. Following in close support came Rear-Admiral Vian with the light cruisers *Naiad* (flag), *Dido*, *Euryalus* and eight fleet destroyers. Next evening after dark three empty merchant ships, the supply vessel HMS *Breconshire*, the cruiser *Penelope* and six destroyers slipped out of Grand Harbour, Valletta, and set course for a mid-voyage rendezvous with Vian.

In the event, although the *Breconshire* and the three empty ships from Malta eventually reached Alexandria safely in company with Vian's returning force, the attempt to re-supply Malta was smashed by enemy air attack. The *Clan Campbell*, badly damaged, had to be diverted to Tobruk; the *Clan Chattan* was set on fire and had to be sunk; the *Rowallan Castle*'s engines were disabled by a near-miss, and although the destroyer *Zulu* took her in tow, her speed was so slow that there remained no chance of her reaching Malta in safety. Back in Alexandria the hapless C-in-C could only order her too to be sunk. In four days of almost continuous action Vian's cruisers fired off some 3,700 rounds of 5.25-inch anti-aircraft ammunition, leaving no more than one and one-third issues for each cruiser remaining in the Mediterranean Fleet.[17]

On 27 February the Chiefs of Staff signalled Cunningham that, since it was at present impossible to supply Malta from the west via Gibraltar, Cunningham must try to run another convoy from Alexandria in March. This operation was to be regarded as the Mediterranean Fleet's primary commitment, to be discharged without regard to the risk to the ships themselves.

The resulting 'Operation MG1', the passing of convoy MW10 to Malta, was to be the last conducted by Cunningham in his present tour as C-in-C, Mediterranean.[18] He deployed his entire remaining strength in cruisers and destroyers under Rear-Admiral Vian's command. From Alexandria would sail three cruisers, an anti-aircraft ship, ten fleet destroyers and seven 'Hunts', while one cruiser (*Penelope*) and one destroyer from Malta would meet the convoy west of Crete. The convoy itself consisted of the Royal Fleet Auxiliary (supply ship) *Breconshire* and three merchantmen, the Norwegian *Talabot*, the *Pampas* and the *Clan Campbell*.

In view of the potentially overwhelming enemy strength Cunningham, Vian and the fleet staff planned MG1 with the greatest care. The 'Hunts' were to search for submarines between Alexandria and Tobruk on the night of 19–20 March (the night before the convoy sailed) and during daylight on the 20th. They would refuel in Tobruk and join the convoy in the forenoon of the 21st. The convoy itself was to sail from Alexandria with a small escort in the forenoon of 20 March, followed by Vian with the main body (Force B) in the evening. Vian would catch up the convoy next morning at the eastern end of the hazardous passage between the airfields of Crete and Libya whence ferocious bombing could be expected. In the morning of the 22nd Vian would pick up the ships from Malta and take the combined force on till dark, steering a course well to the south of the normal route to Malta. As soon as night had dropped its protective curtain over the convoy, Vian was to turn back for Alexandria with his own three cruisers and the fleet destroyers while the convoy itself sailed on to Malta under escort of the warships from Malta, together with the anti-aircraft cruiser *Carlisle* and the 'Hunts'. It was planned that the convoy should reach safe haven in Grand Harbour, Valletta, at dawn on 23 March.

In Cunningham's judgment there was great danger of attack by Italian surface forces during daylight on the 22nd or during the following night. His orders to meet this contingency were admirably clear:

> Should this occur, it is my general intention that the enemy should be, if possible, evaded until darkness, after which the convoy should be sent on to Malta with the destroyer escort, being dispersed if thought desirable,

> and the enemy brought to action by Force 'B'. The convoy should only be turned back if it is evident that the enemy will otherwise intercept in daylight and east of longitude 18°E [some 200 miles east of Malta].[19]

Cunningham posted five submarines on patrol against such surface forces, and arranged for the Royal Air Force to conduct air searches from Malta (prevented in the event by enemy air attack) and Libya; the Royal Air Force was also to bomb the enemy's Cyrenaican airfields, fly fighter patrols over the convoy up to 300 miles from its bases, and provide strike forces of Beaufort torpedo-bombers from Malta and Libya against Italian warships.

Convoy MW10 sailed in the morning of 20 March escorted by the anti-aircraft cruiser *Carlisle* (Captain D. M. L. Neame) and six destroyers. Vian followed in the evening with Force B, the cruiser *Cleopatra* (Captain G. Grantham; flag), *Dido* and *Euryalus* and four fleet destroyers. By this time 'Operation MG1' had already suffered its first casualty – the Hunt class destroyer *Heythrop*, torpedoed by a U-boat off Tobruk, had had to be sunk while in tow. By the forenoon of 21 March Vian had joined with the convoy and the five remaining 'Hunts' from Tobruk (the sixth, delayed by a fouled propeller, joined in the evening) and the combined force was making 12 knots on a westerly course to the north of Tobruk, with relays of Royal Air Force fighters circling reassuringly overhead. At 0800 next day *Penelope* and the destroyer *Legion* joined from Malta, and the convoy (now beyond air cover) steamed on through the passage between Crete and Cyrenaica without incident. Neither inaccurate Italian high-level bombing in the forenoon nor more dangerous German attacks which followed until dusk caused damage. But now came warning via Ultra decrypts of the Italian C38M Enigma signals, confirmed by a British submarine report at 0518 on the 22nd, that an Italian heavy squadron had sailed from Taranto.[20]

For Vian – a hard, long, hatchet face; the outward visor of the ruthlessly tough fighting sailor who had boarded the prison ship *Altmark* in then neutral Norwegian waters in 1940, who had led his destroyers in persistent close-range night attack on the *Bismarck*, who had escorted Arctic convoys to Russia, and who in this same month of March 1942 had had his flagship *Naiad* sunk under him by a U-boat during an abortive sortie against an Axis convoy – for Vian this was the news which he and his C-in-C had feared the most. With just four light cruisers, eleven fleet destroyers and six 'Hunts', he now had to protect his vital convoy from an enemy force at first estimated to comprise three 15-inch gun battleships. The true odds were daunting enough – the new battleship *Littorio*, two 8-inch gun heavy cruisers, a 6-inch gun cruiser and ten destroyers, to say nothing of the enemy air forces, which could range freely over the British convoy now that it lay outside the range of Royal Air Force fighters.

But Vian had carefully worked out and thoroughly practised his tactics with his captains beforehand for just such a crisis, and in particular a manoeuvre 'to move out from a cruising disposition designed to meet air attack into a disposition for surface action with the least possible delay'.[21] In case he chose to avoid close engagement he had arranged a special signal ordering his squadron 'to carry out diversionary tactics, using smoke to cover the escape of the convoy': while the convoy itself was to turn away closely escorted by five 'Hunts' only, the cruisers and fleet destroyers (concentrated in divisions) were to lay smoke at right angles to the bearing of the enemy, but to be ready to reverse course in time to attack with torpedoes when Italian ships approached the edge of the smoke.

At 1230 on 22 March 1942 Vian made the operational signal to his striking force to steer to the north towards the enemy in six divisions (the sixth being charged with the special task of laying smoke) – the opening move in the Second Battle of Sirte.

At 1332 enemy aircraft dropped four red flares as markers ahead of the convoy. At 1410 the cruiser *Euryalus* reported seeing funnel smoke to the north and then, a quarter of an hour later, four warships bearing 015°; at the same time the destroyer *Legion* reported a ship bearing 010°, distance twelve miles. On receiving these reports Vian made his prearranged signal: the convoy hauled away to the south-west while his striking force formed into divisions in line ahead. At 1433 thick black smoke began to belch from funnels as his ships raced to lay a protective curtain between the convoy and the Italian squadron to the northward. For the next hour the four British light cruisers (three with 5.25-inch guns; one with 6-inch) and the fleet destroyers dodged in and out of the fringes of the smoke screen to engage the enemy at long range. But the Italians displayed little appetite for close action, and at 1535 Vian was able to signal Cunningham: 'Enemy driven off.'[22]

In the meantime, however, Ju 88s had been doing their determined best to destroy the convoy by high-level and dive-bombing attacks, only to fail in the face of a storm of anti-aircraft fire and skilful handling of the convoy. This was no Mediterranean summer day of white wave-crests sparkling on a copper-sulphate sea, but the winter Mediterranean – a strong and freshening breeze from the south-east; wind-torn and steeply rolling dark waters. The forecastle guncrews of the destroyers were, wrote Commander Jellicoe of the *Southwold*, 'drenched from the start' and 'fighting their guns under most difficult conditions'.[23] Nonetheless, according to Vian in his subsequent report, the 4-inch fire from the 'Hunts' 'was most impressive, resembling continuous pom-pom fire in sound'.[24] But the cost in ammunition of repelling the Ju 88s proved to be colossal. HMS *Southwold* herself was down to only 40 per cent of 4-inch rounds, while the anti-aircraft ship *Carlisle* had fired off a third of her stocks.

Hardly had Vian come up with the convoy again when Italian ships were freshly sighted to the north-east – and this time the 8-inch gun cruisers *Gorizia* and *Trento* and the 6-inch gun *Giovanni Delle Bande Nere* had been joined by the battleship *Littorio* (45,963 tons full load; nine 15-inch guns; twelve 6-inch).

While the convoy itself steered away to the south (still under air attack), Vian's ships laid a pall of smoke from east to west between it and the enemy. In his report on the action Vian noted 'the enormous area of smoke'

> . . . which lay well in the existing weather conditions of a 25-knot wind from the south-east. The enemy tried to make touch with the convoy by passing round the western end of the smoke, to leeward, and was therefore effectively held away from the convoy, as he would not approach the smoke, which was drifting towards him.[25]

In Vian's professional judgment the Italian commander's best course would have been to pass to windward of the smoke (that is, to the east), but the enemy preferred to take the shortest course to get between the convoy and Malta.[26]

There followed a highly confused action as the British ships manoeuvred in and out of the smoke, catching short-lived sightings of the enemy, while green seas washed over fore and aft, and driving spray drenched even the cruisers' control towers when they were steaming to windward. Yet whenever possible the little British ships went for the Italians: first for the 8-inch gun cruisers and then, from 1700 onwards, for *Littorio* herself, even starting a fire abaft her after 15-inch turret. With rollers sweeping over their heaving forecastles the destroyers replied to 8-inch and 15-inch salvoes with 4.7-inch and 4-inch; torpedoes too when the Italians were close enough. It was a majestic display of tactical skill and sheer aggressive seamanship, absolutely true to the tradition of Hawke and Nelson; and it dominated and daunted the enemy. After two and a half hours the Italian squadron gave up and retired to the north-west. The British cruisers had fired between 1,600 and 1,700 rounds; the destroyers 1,300.

For Cunningham himself, back in a shore operations room in Alexandria instead of in his favourite place on the bridge in the thick of the battle, but listening in to all Vian's signal traffic, it was a time of anxiety sharpened by impotence. 'Never have I felt so keenly,' he wrote in his memoirs, 'the mortifying bitterness of sitting behind the scenes with a heavy load of responsibility while others were in action with the enemy . . . We could imagine it all, yet there was nothing we could do to help.'[27] Yet the C-in-C *was* helping Vian – in the first place by not interfering in Vian's conduct of the action with redundant advice or instructions, and secondly by simply being Cunningham. For Vian knew that stoutly supporting him in his own determination that the convoy should not turn back but (in Vian's words) 'proceed to Malta even if enemy surface forces make contact' there stood a Commander-in-Chief with a clear head, a cool nerve and a steely will. Under another Commander-in-Chief, in another desperate convoy action, Vian would find things very different (see below, pp. 509–10).

Casualties there had been, however, in seeing off the *Littorio* and her consorts. The destroyer *Havock*'s speed had been reduced to 16 knots by a near-miss from a 15-inch shell, while another shell of this calibre had crippled the destroyer *Kingston*. Reckoning that they were not fit to undertake the return voyage to Alexandria in the teeth of a rising easterly gale, Vian ordered them to go on to Malta with the convoy. His own flagship *Cleopatra* had been hit in the bridge early in the action, killing fifteen and temporarily knocking out her radio. But, wrote Vian in his memoirs, 'The damage sustained was of no importance. The leaders of the divisions of the striking force were well aware of my intentions, and communication, for the time, was unnecessary.'[28]

At 1940 on 22 March, with the convoy not yet in sight again and with darkness spreading across the wild sea, Vian turned east for Alexandria as planned with three cruisers and eight destroyers, leaving the convoy to make its own way to Malta under cover of night. At noon on 24 March Vian brought his squadron safely into Alexandria harbour despite constant air attacks on the homeward voyage (the Royal Air Force provided welcome fighter cover on the last leg). As his battered ships steamed slowly to their moorings, he and his ships' companies were, as he put it in his report, 'honoured to receive the great demonstration' for their victory given by the crowds on shore.[29] In the meantime attacks by the Royal Air Force on the homeward-bound Italian warships had proved a total failure, so bearing out

Cunningham's mistrust of its striking power over the sea. However, the submarine *Urge* (Lieutenant-Commander Tomkinson) redeemed the failure by sinking the cruiser *Giovanni Delle Bande Nere* on 1 April.

Vian's superb fight in the Second Battle of Sirte evoked a warm and generous tribute from the Prime Minister, who signalled ('Action This Day') to the C-in-C, Mediterranean:

> I shall be glad if you will convey to Admiral Vian and all who sailed with him the admiration which I feel at this resolute and brilliant action by which the Malta convoy was saved. That one of the most powerful modern battleships afloat attended by four cruisers and a flotilla should have been routed and put to flight . . . in broad daylight by a force of British light cruisers and destroyers constitutes a naval episode of the highest distinction and entitles all ranks and ratings concerned, and above all their Commander, to the compliments of the British nation.[30]

Vian himself was later rewarded with a knighthood of the Order of the Bath: 'I considered,' he wrote, 'that the honour reflected upon all who served with me.'[31]

By the time Vian had turned for Alexandria at 1940 on 22 March, Captain Hutchison of HMS *Breconshire*, the convoy commodore of MW10, had already dispersed the merchant ships for the final run-in to Malta, allotting one or two destroyers to each as escort. But now came a sad, dragging anti-climax to 'Operation MG1'. Owing to losing distance during the evasive daytime manoeuvres the merchant ships proved unable to reach safe haven during the hours of darkness as planned. In the forenoon of 23 March they were still straggling towards Malta under relentless pounding by enemy bombers every last mile of the voyage. The first two ships, *Talabot* and *Pampas*, arrived about 0915, together with their escort destroyers. According to the commander of HMS *Havock*, 'We proceeded up harbour to the cheers of the populace.'[32]

The cheers were all too soon to change to lamentation. A few minutes later the *Breconshire* got within eight miles of harbour when at last the bombers hit and disabled her. Attempts to get her in tow failed because of her deep draught and the heavy swell, and she had to be left at anchor in the open with three destroyers to protect her. At 1020 came the next misfortune: *Clan Campbell* was hit and sunk just twenty miles short of Malta by a bomb dropped from only fifty feet. HMS *Legion* was also so badly damaged that she had to be beached. And this marked only the start of the enemy's avenging of the failure of the Italian Navy. On 24 March the destroyer *Southwold* was sunk by a mine while standing by the stricken *Breconshire*. On the

26th both the *Talabot* and the *Pampas* were hit by German bombers in harbour; the *Talabot* had to be scuttled for fear that her cargo of ammunition might explode, while all but two of *Pampas*'s holds were flooded. That same day HMS *Legion* was bombed again and finally sunk in the naval dockyard. On the morrow the *Breconshire*, hit once more by bombs, sank at Marsaxlokk, whither she had been laboriously towed after three days at anchor outside Malta.

So it was that only 5,000 tons of supplies out of the 26,000 tons originally despatched in the convoy survived for the benefit of the garrison and people of Malta, along with some oil fuel salvaged from the *Breconshire*; a grimly disappointing conclusion to so great and gallant an effort. The consequences of the successful German bombing of the ships in harbour went, however, much further. In Cunningham's words it 'showed all too clearly that there was no further chance of using surface forces from the islands while that scale of attack persisted. The dockyard was a shambles of rubble and twisted girders . . . and they [the surface forces] were nearly out of fuel-oil.'[33] The Vice-Admiral, Malta, Sir Ralph Leatham, therefore began the melancholy process of evacuating to Alexandria all ships as soon as they were patched up enough to steam, starting with the cruiser *Aurora* and the Hunt class destroyer *Avon Vale* on 29 March and ending with the *Penelope* on 8 April – the latter nicknamed 'HMS Pepperpot', so riddled with holes was she.

On 1 April 1942 Sir Andrew Cunningham hauled down his flag as Commander-in-Chief, Mediterranean, on being appointed to head the British naval staff mission in Washington. He was to be replaced in two months' time by Admiral Sir Henry Harwood; in the meantime Admiral Pridham-Wippell assumed temporary command. It was a sad time for Cunningham to go, in the midst of a period of eclipse for the Mediterranean Fleet after the truly heroic days of 1940 and 1941 with their prolonged ordeals unflinchingly borne and their victories resolutely won. Nevertheless his farewell order of the day to the Fleet displayed the authentic Cunningham touch:

> The enemy knows we are his master on the sea, and we must strain every nerve to keep our standard of fighting so high that this lesson never fails to be borne in upon him . . . I look forward to the day when the Mediterranean Fleet will sweep the sea clear and re-establish an age-old control of this waterway so vital to the British Empire. I am confident that day is not far distant, and meanwhile I wish you all good fortune and God speed.[34]

The plight and problem of Malta worsened. The Navy had had to go; the Royal Air Force on the island had been virtually annihilated by the weight of enemy air attack; the future supply position was deeply worrying. In London it was decided that no convoy could be run in May from the Gibraltar direction because British seapower was being globally squeezed – in the Atlantic; in the Arctic where the battleship *Tirpitz* threatened British convoys to Russia from her Norwegian base; in the Indian Ocean where a Japanese raid by Nagumo's fast carrier force had even posed a menace to the sole surviving lifeline from Britain to Egypt up the east coast of Africa to the Red Sea (see below, p. 863). In the meantime only a trickle of vital supplies was reaching Malta by submarine.

If Malta was to survive, the first essential must be to rebuild her fighter defence; and that meant flying the aircraft in from carriers as in 1941. But the Royal Navy lacked the carriers to meet all its commitments. Churchill therefore appealed for help to President Roosevelt, who consented to the employment of the USS *Wasp* (Captain J. W. Reeves, Jr, USN: 21,000 tons full load; capacity 84 aircraft; launched 1939)[35] then already in British home waters. On 13 April 1942 she embarked 47 Spitfires in the Clyde and sailed next day escorted by the battlecruiser *Renown* (Commodore C. S. Daniel), the cruiser *Charybdis* and the anti-aircraft cruiser *Cairo*, and a mixed force of British and American destroyers. The force passed through the Straits of Gibraltar under cover of darkness in the small hours of 19 April and steamed on eastwards – the first time that the Stars and Stripes of the US Navy had flown alongside the White Ensign in the Mediterranean in this war. On 20 April the Spitfires were flown off, all but one safely reaching Malta's airfields, and many of them engaging the Luftwaffe that same day. But the enemy immediately mounted a ruthless effort to eliminate these fighter reinforcements both in the air and by smashing them on their airfields – and he largely succeeded. And so in the first week of May, with Roosevelt's further consent, the USS *Wasp* once again embarked 47 Spitfires and with the same escort as before set course for Gibraltar and the Mediterranean.

At Gibraltar on the night of 7–8 May she was joined by the old British carrier *Eagle* (with seventeen Spitfires aboard) and the fast minelayer *Manxman*, which was to go right through to Malta with a much-needed cargo of special stores and ammunition. 'We are quite likely to lose this ship,' wrote the First Sea Lord to Churchill, 'but in view of the urgency . . . there appears to be no alternative.'[36] In the event, the *Manxman* returned safely, having unloaded her stores and sailed again within seven hours. On 9 May the two carriers flew off their 64 Spitfires, only three being lost en route to Malta. Next day they fought a successful battle against the enemy; the beginning of the turning of the tide in the air over Malta.

In the middle of May the *Eagle* was back again with seventeen more Spitfires; and early in June she made two more such trips, this time ferrying a total of 55 fighters. Through such exertions Malta's fighter defence was at last made equal to its task. By this time too the island's anti-aircraft equipment, including smoke projectors to screen the harbour and dockyard, had also been cumulatively strengthened. The neglect of the inter-war years had finally been made good – but at a period when Britain had lost command of the Mediterranean, and when it looked as if Malta might soon be starved into defeat anyway.

To avert this imminent fate there had now to be mounted a complex operation of maritime war on the largest scale – two convoys to be run simultaneously to Malta from Gibraltar ('Harpoon': six merchant ships) and Alexandria ('Vigorous': eleven ships) in June, although timed to arrive at the island on successive days in order to confuse the enemy. The flying-in of the Spitfires had provided the essential air cover for the convoys during their final approach to their destination. A second serious danger lay, however, in mines, for Malta lacked the vessels and equipment adequately to sweep them.

The plan for 'Operation Harpoon', the western convoy from the United Kingdom via Gibraltar, followed the pattern of late 1941. A covering force (Force W) consisting of the battleship *Malaya*, the old carriers *Eagle* and *Argus*, three cruisers (*Kenya*, flying the flag of Vice-Admiral A. T. B. Curteis; *Liverpool* and *Charybdis*) and eight destroyers, would escort the convoy as far as the Skerki Bank, off Tunisia, then turn back. The close escort (Force X) – one anti-aircraft cruiser (*Cairo*: Acting-Captain G. C. Hardy), nine destroyers and four minesweepers – would shepherd the six merchant ships the rest of the way to Malta.[37] Yet there was a difference between the 'Harpoon' escort forces and those deployed in the late 1941 Malta convoys: the 'Harpoon' forces were much weaker because of the competing demands of the Eastern Fleet in parrying the Japanese, and also of the current Allied invasion of Madagascar (see below, pp. 864–8).

The 'Harpoon' convoy, bearing 43,000 tons of supplies, sailed from Britain on 5 June; passed the Straits of Gibraltar during the night of 11th–12th, and steamed on through a calm and sunlit Mediterranean. Next day enemy aircraft and submarines began to tag the convoy. The 14th proved another glorious – but to ships facing air attack, deadly – Mediterranean summer's day; and the convoy was now well within range of enemy air bases on Sardinia. From 1030 onwards the bombers began their persistent work: at first Italian CR42 fighter-bombers and Savoia torpedo-bombers. A Savoia inflicted the first losses with torpedoes dropped at a height of 100 feet and a range of 2,000 yards, sinking the Dutch merchantman *Tanimba* and hitting the cruiser *Liverpool* in the engine room. Now capable of only 3 to 4 knots on one shaft, the *Liverpool* had to be detached back to Gibraltar under tow by the destroyer *Antelope* and escorted by the destroyer *Westcott*, eventually making port in the evening of 17 June. Then it was the turn of Italian Cant high-level bombers approaching out of the eye of the sun and singling out the carriers, which fortunately survived without damage. So far British carrier-borne fighters had shot down three fighters and three torpedo-aircraft, which was not bad going in the light of what Captain Washbrooke of the *Eagle* called in his report 'the most inadequate measure' of protection afforded by the two small old carriers, able to fly at most only six Hurricanes and four Fulmars at any time.[38]

The day dragged on, the convoy and its escort crawling along naked on the sea's broad surface beneath the bombers and the brilliant sky; the ships' companies sweltering in anti-flash hoods and tin hats. At 1830 the Luftwaffe joined in, ten Ju 88s coming in astern at 10,000 feet and then diving to 6,000 feet for the attack. According to Vice-Admiral Curteis in his report, 'As is usual in the Mediterranean it was very difficult to see these till they had reached the bombing position, and gunfire was ineffective.'[39] Both carriers were lucky to escape damage, especially the *Argus*, which had one bomb pitch fine on her port bow, dive beneath the ship and burst under the starboard bow.

This was merely the overture to an orchestrated onslaught of high-level bombing, dive-bombing and torpedo attacks by both Italian and German aircraft in order to overwhelm the British defences – enemy aircraft swarming round and overhead with ships' tracer curving among them, the puffballs of shellbursts drifting against the blue as thick as thistledown. Yet neither side scored a hit. Meanwhile the convoy had been manoeuvred almost as dexterously as a division of destroyers; a major reason for the enemy failure. The carrier-borne fighters that day shot down eleven aircraft for the loss of seven. As the Director of the Naval Air Division of the Naval Staff remarked later in a minute: 'The results achieved by the small force of naval fighters are most outstanding.'[40] They were the more outstanding because *Eagle* and *Argus* lacked modern fighter-direction apparatus.[41]

At 2100, when the convoy had reached the Sicilian Narrows, four welcome Royal Air Force Beaufighters turned up from Malta. Half an hour later Curteis and Force X hauled round to the west, its part completed. The merchant ships and Force Y – under the command of Captain G. C. Hardy, in the *Cairo* – stood on for Malta; the merchantmen in line ahead screened on all sides by the warships.

That evening, however, Curteis received a report that two Italian cruisers and some destroyers had left Palermo in Sicily, course undetermined. For Curteis, now some fifty miles distant from the convoy, this report presented a dilemma: should he despatch one of his two remaining cruisers to support the outgunned Hardy? His own force still lay within striking range of the enemy's Sardinian airfields, and he was worried about weakening the anti-aircraft protection of his carriers by detaching a cruiser. In any case there would be barely time for her to overtake the convoy before morning. 'With the forces available,' he wrote in his report, 'a decision either way was a gamble: if the LIVERPOOL had been present, there would have been no doubt in my mind.'[42] As it was, he decided that the convoy's own escort should prove sufficient. It was a decision that would be questioned later within the Admiralty.

Next day, 15 June, its good fortune forsook 'Harpoon'. At daybreak British submarines sighted the two Italian cruisers and five destroyers and attacked them without success. At 0620 a Beaufighter reported to Hardy that two cruisers and four (sic) destroyers lay fifteen miles distant on the port beam of the British force. The convoy was then steering south-east at 12 knots, with the merchantmen now in two columns, the *Cairo* ahead, five fleet destroyers to starboard and four 'Hunts' to port, and the four fleet minesweepers and some motor launches astern. Only a few minutes passed before the Italian ships were seen broad on the port beam and hull down against the bright eastern morning sky, and steering a slightly converging course at high speed. They were soon identified as two 6-inch gun cruisers and six destroyers. Hardy, with only an anti-aircraft cruiser, found himself heavily outweighted; a victim (like Curteis too) of the Royal Navy's sheer shortage of cruisers after the losses of nearly three years of war coming on top of crippling reductions of strength in the late 1920s and early 1930s. In previous Malta convoy operations it had been possible to provide a strong cruiser escort to send on to Malta with the merchantmen; not so this time. Hardy would have to battle his way through as best he could.

While Commander B. G. Scurfield (in the *Bedouin*) unhesitatingly led out the five fleet destroyers to attack the enemy force, HMS *Cairo* laid a smoke screen to protect the convoy, which Hardy ordered away to starboard and to shelter in Tunisian waters. At 0640 the Italian cruisers opened fire at 20,000 yards, immediately straddling the *Cairo*.

The 4.7-inch and 4-inch guns of the British destroyers were still completely outranged. In a loose line of bearing the five fleet destroyers steamed for the enemy. At 0645 they opened fire at maximum elevation. But within a quarter of an hour both leading destroyers, *Bedouin* and *Partridge*, had been badly damaged and stopped. The *Ithuriel* held her fire until she had closed the range to 15,000 yards, and succeeded in hitting one of the cruisers at 8,000 yards. The destroyer *Marne* likewise took on an Italian cruiser, and then *Marne* and *Matchless* together attacked the Italian destroyers. After the *Ugolino Vivaldi* was hit, the enemy destroyers followed the customary Italian pattern of discretion before valour, and retired. *Marne* and *Matchless* thereupon turned their guns on the cruisers, which also displayed a reluctance to engage more closely. At 0745 the Italian ships turned away to port; another success for British fighting seamanship.

However, while the bulk of Hardy's strength had been employed in driving off the enemy surface forces, enemy aircraft had taken the opportunity to savage the merchant ships. Ju 88s sank the *Chant* and disabled the *Kentucky*, which had to be taken in tow. At 0745 the convoy commodore, Commander Pilditch, decided to resume the course for Malta in order to join up with Hardy. But since the Italian surface forces were still shadowing Hardy, this could well run the convoy into fresh danger. Hardy therefore ordered the convoy to reverse course again at 0834, while the *Cairo* and the destroyers laid a protective smoke screen which successfully baffled the Italians. At this time *Cairo* took her second hit.

At 1040 the air attacks began again, although at first the enemy was driven off by long-range Spitfires from Malta. Forty minutes later, in the interval before the next relay of Spitfires arrived, Ju 88s and Ju 87s bombed from high and low, crippling the merchant ship *Burdwan*. Yet the convoy still had a hundred and fifty miles to go to Malta. Hardy therefore decided that he must sink the crippled *Kentucky* and *Burdwan* in order that the convoy could make maximum speed. In the afternoon the Italian cruisers tried again – and were driven off again. However, a torpedo-bomber succeeded in sinking the crippled destroyer *Bedouin*, which had been in tow.

The 16th June went better, thanks to constant cover by Malta Spitfires accurately directed against the foe by *Cairo*'s radar and fighter-direction centre. It seemed as though the worst must now have passed. But, by an unfortunate error of timing, the convoy reached the waters round Malta before the minesweepers. Four warships and one merchantman struck mines, although all were able to reach harbour except for the Polish destroyer *Kujawiak*, which sank.

In the evening *Cairo* and the only four undamaged fleet destroyers sailed again for Gibraltar. Back came the relentless enemy air forces, and only after what the captain of the *Ithuriel* in his report described as 'a struggle for existence' did Force Y – amazingly without further damage – rejoin Curteis for a safe return to Gibraltar.

'Operation Harpoon' had been accomplished. Its ships had been attacked by a total of about 200 enemy aircraft, of which the carriers' fighters had shot down thirteen and anti-aircraft fire another sixteen (the *Cairo* was equipped with an American fire-control system). Two destroyers had been lost, and a cruiser, three destroyers and a mine-sweeper badly damaged. And of the six merchant ships despatched, only two finally reached Malta – another disappointing pay-off.

In the meantime the Mediterranean Fleet had been mounting its even bigger operation to try to get eleven merchant ships through to Malta from Alexandria – the first to be carried out under the direction of the new Commander-in-Chief, Mediterranean, Acting-Admiral Sir Henry Harwood, who had hoisted his flag in the *Queen Elizabeth* (now being repaired in a floating dock) on 20 May. Harwood's reputation – especially with Churchill – had been made by his aggressive conduct of action against the *Graf Spee* in December 1939, even though he had earlier been marked down to be passed over for promotion to flag rank.[43] Since December 1940 he had served ashore in Whitehall as Assistant Chief of Naval Staff (Foreign), and therefore when he succeeded Cunningham in the enormous and complex political, strategic and operational responsibilities of the Mediterranean command, his previous experience as a commander had been limited to one small squadron of three cruisers. It was rather as if the owner of a corner shop had suddenly been put in charge of Harrods. No wonder that, when Cunningham heard of the Admiralty's nominee as his replacement, he had written to the First Sea Lord to express a preference for 'someone better experienced and better known to the personnel'.[44] Nonetheless Pound, A. V. Alexander (the First Lord) and Churchill all agreed that Harwood was the man.

It proved, to say the least, a mistaken choice. Harwood lacked the sheer ruthless powers of leadership of his predecessor, the certainty of mind; lacked too the matured grasp of all the problems of the theatre. For the Fleet and its flag officers, it was as if an iron grasp had suddenly relaxed; an animating fire gone cold. And almost as soon as Harwood hoisted his flag, he found himself compelled – by London's direction against his own judgment – to carry out 'Operation Vigorous', a particularly hazardous undertaking the risks of which were vastly increased by the long days and short nights of mid-June.

By 'loans' from the Eastern Fleet, the warship strength available as the main escort for 'Vigorous' was built up to seven cruisers, one anti-aircraft ship, and 26 destroyers. In addition four motor torpedo boats were to be towed by merchant ships, ready to be slipped for action when necessary, while two minesweepers and unarmed rescue ships were also to accompany the convoy.[45] It was a singular mark of the poverty of the Royal Navy's resources that in lieu of a real battleship a dummy *King George V* was to sail in the escort – the old battleship *Centurion*, launched in 1911, stripped of her guns in 1924 and later used as a radio-controlled target ship, and now put back into service again with a light anti-aircraft armament and with her superstructure unconvincingly altered to resemble a 'King George V'. Nor could a carrier be provided.

Harwood therefore looked to Royal Air Force and United States Army Air Force bombers to fill the place of heavy ships and carrier-borne aviation in preventing the Italian battlefleet from attacking the convoy. Because of this he and Tedder moved to a combined command centre in the headquarters of the Naval Cooperation Group, RAF, in Alexandria.

However, the available land-based air forces consisted of a mixed bag of only 40 aircraft: torpedo-armed Wellingtons and Beauforts from Malta, more Beauforts from Egyptian airfields near the Libyan border, and some American Liberator heavy bombers from the Suez area. The joint plan required these varied and widely dispersed forces to launch synchronised attacks on the Italian fleet once it was detected at sea by air search. In his subsequent report Harwood was to write: 'Events proved with painful clarity that our striking forces had nothing like the weight required to stop a fast and powerful enemy force, and in no way compensated for our lack of heavy ships.'[46] This was no more than Cunningham had bluntly pointed out to Pound at the beginning of the year; it hardly needed to be learned afresh by costly experience. Admiral Vian, the flag officer designated to command 'Vigorous' afloat, was of the opinion (according to his post-war recollection) that once Harwood 'accepted a weak, unescorted air striking force as a substitute [for battleships] we were sunk . . .'[47] Vian reckoned that it was not possible with cruisers and destroyers equipped with dual-purpose (anti-ship *and* anti-aircraft) guns to fight a fleet action from dawn till dusk on a June day with what ammunition would be left over after fending off heavy air attacks; and *then* still have enough ammunition for the return passage.[48] Vian therefore went to sea in a frame of mind very different from that in March at the start of 'Operation MG1', for, as he later confessed, he lacked confidence in the plan, in the C-in-C, and the C-in-C's ability to carry out the plan; and, because of all this, he lacked personal confidence too.[49]

In order to mislead the enemy the merchant ships were loaded in various ports between Beirut and Alexandria, and then assembled in two groups in Haifa and Alexandria. At the same time a third group of four ships sailed on 11 June (thirty-six hours ahead of the main body) as far as Tobruk in order – as it was hoped – to draw the Italian fleet to sea prematurely. This ploy failed of its purpose; and it also failed to divert the enemy air forces.

On the evening of 13 June Vian put to sea with the main body, flying his flag in the cruiser *Cleopatra* (Captain G. Grantham). From sunset until 0430 next morning enemy aircraft kept the convoy and its escort brilliantly illuminated with parachute flares. During the night the destroyer screen successfully drove off a marauding U-boat and six E-boats, which success Vian put down to the 'unattractive proposition' presented to the enemy by his dispositions for the dark hours – an anti-submarine screen ahead on the bows of the convoy, a special 'night screen' of two cruisers and four destroyers on each quarter, and a single destroyer five miles out on each bow and quarter. But Rear-Admiral Tennant (the former Captain of the *Repulse*), who was commanding the ships lent by the Eastern Fleet, recalled that 'the flares gave me a very naked feeling when dropped overhead, and it is surprising that the E-boats did not achieve a great deal more success'.[50]

Next day, the 14th – it was the day when far away to the west the enemy air forces began to attack the 'Harpoon' convoy too – the bombers arrived early, and kept it up all day, sinking one merchant ship and damaging another so badly that she had to be detached to Tobruk. Since the bottom of a third ship proved so foul that she could not keep up, the convoy's numbers had already fallen to eight. Now Vian was running the gauntlet of hostile air forces based all along the North African coast as far as Tripoli on one flank, and Crete and Sicily on the other; running deep into the zone where the Italian battlefleet would be likely to strike from its bases in Sicily and the heel of Italy. It was therefore absolutely essential that British air reconnaissance kept Harwood and Vian exactly informed about the enemy's position, course and speed. But, as the Naval Staff History remarks, 'the aircraft available for the purpose were too few to keep the enemy under continuous observation'.[51] Only confusing and sometimes incorrect reports were to reach Harwood and Tedder during the operation; an uncertainty by no means helpful to a novice of a C-in-C in his first crisis of command.

At 2215 on 14 June Vian received a signal from Harwood passing on an aircraft report that two battleships and four cruisers had sailed from Taranto and would probably encounter him on his present course at about 0700 next morning – at almost the beginning, therefore, of the long June day: the very contingency with which Vian knew he could not this time cope. He therefore signalled the C-in-C to ask: 'Do you wish me to retire?'[52] Harwood responded by ordering Vian to keep his course until 0200 (why?) and then to 'turn back along the same track'. At 0145 on the 15th Vian turned the convoy and escort – some fifty ships to manoeuvre on to a reverse course. This cumbersome process gave an opening to an E-boat to infiltrate the escort and torpedo the cruiser *Newcastle* forward, although she still remained capable of 24 knots. A little later a U-boat hit the destroyer *Hasty*, so disabling her that she had to be sunk by a consort.

At the time when Vian turned the convoy the Italian fleet, steering south to intercept, was still more than 200 miles distant to the north-west. At 0224 a further air report gave the Italian strength as one battleship, two cruisers and two destroyers, position 37° 30′N, 19° 35′E, course 190°, speed 20 knots. At 0525 Harwood was signalling once more; this time to order Vian to steer north-westwards again, on the score that 'bomb alley' between Crete and Libya would be more dangerous than the Italian ships. At 0655, Vian, having received this fresh order, duly turned the convoy back towards Malta and the approaching Italian fleet. At 0705 Harwood radioed another instruction to Vian, and not one that could have eased Vian's mind very much:

> Avoid contact until [British] aircraft have attacked, which should be by 1030. If air attack fails, every effort must be made to get convoy through to Malta by adopting offensive attitude. Should this fail, and convoy be cornered, it is to be sacrificed, and you are to extricate your forces, proceeding to eastward or westward.[53]

An hour and a half later Harwood received another air search report according to which two battleships, three cruisers and nine destroyers lay within 150 miles of the convoy, steering south-east. So Harwood signalled Vian yet again: Vian was to steer 105° – that is, eastwards once more. On receipt of the signal at 0940 Vian altered round.

With an Italian squadron including heavy ships known for certain to be at sea and steering to intercept, it was now up to the Allied bombers to fulfil their task of preventing it reaching the convoy. From 0905 to 0940 Beauforts from Malta and Egypt and Liberators from

Suez had a go; and succeeded in landing one bomb on the battleship *Littorio*'s forward 15-inch turret which failed to penetrate the armour, and one torpedo on the 8-inch gun cruiser *Trento*, disabling her. She was to be sunk later that day by the submarine *Umbria* (Lieutenant S. L. C. Maydon). However, the Beauforts wrongly reported at 0944 that they had hit both Italian battleships as well as the cruiser. This apparently marvellous news encouraged Harwood at 1151 to order Vian to resume his course for Malta, although Harwood also repeated by way of caution the broad directive contained in his signal of 0705 that morning. So yet again Vian brought his sprawling and unwieldy command round: further waste of time and loss of distance.

Back in the operations room in Alexandria, Harwood waited anxiously for more aircraft reports on the whereabouts of the Italian fleet; none came. If even Cunningham had found the waiting, the uncertainty and the impotence of 'back-seat' command from on shore hard to bear, the strain on the unfortunate Harwood may be imagined. He began to worry that the Beauforts might only have hit the cruiser. He did not know whether Vian had been attacked or mauled by the Italian fleet; nor what was Vian's present ammunition state. At 1245 he signalled Vian: 'I must leave decision to you whether to comply with my 0705/15, or whether to again retire with hope of carrying out a night destroyer attack, if enemy stand on.'[54]

Vian only received Harwood's earlier signal of 1151 hours at 1345, and soon afterwards came confirmation from a report by 'Aircraft T' that the enemy was indeed standing on. The attempt to substitute bombers for battleships and carriers had thus totally failed to fend off the Italian fleet. So too had the picket lines of eight submarines, whose efforts to screen the convoy had been rendered more difficult by the convoy's changes of course.

By this time both Vian's most modern and powerful cruisers, the *Newcastle* and the *Birmingham* (both 9,100 tons displacement; twelve 6-inch guns; launched 1936 under the rearmament programme)[55] had been damaged; *Newcastle* by the E-boat on the previous day, *Birmingham* by a bomb. Vian therefore decided not to implement for the time being the C-in-C's signal of 1151 ordering him to resume course for Malta: 'My heavy striking force, the Fourth Cruiser Squadron, being somewhat under the weather, I held on to the eastward awaiting [the C-in-C's] reactions to Aircraft T's report.'[56] At 1420 he received Harwood's discretionary signal sent at 1245 hours, which only confirmed him in continuing to steer east. An hour later 30 to 40 dive-bombers escorted by Me 109s roared in from astern. Twelve of the bombers concentrated on the destroyer *Airedale* out in the air-warning screen on the starboard quarter of the convoy, and blanketed her with hits and near-misses. Disabled, she had to be sunk by a consort. Meanwhile another merchant ship had had to drop out because it could not maintain speed, so that the precious convoy was now down to only six ships.

Meanwhile, however, the Italian battle squadron had unexpectedly given up the chase when it got to within about 100 miles of the convoy. At 1515 it hauled round to the north-westward. At 1605 a British aircraft reported that it was by then well on its way to Taranto.

To Harwood this news appeared to change the situation entirely. At 1625 he signalled Vian: 'Now is the golden opportunity to get convoy to Malta. Have Hunts, *Coventry*, minesweepers and corvettes enough fuel and ammunition for one-way trip? If so, I would like to turn the convoy now, cruisers and destroyers parting company and returning to Alexandria.'[57] Two hours later he had still received no reply from Vian to this ebullient signal. For from 1720 onwards Vian was fully occupied with nearly 30 enemy bombers and ten torpedo-bombers, both German and Italian, which sought by a combination of high and low-level attack to do what the Italian fleet had failed to do. Vian wrote in his subsequent report: 'All known forms of attack were employed, the fire of the fleet being fully extended.'[58]

The high-level bombers attacked first, riding unseen at 16,000 feet in the western sun until nearly overhead: near-misses but not hits. Around 1800 it was the turn of the twin-engined Ju 88 dive-bombers. They released their bombs at 6,000 feet, slightly damaging the *Arethusa* and the ancient *Centurion* but crippling the Australian destroyer *Nestor* with a near-miss. An hour later three-engined Savoia 79s (maximum speed 267 mph; range, 1,180 miles)[59] launched torpedoes from both quarters, but again without scoring a hit. At the cost of enormous expenditure in ammunition Vian's ships shot down three Savoias and two bombers.

It was not until 1842, therefore, that Vian replied to Harwood's signal of 1625 about the golden opportunity of getting the convoy through to Malta and also enquiring about ammunition stocks. Vian reported that the destroyers had less than 30 per cent of their ammunition left, that it was being used up fast, and that he calculated it was insufficient for the passage to Malta. His report crossed another signal from Harwood sent at 1830 conveying the C-in-C's second thoughts (something to which he was rather prone) about going on to Malta: only four out of the remaining merchantmen were to continue thither, with the light cruiser *Arethusa* and two fleet destroyers as escort. But when Harwood himself received Vian's report about the depletion of ammunition, he finally ordered at 2053: 'Return to Alexandria with your whole force.'[60]

The enemy had won; the 'Vigorous' convoy had been forced to turn back; Malta would have to survive as best it might. But this did not mark the end of 'Vigorous's' travail. During the night of 15–16 June, a night of angry disappointment for Vian and his squadron, the U-205 torpedoed and sank the cruiser *Hermione* (Captain G. C. Oliver), while the damaged *Nestor* had to be scuttled at 0700 the following morning. That evening Vian's physically battered and morally bruised squadron reached Alexandria. It was some compensation that a Wellington had managed to torpedo the *Littorio* on her way home, inflicting damage that was to put her in the dockyard for several months.

No further convoy was to be run from Alexandria to Malta until November 1942.

Several factors explain this major defeat. The first was undoubtedly, as Harwood wrote (and Cunningham had well realised in his time), that the striking power of the Royal Air Force over the sea in the Mediterranean was simply not capable of stopping a battlefleet. Secondly, 'Vigorous' had to be mounted at a time when Rommel was already winning the Gazala battles – when, therefore, the Royal Air Force was deeply committed to that battle, and when even the airfields in eastern Cyrenaica could no longer be used by Beaufort torpedo-bombers. Coupled with the long June days and Vian's lack of a carrier, this meant that 'Vigorous' was more exposed to enemy air attack and for longer than any previous Malta convoy from Alexandria. Yet the clinching factor in the defeat lay in the C-in-C's dithering which led him to order Vian to turn his convoy no fewer than six times; instructions actually complied with four times, with consequent crucial loss of distance, to say nothing of the expenditure of ammunition. As Vian wrote later, his lack of confidence in the plan, in the C-in-C and in the C-in-C's ability to carry out the plan conduced to his own lack of confidence and hence, in his words, to 'its fatal corollary, irresolution'.[61] Cunningham's own retrospective judgment was that if Harwood had left Vian alone, Vian would have gone straight on; indeed Cunningham wondered why Harwood had not *ordered* him to press on.[62]

Would the convoy have got through if Cunningham had still been Commander-in-Chief? 'The reply is,' wrote Vian in 1954 in answer to this question, 'that no flag officer ever thought of not going through with a direct operation order from Andrew; but he would never issue one not capable of achievement with the forces allocated.'[63]

The end of June 1942 saw the entire Mediterranean strategy pursued by Britain since 1940 dead in the water. All the huge investment in shipping round the Cape, in the equipment, supplies (civilian as well as military), weaponry and military ration-strength poured into the Middle East in that shipping over the last two years, all the swaying Desert campaigns, had ended with a routed 8th Army preparing a last stand in defence of Egypt at El Alamein, only 60 miles west of Alexandria: with the Mediterranean Fleet's pre-war main base, Malta, neutralised; and with the Fleet itself having lost control of the Mediterranean, and even defeated outright in 'Operation Vigorous'. And now, just as the still undaunted General Sir Claude Auchinleck (who had taken personal command of 8th Army) told his soldiers that 'the enemy is stretching to his limit and thinks we are a broken army . . . He hopes to take Egypt by bluff. Show him where he gets off,'[64] his naval colleague, Admiral Harwood, precipitately ordered the Fleet to evacuate its base at Alexandria.

Although Cunningham had previously prepared a contingency plan for such an evacuation, it had taken the form of an orderly withdrawal over three weeks. Now it was carried out in 48 hours, the haste being such that the White Ensign was still flying over the deserted camp at Sidi Bishr while Egyptians looted it at their leisure.[65] The ships retired to Haifa (the submarine depot ship *Medway* being sunk en route by a U-boat) or to Port Said; Harwood himself went back to Ismailia on the Canal. In a letter to the First Sea Lord in November 1942 after his return to Alexandria Harwood claimed that he had ordered the evacuation because of the example of Singapore, where the process of withdrawal from the naval base had been left too late. 'In many ways though,' he admitted, 'I wish I had not left here [Alexandria]. . .'[66]

Yet within a month Auchinleck's hard-won victory over Rommel in the First Battle of Alamein (the first land battle to be conducted thanks to guidance by up-to-date information from Ultra decrypts of Enigma traffic)[67] had ensured that Britain's Mediterranean strategy would not after all finally founder. Hope revived. The Prime Minister (by now obsessed with beating the legendary Rommel and his three under-strength German divisions) and the Cabinet pressed on with fresh military investment in the Middle East on a gigantic scale – enough to build the 8th Army by October up to a strength of nearly 200,000 men, over 1,000 tanks (including 300 new Shermans shipped from the United States), over 900 medium field guns, over 1,400 anti-tank guns, over 8,000 (new) trucks, and more than 18,000 tons of forward stocks of medium and field artillery rounds.[68]

Such a build-up demanded yet another colossal shipping lift, both from the United Kingdom and the United States, at a time of a growing dearth of ships and of dismaying success for the U-boats in the Atlantic. In the three months July to September 1942 no fewer than 262 ships carried military cargoes to the Indian Ocean area (which included the Middle East), as against only 98 in the previous quarter.[69] And this commitment of shipping could only be at the expense of imports into the United Kingdom, both of food and of the essentials for war production, so necessitating recourse to stockpiles.[70]

Meanwhile the problem of Malta remained. Without succour the island could not survive the months that must elapse before this investment produced a victory that won back the vital airfields in the Cyrenaican bulge. Another early attempt to run a convoy to Malta in the meantime there had to be. After the experience of 'Operation Vigorous' it was clear that this attempt could only be made from the west, from Gibraltar. In the early hours of 10 August, the convoy and its escorting battlefleet reached the Straits of Gibraltar under a thick shroud of fog; 'Operation Pedestal' was about to begin.

So high did the War Cabinet place Malta in its global priorities that in order to free ships of the Home Fleet to augment the escort in 'Operation Pedestal' it decided not to run a convoy to Soviet Russia in August even though the Red Army was staggering back towards Stalingrad and the Caucasus in the face of the German 1942 summer offensive. The detachment of the battleship *Nelson*, the carrier *Victorious*, the cruisers *Nigeria*, *Kenya* and *Manchester* and eleven destroyers from the Home Fleet brought the strength of the battle-squadron escorting 'Pedestal' up to three fleet-carriers (the other two being *Indomitable* and *Eagle*), flying a total of 72 aircraft, two battleships (the other being *Rodney*), six cruisers, one anti-aircraft cruiser (*Cairo*), 24 destroyers, an ocean tug, and two fleet oilers with a corvette escort. In addition the carrier *Furious* (escorted by another eight destroyers) was to fly 36 Spitfires into Malta under cover of the main operation. In command of 'Operation Pedestal' was Vice-Admiral E. N. Syfret, flying his flag in the *Nelson* (Captain H. B. Jacomb),[71] who joined the convoy of fourteen merchantmen off the Clyde with the bulk of the escort on 3 August. On the voyage out to Gibraltar Admiral Syfret made the convoy practise emergency turns and other manoeuvres so that, in the words of his report, it 'attained an efficiency in manoeuvring comparable to that of the fleet unit'.[72] At the same time the three carriers practised air defence tactics and fighter-direction.

At Gibraltar most of the escort refuelled. Then, in the forenoon of

10 August Syfret passed the Rock into the Mediterranean, green seas mingling to blue, and set course for Malta. Thanks to fog the enemy only received news of this great armada that afternoon via a report from a Vichy-French commercial airliner. But soon after daylight on 11 August German reconnaissance aircraft were seen circling the horizon round the convoy, the familiar omen of trouble to come. They shadowed Syfret all day despite the attempts of carrier-borne fighters to drive them off. At 1230 the *Furious* (Captain T. O. Bulteel) began flying off her Spitfires to Malta at a distance of some 550 miles, a process which was to take several hours. At 1315 occurred the first disaster – from beneath the sea rather than above it. The U-73 (Lieutenant Helmut Rosenbaum) succeeded in diving undetected beneath the fleet's destroyer screen and through the four columns of merchant ships to fire four torpedoes at the carrier *Eagle* (Captain L. D. Mackintosh) on the starboard quarter of the convoy. The old ship (launched June 1918 as a Chilean battleship, completed 1923 as a carrier) suffered a huge hole blown in her port side, and sank in eight minutes in 38° 05′N, 3° 12′E. Nine hundred out of her complement of 1,160 (including Captain Mackintosh) were rescued by destroyers and the tug *Jaunty*. The four of her aircraft which were then in the air landed on other carriers.

On the evening of 11 August *Furious*, her task accomplished, turned back for Gibraltar with her escort of eight destroyers, one of which, the *Wolverine* (Lieutenant-Commander P. W. Gretton), rammed the Italian submarine *Dagabur* at high speed at 0100 next day, damaging herself badly in the process. Meanwhile the 'Pedestal' convoy and its escorting fleet steamed on towards the waiting enemy air forces. Late in the afternoon of the 11th Syfret received warning that he could expect to see these at dusk. He therefore spread out his destroyers in an all-round air-warning and anti-aircraft screen. At 2045 36 Heinkel He 111 bombers and Ju 88 torpedo-bombers attacked out of the setting sun: no hits, but instead four aircraft downed by the fleet's anti-aircraft fire. This was no more than the apéritif. In the bright midday of 12 August the enemy launched his first main onslaught on 'Pedestal' from his Sardinian airfields with 70 strike aircraft heavily escorted by fighters. For although Air Marshal Sir Keith Park (the airman who in command of No. 11 Group, Fighter Command, had played the leading part in defeating the Luftwaffe in the Battle of Britain, and was now commanding Royal Air Force, Malta) had done his best to suppress the enemy air forces by bombing their bases in Sardinia, Sicily and Pantellaria, he lacked the necessary weight of attack to achieve this.

This time the Luftwaffe and the Regia Aeronautica tried out a new combination of tactics in order to break up the convoy's formation and dislocate the fleet's air defence. Firstly, two Italian torpedo-bombers dropped a fearsome new product of Italian technology ahead of the convoy – the 'motobomba FF', a torpedo which ran round in circles to the bewilderment and dismay, as the enemy hoped, of British skippers. Then 42 torpedo-bombers rode in from each bow of the convoy, followed by dive-bombers and in turn by two Reggiane 2001 single-seat fighters (maximum speed 337 mph; range 684 miles)[73] each armed with an armour-piercing bomb intended for an aircraft carrier. This circus of varied turns went on for nearly two hours, but inflicted no losses beyond the merchant ship *Deucalion*, damaged and sunk later near the Tunisian coast by a torpedo-bomber. For fortunately a heavy bomb which did hit *Victorious*'s flight deck broke up harmlessly on impact.

During the afternoon 'Pedestal' had to fight and dodge its way through a massed submarine ambush. But thanks to the vigilant aggression of the escorting destroyers and frequent emergency changes of course the convoy came through unscathed, while the destroyer *Ithuriel* (Lieutenant-Commander D. H. Maitland-Makgill-Crichton) rammed and sank the Italian submarine *Cobalto*, again with crippling damage to the destroyer; in Syfret's judgment a needlessly expensive method of dealing with a U-boat surfaced after depth-charging.

At 1835 the enemy air forces tried again, this time in a strength of 100 Ju 87s, Ju 88s and Savoia 79s protected by swarms of fighters. And again they sought to confuse and overwhelm the defence by attacks from all directions and all angles – bombers from astern out of the sun, torpedo-bombers coming in from ahead and then splitting up to launch torpedoes against the convoy's starboard bow and quarter. Syfret himself was to pay tribute to the excellence of the timing of these attacks, which proved devastatingly successful. The destroyer *Foresight* (Lieutenant-Commander R. A. Fell) became the first casualty. Disabled by a torpedo, she had to be sunk later. But the onslaught focused on the carrier *Indomitable* (Captain T. H. Troubridge), lying astern of the *Rodney* on the port quarter of the convoy. Four Ju 88s and eight Ju 87s 'appearing', in Troubridge's words, 'suddenly from up sun out of the smoky blue sky' dived steeply down on the carrier from astern, the Ju 87s releasing their bombs from a height of 1,000 feet. Three armour-piercing bombs smashed into the *Indomitable's* 2½ to 3-inch thick deck armour, wrecking her

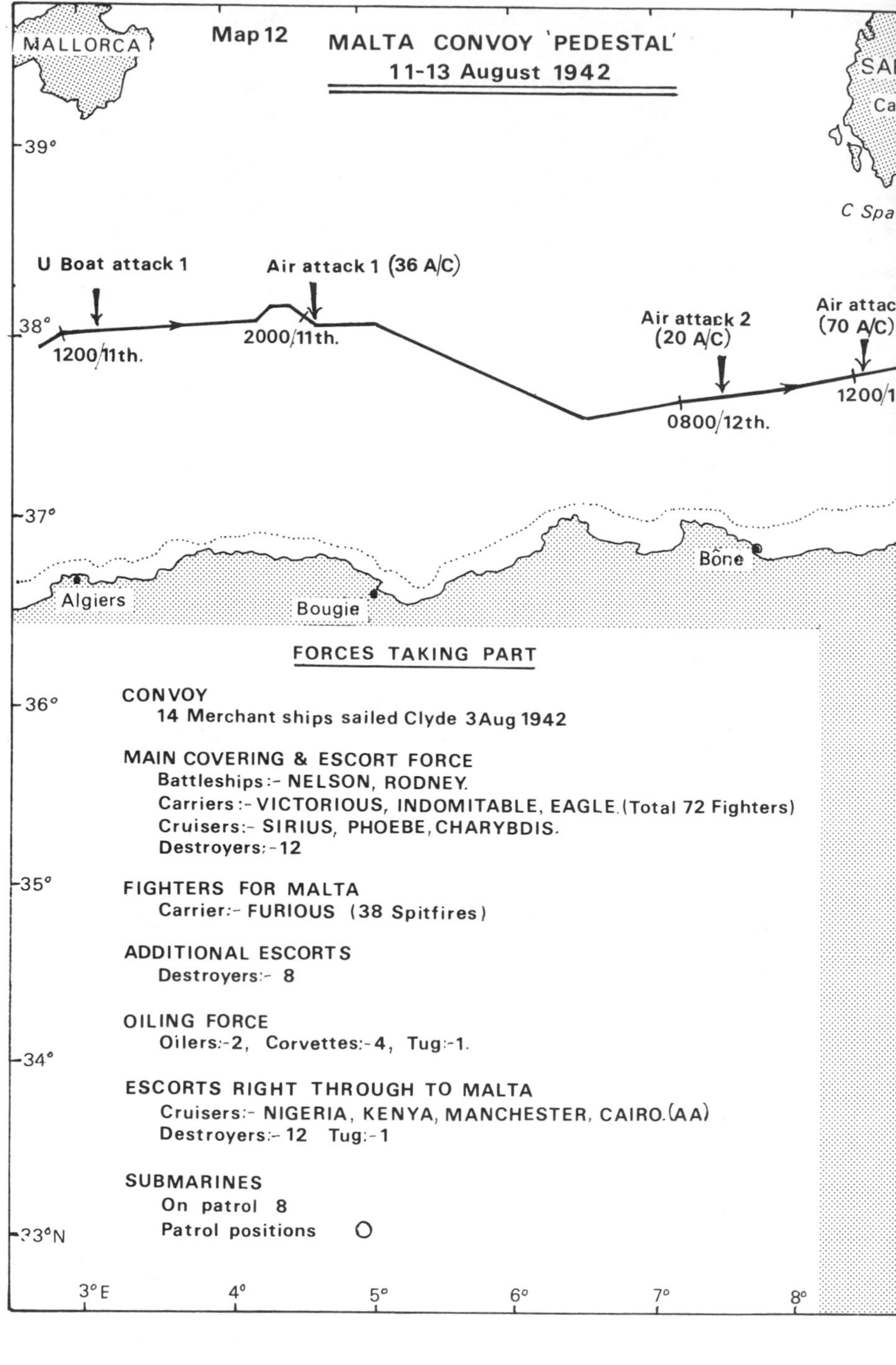
MALLORCA
Map 12
MALTA CONVOY 'PEDESTAL'
11-13 August 1942
SAR
Cag
39°
C Spar
U Boat attack 1
Air attack 1 (36 A/C)
38°
1200/11th.
2000/11th.
Air attack 2
(20 A/C)
Air attack
(70 A/C)
0800/12th.
1200/12
37°
Algiers
Bougie
Bône
FORCES TAKING PART
36°
CONVOY
14 Merchant ships sailed Clyde 3Aug 1942
MAIN COVERING & ESCORT FORCE
Battleships:- NELSON, RODNEY.
Carriers:- VICTORIOUS, INDOMITABLE, EAGLE.(Total 72 Fighters)
Cruisers:- SIRIUS, PHOEBE, CHARYBDIS.
Destroyers:-12
35°
FIGHTERS FOR MALTA
Carrier:- FURIOUS (38 Spitfires)
ADDITIONAL ESCORTS
Destroyers:- 8
OILING FORCE
Oilers:-2, Corvettes:-4, Tug:-1.
34°
ESCORTS RIGHT THROUGH TO MALTA
Cruisers:- NIGERIA, KENYA, MANCHESTER, CAIRO.(AA)
Destroyers:- 12 Tug:-1
SUBMARINES
On patrol 8
Patrol positions ○
33°N
3°E
4°
5°
6°
7°
8°

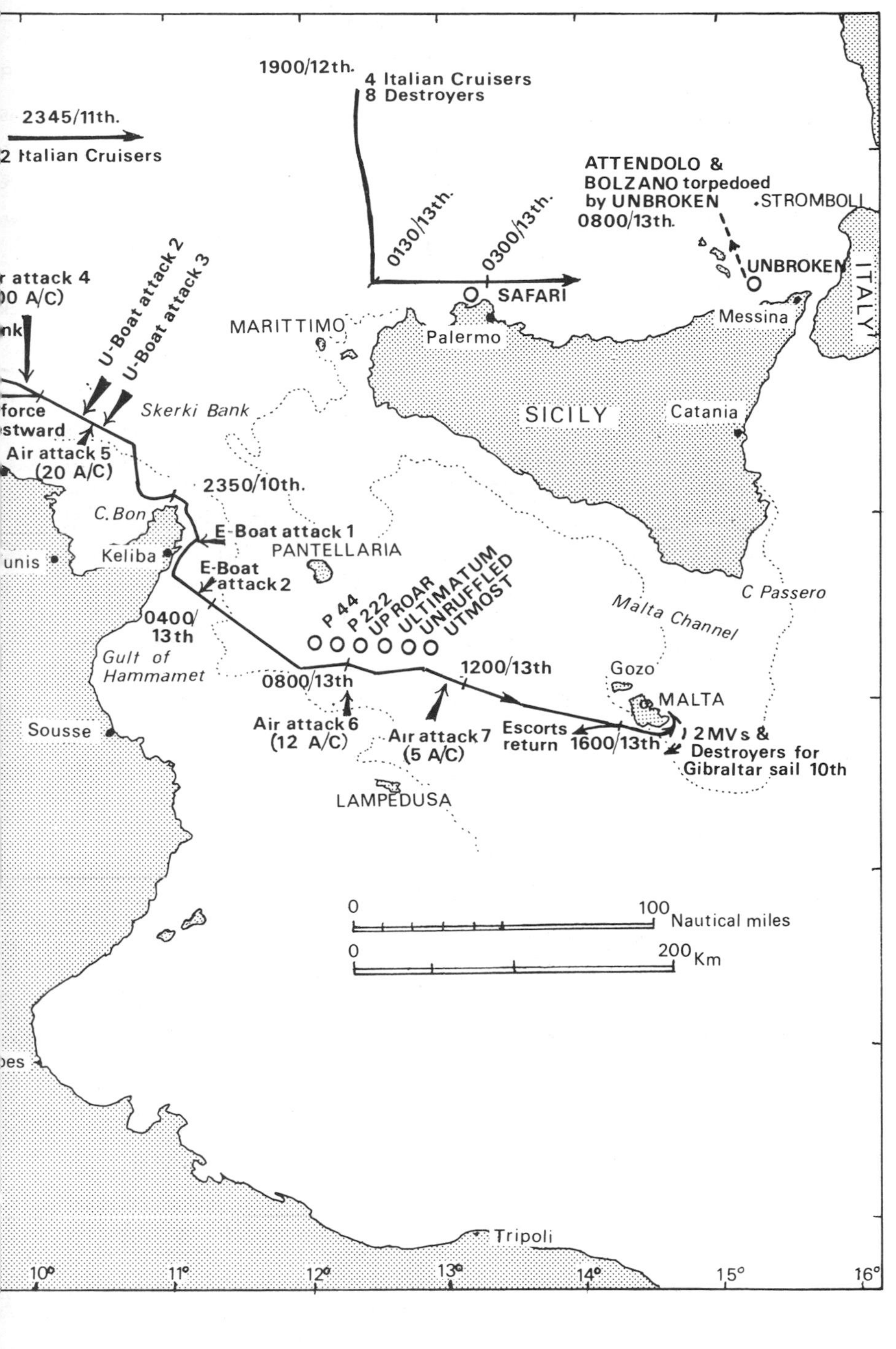

1900/12th.
4 Italian Cruisers
8 Destroyers
2345/11th.
2 Italian Cruisers
ATTENDOLO &
BOLZANO torpedoed
by UNBROKEN
0800/13th.
STROMBOLI
0130/13th.
0300/13th.
UNBROKEN
ITALY
SAFARI
Messina
MARITTIMO
Palermo
U-Boat attack 2
U-Boat attack 3
Skerki Bank
SICILY
Catania
Air attack 5
(20 A/C)
2350/10th.
C. Bon
E-Boat attack 1
Keliba
PANTELLARIA
E-Boat
attack 2
C Passero
P 44
P 222
UPROAR
ULTIMATUM
UNRUFFLED
UTMOST
Malta Channel
0400/
13th
Gulf of
Hammamet
0800/13th
1200/13th
Gozo
MALTA
Sousse
Air attack 6
(12 A/C)
Air attack 7
(5 A/C)
Escorts
return
1600/13th
2 MVs &
Destroyers for
Gibraltar sail 10th
LAMPEDUSA
0
100
Nautical miles
0
200
Km
Tripoli
10°
11°
12°
13°
14°
15°
16°

flight deck and stopping flying operations, so that those of her aircraft then aloft had to land on the *Victorious*.

Having scored this major triumph – although at the cost of heavy losses at the hands of British fighters and anti-aircraft fire – the enemy droned away for home at 1900. The convoy now lay some twenty miles west of the Skerki Channel, off Tunisia, the customary point where the main escort of a Malta convoy from the west turned back for Gibraltar, leaving a close escort to go on with the merchant ships to the island. Syfret therefore now hauled round to the west with his heavy ships and carriers, while Rear-Admiral H. M. Burrough (commanding Force X) continued with three cruisers *Nigeria* (flag), *Kenya* and *Manchester*, the anti-aircraft cruiser *Cairo* and twelve destroyers. It had been planned that Burrough was to be met in the approaches to Malta by a flotilla of minesweepers now based in Malta, while Air Marshal Park was to have twin-engined Beaufighters (maximum speed 303 mph; range 1,470 miles)[74] and Spitfires patrolling as far out as 170 miles west of the island.

Up to this point 'Operation Pedestal' had done well, with only one merchant vessel of the convoy damaged; and in view of the strength and ferocity of the air attacks the ships' companies of convoy and escort were feeling rather pleased with themselves. This happy frame of mind was soon to change. Within an hour of Syfret parting company misfortune started to befall the 'Pedestal' convoy. While the convoy was changing formation from four to two columns in order to follow the minesweepers clearing a channel through shallow water over the Skerki Bank it ran into another underwater ambush. The Italian submarine *Axum* torpedoed Burrough's flagship *Nigeria*, the cruiser *Cairo* and the tanker *Ohio*; a brilliant triple success. The wounded *Nigeria* had to turn back to Gibraltar with an escort of two destroyers, Burrough transferring his flag to the destroyer *Ashanti* (Acting-Captain R. G. Onslow). The *Cairo* (launched 1918; veteran of the Norwegian campaign as well as the Malta convoy run), had her stern blown off and had to be sunk. And it was *Nigeria* and *Cairo* who alone had the kind of radio sets necessary to communicate with Royal Air Force fighters and so guide those from Malta on to enemy aircraft.

As the convoy altered away to the south to escape this underwater danger (at the time it was not known whether from submarines or mines), it became, in the words of naval liaison officers with the merchant ships, 'scrummed up' into a 'heterogeneous mass'.[75] Just when the convoy was in this confused and vulnerable state, and when the fighter cover from Malta had been withdrawn because of the loss of the fighter-direction ships, the enemy air forces struck again at

2030 in the deepening dusk. This time twenty Ju 88s bombed and torpedoed almost at will, sinking the merchant ships *Empire Hope* and *Clan Ferguson* and damaging another, the *Brisbane Star*, which nevertheless managed to struggle on.

Threequarters of an hour later the cruiser *Kenya* took a torpedo from a submarine in her forefoot, but managed to stay with the stricken convoy. At 0040 on 13 August German E-boats and some Italian MTBs took over with torpedo attacks in the dark lasting all the way down the Tunisian coast from Cap Bon to Kelibia. At 0120 one of them hit the cruiser *Manchester* (Captain H. Drew) and damaged her so seriously that her captain decided to scuttle her. Five merchantmen straggling behind the convoy were also hit; and four of them, the *Wairangi*, the *Glenorchy*, the American *Almeria Lykes* and *Santa Elisa* sank. The fifth, the *Rochester Castle*, managed nevertheless to rejoin the convoy.

At 0800 the Ju 88s were back again – twelve of them swooping in for a shallow bombing run to blow up and sink the merchant ship *Waimarama*. The tanker *Ohio* took more damage from a crashing enemy aircraft, but still struggled on. Although British fighters from Malta were now continuously patrolling overhead they could not prevent yet further attrition of the convoy and its escort, when at 1050 the next relay of Ju 88s and 87s arrived. The *Ohio's* engines were stopped by near-misses; the merchant ship *Dorset* was stopped by a direct hit; the *Rochester Castle* was damaged but still able to steam. Admiral Burrough had no alternative but to leave two destroyers with the cripples and press on.

At 1600 he too parted company for Gibraltar (as planned) with his two remaining cruisers and five destroyers. It was now up to the escort forces from Malta, four minesweepers and seven motor launches, under the command of Commander Jerome, to see the three merchant ships that now remained out of the original fourteen the last few miles into Malta. At 1800 on 13 August 1942 these three ships, the *Port Chalmers*, the *Melbourne Star* and the *Rochester Castle* (the latter wallowing very low in the water) steamed at last into Grand Harbour.

Meanwhile there remained the problem of the crippled *Dorset, Brisbane Star* and the *Ohio*. The destroyer *Penn* (Lieutenant-Commander J. H. Swain) took the *Ohio* in tow, while the Hunt class destroyer *Bramham* (Lieutenant E. F. Ramsay) stayed with the *Dorset*. However, the German bombers had not yet finished with 'Pedestal'. At about 1900 that evening they sank the *Dorset* and hit the *Ohio* yet again. At daylight on the 14th the minesweepers *Rye* and *Ledbury* arrived to help *Penn* with *Ohio*, along with some motor launches from

Malta. With the *Ohio* settling deeper and deeper in the water and German bombers complicating matters by parting the tow cable with a lucky bomb hit, this maritime cortège struggled slowly but gamely towards Malta. The tanker was brought safely into Grand Harbour in the morning of 15 August, the Maltese National Holiday, the Feast of Santa Marija. In Malta 'Pedestal' is known as the Santa Marija convoy. Meantime the damaged *Brisbane Star* had made her own way in. Thus 'Pedestal's' final tally amounted to five merchant ships arrived out of fourteen despatched.

In his subsequent report Admiral Syfret wrote:

> Tribute has been paid to the personnel of His Majesty's Ships; but both officers and men will desire to give first place to the conduct, courage, and determination of the masters, officers and men of the merchant ships. The steadfast manner in which these ships pressed on their way to Malta through all the attacks, answering every manoeuvring signal like a well-trained fleet unit, was a most inspiring sight . . .[76]

Captain D. W. Mason, the Master of the *Ohio*, was awarded the George Cross for his outstanding display of courage and seamanship.

It is noteworthy that at least the Italian surface fleet had failed to menace the 'Pedestal' convoy. Its battleships were immobilised in port for lack of fuel. Although five cruisers did put to sea, they were discouraged from energetic action by a British deception plan whereby aircraft illuminated them at night by flares, while alarming radio signals were transmitted in plain language about a forthcoming attack on them by US Liberators and British torpedo-bombers. On 13 August the British submarine HMS P-42 (Lieutenant A. C. G. Mars) torpedoed and seriously damaged the heavy cruiser *Bolzano* and the light cruiser *Muzio Attendolo* – avenging to some degree the losses suffered by 'Pedestal' and its escorting battle squadron.

From the surviving merchant ships were swiftly unloaded 32,000 tons of food and supplies, and in due course *Ohio's* vital fuel – just enough to keep Malta going on iron rations for another couple of months. As the official Naval Staff History comments: 'Five arrivals out of a convoy of fourteen ships with a powerful escort is not a large score, especially at the cost to the escort of an aircraft carrier, a cruiser, an anti-aircraft ship, and a destroyer lost, besides a carrier and two cruisers damaged.'[77]

But the First Sea Lord took a more sanguine view in a letter to Cunningham in Washington at the time: 'We paid a heavy price, but personally I think we got out of it lightly considering the risks we had to run, and the tremendous concentration of everything . . . which we had to face.'[78]

Of what utility was Malta as an offensive base after all the effort and sacrifice of the 1942 convoy operations? The 10th Submarine Flotilla returned to Malta in August and by October had reached a strength of nine boats. It took a steady toll of enemy supply ships on their way to Libya, sinking two vessels and an escort on the night of 19-20 October alone. The Royal Air Force on Malta remained limited in size because of shortage of aviation spirit, but its bombers joined with aircraft based on Egypt and even on Gibraltar in attacking Rommel's seaborne supplies. Yet recent analysis of the Axis logistic problem in North Africa has conclusively shown that British air and submarine attacks on Axis shipping from Malta and Egyptian bases together achieved no decisive effect on Rommel's ability to campaign.[79] Not even the sinking of oil tankers had the impact on Rommel that has been claimed in so many British accounts, for between 2 September and 23 October 1942 only two out of 27 Axis ships sunk were in fact tankers;[80] and Rommel actually received larger quantities of fuel in the months July to October 1942 than in February to June when he was preparing and waging his summer offensive.[81]

The choke-points for Rommel's supply throughout his campaigns from his first arrival in Libya at the beginning of 1941 onwards lay in the limited capacity of Libyan ports and the incompetence of the Italian authorities back in Italy; not in shortage of, or loss of, shipping.[82] His particular problem from July to October 1942 resulted from his own enormously lengthened land communications, which made it impossible with the available trucking lift to bring more than a fraction of the supplies stored in rear bases in Tripolitania up to the army at Alamein.[83] Therefore the damage inflicted on Rommel's communications by the relatively minor air and submarine forces able to operate from Malta in the summer and autumn of 1942 can in no sense be said to justify on objective strategic grounds the grievous losses incurred by the Royal Navy and Merchant Marine in keeping the island going, however much it was a matter of honour. Indeed, it is the judgment of one historian who has rigorously studied all the relevant statistics on Axis North African supply that, in regard to the whole period 1940–42, the importance usually attributed to the 'battle of the convoys'

> is grossly exaggerated. At no time, except perhaps November–December 1941, did the aero-naval struggle in the central Mediterranean play a decisive part in events in North Africa, and even then Rommel's difficulties

> were due as much to his impossibly long – and vulnerable – line of communications inside Africa as to losses at sea . . . the Axis decision of summer 1942 not to occupy Malta was of far less moment to the outcome of the struggle in North Africa than the fact that the port of Tobruk was so small and hopelessly exposed to the attacks of the RAF operating from Egypt.[84]

The key to eventually winning the campaign in the Mediterranean and Middle East and reopening the long-closed imperial route to India via the Suez Canal (the historical reason for Britain's presence in the theatre at all) did not lie in Malta, that strategic burden and moral obligation glorified into a heroic myth; nor in the struggle with Rommel in the Desert. It lay in the decision finally confirmed on 30 July 1942 that the first great Anglo-American maritime expedition in the war against Germany should take the form of an invasion of French North Africa, the coastline of which commanded the sea route through the western basin of the Mediterranean, and capture of which could act as a stepping stone to Sicily and Italy.

On 21 September, D-Day for this invasion was fixed as 8 November. After more than two years of striving and setback by land and sea, and of more loss than profit on an enormous strategic investment, Churchill's Mediterranean 'blue water' strategy was about to flower anew, and on a scale grander yet.

17

Grand Strategy for a Maritime Alliance – I

It was neither an admiral, nor a general, nor even a Chiefs of Staff Committee who, on 30 July 1942, took the crucial decision that an Anglo-American expeditionary force should invade French North Africa as the principal operation of the year. It was a politician, Franklin Roosevelt, President of the United States; and he took it in the teeth of the objections of his own Joint Chiefs of Staff. His directive – which in fact accorded with British wishes – abruptly closed some five months of transatlantic argument over the Allied grand strategy to be pursued in 1942–43; an argument the crucial encounters of which took place between the leading actors across long tables in Washington and London.

The debate followed on from the statement of global strategy, WW1, agreed by the new Allies at the Arcadia Conference in Washington back in December 1941 and largely drafted by the British Chiefs of Staff. For WW1 had for the sake of concord deliberately left vague the actual shape of operations against Germany and her allies in the next two years. It had merely stated broadly that in 1942 a ring was to be drawn round the Third Reich and its allies, running from the Eastern Front in Russia round through Turkey and along the North African shore of the Mediterranean to the seas of Western Europe. The statement had contemplated no major land offensive by the Western Allies in that year. Rather it foresaw a preliminary phase of wearing Germany down by various means of attrition, such as blockade, the bomber offensive, support for Resistance movements, and the shipment of supplies to Soviet Russia in order to keep her going in her struggle with the main power of the Wehrmacht. WW1 looked to 1943 for the début of an Anglo-American grand offensive against the Third Reich. But even here the statement only broadly sketched with the thickest of crayons that 'the way may be clear for a return to the Continent, across the Mediterranean, from Turkey into the Balkans, or by landings in Western Europe. Such operations must be the prelude to the final assault on Germany itself . . .'[1]

WW1 therefore left it still to be decided exactly *what* the Allies should do in 1942–43. The attempt so to decide soon exposed those fundamental divergencies of approach between the Americans and the British over which WW1 had smoothly skated.

The United States was a continental power with a population of 120 million and industrial resources which dwarfed Britain's (and even Germany's). Its military leadership therefore conceived of grand strategy in classic Clausewitzian terms – the concentration of all forces at the decisive point for an offensive directed against the enemy's 'centre of gravity' (that is, his main army or one of his main armies), a decisive victory and finally the occupation of the enemy homeland, so destroying his military, industrial and moral power to resist. General George C. Marshall, the Chief of Staff, forcefully argued to the President in March 1942 that all available Allied resources in the war against Germany should be concentrated on preparing for, and launching, an Anglo-American invasion of France in 1943 (Marshall gave April as the possible month). He envisaged that this invasion would be in an ultimate strength of 48 divisions and 5,800 aircraft.

Thus in essence Marshall wished to create anew the old Western Front. To make this possible all operations elsewhere were to be closed down. In support of this strategy Marshall advanced a convincing case. He contrasted the economy of force and logistics of a cross-Channel front (as in the Great War) with the cost-ineffectiveness of distant peripheral expeditions (such as, although he did not name them, Gallipoli in the Great War and the current Middle East campaign in the Second World War). He argued that France was the only place where Allied airpower could establish overwhelming superiority, thanks to United Kingdom bases and the ability to employ the main striking power of the Royal Air Force. More, it was the only place 'in which the bulk of the British ground forces can be committed to a general offensive in cooperation with the United States forces . . .'[2]

On the other hand, Marshall strongly criticised the possible alternative strategy of attacking Germany by some back-door route – what

General J. F. C. Fuller has called 'the strategy of evasion'. For elsewhere, wrote Marshall, 'the enemy is protected against invasion by natural obstacles and poor communications leading towards the seat of hostile power . . .'[3] Moreover, it was 'impossible, in view of the shipping situation, to transfer the bulk of the British forces to any distant region, and the protection of the British Islands would hold the bulk of the divisions in England'.[4] The United States could also 'concentrate and use larger forces in Western Europe than in any other place, due to sea distances and the existence in England of base facilities'.[5]

This cogent advocacy of a Western Front to the exclusion of diversionary campaigns might have been drafted during the Great War by Field-Marshal Sir Douglas Haig or General Sir William Robertson (the then CIGS) for the enlightenment of the then Prime Minister, Lloyd George. It stood in total contrast to the strategy of evading a fight with the enemy's principal strength on the decisive front, and instead campaigning round the edges of the conflict (the Balkans, the Levant, the Middle East) which Lloyd George and Winston Churchill had urged during that war.

Yet such campaigning around the edges had been favoured since the Elizabethan age by the 'blue water' school of strategic thought in Britain as 'the British way in warfare' (in the phrase of Basil Liddell Hart, an influential military pundit of the 1930s). While some ally was left to bear the brunt of doing battle with the enemy's main army on the continent of Europe, the British (thanks to the Royal Navy) had made profitable colonial conquests at small cost in blood, carried out harmless raids on enemy coastlines, or – more effectively – fought detached portions of the enemy land forces in some secondary theatre, like Wellington in the Iberian Peninsula in 1809–14.[6] No wonder Basil Liddell Hart could contrast this relatively painless 'British way' of the Georgian era with what he saw as the futile and bloody aberration of the 1914–18 Western Front.[7]

By the mid-1930s and under the influence not only of Liddell Hart's preaching but also the harrowing best-selling novels and memoirs by literary veterans of the trenches, British Cabinets had come to accept that never again should Britain commit mass conscript armies to a Western Front, but instead return to the 'British way in warfare'. The task of confronting the German Army was firmly dumped on the French.

Yet what Liddell Hart and the Cabinets who bought his views ignored was that in the Great War the French Army had proved in the event not strong enough alone to deal with the German Army;

and that therefore the deployment of a mass British army alongside the French had proved inescapable. The failure to acknowledge this historical truth in the late 1930s greatly contributed to France's collapse in 1940, when she was left to fight the Wehrmacht virtually single-handed. Thereafter Britain was compelled *faute de mieux* to resort to the 'British way in warfare' by campaigning in the Mediterranean and Middle East – with negligible results so far.

Nonetheless, in 1942 the lure of 'the British way in warfare' and the still painful memories of the Somme and Passchendaele continued to tug powerfully at the minds and emotions of the British leadership, military as well as political.

Thus while Churchill and General Sir Alan Brooke, the Chief of the Imperial General Staff, accepted *intellectually* that Germany could only be finally defeated by an eventual return of the Western Allies to the continent of Europe, they instinctively shrank from any strategic proposal which carried with it a possibility of another prolonged slogging match with the German Army at the peak of its fighting power. In consequence their reaction to General Marshall's Continental and Clausewitzian thinking was somewhat ambiguous; and in the coming years it was to become still more ambiguous.

When in April 1942 Marshall flew to London with Harry Hopkins, the President's confidant, to put his strategy to the War Cabinet Defence Committee, the Committee therefore welcomed it in principle, and agreed that the Allies should indeed work towards an invasion of France in 1943 ('Operation Roundup').[8] But they then proceeded to smudge the black-and-white outline of Marshall's design with references to the need to allot forces to such imperial or 'blue water' concerns as the defence of India, the Indian Ocean and the Middle East. After a COS meeting the day before Marshall's departure for home Brooke confided to his diary his profound misgivings about 'Roundup': it was 'fraught with the gravest dangers' and the chances of disaster were 'great'.[9]

For it was not just a question of committing untried armies against a strongly posted enemy on an *existing front*, as in the case of the Battle of the Somme in 1916, daunting enough a prospect though this would be. 'Roundup' would first of all demand an assault landing on a hostile shore on a scale unprecedented in history, and the winning of an initial lodgement spacious enough to permit the build-up of the Allied armies for an ultimate break-out. These were the 'difficulties and dangers' (Brooke's words) which in his view appeared to be neglected in Marshall's strategic sketch. It was Brooke's standpoint then and later that he would only support an attempt at cross-Channel invasion if and when the balance of forces so favoured the Allies as to minimise the risk of failure or stalemate. But these private hesitations, however reasonable, contrast with Marshall's happy belief that the London discussions had resulted in a firm Anglo-American commitment to launch 'Roundup' in spring 1943, coupled with a renunciation of such 'dispersions' (as Marshall called them) as the Mediterranean and Middle East. Here were the beginnings of a long-festering misunderstanding between the Allies.

In any case, to reach agreement in principle about launching 'Roundup' in 1943 did not provide an answer as yet to what operations, if any, Britain and America should jointly undertake in the war against Germany in 1942. The Soviet Union was locked in struggle with some 200 German divisions; her fate still lay all in doubt; her leaders were urgently demanding a Second Front to drain away German strength. A vociferous section of British public opinion too was demanding 'a Second Front now'. It was therefore as politically unthinkable for the Anglo-Americans to do nothing in 1942 while they painstakingly prepared for 'Roundup' in 1943 as it had been for the unready British Army in France in 1916 to stand idly by while the French Army was being minced at Verdun. A joint offensive operation in 1942 of some kind there simply had to be. But what? And where?

Marshall himself had put forward the suggestion of a *limited* landing in France in 1942, but only if 'the situation on the Russian Front became desperate' or if 'the German situation in Western Europe becomes critically weakened'.[10] The first condition offered the worst possible circumstances for the Anglo-American forces to tackle the German Army in the West, and the second was in the last degree unlikely. Nevertheless 'Operation Sledgehammer' (as Marshall's proposal was somewhat ironically dubbed) was now submitted to rigorous analysis by the British, who would have to supply the bulk of the forces.

On 27 May, a meeting of the Prime Minister and the Chiefs of Staff dismissed 'Sledgehammer' on the score that the available land forces and resources of assault shipping were too small.

This however emboldened Churchill to try afresh to sell to the British Chiefs of Staff his own idea for another intervention in northern Norway, 'Operation Jupiter'. His aim this time lay in occupying the coastline from which the German Navy and Luftwaffe were devastating the Arctic convoys from Britain to Russia. As with his Norwegian schemes of 1939–40, his proposal failed to take account of the operational and logistical problems of either the initial invasion or of long-term occupation and seaborne supply. The Chiefs of Staff had not been enthused, therefore, when they received a personal minute dated 1 May from Churchill with regard to 'Jupiter', telling them: 'High political and strategic importance must be attached thereto.'[11] They had responded by resorting to the First Sea Lord's well tested strategy of procrastination and attrition by weight of detailed facts and figures.

There was left only the alternative of a joint Anglo-American operation in the Mediterranean theatre – the very 'diversion' that Marshall had most feared and which he believed he had scotched during his visit to London in April.

Back in December 1941 Churchill, in his cabin in HMS *Duke of York* plunging and rolling across a stormy Atlantic to the Arcadia Conference in Washington, had drafted a grand statement of future global strategy for the benefit of the Chiefs of Staff. This included a proposal – 'Operation Gymnast' – that American forces as well as British should invade French North Africa in 1942 in conjunction with an offensive into Tripolitania by the 8th Army (then standing on the border of Cyrenaica and Tripolitania).[12] The Allies would thus clear the whole North Africa shore (including Morocco) and open the Mediterranean through route. During the Arcadia Conference, British and American planners had studied the problems and possible timing of 'Gymnast' in detail, especially in terms of naval and shipping resources, but the prospect was put in abeyance because of more urgent needs such as reinforcement of the Far East and the shipment of American troops to Britain.[13] Nonetheless Churchill never lost sight of 'Gymnast'. With the virtual discarding of 'Sledgehammer' and 'Jupiter' by May 1942, he limbered 'Gymnast' up and began to run it again.

On 27 May Churchill telegraphed Roosevelt to inform him of British objections to 'Sledgehammer' (the limited landing in northern France), and remarked: 'We must never let GYMNAST pass from our minds. All other preparations would help, if need be, towards that.'[14] When Vice-Admiral Lord Louis Mountbatten, now an acting Vice-Admiral and Chief of Combined Operations (see below, p. 545), visited Washington in June to explain in person British misgivings about 'Sledgehammer', Roosevelt himself began to take up the 'Gymnast' idea, to the vast unease of General Marshall and also of Admiral King, US Chief of Naval Operations, who feared that it would suck in warships and assault shipping at the expense of the Pacific war, his primary concern.

On 18 June Churchill arrived in Washington with Brooke, after a gruelling 27-hour journey by flying-boat, in order to re-forge agreement on future Allied strategy. It now turned out that at present the fundamental difference of opinion did not lie between the British and Americans, but between the military of both nations on the one hand and the two political leaders on the other. Brooke had for the moment ceased to be in favour of 'Gymnast' – partly because Rommel was currently defeating the 8th Army in the Gazala battles, so putting even Britain's present Middle East position in jeopardy. On 20 June the Combined Chiefs of Staff produced a report calling for the Allies to concentrate on preparations for 'Roundup' (the full-scale invasion of France) in 1943. The report argued against 'Gymnast' on the score that it would weaken the navies in all theatres, but especially the Pacific and the Atlantic; that it would slow up the flow of American troops to Britain ('Bolero'); and that it would disperse the whole Allied strategic effort. The Combined Chiefs warned that 'any 1942 operation would inevitably have some deterring effect upon Continental operations in 1943'. Their uncompromising conclusion was that ' "Gymnast" should not be undertaken under the existing situation'.[15]

Meanwhile, however, the Prime Minister and the President were getting together like old cronies up in New York State at Hyde Park, Roosevelt's neo-Federal-style mansion. At Churchill's persuasion they now agreed to the very opposite to the Combined Chiefs of Staff's conclusions – that some major operation *must* be undertaken in 1942, and that in this context 'Gymnast' ought to be further studied. Next day, 21 June (the day that Tobruk fell to Rommel), the leaders in plain clothes and the leaders in olive drab, khaki and two shades of blue met in the White House to argue it out. Eventually, General Sir Hastings Ismay, the Secretary of the British Chiefs of Staff Committee and a smooth and accomplished fixer, produced a draft for another of those catch-all statements on future strategy that everyone could too easily accept. Although preparations for a cross-Channel invasion in 1943 'on as large a scale as possible' were to be pushed forward 'with all speed and energy', it was nevertheless 'essential that the United States and Great Britain should be prepared to act offensively in 1942'.[16] Therefore plans were to be studied and preparations made for a limited landing in Western Europe ('Sledgehammer') and also for an invasion of French North Africa ('Gymnast'). Even 'Jupiter' was to get a look in by being 'carefully considered'.

On 6 July, at a Chiefs of Staff meeting back in England presided over by Churchill, it was unanimously agreed that 'Sledgehammer' offered no prospect of success. Next day the War Cabinet likewise ruled that a cross-Channel attack in 1942 was 'out of the question'.[17] On 8 July Churchill telegraphed these decisions to Roosevelt, and urged that 'Gymnast' offered 'by far the best chance for effecting relief to the Russian front in 1942'. Spooning on the flattery, he added that this 'has all along been in harmony with your ideas. It is in fact your commanding idea. Here is the true Second Front of 1942.'[18]

Marshall, perceiving here the wreck at the last moment of his own Clausewitzian grand strategy and keenly remembering Churchill's Dardanelles fiasco of a sideshow in 1915–16,[19] rallied the American Joint Chiefs of Staff for a final charge. They stated their conviction to the President that 'Gymnast'

> means definitely no 'Bolero-Sledgehammer' in 1942 and that it will definitely curtail if not make impossible the execution of 'Bolero-Roundup' in the Spring of 1943. We are strongly of the opinion that 'Gymnast' would be both indecisive and a heavy drain on our resources, and that if we undertake it, we would nowhere be acting decisively against the enemy . . .[20]

The American Joint Chiefs of Staff were not alone in realising that an invasion of French North Africa in 1942 would rule out an invasion of France in 1943. On 14 July the British Joint Planners reported to the Chiefs of Staff that 'It is fairly certain that we cannot carry out "Gymnast" and "Roundup" within twelve months of each other. A properly executed "Gymnast" in fact must be regarded as an *alternative* and not in *addition* to "Roundup".'[21]

However, thanks to Auchinleck's defensive victory in the First Battle of Alamein in the first three weeks of July, which transformed British prospects in the Middle East, Brooke himself now changed his mind about 'Gymnast', reverting to his earlier belief that the clearing of North Africa and the Mediterranean was an indispensable preliminary to a cross-Channel invasion.[22] Moreover, in a rare expression of a naval view on the British side, Admiral Sir Andrew Cunningham (then a member of the Combined Chiefs of Staff in Washington) argued to the COS with all the weight of a former C-in-C, Mediterranean, in favour of 'Gymnast'. 'It would,' he wrote, 'go a long way towards relieving our shipping problem once the short route through the Mediterranean was gained.'[23] More, it would 'jeopardise the whole of Rommel's forces and relieve anxiety about Malta. It would shake Italy to the core and rouse the occupied countries . . .'

Now it was the turn of the American Joint Chiefs to fly the Atlantic for a final attempt to trip up 'Gymnast' and instead wield 'Sledgehammer'. On 20 July 1942 Marshall put the case for seizing the Cotentin Peninsula (including the port of Cherbourg) that year and holding it as a bridgehead from which to break out into the heart of France in 1943. On 22 July the War Cabinet rejected the proposal on the advice of Brooke and Portal, who calculated that the land forces which could be put ashore and the air cover which could be provided from British bases would be quite insufficient to deal with the enemy's response.[24] Instead the Cabinet opted firmly for 'Gymnast'.

When Roosevelt learned by cable of this deadlock, he instructed his Joint Chiefs to give up 'Sledgehammer' and come to an agreement with the British on some other operation for 1942. With deep reluctance the Joint Chiefs therefore settled for 'Gymnast', the North African landings, although declaring to their British opposite numbers with some bitterness that they fully realised that this would render the invasion of France in 1943 impossible. The British did not dissent. The Combined Chiefs of Staff were therefore able to submit to the War Cabinet a joint statement on operations for 1942–43, 'CCS94'. Yet even now CCS94[25] fudged the issue. Although it recommended that 'the decision should be taken to launch a combined operation against the North and West coast of Africa at the earliest possible date before December 1942', it made this decision conditional on the news from the Russian front being so bad by 15 September 1942 as to render 'Roundup' (the full-scale invasion of France) incapable of successful execution before July 1943. The document then proceeded to recommend that 'a task force commander for the entire African operation should be appointed forthwith'. As a sop for the American Joint Chiefs it also formally recorded for the benefit of the political leaderships

> That it be understood that commitment to this operation renders 'Roundup' in all probability impracticable of successful execution in 1943 and therefore that we have definitely accepted a defensive, encircling line of action for the continental theatre, except as to air operations and blockade . . .[26]

The Prime Minister would not admit, however, that 'Gymnast' had to be at the expense of 'Roundup'. Far from it: his mind glowed with wider possibilities:

> If, however, we move from 'Gymnast' northward into Europe a new situation must be surveyed. The flank attack may become the main attack, and the main attack a holding operation in the early stages. Our second front will in fact comprise both the Atlantic and the Mediterranean coasts of Europe, and we can push either right-handed, left-handed or both-handed, as our resources and circumstances permit . . .[27]

Now, brushing aside the Joint Chiefs' condition that a decision for 'Gymnast' should only be taken if the state of the struggle in Russia by 15 September ruled out 'Roundup', he pressed Roosevelt via Harry Hopkins to decide without delay in favour of 'Gymnast'. He urged a proviso that the Anglo-American forces would invade French North Africa not later than 30 October. When Roosevelt agreed, the American Joint Chiefs could only acquiesce, albeit repeating in vain that this would kill a cross-Channel invasion in 1943. On 30 July the President told a conference in the White House that

> he, as Commander-in-Chief, had made the decision that 'Torch' [as 'Gymnast' had been renamed] was to be undertaken at the earliest possible date. He considered that this operation was now our principal objective and the assembling of means to carry it out should take precedence over all other operations as, for instance, 'Bolero' [the American build-up in the United Kingdom].[28]

So the two politicians had their way, to the delight of the British Chiefs of Staff (especially Brooke) and the deep gloom of the American Chiefs. Just as in 1940 the British had originally committed themselves to a major campaign in the Mediterranean and Middle East because at the time this theatre provided the only land front where their army could feasibly engage the Axis, so now the Americans were doing the same all over again. But already in Churchill's mind 'Torch' was no mere expedient to get the American forces into battle in 1942, no mere short-term sideshow; it had become the potential first stage in yet more distant developments of his favourite 'blue water' strategy. '*C'est le premier pas qui coûte*'; and now that the Americans had made that step under pressure of circumstances, they had joined the British in making war as they must, not as they ought. They had embarked on a voyage the ultimate destination of which had yet to be charted.

18

'A Quite Desperate Undertaking': 'Operation Torch'

On 1 November 1942 the Naval Commander-in-Chief, the Allied Expeditionary Force, Admiral Sir Andrew Cunningham, Bart, GCB, reached the fortress of Gibraltar in the cruiser *Scylla* (launched July 1940; 5,450 tons; ten 5.25 inch[1] Captain I. A. P. Mackintyre), 'very comfortable but what an armament for a ship of her size',[2] after 'a bit of a volum bolum trip. N.E. gale behind us . . .'[3] Four days later Cunningham was joined by his Supreme Commander, General Dwight D. Eisenhower, who had flown from England in a B-17 Flying Fortress bomber through fog and rain. The Expeditionary Force headquarters, complete with joint Navy/Air Force operations room, was located in old tunnels cut deep into the Rock: airless, dank, dripping, but immune to the heaviest bombardment. Only three days now remained before the launching of the largest and most complicated combined operation in history to that date and in Eisenhower's judgment, an undertaking 'of a quite desperate nature'.[4]

On Eisenhower himself, who had never before commanded a major operation of war, the weight of responsibility, the burden of uncertainty, imposed a strain that tested him to proof. Quite apart from all the operational hazards, so much depended on the reaction of the Vichy French authorities and armed forces – and that lay in doubt to the last minute. Would they cooperate, as was hoped – or would they fight? And what about Franco's Spain, hitherto a neutral country but at whose mercy lay Gibraltar and its exposed airstrip and crowded anchorage, the hub of the entire enterprise? Eisenhower was to confess in a letter to Cunningham in May 1945 that

> the hours that you and I spent together in the dripping tunnels of Gibraltar will probably remain as long in my memory as will any other [episode in the war]. It was there I first understood the indescribable and inescapable strain that comes over one when his part is done – when the issue rests with fate and the fighting men he has committed to action.[5]

Yet Eisenhower, unfledged but already beginning to display the qualities that would make him an outstanding Allied supreme commander, drew strength from his Naval C-in-C, that unshakable veteran of so many desperate ventures, that ever robust optimist. Back in September Eisenhower had confided to Marshall that 'I cannot tell you how strongly and favourably I have been impressed by Admiral Cunningham . . . His frankness, his generous and selfless attitude, his obvious determination and, above all, his direct action methods and impatience with ritual and red tape all come as a refreshing breath of spring . . .'[6] To act as a staunch support to a supreme commander who was still a little unsure of himself constituted not the least of Andrew Cunningham's contributions to 'Operation Torch'.

Cunningham had shown his mettle to the American military leadership during his time as Head of the British Naval Mission (and member of the Combined Chiefs of Staff) in Washington. In particular he had seen off, and thereby won the respect of, Admiral Ernest King, the US Chief of Naval Operations and a man who believed that rudeness cost you nothing. King even regarded the other American armed forces as enemies to be sunk on sight, let alone the armed forces of allies. For the Royal Navy he entertained the underdoggish and now quite anachronistic Anglophobia so prevalent in the United States Navy in the early 1920s. Soon after Cunningham's arrival in Washington the two men engaged in what Cunningham later called 'some straight speaking'[7] over a minor matter of the requested deployment of four or five American submarines for work under British control in the eastern Atlantic. In Cunningham's recollection, King 'was offensive, and I told him what I thought of his method of advancing allied unity and amity. We parted friends . . .'[8]

At the end of July 1942 General Bedell Smith, Chief of Staff designate to the Allied Commander-in-Chief designate, privately asked Cunningham if he would be willing to serve as Naval C-in-C. Cunningham reported this to the First Sea Lord on 31 July, saying that while he did not wish to put himself forward for the post, he 'would be more than willing to serve . . .'[9] In fact, he had had enough of the committees and cocktail parties of Washington, and yearned to return to command and the sea. Pound was however thinking in terms of three separate naval commands under the Supreme Commander – covering the battlefleet, the expedition itself, and Gibraltar – plus a Naval Adviser at Eisenhower's elbow. Cunningham successfully persuaded Pound that this would be unworkable, and that the Supreme Commander must deal with a single overall naval C-in-C. It was a key contribution to Eisenhower's novel design for an integrated Allied command structure.

On 14 August Cunningham was formally appointed Allied Naval Commander, Expeditionary Force (ANCXF), with Vice-Admiral Sir Bertram Ramsay as his Deputy. Commodore R. M. Dick, a most able Deputy Chief of Staff to Cunningham in the Mediterranean in 1940–42, became Chief of Staff. Since April Ramsay had been responsible for the naval side of contingency planning for 'Sledgehammer' and in June had participated in a two-day tri-service study period on the operational problems of a large-scale opposed landing on the Cotentin Peninsula.[10] Now it was he who was to carry the main burden of planning and organising the vast interlocking naval movements involved in 'Torch'. For although Cunningham paid a twelve-day visit to England in September when key decisions were taken, he did not finally return from Washington and take up his new command full-time until mid-October. In any case, Cunningham was no man for detail, as he freely admitted, while Ramsay (as the Dunkirk evacuation proved) was a master organiser. Cunningham provided the broad direction, and also acted as 'facilitator' for Ramsay, such as when he mobilised four outstanding staff officers (including one, Commander M. L. Power, released at his request by Sir John Tovey from command of a destroyer in the Home Fleet) and eight Wren (Women's Royal Naval Service) assistants to type the final and highly complicated naval operation orders for 'Torch' in no more than a week. All the naval planning was carried out within Eisenhower's headquarters in York House, St James's Square, and in the closest liaison with the American services and the Admiralty.

Yet the meticulous routing and scheduling of the 'Torch' armada to the points of assault could avail nothing without success in the landings themselves. This time the lesson had been well learned; this time there was to be no repetition of Gallipoli or Norway in 1940, when troops untrained for landing operations had been shoved into any kind of available boat manned by bluejackets equally unrehearsed for their role, and then simply tipped out on to a hostile shore. For by 1942 the tactics, techniques and specialised craft and equipment for large-scale assault landings had at long last been evolved.

The credit belongs to relatively junior officers of the three services who had jointly studied and solved all the key problems long before the Directorate of Combined Operations was set up in June 1940, long before Churchill's protégé, the glamorous Lord Louis Mountbatten, took over the Directorate in October 1941 as a commodore or as Acting Vice-Admiral became Chief of Combined Operations in March, 1942.[11] The work began in the early 1920s, while the memory of Gallipoli was still wincingly fresh, with 'sand-table' schemes by the three staff colleges for the capture of Singapore and Hong Kong. But there was no money; little interest from on high. This was the period of tight defence budgets under Churchill's Chancellorship of the Exchequer, of the Admiralty's obsession with future fleet battles, the Army's preoccupation with the defence of India, and the Royal Air Force's dream of a strategic air offensive. Yet year by year the three staff colleges together built up a roneoed Manual of Combined Operations comprising all the basic tactical procedures and command and control techniques; the rules of the game as it was eventually to be played by immense armadas of ships and soldiers on the coasts of Africa and Europe.

Meanwhile a new inter-service Landing Craft Committee was pondering the technical problems. By 1930 just three prototype landing craft had been produced – and had proved useless because they drew four and a half feet of water, and the angle of ramp was far too steep for vehicles to negotiate. Not until 1936, and under the spur of the Abyssinian crisis, were six more ordered, but only to be delivered in the post-Munich winter of 1938.

It took the Japanese invasion of China in 1937 to shake the British armed forces into awareness of just how backward they were in developing combined operations, for at Tientsin the Japanese employed 400 landing craft and a special 10,000-ton landing craft carrier. Next year, at the suggestion of the Director of the Naval Staff College, a new Inter-Service Training and Development Centre (ISTDC) was set up, directly reporting to the Chiefs of Staff. The new Centre was modest enough, for it comprised one officer from each service: Captain L. E. H. Maund, RN (Chairman), Major M. W. M. MacLeod, RA, Wing-Commander Guy Knocker, RAF, and Captain P. Picton-Phillips, RM. A proposal that two battalions of Royal Marines should be allotted to the Centre for experimental work was not accepted, since this would cost money, and each service had its own more urgent priorities at a time of hasty rearmament.

In July 1938 (just as the ISTDC was being formed, and when Hitler was winding up the tension in the Sudeten crisis) a major combined operation exercise was mounted off the coast of Devon for which the Royal Navy supplied a battleship, a carrier, two cruisers and a flotilla of destroyers, while the Army furnished three battalions masquerading as two corps. As a gale rose, the troops were rowed to the shore of Slapton Sands by sailors in whalers and cutters in Nelsonian style. The military commander, Brigadier B. L. Montgomery, was to describe the exercise as 'a pitiful exposition of our complete neglect of landing operations'. He remembered: 'There was *one* so-called landing craft, an experimental one made many years before and dug out of some scrap-heap for this exercise . . .'[12] Of this marine demonstration of the truth of Murphy's Law Captain Maund wrote in retrospect: 'The lessons stuck out like tent-pegs. No better start could have been made.'[13]

By way of tapping in these obtrusive tent-pegs, the ISTDC now tackled and solved every kind of practical problem. In particular, it drew up common inter-service codes, procedures and signals arrangements for directing gun fire against shore targets, which were to prove invaluable in 'Torch'. By the end of 1938 the ISTDC had also worked out a complete tactical drill for assault landings – approach under cover of darkness by landing craft carriers (converted merchant ships); despatch of the landing craft to the shore under cover of smoke screens and artillery fire; a floating reserve to feed into the bridgehead in order to secure a position far enough inland to prevent enemy artillery shelling the anchorage; and finally the despatch of personnel, stores and vehicles from the transport ships to the beach in special craft.[14]

Now came the task of designing the ships, craft and equipment themselves. The ISTDC called for fast transport ships (later known as 'Landing Ships [Infantry]') capable of lowering landing craft filled with soldiers from their davits. It proposed a 'silent' armoured landing craft (the LCI or 'Landing Craft [Infantry]') to hold an infantry platoon of 31 men, together with their support weapons and also smoke-projectors; a similar craft, the 'Landing Craft (Support)' (LCS), for weapons and smoke projectors only, and a 'Landing Craft (Mechanised)' (LCM) of 12 tons for the transport of guns, vehicles and stores – all with bow ramps that could be swung down for fast disembarkation.[15] From these original sketches were to proliferate all the varied and ubiquitous vessels of 1942–45. A landing craft mock-up was built, and Authority went so far as to give sanction for £10,000 to be spent on production and trial of prototypes. This was not all; the ISTDC also tackled the problem of the water gap between a landing craft's lowered ramp and the shore, which soldiers could wade, but vehicles could not. Its answer was a design for a floating pier 150 feet long. But for want of further funding none of this inventive effort went beyond the drawing board or the prototype.

And so when in April 1939, with war in the offing, a report was carried out on Britain's present state of preparedness for combined operations it showed that, because of lack of landing craft, no operation even in the strength of one brigade would be possible for six months and no operations large enough to capture and hold territory possible for two years. The report led to a modest order for eighteen 'Landing Craft (Assault)' (LCA), twelve 'Landing Craft (Mechanised)' (LCM) and two 'Landing Craft (Support)' (LCS).

For the officers of the ISTDC this was nevertheless a time of exciting creative endeavour. In summer of 1939 they completed a survey of passenger ships suitable for conversion into 'Landing Ships (Infantry)'. They found the answers to the problems of beach organisation and of quickly laying roadways on sand or shingle; they tried out infra-red beacons for guiding assault craft at night to the correct landing point; they studied how to put tanks ashore, especially in the face of underwater obstacles; decided that a specially equipped tri-service headquarters ship would be necessary for the command and control of a major landing.

Remarkably, the outbreak of war in September 1939 led not to an expansion of the ISTDC but to its disbanding. After all, what with a new Western Front in France and the prospect of fleet battles and the bomber offensive, there was not going to be any such thing as combined operations – or so the service mandarins believed. Only MacLeod was left to carry on, simply because the War Office could find him nothing else immediately to do. Not until January 1940 (when amphibious interventions in Scandinavia and the Baltic had begun to take the fancy of the War Cabinet, and particularly the First Lord of the Admiralty) was Captain Maund ordered to rejoin MacLeod in a revived ISTDC. Further vital development work on the technical apparatus necessary to large-scale combined operations now followed. Heavy-duty davits were ordered for handling loaded landing craft. Proposals were mooted for converting two train ferries to carry LCMs ('Landing Craft [Mechanised]': a 20-ton craft for landing vehicles and stores in shallow water), and for the installation of special gantries in three Admiralty oilers for the purpose of swinging out the LCMs and lowering them into the sea. In March 1940 orders were placed with Thorneycroft shipbuilders for another 30 LCA – 'Landing Craft (Assault)': 10-ton craft able to land troops in eighteen inches of water – and eighteen LCM in addition to the 26 LCA, two LCS and twelve LCM already in production.

Then followed the Norwegian débâcle, when in the haste and muddle all the patient work of the ISTDC, all its carefully evolved rules of the game, were completely ignored. It was left to Maund and his colleagues to note the lessons so harshly taught. Firstly, the commander(s) of a combined operation must receive a clear directive from above. Secondly, the inter-service command system must be based on the precepts laid down in the Manual of Combined Operations. Thirdly (and as again laid down in the Manual) there must be thorough tri-service planning before an operation; thorough training too for the soldiers and sailors. And fourthly, there was the key importance of 'tactical loading' – stowing stores so that what was going to be needed first came to hand first.

The disappearance of the Western Front in June 1940 suddenly lent combined operations a new importance, for it now became the only means by which British forces could again fight on the continent of Europe. The Prime Minister gamely directed that raids should be launched up and down the western coasts of Hitler's empire; and a Directorate of Combined Operations was set up in the Admiralty with Lieutenant-General A. G. B. Bourne, Royal Marines, in charge, Captain Maund as the Navy's representative, and Colonel Hornby as the Army's. The Royal Air Force would send an officer to nod in as required.

Bourne's task now was to press ahead with the construction of landing craft and the conversion of fast merchant and passenger ships into 'Landing Ships (Assault)' and 'Landing Ships (Infantry)' – and recruit and train the crews. In summer 1940 total orders for craft reached 119 LCA, 31 LCM and 8 LCS(M) – as many as the available shipyard space and production resources for engines permitted. By March 1941 a follow-on order for another 104 LCA had been placed. But in this field too Britain had to turn to the vast industrial resources of the United States, placing an order for 136 of the American 'Eureka' design of landing craft. Meanwhile three of the fast 'Glen' passenger ships were being transformed into 'Landing Ships Infantry (Large)' [LSI(L)], each capable of holding three assault battalions. Two 3,000-ton, 22-knot Dutch passenger ferries were also taken up for conversion to carry 450 assault troops. These ships could each despatch 410 soldiers in the first wave with the six LCA and two LCM(I) in their davits.

In close liaison with the Director of Naval Construction a design for a specialised 'Landing Craft (Tank)' was evolved, capable of carrying a 40-ton tank and unloading it over a ramp in the bow. It was to have a speed of ten knots and a draught at the bow of 3 feet 6 inches. Thirty of these LCT(1)s were ordered, and the trial of the first was held on the Tyne in November 1940. There followed an order for a bigger version with a speed of 12 knots, the LCT(2). But here again limited British manufacturing resources imposed their handicap; for want of suitable engines, dangerous Napier Lion petrol aero-engines of 1918 vintage had to be fitted.[16]

In July 1940 the further fiasco of the Dakar expedition, equally neglecting the wisdom accumulated since the 1920s, taught the new Directorate of Combined Operations yet more valuable lessons: the need for exact information about surf conditions and about beaches and their gradients; the urgent need for a special headquarters ship (as envisaged by the old ISTDC), complete with joint operations room and elaborate radio signals equipment, which, unlike a normal flagship, would not be called upon to charge off to engage enemy warships.

Thus by the summer of 1940 the full script and stage directions for combined operations on the grand scale had been written; the production had been designed in almost every detail, and some orders for the kit had already been put in hand. What was now required was an impresario with the drive and personality to enlist the backers and launch the show. Churchill's first choice for this role was that Great War veteran, Admiral of the Fleet Lord Keyes, appointed on 17 July 1940. It proved a mistake, for Keyes, a proud and peppery man as well as an all too senior admiral, upset the three service departments rather than won them over. He did not help his cause by moving Combined Operations out of the Admiralty, its previous base, into separate offices off Whitehall, with the result that the service departments tended to ostracise Keyes's 'private navy'.

Nevertheless, he pushed on the groundwork energetically. In January 1941 a Combined Training Centre (CTC) was created under Captain J. Hughes-Hallett at Inverary, with another at Kabrit in Egypt in the Canal Zone. By February 1941 no fewer than 5,000 officers and ratings had been assigned to the manning of landing craft. A second Royal Navy was coming into existence – but one somewhat disdained by the sea-going Navy. Even in 1943 Admiral Ramsay was regretting in a lecture that

> Service in Combined Operations is, unhappily, still regarded by many of the best Naval officers as a sideshow, and if they are temporarily employed in it their one desire is to get back into normal sea service at the earliest possible moment. This is a most undesirable state of affairs, for circumstances demand the presence in this type of operation of the best officers and men we have got, and we cannot afford always to be changing them and to be conducting operations with inexperienced personnel.[17]

The training was hard and realistic, for it was essential that the landing craft crews got to know their jobs thoroughly before they worked with soldiers on joint exercises, in order that the Army should retain its traditional unquestioning faith in the Royal Navy's seamanship. The trainees would never forget long nights and days spent chilled and wet and tired out on the waters and along the shores of Scottish lochs. Particularly important was the selection and training of naval beach parties. Theirs was the key task of going ashore with the Army's beach groups (the leading assault wave, charged with securing the immediate area of the landing) and organising the orderly flow of men and stores into the beach-head.

In October 1941 Churchill replaced the now seventy-year-old Keyes with an impresario of quite different calibre, Captain (now promoted Commodore) Lord Louis Mountbatten – young, energetic, ambitious, intelligent, charming. Here was the Sam Goldwyn of Combined Operations, eager to promote as his own production the results of twenty years of patient work. As Mountbatten's biographer remarks, by the time the first Americans came to survey his organisation early in 1942, 'they found something to admire and support. He had taken over a directorate with little executive authority and only small resources in men and material. By the spring of 1942 he controlled an important command which enjoyed a virtual monopoly in the skills of amphibious command.'[18] Mountbatten's subordinates rejoiced when Churchill appointed him a Vice-Admiral (although against the First Sea Lord's wishes)[19] and Chief of Combined Operations in March 1942, with a seat on the Chiefs of Staff Committee. Admiral Hallett recalled: 'At one stride our organisation had penetrated the very centre and citadel of Power.'[20]

And certainly Mountbatten was blessed with both the vision of a vast expansion in the resources for seaborne invasions and the power of personality to get what he wanted. Yet it must be also said that he was fortunate in being able to ride the tide of Anglo-American grand strategy as agreed in December 1941, which pinned its hopes in the war against Germany on an eventual major Allied amphibious offensive somewhere or other.

As early as October 1941, when Churchill had first mooted 'Gymnast' to his own Chiefs of Staff, Mountbatten estimated that 16,000 men would be wanted to man the landing craft. He therefore set afoot a hugely expanded programme at the Combined Operations centres at Troon, Dundonald and Inverary. Month by month through 1942 the numbers in this second Royal Navy were to swell, while Mountbatten at the same time pressed on with providing the landing craft. In the last quarter of 1941 the number under construction in Britain totalled 348; the 1942 programme (for completion in May 1943) numbered 1,168.[21] By now Britain had had to resort to America as her main supplier of all kinds of landing craft. In January 1942 for example, Roosevelt approved the production for Britain of 200 'Landing Ships (Tank)' (capable of trans-ocean voyages) and 200 'Landing Craft (Tank)', as well as seven 'Landing Ships (Dock)' – key instruments in the ever more sophisticated orchestra of amphibious operations.[22]

It was under Mountbatten's direction too that, in spring 1942, a start was at last made on fulfilling the old ISTDC's dream of the headquarters ship by the conversion of the armed merchant cruiser *Bulolo* (9,111 tons displacement; 15 knots). This was soon followed by the *Largs* (formerly a French liner: 12,786 tons displacement; 16 knots).[23] Both ships.were to make brilliantly successful débuts during the 'Torch' landings.

Most of these British developments had their parallels, of course, in the United States (where the first manual on combined landings was issued by the Joint Board of the Army and Navy in 1927, and reissued in 1935).[24] In 1934 the first major exercise had been mounted at Culebra Island, east of Puerto Rico. In 1938 there was produced the manual which laid down the American 'rules of the game' as they were to be followed throughout the Second World War – in the Japanese conflict as well as the German.[25] In January 1941 Admiral King, then the C-in-C, Atlantic Fleet, had directed another large-scale exercise at Culebra. Yet even by the time of this exercise specialised tank and vehicle landing craft were still lacking. Moreover, the Americans only came to appreciate much later than the British the need for a headquarters ship, and their own task forces in 'Torch' were to be commanded in traditional style from the fleet flagship, with exactly the disadvantages long foreseen by the ISTDC in Britain. And the United States armed forces, entering the conflict two years after their ally, still had much to learn in the unforgiving school of operational experience.

In contrast, by the time preparations for 'Torch' were well under way from the summer of 1942 onwards the British had already been taught much by two years of attacks on enemy coasts from Western Europe to Crete and North Africa. The attacks ranged in scale from small parties of Commandos to such larger raids as the highly successful sabotage mission to the Lofoten Islands off northern Norway in March 1941, the bold and gallant exploit in destroying the lock gates of the dry dock at St Nazaire in March 1942, and a botched attack on the port of Tobruk in September 1942. In May 1942 took place a major landing on the French island of Madagascar (see below, pp. 864–8). But by far the most painful and valuable lesson of all was learned in the disastrous raid on Dieppe on 13 August 1942.

This was the largest combined operation yet to be launched in the European theatre, with a landing force of two Canadian infantry brigades, a tank battalion, Royal Marine Commandos and a few US rangers – some 6,100 troops in all, most of them carried across the Channel in seven landing ships (infantry). The Royal Navy provided a supporting squadron of eight destroyers, and the Navy crews ferried the assault troops ashore in 24 LCT and 150 LCI. The Royal Air Force deployed 67 squadrons (60 of them fighters as air cover) and the United States Army Air Force seven squadrons. The ostensible aim was to take Dieppe and hold it for a few hours while everything of military value in and around the town was destroyed; the ulterior purpose was to test the German coast defence system in the West. The operation had to be called off in complete and costly failure, with the tanks baulked by a seawall and roadblocks and then knocked out by German fire, and the soldiers slaughtered on the shingle. Only subsidiary flank attacks outside Dieppe achieved any success. Among the Canadians the casualty rate amounted to 68 per cent; gruesome even by Great War standards.[26] The Royal Navy lost a destroyer and 33 landing craft; the Royal Air Force 106 aircraft.[27] The raid fully vindicated General Brooke's apprehensions about the risk of disaster involved in either 'Sledgehammer' or 'Roundup'.

The failure at Dieppe owed itself above all to a faulty plan whereby the main attacking force was committed frontally against the powerful defences of Dieppe itself rather than on the flanking beaches; a blunder for which Mountbatten and the responsible Army commander, Lieutenant-General Sir Bernard Montgomery (GOC-in-C, South Eastern Command), were jointly culpable; Montgomery much the more so.[28]

The lessons of Dieppe for 'Torch' were clear: first and foremost, that heavy and continuous bombardment of shore defences by powerful naval forces was essential during the run-in and landing of the assault waves; secondly, that the most obvious place to land was the wrong place if alternatives could be found. Moreover, Dieppe gave fresh confirmation that a headquarters ship was absolutely vital for effective command and control.[29]

Thus the planners of 'Torch' enjoyed priceless assets denied to all their predecessors in the history of amphibious operations – tactics and techniques thoroughly worked out over many years and tested under fire; a variety of craft and equipment specially developed to serve their purpose. Yet the mounting of a tri-service offensive of such complexity, on so vast a scale, and over such long sea distances presented an entirely novel challenge. General Eisenhower and his commanders and staffs had much to think about.

It hardly helped them that for six weeks, until 5 September, they had to live, in Eisenhower's words, 'under conditions of strain, uncertainty and tension'[30] while they waited for the Allied political and military leaderships to come to a final decision as to exactly how many landings there were to be in French North Africa and exactly where they were to take place. For those leaderships themselves it was six weeks of puzzling how to match desirable strategic objectives with limited available resources – above all, of warships and assault shipping. The process was tortuous and complex; the underlying issues however simple enough. The ultimate aim of 'Torch', as restated by the Combined Chiefs of Staff directive to Eisenhower of 24 August, was

> Complete annihilation of Axis forces now opposing the British forces in the Western Desert and intensification of air and sea operations against Axis installations in the Mediterranean area in order to insure communications through the Mediterranean and to facilitate operations against the Axis on the European continent.[31]

The key to achieving these objectives evidently lay in the swift occupation of Tunisia, so threatening Rommel's main base in Tripolitania at a time when he would be locked in battle with the 8th Army 1,500 miles away to the east at Alamein. To seize Tunisia and especially the ports of Bizerta and Tunis therefore constituted the immediate objective of the Allied landing in French North Africa. As the Joint Planners put it on 5 August: 'Our primary consideration must be to forestall the arrival of Axis forces in Tunisia. The defeat of the [Vichy] French is only a means to an end.'[32]

The obvious operational solution, a direct landing in Tunisia, was out of the question because of enemy land-based airpower in Sicily and Sardinia. The British Chiefs of Staff therefore proposed that

Allied forces should land at Philippeville and Bône in the east of Algeria (as well as at Oran and Algiers) and then carry out a pell-mell advance along the coast to Tunis before the Germans could get there in strength. Eisenhower agreed with this. But Marshall and Brooke both believed that it was equally essential for the Allies to land at Casablanca in French Morocco, so providing the Americans with a direct trans-Atlantic supply route from the United States, and a secure overland line of communication from the Atlantic coast to the Allied expeditionary forces in Algeria. Marshall in particular was anxious about the vulnerability of a single maritime line of communication running through the Straits of Gibraltar, fearing possible attack from Spain or Spanish Morocco. This anxiety was not shared by Cunningham or the Admiralty, who remained cheerfully confident that the Royal Navy could keep open the sea route via the Straits, as it had succeeded in doing in all Britain's previous wars for two and a half centuries.

Calculate and recalculate resources as the planners might, however, there simply was not enough of anything, especially ships and landing craft, to permit five separate landings at Casablanca, Oran, Algiers, Philippeville and Bône. The Royal Navy was already having to strip warships from the Atlantic and the Home Fleet and cancel the next Arctic convoy to Russia in order to provide cover for 'Torch' inside the Mediterranean. Could the United States Navy supply additional ships? Admiral King gave the terse answer: it could not, because it was fully stretched in current operations in the Pacific. Hard choices had therefore to be made.

Eisenhower himself, backed by Cunningham, opted for dropping the landings at Casablanca in French Morocco in order to make possible those at Philippeville and Bône. For him, 'the utmost exertion and ready acceptance of hazards' were worthwhile in order to take Tunis quickly. 'If Axis forces ever beat us to that place,' he wrote on 13 August for Marshall's benefit, 'their later capabilities for building up strength will far exceed our own and will reduce the campaign to another costly and futile defensive venture.'[33] Yet in Washington his patron Marshall and the Joint Chiefs of Staff took the opposite view, recommending to London on 25 August that in order to permit the landing in Morocco not only should the landings at Philippeville and Bône be dropped, but also even that at Algiers. Thus the Mediterranean part of 'Torch' would be restricted to Oran, in western Algeria, so rendering it out of the question to capture Tunis before the enemy.

The JCS memorandum found the British Chiefs of Staff divided in opinion. Brooke reckoned that it would be too hazardous anyway to land at Bône and Philippeville; that it would also be strategically unsound to leave Morocco unoccupied in the Allied rear. Sir Dudley Pound remained anxious about the effects of Atlantic surf on the chances of the Morocco landing; the Chief of Air Staff, Sir Charles Portal, believed like Eisenhower and Cunningham that it was vital to grab Tunis without delay. Nevertheless, the COS reached a compromise view, telegraphing the Joint Chiefs that while forestalling the Germans in Tunis came first and foremost, a landing at Casablanca was certainly desirable 'if it can be done without prejudice to the rest of the operations'.[34]

At this point the Prime Minister directly intervened by telegraphing the President on 27 August (after the Chiefs of Staff meeting) to tell him how 'profoundly disconcerted' they all were by the Combined Chiefs of Staff's proposal to drop the Algiers landing. 'It seems to me that the whole pith of the operation will be lost if we do not take Algiers as well as Oran on the first day – Not to go east of Oran is making the enemy a present not only of Tunis but of Algiers . . .'[35] He added that 'if it came to choosing between Algiers and Casablanca it cannot be doubted that the former is the more hopeful and fruitful objective . . .'[36]

But Roosevelt's reply, though constructive and conciliatory, reaffirmed bluntly that 'under any circumstances one of our landings must be on the Atlantic'.[37] A week of bargaining now ensued in which each ally rummaged again through the cupboard of its naval and military resources to see if enough could be raked together or redeployed to make possible the landing at Algiers as well as those at Oran and Casablanca. President Roosevelt, for his part, offered to reduce the strength of the American assault forces at Casablanca by 5,000 men and make them available together with their shipping for the Algiers landing. The British allotted for the same purpose the forces previously earmarked for Philippeville and Bône, plus 5,000 men from the Oran force, and offered British landing craft for the Casablanca operation. In their calculations of overall resources the British – and Eisenhower – could also now reckon on the US Navy's exact contribution to 'Torch', which had been at last revealed by Admiral King. The sums being done, the Allies decided that Algiers was 'on' as well as Oran and Casablanca. On 5 September the deal was finally struck, to a Presidential 'Hurrah' and a Prime Ministerial 'O.K. Full Blast'.[38]

Yet the deal fudged the original clear strategic axis of 'Torch' eastwards towards Tunisia, Tripolitania and the rear of Rommel's Panzerarmee Afrika. For the immediate objective had now become rather more the occupation of the western half of French North Africa – Algeria from Algiers westwards and Morocco – as a firm base for subsequent operations. This strategic ambiguity is demonstrated by the comparative weight of assault forces finally allotted to the eastern landing at Algiers and to the western in Morocco: the Eastern Assault Force numbered 20,000, whereas the Western Assault Force numbered 35,000. And in any case Tunis, 'the milk of the whole coconut' in Eisenhower's graphic metaphor,[39] lay more than 500 miles to the east of what was now to be the Allies' nearest landing point at Algiers; three times the distance from Bône.

It only remained to decide on D-Day for 'Torch'. The Prime Minister, much concerned about the timing of the next Arctic convoy to Russia in relation to 'Torch's' demand for naval forces, was at first angered when Eisenhower advised on 12 September that the existing provisional date of 31 October could not be met because of the time needed to ship certain American formations and their equipment across the Atlantic, sort them and prepare their loading schedules.[40] Eisenhower offered an earliest date of 4 November and as a latest date a 'best guess' of 8 November, but then only provisionally. Despite heavy personal pressure from Churchill, Eisenhower stoutly refused to guarantee these dates.[41] Being an American national and an Allied commander responsible in the first place to the Joint Chiefs of Staff he was better placed to resist such pressure than British commanders directly under Churchill's authority. A week later, however, he was able to fix D-Day for 8 November – falling 63 days after the final decision to undertake the three landings at Casablanca, Oran and Algiers. It did not, however, give much time in which to plan and organise the deployment of three task forces (one from the United States; two from Britain) comprising more than 70,000 soldiers, more than 400 warships and auxiliaries, and upwards of 60 merchant ships; to say nothing of finalising all the tactical plans for the amphibious assaults on the chosen beaches.

It was on 8 October that Eisenhower's headquarters issued the Outline Plan for 'Torch' incorporating all the work of the previous weeks, first in settling the integrated Allied command structure and then the deployment of forces by sea, land and air.

The land forces were divided into a Western Assault Force under Major-General George S. Patton (35,000 American troops; objective: Casablanca in French Morocco); a Central Task Force under Major-General Lloyd R. Fredendall (18,500 American troops, building up to 39,000; objective: Oran), and an Eastern Task Force under Lieutenant-General K. A. N. Anderson (20,000 troops in the first wave, half American and half British; objective: Algiers). These military commanders reported directly to Eisenhower.

Each of the three assault forces had its equivalent Naval Task Force charged with conveying it safely to the landing point and putting it ashore. The Western Naval Task Force was composed entirely of ships of the United States Navy. It was to proceed in company with the Western Assault Force to Morocco directly from the United States: 91 vessels in all, including 23 'combat loaders' (the equivalent of the British landing ship infantry), twelve of them loaded with 250 tanks, ten auxiliary combat loaders, six cargo ships and a supply train. The Western Naval Task Force itself comprised three battleships, the new *Massachusetts*, the *Texas* and the *New York*; the fleet carrier *Ranger* and four escort carriers newly converted from merchant ships (total: 171 aircraft); seven cruisers; 38 destroyers; eight fleet minesweepers; five tankers.[42] The Task Force ('Task Force 34' in the United States Navy's order of battle) was commanded by Rear Admiral H. Kent Hewitt (flying his flag in the cruiser *Augusta*, which was also to serve as improvised headquarters ship during the landings), a man of calm and massive presence, with a great hook-nosed head and a bulk that would have done credit to an eighteenth-century admiral. Since April 1942 he had been commanding the Amphibious Force, Atlantic Fleet, so he knew his business. By a reluctant concession on Admiral King's part, Hewitt was to pass from the command of Admiral R. E. Ingersoll, C-in-C, Atlantic Fleet, to Eisenhower's once his task force crossed the meridian of 40°W.[43] Although Hewitt would thereby become formally subordinate to Cunningham as Allied Naval Commander, Expeditionary Force (and Cunningham never doubted that this was so), it proved in the event something of a formality, so separate were the Moroccan operations from those along the Algerian coast.

Cunningham's own responsibility as ANCXF therefore really belonged to the Mediterranean landings, where all the naval forces were to be supplied by the Royal Navy, and where the landings stood in danger of attack by hostile heavy squadrons. When Cunningham hoisted his flag in Gibraltar on 1 November, he took over from Admiral Harwood (the C-in-C, Mediterranean) the Mediterranean command west of a line from Cape Bon in Tunisia to the north-western tip of Sicily. Under Cunningham were the Central (Oran) and Eastern (Algiers) Naval Task Forces, together with Force H, the covering battlesquadron, and Force R, its refuelling group of two tankers and escorts.

Force H (Vice-Admiral Sir Neville Syfret) consisted of the battleships *Duke of York* (flag) and *Rodney*; the battlecruiser *Renown*; the fleet carriers *Victorious*, *Formidable* and *Furious* (total: 116 aircraft);[44] three cruisers; seventeen destroyers; four fleet minesweepers.[45] That Force H was to be refuelled at sea provides a mark of the Royal Navy's progress under the goad of war. The Central Naval Task Force (CNTF) (Commodore T. H. Troubridge, the latest of generations of his family to serve in the Royal Navy) comprised the headquarters ship *Largs* (Broad Pendant), the escort carriers *Biter* and *Dasher* (converted merchant ships of 8,200 tons displacement; 17 knots; 15 aircraft);[46] the cruisers *Aurora* and *Jamaica*; the anti-aircraft ships *Alynbank* and *Delhi*; thirteen destroyers; six corvettes; eight minesweepers and various ancillary craft.

The Eastern Task Force (ENTF) comprised the headquarters ship *Bulolo*; the old carrier *Argus* (completed in 1918 as the first carrier in the world with a continuous stem-to-stern flight deck; 22,600 tons displacement; 21 aircraft);[47] the cruisers *Sheffield*, *Scylla* and *Charybdis*; the escort carrier *Avenger* (sister ship to *Dasher* and *Biter*); the auxiliary anti-aircraft ships *Palomares*, *Pozarica* (each 1,895 tons displacement; 16½ knots; six 4-inch AA guns, eight 2-pounder pom-poms, eight 20mm AA guns, and eight 0.5-inch machine-guns),[48] and *Tynwald* (3,791 tons displacement; 18 knots; six 4-inch AA guns, eight 2-pounder AA guns, ten 20mm AA guns);[49] the ancient 15-inch gun monitor *Roberts* (7,970 tons displacement; 12 knots; two 15-inch guns in a single turret);[50] thirteen destroyers; three submarines; three sloops; seven minesweepers and seven corvettes. The force was commanded by Vice-Admiral Sir Harold Burrough, a veteran of the Malta convoys and a man judged by Cunningham a few days after 'Torch' landings to be 'good but obstinate and hasn't yet realised that he is dealing with someone even more pig-headed than himself'.[51]

To find 160 warships for the 'Torch' Mediterranean operations – in particular the fleet carriers and heavy ships for Force H – did not prove at all easy for the Admiralty in the face of global commitments and especially after the loss in the 1942 Malta convoy runs of a fleet carrier, two cruisers, an anti-aircraft cruiser and nine destroyers sunk, and many other ships (including the carrier *Indomitable*) severely damaged. It was compelled to suspend convoys to Russia and also from Britain to the South Atlantic, weaken North Atlantic convoy escorts at a time of soaring U-boat success, and drastically reduce the Home Fleet. The demands of 'Torch' likewise imposed grievous extra strain on Britain's shrinking resources of merchant shipping, for quite apart from the more than 200 vessels required to convoy the Mediterranean assault forces in the first place, it was estimated that 66 ships would be needed each month thereafter up to January 1943 (when the campaign was expected to come to an end) in order to sustain the Allied army in Algeria.[52] In consequence imports into the United Kingdom would have to be still further cut: the British people at home would have to go even hungrier while at the same time drawing even faster on existing stockpiles of food and industrial raw materials in the United Kingdom.[53]

No single Allied air commander equivalent to Cunningham was appointed, but instead two separate area commands were set up directly under Eisenhower – Eastern Air Command (east of Cape Tenez in Algeria: all British aircraft) under Air Marshal Sir William Welsh, and the Western Air Command (west of Cape Tenez: all American aircraft of the 12th United States Army Air Force) under Major-General James Doolittle. In the case of the Western Air Command, Doolittle was placed under the operational control of General Patton, the Assault Force Commander, according to American practice. But in Eastern Air Command the British practice was instead followed of entrusting the effective coordination of air and ground operations to the mutually cooperative spirit of an air marshal and a general; not, as it was to prove, with the happiest results.

With the issue between 3 and 20 October 1942 of the naval operation orders for 'Torch' in eight bulky parts (short titles: 'Ton 1–8'), the planning of a maritime expedition matched for the first time in history the elaboration and exactitude that had long characterised the mounting of great offensives on land.[54] The 'Ton' orders were promulgated over the signature of the Deputy Naval Commander, Expeditionary Force, Admiral Sir Bertram Ramsay – the man who only seven years earlier had resigned as Chief of Staff to the then C-in-C, Home Fleet, Sir Roger Backhouse, because Backhouse remained loyal to the Victorian tradition of command by a one-man-band in admiral's gold sleeve rings, and could not or would not operate a modern staff system. It was another mark of how far and how fast the Royal Navy had finally emerged from the Victorian era since the outbreak of war.

'Ton 1' (issued on 3 October) outlined the strategic plan as a whole. 'Ton 2' (8 October) constituted the core document, for it laid down in detail the routing and scheduling of convoys, escorts and task forces outwards from Britain to the forward assembly area in the Bay of Algeciras; and then the final deployment via the Straits of Gibraltar to the launch points for the landings at Oran and Algiers. 'Ton 3' (also 8 October) added the detailed tactical instructions for the assault landings themselves. 'Ton 4' (issued the same day too) contained instructions for the submarine screens that were to cover the 'Torch' forces from the Italian battlefleet and the French fleet at Toulon. 'Ton 5–8' dealt with various redeployments and convoy arrangements to follow once the initial lodgement had been won.

To ensure that so many separate fast and slow groups of ships of every description (with loads ranging from specialist personnel and equipment to combat troops, tanks, guns, transport and bulk stores) arrived in the assembly area at Gibraltar at the right time and in the right sequence, Admiral Ramsay issued with the 'Ton 2' orders carefully calculated tables of convoy routes complete with lettered routing positions.

The vast, stealthy movement of darkened vessels packed with troops or cargo actually got under way on 2 October, when the first of the two advance convoys, KX1, put to sea from the Clyde with 40 vessels – a mixture of tugs, tankers, colliers and auxiliary craft with an escort of warships, and bearing with it key specialists. KX2 (eighteen vessels, including five ammunition ships, with an escort of thirteen of His Majesty's ships) soon followed. On 18 October the third advance convoy, KX3, consisting of just one ship, the 11,000-ton liner *Clanstephan Castle*, and two escorts sailed with radar, signals, anti-aircraft and other expert personnel.

Meanwhile the 50,000 British and American soldiers of the Oran and Algiers assault forces were stuffing kitbags, donning full marching order, watching their training camps recede behind them as the transport trucks carried them to railway station or straight to dockside, and climbing gangways up into the strange over-crowded, body-smelling shipboard world of messdeck, hammock or bunk, and 'heads'. On 22 October (it was the day before Montgomery launched the Second Battle of Alamein) the first of the big assault convoys, KMS1 (KM = UK to Mediterranean; S = slow) put to sea with 46 vessels escorted by eighteen warships; it was followed three days later by KMS2 with 53 vessels and ten escorts. On 26 October KMF1 (F = fast) followed with 39 ships and twelve escorts; on 31 October KX5 (32 ships and ten escorts); on 1 November, KMF2 (eighteen ships and eight escorts). The last convoy of all to arrive, KX4 (KX = Advance; i.e., first to sail), which was making the passage in two parts, was due to reach Gibraltar on 4 November.

Meanwhile the ships which were to form Force H and the two naval task forces had also been putting to sea. The carrier *Furious* and three destroyers left the Clyde on 20 October; the battleship *Rodney* and three destroyers steamed out of Scapa Flow on the 23rd; four days later the escort carriers *Dasher* and *Biter*, the cruiser *Jamaica* and the anti-aircraft ship *Delhi*, together with four escorts, departed from the Clyde; on the 30th, the main body of Force H sailed from Scapa and the Clyde, rendezvousing to the north-west of Ireland next day – the battleships *Duke of York* and *Rodney*, the battlecruiser *Renown*, the carriers *Furious* and *Formidable* and sixteen destroyers.[55]

This broad stream of convoys and task forces followed a wide sweeping course out into the Atlantic and then south and south-east through the Western Approaches, where the Admiralty knew that up to 50 U-boats could converge on the expedition by the end of October if U-boat Command once detected that it was at sea, and another 25 U-boats by 6 November.[56] The First Sea Lord therefore hardly underestimated the riskiness of the whole gamble when he warned the Prime Minister that the U-boats 'might well prove exceedingly menacing' to 'the most valuable convoys ever to leave our shores'.[57] And U-boats and German aircraft did indeed sight at least two convoys, as well as *Rodney* and two of the carriers. Yet U-boat Command failed to deduce that anything other than normal movements of convoys or warships was afoot, and consequently took no measures to concentrate against this supreme target.[58] Moreover, on 27 October, by a stroke of luck – or intervention of Providence – the U-boats in the key sea area to the west of Morocco and the Straits of Gibraltar located a north-bound convoy of merchant ships from Sierra Leone to the United Kingdom; and this thereafter served as an unwitting sacrificial decoy. Although it lost thirteen vessels, it kept Dönitz's captains entirely occupied.

In the last days of October 1942 and the first of November more than 340 ships were converging on Gibraltar through waters that had witnessed some of the greatest victories ever won by the Royal Navy – past Cape St Vincent which gave its name to Admiral Sir John Jervis's triumph over another Spanish fleet in 1797 ('If there are 50 sail of the line, I will go through them'); past Cadiz, where in 1587 Drake had singed Philip II of Spain's beard by attacking the Armada in harbour; past Cape Trafalgar itself. By 4 November 1942 the grandest assembly of merchant vessels and ships of war in all Gibraltar's turbulent history in Britain's wars since the Rock was first captured in 1704 lay at anchor in Algeciras Bay. 'The harbour is absolutely stiff with shipping, cruisers, aircraft carriers and small fry,' wrote Cunningham to Ramsay (who had remained in Britain to handle all rearward problems). 'How on earth the enemy are expected to take no notice beats me.'[59] In point of fact, the enemy's mind was dwelling on the likelihood of further major Malta convoy operations, or perhaps another attack on Dakar.[60]

On the Rock and in the ships all was now expectation, bustle and the last-minute muddles caused by inevitable human frailty; the latter topic being one on which Cunningham expressed himself with his customary salt breeziness. 'To say that things are chaotic would be an exaggeration,' he told Ramsay, 'but they are certainly a bit confused. The signalmen appear to have made everything so intricate that no one, including themselves, knows what to do.'[61] Not so much of a joking matter, however, was the careless talk about 'Torch' plans prevalent in Gibraltar, as Cunningham reported:

> The chat going on in the bars is most alarming & I have threatened to put the American colonel in *Furious* in a cell for giving the show away by chat in her wardroom. Why on earth did R.A.A. [Rear-Admiral, Aircraft Carriers] ask for them [military liaison officers] – this craze of laison [sic] officers is in my opinion getting quite out of bounds.[62]

But the trouble did not only lie with gabby liaison officers. According to Cunningham, 'a bad mistake had been that some of the Task Force commanders' orders have been distributed with no restrictions as to opening them. The fault lies with the secretariats of Burrough and Troubridge I fear. So even some of the M.L. [motor launches] are aware of the detailed orders.'[63]

For the lucky ones Gibraltar offered the last chance of a run ashore before the voyage to battle. The bars roared with song and laughter; the narrow thoroughfares beneath the Rock witnessed behaviour which aroused the wrath of that formidable disciplinarian, the Naval Commander, Allied Expeditionary Force. 'Things are damned slack in this place,' he reported to his Deputy. 'I want to lay my hands on some of the young officers to be seen in ½ dozens drunk in the streets at night. It is reported to me that they are worse than the sailors.'[64]

While the ward room, the gun room and the lower deck roistered, last-minute high-level secret diplomacy was under way in the hope – vain as it turned out – that the Vichy French administration in North Africa could be won over to the Allied cause and so avert the need for combat. It marked the climax, or rather anti-climax, of months of intrigue in French North Africa by an American diplomat, Robert Murphy (the United States having maintained diplomatic relations with the Vichy French government ever since 1940). On 23 October 1942 the Royal Navy had played its modest part in the cloak-and-dagger work by landing the American General Mark Clark near Algiers from the submarine *Seraph* for a secret meeting with General Mast, the French commander of the Algiers area. Mast was the local representative of General Henri Giraud, an antique French hero who had been captured by the Germans in 1940 but later successfully escaped to the unoccupied zone of France. It was the Allies' illusion that if Giraud could be brought to French North Africa, his prestige was such that the French civil and military authorities would rally to him. This was to be another job for HM submarine *Seraph*, this time flying the Stars and Stripes and under the nominal command of a non-submariner US officer, just in case Giraud still felt bitter about the Royal Navy's attack at Oran in 1940.

On 28 October Murphy (cloak-and-dagger name 'McGowan') signalled urgently to Eisenhower to request that the 'Torch' landings be postponed for a fortnight in order to enable General Giraud to reach Algeria and himself and General Mast, the French commander, to have time to complete their preparations for a coup. This request, with its diplomat's insouciant disregard for military practicalities, served to wind the tension in Eisenhower's headquarters even tighter. Eisenhower furiously signalled Marshall on 1 November that it was 'inconceivable that McGowan can recommend such a delay with his intimate knowledge of the operation and the present location of troops and convoys afloat . . .'[65] Cunningham in a letter to Ramsay on 3 November called Murphy 'that lunatic', and added: 'I got the wind up, not about Eisenhower, but about what might happen in the stratosphere!'[66] But nothing had happened in 'the stratosphere'; 'Torch' would be launched as planned on 8 November.

On 5 November (the first day of Rommel's retreat from Alamein) began the crux of the entire 'Torch' deployment – the passing of upwards of 340 ships through the eight-miles-wide Straits of Gibraltar into the Mediterranean in just 33 hours. According to the Naval Staff History of 'Torch' it was 'a large-scale movement of far-reaching complexity depending for its success, in the case of large vessels, on rigid adherence to a time-table . . .'[67] To complicate the problem even further, smaller vessels had to divert into Gibraltar in order to refuel, so necessitating 'the rapid and flexible execution of a fuelling programme';[68] the tricky responsibility of Vice-Admiral Sir F. Edward-Collins, Flag Officer, North Atlantic Station, and his special assistant for 'Torch', Commodore G. N. Oliver.

At 1930 the van of the armada, Force R (Force H's refuelling group), passed Europa Point. An hour later followed the carrier *Argus*, the cruisers *Sheffield*, *Scylla* and *Charybdis*, the anti-aircraft ship *Tynwald* and their escort. At 2300 it was the turn of the monitor *Roberts*. A quarter of an hour before midnight the first of the assault convoys, KMS(A)1, the slow Algiers convoy, began to head through the narrow neck of water between Europe and Africa, followed at 0100 on 6 November by the fast Algiers assault convoy KMF(A)1, and at 0300 by a group of landings ship (tank) (in this case, converted shallow-draft oilers each carrying 20 tanks or 30 trucks). An hour and a half later the great ships of Force H with their screen of cruisers and destroyers began their passage. At 0445 Force H was followed by three landing ships (infantry) (converted passenger ships) crammed with over 1,000 soldiers and carrying a total of eighteen landing craft (assault). There now elapsed an interval of nearly eleven hours while the Algiers convoys, with miles further to go than those bound for Oran, steamed ahead. At 1600 on the 6th, darkness again, the slow Oran convoy KMS(O)1 steamed eastwards through the Straits, with its fast counterpart KMF(O)1 following astern six and a half hours later. At 0400 on 7 November the Advance Carrier Force for Oran – *Furious*, the anti-aircraft ship *Delhi* and their escort – brought up the rear of the whole armada.

Meanwhile Rear Admiral Hewitt with Task Force 34 and the Western Assault Force, convoy UGF1 (94 ships in all), had safely zig-zagged the Atlantic at a steady 14 knots. In the midnight hours of 6–7 November Hewitt passed to the north of Madeira, feinting in the direction of the Straits of Gibraltar, and then altered south-east for the final approach to the Moroccan coast.[69]

Within the Mediterranean Rear-Admiral Burrough and Commodore Troubridge, in accordance with instructions, assumed on passing the meridian of 3°W the responsibility for the onward routing of their task forces to the 'release' position off Algiers and Oran from which the assault waves would be despatched to the beaches. Force H (less *Rodney*, *Furious* and three destroyers detached in support of the Central Naval Task Force, and the cruiser *Bermuda* detached to the Eastern Task Force) steamed eastwards to cover the landings and the follow-up convoys against attack by either Italian or French heavy ships. Admiral Syfret was under orders, however, not to proceed east of 4° 30′E unless to engage the enemy, and in any event not to jeopardise his force because upon it depended the security of the whole operation. The Malta-based 10th Submarine Flotilla (five boats) had been in place since 5 November off the northern and southern approaches of the Straits of Messina to keep watch for possible sorties by Italian squadrons from either Naples or Taranto; three boats of the 8th Flotilla (based on Gibraltar) were keeping a similar watch on Toulon. The remaining five boats of this flotilla were already on station off the landing beaches at Algiers and Oran, ready to act as rendezvous beacons for the approaching task forces.

On 7 November the Royal Air Force began to fly standing reconnaissance patrols along a line between the eastern coast of Spain and the Bonifacio Strait (between Sardinia and Corsica) in order to detect any southward movement of the French Toulon fleet; between Cape Marittimo in Sicily and Cavoli Island in Sardinia to watch for westward sorties by the Italian fleet; and north and west of Dakar in French West Africa to give early warning of any northward move towards Admiral Hewitt's task force by French warships. In addition the Royal Air Force was flying repeated reconnaissance sorties over French and Italian naval bases, while Catalinas, Hudsons and Swordfish from Gibraltar were providing anti-U-boat escorts for the invasion forces during their voyage to the Algerian coast.

Now, with the long work of preparation over and the task forces steaming eastwards through the Mediterranean, began the worst time for Eisenhower and Cunningham back at Expeditionary Force headquarters in Gibraltar, for Brooke and Churchill in London, and for Marshall and Roosevelt far off in Washington. They could only wait, and weigh again the chances of success or failure. Certainly the Vichy French forces in North Africa presented an immeasurably less daunting proposition than the German Army and the Luftwaffe. The French garrison numbered some 120,000 (about 55,000 in Morocco, 50,000 in Algeria, and 15,000 in Tunisia); and consisted of mostly native rank-and-file with French officers. Though its equipment was obsolete, its discipline was believed to be good. The French Air Force amounted to only 500 aircraft of all kinds, mostly obsolete, against 1,041 Allied aircraft – once these could be deployed forward via Gibraltar to North African bases. It was the French Navy that posed the greatest potential danger to 'Torch'. The Toulon fleet comprised three heavy ships, seven cruisers, 28 destroyers, and fifteen submarines, while at Casablanca lay a 6-inch gun cruiser, eight submarines and the battleship *Jean Bart* (not completed but able to fire her main armament), and at Dakar the modern battleship *Richelieu* and three cruisers.[70] Fortunately only destroyers and smaller craft were stationed at the Algerian base of Oran and the Tunisian base of Bizerta.

How swiftly and how effectively might Axis forces also intervene? In terms of strength in ships fit for sea the Italian fleet remained formidable enough – six heavy ships, nine cruisers, 28 destroyers and 35 submarines. Yet the recent record indicated poor morale and irresolute leadership, while the fleet's mobility was shackled by want of oil fuel. The Axis air forces were another matter, as their relentless and successful attacks on the Malta convoys in June and August had demonstrated. Allied Intelligence estimated their possible strength in Sardinia and Sicily by D-Day as 385 German aircraft (actual on the day 395) and 530 Italian (actual on the day 574),[71] so that the Allies would by no means enjoy air superiority within a radius of some two hundred miles from enemy airfields – a radius which took in Tunisia.

But at least Eisenhower and his colleagues could take comfort from the certain knowledge via Ultra decrypts of Luftwaffe and German Navy Enigma traffic that up to the last moment the enemy had failed to divine the expedition's true destination. On 4 November the enemy was reckoning that the armada now assembled at Gibraltar signified a Malta convoy rather than a landing in the Mediterranean and as late as 7 November the German Navy high command (OKM) was guessing that as well as resupply Malta it might well make a landing either in Sardinia or Sicily, or in the Tripoli–Benghazi area in Libya.[72]

Yet for Allied Expeditionary Force headquarters, uncertainties enough remained: French reactions, Spanish reactions, the surf conditions along Moroccan beaches exposed to Atlantic winds and rollers; the whole unprecedented nature of amphibious operations on the scale of 'Torch'.

'We are standing on the brink,' Eisenhower signalled privately to Marshall in the morning of 7 November, 'and must take the jump – whether the bottom contains a nice feather bed or a pile of brickbats! Nevertheless, we have worked our best to assure a successful landing, no matter what we encounter . . .'[73]

At 1800 on 7 November 1942, Rear-Admiral Burrough (Flag Officer, Eastern Task Force) swung his fast convoy, KMF(A)1, from its easterly course ostensibly for Malta round to just east of south for the Algerian coast. Away to the south-west his slow convoy, KMS(A)1 and its covering force of warships turned south-eastwards at the same time in order to join company with him off Algiers. At 1815 Commodore Troubridge began to turn the Central Naval Task Force column by column from east to south and south-east for Oran. Now ensued the final approach phase of 'Torch' in accordance with 'Ton 2': an intricate routing of fast and slow portions of Burrough's and Troubridge's commands so that they would unite at rendezvous points off the Algerian coast into landing groups ready to launch the assault waves to the beaches. For the officers of the watch and especially the navigating officers these were hours of high vigilance.

At 2145 two of Troubridge's columns were the first to home on an invisible infra-red beam from a submarine already stationed seven miles off shore to mark the rendezvous point; in this case, HMS P-54 to the west of Oran. By 2300 two more columns had picked up the beam from the submarine *Ursula* to the north-east of the port. Meanwhile sections of Burrough's fast and slow convoys had rendezvoused on the submarines P-221 and P-48 to the west of Algiers at 2230 and 2245. To the east of Algiers the remaining portion of his fast convoy homed on the infra-red beam from the submarine P-45 at 2230.

With all six landing groups now stationed on their 'release points' two miles to seaward of their beacon submarines, the work immediately got underway of deploying the assault forces in the water; a time of orderly bustle on bridges, on deck and down below, and for the individual soldier in the ranks a time, according to temperament, for quiet introspection or uneasily boisterous humour.

The product of twenty years of painstaking study by the ISTDC and then Combined Operations Command, of two years of war experience culminating in the Dieppe raid, and of three months of careful planning by Admiral Ramsay and his staff was about to be put to the proof.

At Algiers Burrough's role was to put ashore the American 34th Infantry Division (Major-General Charles W. Ryder), one brigade group of the British 78th (Infantry) Division, and the 1st and 2nd Commandos. A second brigade of 78th Division was to act as a floating reserve. The landing operations would be jointly directed by Burrough, Ryder and Air Commodore G. M. Evelegh from the headquarters ship *Bulolo*, with its elaborate radio communications facilities, ample cabin space for large tri-service staffs, and a central operations room. The invasion plan called for two landings west of Algiers ('A' or 'Apples' Sector and 'B' or 'Beer' Sector) and one to the east ('C' or 'Charlie' Sector).[74] Each sector was further subdivided into specific beaches – Apples Green and White; Beer White and Red; Charlie Green, Blue and Red. From the outer flanking lodgements at Apples and Charlie the assault troops were to drive rapidly inland to encircle Algiers and occupy the airfields at Maison Blanche and Blida.

The Apples Sector landing group consisted of 7,230 soldiers of the British 11th Infantry Brigade (78th Division) and a reconnaissance squadron, embarked in three landing ships (infantry) and four motor transport ships, with an escort of an anti-aircraft ship, two sloops, two corvettes, three minesweeping trawlers and three motor launches.[75] By 2304 on 7 November the 45 landing craft carrying the assault wave had been lowered into the water with the aid of a landing ship (gantry).

It was a dark night with a new moon, fine, a moderate swell, but with 'a very strong set'[76] which was carrying the ships westward at about 4 knots. At 2350 the assault waves chugged away for the beach led by the three motor launches bearing pilots transferred from the submarine HMS P-221, which now lay in its inner beacon position two miles off shore.

Shut within the steel walls of the landing craft, soldiers gripped their rifles in dry-mouthed tension and listened to the rumble of the diesel engines and the slap of the water against the flat sides and bow-ramps; smelt fresh salt breeze after the fug of the ships. Ahead glinted the lights of the coastal town of Castiglione. Four hundred yards from the beach a light flashed seaward from a folbot (folding boat) to guide the landing craft in. The ramps swung down, and despite a 'very bad and dangerous' beach at Apples White because of heavy surf, the troops quickly got ashore and secured a lodgement. There was no opposition from the French. Now the landing craft began to ferry in the rest of the brigade.

On Beer Sector Regimental Combat Teams of the American 34th Infantry Division and the British 1st and 2nd Commandos, 5,420 strong in all (embarked in seven landing ships [infantry] and nine motor transport ships, with an escort of four destroyers, one anti-aircraft ship, one sloop, two corvettes, three minesweepers, three trawlers and three motor launches, as well as the headquarters ship *Bulolo*)[77] had to land on five separate beaches from Sidi Ferruch round to a point just east of Algiers itself. What Clausewitz calls 'friction' soon manifested itself. For a start, an easterly Force 3 breeze pushed the ships some three miles to the west during the disembarkation and also compelled the soldiers in some ships to disembark by the lee side only. There was a failure to transfer a pilot from the submarine P-48 to a motor launch as well as other missed cues. Because of these omissions and the westerly drift, the landing craft crews found it difficult to locate their proper assembly positions for the run in, so that the assault finally went ashore on the wrong beaches, an error which would have been ruthlessly punished had this been a coast defended by German troops. But mercifully there proved to be no opposition here either. Indeed General Mast, the French commander, welcomed the Allied troops at the fort of Sidi Ferruch and even laid on a bus service to ferry them to Blida airfield, so that they could negotiate its surrender with the garrison. However, four Fleet Air Arm Martlet fighters from the carrier *Victorious* led by Lieutenant (A) B. H. C. Nation, RN, just beat them to it, taking the airfield's formal surrender at 0930.

The landing force on Charlie Sector on the opposite flank some ten miles east of Algiers (6,000 soldiers of the 39th Regimental Combat Team of the 34th Infantry Division and five troops of Commandos embarked in three American 'combat loaders', one landing ship [infantry] and one motor transport ship, escorted by an anti-aircraft ship, two destroyers, four minesweepers, two trawlers and two motor launches)[78] likewise suffered from the operation of Murphy's Law – not least because of delays in launching landing craft from the combat loader *Leedstown* and assembling them for the run-in. It did not help that a pall of fog spread from land out to sea and forced the landing craft to slow to 4½ knots in order to keep company. Troops for Blue and Red beaches finished up all on Blue, while the commandos who were to attack the coastal battery at Cape Matifou were landed nearly two hours late, if at least on the right beach. Except for a few rounds from this battery, there was no resistance on Charlie Sector either.

Only within the port of Algiers itself did fighting take place, when the destroyers *Broke* and *Malcolm* attempted to put ashore a party of American infantry to prevent the French from scuttling ships and sabotaging dock installations. At 0345 the *Broke* led the *Malcolm* in towards the harbour's southern entrance. On *Broke*'s bridge eyes dazzled by searchlights and gunflashes sought to locate the harbour entrance at the foot of the dark wall of hills that rose behind the city. At the third approach heavy shells smashed into the *Malcolm*, forcing her to limp away. At 0530, dawn now paling the sky, HMS *Broke* tried again. This time she steamed through the entrance, rammed the boom at high speed, charged through into the harbour, and disembarked her landing party. The soldiers swiftly occupied the power station and the oil storage depot. But all too soon they were pinned down by machine-gun fire, while the *Broke* herself became the sitting target for coastal batteries and field artillery. After enduring four hours of pounding she was compelled to abandon 250 American soldiers on shore and put to sea. But on her way out she was hit so heavily that she sank next day under tow.

From daylight on 8 November the carriers *Victorious*, *Formidable*, *Argus* and *Avenger* began to fly air cover over the invasion area. Troop reinforcements poured into the lodgements, while the spearheads of the assault forces thrust inland fast despite resistance by a handful of obdurate forts and coastal batteries. At 1100 Royal Air Force Hurricanes from Gibraltar flew into Maison Blanche airfield after its capture by the American 39th Regimental Combat Team – the first of many. In the afternoon General Ryder and General Juin (representing

Admiral Darlan, the Commander-in-Chief of all Vichy-French forces by land, sea and air, who happened to be in Algiers visiting a sick son) agreed a local cease-fire. At 1900 American forces rolled into Algiers. The Eastern Task Force had thus triumphed in short order, albeit against either weak opposition or none at all. But in the dusk of that successful day arrived harbingers of a different kind of opponent, in the shape of German bombers sweeping in from the east to attack shipping lying off Charlie Sector. They damaged the destroyer *Cowdray* and the combat loader *Leedstown*, the latter sinking on the morrow.

At Oran too the plan of attack relied on landings on the flanks followed by rapid advances inland to close pincers behind the city and capture the local airfields en route. The operation was to be directed from the headquarters ship *Largs* by Commodore T. H. Troubridge, RN, Major-General Lloyd R. Fredendall and Major-General James Doolittle (commanding the US 12th Air Force and the Allied Western Air Command).[79] Deployed some 30 miles off Oran in support of the landings was Troubridge's covering force: the battleship *Rodney*, the fleet carrier *Furious*, the escort carriers *Avenger* and *Biter*, the anti-aircraft ship *Delhi* and nine destroyers.

In the small hours of 8 November the weather at Oran was 'favourable, calm and dark, with good visibility'.[80] However, 'the unexpected westerly set which so seriously interfered with the landings near Algiers was equally disconcerting . . .'[81] On 'X' Sector, some 30 miles west of Oran, 'Task Force Green' (2,250 soldiers, plus tanks and trucks, of the Western Column of Combat Command B, American 1st Armoured Division) was embarked in three landing ships (infantry), four 'Maracaibo' shallow-draft motor transport vessels and one landing ship (tank), with an escort of the cruiser *Aurora*, one destroyer, two corvettes, a trawler and a motor launch. As the ships approached their 'release point' anchorage, a small French convoy straggled across their bows from starboard to port, causing a delay still further worsened when the landing group ran ahead of its minesweepers, which had also been held up by the French convoy.

As a result the landing began at 0130 instead of 0100. However, all went well, especially on 'White' beach (the westerly of the two in 'X' Sector), where the troops found themselves on a 50-yard stretch of sand in a cove well sheltered from the weather. Yet even here Murphy's Law was operating, for the sea proved so shallow that bulldozers had to be used to push the landing craft off the bottom. The consequent damage to rudders and screws left only three out of the thirteen craft that had carried the assault wave still serviceable. Nevertheless, 458 tanks and trucks and over 3,000 soldiers were to come ashore in 'X' Sector over the next three days, and most of them through that 50-yard wide sandy cove.

On 'Y' Sector, nearly 20 miles closer to Oran, 5,262 soldiers of the 26th Regimental Combat Team of the American 1st Infantry Division, embarked in three landing ships (infantry) and two motor transport ships, and escorted by two destroyers, four trawlers and five motor launches, were to land in the wide bay of Les Andalouses. Of all unlikely things, disembarkation from one landing ship (infantry) the *Monarch of Bermuda*, was seriously delayed because the rungs of the steel ladders down her sides turned out to be too far apart (at two feet) for the soldiers easily to negotiate in full combat kit. More unexpected difficulties followed. When the landing craft got within twenty feet of the shore they grounded on a submerged sand bar running the entire width of the bay, with a strip of water five feet deep inshore of it – too deep for troops to wade through. The landing craft were therefore compelled to bludgeon their way over the sand bar, thereby damaging their rudders and screws also.

By this time a northerly swell had begun to rise, causing many craft to broach to on top of the bar. With some soldiers trying to swim for the shore and with jeeps and guns submerging as soon as they left the bow ramps, it was fortunate indeed that neither a storm of fire nor a swift counter-attack descended from the rocky high ground dominating the beach on to the hapless landing forces. This potentially disastrous hold-up resulted from the Expeditionary Force headquarters' decision not to permit reconnaissance parties to land from canoes to survey beach conditions on the spot, but instead rely on observation through submarine periscopes.

Only east of Oran, in 'Z' Sector, did the landings go with complete smoothness. Here 10,472 soldiers of the 1st US Ranger Battalion, the 16th and 18th Regimental Combat Teams of the 1st Infantry Division and the Western Column of Combat Command B of the 1st Armoured Division were to disembark with their tanks and transport from nine landing ships (infantry) and two landing ships (tank), assisted by a landing ship (gantry), plus 22 motor transport ships. Because this was to be by far the largest of the Oran landings, Troubridge, Fredendall and Doolittle were themselves present offshore in *Largs*. The naval escort force comprised the cruiser *Jamaica*, the anti-aircraft ship *Delhi*, three destroyers, five corvettes, one sloop, two cutters, eight minesweepers, three trawlers and four motor launches.[82]

Punctually at 0016 the 'Z' Sector assault forces poured ashore from 68 landing craft on beaches Green, White and Red south of Arzeu, a little port nestling beneath a rocky headland and overlooked by the Fort de la Pointe, and on 'R' beach to its north. From 'R' beach the Rangers advanced swiftly overland to take the fort (it fired a few shots during the night) and Arzeu.

But the successful landings on the flanks had by now been accompanied by a bloody repulse in the centre, where (as at Algiers) an attempt had been made to rush the harbour and land a party of soldiers to prevent the French sabotaging installations or scuttling warships. At 0240 HMS *Walney* and *Hartland*, two ex-American coastguard cutters carrying Rangers and wearing both the Stars and Stripes and the White Ensign, steered for the harbour entrance starkly lit by hostile searchlights and with tracer swinging towards them. At 0310 *Walney* broke through the boom into the harbour, only to be reduced to a flaming hulk by the French sloop *La Surprise* and cross fire from submarines and the destroyer *Epervier*. *Walney* later sank. The *Hartland* fared no better, for the destroyer *Typhon* shattered her at point-blank range, leaving her to blaze from stem to stern in the middle of the harbour until she blew up after daylight. Captain F. T. Peters, RN (who planned and commanded the assault), one of the few survivors from either ship, was by a tragic irony killed a few days later in an air crash. He was posthumously awarded the Victoria Cross and the American Distinguished Service Cross. The attempts to rush the harbours at Oran and Algiers were just like the 1918 Zeebrugge raid all over again – desperate ventures, gallant and futile.

With the destruction of the *Walney* and the *Hartland* the outnumbered and outclassed French Navy, Army and Air Force now began to fight back. The destroyers *Tramontane*, *Tornade* and *Typhon* courageously put to sea to engage Troubridge's powerful task force, but the first two ships quickly succumbed to the accurate shooting of the cruiser *Aurora*, whereupon the *Typhon* temporarily sought shelter in harbour. The sloop *La Surprise* attempted to follow up her success against the *Walney* by attacking Allied shipping off 'Y' Sector, but was sunk by the destroyer *Brilliant*. Next day, 9 November, a fresh sortie by the *Typhon*, this time in company with the *Epervier*, ended with *Epervier* driven ashore engulfed in flames and *Typhon* beached after struggling back into harbour, both of them victims of the cruisers *Aurora* and *Jamaica*.

On land on 8 November a French field battery on high ground behind Arzeu shelled after first light the mass of shipping large and small lying off the shore, and hit the 17,000-ton landing ship (infantry) *Reina del Pacifico* before making off in the face of fire from the destroyer *Vansittart*. At 0900 the coastal battery Du Santon on the promontory behind the Mers-el-Kebir naval base opened accurate fire on ships lying off 'X' Sector; it took *Rodney*'s 16-inch guns to persuade it to cease fire, but then only temporarily. *Rodney* and the battery were later to resume lobbing shells at each other at extreme range, without effect. Throughout this day and the next the French field forces continued stoutly to defend the approaches to Oran from west and east.

Although it had been planned that American parachute troops should capture the airfields at Tafaraoui and La Senia at dawn on the 8th, none arrived owing to bad weather, poor visibility and errors of navigation. Albacores from HMS *Furious* escorted by Seafires and Sea Hurricanes therefore attacked both airfields, destroying some 70 French aircraft at La Senia. At noon that day the armour of Task Force Red from the 'Z' Sector beaches took Tafaraoui, and 28 British and American Spitfires from Gibraltar began to fly in. But the French Air Force was not yet finished. Dewoitine DW 520 fighters (maximum speed 332 mph)[83] attacked the last four Spitfires to arrive, shooting down one of them for the loss of three aircraft. Not until 1600 on 9 November did the armour of Task Force Green succeed in fighting its way through from 'X' Sector to take La Senia airfield. Meanwhile the American 1st Infantry Division had been slowed by tough resistance at St Cloud on the road from Arzeu to Oran. It took a general attack at 0800 on 10 November supported by a bombardment of the coastal batteries by *Rodney*, *Aurora* and *Jamaica* to bring about the final surrender of Oran to the Allies.

Back at Expeditionary Force headquarters in Gibraltar the setbacks and delays in taking the city had momentarily shaken Eisenhower, new as he was to the stress of high command in war. 'Eisenhower is good, but terribly mercurial,' wrote Cunningham to Ramsay on 12 November. 'He was in the depths of despair because Oran did not fall at once . . .'[84] It was fortunate, perhaps, that Eisenhower had 'A.B.C.', that man of battle-hardened steel, at his side.

The operations of Rear Admiral Kent Hewitt's Western Naval Task Force in landing the Western Assault Force on the coast of Morocco north and south of Casablanca belong to the history of the United States Navy.[85] Suffice to say that after incidental errors, mishaps and delays similar to those experienced in the Algerian landings, but here complicated by pounding Atlantic surf and fierce but short-lived fighting against the French Navy and ground troops, Casablanca fell early on 11 November. It is noteworthy, however, that because of the American lack of a headquarters ship General Patton (commanding the assault force) found himself carried helplessly away in Hewitt's flagship *Augusta* just as he was about to go ashore to set up his command post, simply because *Augusta* was needed to repel an attack by French warships.[86]

In hardly more than three days the Allied Expeditionary Force had thus accomplished 'Torch's' first objective of occupying French North Africa from Algiers (inclusive) westwards to the Atlantic. But now came the challenge of beating the Germans and Italians in the race for Eisenhower's 'the milk of the whole coconut' – Tunisia, and, above all, the ports of Bizerta and Tunis.

General Giraud proving on his arrival in Algiers to carry no weight at all with the French civil and military authorities, Eisenhower struck a deal with Admiral Darlan who did. By this deal the Allies recognised Darlan as the High Commissioner for North Africa. All French African territories (except Tunisia) were thereby aligned on the Allied side, including the Dakar naval base in West Africa, a strategic key to the South Atlantic, and the French battle-squadron stationed there. Nevertheless the deal was quickly criticised by prigs in the House of Commons on the grounds of having truck with a former collaborator with the Nazis and so betraying the high principles of the United Nations cause. What mattered to the pragmatic Eisenhower and his military and naval colleagues was that the deal secured the Expeditionary Force's base, and saved it from having to provide precious resources for a complete military occupation of French territories.

Darlan's defection provoked Hitler into ordering the German Army into the unoccupied zone of France, and, on 27 November, into attempting to seize the French fleet at Toulon. Nevertheless, just as Darlan had promised ever since 1940, the fleet – one battleship, two battlecruisers, four heavy and three light cruisers, 24 destroyers, sixteen submarines – scuttled itself.[87] So, after all, the French battle-fleet passed neither to the Allied side nor the Axis, but simply disappeared altogether from the naval balance in the Mediterranean.

On 15 November Admiral Syfret had taken Force H back to Gibraltar after cruising in defence of the 'Torch' landings against a possible Italian sortie that in the event never came, Force H's only victim during its patrol being the Italian cruiser *Attilio Regolo*, torpedoed and crippled by the submarine *Unruffled* (Lieutenant J. S. Stevens). The Admiralty promptly ordered the *Duke of York* and *Victorious* to return to the denuded Home Fleet. Now that the 'Torch' landings had been accomplished, the Naval Staff in London were in any case keen to strip ships away from the Mediterranean and redeploy them on the hard-pressed Atlantic convoy routes. Cunningham, however, found their keenness all too precipitate, confiding to Ramsay on 21 November:

> Not a few of the Admiralty signals are pretty futile. I got one today which indicates that someone has it in what he doubtless calls his head that you can turn Operation Torch off like a tap. Wanting to know when we can cut down on Torch commitments, when I can part with Force H destroyers and when I can part with the Gib escort force.
>
> I just sent a long signal to CNS giving our appreciation of the naval forces required but I doubt it went into his drawer and no one saw it otherwise the above signals could not have been made.[88]

The successful establishment of the Allied Expeditionary Force in Algeria added yet another continuing maritime supply route to the burdens of the Royal Navy and the merchant marine, and at the same time offered a fresh target to the U-boat. Only four days after the landings Cunningham was reporting to Ramsay: 'We have started having heavy losses from the U-boats and air attacks . . . There is I think a concentration of 20–30 of the former between here [Gibraltar] and Algiers and they are picking off our shipping rather too rapidly . . .'[89] Already picked off by the time of this letter were the 19,600-ton *Viceroy of India*, the 11,600-ton *Nieuw Amsterdam* troopships, and destroyers HMS *Martin* and HNLMS *Isaac Sweers*.[90]

In any event the race for Tunis depended on seapower because overland routes were limited to two narrow roads (only one of which was metalled), a single standard-gauge railway meandering through the hills inland and a metre-gauge line along the coast, both with worn-out locomotives and rolling-stock. It was therefore decided to land assault forces at Bougie and Bône, as staging posts along the coast to Tunis. The landing at Bougie, planned for 9 November, had to be postponed for two precious days by bad weather. Although the assault force landed safely without opposition the Luftwaffe (already operating from Tunisian airfields) proceeded ferociously to attack its shipping and escorts, sinking the landing ships (infantry) *Cathay*, *Awatea* and *Karanja* and seriously damaging the old Monitor *Roberts*. The anti-aircraft ship *Tynwald* succumbed to a mine. Where was the RAF? Its fighters were delayed in arriving at a nearby airfield because their petrol was at sea in the assault convoy.

On 12 November Bône was occupied in a joint operation by the British 3rd Parachute Battalion dropped from the air and the 6th Commando landed from the destroyers *Lammerton* and *Wheatland*. By this time the Luftwaffe in Tunisia had reached a total of 81 fighters and 28 dive-bombers, and a handful of parachute troops and panzer-grenadiers were already on the ground. Very soon the sturdy tri-motor Junkers Ju 52s began to fly in troops at an average rate of 750 a day. By sea across the narrow channel between Sicily and Tunisia (and despite British forces based on Malta) followed tanks, including the formidable new 'Tiger', 88mm dual-purpose anti-aircraft/anti-tank guns, field artillery, transport. The Italians too were moving troops and weapons in piecemeal as fast as possible.[91] The scale and pace of this enemy build-up, so much greater and faster than was expected beforehand, was fully revealed to the Allied command by Ultra decrypts of Enigma. On 16 November General Nehring (once commander of the Afrika Korps) arrived to set up a corps headquarters and direct the defence of Tunisia. With the customary German speed and enterprise, he threw forward a screen of ad hoc battlegroups of the kind which, thanks to standard tactical training, always proved so formidable. The Anglo-Americans had very little time left.

What the Allies therefore needed to lead the chase to Tunis was a Rommel or a 'Fast Heinz' Guderian who would take every risk to pre-empt and disconcert the enemy. What they had was Lieutenant-General Kenneth Anderson, a conventional British soldier judged by Eisenhower before 'Torch' to be 'straightforward, direct', but 'inclined to be too meticulous. He studies the written word until he practically burns through the paper.'[92] As early as 12 November, Cunningham, a bold enough thruster himself, was reckoning that 'we are not moving fast enough. Tunis is anyones [sic] who cares to walk in but the Huns are beating us in the race. I cannot understand why our soldiers do not embus and get on but they are methodically piling up POL [petrol, oil, lubricant] and amun [ammunition] and haven't really got going yet.'[93] Yet the logistic problems remained crippling, as even Cunningham had to acknowledge at the beginning of December: 'Rail head is choked, the wharfs are littered up all for want of transport to take the stuff away.'[94]

By the time Anderson's 1st Army (as his command had now become) and the Allied air forces were ready to launch a major offensive towards Tunis on 22 November, the German–Italian forces under Nehring were strong enough to defeat it, launch counter-strokes and throw the 1st Army back. In December the Mediterranean winter rains hosed down on the battlefield, turning roads and tracks to swamp, forcing a postponement *sine die* of a renewed Allied offensive and bogging the campaign down in stalemate. In January 1943 local Allied and German offensives equally failed to break the stalemate.

At the beginning of February (the month when, according to the original 'Torch' planning, the North African campaign was supposed to end in victory) Tunis still lay well beyond the Allied grasp behind a mountainous front strongly held by the 5th Panzer Army (created on 8 December 1942, when General von Arnim superseded Nehring). The grand strategy agreed by the Prime Minister and the President back in July 1942 had thus finished up (at least for the time being) in a cul de sac, so bearing out all Marshall's worst fears.

But much more dangerous to the Allied cause than this military stalemate was the colossal and continuing demand on shipping lift made by the campaign. It had been originally estimated that 66 ships a month would be needed until January 1943, and thereafter only a much reduced figure for the maintenance of an occupation force.[95] Even at the end of December 1942 it was still being assumed that the enemy would be thrown out of both Tunisia and Tripolitania by the end of January. But instead military demand constantly increased, so that in the event an average of 106 ships instead of 66 were despatched each month to North Africa between October 1942 and January 1943,[96] and in February 92 ships as against the original estimate of 30.[97] And it was on the Royal Navy that the strain of protecting this traffic principally fell, amounting to as many as 23 outward-bound and 22 homeward-bound convoys between 8 November 1942 and 20 February 1943 alone.[98] On top of the naval, military and air force investment in 'Torch', the total investment of merchant shipping came to 1,781,809 tons between August and December 1942[99] – all for a present strategic pay-off of a stalemated campaign against just 100,000 Axis soldiers.[100] And shipping losses on the North African route at the hands of the U-boat and the Luftwaffe amounted to 208,824 tons from October 1942 to February 1943 inclusive.[101] Taken all in all it so far hardly added up to cost-effective strategy.

But this was not the whole of it. The unexpectedly large tonnage of merchant vessels drawn into the North African campaign and the accompanying losses greatly worsened the current world shipping crisis that had been brought about by the competing demands of conducting maritime warfare against Japan as well as Germany and Italy, of supplying British war industries, of transporting American troops to the United Kingdom, and of feeding the peoples of Britain and the Indian Ocean Area countries.[102]

Such then were the costs of embarking on this grander version of Mediterranean 'blue water' strategy; costs which the Royal Navy and the Merchant Marine were having to meet just when the Battle of the Atlantic was mounting to its crisis, and when it seemed more and more possible that Britain and North Africa (and the Allied armies along with it) could be effectively cut off from the rest of the world.

19

'The Battle of the Atlantic Is Getting Harder'

In the North Atlantic the year 1942 had ended and 1943 had begun deceptively well for the Allies. Ferocious winter gales hampered the U-boats' ability to track convoys and then mass for the attack. For while cruising on the surface the U-boats were violently thrown about by huge Atlantic seas topped by breaking crests and while seeking tranquillity beneath the surface their electric motors gave them insufficient speed and range to overtake their victims. In the meantime the merchant ships steamed sturdily on though continually swept by green water. In December 1942 the Allies lost 46 ships totalling 262,135 tons in the North Atlantic as against 124 ships of 623,545 tons in the peak month of June.[1] In return the convoy escorts sank three U-boats, and shore-based aircraft another two.[2] In January 1943 the figures were even more encouraging: only 27 ships totalling 172,691 tons lost.[3]

Yet the cumulative losses of 1942 in the North Atlantic were appalling enough: 5,471,222 tons of shipping; 70 per cent of losses in all theatres of war.[4] And even though December 1942 looked so encouraging, it was ominous that convoy ONS154, although protected by six, later seven, escorts, lost fourteen out of 45 ships in a four-day battle with a pack of twenty U-boats, while the escorts sank only one U-boat and damaged another. This demonstrated that surface escorts simply could not fight off twice their own number of submarines; that the convoy system itself in these circumstances might fail. The experience of ONS154 bore out the First Sea Lord's prediction at the end of October about 'the exceedingly difficult and dangerous situation which is arising in consequence of our being unable to make the full naval provision required to tackle effectively the problem of the U-boat menace'.[5] Against a requirement of 1,050 ocean escorts of all types, only 445 were then available, and 100 of these dated from the Great War.[6] The Admiralty's Monthly Anti-Submarine Report for January 1943 therefore did well to warn that the U-boats were now deployed primarily so as 'to cut the main artery from the United States to Great Britain . . . most of them between Newfoundland and the longitude of Central Iceland . . .'; that 'the tempo is quickening, and the critical phase of the U-boat war in the Atlantic cannot be long postponed'.[7]

Nevertheless the balance sheet of the U-boat offensive against Allied shipping was much more complicated than the comparative totals of lost tonnage and sunk U-boats might indicate. In the first place shipping losses had to be set against new construction – and here the picture was very different from that during the U-boat offensive back in the Great War. As the First Sea Lord pointed out to the Prime Minister on 10 February 1943, the total tonnage of non-enemy new construction during the first 41 months of the Great War amounted to 6,840,000 tons; in the first 41 months of the present war to 10,790,000 tons.[8] Thanks to this prodigious output of new merchant ships, total *net* losses in 1942 amounted to about 700,000 tons, as against 3,700,000 tons in 1917. Better still, according to the First Sea Lord, the Allies had enjoyed an average *net* gain of something over 160,000 tons per month during the second half of 1942. 'In fact,' he told Churchill, 'despite the infinitely more difficult situation . . . [we] have brought the country through with considerable success.'[9]

That the cumulative output of new shipping in the first 41 months of the war was some 4 million tons greater than in the equivalent period of the Great War did not redound to the credit of the British shipbuilding industry, however. In fact its production and productivity record caused the government deep concern.

In September and October 1942 a small team of technical experts appointed by the Ministry of Production submitted two detailed reports on the deficiencies of the industry. The team found that with few exceptions the yards were cramped, the layouts confused, the equipment ancient, the workforce idle or strike-prone, and the whole production process slowed up by incompetent management, overmanning, and by the unions' restrictive practices and inveterate opposition to new technology and methods. The team reported that 800 new machines and nearly 200 heavy-lift cranes were needed, at a cost of over £2 million, to modernise the yards.[10] British output of merchant ships in 1942 amounted to 1.3 million gross tons – as against Allied and neutral losses of 7,790,697 tons in all seas.[11] In any case even the targets for output of new merchant ships had had to be cut back because much capacity was tied up in repairing damaged ships – and doing this so slowly and incompetently that a backlog had grown up of some 2 million tons under repair.[12]

The explanation for this hugely greater Allied output of ships in the present war lies in the American shipyards. Throughout 1942 an ever bigger procession of standardised cargo vessels, the 'Liberty ships', to a total of some 7 million tons, had been coming off the production lines of new American yards equipped with the latest technology and laid out for flow-line assembly. In 1943 American output would reach the staggering total of 13.6 million deadweight tons of dry-cargo ships.[13] American machines and American managerial excellence was therefore presenting Dönitz with the ever more difficult task of out-sinking this soaring new production.

Dönitz's answer too lay in flow-line assembly methods and standard products. From inland workshops prefabricated sections of U-boat hulls were transported by canal to Germany's excellently equipped shipyards, there to be welded together and fitted out with diesel and electric motors manufactured by great engine and electrical firms like M.A.N. and Siemens-Schuckert. Dönitz's main industrial problem lay in securing enough steel in the game of competitive scrounging which in the chaotic Nazi war economy took the place of planning. In 1942 completion of new U-boats reached seventeen per month, as against the target of twenty.[14] Meanwhile U-boat Command's training schools were batch-producing crews for the new boats. The British Monthly Anti-Submarine Report for January 1943 estimated that Dönitz now had some one hundred boats at sea, half of them in the Atlantic.[15]

However, the recent ability of Allied shipyards (above all, American) to outbuild losses of merchant ships did not mean the Allies faced no shipping crisis at the beginning of 1943 comparable to that of 1917. A further factor in a complex equation lay in the huge scale of demand for shipping in the present war.

In the first place, Britain in particular was again paying the penalty for a hundred years of Free Trade policy. This had rendered her dependent on enormous quantities of imported foodstuffs (to the ruin of British agriculture, only now being once more resuscitated in wartime by emergency measures). Free Trade had also reduced her general economic and industrial self-sufficiency by exposing her home market to massive imports of foreign technology, all of it paid for in peacetime by British exports (now reduced to only a third of the peacetime figure) or by income from foreign investments (now all liquidated). In the Victorian era this national dependence on a high volume of seaborne imports and exports had seemed the formula for unexampled prosperity. Now, in the crisis of a world war, it constituted, as in 1914–18, a strategic vulnerability that menaced the country's very survival. Britain's estimated minimum (and that meant cut to the bone) import requirements for 1943 still amounted to 27 million tons.[16]

Yet, on top of Britain's own requirements, the global civilian and strategic claims on shipping in the present war were so much larger than in the Great War. In 1917, at the height of the then U-boat offensive, the Allies were conducting a single major conflict, against a European coalition led by Germany. The overriding problem had therefore lain in supplying Britain and transporting American forces to France. The British armies on the Western Front were being maintained by the cross-Channel sea routes at maximum economy in shipping space. Large-scale military demand for merchant shipping tonnage had therefore been limited to the Atlantic and the Mediterranean (in support of the fringe campaigns against Germany's allies Bulgaria and Turkey). In 1942–43 by contrast Britain and America were fighting two separate major maritime wars at opposite ends of the globe, against Germany and Japan, while also again conducting a campaign (but even more costly in shipping than in the Great War) in the Mediterranean and Middle East.

Nor was this all. The swarming populations of India and the Middle East had to be fed (an aspect of that burden of Empire which Britain had failed to shed in the 1920s and 1930s), and in the case of India in 1942, rescued from outright famine – more heavy demands therefore for cargo ships.

It was in these vast, cumulative demands for merchant shipping, greatly exceeding available resources, that there lay the root cause of the deepening world shipping crisis at the start of 1943. Thus the rate of loss inflicted by the U-boat was not decisive in itself, as it had been in 1917 when month by month it hugely shrank the total merchant tonnage available to the Allies. Instead it was decisive in relation to the minimum amount of shipping needed by the Allies for the conduct of a global maritime war and at the same time for the civilian supply of Britain, India and the Middle East. As the British and Americans juggled their shipping budgets to make possible this campaign and that, this military build-up and another, this or that country's nourishment, Dönitz's U-boats in the Atlantic therefore supplied the marginal factor which determined whether the Allied sums would come out right or not. And herein lay the crucial significance of the Battle of the Atlantic in 1943.

The battle itself was waged at several different levels, all closely inter-connected – from the murderous front line out there in the mid-ocean spaces, through the industrial competition between the production and the sinking of merchant ships and U-boats, to the struggle for supremacy between rival technologies. This last struggle was fundamental to the outcome of the battle, for the shark, however ruthless in pursuit of prey, is impotent without lethal teeth; its hunter, however relentless, impotent without lethal harpoons; while both must have sharp eyes and acute hearing in order to track and kill – and best of all, the ability to read their antagonist's purposes in advance. In the continued striving for this ability lay the most secret technological competition of all; its swaying fortunes, indeed its very existence, unknown until 30 years after the war had ended. For in rooms quiet with mental concentration the rival cryptographers and electronics experts of the Government Code and Cypher School at Bletchley Park (GC and CS: 'Ultra') and of B-Dienst were now engaged in the climactic phase of their own battle of the Atlantic.

Back at the beginning of February 1942 GC and CS had suffered a major defeat when U-boat Command adopted a new and more complex four-rotor Enigma cypher, codenamed 'Shark' by the British (see above, p. 456).[17] It became no longer possible to divert convoys on to evasive routes away from wolf packs according to exact prior knowledge of Dönitz's instructions. Nevertheless the operational effect was less serious for several months than it might have been, because the U-boats were then concentrated along the American seaboard or working individually against ships still sailing independently.[18] When in the second half of 1942 U-boat Command again stepped up its concerted offensive against the North Atlantic convoys, the inability to read 'Shark' left the Admiralty's Operational Intelligence Centre and the tracking rooms in London, Ottawa and Washington half-blinded – but *half*-blinded only, because they now knew so much about the pattern of U-boat operations and U-boat Command's habits of mind that they could make brilliant guesses as to impending wolf-pack deployments from scraps of information from other sources, such as the German Navy Home Waters Enigma, or sightings by Allied aircraft and ships.

Nevertheless, losses to the U-boat of merchantmen in convoy had reached 50 in August 1942, 29 each in September and October, and 39 in November.[19] And it was of course in November that 'Torch' began to lay a heavy overload on Allied resources of shipping. With the prospect that in 1943 shipping available after other needs had been met would not even suffice to provide Britain with the absolute minimum level of imports needed for survival, Rear-Admiral J. Clayton, head of the OIC (Operational Intelligence Centre) on 22 November 1942 pressed GC and CS at Bletchley Park to devote 'a little more attention' to breaking the 'Shark' Enigma. He remarked that the battle with the U-boats was 'the one campaign which Bletchley Park are not at present influencing to any marked extent – and it is the only one in which the war can be lost unless BP *do* help. I do not think that this is any exaggeration.'[20]

Yet only three weeks later, on 13 December, Bletchley Park did the trick thanks to a new four-rotor electronic 'Bombe' for trial and error testings of all possible Enigma settings which had been devised by the Telecommunications Research Establishment;[21] and 'Shark' yielded the essential secret of its million-fold encyphering combinations. Yet it was still to take time before GC and CS could always read 'Shark' fast enough to enable the information to be put to immediate operational use. By the beginning of 1943 Bletchley Park had read the settings for eight days in November and also for early December, and on some occasions even the current settings. Step by step between now and August 1943 Bletchley Park, in collaboration with the US Navy Department's cryptographers, would work their way to complete and rapid mastery of 'Shark'. In the meantime they veered between periods of clear vision, when 'Shark' was being read at delays of 24 hours or less, and temporary loss of sight when the settings defied solution. Even by 17 February, for instance, the settings for the first seventeen days of January had still not been cracked, and between 10 March and 30 June settings for a further 22 days were either never broken or only at long delay.[22]

The task of decyphering 'Shark' fast enough to enable its secrets to be used operationally was rendered much harder by U-boat Command's system (introduced in November 1941) by which coded equivalents of the digraphs of the German naval grid could be frequently changed according to tables identified to the U-boats by the first name and address of imaginary persons[23] (see above, p. 456). Every time U-boat Command changed the 'address' Bletchley Park had to puzzle out the meaning by *ad hoc* brain work. And even a delay of three days in reading U-boat Command's signals directing U-boats to a new position meant that it would by then be too late to re-route a threatened convoy away from an ambush, because whereas U-boats on the surface could make 320 to 370 miles in 24 hours, a convoy could at best make only 240 miles. Add to these problems an increase in the total number of U-boats to be tracked from 212 in January 1943 to 240 in May, with some 60 usually on station in the North Atlantic, and it can be seen that the breaking of 'Shark', though a considerable help, could not yet enable the OIC and the tracking rooms promptly to locate all U-boats or route all convoys clear of them.[24]

At the same period, moreover, B-Dienst had scored its own success against the British Naval Cypher No. 3 – 'the convoy cypher'. In December 1942 the Admiralty had changed this and other cyphers, so blinding B-Dienst and leaving the U-boats groping for targets. But by February 1943 B-Dienst had broken Naval Cypher No. 3 again: once more it was as if Dönitz were present in British operation rooms, observing the flagged dispositions and routes of convoys on the wall charts, reading Admiralty movement signals in advance, and deploying his wolf packs accordingly.[25]

Yet the very sophisticated means by which Dönitz directed these far-off deployments made him peculiarly vulnerable to GC and CS's increasing mastery of 'Shark'. By 1943 Dönitz had perfected his system of detailed centralised conduct of the U-boat offensive from his command bunker near Lorient. The freebooting U-boat skippers of 1917 and of 1939–40 had now given way to captains who could hardly kill the lice in their shirts without a radio signal from U-boat Command. They had to report constantly in detail throughout their sorties – on their way out when they had cleared Biscay or (if sailing from Norway or the Baltic) 60°N; while at sea their positions and fuel states; at the end of a sortie their estimated times of arrival home. In return U-boat Command minutely directed the captains by radio in the search for convoys, in the concentration for the attack, even the time and method of attack; likewise when and where to refuel from 'milch cow' U-boats. This was how Dönitz sought to wield maximum striking power in the most effective and most economical way possible.

But this unique and unprecedented command and control system demanded an immense volume of radio traffic, handled by what one historian has called 'a signals network which for complexity, flexibility and efficiency, was probably unequalled in the history of military communications'.[26] It marked the complete reverse of the radio silence traditionally observed for security reasons by naval forces at sea, and it was founded on Dönitz's never-to-be-shaken belief that the U-boat Enigma cypher was unbreakable. But as GC and CS gradually mastered 'Shark', Dönitz's system would present his enemy with an overflowing treasure house of secrets; indeed the complete and detailed picture, constantly updated, of all U-boat operations and future tactical moves.

The escort forces too had their own means of exploiting the dependence of the Dönitz system on frequent radio-signalling back from U-boats to U-boat Command, for since July 1942 High Frequency Direction Finders (HF/DF) had been steadily fitted to more and more ships until at the beginning of 1943 this equipment had become standard. It enabled the escorts to fix the direction of a transmitting U-boat and even to estimate its range; they could then choose whether to close on the U-boat or divert their convoy clear of it.[27]

Nonetheless, even with Bletchley Park's gradually improving mastery of 'Shark' and the escorts' use of HF/DF it still needed short-wavelength radar mounted in ships and aircraft to pin-point a U-boat on the surface for the kill. The 10cm Type 271 ship's radar had been successfully tested as long ago as March 1941[28] and installation began in May that year. Able to pick up even a U-boat's periscope, it became the electronic eye of the escorts. To quote one appreciative customer, the commanding officer of HMCS *Brandon*, in a report to the Commodore (D) at Londonderry in March 1943: 'I have no hesitation in saying that the Mk IV Type 271 on the outward voyage very definitely saved some thousands of troops from an unpleasant swim . . .'[29]

However, only aircraft could speedily sweep the broad sea areas where 'Shark' decrypts or other information indicated that U-boats would be lurking; only airborne 10cm radar could enable these aircraft to pinpoint a U-boat or even just its periscope amid the clutter of the waves. Airborne 10cm radar was under development at the Telecommunications Research Establishment by mid-1941.[30] Yet the first operational sortie with ASV Mark III (the production version) did not take place until March 1943.[31] This protracted delay in bringing 10cm airborne radar into service – a delay which could have cost the Allies the Battle of the Atlantic – owed itself to a gruesome combination of bureaucratic and industrial muddle; to the priority given to Bomber Command's H2S (technically almost identical to ASV Mk III); and to the shortcomings of Britain's electronics and precision-engineering industries.[32] Two thoroughgoing reports on radio and radar production, the first by Lord Justice du Parcq (appointed by the War Cabinet) in August 1942 and the second to the Radio Board in April 1943, excoriated the wasteful overlaps in R and D and production programmes for the three services; the proliferation of different types of the same component because of the total lack of standardisation; the shortage of skilled technical personnel and managers in the radio firms; the muddles and delays in manufacture owing to the failure to plan and schedule the work properly; the 'crash' programmes by which urgently needed equipment was hand-built on benches rather than manufactured on a line.[33]

But the fundamental deficiency lay in the limited technological capabilities of the British radio and precision engineering industries. These had sufficed to produce early crude radar systems such as the 8–13 metre wavelength Fighter Command Home Chain, the 1.5 metre ASV Mark I fitted to Coastal Command Hudsons in 1940, and the 1 metre air-warning radars in warships (the early versions of the latter being 'something of a lash-up', according to one gunnery expert).[34] But the manufacture of the new 10cm radars and H2S and their sophisticated thermionic valves, the Klystron and Magnetron, presented immense difficulties because of the advanced technologies involved. The Klystron and Magnetron, British inventions, had had to be handed over to the Americans to manufacture, while the wartime development of the British electronics industry itself came to depend on American supplies of machine tools as well as components.

The Cabinet decision to give Bomber Command's H2S first call on the British radio and precision-engineering industries' limited resources meant that Coastal Command had to wait interminably for its 10cm ASV Mark III, for throughout 1942 production of H2S was held up by all kinds of teething troubles and bottlenecks.[35] Only in August 1942 (as a result of one success by the Admiralty in 'the Battle of the Air') did the government decide to divert some H2S sets into Leigh Light Wellingtons as ASV Mark IIIs. But the conversion itself presented problems because the scanner had to be redesigned for an aperture of 28 inches, instead of the 36 inches in Bomber Command's big bombers, so that it could fit under the nose of a Wellington. Other modifications were also needed because the ASV Mark IIIs would be operated at 2,000 feet instead of 20,000 as H2S.[36] It was not until December 1942 that two prototype ASV Mark IIIs could be fitted to Wellington VIIIs; not until 30 January 1943, after more technical and electronic teething troubles, that sets had been fitted to two Wellington XIIs and another Wellington VIII.[37] At this point it was found that a modification of the aerial system was urgently needed. Thanks to the zeal of the Telecommunications Research Establishment at Malvern, twelve ASV Mark IIIs had been fitted to Wellingtons by 27 February 1943, and in the evening of 1 March (a month after Bomber Command's first use of H2S) two ASV Mark III Wellingtons took off on their inaugural sortie; and on the 17th the new radar detected its first U-boat in the Bay of Biscay at a range of nine miles.[38] It enjoyed the immense extra advantage that because of its short wavelength it could not be detected by the U-boats' Metox equipment.

Yet the Wellingtons could only cover the Bay itself. Mid-ocean detection demanded VLR aircraft fitted with 10cm radars; it demanded too that aircraft from the small new escort carriers about to come into service should likewise be equipped. In January 1943 the United States began delivering to Coastal Command (by grace of the air staff and with the grudging acceptance of Bomber Command) VLR Liberators equipped with the SCR 517, the American equivalent of ASV Mark III.[39] This had been developed by the lavish human and technical resources of the Radiation Laboratory of the Massachusetts Institute of Technology and built by the US radio industry.

But fitting 10cm radar into the small single-engined aircraft that would work from the cramped flight decks of escort carriers had proved a hard technical problem to solve ever since R and D began in 1941. Most importantly the equipment for such aircraft had to be lightweight and compact; none such then existed.[40] At the end of 1941 design work was started on a set, the ASV-X, to be fitted in the Royal Navy's new carrier aircraft, the Fairey Barracuda, but since this was not yet in production the choice shifted to that old stand-by, the Swordfish. The problem of where to install the set was solved by dispensing with the third member of the aircrew and stowing the set in his place.[41] However the Swordfish was not a very suitable aircraft to work off escort carriers pitching steeply over the Atlantic, because, in the words of a report by the commanding officer of the carrier HMS *Fencer* to the C-in-C, Western Approaches, on 26 December 1943, it was 'a very tender aircraft', liable to damage throughout its fuselage in a heavy landing.[42]

The first aircraft to be fitted with a trial ASV-X set did not arrive at Faireys (the manufacturer of the Swordfish) until July 1942. The first aircraft was not fitted with a preproduction prototype set until February 1943. March passed in trials; July and August in operational trials and exercises, while in the meantime the sets were slowly being pushed out of the factories. Then came the formation of a nucleus training squadron, and finally, but finally, in November 1943 the first operational squadron of Swordfish equipped with 10cm radar was ready to embark in an escort carrier – by which date the crisis of the Battle of the Atlantic was many months past.[43] Yet had it been available in good time it would have transformed the task of the escorts and support groups, because the ASV-X Swordfish could patrol an area within a forty-mile radius of the carrier and pick up a U-boat with its decks awash or even its periscope by sweeping a lane fourteen miles wide.

But in any case there were equivalent delays in deploying the escort carriers (CVEs) that would carry the 10cm ASV aircraft. Even before the regrettably short-lived success at the end of 1941 of HMS *Audacity*, the first of all CVEs to enter service (see above, pp. 275–6), the Admiralty and the Navy Department had decided on an initial programme of building very simple carriers on existing standard American cargo-ship hulls. Four of these vessels were allotted to the Royal Navy. HMS *Archer* (the name ship of the class: 9,000 tons; diesel driven; 17 knots; 15 aircraft)[44] was completed on 17 November 1941, but did not become operational until March 1942; *Biter* (8,200 tons; 16½ knots)[45] was completed on 1 May 1942 but did not become operational until September; and *Dasher* (also 8,200 tons) was completed on 1 July 1942, but did not enter service until October. The fourth ship, *Avenger*, though completed in America on 2 March, only made her operational début with an Arctic convoy in September.[46] However, all four British CVEs were soon pulled away to provide close air support to the November 'Torch' landings in Algeria, and while escorting a 'Torch' convoy west of Gibraltar HMS *Avenger* was blown up and sunk by a torpedo from the U-155.

The United States had by now begun the series production of 11,420-ton standardised CVEs, Model Ts of the sea;[47] and Britain was provisionally to receive under Lend-Lease a total allotment of 28 vessels.[48] But whereas the United States Navy was happy to accept such CVEs into service simply equipped for the principal role of anti-submarine operations, the Royal Navy wanted them as poor man's fleet carriers. For Britain had had to abandon further large-scale construction of big fleet carriers for want of financial and industrial resources (see above, pp. 437–8). The Royal Navy therefore put their new CVEs through a three to four month refit after delivery from American yards in order to extend the flight decks, improve fire precautions, strengthen the structure, and – the most important of all – install fighter-direction radars. In the words of an Admiralty signal to the British Admiralty Delegation in Washington on 7 September 1943, 'the main cause of delay in getting our carriers into service is our endeavour . . . to get all these carriers capable of full fighter operation and not merely fit for A/S work':[49]

> It must be remembered that we differ from the United States Navy since we have not in sight so large a force of Fleet and Light Fleet Types. For

> this reason we shall in future have to depend more than the Americans upon fighters operated from Escort Carriers in support of amphibious operations . . . We have also to consider the anti-aircraft protection of trade (e.g. in the Bay and possibly North Russian routes) . . .[50]

At the time of this signal the Admiralty reckoned that the current demands of the landings at Salerno in Italy (see below, pp. 659–60) for CVEs capable of 'full fighter operation', together with future needs in the Indian Ocean in 1944, completely justified the delays in getting them into service. Nevertheless Admiral 'Ernie' King, who at this time was providing all the CVEs on anti-U-boat operations in the Atlantic, was so incensed by British dilatoriness in getting American-supplied CVEs into service that it was formally intimated to the Admiralty that unless the delays were drastically reduced the next British allotment of seven ships would be stopped, and the ships deployed straight away in the Atlantic under the US ensign: hence the pained Admiralty signals of self-justification to Washington.[51] A report by the Allied Anti-Submarine Survey Board on 27 August 1943, signed by Rear-Admiral J. M. Mansfield, RN, and Rear Admiral J. L. Kauffman, USN, noted that out of Britain's current total of 13 escort carriers (CVEs), only six were operational; four of these allotted to the Mediterranean; and not one to anti-submarine operations in the Atlantic.[52] Little scope here, then, for Swordfish equipped with 10cm ASV, even if these had not still been in the stage of squadron training.

In the opening months of 1943 the looming crisis in the Battle of the Atlantic had consequently to be faced by the Allies without benefit of escort carriers equipped with 10cm ASV aircraft; indeed without benefit of CVEs at all to begin with, for it was not until mid-March that the first, the USS *Bogue*, joined in the battle. The Admiralty had made an ingenious attempt to fill the gap before the CVEs entered service by embarking on the construction of 'Merchant Aircraft Carriers' (MACs) – ordinary merchant ships or tankers topped by a flight deck 400 to 490 feet by 62 feet, but without hangars and able to carry only four Swordfish. The idea had been mooted in April 1942, but the first keel out of six ships was not laid until August. In November the Cabinet Anti-U-boat Warfare Committee agreed to the construction of a further twelve, possibly eighteen. It had been hoped that the initial six would be in service by the early spring of 1943, but in the event it was May before the first ship, *Empire MacAlpine*, sailed with an Atlantic convoy. The programme had miscarried in the congestion of the shipyards and because of a bottleneck over arrester gear.[53]

Eventually these invaluable escorts, flying the Red Ensign and commanded by Merchant Navy masters, were to spend 4,447 days at sea escorting 217 convoys, of which only two lost any ships while a MAC ship was in company.

But at the beginning of 1943 all this was in the future. In the meantime there were not enough destroyers or other suitable escort vessels, let alone CVEs, to enable the formation of 'support groups' for the rescue of convoys under heavy attack. Although in September 1942 an experimental 'killer group' had proved its worth in the Atlantic, thereafter the demand for destroyers on the Arctic convoy routes and then for the 'Torch' operations had taken precedence. Only in mid-February 1943 did the Admiralty judge that there were enough suitable ships to allow the C-in-C, Western Approaches, to begin planning the creation of support groups (to be titled 'Escort Groups'); and only in mid-March did the Allies decide at the Atlantic Convoy Conference in Washington that four such escort groups should be deployed as soon as possible – one American, with a CVE (*Bogue*) and five destroyers; one Canadian and two British (to include the CVEs *Dasher* and *Biter*).[54] Here was another dangerously last-minute development. On the British side, this belatedness stemmed partly from the unexpectedly long-drawn-out demands of the North African campaign, partly from shortfalls in the production of new destroyers and other escorts by British shipyards.[55]

In any case, such grim experiences as that of Convoy ONS154 in December 1942 (see above, pp. 573–4) made it all too plain that the convoy escorts themselves were not strong enough either in numbers or type of ship to fight off massed U-boats. As the commanding officer of a support group was to put it late in 1943, '. . . although the corvettes did excellent work, they were handicapped by insufficient speed, lack of plotting facilities, and their size and movement in rough weather, which imposed great strain on the personnel after long periods at sea'.[56] Only gradually in the course of that year did new classes of escort, such as the 1,350-ton, two-shaft steam turbine 'Modified' Black Swan escort sloops and the 1,370-ton River class frigates (each type with a speed of around 20 knots)[57] provide the Royal Navy in the Atlantic with vessels with the right sea-keeping qualities and the speed to chase U-boats to the death. Yet British output fell far short of the Royal Navy's needs for escorts, fewer than 50 corvettes and destroyers being completed in 1943;[58] and by now Britain had become 85 per cent dependent on North American yards for new escorts of all types.[59]

In that other technological competition to develop more and more lethal weapons, each side had so far managed to match the other in muddle, delay and designs that would not work. Dönitz's U-boats only found themselves equipped with reliable magnetic pistols for their torpedoes instead of Great War type contact pistols by the end of 1942; and only then was the problem of maintaining the torpedo's run at the correct depth also solved. It was only in September 1942 that the U-boats began to be armed with a new torpedo (FAT, or *Feder-Apparat Torpedo*) that would keep changing course according to a predetermined pattern after travelling a preset distance, and so be almost certain to hit a target within the sprawling columns of a convoy. It had therefore taken three years of war for the U-boats to come to enjoy what Dönitz called an 'unsurpassed level of excellence' in its weaponry.[60]

Why had it taken German technology, for all its resources and proven record, so long? Dönitz himself blamed it on the stultifying effects of bureaucracy within the relevant departments of the German Navy, especially the Torpedo Experimental Department that for years had been in sole charge of the whole process of torpedo development. In his view this was 'fundamentally wrong in principle':

> The Armed Forces should themselves have nothing whatever to do with the construction of the weapons they require, but should pass on their requirements to private industry. They should then submit the best weapons which emerge as the result of very keen industrial competition to most rigorous tests under as near to war conditions as possible and should then accept them only if they prove satisfactory.[61]

British experience up to 1943 in developing air and sea anti-submarine weaponry entirely bears out Dönitz's shrewd judgment. Bureaucratic rigidity of mind and structure within the various R and D departments of the Admiralty coupled with the technical conservatism of men too long in the job fouled the screws of progress. It took a year to meet a need for a shallow setting on the existing depth-charge pistol that had been first stated to the Director of Torpedoes and Mines in July 1941 – all because of lack of liaison between the development team and the end-user, lack of proper briefing as to the operational basis of the requirement, and finally to officious middle-men altering the requirement to include deep setting on the same pistol.[62] In another case, the Admiralty (and Admiral Sir Max Horton, the then C-in-C, Western Approaches) refused to believe that U-boats could dive as deep as they in fact did, well beneath the level at which the existing British 'deep' setting pistol detonated. As a result it took until June 1943 to equip the Mark X

200-pound depth-charge with a deep setting designed to detonate well below 500 feet. In any event the 200-pound Mark X depth-charge itself had not appeared until May 1942.[63]

The Air Ministry development departments proved no more fast moving. Only from May 1942 were Coastal Command aircraft equipped with Torpex-filled Mark VII 250-pound depth-charges; only from July 1942 were these depth-charges fitted with a reliable 25-foot setting pistol for destroying U-boats at the beginning of their dive to escape. It had therefore taken nearly three years of war to equip Coastal Command with a truly deadly anti-U-boat weapon.[64] But still under development at the beginning of 1943 were a 600-pound anti-submarine bomb and an air-launched rocket.[65]

However, it was the 'Hedgehog' device for throwing anti-submarine warheads forward over the bows of escorts which provides the most dismaying case-history of bureaucratic stone-headedness. By early 1940 it had already become apparent that the traditional method of discharging depth-charges over the stern suffered from the drawback that the attacking vessel necessarily lost sonar contact with her victim, often never to regain it; and that what was needed was a device for lobbing high-explosive *ahead* (see above, p. 256). A struggle now ensued between the departmental stone-heads and a group of energetic and bright-minded young officers and scientists.[66] Captain G. H. Oswald, RN, of the Department of Naval Ordnance, later recalled how a 36-year-old scientist and Fellow of the Royal Society, Charles Goodeve, then serving in the rank of Commander, RNVR, in the new Admiralty Anti-Aircraft Weapons and Devices Department, and the group of eager doers which Goodeve recruited from no matter what bureaucratic 'box'

> pursued the problem with the greatest zeal and it soon became evident that a solution would be available in months. I regret to say however that others put every obstacle in the way; for example D.N.O. [Director of Naval Ordnance] said if a mortar system was adopted the whole scheme should go back to D.T.M. [Director of Torpedoes and Mines] but that the Ordnance Board must be closely associated with the ammunition; the O.B. said the required fuze was so novel that five years were required for its design and adequate test; Fairlie [the Anti-Submarine Warfare Establishment] who were busy on their own Mortar would have nothing to do with Hedgehog and would not even lend their Underwater Range in the Clyde for our trials. Incidentally we requisitioned and commissioned Western-Super-Mare Pier for this purpose.
>
> In other words, the Obstructors were many and the Faint-hearts not a few but the enthusiasts outnumbered them.[67]

Thanks to the creative energy of these young scientists, soldiers and sailors from different departments but all working together as a team, the basic design of the Hedgehog (a ripple-firing multiple spigot mortar throwing a spread of 24 projectiles weighing 65 pounds and with 35-pound Torpex warheads) went forward well. The trouble started when the conventional departmental hierarchies took a hand, their standards of science and engineering being both second-class and out of date. The Chief Inspector of Gun Mountings designed a mounting which did not even take into account the elementary need to resist the recoil, and in his calculations used cordite tables dated 1905.[68] The Ordnance Board proposed a design for a fuze with 127 parts which, owing to inherent defects, could not possibly succeed.

The Head Scientist at the Anti-Submarine Warfare Establishment at Fairlie in Scotland, one B. S. Smith, an able man back in the 1920s in developing Asdic but now ossified into bureaucratic authoritarianism, did his best to thwart the Hedgehog team because of his own alternative project, the so-called 'Fairlie Mortar' which eventually turned out to be a complete failure.[69] Smith proposed to train his device on to its target by means of two electric motors and a differential gear box; and insisted on building a trial apparatus even though junior scientists on his staff pointed out on theoretical grounds that it could not work.[70] This was by no means the only example of Smith's opinionated mediocrity, and he eventually provoked a mutiny among the scientists drafted into his department because he took new ideas 'as criticism of existing apparatus' and therefore 'frequently discouraged' them.[71] Anyone who has worked in large bureaucratic organisations will recognise the dreary pattern. The Director of Naval Ordnance himself turned his back on the Hedgehog project, while the Director of Naval Construction gloomed fallaciously about the effect of the deck thrust.[72]

The whole Hedgehog project might well therefore have been obstructed into oblivion but for the enthusiastic backing of the Controller of the Navy, Admiral Sir Bruce Fraser.[73] Thanks to him and their own determination to succeed, the 'young Turks' finally had their way. Industry, in the form of the Hall Telephone Company, manufactured the novel hydro-dynamically armed fuze (the solution to the problem which had so baffled the Ordnance Department).[74] Hedgehog finally went to sea operationally in January 1942, nearly two years after the first gleam in its creators' eye, and by the end of the year over 100 ships had been equipped with it.[75]

In February 1942 there began a reworking of the Anti-Submarine Warfare Department's abortive 'Fairlie Mortar', this time with three

ove) Atlantic Convoy (Crown copyright)
low) Atlantic Convoy OB (Outward Bound) 331, e 1941. '. . . the convoys which in constant progression bore the North American supplies across the ocean to Britain, without which she could neither wage war nor even live.' (IWM)

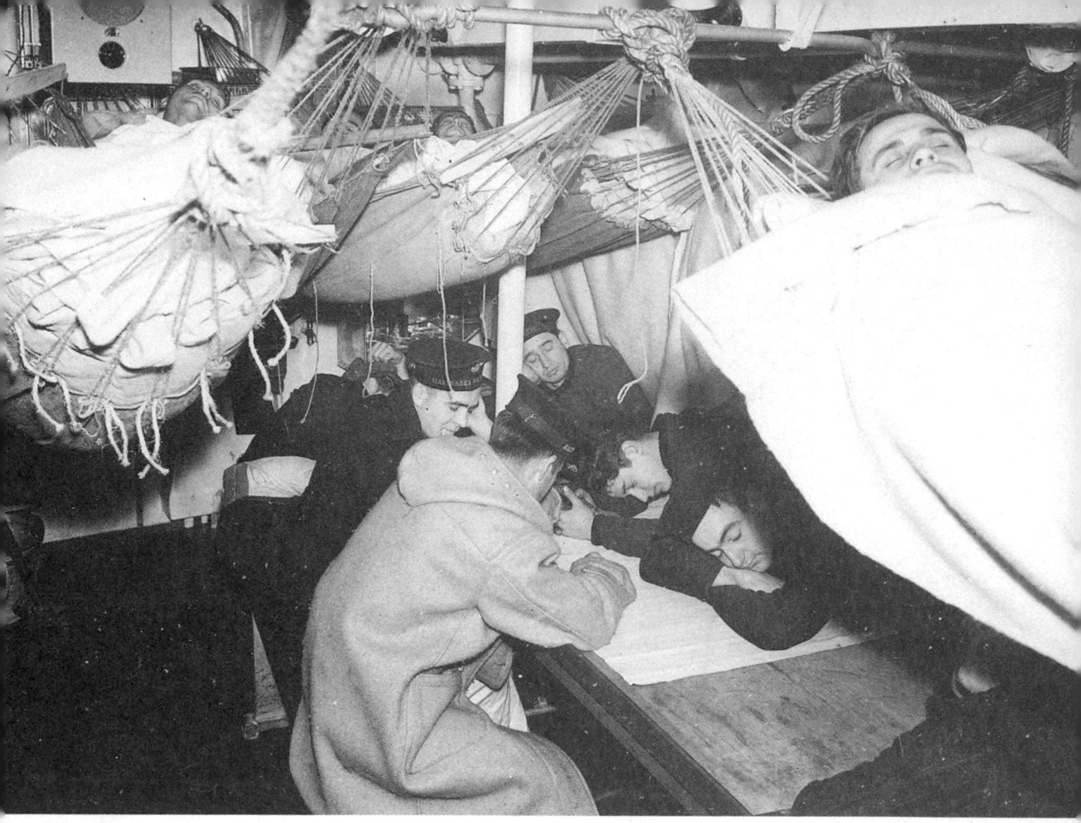

(Above) '. . . the bulkheads running with condensation; the air thick with human exhalations. . . .' A mess-deck scene typical of a destroyer or escort vessel; here the ship is the Polish-manned destroyer *Piorun.* (Crown)

(Below) A U-boat sinking. 'They felt more and more naked beneath a sky out of which an aircraft would suddenly thunder to smother their boat with 250-pound depth charges.' (IWM)

ɔove, left) 'The most secret technological competition ıll.' A German Enigma encyphering machine. Dönitz ieved its cyphers to be unbreakable, yet the vernment Code and Cypher School at Bletchley Park ıstered them. But the German B-Dienst read British ·val cyphers too. (IWM) *(Above, right)* 'HF/DF (High ·quency Direction Finders) mounted in the convoy escort could reveal the presence and bearing of a U-boat.' The first set came into use in mid-1941. (IWM) *(Below)* 'Across one wall was displayed the current Operational Plot of the Battle of the Atlantic.' The operations room of Western Approaches Command beneath a thick concrete roof in Derby House, Liverpool. (IWM)

(Top) 'A new means of locating the surfaced U-boat in all conditions of weather and light.' The Type 271 radar set, installed in fifty escort ships by the end of 1941. (IWM) *(Middle)* The 'Squid' anti-submarine mortar. Under development from February 1942, it did not kill its first U-boat until July 1944. (IWM) *(Left)* The 'Hedgehog' anti-submarine mortar, housing a spread of 24 projectiles with 35-pound warheads over a ship's bow. It only saw service thanks to a protracted campaign by young scientists and serving officers against the 'bureaucratic stoneheadedness' of the Admiralty research 'establishment'. (IWM)

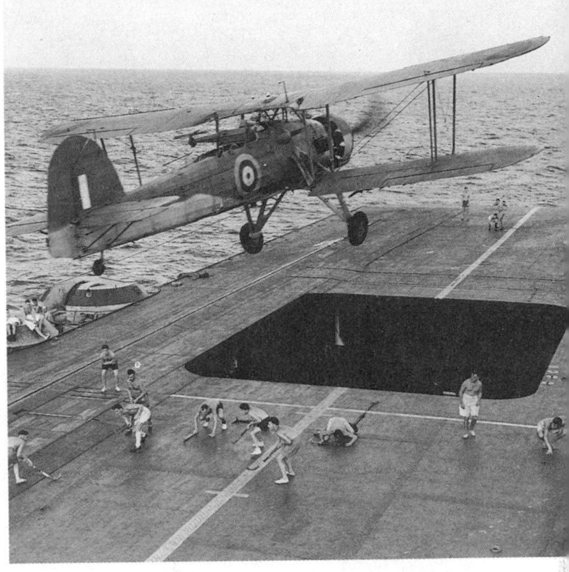

bove) Admiral Sir Percy Noble *(left)*, C-in-C, Western
pproaches, 1941–42 with Noble's opposite number,
r Vice-Marshal J. M. Robb, Commanding No. 15
roup, RAF Coastal Command. (IWM) *(Above, right)*
enjoyed the affection and respect of its crews because
its sturdiness . . . and its stability as a weapons
atform.' The Blackburn Swordfish (maximum speed
4 mph), the Royal Navy's torpedo-bomber in the early
years of the war. In November 1940, a Swordfish strike crippled the Italian Fleet in Taranto harbour. (IWM) *(Below)* The Fairey Barracuda Mark II (maximum speed 228 mph), the Fleet Air Arm's first monoplane torpedo bomber, did not see action until the landings at Salerno in September 1943. In 1944, Barracudas inflicted serious damage on the battleship *Tirpitz*. (IWM)

(Above) 'We have the gap between Newfoundland an Iceland in which our convoys are at the mercy of the U-boat. At the moment, the main weight of the air escort work is being carried by 17 Liberators.' A Very Long Range (VLR) Liberator equipped with the Leig Light – subject of the 'Battle of the Air' between the Admiralty and the Air Ministry. (IWM) *(Below)* The Leigh Light, which enabled aircraft to illuminate U-boats at night, had its successful trial in May 1941 b bureaucratic obstruction and technical problems delaye its first 'kill' to July 1942. (IWM)

ove) 'Such desolate and dangerous voyages.' Arctic voy JW53 passing through pack ice on passage to rth Russia, February 1943. (Crown) *(Below)* 'All too iliar and routine to every ship's company in the Arctic convoys was the mustering of all hands to chip away the enveloping crusts of ice. . . . In a small ship this could make all the difference between capsizing or not if hit by a torpedo.' (IWM)

'The hull was carried up to the flight deck, making an integral box-like structure of immense strength.' HMS *Illustrious* (23,000 tons displacement; designed to carry 36 aircraft), one of four new carriers laid down under the pre-war rearmament programme. (IWM)

barrels in tandem instead of five abeam. Known later as the 'Squid', it was not mounted in a ship until September 1943 and did not kill its first U-boat until 31 July 1944.[76]

All this time another 'Battle of the Atlantic' was being fought in the training schools. Since the early days of the war the Royal Navy had trained individual anti-submarine officers and lower-deck personnel in manoeuvring a ship and operating weapons and Asdic by means of the Attack Teacher House, an elaborate simulator of an escort ship at sea. Attack Teacher Houses were gradually set up at all British fleet bases and throughout the Commonwealth. In summer 1941 one was supplied to America and by June 1942 the United States Navy had put them into quantity production. The Royal Navy even installed mobile Attack Teachers in converted buses so that they could be used by smaller bases. Meanwhile the Anti-Submarine School – transferred from Portland on the south coast of England to the Clyde during the invasion months of 1940 – had grown into a great complex of training establishments for batch-producing specialist officers and ratings. The job of 'working up' such trained individuals into ships' companies who could work smoothly together to fight the ship was performed by HMS *Western Isles*, a sea training establishment at Tobermory in the Inner Hebrides. This had been opened by Commodore (Vice-Admiral retired) G. O. Stephenson in July 1940. Stephenson – 'the Terror of Tobermory' – proved a hard and brilliantly imaginative trainer, putting his fledgling crews through a relentless month of fictitious emergencies such as towing damaged ships, putting out a fire in an abandoned merchant ship or fighting their own ship with half the crew and equipment out of action.[77]

But despite all this immense and innovative training effort it had become apparent to Western Approaches Command by early 1942 that while some convoys were getting through safely or with small loss, others were sustaining heavy losses even though their escort was just as strong. This clearly indicated that wide differences existed among the escort forces in the quality of teamwork and the skill of group command.

In March 1942 Western Approaches Command therefore set up the Western Approaches Training Unit in Liverpool, followed in December by another in Londonderry. Each consisted of a large room, the floor of which represented a stretch of the mid-Atlantic, and across which Wrens moved symbols of U-boats, convoys and escorts as the training exercises proceeded. The 'U-boats' were commanded with the maximum cunning and aggression by the training officer. The escort commanders under training were shut in small cubicles off the main floor, able to see just so much of the 'Atlantic' through a slit in the wall as from the bridge of a ship. In response to U-boat attacks or sightings (either directly or as reported to them) they had to issue appropriate orders to the 'escort force' under their command. This ingenious simulator could also be used for experimental exercises in tactics and organisation.[78] In the same year the Royal Canadian Navy created its own realistic simulator for teaching night escort tactics, complete with a pitching and rolling ship's bridge and a horizon on which could be projected the silhouettes of ships, U-boats, aircraft or such illuminations of battle as star shell, searchlights and burning vessels.[79]

Nonetheless, and despite all their ingenuity, simulators could not substitute for command training at sea. In January 1943 the C-in-C, Western Approaches, therefore set up a new establishment at Londonderry round HMS *Philante*, formerly the millionaire industrialist Tom Sopwith's luxury yacht. While *Philante* served as a 'convoy' and two old submarines played the parts of U-boats, British and Canadian escort commanders in their own ships could practise escorting the 'convoy' safely through the most craftily devised attacks.[80] But only in April 1943 – as it proved, the critical month of the whole Battle of the Atlantic – was a Combined Service Anti-Submarine Training Centre set up to promote intimate cooperation between Royal Air Force Coastal Command, the Fleet Air Arm and surface escorts. The RAF stations at Eglington and Maydown in Northern Ireland were turned over to the Royal Navy for this purpose.

Yet it was beyond the reach of even sea training exercises to mimic such realities as the appalling weight of responsibility bearing down on the mind and will of an escort commander when on a night lit by the flames of dying ships he must make almost instantaneous decisions on the basis of incomplete and possibly false information; decisions which if mistaken could so easily lead to the massacre of his convoy. Nor could exercises mimic the insidious assault on the mind mounted by sheer exhaustion after days at sea and hours on the bridge; the wearing out of bodily strength by almost continuously bad weather that forced sailors to brace themselves against the violent movement of the ship 24 hours a day, waking, eating, trying to sleep. And nor could training simulate the grinding away of courage by the attrition of constant danger. In Allied escort ship and German U-boat alike duty and discipline fought a constant battle with fear – and on occasion with outright terror.

For however important were the 'battles' between rival technologies and industrial resources and cryptographic brains, the issue of the struggle out there in the Atlantic front line must in the end turn on the seamanship, the fibre and the fighting spirit of the men who crewed the merchant ships and escorts – and the U-boats. On that, and on the admiralship and willpower of those who on the opposing sides directed the battle.

Karl Dönitz, a submariner admiral to rank with the greatest fleet commanders of history, held the U-boat offensive in his single grasp. He wielded it like a cutlass, hacking relentlessly and skilfully at his enemy, thrusting swiftly through any momentary opening in his enemy's guard; a nimble killer with an incisive operational brain and a will of Krupp steel.

On the Allied side, direction of the battle remained divided – in the first place between the Royal Navy, the Royal Canadian and United States Navies, even though liaison remained close and the 'chop-lines' (marking changes in operational control) clear cut. In January 1943, in another perilously late development, the First Sea Lord and Chief of Naval Staff and COMINCH (C-in-C, US Fleet, and also Chief of Naval Operations) set up the Allied Anti-Submarine Survey Board with the task of standardising training, operational procedures and the overall deployment of the Allies' available pool of escorts. In the opinion of an Admiralty report in August 1943, the new board 'has made a great contribution in every sphere of the Anti-U-boat war . . .'[81] Nonetheless it failed to lull British suspicions that Ernie King as COMINCH (C-in-C, United States Fleet) was more concerned with finding ships for the Pacific than the Atlantic.

Nor in any case did British responsibility itself lie in single hands. At the top the War Cabinet Anti-U-boat Warfare Committee (created in November 1942) acted as a forum where major questions of policy, such as the provision of Very Long Range (VLR) aircraft, could be thrashed out and decided; it also kept a watching brief over the whole field of strategy and operations. The committee was gradually to stale into a routine chore for its members. Rear-Admiral C. D. Howard-Johnston (then Director of the Anti-U-boat Division of the Admiralty) was to recall:

> . . . the highlight of the month was the Cabinet Anti-U-Boat Meeting with the Prime Minister in the Chair. We used to lose an awful lot of time with Winston who was often miles off the point with things thought up by Professor Lindemann (later Lord Cherwell) . . .[82]

On one occasion when the Premier asked why it took so many

depth-charges to sink one U-boat, it turned out that Lindemann had simply divided the total world stocks of depth-charges at sea and on shore by the number of U-boats sunk.[83]

Under Admiral of the Fleet Sir Dudley Pound, who as First Sea Lord was in supreme executive command of all British naval operations, the day-to-day conduct of the battle against the U-boat in the Atlantic continued to lie with the Commander-in-Chief, Western Approaches, now Admiral Sir Max Horton, who had succeeded Sir Percy Noble in November 1942. Noble, an elegant, courteous, charming man, lacked aggressive drive either in regard to his own command or London's naval and political hierarchies. Horton could hardly have stood in greater contrast. Himself a veteran submariner, his last appointment that of Flag Officer, Submarines, he could match Dönitz in first-hand understanding of U-boat operations – and the psychology of U-boat crews. He no less matched Dönitz in ruthless will to win, though perhaps not in power of mind. Horton drove his command hard, his displeasure expressed in ways which reduced his less robust subordinates to nervous wrecks; and only the bravest dared approach him on days when he had lost at his regular game of golf. Every ship's company in Western Approaches Command could feel the grip and impulse of such harsh leadership.

From February 1943 the Royal Navy worked with a new Air Officer Commanding-in-Chief, Coastal Command, in Air Marshal Sir John Slessor, an able and ambitious officer, subtle of mind to the point (as some believed) of deviousness, but a committed exponent of close cooperation between the two services. From Coastal Command's operations theatre deep under a park at Northwood in the north-west London suburbs, with galleries for commander and staff facing a vast wall board where WAAFs (Women's Auxiliary Air Force) constantly updated the positions of convoys, escorts and U-boats – Slessor now directed the shore-based air offensive against Dönitz's submarines in the closest telephone and teleprinter liaison with the Naval Staff and the Admiralty Tracking Room.

Sadly, however, it was exactly in the strategy of the shore-based air offensive that the British now repeated probably their worst single misjudgment of the long Atlantic battle. For in February 1943, and once again at the Admiralty's urging though with Slessor's full concurrence, Coastal Command resumed its offensive against U-boats in transit outwards and homewards across the Bay of Biscay.

The earlier 'Bay offensive' had collapsed in October 1942 when the U-boats' new Metox device enabled them to detect an aircraft's 150-centimetre wavelength radar. But in any case the offensive had never proved cost-effective. From June 1942 to January 1943 an average of 3,500 patrol hours a month had been flown; some 100 aircraft lost; and only seven U-boats destroyed.[84] Now, it was decided to resume the 'Bay offensive' on the old fallacious supposition that it could throttle Dönitz's effort almost at source. Between 6 and 15 February 1943 eighteen U-boats were sighted out of the 40 known (thanks to Sigint) to have crossed the Bay, but only one, the U-519, sunk, and that by a US Liberator with American 10cm radar. On 20 February a Leigh Light Wellington sank the U-268. That was all. Early in March the Americans transferred the only available Liberators to Morocco in order to deal with a U-boat concentration off its coast; a serious weakening in the Allied effort. However, for eight days towards the end of March, No. 19 Group, Coastal Command, at last equipped with ASV Mark III Wellingtons, had another go. Out of 41 U-boats crossing the Bay area patrolled by the Wellingtons thirteen were sighted but only one was sunk and another seriously damaged. Meanwhile the U-333 had managed to shoot down an ASV Mark III Wellington which had attacked her, reporting back to Dönitz that her Metox had failed to give warning of the enemy's radar – Dönitz's first intimation that Allied technology had jumped past him.

The Admiralty's only response to these disappointing results was to plead in the Anti-U-boat Warfare Committee for more aircraft over the Bay – 190, no fewer. The Chief of Air Staff would only offer 70. So the 1942 'Battle of the Air' resumed in the committee. While the arguments droned on, the aircrews of Coastal Command tried again for a week in April in response to a plea from the First Sea Lord to Slessor: 'I feel that enough has been written about the poor old Bay offensive, and that what we want to do is to collect the necessary aircraft . . . and get on with the job.'[85] They had got on with the job; result: U-376 sunk and one more damaged.[86] And these were the months when the convoy system itself was coming ever closer to breakdown in the Atlantic as Dönitz relentlessly pressed his onslaught.

In December Ultra decrypts of 'Shark' signals had warned of the storm to come by revealing that U-boat Command was making radio-signalling arrangements for 'two convoy battle circuits';[87] and by 18 January Dönitz had raised the total of U-boats on the North Atlantic routes from 25 to 40.[88] Yet January like December passed deceptively well for the Allies. The weather – wild to the limits of ferocity – again played its part in hampering U-boat operations. GC and CS's partial success in reading the 'Shark' Enigma enabled the Admiralty once more to route many convoys far out of the way of Dönitz's concentrations, so that the storm-shaken U-boats searched the mountainous seascape in vain. The puzzled Dönitz and his staff sensed that the 'game of chess had become more complicated',[89] but could not make out why or how. In the whole month the U-boats sank only fifteen ships in convoy in the North Atlantic and fourteen sailing independently,[90] while one U-boat was sunk by a Coastal Command aircraft in the North Atlantic itself, and another by an American aircraft off the coast of Brazil.

And yet for the Admiralty there was a disquieting feature in the month's apparently favourable record. Of the fifteen ships lost in convoy no fewer than seven belonged to convoy TM1 of nine tankers bound from Trinidad to Gibraltar and North Africa. It is now known that the fate of TM1 had been determined by a British defeat in the covert war of Sigint. While B-Dienst had identified the convoy's course through the Admiralty 'convoy cypher', GC and CS for its part had failed to decypher fast enough the 'Shark' signals deploying the U-boat ambush, so that the Admiralty was unable to route the convoy clear.[91]

On 30 January Dönitz hoisted his flag as Commander-in-Chief of the German Navy in succession to Grand-Admiral Raeder, in whom Hitler had now lost all faith. Dönitz's new appointment did not mean a weakening in the U-boat offensive; quite the contrary, because as well as retaining his old post as *Befehlshaber* (Flag Officer), U-boats, he could now switch the balance of the whole German naval effort away from the surface fleet so prized by Raeder. To conduct day-to-day operations he appointed his former Chief of Staff, Rear-Admiral Godt. In the words of Admiralty's February report to the War Cabinet Anti-U-boat Warfare Committee, the enemy 'continued with remarkable singleness of purpose to concentrate against supplies from America to Great Britain'.[92] The daily average of operational U-boats in the entire Atlantic rose to 116, and on the northern routes to about 60.[93] In the Sigint struggle B-Dienst remained for the time being well ahead of GC and CS, able to read the British convoy cypher with such mastery that it was all too simple for Dönitz and Godt accurately to deploy their massed ambushes. Moreover they were now concentrating against eastbound convoys at the beginning of their voyage, with U-boats patrolling in a layered screen across their course.

According to the monthly Anti-Submarine Report for February 1943, nine convoys comprising 242 merchant ships suffered U-boat attack during the month; 34 ships were lost. But almost all these went down in just two convoys when GC and CS again failed to read 'Shark' quickly enough for the Admiralty to reroute them.[94]

On 4 February convoy SC118 of 63 merchantmen ran into a patrol line of 21 U-boats hastily deployed by U-boat Command according to B-Dienst decrypts of British signals in the convoy cypher. During five harrowing days of a battle fought along a track of over 1,000 miles thirteen ships went down, for the loss of three U-boats destroyed plus two more badly damaged. In Dönitz's opinion this was 'perhaps the hardest convoy battle of the whole war'.[95]

For the Allies it presented alarming portents. The convoy escort had been reinforced to a total of twelve ships, twice as strong as usual. The convoy enjoyed constant shore-based air cover during daylight hours – but this did not present surfaced U-boats, diesels pounding, from catching up the convoy and attacking it during the long winter nights. And the expenditure of depth-charges had been so colossal as almost to empty the escorts' magazines. The Admiralty drew the lessons: Leigh Lights for Liberators and Wellingtons; the importance of escorts highly trained as teams rather than spatchcocked together at the last moment; the need – long perceived but now desperately urgent – for support groups to reinforce attacked convoys and to hunt down U-boats once located. The lesson with regard to team training was rammed home by the success of the veteran escort with convoy ONS165 in mid-February, which for the loss of only two merchantmen sank two U-boats. These were the same ships of the Liverpool Escort Force – the destroyers *Fame* and *Viscount* – which had so magnificently brought SC104 through in October 1942 (see above, pp. 483–90). In Admiral Horton's words to an Admiralty conference, 'it could not be too often stressed that the trained group was the basis of protection, not mere numbers of escort vessels'.[96]

On 21 February began the second calamity of the month, when convoy ON166 ran into a U-boat ambush again deployed thanks to B-Dienst decrypts of the British convoy cypher, and when again GC and CS read 'Shark' too late to be of corresponding use to the Admiralty.[97] In another five-day span of relentless fighting convoy ON166 lost fourteen ships for only two U-boats sunk. When February closed in squalls of snow and hail, Allied losses in the month at the hands of the U-boats had reached a total of 63 ships (29 of them independents) of 359,328 tons.[98]

March brought the onset of the grand crisis of the Battle of the Atlantic. Dönitz well recognised through B-Dienst readings of Admiralty 'U-boat Situation Reports' that his enemy enjoyed an uncanny knowledge of latest U-boat deployments, but, after much cogitation, he and his staff attributed this to long-distance airborne radar surveillance for which he had no answer.[99] By an irony, however, it was during this month that GC and CS actually suffered severe setbacks in its ability to read the 'Shark' Enigma, with more than average delays for seven out of the first ten days, and a complete blank between the 10th and 19th.[100] Meanwhile B-Dienst continued regularly to place on the desks of Dönitz and Rear-Admiral Godt complete pictures of Allied dispositions and intended convoy courses and timings. This current German superiority in Sigint was the more operationally significant because of continuing Allied weaknesses out in the ocean front line.

It was only on 1 March that the British, Americans and Canadians held an 'Atlantic Convoy Conference' in Washington to sort out the organisation of the Atlantic battle and remedy the deficiencies in ships and aircraft bequeathed by earlier dilatoriness or (in the case of VLR aircraft) purblind policy. Admiral King, COMINCH and Chief of Naval Operations, now sprang an unwelcome surprise to the conference by wishing to withdraw American ships altogether from the North Atlantic convoy routes in order to concentrate them on routes further south between America and the Mediterranean theatre where the American forces, currently stuck in the Tunisian stalemate, were dependent on seaborne logistics. A bargain was eventually reached whereby the United States Navy would furnish a support group with an escort carrier (CVE) to work under British control on the North Atlantic route and also take over the task of convoying traffic between Britain and the Dutch oilfield islands in the Caribbean, while the Royal and Royal Canadian Navies would assume sole general responsibility for the North Atlantic.

The conference also agreed that the number of American and Canadian VLR aircraft based in Newfoundland should be raised to 48, as against a present operational total for the whole Atlantic of only eighteen; a dangerously belated decision. Canada agreed to create a North-West Atlantic Command (equivalent to Western Approaches Command) to control her side of the 'chop-line', which was to be shifted eastwards to 47° West. This marked the advent of Canada as a senior partner in the conduct of the 'grey water' strategy on which Allied victory in the German war so completely depended.

Yet these new command arrangements and reallotments of operational responsibility were only to come into effect on 1 April. Even by that time the number of VLR aircraft over the Atlantic had in fact risen to no more than twenty. The promised American support group (USS *Bogue* and five destroyers) did not go to sea with a convoy until the second half of March. Furthermore, it was only gradually in the course of March that ASV Mark III Wellingtons came into service over the Bay area. It was all desperately last-minute, and in the meanwhile Dönitz and his crews were inflicting savage punishment on the Allies. The March statistics starkly delineate the German success. The U-boats alone sank 108 ships of 627,377 tons in all waters; the Luftwaffe added another twelve of some 65,700 tons; the worst figure since the ghastly month of November 1942.[101] Worse, the proportion of convoyed ships lost was up 68 per cent on February.[102]

The most appalling losses fell within the first twenty days of the month. From 7 to 10 March seventeen U-boats hung on the flanks of convoy SC121 as it struggled through the storms, and picked off the stragglers one by one. In all SC121 lost thirteen ships of about 62,000 tons; not a single U-boat was sunk in return. From 7 to 14 March convoy HX228 also came under attack, but here the U-boats found no easy prey, sinking only four ships. The senior officer of the escort (Commander A. A. Tait, RN) in the destroyer *Harvester* rammed and sank the U-444 (Lieutenant Langfeld). *Harvester* having disabled herself in the process, she was torpedoed and sunk by the U-432 (Lieutenant-Commander Eckhardt), with Commander Tait lost with his ship. In turn, the U-432 was destroyed by the French corvette *Aconit*.[103]

The frantic violence of such encounters, their stabbing moments of terror, contrast strangely with the battle of brains between Bletchley Park and B-Dienst, with the wall-chart chess game between the Allied and German operation centres, or with the competition between the scientists of each side in laboratory and testing shop.

> March 10, 1943 . . . 30° West, 51° North [begins the war diary of Lieutenant-Commander Trojer of U-121 in describing his successful part in the attack on HX228]. In a snow squall [I] came up at right angles to course of the enemy, surfaced as soon as latter emerged from the snow squall . . . 2131. Fired two torpedoes at two large, overlapping merchant ships. First torpedo hit. Ship disintegrated completely in flames and a vast cloud of smoke. Hundreds of steel plates flew like sheets of paper through the air. A great deal of ammunition exploded.
>
> Shortly afterwards scored another hit on a freighter, which also exploded. From bows to bridge the ship was under water. Heavy debris crashed against my periscope, which now became difficult to turn. The whole boat re-echoed with bangs and crashes . . .[104]

When Trojer torpedoed another freighter from periscope depth, he had to go full astern in order to avoid running into the exploding ship:

> My periscope suddenly went completely black. I could hardly see a thing, while all the time heavy fragments of debris continued to shower down on us. The noise inside the boat was terrific. It felt as though we were being hit by a stream of shells. Heard clearly the noise of a sinking ship, and then all was quiet. Tried to lower my periscope in order to clean the lens. It came down about five feet and then stuck. It was absolutely bent.

At this moment Trojer's hydrophone operator reported the sound of approaching retribution – the propellers of a destroyer at high speed. Trojer raised his periscope:

> Thanks to the swell and the smeared lens I could see very little. Then I myself heard the noise of the destroyer's propellers where I stood in the conning tower and at once gave the order: 'Dive! – full ahead! Both!' Depth charges, two patterns of four, were already falling, and pretty close to us. The conning tower hatch started to leak, and a mass of water came down into the boat. The boat plunged and jumped, but she gained depth steadily.[105]

The generally unprofitable attack on convoy HX228 was followed by complete failure against convoy ON170, which had been successfully diverted away thanks to detection of the ambush by shore-based and shipborne HF/DF. But these setbacks served only as the prelude to the U-boats' greatest single convoy victory of the whole war.

During 14–15 March 1943 the Allied command sought to reroute the eastbound convoy HX229 away from an ambush that had also been detected by HF/DF. However, U-boat Command now signalled two reserve groups of boats in mid-Atlantic to make utmost speed to reinforce the western patrol line which, thanks once again to copious B-Dienst decrypts, had already been ordered to intercept the convoy. By noon on 16 March eight U-boats were clinging to HX229 and its 38 ships, while the reserve groups had run into a slow eastbound convoy of 51 assorted vessels, SC122, then about 120 miles ahead of HX229. To complicate the battle even further, a third convoy, HX229A, composed of 25 fast ships of various types, was also making an eastbound crossing, although on a diversionary course well to the north, near Greenland; and the U-boats confused this group with HX229. As the fast HX229 closed on the slow SC122, there was to ensue a single struggle by the two escort groups to protect a vast sprawl of shipping against 38 U-boats, described by Operational

Intelligence Centre after reading belated 'Shark' decrypts as 'the largest pack of U-boats which has ever been collected together into one area for the same operation'.[106] It could be said that for the first time an encounter in submarine warfare attained the scale and decisive character of the great fleet battles of the past.

Action was joined on 16 March. Through the night of 16–17 March – nearly full moon – the convoys entirely lacked air cover, for the escort forces did not include a carrier, and nor were there shore-based VLR aircraft, which, lacking Leigh Lights, were useless in the dark. The U-boats took full advantage, hitting or sinking twelve ships in one murderous night. During daylight on the 17th three Liberators of No. 120 Squadron, Coastal Command, turned up over SC122 and attacked six out of the eleven U-boats they sighted, but without success. Only one freighter was lost. Meanwhile HX229, with no air cover, lost two ships. At dusk the Liberators had to abandon SC122. The U-boats sneaked in again in the moonlight and sank two more ships. Next day five Liberators from No. 120 Squadron were patrolling over SC122; no ships were lost. But the unfortunate HX229, still without air cover, saw two more of its freighters go down. It was during the following night that HX229 finally caught up with SC122 to form one vast area of shipping defended by a total now of eighteen escort vessels. By now the convoys had got within the operational orbit of medium-range shore-based aircraft, and so on the 19th the air cover was boosted to seven Fortresses and three Sunderlands as well as six Liberators. On this day a Sunderland of No. 201 Squadron sank the U-384 and damaged another (the first and only kill of the battle). Nevertheless the U-boats again made the most of the hours of darkness after the aircraft had returned to base, sinking two more merchantmen.

Only on 20 March, with his U-boats under heavier and heavier combined attack by Coastal Command and the escorts, did Dönitz close down the battle. It had been a triumph for him – twenty-one ships sunk in convoy for the loss of only one U-boat sunk and three badly damaged. The storms of that appalling March helped to do Dönitz's work, for another ten ships of HX229 and SC122 either foundered on passage or had to put back to port.

The disaster which had overtaken these two convoys merely formed the central episode in what had proved a catastrophic three weeks. In all waters and from all causes the Allies had lost 97 ships totalling more than half a million tons – and what was so profoundly disquieting was that threequarters of this total had been lost in convoy, the cornerstone of anti-U-boat warfare in two world wars. On 22 March, in the immediate aftermath of the disaster to HX229 and SC122, the First Sea Lord reported to the Cabinet Anti-U-boat Warfare Committee that 'we can no longer rely on evading the U-boat packs and, hence, we shall have to fight the convoys through them'.[107]

But how? For, as the Prime Minister had informed his Cabinet four days earlier, Britain's naval resources 'were stretched to the uttermost, and the strength of the escorts to our Atlantic convoys was inadequate to meet the enemy's concentration of U-boats'.[108] It was no longer a question of the U-boat eventually torpedoing the Allies' delicately balanced shipping budgets by sheer attrition; it was a question of the Atlantic soon becoming impassable. From the consequent severing of communications between North America and Great Britain – and also with the Allied forces committed to the Mediterranean – would ramify cataclysmic effects on the whole course of the war.

It was, as the Duke of Wellington said of Waterloo, a damned near run thing. But in the case of the Battle of the Atlantic relief did not arrive in the form of a single Blücher turning up at the last moment to save the day; it arrived in a cluster of operational and technical innovations, in piecemeal increases of strength on and over the ocean – though all of them just as last-minute and long-awaited in the circumstances as Blücher's appearance on the field of Waterloo.

In the final week of March 1943 the USS *Bogue* became the first of the new escort carriers to make its début in the North Atlantic, when together with two American destroyers it escorted the eastbound convoy SC123 to a position 175 miles south-east of Cape Farewell (the southernmost tip of Greenland).[109] A utilitarian ship, with all the grace of a floating coffin, *Bogue* and her aircraft signified the beginning of a new era in convoy warfare – continuous air cover even when shore-based VLR aircraft could not be present. Moreover convoy SC123 also enjoyed the protection of the first permanent destroyer escort group to be formed by Western Approaches Command. No merchant ships were lost; and only one straggler from HX230, in order to protect which the *Bogue* group turned back after escorting SC123.

By the end of the month the Royal Navy had organised its own first three escort carrier support groups round *Bogue*'s British sister ships HMSs *Biter*, *Archer* and *Dasher*. In a major setback, however, *Dasher* blew up and sank while on exercise on 27 March; probably because aviation fuel vapour had been ignited by a member of the crew smoking a cigarette or dropping a cigarette through a grating.[110] This disaster led to modifications in American dockyards to the aviation fuel system (always regarded by the Admiralty as unsafe) in new CVEs (escort aircraft carriers) under construction.

The deployment at long last of these CVE escort groups had only been possible because for the first time since November 1942 the carriers were no longer urgently needed for 'Torch' operations in the Mediterranean. This was also true of some of the destroyers that made up the CVE escort groups and the other new escort groups. So whereas at the beginning of March 1943 the C-in-C, Western Approaches, had not a single escort group at sea, at the beginning of April he had five plus one American under command – three composed of a CVE and three destroyers each, and the remainder of five to seven destroyers or other types of small ship each. At this time too the Royal Navy began to reap the reward in operational efficiency of much more thorough group training.

A no less swift and radical revolution was taking place in the effectiveness of Royal Air Force Coastal Command and the Royal Canadian Air Force. By mid-April the available strength in VLR aircraft had risen from the winter low point of six to 41, all equipped with 10cm ASV Mark III radar. The Atlantic air gap south of Iceland and north of the Azores, so long the U-boats' rich hunting ground, was now swiftly shrinking. From 14 March Coastal Command changed the spacing of the pattern in which its aircraft dropped the 250lb Torpex depth-charge from 36 feet to 100 feet, after operational research had indicated that this wider spacing gave the optimum chance of achieving a hit or a damaging near-miss. Along with the concurrent introduction of 10cm radar this new method was in a few weeks to transform the effectiveness of air attack on U-boats. Over the Bay of Biscay too the number of ASV Mark III Wellingtons was growing rapidly from just three in March. And the airmen in the cockpits and the sailors on the bridge had now learned to work closely together in spotting and hunting U-boats.

Only in the battle of Sigint did April 1943 see little change. B-Dienst continued to supply U-boat Command with a stream of decrypted Allied secret signals. GC and CS at Bletchley Park for its part certainly read the 'Shark' Enigma much more continuously and at shorter delays than in March, but this only enabled the Admiralty successfully to reroute a few of the convoys, so numerous now were the patrolling U-boats, with as many as 98 new or refitted boats coming out from German or French bases during the month.[111]

Dönitz's total operational strength now stood at 240 U-boats;[112] the bulk of them Type VIICs (769 tons surfaced; 871 tons submerged) with a crew of 44 packed into the narrow, machinery-crammed hull.

The Type VIICs were oceanic submersible Volkswagens, rugged and reliable. On the surface their diesel-electric motors could push them to nearly 18 knots; when submerged they could manage a maximum of 7.6 knots, but only for an hour. Their range was enormous – nearly 10,000 miles on the surface at 10 knots; 3,450 miles at maximum speed. This could be extended much further by refuelling from milch-cow tanker U-boats. Beneath the surface, however, their endurance was poor – only 130 miles when creeping at 2 knots; only 80 miles at the modest speed of 4 knots. The Type VIICs could dive to 309 feet, and much deeper still in dire emergency, while later versions enjoyed a standard diving depth of 394 feet, and could actually reach well over 700 feet. The Type VIIC U-boat was essentially a platform to carry five torpedo tubes (four in the bow, one at the stern) from which to launch a maximum stock of twelve torpedoes at Allied ships. However, the boat's only protection against Allied aircraft at this time consisted of one 37mm and two 20mm anti-aircraft guns.[113]

But it would not be the shipwrights and armourers of the opposing sides, any more than the codebreakers, who would ultimately decide which way the balance of the battle would tip that critical April and May; it was the sailors ranged against each other in the Atlantic front line itself and their willingness to endure and dare. In the event the attackers, especially the novice captains and crews batch-trained in Dönitz's schools to man the new boats coming off the production lines, were the first to flinch. From the end of March onwards U-boats were signalling U-boat Command to offer ingenious excuses for failing to press their attacks or for aborting sorties; and U-boat Command was sternly signalling back to the boats to stiffen morale and resolve. All these signals were decrypted by GC and CS for the benefit of the Admiralty Operations Intelligence Centre and to the great encouragement of Western Approaches Command. The mind-numbing boredom of keeping the sea between convoy battles, the days and days spent pallid, haggard and stinking in a narrow steel tube under electric light, corroded the morale and the operational efficiency of the U-boat crews. They felt more and more helpless and naked beneath a sky out of which an enemy aircraft could suddenly thunder without warning to smother their boat with a devastating pattern of 250lb depth-charges. They had come to dread the long claustrophobic periods when lying stationary deep down, silent and listening to the screws of the hunting destroyers thrashing the water above them or to the hull-creaking thunder of the depth-charges. Dönitz's cutlass was beginning to bend in his hand.

He sustained his first major defeat at the turn of March and April when the escorts of convoy HX230 supported by the USS *Bogue*'s escort group drove off a mass attack by 40 U-boats for the loss of only one ship, and that a straggler (see above, p. 600). In the first week of April the failure by another mass U-boat ambush to sink more than six ships in convoy HX231 elicited a harsh reproach from U-boat Command. Four days later another group of U-boats managed to sink only two ships in convoy ON176. When on 11 April the next victim, convoy HX232, was sighted, a perturbed U-boat Command again signalled its suspicions to its captains that they were not pressing home their attacks as they ought. It called on the two groups now deployed against HX232 to display what it called 'the healthy warrior and hunter instincts'.[114] Nonetheless the group's instincts proved far from healthy enough, for they sank only three ships.

So it went on through the month, with some convoys successfully diverted clear of ambushes thanks to timely Ultra decrypts of the 'Shark' Enigma, and others attacked with small loss. In a combined battle against three convoys from 20 April onwards the U-boats sank only four merchantmen for the loss of three of their own number; hardly a profitable exchange rate. Already, on 19 April, the Operational Intelligence Centre tracking room on the basis of decrypts of signals traffic between U-boat Command and its boats had remarked on 'the incipient decline in U-boat morale', and particularly the crews' 'concern for vulnerability to air attack'.[115] As it happened, it was on that same day that U-boat Command conceded that it could no longer effectively employ wolf-pack tactics against convoys with air support.[116] On 26 April the OIC was stressing the success of HMS *Biter* and her escort group in completely defeating a mass attack on convoy ONS4, and reckoning that most U-boat captains had now yielded to a lack of boldness.[117]

The strengthened power of the Allied anti-submarine forces and this resultant waning in U-boat skippers' willingness to risk their boats and crews stare out of the April balance sheet of battle – 56 ships of 327,943 tons of merchant shipping sunk by U-boats in all seas; barely half the March loss.[118] 'This,' wrote the Admiralty, 'shows what our counter measures can achieve against the enemy's most strenuous efforts.'[119] It was all the more encouraging that the number of U-boats destroyed in the whole broad Atlantic or in transit through the Bay of Biscay rose from twelve in March to fourteen in April – and six of these in the last week of the month alone.[120]

Dönitz characteristically responded to these disappointing results by driving his crews still harder, his own will to victory in no degree diminished. With his numerical strength – 128 U-boats actually at sea; more than 60 of them across the North Atlantic convoy tracks – climbing to its peak,[121] he and his deputy, Rear-Admiral Godt, now launched their climactic offensive. Their purpose and strategic deployment were divined by GC and CS even though from 26 April onwards there had been great difficulty in solving the 'Shark' Enigma. The Admiralty Operational Intelligence Centre warned: 'On the basis of available information and an appreciation of the new pattern [of U-boat patrol lines] it was estimated on 1 May that by 3 May all routes would be blocked from 53°N, 48°W around to 46°N, 38°W.'[122] Two groups of seventeen and fifteen U-boats now lay spread on the western fringes of the mid-Atlantic air gap; two more of thirteen each on its eastern fringes, one of them off Cape Farewell on the northern flank of the convoy tracks, the other on the southern flank west of the Bay of Biscay.[123] On 29 April 1943 a U-boat near Cape Farewell picked up on her hydrophones the sound of the ships' screws of convoy ONS5; the decisive battles were about to be joined.

Yet the advantage in numbers of vessels, in operational technique and in technology was by this time swinging fast to the Allies. Admiral Horton, the C-in-C, Western Approaches, now disposed of six escort (support) groups, three of them with CVEs carrying a total of some 45 aircraft. At the end of May the first MAC (Merchant Aircraft Carrier, see pages 584–5), the grain ship *Empire MacAlpine* (7,950 tons), was to take her four Swordfish to sea with convoy ONS9. Thanks most of all to the prodigious output of American shipyards and the current slackening of demand from the Mediterranean for destroyers, Horton could now allot an average of eight ships to each close convoy escort, as against five in 1942. The much larger pool of such vessels had also made it possible to give more time to training captains and crews thoroughly in anti-submarine tactics, with the result that the close escorts themselves were much more effective than hitherto. In the case of convoy ONS5, now about to fight its way westwards against a swarm of U-boats, the particularly experienced escort consisted of three destroyers, a frigate, two corvettes and two rescue trawlers under a ruthlessly determined commander, Commander P. W. Gretton in the destroyer HMS *Duncan*. Moreover, the equipping of the close escorts and the escort groups alike with the Hedgehog forward-throwing anti-submarine mortar (100 ships by the end of 1942) and the new Torpex-filled depth-charge had enormously enhanced their power to kill U-boats once detected by air search or their own HF/DF, Type 271 10cm radar and sonar, or in the last resort the keen eyes of their lookouts.

But it was the advent of the escort (or support) groups, still barely a month old, which was transforming the tactical battle, and in unexpected ways. In the summer of 1943 an Admiralty Operational Research Department analysis of U-boat hunts for all 1941 and from July 1942 to March 1943 found that in the middle stage of a hunt the chances of a kill dropped away, while after the sixth attack by the escorts the chances climbed steeply to three times the average expectation.[124] The study pointed out that, following an attack by a U-boat, some 90 minutes sufficed for locating the enemy, yet the escorts had to close on their convoy again to protect it before they had time to carry out 'adequate search'. The study had ascertained that 'the number of U-boats destroyed would probably have been increased by about 30 per cent if searches up to 90 minutes could have been carried out after [initial] loss of contact. In the majority of cases contact could have been regained in a very much shorter time than 90 minutes.[125]

Thus the value of the new support groups lay in their ability to make prolonged searches and conduct protracted hunts, which served to increase the total kills by all surface ships by 30 per cent.[126] Another study, this time of support group operations between 5 May and 12 June 1943, estimated that the groups actually raised total kills by 45 per cent, even though they spent less than half their sea-time actually supporting convoys.[127] With one exception, noted this study, all kills by support groups were made in the vicinity of a convoy rather than on passage. Thus these groups of 1943, for all their offensive purpose, were in no sense successors to the 'hunter' groups which had vainly swept the seas in 1939–40 on the off-chance of encountering a U-boat (see above, pp. 68–9).

In the air dimension of what had now become a single closely integrated anti-submarine effort, the number of 10cm radar VLR aircraft available to cover a convoy for three to five hours up to 650 miles from bases in the United Kingdom, Iceland and Newfoundland had risen by 1 May 1943 to 49, out of which twelve to fifteen were operational at any one time.[128] In medium-range aircraft all Coastal Command's ageing Whitleys had been re-equipped by mid-May with Leigh Light Wellingtons (more and more of which were fitted with 10cm ASV Mk III radar) or Liberators. This changeover coincided with a mistaken new instruction by Dönitz that his boats were to evade night-time Leigh Light Wellington attacks by surfacing to charge their batteries by day.[129] Sightings of U-boats in transit across the Bay of Biscay rose from 24 in April to 100 in May;[130] sinkings from two to six. And this month, for the first time, Coastal Command and the Royal Canadian Air Force aircraft began to carry three revolutionary new items of U-boat killing technology – the new American acoustic torpedo which once in the water homed on the sound of its submerged victim's screws and motors; a 600lb-bomb (350lbs heavier than the existing standard Coastal Command bomb); and an air-to-sea rocket.[131]

Thus it was that Dönitz's supreme effort to bar the North Atlantic encountered the Allied navies and air forces when they at last enjoyed adequate strength in the right kinds of ships and aircraft, were trained to high efficiency and equipped with a comprehensive armoury for finding and destroying U-boats. The Allies – and this means above all Great Britain – had repaired two decades of neglect and mistaken policy just in time, and Dönitz was too late, thanks to Grand Admiral Raeder's and Hitler's long-standing failure to perceive that the U-boat if given sufficient industrial priority could win the war. In truth, Dönitz was too late by years, as he himself was later bitterly to admit.[132]

The turning-point arrived with the week-long effort by Commander Gretton and his eight escort ships to pass the 42 merchantmen of ONS5 through a patrol line of 31 U-boats (later 41) deployed by Dönitz to intercept the convoy. On 28 April the U-258 sighted the convoy, and Dönitz ordered his concentration against it. The weather would have done justice to January – a full gale, a colossal seaway, low cloud, squalls of rain. It was impossible for VLR aircraft to fly air cover; difficult enough for the 3rd Escort Group, which had been ordered out to the rescue from St John's, Newfoundland, even to find the convoy. Happily on 1 May the U-boats lost contact, to the lamentations next day (decrypted by Bletchley Park) of U-boat Command: 'With 31 boats something can and must be accomplished.'[133] From 1 to 3 May the U-boats searched for ONS5 and three other convoys, thus far in vain. On the 4th they managed to find ONS5 again.

By this time the 3rd Escort Group, composed of five destroyers commanded by Captain J. A. McCoy, RN, in HMS *Offa* (1,540 tons; designed 1939, launched 1941)[134] had joined the convoy. The weather was now so foul – complete with icebergs and pack-ice – that the escort ships could not be refuelled at sea. On 3 May Gretton's own ship *Duncan* (1,375 tons; 35½ knots; launched 1932)[135] had been forced to part company to St John's for oil, and command of the convoy escort passed to Lieutenant-Commander R. E. Sherwood, RNR, in the River class frigate *Tay* (1,370 tons; 20 knots; launched 1942).[136] On the morrow two ships of the 3rd Escort Group also had to make for port in order to refuel their tanks.

When the U-boat pack began its mass attack that same day, the

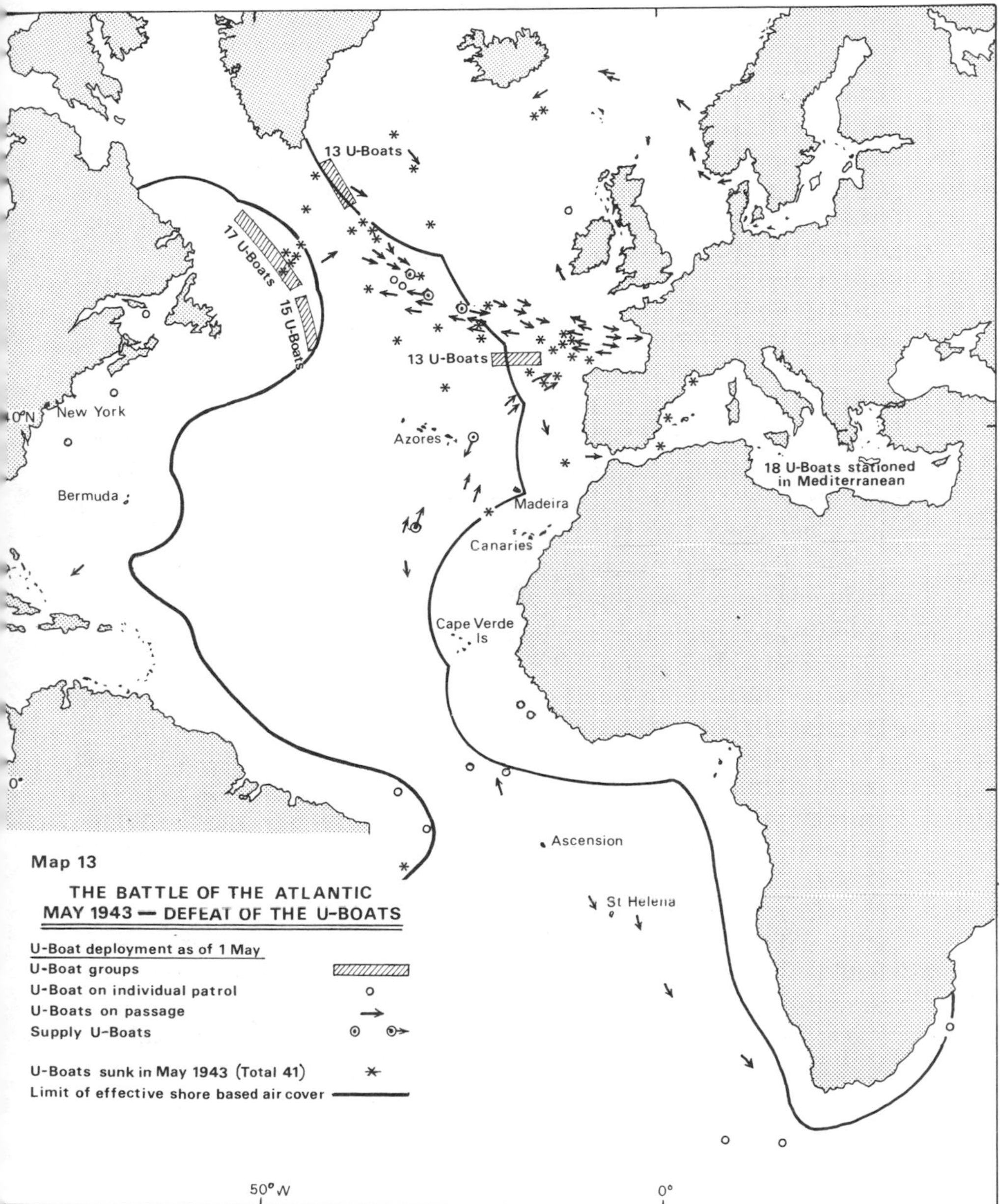

Map 13

THE BATTLE OF THE ATLANTIC
MAY 1943 — DEFEAT OF THE U-BOATS

convoy's escort was thus perilously weakened. Fortunately Horton had already ordered out the 1st Escort Group (Commander G. N. Brewer, RN) from St John's as further reinforcement. Comprising the sloop *Pelican* (1,200 tons; 19½ knots; launched 1938 as part of the pre-war rearmament programme),[137] three frigates and an ex-United States coastguard cutter, it did not join the convoy until 6 May. Meanwhile ONS5 had to fight a running battle with 30 U-boats ranged across its track, with yet another group of eleven lying in reserve further to the west. It heartened the convoy and its escort that Royal Canadian Air Force flying boats managed to find them on 4 May; and two flying boats searching ahead of the convoy sank the U-630. But with the fall of darkness over a wild sea, the convoy was on its own again with its surface escort now down to the *Tay*, four corvettes and, from the 3rd Escort Group, the destroyers *Offa* and her sister ship *Oribi*. The U-boats closed in and during a night fierce with attack and counter-attack succeeded in sinking five freighters, including a straggler, despite all the escort's endeavours.

During daylight on 5 May the weather moderated enough to enable the escorts to refuel. Four more merchantmen went down; four more ships' companies of merchant seamen to seek survival in open rowing boats in the icy Atlantic swell. However, the Flower class corvette *Pink*, having rounded up half a dozen stragglers into a little convoy of her own, sank the U-boat U-192 by way of revenge. On this day a VLR aircraft from Iceland flying at its uttermost range stayed with the hard-pressed convoy for a time. During the next night the action resumed with even greater ferocity. According to the Senior Officer of the escort in his report, 'about twenty-four attacks took place in every direction except ahead'; the fighting continued 'without a stop' until 0420 on 6 May. With some understatement the Senior Officer described the situation as 'confused'.[138]

Yet the escorts won decisively. The corvette *Loosestrife* sank the U-638; the destroyer *Vidette* (a Great War veteran, launched 1918; 1,090 tons; 24½ knots)[139] put the U-125 down with her Hedgehog mortar; the *Oribi* rammed and sank the U-531 when she suddenly slid out of the fog nearby; and the sloop *Pelican* located the U-438 by radar and destroyed her under water by repeated patterns of depth-charges. On the morning of the 6th the local Canadian escort joined, and the U-boats gave up.

In the course of their three-day assault the U-boats had sunk twelve ships, but at the cost of no fewer than seven of their own number (including one destroyed early on by a Coastal Command Flying Fortress) – five of them at the hands of the Royal Navy. Dönitz had lost some 300 of his precious highly trained submariners killed outright or trapped and drowned in the riven hulls of their boats. Five more U-boats were also badly damaged. From Dönitz's point of view this constituted a disastrous rate of exchange; a rate which, thanks to Ultra decrypts of 'Shark', was soon exactly known to his enemy.

Now the cryptographers began to take an active part in shaping the manoeuvres of the May battle. Theirs was a curious game of trick and trump. GC and CS read 'Shark' in time for Western Approaches Command to signal convoys HX237 and SC129 to alter course away from ambushes, whereupon B-Dienst in turn read these signals sent in the 'convoy cypher' and so enabled U-boat Command to redeploy the ambushes. Convoys HX237 and SC129 therefore failed to evade attack by as many as 36 U-boats between 7th and 14 May.

This time, however, the U-boats encountered the full panoply of British air and sea power over the Atlantic. HX237 enjoyed the protection of the 5th Escort Group (Captain E. M. C. Abel-Smith, RN), including the escort carrier HMS *Biter* and her aircraft, while shore-based VLR aircraft sank one U-boat and aided warships to destroy another. Despite hazardous flying conditions *Biter*'s aircraft attacked six U-boats and sank one in conjunction with surface escorts; one of her aircraft was lost, and three more damaged by forced landings. The German attack on HX237 ended in a score of three freighters sunk in return for three U-boats – another disastrous result for Dönitz.

The onslaught on SC129 fared no better. On 12 May, when the convoy was still out of range of shore-based air cover, the escort sank their first U-boat. Next day a VLR aircraft, 1,200 miles from base, attacked two U-boats patrolling ahead of the convoy (which was itself still out of air range). On the 14th the convoy came under the cover of VLR aircraft; it was also joined by HMS *Biter* with 5th Escort Group from convoy HX237. The final score of sinkings for this encounter came to two merchantmen and two U-boats, plus several other U-boats seriously damaged. Wailed U-boat Command to its captains: 'We can see no explanation for this failure.'[140] The Operational Intelligence Centre drew the cheering lesson that the failure 'provides further evidence that U-boat efficiency and morale were declining'.[141]

On 18 May began the first of the two final major convoy actions of the whole war. Guided by 'Shark' decrypts giving the secrets of Dönitz's deployment the Admiralty sought to steer convoy SC130 (38 ships) through a gap in the U-boat patrol line. It was sighted nonetheless by one of the 33 U-boats spread across its course. This time the action ended in utter failure for the U-boats. Continuous air cover was flown by Liberators of No. 120 Squadron, Coastal Command, which sank the U-954 and the U-258, and by Hudsons of No. 269 Squadron which sank the U-273. Commander Gretton (commanding the convoy's close escort) in the *Duncan* took part in destroying the U-381. And the frigate *Jed* and the escort sloop *Sennen* (ex-US coastguard cutter; 1,546 tons; 16 knots; launched 1928)[142] of the 1st Escort Group accounted for U-209. Not a single merchant vessel was lost. The convoy steamed on to Londonderry with such despatch as to fulfil the keen wish Gretton had expressed to the convoy commodore not to be late for his wedding.[143]

By this time U-boat Command had become profoundly anxious about the enemy's ability 'to deprive the U-boat of its most important attribute, its invisibility',[144] and it ordered its captains to make dummy radio signals to disguise their position.[145] Now occurred the second of the two last grand encounters of the Battle of the Atlantic; one in which all the operational and technological threads were aptly woven together. First of all B-Dienst detected the location and course of convoy HX239, so that U-boat Command was able to deploy 22 U-boats to attack it. Then GC and CS at Bletchley Park detected the ambush, thus making it possible for the Admiralty to reroute the convoy. But B-Dienst in turn decyphered the details of the rerouting, so that U-boat Command could accordingly make a fresh deployment of its boats. Now it was up to the seamen of both sides and their weaponry. On the evening before the convoy was actually sighted on 22 May U-boat Command made an almost despairing signal of supposed encouragement to its captains:

> If there is anyone who thinks that combating convoys is no longer possible, he is a weakling and no true U-boat captain. The battle of the Atlantic is getting harder but it is the determining element in the waging of the war.[146]

This signal, once decrypted, made astonishing reading for the Admiralty and for Western Approaches Command. For the first time in history the victor literally read the mind of the vanquished at that moment when hope dies and the will begins to break. In any case, U-boat Command's exhortation proved of no avail. For HX239 enjoyed powerful and continuous air cover from the USS *Bogue* and HMS *Archer*. The *Bogue* accounted for the U-569 and the *Archer* for the U-752, three of the *Archer*'s aircraft having been just fitted with the new air-to-sea rocket. Not a single merchant ship was sunk.

The very last convoy to be seriously menaced that month, SC130, arrived in the United Kingdom on 25 May also without loss. It had been continuously protected by VLR aircraft for three days and two nights, and these had made 28 sightings of U-boats, launched ten attacks on them, and sunk two.[147] By this time Dönitz's total losses for the month of May in all waters had already reached the catastrophic total of 33 U-boats; by 31 May they would rise to 41. Like Villeneuve's fleet at Trafalgar Dönitz's crews had simply been outfought and outclassed by the foe who had engaged them far more closely than they cared for.

For all his tenacity and resolve Dönitz was a cool realist. On 24 May he wrote:

> In the last few days, circumstances have arisen which give a particularly strong indication of the present crisis in the U-boat war. These circumstances are:
>
> a) The confirmation of further heavy losses.
>
> b) The complete failure of the operation against SC130 as well as the conditions encountered during the attack on Convoy HX239 . . .
>
> We have to accept the heavy losses provided the amount of enemy shipping sunk is proportionate. In May, however, the ratio was one U-boat to 10,000 gross tons of enemy shipping, whereas a short time ago it was one U-boat to 100,000 gross tons . . . The U-boat losses in May 1943 therefore reached unbearable heights . . .

As for the cause of these losses,

> . . . the enemy Air Force therefore played a decisive part . . . This can be attributed to the increased use of land-based aircraft and aircraft carriers combined with the advantages of radar location . . . To a very great extent, the enemy aircraft brought about the failure of our U-boats against Convoys SC130 and HX239. In the former they prevented the U-boats from manoeuvring into an attacking position ahead of the enemy. In the case of HX239, the enemy aircraft precluded all contact.[148]

Although Dönitz failed to mention it in this report, the Luftwaffe had throughout wholly failed to provide the U-boats with equivalent air support, either by way of VLR reconnaissance or in cooperating in attacks on Allied convoys, or providing a defence to the U-boats against Allied aircraft. Whereas the British Air Staff had relented in its doctrinaire concentration on the bomber offensive just about in time to enable Coastal Command to become a fully effective partner of the Royal Navy, the Luftwaffe (in the ample person of Reichsmarschall Göring) remained aloof and apart from the U-boat war. Indeed Göring was openly hostile to his sister service.[149] In particular the failure of the Luftwaffe to put the Heinkel He 177 four-engined bomber into production, let alone the projected very long range 'Amerika' bomber, meant that the Luftwaffe had no aircraft to match the VLR Liberator.[150] As Dönitz was sourly to remark in his memoirs, 'In this Second World War Germany was waging war at sea without an air arm; that was one of the salient features of our naval operations, a feature that was as much out of line with contemporary conditions as it was decisive in effect.'[151]

Now, in that third week of May 1943, Dönitz had to accept that for the time being at least he had been beaten. On the 24th he wrote in his log:

> The situation in the North Atlantic now forces a temporary shifting of operations to areas less endangered by aircraft . . . the Caribbean Sea, the area off Trinidad, the area off the Brazilian and West African coasts . . . With the boats at present in the North Atlantic, operations will be made against the traffic between the U.S.A. and Gibraltar – as far as these boats are able to do with their fuel. The North Atlantic cannot, however, be entirely denuded of boats. It is necessary, by means of single boats, to leave the enemy in ignorance as long as possible of these alterations in tactics . . .[152]

However it did not at all occur to Dönitz's mind that he had finally lost the Battle of the Atlantic:

> These decisions comprise a temporary deviation from the former principles for the conduct of U-boat warfare. This is necessary in order not to allow the U-boats to be beaten at a time when their weapons are inferior, by unnecessary losses while achieving very slight success. It is, however, clearly understood that the main operational area of U-boats is, as it always was, in the North Atlantic . . . It is . . . anticipated that after equipment with quadruples [quad 20cm flak guns], i.e., from the autumn, the Battle of the North Atlantic will be completely resumed once more.[153]

So the signal went out to his captains to withdraw from the fray. The North Atlantic suddenly emptied of U-boats. The convoys began to steam across unscathed – only one ship lost in convoy between 1 June and 18 September 1943; and only fifteen ships lost in total in the North Atlantic.[154] It was as if a steel gauntlet had relaxed its grip on the Allied throat.

But this victory so hard won by the crews of the escorts and merchantmen and maritime aircraft came only just in time for the Allies. For even despite the consequent falling-off in sinkings by the enemy from June onwards, even despite the soaring output of new ships by American yards, the problem of a global deficit in shipping resources actually continued to get worse for the rest of 1943 and into 1944, so great and rising were the competitive demands.[155] And during late May and June 1943, as the U-boats slunk away from the North Atlantic, the Allies were preparing to add to these demands by embarking on a further extension of 'blue water' strategy in the Mediterranean – more amphibious landings on the grand scale (this time on a hostile shore) calling for a mass of shipping and warships; and the entire venture dependent for its continuing success on uninterrupted long-distance sea communications.

20

Grand Strategy for a Maritime Alliance – II

On 13 January 1943 the Prime Minister had arrived in Casablanca to join the President in another summit conference (codenamed 'Symbol') to decide the maritime alliance's global strategy for the current year and after. For Churchill and his entourage it had been a somewhat harrowing flight in a converted bomber, for he had woken up to find a heater point next to his makeshift bed so hot as to threaten to ignite the bed-clothes and after them the aircraft, whereupon he ordered the entire heating system to be turned off. The cargo of distinguished personages was left to shiver in winter skies at 8,000 feet. 'I am bound to say,' he was to record in his memoirs, 'this struck me as a rather unpleasant moment.'[1] Pleasanter ones were now to follow, as Premier and President and attendant suites of the gold-braided or merely business-suited type took up residence in luxurious villas grouped round a hotel in sub-tropical gardens, while HMS *Bulolo*, at anchor in Casablanca harbour, provided the cypher and signals facilities.

The conference sessions proved long and tough, partly because of the deep divisions of view about grand strategy between the delegations, partly because of the nature of the participants themselves: Admiral 'Ernie' King, a curmudgeon of a sailor for whom the Pacific as always took absolute priority; Marshall, still massively resolved on a cross-Channel invasion ('Roundup') in 1943; Alan Brooke, a sharp mind behind a sharp face, stubbornly in favour of pursuing still further the existing Mediterranean 'blue water' strategy; Churchill himself, resplendent in private in a dragon-embroidered silk dressing-gown and in public in the uniform of an air commodore of the Royal Air Force, by now convinced that Brooke was right, and determined to win the argument for Britain; Roosevelt, much less closely involved in the strategic argument, but a final arbiter of decisive authority. The First Sea Lord, Admiral of the Fleet Sir Dudley Pound, was of course present too; a prematurely aged man leaning on a stick and prone to doze off in committee, he was less concerned with the grand strategic issues than with the executive detail of naval operations as such, and above all the crucial Battle of the Atlantic.

The 'Symbol' Conference met when the tide of the Axis fortune had just passed high water and begun to ebb. In Russia the great German offensive of 1942 had ended in total failure with the Soviet counter-offensive at Stalingrad on 2 November 1942; and General Paulus's 6th Army, cut off in the ruins of the city, was now in the last hopeless days of its resistance (he was to surrender on 2 February with the 90,000 survivors out of his original strength of a quarter of a million). In the Pacific the United States Navy's victory over the Japanese Combined Fleet in the Battle of Midway on 3–6 June 1942 (a decisive naval battle to rank in history with Salamis, Lepanto, the thwarting of the Spanish Armada, and Trafalgar) had thrown the Japanese ineluctably on to the strategic defensive. American and Australian troops were gradually pushing back the Japanese invaders of New Guinea. Ten days before the opening of the 'Symbol' Conference the Japanese high command had ordered the evacuation of the island of Guadalcanal in the Solomons (it was completed by the end of the month), signifying America's first success on land in the Pacific theatre. In North Africa General Montgomery, plodding forward from Alamein with extreme caution (even though he was well aware through constant Ultra decrypts that Rommel was reduced to a mere handful of tanks and was shackled by dearth of fuel)[2] had now reached Buerat on the Gulf of Sirte, some 80 miles east of Tripoli. It was therefore evident that within a few weeks Rommel would have fallen back into Tunisia in order to unite with von Arnim's 5th Panzer Army in a single Axis North African perimeter. The Royal Navy had played its familiar role in the 8th Army's advance by ferrying forward supplies along the coast, and by opening the harbours of Bardia, Tobruk and Benghazi as quickly as possible after their capture despite sunken wrecks and sabotaged dockside installations.

And thanks to Royal Air Force fighter cover from Libyan bases captured by Montgomery, the first convoy to Malta from Alexandria since the June failure had been successfully run by the Royal Navy on 17–20 November 1942 – but still at a cost, for an escorting cruiser, *Arethusa*, had been torpedoed by an enemy aircraft on the outward voyage, and she only made it back to Alexandria thanks to a stern tow in heavy seas while on fire.[3] The flow of convoys to Malta continued, putting an end to her long blockade. The Royal Navy's Force K – now the cruisers *Cleopatra*, *Orion* and *Euryalus* and some four destroyers – returned to the island to savage Axis traffic between Sicily and Tunis and Tripoli in conjunction with Force Q, usually based at Bône in Algeria. In the small hours of 2 December 1942 Force Q (the cruisers *Aurora*, flying the flag of Rear-Admiral C. H. J. Harcourt, *Argonaut* and *Sirius* and the destroyers *Quentin* and HMAS *Quiberon*) sank a complete convoy of four merchant ships and four escorting destroyers off the Gulf of Tunis by point-blank gunfire in a hellish scene of ships blazing and exploding amid luridly lit billows of smoke and steam.

The 8th Submarine Flotilla continued to work out of Malta, as it had done through the worst of enemy air attack in 1942; the 10th Flotilla, now based at Algiers, also contributed to the relentless attrition of enemy convoys. This was hazardous service, for seven boats were lost between January and May 1943, including the *Turbulent*, commanded by one of the Royal Navy's veteran submarine 'aces', Commander J. W. Linton, who was awarded a posthumous Victoria Cross. The Royal Air Force too had rebuilt its striking force based on Malta, to a total of eight squadrons of torpedo bombers – Wellingtons, Beauforts and Albacores.

Now it was the Axis which had lost control of the central Mediterranean convoy routes. Tanker after tanker went down to British attack beneath the sea, on its surface and from the air, starving Rommel in particular of the fuel he needed in order freely to manoeuvre in retreat in the face of superior forces. Thus, and entirely as a consequence of the 8th Army's advance along the Libyan coast, which had evicted the Luftwaffe from the airfields in Cyrenaica that commanded the waters between Italy and Africa, and installed the Royal Air Force instead, Malta had at last become once again a strategic asset to Britain.

In Tunisia, however, as the 'Symbol' Conference met in January 1943, the stalemate still continued along the north–south front through the mountains west of Bizerta and Tunis. Enemy bombers unrelentingly attacked supply vessels and warships in the Allied advanced base of Bône, despite the efforts of the Eastern Air Command, and between 13 December 1942 and 1 February 1943 there were 68 red alerts and more than 2,000 heavy bombs dropped,[4] the most recent casualty being the cruiser *Ajax*, so badly damaged on New Year's Day as to require her to leave the station for repairs.

The land stalemate had laid a heavy and unexpected burden on the Royal Navy and the Merchant Marine, for an average of 100 ships every month was sailing from Gibraltar to Algerian ports instead of the estimated 60, all requiring defence against numerous and resolute U-boat attacks. According to the original 'Torch' calculations Tunisia was to have been occupied by the end of January 1943, so releasing Allied land, sea and air forces (and shipping lift) for other offensive projects. But now the 'Symbol' Conference had to accept that Tunisia was not likely to fall until April at the earliest. This delay bore acutely on the conference's discussions of grand strategy, which turned on two inter-related issues – the proportion of resources to be allotted respectively to the German war and the Japanese war; and the rival merits of making the main Allied effort against Germany in 1943 in the Mediterranean or across the Channel ('Operation Roundup').

The war against Japan (except for the Burma front and the Indian Ocean) had become an exclusively American preserve controlled by Admiral King as Commander-in-Chief of the US Fleet (COMINCH) and Chief of Naval Operations. Grappling as he was with the problems of 'triphibious' warfare at the end of 3,000 miles-long sea communications, King believed that the Pacific theatre was being dangerously starved of resources in favour of the German war, and that there was a consequent risk that the Japanese would be given leisure to establish a perimeter defence round their conquests so strong that the Allies might later find great difficulty in overcoming it. King therefore demanded a bigger proportion of Allied resources for the Pacific, even mentioning a figure of 30 per cent as against the present 15 per cent. This would permit him to mount a series of step-by-step or island by island offensives aimed at retaining the initiative over the Japanese and denying them the opportunity to dig in. The British, being naturally preoccupied with Germany and enjoying little or no say over operations in the Pacific, suspected King of seeking to overturn the order of strategic priority decided at the Washington Conference in December 1941 whereby Germany was to be beaten first (see above, p. 434). They wanted to see this priority clearly reaffirmed, with only minimum force going to the Pacific in the meantime. In any event, the key to Allied offensive strategy everywhere lay in landing craft lift, and thanks to American mass production of these articles, 'Ernie' King firmly held that key.

With regard to grand strategy in the German war, Churchill and the Chiefs of Staff came to Casablanca agreed that to follow the conquest of North Africa with a cross-Channel invasion ('Roundup') in 1943 (as agreed in July 1942) was not a practicable operation of war after all. But it had taken Brooke's utmost powers of persistent argument to convince Churchill that to launch 'Roundup' in 1943 would invite catastrophic failure. From the very moment when the original decision for 'Torch' was reached in July 1942, the Prime Minister had refused to accept that opting for 'Torch' in 1942 ruled out 'Roundup' in 1943, as Marshall for one had already feared must be the case. Instead Churchill had optimistically envisaged a two-handed strategy against Germany, punching with the right through the Mediterranean and with the left across the Channel.[5]

By October 1942 he had come to see 'Roundup' as following after a further development of 'blue water' strategy in the Mediterranean once the occupation of Tunisia consummated the objectives of 'Operation Torch'. The Allies, he minuted to the Chiefs of Staff, would then be in a position

> . . . to attack the underbelly of the Axis at whatever may be the softest point, i.e., Sicily, Southern Italy or perhaps Sardinia; or again, if circumstances warrant, or, as they may do, compel, the French Riviera or perhaps even, with Turkish aid, the Balkans. However this may turn out, and it is silly to try to peer too far ahead, our war until the summer of 1943 will be waged in the Mediterranean theatre.[6]

An each-way bet then – more 'blue water' strategy *and* later in 1943 a Continental campaign in France by means of 'Roundup'.

The Prime Minister was therefore much peeved when the Chiefs of Staff replied with a powerful report arguing that 'Roundup' would not be a practicable operation of war in 1943, and must wait until 1944: 'Sufficient experience has already been gained [i.e., at Dieppe] that it will not be tactically possible to establish and maintain a large Allied Army in France until German military power has been undermined . . .'[7] In the opinion of the COS, only the Red Army on the Eastern Front could achieve this: 'It cannot be too clearly recognised that it is the war in Russia which is most rapidly sapping Germany's strength.' They therefore saw the Red Army as 'the primary means by which the German army can be defeated on land'. It followed that Anglo-American operations in 1943 must be 'shaped so as to assist Russia . . .'

The COS listed the means of assistance: the bomber offensive against the German industrial machine; copious military supplies via Persia and the Arctic convoys (see below, Chapter 23); subsidiary campaigns in the Mediterranean to draw off German strength. 'In short,' summed up the COS, 'it should be possible to turn the

Mediterranean as a whole, and Italy in particular, into an immense liability for Germany . . .' Thanks to the Red Army as assisted in these ways by the Western Allies, the German Army could be weakened enough to make 'Roundup' a runner in 1944.

But Churchill did not readily give up 'Roundup' for 1943. He reminded the COS that, by the original deal with the Americans in July 1942, there were supposed to be 27 United States and 21 British divisions ready in the United Kingdom by April 1943 to launch an invasion of France, along with the necessary landing craft. Since 'Torch' had absorbed only 13 divisions, the hoped-for Anglo-American offensive effort had been effectively cut by 35 divisions. 'There is a frightful gap,' wrote the Prime Minister, 'between what the Chiefs of Staff contemplated as reasonable in the summer of 1942 for the campaign of 1943 and what they now say we can do in that campaign.'[8]

And he went on: 'We have in fact pulled in our horns to an almost incredible extent, and I cannot imagine what the Russians will say or do when they realise it. My own position is that I am still aiming at a "Roundup" retarded until August [1943] . . ."[9]

The successful Russian counter-stroke at Stalingrad in November 1942 encouraged Churchill in his hopes for 'Roundup' in 1943 for, as he pointed out to the COS, no longer would the Germans be able to transfer divisions from the East to meet an invasion in the West, 'a new fact of the first magnitude'.[10] Assuming that present operations in the Mediterranean could be wound up by June 1943, he wanted all shipping and landing craft back in Britain by the end of that month so that 'Roundup' could be launched in August and September. He counted on fifteen to twenty US and British divisions (twelve of them armoured) then being available in the United Kingdom and another fifteen (five of them armoured) in the United States. But on his reckoning no fewer than 31 divisions (including French, New Zealand and Indian) would still be required in the Mediterranean. Here was a measure of the inescapable minimum continuing cost that must result from the original Allied decision to undertake 'Operation Torch'.

The Chiefs of Staff challenged his arithmetic, however. They reckoned that only thirteen British and American divisions (or seventeen at most) would be available for 'Roundup' in July 1943, as against 40 German divisions already in France, to say nothing of reserves elsewhere.[11] The Joint Planners had already calculated that only five extra divisions could be found for 'Roundup' if all Mediterranean operations were suspended.[12]

> It is certain [wrote the COS] that our resources in manpower, shipping and landing craft are wholly inadequate to build up 'Torch', re-open the Mediterranean and carry out the operations we contemplate in the Mediterranean next spring and summer, in addition to 'Round-up' in July 1943.[13]

The total Allied expeditionary force in the United Kingdom by August 1943 would be only half the size of that originally deemed necessary, while only six divisions could be organised as an assault force because of limited shipping and landing craft lift. Even this lift, they wrote, could only be found by closing down all Mediterranean amphibious operations and cancelling a cherished Allied project for a seaborne invasion of southern Burma ('Anakim'). Meanwhile the Russians would have to fight on alone for the first eight months of the year before 'Roundup' could be launched.

The Chiefs of Staff wound up their memorandum with a heavy sales pitch in favour of pursuing instead 'blue water' strategy in the Mediterranean. They laid out for the Prime Minister an enticing array of possible operations – against Sardinia, Sicily or the toe of Italy, even Crete and the Dodecanese (so encouraging Turkey to abandon her neutrality). All of these, averred the COS, would serve to drain off German strength while at the same time the mere threat of invasion kept 40 German divisions pegged down in France. Such a strategy would also allow 'Anakim' (the Burma landing) to go ahead, and permit the Anglo-American bomber force in Britain to be vastly expanded.[14]

On 16 December 1942 the CIGS, General Sir Alan Brooke, expounded this paper to a COS meeting chaired by Churchill as Minister of Defence. Brooke in fact gave the meeting a veritable staff college lecture, complete with maps and diagrams, in order to show the rate at which enemy divisions could be switched from east to west by means of the 'magnificent lateral railway system'.[15] He compared this system with 'the two vulnerable lines leading south through Italy and the single track through Nish into Greece'. The minutes do not record that he similarly dilated on the long and circuitous Allied sea communications to actual or potential Mediterranean fronts, or on the needed shipping lift and naval deployment.

If, concluded Brooke, the Allies held 40 German divisions in France by threat of a comparatively small-scale invasion, 'and could at the same time force Italy out of the war and perhaps enter the Balkans, there was no doubt that this was the better strategy, from the Russian point of view, than for us to stake everything on "Roundup", which could, at best, afford Russia no relief before August . . .'

The First Sea Lord's only contribution to this crucial meeting which so much concerned the future employment of the Royal Navy was to remark that 'it was essential that the Americans should provide a share of the Naval Forces required for amphibious operations in the Mediterranean. There was a tendency at present for all American new construction to disappear into the Pacific . . .'[16]

Churchill, for his part, at last gave way to Brooke's pertinacious argument, saying that he 'found nothing to quarrel with in the COS paper . . .' and acknowledging that 'unless the Americans could vastly improve on the estimates [of their rate of build-up for 'Roundup'] in the Memorandum, he saw no alternative to the strategy recommended by the Chiefs of Staff . . .'[17] The meeting broke up with the Prime Minister's blessing to Brooke's proposals for major operations against Sicily or southern Italy aimed at knocking Italy out of the war.

It seemed as though the Chiefs of Staff, and Brooke in particular, had won, but, a fortnight later, Churchill put in a final counter-attack which hit the very nub of the whole grand-strategic issue of the relationship between reopening a Western Front and further pursuing a Mediterranean 'blue water' strategy:

> . . . unless . . . during the summer and autumn we *also* [emphasis added] engage the enemy from the West, we shall not be able to bring the most important part of our forces into play . . . Our resources in small shipping will not be utilised. The weight of the British Home Army and of the American forces to be gathered in Britain will not count. Thus we shall have failed to engage the enemy with our full strength, and may even fail to keep him pinned down in the West while we attack in the South.[18]

Marshall himself could not have put it better. But next day, 29 December 1942, the War Cabinet Defence Committee with Churchill in the chair nevertheless approved for transmission to Washington a 'Memorandum on Future Strategy' which fully endorsed the views of the Chiefs of Staff. The Memorandum stated that the defeat of the U-boat was to remain 'first charge on our resources' and placed second on the list the expansion of the bomber offensive. Third came 'the exploitation of our positions in the Mediterranean' with a view to knocking Italy out of the war and bringing Turkey into it; and fourth the maintenance of supplies to Russia. Subject to these and other prior claims on resources, such as limited offensives in Burma and the Pacific, there was to be (according to an extra paragraph inserted by the Defence Committee) the greatest possible build-up of forces in the United Kingdom with a view to 're-entry' on the Continent in August or September 1943, 'should conditions hold out a good prospect . . .'[19]

This last inserted phrase reflected the Prime Minister's deep reluctance to abandon 'Roundup' altogether for 1943, but it was no more than a sop to him. So far as the British were concerned, 'Roundup' in 1943 was dead; the 'push' of existing commitments in the Mediterranean coupled with the 'pull' of enticing future prospects there had finally rendered the further pursuit of 'blue water' strategy irresistible.

What the prolonged debate had left almost entirely out of account, however, was the likely tonnage of merchant shipping needed to sustain extended operations in the Mediterranean; where that tonnage was to be found in the midst of a world shipping crisis; and at what cost in other directions, such as imports into Britain, the feeding of the Middle East and the averting of famine in India. To quote the official historian of merchant shipping in the Second World War, 'most of the British commitments were entered into without calculating the cost in ships . . . Yet at this time the stringency was so acute that the Ministry of War Transport was haggling over single ships on the routes to India and the Middle East . . .'[20]

The British went to Casablanca knowing that they would have a battle on their hands, for on 23 December 1942 the American Joint Chiefs of Staff had despatched to London a memorandum, 'Basic Strategic Concept for 1943', which stood in fundamental contradiction to the strategy Brooke had successfully sold to Churchill. For General George Marshall wanted even now, despite the Allied commitment to 'Torch', to arrest if he could the slide deeper and deeper into what he saw as a peripheral theatre of war. He wanted instead to pull Allied strategy back to the Clausewitzian principle of concentration of force at the decisive point. The JCS memorandum therefore called for the 'primary effort of the United Nations' to be 'directed against Germany rather than her satellite states'.[21]

This effort was to take the form of a bomber offensive 'on the largest practical scale' against German war production from bases in Britain and North Africa, coupled with building up 'as rapidly as possible adequate balanced forces in the United Kingdom in preparation for a land offensive against Germany in 1943'. The memorandum recommended closing down Mediterranean operations (except for bombers based there) once North Africa had been cleared, and transferring all surplus forces back to Britain for 'Roundup'. In short, Marshall advocated 'the strategic offensive with maximum forces in the Atlantic–Western European theatre directly against Germany at the earliest practicable date'.[22]

With so vast a gulf between the two Allies' concepts of grand strategy to bridge, it is no wonder that Brooke was to write to his wife afterwards: 'I have seldom had a harder week or one with a heavier strain.'[23] Yet in the Combined Chiefs of Staff committee sessions Marshall from the start was in the weaker position. '*C'est le premier pas qui coûte*'; and that step had been taken in July 1942 with the original decision for 'Torch'. The second step now became all too inevitable. As Marshall admitted, 'one of the strongest arguments for undertaking such an operation [as landing in Sardinia or Sicily] is that there will be an excess of troops in North Africa once Tunisia has been cleared of Axis forces'.[24] Against Brooke's eloquent repetition of the same arguments that had worn down Churchill earlier, Marshall could only fight a rearguard action, asking Brooke and his colleagues whether the Mediterranean strategy was to be a means to an end or an end in itself. Was it simply opportunism, he wished to know, or was it part of an integrated plan to win the war? Brooke had his well-rehearsed answer to this of course. He deftly soothed Marshall's fear of 'interminable operations' in the Mediterranean by warning that the Allies should be very careful about invading Italy, even in support of an anti-fascist coup. Nonetheless Churchill in the previous November had already scorned Sicily or Sardinia as an ultimate Mediterranean objective and instead looked beyond to 'a decisive attack on Italy'.[25]

And so Marshall finally came to accept Brooke's contention that the forces available for 'Roundup' in 1943 were insufficient to offer hope of success, that it was better therefore, in Brooke's words, 'definitely to count on re-entering the Continent in 1944 on a large scale',[26] and in 1943 to exploit Mediterranean possibilities instead. Of these Roosevelt for his part liked best a landing in Sicily. The conference duly settled for this operation, codenamed 'Husky'. It was Marshall himself who explained to Roosevelt and Churchill when they met the Combined Chiefs of Staff that he and his colleagues had agreed to undertake 'Husky' 'because we will have in North Africa a large number of troops available . . .'[27] – in other words that the Allies were once again to wage war as they must rather than as they ought.

Only in a later session, concerned not with grand strategy but with the particular operational problems of the war against the U-boat, did the conference touch on the implications of 'Husky' in regard to shipping and naval escorts. The First Sea Lord took the opportunity to warn his colleagues that they might be trying to have it both ways, in that the decision to go ahead with amphibious operations in the Mediterranean as well as in the Pacific was not compatible with the principle that 'the defeat of the U-boat remains first charge on resources'.[28] Pound's apprehensions were to be borne out at the end of February when Eisenhower reported that, if 'Husky' were to be launched in June, he would need enough extra shipping, including 30 merchant ships, to carry an additional 38,000 soldiers earmarked for the expeditionary force.[29]

On 24 January the 'Symbol' circus left town by aircraft and ship, the star turns generally well satisfied with the final agreed memorandum on 'The Conduct of the War in 1943', which was based on a subtle compromise drafted by that wily diplomat of an airman, John Slessor.[30] 'Ernie' King was given essentially all he needed for his Pacific theatre; Dudley Pound had the defeat of the U-boat confirmed as the Allies' first priority; 'Hap' Arnold, the US Chief of Air Staff, and Charles Portal had 'the heaviest possible bomber offensive' confirmed as the Allies' main direct mode of attack on Germany in 1943; Brooke the ringmaster carried away the strategic box-office. Marshall for his part could only stifle his mistrust of British commitment to an eventual cross-Channel invasion and resolve that, whatever happened, Brooke's 'blue water' strategy would not be allowed to wander further than Sicily.

In the meantime the Allies still remained far from even fulfilling the objectives of 'Torch'.

On 12 February 1943, the second anniversary of Rommel's arrival in Africa, the rearguards of Panzerarmee Afrika retreated across the Libyan frontier into Tunisia, so closing the Desert campaign as such. It can be said that, except for his one major error, that of trying to reach Alexandria in the summer of 1942, Rommel had mounted one of the most successful diversionary campaigns in history. He had been sent to Libya in January 1941 simply to rescue the defeated Italians and hold the British off in a passive defensive. By his genius for taking risks and leading marvellous spoiling offensives, by the power of his own striking personality, he had wonderfully played on the obsession of the British with the Middle East, inducing them (and especially Churchill) to pump ever larger forces, ever more tanks and guns and aircraft into the effort to beat him – which equally meant an ever increasing procession of convoys trundling 13,000 miles round the Cape and up the Red Sea from Britain. By his domination of the Libyan coastline (and, except for brief intervals, the Cyrenaican airbases) he had stretched the Mediterranean Fleet to the limit in its attempts to keep Malta going. Rommel had, in sum, kept in play the major active war-waging effort of the British Empire for two years – and all with a shipping lift across the Mediterranean narrows that had been the merest fraction of the comparable British shipping investment; all with just three (later four) under-strength German divisions and some largely second-rate Italian formations. This and not the equivalent British Middle East and Mediterranean campaign had proved the profitable exercise in 'blue water' strategy; an irony of which British myth takes little account.

On 14–22 February 1943 Rommel's and Arnim's now united forces launched a major offensive westwards through the Tunisian mountain passes. Though compromised by Arnim's cautious orthodoxy, the offensive dealt a heavy blow on green American formations (this was Rommel in the Battle of the Kasserine Pass), and temporarily threw the Allied armies into disarray. Up to this point, therefore, the Axis intervention in Tunisia in opposition to 'Torch' had likewise proved a profitable diversionary exercise, bogging the Allied expeditionary force down in stalemate and dislocating the Allies' timetable for the clearance of North Africa. Moreover, it had compelled them to invest nearly twice the expected monthly total of ships in order to sustain the protracted land operations; between D-Day on 8 November 1942 and 12 March 1943 'Torch' had demanded the colossal cumulative total of 8,029,929 tons of shipping.[31]

But the successful spoiling offensive of 14–22 February marked the moment when a wise Axis leadership would have decided to liquidate its investment in Tunisia before superior Allied strength by land, sea and air could trap and destroy the German and Italian armies. However, Hitler, as is the way with political leaders when wars are going badly, had already got into the suicidal habit at Stalingrad and Alamein of ordering his forces to stand fast and fight to the bitter end. From March to the beginning of May 1943 von Arnim (Rommel had gone home sick) fought on obediently while the Royal Navy sought to throttle his sea communications.

In Cunningham's judgment, the Royal Air Force in the Mediterranean was still not being as helpful or effective in supporting the Navy in this task as it ought. He reported to the First Sea Lord on 15 March 1943 that he had 'had a collision with Tedder over a sea striking force permanently attached to the Coastal Group and he gave way'. But this was not the only difficulty:

The Air have reached the decision that no reconnaissance over the

Sicilian narrows in daylight is possible with which I don't agree and the reconnaissance in the Tyrrhenian Sea is still quite inadequate.

Fortunately we get on very well with the Americans who are always ready to place squadrons at our disposal. They seem to realise the importance of sinking ships *at sea* much better than do our R.A.F.

The Coastal Group *will* function satisfactorily but it's hard slogging getting them going. Neglect to make an all weather aerodrome between Bône and Algiers is also exposing our shipping to most unnecessary risks. Yesterday, Sunday, the cruisers and the L.S.I.s carrying troops to Bône spent the day dodging torpedoes fired by T/B aircraft boldly within 10 miles of our coast. Eisenhower has got on to this himself and his Chief Engineer has orders to give this aerodrome first priority.[32]

But gradually, as the Axis air effort waned and the Allied air effort grew and the Royal Navy's little ships hunted for victims, von Arnim's shortfall of supplies of every kind grew more and more crippling. On 6 May the Allied armies (now the 18th Army Group, under the command of General Sir Harold Alexander) launched their final onslaught against the Axis bridgehead, burst through after an initial repulse, and took Bizerta and Tunis. On the 12th von Arnim surrendered with some 230,000 men (of which about 100,000 were German). Very few enemy troops had attempted to escape by sea in the face of the destroyers and light craft scraped up by Cunningham from all over the Mediterranean and deployed in 'Operation Retribution' with the order: 'Sink, burn and destroy. Let nothing pass.'[33] Nor did the Italian Navy emulate the Royal Navy's self-sacrifice off Greece and Crete in 1941 and attempt to rescue von Arnim's stranded soldiers.

So at long last, by gift of Hitler's misjudgment, had arrived the crowning triumph of 'Torch' and indeed of the entire campaign along the North African shore since June 1940; and at long last too, after all the fleet actions and all the convoy battles, the Mediterranean lay open again to through military traffic. The first such convoy passed the Straits of Gibraltar on 17 May, and steamed into Alexandria harbour on the 26th. Two days earlier the first convoy to make an unopposed voyage to Malta since Italy's declaration of war reached the island.

By now planning for 'Operation Husky', the invasion of Sicily, was well in hand; its original target date the June new moon period.

21

The Invasion of Sicily: 'Operation Husky'

The Combined Chiefs of Staff Committee had set up the higher command structure for 'Operation Husky' at the 'Symbol' Conference in Casablanca. Eisenhower was again to be Allied Commander-in-Chief, with Air Marshal Sir Arthur Tedder (previously British AOC-in-C, Middle East) as his air C-in-C, General Sir Harold Alexander (currently commanding the 18th Army Group in Tunisia) as ground forces C-in-C, and Admiral Sir Andrew Cunningham once again his naval C-in-C.

On 20 February 1943 the Admiralty had reorganised the British naval commands in the Mediterranean, with Cunningham hoisting his flag for the second time as Commander-in-Chief, Mediterranean, and Admiral Harwood becoming C-in-C of a new Levant Command. The boundary between the two commands ran north from the frontier between Tunisia and Tripolitania to 35°N, 16°E, and thence to Cape Spartivento on the toe of Italy.

In March the Admiralty in any case relieved Harwood on the grounds of ill-health, largely because of an intrigue against him by General Montgomery, the 8th Army Commander. Montgomery had conceived a spite for the corpulent Harwood, a man who – although Pound's and Churchill's choice – certainly lacked the mental and physical drive desirable for the job. Alleging slothfulness and neglect on the Royal Navy's part in opening up the port of Tripoli, and on the score that the Army had lost confidence in Harwood, Montgomery virtually demanded that he should go. As so often with Montgomery's tales out of school, the record does not bear out these allegations.[1] Nevertheless once doubts about Harwood's capacity had been conveyed to Pound via the Prime Minister, Pound was quick to sack him. As Cunningham was to write privately after the war, 'I fear D.P. was inclined to condemn officers, without hearing what they had to say, in reply to reports and rumours backstairs and otherwise.'[2]

Planning for 'Husky', from its very start in mid-February 1943, yawed rudderless while on the bridge all was argument, confusion and increasingly bad blood. Until May Eisenhower, Cunningham, Tedder and Alexander had their minds and energies almost entirely engaged in the conduct of the Tunisian campaign. This was also true of the designated military commanders of the Western and Eastern Task Forces, Generals Patton and Montgomery. Meanwhile an undirected and relatively junior team of planners, entitled 'Force 141' and set up in Algiers on 10 February, struggled on unhappily to produce an acceptable outline plan. It hardly helped that the nucleus Western Task Force headquarters lay in Rabat, Morocco, while the equivalent Eastern Task Force headquarters lay in Cairo (where the Naval Commander, Eastern Task Force, Admiral Sir Bertram Ramsay, had hoisted his flag on 2 March). Moreover, other planners in Washington and London also had their say in the steering of 'Husky' plans, because some American troops were to travel directly from the United States and some British and Canadian troops directly from the United Kingdom.

All this fell far short of an ideal way to tackle for the first time the problem of mounting assault landings on the grand scale against German and Italian opposition; a very different prospect from the Vichy French. Montgomery, a clear-headed military realist if ever there was one, was reckoning in April that they 'must plan the operation on the assumption that resistance will be fierce and that a prolonged dogfight will follow the initial assault'.[3] A month earlier Eisenhower even conveyed to the British Chiefs of Staff and the American Joint Chiefs of Staff his own and his fellow Commanders-in-Chief's convictions that 'if substantial German ground troops should be placed in the region prior to the attack, the chances for success become practically nil and the project should be abandoned'.[4] This fainthearted signal blew into flame the Premier's always smouldering fighting spirit, and he blazed out at the Chiefs of Staff:

> . . . if the presence of two German divisions is held to be decisive against any operation of an offensive or amphibious character open to the million

> men now in North Africa, it is difficult to see how the war can be carried on . . . I trust the Chiefs of Staff will not accept these pusillanimous and defeatist doctrines, from whoever they come . . . I regard the matter as serious in the last degree . . . What Stalin would think of this, when he has 185 German divisions on his front I cannot imagine . . .[5]

In due course the Combined Chiefs of Staff signalled their own displeasure to Eisenhower, who meekly replied that he and his colleagues would prosecute 'Husky' 'with all means at our disposal. There is no thought here except to carry out our orders to the ultimate of our ability . . .'[6]

But fighting spirit alone did not supply answers to the problems of successfully landing in Sicily. A balance had to be struck between clashing service interests. Tedder and Cunningham both wanted the cluster of airfields in the south-western corner of Sicily to be captured early on in order to deprive the enemy of air striking power over the invasion shipping and the beach-heads. They could hardly forget that it was from Sicilian fields that the Luftwaffe had so successfully dominated the central Mediterranean since spring 1941. Moreover Cunningham wished landings to be made at widely separated points round the eastern and western coasts of Sicily in order to exploit the flexibility of seapower and so distract the enemy ground forces.

In late March 'Force 141' produced its own outline plan for landings by three British divisions at several points strung along 100 miles of the southern coast from Syracuse round to Gela, while an American division went ashore on the west coast some 60 miles distant from the nearest British beach-head. On D + 2 another American landing was to take place near Palermo in the north-west of the island, and on D + 3 a further British landing on the west coast at Catania. Because of its dispersion and its promise of early capture of enemy air fields, both Cunningham and Tedder rather liked this plan. So too did Eisenhower and Alexander. It was therefore duly approved in principle.

However, when Montgomery learned in mid-March about the plan it was the very dispersion that horrified him. He signalled Alexander: 'In my opinion the operation breaks every common-sense rule of practical battle fighting and is completely theoretical. It has no hope of success and should be completely re-cast.'[7] It was, and remained, Montgomery's conviction that 'To operate dispersed means disaster'[8]; and he began to use all the power of his ruthless will to rescue 'Husky' from being in his words 'a real dog's breakfast' and 'a very high-class mess'.

Fortunately Admiral Ramsay in Cairo and Major-General Miles Dempsey, the corps commander deputed by Montgomery to work with him, got on well, as Ramsay confided to his wife in a letter of 19 March: 'I like my general immensely and we see eye to eye on things, which makes life easier. But we don't see eye to eye in all things with those above us! . . .'[9] In particular Ramsay did not see eye to eye with his Commander-in-Chief, Andrew Cunningham, who, superb fighting sailor in command of a fleet though he was, now showed serious limitations in terms of an inter-service amphibious operation of the new kind. In brief, he revealed himself as an old-fashioned and authoritarian centraliser. As Ramsay expressed it in his letter home on 19 March:

> A.B.C. has his own very definite views, which are based on wishful thinking rather than facts. His judgment is excellent but his facts are often wrong. There may be trouble later on, owing to his way of centralising command, in the same way as when he and I play together in Ping Pong he takes 4/5ths of the balls. He's very good too.[10]

The problem, exacerbated by distance and communication by signal, grew trickier. On 7 April 1943 Ramsay was writing to his wife:

> I am not awfully happy about the way things are taking shape between A.B.C. and his party and myself and mine. I find him most unsympathetic towards suggestions put up to him, making it appear as though he was at pains to find an excuse to knock them down instead of a way of meeting them. The fact is that he wants to keep everything very tight in his own hands and doesn't welcome suggestion or anything that doesn't emanate from himself and his staff. It will lead to a cleavage sooner or later, which is most undesirable. It seems that he regards anything to do with Combined operations as anathema & that the R.N. must keep well clear & all to themselves. I on the other hand have had diametrically opposite views and consider the army & Navy as one for thinking, planning and action. He is of the 'true blue' school and I suppose I am not. I hope for the avoidance of trouble but am afraid it is going to be difficult.[11]

Trouble shortly arrived, when Cunningham, in Ramsay's words, allowed

> the army [that is, the military staffs in Algeria] to make plans without prior consultation with the Navy and in particular accepting plans which I should have to carry out, without my knowing anything about it . . . In this respect I was confronted a few days ago with a plan which had been concocted and approved right up to the highest plane; in fact a 'fait accompli'.[12]

The plan in question represented the latest attempt by the staffs in Algeria to amend the original strategy in order to assuage Montgomery's horror of dispersion, and it too had won the approval of Eisenhower, Alexander, Tedder and Cunningham. Ramsay was so horrified at its operational implications that he protested to Cunningham, who replied that the plan had his full approval – 'meaning,' wrote Ramsay, 'that he had not properly gone into it'.[13]

> At the end of a long passage [he] added grudgingly that if I liked to try and persuade a certain prominent person [Montgomery] to change it I might do so! I did try and got his immediate & hearty consent (& almost thanks) and have just had the great satisfaction of telling him [Cunningham] so. But the work entailed in changing the plan now is almost heartbreaking to the wretched staffs. If only I'd been consulted at the right time & the plan made jointly or if A.B.C.'s staff had done their job properly the necessity would never have arisen.[14]

Montgomery, with Ramsay's full concurrence, now produced a completely novel plan by which his 8th Army was to land shoulder to shoulder in a single extended lodgement on the eastern coast of Sicily south of Syracuse. This entailed abandoning the proposed British landings in the Gulf of Gela in the south-west, aimed at quickly securing three vital airfields. Incensed by all the bumbling, Montgomery added to the brief statement of his plan a crisp ultimatum that 'I have given the orders that so far as the army is concerned all planning and work is now to go ahead along the lines indicated'.[15]

Montgomery's thinking might be clear and his action decisive, but his personality now served to obstruct rather than further his purpose, which Ramsay sought as best he could to overcome by judicious lubrication:

> Monty has thrown a spanner of considerable size into the works & in doing so has caused almost complete disruption of work besides increasing, if possible, his unpopularity. It is really most unfortunate that he should do so many things that make him unpopular and so few the contrary. It means, naturally, that I have all the time to try & modify his remarks to suit his audience & it is curious how quite unable he is to see the effect he causes or in fact to care in the least what that effect is. It requires all the tact I can gather in to deal with him in this way, though he and I are on the best possible terms. I have got him just where I want him as regards the Navy & there is complete understanding between us. I can however foresee that he will for ever be putting me in the midst of most difficult circumstances which, with someone like A.B.C., produces difficulties I would prefer to avoid. It's all a great pity for Monty is a great success.

> The trouble is that he adopts the attitude that he is now omnipotent.[16]

Cunningham did indeed take exception to Montgomery's new plan, judging it to be 'unsound' partly because it left the airfields in enemy hands, 'and we are landing from a mass of shipping a mere thirty miles off', partly because it 'also seems to surrender our greatest asset – that of being able to assault the island in numerous places at once at will'.[17] Yet in his retrospective report on 'Husky' to Eisenhower in 1944 he followed Ramsay in acknowledging that the fundamental principle of amphibious warfare must be that

> . . . a combined operation is but the opening, under particular circumstances, of a purely army battle. It is the function of the navy and of the air to help the army establish a base or bases on the hostile coast from which the military tactical battle to gain the object must be developed. It is upon the army tactical plan for the fulfilment of its object that the combined plan must depend. The navy and the air commanders must join with the army commander to ensure that the base or bases for seizure are capable of achievement without prohibitive loss in their respective elements, and that, when seized, they will fulfil the requirements of the force; but it is of no use to plan on the seizure of bases unrelated to the realities of the military situation when ashore.[18]

This exactly mirrored the views of Admiral Ramsay, the acknowledged master planner of amphibious operations, who had agreed from the first with Montgomery over 'Husky'.

It was therefore entirely proper that Montgomery's clear-cut military plan should prevail; and impossible in retrospect not to applaud his insistence on concentration instead of dispersion. But the resentment which he aroused in other equally strong personalities contributed yet another complicating factor in a planning process already bedevilled by human as well as purely operational problems. On 28 April Cunningham complained to the First Sea Lord that 'Montgomery is a bit of a nuisance; he seems to think that all he needs to do is to say what needs to be done and everyone will dance to the tune of his pipings'.[19] Cunningham went on:

> But the seriousness of it all is that here we are with no fixed agreed plan, just over two months off D-day and the commanders all at sixes and sevens, and even if we do get a final agreement, someone will be operating a plan he doesn't fully agree with. Not the way to make a success of an operation . . .[20]

It worsened the impasse that Eisenhower as overall Commander-in-Chief chose to act the role of remote chairman of the board, while Alexander, his ground forces commander, was a man weak of will and dim of brain who would take no decisive lead.

This collective vacuum in leadership Montgomery took it upon himself to fill, and just as well he did. At a meeting in Algiers at the end of April he convinced Eisenhower and his Chief of Staff, Bedell Smith, of the merits of a revised version of his own plan. As Ramsay reported to his wife with qualified jubilation: 'We managed to get our way, however, in Algiers which has simplified things though causing us and everyone else an immense amount of work . . .'[21] Under Montgomery's new plan the American landings near Palermo would be abandoned altogether in favour of one in the Gulf of Gela only twenty miles distant from the 8th Army's left flank. This would make it possible to capture early the south-western airfields of so much concern to Tedder and Cunningham while, at the same time, both Allied armies would be enabled to consolidate a strong single lodgement astride the southern tip of Sicily from which to break out later. Montgomery conceived that it would be he who did this breaking out (towards Catania) with Patton acting as his left flank guard. In the event Patton's thrusting leadership was to make its own comment on this wishful thinking.

The major drawback with Montgomery's plan lay in that instead of Patton's 7th Army being able quickly to make use of the port of Palermo, it would for a time have to be supplied with 3,000 tons of stores a day over open beaches, which Admiral Hewitt (Naval Commander, Western Task Force) doubted could be done. Moreover the nature of the plan, reducing Patton to a secondary role, and the pushy manner by which Montgomery successfully sold it, left Hewitt and Patton 'very sore', in Cunningham's words.[22]

On 12 May the plan, already blessed by Eisenhower and Alexander, was formally approved by the Combined Chiefs of Staff at the Washington ('Trident') Conference – three months after the 'Symbol' Conference at Casablanca, and only two months before 'Husky's' currently projected launch date in July. With all the detailed operational plans for this daunting triphibious operation still to be worked out, time was houndingly short. Ramsay wrote that although his staff was 'excellent' it was 'proving too small and some members are grossly overworked. Compared with Monty's staff mine are in the proportion of about 1 to 8. The army doesn't know what work is for us.'[23]

In January 1943 the Joint Intelligence Committee in London had guesstimated that, after the conclusion of the Tunisian campaign, enemy strength in Sicily could rise by the time of the landings to between five and eight field divisions, of which two or three could be German, and that reinforcements by ferry across the Straits of Messina could reach a total of one German and one and a half Italian divisions per week.[24] These guesstimates governed Allied planning, which throughout was based on the need for an expeditionary force of at least eight divisions. This figure in turn determined the quantity of shipping and landing craft that would be required – no fewer than 1,365 warships and merchant ships and 715 British and 510 American landing craft; a grand total of 2,590 ships and craft of all descriptions for the operation itself and thereafter for the expeditionary force's seaborne logistics. In the event the total was to climb close to 3,000.[25]

That various portions of the expedition were to sail from the United States and Britain as well as from Mediterranean bases as widely separated as Egypt and Tunisia immensely complicated the staff problems both of concentrating the assault forces off the coast of Sicily and also of training the troops and crews. In particular, Bizerta and Tunis, the bases for the Western Task Force (American), only fell into Allied hands on 12 May, and much damage had then to be repaired. A section of the Eastern Task Force faced similar problems at Sfax and Sousse. Moreover a very large number of landing ships and craft new to the theatre had to be received and allotted base facilities, while their officers and crews (many of them newly recruited and trained) had to be put through crash training programmes in the specialised task of disembarking troops on beaches. Their initial inexperience caused some temporary wavering in the soldiers' confidence in the sailors.

The problems of training and rehearsal were worsened because vessels such as landing ships (tank) were late to arrive in the theatre, and crews had little opportunity to practise with the pontoons by which tanks were transferred to shore.[26] A further handicap to training lay in the need to employ landing craft in heavy and continuous running simply in order to transport troops, airmen and vehicles from widely scattered points round the Mediterranean to the assembly bases for the attack. Would the landing crafts' engines stand the strain? According to Cunningham later, 'These fears were happily disproved, and in fact the sea training provided by these voyages must have stood them [the crews] in good stead. That the craft themselves withstood the extra wear and tear is a tribute to those who designed and built them.'[27]

The problem of repair and maintenance of these overworked craft before the launch of 'Husky' was aggravated by what Cunningham called 'one of the most disappointing things, pre "Husky"'[28] – that 'not a single one of all the landing craft maintenance equipment, docks, slips, etc, etc, functioned before the operation . . .'

> The craft were only just got ready by suspending repairs and maintenance to every other type of vessel in every port in North Africa and Malta and Gibraltar. If it had not been for this and for a most astonishing and, to me, previously unknown tidal rise and fall of 8 ft at Sfax, which enabled us to dock the landing craft on a sand bank, we should have been badly caught.[29]

A military decision that airborne forces must serve as a key to quick seizure of lodgements ashore further complicated the task of Cunningham, Ramsay and Hewitt and their staffs. In plotting the complex routing tables for the assault convoys from their various bases they had to leave corridors clear for the flight paths of Allied transports in order to avoid confusion with enemy aircraft, and possible mistaken anti-aircraft fire by Allied ships. The intended use of airborne forces also made the navies' role more difficult in regard to the timing of the actual assaults, for while moonlit nights were needed for the parachute drops and glider landings, the navies would have preferred a new-moon period, giving them the cover of darkness against air attack during the initial run-in and on every night thereafter. On the finally decided launch date for 'Husky', 10 July 1943, there would be a waxing moon which set about 0200, with full moon on the 17th.[30] In the event, the airborne troops were not employed as originally intended, but the change was made too late for the timing of the landings to be altered. The navies therefore had to operate at night in disadvantageous light conditions for no good purpose. Admiral Kent Hewitt in his report on 'Husky' was to vent angry criticism of the decision to time seaborne landings according to the needs of airborne troops, and Cunningham agreed with him, writing:

> A seaborne assault is unalterably committed to a date for some days in advance of D-day. In tidal waters it is even more inflexibly bound by time and tide. It may well be that, on the selected date, airborne troops are weatherbound and cannot operate. It does therefore appear most necessary that airborne troops should be considered as a useful auxiliary rather than as a governing factor which may react to the disadvantage of other services . . .[31]

More generally, the air plans for 'Husky' appeared all along to the naval commanders to be, in Cunningham's phrase, 'somewhat nebulous'.[32] It did not help that Tedder and his HQ remained at La

Marsa in Tunisia, while the naval and ground forces Cs-in-C moved to Malta.

Also to be dovetailed into the overall plan were naval covering forces against the Italian battlefleet. Although its morale and state of training were known to be low, it still remained formidable enough in numbers – six battleships, seven cruisers, 48 destroyers and torpedo boats, 50 submarines (plus twenty German U-boats) and some 115 Italian and 30 to 35 German E-boats.[33] 'It must be recognised,' stated Cunningham's 'Husky Orders Naval', 'that if it is ever going to fight, it must fight now in defence of its country . . .'[34]

And finally all aspects of the 'Husky' deployment had to be planned so that they fitted in with the deception plan being sold to the enemy – that the Allies were intending to land in Greece.[35] Cunningham therefore instructed that in order to disguise the direction of attack the concentrating of ships in the central Mediterranean should be delayed as long as possible, while the 'approach march' of assault forces from great distances to their assembly areas were to conform with the normal pattern of through Mediterranean convoys. Yet further complications were posed to the planners by the bottleneck through the Tunisian channel, and by the need to schedule movements so that escort vessels could refuel before they finally deployed for the landings.

On 20 May 1943 Cunningham issued the bulky 'Husky Orders Naval' ('HON') which embodied the meticulously thorough answers to this whole vast and intricate strategic conundrum. In the opening words of the Introduction to 'HON', 'This is a large and complicated operation involving in all the movement of some 2500 ships and major landing craft. The operational orders are necessarily voluminous.'[36] It had taken twenty typists seven days to type the originals, after which 800 copies had to be run off.[37] In his own words in reporting to Eisenhower in January 1944:

> Very detailed orders were issued regarding the routes and timing of the approach, backed up by track charts and the inevitable 'Mickey Mouse' diagrams which are in my view essential to the clear understanding of a problem of this nature. Even so, everything depended, as always, on the seamanship and good sense of individual commanding officers and on the smooth working of the berthing and fuelling organisations of the several ports concerned. My confidence in their abilities was not misplaced. The operation ran like a well-oiled clock.[38]

The sea movements began on 28 May when the first convoy from the United States for Oran and Algiers sailed with troops and stores for the Western Task Force. Between 20 June and 1 July two slow convoys (KMS18 and KMS19) and one fast convoy (KMF18), making up Force V, steamed out of the Clyde with tanks, stores and fuel for the Eastern Task Force. Movements within the Mediterranean itself got under way on 3 June, when the 30 motor transport stores ships, fifteen landing ships (tank), and two landing ships (gantry) of convoy MWS36 put to sea from Alexandria and headed westwards at an average speed of advance of 8 knots. Three more convoys from Alexandria followed on 6–9 July. These convoys, making up Force A of the Eastern Task Force, comprised in all 60 motor transport ships and 32 personnel ships, as well as fuel carriers and the fighter direction ship *Antwerp* (see below, p. 638). Only one vessel was lost on passage, falling victim to a U-boat off Derna on the Libyan coast.

Meanwhile the American assault convoys of the Western Task Force (TJS1, TJF1 and TJM1) had sailed from Bizerta and Sousse, and the convoys from the United States (NCF1 and NCF2) had put to sea again from Algiers and Oran. More than 800 major vessels were converging on the sea area south of Malta from west, south and east at speeds varying from 6 knots to 13, bearing with them some 115,000 British Empire and 66,000 American troops, together with a mass of tanks, artillery, motor transport, ammunition and every kind of stores: their purpose the destruction of two under-strength German panzer-grenadier divisions, four Italian field divisions (only one of which was fit for battle) and five Italian coastal divisions of largely low quality and poor equipment.[39]

By way of an overture to 'Husky' the Italian island base of Pantellaria west of Malta (the object of Churchill's cherished 'Workshop' project in 1940–41; see above, pp. 202–3 and 324) was attacked on 19 June. Allied bombers had already dropped 6,400 tons of bombs on it in three weeks; a lavish expenditure of ordnance on so tiny a target. On 10 July cruisers added their mite of high explosive, watched by Eisenhower and Cunningham from HMS *Aurora* (wearing Cunningham's Admiral of the Fleet's Union Flag). Next day the garrison of 11,000 war-weary Italians surrendered even before the landing craft could reach the harbour. The only Allied casualty was a British soldier bitten by a donkey. On the 12th the neighbouring island of Lampedusa also surrendered. The capture of Pantellaria not only removed a potential menace to Allied sea communications but it also provided a much needed extra advanced airbase from which Allied fighters could cover the 'Husky' landings.[40] Already 600 Allied fighters had been concentrated on Malta and its neighbouring island of

Gozo; a further belated return on the past British strategic investment in their defence.[41]

On 1 July 1943 Admiral Ramsay sailed from Alexandria to join Cunningham in Malta. At 0630 on 9 July, the eve of D-Day for 'Husky', he put to sea from Grand Harbour in a sun-sharp Mediterranean morning, white foam sparkling against the blue, in the fighter direction ship *Antwerp* (2,957 tons gross) in order to witness the culmination of his own and his staff's labours – the rendezvousing south of Malta between Force V from Britain, Force A from Egypt and Force B from Sousse, Sfax, Tripoli and Malta. At noon he assumed operational command of all these components of the Eastern Task Force. 'After the months of tiresome planning,' he wrote to his wife two days later, 'it is a treat to *do* things instead of write or talk about them.'[42] The past irritation of signals from Cunningham 'worded most rudely'[43] gave way to the exhilaration of being at sea 'with my flag flying'[44] and in command of a great enterprise.

In the course of the forenoon the wind had freshened; the landing craft loaded with soldiers on the haul from Sousse and Sfax began to pitch sickeningly in the short, steep sea for which the Malta channel is notorious, forcing them to slow down; and the flagship groaned in its twenty-four-year-old joints as it took the strain.

Far off, the covering forces to protect the expedition against the Italian battlefleet were already on station. Five submarines of the 8th Flotilla were patrolling on a line between Corsica and the Italian mainland in order to intercept any fleet units making sorties from the bases of La Spezia, Genoa or Leghorn, while three boats of the 10th Flotilla (including the Polish *Sokol*) lay north of the Strait of Messina and five more (including the Polish *Dzik*) were off Taranto watching out for the two battleships stationed there. Well away to the east of Sicily Force H (Vice-Admiral A. U. Willis), comprising the battleships *Nelson* (flag), *Rodney*, *Warspite* and *Valiant*, the fleet carriers *Indomitable* and *Formidable*, six light cruisers of the 12th Cruiser Squadron and eighteen destroyers, had concentrated in the Ionian Sea in order to protect the eastern flank of the landings from attack by Italian ships based on Taranto. As part of the cover plan, Force H feinted towards the west coast of Greece on 9 July (D – 1); then closed the assault area by dawn on D-Day. Force Z (Captain C. H. L. Woodhouse, RN), consisting of the battleships *Howe* and *King George V*, two cruisers and six destroyers, lay to the west of Sicily with the role of reserve force. Force K (four cruisers and six destroyers under Rear-Admiral C. H. J. Harcourt) was to provide close fire support to the landing operations of the Eastern Task Force.[45] Force Q (detached from

Force H) was to provide nightly cover to the north of the British landings.

The painstaking assembly of a maritime steamhammer was thus complete. How easily would the continental walnut crack? At the end of May GC and CS (Ultra) had broken into the teleprinter link between the German high command in Italy and the German Army high command (OKH), and from now on to the end of the Italian campaign in 1945 this was to yield even more comprehensive information than the Luftwaffe or Army Enigmas.[46] Thanks to such sources the Allies calculated with fair accuracy on the eve of 'Husky' that the Axis forces defending Sicily consisted of the Hermann Göring Division (a Luftwaffe field division), and the 15th Panzer-Grenadier Division, plus four Italian field divisions and five coastal.[47] Of the Italian field divisions only the Livorno was thought to be worth much, while the coastal division on the front of the Eastern Task Force's landings was known to be poorly equipped. The two German divisions had been divided into four battlegroups to act as stiffeners to the lacklustre Italians.

The Hermann Göring Division presented neither a great advertisement for its namesake nor for the German armed forces, for it had no battle experience and in the main its leadership was slack. However, in its commander, Lieutenant-General Paul Conrath, it enjoyed a standard issue German general – that is, experienced, thoroughly well trained, tough, resourceful. The 15th Panzer-Grenadier Division had only been cobbled together since its elements arrived in Sicily, but its commander, Major-General Eberhard Rodt, was another standard issue German general with similar attributes. The liaison officer to General Guzzoni, commanding the Italian 6th Army (responsible for the defence of Sicily) was General Frido von Senger und Etterlin, an outstanding soldier against whom the Allies were to break many lances in the Battle of Cassino.

Luftwaffe strength was calculated by Allied Intelligence to amount to 135 fighters in Sicily and 130 fighters and fighter-bombers in Sardinia (actual figures: some 300 fighters in Sicily and the toe of Italy, 70 in Sardinia, together with a total of some 130 fighter-bombers in the whole region).[48] As against this the Allied air forces deployed 4,328 aircraft of all kinds, including some 700 fighters based on Malta, Gozo and Pantellaria.[49]

Sigint guided the Allies in other important respects too. It revealed that the enemy had not been deceived by the Allied cover plan of a landing in Greece, but instead was correctly expecting an attack on Sicily, and along the southern and south-eastern coasts (though the

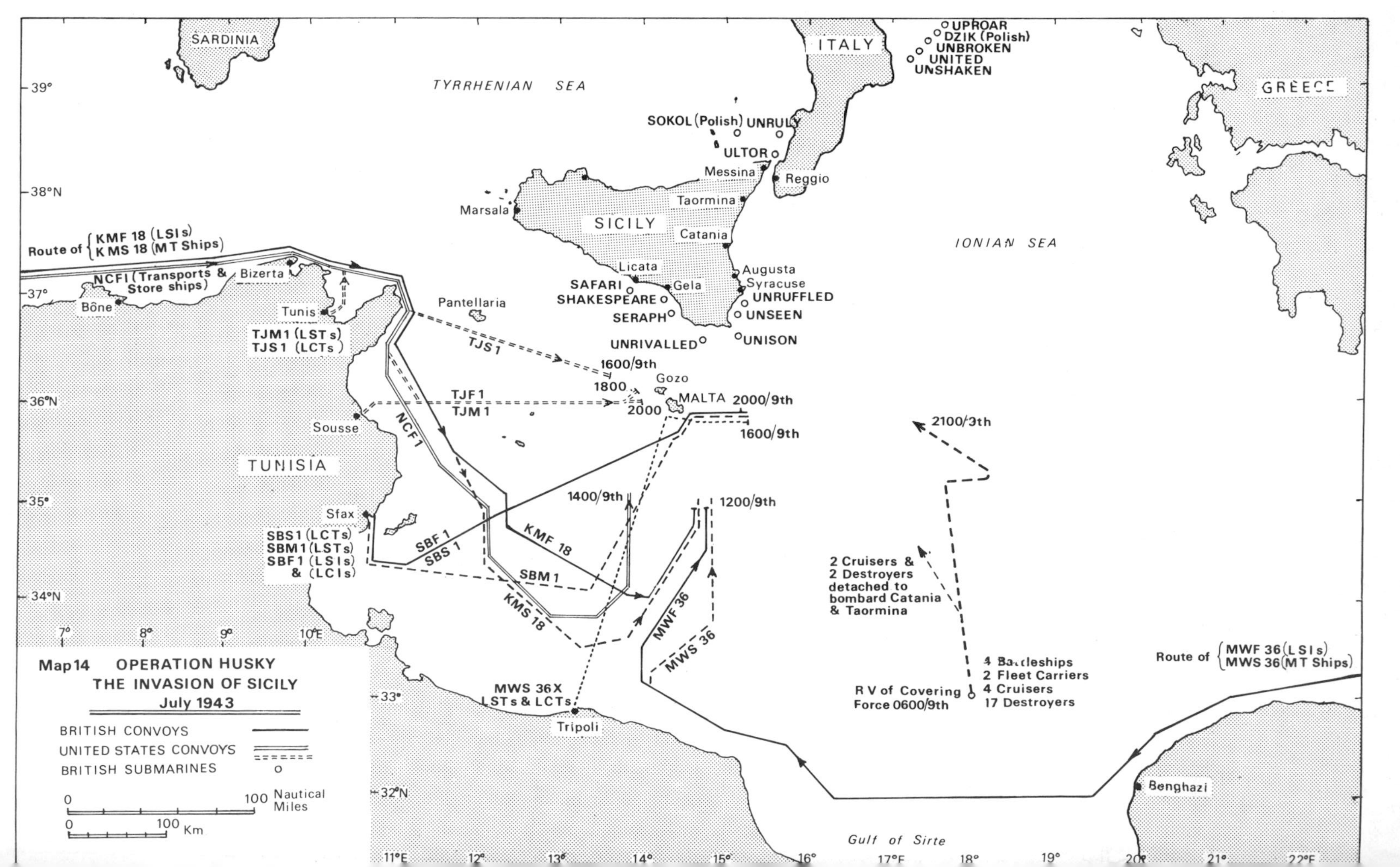

SARDINIA
TYRRHENIAN SEA
ITALY
GREECE
IONIAN SEA
SICILY
TUNISIA
Gulf of Sirte
UPROAR
DZIK (Polish)
UNBROKEN
UNITED
UNSHAKEN
SOKOL (Polish)
UNRULY
ULTOR
Messina
Reggio
Taormina
Catania
Marsala
Licata
Gela
Augusta
Syracuse
SAFARI
SHAKESPEARE
SERAPH
UNRUFFLED
UNSEEN
UNISON
UNRIVALLED
Pantellaria
Gozo
MALTA
Route of {KMF 18 (LSIs) / KMS 18 (MT Ships)}
NCFI (Transports & Store ships)
Bizerta
Bône
Tunis
TJM1 (LSTs)
TJS1 (LCTs)
TJS1
TJF1
TJM1
NCF1
Sousse
Sfax
SBS1 (LCTs)
SBM1 (LSTs)
SBF1 (LSIs)
& (LCIs)
SBF 1
SBS 1
SBM 1
KMF 18
KMS 18
MWF 36
MWS 36
1600/9th
1800
2000
2000/9th
1600/9th
1400/9th
1200/9th
2100/9th
2 Cruisers &
2 Destroyers
detached to
bombard Catania
& Taormina
4 Battleships
2 Fleet Carriers
4 Cruisers
17 Destroyers
R V of Covering
Force 0600/9th
Route of {MWF 36 (LSIs) / MWS 36 (MT Ships)}
MWS 36X
LSTs & LCTs
Tripoli
Benghazi
39°
38°N
37°
36°N
35°
34°N
33°
32°N
7°
8°
9°
10°E
11°E
12°
13°
14°
15°
16°
17°E
18°
19°
20°
21°
22°E
Map 14 OPERATION HUSKY
THE INVASION OF SICILY
July 1943
BRITISH CONVOYS
UNITED STATES CONVOYS
BRITISH SUBMARINES
0
100 Nautical Miles
0
100 Km

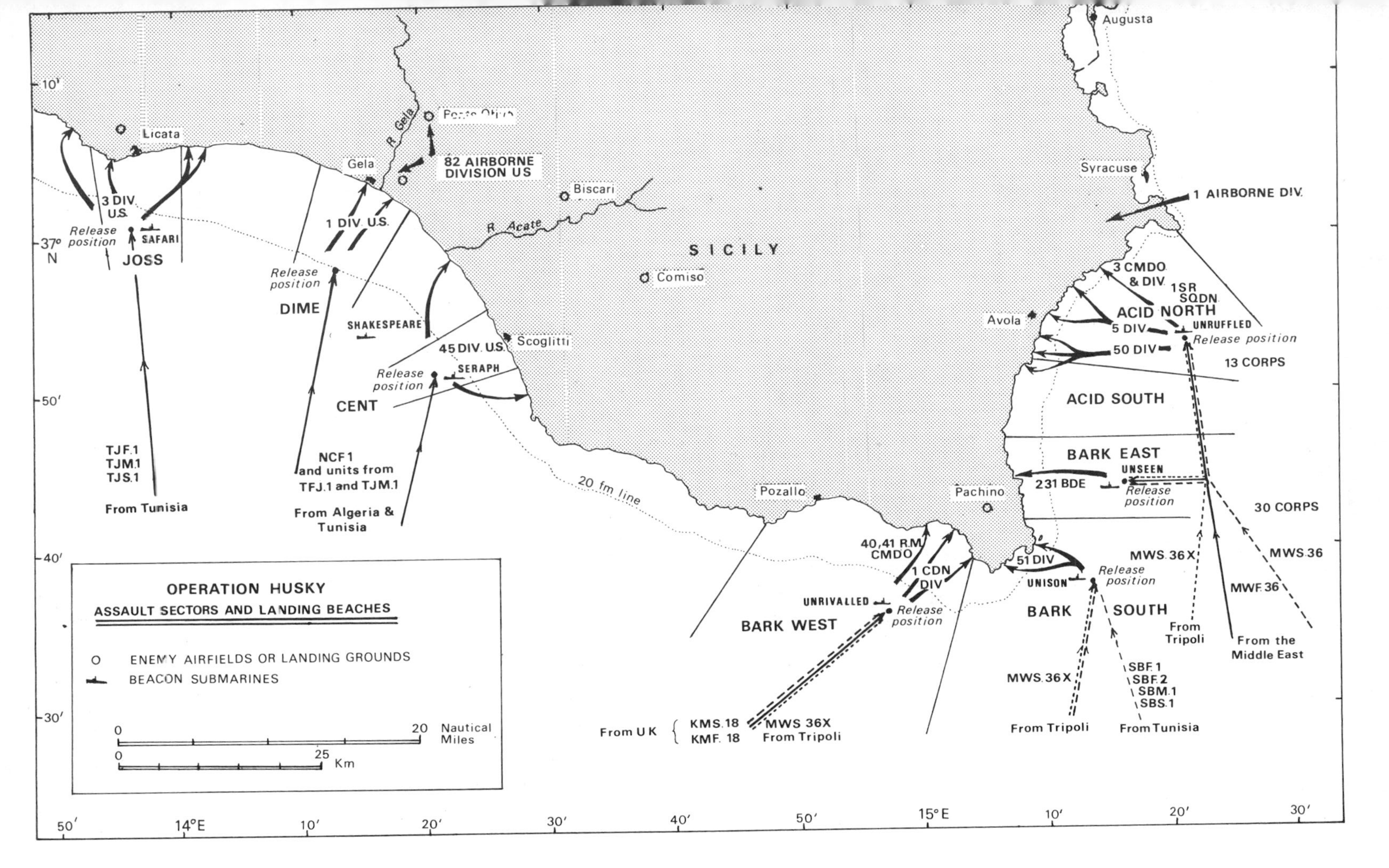

OPERATION HUSKY
ASSAULT SECTORS AND LANDING BEACHES
ENEMY AIRFIELDS OR LANDING GROUNDS
BEACON SUBMARINES
0
20
Nautical Miles
0
25
Km
SICILY
Augusta
Syracuse
Avola
Pachino
Pozallo
Comiso
Biscari
Scoglitti
Gela
Licata
R. Gela
R. Acate
20 fm line
1 AIRBORNE DIV.
82 AIRBORNE DIVISION US
3 CMDO & DIV.
1SR SQDN
ACID NORTH
5 DIV.
50 DIV.
UNRUFFLED
Release position
13 CORPS
ACID SOUTH
BARK EAST
UNSEEN
231 BDE
Release position
30 CORPS
MWS.36
MWF.36
MWS.36 X
From Tripoli
From the Middle East
51 DIV
UNISON
Release position
BARK
SOUTH
MWS.36 X
From Tripoli
SBF.1
SBF.2
SBM.1
SBS.1
From Tunisia
40,41 R.M. CMDO
1 CDN DIV
UNRIVALLED
Release position
BARK WEST
From U K
KMS.18
KMF. 18
MWS 36X
From Tripoli
45 DIV. US.
SERAPH
Release position
CENT
SHAKESPEARE
NCF1 and units from TFJ.1 and TJM.1
From Algeria & Tunisia
1 DIV. U.S.
Release position
DIME
3 DIV. U.S.
Release position
SAFARI
JOSS
TJF.1
TJM.1
TJS.1
From Tunisia
10′
37° N
50′
40′
30′
50′
14°E
10′
20′
30′
40′
50′
15°E
10′
20′
30′

western coast was not excluded). Allied Intelligence also knew from the latest decrypts of the medium-grade Italian C38M naval Enigma cypher that the enemy had ordered their forces to a state of readiness in the early evening of 9 July, having observed by air the approach of some of the assault convoys.[50]

Given that on top of all other deficiencies the German and Italian commands had failed to agree on a joint strategy for the defence of the island, the Axis was ill-prepared in every sense to meet an invasion of such weight and power as 'Husky'. Their one advantage lay in the classic strategic position of 'interior lines', with communications running back via the two to five-miles-wide Messina Strait and then direct road and rail links through Italy to the Reich – in contrast to the Allies' 'exterior lines', with forces and logistic communications converging from vast distances.

During the afternoon of 9 July, as the various components of the Western and Eastern Task Forces advanced according to their intricately woven net of routings towards the assembly areas from which the assault forces would be launched, the weather grew gradually worse, with the wind rising to force 6, and the landing craft struggling in a choppy sea to make 3½ knots.[51] In Force B of the Eastern Task Force the craft were driven to leeward, as well as losing formation in trying to make up for lost ground, so that the final stages of the approach 'resembled a general chase',[52] with landing craft (tank) arriving two hours late at the release position. In Force A also the majority of smaller craft were compelled to drop astern; and the Force commander, Rear-Admiral Troubridge (as he now was), resolved that even if his landing craft (tank) had had to heave to, he would launch his assault without the supporting arms. In the headquarters ship *Antwerp* and back in Cunningham's and Alexander's headquarters in Malta 'considerable anxiety' was felt on account of the plight of the small craft, especially since it was 'manifestly too late' to postpone the landings.[53] But, thankfully, the wind began to drop as the sun westered, the sea subsiding into a heavy swell that still promised thunderous surf on the beaches.

At 2030 Force A (the right flank of the Eastern Task Force) made the most dramatic landfall of any of the British or American task forces that evening as they approached their release positions for the assault – the conical mass of Mount Etna rising black against a clear starlit sky. At 2200 British and American aircraft towed gliders carrying 2,000 soldiers of the British 1st Airborne Division over the assembled ships of the waiting Eastern Task Force towards the coast. The mission of this airlanding brigade was to capture the Ponte

Grande Bridge, a key to a swift advance on Syracuse. Now, however, a tragic combination of high winds, poor navigation owing to inexperience, and the bewildering effects of Italian anti-aircraft fire and flares caused the glider formations to disintegrate into total confusion. Sixty-nine gliders crashed into the sea, ten were towed back to Tunisia, two were shot down, 59 landed in Sicily in a 25-mile scatter, of which only twelve grounded in the intended landing zones. Nonetheless, a handful of survivors took the Ponte Grande Bridge and held it until British ground forces from the beaches came to the rescue next day.

In the meantime a similar disaster overtook the drop of American parachute troops of the 82nd Airborne Division in the Gela area, when again the pilots became entirely lost in darkness and strong wind, and the soldiers landed in small parties all over the place; none of them in the designated dropping zones. With commendable leadership and enterprise these parties transformed themselves into guerrillas and for several days spread alarm among the German and Italian defenders. Nevertheless this first great Allied airborne operation of the war, the routing of which had added to the problems of the naval planners and commanders, lamentably failed to fulfil the role allotted to it.[54]

About an hour and a half after the Allied transport aircraft had rumbled overhead at 2200 on 9 July, the assault forces parted company from their parent convoys and headed off towards their release positions. This time it was hoped that the confusions and mishaps of the 'Torch' landings could be avoided. In reconnoitring the beaches in the weeks beforehand the hard lessons learned on the Algerian shore had been applied as best possible. According to Cunningham, 'the estimation of beach conditions and gradients by air photography and study of wave velocities have now reached a fine pitch of efficiency . . .'[55] Unfortunately the results of this photo-reconnaissance had not reached the staffs in time to be of much value.[56] COPP parties (Combined Operations Pilotage Parties) had this time been put ashore or had swum ashore from submarines (all of them Royal Navy, even on American beaches) and from folbots (folding boats) to obtain details of beach gradients and sand bars. As Cunningham reported afterwards, 'where sand bars exist there is no present substitute for swimming reconnaissance, so the service of these gallant parties will continue to be necessary. Their casualties in this operation were unfortunately heavy . . .'[57]

As in 'Torch', submarines (again all of them British) marked the release positions for the assault waves; their names a roll call of hazardous service: *Safari*, *Shakespeare* and *Seraph* on the Western Task Force Front; *Unrivalled*, *Unison*, *Unseen* and *Unruffled* on the Eastern Task Force Front. Sonic buoys and folbots again served to guide the landing craft into the beaches. Once more, however, the utmost care and foresight failed in the event to avert the operation of Murphy's Law. For delays caused by the bad weather and difficulties in joining separate elements of the assault waves and forming them up in correct order for the run-in caused some problems in getting craft to the right beaches on time.

In the Eastern Task Force (British) the assault on the right flank, nearest to Syracuse, touched down on Acid North beach at H-Hour + 10 minutes, and met only slight opposition, a coastal battery being soon silenced by the destroyer *Eskimo*. On Acid South everything went well even though on some stretches of beach the sonic buoys were either missed or not present. On Bark East (the southernmost beach on the eastern coast of Sicily) all flights touched down on time despite a somewhat ragged run-in, and fire from warships suppressed an attempt by an Italian coastal battery to engage the landing craft when some 200 yards out from the shore. On Bark South and West (astride the southern tip of the island) the heavy swell made it difficult to lower the landing craft (mechanised) or for landing craft to embark soldiers from the big landing ships (infantry). And despite all the efforts at accurate beach reconnaissance, surprises were sprung on Bark West by off-lying sandbanks; and an attempt to blast openings through them proved only a short-lived answer. On another stretch of Bark West, however, the swell simply heaved the landing craft over the false beach.

On every beach of the Eastern Task Force the assault forces enjoyed complete surprise and virtually no opposition. Cunningham attributed this 'unexpected success' partly to the 'little blow' during the day of 9 July, coupled with the enforced choice of an unfavourable phase of the moon. These, he reckoned, had 'actually the effect of making the weary Italians, who had been alert for many nights, turn thankfully in their beds saying "tonight at any rate they can't come!"'[58]

But the morning broke fine and calm, the prelude to a 'most lovely day', as Ramsay recounted to his wife:

> It was almost unreal to find oneself off Sicily with Etna looking down on the scene of the landings. Hundreds literally of ships of the largest size down to the smallest & one had to pinch oneself to make sure one was not in a dream. The coast looked so sleepy and peaceful.
>
> The opposition was surprisingly poor but there was just sufficient to

make it clear that we really were undertaking a warlike operation . . .[59]

So Montgomery's army was solidly ashore; and the admiral responsible for putting it there could well write that launching 'Husky' 'has all been a great thrill and an outstanding success so far . . . I wouldn't have missed it for the world.'[60]

It was on the Western Task Force (American) front along the Gulf of Gela that the toughest opposition was encountered, as well as the worst conditions of sea and beach. In the Joss area on the left flank, even though here the Italian 207th Coastal Division offered only unenthusiastic resistance, the beaches sprang nasty surprises. Two of them combined narrow rocky entrances with shallow sand beyond, features which in conjunction with a north-westerly cross-sea left most of the landing craft stuck in the sand and impossible to pull off.[61] At another Joss beach soft sand and a difficult gradient thwarted attempts to unload tanks. On Dime beach, in the centre astride the town of Gela itself, the Americans ran into heavy fire, but here too the main problem lay in the breaking surf rolled on to a dead lee shore by a Force 4 westerly wind, causing many landing craft to broach. Only on the Cent beaches, on the right flank, did everything go smoothly.[62]

While joint army and navy beach groups sorted out the beach-heads and strove to organise the smooth inward flow of supplies, reinforcements and vehicles, the British and Canadian troops of the Eastern Task Force (now constituted as the 8th Army under Montgomery) and the Americans of the Western Task Force (now the 7th Army under Patton) consolidated their lodgements. By 2100 on D-Day the 8th Army had captured the ports of Syracuse and Augusta, and within three days Royal Navy harbour parties had put them into full working order. On the west coast the 7th Army had taken the port of Licata and the airfields behind Gela, and – thanks partly to its own stout resistance and partly to the devastating fire of the US cruisers *Savannah* and *Boise* – had repulsed a counter-attack by the Hermann Göring and Livorno Divisions which at one point almost reached the beaches.

The two navies had now done their job, landing in three days 80,000 men, 7,000 vehicles, 300 tanks and 900 guns.[63] His own task complete, Ramsay struck his flag as Naval Commander, Eastern Task Force, on 19 July and returned to the United Kingdom, while Hewitt handed over command of the Western Task Force to Rear Admiral Connolly before proceeding to Bizerta. From now on the navies' role was to provide flank guards against enemy ships and E-boats and to bombard coastal targets in support of military operations. On D + 1 the battleships *Howe* and *King George V* shelled Levanzo and Trapani on the western tip of Sicily by way of seeking to arouse enemy apprehensions that another landing was about to take place there; the cruisers *Sirius* and *Dido* performed the same service at Marsala. On 17 July HMS *Warspite*, showing a remarkable turn of speed for a veteran of Jutland, raided Catania, pouring in a storm of 15-inch shells. Her exploit elicited the appreciative signal from the Commander-in-Chief to his one-time flagship: 'Operation well carried out. There is no question that when the old lady lifts her skirts she can run.'[64]

Throughout the campaign the light forces of both Royal and US Navies fought off sorties by enemy cruisers, submarines and E-boats, sinking in all four German and three Italian submarines,[65] for the loss of only four British and two American merchantmen and two American landing ships (tank), and damage to a further three merchantmen and the cruisers *Cleopatra* and *Newfoundland*. But as during the North African campaign it was the Luftwaffe which posed the most dangerous threat to the Allied navies and shipping, arriving early on D-Day and keeping it up to the end. The first victim was the brilliantly lit hospital ship *Talamba* on the night of the 10th. The Eastern Task Force lost merchant vessels and landing craft to a total of 41,509 tons in the course of the campaign; the Western Task Force a destroyer, a minesweeper, two landing ships (tank) and one merchant vessel.[66] The Luftwaffe also seriously damaged the fleet carrier *Indomitable*, the monitor *Erebus* and two destroyers.[67]

The Allied air forces, although so numerous, failed to prevent these enemy strikes – possibly because, as the navies believed, the command and control links between sea and air forces remained slow and cumbersome.[68] And yet fresh innovations had been made in this regard, with air controllers in each headquarters ship to direct forward fighter operations, and a fighter direction ship (equipped with long-range radar) with each headquarters ship to provide the controllers with battle information. For the control of night fighters three seaborne ground control interception centres were lodged in landing ships (tank).[69] Nevertheless the navies still found that the air forces were failing to deploy aircraft quickly enough where most urgently needed.

Both navies rendered an essential if humdrum service to the developing campaign by running a dense traffic of ships and landing craft under their protection between North Africa and the Allied lodgements in Sicily. The two armies had to rely for some time partly on supplies fed through open beaches because port capacities were not large enough. The American 7th Army, with at first only the small harbour of Licata, particularly depended on the beaches; and it was here that the ingenious American invention, the DUKW or 'Duck' (DUKW stood for the factory serial letters of production: 'D' for the year of origin, 1942, the fourth year of war; 'U' for utility; 'K' for front-wheel drive; 'W' for six-wheeled) proved invaluable. The Duck was an amphibious 2½-ton truck, able to ferry stores or troops from ships off shore and then trundle straight out of the sea and up the beach to the unloading point; and it proved the key tool in keeping the 7th Army supplied and on the move. As Admiral Vian put it, 'the DUKWs first and last were the outstanding success of the operation'.[70]

Yet much reliance had also been placed on ordinary landing craft for transport, especially the big seagoing landing craft (tank). For the first time repair ships were taken to the assault area so that each beach could have its own repair and maintenance facilities for landing craft. Nonetheless Cunningham was not at all happy about working so hard as supply transport craft that were really designed for assault operations; and he drew afresh the lesson 'which we have learnt time and time again but neglected on every new occasion' that, as part of the equipment of an amphibious assault, 'one must provide an ample supply of tugs and lighters to take over from the landing craft so that they can be serviced for the next operation . . .'[71]

In 'Husky' just as in 'Torch' the complete success of the initial landings was swiftly succeeded by stalemate in the land campaign, as Hitler fed in the 1st Parachute and 29th Panzer-Grenadier Divisions as reinforcements, and Lieutenant-General Conrath sharpened up the Hermann Göring by means of ferocious orders of the day coupled with courts martial and the sacking of senior officers.[72] On 14 July Montgomery found himself blocked in his frontal push on Catania, and blocked again a week later in trying to carry out a left-hand hook round the western skirts of Mount Etna. There he stuck until a fresh push by his left wing on 29 July – also abortive. Although Rear-Admiral R. McGrigor (Flag Officer, Sicily) had available a force of small landing ships (infantry) and landing craft complete with Commando troops, Montgomery failed to make use of them to outflank the strong German defensive positions, except on one occasion (on 15–16 August) when the Commandos were anyway put in short of the by now retreating enemy. Cunningham later commented acidly in his report to Eisenhower on 'Husky':

> There were doubtless sound military reasons for making no use of this, what to me appeared, priceless asset of seapower and flexibility of manoeuvre; but it is worth consideration for future occasions whether much

> time and costly fighting could not be saved by even minor flank attacks which must necessarily be unsettling to the enemy. It must always be for the General to decide. The Navy can only provide the means and advice on the practicability from the naval angle . . . It may be that had I pressed my views more strongly more could have been done.[73]

It was otherwise with Patton's 7th Army and the United States Navy. Freed by Alexander on 19 July from the shackling role of flank-guard to the deliberate Montgomery, Patton thrust swiftly up into the north-western tip of Sicily, took the port of Palermo on 22 July, and swung east along the northern coastline towards Messina. All through his operations Patton sought to make use of the US Navy and its landing craft lift, as the Allied naval Commander-in-Chief was to praise in reporting to Eisenhower:

> The whole of these operations [wrote Cunningham] both before and after the capture of PALERMO was a model of amphibious tactics by the Western Task Force.
>
> In particular, after the capture of PALERMO . . . U.S. generalship showed that it had nothing to learn of the value of sea power and Task Force 86 [the US Navy component of the Western Task Force] under Rear Admiral DAVIDSON, U.S.N., that it had nothing to learn of the rapid planning and execution of outflanking operations.[74]

In point of fact Cunningham was being over-generous to Patton, possibly because Montgomery's failure to exploit seapower still rankled. Patton's navy-borne left-hooks achieved little, and on one occasion landed behind the American front, to be greeted by General Lucian Truscott's staff on the beach.

On 25 July 1943 Mussolini was dismissed from office thanks to a revolt within his own Fascist Grand Council, and replaced by an interim government under Marshal Badoglio. Hitler had now to take into account the possible defection of Italy from the Axis, and he laid long-term plans accordingly. But as an immediate consequence of Mussolini's fall OKW ordered Field-Marshal Kesselring (Commander-in-Chief, South) on 26 July to prepare to evacuate German troops from Sicily. So this time there was to be no repetition of the Tunisian débâcle; no last stand ending in a free gift to the Allies of a colossal bag of prisoners. By 1 August the plans were ready, and a preliminary evacuation began. The German forces on the ground, now constituted as the 14th Panzer Corps under General Hans Hube, and such Italian formations as still wished to fight, now carried out a characteristically skilled and stubborn step-by-step withdrawal on Messina.

On the night of 11 August the main evacuation ('Operation Lehrgang') began; it was completed on 16 August. Thanks to the efficiency with which Captain von Liebenstein of the German Navy organised the German ferry operation (mostly by Siebel ferries, mass-produced diesel-driven craft 80 feet long and 50 feet in the beam), nearly 40,000 German troops and 15,000 wounded, 10,000 vehicles, 51 tanks, 163 guns and about 20,000 tons of ammunition and equipment were safely brought back to the mainland.[75] The Italian evacuation, conducted by Admiral Barone (Naval Commander, Sicily) and Brigadier-General Monacci (land force commander) proved similarly successful, bringing away a total of 62,000 soldiers and sailors.[76] 'Operation Lehrgang' marked the model ending of what became, after a shaky start, a model defensive and delaying campaign; it rendered hollow and sour the Allies' eventual Sicilian victory. And 'Lehrgang' was carried out virtually without interference from the Allied air forces or navies – or armies, whose medium artillery had sufficient range if pushed forward. Yet the Allied command had been forewarned by cumulative indications from Sigint.[77]

Part of the problem lay in delays within the cumbersome Allied organisation in passing the Sigint indications on to the operational commands. It was only on the third day of the main enemy evacuation that Alexander signalled Tedder that 'it now appears German evacuation has really started'.[78] Even now, the Allied bomber forces (only a fraction was deployed) achieved little in the face of the immense concentration of anti-aircraft batteries organised by the enemy on both sides of the Messina Strait – 123 heavy and 102 light anti-aircraft guns in fixed batteries, plus another 150 mobile dual-purpose guns.[79] Neither was it thought possible for heavy ships, cruisers or even destroyers of the Allied navies to penetrate up the Strait, a two to five-miles-wide winding strip of water between mountainous coasts bristling with heavy cannon.[80] Certainly no such attempt was made: a unique occasion where Cunningham failed to show boldness, fiery aggressive spirit and disregard for loss. It may well be that Cunningham was remembering Admiral Sir John de Robeck's disastrous attempt to take a fleet up the Dardanelles in 1915, with the loss of three battleships. It fell to the light craft (motor torpedo boats and motor gunboats) gallantly to do what they could, which was little; and in the course of 'Lehrgang' the Axis lost only fifteen ferry craft from all causes and not a single man.[81]

On 17 August Patton consummated the Allies' conquest of Sicily after a 38 day campaign by entering Messina. What then was the final balance sheet of 'Husky'? The Allies committed nearly 3,000 warships, transports and landing craft, nearly 2,000 aircraft, and 450,000 men. These forces brought to battle a total of never more than 65,000 Germans at any one time,[82] inflicting losses of about 5,000 killed and between 5,500 and 6,600 captured, at a cost to themselves of nearly 5,000 killed and missing, and 13,083 wounded.[83] In addition the Allies inflicted on the 200,000 Italian troops on the island losses of 2,000 killed, 5,000 wounded and 137,000 prisoners.[84] By way of a benchmark as to comparative scale, in the same month of July 1943 the Red Army had defeated seventeen panzer divisions in the course of repelling the German summer offensive on the Eastern Front ('Operation Zitadelle', 5–13 July 1943), and inflicted losses of between 2,000 and 3,000 tanks and 70,000 killed.[85]

All that can be said in mitigation of the Sicilian campaign's poor return on a large investment is that it certainly helped to topple Mussolini, and thereby brought Brooke's original aim of knocking Italy out of the war a step nearer.

And now what? That had already been decided, not without acrimony, by another summit conference ('Trident'), held in Washington on 11–19 May 1943, when the North African campaign was coming to a victorious close.

The British delegation had profited by the five-day voyage across the Atlantic in the liner *Queen Mary* to agree the strategic case to be put to their allies. It was a case that was to fulfil General Marshall's glummest apprehensions, for it argued in favour of an open-ended extension of 'blue water' strategy in the Mediterranean after the capture of Sicily. In the words of a Joint Planners' memorandum, adopted almost completely by the Chiefs of Staff and the Prime Minister:

> Our final conclusion is that the Mediterranean offers us opportunities for action in the coming autumn and winter which may be decisive, and at least will do far more to prepare the way for a cross-Channel operation in 1944 than we should achieve by attempting to transfer back to the United Kingdom any of the forces now in the Mediterranean theatre. If we take these opportunities, we shall have every chance of breaking the Axis and bringing the war to a successful conclusion in 1944.[86]

During the previous month the Joint Planners, the Chiefs of Staff and the Prime Minister had revolved in detail how best to exploit these apparent Mediterranean opportunities. What about invading

Italy, not least to gain air bases from which to bomb southern Germany? The Joint Planners, much in favour of this invasion, calculated that if Italy defected from the Axis then the Germans would have to find 24 divisions to hold Italy itself, the Balkans and southern France, which they could not do 'without disastrous consequences elsewhere'.[87] The COS, however, were not yet willing at this point to buy an invasion of Italy, for they were still bothered about the cost of a protracted campaign in all kinds of resources.

What about Sardinia (and perhaps Corsica) instead, as advocated by Eisenhower and Cunningham? The case for these was well put in a paper by Eisenhower's Chief of Staff, General Bedell Smith, which criticised an invasion of Italy on the grounds that 'we might be involved in a campaign against superior German forces in a country where superiority in numbers would have full weight',[88] with a consequent heavy drain on shipping resources. To invade Sardinia, on the other hand, would only take five infantry divisions and one armoured; and only two infantry divisions to hold it afterwards. Sardinian air bases would enable the Allied air forces to dominate the whole of Italy while at the same time reducing the enemy air threat to sea communications in the western basin of the Mediterranean. But Air Chief-Marshal Tedder disagreed: an invasion of Sardinia would lie beyond the cover of shore-based fighters, while Sardinia's airfields were in any case really not needed for a bomber offensive against Italian targets, all of which could be reached from present Allied bases.[89]

Or what about the Aegean and the Balkans, the old favourites of the Great War 'easterners' like Lloyd George and Churchill, and taken up again by Churchill in 1941? This was the choice of GHQ, Middle East, although old hankerings stirred in Churchill too. An attack on the Dodecanese might bring in Turkey, might it not, and so open the way for a major offensive thrust via Greece into the Balkans. Or the occupation of southern Italy might itself serve as the preliminary to amphibious landings in the Balkans directly across the Adriatic.

Common to all this strategic picking and choosing was the conviction, just as with 'Torch' and 'Husky', that Allied forces could not simply be left idle until the launching of a cross-Channel invasion a year ahead; and hence in the present situation should be freshly employed as soon as possible after 'Husky' in further Mediterranean operations. In view of Soviet Russia's struggle with some 200 German divisions, the political and moral pressure on the Western Allies to campaign actively and on the largest possible scale somewhere during the current year was certainly enormous, perhaps irresistible; another case of waging war as one politically must, rather than militarily ought.

Yet the drawback with all these ample gestures over the map of southern Europe was that they depended for fulfilment on long-distance sea communications and consequently major investments in assault and merchant shipping. The participants in these British discussions were more aware of this problem now than they had been when advocating 'Husky' at Casablanca. But they were quite happy that this shipping should be found at the expense of 'Bolero' (the movement of US forces across the Atlantic to Britain in preparation for the invasion of France). A paper drafted by General Ismay in the *Queen Mary* pronounced that the disadvantage of taking shipping from 'Bolero' 'will be greatly outweighed by the fact that successful Mediterranean operations, and still more the elimination of Italy, will ease the task confronting an army landing in Europe from the United Kingdom'.[90] The British delegation as a whole endorsed this. As the Prime Minister wrote in his cabin while the 81,000-ton bulk of the *Queen Mary* thrust its way towards the new world, 'We want them to agree to the exploitation of "Husky" and the attack on the underbelly taking priority of the build-up for "Bolero", as it must necessarily do for the execution of "Round-up".'[91] Brooke, for his part, although recognising that the pursuit of Mediterranean strategy would mean taking shipping from the Pacific theatre or 'Bolero', reckoned that 'Bolero' 'could afford a cut'.[92] Portal even went so far as to suggest that the British delegation should seek an agreement that the requirements of Britain's import programme and of the Mediterranean should be 'sacrosanct', after which it might be discussed whether 'Bolero' or the Pacific should suffer the necessary cuts.[93]

In total contradiction to all this renewed British enthusiasm for 'blue water' strategy General Marshall came to the Washington Conference even more strongly determined than at Casablanca to put a stop to the ever deeper slither into the mire of peripheral warfare in the Mediterranean at the expense of 'Roundup' – the direct cross-Channel invasion and the defeat in battle of the main German Army in the West. Already by the beginning of May 1943 he had seen the commitment of US forces to the Mediterranean rise to 388,000 men and 37 Combat Air Groups, while US forces in the United Kingdom had sunk from 168,000 at the beginning of the previous November to only 59,000.[94] Marshall wondered whether a cross-Channel invasion would ever be possible if such a haemorrhage continued; certainly he could not conceive how the grand ideas entertained by the British about the Mediterranean in 1943 could be reconciled with 'Roundup' in 1944.

The United States Joint Chief of Staff's policy position for the conference (endorsed by the President) therefore ruled out further operations in the Mediterranean after Sicily, except such limited ones as would enable Allied forces there to be actually reduced. It totally ruled out too adventures in the Aegean, leaving the British to have a go on their own if they were so minded. As the Joint Chiefs roundly briefed themselves for the conference:

> . . . in the event the British insisted on Mediterranean commitments that in American opinion would jeopardise the early defeat of Germany and the ultimate defeat of Japan the U.S. representatives were to inform the British that the United States might be compelled to revise its basic strategy and extend its operations and commitments in the Pacific.[95]

In furtherance of these aims, the Joint Chiefs submitted a memorandum to the British Chiefs of Staff which uncompromisingly laid down:

> . . . from our standpoint the concept of defeating Germany first involves making a determined attack against Germany on the Continent at the earliest practical date; we consider that all proposed operations in Europe should be judged primarily on the basis of their contribution to that end . . . It is the opinion of the United States Chiefs of Staff that a cross-Channel invasion of Europe is necessary to an early conclusion of the war with Germany . . .[96]

There resulted a dourly fought encounter-battle between the US Joint Chiefs of Staff and the British Chiefs of Staff and their opposed philosophies of war. The issuc turned on guesstimates as to whether further Mediterranean operations in 1943 such as the invasion of Italy would weaken German forces available to meet a cross-Channel invasion in 1944 more than it would weaken the Allied forces (including assault shipping) available to launch that invasion. Marshall, for example, reckoned that every further Mediterranean operation would reduce the number of landing craft for 'Roundup' by 1,000.[97]

But there was also a clash between the Americans' Germanic preference for a clear 'overall strategic concept' and British opportunism. Thus Brooke threw in the thought that a collapse of Mussolini's régime or an invitation to the Allies by some other Italian political party to enter Italy could present thc Allies 'with a decision as to what action was necessary to take advantage of this situation'.[98] But Marshall in response wondered whether the British were underestimating the likely strength of a German defence of Italy, and he uttered a prophetic warning:

> In this very connection it must be remembered that in North Africa a relatively small German force had produced a serious factor of delay to our operations. A German decision to support Italy might make intended operations extremely difficult and time-consuming.[99]

There finally emerged from this collision of minds in Washington yet another fudge. On the one hand it was agreed by the Combined Chiefs of Staff in their final report to the President and the Prime Minister

> That forces and equipment shall be established in the United Kingdom with the object of mounting an operation with target date 1st May, 1944, to secure a lodgement on the Continent from which further offensive operations can be carried out.[100]

The required forces were put at nine assault divisions and twenty follow-up divisions.

But on the other hand, the Combined Chiefs of Staff also resolved:

> That the Allied Commander-in-Chief, North Africa, will be instructed, as a matter of urgency, to plan such operations in exploitation of 'Husky' as are best calculated to eliminate Italy from the War and to contain the maximum number of German forces. Which of the various specific operations should be adopted, and thereafter mounted, is a decision which will be reserved to the Combined Chiefs of Staff. The Allied Commander-in-Chief in North Africa may use for his operations all those forces available in the Mediterranean area except for four American and three British divisions which will be held in readiness from the 1st November onwards for withdrawal to take part in operations from the United Kingdom, provided that the naval vessels required will be approved by the Combined Chiefs of Staff when the plans are submitted. The additional air forces provided on a temporary basis for 'Husky' will not be considered available.[101]

In other words, a continuation of 'blue water' strategy but supposedly under tight rein. Even so, Brooke essentially got his way, for the Mediterranean theatre was to be left with 27 divisions (virtually equal to those at present allotted to 'Roundup' in 1944) and 3,648 aircraft.[102] This figure of 27 Allied divisions may be compared with a British Joint Planners' estimate this same month that 24 German divisions would have to be diverted from other fronts for the defence of Italy and the Balkans in the event of Italian defection from the Axis.[103]

Marshall had to draw what comfort he could from the 'Trident' conference's other decision to instruct COSSAC – the Chief of Staff to the Supreme Allied Commander designate, Lieutenant-General Sir Frederick Morgan – to prepare by 1 August 1943 an outline plan for a cross-Channel invasion with the target date of 1 May 1944.

Italy was therefore to be knocked out of the war. But the 'Trident' Conference left it to Eisenhower and his colleagues to recommend to the Combined Chiefs of Staff the appropriate means, whether direct invasion or other. The Prime Minister himself, flying to Algiers immediately after 'Trident' to confer with Marshall, Eisenhower, Alexander, Cunningham and Tedder, was 'determined to obtain before leaving Africa a decision to invade Italy should Sicily be taken'.[104] Eisenhower, for his part, advocated setting up two planning staffs, one to consider the problems of invading Sardinia, the other of the Italian mainland; a final decision to be deferred until after Sicily had fallen into Allied hands and the quality of German opposition could be gauged. This proposal was backed by Marshall and adopted by the conference. Nevertheless Churchill put in a last emotional plea in favour of invading Italy itself and seizing Rome: 'the alternative between Southern Italy and Sardinia,' he proclaimed, 'involved the difference between a glorious campaign and a mere convenience.'[105] At this Marshall raised the sordid question of shipping lifts and shipping shortages. But Churchill had his answer: he would, he averred, cut the rations of the British people in order to provide the ships.[106]

The arguments as to the best means of laying Italy low rumbled on through July, Churchill's strategic visions being given new wing by the success of the Allied landings in Sicily. He kept up relentless pressure on his own Chiefs of Staff and on Eisenhower in favour of far-reaching operations in Italy with Rome 'as the bull's eye'. Brushing aside American concerns about availability of landing craft in the context of global strategy, he asked on 13 July '. . . why we should crawl up the leg like a harvest-bug from the ankle upwards? Let us rather strike at the knees . . .'[107] He instructed the British Joint Planners immediately to 'prepare the best scheme possible for landing on the Italian west coast with the objective the port of Naples and the march on Rome . . . It would seem that two or three good divisions could take Naples and produce decisive results . . .'[108]

Here was the first sketch of what became 'Operation Avalanche', the Allied landings in the Gulf of Salerno. Churchill was resolved that in any event, as he wrote to Field-Marshal Smuts on 15 July 1943, he would 'in no circumstances allow the powerful British and British-controlled armies in the Mediterranean to stand idle . . .'[109]

His imagination flew even further: 'Not only must we take Rome and march as far north as possible in Italy, but with our right hand must give succour to the Balkan patriots . . . I shall go to all lengths to procure the agreement of our Allies. If not, we have ample forces to act by ourselves.'[110] Four days later visions of marching on Vienna from northern Italy blazed before him, relegating 'Overlord' (as 'Roundup' had now been re-named) to the shadows.[111]

In any case Marshall, as well as Eisenhower, had by this time become convinced by the collapse of Italian resistance in Sicily that mainland Italy and not Sardinia should indeed be the next Allied objective; and on 18 July Eisenhower's formal recommendation to this effect was promptly approved by the two governments (hence Churchill's Napoleonic vision next day of a march on Vienna).

So by the familiar process of the 'push' of existing commitment (coupled with the pressing political need to support Soviet Russia during the current year) and the 'pull' of the next enticing prospect, the Allies finally opted for an offensive campaign in the perfect defensive terrain of Italy; another campaign to be opened by large-scale seaborne landings protected by major Allied naval task forces and thereafter nourished by ships in slow procession from Britain and the United States and back again.

Yet in their pertinacious and eventually successful advocacy of an invasion of Italy Churchill and Brooke had astonishingly ignored one key factor – German fighting prowess on land. They had reckoned without such formidable opponents as the 1st Parachute Division and the 14th Panzer Corps (already encountered in Sicily), or such redoubtable leaders as General von Senger und Etterlin, future defender of Cassino, and Field-Marshal 'Smiling Albert' Kesselring who, as Commander-in-Chief, South, and later of Army Group C, would prove himself a grandmaster of the strategic defensive. The capture of Rome, let alone the march on Vienna, might be somewhat delayed.

22

'Some Underbelly; Some Softest Part': The Mediterranean, 1943–1945

By the time this final decision to undertake a campaign in Italy had been taken, the implications in terms of resources had already begun to sink in. Eisenhower, in a signal to the COS and Combined COS on 30 June outlining various proposals for invading Sardinia or landing on both sides of the toe of Italy, had asked for more long-range fighters to cover the beaches; and also asked to retain thirteen American combat loaders (landing ships) and eighteen American destroyers due to depart from the theatre.[1] Three weeks later the Admiralty signalled the Chief of Naval Operations to request that the US carrier *Ranger* be lent to the Home Fleet because the Home Fleet carrier, HMS *Illustrious*, had to be sent to the Mediterranean to replace the damaged *Indomitable*. The Admiralty added that it was proposing to send out four escort carriers for the forthcoming invasion of Italy, leaving only one in the Atlantic on convoy duties – a risk that it reckoned it could now accept because of Dönitz's withdrawal of his U-boats.

Because the British COS doubted whether Eisenhower would have enough assault shipping, they now urged their American colleagues to agree that, for the time being, none should leave the Mediterranean for South-East Asia as had been decided at the 'Trident' Conference; and on 20 July the Admiralty unilaterally ordered Cunningham not to allow any shipping to leave the theatre except such as was needed for Atlantic convoys. Cunningham, conscious of his awkward position as an Allied commander, at first asked the Combined Chiefs of Staff to issue a confirming order to Admiral Hewitt but then, on 23 July, gave the order himself in accordance with his instructions from the Admiralty.[2] Meanwhile the Combined Chiefs of Staff had replied to Eisenhower's requests, telling him that he was to get no more long-range fighters even as a temporary loan, because they were needed in the United Kingdom for the bomber offensive. Nevertheless, they consented to eighteen US destroyers remaining in the Mediterranean and up to three cruisers, but reiterated that fifteen destroyers would have to leave the theatre by 31 July and another fifteen by 12 August. They also informed Eisenhower that he could retain thirteen American combat loaders, and that a total of 90 cargo ships would be allotted to support the landings. A convoy carrying extra troops asked for by Eisenhower would sail in late August.

Thus the agreement to limit resources committed to the Mediterranean, which Marshall had stitched up (as he had hoped) in Washington, was already beginning to unravel. The disputes between London and Washington began all over again, but this time not just as an intellectual debate as to the best grand strategy, but over the real material questions of quantities of shipping and troops and aircraft needed for the strategy chosen. On 22 July the COS signalled the British Joint Staff Mission in Washington that Eisenhower would need an extra 40 stores ships, as well as retaining some amphibious craft at present due to leave the Mediterranean. They recommended that he be instructed to plan the landing on the west coast of Italy on the basis that all necessary resources *would* be provided, and that he should report as soon as possible on just what resources he would require. The COS again urged the American Joint Chiefs to agree that in the meantime all movement of shipping out of the theatre be halted.

But the Joint Chiefs would have none of it. They insisted that Eisenhower must plan his landings on the basis of resources at present allocated, otherwise operations elsewhere would be prejudiced. General Arnold, Chief of Staff of the US Army Air Force, wanted the three heavy bomber groups lent to Eisenhower for 'Husky' to be returned to the United Kingdom. He did not reckon that to eliminate Italy would directly threaten Germany, and he did not consider Italian airbases would be of much help to the bomber offensive; and he thought that Eisenhower's demands for resources could compromise 'Overlord' in 1944. Arnold, King and Marshall were all agreed therefore that Eisenhower's requests were excessive, indeed would prejudice the seaborne landings in Burma (now 'Bullfrog') also decided on at the 'Trident' Washington Conference; and in this they were to be proved right enough, for 'Bullfrog' was not merely delayed until 1944 but even into 1945. In short, the Americans were prepared to take a risk over the invasion of Italy on the grounds that Italy might soon collapse, while the British, remembering such débâcles as Gallipoli, wished to be well insured against failure.

Nevertheless, the US Joint Chiefs were not to be budged further, even though the British COS played their well-worn record that 'it would be a profound mistake to allow anyone or anything, which General Eisenhower might need, to move from the Mediterranean area until we know . . . his precise requirements for whatever operation might be decided upon'.[3] And the First Sea Lord, in repeating this signal to the Commander-in-Chief, Mediterranean, added: 'In view of the effect this proposal will have on "Overlord" and "Bullfrog" there may be objections from Washington but meanwhile you should hold everybody and everything you think may be required for "Priceless" [the invasion of Italy] whatever form it may take.'[4]

No wonder, then, that an angry Marshall was reported by the British Joint Staff Mission as having expressed disquiet lest the initial landing near Naples 'might well be the first step to similar demands as success after success opened further possibilities'.[5]

From the Allied Mediterranean command itself the pleas to retain ships and aircraft or even be sent more of them still mounted. Eisenhower, like his colleagues, was worried about the weakness of the land-based air cover to be provided over the beaches. On 28 July he asked for four groups of B-17 'Flying Fortress' heavy bombers to be lent by the 8th Army Air Force in Britain in order to smash the Luftwaffe on its airfields. But the request was turned down by the COS and JCS on the score that it would enfeeble the bomber offensive against Germany, and that in any case it would take a month to transfer the 4,000 groundcrew. They similarly turned down a later proposal by Eisenhower on 10 August that he be allowed to keep the three B-24 Liberator groups lent to him for 'Husky'.

Meanwhile the Admiralty had acceded to Cunningham's request for escort carriers in order to provide seaborne air cover over the landing areas, signalling him on 25 July that as well as the fleet carrier *Illustrious* for Force H, the American-built ex-United States Navy escort carriers *Attacker*, *Battler*, *Hunter* and *Stalker* (11,420 tons displacement; 17 knots; 18 aircraft)[6] were sailing for the Mediterranean. As Cunningham explained to the First Sea Lord:

> I am most unwilling to use the escort carriers for AVALANCHE but I made Tedder produce an estimate of the fighters he could maintain over the assault and found it was only nine. This miserable figure made it essential that ship-based fighters should be used . . . Although it would appear natural that they should form part of the assault force I am not prepared to put them under Hewitt's command. As the U.S.A. troops are in the majority he has been nominated task force commander.
>
> I intend to form the escort carriers, 3 DIDO class cruisers and 8–10 Hunts, if I can collect them, into one force with the job of fighter support on the beaches. Unless you have any objections I propose to make Vian hoist his flag in command of this force . . .[7]

At Cunningham's urging the Admiralty dropped a proposal that he should return one of his only two modern battleships (*Howe* and *King George V*) in a swap with the old *Malaya*, which Cunningham argued would only prove a liability. The Admiralty also acceded to his request that the cruisers *Scylla* and *Charybdis* be sent out as replacements for the *Cleopatra* and *Newfoundland*, damaged in Sicilian waters.[8] It can be seen that the First Sea Lord and the naval staff were doing their best to meet Cunningham's wishes over naval forces for 'Avalanche'. But, after all, this was Britain's own cherished 'blue water' project, and it was being driven by the full power of the Prime Minister's enthusiasm.

On 13 August there opened yet another of the 1943 summit conferences ('Quadrant'), this time in Quebec; a fresh opportunity for General Marshall and his fellow American Joint Chiefs of Staff to restitch the limits on resources for the Mediterranean. In consequence the Combined Chiefs of Staff proceeded to revoke the British stand-still order on the movement of assault shipping from that theatre to South-East Asia. They ordered Eisenhower *not* to detain the ten landing ships (tank) due to leave Oran for India. Such decisions caused further anguish in Malta and Algiers. Cunningham in particular remained uncharacteristically gloomy, signalling the Admiralty on 29 August that, in his view, the Combined Chiefs were being altogether too sanguine about the prospects for 'Avalanche'. Had they realised how difficult the operation would be? 'I believe that we can and shall succeed but only if we go flat out. If we whittle away our resources now to build up "Overlord" our chances of success will be greatly reduced, and if "Avalanche" fails "Overlord" may be stillborn.'[9]

He particularly protested at the removal of the three groups of B-24 heavy bombers (to be followed by three Wellington squadrons on 15 September, six days after D-Day of 'Avalanche'), stressing that 'Avalanche' depended on the Allies being able to pass a mass of ships and craft right up to an enemy coast on a moonlit night, with only carrier-borne fighters for protection against the Luftwaffe. This, he remarked, was a calculated risk taken on the assumption that the Luftwaffe would have been beaten into impotence, but the removal of powerful bomber forces rendered this assumption doubtful.[10]

Cunningham was also worried about the capacity of his landing craft lift, in this case, in regard to shuttling supplies and reinforcements to the armies. He pointed out to the Admiralty that even if the Allies held every port in Italy south of Naples, it would only be possible to build up to twelve divisions by December, as against the elements of seventeen German divisions at present on Italian soil. The Admiralty having forwarded this signal on to Churchill in Quebec, the First Sea Lord signalled Cunningham the answers on 31 August: while the Premier agreed that 'nothing should be removed which is necessary for victory in "Avalanche" ', it had been decided that the three B-24 groups (now in any case back in the United Kingdom) would not be made available, although the Wellingtons might be retained after 15 September if need be. But Cunningham was given discretion to retain landing craft due for withdrawal 'if this was considered essential'.[11]

Just two days before the first assault convoy was due to sail for the 'Avalanche' beaches even Marshall, that stern refuser of further resources for the Mediterranean, began to have anxious second thoughts and offered Eisenhower extra shipping. However, Eisenhower's Deputy Chief of Staff replied that the problem in speeding the build-up of Allied armies lay in port capacities rather than shipping – not Cunningham's view. On the same day the First Sea Lord (now in America) signalled the Vice-Chief of Naval Staff in London to ask if he was satisfied that the Commander-in-Chief, Mediterranean, was getting all he needed, even at the expense of other theatres.

This tug-of-war prolonged to the last minute serves to illustrate afresh the essential paradox of maritime warfare waged against a continental foe. On the one hand Eisenhower and Cunningham were perfectly justified in their calculations of the resources of all kinds needed to ensure success in a risky, opposed, large-scale amphibious operation virtually beyond the range of Allied land-based airpower; yet on the other hand the size of the total Allied commitment to the coming campaign in southern Italy was out of all proportion to the eight German divisions which according to Sigint were at present deployed in that region – two panzer, four panzer-grenadier and two parachute.[12] For the Combined Chiefs of Staff had allotted Eisenhower a total of 27 divisions (excluding seven due for return to the United Kingdom at the end of November in preparation for

'Overlord', and two British divisions earmarked for Turkey if required). The Allied Mediterranean air forces would (according to a Combined Chiefs' estimate in May) amount to 242 heavy bombers, 519 medium bombers, 296 light or dive-bombers, 2,012 fighters and 576 transport and Army Cooperation aircraft;[13] a vast margin of numerical superiority over the dwindling Luftwaffe in the Mediterranean. To deal with the Italian Navy in its present moral and professional decrepitude, the British Mediterranean Fleet alone would comprise six capital ships, two fleet carriers, five light carriers, ten cruisers, six anti-aircraft ships and cruisers, 27 fleet destroyers, 44 escorts of all kinds, 24 submarines, two headquarters ships, twelve landing ships (infantry), and well over 300 ancillary vessels and craft from minesweepers and tugs to repair and depot ships.[14] And there has also to be weighed in the balance the merchant shipping which would provide the essential foundation of a protracted campaign – no fewer than 3½ million deadweight tons or 900 ships over the remaining months of 1943, according to Ministry of Transport estimates in August.[15]

The uncertainties and disputes over resources hardly helped the Allied staffs in trying to work out in exact detail the mustering and launching of another complex 'triphibious' operation; and neither did the short span of time available. It was only seven weeks before the eventual D-Day for 'Avalanche' that Eisenhower received instructions to consider Naples as his objective, and was first told that an invasion of Italy was to follow immediately after the fall of Sicily rather than in November or even early in 1944.[16] The date of 9 September was only confirmed as D-Day for a landing on the Italian west coast at a conference between Eisenhower and his commanders-in-chief on 17 August. Since 17 August happened also to be the day that Patton's entry into Messina brought the Sicilian campaign to an end, only now could the Allied commanders and staffs free themselves from involvement in current operations and so wholly concentrate on 'Avalanche' and 'Operation Baytown' (a crossing of the Straits of Messina into the toe of Italy by the 8th Army). In any event, it was only on 19 August that 'Avalanche' took priority with the planners over 'Buttress', a now discarded project for landing on the west coast of the toe of Italy. From the very beginning the planning of 'Avalanche' therefore became a frenzied scramble.

Yet at least it looked as if the Italian Navy, Army and Air Force would be out of the fight. Already secret negotiations for Italy's surrender, clandestine meetings, were in progress between the Allies and the Italian government that had replaced Mussolini. It proved a story of remarkable muddle, sometimes farce, which dragged on until 3 September (final D-Day for 'Baytown'), when the Italians signed an instrument of unconditional surrender, to come into effect on 8 September, the night before 'Avalanche'. Here then was another uncertainty to plague the planners in the meantime.[17]

Their tasks were rendered all the harder because (just as in the case of 'Husky'), commanders, headquarters, military formations and assault shipping lay scattered at various points round the Mediterranean. Eisenhower was in Algiers and, in any case, deeply entangled in the clandestine negotiations with the new Italian government; Cunningham was in Malta; Alexander (Deputy Supreme Commander, and army group commander, Allied 15th Army Group, comprising the American 5th and the British 8th Armies) was in Syracuse; Tedder (Allied Air Commander-in-Chief) was in Tunis; Admiral Hewitt (Allied Naval Commander, Western Task Force) was at first at sea off Sicily, then in Malta and finally Algiers. General Mark Clark (commanding the 5th Army, and Ground Force Commander, 'Avalanche') was at Mostaghanem in Algeria, while Montgomery was in the field in Sicily. Commodore Oliver (Naval Commander, Northern Attack Force, 'Avalanche') was in Algiers, while his military opposite number (Horrocks; later McCreery) was in Tripoli.

It all made for severe strain on a signals net already stretched by the Sicilian campaign – as well as for intense competition for aircraft seats. As Cunningham confided to the First Sea Lord on 5 August:

> I travel madly between Malta and Algiers . . . There is a suggestion in the wind that when taken A.F.H.Q. [Allied Forces Headquarters] should move to Naples and I think this will solve the problem. Meanwhile continual air travel, in spite of the irritating difficulties and delays that appear to be inseparable from getting a plane to take you or your staff, appears to be the best we can do.[18]

The limited capacity of available ports in relation to the mass of vessels to be brought together for 'Avalanche' meant that the preliminary mustering of shipping and their loads had to be dispersed over every usable harbour on the North African coast from Oran to Alexandria – another conundrum for the staffs to solve.[19] Fortunate indeed by comparison are the commander and staff planning a classic land offensive, all tidily together in a single headquarters, and with subordinate formation commanders only a brief journey away by air, road or rail.

Because of the pressure of time, naval planning for 'Avalanche' had to proceed simultaneously at three different levels of command –

Allied Force Headquarters, Naval Commander, Western Task Force (Admiral K. Hewitt), and under him, the Naval Commanders, Northern Attack Force (Commodore G. N. Oliver, RN) and Southern Attack Force (Rear Admiral John Hall, USN). In Commodore Oliver's words, 'Orders were coming in from three authorities more rapidly than they could be disseminated, and, due to hurried and simultaneous production amendments and addenda kept pouring in up to the last moment . . . a most undesirable, but in the circumstances, unavoidable state of affairs.'[20]

It added to the naval staff's problems that military requirements were frequently altered, upsetting for example the tactical stowage that had been painstakingly worked out in relation to the exactly measured dimensions of vessels' internal spaces. Oliver put these alterations down to the 'inability of the Army Command to reach a final decision as to what troops should be employed in the operation and how they should be distributed between the two Task Forces . . .'[21] On 24 August General Clark made his own helpful contribution by advancing H-Hour by 30 minutes, so compelling changes to the navies' sailing and routing schedules.

It is hardly surprising that personal relations between commanders could become somewhat strained, causing more dry bearings in an already hot-running staff machine. In the case of D-Day for 'Baytown', the 8th Army's crossing of the Straits of Messina, Montgomery brought on a blazing row between himself and Cunningham by exercise of his habit of instant lying if convenient. When Eisenhower asked at a conference on 23 August 1943, why D-Day for Baytown could not be advanced to 1 September, Montgomery answered that the Navy refused to carry out the operation until 4–5 September. Montgomery also asserted that the Navy was unwilling to undertake the operation at night. As Cunningham wrote furiously to Montgomery's superior, General Alexander, three days later:

> So serious did it appear to me that I decided . . . to fly to Sicily at once as the only means of clearing up the situation. I found that, not only were the statements incorrect, but that General Montgomery had at no time been in direct touch with the Senior Naval Officer of the Expedition [Rear-Admiral R. McGrigor] and that his statements were, in fact, completely unfounded . . .[22]

Cunningham discovered that McGrigor had in fact been given the date of 4–5 September by the responsible corps commander, Lieutenant-General Dempsey, although McGrigor was instead working to the earlier date of the 3rd as decided in a staff conference (and confirmed by a signal from Alexander on 20 August). Cunningham now instructed McGrigor to advance the date to 2/3 September in accordance with Eisenhower's known wish. But, as Cunningham pointed out to Alexander, 'Had I or Rear-Admiral McGrigor been made aware some days previously that the Army could be ready on 1st September I have no doubt another valuable day could have been saved.'[23] And he also pointed out that while McGrigor had certainly told Dempsey that there were naval disadvantages in a night operation, McGrigor had also said that the final decision must rest with the Army: '. . . again a complete contradiction to General Montgomery's statement that the Navy insisted on a day assault.'[24]

While Montgomery's latest victims fumed and wasted time, the staffs toiled on with their piles of paper; and sailors, soldiers and local labour in djellaba or galabieh humped stores into ships under the keen eyes of the quartermasters, and drivers manoeuvred trucks and armour into the narrow decks of landing craft (tank). The naval planners themselves derived great help from the system of Mediterranean Naval Planning Memoranda, which were promulgated regularly by the Commander-in-Chief. As he wrote later, 'It is no exaggeration to say that without this system, these subordinate commanders could never have produced their own orders in time for the operation . . .'[25] Even so, the orders proved so voluminous, the amendments and annexes so numerous that, according to Oliver, it was only 'by superhuman efforts of all concerned and under conditions in which I hope a combined operation will never again have to be concerted', that the various commands managed to issue their final orders by 29 August.[26]

Many discrepancies and gaps still remained. Only a fortnight before D-Day for 'Avalanche' Intelligence revealed a probable enemy minefield in the assault area,[27] but in order to avoid compromising the source of the information the task forces were not told until the last minute. So the brain-weary staffs had to set to and revise the intricate landing craft schedules because the lowering points for the assault waves now had to be nine miles off shore for the British landing ships (infantry) and twelve miles for the American combat loaders. And this was not the only last-minute development demanding that schedules be rejigged. It turned out that there would be a larger number of landing craft available than expected, both because of successful repair work and because losses in 'Baytown' (launched on 3 September) were less than expected, so enabling more craft to be transferred to 'Avalanche'. No wonder Cunningham's own set of orders bears innumerable annotations; no wonder Rear Admiral Hall of the United

States Navy (Commander, Southern Attack Force) was to write in his report that even when he entered the assault area in the evening of 8 September, he still did not know the exact number of landing craft under his orders, 'the designation of the individual craft assigned, or the designation of all the units embarked therein'.[28]

On 30 August Eisenhower submitted the overall 'Avalanche' plan for approval to the Combined Chiefs of Staff and COS. Of three possible landing areas, Eisenhower and his colleagues ruled out the coast north of Naples because it lay beyond the range of land-based Spitfires and in any case the beaches were poor; and they ruled out the Bay of Naples itself because of its powerful coastal defences. Instead they selected the Gulf of Salerno, the nearest point to Naples that could be covered by fighters from Sicilian airfields, and blessed with superb beaches conveniently weak in fixed defences. Its sole disadvantage lay in that Naples, the Allies' strategic objective, lay 30 miles distant to the north on the far side of a mountain bottleneck.

According to the air plan the beaches were to be covered on D-Day by 36 land-based fighters at one time, flown in rotation by three groups of American Lightnings, one group of American Spitfires and eighteen squadrons of Royal Air Force Spitfires – a great improvement on Tedder's original offer of only nine aircraft aloft at any one time. The light aircraft-repair carrier HMS *Unicorn* (14,750 tons displacement; 24 knots; 35 aircraft)[29] and the four escort carriers of Force V (Rear-Admiral Vian, with his flag in the cruiser *Euryalus*) would keep another 22 fighters over the beaches on D-Day. However, the air plan critically depended on the soldiers capturing Montecorvino airfield, less than two miles from the sea, on the first day so that Spitfires could be flown in.

With regard to ground forces, Eisenhower estimated on the basis of Sigint that on D-Day the Allies would meet one panzer division and two to five parachute battalions; that by D + 5 enemy strength would rise to two and a half panzer divisions, one and a half motorised (panzer-grenadier) divisions and one parachute division; and by D + 22 by another panzer division, and half a motorised.[30] By the latter date Allied forces ashore would amount to one armoured division, three tank battalions, one airborne division and four infantry divisions. This was by no means a comforting balance, even allowing for the 8th Army coming up overland to the rescue from Messina.

The British return to the mainland of Europe after two and a half years, and this time to stay, began at 0430 on 3 September 1943 with a bombardment by massed artillery of the 8th Army across the Straits of Messina, augmented by the fire of fifteen warships on Reggio di Calabria at the southern end of the Straits and by strikes inland by heavy bombers. This impressive Montgomeryian overture was followed by anti-climax when British and Canadian soldiers, crossing the Straits in some 300 landing craft, found the far shore devoid of enemy, for the German forces had prudently withdrawn two days previously. In the next fortnight cunningly located demolition of bridges and the blowing of precipitous roads in the wild mountain country of Calabria effectively put the brake on the 8th Army, which now needed mules and pack artillery rather than masses of motor transport dependent on copious fuel supplies. On 8 September, when his advanced guard had got as far as the narrow neck of land where the toe of Italy joins the instep, Montgomery halted his army in order to bring up stores and fuel and put his line of communication in order.

On the same day, at Cunningham's initiative, the cruisers USS *Boise* and HMSs *Aurora*, *Penelope*, *Sirius* and *Dido*, and the fast minelayer *Abdiel* put to sea from Bizerta loaded with troops of the British 1st Airborne Division. They rendezvoused at sea with the battleships *Howe* (flying the flag of Vice-Admiral Arthur Power) and *King George V* from Malta, and on 9 September entered Taranto harbour and put the soldiers ashore to occupy the port and city. Sadly the *Abdiel* struck a mine and sank in a few minutes, with heavy loss of life.

While Power's squadron was steaming towards the 'instep' of Italy on 8 September, the 'Avalanche' convoys were approaching the 'knee', in Churchill's word – the Gulf of Salerno.[31] The first convoy, consisting mainly of landing craft (tank), had left Tripoli for the Sicilian port of Termini on the 3rd, and by dusk of the 8th all the assault convoys had been staged through Sicilian ports and refuelled as necessary. Over a calm sea under a brilliant moon the sprawl of shipping headed northwards like some giant regatta towards the waiting folbots and beacon submarines off shore. In the afternoon of 7 September Force H had steamed out of Grand Harbour, Valletta, in two divisions – *Nelson*, *Rodney* and *Illustrious*, escorted by the 4th and 24th Destroyer Flotillas; and *Warspite* (wearing the flag of Rear-Admiral A. W. de la T. Bissett), *Valiant* and *Formidable* – to take up its role of protecting Vian's Force V, the five light carriers which were to fly air cover over the beaches. During the night of 8–9 September Force V steamed north through the Straits of Messina and, as Vian remarked in his report later, 'H.M. Ships *Scylla* and *Charybdis* made a bowing acquaintance with their famous forbears.' Meanwhile the battleships and destroyers of Force H and night fighters flown by *Formidable* and *Illustrious* beat off an attack by 30 German torpedo-bombers; and by daylight on the 9th fighters from *Illustrious* and *Formidable* were circling high above Force V.

Meanwhile a swarm of British, American and Dutch small ships and craft from Palermo had been shelling and raiding islands off Naples and the Gulf of Gaeta (north of Naples) in order to deceive the enemy about the location of the Allied landing – but without success.[32] As Ultra decrypts of the Luftwaffe Enigma traffic had revealed, the German command had for some time been expecting the Allies to land near Naples; and at 2200 on the 8th it signalled '*Orkan*' ('Hurricane'), the codeword to alert its forces to repel a landing next day in the Naples–Salerno area (a signal also quickly decrypted by Ultra). This time the Anglo-American assault waves would not come ashore against little or no opposition, but would run into the 16th Panzer Division.

For while the Allies had been bumbling away at their negotiations for Italy's surrender, and dickering with a project for landing the US 82nd Airborne Division to seize Rome, Hitler and the OKW had prepared complete contingency plans to deal with Italy's likely defection and to defend Italian territory. When in August Rommel, now C-in-C of Army Group B in northern Italy, had recommended that Italy south of the River Po should be abandoned, Kesselring had successfully convinced Hitler that instead battle could and should be given to the Allies south of Rome. Kesselring's plan was that such formations as he had at hand in southern Italy should delay the Allies for as long as possible, while his engineers surveyed and constructed a formidable defence in depth (to be called the *Gustavstellung* or Gustav Line) sited in ideal mountainous country across the narrowest point of the waist of Italy, from Gaeta to the Adriatic. In parallel Hitler and the OKW had perfected arrangements for disarming the Italian forces both in Italy and Greece and the Balkans, should Badoglio's government 'treacherously' surrender to the Allies.

'Operation Axis' (as this plan was codenamed) was precipitated in the event by an ill-judged radio broadcast by Eisenhower from Algiers on 8 September announcing that Italy was surrendering. The OKW thereupon issued the prearranged signal 'Bring in the harvest' to all German units, and the Wehrmacht pounced on the Italian armed forces with all the old ruthless speed and boldness of 1940. Within two days it had disarmed them all on pain of being shot, and had occupied Rome. Only the Italian Fleet escaped, its main body sailing from La Spezia at 0300 on the 9th for a rendezvous off Tunisia with Rear-Admiral A. W. de la T. Bissett's battle squadron detached from

Force H (*Warspite*, *Valiant*, and five British, one French and one Greek destroyer; the old Allies). The Italian Fleet was then to be escorted into Grand Harbour, Valletta, to surrender. But events did not go entirely according to expectation.

At about 1600 on 9 September the Italian Fleet, consisting of the battleships *Roma*, *Vittorio Veneto* and *Italia* (formerly the *Littorio*), six cruisers and eight destroyers under the command of Admiral Bergamini (flying his flag in the *Roma*) was attacked west of the channel between Corsica and Sardinia by eleven Dornier Do-17 bombers of a special unit from an airfield in southern France. Mistaking them for Allied aircraft the Italians failed to fire on them. The attack marked the opening of a new era in the technology of naval warfare, for the Do-17s were equipped with the first ever air-to-sea guided missile – the free-falling FX-1400 radio-controlled armour-piercing bomb filled with 1,400 pounds of high explosive, released at heights of between 12,000 and 19,000 feet, and attaining a terminal velocity of 800 feet per second.[33] The FX-1400 had already been tried experimentally but unsuccessfully against Allied ships in Malta and off Sicily. Thanks to Ultra, however, neither its existence nor the enemy's intention to use it in current operations was a secret to the Allies.[34] Now a single FX-1400 smashed its way deep into Bergamini's flagship, the 41,000 ton *Roma*, blowing it up in a storm of flame with the loss of nearly all hands, including Bergamini himself.

At 0600 next morning the surviving Italian ships (*Italia* too was damaged by an FX-1400) made their rendezvous with Admiral Bissett's squadron. Cunningham was there with Eisenhower to witness this consummation of his outstanding leadership of the Mediterranean Fleet since 1940, having come out from Bizerta for the occasion in the destroyer *Hambledon*. The meeting of the two fleets was resonant with historical echoes; an occasion when even Englishmen might display their feelings. At the head of the British line steamed Cunningham's old flagship *Warspite* – 'in her appointed station', as Cunningham signalled her with pride and pleasure – the veteran not only of the victories over the Italian battlefleet at Cape Spartivento in 1940 and Cape Matapan in 1941, but also of the Battle of Jutland. And both *Warspite* and *Valiant* had been at sea that grey November day in 1918 when Beatty's Grand Fleet had conducted the Imperial German High Seas Fleet into internment. Now it was an Italian flagship, the cruiser *Eugenio di Savoia* (flying the flag of Admiral Romeo Oliva, who had taken the place of Bergamini) which led the line of a vanquished fleet astern of the same great battleships flying the White Ensign at the truck. Captain H. A. Packer of the *Warspite*, who had also served in her at Jutland, recorded the moment of meeting in his diary:

> Presently they came in sight at about 15 miles, and we steamed towards each other at 20 knots. It was in November 1940 in the Battle of Spartivento that I had last seen the Italian battleships. Our feelings were queer. Curtis, the Officer of the Watch (a South African), was mumbling to himself 'To think that I should be here to see this', and I felt the same. 'Guns' was busy comparing their silhouettes with his [identification] cards, and remembering his many tussles with them. As they took station astern the Padre said 'It's pathetic somehow'; and Pluto [the ship's dog] raced up and down the fo'c'sle barking . . .[35]

For Cunningham personally it was, in his own words 'a most moving and thrilling sight':[36]

> To see my wildest hopes of years back brought to fruition, and my former flagship the *Warspite*, which had struck the first blow against the Italians three years before, leading her erstwhile opponents into captivity, filled me with the deepest emotion and lives with me still. I can never forget it.[37]

When the British battleships escorted the Italian Fleet into Grand Harbour in the morning of 11 September, they found the Italian squadron from Taranto – the battleships *Andrea Doria* and the *Caio Duilio*, two cruisers and a destroyer – already there. Except for a few stray ships that came in to surrender in the following days, the entire Italian Navy was now moored in waters ringed by the cumulative ruin left by the Axis's three-year effort to bomb Malta into submission, and within the joyful sight of the celebrating population. Cunningham had now only one more duty to perform in the war against Italy, and that was to make this signal to the Admiralty:

> Be pleased to inform their Lordships that the Italian Battle Fleet now lies at anchor under the guns of the fortress of Malta.[38]

So, at a total cost to the Royal Navy since June 1940 in ships sunk of one battleship, two aircraft carriers, fourteen cruisers, a monitor, two anti-aircraft ships, two fast minelayers, 44 destroyers, 41 submarines, seven corvettes, eight fleet minesweepers, 94 other ships and craft of all kinds[39] and all the killed, drowned and wounded of their ships' companies, the Italian menace so quixotically and unnecessarily raised up by British diplomacy (and British public opinion) in the Abyssinian crisis of 1935–36 had at last been removed. The middle prong of the triple threat to the global sprawl of the British Empire had been broken.

ɔove) The fortress and harbour of Gibraltar, in 1939. ʻas the key to British control of the western diterranean and the eastern side of the Atlantic. re the Anglo-American armada was concentrated ore the 'Torch' invasion of French North Africa, November 1942. (IWM) *(Below)* '*Ark Royal* owed her demise primarily to flaws in her own design. . . .' The aircraft-carrier sinking after being torpedoed by U-81 some thirty miles from Gibraltar, 13 November 1941. (IWM)

(*Left*) 'Cunningham's most conspicuous quality was his intense spirit of attack.' Sir Andrew Cunningham, Commander-in-Chief, Mediterranean Fleet, 1939–42 and 1943; Allied Naval Commander Expeditiona Force in 'Operation Torch,' 1942; First Sea Lord, 1943-45. (Hulton) (*Below*) 'The enemy was at a range of no more than 3,80 yards – point-blank.' The sinking of three Italian cruisers by the Mediterranean Fleet, 28 March 1941, in the Battle of Cape Matapan, from a painting by Roland Langmaid. (IWM)

ove) 'The steadfast way in which these ships pressed
heir way to Malta through all the attacks . . . was a
st inspiring sight.' *(Below)* The oil tanker *Ohio* hit
torpedo in the Malta convoy 'Operation Pedestal',
gust 1942. She finally reached Malta safely. (Crown)

(*Above*) 'The dull rumble of a terrific explosion. . . .' The battleship HMS *Barham* blows up in the Mediterranean, 25 November 1941, after being struck by three torpedoes from U-331. (IWM) (*Below*) 'The Italian Battle Fleet now lies at anchor under the guns of the fortress of Malta.' Admiral Sir Andrew Cunningham's signal to the Admiralty on 11 Septem[ber] 1943 after the surrender of the Italian Navy. (IWM)

The imperial lifeline through the Mediterranean to the dependent territories of the East lay open again to civilian as well as military traffic, so offering an immense economy in shipping tonnage as compared with the circuitous Cape route.

Yet how much nearer did the fall of Italy bring the defeat of Nazi Germany, the only prong of the triple threat that posed a mortal threat to the United Kingdom itself? Not much so far, to judge from the experience of the 'Avalanche' assault forces in the beach-heads of Salerno at the hands of the 16th Panzer Division.

> It is important that the Military plan for the subsequent land campaign should be worked out first, and that the assaults should be solely designed to position our forces for the commencement of this. A sound Military plan subsequent to the assaults must be the basis of the whole operational plan . . .

So in September 1943 wrote Admiral Ramsay, the brilliantly successful naval planner of 'Torch' and 'Husky', and now home in the United Kingdom engaged in preliminary studies for 'Overlord'.[40]

Unfortunately General Mark Clark's 5th Army staff produced a military plan for 'Avalanche' that was flawed in overall design and defective in detail.[41] There were to be two separate landings some ten miles distant from each other; a clear invitation to a German commander to thrust in between them if the Allies failed to link up quickly. The British 10th Corps (General R. McCreery) formed the Northern Attack Force, with the British 46th and 56th Infantry Divisions, and two special brigades of Commandos and US Rangers under command. Its task on D-Day was to seize a lodgement running from the mountains fringing the northern coast of Salerno Bay (in order to command the road to Naples) and just north of the town of Salerno itself and then inland beyond the little town of Battipaglia, giving a maximum depth of about ten miles. The plan required the 46th Division to wheel north after landing in order to capture Salerno, a manoeuvre which must therefore expose its right flank to German counter-attacks; it required the 56th Division to advance inland ten miles and then extend its right flank southwards in order to link up with the American 45th Infantry Division from the southern beach-head. This would give the 56th Division a weak and vulnerable front some fifteen miles wide.[42]

Clark's plan allotted the Southern Attack Force (the US 6th Corps, with the 45th and 36th Infantry Divisions under command) a much narrower frontage both of initial landing and of objective line for D-Day, which ran from Ponte Sele some ten miles inland round to the coast just south of Paestum. However, the little river Sele and its tributary the Calore, both impassable except by bridges, sliced the hoped-for lodgement right to the sea; another opening for a German counter-attack.[43]

The 'Avalanche' lodgement area consisted of an undulating plain filled with tall crops, villages and olive groves and overlooked by a ring of mountains offering the German defenders marvellous observation and siting for artillery. In the words of two authorities on the Battle of Salerno, an invader 'was in effect thrusting his head into a bag'.[44]

The Allied landing forces appear formidable enough in numbers of men and heavy weapons – two special brigades of Commandos and Rangers, 27 battalions of infantry supported by 150 tanks, plentiful anti-tank guns, 144 field guns, 200 medium guns and howitzers, and 24 self-propelled howitzers, all to be put ashore by nightfall on D-Day. The defending 16th Panzer Division – 100 tanks, 55 assault guns, 36 medium howitzers, eight dual-purpose 88mm guns (as well as light anti-tank guns) – was therefore heavily outweighted.[45] Yet on the accepted rule-of-thumb that attackers should outnumber defenders by between 2.5 to 1 and 4 to 1 (and enjoy a faster rate of reinforcement) the Allied margin was slender, especially as the Allied infantry divisions as a whole could not compare in fighting efficiency with 16th Panzer. All four Allied divisions had originated as Territorial or National Guard civilian volunteer formations, and were now filled out with conscripts. Their own training and the quality of their officers and staffs did not always match the rigorous demands of an assault landing like 'Avalanche'. Moreover, while the two British infantry divisions (or some units within them) had had previous experience of battle (the 46th had been in the field in Tunisia from February to May), the two American divisions in the Southern Attack Force came largely new to it. The most effective arm of the Allied forces lay in their abundant and excellent artillery, and the well-trained gunners who served it.[46]

In the 16th Panzer Division the Allies confronted a veteran, if battered, formation of the Stalingrad campaign, with a core of war-hardened survivors around which a mass of new recruits had been quickly turned into competent soldiers by means of the excellent German training system and standardised tactical drills. Its officers and NCOs would know what to do, and they would do it with the customary unhesitating initiative;[47] and on the night of 8–9 September 1943 the four battlegroups of 16th Panzer were already in position around the Gulf of Salerno, watching and waiting for the Allied armada to loom into view across a moonlit sea.

The assault convoys deployed before dark for the final approach. From the British vessels of the Northern Attack Force the island of Capri could be clearly seen in the moonlight on the port beam. At 2155 the Southern Attack Force sighted the beacon light from the submarine HMS *Shakespeare*. At 2357 the moon set; by 0053 on the 9th all transports were anchored in their lowering positions nine to twelve miles off shore, and unloading began according to the now familiar routine. At 0217 the Commandos and Rangers set off for the northern shore of Salerno Bay. Soon the mass of infantry and support landing craft (many of them had voyaged from Sicily or North Africa under their own power) were heading for the beaches through enemy shell splashes with the main bodies of the two attack forces. In the vain hope of achieving tactical surprise the Allied command had decided not to lay on a preliminary naval or air bombardment of the German defences. Morning twilight was just beginning to lighten the sky behind the mountains inland when the ramps of the assault craft dropped on to the sand at about 0300.[48]

In the Northern Attack Force area (Commodore G. N. Oliver, with his broad pendant in the headquarters ship HMS *Hilary*) the Royal Navy put 10th Corps ashore with relatively few foul-ups. On the extreme left flank the Commandos and Rangers found their beaches empty of Germans, and they hastened into the mountains in order to secure the vital ground commanding the roads and railway from Naples to Salerno. On the adjacent Uncle Red beach part of the British 46th Division also came ashore free of mishap; a deceptive beginning. On Uncle Green beach the landing craft guides steered the assault wave towards a stretch of sand where rockets from support landing craft could be seen exploding. But the landing craft had mistaken the target, and the assault went ashore on the wrong part of the beach. The error led to congestion and confusion; it made it impossible to use Uncle Green for unloading that day.

The error also produced a knock-on effect on the neighbouring Sugar beaches to the south, by shouldering the assault waves of the 56th Division sideways. Nevertheless the beach parties managed quickly to sort out the resulting crowd scenes. On Roger Amber and Roger Green (the right flank beaches of the 56th Division) another error of navigation turned out to be a stroke of luck, Murphy's Law in reverse, for by landing 1,500 yards south of the correct point the first wave of landing craft evaded the fire of a German battery.

On the Southern Attack Force sector (Rear Admiral J. L. Hall,

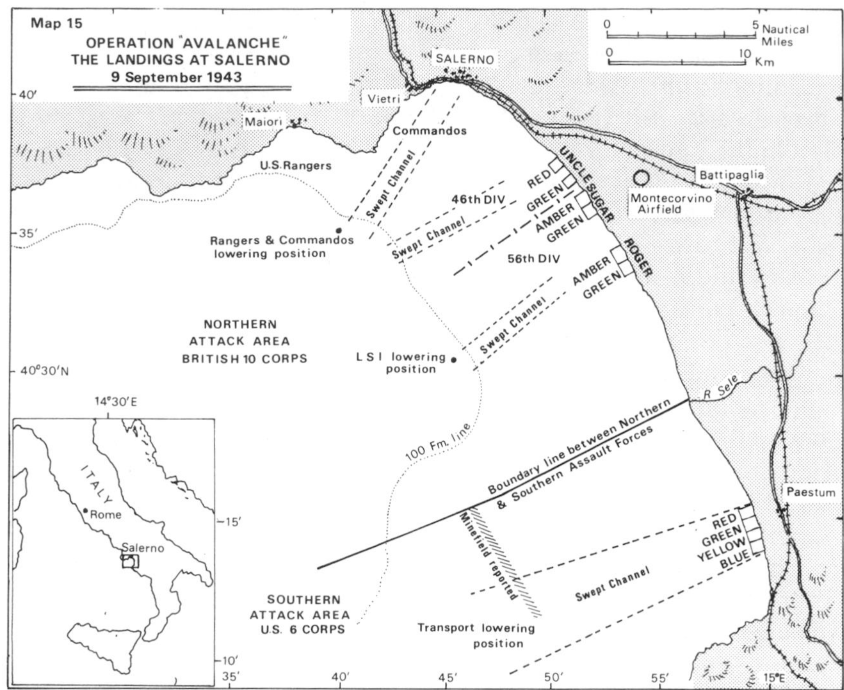

flying his flag in the transport *Samuel Chase*) the United States Navy put the US 45th and 36th Infantry Divisions (6th Corps) ashore on a narrow and continuous front without mishap except for delays in sweeping a channel through a suspected minefield. However, the very narrowness of the beach-head (the result of a shortage of landing craft) now began to cause major problems in deploying troops and feeding in supplies.

As a whole, therefore, the landings themselves had gone better than those in 'Torch' or 'Husky'. It was from now on, with the coming of daylight, that the trouble started. When Allied troops tried to push inland towards their D-Day objectives, the 16th Panzer offered the kind of resistance behind the beaches never before encountered in major amphibious operations in the Mediterranean. At the same time 16th Panzer put down a fierce bombardment on the crowded beaches themselves and on the follow-up waves of landing craft bringing in reinforcements and heavy weapons such as tanks. Luftwaffe fighter-bombers and dive-bombers roared in to make their own contribution of high explosive. The 'Avalanche' beaches all too soon presented a very different picture from the relatively undisturbed and systematic process of sorting out initial confusions that had characterised 'Torch' and 'Husky'. Instead, here was the classic picture of a battlefield – continual explosions, a litter of wrecked guns and transport and abandoned kit, damaged landing craft, corpses and wounded; frenzied, fear-driven activity.

On the Northern Attack Force sector the destroyers HMS *Laforey*, *Lookout* and *Loyal* closed the shore astern of the first assault waves according to plan in order to provide immediate floating artillery-support to the hard-pressed army, their fire called down on to specific targets by Bombardment Liaison Officers (BLOs) ashore with the troops. Direct duels took place between destroyers and German tanks and batteries, in which *Laforey* was hit five times and forced to retire temporarily for repairs. Under cover of smoke screens belched out by smoke-projectors in specially equipped landing craft, the follow-up waves continued to feed in troops, supplies, tanks and guns. By 1030 that morning the first of the big landing craft (tank) had beached; and in the next eleven hours no fewer than 38 of those valuable carriers unloaded on Sugar and Roger beaches.

On the Southern Attack Force sector no prior plans for destroyers to give the two American divisions fire support immediately on touch-down had been made, because of the US Army's mistaken hope of achieving surprise by a 'silent' landing. The green and not very well trained troops of the 45th and 36th Infantry had to struggle forward off the beaches in the face of the crackle and thunder of accurate enemy fire; a terrifying initiation to battle. But later in the day the monitor HMS *Abercrombie* (7,850 tons; two 15-inch guns),[49] the cruisers USS *Savannah* and *Philadelphia*, and several US destroyers came up to the rescue. By smothering positions held by 16th Panzer with 15-inch, 6-inch and 5-inch rounds, they decisively helped to prevent 6th Corps being trapped and destroyed on the beaches that first day.

Above this 30-mile-wide sunlit scene of smoke, fire, flashes from guns and bursting shells and bombs, packed beaches and a wide blue bay filled with shipping of all shapes and sizes, flew the Seafires from Admiral Vian's five light carriers. That day they made 265 sorties, keeping an average of 20 aircraft aloft at any one time. From bases in Sicily American Lockheed P-38 Lightnings with long-distance tanks also joined in the fight to keep the Luftwaffe away. But the Allied air plan went into a fatal spin when the British 56th Division failed to capture Montecorvino airfield as planned.

For in the course of D-Day the armies' battle had already gone desperately wrong – and with dangerous repercussions for the navies as well. On the extreme left of the landings, on the peninsula where the resort villages of Amalfi, Positano and Sorrento cling to the sides of mountains tumbling steeply into a copper sulphate sea, the Rangers and Commandos had fought their way inland and secured an objective line giving command of the key roads and the railway from Naples. But on the main British 10th Corps front, and despite the capture of the port of Salerno itself, 16th Panzer had the best of a confused 'soldiers' battle' at close quarters amid the sweetcorn and tobacco plantations, its battlegroups putting in a successful counter-attack that completely dislocated 10th Corps' plan. At the end of D-Day the Corps had been stopped well short of its objective line, and holding only a narrow lodgement less than five miles deep. The American 6th Corps (Southern Attack Force) had a truly terrible day, for the Corps attracted the heaviest German artillery fire and air attack, and its inexperience and clumsy tactics fared ill against 16th Panzer's determined battlegroups. By the end of D-Day 6th Corps too lay cramped into a narrow lodgement far short of its objectives. Most dangerous of all, the British and Americans had failed to link up their two beach-heads.[50]

The inability of the armies to get rapidly forward and the weight of enemy fire on the beaches (causing some to be closed) created a waterborne traffic jam of the big landing craft (tank) that were trying to put urgently needed armour ashore. This situation worsened the next day when enemy artillery fire forced the British to give up using the port of Salerno. By now the 14th Panzer Corps (with three panzer-grenadier divisions) was on its way to help 16th Panzer, and the 10th Army (General von Vietinghoff) had taken control of the German forces.

Between 10 and 15 September, the struggle at Salerno mounted to a crisis in which the Allied 5th Army appeared to Clark to be near to disaster. On land the enemy first fought the British and American troops to a standstill and then launched a classic counter-stroke intended to split the American 6th Corps front in two, and reach the sea. In the air the effort of carrier-borne Seafires waned each day until on 12 September Vian withdrew his light carriers to Palermo, while Admiral Hewitt ordered the remaining 26 aircraft to transfer to an improvised airstrip near Paestum. The Seafires (adapted Spitfires) were not really suitable for carrier operations, having weak undercarriages which led to 32 of those at Salerno being damaged by deck landings. At a maximum speed of 341 mph[51] they lacked the pace easily to intercept the German fighter-bombers. They also had difficulty in reaching the 19,000-feet altitude from which the special unit of Do-17s which had sunk the *Roma* were launching FX-1400 radio-guided bombs.[52]

And the radio-guided bombs once again were proving dismayingly effective. On 11 September the USS *Philadelphia* was badly shaken by a near-miss, the *Savannah* heavily damaged, and HMS *Uganda* damaged so severely as to need towing back to Malta. Cunningham forthwith ordered the cruisers HMS *Aurora* and *Penelope* to replace the damaged ships, while the US Navy sent in the cruiser *Boise*. Shortly before 1500 on 14 September Hewitt signalled Cunningham to report his anxiety about the critical military situation, and asked for heavy ships which could lay a protective curtain of fire between the recoiling Allied troops and the enemy. Cunningham immediately ordered *Warspite* and *Valiant* to sail forthwith. On 16 September the *Warspite* (which had arrived off Salerno with *Valiant* the previous day) was attacked at 1410 by an FX-1400-carrying aircraft which was neither detected by radar nor sighted. Two FX-1400s near-missed; a third penetrated to *Warspite*'s No. 4 boiler room and burst with tremendous concussion. At once five out of six boiler rooms filled with sea water, and the ship could only steam at slow speed on her starboard engines. Then at 1500 the last boiler room filled and all steam was lost. *Warspite* lay dead in the water in a crowded sea under enemy air attack; a situation which was indeed, as Captain Packer wrote in his subsequent report, 'unattractive'. Ignominiously this renowned fighting ship had to return to Malta wallowing astern of British and American tugs.

Meanwhile British and American cruisers and destroyers had been doing their own best to bloody the nose of the German offensive. Between 10 and 13 September the cruiser HMS *Mauritius* alone fired over 1,000 6-inch rounds. Nevertheless, by 14 September the Allied armies were everywhere stuck fast. Attacks rashly ordered by General Clark had been smashed by the enemy, and battlegroups of the 16th Panzer-Grenadier and 15th Panzer-Grenadier had thrown the Americans back to within three miles of the sea (this was the day that the much-needed fire of *Savannah* and *Uganda* was silenced by radio-guided bombs).

The German command believed on the 14th that the Allies were about to admit defeat and re-embark.[53] This was by no means fanciful. For that day a major crisis, even a panic, was taking place in the headquarters of General Clark's 5th Army. According to Admiral Sir Geoffrey Oliver (then Commodore Oliver, Naval Commander, Northern Attack Force):

> Rather late on in the afternoon on D + 5, Hewitt asked me to come down and see him in BISCAYNE [his headquarters ship]. I duly went in the

> barge and found an atmosphere of intense gloom . . . To my surprise and misgiving, I was told that General Clark wanted two emergency plans immediately prepared . . . One was to withdraw the British X Corps and disembark it again through the American VI Corps beaches; the other was vice versa and was stated to be the most likely alternative. I was also asked to find room in HILARY for General Clark and his numerous Headquarters in the event of their leaving to be re-embarked, since ANCON [the big and vulnerable American headquarters ship] had departed.[54]

In other words, Clark and his staff were seriously considering giving up the American lodgement. In fact, at Clark's request Hewitt had already ordered all available craft to stand ready to lift the troops, and stopped the unloading of cargo ships in the Southern Attack Force sector. On hearing this defeatism as reported by Admiral Hewitt, Oliver was horrified:

> I protested to Hewitt that re-embarkation of heavily engaged troops from a rather shallow beach-head, followed by disembarkation again, was simply not on, quite apart from other considerations. I also said that in my view it would be suicidal to so shorten the front, which would allow enemy artillery to rake the beaches from end to end, and that we should lose an immense amount of ammunition and stores already ashore.
>
> I asked whether my Corps Commander [McCreery] had been consulted, but no one seemed to know.[55]

General Mark Clark, inexperienced as he still was, had so far proved in his first battle crisis a commander more notable for his imposing eagle profile and his personal courage under fire than his operational competence. As for Commodore Oliver, he returned to his ship 'very angry', and got in touch as soon as he could with McCreery through his liaison officer at 10th Corps headquarters. He learned later that night that McCreery knew nothing of Clark's project, 'was furious and was last seen making tracks for Army Headquarters to expostulate. I reported the position by signal to A.B.C. to enlist his support against any such plan being pursued further.'[56] McCreery himself signalled Clark and Hewitt to say that he considered there was no question of such re-embarkations taking place. Cunningham fully supported Oliver; he too perceived that if the Allied lodgement were narrowed, the enemy would be able to enfilade the entire length of shore from either flank. Nothing further was heard about the project, which would have resulted in a catastrophe of the first magnitude. As Admiral Hewitt remarked in retrospect, 'Fortunately, very fortunately I believe, subsequent developments made it unnecessary to attempt it.'[57]

Since the British 10th Corps, although stuck fast, was at this time not so hard-pressed by enemy attack as the American 6th Corps, McCreery remained confident that with the mass of reinforcements, tanks, guns and ammunition still pouring into the lodgement the Allies could stop the enemy and force him back. And so it proved. The German onslaught on the Americans faltered in the face of the immense weight of fire put down by the American gunners, supplemented by the heavy ships, cruisers and destroyers off shore. A fresh attack on the 10th Corps was similarly smashed by British artillery. By 16 September the crisis was over; the Allied lodgement was secure. Meanwhile, on the 13th, Montgomery had started off again with the main body of the 8th Army in response to anxious proddings from Alexander, at the same time sending light troops on ahead to make contact with the 5th Army and threaten the rear of the enemy. In the event, it was a party of journalists with the 8th Army who were first to penetrate through to the Salerno beachhead.[58]

Field-Marshal Kesselring was nevertheless well pleased with the performance of his 10th Army at Salerno. For eight days it had held, and even forced on to the defensive, a much more powerful Allied army backed by a fleet. Mere platoons of panzer-grenadiers had seen off whole companies of Britons and Americans. Now it was time to put into operation his well-pondered strategy for a protracted campaign. He ordered the 10th Army to wheel back, pivoting on its right (on the north coast of Salerno Bay) in order to form a front with a new 14th Army extending from the Mediterranean across to the Adriatic, and then make a step-by-step fighting withdrawal to the *Gustavstellung* (Gustav Line).[59]

The Allies took much delight in their prize of Naples, occupied on 1 October. It seemed for a happy moment that the grand hopes entertained by Churchill and Brooke of their Mediterranean strategy were now in the course of being realised. The moment swiftly passed. Instead the 5th and 8th Armies now began dragging months of dreary campaigning against a skilled and stubborn German retirement, as the weather worsened week by week; one mountain ridge after another to fight for, one river after another to battle a way across. An attempt to employ seapower to land commandos and two infantry brigades behind the German front on the Adriatic at Termoli on 3–6 October narrowly succeeded after a stiff fight against battlegroups of the 16th Panzer counter-attacking straight off the march from their rest camps;

a repetition in miniature of the lesson of Salerno that seapower is merely a defended transport service, not a magic formula of victory, and that what counts is the subsequent land battle.

In November the Allies came up against the *Bernhardstellung*, the formidable outwork of the *Gustavstellung*; more grim attrition battles and slow advances against the German 10th and 14th Armies (now constituted as Army Group C). By now the Italian winter had broken in all its bleakness, and the Allied troops began to suffer from attrition by sickness and frostbite as well as German fire. In December the 5th and 8th Armies found themselves before the *Gustavstellung* itself – the most ingenious use of ideal defensive terrain in order to create a virtually impregnable defence system since Wellington's Lines of Torres Vedras in Portugal in 1810.[60] On the Adriatic sector Montgomery's frontal pushes across the River Sangro, intended to break through the *Gustavstellung*, bogged down in mini-Sommes of clinging mud, floods, lashing rain and a tenacious German defence in depth. In the Mediterranean sector Clark's 5th Army gnawed away at a massive chain of fortified mountain ramparts largely held by an outstanding frontline soldier, General von Senger, and his valiant 14th Panzer Corps.

By the end of December 1943 the Italian front had become locked fast in a stalemate reminiscent of such earlier essays in 'blue water' strategy as Gallipoli in 1915 or the Allied Salonika front in 1916–18. Rome, the prize Churchill had dreamed of in July, still lay securely under the Swastika some 80 miles beyond the *Gustavstellung*, with far distant Vienna unimaginably out of reach. Some 'underbelly'; some 'softest part'!

As for the Royal and United States Navies, their major role in Mediterranean 'blue water' strategy had come to an end with the successful establishment of the Allied armies on the Italian mainland in September 1943. On 6 October Admiral Kent Hewitt struck his flag as Commander, Western Naval Task Force, upon the dissolution of that force. Henceforward Rear-Admiral J. A. V. Morse of the Royal Navy, flying his flag ashore in Naples as Flag Officer, Western Italy, would be responsible for naval operations in the Tyrrhenian Sea. On 14 October Vice-Admiral Sir Algernon Willis struck his flag as Flag Officer, Force H, and a few days later this famous battle squadron, whose record of battle encompassed the attacks on the French Fleet in 1940, the hunt for the *Bismarck*, the hard-fought convoys to Malta, and the 'Torch', 'Husky' and 'Avalanche' landings, was also disbanded. Its badly needed heavy ships could now be deployed against the Japanese in the Indian Ocean or brought back to England to strengthen the Home Fleet.

And at sunset on 17 October 1943 the Union Flag of Admiral of the Fleet Sir Andrew Cunningham, Bart, GCB, Commander-in-Chief, Mediterranean, was struck in HMS *Maidstone*. The Admiral had already flown back to London two days earlier to take up the post of First Sea Lord in succession to the dying Sir Dudley Pound (see below, pp. 731–4). Cunningham's departure from the Mediterranean marked the end of the sea-going career of England's greatest fighting sailor since Nelson – who, like him, was ever eager to engage the enemy as closely as possible.

> I leave you all in the Mediterranean with keen regret [he signalled in farewell]; but also with pride. It has been my privilege to command a great fleet of ships of the Allied nations of every category from battleships to the smallest craft. We may well look back with satisfaction to the work which has been performed . . . To you all who have fought and endured with such courage, tenacity and determination, I send my heartfelt thanks and appreciation . . .[61]

He was succeeded by his namesake (but no relative) Admiral Sir John Cunningham, formerly C-in-C, Levant Command, who at first flew his flag ashore at Algiers, and then, from the beginning of January 1944, at Naples. With the Mediterranean now dominated by Allied seapower from end to end, and no longer an enemy battlefleet to fight, the tasks of the Allied navies henceforward would be to protect convoys against U-boats, E-boats and the Luftwaffe ranging down from French or North Italian airfields; to run supplies up both coasts of Italy to the Allied armies; and to attack the enemy shipping that still plied in the Aegean, Adriatic and in Mediterranean waters off France and Italy. It was a war now of smaller vessels and craft instead of heavy ships and fleet carriers, of workaday but essential service instead of desperate sea fights.

However in the autumn of 1943, while the Allies were landing in Italy and struggling north towards the *Gustavstellung*, the Royal Navy had been put through an exercise in instant 'blue water' strategy in the Aegean that marked a throw-back to the Greek adventure of 1941, the trip to Dakar and the intervention in Norway in 1940, and even the expedition to the Dardanelles in 1915.

On 10–14 September 1943, British forces had landed on the Dodecanese islands of Kastellorizo, Kos and Leros. By 18 September seven of the islands were in the hands of scratch British garrisons, but not Rhodes, the biggest and the military key to all the rest. On the 13th Churchill had made a signal to General Sir Henry Maitland Wilson, the C-in-C, Middle East, which struck a familiar enough note:

> The capture of Rhodes by you at this time with Italian aid would be a fine contribution to the general war. Let me know what are your plans for this. Can you not improvise the necessary garrison out of the forces in the Middle East? What is your ration strength?[62]

The capture of Rhodes ('Operation Accolade') had been a favourite in the Prime Minister's toy-box ever since 1942, taken out and played with from time to time by him and the British Chiefs of Staff, even offered to the Americans at various summit conferences as one of the attractions for pursuing a Mediterranean strategy throughout 1943.[63] In May 1943, at the Chiefs of Staff's request, General Maitland Wilson had submitted in time for the 'Trident' Washington Conference a grand proposal by which 'Accolade' became the mere preliminary to 'possible major operations based on Salonika and Istanbul with objectives up to the line of the Danube'.[64] In July, with the fall of Mussolini, the Prime Minister took 'Accolade' out of the box again, minuting the Chiefs of Staff: 'Here is a business of great consequence, to be thrust forward by every means . . .'[65] In turn the Chiefs of Staff on 3 August prodded Maitland Wilson, authorising him to ask Eisenhower for the necessary landing craft and air cover.[66] But Eisenhower refused to divert resources from the task given him by directive of the Combined Chiefs of Staff.

> I view with considerable concern [he signalled the British Chiefs of Staff on 12 August] possibility that in practice requirements of this operation will draw on resources urgently required for main business in hand which is to knock Italy out of the war. Fact is that in Mediterranean there are many critical items such as AA, landing craft, air forces which are barely sufficient for present operations. Operations such as Accolade cannot be staged without drawing to some extent upon these resources.
>
> In my opinion, with which the D.C-in-C [Alexander], C-in-C, Mediterranean [Sir Andrew Cunningham] and Air C-in-C [Tedder] agree, we should concentrate on one thing at a time and Accolade should be abandoned for the present.[67]

Eisenhower, strong in his position as an Allied commander and an American officer, was not to be budged by further pleading and pressure from the British. If they wanted to adventure in the Aegean, they would therefore have to do it on their own resources. General Maitland Wilson therefore netted his now backwater of a Middle

East command for resources. On 9 September, D-Day of 'Avalanche' and the morrow of the Italian surrender, Churchill signalled Wilson on learning that his attack on Rhodes with improvised forces was imminent: 'Good. This is the time to play high. Improvise and dare.'[68]

But on 14 September the Italian garrison on Rhodes surrendered to the Germans. To take the island would now require a major amphibious operation and a hard fight. By no means discouraged, however, the Premier now evoked for his colleagues and Allies a vision of the Balkans set aflame by the igniting agent of an Allied occupation of Rhodes. Turkey might thereby be encouraged to enter the war; the Allies might land a small force in Greece; the Allies might then open the Dardanelles and pass ships through into the Black Sea; an Allied expeditionary force (perhaps the 80,000 strong Polish Army in exile, now in the Middle East, plus the New Zealand Division) might land on the Dalmatian coast.[69]

However, it soon became obvious that the British forces in the Aegean were neither strong enough to attack Rhodes, nor even withstand for long a German counter-offensive aimed at recapturing the other islands of the Dodecanese. In particular the Luftwaffe enjoyed complete air superiority (the Dodecanese being virtually out of range of British aircraft from the Middle East) and was using it to full effect – another throw-back to 1941.[70] From the British Chiefs of Staff, from the Prime Minister himself, there now came a succession of pleas to Eisenhower for troops, ships, bombers, transport aircraft and long-range fighters.[71]

But Eisenhower steadfastly refused more than a trickle of help. On 12 August he signalled the British Chiefs of Staff: 'In my opinion we should concentrate on one thing at a time and Accolade [the projected attack on Rhodes] should be abandoned at present.' In a further signal of 1 September he listed the 'limit of resources provide for Aegean in view of absolute necessity for concentrating on main battle in Italy . . .'[72]

This signal caused dismay among the British Middle East Cs-in-C, for they estimated that 350 German aircraft were now thrashing the weak British garrisons in the Dodecanese and the Royal Navy in the Aegean Sea. A minimum of four Lightning fighter squadrons and a heavy bombing effort against Greek airfields was required 'forthwith', they signalled London in reply to a COS signal of 20 September, 'otherwise position in Leros and Cos [sic] may become untenable . . .'[73] But on 5 October Eisenhower (backed by Tedder) insisted that likely German resistance in Italy meant that he 'must employ the whole available air effort'; and he pronounced against a major operation to take Rhodes;

> . . . if Accolade is undertaken the operation however desirable in itself is bound to place calls on us for a very considerable and continuing diversion of air effort from the main operations in Italy. I consider any material diversion highly prejudicial to the success of Italian operations . . .[74]

And that was that. Eisenhower's devotion to the classic strategic principle of the concentration of force and the avoidance of dispersion (as well as his obedience to the directives of the Combined Chiefs of Staff) cannot be faulted. Now the British armed services had once again to pay the consequences of strategic opportunism. By 3 October Kos had already come under German assault, eliciting a message from the Prime Minister to the British garrison commander that might easily have been reprinted from those despatched just before the fall of Singapore or Tobruk: 'We rely on you to defend this island to the utmost limit . . .'[75] Next day Kos was overrun.

In the face of the Luftwaffe the British had to resort to the submarines *Severn* and *Rorqual* to run supplies to the British garrison on Leros from Haifa. During one trip the *Rorqual* had to dive with a jeep and six Bofors guns lashed to the casing when it was attacked by German aircraft; hardly to the benefit of the jeep's engine. Four Italian submarines were also employed to ferry stores. But such frantic improvisations proved of no avail. On 13–14 November the German Army landed on Leros supported by the Luftwaffe enjoying its brief local return to total air superiority. By the 16th Leros was in enemy hands. On the night of 19–20 November Samos was evacuated, and on the 28th Kastel/lorizo. So ended this replay in miniature of Greece and Crete in 1941.

For the Royal Navy, as it braved the Luftwaffe in order to succour the troops and then eventually bring them away, the sense of *déjà vu* was especially keen, for the Dodecanese gamble too cost them dear. The Royal and Royal Hellenic Navies suffered four cruisers damaged (one of them, HMS *Carlisle*, beyond repair), six destroyers sunk and four damaged, and ten coastal craft and minesweepers sunk.[76]

The unfolding débâcle by no means quenched Churchill's enthusiasm for maritime offensives in the Aegean. Even while the Dodecanese islands were falling to the enemy he was urging that fresh operations be mounted to retake Kos and take Rhodes. What was more, in his mind such operations remained only the opening gambit in carrying the war into the Balkans.[77] Did Brooke, that other convinced proponent of 'blue water' Mediterranean strategy, concur? He certainly disapproved of Churchill's 'Rhodes madness', as he termed it on 7 October 1943, characterising it as 'another of those typical examples of dispersal of effort for very problematic gains'.[78] But on the much larger issue of extending the scope of present Mediterranean operations from Italy into the Balkans, he was much of the same mind as the Premier, confiding to his diary on 20 November (during another summit conference, this time in Cairo: 'Sextant') that 'the drag' of the Americans

> ... has seriously affected our Mediterranean strategy and the whole conduct of the War. If they had come wholeheartedly into the Mediterranean with us we should by now have Rome securely, the Balkans would be ablaze, the Dardanelles would be open, and we should be on the highway to get Rumania and Bulgaria out of the war.[79]

Did Brooke in his heart hanker like Churchill for a Mediterranean solution to beating Germany which would avoid the necessity for 'Overlord', that dreaded encounter with a main body of the Germany Army?[80] His biographer has to answer that this remains an enigma.[81] Certainly Brooke and Churchill fought as hard as they could with their American allies before and at the Cairo Conference to persuade them not to weaken Allied resources in the Mediterranean in order to build up strength in the United Kingdom for 'Overlord', and successfully cajoled them into allowing General Alexander (now Allied Commander, 15th Army Group, in Italy) to retain 68 landing craft due to go to England.[82] Certainly too both men (and the British Chiefs of Staff) were willing to see 'Overlord' postponed in order to ensure success in Italy.[83]

At the second plenary meeting of the Cairo Conference on 24 November 1943 Churchill put to Roosevelt 'the programme he advocated':

> Rome in January, Rhodes in February, supplies to the Yugoslavs, the opening of the Aegean subject to the outcome of an approach to Turkey, and all preparations for 'Overlord' to go ahead full steam within the framework of the foregoing policy for the Mediterranean.[84]

A paper by the British Chiefs of Staff wrapped meat round these bare bones, but no final decision was taken. That had to wait for the Teheran Conference ('Eureka') held immediately after 'Sextant'. Here Churchill presented a deftly turned sales pitch to Stalin on the next stage of Mediterranean strategy:

> . . . we had not contemplated going into the broad part of the leg of Italy, still less of invading Germany across the Alps. The general plan was first to capture Rome and seize the airfields north of it, which would enable us to bomb Southern Germany, and then to establish ourselves on a line towards Pisa–Rimini. After that the possibility of establishing a Third Front in conformity with, but not in substitution for, the cross-Channel operation would have to be planned.[85]

This 'Third Front' might take the form, he said, of a move into southern France or 'from the head of the Adriatic north-west towards the Danube'.[86] Beguilingly he assured the conference that there was 'no question' of using large forces in the Mediterranean or the Aegean. But neither he nor Britain any longer weighed in the scales of Allied decision-making as once they had, for in different ways the war efforts of the United States and Soviet Russia, the two continental powers, now dwarfed that of Britain, an island state of only 45 millions with an industrial base too small and backward to equip her own forces, and an economy kept going by an American life-support machine. It was Stalin who – with Roosevelt's tacit support – ruthlessly decided the outcome of the conference: 'Overlord' in May 1944; a Supreme Commander for it to be nominated immediately; a subsidiary Mediterranean operation into southern France rather than towards the Danube.

The Anglo-American Combined Chiefs of Staff in their own closed sessions in Teheran did however agree that there should be a limited further offensive in Italy aimed at the capture of Rome and an advance to the Pisa–Rimini line, as well as the supply of modest rations of support for the Yugoslav partisans. So once again the Western Allies decided to take their Mediterranean strategy forward one more step, and once again supposedly under tight limits. Yet Brooke took comfort from the fact that the theatre was now going to retain landing craft for the invasion of southern France ('Anvil'); resources which he reckoned (according to his biographer) that General Alexander, 'once they were to hand, might use to better effect as the situation developed'.[87] In other words Brooke still saw a chance that the tight limits might again in the event be stretched, just as they had been stretched to General Marshall's discomfiture and dismay after 'Torch' and after 'Husky'.

In December 1943 the Prime Minister suggested to the Chiefs of Staff that the 'stagnation' on the Italian front could be ended and Rome swiftly taken if Allied seapower were used to land a powerful force behind the German front.[88] Such an operation, reckoned the COS, would require at least 88 landing craft. However, of the 102 at present in the Mediterranean, 68 (56 of them British) were due to return to England in mid-January in preparation for 'Overlord'. Could the Americans be persuaded to consent to all craft remaining in the theatre for another three weeks for the sake of a stroke which would enable the Allies to advance to the Pisa–Rimini line? They could: Roosevelt telegraphed their agreement on 28 December.[89]

On 21 January 1944 the expedition to carry out 'Operation Shingle' (a landing on the west coast of Italy astride the port of Anzio) put to sea from Naples, the force commander, Admiral F. J. Lowry (of the United States Navy) flying his flag in the headquarters ship USS *Biscayne*.[90]

The Northern Assault Force ('Peter' Force) consisted of the British 1st Infantry Division and two Commandos embarked in three landing ships (infantry), 33 landing ships (tank) and 56 infantry and other types of landing craft, all escorted by the cruisers *Orion* and *Spartan* (15th Cruiser Squadron: Rear-Admiral J. M. Mansfield), the anti-aircraft and fighter-direction ship *Palomares*, eleven destroyers, sixteen minesweepers, four anti-submarine/minesweeping trawlers, three tugs and some twenty miscellaneous smaller craft.[91] The majority of the shipping and warships were British. In command of Peter Force was Rear-Admiral T. H. Troubridge, flying his flag in the headquarters ship HMS *Bulolo*, the veteran of 'Torch'.

The Southern Attack Force ('X-Ray') comprised three battalions of Rangers and the US 3rd Infantry Division, transported in five British landing ships (infantry), 40 British and ten American landing ships (tank), and 104 assorted types of landing craft. X-Ray Force was escorted by the cruisers HMS *Penelope* and USS *Brooklyn*, thirteen destroyers (ten American, two Greek and one British), two Dutch gunboats and 23 American minesweepers.[92] The Royal Navy supplied the two beacon submarines for the landing, HMS *Ultor* ('Peter' beaches) and HMS *Uproar* ('X-Ray' beaches). In the event the expedition's strength in landing craft of all kinds had been built up to a total of no fewer than 162. 'Operation Shingle' therefore represented a very major investment of maritime resources.

From the navies' point of view the Anzio landings on 22 January 1944 (H-hour at 0200) proved much like the first day of 'Avalanche', there being few major mishaps or errors, thanks to the excellent prior reconnaissance of the beaches and painstaking staff work carried out against the clock; and even though the beaches 'with their shallow approach and offshore sandbars were,' wrote Troubridge in his report, 'the worst in my experience.' Within a week 68,886 men, 508 guns, 237 tanks and 27,250 tons of stores had been unloaded – and despite a gale which forced the closure of the beaches for two days.[93] But, again as in 'Avalanche', German fighter-bombers, torpedo-bombers and a special unit equipped with glider bombs (this time the Hs.293 radio-controlled, rocket-boosted, winged missile with a speed of 300 to 400 mph and a warhead of 1,000 pounds of explosive)[94] came early and stayed late. In that first week the destroyer HMS *Janus* was sunk and HMS *Jervis* and USS *Plunkett* badly damaged; one of three brilliantly illuminated hospital ships, the *St David*, was also sunk – a repetition of the Luftwaffe's similar feat of arms on D-Day of 'Husky'; the US destroyer *Mayo* struck a mine and had to be towed back to Naples; and, worst loss of all, HMS *Spartan* capsized inshore after being hit by a Hs.293 guided missile.

On 2 February Admiral Sir John Cunningham, C-in-C, Mediterranean, ordered Lowry to hand over command of the naval forces to Rear-Admiral Morse, Flag Officer, Western Italy, in Naples. It was a sign that the navies' principal task in landing the 'Shingle' forces was done; now began the hard grind of running in supplies and reinforcements and providing fire support to the Army. For it was on the soldiers and the land battle that depended the success of 'Shingle', as of all amphibious operations.

According to General Clark's offensive plan, the 'Shingle' forces were to strike immediately and rapidly inland to cut the communications of the German 10th Army in the *Gustavstellung* while the 5th Army attacked it frontally and broke through towards Rome. None of this happened. The 5th Army's offensive was stopped in its tracks with heavy loss, largely owing to Mark Clark's faulty planning and operational mistakes. Owing to feeble leadership on the part of the commanding general, the American John Lucas, the 'Shingle' landing forces contented themselves with establishing a defensive perimeter round their beach-head. Both he and Clark himself had strongly disliked the 'Shingle' venture; and Clark had even told Lucas to dig in rather than take risks. The initiative was promptly seized by the Germans; the invaders became the besieged and in desperate danger of being heaved into the sea – 'Avalanche' all over again. But just as in 'Avalanche', the enemy attacks were eventually held in savage fighting and partly thanks to naval gunfire, and the Allied lodgement made secure.

This time, however, no strategic retreat by the enemy followed. Instead the front at Anzio became as frozen in stalemate as the main

Italian front – a vain exercise in seapower, indeed a veritable Gallipoli. This four-month stalemate laid a severe strain on the Allied navies, for the planning for 'Operation Shingle' had originally assumed that the expeditionary force would only have to be supplied by sea for fifteen days, after which it had been expected that overland supply would be opened from the main Allied front.

On that main front, the cutting edge of Churchill's and Brooke's Mediterranean strategy, the 5th Army continued to hew in vain at the iron shield of the *Gustavstellung*. American, British, Indian and New Zealand troops in turn all pitted their military skills and military virtue in vain against the 14th Panzer Corps in a narrow killing ground around Monte Cassino, and beneath in the ruins of the town of Cassino itself (defended by the 1st Parachute Division). Here – and at Anzio – was fought the Verdun, the Stalingrad, the Passchendaele of the Italian campaign.[95] The stalemate endured through February, through March, through April and into May, despite one Allied offensive after another – and these were the months of preparation for 'Overlord', when according to Churchill's and Brooke's strategic thinking the Italian front should have been weakening the forces available to the enemy to meet a cross-Channel invasion. That, after all, had supplied them with a central argument in support of their 'blue water' strategy.

But in fact the long-drawn-out campaign in Italy was costing the Allies far more dear in resources than the enemy, not least because again they were fighting in a detached theatre of war dependent on long sea communications.

According to two authorities on the campaign, Dominick Graham and Shelford Bidwell, the Allied commitment of manpower for land and air forces (including infrastructure and logistics) was to rise by 1944 to a total of 1,677,000.[96] This figure compares with Kesselring's 195,000 men in July 1943 and 411,000 in July 1944.[97] As for the high British hopes that the collapse of Italy would force the Germans to drain away troops from their other fronts to a possibly disastrous extent in order to hold the Balkans, the truth is that the German deployment in Yugoslavia increased by a net total of only seven divisions (mostly second-class and ill-equipped) between the time of Italy's surrender up to February 1944, and only one of these divisions came originally from the Russian front.[98]

Moreover, to supply the Allied forces in the whole western Mediterranean area (including Italy) called for the commitment of over 1 million deadweight tons of British shipping alone.[99] Kesselring by contrast drew his supplies direct from Germany, only some 600 miles distant, along direct road and mainline rail links through the Alps – including the railways of neutral Switzerland. As Graham and Bidwell acknowledge: 'It could be said, therefore, that it was not Alexander who was drawing forces that would otherwise be employed against Allies in north-west Europe, but Kesselring who was containing Alexander.'[100]

On 18 May 1944 Alexander launched the 15th Army Group into a grand offensive on the front from Monte Cassino to the sea. Thanks to a brilliant plan designed by Major-General John Harding, Alexander's Chief of Staff, and the sheer weight of cleverly concentrated manpower, airpower and metal the *Gustavstellung* now gave way at last. Polish troops took Monte Cassino. Reinforced Allied forces in the Anzio beach-head broke out with the task of cutting off the 10th Army's retreat and so turning victory into total annihilation. However, General Clark, the 5th Army commander, in his vanity and egoism, diverted the Anzio forces north-westwards in order to award himself the prize of the city of Rome, rather than north-eastwards across the German lines of communication. The 10th Army escaped to fight another day. Rome fell on 6 June – D-Day for Overlord.

Now, while the 15th Army Group pressed on after the retreating enemy, Churchill and Brooke tried for the last time to persuade the American leadership to make a further investment in their Mediterranean strategy. They wished them to cancel the proposed seaborne invasion of the French Riviera (now codenamed 'Dragoon' instead of 'Anvil') so that Alexander could keep the two divisions and the landing craft earmarked for it. Alexander even revived Churchill's vision of marching to Vienna (and getting there before the Russians) from northern Italy via the so-called 'Ljubljana Gap' in Yugoslavia. Brooke himself, however, regarded this less as strategy than as mere 'dreams' or 'hopes',[101] since the 'Ljubljana Gap' actually consisted of a long and tortuous route with bad road and rail communications through mountain country; ideal terrain for a German army on the defensive.[102]

But the Americans would not hear of cancelling 'Dragoon'. Eisenhower (whose Allied Expeditionary Force was by now on the verge of final victory in Normandy), Marshall and Roosevelt all turned down the proposal flat, much to Churchill's chagrin.[103] 'Dragoon' duly took place on 15 August, so securing in Marseille a major and undamaged port which Eisenhower badly needed for the supply of his armies via the Rhone valley (see below pp. 842 and 849).

After the fall of Rome the elation of victory in the 15th Army Group once more gradually gave way to curdling disappointment as the retreat of Kesselring's Army Group C slowed down to another step-by-step fighting withdrawal through the mountains. It took August and September to crumble away the stubborn defence of the Gothic Line, running across Italy north of Pisa and Florence to Pesaro on the Adriatic. By December 1944 after months of grim slogging, of huge expenditure of shells and steeply mounting casualties, and despite total command of the air, the Allied armies found themselves once more stuck fast in stalemate: and still short of the wide plains of northern Italy. There they remained until April 1945.[104]

And every shell, every cartridge, every man's daily rations, every gallon of fuel or aviation spirit, every spare part and every bandage reached the Allied front by grace of the convoys still making the 8,000-mile round voyage between America and the Mediterranean ports and the 3,000-mile round voyage between Britain and those ports – and by grace also of the Allied warships that protected the merchantmen against the U-boat, the E-boat and the marauding bomber. Albert Kesselring could well smile, for his diversionary campaign was proving as profitable as Rommel's in Africa.

While the Allied armies had been hammering their way north, the navies had been keeping pace along the west and east coasts of Italy, busy with the routine tasks of ferrying up supplies, bombarding enemy troops and communications, attacking his convoys, landing raiding parties to keep alive the enemy's fear for his flanks. In the Adriatic a kind of guerrilla war at sea was fought by the Royal Navy and the French Navy, their destroyers and coastal craft sneaking into the channels running between the myriad islands strung along the Dalmatian coast in order to prey upon enemy coastal traffic. In the Aegean British and Greek ships were waging a similar buccaneering war amid the archipelagoes.

Yet it was the Russian victories on the Eastern Front in autumn 1944, leading to the collapse of the whole German position in the Balkans, which opened the way for the Royal Navy to return to the waters north of Crete for the first time since May 1941. On 5 September the Germans began to thin out their troops in southern Greece, Crete and the Aegean islands. On 3 October they decided to pull out of Greece altogether, although they still left reduced garrisons in Crete, Rhodes and elsewhere to fight it out to the last. Next day British commandos landed at Patras in the Peloponnese; the first British troops to stand on the Greek mainland since the débâcle of 1941. On 13–14 October parachute troops seized Athens airport in the wake of the decamping Germans and entered Athens. On the

15th a task force of two British infantry brigades escorted by the 15th Cruiser Squadron and two escort carriers commanded by Rear-Admiral J. M. Mansfield, flying his flag in HMS *Orion*, arrived in the Gulf of Athens; and by sunset, after a mass of shallow mines had been swept, Mansfield brought his ships to anchor off Piraeus. So after three and a half years the Royal Navy and the British Army returned again to Greece by the grace of the continental victories of the Red Army; and two veterans of the desperate evacuation of April 1941, HMS *Orion* and her sister ship *Ajax*, lay moored amid a mass of British and Greek ships of war beneath a sky whence never again would Stukas howl down to loose their bombs.

On 8 April 1945 the 8th Army in Italy in a new offensive smashed through the Adriatic sector of the German front; on the 14th (it was two days before the Red Army opened its final offensive across the Oder towards Berlin) the 5th Army Group pursued a disintegrating Army Group C to the foothills of the Alps. On 29 April (far away to the north the Russians were now fighting in the very heart of Berlin) was signed the unconditional surrender of Army Group C, to come into effect on 2 May. It marked the final consummation of the 'blue water' strategy espoused by the British since June 1940.

Yet after all the land campaigning from the Nile to the Po and beyond, all the Royal Navy's fleet actions and convoy struggles, all the sunk and shattered ships, all the arguments in London and Washington, this strategy had ended in a cul-de-sac. For ahead of 15th Army Group towered the barrier of the Alps, stretching in a vast semi-circle from the French Riviera round to Trieste on the Adriatic. This barrier German soldiers could have defended indefinitely if there had not been already behind it in southern France the forces of the Anglo-Americans, and behind it in northern Yugoslavia and Austria the forces of the Yugoslavs and Russians – and if the Third Reich had not itself been within six days of extinction when the surrender of Army Group C to Alexander came into effect.

For the ultimate victory in the Mediterranean was a mere by-play in the conclusion of a war that had been won in mass battles on the Eastern and Western Fronts. And the Western Front owed its existence to what remains to this day by far the grandest amphibious operation ever, and one executed under the command of an admiral of the Royal Navy.

23

'Such Desolate and Dangerous Voyages': the Arctic Convoys, 1941–1945

Ever since 22 June 1941, when 143 German divisions (including seventeen panzer) launched 'Operation Barbarossa' – Hitler's war to conquer and colonise the Soviet Union west of the Urals – it had been clear to the British leadership that in the Red Army lay the one potential means of tearing the guts out of German military power. For in contrast to the Great War the Eastern Front now constituted the *only* front in the present war where mass battles of attrition were taking place; it would remain the only one until the Western Front could be eventually reopened by an Anglo-American landing in France. At first, during the initial German onrush into the Soviet Union in the summer of 1941, British military opinion doubted the Red Army's ability to survive. Nevertheless, in order to help the Soviet Union as best she could, Britain quickly began to despatch aircraft, tanks, trucks and other war supplies which she could ill spare at this time of her own weakness. In August 1941 the first convoy to Russia (codenamed 'Dervish'), sailed for Archangel with seven freighters, followed by a second in September (PQ1). By the end of the year eight outward convoys had been despatched, all arriving without loss; a short-lived 'happy time'.

When the successful Soviet counter-offensive during the winter of 1941–42 proved that Hitler was after all not going to win his Russian war outright, the Western Allies (America by now having been bombed into the war by the Japanese attack on Pearl Harbor) came to base their entire grand strategy against Germany on the Red Army. As the British Chiefs of Staff summed it up in October 1942: 'It cannot be too clearly recognised that it is the war in Russia which is most rapidly sapping Germany's strength.' In their view, the Red Army constituted 'the primary means by which the German army can be defeated on land'. Only when the Red Army had finally undermined German military power would it be possible 'to establish and maintain a large allied army in France . . .'[1] It therefore followed, according to the COS, that the Western Allies must shape their own war-making first and foremost 'so as to assist Russia'.

The postponement of 'the Second Front' from 1942 to 1943 and then to 1944, meant, however, that there was relatively little that Britain and the United States could do militarily to take the pressure off the Red Army – only the bomber offensive and the secondary campaigns in North Africa and Italy. The Western Allies' most useful direct contribution therefore took the form of sending copious military supplies, the bulk of them American (and including thousands and thousands of trucks to move and supply the Red Army in the vast campaigns of movement that sprawled across the Russian plains). Although the overland route through Iran from the Persian Gulf ports carried some of this material, capacity was restricted by poor road and rail links, and most of the supplies had to go by sea from Britain through the Arctic to North Russian ports.

From August 1941 to the end of the war a total of 40 outward convoys were despatched on what was probably the most hazardous and horrible convoy route of them all – Arctic pack ice; fog; ferocious storms; perpetual night in winter, perpetual day in summer; compasses, even gyro compasses, unreliable because of the high latitudes, so making large navigational errors an extra hazard; all this plus the constant menace of attack by the Luftwaffe, the U-boats and the German heavy ships (including the *Tirpitz*, sister ship of the *Bismarck*) from their strategically dominating Norwegian bases. A total of 811 merchant ships sailed from Britain to Russia, the majority of them American or Panamanian-registered; 33 returned to port for various reasons such as weather or damage from ice; 58 were sunk by the enemy (plus another five lost in the Kola Inlet after arrival); and 720 arrived safely. The convoys carried a total of 4 million tons of supplies, including 5,000 tanks and over 7,000 aircraft; of that huge total despatched only about 300,000 tons (7.5 per cent) went down with sunken ships. The return journey was made by 35 convoys of 717 ships in all; eight ships had to return to harbour, while 29 ships were sunk, including one foundered and four lost in British minefields. Of thirteen ships which sailed independently to Russia from Iceland, five were sunk, and three had to turn back; in the reverse direction, 28 independents sailed, but only one was lost. Given all the dangers, these are remarkably small losses.

From start to finish the Arctic convoy shuttle cost the Royal Navy two cruisers, six destroyers, two sloops, one frigate, two corvettes, four minesweepers and one armed whaler; a Polish submarine was also lost.[2] Although American warships served with the Home Fleet during certain operations to support convoys, and Russian destroyers occasionally met convoys on their arrival, almost all the escorts and covering forces were furnished by the Royal Navy, which also carried the sole operational responsibility.

This heavy new burden began to fall on the Royal Navy when its resources were already painfully stretched by Dönitz's 1941 offensive in the Atlantic and by the battles that year to run convoys through the Mediterranean; when the Admiralty was also having to take anxious note of the growing Japanese menace. In 1942 the strain was to grow worse. The war in Russia still lay in the balance, for this was the year of the second great German summer offensive, which by September had reached the Volga at Stalingrad and the foothills of the Caucasus. The Western Allies consequently tried their uttermost to swell the flow of supplies to Archangel and Murmansk, with no fewer than twenty outward convoys despatched in the course of the year. The Germans equally recognised in 1942 how important these convoys had become to the issue of the campaign on the Eastern Front, and this year they mounted their most ferocious and sustained attack on the Arctic traffic. Yet 1942 saw the Admiralty even more hard pressed for ships than 1941. There were Dönitz's mounting successes in the Atlantic. There was the need to reconstitute British seapower in the Indian Ocean after the destruction of the *Prince of Wales* and *Repulse*. There were the most desperate of all the Malta convoy battles. And finally, from October onwards the demands of the 'Torch' expedition and the subsequent campaign in North Africa had to be met. As the Admiralty juggled its resources as best it could between all these urgent requirements, the same ships were to see service in turn in the Arctic, the Atlantic and the Mediterranean.

If the Arctic convoys added enormously to the Admiralty's global strategic problems, they presented Sir John Tovey, the Commander-in-Chief, Home Fleet, the admiral responsible for routing and protecting the convoys, with a baffling operational conundrum. In the first place, Tovey had to face both ways – to cover the convoys to the eastward while at the same guarding against a breakout westward by the German heavy ships. For from the end of February 1943, as Ultra decrypts recorded, Hitler moved both the *Tirpitz* and the pocket battleship *Admiral Scheer* to Trondheim in Norway. Parrying the threat of so formidable a battleship as the *Tirpitz* – in view of what it had taken to trap and sink her sister ship *Bismarck* – became a major preoccupation, not only for Tovey but also for the Admiralty and the government. In the second place, the Arctic convoys' Russian destination lay 2,000 miles distant, yet exposed to U-boat attack all the way, while the convoys' sea-room was restricted to a relatively narrow corridor by ice to the west and north and by the German-held coast of Norway to the south and east. This coast was blessed with numerous anchorages and well-placed airfields. From the airfields the Luftwaffe could dominate 1,400 miles of the voyage, while British shore-based aircraft were limited to bases no further to the north and east than Iceland and Sullom Voe in the Shetlands. The Luftwaffe also kept the ports at both ends of the route under constant surveillance. It is hardly surprising in the circumstances that differences of professional judgment should sometimes arise between Tovey and the First Sea Lord, Sir Dudley Pound, or that the latter, the arch-centraliser in the old naval tradition, should sometimes directly intervene in operations – on one occasion with catastrophic results.

Nevertheless at the beginning, from August 1941 to the end of February 1942, the Arctic convoys encountered small enemy opposition and sustained only minor loss. At this period the German Army hoped to take Murmansk, which would have effectively put a stop to the convoys. The failure to take the port compelled the German high command to look to its air and naval forces in Norway instead to stop the traffic of goods to Russia. It was from March 1942 onwards, with both sides coming fully to recognise the relevance of the convoys to the now protracted struggle on the Eastern Front, that Tovey's troubles really commenced. All factors were against him. The *Tirpitz* and *Scheer* lay at Trondheim ready to strike. The hours of daylight – the Luftwaffe's hunting time – were lengthening, and yet the pack ice still lay at its furthest extent southwards, so compelling convoys to pass south of Bear Island and therefore within 250 miles of the Norwegian coast. From 19 April to 6 May there would be no hours of darkness, only all-night twilight; between 6 May and 5 August the sun would always remain above the horizon.[3]

On 26 February, with an outward and a homeward convoy (PQ12 and QP8) due to run shortly, Tovey submitted his general proposals to the Admiralty for the future protection of the Arctic traffic. Firstly the voyages of the PQ and QP convoys were to be synchronised so that they passed together (on opposite courses) through the area of greatest danger of attack by German warships between longitude 5°W and 14°E; convoys were therefore to sail on the same date at minimum intervals of fourteen days.

'Such a programme,' Tovey wrote, 'would involve Home Fleet forces being in northern waters about five days in every 14; and it cannot be managed with the present number of destroyers, if a proper screen is to be provided for capital ships and an escort of two destroyers for each convoy. Another four destroyers will be required.'[4]

Tovey informed the First Sea Lord that he intended 'normally to cover these convoys with two capital ships, and sometimes with a carrier as well'. He accordingly proposed sending his second-in-command, Vice-Admiral A. T. B. Curteis, with the battlecruiser HMS *Renown* and the modern battleship HMS *Duke of York*, together with a cruiser and a destroyer screen, to support the convoys between 5°W and 14°E. He himself would remain at Scapa Flow with HMS *King George V*, the fleet carrier *Victorious* and another cruiser, ready either to join Curteis if necessary or to deal with a German attempt to break out into the Atlantic. Tovey acknowledged that the protection of the Arctic convoys constituted 'a major commitment for the Home Fleet, but in it lies the hope of bringing enemy surface ships to action'.[5] He nonetheless pronounced himself against employing the whole of the Home Fleet in this role, on the grounds that it would 'lead to a steady decline in efficiency' by interrupting the cycle of refits and leave.[6] But Pound and the Naval Staff overruled him. He was instructed instead to concentrate his entire fleet in support of the convoys – *King George V*, *Duke of York*, *Renown*, *Victorious*, the cruiser *Berwick* and nine destroyers. 'Their Lordships,' Tovey was informed on 3 March 1942, 'took full responsibility for any breakout of German ships which may occur while you are covering PQ and QP convoys.'[7]

On 1 March 1942, PQ12 (fifteen freighters and one oiler) left Reykjavik and QP8 (fifteen freighters) the Kola Inlet.[8] In the afternoon of the 5th a Luftwaffe Focke-Wulf Condor located PQ12 and reported its course and position; as it was to prove, the last useful reconnaissance by the Luftwaffe during this particular convoy action. On receipt of the Condor's report the *Tirpitz* (flying the flag of Vice-Admiral Ciliax) and three destroyers put to sea from Trondheim. Ciliax's orders were to avoid action with superior enemy forces but to engage equal British forces if need be in order to accomplish his main task of destroying the convoy.[9] *Tirpitz*'s departure escaped the vigilance of Coastal

Command reconnaissance patrols; nor did Sigint give the British any warning.[10] However, at 1730 on 6 March, Lieutenant I. F. Raikes, RN, in the patrolling submarine *Seawolf* sighted a faint smear of smoke to the south, and then the foretop and funnel of a large warship steaming fast up the Norwegian coast. According to his later report, 'I was certain in my own mind that it was the *Tirpitz*.'[11] But whereas Tovey now knew that *Tirpitz* was hunting for the convoy, Ciliax still had no idea that the Home Fleet was at sea.

The *Tirpitz* presented one lethal hazard; another lay in the ice encountered by the convoy that evening, causing it to alter from north-east to south-east. Even though this was only loose pack ice the experience led Captain M. M. Denny of the cruiser *Kenya* to conclude that 'I would never take a convoy anywhere near ice, accepting almost any other risk in preference'.[12] During the night, as vessels butted their way through the heaving islets of ice, the *Oribi* (Commander J. E. H. McBeath, RN) sustained considerable damage to her destroyer's light hull. (As destroyers went in for a refit, they had their hulls strengthened forward by lining with wood, and the whole hull lined with sprayed limpet asbestos in order to insulate against the cold and prevent condensation, which was a curse in closed down mess decks full of men.)

Next day, while Arctic fog rose eerily from the icy sea like a special effect in a horror film, the two sides played hide-and-seek with each other, the *Tirpitz* and her destroyers hunting for QP8 and PQ12, and especially PQ12 (crammed with supplies for the Red Army), but fortunately always to the south of the convoy's track; the Home Fleet in turn hunting for *Tirpitz*, but always to the south-west of her. Even so, all four groups of ships were steaming within 100 miles of one another for most of the day, and the convoys only narrowly escaped discovery. Because of poor visibility and icing *Victorious* was unable to fly air searches as intended to the south of the convoys which would in all likelihood have picked up the *Tirpitz*, while the *Tirpitz* herself was similarly unable to use her four Arado reconnaissance aircraft. The only contact of the day, a violent one, took place between a German destroyer and a Russian straggler from QP8, sunk by the destroyer.

The Russian's garbled and unintelligible distress signal, coupled with HF/DF bearings of an enemy ship which might be the *Tirpitz* (in fact it was a U-boat), persuaded Tovey that the enemy would now regard his position as being compromised and would be making for home. Tovey therefore altered to the east at 1750 and then north-east at 2000 in order to intercept him, ordering six destroyers to sweep

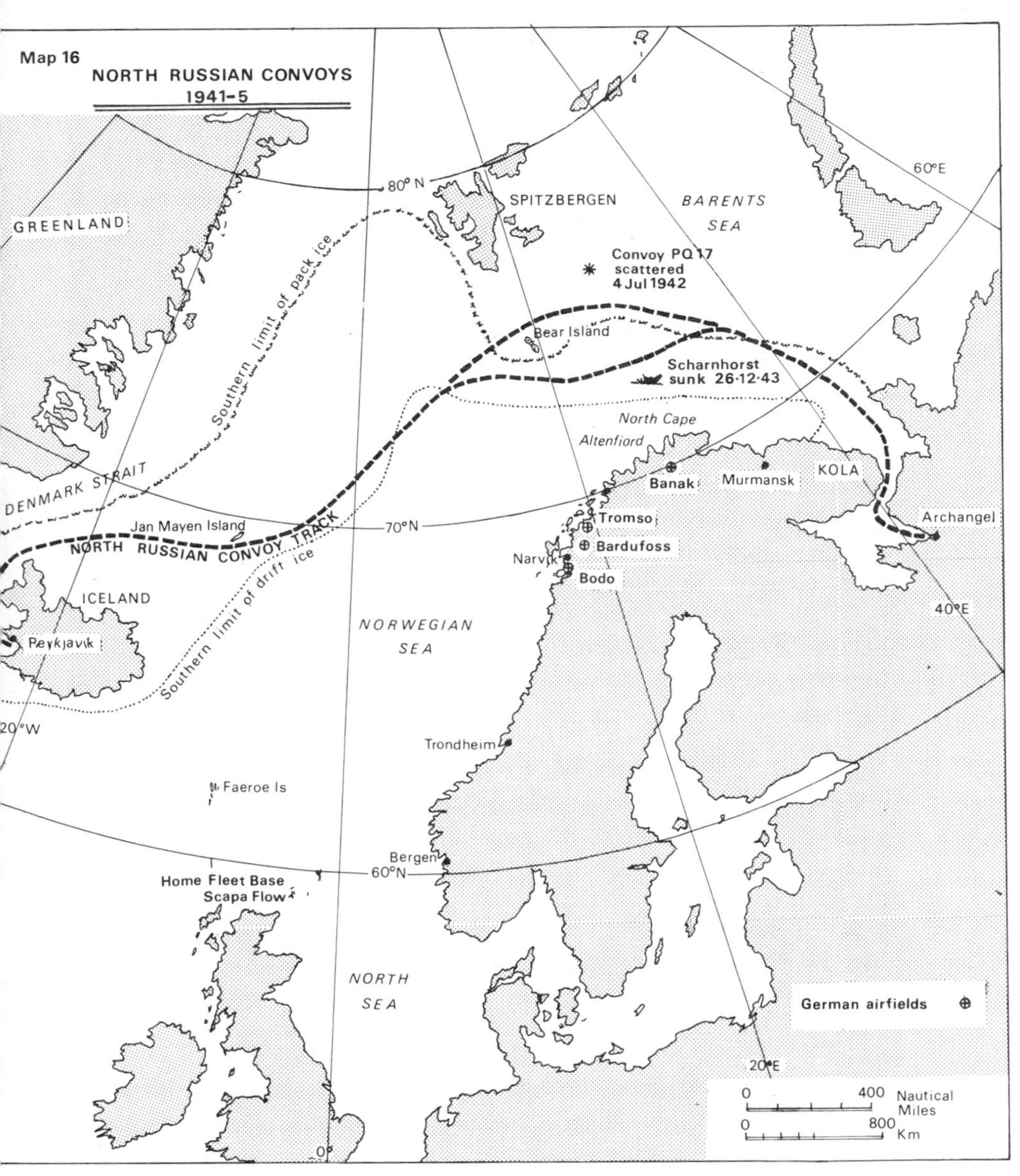
Map 16
NORTH RUSSIAN CONVOYS
1941–5
GREENLAND
80° N
SPITZBERGEN
BARENTS
SEA
60°E
Convoy PQ17
scattered
4 Jul 1942
Southern limit of pack ice
Bear Island
Scharnhorst
sunk 26·12·43
North Cape
Altenfiord
Banak
Murmansk
KOLA
Archangel
DENMARK STRAIT
Jan Mayen Island
70°N
Tromso
Bardufoss
Narvik
Bodo
NORTH RUSSIAN CONVOY TRACK
ICELAND
Southern limit of drift ice
Reykjavik
NORWEGIAN
SEA
40°E
20°W
Trondheim
Faeroe Is
Bergen
60°N
Home Fleet Base
Scapa Flow
NORTH
SEA
German airfields
20°E
0
400
Nautical
Miles
0
800
Km
0°

ahead across Ciliax's most probable course. There now followed a complex interaction between Ultra decrypts of the Luftwaffe and German Navy 'Home Waters' Enigmas (at around 16 to 24 hours' delay), consequent Admiralty signalling of information and even instructions to Tovey, and Tovey's own evolutions at sea.[13]

Meanwhile Ciliax had in fact not passed the Home Fleet on a homeward course, but instead was searching to the north and then to the west for PQ12; *Tirpitz* now being on her own, the destroyers having to return to port for want of fuel. Around noon on 8 March Ciliax came within 80 miles of the convoy. The Admiralty, recognising the danger from intercepts, signalled the convoy commodore to steer north of Bear Island. A sensible enough solution on the wall chart in the Admiralty War Room, it did not appeal to the commodore in view of the dangerous mass of ice lying even to the south of Bear Island, and he disregarded the order, continuing instead to follow the southern edge of the ice.

On the same day came a stroke of good fortune: at only three hours' delay GC and CS cracked an Enigma signal ordering Ciliax to return to Trondheim if he had not found the convoy by nightfall. At 1500 the Admiralty made a signal to Tovey accordingly, who on receiving it hauled round to make for Bear Island. The flow of intercepts continued. At 0102 on 9 March the Admiralty received a decrypt of a signal from *Tirpitz* as repeated back to her by Group North and timed 2232 on 8 March, cancelling her proposed search for the convoy on the 9th and stating that she would rendezvous with destroyers off the Lofoten Islands at 0700 that day.[14] The Admiralty thereupon made the terse and peremptory signal to Tovey: 'Steer 120° maximum speed'.[15] A later signal filled in the reasons.

Tovey now lay some 200 miles west of his quarry. At 0640 on 9 March *Victorious* flew off her reconnaissance aircraft. To the torpedo-carrying Albacores that followed, Tovey made the signal: 'A wonderful chance. God be with you.'[16] At 0800 a reconnaissance aircraft sighted *Tirpitz*; at 0840 the Albacores rode in to attack her great, graceful bulk. Yet not a single torpedo struck home, all passing astern, while two Albacores were shot down by *Tirpitz*'s fearsome array of anti-aircraft batteries of assorted calibres. Here was a fresh repetition of one of the oldest lessons of war – that success demands more than courage and determination; it demands group training to the highest standards of performance. The Albacore crews were relative novices, and the flight commander himself new to his squadron, having never flown with it before. By attacking from astern and into the wind rather than ahead and from windward the aircrafts' speed relative to the battleship was much less than it might have been, so giving the enemy time to take effective evasive action. Never again was the opportunity to occur for carrier aircraft to slow *Tirpitz* in the open sea so that the Home Fleet could bring her to action and destroy her like her sister ship.

In the evening of 9 March *Tirpitz* reached harbour in Narvik; on the following day Tovey brought the Home Fleet into Scapa Flow. Despite all the gropings and confusions Convoys PQ12 and QP8 had made safe passage in the face of the first sortie by the German heavy squadron now based in Norway.

Nevertheless the episode caused Tovey to think again about the whole problem of covering the Arctic convoys; and on 14 March he signalled a new appreciation to the Admiralty. In particular he now expressed pungent dissatisfaction with the Admiralty's directive of 3 March (see above, p. 697). In the first place Tovey was convinced that the German policy for their heavy ships must be to avoid at all costs action with British heavy forces:

> The *Tirpitz*, by her existence, contains very large British and United States forces and prevents their transfer to the Far East or the Mediterranean. She is so valuable an asset to all the Axis Powers that I am convinced that the enemy will not willingly expose this unique and irreplaceable asset to any unnecessary risk. The promptitude with which she entered the nearest harbour when attacked by aircraft from the *Victorious* . . . supports my conviction . . .[17]

In this Tovey guessed exactly right: in their own post-mortem on the PQ12 and QP8 operation the enemy were ruefully acknowledging that only 'sheer good fortune' had saved *Tirpitz* from damage, and both Ciliax and Raeder were determined in future to husband rather than hazard the ship.[18] On the assumption that the enemy would not risk the *Tirpitz* in future Tovey wrote that he preferred his own original suggested disposition of his resources. He argued that the Admiralty instructions of 3 March compelled him to operate his three capital ships and his carrier as a single unit in far-distant U-boat ridden waters where his destroyers' lack of endurance (for refuelling at sea remained in 1942 a relatively limited practice in the Royal Navy) would force him to keep the sea for long periods without a screen. All of this amounted in his view to 'a risky proceeding'.[19] He also bluntly stated to the Admiralty – really to Pound himself – that throughout the recent operation he 'had been seriously embarrassed' by the Admiralty's instructions. He reckoned that to sink the *Tirpitz* was 'of incomparably greater importance to the conduct of the war than the safety of any convoy'.[20] He claimed that if it was known that she was at sea he must be at liberty to take her destruction as his object. And he requested an assurance that the Admiralty agreed with this analysis, adding that in any case he believed that it was the U-boat that offered 'by far the most serious threat' to the convoys.

This was not all Tovey had to say. He strongly complained about the Admiralty signalling to him 'detailed instructions for the handling of his forces'. However here, in this particular case, he was on unsafe ground, because the Admiralty had known much more about Ciliax's intentions and movements thanks to Ultra than Tovey had at sea, while because of signalling difficulties on a secure link Tovey himself had at one point to ask the Admiralty to manoeuvre his cruisers and destroyers for him.

The First Sea Lord and the naval staff still believed, for their part, that two battleships, as proposed by Tovey, did not constitute enough force to cover a convoy against the *Tirpitz*, especially in view of experience with the *Bismarck*. Nonetheless, they did agree that the Home Fleet should not go east of 14°E without a destroyer screen; and also that Tovey's main objective should be to destroy the *Tirpitz*. But they considered that the best way of bringing this about was to provide a strong escort to the convoys. It is not clear whether they actually conveyed these views back to Tovey, for no reply to the latter's letter remains on the file.[21]

In the last week of March it was the turn of PQ13 and QP9, each of nineteen ships, and again supported by the whole of the Home Fleet during the most dangerous part of their passage. This time, however, the German heavy ships stayed in harbour – even though they had now been reinforced by the heavy cruiser *Hipper* – leaving the convoys to the Luftwaffe, the U-boats and the big German destroyers. All went well with QP9, but not so with PQ13, which on 24 March ran into a storm so violent that by the 27th not one merchantman remained within sight of the escort. Next day, with the convoy scattered along 150 miles of sea south of Bear Island, offered the Luftwaffe a superb opportunity to massacre the defenceless, and yet it only managed to destroy two vessels.

On the 29th German destroyers from Kirkenes took a hand, encountering the British escort at around 0900 in appalling weather. At 0922 the cruiser HMS *Trinidad* (flying the flag of Rear-Admiral S. S. Bonham-Carter: 8,000 tons; twelve 6-inch guns; launched March 1940)[22] fired torpedoes at the German destroyer Z26, but two of them failed to leave the tubes because of icing. With ships looming momentarily out of the snowy murk, two British destroyers even fired at each other. The report of proceedings by the captain of HMS

Eclipse (1,375 tons; four 4.7-inch guns; launched 1934)[23] described how spray sweeping over the guns and bridge froze instantly; how the gun decks became a sheet of ice; how the gun wells filled with sea water and ice. It was almost impossible to use binoculars because frozen spray immediately obscured the lenses.[24]

When the action petered out Z26 had been sunk, but HMS *Trinidad* herself had been seriously damaged by a torpedo. She finally struggled into Murmansk on 30 March. Here on 7 May a stoker fished out of a boiler furnace part of a torpedo pistol identifiable as belonging to *Trinidad*. She had thus torpedoed herself owing to the effect of intense cold on the oils in the torpedo's motor and gyroscope.[25] This was unique. But all too familiar and routine to every ship's company on the Arctic convoys was the mustering of all hands to chip away the enveloping crusts of ice on decks and gear and guns with pick and maul, in order to reduce the top weight of ice. In a small ship this could make all the difference between capsizing or not if hit by a torpedo. Only later in the war were technical measures introduced to keep the working parts of deck machinery, the muzzles and chases of guns, and the torpedo tubes free of ice, such as a coating of special grease, steam or electric heating, and insulating jackets.[26]

The attacks on PQ13, costing five merchantmen, convinced Tovey that the enemy was 'determined to do everything in his power to stop this traffic. The U-boat and air forces in Northern Norway had been heavily reinforced, the remaining three destroyers were disposed offensively at Kirkenes and the heavy forces at Trondheim remained a constant, if reluctant, threat.'[27] At his request the Admiralty transferred sufficient destroyers, corvettes and trawlers from Western Approaches Command to bring the close escorts of each convoy up to ten. The Russians were asked again and again, even at the highest level, to supply air and naval support, but so pressed were they that in Tovey's words 'little was forthcoming'.[28] Nonetheless two Russian destroyers did join the escort of the next outward convoy, PQ14, for the last few days before arrival in Murmansk.

With the arrival of the season of perpetual sunlight in the Arctic Tovey urged that the convoys should be run less frequently. His view was shared by the First Sea Lord, who submitted a memorandum on 8 April 1942 to the War Cabinet Defence Committee listing the threats to the convoys from German air and naval forces in Norway. He argued: 'Geographical conditions are so greatly in favour of the Germans that losses . . . may become so great as to render the running of these convoys uneconomical.'[29] Indeed the Naval Staff wanted to stop the traffic altogether during the summer months. Yet April was the month when the Russians launched a series of spring counter-offensives in the Crimea and Ukraine, while at this same period the British government knew from Ultra decrypts that the German Army was preparing its own summer offensive on the Eastern Front in prodigious strength. The Prime Minister had already assured Stalin in the previous month that he had given 'express instructions' that supplies to Russia 'shall not in any way be interrupted or delayed'.[30]

But now occurred a near-disaster to the joint passages of PQ14 and QP10, which left their departure ports on 8 April. PQ14, enlarged to 24 freighters in response to pressure from Roosevelt on Churchill, ran into a maze of thick drifting ice and became hopelessly scattered as each ship sought its way out through channels of clear water, only to find themselves blocked ahead or with ice closing in astern. Forepeaks crumpled against the jagged shelves; propellers and rudders were damaged and distorted by submerged ice. Several ice-damaged escorts had to return to Iceland, while only eight out of the 24 freighters were eventually able to make their way on towards Kola. Then came the Luftwaffe. The convoy commodore's own ship, *Empire Howard*, succumbed to two torpedoes, and the commodore himself, Commodore Rees, RN, was lost with her. Seven ships out of the original 24 reached harbour on 19 April. The commander of the escort, Rear-Admiral Bonham-Carter, who was flying his flag in the cruiser *Edinburgh* (10,000 tons displacement; twelve 6-inch guns; a 'rearmament' ship launched in March 1938)[31] explained in his report of proceedings why the enemy only managed to sink the *Empire Howard*:

> The remains of PQ14 were extremely lucky in the weather in that when the first heavy air attack developed on Friday, 17th April, fog suddenly came down . . . on the following day . . . when a combined surface, submarine and air attack was expected, the weather again was on our side, fog and snow showers persisting all day, and on the final run into the Kola Inlet a strong gale from the north-west sprang up. I consider it was due to the fine work of the Anti-Submarine Escort Force (under Commander M. Richmond) that only one ship was lost.[32]

Bonham-Carter could only draw a depressing lesson from the experience of the PQ14:

> Under present conditions with no hours of darkness, continually under air observation for the last four days, submarines concentrating in the bottlenecks, torpedo attacks to be expected, our destroyers unable to carry

out a proper hunt or search owing to the oil situation, serious losses must be expected in every convoy.[33]

Yet the political pressures to continue the convoys, even increase the traffic, were mounting. When on 26 April Churchill sought to make Roosevelt understand 'the serious convoy situation' Roosevelt replied that any stoppage of supplies, 'for any reason', would have 'a most unfortunate effect'.[34] Although the Prime Minister explained how short the Royal Navy was of escorts and that each convoy meant a major fleet operation, the President remained adamant that Britain must recognise 'the urgent necessity of getting off one more convoy in May in order to break the log-jam of ships already loaded or being loaded for Russia'.[35] Courteously but unshakably Churchill answered on 2 May: 'With very great respect what you suggest is beyond our power to fulfil.' After going on to list all the operational problems, he concluded: 'I can assure you, Mr President, we are absolutely extended and I could not press the Admiralty further.'[36] The question being then referred to the joint professional opinions of the First Sea Lord and COMINCH (Commander-in-Chief, United States Fleet), the latter agreed with his British colleague; whereupon Roosevelt at last accepted the British view.[37]

By this time, however, further calamities had befallen the Royal Navy on the Arctic route while escorting PQ15 (of fifteen merchantmen) and QP11 (of thirteen). From 29 April onwards the homeward-bound QP11, with a strong close escort of six destroyers, four corvettes and a trawler under the command of Rear-Admiral Bonham-Carter (again flying his flag in HMS *Edinburgh*), came under heavy attack by U-boats, destroyers and aircraft. *Edinburgh*'s stern was blown off and her steering wrecked by two torpedoes from the U-456. For 23 hours she steered back to Murmansk in the company of two British and two Russian destroyers on her engines only at about two knots average speed of advance, all the time swinging from port to starboard and back. According to her engine-room register no fewer than 64 engine orders were issued in one watch on one propeller shaft alone.[38] On her way she still managed to hit and stop the German destroyer *Hermann Schoemann* in a fight with three enemy destroyers hungry for an easy victim, but sadly then succumbed to another torpedo which almost cut her in two. *Edinburgh* was finally sunk by a torpedo from HMS *Foresight* (Commander J. Salter) after the minesweepers *Harrier* and *Gossamer* had rescued all 790 survivors. In the same fight the destroyers *Forester* and *Foresight* (each 1,350 tons displacement; four 4.7-inch guns; launched 1934)[39] were in turn hit, stopped and badly damaged by the big German destroyers with their 5.9-inch guns. Fortunately the remaining two enemy ships chose to go to the aid of their wounded sister rather than finish off their enemies. Once the *Hermann Schoemann* had sunk, they withdrew; another German case of not engaging the enemy more closely. The British destroyers now slowly got under way again.

On 1 May the three German destroyers before turning their attention to the *Edinburgh* had tried five times to break through QP11's weakened escort and get at the convoy – and each time were foiled by the aggressiveness of the British escort, even though the German ships mounted a total of ten 5.9-inch guns and five 5-inch to the six 4.7-inch and three 4-inch in the four smaller British ships remaining with the convoy. The convoy itself sought refuge within the pack-ice, picking its way in single file through heavy drifting slabs. According to the report of Commander Richmond, commanding officer of the escort, in HMS *Bulldog*: 'in order to maintain touch the destroyers were led through lanes of open water as opportunity offered, bearing in mind that sufficient sea-room to manoeuvre in action must be maintained. This presented a nice problem.'[40] The enemy destroyers finally gave up and disappeared behind a smoke screen as the British ships headed towards them. When Commander Richmond signalled his congratulations to his little force, one captain instantly replied: 'I should hate to play poker with you!'[41]

The outward convoy, PQ15, supported by the Home Fleet and with a strong close escort, proved to have better luck. Although aircraft and U-boats attacked it from 2 to 4 May only three merchantmen were lost, victims of torpedo-bombers. Then on the 4th dense fog closed protectively round the convoy and shrouded it for the rest of the voyage. The total losses in both convoys amounted therefore to no more than four out of 38 ships. But the Royal Navy's own losses had been dismayingly high. In addition to the cruiser *Edinburgh* sunk and the destroyers *Forester* and *Foresight* damaged, the destroyer *Punjabi* was rammed and sunk by HMS *Duke of York* in fog on 1 May and the Polish submarine *Jastrzab* destroyed in error by British warships when she was suddenly encountered 100 miles away from her expected patrol area. Nor was this all. On 14 May the damaged cruiser *Trinidad* was hit by a bomb while on her way home from Murmansk and set on fire. The fire spread out of control and she had to be sunk by a British torpedo. Rear-Admiral Bonham-Carter thus lost two flagships in succession. In his report of proceedings he drew an even more sombre lesson from the experiences of PQ15 and QP11 than from those of PQ14 and QP10:

> I am still convinced that until the aerodromes in North Norway are neutralised and there are some hours of darkness that the continuation of these convoys should be stopped. If they must continue for political reasons, very serious and heavy losses must be expected. The force of German attacks will increase not diminish. We in the Navy are paid to do this sort of job, but it is beginning to ask too much of the men of the Merchant Navy. We may be able to avoid bombs and torpedoes with our speed, a six or eight knot ship has not this advantage.[42]

Tovey fully endorsed these views in conveying them to the Admiralty. In any case the First Sea Lord was of the same mind, writing to COMINCH, 'Ernie' King, on 18 May that the Russian convoys 'are becoming a regular millstone round our necks and cause a steady attrition in both cruisers and destroyers'. He added that 'the whole thing is a most unsound operation with the dice loaded against us in every direction . . . but I do . . . recognise the necessity of doing all we can to help the Russians at the present time'. 'Ernie' King answered on 21 May: 'I am very much in sympathy with your views . . .'[43] The political pressure to continue, even to enlarge, the operation proved irresistible. By now the Russian spring offensives on the Eastern Front had become stuck, and on the very same day that the First Sea Lord was writing to COMINCH the Germans launched a smashing counter-stroke in the Ukraine which threw the Russians back in disorder. And all the time, as the Western Allies well knew through Ultra, the Germans were slotting into place the panzer armies for their own coming summer offensive on the Eastern Front. The Arctic convoys would have to go on, as the Red Army would have to go on.

On 21 May 1942, now the most unfavourable season of the year with perpetual Arctic daylight, the largest ever outward convoy to Russia, PQ16 of 35 merchantmen, put to sea from Iceland. Although the Commander-in-Chief, Home Fleet, had asked for Royal Air Force reconnaissance aircraft and fighters to be stationed in North Russia to provide air cover over the Barents Sea, Coastal Command simply could not find the resources.[44] The Arctic skies would therefore belong to the Luftwaffe 24 hours a day. It was known through Ultra that the two pocket battleships *Scheer* and *Lützow* now lay at Narvik, in addition to *Tirpitz* and *Hipper* at Trondheim. Tovey therefore deployed four cruisers, HMS *Nigeria*, *Norfolk*, *Kent* and *Liverpool*, and three destroyers under Rear-Admiral H. M. Burrough as close cover while the whole Home Fleet provided distant cover against the German heavy ships, especially the *Tirpitz*. As was usually the case, submarines were also deployed as cover for the convoy in the hope that they might intercept and sink the German heavy ships if they should put to sea to attack it. The escort of PQ16 comprised HMS P-614, the Dutch submarine 010, HMS P-46 (*Unruffled*), HMS P-37 (*Unbending*) and the Norwegian *Uredd*. Serving as close escort to the convoy were HMSs *Trident* and *Seawolf*, the former submarine firing off all her ammunition in the course of the convoy's fight against enemy air attacks.

On 25 May a Luftwaffe shadower appeared on the horizon, and for the next five days the merchantmen were never without a watcher circling maddeningly out of gun range; as always, an experience cumulatively depressing to morale. After the homeward convoy QP12, of fifteen ships, had passed safely to the westward of PQ16, the Luftwaffe started work on PQ16 and kept it up almost without pause throughout the remaining five days of the voyage, Heinkel He 111 torpedo-bombers alternating with Ju 88 dive-bombers in the tactics already so familiar in the Mediterranean. Their first victim was the freighter *Carlton*, which suffered a fractured steam pipe from a bomb hit; she had to be detached to Iceland under tow by the *Northern Spray*. The commander of the close convoy escort, Commander R. G. Onslow, RN, was to write in his report: 'I was greatly impressed by the spirit and determination of the Master and crew of the *Carlton*, also by the calm acceptance by *Northern Spray* of a long and difficult voyage with no hope of support against air attack.'[45]

Early on 26 May came the convoy's first loss – a freighter torpedoed by a U-boat. Then it was the Luftwaffe's turn again, only to be thwarted by the storm of fire put up by the combined close and cruiser escort forces. Making her début on the Arctic run was the catapult aircraft carrier *Empire Lawrence*, whose single Hurricane shot down one enemy aircraft and damaged another.

Next day, however, after Burrough had turned back with his cruiser force according to instructions, the Luftwaffe hammered the convoy with unrelenting strikes, the German aircraft giving their customary but unadmired imitation of a swarm of furious hornets buzzing round the head of an intruder. The anti-aircraft ship *Alynbank* counted attacks by 108 aircraft. Six ships went down, including the *Empire Lawrence*. The convoy commodore's own ship, the *Ocean Voice*, received a direct hit from a bomb which set her on fire and stripped away about twenty feet of side plating abreast of No. 1 hold within two feet of the waterline. Two other ships and the Polish-manned destroyer *Garland* were badly damaged. Fortunately for the *Ocean Voice* the sea remained calm. Yet Commander Onslow, the escort commander, later confessed that he 'had little hopes of her survival, but this gallant ship maintained her station, fought her fire, and with God's help arrived at her destination'.[46]

Nevertheless it had been a terrible day. 'With another three days to go', wrote Onslow,

> . . . and 20 per cent of the convoy already lost, I felt far from optimistic. I ordered all ships to exercise strict economy [of ammunition] and restricted controlled fire in *Ashanti* to one mounting at a time. We were all inspired however by the parade ground rigidity of the convoy's station-keeping, including *Ocean Voice* and *Star Bolshevik* who were both billowing smoke from their holds.[47]

Thankfully this proved to have been the worst day. Only an already damaged ship was lost on 28 May, while the escort was strengthened by three Russian destroyers. In the evening of the 29th six British minesweepers also joined, and next day Russian Hurricanes flew in to provide air cover. That afternoon the convoy passed Toros Island into the Kola Inlet, 'reduced in numbers,' wrote Onslow, 'battered and tired, but still keeping perfect station'.[48] That PQ16 had got through without disaster in fact owed much to Onslow's own leadership as an outstandingly skilful and resolute close escort commander. The two previous convoys had had a cruiser and an admiral in their close escorts, and lost both cruisers.

He now had his own recommendations to make to his superiors: the importance of including an escort carrier or a catapult aircraft carrier in the escort in order to deal with shadowing aircraft; likewise an anti-aircraft ship; the need for stronger anti-aircraft armament in the destroyers and for reserves of ammunition to be held in the convoys and at Kola; the desirability of as many long-range radar sets as possible.[49] Onslow also suggested that convoy escorts should include a high-powered salvage tug with good fire-fighting appliances which could save damaged ships; special rescue ships as well. But how was the Royal Navy, with its desperately straitened resources, to honour these requests?

The Commander-in-Chief, Home Fleet, gave vent to immense relief that PQ16 had completed its passage with such small loss:

> This success was beyond expectation; it was due to the gallantry, efficiency and tireless zeal of the officers and men of the escorts and to the remarkable courage and determination of those of the merchant ships. No praise can be too high for either.[50]

Dönitz, for his part, could only confide glumly to his war diary that the attacks against the convoy 'must be accounted a failure'.[51]

Thus Tovey's and Pound's forebodings about the appalling risks being incurred in continuing to run the Arctic convoys had so far failed to be borne out in the event. They could only pray that the next outward convoy, PQ17, would be equally fortunate.

Convoy PQ17, of 36 merchantmen, did not sail for Russia from Iceland until 27 June 1942. The Admiralty had been compelled to suspend the Arctic convoy traffic for a month because the cruisers *Kenya* and *Liverpool* and eight destroyers had had to be despatched to the Mediterranean for 'Harpoon', the hazardous operation to run a convoy through to Malta from Gibraltar in order to relieve Malta's now extreme plight (see above, pp. 505–9). This redeployment of ships serves as a demonstration both of the flexibility of seapower and of the Home Fleet's role as the Royal Navy's central strategic reserve. Unfortunately *Liverpool* and the destroyer *Matchless* were reduced to dockyard cases by enemy action during 'Harpoon', and the destroyer *Bedouin* (Commander B. G. Scurfield, a close friend of Onslow) was sunk. The Mediterranean Fleet also lost a destroyer and had two destroyers and a minesweeper damaged. Such weakening of resources could only sharpen Pound's and Tovey's anxieties about the prospects for the next convoy to North Russia. As Tovey was to write in his despatch, the strategic situation

> . . . was wholly favourable to the enemy. His heavy ships would be operating close to their own coast, with the support of powerful shore-based air reconnaissance and striking forces, and protected, if he so desired, by a screen of U-boats in the channels between Spitzbergen and Norway. Our covering forces, on the other hand, if they entered these waters would be without shore-based air support, one thousand miles from their bases, with their destroyers too short of fuel to escort a damaged ship to harbour.[52]

Tovey wished to solve the problem by means of deceptive manoeuvre rather than simply trying to fight PQ17 through the enemy's ambushes. Reckoning that 'a more favourable disposition could be brought about only by inducing the enemy heavy ships to come further to the westward to deliver their attacks',[53] he proposed that when PQ17 reached longitude 10°E it should put back for twelve to eighteen hours, unless the German heavy ships were known to be still safely in harbour or unless the weather proved thick enough to prevent enemy aircraft from shadowing. Tovey hoped that 'this temporary turn back would either tempt the German heavy ships to pursue, or cause them to return to harbour, or cruise for an extended period among our submarines . . .'[54]

The Admiralty – the First Sea Lord and the naval staff – disagreed with Tovey's proposal, issuing instructions to Tovey on 27 June which, in the words of the Naval Staff History, 'envisaged the possibility, under certain circumstances, of the convoy being temporarily turned back by the Admiralty; but not of this turn being timed to achieve [Tovey's] object'.[55] Instead the Admiralty instructions laid down that British surface forces were to defend the convoy against enemy heavy ships to the west of Bear Island, but not beyond, where the task would fall to submarines alone. The Admiralty emphasised that even the cruiser covering force was not intended to go east of Bear Island unless the convoy was threatened by surface forces capable of being fought by cruisers, and in any case not beyond 25°E.

This was not the only point of disagreement between the Admiralty and the Commander-in-Chief, Home Fleet. The other related to contingency plans should German heavy ships attack the convoy when it was no longer supported by the Home Fleet. On 16 March 1942 Tovey had issued a new directive, subsequently incorporated into the Home Fleet's 'Instructions for Escorts of North Russian Convoys',[56] in which he stated:

> I wish it to be clearly understood that in the event of a Russian convoy being attacked by a force overwhelmingly superior to the escort, the primary object of the escort is to ensure the enemy being shadowed to enable them to be brought to action by our heavier forces or submarines or to be attacked after dark, or under more favourable conditions, by the escort itself.[57]

The Atlantic Convoy Instructions (ACIs) of April 1942 indeed specifically forbade scattering in the face of attack, 'until or unless the escort is overwhelmed'; and on 21 June, a week before PQ17 put to sea, Tovey issued a Home Fleet memorandum that Arctic convoys were to follow ACIs.[58]

Tovey was therefore seriously perturbed to learn, during a telephone conversation with Pound, that the Admiralty now contemplated ordering PQ17 to scatter under certain circumstances. Tovey pointed out to Pound how recent operations had shown the importance of convoys remaining concentrated for the sake of mutual support against aircraft. According to the Naval Staff History, Tovey 'strongly deprecated such an order being given, except as a last resort in the actual presence of attack by overwhelming surface forces'.[59]

The deployment of warships in support of PQ17 and QP13 followed the pattern for PQ16 and QP12. PQ17's close escort, all British or French ships, consisted of six destroyers (plus the US destroyers *Wainwright* and *Rowan*, which joined on 4 July), the anti-aircraft ships *Palomares* and *Pozarica*, four corvettes and two submarines under the command of Commander J. E. Broome, RN, in the old destroyer *Keppel* (1,480 tons displacement; two 4.7-inch guns; four 20mm anti-aircraft guns).[60] Three rescue ships also accompanied the convoy, which initially numbered 36 merchantmen. Commander Jack Broome was one of the Royal Navy's colourful characters, an able and witty cartoonist, a man with a sense of humour buoyant even in the most hazardous of circumstances; a skilled and resolute fighting sailor in the best tradition of convoy escorts. Close cover to PQ17 as far as Bear Island would be provided by the 1st Cruiser Squadron, composed of the cruisers HMS *London* (flag), HMS *Norfolk*, USS *Tuscaloosa* and USS *Wichita*, and three destroyers under Rear-Admiral L. H. K. Hamilton. Tovey, with two battleships, HMS *Duke of York* (flag) and USS *Washington* (flying the flag of Rear Admiral R. C. Giffen, commanding the United States Navy's Task Force 39), the fleet carrier *Victorious*, the cruisers *Nigeria* and *Northumberland* and fourteen destroyers (including the USSs *Mayrant* and *Rhine*), would give distant support against the German heavy ships to the north-east of Jan Mayen Island. In addition, thirteen submarines were now patrolling off the exits to the bases of German surface forces.

Rear-Admiral 'Turtle' Hamilton, 'a fighting puckish little bachelor' according to his Staff Officer (Operations), 'a destroyer officer in the classic mould',[61] all too soon found himself having to manoeuvre to the whistles of two masters. Around noon on 4 July, when PQ17 had been at sea for a week and had already passed east of Bear Island into the zone of greatest danger, Hamilton received a signal from the Admiralty that 'unless otherwise ordered by the C-in-C, HF, you may proceed eastward of 25°E [NB: five degrees east of Bear Island] should the situation demand it. This is not to be taken by you as urging you to proceed eastwards against your discretion.'[62] The C-in-C, Home Fleet, thereupon signalled Hamilton with his own gloss on this Admiralty instruction: 'Once the convoy is to the eastward of 25°E or earlier at your discretion you are to leave the Barents Sea unless assured by the Admiralty that the *Tirpitz* cannot be met.'[63] Longitude 25°E runs almost exactly through Norway's North Cape, where the jagged coastline bends from a SW–NE alignment to NW–SE towards Russia, and some 2° east of Altenfiord.

The C-in-C's signal to Hamilton crossed one from Hamilton to him at 1520 stating that he, Hamilton, would remain with the convoy until the situation with regard to enemy surface forces had been clarified, but certainly no later than 1400 on 5 July.[64] At 1809 Hamilton informed the C-in-C that he intended withdrawing the 1st Cruiser Squadron to the west about 2200 that evening after refuelling his destroyers. But about 1930 Hamilton received a fresh order from the Admiralty telling him to remain with the convoy pending further instructions. It could not be said therefore that Hamilton was enjoying a Nelsonian standard of decisive leadership from above. But the explanation alike for these uncertainties of mind and for the 'second-guessing' of the C-in-C by the Admiralty is to be found in the amount and reliability of the available Sigint (and especially Ultra decrypts) about German movements and intentions. In the first place, the Admiralty – that is, the Operational Intelligence Centre, the War Room, the Naval Staff, the First Sea Lord himself – enjoyed the fullest first-hand access to Ultra decrypts, which Tovey at sea to the north-west of Bear Island did not, so providing in this case a powerful and genuine justification for Pound's own temperamental itch to centralise decision in his own hands. In the second place, Sigint – even Ultra – was failing to give a clear and certain picture of the most dangerous single threat facing PQ17, that of the *Tirpitz*.[65]

By the time PQ17 sailed, GC and CS at Bletchley Park had certainly provided full information about the intended deployment of U-boats against the convoy and also about the Luftwaffe's operational plans. As for the German surface forces, decrypts of the naval Enigma had provided no evidence that the *Tirpitz* had left Trondheim for the north; they also indicated that it was 'probable' that the pocket battleships *Scheer* and *Lützow* were still in Narvik.[66] In the afternoon of 1 July the Admiralty informed Tovey and Hamilton that, while it was known that the enemy expected the convoy to pass Jan Mayen Island about this time, 'on negative evidence it would appear that there had been no movement of main units and no sighting of PQ17 up to 1200 on 1 July'.[67] At 1900 that day the Admiralty was able to report further to the C-in-C and the Flag Officer, 1st Cruiser Squadron, that the convoy had now been sighted by the enemy; and that at 1313 on 2 July a torpedo-bomber attack had been ordered. At 2349 the Admiralty confirmed to the two flag officers that there was still 'no direct indications of movements of enemy main units', but only possible inferences to be drawn from the fact that the Luftwaffe had located the Home Fleet (it soon lost it again).[68]

Next day, 3 July, however, it became clear through Ultra that the *Scheer* was now on the move to some base north of Narvik, probably

Altenfiord, and that the *Tirpitz* and *Hipper* too were steaming north from Trondheim, though it seemed that *Lützow* was not in company with *Scheer* (in fact, the *Scheer* and three destroyers ran aground and took no further part in the operation).

Now, just as German movements were under way, there occurred a tantalising delay in decrypting the naval Enigma, for not until 1837 on 4 July were the signals for the period 1200 on 3 July to 1200 on 4 July read by GC and CS. To fog the situation still further, Coastal Command reconnaissance patrols off the North Cape were interrupted by an accident to an aircraft. Only two pieces of Ultra guidance reached Tovey in *King George V* during this lapse of time – confirmation that the *Scheer* was moving to Altenfiord; and that an hourly sequence of indecipherable Enigma signals 'may indicate the commencement of a special operation by main units'.[69] Tovey was thus for the moment reduced to the same kind of anxious guessing as his predecessors as fleet commanders in earlier wars such as Jellicoe steaming towards the High Seas Fleet in 1916, or Nelson hunting for Villeneuve in 1804–5. This accounts for Tovey's signal to Hamilton ordering him to leave the Barents Sea when the convoy was east of 25°E or earlier at his discretion, unless the Admiralty could assure him that the *Tirpitz* could not be met.

During the afternoon of 4 July a Luftwaffe Enigma decrypt indicating that aircraft from Bardufoss airfield were preparing to attack the convoy led the Admiralty to signal directly to Commander Broome (commanding PQ17's close escort), who was not in on the Ultra secret, in plain language: 'Most immediate. Blue Pendant', Blue Pendant in the signal code meaning air attack imminent.[70]

In the warren of fusty offices adjacent to the Admiralty War Room in 'the Keep' (the huge block-house on the corner of Horse Guards' Parade and the Mall) uncertainty was winding nerves taut, sharpening minds. Since the convoy had put to sea, Commander Norman Denning, the officer in the Operational Intelligence Centre responsible for reading the intentions of the German surface fleet, had been visited ever more frequently by various members of the Naval Staff – the Assistant Chief (Rear-Admiral E. J. P. Brind), the Director of Operations (Home) (Captain John Eccles); and the Vice Chief (Vice-Admiral Henry Moore). Not until late on 3 July, however, did the First Sea Lord and Chief of Naval Staff, Sir Dudley Pound, himself limp into Denning's room for the first time.

Now, 24 hours later, as the Naval Staff waited eagerly and in trepidation for the latest Enigma decrypts to come through, Pound's homely face and bent figure of a weather-worn old sailorman came through Denning's door again. With him were Brind and Eccles. Rear-Admiral Clayton, the Director of the OIC, was already in the room with Denning, who recalled:

> Pound sat down on a stool in front of the main plotting table. The plot showed the planned convoy route, the position of the convoy, our own forces and as far as was known or estimated, the position of U-boats and German surface forces.
>
> Bletchley had not yet broken the new keys.
>
> Luftwaffe reconnaissance had still not relocated Tovey's force, and had not yet located Hamilton's cruiser force.
>
> Almost immediately Pound asked what would be the farthest on position of TIRPITZ assuming she had sailed direct from Trondheim Fjord to attack the convoy . . . someone – I think it was Brind – plotted a rough course and estimated that she could then be within striking distance of the convoy.
>
> I interjected that it was unlikely in any event that she would have taken a direct course from Trondheim Fjord as she would almost certainly have made as much use as she could of the Inner Leads and proceed via Vest Fjord: I also considered that she would put into Narvik or Tromso to refuel her escorting destroyers before setting out on a sortie.[71]

The roomful of officers fell silent while Pound 'gazed at the plot for some time but said very little'.[72] Denning then broke into 'his apparent reverie' to say that within a few hours Bletchley Park would probably have broken the naval Enigma for the previous twenty-four hours. Pound then left the room. Shortly afterwards Denning was telephoned from Bletchley Park by Dr (now Professor Sir Harry) Hinsley of the Naval Section of GC and CS with the news that a break was imminent. This prompted the signal, drafted by Eccles and presumably approved by Pound, to Hamilton (and repeated to Tovey at 1930): 'Further information may be available shortly. Remain with the convoy until further instructions.'

At 1900 the teleprinter began to clack out two decrypts: a report timed 0040 that morning that the Luftwaffe had located a force composed of a battleship and three cruisers (which the Admiralty knew from the position given must be Hamilton's 1st Cruiser Squadron); and an order timed 0740 that morning from Grand Admiral Raeder to the Admiral Commanding Cruisers. This read:

> Immediate. Arriving Alta [Altenfiord] 0900. You are to allot anchorage to TIRPITZ . . . Newly arrived destroyers and torpedo boats to complete with fuel at once.[73]

Denning was in the midst of drafting a signal to convey this information to Tovey and Hamilton when Pound came in with several members of the Naval Staff, followed shortly by the VCNS and the Assistant Chief of Naval Staff (Trade), Vice-Admiral E. L. S. King. 'I was immediately asked,' writes Denning,

> what I was proposing to say. I gave the gist of the two intercepts and a proposed comment that all indications pointed to TIRPITZ and accompanying ships still being in harbour at Alta. Pound apparently considered the comment premature and my proposed 'Ultra' was whittled down to the bald facts that TIRPITZ had arrived at Alta at 0900 that morning and that Admiral SCHEER was already there.[74]

All decisions now turned on whether the *Tirpitz* was or was not by now at sea heading for PQ17. These decisions Pound, the executive head of the Navy, took upon himself in the most critical hour of his entire service as First Sea Lord. He suffered from the handicap that he had never flown his flag at sea in the present war, and knew nothing of modern naval operations at first hand; from the further handicap that his habits of mind had been shaped by the rigidities and artificiality of peacetime fleet manoeuvres. Now he had to resolve an operational puzzle on the basis of negative rather than positive Intelligence indications.

> Pound resumed the seat on the stool at the head of the plotting table and enquired how long it would take for the destroyers to top up with fuel. I had already mentally calculated this as about three hours. Then he asked what was likely to be the speed of TIRPITZ. I replied probably 25 or 26 knots provided the weather was favourable for the destroyers but two or three knots less if pocket battleships were also in company.
>
> Taking up the dividers and using a smaller chart of the area for plotting, Pound remarked that if TIRPITZ had sailed from Alta that morning, she could be up with the convoy about midnight. He then asked me why I thought TIRPITZ had not yet left Alta?[75]

In reply Denning drew Pound's attention to the cautious pattern of *Tirpitz*'s sortie against PQ12; noted that up to noon that day no decrypt had been received ordering U-boats to keep clear of the convoy (in order to avoid possible mistaken attack on *Tirpitz*), and that HF/DF showed that the U-boats were still clinging to the convoy. Moreover, the Luftwaffe had not yet relocated Tovey, while its having reported Hamilton's cruiser squadron as including a battleship could only increase the German naval command's apprehensions. The Luftwaffe had also reported seeing an aircraft in the vicinity of Hamilton's force, so probably raising the spectre for the German command that a British carrier might be present. Then again, the pattern of German naval radio signalling showed none of the characteristics typical of surface ships at sea. Finally, no sighting report of enemy heavy ships had been received from the British submarines patrolling off the North Cape.

Though other members of the Naval Staff made comments or put questions to Denning, Pound himself 'spoke very little and played idly with the dividers, and apparently sunk in thought'.

> After a time Pound got up to proceed to the U-boat tracking room but before leaving he turned to me and asked: 'Can you assure me that TIRPITZ is still in Altenfjord?'
>
> My reply was to the effect that although I was confident she was, I could not give absolute assurance but fully expected to receive confirmation in the fairly near future when Bletchley had unbuttoned the new traffic.[76]

At 2031 the teleprinter clattered out a fresh decrypt of a signal timed 1130 that forenoon from Admiral Commanding Group North to the U-boats operating against PQ17: 'No own forces in operational area. Position of heavy enemy group not known at present but is main target for U-boats when encountered . . .'[77]

This new decrypt resolved all possible doubts in Denning's mind; in his own words, 'Clearly TIRPITZ had not sailed that morning.'[78] He hastened to find Clayton, only to bump into him in the corridor while he was on his way to a meeting called by Pound. They exchanged a quick word, and Clayton took the teleprinter message with him to the meeting. Back in his own room, Denning 'tried to sum up the situation as it appeared in the eyes of the German Naval Staff from such information as was available to them . . .' Denning came to the firm conclusion that with Tovey's heavy ships and the possible carrier still not relocated, with the chance that there might be a second British heavy group with a carrier at sea (that is, Hamilton as reported by the Luftwaffe), he as a German admiral would judge that 'it would be taking an unjustifiable risk to commit our only worthwhile surface force to attack the convoy at present. Thus for the time being we will continue to attack and harass the convoy by U-boat and aircraft.'[79]

This appreciation chimed, of course, with Tovey's general judgment in his letter to the Admiralty on 14 March that the Germans would take no risks with so precious and irreplaceable an asset as the *Tirpitz*.

Denning now began to draft a signal to Tovey and Hamilton based on his appreciation. The draft stated, according to Denning's recollection, that 'it was considered TIRPITZ and accompanying ships were still in Altenfjord at 1200/4. Indications strongly pointed to them not having yet sailed. It was unlikely they would sail until Germans have located and established location and strength of the forces in support of the convoy.'[80]

Tovey back in March and Denning now had in fact accurately read the enemy's mind. For although Admiral Raeder had ordered the movement of the heavy ships to northern Norway, Hitler consistently refused to allow them to go to sea to attack the convoy until and unless the whereabouts of British aircraft carriers had first been established.

In the normal course of events Denning would have despatched his signal on his own responsibility. This time he felt he must await Clayton's return from a meeting with the First Sea Lord. Meanwhile he was visited by Commander Rodger Winn, RNVR, in charge of the U-boat tracking room, who on reading Denning's draft remarked that he understood from discussion going on in his room that 'the TIRPITZ was already at sea and there was talk of dispersing the convoy'.[81] It did not relieve Denning's 'grave concern' at such a decision being taken, and on unsound grounds, when Clayton returned at about 2130 and confirmed that 'because of the U-boat threat Hamilton had been ordered to withdraw to the westward at high speed and because of the possible threat of attack by surface forces on the convoy, Pound had decided to disperse it'.[82]

Denning now showed his draft signal to the equally perturbed Clayton, who fully agreed with its contents. With some hesitation he fell in with Denning's suggestion that he should take it to Pound. All too soon, however, Clayton was back again: 'Father says he's made his decision and is not going to change it now.'[83]

Three fateful signals resulted from Pound's irrevocable decision, each bald of language and without explanatory comment, certainly without the comment Denning had wished to include, that is, to the effect that the *Tirpitz* was most probably still in harbour.

> Most Immediate. Cruiser force withdraw westward at high speed. (Despatched at 2111.)
>
> Immediate. Owing to threat from surface ships, convoy is to disperse and proceed to Russian ports. (Despatched at 2123.)
>
> Most Immediate. My 2123/4. Convoy is to scatter. (Despatched 2136.)[84]

It cannot be doubted that in the absence of positive Intelligence as to whether the *Tirpitz* was or was not at sea, the First Sea Lord had confronted an unpleasantly hard choice, and one fraught with heavy consequences. Nevertheless Pound's performance during this crisis shows up his characteristic limitations. Why did he not allow Denning to send his signal to Tovey and Hamilton as drafted, complete with Denning's appreciation that the balance of the evidence indicated that *Tirpitz* had not left Altenfiord – and then leave it to the responsible Commander-in-Chief at sea to act as he judged best? Instead Pound had arrogated operational direction to himself once again, despite Tovey's vehement objections to such interference after the PQ16 episode in May. Why did Pound during his first meeting with Denning already find it easier to think that *Tirpitz* might be at sea heading for the convoy than not? Why did he thereafter close his mind firmly to the later Ultra evidence that she was still at Altenfiord? And why, even given his own assumption that she might well be heading for the convoy, did he order Hamilton so urgently to withdraw at high speed simply because of U-boats? This order stood in glaring contradiction to Tovey's own directive in March that in the face of enemy heavy ships convoy escorts should remain in the vicinity to shadow and even to attack the enemy if opportunity should serve.

And why also, given again Pound's assumption that *Tirpitz* could well be at sea, did he order the convoy first to disperse (meaning spread out) and then, a quarter of an hour later, to scatter? These orders stood in contradiction to both Atlantic Convoy Instructions and Tovey's own directive, which alike stated that a convoy was only to scatter if the escort had been overwhelmed. Why in any case was Pound so much more concerned with the danger posed by the *Tirpitz* to the convoy while concentrated than with the danger from U-boats and aircraft once it was scattered? Yet Pound's decision only fulfilled what had already been in his mind when he first mentioned scattering to Tovey on the telephone between Whitehall and Scapa before PQ17 sailed, and to which Tovey had then objected so strongly.

It is not unjust to see in all this a combination of Pound's old-fashioned naval authoritarianism and his well-known stubborn closed-mindedness – coupled with a lack of that imaginative insight into the enemy's mind which is the mark of great commanders. After all Tovey, long before the sailing of PQ17, and Denning, at the critical hour, both rightly divined that the Germans would not hazard the *Tirpitz* in waters where she might encounter unlocated British heavy forces.

Nor did the very language of the three signals, with their almost panicky tone of imminent emergency, do Pound any credit as a leader in a crisis. He, or his staff, ought to have realised the impact such signals must have on the recipients at sea.

Thus far PQ17 had come through almost unscathed and in high fettle. Two merchantmen had dropped out because of ice damage and grounding. On 1 July the escort beat off U-boat attacks without loss to the convoy; on 2 July PQ17 and the homeward QP13 passed each other in 73°N, 3°E, and that evening torpedo-bombers attacked PQ17, which again sustained no loss. By now Rear-Admiral Hamilton's 1st Cruiser Squadron had caught up with the convoy, and was steaming some 40 miles off its port beam (that is, on the far side from a likely approach by German surface ships). Early on 4 July a torpedo-bomber suddenly swept out of a hole in the then prevailing fog to inflict PQ17's first casualty, an American freighter. At about 2000 came a determined attack by some 20 torpedo-bombers (as Broome had been forewarned by the Admiralty thanks to Ultra), which were welcomed with heavy anti-aircraft fire by convoy and escort, in which the USS *Wainwright* (Captain R. H. Gibbs, USN) played a particularly effective part. Three ships were hit, and two of them had to be scuttled. The third, a Russian tanker, survived 'holed but happy and capable of nine knots', as Commander Broome expressed it in his later report of proceedings. That evening of 4 July a feeling of elation buoyed up the ships' companies of PQ17 and its escort. 'My impression,' recorded Broome, 'on seeing the resolution displayed by the convoy and its escort was that, provided the ammunition lasted, PQ17 could get anywhere.'[85]

Then, at around 2200, with the convoy in 75° 55′N, 27° 52′E, arrived the Admiralty's 'Most Immediate' order to scatter the convoy. Just as Denning and Clayton had feared back in Whitehall, the urgency of the language led Broome to expect to see at any moment Hamilton's cruisers open fire and the enemy's masts appear on the horizon.[86] Fifteen minutes later Broome passed on the order to scatter the convoy, and he himself steered to join Hamilton in compliance with Tovey's standing instructions. His decision to do so was later approved both by Hamilton and Tovey. At 2230 Rear-Admiral Hamilton, on receipt of the Admiralty's order to him to 'withdraw westward at high speed', turned south-west to get between the convoy and the apparent enemy. 'Assuming as we all did assume,' he later wrote, 'that the scattering of the convoy heralded the imminent approach of enemy surface forces, we were – in the eyes of all who did not know the full story – running away, and at high speed.'[87]

The commodore of PQ17, Commodore J. C. K. Dowding, RNR, on receiving the order to scatter signalled Broome in HMS *Keppel*: 'Many thanks, goodbye and good hunting.' Broome could only reply: 'It is a grim business leaving you here.'[88] The convoy then proceeded to scatter, in Dowding's words, 'as laid down ... in perfect order, though it must have been apparent to the ships that had to turn to the south-west that they were heading towards where trouble might be expected'.[89] So the defenceless merchant ships steamed away, each on her lonely course under the Arctic summer daylight, the numerous patches of fog 'made all the more interesting by the presence of growlers [small icebergs]'.[90] The nearest Russian landfall lay 600 miles distant.

The Commander-in-Chief, Home Fleet, was to write in his despatch:

> The order to scatter the convoy had, in my opinion, been premature ... its results were disastrous. The convoy had so far covered more than half its route with the loss of only three ships. Now its ships, spread over a wide area, were exposed without defence to the powerful enemy U-boat and air forces. The enemy took prompt advantage of this situation, operating both weapons to their full capacity.[91]

Tovey also retrospectively criticised Rear-Admiral Hamilton for failing to release Broome's escort force back to the merchant ships once he, Hamilton, was clear of the convoy 'and in default of information that the *Tirpitz* was near'.[92] Tovey judged that the value of Broome's destroyers 'for anti-U-boat purposes, for rounding up scattered ships, and, if the *Tirpitz* had appeared, for diverting and delaying her, would have been considerable ...'[93] This was hardly fair on Hamilton, for the destroyers' oiler had been sunk, leaving them without fuel for extended operations in the Barents Sea.

In the event, the *Tirpitz* did put to sea next day, 5 July, only to be quickly recalled by the German naval command (as revealed to the Admiralty by Ultra), and for the very reason guessed by Denning on the 4th: a decision to leave the convoy to the U-boats and the Luftwaffe. And for these to massacre the scattered merchantmen in the following days proved as easy as shooting rabbits in a stubble-field. Twenty-three ships went down, including the Commodore's ship *River Afton*, although happily Dowding and her master survived. The rescue ship *Zaafaran* was also sunk.[94]

That eleven merchantmen still managed to reach Kola owed itself to the courage of their crews and the cunning of their masters in navigating along unlikely shores and exploiting the recurrent fogs – as well as to the devotion of Allied escort ships in defending small groups against the Luftwaffe. Lost with the sunk ships were 210 crated aircraft, 430 tanks, 3,350 vehicles and nearly 100,000 tons of stores.[95] This huge loss was the more serious because on 18 June the

German Army had begun its summer offensive on the southern half of the Eastern Front with the first of a succession of grand attacks over the next two weeks that smashed the Russian defence to fragments. On the very days that PQ17 was scattering in obedience to the Admiralty's order the German panzer armies reached the River Don at Voronezh. Once again battle had been joined on a scale and of a savagery not experienced by armies of the Western democracies since the Great War.

On 1 August the First Sea Lord reported to the War Cabinet on the disaster to PQ17. His version of events was, to say the least, somewhat disingenuous. He alleged (according to the minutes of the meeting) that the Admiralty 'had had information on the night before the order to disperse was given that the TIRPITZ, having eluded our submarines, would, if she continued on her present course, be in a position to attack the convoy early the following morning . . .'[96] Of the three forms of attack, air, U-boat or surface ships, proceeded Pound, 'the most dangerous threat' if the convoy remained concentrated 'appeared, in the circumstances as then known to the Admiralty, to be from surface ships'; hence the order to scatter.

The massacre of PQ17 aroused the Prime Minister's pugilistic instincts, and on 12 July he urged on the Admiralty that 'assuming all goes well in Malta' the Mediterranean Fleet's two modern fleet carriers *Indomitable* and *Victorious*, the older carriers *Argus* and *Eagle*, at least five of the new escort carriers, all the Dido class cruisers (5,450 tons displacement; ten 5.25-inch dual-purpose guns; 33 knots)[97] and at least 25 destroyers should be concentrated to protect PQ18. This vast concourse of ships should, he suggested, proceed to Archangel 'keeping southward, not hugging the ice, but seeking the clearest weather, and thus fight it out with the enemy'.[98] With the supply ships moving 'under an umbrella of at least 100 [carrier] aircraft,' wrote Churchill, 'we ought to be able to fight the convoy through and out again, and if a Fleet action results, so much the better.'[99]

Neither the First Lord, A. V. Alexander, nor the First Sea Lord were attracted to this grandiose concept, especially at the price of denuding the Mediterranean Fleet at a time when all was *not* going well in Malta. Next day the Defence Committee agreed to the recommendation of the Chiefs of Staff that 'convoys should not be run to North Russia in present circumstances' – no attempt therefore to fight PQ18 through by means of a great fleet; indeed, no further convoys at all for the remainder of the Arctic summer of 1942.[100] It fell to Churchill himself to telegraph this disagreeable news to Stalin at a time when the Russian defence in the Ukraine had already crumbled under the weight and power of the German summer offensive.

In the event, instead of the Mediterranean Fleet releasing major ships for the Arctic in August, the Home Fleet had to release the battleship *Nelson*, the carrier *Victorious*, the cruisers *Kenya*, *Nigeria* and *Manchester* and eleven destroyers to the Mediterranean for another Malta convoy – 'Pedestal' (see above, pp. 517–25), the supreme effort which alone enabled Malta to survive into the autumn. Of these Home Fleet ships, the *Manchester* and a destroyer were sunk during 'Pedestal', and *Nigeria* and *Kenya* damaged, so materially adding to Admiral Tovey's troubles. The anti-aircraft cruiser *Cairo* had also been sunk. In mid-July the battleship *Washington* and four American destroyers were withdrawn from service with the Home Fleet, Admiral Giffen transferring his flag to the heavy cruiser *Wichita*. In August the *Wichita* and then the *Tuscaloosa* also departed. 'Task Force 39' thus came to an end, much to the regret of the Home Fleet and of Tovey, its Commander-in-Chief, who was to pay a heartfelt tribute in his despatch:

> This force had provided a welcome reinforcement to the Home Fleet of a time when its strength was much reduced. The conduct of officers and men had been admirable, and the ships displayed a very high degree of weapon efficiency. In Admiral Giffen I had a loyal and enthusiastic colleague whose tact and good humour never failed. I was very sorry to see them go.[101]

To fill the place of the departing *Washington* there had already arrived HMS *King George V*, fresh from a refit. In August the recently worked-up new battleship *Anson* (another 'King George V': 38,000 tons displacement; 29 knots; ten 14-inch guns; launched February 1940)[102] joined the Fleet, bringing its strength in heavy ships up to three battleships and the battlecruiser *Renown*.

To Churchill's news that no further convoys were to be despatched to North Russia during the summer and the concurrent and equally unpalatable news that the Western Allies had finally decided that a 'Second Front' in France in 1942 was not a feasible operation of war, Stalin objected furiously on 23 July, pointing out the present critical position on the Eastern Front (where German panzer forces had now got as far as the southern reaches of the River Don). In the course of August these forces were to hammer their way closer and closer to Stalingrad and to the Volga crossing, while a second army group was to drive deep into the Caucasus. With the Red Army fighting desperately to slow and stop these divergent offensives and in ever more urgent need of tanks, trucks, aircraft and ammunition from the Anglo-Americans, it was therefore decided after all that PQ18 must be run in September.

Although the Admiralty had torpedoed the Prime Minister's suggestion of escorting the convoy all the way through with a great fleet, nevertheless arrangements for protecting PQ18 were on an unprecedented scale. Accompanying the convoy (of 39 merchantmen, a rescue ship, an oiler, three minesweepers for Russia and two fleet oilers) would be a close escort of two destroyers, two anti-aircraft ships, two submarines, four corvettes, three minesweepers and four trawlers. This in itself was not very different in strength from PQ16's or PQ17's close escorts. But this time there would be two other escort forces with the convoy as well during the most dangerous stretches of the passage – a Carrier Force comprising the escort carrier *Avenger* (Commander A. P. Colthurst, RN: American-built; 8,200 tons displacement; Diesel motors giving 17 knots; 15 aircraft),[103] making her operational début, and two destroyers; and a Fighting Destroyer Force consisting of no fewer than sixteen fleet destroyers and the light cruiser *Scylla* (5,450 tons displacement; 33 knots; ten 5.25-inch dual-purpose guns; launched August 1940).[104] Rear-Admiral R. L. Burnett (flying his flag in *Scylla*) was to command all three escort forces.

As in previous operations there was to be a cruiser covering force, this time made up of the *Norfolk* (flag of Vice-Admiral S. S. Bonham-Carter, recently promoted), *Suffolk* and *London*. The distant covering force of heavy ships would be based on Akureyri in northern Iceland and commanded by Vice-Admiral Sir Bruce Fraser, Second-in-Command, Home Fleet, flying his flag in the new battleship *Anson*. With him would be one other battleship (*Duke of York*), the cruiser *Jamaica* and five destroyers, all of the latter being of limited range because the fleet destroyers had been allotted to the Fighting Destroyer Force.

This time the homeward-bound convoy (QP14) was not to pass the outward convoy just west of Bear Island, but in the Barents Sea where, as experience had painfully taught, both would stand in the greatest need of protection.

With so many warships therefore going so far, elaborate arrangements had to be made to fuel them *en passage*. As well as the two fleet oilers sailing with the convoy, two more were to be sent under escort by four destroyers to a rendezvous in Lowe Sound, on the coast of the island of Spitzbergen. The Royal Navy had indeed come a long way since Admiral Sir Charles Forbes's operations during the Norwegian campaign in 1940 had been shackled by the need frequently to return ships to Scapa to refuel. One further force was also involved: the cruisers *Cumberland* and *Suffolk* and one destroyer were to carry reinforcements and stores to the Allied garrison on Spitzbergen.

By the beginning of September 1942, at long last, and by dint of much effort – not least in eliciting the necessary Russian cooperation – Royal Air Force Coastal Command had been able to set up an advanced striking force in North Russia, the necessary ground staff and equipment being transported by the USS *Tuscaloosa* (on her last operation in Arctic waters) and three destroyers in August. The force, under the command of Group Captain F. L. Hopps, consisted of 24 Hampden torpedo-bombers of Nos. 144 and 455 Squadrons, four photographic reconnaissance (PR) Spitfires and long-range reconnaissance Catalinas of No. 210 Squadron. A joint Navy–Air Force Combined Area Headquarters was created at Polyarnoe on the Kola Inlet leading to Murmansk, the Navy's representative being Rear-Admiral D. B. Fisher, the Senior British Naval Officer in North Russia.[105] No longer would the Luftwaffe enjoy that undisputed mastery of the Arctic skies which it had wielded with such success against previous Allied convoys.

In the air as well as on the surface, therefore, PQ18 was to be immensely better protected than the unfortunate PQ17 or the triumphant PQ16 and its gallant escort. And this time Sigint posed no taxing operational puzzles for the Admiralty or the Commander-in-Chief, Home Fleet (who coordinated his different task groups from a shore headquarters at Scapa). The British Naval Attaché in Stockholm, the able and assiduous Captain H. M. Denham, was receiving through the Deputy Chief of the Swedish General Staff information derived from the tapping of the supposedly secure teleprinter landline through Sweden from Berlin to the Wehrmacht in Norway.[106] From this source and from Ultra it was known that the pocket battleship *Lützow* had been withdrawn from Norway and the 6-inch cruiser *Köln* transferred from the Baltic to Trondheim, and then, later in August, to Narvik. The Admiralty also knew the location of the twenty U-boats deployed to attack the convoy; it estimated the Luftwaffe's strike forces at 65 torpedo-bombers (actually 92) and 120 bombers.[107] On 11 September (eight days after PQ18 put to sea from Iceland) Ultra decrypts confirmed sightings by British submarines on the day before that the *Scheer*, *Hipper* and *Köln* had been moved north to Altenfiord. From hints in Enigma signals and the results of photo-reconnaissance by Spitfires from North Russia the Operational Intelligence Centre concluded that *Tirpitz* probably remained in Narvik. Later photo-reconnaissance confirmed that the three smaller ships remained in Altenfiord, while on 15 September Ultra decrypts revealed that on the previous day the *Tirpitz* had still been in Narvik. On the 16th came fresh news from Captain Denham's impeccable source that the German naval command only proposed to employ the three smaller ships against PQ18 and that *Tirpitz* was suffering from a technical defect (later confirmed through decrypts as bearing trouble). By this time, as it happened, the enemy had in any case decided not to take unnecessary risks even with the smaller ships in view of their importance to the defence of Norway.[108]

Yet for all the strength of PQ18's covering forces under the command of no fewer than three admirals afloat and one ashore, the Luftwaffe and the U-boats gave the convoy as hard a time as PQ16, which had nevertheless finally reached its destination with the loss of only seven ships out of 35.

The air attacks on PQ18 began at 1530 on 13 September 1942, after the convoy emerged from the cover of fogs and snowstorms. Over 40 twin-torpedoed Ju 88s and He 111s flying in the 'Golden Comb' formation line abreast came in, according to Commodore (Rear-Admiral, retired) E. K. Boddam-Whetham, the convoy commodore, like 'a huge flight of nightmare locusts'.[109] At the time HMS *Avenger*'s aircraft were all chasing shadowers and high-level bombers, so that in less than ten minutes the 'locusts' succeeded in sinking eight ships.[110] The experience decided the captain of *Avenger*, Commander A. P. Colthurst, that

> . . . with the small number of obsolete fighters at our disposal, and with their slow operation in an auxiliary carrier, we must use them only to break up large attacking formations rather than to destroy individuals; further we must endeavour to maintain a continual cycle of sections taking off, landing to re-arm and re-fuel, and taking off again. The achievement of this would avoid congestion in the carrier and ensure that there were always some fighter sections available ready to counter-attack striking forces.[111]

Next day *Avenger* was to live up to her name – partly owing to Colthurst's revised operations system, partly owing to the 'Headache' party installed in Rear-Admiral Burnett's flagship *Scylla*. 'Headache' was the codename for the shipborne sections of 'Y' Intelligence (charged with intercepting and reading the enemy's low-grade radio-telephone traffic) which had been steadily introduced since 1941.

Now 'Headache' gave *Avenger* advanced tactical warning of impending Luftwaffe attack.[112] The combined results of 'Headache' and Commander Colthurst's change of method proved impressive, as Rear-Admiral Burnett recounted:

> It was a fine sight to see *Avenger* peeling off Hurricanes, whilst streaking across the front of the convoy from starboard to port inside the screen with her destroyer escort [HMS *Wheatland* and *Wilton*] blazing away with every gun that would bear, and then being chased by torpedo-bombers as she steamed down on the opposite course to the convoy to take cover . . . Altogether a most gratifying action . . .[113]

That day, 14 September 1942, *Avenger*'s Hurricanes and the guns of the escorts shot down 22 enemy aircraft for the loss of three Hurricanes – and even those three in fact fell victim to their own pilots' courage in flying through the ships' anti-aircraft fire to reach the enemy. Happily all of the pilots were rescued from the icy water. For the next five days the Luftwaffe tried again and again, though not on the same scale, despite the fact that the *Avenger* and other covering forces turned back on the 16th to protect the homeward QP14 convoy. The Luftwaffe's final attack coincided with a full gale. When the battle died down at last on 20 September, the enemy had lost 33 torpedo-bombers, six dive-bombers and two long-range reconnaissance aircraft – 41 in all, one of them falling to the Hurricane pilot from the Catapult Aircraft Merchant Ship *Empire Morn*. Thus the introduction of the CVE began to close the air gap over the Arctic in 1942 six months before it served the same vital purpose in the Atlantic in March 1943; and the Luftwaffe in northern Norway was left permanently winged.

Nor were the U-boats successful against PQ18, partly because of the presence of patrolling Catalinas from Russia from 18 September onwards. They sank only three ships for the loss of three of their own number. Of the 40 ships which had set out, 27 reached safe haven in Russia after eighteen days of constant strain, exertion and peril. For the ships' companies of the merchantmen, there was (as in all convoys) the added stress occasioned by the often hazardous nature of their cargoes. As Commodore Boddam-Whetham remarked in a private letter later to Rear-Admiral Burnett:

> It's a funny feeling to realise one is sitting on top of 2,000 tons of T.N.T., but we nearly all carry between that and 4,000 tons. I don't think the bigger amount would make much more than a tiny fraction of a second difference to the time one entered the next world . . .[114]

PQ18's escort and covering forces had not merely got the convoy through without crippling losses (though they were still greater than those of PQ16), but also scored a damaging victory over the Luftwaffe. Nevertheless Burnett reckoned that they had been lucky. In his report of proceedings he wrote: 'I do not know how far this operation may be considered a success or a failure, but I am convinced that had any of six circumstances been otherwise it must have been a tragic failure . . .'[115] For instance, if the weather had been bad, no oiling at sea would have been possible, forcing the escorts to turn back – as would also have happened if one or two of the oilers had been torpedoed early on. Delays in refuelling part of the Fighting Destroyer Escort at Spitzbergen or delays if it had had to be oiled at sea would have meant its absence during the crisis of the battle. Burnett also pointed out that had the enemy synchronised his air and sea attacks the losses would have been heavy. Then again, if the enemy had kept up his torpedo-bomber attacks, the stocks of anti-aircraft ammunition would have become critical, with little left with which to defend the homeward QP14.[116]

QP14 (fifteen merchant ships) in any case ran into trouble – partly because en route Burnett detached *Avenger* for home rather than expose her to further risk of U-boat attack. Although he asked for shore-based air cover, Coastal Command was too stretched by simultaneous demands in the Battle of the Atlantic and too hampered by bad weather to provide more than intermittent protection. This time it was the U-boats that did the damage, sinking three merchant ships and a fleet oiler. The Tribal class destroyer *Somali* also took a torpedo from a U-boat, but was taken in tow by her sister ship *Ashanti*. Thanks to prodigious seamanship they made 420 miles westwards in eighty hours before that ever-present enemy, the weather, intervened with a full gale. *Somali*, her weakened hull severely stressed by motion through huge seas, broke in two and sank.

Taken together, the battles of PQ16/QP12 and PQ18/QP14 mark the turning point for the Arctic convoys, for with the exception of the heavy ships the German forces in northern Norway had done their utmost to stop the traffic, and yet failed first against PQ16 and then, after a misleadingly easy triumph over PQ17, failed once more against PQ18. Henceforward the German effort would wane. In particular the Luftwaffe's strike forces were drawn away to the Mediterranean in November 1942 to deal with the Anglo-American 'Torch' landings (an uncovenanted benefit of that operation to the Royal Navy in the Arctic), and were never fully rebuilt.

Yet it was the demand of 'Torch' for warships from the Home

Fleet that prevented any further outward convoy to Russia until 15 December, despite renewed attempts by Stalin and Roosevelt to bully Churchill. In fairness to Stalin, this was another time of crisis on the Eastern Front. In October the German offensive against the Soviet garrison of Stalingrad was entering its final and appalling phase of street-fighting amid the ruins. On both flanks of the German 6th Army, Red Army reserves were moving into place in readiness for the coming Soviet counter-offensive. This was launched on 19 November 1942, leading within a week to the encirclement of the 6th Army.

On 15 December – by now the trapped 6th Army under General Paulus was dying fast of hunger and frostbite – the Royal Navy resumed the Arctic convoys with JW51A (first of a new numerical series in replacement of the PQ/QP series) of fifteen ships; at Tovey's insistence half the size of the last three PQs. The threat of the German heavy ships remained, but their sorties proved to be rare and timid. On 30 December 1942, for instance, Vice-Admiral Kummetz put to sea with the pocket battleship *Lützow* (six 11-inch guns), the 8-inch gun cruiser *Hipper* and six destroyers to attack outward convoy JW51B south-east of Bear Island in the Barents Sea. In a confused sequence of encounters amid snow storms the German squadron was seen off by the convoy's escort of destroyers and two 6-inch light cruisers, all of which steered to engage closely a cringing enemy whenever he was sighted; a familiar enough pattern. The close escort of five destroyers under Captain R. St. V. Sherbrooke in HMS *Onslow* themselves held off the German heavy ships for an hour in yet another unhesitatingly aggressive destroyer action. Sherbrooke himself, badly wounded, later received the Victoria Cross. As Admiral Tovey remarked in his despatch:

> . . . that an enemy force of at least one pocket battleship, one heavy cruiser and six destroyers, with all the advantages of surprise and concentration, should be held off for four hours by five destroyers and two 6-inch cruisers without any loss to the convoy is most creditable and satisfactory.[117]

In March 1943, after two more outward convoys had been despatched, the current danger of catastrophe in the Atlantic at the hands of the U-boat, with the Royal Navy desperately short of escort vessels to take on the wolf packs, compelled the War Cabinet to cancel the next two Arctic sailings. Even Roosevelt had to agree when Churchill told him that the disasters to the Atlantic convoys HX229 and SC122 (see above, pp. 598–600) offered a 'final proof that our escorts are everywhere too thin. The strain upon the British Navy is becoming intolerable.'[118] It was thanks to the cancellation of further Arctic convoys that the Home Fleet was able to release enough destroyers and corvettes to enable the creation of the new 'escort groups' in the Atlantic which helped so much in April and May 1943 to break Dönitz's U-boats.

The hiatus in the Arctic convoy traffic also simplified the Home Fleet's role as the Admiralty's central strategic reserve, enabling it to release the new battleship *Howe* (another 'King George V') and the *King George V* to the Mediterranean for 'Husky', the invasion of Sicily, in June 1943 (see above, Chapter 21). In return the elderly *Rodney* and the Great War veteran *Malaya* came home. To augment the Home Fleet's strength in the face of the modern German heavy ships still based in northern Norway – *Tirpitz*, *Scharnhorst*, *Lützow* – the United States Navy again contributed a task force, this time composed of the battleships *Alabama* and *South Dakota* and five destroyers under Rear Admiral O. M. Hustvedt.

On 8 May 1943 Admiral Sir John Tovey struck his flag as Commander-in-Chief, Home Fleet. He was later appointed C-in-C, The Nore. No diplomat but a forthright sailor of unbendable integrity, he fell into that same category as Generals Wavell and Auchinleck of commanders-in-chief serving in the most difficult period of the war whom the Prime Minister found uncongenial in their stubborn realism. Churchill had indeed manoeuvred to oust Tovey as long ago as April 1942 when Cunningham had been called home at short notice from the Mediterranean Fleet ostensibly to become head of the British Naval Mission in Washington. On Cunningham's arrival Churchill told him that he wanted him to relieve Tovey, to which 'A.B.C.' had angrily retorted: 'If Tovey drops dead on his bridge I will certainly relieve him. Otherwise not.'[119] So Cunningham went to Washington after all, before returning to the Mediterranean as Naval Commander, Allied Expeditionary Force (see above, pp. 538–9).

The new Commander-in-Chief of the Home Fleet, previously its Second-in-Command, Admiral Sir Bruce Fraser, had no doubt that the Russian convoy traffic should not be resumed even in September (the earliest feasible month in terms of ice and light) unless German surface strength could be reduced, or unless to operate this route in addition to the trans-Iranian route was considered 'vital to the prosecution of the war', which he wrote in a letter to the First Sea Lord on 30 June he had 'no reason to suppose'.[120] In fact by this time the danger that Soviet Russia might collapse had passed for good with the destruction of the German 6th Army at Stalingrad (Paulus and the remnant of his army had surrendered on 2 February 1943) and the sweeping Russian advances in the Ukraine and the Caucasus which had followed. The German Army on the Eastern Front had now been forced ineluctably on to a strategic defensive which was to end two years later in the ruins of Berlin. Moreover, Russia's own factories were now pouring out crude but effective weapons to equip her massed soldiery – T.34 tanks, heavy artillery and 'Katushka' rocket batteries, Stormovik ground-attack aircraft. The British and American Armies were beginning to take some of the weight off the Red Army by their campaign in the Mediterranean, for von Arnim surrendered in Tunisia on 13 May and the invasion of Sicily was scheduled for July. The possible invasion of Italy thereafter was already under debate. There was no longer, therefore, the hounding need of 1941–42 to keep the Arctic convoys going at any hazard; and in the event no further convoy was to be run until November 1943.

Yet the existence of the German heavy ships as a 'fleet in being' – and especially the *Tirpitz* – continued to weigh on the Admiralty. It was only partial comfort that Fraser, like his predecessor, judged that these ships would not put to sea 'unless they either could attack a convoy while it was not covered by British heavy forces', or unless those forces 'suffer damage from underwater or air attack'.[121] The German heavy ships, enjoying as they did the choice of the time and direction of a sortie, compelled the Admiralty to keep a disproportionate number of capital ships at Scapa and preferably a fleet carrier as well in order to parry a breakout into the Atlantic. This in turn affected the Admiralty's entire global deployment. And so during the months April to September 1943 the Royal Navy was patiently, thoroughly, preparing an entirely novel weapons system for destroying the *Tirpitz* and the other two heavy ships; one which for success merely required superlative skill and dauntless audacity on the part of its operators. On 11 and 12 September the task force put to sea to launch 'Operation Source'.

One day earlier, on 10 September, Admiral of the Fleet Sir Dudley Pound had ceased to be First Sea Lord. So long an evidently very tired man prone to drool down his pipe in a doze during Chiefs of Staff meetings, worn down by the ceaseless pain of his arthritic hip, Pound suffered a stroke while in Washington with the Prime Minister after the Quebec ('Quadrant') summit conference. By the night of 9 September, when he was being questioned by the Premier and President Roosevelt after dinner in the White House Pound showed clear signs of being, in Churchill's words, 'very ill'.[122] Next morning Pound went to see Churchill in his bed-sitting room, and told him: 'Prime

Minister, I have come to resign. I have had a stroke and my right side is largely paralysed. I thought it would pass off, but it gets worse every day and I am no longer fit for duty.'[123] Brought home in HMS *Renown* he was reduced by a second stroke to total paralysis. He lingered on until 21 October, Trafalgar Day, 1943.

Unlike his opposite numbers, the Chiefs of the Imperial General Staff and Air Staff, Pound had carried a double burden and had done so for four years of war. As well as bearing in his capacity as Chief of Naval Staff a responsibility similiar to theirs in terms of general policy and strategic advice to the Prime Minister, Pound in his other capacity as First Sea Lord was also supreme commander of the Royal Navy. For the Admiralty – unlike the Army and Air Councils, which were purely administrative bodies – was an operational headquarters, its radio net giving it direct access to British fleets, squadrons and individual ships in all oceans. To discharge effectively these twin roles called for high managerial talent, not only for delegation, but also especially for selecting the big questions from the detail. This talent Pound sadly lacked. He ran the Navy as if he were the executive officer of a ship, endlessly prying into and arranging matters of detail, drafting signals himself, second-guessing his staff and commanders-in-chief; even on one occasion, when on passage home from the first Washington Conference in August 1941 in the *Prince of Wales*, signalling a rebuke to two escorting destroyer captains for failing to carry out a minor evolution according to the book.[124] Admiral Sir Ralph Edwards, then, as a Captain, the Deputy Director of Naval Operations (Home), was to bear witness after the war:

> He was an arch meddler and I could not have believed that any Admiral could interfere with his Commanders at sea as the First Sea Lord then did. Over and over again I was instructed by him to make signals to the Fleets and ships how fast to go and where to put the Cruiser screen . . . I do not agree that Winston was invariably the nigger who interfered. Far from it; I regard his interference as negligible when compared with Dudley Pound.[125]

Pound's direct order to PQ17 to scatter stands as the supreme case of such operational intervention – and not least because of his rigid refusal to change his mind about scattering in the face of new evidence from Ultra that *Tirpitz* was not at sea (see above, pp. 717–8).

The double functions of First Sea Lord and Chief of the Naval Staff as Pound chose to interpret them could only be discharged by unceasing desk work; and in accomplishing this the elderly admiral simply wore himself out. Happiest when immersed in administrative and operational detail, Pound allowed the larger issues of grand strategy in a maritime war to become dominated by soldiers in the shape of the Chiefs of the Imperial General Staff. For all his sense of duty he was therefore far from being another Lord Barham or a Beatty (in the latter's full professional maturity as First Sea Lord after the Great War); rather an industrious journeyman, a narrow professional sailor, not very well informed about wider issues.[126] Nonetheless, he did grasp a single simple truth, one which cleverer minds in high places lost sight of from time to time – that Britain's survival and the Western Allies' ultimate victory alike depended totally on keeping the Atlantic convoy routes open; and that therefore the defeat of the U-boat ought to override all other considerations in framing grand strategy.

It is possible to admire Pound's devious tactics in handling his headstrong Prime Minister and putting to sleep some of his wilder schemes, such as 'Operation Catherine' (see above, pp. 93–5). Thereby he never incurred the smouldering hostility that Churchill evinced towards those who openly crossed him, such as Wavell and Auchinleck among soldiers and Tovey and Cunningham among sailors. However it also meant that Pound never enjoyed the independent stature of his predecessor, Admiral of the Fleet Lord Fisher, as First Sea Lord during the Great War (which Churchill all too keenly remembered), or of General Sir William Robertson, the Chief of the Imperial General Staff during the same conflict, or Alan Brooke in the present one. Too often Pound acquiesced in Churchill's interventions, such as the signals to Warburton-Lee and Lord Cork during the Narvik operation in April 1940 (see above, pp. 114–116 and 124), or the fatuous order (on the face of it issued by the Admiralty) to Tovey during the *Bismarck* chase to the effect that *King George V* was to continue to pursue even if it meant towing her home later for want of fuel.

This compliance with Churchill's wishes, coupled with a manner towards subordinates that varied between aloofness and bullying ill-temper, meant that Pound by no means enjoyed wide trust and confidence among his flag officers and staff, although he always remained on cordial relations with Andrew Cunningham. There was a feeling that he was too ready to listen to criticisms of naval officers via the backstairs or from outsiders such as the Prime Minister, as in the case of the enquiry into Somerville's conduct in the face of the Italian Fleet while escorting a Malta convoy in November 1940 (see above, pp. 241–3), or the precipitate relief of Harwood in 1943 on the basis of Montgomery's tittle-tattle. Some even suspected that

Pound was not always quite 'as high principled' in his dealings as could be wished.[127] If so, was this unwitting? It is curious that he once wrote to Churchill that he could 'quite definitely' tell his critics in the Navy that the *Prince of Wales* and *Repulse* had been sent to Singapore 'in accordance with my advice',[128] whereas the documentary record clearly shows that Pound opposed the move but allowed himself to be overborne (see above, pp. 393–400).

Thus, taking Pound's record as First Sea Lord all in all, there is an unintended resonance in Churchill's tribute in his war memoirs when he writes that Pound 'had been a true comrade to me, both at the Admiralty, and on the Chiefs of Staff Committee'.[129]

Churchill wanted Admiral Sir Bruce Fraser to replace Pound, out of fear of getting Andrew Cunningham instead, whose powerful and independent character he had encountered since 1940 in the course of Mediterranean operations. But Fraser told the Prime Minister that whereas he believed he enjoyed the confidence of his own fleet 'Cunningham has that of the whole Navy'.[130] So for the second time Cunningham struck his flag as C-in-C, Mediterranean, and returned to London (see also above, p. 681). In the Chiefs of Staff Committee and the War Cabinet Defence Committee Churchill no longer looked across the table at an admiral content to be his loyal sea-dog, but one with the high stature conferred by victorious command of a fleet in battle; a man of dominating presence, well able with his blue-eyed glare to outface even the Prime Minister.

Between 1600 on 11 September 1943 and 0100 on the 12th the submarines *Thrasher*, *Truculent*, *Stubborn*, *Syrtis*, *Sceptre* and *Seanymph* put to sea from Loch Cairnbawm on the north-west coast of Scotland in the first phase of 'Operation Source'. Each towed an 'X-Craft', the Royal Navy's latest technological innovation: a 51-foot-long midget submarine of only some 30 tons, with a beam of only 5¾ feet and a height from upper deck to keel also of only 5¾ feet. A 42 brake-horsepower diesel engine gave her a maximum speed of 6½ knots on the surface; a 25 horsepower electric motor a maximum speed of 5 knots submerged. Cruising on the surface at a speed of 4 knots the X-Craft had a maximum range of 1,500 miles.[131] Each operational crew consisted of three officers and one engine room artificer, all volunteers, who were expected to endure in the tiny coffin-like interior for up to a fortnight if need be. During the outward voyage the boats were manned by a 'passage crew' of three. The X-Craft's armament consisted of two 1-ton high-explosive charges carried on each side of the hull. These could be either detached on to the seabed beneath an enemy ship or be fixed to the enemy's hull with magnetic clamps and lines by a diver exiting from the submarine from a special chamber. After the X-Craft had been released by the towing submarines off the enemy coast, it would be the task of the four-man crews to navigate through confined and tortuous rocky channels towards their victims, penetrate through elaborate net defences, dive under the enemy's hulls, detach the charges, and then make good their escapes before the charges were blown by clockwork time-fuzes.

Three prototypes had been successfully tested in 1942.[132] In April 1943 the 12th Submarine Flotilla was formed under Captain W. E. Banks, RN, to train the crews of the six operational X-Craft. All that summer the crews rehearsed and rehearsed again what they would have to do. Thanks to three photo-reconnaissance Spitfires temporarily based in North Russia at the end of August the planners of 'Operation Source' possessed complete and detailed pictures of the location of the German ships and the protective measures round them.[133] At the last minute Ultra decrypts of the naval Enigma together with air reconnaissance by Catalinas gave confirmation that *Tirpitz*, *Scharnhorst* and *Lützow* should indeed all be present as expected in inlets off Altenfiord rather than in some alternative base such as Narvik or Trondheim.

Yet the voyage from Scotland to Norwegian waters proved tricky enough in itself. Tows parted; the X9 tragically foundered in unknown circumstances; the X8 had to be scuttled after damage from the premature explosion of her charges, ditched because of leaks; a third (X7) impaled herself on a mine, and was only safely got free by a gambler's kick against the mine-casing by the boat's commander. In the small hours of 20 September 1943 the crews who were to carry out the attacks took the place of passage crews in the four X-Craft that remained. Between 1830 and 2000 that day X5 (Lieutenant H. Henty-Creer, RVNR), X6 (Lieutenant D. Cameron, RNR), X7 (Lieutenant B. C. G. Place, RN) and X10 (Lieutenant K. R. Hudspeth, RANVR) parted from the parent submarines and began the run-in through Sorby Sound between the outer Norwegian islands and thence deep into Altenfiord.

X10, detailed to attack the *Scharnhorst* in Kaa Fiord, off Altenfiord, fell early victim to Murphy's Law, for technical troubles left her without effective compass or periscope and lying low on the bottom of the fiord while the crew tried to remedy the defects. As it happened, however, the *Scharnhorst* had anyway gone to sea for firing practice, a fact revealed by Ultra too late for the news to be relayed forward to the task force. Lieutenant Hudspeth nevertheless managed to get X10 to sea again, but took six uncomfortable days to locate one of the parent submarines. On 3 October, when on tow within 400 miles of the Shetlands, X10 had to be scuttled because of an imminent gale; a sad end to a gallant effort.

Of the three X-Craft making for the *Tirpitz*, X5 simply disappeared, her fate unknown, although it is possible that she fell victim to German gunfire outside the net defences. As for the surviving midget submarines X6 and X7, their experiences might have come from a boy's adventure story. After slipping past the anti-submarine boom in Kaa Fiord on the surface early on 22 September Lieutenant Place in X7 was forced to dive when a patrolling German motor boat neared him, only to become tangled up in defensive nets. It took him two hours to get his boat free. Lieutenant Cameron in X6, for his part, had to creep his way through the German defences with a periscope operated by hand because the electric motor had burnt out. When X6 accidentally broke surface at 0707 that morning of the 22nd on going aground, she was sighted from the *Tirpitz*, becoming the target for frenzied small-arms fire. By this time Cameron was feeling his way blind because his periscope and compass had both failed. Nevertheless he managed to surface alongside the battleship, detach his explosive charges and scuttle his boat. He and his crew were picked up from the water by a German motor boat and taken on board the *Tirpitz*, there to await the detonation of his own charges.

Meanwhile Lieutenant Place in X7, with his compass too now useless, had continued to struggle through one entangling net after another. He finally bumped into *Tirpitz*'s towering side before diving beneath her to drop his charges. When all four charges exploded shortly afterwards X7 was temporarily trapped nearby in yet another net, and the shock of the explosions damaged her controls. After helplessly plunging and surfacing like a porpoise while under heavy fire, X7 finally ran alongside a German gunnery practice target, then sank. Lieutenant Place and one other officer survived to be taken prisoner.

On board the *Tirpitz* the shock of sighting the approaching X-Craft close by within her supposedly impenetrable anchorage caused near panic. Even though the battleship was winched on her cables away from the point where the X6 had sunk, at least one charge dropped by X7 went off exactly beneath the battleship's engine rooms. According to one report, the force of the explosion caused 'the whole ship to heave several feet . . .' The lights went out; unstowed or unsecured gear crashed about; hatches jammed. But these were only the immediate and outward signs of the crippling inner blow which the *Tirpitz* had sustained, for inspection was to discover that her main turbines and her fire-control system had been put out of action.

Although Ultra decrypts were not able to tell the Admiralty the exact nature of the damage, they did make it clear that the enemy expected it to take until mid-March 1944 to repair the ship, and that the work was going to have to be carried out in Norway rather than back in Germany.[134] On 2 January 1944 a further decrypt was to specify 15 March as the date when the work on the hull, machinery and electrical systems would be completed.[135] Thus although *Scharnhorst* and *Lützow* had escaped attack and *Tirpitz* had not actually been sunk, 'Operation Source' had nonetheless achieved a stunning success. For their audacity, courage and skill in the face of such immense hazards, Lieutenants Place and Cameron were both awarded the Victoria Cross.

By putting the German Navy's most valuable single asset out of action for six months, 'Operation Source' had also transformed the whole strategic situation in home waters and the Arctic. The Admiralty and the Commander-in-Chief, Home Fleet, could now contemplate reopening the Russian convoy traffic, the more so as the enemy brought the *Lützow* back to Germany in the last week of September. *Lützow*'s homeward voyage, however, occasioned yet another demonstration of the limited effectiveness of Britain's shore-based maritime airpower in attacks on enemy surface ships. Just as with the escape of the German battleships up Channel in 1942 the strike force against the *Lützow* had to be cobbled together at the last moment from such aircraft as were serviceable. The Fleet Air Arm and Coastal Command crews enjoyed no common doctrine and had never worked together. To mount and carry out the operation itself called for much telephoning between the C-in-C, Home Fleet and his Chief of Staff, the AOC, No. 18 Group, Coastal Command, and Headquarters, Coastal Command; another case of clumsy and creaking liaison links instead of a proper joint command organisation. Despite advance warning from Ultra and an SIS agent that *Lützow* was about to move, and then was on the move, the small strike force failed even to locate the pocket battleship, let alone attack her, let alone sink her – not least because a wrong guess by Admiral Sir Henry Moore, Chief of Staff, Home Fleet, led the force to search too far to the north, and actually astern of the pocket battleship on her voyage south.[136]

These fresh muddles and confusions in shore-based air operations against an enemy surface ship provoked a report by yet another heavyweight Navy and Air Force Committee in November 1943.[137] This recommended that Coastal Command's strike forces be expanded to three strike wings, each of twenty torpedo-bombers and twenty twin-engined fighters; and that Coastal Command and the Fleet Air Arm should hammer out a common operating procedure and tactical doctrine. Would this report, coming as it did at the end of the fourth year of war, have been needed if all air operations over the sea had continued to be vested in the old Royal Naval Air Service? Coastal Command under its successive Air Officers Commanding-in-Chief had certainly done its loyal best to become an effective all-purpose maritime air force, but the Command had always been, and still was, shackled by lack of resources in numbers and modernity of aircraft, thanks to an Air Staff doctrinally committed to putting the bomber offensive first and foremost and to the War Cabinet's endorsement of this priority. It is a depressing irony, therefore, that just at this period, autumn 1943 into winter 1943–44, Sir Arthur Harris's heavy bombers were in the course of being defeated in the Battle of Berlin by the Luftwaffe's night-fighter defence, as well as suffering insupportable losses in the bomber offensive as a whole without commensurate effect on German war production.[138]

The renewal of the North Russia convoy traffic after the crippling of the *Tirpitz* and the departure home of the *Lützow* would no longer represent – as in the past – the Western Allies' principal effort to save Soviet Russia from defeat, but instead an investment in her victorious forward march. Since smashing the German summer offensive at Kursk ('Operation Zitadelle') in July 1943 the Red Army had recovered about half the Soviet territory initially conquered by the Germans in 1941. The first of the new series of convoys to sail, the homeward-bound RA54A of thirteen empty ships marooned at Archangel since traffic was suspended in the spring, made a safe voyage at the beginning of November. On 15 November the first outward convoy (JW54A, of eighteen merchantmen) followed, with close escort and covering forces of the well-established pattern. Neither JW54A, nor its successor JW54B sailing a week later, suffered any form of enemy attack.[139] In the middle of December Admiral Fraser even took his flagship *Duke of York* all the way through to Kola with convoy JW55A, so insignificant now was the German air threat owing to the demands of the Eastern Front; and there conferred with the Soviet Commander-in-Chief, Admiral Golokov.

Sir John Tovey had vainly hoped during his command of the Home Fleet that the passage of an Arctic convoy would give him an opportunity to bring German heavy ships to action. Now the opportunity was to fall to his successor, for the enemy had come to the decision to send out the *Scharnhorst* to attack the renewed Arctic traffic when the time seemed ripe. This decision had been maturing for almost a year. On 26 February 1943 Dönitz had successfully persuaded Hitler to delegate to himself the responsibility for choosing whether or when to risk the heavy forces against convoys. In April Hitler had sanctioned the transfer of *Scharnhorst* to northern Norway in order to 'provide a significant reinforcement', so ran the German Naval Staff directive, 'for attacking the convoys running to North Russia. This task is to be given priority, and it is not to be hampered by the secondary considerations of the defence of Norway.'[140] As Commander-in-Chief of the German Navy Dönitz remained committed to keeping the heavy ships in Norwegian bases in order either to induce the British to suspend the convoys (as they did from May to November 1943) or to attack the convoys should they still continue to run.

On 20 November 1943 the German Naval Staff in a new directive appreciated (a little late) that the British might resume the traffic to Russia in the dark winter season, even if only in the form of single ships: 'Against this traffic both the Northern Task Force and the U-boats are to be operated.'[141] According to the directive such deployment compelled the Royal Navy to hold capital ships in home waters, and so took the pressure off Germany's Japanese ally.[142] After B-Dienst decrypts and air and U-boat sightings confirmed that in November the Arctic traffic had indeed been resumed, Dönitz reaffirmed his decision to send the Northern Task Force into action, not least because supplies were being sent to Russia 'under our very noses' at a time when the German Army on the Eastern Front was under heavy pressure. Dönitz rated the chances of success as 'not inconsiderable'.[143]

From 22 December U-boats and Luftwaffe reconnaissance repeatedly reported sightings of the outward convoy JW55B (22 ships), which had left Loch Ewe on 20 December. On the 22nd *Scharnhorst* was brought to three hours' notice for steam. Late on Christmas Eve Group North at Kiel asked Dönitz for a decision by noon on Christmas Day as to whether *Scharnhorst* should be ordered to attack the convoy. The German naval hierarchy being in fact riven with dissent over the question, the teleprinters clattered with last-minute argument. Admiral Otto Schniewind, Fleet Commander and Flag Officer, Group North, remained (as previously) sceptical of *Scharnhorst*'s chances of braving the escorts' torpedoes and then cutting up the convoy at a season when there was only one hour of maximum visibility for gunfire in the day: 'On the whole the chances of a major success are slender, and the stakes high.'[144] Admiral Erich Bey in Altenfiord, the Flag

Officer, Northern Task Force, was of the same mind; himself a destroyer man, he agreed with Schniewind that the convoy should be attacked by destroyers only. In any case he was very unhappy about the 'completely inadequate' air reconnaissance, and wanted a further search to establish whether or not the British heavy ships were covering the convoy.[145]

Nevertheless Dönitz (who had returned to Berlin from Paris on Christmas Day) completely overruled his subordinates, so demonstrating that he yielded nothing to Dudley Pound when it came to taking operational decisions into his own hands. At 1412 (actually before Dönitz himself arrived back in Berlin) the naval staff passed on his instructions to Admiral Bey to take the *Scharnhorst* and six destroyers to sea.

At 1900 the *Scharnhorst* (Captain Fritz Hintze) weighed anchor in Altenfiord and headed for the open sea, her mess decks still festive with Christmas trees, her ensign a tiny splash of red, white and black against the snowbound granite cliffs. Her ship's company were in high spirits at the prospect of action at last. But even in the deep shelter of the fjord the wind howled in the rigging, a witness to the accuracy of the latest weather forecasts:

> Southerly gale, Force 8–9, increasing sea 6–7. On 26.12. veering south west 6–8, with heavy S.W. swell. Overcast with rain, visibility 3–4 miles, only intermittingly improving to 10 miles. Snow-falls in Barents Sea.[146]

Rightly fearful of the effects of such weather on the destroyers, Schniewind (as Flag Officer Group North and Fleet Commander) telephoned the Naval Staff in Berlin to ask that 'Operation Ostfront' be cancelled while the task force was still within the fjords. But the Naval Staff adamantly ordered that even if heavy seas prevented the destroyers from keeping station, *Scharnhorst* was to carry out the attack in the form of 'cruiser warfare', that is, as a lone raider. The final decision as to how to operate was left to Bey. It seems clear that Dönitz stuck to his resolve largely because of the current plight of the German Army on the Eastern Front. In the words of his signal to Bey earlier for benefit of ships' companies: 'In sending an important convoy of supplies and weapons to Russia the enemy hopes to increase the difficulties of the heroic struggle of our Eastern Army. We must help.'[147]

In its report later on *Scharnhorst*'s sortie, the German naval staff justified the decision to carry 'Ostfront' through on the grounds that there was a chance of surprising the British after two convoys had gone through unmolested, and that 'No heavy ships had been reported among the enemy's covering force, either by air reconnaissance or by other sources . . .'[148]

But in point of fact Admiral Sir Bruce Fraser was at sea with the *Duke of York* (flag), the cruiser *Jamaica* and four destroyers, in addition to the cruiser covering force under Vice-Admiral R. L. Burnett (*Belfast*, *Sheffield* and *Norfolk*). The outward convoy JW55B and the homeward RA55A themselves each enjoyed a powerful escort of ten destroyers and several smaller vessels.

The *Scharnhorst* (32,000 tons displacement; 39,000 tons full load)[149] with her nine 11-inch guns could therefore find herself fighting the heavily armoured *Duke of York* (38,000 tons displacement; 44,460 tons full load)[150] with ten 14-inch guns, as well as one 8-inch cruiser and three 6-inch cruisers. She would also face the hazard of torpedo attack by the cruisers and by up to 24 destroyers.

Throughout the coming action the German command ashore and Bey himself remained in a complete fog as to British strength and movements – partly because of the poor liaison between the Luftwaffe and the naval headquarters, leading to a failure to pass on news of a sighting of a force of several ships, including 'a big one', by reconnaissance flying boats on the 26th. B-Dienst indications that a British heavy force might be at sea were also ignored.[151] GC and CS on the other hand provided the Admiralty with the texts of all signals between the German naval command and *Scharnhorst* at relatively short delay. Thus it was that at 0217 on 26 December the Operational Intelligence Centre issued the urgent Ultra signal: 'Emergency: *Scharnhorst* probably sailed 1800 25 December.'[152]

At 0339 and for the benefit of the convoy escort and other ships not in receipt of Ultra, the OIC broadcast the general message: 'Admiralty appreciates *Scharnhorst* at sea.'[153]

Thereafter the flow of Ultra decrypts, coupled with intercepts of low-grade Luftwaffe radio traffic by airborne Royal Air Force 'Y' parties, kept Admiral Fraser fully informed about his enemy's intentions and – just as useful – the enemy's current state of knowledge about British strength and movements. This invaluable Intelligence, undreamt-of by admirals in earlier wars, enabled Fraser to manoeuvre his own force, the cruiser force and the convoy escorts as components in a single evolving operational design. In order to coordinate the operation in this way Fraser took the risk of breaking radio silence, so that he could signal instructions and also so that his separate groups could be kept fully informed as to each other's current positions.[154]

In the early hours of 26 December the enemy and the British forces were converging within the sea area between Bear Island and the North Cape – Admiral Bey in *Scharnhorst* coming up from the south, Burnett and his cruisers down from the north-east in order to intercept Bey; convoy JW55A steaming from the west; and Fraser in the *Duke of York* from the west also, but still some 200 miles distant from the convoy. In order to narrow the gap Fraser ordered the convoy to put about for three hours before resuming course eastwards; he also ordered it to steer further north away from the *Scharnhorst*. It would be a day of virtual darkness, with Arctic twilight providing the merest paling on the horizon between 0830 and 1530. The wind was now blowing hard from the south-west, the sea rough and rising. Fraser's and Bey's destroyers alike were having a particularly uncomfortable time, the following wind and sea making it hard for their helmsmen to keep them on course. An officer in HMS *Scorpion* describes how the destroyer

> . . . running downwind of a gale broached to at 24 knots, and charged along a giant trough with her funnel nearly in the water. Thank God the Quartermaster kept hold of the wheel which of course had full opposite rudder on. I tried to hold on to the binnacle but was flung down on my back in one corner of the bridge . . .[155]

The big German destroyers, being not such good sea-boats, generally suffered worse than the British. At about 0730 Bey spread them to the south-west to search for the convoy, so plunging them straight into a head sea. In the event they found nothing thanks to Fraser's diversion of the convoy to the north; and Bey later ordered them back to base. So *Scharnhorst* steamed on alone while Admiral Fraser drew his net round her.

At 0840 Burnett's cruisers picked up the distant battleship by radar; at 0921 *Sheffield* (Captain C. T. Aldiss) sighted her at 12,000 yards in the faint twilight. Three minutes later Burnett's flagship *Belfast* (Captain F. R. Parham) fired a starshell; at 0939 the *Norfolk* (the only cruiser that could bear, the others being masked by their fellows in quarter line) crashed out a salvo. Like a silent ghost in the shadows *Scharnhorst* immediately hauled round to the south without returning the fire and at 30 knots soon outran the British cruisers struggling at 24 knots against wind and sea. She had been hit at least once.

Burnett now steered to place himself ahead of the convoy in order to guard against any enemy attempt to work round and attack it. He was reinforced by Fraser with four destroyers switched from the escort of the homeward RA55A, which was now out of the danger zone to the westward. Fraser himself was now coming up in *Duke of York* at 24 knots, the flagship taking as usual in a sea-way masses of water over her flat forecastle (the lack of sheer in her bows being a fault in the design of this class of ship).

For the Commander-in-Chief the worry now lay in that his destroyer screen might run short of fuel before *Scharnhorst* could be brought to action, so giving him the difficult choice of turning back or running all the way on to Kola. The German admiral solved his problem for him, however, by turning north in the hope of finding the convoy – only to run into Burnett's cruisers again. Just after noon the *Belfast* detected the *Scharnhorst* on her radar, and twenty minutes later the *Sheffield* reported: 'Enemy in sight'. For Fraser this was glad news indeed, for he now lay only 160 miles distant from the scene to the west. At a range of about 11,000 yards Burnett's three cruisers opened fire. As the *Scharnhorst* turned south and sped for home she smashed back with 11-inch salvoes, putting out of action one of *Norfolk*'s main turrets and all but one of her radar sets.

Burnett now shadowed the enemy by radar just out of visibility range, secure in the knowledge that *Scharnhorst*'s southerly course was delivering her to Admiral Fraser as he came up on a converging course from the west. At 1617 *Duke of York*'s own radar picked up *Scharnhorst* at 20 miles range, and the C-in-C deployed his force for action. At 1650 the flagship and *Belfast* fired a starshell; a lurid white glare in a charcoal sky. An eye-witness in HMS *Scorpion* was to recall:

> . . . when the starshell first illuminated *Scharnhorst*, I could see her so clearly that I could see her turrets were fore-and-aft (and what a lovely sight she was at full speed). She was almost at once obliterated by a wall of water from the *Duke*'s first salvo – quite like the spotting table! When she re-appeared her turrets wore a different aspect![156]

For the next two and threequarter hours *Scharnhorst* twisted and turned in her attempts to shake off her hunters while steering for home, her guns again and again straddling *Duke of York* without inflicting damage. In this war, unlike the Great War, it was German shells that proved unreliable, too often failing to explode at all. Not least owing to the superior British gunnery radar the *Duke of York* scored probably as many as thirteen 14-inch shell hits on her enemy in the course of the battleship action – and yet still the German ship floated and steamed. At 1830 the *Scharnhorst*'s guns stopped firing. At about 1850 HMS *Scorpion* and the Norwegian destroyer *Stord*, labouring in the heavy seas, at last gained enough bearing to launch torpedoes. Just at that moment *Scharnhorst* sighted them in the light of starshells, and her captain put his wheel over in an instinctive but fatal evasive move, so that, in the words of an officer in *Scorpion*, 'an onrushing target at a fine inclination became a sitting bird'.[157] *Scorpion*, *Stord*, *Savage* and *Saumarez* were able to fire a total of twelve torpedoes at the *Scharnhorst*'s beam, of which probably three struck home.

With her speed down to only five knots, *Scharnhorst* now became merely a hapless target for more torpedoes, for 8-inch and 6-inch salvoes from the cruisers and 14-inch salvoes from *Duke of York* at a range of only 10,000 yards. Last seen as a dim red glow within a pall of smoke, the *Scharnhorst* finally succumbed to torpedo attack from all sides by the cruisers and destroyers. She went down with Admiral Bey and Captain Hintze in 72° 16′N, 28° 41′E. Only thirty-six survivors from her complement of 2,000 were plucked from the ice-cold rollers.

Scharnhorst's lone fight for so long against such odds reflects the greatest credit on her ship's company and also on her designers and builders, who enabled her to withstand hits from some thirteen 14-inch shells, about a dozen 8-inch or 6-inch shells and at least eleven torpedoes before foundering. But her fight reflects little credit on liaison between the German Navy and the Luftwaffe, nor on the German ability to make good operational use of available Sigint; and it reflects none at all on Dönitz's strategic judgment and exercise of command.

Henceforward it was left to the U-boats virtually alone to try to interrupt the Arctic traffic. But in the face of very large escorts that included on occasion as many as two escort carriers and two of the Western Approaches Escort (Support) Groups, they could achieve little. In a battle in March 1944 with outward convoy JW58, of 49 ships, closely escorted by the light cruiser *Diadem*, twenty destroyers, four corvettes, five sloops and the CVEs *Activity* and *Tracker*, the enemy lost six shadowing aircraft and four U-boats without sinking a single ship. Here was a very different scene from the desperate convoy fights of 1942 against great odds above and below and on the surface of the sea.

Yet the *Tirpitz* still remained a potential menace, her wounds slowly healing. In January and February 1944 Intelligence from Ultra and other sources indicated that she could be seaworthy by mid-March.[158] By mid-March further decrypts of Enigma revealed that she was undergoing sea trials. On 21 March the Operational Intelligence Centre suggested that because of the worsening plight of the German

Army on the Eastern Front (during the previous five weeks the Russians had smashed through in the Ukraine towards the Carpathians), the enemy might risk the *Tirpitz* against an Arctic convoy if it were not covered by heavy forces. The Admiralty therefore decided that the Home Fleet should cover JW58, strongly escorted as it in any case would be (see above). Admiral Fraser would have with him the battleships *Duke of York* and *Anson*, the fleet carriers *Victorious* and *Furious*, and the escort carriers *Emperor*, *Searcher* and *Pursuer*. But the carriers were to operate as a separate task force with the separate mission of crippling the *Tirpitz* in her anchorage in Altenfiord.[159]

In the small hours of 3 April 1944 the task force (under Vice-Admiral Sir Henry Moore) had reached the launching point 120 miles from Altenfiord. By 0437 the bombers and fighters of the first strike were aloft and heading for *Tirpitz*; at 0525 the second strike followed: a total of 42 bombers and 80 fighters. The bombers, Fairey Barracudas (cruising speed 172 mph; range 1,150 miles; the Fleet Air Arm's first monoplane torpedo-bomber)[160] were all flown from the two fleet carriers. The fighter cover, American-built Grumman Wildcats and Hellcats (maximum speeds respectively 318 and 380 mph; armament six forward-firing 0.5-inch Browning machine-guns, or, in the case of the Hellcat, two 20mm cannon plus four 0.5-inch machine-guns)[161] was largely provided by the three escort carriers.

The *Tirpitz* presented a difficult enough target, ensconced as she was behind torpedo nets close under the cliffs of the fjord and heavily defended by her own 68 anti-aircraft guns of various calibres and by numerous shore batteries tactically sited round the fjord. However, thanks to detailed photo-reconnaissance pictures and repeated rehearsal of the attack with uttermost thoroughness by the strike forces, both attacking waves swept in and over and out in just a few minutes with the loss of only three aircraft. As they flashed over the ship they dropped a mixture of ten 1,600-pound armour-piercing bombs (from a height of 3,500 feet), sixty-six 500 pound semi-armour-piercing bombs (from a height of 2,000 feet) and some high-explosive and anti-submarine bombs for good measure. The first wave swept in before smoke from smoke candles had time to shroud the ship, even before all *Tirpitz*'s water-tight doors could be closed.[162] By attacking from port and starboard simultaneously, the Barracudas confused a defence already taken by surprise. As the German battle report later ruefully described:

> . . . The aircraft flying in to port (about 20 in number) flew along the ridge of the mountains, making use of every dip, and so low parallel to

> the ship that they themselves could only see the Foretop, thus making it impossible for the lower lying guns and controls to fire at them. When these aircraft were in a position between 220° and 240° from the ship, they suddenly (from a distance of 6,560 feet), 'hedge-hopped' over the mountains and dived on to the ship, firing with all their guns. The bombs were released from a height of 600–1,000 feet. At this time the main Flak battery with both Forward Flak fire controls had already been put out of action by gunfire . . .[163]

Tirpitz took a total of fifteen bomb hits, causing internal fires and widespread damage, some of it structural,[164] putting her out of action again for three months.

The Fleet Air Arm was to attack her four more times, on 17 and 22 July and 24 and 29 August 1944, with varying success. However, carrier aircraft could not carry an armour-piercing bomb of sufficient weight to penetrate the *Tirpitz*'s main armour and so inflict mortal damage. It finally took four-engined Lancasters of Bomber Command to do the trick with their recently developed ability to hit small targets.[165] On 15 September 1944, 28 Lancasters took off from North Russian airfields, dropped their own number of monster 12,000-pound armour-piercing bombs, and flew on to Britain. One direct hit and two near-misses left *Tirpitz* with severe damage to her bow. Dönitz now decided that her sea-going days were finally over, and he ordered her to be moved to Tromsö harbour to serve as a floating coastal defence battery. Here the German naval authorities sought to find shallow water with a suitable bottom for her berth so that she could not capsize even if badly holed, but simply settle on even keel. They failed, for calculations showed that the depth of water under her, according to a German report, 'would not give complete security against capsizing, but that safety was likely'.[166]

Before the unfavourable contours of the bottom could be filled by dredger Bomber Command struck again on 12 November with 32 Lancasters, with results tersely summarised in the report of the Sea Defence Commandant at Tromsö, Captain Krüger:

> Eye-witness accounts reveal that the port-side outer hull was ripped open by a direct hit and several near-misses. This caused heavy inrush of water. The Captain's order for counter-flooding could not be carried out. As a result of the explosion [in her magazines] when the ship heeled over 60–70°, C turret [the after turret] shifted 20–25 metres from its mounting – confirmed by divers. This immediately caused heavier inrush of water and further rapid heeling over of the ship, resistance to further heeling over

> was small, so that, in spite of the bilge keel, which broke off, the ship finally turned over.[167]

Of the 1,000 members of her ship's company trapped in the capsized hull, 85 were rescued thanks to the prompt initiative of an engineer captain and his men in at once cutting a hole through the plating of the bottom.

With the capsizing of the *Tirpitz* was finally ended that menace from the German heavy forces that had weighed so much on the minds of the Admiralty and the Commanders-in-Chief, Home Fleet, ever since the outbreak of war, with consequent ramifying effect on the global deployment of Britain's inadequate resources of capital ships and fleet carriers. Only the pocket battleships *Scheer* and *Lützow* were now left to Dönitz, and henceforward they were to be fully committed in the Baltic in support of the struggling German troops on the northern flank of the Eastern Front as they fell back into Germany itself.

For the Arctic convoys and their escorts the principal enemies in 1944 and 1945 were therefore the U-boats – and the weather and the latitude, both particularly hard on the ships' companies and the flying crews of the escort carriers that now often sailed with the convoys. The Arctic run meant operating aircraft on a gruelling schedule of twelve hours flying and twelve hours maintenance, in light conditions ranging from perpetual daylight to perpetual dark, in extreme cold with deck gear frozen, and in seas that could be gigantic. Some escort carriers buckled the fore-ends of their flight decks 60 feet above the waterline, and one even recorded a green sea rolling the full length of the flight deck.[168] Convoy RA64 in February 1945 met constant gales of up to 80 knots from dead ahead, and Rear-Admiral McGrigor, the covering force commander, reported '. . . much difficulty in keeping stragglers with the convoy. Engine troubles, defective steering, ice-chipped propellers, shifting cargoes, and splitting decks were among the very genuine reasons for dropping astern and at times stopping.'[169]

During this particular but by no means untypical passage the escort carrier HMS *Campania* (12,450 tons displacement)[170] was compelled to heave to after rolling 45° each way; and the convoy's average speed of advance dropped to 3½ knots.[171]

For the ships' companies – Merchant Marine as well as Royal Navy – life on the mess deck of a closed-up vessel in such weather was wearing enough in itself to body and spirit, just as it was on the North Atlantic too. Packed into the steel box of the mess deck, deadlights screwed down over the scuttles, with a mass of hammocks swinging only some five feet above the deck, the crews breathed a damp fug of their own stale exhalations and the rising vapour from wet serge slowly drying; a fug stinking of sweat, vomit and the all-pervasive reek of fuel oil. Above them in the dim electric lighting the deck-head dripped and dripped with condensation, while the thin steel plating separating them from the icy sea resounded regularly to the crashing of green water on to the forecastle.

When exhausted crews at last made landfall at Murmansk after such desolate and dangerous voyages, they found – like their predecessors of 1941–43 – no warm welcome, no chance of a jolly run ashore, as in Canada and America at the end of the North Atlantic run, but instead one of the bleakest, most poverty-stricken corners of Stalin's tyranny, and the surly face of Soviet authority. Perhaps the sourest example of the Stalinist state's hospitality to the Royal Navy during 1941–45 is offered by its refusal in 1942 to allow a medical unit (sent out with PQ18 to care ashore for wounded sailors from earlier convoys) to enter the Soviet Union, insisting that it return to Britain with the next convoy. Tovey was to write in his despatch:

> The reason for this astonishing decision by our Allies could not be discovered, but I renewed my representation for the strongest pressure to be brought to bear to induce them once more to change their minds. That British seamen, wounded while carrying supplies to Russia, should be exposed unnecessarily to the medieval treatment prevalent in Russian hospitals, was intolerable.[172]

Eventually the Soviet authorities did relent.

On 29 April 1945 the final wartime outward North Russian convoy, JW66 of 22 ships, sailed for North Russia. Powerfully escorted by the CVEs *Vindex* and *Premier*, the cruiser *Bellona* and eighteen escort ships, and with the 19th Escort Group deployed ahead to deal with waiting U-boats, it reached Kola without loss after attack by only one U-boat. The homeward RA66 suffered the very last casualty of the Arctic convoy run – the frigate *Goodall* torpedoed and sunk.

The decisive nature of the Royal Navy's Arctic victory is demonstrated in stark brevity by the statistics. Between December 1942 and May 1945 sixteen convoys made the outward voyage to North Russia, and yet in 1943 not one ton of 450,000 tons despatched was lost; in 1944 only 10,000 tons out of 1.25 million; and in 1945 10,000 tons out of 650,000.[173] Such was seapower's contribution to the Red Army's advance from the depths of European Russia to Berlin. Yet by this time seapower had done much, much more than this to aid in the destruction of the Wehrmacht. For it had been instrumental in creating a Western Front once again, where American, British and Canadian armies too could join in the work of smashing the enemy in mass battles; it had nourished the victorious march of the Allied Expeditionary Force of up to ninety divisions across France and Belgium and on into the German heartland.

PART IV

VICTORY

24

'Neptune': Problems, Puzzles and Personalities

In October 1943 Admiral Sir Bertram Ramsay, an officer still on the retired list, entered Norfolk House, the London mansion of the Dukes of Norfolk and now the headquarters of COSSAC (Chief of Staff to Supreme Allied Commander), in St James's Square to take up the post of Allied Naval Commander, Expeditionary Force (ANCXF) for the second time. He had first been appointed in May 1942 when a 'Combined Commanders Committee' was set up to study the possibility of invading France that year in operations 'Roundup' or 'Sledgehammer' (see above, pp. 530–1). The post had lapsed when these projects were shelved in favour of 'Operation Torch' and he became instead deputy to Andrew Cunningham as ANCXF for 'Torch'. COSSAC had been set up since then by the Casablanca Conference in January 1943, as an inter-Allied planning staff under Lieutenant-General F. E. Morgan with the title of Chief of Staff, Supreme Allied Commander (designate). His task was to produce an outline plan for the invasion of France in 1944. In August 1943 the combined Chiefs of Staff at the Quebec Conference approved this outline and instructed Morgan to get on with detailed planning and preparations for 'Operation Overlord', as it was now dubbed, with the target date of 1 May 1944.

During the Quebec Conference the then First Sea Lord, Sir Dudley Pound, recommended to the Prime Minister that Admiral Sir Charles Little, the Commander-in-Chief, Portsmouth, and at that time also the ANCXF (designate), be confirmed as ANCXF. But Churchill trenchantly objected – on this occasion with every justification – arguing that he was 'sure that Admiral Ramsay would be a far better appointment for this purpose on account not only of his natural abilities but his unique experience in conducting a great overseas descent . . .'[1] Pound reluctantly gave way, although why he should have preferred Little will never be known. Was it a pedantic belief that Ramsay, being on the Retired List, was not suitable as a C-in-C, but only as a Chief of Staff (as in 'Torch')?

In Norfolk House – elegant Georgian chambers contrasting with standard-issue Whitehall desks and filing cabinets; the grand saloon now a conference room – Ramsay found himself the only one of the Allied Expeditionary Force commanders already in post. Eisenhower, the Supreme Commander, and Montgomery, C-in-C, 21st Army Group and overall land forces commander (Ramsay's opposite number), were still in the Mediterranean conducting the Italian campaign, where the Allied armies were struggling after Kesselring's troops as they retreated from Salerno towards the *Gustavstellung*. It would be several weeks before the Allied Expeditionary Air Forces Commander, Air Chief-Marshal Sir Trafford Leigh-Mallory, was even appointed. And not until January 1944 would Air Chief-Marshal Sir Arthur Tedder become Deputy Supreme Commander. Ramsay and his new Chief of Staff, Rear-Admiral G. E. Creasy, had to begin work with General Morgan in a mist of uncertainty.

Although Ramsay brought to his new task the experience and confidence acquired during the desperate improvisation of the Dunkirk evacuation and the successful mounting of 'Torch' and 'Husky', he now confronted a supreme professional challenge, for 'Neptune' (codename for the maritime first phase of 'Overlord': the whole operation of transporting the Allied Expeditionary Force across the Channel and putting it ashore on D-Day) had no precedent in terms of scale, risk and strategic importance. In the first place, it would not be another 'blue water' expedition in a secondary theatre of war like 'Torch' or 'Husky'; it would be the Anglo-Americans' one and only opportunity of re-establishing the Western Front, thereby defeating a main body of the German Army in battle and opening the way for the eventual invasion of the Third Reich. The outcome of the war was therefore to be staked on this one card. Operationally too 'Neptune' presented a far greater gamble than 'Torch' or 'Husky'. Instead of the tideless Mediterranean with its often fine weather, there would be the English Channel in all its unpredictability of wind and sea even in summer; the rise and fall of the tide and the tricky tidal streams and currents, changing from hour to hour, day to day and place to place. 'Neptune' would moreover far exceed the Mediterranean landings in sheer size and complexity, and in the consequent problems of dovetailing sea, air and land forces into a single enterprise.

Only by the efficient functioning of the vast machine on D-Day could the gamble therefore succeed. Such functioning in the face of the inevitable rule of Murphy's Law depended on the thoroughness and professional skill of the prior staff work in designing and putting together the machine. It depended on rigorous joint training of the soldiers and sailors; on the rehearsal again and again, of the landing process – and also of the complicated prior assembly of invasion forces that were scattered in ports and harbours right round the southern coasts of England.

Nor would Ramsay's problems come to an end on D-Day, for the Allied Expeditionary Force would depend on an uninterrupted seaborne flow of troops, stores, weapons, transport and fuel *en masse* for its expansion into a great field army capable of breaking out of the initial lodgement. Yet there was little prospect of immediately capturing intact a major port, let alone *ports* as in 'Torch', since the Germans had encased every such port along the Channel and North Sea coasts in reinforced concrete defences formidable alike in their density, clever tactical siting and firepower.

These stupendous problems facing the navies are sometimes ignored by some historians of the land campaign in Normandy, who commence their narratives on the beaches, almost as if all that lay between southern England and Normandy were a No Man's Land swiftly and easily traversed by the attacking armies.[2]

Nonetheless, as Ramsay was aware, a mass of crucially important preliminary work on all the operational problems had already been done before he became ANCXF in October 1943. As early as October 1941 the General Staff Intelligence section of GHQ, Home Forces, had moved into Norfolk House with the new responsibility of gathering information about the Continental coast from Den Helder in the Netherlands to the Loire, together with a zone extending thirty miles inland.[3] Later it was joined by the section of the Naval Intelligence Department concerned with German coastal defences; and early in 1942 both sections were amalgamated into the Combined Intelligence Section (CIS) of GHQ, Home Forces. After COSSAC also took up its quarters in Norfolk House in 1943 the CIS (renamed 'Theatre Intelligence Section' or TIS) continued to remain responsible for collating, updating and disseminating the Intelligence needed for the planning of a cross-Channel invasion.

To the desks of CIS had flowed since 1941 information about winds and tides from the service meteorological departments and from the Hydrographer of the Navy; about Continental airfields and airfield sites from the Air Intelligence Branch; about port capacities from the Transportation Branch of the War Office. The CIS itself had examined the advantages and disadvantages of every potential landing beach between Den Helder and the Loire, both in terms of the assault itself and of later tactical and strategic exploitation, including the relative prospects of capturing a major port.

As early as summer 1942 the CIS had been able to provide the Combined Commanders Committee with a complete dossier on the relative merits of all possible invasion shore-lines. To the Chief of Combined Operations (Vice-Admiral Lord Louis Mountbatten) and his staff the CIS dossier clearly pointed to the Bay of the Seine as the most favourable shore to assault – 50 miles of sandy beaches backed by easily accessible low-lying countryside stretching between the base of the Cotentin Peninsula in the west and the Caen area in the east. But Mountbatten's fellow members of the Combined Commanders Committee in 1942 – General Sir Bernard Paget (Commander-in-Chief, Home Forces) and Air Chief-Marshal Sir Trafford Leigh-Mallory (then Air Officer Commanding-in-Chief, Fighter Command), as well as Sir Alan Brooke, the CIGS – preferred the obvious choice from the map: the Pas de Calais, just across the nar0rowest part of the English Channel, within close range of United Kingdom fighter bases, and on the shortest strategic axis to the Ruhr and the heart of Germany.[4]

By April 1943, however, when the CIS had gathered together an even more comprehensive dossier on the topography and defences of the entire Channel coast of France, the Combined Commanders Committee had after all come round to the Combined Operations view that the Bay of the Seine offered the better location. Nevertheless, no formal decision was recorded; no directive issued. As a result, the newly created COSSAC found himself, in Morgan's own words, in 'an appalling quandary'.[5] From it he was rescued by the Royal Navy in the person of Admiral Mountbatten, who invited twenty generals, eleven air marshals and air commodores, and eight admirals (including five Canadians and fifteen Americans) to a conference ('Rattle') at Largs, the Combined Operations training base in Scotland. The most important participants were however Paget, Little, Leigh-Mallory and Morgan himself. The conference bent its collective mind to the task of making a final choice of invasion coast.

The Pas de Calais, despite its superficial attractions, suffered from the drawback of narrow beaches bounded by high cliffs with relatively few – and narrow – exits, so restricting the assault wave to two divisions, while the hinterland did not favour the swift build-up of an expeditionary force. Moreover road and rail communications in the region as well as the location of airfields would facilitate a German concentration and counter-stroke. In any case this stretch of coastline was for evident reasons the most densely fortified of all. And finally a landing here would, for equally obvious reasons, forfeit all hope of strategic or tactical surprise. From the naval point of view too the Pas de Calais was not a runner. Its apparent advantage of offering a short sea crossing was illusory, because the invasion forces would in any case have to be mustered from English ports as far distant as Yarmouth and Milford Haven. It offered no prospect of the early capture of a major port capable of handling the massive flow of stores and reinforcements required by a great army on the offensive, for the nearest ones, Le Havre and Antwerp, lay some 100 miles distant.

After much wearisome argument the view of Mountbatten and the Combined Operations staff carried the day. The Pas de Calais was finally sunk: the Normandy coast it was to be.[6] COSSAC could now proceed to work out – with the benefit of the CIS's invaluable dossier – the outline operational plan that was approved by the Quadrant Conference at Quebec in August 1943, and which Ramsay found awaiting him on his arrival in Norfolk House in October.

By this time the logistics conundrum fundamental to the success of 'Overlord' had also been solved – and again thanks largely to Mountbatten and his staff. The conundrum is easily stated. To expand the Allied Expeditionary Force fast enough to outweigh the flow of German reserves and enable it to break out into the interior of France demanded use of a major port. Yet there was little hope of capturing the nearest to the Bay of the Seine – Cherbourg – quickly enough; and in any case the enemy would certainly have destroyed the docks and obstructed the harbour with his customary dismal thoroughness. The German high command was indeed calculating that, with all the Channel ports fortified to the point of impregnability, the Allied invasion force would simply wither in its lodgement for want of supplies. The solution to this crucial problem was magnificently simple: the Allies would tow over the Channel two prefabricated harbours in sections and install them off the American and British invasion beaches.

It all began with limited studies of the engineering problems in designing prefabricated piers that could be erected in the open sea off a beach. On 28 April 1942 the Director of Transportation at the

War Office wrote to the Combined Development Centre to point out the potential of the so-called 'spud' system of mooring (that is, piers mounted on adjustable legs and floating up with the tide) for berthing large ships. Mountbatten's questing mind having seized on the operational possibilities of such piers, he sold the concept to the Prime Minister who, in a now famous minute of 30 May 1942 on the topic of 'piers for flat beaches', grandly directed:

> They must float up and down with the tide. The anchor problems must be mastered. The ships must have a side-flap cut in them, and a drawbridge long enough to overreach the moorings of the piers. Let me have the best solution worked out. Don't argue the matter. The difficulties will argue for themselves.[7]

By the end of September 1942 and under the aegis of Combined Operations three prototype designs were developed by the War Office Directorate of Transportation. The Directorate's own design consisted of a pierhead unit mounted on adjustable legs (the 'spud' system) and flexible steel bridges to the shore on floating steel or concrete pontoons. A second scheme by a Mr Lorys Hughes proposed steel bridges mounted on concrete caissons towed to the site and sunk on to the seabed. Finally there was the 'Swiss Roll', a floating mat bridge sponsored by the Director of Miscellaneous Weapons Development at the Admiralty, and consisting of a flexible timber and canvas mat supported on wire cables and secured to both shore and sea anchor-points. In that same month Mountbatten submitted to the Chiefs of Staff his own ideal specification: a pier one mile long that was capable of withstanding gale-force winds and berthing large coasters. Churchill, his boyish enthusiasm for imaginative inventions further roused by Mountbatten's memorandum, wrote on 26 September: 'It seems to me that we ought to have 3–4 miles of this pier tackle. It could of course be used in many places as short sections. Pray do not lightly turn this aside . . .'[8]

But thereafter impetus sagged in delays in developing and testing the three prototype systems. On 10 March 1943 Churchill was angrily minuting the Chiefs of Staff, the Chief of Combined Operations and the War Office Director of Transportation: 'This matter is being much neglected. Dilatory experiments with varying types and patterns have resulted in our having nothing. It is now nearly 6 months since I urged the construction of several miles of pier.'[9]

Despite this Prime Ministerial boot in the bottom, it was not until June 1943 that two miles of the Directorate of Transportation's design was at last ordered in preference to the others. Further trials proving satisfactory, the Chiefs of Staff on 12 July ordered four miles of pier and six pierheads (1,200 feet) for delivery in February 1944. If steel supplies permitted, the Chiefs wanted the order to be increased to ten miles of pier and fifteen pierheads. But even now it took until the autumn of 1943 finally to discard the Hughes pier, while as late as the beginning of 1944 and despite unfavourable trial reports an order was placed for two and a half miles of 'Swiss Roll'.

Yet the original intention behind these developments had been that the piers were to be erected in invasion anchorages open to the sea, as in 'Torch' or 'Husky'. It was not until 26 February 1943 that the Admiralty Director of Miscellaneous Weapons Development suggested to the War Office Director of Transportation that artificial breakwaters might be used to protect such an anchorage. During the summer two alternative designs were tested – the 'Bubble' breakwater, where a curtain of air bubbles rising from a submerged pipe was supposed to destroy the rotary motion of water particles and so damp the waves; and the 'Lilo', compartmented canvas bags filled with air and anchored so as to extend fourteen feet below the water and eight feet above, and at an angle to the sea. The 'Lilo' was supposed to yield to the pressure of the waves on its seaward side and so damp the transmission of the wave motion past it.

By the end of October 1943 these ingenious fancies had been abandoned in favour of Admiralty-sponsored cruciform hollow steel structures, each 198 feet long and 25 feet high, dubbed 'Bombardons'. Despite misgivings on the part of the Army as to whether in gale-whipped seas the Bombardons would protect or demolish the piers, an order was placed for 75, later raised to 115 and then reduced again to 93. Meanwhile, Combined Operations had gone its own way and built a prototype concrete caisson ('Hippo') to be sunk on the seabed.

It was Captain John Hughes-Hallett, RN, of Mountbatten's staff, whose mind first soared beyond mere technical development of piers and breakwaters to conceive the all-embracing idea of artificial harbours.[10] Mountbatten took the idea up and became its dynamic and successful impresario in high places, with the result that on 4 August 1943 General Morgan (COSSAC) informed the Chiefs of Staff that two artificial harbours were indispensable to 'Overlord'. The Chiefs forthwith decided to proceed with planning and developing the harbours (codenamed 'Mulberries'); a decision ratified by the Combined Chiefs of Staff at the Quadrant Conference at Quebec. The conference also set up an Anglo-American 'Combined Committee' to recommend a general specification for the Mulberries; it reported on

2 September 1943 calling for a minimum total throughput of supplies (excluding motor transport) of 12,000 tons per day – 5,000 in the American port and 7,000 in the British. The harbours would have to function for 90 days.

In both harbours a deep-water breakwater parallel to the beach capable of coping with mean high water tides would be needed. The American harbour would also require two side breakwaters in shallow water; the British an extension eastwards into shallow waters of the deep-water barrier and a further shallow-water breakwater running inshore. All this would demand 10,000 feet of deep-water breakwater 40 to 50 feet deep, and 13,000 feet of shallow-water breakwater averaging 25 feet deep. The committee also decided that concrete caissons, as under development by Combined Operations since 1942, should form the main breakwaters and that Britain would have to build them. Four days later the Chiefs of Staff instructed the War Office to supervise construction of the caissons, now codenamed 'Phoenix', and by the end of September 147 were on order in six different sizes, the work being sub-contracted by the Ministry of Supply to 24 firms.

But now the development of the Mulberries ran into the same kind of bureaucratic demarcation dispute that had bedevilled the design of an effective anti-submarine mortar (see above, pp. 256 and 588–9). Thus far, by a traditional division of engineering responsibility, the Admiralty had overseen most of the breakwater work and the War Office the piers, with Combined Operations acting as liaison link and nursery of ideas. At this point, Combined Operations suggested that a clear-cut management structure was needed to run the complete Mulberry project as now adopted. Unfortunately neither the Admiralty nor the War Office would accept the other as project leader, nor relinquish its traditional prerogatives. A civilian coordinator without executive powers, Sir Harold Wernher, was therefore appointed to try to resolve differences and agree divisions of responsibility. But the War Office and the Admiralty fiercely pursued their trade-union style battle as to who should do what into January 1944. In fact Ramsay himself forcefully entered the dispute in December 1943, asserting that the Admiralty was the responsible body; according to him, the Army said where they wanted the artificial harbours, and the Navy provided them. Such development work as the Army had done, Ramsay argued, took the form of a sub-contract from the Navy. Hardly surprisingly, the War Office stoutly repudiated this interpretation. It took a meeting held by COSSAC on 15 December and a final decision by the Chiefs of Staff on 3 January 1944 to settle the matter – in favour of the Admiralty, which was charged with drawing up the final plan for the Mulberries.[11]

The Mulberries were not the only imaginative answer to 'Overlord's' supply problems to be already well in hand by the time Ramsay took up his duties as ANCXF. Modern mechanised armies – especially the American, with its lavish scales of motor transport – gulped petroleum fuel. How was it to be delivered to the shores of Normandy without the use of a large port's oil terminal? Once again the simple but bold answer was provided by an ingenious mind in Combined Operations Headquarters,[12] when in spring 1942 Commander Thomas Hussey, RN, suggested to Mountbatten that a petroleum pipeline could be laid across the bed of the English Channel. Mountbatten, in his valuable role as marketing man for original ideas, passed Hussey's suggestion on to Geoffrey Lloyd, the Minister of Fuel, who in turn handed it to his experts, who soon produced the technical answers.

Mr A. C. Hartley of the Anglo-Iranian Oil Company proposed a pipeline like a submarine telegraph cable with the copper and gutta-percha core omitted; a trial order was placed with the British (originally German) firm of Siemens; and soon the HAIS Cable (Hartley, Anglo-Iranian, Siemens) had been successfully laid and tested in the Thames. By December 1942 a trial line had been laid by cable ship across the widest part of the Bristol Channel, and by 1 June 1943 Lloyd was able to report to Churchill that motor spirit had been continuously pumped across for two and a half months. By this time too an alternative technical solution, the HAMEL pipe (from its inventors, H. A. Hammick, Chief Engineer of the Iraq Petroleum Company, and B. J. E. Ellis, the Chief Oilfields Engineer of the Burmah Oil Company) had been tested. It consisted of a 3-inch welded steel pipe capable of being wound on to a rotating drum 50 feet in diameter mounted on a hopper barge.

In June 1943 Lloyd ordered the manufacture of both these versions of 'Pluto' (Pipe Line Under the Ocean). Responsibility for laying the pipelines would fall to the Admiralty, and so one of the more unusual branches of the Royal Navy to come under Ramsay's command was 'Force Pluto': one hundred officers and one thousand sailors from the Merchant Marine now serving beneath the White Ensign.

'Pluto' also comprised two further ingenious, though less ambitious, schemes which inspired greater confidence in the Army that they would actually work on the day than the cross-Channel pipelines. 'Tombola' consisted of a 6-inch pipeline up to 3,000 feet long to be laid on the seabed from storage tanks on the invasion shore to buoyed flexible connections to seaward which would be picked up by discharging tankers; 'Amethea' was a similar concept based on a 10-inch steel pipe towed from England and laid in places where the shore was unsuitable for 'Tombola'. The installation of these systems too would be the task of the Royal Navy's Force Pluto. Mulberry and Pluto stand as twin triumphs of the British genius for improvisation and adaptation using essentially 'low technology' components, materials and engineering methods. Nevertheless the two projects – and especially all the components of the Mulberries such as breakwaters, pierheads and piers – constituted a colossal manufacturing task to be undertaken in haste by a country already stretched to the limit.

Meanwhile the Commanders-in-Chief of the naval commands in southern England – Plymouth, Portsmouth and the Nore – had been busy preparing the elaborate infrastructure necessary for training the 'Overlord' forces and then launching them across the Channel, as well as running the actual training programmes. As Admiral Sir Charles Little, C-in-C, Portsmouth, put it in his later report on 'Neptune': 'Rome was not built in a day, and so it has been with our work of preparation . . . Broadly speaking the whole Command became involved in the preparations, many of the older establishments performing extraneous services without interfering with continuity of training . . .'[13] Early in 1942, in the little harbours of southern England, round from Yarmouth and Lowestoft in East Anglia to Fowey and Falmouth in Cornwall, the work was begun of laying down hards for landing craft and building Nissen-hutted camps for their joint-service complements and the training units. The churning of the cement-mixers preceded the rumble of landing-craft diesels; the cries of workmen, the shouts of petty officers; the clatter of hammers and the clang of corrugated iron anticipated the rattle and roar of practice small arms and ordnance.

In 1943 new repair and maintenance shops for landing craft followed; more amphibious training bases – especially in Plymouth Command after it learned in June that all the assault forces within its boundary would be American. In the words of Admiral Sir Charles Leatham, the C-in-C, Plymouth: 'From the summer of 1943, S.W. England became an American training area.'[14] American naval bases were opened at the principal ports of the Command, and the United States Navy took over its landing craft maintenance and repair centres. Between 11 October and 24 December 1943 alone the Stars and Stripes were hoisted over six new amphibious bases in this region of estuaries and fishing ports, tiny green fields and tumbled cliffs whence settlers of New England had set sail for America three centuries before, which now teemed with the soldiers and sailors of the mighty nation founded by the settlers. In November the British Cabinet requisitioned Slapton Sands in Start Bay, Devon, and its hinterland as an important American assault training area, and by 1 January 1944 it was ready for use. 'To be suddenly evacuated from their homes and means of livelihood at short notice,' wrote Admiral Leatham, 'was not a pleasant prospect for the inhabitants, but they took it in good part, realising their sacrifice was a necessary contribution to the success of the Second Front.'[15] But such requisitioning and enforced evacuation – and the cheerful acceptance of it – had long been common enough in the coastal areas of wartime Britain.

Even after Ramsay took up his new appointment as ANCXF the Commanders-in-Chief of the area naval commands retained their customary responsibilities, and continued to provide the 'Neptune' forces with administrative services and logistical support, especially with regard to infrastructure such as new hards and training centres. Only when the 'Neptune' armada was about to put to sea would Ramsay, as ANCXF, assume command. By this division of responsibility the Admiralty left Ramsay free to concentrate on all the complexities, human as well as technical, of the 'Neptune' operation itself; a task he was all too soon to find more than enough to keep him busy.

After his experiences in 'Torch' and 'Husky' Ramsay was absolutely clear in his mind as to the fundamental principle that must guide him. He laid it down that autumn of 1943 in a lecture which he wrote on 'Combined Operations' but which, on security grounds, he was not allowed by the Admiralty to deliver:

> It is important that the military plan for the subsequent land campaign should be worked out first, and that the assaults should be solely designed to position our forces for the commencement of this. A sound military plan subsequent to the assaults must be the basis of the whole operational plan. There is a danger that administrative considerations may cause the adoption of an assault plan solely based on them, which, while appearing essentially sound, will not give effect to the military requirements for the land battle later on . . . it must always be remembered that the guiding rule must be the operational plan first, and the administrative plan later, rather than the other way round. Once the Army have decided how they wish to fight the land battle it is necessary to examine how the troops can best be put ashore to give effect to the Army plan. In general it is the responsibility of the Navy to land the Army as they require, but as the plan develops Naval considerations will arise which must be discussed and agreed upon . . .[16]

Yet in the existing military plan for 'Overlord' there was a basic flaw. Because of the then probable limit of available military forces and landing craft lift, COSSAC had been originally instructed by the Combined Chiefs of Staff to plan on the basis of a three-division assault only. Morgan himself was well aware that an assault in this strength, with a front of only some 30 miles, had little chance of winning a secure lodgement in the face of German resistance, but he proved unable to win consent for an assault in greater strength. At a meeting in Algiers on 27 December 1943 to discuss the COSSAC plan, Eisenhower, Montgomery and Bedell Smith all agreed that three divisions were indeed not enough; that at least five were required in the first assault wave.[17] Montgomery omits to mention this consensus in his memoirs, characteristically claiming all credit for himself for seeing the need to widen the front of assault.[18]

On 2 January 1944 – 'two months too late', in Ramsay's opinion[19] – Montgomery flew into London to begin his customary 'Military Messiah' act on taking over a new command, and two days later Ramsay and Montgomery held their first meeting on 'Overlord' in Norfolk House. 'Monty is being perfectly sensible,' Ramsay wrote to his wife in Scotland, '& is creating a good impression.'[20] That night they dined together at Claridge's, and had 'a full and free discussion of things & found ourselves in complete agreement. I always find him [Montgomery] easy & amenable . . .'[21]

The two men on whose intimate professional cooperation the success of 'Overlord' primarily depended had forged a mutual respect during the planning of 'Husky'. They shared a 'big business' attitude to the mounting of great operations of modern war – a belief in careful, elaborate preplanning so that as little as possible was left to chance. They also shared a belief in employing the greatest possible strength as an insurance against the unexpected setback. Montgomery had paid Ramsay the high compliment that 'you understand us soldiers and know more about the land battle than any other sailor'.[22] Yet personally they could not have been more different – the fox-muzzled English general of Anglo-Irish descent, all egotism and wiry tensions; the Scots admiral with his broad, open features, a man imbued with the spirit of allied teamwork, a man commonsensical, steady, but a stout fighter for what he believed to be right, and a stickler for protocol and punctilio – 'ritualistic' was Eisenhower's word for it[23] – in the stiffest tradition of the Royal Navy.

Ramsay was well aware that Montgomery could set back their common purpose by upsetting colleagues or superiors in his blindness to other men's susceptibilities, and he sought in the coming months to steer Montgomery clear of the shoals. In order to forge the closest possible personal links with his colleague, Ramsay moved into the same mess in Latymer Court, a block of flats near Montgomery's headquarters in St Paul's School, Hammersmith, West London. 'He is not the ideal messmate, Monty,' he confided to his wife, 'as he apparently must always lead the stage, which gets a bit boring. But he is almost always interesting. He & I get on well together & he listens to my advice & generally acts on it.'[24]

On 5 January 1944 the struggle for an 'Overlord' plan that would be a sound operation of war began, and life for the ANCXF immediately became 'both hectic and exhausting'.[25] That day Montgomery made a formal presentation in Norfolk House of his initial proposal to increase the three division assault plus one division afloat in reserve under the COSSAC plan to four divisions plus one in reserve. 'Monty has struck out a new line of action,' Ramsay wrote to his wife, 'and it is my part to keep him within bounds. This requires accurate statement of fact & clear reasoning because much of it is of a nature which must curb his ambitions. He skates lightly over what I know to be dangerous or impossible ice and it's all got to be carefully reasoned . . .'[26]

Nonetheless, true to Ramsay's principle that the Navy must meet the needs of the Army's battle if it possibly could, he accepted Montgomery's additions, although pointing out 'the cost of what it implied & that the bill must be met by the Admlty [sic] for increased forces or it would not be possible. We then drew up a directive given to ourselves as from the Supreme Comdr [sic]. This was for a 4 Div assault & 1 in reserve.'[27] Next day Ramsay presented the new proposal to the First Sea Lord and Chief of Naval Staff, Admiral Sir Andrew Cunningham, and other members of the Naval Staff and pointed out the implications for the size of the assault shipping lift, 'which were considerable'.[28] Cunningham, never a man for difficulties, was (noted Ramsay in his diary) 'favourable to the proposals, & the consensus of opinion was that additional requirements could be met'.[29] These amounted to no fewer than 216 landing craft, 54 assault ships, three cruisers, 27 destroyers and many more smaller vessels.[30]

Yet there was a crucial proviso. The Allies did not possess in the European theatre enough landing craft to cover the requirements of the enlarged 'Overlord' plan as well as further landings along the Italian coast after the Anzio operation (then in preparation) and the Americans' cherished project of a two-division landing on the French Riviera ('Anvil') to take place simultaneously with 'Overlord'. Admiral 'Ernie' King, however, would not look kindly on any suggestion that his island-hopping war against Japan should yield up landing craft for

'Overlord'. Although the British were already seeking to persuade the Americans to drop 'Anvil' for the sake of retaining amphibious capacity in Italy, Cunningham pointed out to his colleagues that it was by no means certain that 'Anvil' *would* be abandoned, and as Ramsay recorded his words, 'without that we should not be able to carry out the whole new plan'.[31] This same day of Ramsay's discussions with the First Sea Lord, COSSAC formally recommended to the Chiefs of Staff that 'Anvil' be abandoned and the landing craft reallocated to 'Overlord': 'In view of the shortness of time available in which to complete planning, I request the early concurrence of the Combined Chiefs of Staff to this proposal.'[32]

Ramsay and the Naval Staff now proceeded urgently to examine all the naval implications (and not merely extra shipping lift and warships) of Montgomery's proposal. These implications, in Ramsay's words, proved 'very extensive, & absolutely devastating to progress in planning, in which direction we are already badly adrift. The staff are a bit frantic about it.'[33] But worse was to come on 8 January:

> Monty came to see me at 0930 & put up a proposition for an increased width of assault, including a departure from what had been proposed at our previous meeting on 5th January. This was not unexpected as I felt certain that (as in Egypt) he would not reach a decision on a final plan without several false starts. I promised to investigate the implications of his proposal & give him an answer . . . he should have, but didn't, put the same proposition to L.M. [Leigh-Mallory], as it largely affects the air forces.[34]

Montgomery's 'increased width of assault' now embraced a 50-mile front from Cabourg, east of the River Orne, to Varreville on the eastern coast of the Cotentin Peninsula, within reach of Cherbourg: this meant five divisions landing together instead of four plus one in reserve. It disturbed Ramsay that Montgomery would not pay sufficient attention to the naval problems involved although these were 'forcibly' put by himself.[35]

On 12 January, Ramsay, Leigh-Mallory and Montgomery took part in a large conference at 21st Army Group Headquarters in St Paul's School which included the commanding generals of the 1st United States Army and 2nd British Army and corresponding air force officers. The purpose of the conference was to settle the joint questions of the size of the assault wave and the width of the front, the key to all future planning as well as to the ultimate success of 'Overlord'. Montgomery did not help by stage-managing the seating arrangements in order, in Ramsay's words, 'to imply that Monty was the supreme commander & L.M. & myself subsidiary to him, which was absurd as we are not in the least . . .'[36]

Ramsay forthrightly told the conference that the implications for the five-division assault were 'very serious' from his point of view as ANCXF and that 'it could not be recommended whereas the 4 Div & 1 staggered could. As however the 5 div assault was so important from the army pt [sic] of view, I was prepared to agree to it, provided the additional naval forces and lift were provided . . .'

By now he felt deep and growing anxiety about the whole prospect for 'Neptune'/'Overlord', especially in view of the continued absence of Eisenhower as Supreme Commander, not due to arrive from Washington until 16 January. On the night before Eisenhower's arrival Ramsay confided his misgivings to his diary:

> Monty has come down firmly with request for 5 Div assault. I have agreed, subject to necessary lift *and* naval forces for Bombardment, Minesweeping & escort being available. In doing so I am under no delusions as to the complexity of the naval operations entailed by this requirement & as to the extent to which success will be a gamble with fortune. The weather both for air and surface participation could of itself mar success. The Mine menace is very real, and the degree of training of the thousands of craft will be unknown until a late date. The capacity of the beaches & their suitability for receiving the craft & ships of all kinds is also largely guesswork. The making of the artificial harbours is also in the realm of fairyland & may or may not be a practical proposition. We now await information from Chiefs of Staff whether we are to get the extra lift or not. Until then we just cannot plan on any firm foundation.[37]

Nor was he cheered by his first meeting with the Supreme Commander two days later:

> He was pleasant as usual. He is obviously keen that Anvil should not be cancelled but agrees that Overlord must be increased. Like everyone else on the highest plane he wants to have his cake and eat it. I assured him that the two things couldn't go together & the only means of making Overlord go properly was to cancel Anvil.[38]

Nonetheless, on 23 January Eisenhower did signal the Combined Chiefs of Staff to say that while the 'ideal would be to mount a five-division Overlord assault and a three-division Anvil simultaneously', he would accept 'as a last resort' a one-division 'Anvil' to serve merely as a threat. He would also accept a postponement of 'Overlord' for a month 'if I could then be sure of obtaining the required strength [in assault shipping] . . .'[39] Although the Supreme

Commander too asked for a speedy decision, his signal proved only the first salvo in yet another protracted inter-Allied battle over grand-strategic priorities. For although the British Chiefs of Staff promptly responded by advocating that 'Anvil' be cancelled altogether and 'Overlord' postponed by a month, the Joint Chiefs of Staff in Washington refused to countenance either proposal. They merely offered three extra landing ships and 57 extra landing craft for 'Overlord', which addition they reckoned would enable a five-division assault to be lifted – given 95 per cent serviceability and more economical loading. The JCS's reply 'has driven everybody mad', wrote Ramsay in his diary, 'as it consists of a series of questions bearing upon the figures we were working to . . . *Just* what we did *not* want as it starts a cross Atlantic game of ball . . .'[40]

Between 29 January and 3 February the Prime Minister and the Chiefs of Staff discussed their next play in the trans-Atlantic ball game, finally seeking to persuade the Americans that 'Anvil' should be cancelled as much for the sake of the Italian campaign as of 'Overlord'; not an argument likely to appeal to men such as General Marshall. The Joint Chiefs would only concede that 'Overlord' should in fact be postponed until the first week of June in order to gain an extra month's British production of landing craft; but they stubbornly insisted that 'Anvil' must take place and at the same time as 'Overlord'. Thus in different ways the Mediterranean theatre continued to distract Washington and London alike, and to threaten to divert amphibious strength from the Allies' true *Schwerpunkt*, 'Overlord'.

Meanwhile those responsible for planning 'Overlord' could only pursue their course 'uneasily', in Ramsay's word. 'It is outrageous,' he noted in his diary on 4 February, 'that we should still be unable to issue a firm plan.'[41]

At British request an Anglo-American conference opened on 13 February in London to try to settle this fundamental question of assault shipping lift. The American Joint Chiefs declined to attend in person because they were themselves in the midst of a grand conference on American strategy in the Pacific. Eisenhower therefore represented the United States, together with two members of the Washington planning staffs, General J. E. Hull and Rear Admiral C. M. Cooke, as his advisers. After Ramsay had presented an outline of his naval proposals, Hull and Cooke argued the Washington view that the British were asking for a greater lift than was really needed, 'forgetting,' wrote Ramsay, 'that we have to load tactically to assault a strongly defended coast & any arithmetical calculation is bound to be impractical operationally'.[42] The meeting thus turned on technicalities about load capacities, tactical loading, and probable rates of serviceability; it ended in a compromise by which the Americans offered some extra lift from their own production and the British accepted that a five-division 'Overlord' could be managed with a smaller lift than they had originally asked for. This compromise would make it possible to leave a lift in the Mediterranean for two or three divisions. The compromise infuriated Ramsay, the more so since he was forced to accept it because Montgomery had already surrendered to American pressure – 'an iniquitous thing to do'.[43]

The new decision compelled Ramsay and his staff to go through 'a series of contortions' in order to adjust their operational planning to the reduced lift. He warned the Allied Supreme Commander during a meeting of AEF Commanders-in-Chief: '. . . I would like to make it clear that the reduction agreed to will inevitably add to the complexity of what are already ultra-complex naval operations & as such is not welcome . . .'[44]

On 25 February – the weeks towards D-Day were slipping away – the British and Americans agreed that a final decision over 'Anvil' should be postponed until 20 March. They did now decide, however, that unless the Combined Chiefs of Staff concluded on 20 March that it could take place after all, only sufficient lift for one division would thereafter remain in the Mediterranean, all the surplus assault shipping being brought back to Britain for 'Overlord'. Thus the question of the total lift to be available for 'Overlord', so crucial to the planning of 'already ultra-complex naval operations' was to be left hanging for nearly another month without final answer. No wonder Ramsay groaned in his diary on 22 February that this was 'highly unsatisfactory'.[45]

In the meantime the debate and the lobbying went on. Gradually Eisenhower himself came to accept that 'Anvil' must be cancelled as an operation simultaneous with 'Overlord' because, as he signalled the Joint Chiefs on 9 March, 'we actually have, in sight, on a reasonably assured basis, fewer LST's [Landing Ships Tank] than we considered our minimum requirement for a successful OVERLORD operation. The uncertainty is having a marked effect on everyone responsible for planning and executing Operation OVERLORD.'[46]

This signal, which bears all the signs of Ramsay's advice,[47] pointed out that theoretical calculations of lift did not take into account the needs of tactical loading for assault on a strongly defended beach. Eisenhower went on to remark that it seemed to him 'that all except ourselves [in SHAEF] take it for granted that the actual assault will be successful and relatively easy whereas we feel that it will be extremely difficult and hazardous'.[48] He therefore pleaded with the JCS that the 'minimum requisite lift and flexibility for OVERLORD' made it 'inevitable' to draw on shipping so far hypothecated for a possible 'Anvil'. 'This being the case, I think it is the gravest possible mistake to allow demands for ANVIL to militate against the main effort even in the matter of time and certainty of planning.'[49]

Still Washington refused to give a prompt and satisfactory answer, and a fortnight later Eisenhower was urgently signalling General Marshall 'for eyes only' to insist that 'Anvil' must be abandoned for the sake of a badly needed 'bit of margin and more flexibility for Overlord'.[50]

It was only on 24 March, now barely more than two months to the new D-Day target of 1 June, that after yet further urging by Eisenhower and the British Chiefs of Staff the JCS finally consented to the postponement of 'Anvil' until July,[51] so that most of 'Anvil's' ration of assault shipping could in the meantime be returned to Britain for 'Overlord'.

Yet shipping lift did not pose the only question of naval resources to drag on for weeks without decision because of Washington's obduracy – or rather, Admiral Ernest King's obduracy. In view of the strength – still increasing – of German shore batteries in their concrete casemates commanding the invasion beaches, Ramsay wanted his bombarding forces to be enlarged by one battleship, seven cruisers and fourteen destroyers to a total of six battleships or monitors, 25 cruisers and 56 destroyers: 'a huge force but not great in respect for the issues at stake',[52] although even the First Sea Lord, Admiral Sir Andrew Cunningham, had felt that Ramsay's demands exceeded what was necessary, and told the Prime Minister so.[53] Ramsay himself recognised that 'the Royal Navy can't possibly meet this bill & it can only be provided by the U.S., as indeed is only right and proper'.[54]

For the Royal Navy – like every part of Britain's war effort – had now bumped up against the limits imposed by the British population of only 45 million, a third of that of the United States or Soviet Russia, and half that of Greater Germany. By October 1943 the Navy had swelled from its complement of 127,000 officers and men at the outbreak of war to some 750,000, together with over 55,000 Wrens (Women's Royal Naval Service). The Navy's slice of industrial resources, including shipbuilding, accounted for 900,000 workers.[55] 'Overlord' itself was expected to require a further 35,000 sailors and 10,000 Wrens. On top of all this there were all the new escort carriers to be manned as well as the fast-expanding Fleet Air Arm, while the technical revolution in the Royal Navy since 1939 had called for far greater numbers of electrical and radar personnel in ships' companies. And this many-faceted expansion of the Navy necessarily carried with it an ever bigger training effort, demanding in turn yet more manpower.

At the end of 1943, after a merciless review of ships and naval establishments, the Admiralty had decided on drastic measures – measures which were only possible because of the end of the Italian threat, the defeat of the Atlantic U-boats in the spring and the two-to-one superiority now enjoyed by the United States Navy over the Imperial Japanese Navy. The four unmodernised Great War battleships *Resolution*, *Ramillies*, *Revenge* and *Malaya* were to be laid up; so too were five of the 'C' and 'D' class cruisers dating from the end of that war, and 40 old destroyers. However, even these measures could not solve the Royal Navy's manning crisis, and soldiers and airmen found themselves in navy blue serge and being introduced to the mysteries of the sea service.[56]

In any case Britain lacked both the money and the shipyard resources to expand the Royal Navy as the United States Navy was expanding. At the end of 1942 the naval staff had prepared proposals for 'a correctly balanced Navy' in order to guide future building policy. The report called for 22 fleet carriers, nineteen light fleet carriers, 83 escort carriers, nine battleships, 50 cruisers, 191 destroyers, 300 submarines and 50 fleet oilers; a pattern that reflected the declining importance of battleship and cruiser in comparison with carrier-borne aviation.[57] In spite of its eloquent strategic and operational justification of this ambitious shopping list, the report was no more than fantasy, harking back to the nineteenth century when Britain had been the richest and industrially most successful country in the world as well as the world's greatest seapower; it was quite irrelevant to the present wartime reality of a bankrupt second-rank nation. Two and a half years later, at the end of the European war, the Royal Navy's strength in ships of these categories in commission was only to amount to six fleet carriers, four light fleet carriers, some 30 escort carriers, five battleships, some 40 cruisers, 108 fleet destroyers and some 120 submarines.[58]

So it was that the Royal Navy could not meet Ramsay's enlarged bill for naval forces in 'Neptune' on top of its remaining commitments in the Mediterranean, the Eastern Fleet in the Indian Ocean, the Arctic convoys and all its other duties in the war against Germany. The bill would have indeed to be met by the new mistress of the seas, the United States Navy. But it took a month after Ramsay's request was forwarded to the Joint Chiefs of Staff in Washington before Admiral King boxed his compass and offered to send three battleships, two cruisers and 34 destroyers: a more powerful force than he had been asked for.[59]

All this time, and under a pall of anxiety about the shipping lift, that essential key to the entire enterprise, Ramsay and his staff had been at full stretch in their efforts to solve 'Neptune's' operational problems and work out their detailed plans. Although Ramsay consulted frequently with the Supreme Commander and with Leigh-Mallory, the Expeditionary Air Forces Commander, it was with his opposite number as land force commander, General Montgomery of 21st Army Group, that he needed to work most closely. By and large their relationship worked well, not least because of Ramsay's guiding principle that the Navy's task was to enable the Army to win the land battle. But their methods differed sharply. Whereas Ramsay immersed himself in the transaction of business, Montgomery spent much time away from London inspecting troops, and left even participation in important meetings (such as some of those on the landing craft lift) to his Chief of Staff, the invaluable 'Freddie' de Guingand. 'It really is quite wrong,' Ramsay confided to his diary on 17 February in a moment of irritation, 'that he [Montgomery] should take no part in these high policy negotiations. His knowledge of the technique of the operation is very small and he leaves everything to Freddie & his staff, with whom, in consequence I have to negotiate. He does *no* work at all.'[60]

Of Rear Admiral Alan Kirk, the American admiral in command of the Western Task Force which would put ashore and support the 1st American Army, Ramsay as ANCXF did not entertain a high opinion, regarding him privately as a fuss-pot and a whinger, and too much under the influence of his Chief of Staff, Rear Admiral A. D. Struble. Ramsay recorded in January how Kirk, having been satisfied with the latest telegram to Washington over landing craft, came to see him 'wearing his discontented face'; and Ramsay added: 'as usual after Struble has been at him, he entirely changes ground'.[61] Ramsay's judgment of Kirk was not to soften as the strains of organising 'Neptune' grew more severe. At the beginning of May he characterised as 'hysterical' two letters from Kirk on the topics of salvage craft and the threat from E-boats: 'He has quite lost his sense of proportion besides being rather offensively rude. My opinion of him decreases steadily. He is not a big enough man to hold the position he does.'[62]

But then Ramsay, whose standards were rigorous in the quietest of times, was also to have his doubts about Rear-Admiral Sir Philip Vian, the commander of the Eastern Task Force charged with landing the British 2nd Army, whom he had personally asked the First Sea Lord to appoint.[63] During a long discussion with Vian on 3 March about his functions, Vian struck Ramsay 'as being a little helpless & requires to be given so much guidance on matters which I feel he could work out for himself. In fact I feel that I am organising his part of the show as well as my own, which gives me unnecessary additional work to do. I don't think he uses his Staff enough.'[64] It has to be said that Vian, a man of notoriously dark and difficult nature, had only accepted the post with reluctance and out of a sense of necessity.[65] However, the ANCXF's judgments were not always so critical. He found Admiral Harold Stark, the US naval representative in Britain since 1941, 'a shrewd old man';[66] the newly arrived (in March) Rear Admiral D. P. Moon, who was to command Force U ('Utah' beach), 'a fine type of U.S. officer. Efficient & alert. He should do well . . .'[67]

No great military enterprise can be immune from friction caused by individual human personality, least of all one so vast and intricate as 'Neptune'. What is remarkable in such a joint undertaking between two Allies – and is unprecedented in the history of alliances – is how relatively unimportant were such incidental gratings of personality. It is no less remarkable that they were never based on nationality. This melding of British and Americans into a common command structure – more, a single team – is rightly ascribed to Eisenhower's determination that it should be so, and his skill in bringing it about. Yet the task of planning 'Neptune' and 'Overlord', so daunting and so urgent, imposed its own discipline and provided its own drive towards unity. Nor, thanks to the patient acquisition and collation of Intelligence about the enemy, could anyone concerned with planning the invasion fail to recognise that what lay ahead must be, in Eisenhower's words, 'extremely difficult and hazardous'.

From Ultra decrypts – including a telegram home from the Japanese ambassador in Berlin in November 1943 passing on the complete order of battle of the German Army in the West as given him in a briefing by General Blumentritt, Chief of Staff to the C-in-C, West[68] – the Joint Intelligence Committee in January 1944 was able to give an estimate of the German forces that could confront the Allies on D-Day and after. It reckoned that the Luftwaffe in the West could number 2,530 aircraft, and be able to fly 1,750 sorties on D-Day against embarkation ports in England, the 'Neptune' armada on passage and the beaches. The German Army in the West could muster 45 divisions, including twelve high-quality attack formations. By D-Day evening one SS panzer division and one infantry division could have moved into place opposite the Allied lodgement; by D +

2, two panzer divisions, one panzer-grenadier, two SS divisions and one infantry field division, plus elements of two coastal defence divisions – some six in all. By D + 7 the total could be up to more than nine divisions, including four panzer and two panzer-grenadier.[69] These were the intimidating figures which clinched the decision to enlarge the 'Overlord' assault from three to five divisions, with a 50-mile front stretching from the River Dives (east of Caen) to Varreville at the base of the Cotentin Peninsula, with all that this implied for the two navies.

Month by month through the spring of 1944 Sigint, Army 'Y' radio intercept Intelligence and secret agents continued closely to monitor the ebb and flow of German divisions in the West according to the degree of pressure being exerted by the Red Army on the Eastern Front. By the end of March it had become alarmingly clear that the enemy was moving formations nearer the coast – most of them in the Pas de Calais but also some into Normandy and Brittany. A month later the JIC was putting the total number of German divisions in the West at 53, rising to 55 by D-Day. This included eight panzer or panzer-grenadier divisions and fourteen high quality infantry field divisions.[70] The JIC now conjectured that from D-Day evening to D + 1 the 'Overlord' forces would face two panzer divisions, one infantry field division and four coastal defence divisions; and that by D + 3 to D + 7 the total would have risen to no fewer than seven panzer and seven infantry field divisions, as well as the four coastal defence divisions.[71]

These constantly updated calculations determined not only the initial necessity for the Allies to land five divisions on D-Day, but also the essential pace and scale with which the follow-up formations flowed into the lodgement. On 1 February the 'Initial Joint Plan' for 'Neptune' issued by Eisenhower (giving the broad framework for detailed planning by the air, sea and land commanders) therefore set a target of nine follow-up divisions by D + 3 and twenty by D + 14.[72] And this target in turn determined the scale of shipping lift that Ramsay believed 'Neptune' would require, and which Eisenhower had by the end of March at last successfully obtained. It also gave the measure of the problems of scheduling and routing the cross-Channel traffic on and after D-Day that must be solved by the ANCXF and his staff.

Intelligence also forewarned the ANCXF about the dangers that the 'Neptune' armada on D-Day and the follow-up forces later would face while at sea. As always the German Navy Home Waters Enigma served as a marvellous window into enemy secrets, for a new key was broken by GC and CS at Bletchley Park in March 1944. 'Y' stations along the English coast eavesdropped on German radio-telephone traffic and also began to pick up easily decoded ship-to-ship tactical signals called 'PP'.[73] This electronic watch was supplemented by constant surveillance by photo-reconnaissance aircraft of enemy naval movements and bases along the French coast.

The least of Ramsay's concerns lay in the remaining serviceable ships of the German surface fleet: the pocket battleships *Scheer* and *Lützow*, the 8-inch cruisers *Hipper* and *Prinz Eugen* and the light cruisers *Leipzig*, *Köln*, *Nürnberg* and *Emden*. All of them were currently stationed in the Baltic in support of the German Army on the Eastern Front. On 10 May the British and American Joint Intelligence Committee did produce a 'worst case' scenario in which the heavier German ships would move to Norway and try to divert Allied warships from 'Neptune' by threatening to break out into the Atlantic, while the light cruisers raided convoys along the east coast of England. Four days later Ramsay, his staff and Vian met to discuss the alternative contingency of the German surface fleet making a dash into the Channel. 'P. Vian shall have the command of the forces I shall concentrate to deal with them = 2 BB [battleships], 8 Cr [sic] & 20 DD [destroyers]. It would be a glorious thing to wipe out the German fleet . . .'[74] However, an Operational Intelligence Centre report appreciated that westward sorties by the German surface fleet would depend on the military situation in the Baltic; and in the event that was where the German ships stayed, except for four heavy 'Z' class destroyers based in Brest.

The U-boats and E-boats, almost invulnerable from air or sea bombardment while within their concrete pens in their base ports, were another matter. In particular Ultra decrypts had revealed that when at the end of January a Luftwaffe aircraft falsely reported that some 200 to 300 landing craft were heading for the Gironde estuary, U-boat Command had ordered U-boats as far off as Rockall to close on the threatened area at utmost speed and ignoring all hazards.[75] At the beginning of March (when ANCXF and his staff were entering their most hectic planning period) the Operational Intelligence Centre was gloomily reckoning that no fewer than 75 500-ton U-boats could be deployed on the western flank of the cross-Channel invasion traffic by D-Day + 4 or 5.[76]

Nevertheless Ramsay appreciated that 'Neptune's' worst hazard while on passage lay in minefields, destructive and invisible obstacles waiting in ambush beneath the innocently empty surface of the sea, and which if undetected and unswept could disrupt the finely timed movements of the assault forces. On 21 February the Operational Intelligence Centre first gave warning that the enemy had begun to lay a major deep-water barrier in the Bay of the Seine. In March 'PP' decrypts revealed that an experimental inshore minefield had been laid off the little port of Ouistreham on what was to be the left flank of the British 2nd Army's landing area. But by early April, when Ramsay and his staff were busy drafting the final naval orders for 'Neptune', the OIC was still unable to give the location of inshore fields with any precision. Ramsay was particularly worried about the question of ensuring clear passage for the warships that were to provide fire support to the assaulting troops. On 24 March after a long discussion with Vian about the problems of minesweeping, Ramsay wrote in his diary:

> It is a most complicated operation & however we looked at it we could find no satisfactory solution of how best to sweep the channels of the faster groups & bombarding ships. In the end I decided that the only way out was to find 2 more flotillas made up from existing flotillas & to employ them to sweep the cruisers through to their bombarding positions. There is no doubt that the mine is our greatest obstacle to success, and if we manage to reach the enemy coast without becoming disorganised & suffering serious loss we shall be fortunate.[77]

The problem was the more perplexing because the OIC found difficulty in distinguishing inshore minelaying from the simultaneous erection of submerged beach obstacles. In February 1944 Field-Marshal von Rundstedt, the German C-in-C, West, told the press that Allied landing forces would run into a wide zone of fixed obstacles as well as mines.[78] British photo-reconnaissance confirmed from 20 February onwards that, beginning with the Bay of the Seine, these obstacles were sprouting on every beach in France and Belgium suitable for a landing. If this belt were widened from the present limit of 100 metres below the high-water mark down to the low-water mark, it would render the Allies' selection of H-Hour even more difficult than it already was. Effective counter-measures therefore depended on exact information about the obstacles themselves, and the physical characteristics and gradients of the beaches. Although by April an accurate enough picture had emerged from aerial photo-reconnaissance of the beaches at all states of tide, it had needed COPP (Combined Operations Pilotage Parties) to bring back samples of sand and shingle, as well as data about tidal flows and the widespread inundations carried out by the enemy behind key sectors of coastline, especially in the American area of assault.

One particularly valuable reconnaissance, enabling a mock stretch of German sea and shore defences to be constructed later on the Norfolk coast for experiment and training, was carried out by a force including two midget submarines, or X-Craft. The C-in-C, Portsmouth, Admiral Sir Charles Little, described their feats as a 'sustained and impudent reconnaissance under the very nose of the enemy'.[79] The sorties proved as uncomfortable as they were dangerous, as the force commander, Lieutenant-Commander H. N. C. Willmott, RN, described in his report:

> It was found desirable for the naval officer on watch on the casing to be able to lift his head above water for breathing purposes. He is strapped to the induction pipe, and has a bar to which he clings, with fervour, while floating on his front like a paper streamer on the bosom of the ocean, which has submerged the rest of the craft beneath him. Legs are liable to injury. There is a vacancy in the complement for an intelligent merman to fill this role.[80]

Human daring and advanced electronic and photographic technology would continue up to the eve of D-Day to feed SHAEF and its commanders with ever more abundant information about the enemy's evolving defence and deployment. But it was the Intelligence already at hand up to April that had to guide them in framing the plans for 'Neptune'/'Overlord'. For Ramsay and his staff in particular the issue by Eisenhower on 1 February 1944 of his 'Initial Joint Plan' served as the signal to accelerate their work to utmost speed – exhaustive operational studies and discussions; meetings that took in at one time or another the Prime Minister and all the senior Allied sea, land and air commanders, including the commanders-in-chief of the Royal Navy's Home commands. In Ramsay's words

> The Naval problem that had to be faced can be briefly summarized as, first, the breaking of the strong initial crust of the coast defences by assault, together with the landing of the fighting army formations; and, secondly, to commence, and continue without a pause for five or six weeks, their reinforcements at as high a rate as possible. The first required the co-ordination of the movement of thousands of ships and landing craft and aircraft, and then of the firepower; the second the co-ordination of the activities of hundreds of thousands of men and women of all services, both in the United Kingdom and off the French coast, marshalling, loading, sailing, unloading and returning at least eight ship convoys a day, in addition to 10 or 12 landing craft groups. Considerations of time and space did not permit the use of any unexpected manoeuvre to confuse the enemy; we had simply to drive ahead in great strength and to ensure that

> the organisation was as efficient as it could be, as the time factor was all important.[81]

On 2 March Ramsay issued the Naval Plan for 'Neptune', the comprehensive solution to all these problems and the blueprint for the next colossal task of preparing detailed operation orders. The round of meetings, of visits to training centres and exercises, spun faster. When Ramsay was in his room in Norfolk House he found himself beset by a 'queue of people waiting to see me, headed by Creasy [his Chief of Staff]'; and all of them seemed to have 'an insoluble difficulty to present to me'.[82] He wrote to his wife in Scotland on 2 April: 'Life is a great rush, & I am near up to date. Perhaps there is a lot in Monty's method of never reading anything or attending to any details but concentrating on main essentials . . .'[83] As it was, he acknowledged that his own mind was 'obsessed with current & future operations. How relieved I shall be when things are over and either one will be feeling frightfully bucked or we are back behind where we started from. One hopes & believes all will be abundantly well.'[84]

Yet in the midst of all this effort and strain came marvellous encouragement – a letter from Their Lordships of the Admiralty dated 30 March 1944 to tell him that he had been restored to the active list of flag officers of the Royal Navy, and in the rank of admiral. His pride and pleasure were however tempered by the circumstances of his reinstatement. As he confided to his wife, 'Everyone says how splendid of the Admiralty to reinstate me & acknowledge an error, little knowing that it had nothing really to do with them or rather that unless the P.M. had made a move about it, they would never have acted in the matter.'[85]

Outwardly he bore the stress well. 'One could not have worked for a more considerate or more patient master,' recalled his meteorological adviser, Captain J. Fleming, RN. 'Calm and unhurried in his duties, friendly and kindly in his personal relations, he welded us into a team . . .'[86] Inwardly the stress was beginning to tell – a repeatedly upset stomach; a 'muck sweat' while trying to prepare his hour-long briefing on the naval side of 'Neptune' to a grand two-day conference, 'Thunderclap', which opened at 21st Army Group headquarters in St Paul's School on 7 April.

'Thunderclap' began with an hour and a half long exposition of the land battle plan by Montgomery; the battle it was Ramsay's task to serve: 'The intention is to assault simultaneously: immediately north of the Carentan estuary and between the Carentan estuary and the

River Orne with the object of securing as a base for further operations a lodgement area which will include airfield sites and the port of Cherbourg.'[87]

Montgomery reckoned that by D + 5 the enemy could have concentrated six 'panzer type' divisions against the lodgement, by which time the Allies should have landed 15 divisions: 'The enemy build-up can become *considerable* from D + 4 onwards; obviously therefore we must put all our energies into the fight and get such a good situation in the first few days that the enemy can do nothing against us.'[88]

Therefore (and this reflects the intimate cooperation between Ramsay and Montgomery and their staffs):

> The general principle on which the build-up has been planned is to land on the continent the maximum number of fighting formations in the first few days . . . Flexibility has been introduced at the earliest possible moment so that the priority of fighting formations . . . can be varied to suit operational conditions as they develop . . .[89]

Montgomery's address was followed by Ramsay and Leigh-Mallory on the naval and air plans, and in the afternoon by detailed descriptions of the American 1st Army and British 2nd Army plans by Generals Omar Bradley and Sir Miles Dempsey. 'Thunderclap' ended at 1345 next day with the Allied master plan for 'Neptune'/'Overlord' finally settled and approved.

Now came the task of issuing the actual operation orders. 'Things have reached the intense stage of getting orders into print,' Ramsay wrote to his wife on 11 April, '& all the staff are stretched beyond the limit . . .'[90] It hardly helped that Creasy, his Chief of Staff, was suffering from back trouble and likely to go sick.[91] Nonetheless, thanks to a final sustained burst of work by a production line of typewriters driven by a team of Wren typists, 'Operation Neptune – Naval Orders (Short Title: ON)' went to press on 10 April 1944.[92] The introduction stated:

> This is probably the largest and most complicated operation ever undertaken and involves the movement of over 4,000 ships and craft of all types in the first three days. The Operation Orders are therefore necessarily voluminous.

This was no exaggeration. 'ON' comprised 22 parts covering every conceivable aspect of the operation, and numbered 579 pages even without the numerous appendices giving even more intricate detail. But on top of 'ON' there was also 'ONAD' (Operation Neptune

Administrative Orders) and 'ONCO' (the Communications Orders), bringing the total package to more than 1,000 pages of foolscap print. It constituted a remarkable achievement for a Navy that had been so very late in fully adopting a staff system. It was, after all, only nine years previously that Ramsay, the principal architect of the 'Neptune' plans, had retired from the Navy in the face of the then Commander-in-Chief Home Fleet's refusal to allow him to function properly as a Chief of Staff; a retirement which the Admiralty, siding with the C-in-C and his obsolete 'one-man-band' style of command, had been happy to accept.

Yet 'Operation Neptune – Naval Orders', taken together with Ramsay's preceding Naval Plan, constitute much more than a remarkable achievement in terms of just the Royal Navy's own history. In scope and thoroughness, in the complexity and scale of the problems solved, they eclipse the renowned performances of the German General Staff from 1866 onwards. They stand to this day as a never surpassed masterpiece of planning and staff work.

25

'A Never Surpassed Masterpiece of Planning'

> The object of Operation Neptune is to carry out an operation from the United Kingdom to secure a lodgement on the Continent from which further operations can be developed. This lodgement area must contain sufficient port facilities to maintain a force of 26 to 30 divisions and enable this force to be augmented by follow-up formations at the rate of three to five divisions in a month.[1]

So began the introductory opening section and summary (ON1) of 'Operation Neptune – Naval Orders'. It defined the task of the Allied navies as 'The safe and timely arrival of the assault forces at their beaches, the cover of their landings, and subsequently the support and maintenance and the rapid build-up of our forces ashore', emphasising that this was 'a combined British and U.S. undertaking by all services of both nations'. ON1 went on to restate command responsibilities. Under Eisenhower as Supreme Commander were three equal sea, land and air Commanders-in-Chief: Ramsay (ANCXF), Montgomery (C-in-C, 21st Army Group), and Leigh-Mallory (C-in-C, Allied Expeditionary Air Forces). The ANCXF 'will exercise general command and control over the naval forces other than those providing distant cover . . . He will exercise direct command within an "assault area" off the French coast.' The Cs-in-C, naval home commands, would continue to carry out their normal functions of command and administrative support except within the assault areas.

Under ANCXF the two naval task force commanders, Rear Admiral Kirk (Western Task Force = NCWTF) and Rear-Admiral Vian

(Eastern Task Force = NCETF) would 'initially exercise command of their forces [i.e., for training and rehearsal] and later operational control within the assault area'.[2] Each task force was divided into naval forces corresponding to the assault waves of the British 2nd and American 1st Armies which it was their role to put ashore and support. In Kirk's Western Task Force, Force U ('Utah' beach at the base of the Cotentin Peninsula; the westernmost Allied landing; 4th US Infantry Division) was commanded by Rear Admiral D. P. Moon, USN; Force O ('Omaha' beach to the eastwards; 1st and 29th US Infantry Divisions) by Rear Admiral J. L. Hall, USN. In Vian's Eastern Task Force, Force G ('Gold' beach, ten miles east of 'Omaha'; 50th British Infantry Division) was under the command of Commodore C. E. Douglas-Pennant, RN; Force J ('Juno' beach, on 'Gold's' eastern flank; 3rd Canadian Division) under the command of Commodore G. N. Oliver, RN; Force S ('Sword' beach, the easternmost Allied landing; 3rd British Infantry Division) under the command of Rear-Admiral A. G. Talbot, RN. The seven follow-up divisions to land on the second tide of D-Day (2nd, 9th, 29th and 90th US Infantry; 49th, 51st British Infantry and 7th Armoured) were the responsibility of Forces B (Commodore C. D. Edgar, USN) and L (Rear-Admiral W. E. Parry).

Having set the scene in 'ON1', Ramsay's orders, section by section, tackled each phase or facet of 'Neptune' chronologically, starting with minelaying operations off enemy ports from the Baltic to the Bay of Biscay from D − 45 onwards by the Royal Navy and Royal Air Force Bomber Command (ON2), and with naval diversions with air support against the Pas de Calais and elsewhere around the time of D-Day (ON3). These diversions formed part of an elaborate plan ('Fortitude') to hoax the enemy into believing that the Allies were in fact to land in the Pas de Calais, and at a later date than D-Day. A signal net had been set up in Kent to simulate the traffic of a '1st American Army Group' under the command of General Patton,[3] and feed German Intelligence with appropriate clues about this bogus formation and its preparations to invade the Pas de Calais. Thanks to Ultra it was possible for SHAEF to monitor just how successful the hoax was proving, especially in terms of the relative weight of deployment of German divisions north of the Seine and south of it.[4] In Ramsay's own retrospective judgment:

> Had the enemy not been deceived by our cover plan and the latent threat to the Pas de Calais, it would have been possible for him to have built up his forces against us at a rate at least equal to that of which we were

> capable with the craft and shipping at our disposal, assuming optimum conditions on our part and minimum turn-round times . . .[5]

ON4 dealt with the mammoth business of loading and assembling the 4,000 vessel-strong D-Day Armada and the immediate follow-up forces and supplies in comprehensive detail, complete with tables and 'Mickey Mouse' diagrams. The five assault forces were to assemble and load – together with their escorts and minesweepers – in south-coast ports from Plymouth round to Newhaven; the two follow-up forces in Felixstowe on the east coast, in the Thames, and in south-western ports to the west of Plymouth. The first build-up groups – and Ramsay reckoned the build-up plan to be of 'unique and major importance' – were to be brought together and pre-loaded in the Bristol Channel (American) and the Thames (British). The naval covering forces charged with protecting the flanks of 'Neptune' were to assemble in the Bristol Channel and the Thames; the heavy bombardment forces in the Clyde and Belfast Loch, except for one battleship and two monitors stationed in the south. All the varied ships, craft and equipment needed for maintenance services off the French coast after D-Day were to be slotted into ports from Falmouth to Harwich; the unwieldy components of the Mulberries were to be brought together in anchorages between Portland and Felixstowe, but clear of other shipping. ON4 laid down that the supply ships on which the logistics of the Allied Expeditionary Force would completely depend in Normandy were to start loading on D – 21: 89 of them in the Thames (33 of which were to sail to the Solent when loaded); 24 at Grimsby up on the east coast, later removed to Southend in the Thames Estuary; 104 in the Bristol Channel ports, of which 22 were then to sail to the Solent. It had been a jigsaw puzzle in which the pieces seemed larger and more numerous than the vacant spaces on the board; and yet the ingenuity of the planners had now found a place for all.

The deployment at sea of the naval covering forces was laid down in ON5. Distant cover outside the English Channel would be provided by the Commanders-in-Chief, Home Fleet, Western Approaches and Plymouth, under Admiralty direction. Should U-boats enter the Channel the Admiralty would probably transfer some support groups to the ANCXF. Close cover against German destroyers, E-boats and R-boats (motor minesweepers) would be the responsibility of the Cs-in-C, naval home commands: Plymouth, with eight British and four US destroyers; Portsmouth with four British destroyers and four frigates; Dover with four destroyers. All three commands would also have at their disposal coastal forces such as MTBs and motor launches equipped to lay smoke screens. The two 'Neptune' naval task force commanders would in addition deploy their own protective light forces.

In ON6 Ramsay gave orders for overcoming the German minefields, and especially the barrier known to have been laid from about latitude 50°N to within seven to ten miles of the Normandy coast. Although to the south of it lay a coastal channel left clear by the enemy for his own use, and which the 'Neptune' plan counted on for the final deployment of the assault and bombarding forces, even this might be mined at the last moment. Inshore mining also had to be taken into account. After much thought and long discussion with Vian and Kirk, Ramsay formulated a minesweeping plan in four main phases, of which the first would amount to the largest single minesweeping operation of the war.[6] Under his direct control two channels, each two miles wide, were to be swept simultaneously through the main German barrier for each of the five assault forces. One fleet minesweeping flotilla would be employed for each channel, giving a total of 255 vessels. The swept channels were to be marked by Dan buoys (small buoys bearing a flag or light on a pole) at one-mile intervals along both of their sides. In phase two, which would be carried out under the command of the task force commanders, a British inshore minesweeping flotilla would precede each bombardment group on D-Day in order to locate or, if necessary, sweep clear areas and anchorages close inshore. In phase three, the approach channels were to be widened to give more sea-room, while phase four provided for the sweeping of any mines laid after the Allied landings had taken place. Ramsay's orders emphasised that 'good navigation on the part of the Fleet minesweepers is of the utmost importance', and laid it down that they must keep to their sweeping courses even if 'heavily engaged', because the assault forces following the minesweepers relied 'solely on them for safety'.

The exact positions of all channels and areas to be swept were specified later in ON17, which also detailed swept routes across the Channel to the northern limit of the German mine barrier. From the permanently swept channels along the south coast of England four special channels were to be swept and marked with light buoys converging southwards to 'Position Z', a circle five miles in radius centred on 50° 25′N, 0° 58′W, some fifteen miles south-east of St Catherine's Head, Isle of Wight. 'Position Z' formed the entrance lobby, as it were, to 'The Spout' down which all 'Neptune' vessels would pass to the Normandy coasts. The Spout itself, as far as the northern limit of the German mine barrier, would consist of eight designated routes, not all of which would be swept unless there was evidence of minelaying.

In all, the minesweeping orders provided for a programme of as many as 76 'serials', each to be put in hand by order of the task force commanders as soon as the previous one had been completed.

Admiral Kirk, who along with other American flag officers criticised Ramsay in general for laying down the 'Neptune' plans in too much detail rather than devolving the work to commanders of task forces, was to acknowledge:

> It can be said without fear of contradiction that minesweeping was the keystone of the arch of this operation. All of the waters were suitable for mining, and minesweeping plans of unprecedented complexity were required. The performance of the minesweepers can only be described as magnificent . . .[7]

The bulk of these minesweepers was provided by the Royal Navy even in the Western Task Force area of operations; a heavy burden. At Kirk's request a British officer, Commander J. G. B. Temple, RN, was appointed Commander, Minesweeping West, with the USS *Chimo* as his headquarters ship. His opposite number, Captain, Minesweeping East, was Captain R. B. Jennings, RN.[8] In addition ANCXF would deploy a reserve force of minesweepers for work with the Mulberries, for escort duties on D-Day and to relieve the task force sweepers. Because it was so important that the swept channels through the mine barrier be clearly marked, the small Dan buoys were to be replaced between D-Day and D + 1 by large ocean light buoys laid by the Royal Navy and Trinity House (the institution responsible for lighthouses, lightships and light buoys).[9]

Next, in ON7, came Ramsay's orders to the task and assault forces for the 'approach march' from British ports to the touchdown on the Normandy beaches at H-Hour. On receipt of his signal 'Carry out operation', the Cs-in-C, naval Home commands, were to sail the invasion forces within their areas. The X-Craft X20 and X23, serving as markers for Forces J and S in the British sector, were to leave Portsmouth probably about sunset on D – 3, be towed as far as possible, and arrive off the beaches early in daylight on D – 1. The northern approaches to the swept channels were to be marked by motor launches and by radio beacons laid by the launches. Other launches were to mark the route over which American airborne divisions were to fly to land behind the German defences in the

Carentan area. Once the assault forces had entered the swept channels smoke was not to be used during the night hours, and nor were navigation lights except in an emergency and then only dimmed.

Ramsay was much concerned about the danger of friend firing on friend if vessels were sighted out of their expected positions; an eventuality all too probable in view of what he called in ON7 the 'stress of weather ... and general unhandiness of many of the units . . .' He sought to reassure the recipients of his orders that 'The chances are that an unrecognised ship or object sighted in the Channel is friendly'; and he instructed that fire was not to be opened on ships by day unless clearly recognised as hostile. By night only the escorts on the outer flanks were to be permitted to open fire, and then only in an outward direction after a prior challenge. Assault shipping was ordered not to leave the swept channels if it came under enemy surface attack, but to keep driving ahead for the shore, leaving the escorts (whose orders, complete with escort diagrams, were given in ON15) to tackle the threat.

The standard procedure in the final approach and landing of each assault force took the form of sixteen carefully timed stages, ranging from H-Hour − 120 minutes (arrival at the lowering points of the first landing ship [tank] group loaded with amphibious tanks) to H − 60 (bombarding ships open fire), H − 10 (first group of rocket-equipped LCTs open fire), H − 7½ (amphibious tanks touch down on the beach) and to H-Hour itself, the infantry assault. At H + 30, assault landing craft would bring in the first infantry reserves and the obstacle clearance units; between H + 75 and H + 105 it would be the turn of LCTs with self-propelled artillery and priority motor transport to touch down.[10] The assault, ordered the ANCXF, was to be 'pressed home with relentless vigour and determination, regardless of loss or difficulty'.

ON7 also briefed recipients that fighter patrols would be flown over the assault forces on passage and on the beaches, and that they would be controlled by GCI (Ground Coastal Interception) from England and by Fighter Direction Ships with Forces O, S and G; later by ground stations.

In ON8 Ramsay turned to the bombardment forces whose task was 'to assist in ensuring the safe and timely arrival of our forces by the engagement of hostile coast defences, and to support the assault and subsequent operations ashore'. Their firepower was weighty indeed – in Kirk's Western Task Force, three battleships (all American), one British monitor, nine cruisers (of which two were American and two French; the rest British), and 25 destroyers (21 American, three

British and one Dutch); in Vian's all Royal Navy Eastern Task Force, two battleships, one monitor, eleven cruisers and 40 destroyers, plus one battleship (HMS *Nelson* in Portsmouth) and one cruiser in reserve. The bombardment forces were divided into five groups each allotted to an assault force.

It had not proved easy to agree with 21st Army Group and the Allied air forces on arrangements for an integrated air and naval bombardment. Montgomery had claimed that it was for the Army to determine the type and quantity of fire support, but Ramsay had firmly and successfully insisted that, although the fire plan itself should be jointly settled, the 'prime responsibility for calculating the type and quantity of fire support required until the beaches are captured, and for deciding upon its application must rest with the Navy, because the Navy bears the responsibility for the safe arrival of the assault convoys'.[11] The Royal Air Force and the United States Army Air Force, for their part, declined to commit themselves until late as to the weight of bombing they would provide or as to the times relative to sunrise on D-Day when the bombers should operate – hardly helpful.[12] Nevertheless a coordinated bombardment plan was finally framed by which, as ON8 described in detail, certain German batteries were to be bombed in the run-up to D-Day, others were to be attacked by Bomber Command heavy bombers the very night before D-Day, and six more batteries in key tactical positions were to be hit by medium bombers soon after daylight on D-Day itself. Starting at H – 45, heavy and medium bombers would also deliver a total of 4,200 tons of bombs on the enemy beach defences, after which the guns of the warships would take over.

In the case of the German coastal defence batteries, ON8 allocated targets to ships according to an elaborate fire plan based on photo-reconnaissance data. Bombarding warships were not to open fire before daylight except as an emergency, but wait until the assault convoys had come within range of enemy guns and spotter aircraft had arrived overhead. Fire was to be continued until the target batteries had been silenced or captured. A similar fire plan had been drawn up for the close support of the assault forces as they attacked the enemy beach defences. ON8 defined the object of close support bombardment as 'To neutralise defences and demoralise the defenders preparatory to the final assault'. Concrete bunkers were to be engaged with armour-piercing shell from as close inshore as possible. Battleships, monitors and cruisers were ordered to support thereafter the armies' advances inland by bombarding enemy troops and positions by day and night.

The fall of shot on D-Day was to be monitored by Forward Observers, Bombardment, on shore with the troops, by shore fire-control parties, and by single-seat fighter patrols. These latter, numbering 104 Mustangs and Spitfires, would work in pairs, one spotting and the other acting as escort. Further aerial spotting would also be provided after the landings by light aircraft such as Austers or Piper Cubs normally employed as spotters for the armies' artillery.

'It is in the rapid follow-up of reserves and on the swift unloading of stores that the attack relies for its impetus which alone can sustain it and give it complete success.'[13] With these words began ON9, the orders to task and assault forces for the rest of D-Day after H-Hour, and which detailed the English ports to which ships and craft must return from the beaches for reloading. This stress on the need for speed and impetus applied no less to ON10, dealing with follow-up forces: Force L (British) was to be sailed in five groups by the C-in-C, Nore, and Force B (American) in three groups by C-in-C, Plymouth. Since all LSTs could not discharge on the second tide of D-Day, some of them, so ordered ON10, would have to arrive on the third tide with the first of the build-up convoys.

Next, in ON11, Ramsay briefed his commanders about the air plan, an absolutely crucial aspect of the entire 'Neptune'/'Overlord' operation. For the Allies had always accepted that it would be impossible to launch an invasion of France until and unless the Allied air forces enjoyed mastery of the air over the Channel and the Normandy coast. By the time Ramsay and his staff were drafting 'Operation Neptune – Naval Orders', this mastery had in fact been won, and the two air forces had begun to concentrate their heavy bombers under SCAEF direction against the French transportation network. Yet these things had only come to pass in the teeth of the bomber chieftains' doctrinaire opposition.

By decision of the Washington Conference in May 1943, the Allied heavy bomber forces were to give high priority to destroying the Luftwaffe's fighter force and the German aircraft industry.[14] But by January 1944 this 'Operation Pointblank' had failed of its purpose. Air Marshal Sir Arthur Harris's Bomber Command had suffered unsustainable losses at the hands of enemy night-fighters without decisive effect on German industry or morale.[15] The United States 8th Air Force had done its best in daylight raids to demolish enemy ball-bearing and aircraft factories by precision bombing, but German aircraft production had continued to climb. By the beginning of 1944 the 8th Air Force too was suffering from such an appalling rate of loss as to constitute a strategic defeat as decisive as that of Bomber Command.

Then, in January 1944, a new phase of the 8th Air Force's offensive opened, with its fleets of Flying Fortresses and Liberators now escorted all the way to the target by long-range Merlin-engined Mustang fighters. The Luftwaffe, compelled to give battle in defence of the Reich, was rapidly gutted of combat effectiveness by the Mustangs – above all, through attrition of irreplaceable highly trained and experienced pilots. By April 1944 the Luftwaffe in France had been reduced to a wasted invalid. Thus mastery of the air over the Channel had been won in the skies of Germany – although not by means of the heavy bomber itself wrecking German aircraft production, but instead its fighter escort killing German pilots.[16] This was why Ramsay's ON11 was able to contrast the 5,886 Allied bombers and fighters to be operational on D-Day (3,612 American and 2,274 British) with an estimated Luftwaffe strength in the West of 1,515 aircraft, of which only some 590 were likely to be available for close support against the 'Neptune' forces.

Nevertheless the early months of planning for 'Neptune'/'Overlord' also saw another 'battle of the air', rather like that in 1942 over VLR aircraft for the Battle of the Atlantic. Eisenhower and his air commanders (Air Chief-Marshal Sir Arthur Tedder, his deputy, and Air Marshal Sir Trafford Leigh-Mallory, the C-in-C, Allied Expeditionary Air Force) wanted both Bomber Command and the 8th Air Force to be placed under SCAEF direction for an offensive to smash the French transportation network, so that German reserve divisions moving to the invasion front would be slowed up by a morass of wrecked railways, destroyed bridges and cratered road junctions. It eventually took a decision by the American and British governments in March to overcome the stubborn reluctance of the bomber chieftains, Harris and General Carl Spaatz (C-in-C, 8th Air Force) to give up their attacks on Germany in favour of the so-called 'Transportation Plan', and at the same time yield control of their commands to Eisenhower.[17] Henceforward Bomber Command in particular was vigorously to devote itself to French marshalling yards and similar targets, with an effect similar to hobnailed boots trampling over a child's toy railway. The accuracy and destructiveness of these attacks made their own ironic comment on Harris's inveterate belief that his aircraft could not and should not attack targets smaller than cities. The Allied tactical air forces – under Leigh-Mallory's command – also joined in the 'Transportation Plan', striking at road and rail traffic on the move.

Although the ultimate success of 'Neptune'/'Overlord', especially in the key matter of the relative rates of Allied and German military build-up in Normandy after D-Day, depended so much on this sustained air offensive deep into France, the air forces would also directly serve the Allied navies and armies on D-Day itself: the heavy bombers as part of the combined bombardment plan (ON8; see above, p. 786), and the tactical air forces as air cover. Leigh-Mallory was to deploy five squadrons of day fighters over the cross-Channel 'Neptune' routes and another ten (half at a time) over the beaches. According to ON12 ('Air Defence') three Fighter Direction Centres installed in converted landing ships (tank) would direct the fighters against incoming enemy air strikes. If these FDCs were knocked out, their role would be taken over by four appropriately equipped warships.

In this refined system of fast-reacting cooperation between the Navy and the Air Force and the similar system now perfected between Army and Air Force lies another irony. Had not the British air staff before the war and during its opening years viewed the very idea of a 'tactical air force' taking part in the Navy's or the Army's battles as heresy? It had taken much pressure from the Army and the Royal Navy, as well as the bitter lessons taught by the Luftwaffe in 1940–42 gradually to break down the Air Staff's doctrinal insistence on the 'independence' and 'unity' of airpower, although in the field – especially in North Africa – the Royal Air Force itself had contributed greatly to the development of the advanced technical and command systems for air/sea and air/land cooperation that were to be deployed on D-Day. In this process Air Chief-Marshal Sir Arthur Tedder's own enlightened advocacy since his time as AOC-in-C, Middle East, had been of crucial importance (the very title 'tactical air force' was his invention).

Coastal Command had of course always provided an exception to the Air Staff's cult of 'independent airpower', although even here it had taken some two years to overcome mutual suspicions and differences of operational opinion between it and the Royal Navy. But by 1944 they had matured the closest of professional partnerships. It helped that Admiral Ramsay personally got on well with present Air Officer Commanding-in-Chief, Air Marshal Sir Sholto Douglas. There was no question that Coastal Command would full-heartedly serve the Allied navies during 'Neptune'. It was to concentrate its effort, as ON11 explained, in the south-western approaches in order to put the 'cork in the bottle' and thereby prevent the U-boats passing through from Biscay to attack the 'Neptune' convoys. The Command hoped to maintain a 30-minute 'density' of cover in order either to catch U-boats on the surface or force them to remain submerged and so exhaust their batteries. Under the direction of Coastal Command the Fleet Air Arm would fly cover in the western and eastern exits of the Channel against U-boat or E-boat incursions. The Fleet Air Arm and Coastal Command would jointly fly night and dawn/dusk sweeps with Albacores, Swordfish and Beaufighters against enemy shipping and warships.

Also included in ON11 was a summary of Allied plans for airborne landings – the British 6th Airborne Division east of the River Orne on the night before D-Day in order to secure the Allies' eastern flank; the United States 82nd and 101st Airborne Divisions behind the German defenders at the base of the Cotentin Peninsula.

These briefings on the air and air-defence plans concluded ON's coverage of the opening phase of 'Neptune' – its mounting and launching. Next, in ON13, began the orders for the build-up phase which Ramsay had characterised in his earlier Naval Plan as 'of unique and major importance',[18] for the armies' ability to retain and expand their lodgement in Normandy depended entirely on the rate at which the navies could bring in stores, fuel, ammunition, weapons, transport and reserve formations. In the first few days especially very large numbers of convoys would have to rotate between England and France according to exact scheduling and routing – all under the operational direction of the ANCXF.

At the English end, responsibility for loading and despatching ships would lie with the Cs-in-C, naval area commands. To assist them, combined service handling agencies were to be set up: at Portsmouth a 'Build-up Control Organisation' (BUCO) to adjust the movements of ships and craft of all types and their military loads as needed; in the Nore, Portsmouth and Plymouth commands 'Turn Round Controls' (TURCOs) to speed the reloading and return of vessels to Normandy, using designated ports from the Thames to the Bristol Channel. Each convoy was code-lettered by country and place of departure, nature of cargo and its number in order of sailing; for example, 'ETM1' stood for 'England, Thames, Motor Transport Convoy No. 1'. On D + 1 and D + 2 because of the density of traffic the convoys were to traverse the Channel strictly according to the routes and times laid down in ON13. All Ramsay's orders for the loading, sailing and unloading of different kinds of vessel during the first few days reiterated the urgent need for 'sustained movement'.

Later, when the swept channels had been widened, ships were to be despatched as soon as they were ready and make the best speed on passage possible. No fewer than eight build-up convoys a day would then continue to run. Their reception off the Normandy coast, and despatch when empty back to England, were to be controlled by two officers stationed to seaward of each task force area, 'Captain, Southbound Sailings' and 'Captain, Northbound Sailings'. The unloading itself would be in the hands of a Senior Officer, Ferry Craft (SOFC) on each beach, working with the Principal Beach Master and Beach Group Commander.[19] In this build-up stage there would also be installed a complete salvage organisation ashore under the Chief Salvage Officer (Commander T. McKenzie, RNVR, seconded from Metal Industries Ltd) on ANCXF's staff. To help keep flowing the movement of vessels Ramsay's orders set up two other agencies: 'Control Organisation for Repair' (COREP) and a Tug Organisation (COTUG). The latter was particularly important because the ANCXF was anxious lest there should not be enough tugs to meet 'Neptune's' colossal need for them.

And then in ON14 came instructions for organising on D-Day and afterwards the traffic of an astonishing regatta of ancillary vessels: depot and repair ships; salvage and wreck disposal vessels; explosives carriers; rescue tugs; colliers, oilers and water tankers; telephone cable-laying vessels; despatch boats; ammunition barges; American naval pontoons to create sunken causeways; smoke-projector trawlers; ships for evacuation of casualties; air/sea rescue craft; a swarm of Royal Army Service Corps and Royal Engineers small craft; anti-aircraft ships for defence of the Mulberry harbours; mooring vessels for the components of the Mulberries.

Indeed, the transport and installation of the Mulberries – some 400 units totalling 1½ million tons – presented a colossal undertaking in itself. It merited an entire part (ON16) of 'Operation Neptune – Naval Orders'. When Ramsay had first seen 'Phoenix' concrete caissons, each 400 feet long and 2,000 to 6,000 tons displacement, at the beginning of February, he found them 'even more formidable and abortion-like than I anticipated. They will be the devil to tow into position & get round the coast.'[20] According to ON16, the process would demand 35 heavy tows daily for more than a fortnight, and a total of 158 tugs and 10,000 men. To take complete charge of this 'devil' of a task, Rear-Admiral W. G. Tennant (who as a Captain, RN, had been in command of the Dunkirk beaches in 1940) had been appointed to Ramsay's staff in January 1944.[21]

Tennant immediately doubted whether the Phoenix breakwaters could withstand even a moderate gale. Moreover, since it would be nearly three weeks before all had been towed over and put in place, he thought that in any case some other kind of shelter must be immediately provided for small craft off the beaches. He therefore proposed that obsolete ships should be sunk stem to stern as breakwaters. The Prime Minister approved; 55 old merchant ships and four redundant warships were to be prepared as blockships (codename: 'Corncobs') to be scuttled to form five shelters (one in each of the five assault areas, including the two Mulberries) codenamed 'Gooseberries'.

ON16 emphasised that the Mulberry, 'an artificial harbour erected primarily for the landing of stores off the enemy beaches', was essential to the success of 'Neptune'; and laid down that Mulberry 'A' (American) at St Laurent and 'B' (British) at Arromanches were to be completed by D + 18. The breakwaters were to enclose a harbour two miles long by one mile wide; as big as Dover. The outermost breakwaters were to consist of 25 of the 200-feet-long steel 'Bombardons' moored end to end in ten fathoms, giving shelter to eight big ships of up to 25 feet draught. Next were to come 30 to 40 coasters at anchor; nearest the shore (but first to be installed) and sunk in up to two and a half fathoms would be the 'Gooseberries' (each made up of twelve 'Corncobs'), as shelters for landing craft. The 'Gooseberries' were to be all sunk in place by D + 3.

Within this triple shelter each Mulberry would be equipped with a large floating pierhead on the 'spud' system for stores coasters drawing up to seventeen feet, and other pierheads for unloading motor transport from landing ships (tank) and landing craft (tank). The pierheads were to be linked to the shore by floating piers (some seven miles of them in all). The combined system of floating pierheads and piers was codenamed 'Whales'. In the British Mulberry, stated ON16, the Royal Navy would be responsible for putting the breakwaters in place and the Army the 'Whales' (though these were to be delivered to the Army by the Navy). In the American Mulberry, the United States Navy would carry sole executive responsibility for the entire undertaking, although with the assistance of the United States Army.

The assembling of all these cumbersome novelties in British ports and their movement across the Channel supplied yet another of the brain-heating puzzles solved by ANCXF's staff. The 'Gooseberry' blockships were to assemble in Scottish ports and proceed to Normandy under their own steam (except for one old French cruiser on tow); the 'Phoenix' caissons were to be assembled in Selsey, Dungeness and the Thames (with a final 'park' established off Selsey); the 'Bombardons' at Portland; and the 158 British and American tugs between the Thames and Portland. Towage of Mulberry units – at about three knots – was to begin in the forenoon of D-Day, using a reserved channel down 'The Spout' and through the main German mine barrier; it would continue according to a strict timetable of sailings over the following seventeen days. Survey units would mark the positions of the Mulberry components with buoys before mooring units under the direction of officers, dubbed 'Planters', put the components in place as ordered by control officers located in five HQ ships. ON16 remarked that 'Good seamanship and teamwork' would be essential; a classic of naval understatement.

Once in place the Mulberries were for administrative purposes to constitute 'ports operated by a N.O.I.C. [Naval Officer In Charge]' under the appropriate task force commander. Their daily handling capacities would amount to 5,600 tons and 1,400 vehicles in the American Mulberry and 6,000 tons and 1,250 vehicles in the British. They would have their own anti-aircraft defences mounted on the Phoenixes and Gooseberries in addition to anti-aircraft ships. Barrage balloons would be flown at 1,000 feet. All that was missing in ON16's instructions in order to make each Mulberry the complete port at war was a prefabricated dockside pub.

In striking contrast ON18 (for ON17, swept channels, see above, p. 784) simply provided compendious navigational and meteorological information – another necessary key to 'Neptune's' success. It listed the charts to be issued to ships, and stated that all landing-craft skippers were to receive a shoreline sketch prepared by the United States Navy and a 'Small Ship Folio' of useful information. ON18 also provided comprehensive astronomical data all tabulated for the period 1 June to 4 July 1944, including moonrise, moonset, sunrise and sunset on 5 and 6 June. An appendix on tidal data covered the times and heights of high and low water along the assault beaches (including Arromanches on 5 and 6 June) and also the tidal streams, although it warned that the latter were based on French predictions and might prove inaccurate. ON18 further provided a brief on the 'Neptune' meteorological organisation, with offices at the headquarters of ANCXF in England, the Flag Officer, British Assault Area, and in certain French ports after capture. The ANCXF, it noted, would issue special weather forecasts daily.

Next, in ON19, were laid down how naval command responsibilities for the assault areas were to evolve as the Allied armies consolidated their lodgement. In the British assault area the Naval Commander, Eastern Task Force himself (Vian) was to exercise direct operational command during the initial phase, assisted by a Rear-Admiral, Administration (Rear-Admiral J. W. Rivett-Carnac). Once the lodgement was secure and naval headquarters and communications nets had been set up ashore, NCETF would hand over command to a Flag Officer, British Assault Area (FOBAA: Rivett-Carnac in a new role). Each British landing area, Sword, Juno and Gold, was to be self-contained under its Naval Officer In Charge (NOIC) with regard to beach and repair organisations, salvage and fire-fighting. A depot ship organisation under a Commander, Depot Ship, based in the Mulberry harbour, was to be set up to look after such needs as accommodation for the crews of ferry craft.

In the American assault area, and in accordance with United States Navy procedures, operational command in the initial phase would lie with the Commanders, Omaha and Utah beaches (under the authority of the Naval Commander, Western Task Force: Kirk). The Commander of Force O would also be responsible for Mulberry 'A'. Once the United States Army was solidly established ashore, the NCWTF would withdraw one landing area commander, leaving the other in overall control. In the third phase the second commander too would be withdrawn and naval responsibilities in the American area would be devolved to a Commander Service Force.

ON19 also dealt in detail with procedures for opening captured ports; in the first instance, the nine small fishing or yachting harbours along the immediate invasion coast. But ON19 also looked ahead to the capture of Cherbourg and even further afield to those other major ports from St Nazaire to Dieppe which would fall into Allied hands after the eventual breakout of the armies from the Normandy lodgement. It specified the sequence of operations to be followed in clearing a port, from the first arrival of a Navy/Army reconnaissance party to the work of the main port party (there were to be four of them, all Royal Navy), and of specialist units such as would be needed to deal with underwater explosive devices or undertake salvage work – not forgetting a hydrographical party for sounding and marking channels and obstructions.

In ON20 were listed no fewer than seventeen 'Mickey Mouse' diagrams plotting the intricate web of all movements of the Neptune Armada from H – 24 hours to D + 3.

'Force Pluto,' began ON21, 'consists of ships and craft which, in cooperation with the Army and the Ministry of Fuel and Power, provides means of supplying petrol to the Army on the far shore.' Having described the HAIS and HAMEL systems (see above, pp. 761–2), it instructed that ten such cross-Channel pipelines were to be laid from Sandown Bay to Querqueville near Cherbourg: the first on D + 20 and the tenth on D + 75, so giving a maximum throughput of 2,500 tons of fuel per day. With regard to 'Tombola' and 'Amethea' (the pipelines between buoyed connections for tankers to seaward and storage tanks on shore), four discharge points were to be operating off Port en Bessin by D + 18. Each line would be capable of discharging 150 tons of fuel per hour. The entire 'Pluto' operation was to be carried out under the direction of the SNO (Senior Naval Officer), Pluto, Captain J. F. Hutchings, RN, in the corvette *Campanula*. The 'Pluto' craft and equipment were to assemble at Southampton (the Pluto depot), Milford Haven, London River and Exmouth.

'Operation Neptune – Naval Orders' concluded its encyclopaedic coverage with a glossary in ON22 of all the terms and acronyms employed: five pages of initials standing for different types of ships and craft both British and American; six pages of terms and definitions; three and a half pages of British abbreviations and their American equivalents.

ON thus added up to a formidable package for its recipients to digest, especially when ONAD and ONCO were included as well. However, only a limited number of 'Need-to-know' officers were authorised to open the orders immediately on receipt. The problems would arise when all the remaining thousands of officers would open them before D-Day upon being ordered to do so. In May the Commander-in-Chief, Home Fleet, Admiral Sir Bruce Fraser, was to signal Ramsay with suggestions 'to avoid consternation and possible outcry from ships when these and other orders are opened by them . . .'[22] Ramsay himself confessed afterwards that he had been 'gravely concerned at the problems likely to arise in smaller vessels when, shortly before D-day, not only my orders but in addition the orders of the Task Force and lower commanders would be opened'.[23] In the event, oral briefings were arranged for all subordinate commanders before they began to read their orders, and they were advised only to study the sections of ON relating to their own tasks.

Had Ramsay preplanned 'Neptune' from the top in too great a detail? Certainly Kirk and his fellow American admirals believed so on the basis of US Navy practice and experience in the Pacific, although it must be said that landings on Pacific islands were weekend boating trips in comparison with 'Neptune's' scale and complication. In retrospect Ramsay himself had no doubts, writing in his official report:

> The very considerable detail to which A.N.C.X.F.'s operation orders descended . . . was foreign to the practice of the U.S. Navy, where the orders of the higher levels of command are largely confined to the definition of tasks and the issuing of directives. Despite their frank

> criticisms, before and after the operation, it is still believed that the large size of the operation orders was unavoidable . . . The attack had to be made on a narrow front and the ports and anchorages in the Isle of Wight area were jointly used by the British and the U.S. Coordination could only therefore be achieved on the highest command level.[24]

'Neptune', like its smaller precursors 'Torch' and 'Husky', had no precedent as an exercise in seapower. From the decisive battles of the sailing era to the Royal Navy's fights with the Italian Fleet and the German heavy ships in the present war or the United States Navy's victory over the Japanese Combined Fleet at Midway in 1942, the outcome of a great naval encounter had always been determined at the time by the weather, by luck and by the orders of the opposing admirals. In 'Neptune', by contrast, the commanding admiral's orders written two months beforehand provide a detailed history of the operation as it actually took place. 'Operation Neptune – Naval Orders' constitute a painstaking and brilliantly successful exercise in operational predetermination; and it is this that lends all 22 parts of 'ON' their outstanding interest and importance.

Yet their completion and issue did not conclude the labours of the ANCXF and his staff or assuage his own anxieties. Key questions had still to be settled, such as the final choice of D-Day and H-Hour. Fresh problems continued to rear ahead like uncharted rocks. Personal relationships grew frayed with strain. The pace of preparation relentlessly quickened.

For all their comprehensive forethought, Ramsay's orders depended for successful fulfilment on the combined training of the soldiers and sailors of the 'Neptune' assault forces. Ramsay and Vian were agreed that five to six months offered the ideal time for an assault force to work up to maximum efficiency, but the reality did not always match the ideal. In the Eastern Task Force, Force S ('Sword' beach) had been based on Inverness in Scotland, since October 1943, but for three months had lacked slipways or docks for underwater repairs. Although it began work with the 3rd (British) Infantry Division in December, it could not carry out assault and live firing exercises until March because of restrictions on its training area. In April it moved with its division to the Portsmouth area.

Force G ('Gold' beach) was not formed until March 1944, being a result of the decision to widen the front of the D-Day assault from three divisions to five. It trained with the 50th (British) Infantry Division in the Portland–Poole area until the end of April when it was transferred to the Southampton–Solent area. Its headquarters ship, HMS *Bulolo*, did not return from the Anzio operation until mid-April and, because extra communications equipment had to be installed, she was not available for training until the final 'dress rehearsal' in the first week of May.[25]

Force J ('Juno' beach), however, had been training and exercising with the 3rd Canadian Division in the Isle of Wight since it had returned from the Mediterranean in September 1943. Of the American assault forces, Force U ('Utah' beach) was another belated creation as a result of the widening of the front, and so did not start training until March; even in mid-April it still lacked some of its units.[26]

Therefore although all five Allied assault forces were now training rigorously by day and by night, in good weather and foul, Ramsay was by no means always heartened by what he saw on his visits to exercises. On 27 April he and Montgomery watched the first day of 'Exercise Tiger', the final rehearsal by Admiral Moon's Force U at Slapton Sands in Devon. Because of a signals muddle over postponing the start only two companies of infantry landed after the warships had carried out their bombardment. The exercise, wrote Ramsay in his diary, was 'a flop' with 'much to criticise', especially 'the lack of senior naval officers on the beach to take charge and supervise'.[27] But after the flop came outright tragedy, for at 0020 next morning eight landing craft (tank) and two pontoons of Force U escorted by the corvette HMS *Azalea* were jumped fifteen miles off Portland Bill by a swarm of E-boats, who sank two of the LCTs and damaged a third in an encounter of utter confusion and blind firing into the night. The American casualties amounted to 638 killed (many of them much-needed engineers) and 89 wounded.[28] Here was a cruel reminder that the enemy too would have his part to play in 'Neptune'; a reminder also of the price that would be paid on D-Day for error or misfortune.

On 29 April Ramsay moved to his operational headquarters in Southwick House, a mansion seven miles north of Portsmouth. Eisenhower's command post and Montgomery's Tactical Headquarters had been installed in a sprawl of caravans and huts in the park. In the first week of May the final rehearsals of the rest of the assault forces ('Exercise Fabius') took place. Ramsay observed Forces S, G and J go ashore, and this time was 'very favourably impressed by all that I saw . . .'[29]

But he was far less impressed with the situation prevailing over the components of the Mulberries. By 1 May it had become plain that production was falling behind schedule. Nor was this all. Transport of the 'Phoenix' concrete caissons was presenting special problems.

When in mid-April a 'Phoenix' had been accidentally stranded on a sand bank, it had taken a salvage vessel a week to refloat it, so boding ill for cross-Channel towage to Normandy. There was a more general problem. After construction the 'Phoenixes' were filled with sea water and sunk in order to save berthing space. When they needed to be moved they therefore had to be pumped out in order to regain buoyancy. Regrettably the pumping gear supplied by the War Office (responsible for production of the 'Phoenixes') proved 'totally ineffective'.[30] In order to pump them out even the London Fire Brigade's Thames fire-fighting tenders had to be mobilised. In any case, as Ramsay sourly noted in his report later, the 'Phoenixes' and also the 'Whales' (another War Office production responsibility) were 'in no state to be towed, nor was towing gear provided. All the riggers in Chatham Dockyard were put on to this at high pressure to make good the deficiency. This shows how essential it is for the Admiralty to be concerned at the outset of any seagoing project.'[31]

This still left unsolved the other basic headache with the Mulberries – the shortage of tugs to tow the components to Normandy. As late as 31 May only 48 out of 72 large tugs (allocated to 'Whales' and 'Phoenixes') and four out of 44 small tugs had become available. Ramsay therefore gave the Mulberries overriding priority for tugs and appointed Captain E. J. Moran, USNR, as 'Tug Controller' of the total 'Neptune' pool of 200 tugs.[32]

All this time the picture presented by Allied Intelligence sources of the German beach and coastal defences and the enemy's deployment of sea and land forces kept altering, with consequent need to adjust 'Neptune' plans. It was especially important to establish the exact location and nature of the latest beach and underwater obstacles (as uncovered at low tide) in order to select the best phase of tide for clearing them – which in turn would determine H-Hour, about which many were the anguished discussions. Then, at the end of April, a new technique of low-level oblique-angle photo-reconnaissance with a moving camera enabled American Mustangs to bring back pictures which told Ramsay and his colleagues exactly what they needed to know.[33]

On 1–2 May he, Eisenhower, Tedder, Montgomery and Leigh-Mallory met at 'Widewings' (codename for Eisenhower's residence in Bushey Park, West London) finally to 'settle the relationship between H-hour and obstacles', with the result, as Ramsay noted in his diary, 'that my revised dates and timing were accepted . . .'[34] The obstacles were to be dealt with 'dry shod', that is, in less than two feet of water, which fixed H-Hour as three hours before high water on any given beach. D-Day was provisionally fixed for 5 June, that and the 6th being the earliest acceptable dates from the naval point of view in terms of phases of the moon, although, as Ramsay told his colleagues, the 7th would serve in case of extreme necessity.

On 9 May Ramsay formally notified Eisenhower that the naval plan would be 'frozen' at 0900 on the 12th.[35] By now the pace of work and the approach of D-Day were beginning to tell on the 61-year-old ANCXF, his staff and his fellow commanders. After one meeting Ramsay recorded that Vian and Hall had been 'sticky', and Vian in particular 'most irritating', his attitude 'one of criticism'.[36] Ramsay confided to his wife on 11 May:

> There are so many pitfalls and in an allied operation there are bound to be jealousies. Kirk is being troublesome & stupid & pompous & though I've been very patient with him & with all the Americans, most of whom are excellent in every way, one can never be certain things will continue to go well when people's nerves are strung up.[37]

In the last week of the month Ramsay's Chief of Staff, Creasy, finally went sick with his bad back:

> At this hour it is not a good situation. Luckily most people are standing up pretty well . . . I have my better & less good days . . . I suppose that it is only to be expected when one is head of a big concern that when everything goes wrong or when they have moans, people must put it on my shoulders. One ought to be a hard, ruthless callous character I'm sure, as it would be so much easier to deal ruthlessly with people . . .[38]

On 30 May Admiral Vian, CETF, went down with quinsy, putting his fitness to command on D-Day in doubt.

Fortunately the First Sea Lord's country home was at Bishop's Waltham, not far from Southwick House, and Ramsay visited him whenever he could, to find like others before him that morally 'A.B.C.' was worth a battle-squadron. He wrote to his wife after dining one night with Cunningham: 'He was in good form & nothing seems to concern him which is a wonderful attitude!'[39]

On 25 May all holders of 'Operation Neptune – Naval Orders' were ordered to open them. Three days later D-Day was notified to them as 5 June, along with the H-Hour relating to their particular beach.[40] Although thousands of Allied officers now shared these tremendous secrets, no leak occurred, while so complete was the Allied air forces' domination over the Luftwaffe that the enemy could glean little information by air reconnaissance about the colossal concourse of naval and military power gathering along the southern coasts of England. Every suitable stretch of water was now crammed with shipping and craft. How crammed is recounted by C-in-C, Portsmouth, in his report:

> It is a commonplace expression to say that an anchorage is 'full of ships', but in the case of the East and West Solent, with an available area of approximately 22 square miles in which to anchor ships, it was literally true. On 18 May, the Admiralty offered the C-in-C Portsmouth the services of H.M.S. *Tyne* [10,850 tons displacement; destroyer depot ship], but it was only possible to accept her because H.M.S. *Warspite* was not being sent to Portsmouth till D-Day, which gave us one berth in hand.[41]

Inland from these anchorages and harbours now boarded over with vessels were concentrated 37 Allied divisions, ten of them armoured,[42] filling up the countryside so that Southern England could truly be described as one vast encampment; the Expeditionary Force's thousands upon thousands of vehicles, tanks and guns ranged *en masse* along roads turned into parking lots. A Cabinet Committee chaired by the Prime Minister made sure that everything the Supreme Allied Commander asked of British society would be granted.[43] In these last days of May 1944 a muscle of gigantic power, years in development, was tautening in a final contraction before it struck its blow.

For the Royal Navy and the British Merchant Marine, 'Operation Neptune' marked the consummation and reward of all their endeavour since 1939. The invasion armies' supplies would be carried to the pierheads of the Mulberry harbours by the coasters which, during four and a half previous years of war, had plied in convoy between the harbours of Britain, an essential part of the United Kingdom's overloaded transport system. These humble ships, escorted by the Royal Navy's oldest destroyers and by armed trawlers, had constantly braved the marauding Junker or Heinkel bomber and more recently U-boats redeployed from the Atlantic. The minesweepers which, crewed by 'Hostilities Only' officers and men or by fishermen, month in, month out, in all weathers had kept British coastal waters clear of the magnetic mines scattered by German aircraft – they too would have their valuable role in 'Neptune'. The small craft of the Royal Navy's Coastal Forces – motor torpedo boats and motor gunboats also often manned by the RNVR – which had helped to protect coastal convoys, had skirmished with enemy E-boats, and attacked enemy shipping in the Channel and North Sea – would be laying mines and covering the invasion armada against German light forces.

Then again, it was thanks to the destruction of the *Graf Spee*, the *Bismarck* and the *Scharnhorst* by the Royal Navy's battleships and cruisers, and the Fleet Air Arm's crippling of the *Tirpitz*, that the enemy no longer possessed a surface fleet capable of posing a serious threat on D-Day. But, most of all, 'Operation Neptune' represented the ultimate reward for the hard-won victory by the Royal Navy, by Royal Air Force Coastal Command and by their Canadian and American sister services over the U-boat in the Atlantic in May 1943. This victory alone had enabled Britain herself to survive and thereafter serve as the Anglo-American base for the invasion; it alone had made it possible to transport by sea to that base an American expeditionary force of twenty divisions.

In the event the victory in the Atlantic had proved final even though Dönitz and the Admiralty alike had expected the U-boat offensive to resume in the autumn of 1943 with renewed ferocity. Dönitz had pinned his hopes on new technology – the acoustic torpedo (thwarted in the event by a towed decoy), a radar detector called 'Hagenuk' (it failed of its purpose), a radar decoy called 'Aphrodite' (no more successful), and the fitting of U-boats with armour and quadruple 20mm flak guns against air attack.[44] But in September and October 1943 his fresh offensive had been smashed by close cooperation between surface escorts, Very Long Range aircraft and the aircraft of the escort carriers. In October alone Dönitz lost 23 U-boats in the North Atlantic.[45] Even top-loading his Type VIIC boats with so much armour and anti-aircraft armament that they rolled 30° continuously in rough weather availed him nothing; nor did the laying of radar decoys ('Thetis') at 25-mile intervals across the Bay of Biscay. In January 1944 he lost nine U-boats in the Atlantic; in February he lost twelve, and in March another twelve.[46] Six of those lost in January and February were sunk by Captain F. J. Walker, RN, most renowned of all escort group commanders, whose total wartime bag came to twenty U-boats thanks to a personal technique of the 'creeping attack'. He once remorselessly hunted a victim for 38 hours.[47]

For 1944–45 Dönitz had cherished hopes of a new technological generation of U-boats, no longer 'submersibles' but true underwater vessels – the 1,600-ton Type XXI and the 850-ton Type XXIII with streamlined hulls and very powerful electric motors driven by a new kind of battery which together gave them underwater speeds of 18 knots for one and a half hours or some 12 knots for as long as ten hours. Also under development was a similarly streamlined boat designed by Dr Walter, powered by a hydrogen peroxide-fuelled turbine which could attain the astounding underwater speed of 25 knots.[48] These were performances which would destroy the whole basis of current Allied anti-submarine deployments and hunting tactics. The standard Type VIIC U-boats as well as the new designs were being fitted with the 'Schnorchel', a vertical pipe containing air inlet and exhaust outlet so that they could use their diesels under water and so avoid surfacing to recharge their batteries.[49]

Yet to bring the Type XXIs and XXIIIs, to say nothing of the Walter boats, into series production took time. All the complex working drawings for construction were ready by mid-November 1943. A month later a wooden mock-up of a Type XXI had been built. In spring 1944 the first four experimental boats were commissioned for trials; and on 26 May contracts were placed for 100 of the 850-ton Type XIIIs for delivery in 1945.[50] As for Schnorchel-equipped standard Type VIIC U-boats, only nine were based on Biscay ports by D-Day,[51] even though the original Dutch invention dated back to 1937. It was only after his defeat of May 1943 in the Battle of the Atlantic that Dönitz woke up to the Schnorchel's possibilities, and only in July that he won Hitler's sanction for its mass production – a year, two years, too late, especially under the flail of Allied bombing even if that were more disruptive than devastating.[52]

By the time 'Neptune' preparations were getting under way at the beginning of 1944 Dönitz had finally come to abandon all thoughts of retrieving the lost Battle of the Atlantic that year: 'All we could now hope to do was to fight a delaying action . . . and continue to tie down forces of the enemy.'[53] So it was that in the months before D-Day the Allies were able to run convoys between North America and Britain comprising as many as 100 ships each, which allowed the Royal Navy to strip escort groups and escort carriers from the Atlantic for the protection of the western flank of 'Neptune'. Here was a final dividend from the victory in 1943 over Dönitz's wolf packs; another aspect of 'Operation Neptune' as the crown and climax of previous endeavour.

From 20 May onwards Allied Intelligence formulated its final updates of German strength and deployment by land, sea and air opposite 'Neptune'. On 25 May the Joint Intelligence Committee (employing Operational Intelligence Centre figures) guesstimated that by D-Day there could be 70 of the Type VIIC U-boats based on Biscay ports, and perhaps ten or more from the Atlantic in the western and central English Channel; that by D + 2 the number in the Channel might climb to 45, and by D + 5 to 60.[54] Uncertainty remained about German intentions for these U-boats. How far would they be launched against the 'Neptune' armada on D-Day and how far against the follow-up convoys? No chances could be taken: the Admiralty re-deployed its anti-submarine forces in order to strengthen the protection of 'Neptune's' western flank, and Coastal Command did likewise, thanks to the willing cooperation of the AOC-in-C, Air Marshal Sir Sholto Douglas:[55]

> Coastal Command [wrote Ramsay in his later report] threw themselves into the preparations for 'Neptune' with as much enthusiasm as any unit in the Allied Expedition, and I personally and the whole Naval Expeditionary Force are deeply indebted to them for the efficiency of the measures they adopted which was reflected by the very small scale of U-boat attack which eventuated.[56]

On 31 May the OIC was able to define the exact limits of the mine-free water in the Bay of the Seine and near Le Havre where the 'Neptune' bombardment and assault forces were to deploy. An Ultra decrypt of a signal in the 'Offizier' Enigma key had enabled Allied aircraft and MTBs to intercept and cut up a German minelaying force on 23 May to the north of the previously supposed southern limit of the main mine barrier, inflicting such losses as to put an end to any further minelaying. The interception in itself thus served to amend the British estimate of the barrier's extent. But it was the frenzy of 'PP' signals after the encounter specifying safe courses home for the surviving German vessels which yielded to Allied cryptographers the precise limits of mine-free waters.[57] At the same period other decrypts, together with photo-reconnaissance pictures, enabled the OIC to assure ANCXF and his staff that there was no evidence that ground-mines had been laid inshore of the main mine barrier.[58]

With regard to the Luftwaffe, the final OIC appreciation of 25 May put its total first-line strength against 'Neptune' on D-Day at 900 aircraft, with reinforcements of 530 arriving by D + 4;[59] a shrunken total indeed compared with the January estimates of a total strength of 2,530 and 1,750 D-Day sorties; a measure of the crushing victory won over Germany by the 8th Air Force's Mustangs (see above, p. 789). The OIC reckoned that the Luftwaffe's sorties against 'Neptune' from dawn on D-Day to D + 1 could amount to 1,150 to 1,250, but that 'in view of the low morale and operational efficiency of the G.A.F. [German Air Force]' such a scale of effort might not be reached in the face of Allied mastery of the air.[60]

The German Army in the West was, however, another matter – and it was the German Army whose defence of the coastline and whose panzer counter-strokes presented the greatest danger to the success of 'Neptune', especially in the precarious first few days after the Allied land forces had been put ashore. Monitoring of the movement and deployment of German divisions in France by Sigint and by secret agents worryingly showed that powerful formations were beginning to gather on the flanks of the intended Allied lodgement. By 22 May the Joint Intelligence Committee was even wondering whether the enemy had guessed that the Le Havre–Cherbourg area would be 'a likely, and perhaps the main point of assault'.[61] The 21st Panzer Division was somewhere near Caen, a key objective of the British 2nd Army, though unfortunately its exact whereabouts were unknown, while an Ultra decrypt revealed that the Germans were reinforcing the Cotentin Peninsula, in the American assault area.[62]

On 26 May – ten days to go to D-Day as then fixed – Ramsay noted in his diary: 'Disturbing features of Overlord have arisen in the strengthening of German Divisions in the Neptune area, particularly opposite the west flank of the Americans. This makes their task very much more difficult & particularly that of their Airborne Divs [sic] & may necessitate a change of plan.'[63] It did – and that meant selecting new dropping and landing zones and flying-in routes over the sea, which led Admiral Moon strenuously to object to troop-carriers flying in the vicinity of his ships[64] for fear of confusion of identity and consequent firing on friendly aircraft. Here were more unwelcome problems needing to be sorted out at the last moment.

In its final appreciation of 25 May the Operational Intelligence Centre put the total strength of the German Army in the West on D-Day at 62 divisions, of which ten would be panzer or panzer-grenadier and fourteen infantry field. In the forenoon of D-Day the Allied assault forces could encounter three coastal defence (static low establishment) divisions and one infantry field division (352nd; exact whereabouts unknown). By last light the whole of 21st Panzer could be engaged, plus elements of 12th SS Panzer. On D + 1, two more panzer divisions could be present. Between D + 17 and D + 25, the period judged most likely for a classic German counter-stroke in depth, no fewer than ten or eleven panzer or panzer-grenadier divisions, thirteen infantry field divisions and eight 'low establishment' divisions could have been concentrated.[65] These were formidable (and as the event proved, closely accurate) numbers. They showed how narrow must be the margin between victory and defeat for the Allied armies – how critical therefore the performance of the navies in landing and building up those armies on D-Day and after.

On 27 May the 'slow ahead' for 'Operation Neptune' was signalled by the imposing of restrictions on air attack on surface ships in the

Channel to the west of a line from the North Foreland to Walcheren Fort near Dunkirk except by Coastal Command. From now onwards the huge 'Neptune' machine would gradually, inexorably, gather way according to plan. On 28 May Allied minelaying operations off enemy bases were completed five days ahead of schedule, the mines accounting eventually for sixteen enemy vessels sunk and 37 damaged.[66] Two days later Ramsay was briefing Vice-Admiral Glennie (the new Vice-Admiral, Destroyers) on his role, should he have to take the place of the quinsy-stricken Vian.[67] Now that the count-down to D-Day had begun, Ramsay himself could record:

> Things are becoming a little more calm & a distinct lull in our activities is noticeable today. I took the occasion to address the Wrens of the Secretariat, amounting to about 60, & thank them for their hard & good work. Only a few days to go & everyone is thankful for that.[68]

On 31 May the Royal Navy laid ten underwater sonic buoys to mark the edge of the enemy mine barrier in the assault approach channels ('Operation Enthrone'). The buoys were laid dead to come alive on D – 1 in order to guide the motor launches which would act as marker boats enabling the minesweepers to start their work from the precisely correct positions. On this day also began the whole colossal operation of loading the assault shipping and concentrating it into assault convoys. All too soon came the first symptoms of Clausewitzian 'friction' in the functioning of a military machine. In Forces S ('Sword' beach) and J ('Juno'), both of them British, loading fell behind schedule because of a shortage of experienced military loading personnel, and in the case of Force J also because it proved difficult to back heavy trailers down the Southampton hards at low states of tide.[69]

On 1 June Ramsay assumed operational command over the 'Neptune' forces and the sea area of the English Channel. One of his first tasks was successfully to persuade the Prime Minister and King George VI that they should not go over to France with the assault forces on D-Day as they wished, because the risk was 'unacceptable'.[70] Churchill's eagerness did him credit, though hardly his commonsense: after all, 'Neptune' constituted the consummation of his war too; and, ever a man for the sound of guns, he itched to be at sea under the White Ensign to witness it.

In the evening of 2 June the first of the bombardment forces steamed out of the Clyde and headed south; and the midget submarines X23 and X20 were towed out of Portsmouth towards the French shore. By now in all the ports and estuaries of southern England, on quayside and on hard, the bustle of loading was reaching a fury of physical effort and mental concentration, of roaring engines and crashing gears, of shouted orders and curses of impatience and irritation. However, as Commodore Oliver (Force J) remarked in his report, 'the knowledge that they were "off at last" acted as a great incentive'.[71] To Ramsay 'who was not feeling at all fit today'[72] it was one relief that Vian was making a good recovery.

The ANCXF spent 3 June watching the loading at Gosport, Portsmouth and Shoreham, only to be dismayed at the blunder committed by the 50th (British) Infantry Division at Gosport, where tank landing craft were

> . . . being much overloaded, resulting in TLCs being too low in the water, with a risk of grounding too far out & thus drowning vehicles on their way out . . . [the Army's] one idea was to cram as many vehicles into ships & craft & as much into each vehicle as possible, without regard to the disastrous results which must ensue.[73]

He therefore made a signal to all 'Neptune' forces ordering that correct draughts must not be exceeded.

In the evening the weather chart was, in Ramsay's laconic word, 'unpromising';[74] unpromising enough indeed to raise the possibility of having to postpone the landings. Yet if Force U ('Utah' beach), sailing from the West Country ports of Dartmouth, Brixham and Salcombe, were to reach its assault area on time on the present D-Day of 5 June, its departure could not be delayed. At 2130 Eisenhower met his commanders-in-chief to consider whether or not to postpone; he decided, so wrote Ramsay later that night in his diary, 'to order the operation to proceed, in *spite* of a bad weather forecast. This was only done because Ike was over impressed with the frightful results of postponement . . .'[75] In fact the possibility of postponement had been written into Ramsay's naval orders, and all the 'Neptune' forces knew what they had to do in such an event. A further meeting was arranged for 0415 next morning, 4 June. In the meantime Force U put to sea according to its existing instructions.

Punctually at 0415 on 4 June, a deceptively calm and lovely morning, the Supreme Commander and his senior subordinates met as arranged to consider the latest weather report, 'which was *bad*,' wrote Ramsay in his diary,

> . . . The low cloud predicted would prohibit use of Airborne Troops, prohibit majority of air action, including air spotting. The sea conditions were unpromising but not prohibitive. I pointed out that we had only

> accepted a daylight assault on the understanding that our overwhelming air & naval bombardment would be available to overcome the enemy coast & beach defences. S.A.C. decided therefore to postpone assault for 24 hours. Forces U & O would have started and must be recalled. The weather got progressively worse after midday . . . as the day went on and the forecast became more fully justified.[76]

The order to postpone D-Day until 6 June was issued from SHAEF at 0515 – just about the time when the midget submarines X23 (Lieutenant K. R. Hudspeth, RANVR) and X20 (Lieutenant G. B. Honour, RANVR) arrived on station off the Normandy coast, the tiny advanced guard of a vast armada. From ANCXF's headquarters signals were made to the convoys already at sea to put back; and to divert the 'Corncob' blockships for the Mulberry harbours into Poole Bay to await the new departure time.

Unfortunately Group U2A of Force U, consisting of 128 landing craft crammed with American troops and their equipment, four escorts and a rescue tug missed the signal of recall. At 0900 they were 25 miles south of the Isle of Wight and still chugging southwards for Normandy and – as they believed – battle. The C-in-C, Portsmouth, thereupon sent two destroyers at utmost speed to catch them up and turn them back before they were detected by enemy radar. Ordered to shelter in Weymouth Bay and there refuel, Group U2A struggled all day to make to the westward against a Force 5 to 6 west-south-west wind and a nastily short, steep sea on the port bow. It was after midnight on 4–5 June before any of the group's clumsy landing craft came to anchor, and for the chilled, tired and seasick soldiers a voyage that had begun in apprehension of death ended in futility and anti-climax.

At 2100 on 4 June there opened another and perhaps even more fraught commanders' conference chaired by Eisenhower, as a gale of wind rattled the sash windows of the library in Southwick House and rain squalls splattered against the panes.

> A postponement of one more day, [wrote Ramsay in his later report], e.g., till 7th June would, in the event, have proved disastrous owing to conditions of sea off the beaches. The problems arising out of postponement of 12 or 14 days to the next suitable period [of moon and tide] are too appalling even to contemplate.[77]

No record was taken of this meeting, and recollections differ as to its outcome. According to Montgomery, a final decision was put off until another meeting at 0400 next morning, in view of the continuing unfavourable weather forecasts.[78] But in fact the meteorologists were predicting that a gap would occur in the windy and overcast weather by the forenoon of Tuesday 6 June.[79] Ramsay himself recorded in his diary after the meeting that 'the weather prophets were more optimistic & we decided to continue the operation as ordered . . .'[80]

So certain was he that the great decision *had* been made, even though he recognised that it meant taking 'a big chance',[81] that he forthwith issued the necessary naval orders,[82] including the final fixing of H-Hours – Sword and Gold beaches 0725; Juno right wing 0735; Juno left wing 0745; Omaha and Utah 0630, by American wish about an hour earlier than the British landings.

At 0415 on the 5th Eisenhower and his commanders conferred yet again. 'This time,' recorded Ramsay, 'the prophets came in smiling, conditions having shown considerable improvement.'[83]

> It was therefore decided to let things be & proceed. The wind was still fresh & it is clear that forces will have an uncomfortable initial journey, improving as the day proceeds. Thus has been made the vital and crucial decision to stage & start this great enterprise which will, I hope, be the immediate means of bringing about the downfall of German fighting power & Nazi oppression & an early cessation of hostilities. I am under no delusions as to the risk involved in this most difficult of all operations & the critical period at around H-hour if when initial flights are held up success will be in the balance. We must trust in our invisible assets [a reference to the 'Fortitude' deception plan?] to tip the balance in our favour & to allow the landings to proceed without interruption. We shall require all the help that God can give us & I cannot believe that this will not be forthcoming.

26

'This Great Enterprise': 'Operation Neptune'

At 0900 on 5 June the force commander of Force S, Rear-Admiral A. G. Talbot, made the flag signal from his flagship HMS *Largs*: 'Good luck: drive on' (he kept it flying until he himself sailed in the evening); and the first landing craft (tank) put to sea from the Solent and Spithead.[1] Soon the landing crafts' flat bows were butting into a short, steep sea, the wind west-south-west Force 5 on the Beaufort scale: sixteen to twenty nautical miles per hour, causing (according to the definition) 'large waves to begin to form; the white crests become more and more extensive'.[2] For the British, American and Canadian soldiers voyaging to war packed with full kit into these vessels, it was going to be a day and a night of harsh physical discomfort as well as mental stress – the heave of seasickness mirroring the heave of apprehension at the prospect of battle and mutilation or death.

Throughout the day the log-jams of shipping of all descriptions, fast and slow, in the estuaries and harbours of southern England gradually broke up and cleared as the 'Neptune' armada sailed in due sequence according to Ramsay's orders. The coastal waters from Cornwall to Kent filled with traffic forming into assault and follow-up convoys and converging from west and east towards 'Position Z', the concentration area south of the Isle of Wight already dubbed 'Piccadilly Circus'. Some 2,700 vessels (not counting the 1,897 smaller landing craft carried in the landing ships) were on the move, ranging from battleships of over 30,000 tons displacement to Thames barges on tow and making their hazardous début on the open sea. No fewer than 195,000 sailors, navy and merchant marine, more than half of them British, manned this invasion fleet with its cargo of some 130,000 soldiers, 12,000 vehicles, 2,000 tanks and nearly 10,000 tons of stores.[3]

Thanks to ANCXF and his staff's meticulous scheduling and 'Mickey Mouse' diagrams the forward movement of the assault convoys through 'Piccadilly Circus' and southwards down the ten designated channels of 'The Spout' was accomplished without muddle or delay. Admiral Vian, CETF, sailed from Spithead at 1630 in his flagship HMS *Scylla* (5,450 tons displacement, Captain T. M. Brownrigg, RN), and for the next few hours watched the passing of this huge procession into 'The Spout'. In early evening the minesweepers began sweeping the ten two-mile wide approach channels through the German mine barrier, marking the boundaries with Dan buoys as they went. Despite the west-south-west wind and a 2½-knot tidal stream running dead abeam, which compelled some vessels to make as much as 40° allowance in order to keep a true course, the assault forces followed the minesweepers on through the night hours with few errors of navigation.

And still the enemy had not stirred. The only Allied casualties had been the minesweeper USS *Osprey* sunk and the destroyer HMS *Wrestler* and a landing craft damaged by mines, and some 50 smaller craft swamped by the rough seas. That long day of mass movement had passed without attack by German aircraft or U-boat or E-boat. Ramsay, waiting in his headquarters at Southwick House for news, could hardly believe their luck:

> There was an air of unreality [he wrote in his report] during the passage of the assault force across the Channel curiously similar to that on D – 1 in 'Husky' as our forces approached Sicily. The achievement of strategical surprise was always hoped for in 'Neptune' but was by no means certain, whereas that of tactical surprise had always seemed extremely unlikely. As our forces approached the French coast without a murmur from the enemy or from their own radio the realisation that once again almost complete tactical surprise had been achieved slowly dawned.[4]

The German command had in fact been blinded – in the first place by the inability of the Luftwaffe to maintain constant or comprehensive surveillance of Allied shipping concentrations and movements during the past weeks, and secondly by lack of accurate forecasts of weather conditions for several days ahead, now that the German weather ships had been swept from the Atlantic. Noting the immediately unfavourable state of wind, sea and cloud in the Channel and Biscay on 4 June but ignorant that an interval of better weather was on its way for the 6th and after, the German Navy's Group West pronounced on the 4th that 'at the present moment a major invasion cannot be assumed imminent'.[5] The C-in-C of Army Group B, responsible for the defence of France between the Seine and the Loire, Field-Marshal Rommel, was himself absent in his home town in Germany for his wife's birthday. Nor did coastal radars pick up the advancing armada, thanks to Bomber Command (again in the tactical role) having knocked out several stations, including the one on Cap Barfleur commanding the western flank of the approaches to the Bay of the Seine; and thanks also to electronic jamming which had blinded the station at Arromanches and others.

That night the German coastal defence divisions (many of the soldiers being non-Germans such as ex-Russian prisoners) and the gunners of the batteries behind the beaches took to their bunks in their deep shelters in customary peace of mind, while those on watch and peering into the darkness to seaward saw as usual nothing but the faint gleam of waves.

At midnight Bomber Command shattered this German tranquillity with the first of the 5,000 tons of bombs that were going to be dropped by 1,056 aircraft during the next five hours on to ten of the most powerful and tactically important German batteries. Soon after midnight the British 6th Airborne Division began to land by glider and parachute east of the River Orne, with the objective (successfully accomplished) of capturing the bridges over the River Orne and the Caen Canal in order to secure the left flank of 'Sword' assault force from counter-attack. At 0130 the American 82nd and 101st Airborne Divisions began to land in the south of the Cotentin Peninsula behind the German defences along Utah beach. Yet it was not until 0300, when some large ships were sighted, dark shapes against the moon-glow, off Port en Bessin, that Group West realised that an Allied invasion, if not *the* Allied invasion, was about to take place, and signalled orders accordingly.

In the meantime the 'Neptune' assault convoys had been following astern of the minesweepers through the German mine barrier, the wind now north-north-westerly: for the sailors a night of tense navigation by the dim lights of the Dan buoys; for the soldiers in closed-up ships or landing craft amid the smells of diesel oil, vomit and the sweat of men afraid, an uneasy night of fitful sleep. On debouching from the southern exits of the swept channels the assault forces spread out to their lowering or bombarding positions along the courses laid down in ANCXF's orders. Ahead could be seen the flash of bomb explosions, the glow of fires and the sparkle of German anti-aircraft fire as Bomber Command did its work.

Responsibility for planning the final deployments and the actual assault landings had lain with the commanders of the two naval task forces, their subordinate commanders of Forces U, O, J, G and S, and all their military opposite numbers. In the Western Task Force American procedures were followed; in the Eastern, British. The United States command chose to locate its lowering positions some eleven miles off shore as against some seven to eight miles out for the British, in order that their 'attack transports' (landing ships infantry) might be out of range of German heavy shore batteries. Ramsay regarded this as a needless precaution, given the weight of Allied counter-bombardment available to suppress the enemy guns.[6] The decision meant that the American assault divisions would take some three hours to reach the beaches, against two for the British, so necessitating much earlier lowering and despatch. Moreover, the US command had also elected to make its H-Hour 0630, an hour before the British, so demanding an even earlier start to the run-in. It was therefore shortly after 0230, full darkness, when the Western Task Force began hoisting out landing craft, followed by the Eastern Task Force at 0530, in the growing light of morning.

The amphibious warfare pioneers of the 1920s and 1930s could not have imagined that their paper schemes and few experimental craft would lead to a landing fleet of the size and astonishing variety now massed in the Bay of the Seine. The sea-going vessels comprised six headquarters ships of 7,000 to 8,000 tons, each of them draped with radio aerials; 55 landing ships (infantry) (converted passenger ships) of 3,100 to 14,000 tons; six specialised landing ships (dock) and (repair); 236 landing ships (tank), ugly, utilitarian 4,000 tonners with bow ramps, and carrying up to 60 tanks and 300 soldiers; 248 landing craft (infantry), up to 160 feet long and taking some 200 soldiers, and in some cases converted to serve as tactical headquarters craft off the beaches; and 837 landing craft (tank), carrying up to eleven vehicles and 55 soldiers, plus others adapted for special purposes such as the 29 landing craft (flak) and the 36 landing craft (rocket). And then there were all the small craft carried in the ships and now lowered by davit into the water for the run-in – 502 landing craft (assault), carrying 30 soldiers and their kit, some being equipped to clear beach obstacles; 464 landing craft (mechanised), to supply a ship-to-shore ferry service for armoured vehicles and motor transport; 189 landing craft (personnel) carrying 22 soldiers, but also sometimes converted for special roles, in this case smoke-laying or survey work; 121 landing craft (support), equipped with machine-guns and smoke-projectors; and the invaluable 'Duck' (DUKW), the 2½-ton, six-wheeled amphibious truck carrying 25 fully equipped soldiers, and capable of 6.4 mph in water and up to 50 mph on land.[7]

At 0430 on 6 June 1944 Forces U and O, the first assault forces to be despatched, began to heave and bump over choppy seas towards the coast some eleven miles distant. For the Western and Eastern Task Forces it marked the start of what was afterwards to become the most often and most minutely described day in the history of warfare, except perhaps for the Battle of Waterloo.[8]

While the bombarding force supporting Force S, on the extreme left of the Allied line, was deploying on station, the enemy made his one and only attempt – by E-boats – to attack the 'Neptune' armada at sea before the landings could take place. Two torpedoes passed harmlessly between HMS *Warspite* and HMS *Ramillies*, but a third hit the destroyer HNorMS *Svenner* under the boiler room, breaking her back. Although she sank quickly, most of her company were safely picked up. Another torpedo was seen driving straight for the headquarters ship *Largs*, flagship of Force S, and she had to put her engines emergency full astern to evade it. *Warspite* fired back with her 15-inch and 4-inch guns, crumpling up one E-boat which sank by the stern. The remainder of the flotilla retired behind a smoke screen.[9]

At 0500 the X-Craft X20 and X23 three miles off Juno and Sword beaches began flashing their green lights to seaward to guide the approach of the British and Canadian assault waves. The two X-Craft had been waiting offshore for 76 hours, 64 of them lying on the bottom, a gruelling experience for their five-men crews (including two COPP officers); their mission, as Ramsay paid tribute in his report, a feat of 'great skill and endurance . . . Their reports of proceedings, which were a masterpiece of understatement, read like the deck log of a surface ship in peacetime; and not of a very small and vulnerable submarine carrying out a hazardous operation in time of war.'[10]

At 0530, light enough now for aircraft to spot for the warships' guns, the Royal Navy's broadsides crashed out against German shore batteries along the Eastern Task Force front. The Western Task Force did not however open fire until 0550, even though H-Hour for the American 1st Army was one hour earlier than for the British 2nd Army. For Admiral Kirk had opted for a preliminary bombardment lasting only 30 to 40 minutes instead of the two hours preferred by

Ramsay and Vian, hoping thereby to gain the advantage of surprise; he was to be keenly disappointed.

Off Sword beach, on the left of the Allied invasion front, the Great War veterans HMS *Warspite* and *Ramillies* and their contemporary the monitor HMS *Roberts* threw salvo after salvo of 15-inch shells at the enemy shore batteries between the rivers Orne and Seine.[11] HMS *Warspite* was present with one boiler room and one turret still out of action as a result of being hit by an FX-1400 radio-controlled bomb at Salerno; *Ramillies* because she and her sister ship *Revenge* had been reprieved from the laying-up planned in late 1943. Further west along the Sword sector the cruisers HMS *Danae*, *Frobisher* and *Arethusa*, and the Polish cruiser *Dragon* bombarded gun positions astride the River Orne and behind the beaches. In Juno and Gold sectors the cruisers HMS *Ajax* (of River Plate fame), *Argonaut*, *Emerald*, *Orion*, *Belfast* and *Diadem*, and the Dutch gunboat HNLMS *Flores* concentrated their fire on seven tactically important shore batteries.

In the Western Task Force the 14-inch battleships USS *Texas* and *Arkansas*, the cruisers FS *Montcalm* and *Georges Leygues*, and HMS *Glasgow* carried out forty-minute bombardments along Omaha beach against German positions round the little harbour of Port en Bessin, beach defences and a major German heavy battery at Pointe du Hoc. On the far right of the Allied line, Utah beach, the 14-inch battleship *Nevada*, the 15-inch monitor HMS *Erebus*, and the cruisers USS *Tuscaloosa* and *Quincy*, HMS *Hawkins*, *Enterprise* and *Black Prince*, and the Dutch gunboat HNLMS *Soemba* sought to knock out or suppress German batteries extending from St Martin de Varreville northwards to Cap Barfleur. When the assault waves began to near the shore it was the turn of the destroyers – 57 in all – to blast the German bunkers behind the beaches with close-range low-trajectory fire. Never before had such a weight of fire been put down by warships before a landing.

The Allied air forces had also been joining in again. A little before 0600, half an hour before H-Hour for the Americans, 269 Martin Marauder medium bombers of the US 9th Air Force flew in under the 2,000-foot cloud base to launch an accurate attack on German positions behind Utah beach. Next 329 Liberators and Flying Fortresses of the 8th Air Force dropped 1,285 tons of bombs through the cloud in an attempt to obliterate the enemy defences behind Omaha beach. Yet this impressive tonnage fell harmlessly in the fields beyond, owing to a mistaken decision to delay the timing of the blind, instrument-guided, drop for 30 seconds for fear of hitting the American assault waves as they neared the shore.[12] In the British sector, over 1,000 Flying Fortresses and Liberators of the 8th Air Force also bombed from above the clouds, again relying on the guidance of pathfinders fixing the moment of release by instrument. Most of the 3,000 tons of bombs simply made craters in Norman pastures, although some damage was usefully done to German defences.

From this colossal and cumulative delivery of explosive from sea and air the German coastal defence batteries and defensive positions emerged largely unscathed even though the defenders themselves had been badly shaken and their communications disrupted. This was a tribute to the effectiveness of reinforced concrete up to seven feet thick under piled earth and gun embrasures angled to enfilade the beaches and inshore waters rather than towards the open sea.[13] The Western Task Force's fire also proved far less damaging than that of the Eastern Task Force. This was partly because it was spread evenly along the coast instead of being concentrated on key enemy positions; partly because the targets proved difficult to identify because of the lie of the shoreline; and partly because some American warships had been firing at German gun-flashes some 100 feet above the actual guns.[14] In any event, as Kirk and his fellow American admirals agreed afterwards, a bombardment of forty minutes was far too brief.[15]

Thus the Allies' hope that the warships and bombers would have crushed the defence before the attackers reached it was to prove vain, just like the comparable hope entertained by Sir Douglas Haig and his generals with regard to preliminary bombardment before the Battle of the Somme in 1916.

At 0630, preceded by a final storm from rocket-launchers mounted in adapted landing craft, Forces U and O put down the 4th US Infantry Division on Utah beach and a regimental combat team (brigade group) each from the 1st and 29th US Infantry Divisions on Omaha beach. In the case of Utah at the base of the Cotentin Peninsula (and lying to the north of the estuary of the River Vire) the troops came ashore on the wrong beach, a mile south-east of the correct one; an error due to the loss of guide vessels and the veiling of the low shoreline by haze and the smoke of explosions. It proved a lucky mistake, for this stretch of coast was less strongly defended. The 4th Infantry Division pushed fast inland on to high ground and by evening had established a firm lodgement five miles deep close to elements of the 82nd Airborne. By the end of D-Day Admiral Moon's Force U had landed 21,328 soldiers, 1,742 vehicles and 1,695 tons of stores. It had been a copybook operation.[16]

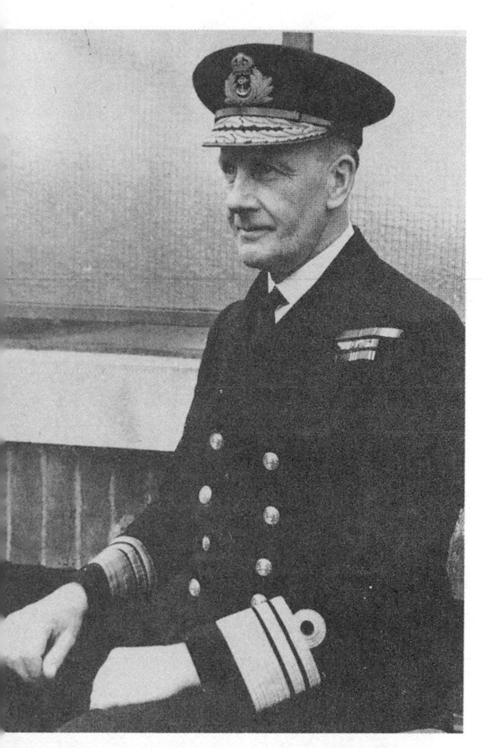

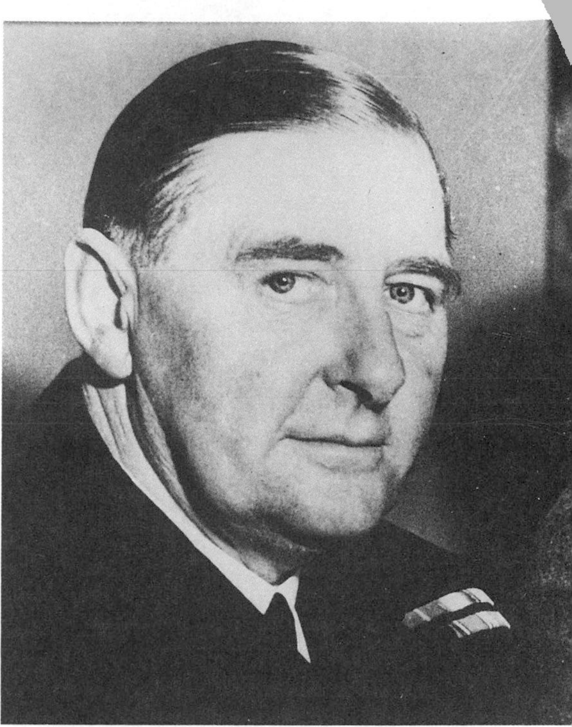

(Top, left) 'Bouncy bonhomie consorted with a high professionalism. . . .' Admiral Sir James Somerville – Flag Officer, Force H, 1940–42; Commander-in-Chief, Eastern Fleet, 1942–44. (Crown) *(Top, right)* 'Harwood lacked the sheer ruthless powers of leadership of his predecessor.' Admiral Sir Henry Harwood, who replaced Cunningham as Commander-in-Chief, Mediterranean Fleet, in May 1942, is pictured here in 1939 when, as a Commodore, he commanded the three British cruisers which defeated the pocket battleship *Admiral Graf Spee*. (Hulton) *(Below)* 'A man of notoriously dark and difficult nature. . . .' Admiral Sir Philip Vian *(left)*, victor of the second Battle of Sirte, March 1942, Naval Commander, Eastern Task Force, in 'Operation Neptune', June 1944; commanded Pacific Fleet's aircraft carriers, 1945. (Hulton)

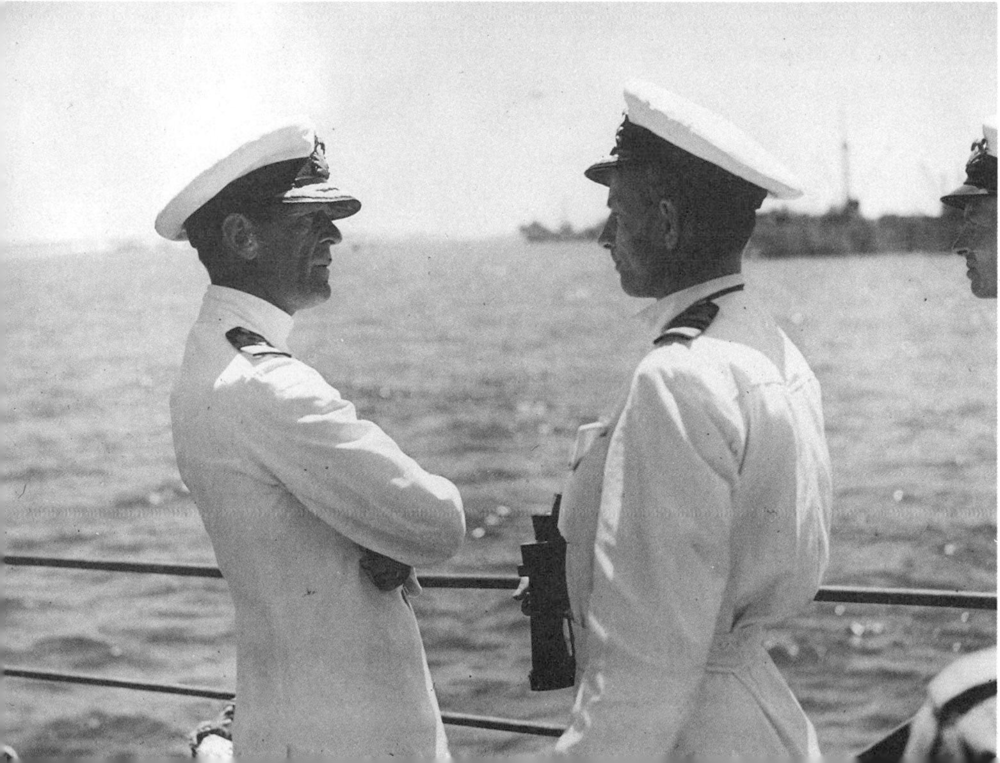

(Top, left) 'A belief in careful, elaborate pre-planning so that as little as possible was left to chance.' Admiral Sir Bertram Ramsay. As Vice-Admiral, Dover, he commanded 'Operation Dynamo' (the Dunkirk evacuation) in 1940, and, as Naval Commander Allied Expeditionary Force, planned and carried out 'Operation Neptune', the D-Day landings in Normandy on 6 June 1944, the most complex combined operation ever. (IWM) *(Top, right)* 'A man of calm and massive presence.' Rear Admiral H. Kent Hewitt, United St Navy, commander of the Western Naval Task Force 'Operation Torch', 1942; the Western Task Force in 'Operation Husky', Sicily, July 1943, and 'Operation Avalanche' (Salerno) in September 1943. (IWM) *(Below)* 'Some 2,700 vessels were on the move. . . .' Landing craft on passage down 'The Spout' towards Normandy beaches, June 1944. (Crown)

›ove) 'The transport and installation of the lberries presented a colossal undertaking in itself.' : 'Mulberry' artificial harbour at Arromanches, as ;e as Dover, showing floating pierhead and pier and, he foreground, the 'Corncob' breakwater of scuttled old ships. (Crown) *(Below)* '. . . a chaos of wrecked equipment, corpses and wounded. . . .' Omaha Beach, where poor American joint army-navy planning and an ineffective naval bombardment led to an initial repulse on D-Day, 6 June 1944. (Hulton)

(Above) 'The wonderful little DUKWs, manned by Royal Army Service Corps men, wallowed like hippopotami between the coasters and the shore.' DUKW amphibious trucks in the British 'Mulberry' harbour at Arromanches. (Hulton) *(Below)* '. . . an immeasurably more destructive force than U-boats c E-boats or mines. . . .' The Arromanches 'Mulberry harbour after the great gale of 19–22 June 1944, showi damage to piers and other components. (Crown)

But on Omaha beach, between Vierville (inclusive) in the west to just short of Port en Bessin, Admiral Hall's Force O and the two regimental combat teams from the 1st and 29th Divisions proved not so fortunate.[17] Riding the eleven miles into this more exposed north-facing coast the assault formations had suffered much more from wind and waves than the relatively sheltered Force U. Out of 32 amphibious tanks launched at sea to spearhead the assault, all but five foundered. Thirty-two out of 50 howitzers to be landed to support the infantry attack went down in swamped 'Ducks'. Many landing craft also foundered, including – disastrously – those equipped for clearing beach obstacles.

As a result, the dense belts of obstacles ('Rommel's asparagus') installed thanks to Field-Marshal Rommel's ingenuity and energy here did their job well – not least because the Americans had declined to use the tanks especially adapted by the British for smashing paths through obstacles and minefields by means of rotating chain flails. Despite the extra time available for clearing obstacles during low states of tide because of the earlier H-Hour chosen by the American command, only a few paths could be opened through them before the water rose and covered them again. Thus unable to reach the shore, the waves of landing craft began to jam up to seaward, their orderly organisation and sequence disintegrating into a formless mass. Those troops who did manage to reach the beaches now found themselves pinned down before high bluffs and a concrete sea-wall supposed to have been demolished by the air and naval bombardment but actually largely intact.

For on Omaha beach the preliminary bombardment had proved the least effective of anywhere. The USS *Texas* had fired 250 rounds of 14-inch shell at the commanding battery on Pointe du Hoc to the west of the beach, but in vain, because, as US Rangers discovered when they occupied the battery later after a stiff fight, the enemy had shifted the guns to another position. The landing craft (rocket) fired too early, their projectiles falling short of the German beach defences. Trapped now without artillery support between the high water mark and the sea-wall or the bluffs, the hapless forward elements of the 1st and 29th Divisions were raked with German artillery, mortar and small arms fire. The beach became a chaos of wrecked equipment, corpses and wounded: a scene of paralysing terror only redeemed by individual acts of initiative and bravery. Offshore in the milling mass of landing craft, the confusion and leaderlessness among the American bluejackets and seasick soldiers verged on panic.

All in all Omaha beach that forenoon of D-Day offered exactly the scene of disastrous repulse which Rommel had hoped to arrange for the entire Allied Expeditionary Force. It reflected the lack of training and experience of the crews of the 'control vessels' responsible for directing the landing craft.[18] It also reflected poor joint planning and staff work on the part of Rear Admiral Hall and Force O and his opposite number, Major-General L. T. Gerow, and the US V Corps.[19] If a panzer or panzer-grenadier division had been present or within striking distance rather than the static 716th Infantry Division (lacking any transport at all) and some elements of the 252nd Infantry Division, Omaha beach could easily have seen a repetition of the dismal opening phase of the American landing at Salerno, if not an outright catastrophe. As it was, by the afternoon the mass of landing craft offshore had been sorted back into assault formation and more gaps cleared through the obstacles. With the American forces ashore now growing steadily stronger, German resistance weakened, not least because of close-range fire by destroyers. By the end of D-Day troops of the 1st and 29th US Infantry Divisions had gained a firm lodgement after all, even though it was barely a mile deep and five miles wide.

In the Eastern Task Force area the three assault forces completed their much shorter runs-in without losing formation despite the short, steep sea: a tribute to the conning of the unhandy landing craft. On the flanks of the landing craft groups as they headed for the shore steamed the big fleet destroyers, their 4.7-inch guns constantly engaging enemy batteries of defences behind the beaches. Ahead of them the smaller 'Hunts' moved as close inshore as possible to support the assault with fire from their 4-inch guns. Rocket-firing Typhoons of the 2nd Tactical Air Force ranged low along the coast beyond, blasting German positions. About 45 minutes before touchdown sixteen landing craft (gun) opened furious close-range fire on the actual beach defences with their 4.7-inch, 6-pounder and 2-pounder armaments. Fifteen minutes later the bombardment mounted to its climax when 22 landing craft (rocket) launched flights of 5-inch rockets at the rate of a thousand per craft per minute and a half.

'The air,' wrote Rear-Admiral Talbot (Force S) in his report, 'was full of bombers and fighters, and of the noise and smoke of our bombardments. The enemy was obviously stunned by the sheer weight of support we were meting out.'[20] And certainly German artillery fire on the vast, sprawling gift of a target of landing ships, warships and massed columns of landing craft was everywhere sporadic and ineffective. There was, however, a good reason for this, as the assault forces discovered later.

As the first landing craft neared the beaches, their crews could see the waves breaking against the German beach obstacles in fountains of white spume. Beyond lay the low shoreline of dunes overhung by thick palls of smoke and dust: a scene much resembling the Dunkirk beaches in 1940. But now the bombs and shells were British, and the Royal Navy was landing the British Army in France, not rescuing it.

In Gold sector, ten miles east of Omaha, the 50th (Northumbrian) Division landed by Force G (Commodore C. E. Douglas-Pennant flying his broad pendant in the HQ ship HMS *Bulolo*) quickly ran into trouble.[21] In the centre of the sector (Jig beach) amphibious tanks could not be launched to spearhead the assault because of the rough sea; instead they were put ashore directly from their landing craft (tank), but behind instead of ahead of the obstacle clearance parties. Ten other tanks were landed late, and in any event all but one were soon knocked out. The enemy's destruction of a shore radio-link made it impossible for the troops to call in the fire of the warships as arranged. The leading infantry therefore had to attack without fire support against a vigorous defence by units of the 915th and 736th Infantry Divisions, supported by accurate enfilade fire from shore batteries. Here as everywhere else the enemy had angled the embrasures of his concrete gun emplacements towards the beaches instead of out to sea.

This cardinal fact had not been revealed by interpretation of photo-reconnaissance pictures. It largely nullified the impact of the naval bombardment designed by the 'Neptune' fire-plan to destroy or suppress shore batteries firing out to sea. Against the blind seaward faces of thick concrete, naval gunfire could do little. As Ramsay was to remark in his report: 'One of the striking intelligence lessons of the operation was that no Staff is complete without the services of a photographic interpreter ... *At the last moment* [author's emphasis] the services of a Photographic Interpretation Officer were lent to A.N.C.X.F. and his work proved invaluable.'[22]

This was not the sum of the travails on Jig beach. The clearance parties found the tide higher than expected, and had to wait for it to fall before they could begin their work. In any case the 'Rommel's asparagus' along most of this sector was particularly formidable – no fewer than 2,500 of them along three and a half miles of shore, many fitted with fuzed mines or shells. By the time the tide rose again the clearance parties had only managed to open one gap. Reserve battalions of the 50th Division found getting ashore on Jig a hard and hazardous business; many craft were damaged.

Fortunately elsewhere along the Gold sector the landings started better. In the west (Item beach) flail tanks (equipped with rotating

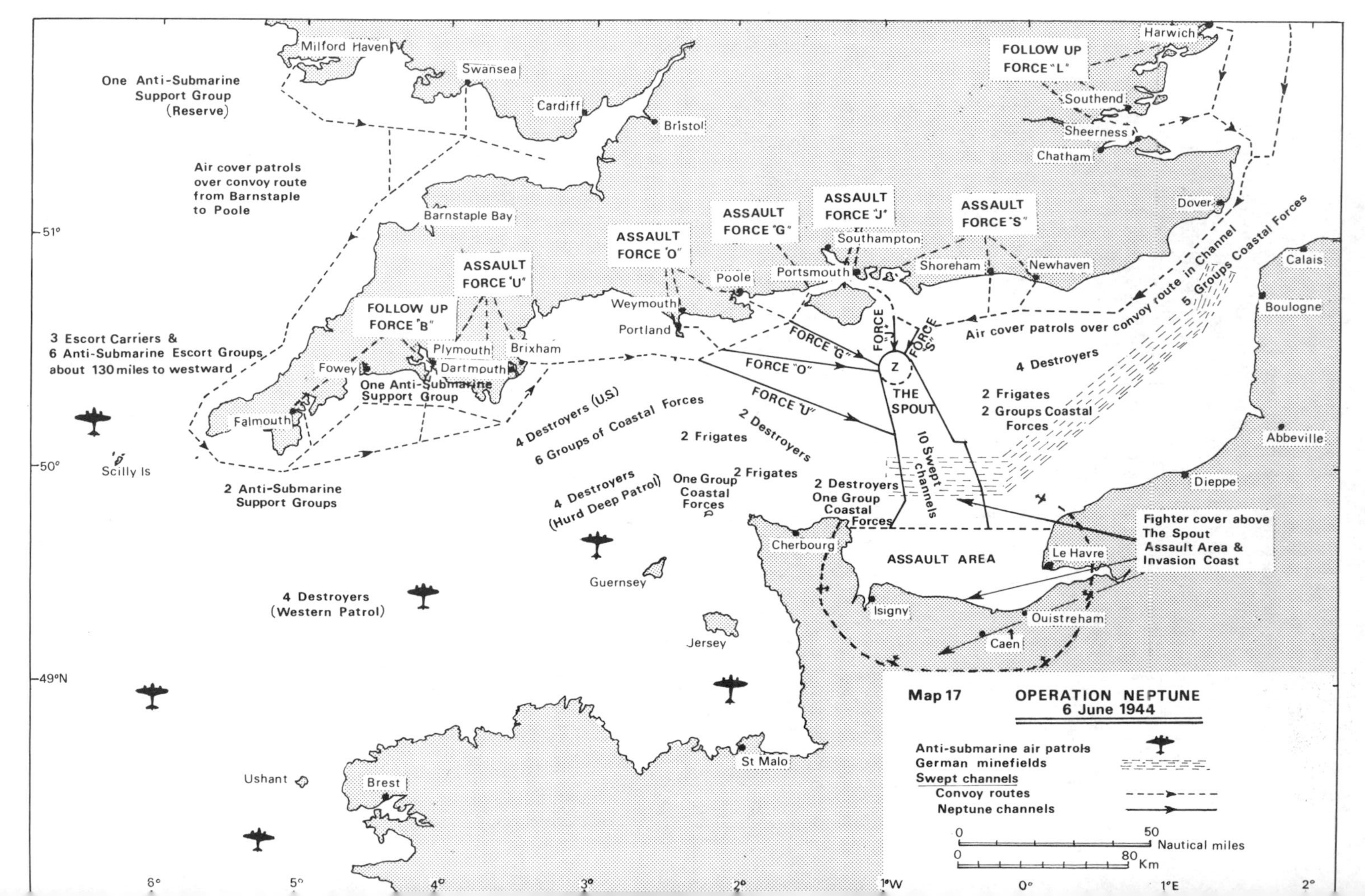
Map 17
OPERATION NEPTUNE
6 June 1944
Anti-submarine air patrols
German minefields
Swept channels
Convoy routes
Neptune channels
0
50
Nautical miles
0
80
Km
Milford Haven
Swansea
Cardiff
Bristol
Barnstaple Bay
Harwich
Southend
Sheerness
Chatham
Dover
FOLLOW UP FORCE "L"
One Anti-Submarine Support Group (Reserve)
Air cover patrols over convoy route from Barnstaple to Poole
ASSAULT FORCE "U"
ASSAULT FORCE "O"
ASSAULT FORCE "G"
ASSAULT FORCE "J"
ASSAULT FORCE "S"
FOLLOW UP FORCE "B"
Southampton
Portsmouth
Shoreham
Newhaven
Poole
Weymouth
Portland
Plymouth
Brixham
Fowey
Dartmouth
Falmouth
3 Escort Carriers & 6 Anti-Submarine Escort Groups about 130 miles to westward
One Anti-Submarine Support Group
Scilly Is
2 Anti-Submarine Support Groups
4 Destroyers (Western Patrol)
4 Destroyers (U.S.)
6 Groups of Coastal Forces
4 Destroyers (Hurd Deep Patrol)
2 Frigates
2 Destroyers
One Group Coastal Forces
2 Frigates
2 Destroyers
One Group Coastal Forces
FORCE "G"
FORCE "O"
FORCE "U"
FORCE "J"
FORCE "S"
Z
THE SPOUT
10 Swept channels
Air cover patrols over convoy route in Channel
5 Groups Coastal Forces
4 Destroyers
2 Frigates
2 Groups Coastal Forces
Calais
Boulogne
Abbeville
Dieppe
Fighter cover above The Spout Assault Area & Invasion Coast
Le Havre
ASSAULT AREA
Cherbourg
Isigny
Ouistreham
Caen
Guernsey
Jersey
St Malo
Brest
Ushant
51°
50°
49°N
6°
5°
4°
3°
2°
1°W
0°
1°E
2°

chains to explode mines or demolish obstacles) and armoured bulldozers landed punctually and began to smash gaps through the obstacles for the first assault wave. But a second wave landing further westwards later had trouble getting through intact obstacles. By the time No. 47 Marine Commando tried to get ashore on this same beach the obstacles had been submerged again by the returning tide. The Commandos lost three out of five landing craft together with vital radio kit. Meanwhile on Gold's eastern beach (King), flail tanks together with successful work by obstacle clearance parties and naval gunfire called in by Forward Observers Bombardment all enabled the 50th Division's 69th Brigade to land without problems and fight their way inland, albeit against some tenacious resistance. By early afternoon the Division's two reserve brigades had also landed. By midnight on D-Day its lodgement extended westwards to include Arromanches, future site of Mulberry 'B', and inland to within a mile of Bayeux, which it had however failed to take as required by Montgomery's master plan.

On Juno beach in the centre of the British front (lying between La Rivière and St Aubin-sur-Mer) Force J (Commodore G. N. Oliver, flying his broad pendant in the HQ ship HMS *Hilary*) and the 3rd Canadian Division faced the additional barrier of an off-shore reef, exposed at low tide.[23] The only gap, a mile wide, lay opposite the little harbour of Courseulles. In this gap the enemy had concentrated his strongest defences of the sector – beach obstacles, dense barbed-wire belts, minefields, houses strengthened as strong points, concrete gun emplacements commanding the harbour entrance. Partly in order to make sure that the tide had risen high enough to give the landing craft clearance over the reefs, it was decided to delay H-Hour on Juno by ten minutes. This, coupled with the delayed arrival of some landing craft (including those carrying flail tanks), meant that the rising tide had already begun to engulf the German beach obstacles by the time the assault forces reached the shore. Instead of being able to disembark forward of them and clear them 'dry shod' as planned, the assault forces found themselves landing among the obstacles. With skill and determination the crews of the smaller landing craft sought to weave their way through; the big landing craft (tank) simply bludgeoned ahead. All too soon the tide covered the obstacles altogether, so halting the work of the clearance parties. An officer of the Royal Canadian Naval Reserve describes how after two out of five landing craft under his command had been holed by mines attached to posts or by mortar bombs, and their complements of soldiers rescued . . .

> . . . Another explosion holed L.C.A. 1137 and stove in the starboard bow. All troops were cleared from the craft without casualties. All troops had been disembarked from L.C.A. 1138 and the craft was about to leave the beach when a wave lifted it on to an obstruction. The explosion which followed ripped the bottom out of the craft . . . the boat officer in the craft suffered several shrapnel wounds in his legs, a fracture of the right fibula and slight head injuries. All troops were discharged from L.C.A. 1151 without loss . . . I ordered the crews of the sunken craft to embark for return passage to the ship. By this time there was a cleared channel through the obstructions . . . but as we were leaving, an approaching L.C.T. forced us to alter course. An obstruction ripped out the bottom of L.C.A. 1151. The crews then transferred to an L.C.T. and were eventually brought back to the ship.[24]

This was the kind of operational reality against which no planning, however thorough, could provide. Ninety out of 306 landing craft employed by Force J that forenoon were lost or damaged. And except on one of the Juno beaches the amphibious tanks launched at sea failed to arrive on the shore before the infantry whose assault they were supposed to spearhead.

Once again the enemy reserved his fire for that moment of scrambling confusion after landing when the assault forces were at their most vulnerable. On all three Juno beaches it was only after hard fights that the assault forces eventually managed to escape from this killing ground by advancing inland. By the close of D-Day the 3rd Canadian Division and part of the 51st (Highland) Division, the Juno follow-up formation, held a lodgement up to six miles deep, extending from the left flank of 50th Division (Gold sector) through Villons les Buissons to the right flank of No. 48 Royal Marine Commando in Langrune-sur-Mer.

On Sword beach to the east of Juno, extending from Lion-sur-Mer to Ouistreham at the mouth of the Caen Canal inclusive, Force S (Rear-Admiral A. G. Talbot, flying his flag in the HQ ship HMS *Largs*) and the British 3rd Infantry Division confronted perhaps the most crucial task of all the 'Neptune' forces on D-Day.[25] According to Montgomery's military plan, the 3rd Division was to take the city of Caen, eight miles from the coast, and secure bridgeheads over the River Orne. Caen was needed as a bastion to secure the left flank of the entire Allied lodgement against German strategic reserves coming in from northern or central France. It was also needed as the launching point for a further British advance to occupy the good airfield country southwards towards Falaise. The 21st Panzer Division was somewhere in the Caen area, though its exact whereabouts were not known.

Montgomery therefore planned (as he hoped) an initial onslaught on the coast defences in overwhelming strength. All three brigades of the 3rd Division were to land in succession on a single Sword beach ('Queen') on a one-brigade front of barely more than two miles in width between Lion-sur-Mer and the little seaside resort of La Brèche (inclusive). Once a gap was blown in the German defence the 185th Infantry Brigade with an armoured regiment under command was to thrust swiftly into Caen.

Along this flat and duny shore and its coast road sprinkled with holiday villas Rommel had installed the 736th Infantry Division in the usual cunning defence system. Lion-sur-Mer and La Brèche had been transformed into formidable strong-points, their guns raking the beaches in between them. These beaches had been thickly planted with the standard obstacles, and their exits inland barred by a wilderness of mines, barbed wire, tank traps and machine-gunners and mortar crews in fox-holes. On the high ground of the Périers Ridge some three miles inland lay two powerful subterranean defence complexes which commanded the entire sweep of the coast from St Aubin round through Ouistreham to the Caen Canal north of Caen. And on Sword as on all the other 'Neptune' beaches on D-Day the state of wind and tide served greatly to enhance the effectiveness of 'Rommel's asparagus'.

Covered by the fire of the destroyers from as close inshore as possible, the 3rd Division's leading brigade, the 8th, began to land on time. Of 34 out of 40 amphibious tanks launched at sea all but two safely reached the beach; the remaining six landed from landing craft. However, German 88mm anti-tank guns which had held their fire during the run-in quickly knocked out ten tanks amid the surf. By this time the planned landing sequence had already gone astray, for the tanks had come ashore after instead of in advance of the infantry, the assault engineers and the clearance teams. The brisk west-north-west wind swept the tide in so fast that the clearance parties only had time to open one passage through the obstacles before these became submerged. On Queen beach as on others the landing craft therefore had to manoeuvre or butt their way ashore. That the 8th Brigade was nevertheless able to land and deploy was yet another tribute to the cool nerve, presence of mind and seamanlike skill under fire displayed by the crews of the landing craft, mostly Royal Marine or Royal Naval Volunteer Reserve.

But now came the task of breaking out of the fifteen-yard-wide strip of sand left between the rising sea and the coast defences – a strip swept by enfilade fire from La Brèche. Not until past 1000, after three hours of fighting, did this strongpoint fall. Meanwhile, just as Rommel intended, the beach obstacles and the defences barring the beach exits together choked the flow of assault troops, follow-up troops and stores into and out of the beach. To clear the exits under fire here proved a particularly hard job for the engineers, and for a whole hour the armoured regiment (the Staffordshire Yeomanry) that was supposed to lead the advance on Caen remained stuck fast on the shore. So tightly jammed were tanks, guns and transport in the ten-yard-wide strip now remaining between sea and dunes that it was hard to manoeuvre to reach the exits even when these had been eventually cleared. When at last inland beyond these exits the armour still found itself jammed nose to tail on the few available routes.[26]

By the mid-forenoon Montgomery's timetable had gone well astray, even though on the left of the 3rd Division front Ouistreham had been successfully cleared. On the right of Queen beach No. 41 Royal Marine Commando had failed to take Lion-sur-Mer; and at the end of the day a gap was still to remain between it and No. 48 Commando in Langrune (Juno beach). Much more serious, the main attack by 3rd Division, the centre, on Caen had been fatally compromised by the mishaps and confusions on the beach. Not until 1230 did 185th Brigade begin its southward advance – without the armour. Not until 1400 did the Brigade's leading elements approach the Périers Ridge and the powerful field fortification on it which barred the way to Caen. Not until around 1600 had it bypassed this position (which did not fall until 2000) and reached Biéville, four miles north of Caen. But by this time the 21st Panzer had arrived. The British advance sputtered out in a brisk action with German tanks. Caen was not to fall for another month.[27]

While the armies were everywhere struggling to get on and then off the beaches, the navies and tactical air forces had been putting down an immense weight of high-explosive on the defenders, whose reports were movingly eloquent about the distress thus caused them. Nonetheless, the evidence suggests that the effect of the naval fire support did not match its weight. Sometimes the communication links between spotting fighters and the ships broke down; sometimes lack of suitable observation posts for Forward Observers, Bombardment, or loss of FOBs in action equally left the guns without guidance. Then again, as the Naval Commander, Force J, pointed out in his report, 'the extremely fluid state of the battle . . . often left the HQ ship and bombarding ships in doubt as to the position of our own troops and with which [state] the general standard of communications between F.O.B.s and firing ships was not always able to compete'.[28]

The skill with which the Germans concealed their guns and hoaxed spotters with false flashes, coupled with the adroitness with which they switched positions, likewise lessened the effectiveness of naval gunfire.[29]

At the end of D-Day the Allied Expeditionary Force had won four firm but shallow and isolated footholds, the gap opposite 21st Panzer between the 50th Division on Juno and the 3rd Division on Sword being particularly vulnerable. This was far short of Montgomery's D-Day objective of a continuous lodgement from the east of the River Orne to the River Vire up to ten miles deep and including Caen and Bayeux, with a second lodgement north of the Vire reaching half way across the Cotentin Peninsula. However, despite the hazards and hard fighting of the day Allied casualties proved remarkably light. The British airborne and seaborne forces suffered about 3,300 killed, wounded and missing; the Canadians about 1,000; the Americans some 6,000.[30] The Royal Navy alone had had 258 landing craft sunk or damaged by the combination of rough seas and German obstacles.[31]

On balance therefore D-Day had proved a solid success when it might well have resulted in the total disaster imagined by General Eisenhower when he drafted on 5 June for use in such a contingency a communiqué announcing that the invasion had failed and that he had withdrawn the Allied forces.[32] As Admiral Sir Bertram Ramsay, Naval Commander, Allied Expeditionary Force, justly summed it up in his official report, 'the outstanding fact was that, despite the unfavourable weather, in every main essential the plan was carried out as written'.[33]

But all still turned on whether the two navies – above all, the Royal Navy – could enable the armies to build up their strength fast enough to repel the German panzer counter-strokes that must surely come.

The follow-up forces 'B' (American) and 'L' (British: 7th Armoured Division for the Caen sector) arrived as planned on the second tide of D-Day and safely disembarked. Nonetheless the muddle and wreckage on the beaches and the hindering effects of wind and rough seas meant that the whole process of landing stores and equipment was, as Ramsay glumly noted, '24 hours adrift'.[34] While the armies were fighting their way inland the naval beach parties and their military equivalents had already begun working valiantly to sort out the mess. The army beach groups set about clearing wreckage and organising the beaches into base areas complete with stores dumps, field dressing stations and all-weather roadways. The naval beach parties swung into their role of managing the flow of landing craft to and from the

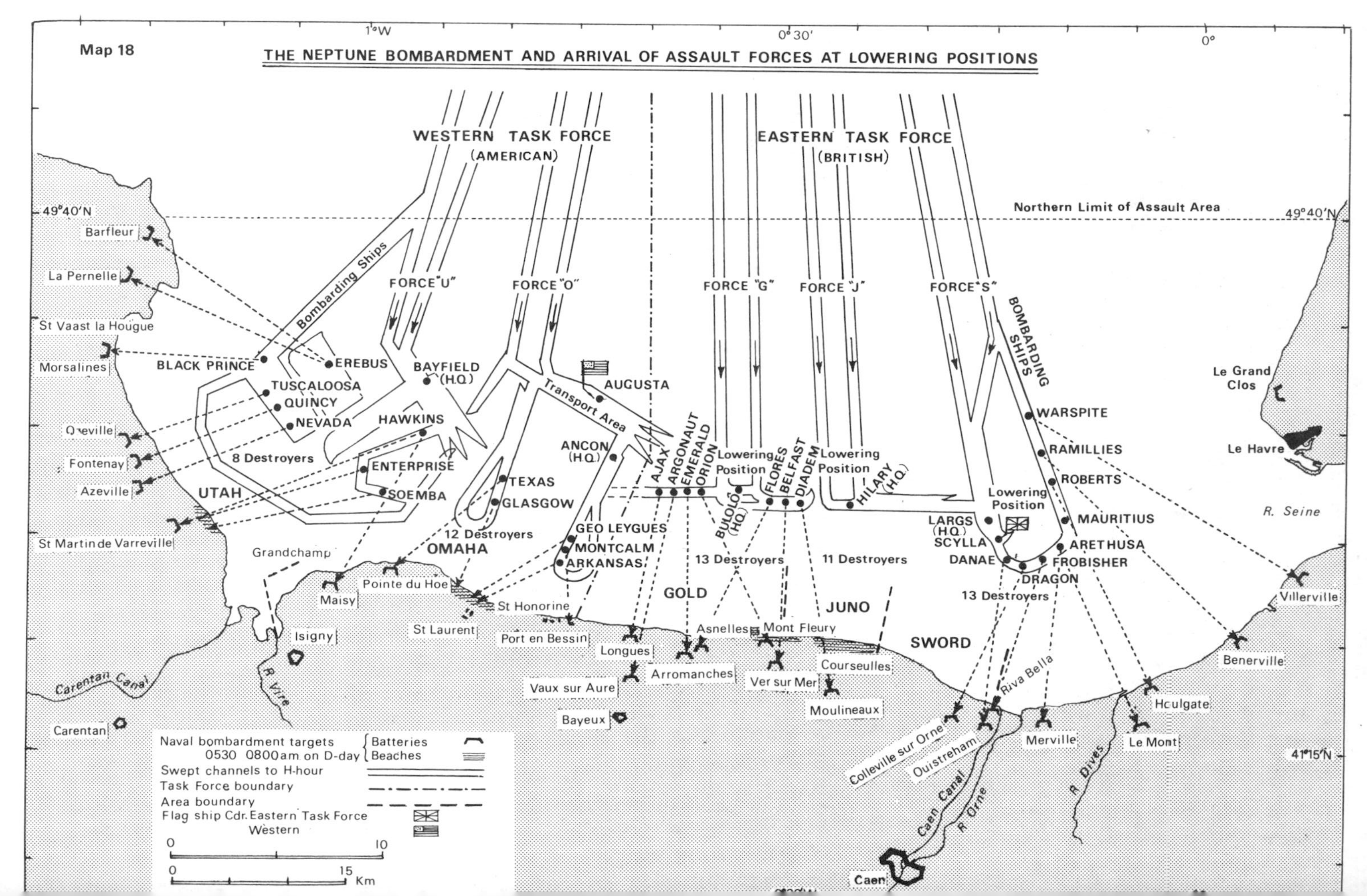

Map 18
THE NEPTUNE BOMBARDMENT AND ARRIVAL OF ASSAULT FORCES AT LOWERING POSITIONS
1°W
0°30'
0°
49°40'N
41°15'N
Northern Limit of Assault Area
WESTERN TASK FORCE
(AMERICAN)
EASTERN TASK FORCE
(BRITISH)
FORCE "U"
FORCE "O"
FORCE "G"
FORCE "J"
FORCE "S"
Bombarding Ships
BOMBARDING SHIPS
Transport Area
Lowering Position
BLACK PRINCE
EREBUS
TUSCALOOSA
QUINCY
NEVADA
BAYFIELD (H.Q.)
HAWKINS
ENTERPRISE
SOEMBA
8 Destroyers
AUGUSTA
ANCON (H.Q.)
TEXAS
GLASGOW
12 Destroyers
GEO LEYGUES
MONTCALM
ARKANSAS
AJAX
ARGONAUT
EMERALD
ORION
BULOLO (H.Q.)
FLORES
BELFAST
DIADEM
HILARY (H.Q.)
13 Destroyers
11 Destroyers
WARSPITE
RAMILLIES
ROBERTS
MAURITIUS
ARETHUSA
FROBISHER
DRAGON
DANAE
SCYLLA
LARGS (H.Q.)
13 Destroyers
UTAH
OMAHA
GOLD
JUNO
SWORD
Barfleur
La Pernelle
St Vaast la Hougue
Morsalines
Q.eville
Fontenay
Azeville
St Martin de Varreville
Grandchamp
Maisy
Pointe du Hoe
St Laurent
St Honorine
Port en Bessin
Isigny
R. Vire
Carentan Canal
Carentan
Longues
Arromanches
Vaux sur Aure
Bayeux
Asnelles
Mont Fleury
Ver sur Mer
Courseulles
Moulineaux
Riva Bella
Colleville sur Orne
Ouistreham
Caen Canal
R. Orne
Caen
Merville
R. Dives
Le Mont
Houlgate
Benerville
Villerville
R. Seine
Le Havre
Le Grand Clos
Naval bombardment targets 0530 0800am on D-day
Batteries
Beaches
Swept channels to H-hour
Task Force boundary
Area boundary
Flag ship Cdr. Eastern Task Force
Western
0
10
0
15
Km

beaches, so that the follow-up and build-up forces and the huge tonnages of stores and equipment could move smoothly into the lodgements. For this purpose Forces S, J and G each deployed a beach party of four officers, six petty officers and 67 ratings, as well as a signals unit numbering thirty.[35] Despite all the congestion, despite the steep waves breaking along the shore, the Royal Navy and the Merchant Marine landed over 75,000 soldiers, over 6,000 vehicles (including nearly 1,000 tanks) and over 4,000 tons of stores in the British sector during D-Day.[36]

In the course of the day Admiral Vian, NCETF, had visited each of the British beaches to assess the problems for himself. His flagship HMS *Scylla* had added her ten 5.25-inch guns to the bombardment of the German defenders of Sword and Gold. That evening he held a meeting of his three force commanders in *Scylla* off Juno beach to coordinate measures to defend the mass of shipping and landing craft against German E-boat or U-boat attack or enemy mining during the night and the nights to follow. Minesweepers were to be anchored at half-mile intervals in a cordon parallel to the shore and some six miles from it. Inshore of this cordon a patrol line of MTBs and destroyers was to be deployed. On the eastern flank the cordon was to be brought shorewards into shallow water just beyond the River Orne by landing craft (support) anchored two hundred yards apart, the so-called 'Trout Line'. Vian's flagship would be anchored on this flank as extra support. Out to sea the approach channels from 'The Spout' were to be patrolled by more destroyers and MTBs. Close defence of the offshore anchorages would be the responsibility of each force commander. The United States Navy, for its part, preferred to do without such a fixed cordon of ships in the Western Task Force area and rely instead entirely on roving patrols.

In the forenoon of 7 June Admiral Ramsay (flying his flag in the minelayer HMS *Apollo*) and General Eisenhower crossed the Channel to monitor the state of the battle for themselves. They had spent D-Day itself in that nerve-twisting limbo of impotence peculiar to high commanders when they have launched their forces into action and can do nothing more but wait for news. When at 1145 on the 7th HMS *Apollo* anchored off Omaha beach Ramsay was dismayed by 'the scene of great confusion' that met his eye:

> The blockships had just arrived & were hanging about awaiting someone to tell them what to do. L.S.T.s & ships & craft of all sizes anchored anywhere. No L.S.T.s unloading, the beaches littered with stranded craft and no traffic going on between beach & ships. *Augusta* was anchored 1½

> miles from shore & other bombarding ships firing. But a complete absence of activity prevailed. Kirk & Bradley came over & discussed the situation & did nothing to relieve my anxiety. Situation a little better than yesterday but bridgehead still very shallow . . .[37]

A huge backlog of ships and craft built up in the next three days off Omaha, partly because of the bottleneck on the beaches caused by wreckage, but partly also because of the arthritically bureaucratic nature of the joint US Navy and Army arrangements for handling the inflow of supplies and reinforcements.[38] Finally Ramsay with Scots commonsense ordered that such pedantic adherence to set procedures for establishing priorities for unloading should be abandoned. He told the responsible American naval officer instead to 'empty the ships and the priorities will take care of themselves'.[39] So it proved: within 36 hours the backlog had cleared, and Omaha was on its way to becoming the busiest of all the 'Neptune' beaches.

After his discouraging visit to Omaha in the forenoon of 7 June Ramsay was glad to find Commodore Douglas-Pennant (Force G) off Gold beach 'in excellent form' and reporting that 'everything was fine' except for a lag of about twelve hours in landing vehicles and stores because of the weather. In a letter next day to his wife Ramsay wrote that Douglas-Pennant 'cheered me up a lot'.[40] But Vian, whom Ramsay met along with Commodore Oliver (Force J) off Juno beach, 'was looking tired & was a bit querulous, but that is hardly surprising in view of the fact that he is only just recovering from Quinzy [sic] & had been up 2 days & nights under considerable strain. Oliver was in good shape & his beach going well, after trouble owing to the weather . . .'[41] Ramsay was further reassured when Montgomery came aboard *Apollo* to give 'a quite cheerful description of the land battle'.[42] No less heartening to Ramsay was the spectacle from his flagship of the Allied (but overwhelmingly British) seapower in the Channel that was now sustaining and strengthening the Expeditionary Force's lodgements. 'The sea between here & there,' he wrote to his wife, 'was packed with returning craft who'd emptied their loads on the beach, craft who were going over . . .'[43]

Among this traffic were the first convoys of the strangest floating objects ever to go to sea – the unwieldy steel Bombardons and huge 'Phoenix' concrete caissons slowly wallowing across under tow to form the breakwaters of the Mulberry harbours. Next day the components of the 'Whale' piers and pierheads joined the procession. On 9 June, when the work of surveying the Mulberry sites was well under way, the first 'Phoenixes' were sunk in place. This proved no simple task.

After their flooding valves had been opened the 'Phoenixes' took at least half an hour to settle on the seabed. During that time their thousands of tons had to be held in place by tugs against the pull of a 2½ knot tidal stream and the push of the wind on their towering sides. Next day the 'Gooseberry' breakwaters were completed by the scuttling of the last of the 'Corncob' blockships by means of explosive charges. The 'Gooseberries' immediately provided very welcome shelter for the unloading of vessels on the beaches.[44]

According to Ramsay's 'Operation Neptune – Naval Orders' no small vessel was to 'dry out' (i.e., become beached with the fall of tide) for fear of breaking their backs. But so serious had become the backlog of landing craft (tank) and coasters waiting off shore for their turn to be discharged that on 7 June Ramsay instructed that they should all be beached. Left high and dry for unloading straight on to the sand as the tide receded, they were floated off again on the next tide. Soon the discharging of vessels and their return to England for fresh cargoes settled into a smooth and accelerating rhythm thanks to the efforts of the inter-service beach organisations. In his report as ANCXF Admiral Ramsay was to pay them high tribute:

> . . . What they achieved was really remarkable. It has been said that on the stores side alone the tonnages handled daily into France were over one-third of the normal import capacity of the United Kingdom. On an average day during the first week the following number of ships and craft arrived off the assault area:–
> 25 'Liberty' ships
> 38 coasters
> 40 L.S.T.
> 75 L.C.T.
> 9 Personnel Ships
> 20 L.C.I. (L)
> The identification, unloading, marshalling and sailing of such a volume of shipping off an open coast was a gigantic problem, which was rendered more difficult by the adverse weather . . .[45]

During the first six days of 'Operation Neptune' 326,547 men, 54,186 vehicles and 104,428 tons of stores were brought across the Channel and unloaded over the beaches.[46]

The Luftwaffe and the German Navy failed to hinder, let alone interrupt this traffic, either in these first critical days of the invasion or the weeks that followed. Their most effective means of nuisance lay in the new 'oyster' mine, which was detonated by the changes in water pressure caused by the passing of a vessel and therefore virtually impossible to sweep. On the night of 6–7 June German light craft laid a mixture of oyster and conventional mines in the western and eastern fringes of the Bay of the Seine, and from 9 June onwards the Luftwaffe too began laying mines, flying in fast and low at night. In the particularly exposed Utah sector Admiral Moon lost four destroyers and two minesweepers during the first ten days of 'Neptune' and another 25 vessels and craft damaged. Later in the month it was the Royal Navy's turn to suffer from the Luftwaffe's nightly sowing of oyster mines. Between 22 and 29 June five warships and four other vessels went down and another seven were damaged. Most of them were small ships, but Admiral Vian's own flagship HMS *Scylla* struck a mine on the 23rd, putting both engine rooms out of action. *Scylla* had to be towed back to Portsmouth, Vian transferring his flag to the HQ ship HMS *Hilary*. The minesweepers (the great majority of them from the Royal Navy) did valiant work in all weathers sweeping conventional mines, their total bag off the invasion coast in the three months after D-Day amounting to one-tenth of all the mines swept in all theatres from the beginning of the war to 6 June 1944.[47] But for the time being there was no answer to the oyster mines except to slow ships' speed to the point where the change in water pressure was too small to detonate them.

In the first week of the invasion German E-boats for their part managed to sink only three small ships, two landing ships (tank) and six smaller craft out of all that mass of shipping lying off the beaches or in transit across the Channel. Two E-boats succumbed to British mines off Barfleur in the same period, and a third was sunk by Royal Navy surface ships. Every E-boat sortie had to brave the hazard of attack by Coastal Command Beaufighters and Wellingtons; and on 13 June Beaufighters of Nos. 143 and 236 Squadrons sank three and one R-boat (motor minesweeper) off Le Touquet. At Admiral Ramsay's request Bomber Command took a hand on 14 June, sending in 325 Lancasters just before dusk to attack a mass of light craft revealed by air reconnaissance to have been concentrated in Le Havre. The 12,000-lb 'Tallboy' bombs smashed through the concrete roofs of the E-boat pens (much less thick than those of the U-boat pens) and sank thirteen boats and damaged three others. Three torpedo boats and about 40 other craft were also destroyed in the harbour. The German naval command judged this to have been 'a catastrophe', and reckoned that as a result 'the naval situation in the Seine Bay had completely altered'.[48]

On the night of 8–9 June eight ships of the 10th Destroyer Flotilla (Captain B. Jones, RN) had smashed a sortie by four ships of the

German 8th Destroyer Flotilla (Captain Baron von Bechstolsheim) west of Cherbourg. Exactly forewarned as to the enemy's course, speed and intentions by Ultra decrypts of Enigma signals,[49] Ramsay deployed the 10th Flotilla to intercept him. At 0115 radar contact was made, and ten minutes later Captain Jones's ships opened fire. There ensued a ferocious high-speed action in the dark lasting several hours. HMCS *Haida* and *Huron* chased two German destroyers westwards until they escaped in the dark, one of them so badly damaged as to be out of action for weeks. Jones's own ship HMS *Tartar* was hit by four shells round the bridge, starting a fire and bringing down the trellis foremast and radar gear. According to Captain Jones's report of proceedings, 'the conditions of fire, noise, smoke and casualties were distracting but the enemy was soon silenced'.[50] While the *Ashanti* was standing by the burning *Tartar*, whose damage looked worse than it was, the *Ashanti*'s 'Y' (radio-intercept) operator heard a German destroyer announce that he was steering 140 degrees towards the burning ship. Heading out on a reciprocal course the *Ashanti* fired four torpedoes as the two ships passed. Two of them hit home, blowing off the enemy's bow and stern. The German destroyer subsequently blew up with a 'spectacular explosion'.[51] The enemy flotilla leader was now intercepted by the two Canadian destroyers returning from their chase to the westward. Hunted down by Allied ships (the Polish destroyer *Blyskawica* was there too) and engaged ever more closely, the enemy was finally driven ashore in a flaming wreck.[52] Thus ended the attempt by the last German destroyers serviceable in Group West to attack 'Neptune' shipping.

The U-boats fared little better than the E-boats and destroyers, not least because their patrol areas and orders were throughout largely revealed to the Admiralty by Ultra.[53] In any event the density of Coastal Command patrols and surface escort groups in the western English Channel gave the U-boats little chance. It was only in the small hours of D-Day that U-boat Command ordered its anti-invasion groups in Biscay and Norway to sea – about a week too late for them to be in a position to attack the 'Neptune' armada on passage. Of nine 'Schnorchel' boats ordered out of Brest and La Pallice that morning just one finally reached her station (on 15 June) off the Isle of Wight, but even she only sank a landing craft (tank) before abandoning her mission in the face of repeated attacks by Coastal Command aircraft, and returning to Brest. On the same day, however, a 'Schnorchel' boat from Norway sank the frigate HMS *Mourne* off Land's End. Of the other eight 'Schnorchel' boats from Biscay ports, one was sunk on 10 June and two others forced to return to harbour because of damage; a fourth had to be put back because of technical defects; two more (one of them with flat batteries) entered St Peter Port, Guernsey, thereafter to return to Brest as well; and although the U-764 torpedoed the destroyer HMS *Blackwood* (who later sank while in tow), she was herself so badly damaged by the avenging counter-attack that she like her sisters made for home.[54] Of seven non-'Schnorchel' U-Boats ordered on D-Day to patrol between Start Point in Devon and the Scillies four were sunk (two of them by Coastal Command) and the remaining three forced back because of damage. The disheartened Admiral Kranke, Flag Officer, Group West, now ordered all remaining eighteen non-'Schnorchel' boats at present deployed on a patrol line in the Bay of Biscay to return to base.

In the whole of June as many as 25 U-boats were sunk in all seas, twelve of them in the Channel or the Bay of Biscay:[55] a masterful demonstration of the teamwork of Coastal Command and the Royal Navy at the zenith of its wartime evolution. Apart from the *Mourne* and the *Blackwood* and one landing craft (tank), the only success which U-boat Command could set against this gruesome writing-down of its strength were four Liberty ships torpedoed in convoy off Selsey Bill on 29 June, and even one of these successfully limped into port.[56] It was a pitiful performance for a weapons-system and a service which had come so near to winning both world wars; the last limp punch of a beaten prizefighter whose legs were already buckling.

The flow of Allied build-up formation and all their matériel into the lodgements continued to gather momentum. After ten days the strength of the Expeditionary Force had swelled to thirteen infantry divisions, three airborne and three armoured, plus abundant artillery.[57] By this time the German Army had already lost the reinforcement race, and with it all hope of driving the Allies into the sea. This was by no means only because of the failure of the German Navy and Luftwaffe to impede, let alone halt, cross-Channel traffic, or because of the Allied air forces' destruction of the French transport network. In the first critical twelve hours of the invasion the reaction of the German Army in the West itself had been paralysed because of divided command responsibilities and unresolved disputes over strategy. Rommel (C-in-C, Army Group B) wanted to post all the panzer divisions close to the coast in order to 'Dunkirk' the Allied assault forces on the beaches while they were in greatest disarray. Field-Marshal von Rundstedt (C-in-C, West) instead had urged the classic strategy of holding the armour well inland for a grand counter-stroke once the Allies had revealed their axis of advance – a strategy which in Rommel's view took no note of the power of the Allied air forces to paralyse movement. The outcome of the debate, thanks to Corporal Hitler's decision, had been a disastrous compromise. Three panzer divisions were allotted to Rommel; four others to a central reserve under Hitler's direct control. Neither Rundstedt nor Rommel enjoyed authority to commit a panzer division to battle.

In the event it was nearly 1600 on D-Day before Hitler ordered two of Rommel's panzer divisions to move up to the invasion area. Only 21st Panzer was on the spot to attack the precarious Allied lodgements. Although it cleaved its way to the coast between Juno and Sword beaches and prevented Montgomery from taking Caen, it lacked the weight to drive the British and Canadians into the sea. By the time the two panzer divisions ordered up by Hitler arrived, the German opportunity had passed. By 10 June the Allies had expanded their four beach-heads into a continuous and solidly-held lodgement from beyond the River Orne westwards to the eastern coastline of the Cotentin Peninsula. Rundstedt's war diary dolefully recorded that 'the Seventh Army [on the invasion front] is everywhere on the defensive'.[58]

In this defensive against limited Allied attacks aimed at deepening the lodgement area, the 7th Army suffered much from the broadsides of British and American battleships and cruisers (including two French cruisers) as well as the constant onslaught of the Allied tactical air forces. HMS *Ramillies* and *Warspite* carried out daily shoots with their 15-inch guns; *Rodney* and *Nelson* with their 16-inch. With corps and divisional headquarters calling down the fire on German positions and troop concentrations on their front, and aircraft monitoring the fall of shot, the salvoes from the battleships' great guns plunged accurately down with crushing moral and material effect. On 30 June German armour lying some seventeen miles south of Gold beach was astonished and disconcerted by the delivery of several tons of 16-inch high-explosive shell from the *Rodney*. In the American sector the USS *Nevada*, *Arkansas* and *Texas* were performing similar services for the US 1st Army with their 12- and 14-inch main armaments. On 11 June Rommel glumly reported to the Führer that 'the effects of heavy naval bombardment are so powerful that an operation either with infantry or armoured formations is impossible in an area commanded by this rapid fire artillery'.[59]

On 17 June troops of the American 1st Army reached the west coast of the Cotentin Peninsula, so isolating the great port of Cherbourg, which the Allies urgently needed to supplement supply across open beaches and through the two Mulberries, which were now almost complete. Two days later that existing method of supply, on which the continuance of the campaign absolutely depended, was attacked by an immeasurably more terrible destructive force than U-boats or E-boats or mines:

> All Sunday, 18th June, the barometer held steady, the sea was flat, the sun shone, and the beaches had a holiday look; they were black with men and vehicles, and the masts of the landing-craft and bigger ships were like little copses growing up off shore as far as the eye could see . . .
>
> Towards evening the barometer – how anxiously we watch that barometer – began to betray a faint tremor. It wasn't much. It wasn't anything to worry about, we told ourselves, and we went to bed.
>
> But by 0300 on Monday morning it began to blow. We didn't get our usual dawn visit by the snooping F.W.s nor hear the Spits and the Marauders streaming over; for the cloud was down to 500 feet, the balloons were faint grey shadows overhead, and the wind was whipping up white horses on the pewter-coloured sea.
>
> It blew all the morning and all the afternoon; but the sky seemed brighter in the north, and we told ourselves: 'It can't last. A gale can't possibly last long, in June.'
>
> By now it was indeed a gale . . . Force 8, and stronger in the gusts. It came from the north, with a touch of east in it, and that was the worst direction, for it piled up the seas on our north-facing beaches and created the very condition which is the mariner's ancient peril and ancient dread: a lee shore, on which even great ships can meet their doom, and small ones are smashed to matchwood.
>
> Most of ours were small ones, and they stood offshore, head to wind, riding it out. There must have been hundreds in peril there . . .
>
> The full flood of our supplies had dried up to a trickle . . . Here and there, when the tide served, the wonderful little DUKWS, manned by R.A.S.C. [Royal Army Service Corps] men, wallowed like hippopotami between the coasters and the shore. They carried ammunition mostly . . . a priority.
>
> In places, from time to time, a few landing-craft beached. Some broke their backs. It is terrible to watch a craft broached-to and to see the surf savage it, crunch it like a dog with a bone . . .[60]

The huge seas ripped the Bombardons from their anchorages and smashed them against the breakwaters of the Mulberry harbours; rolled and pounded 'Phoenix' caissons to pieces, especially where sunk in deep water as in the American Mulberry off St Laurent; broke up the nearly completed 'Whale' pierheads and piers and flung the segments against the ships and landing craft along the shore. Only the 'Gooseberry' shelters composed of 'Corncob' blockships stood firm against the violence and power of the waves. The American Mulberry suffered worse because the blockships had been planted from the outer ends of the breakwaters, so leaving a wide unprotected gap in the middle. It was here that the gigantic seas rampaged over the 'Phoenix' caissons and scoured under their bottoms, heaving them about as if they were mere bricks.

> On Tuesday, when it blew just as hard as ever, somebody said: 'I reckon this'll be the second most famous gale to the Armada . . .'
>
> It had blown now for forty hours; some of the ships out to sea began to get into trouble. They dragged their anchors, or their anchors carried away . . .
>
> A destroyer hit a mine, and with her engines, steering-gear, and anchors out of action, hove ashore . . . And at dusk a big coaster, attended by frantic tugs, bore down on us, and we got a frantic signal from another ship: '*If* the vessel on your port bow is 269, she contains 3,000 tons of ammunition!' The tugs held her, held on to her all night like terriers, and she was saved.
>
> Wednesday was the third day. Perhaps the wind was slightly less fierce; but in some ways Wednesday was the worst day, for we were all tired, the situation ashore was obviously more critical . . . And we began to get a terrible lot of flotsam and jetsam on our beaches: upturned boats, which are always a disquieting sight, lorries, a 25-pounder gun, motor bicycles, rhino ferries – and dead men.
>
> . . . But on Wednesday evening the clouds lifted a bit and the shriek of the wind in the shrouds was less of a shriek than a long-drawn sigh. We heard a murmur in the sky that grew to a great roar and watched the Dakotas going over to bring supplies and carry back the wounded . . . And then suddenly – it was as if we saw it for the first time – the sun shone.[61]

In the three days before the gale a daily average of 34,712 men, 5,894 vehicles and 24,974 tons of stores had been landed through the Mulberry harbours and the beaches. From 19 to 22 June the daily totals dropped to 9,847 men, 2,426 vehicles and 7,350 tons of stores.[62] The build-up of the British 2nd Army alone fell three divisions behind schedule, and Montgomery was compelled to postpone his next push near Caen, due on 22 June. With the Americans now sweeping up the Cotentin Peninsula towards Cherbourg, a strong fortress as well as a port, it was desperately urgent to sort out the aftermath of the storm and get the flow of supplies back to full spate. On 23 June Ramsay went over to Normandy to put his personal weight behind this work. Although he found the damage to the British Mulberry 'not too bad', he was dismayed by the evident exhaustion of all the men on the spot: '. . . there were many craft inactive for one reason or another & a general air of floppiness prevalent. However, Harold

[Hickling, Captain, RN, whom Ramsay had just appointed as replacement Naval Officer In Charge of the Arromanches Mulberry] will soon put that right.'[63] When Ramsay later inspected the Omaha beach and the American Mulberry with Admiral Kirk, the sight struck him as 'frightful, with so many craft ashore. Much worse than Gold beach. As for the Mulberry gooseberry [sic] it was in a frightful state . . .'[64]

Back again in England Ramsay immediately concerted emergency measures with the Cs-in-C, naval home commands. Teams of skilled men were mobilised and rushed to Normandy to help in clearing the beaches and making good damage. Extra repair ships were despatched. The existing salvage organisation was strengthened. The scene of destruction and exhaustion gave way to one of energetic effort. Stranded vessels and craft were swiftly repaired and refloated, even those left high and dry far up the shore by the storm. At the same time the inter-service beach organisations, well aware that the armies were running critically short of ammunition and other supplies, made prodigious and successful efforts to restore the unloading cycle by using every available ship and craft and (thanks to the now favourable weather) every available stretch of shore. In the first week after the gale the daily average numbers of vehicles landed was actually higher than in the week before the gale; the tonnage of stores as much as a

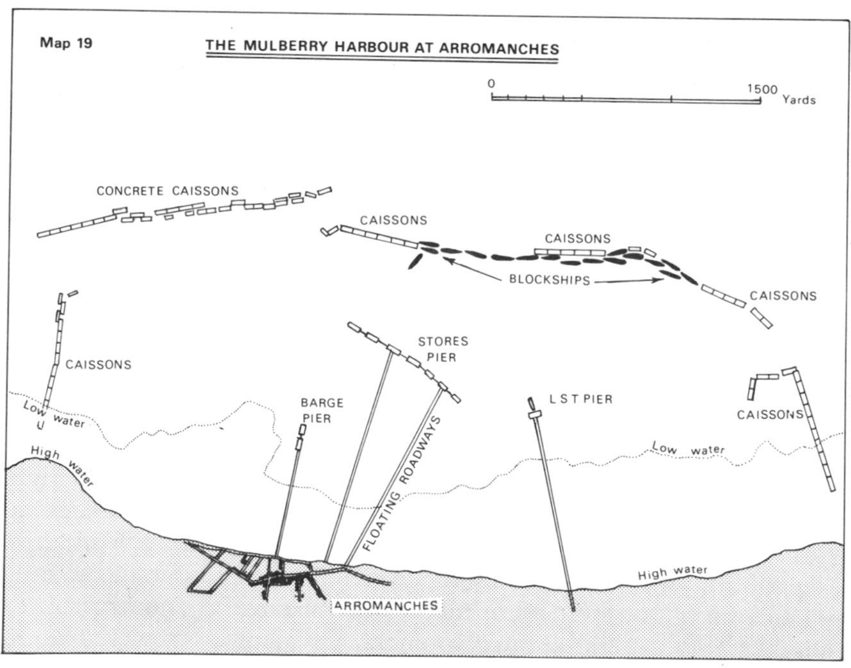

third higher.[65] In the same week (on 26 June) Force Pluto brought the first of the 'Tombola' ship-to-shore pipelines into action at Port en Bessin. Thus was swiftly overcome a crisis that could have endangered the whole campaign.

On the advice of ANCXF and the American admirals Eisenhower decided that no attempt should be made to repair the wrecked Mulberry harbour at Omaha, and instead all spare components used to make good the relatively light damage to the British Mulberry and strengthen it against the winter weather. Henceforward the Americans would largely rely on pontoon piers extending off open beaches – with astonishing success, as it was to prove. On 29 June the first cargoes were discharged on to the main stores pier of the British Mulberry. When on 19 July the landing ship (tank) pier came into operation, it marked the completion of the project at long last. On that day a total of 7,000 tons of stores, the figure originally planned for the Mulberry, was unloaded. Ten days later the daily total of stores landed in the Mulberry reached a record 11,000 tons, together with nearly 4,000 men and over 400 vehicles.[66]

On 24 June Admiral Ramsay formally wound up 'Neptune' as an operation distinct from 'Overlord'. Since D-Day the Allied navies and the Merchant Marine had landed 714,000 men, 111,571 vehicles and 259,724 tons of stores.[67] When he had had the time to reflect, Ramsay was to record in his pocket diary a private 'Thought on Neptune': 'Because it all went so smoothly it may seem to some people that it was all easy & plain sailing. Nothing could be more wrong. It was excellent planning & execution . . .'[68]

Rear-Admiral J. W. Rivett-Carnac, Flag Officer, British Assault Area, hoisted his flag in a shore headquarters at Courseulles in succession to the three British assault force commanders, who returned to England during the next week. In the same period Admiral J. W. Wilkes of the United States Navy similarly took over from Rear Admirals Moon and Hall in the American assault area. The NCETF, Vice-Admiral Sir Philip Vian, returned to England on 30 June; Admiral Kirk, NCWTF, on 3 July. Two days later the millionth Allied soldier stepped ashore in France; apt and timely enough testimony to 'Neptune's' success.

The winding-up of 'Operation Neptune' signified the tremendous fact that the Western Front had now been firmly re-established – four years almost to the day after its collapse because of the French Army's capitulation. On this new Western Front was being fought a bloody struggle of attrition amid the high hedgerows of the *bocage*; a struggle in which for the time being both sides remained evenly balanced. Yet it was vital for the Allies that this should not bog down in long-term stalemate, as Hitler and his generals now hoped. Instead the limited German resources must first be ground away by attrition until only a fragile defensive crust remained, whereupon the Allied Expeditionary Force must (as envisaged in Montgomery's master plan) break out into open country and destroy the enemy in a great offensive. But this whole process depended on a continuing copious flow of tanks, guns, trucks, stores, fuel and reinforcements into the Normandy lodgement, to say nothing of all the elaborate base facilities needed by modern armies.

For the Western Allies, therefore, seapower remained as ever the midwife of victory on land.

27

Victory in Europe

On 26 July the German garrison commander of Cherbourg surrendered after troops of the American 1st Army had fought their way into the city. A bombardment of two coastal batteries the day before by two groups of ships under the command of Rear Admirals M. L. Deyo and C. F. Bryant of the US Navy had served to repeat yet again the ancient lesson first learnt by the Royal Navy at the siege of Havana in 1762 that naval gunfire is not particularly effective against casemated cannon ashore. The battery at Querqueville remained in action despite the attempts to silence it by a battleship (the 14-inch USS *Nevada*), four heavy cruisers (the USS *Tuscaloosa*, flying the flag of Rear Admiral Deyo, and *Quincy*, and HMS *Glasgow* and *Enterprise*) and six destroyers.[1] A second bombarding group consisting of the battleships USS *Texas* (flying the flag of Rear Admiral Bryant) and *Arkansas* and four American destroyers took on the 11-inch guns of 'Battery Hamburg'. After *Texas* had fired 206 14-inch rounds, *Arkansas* 58 12-inch and the destroyers a total of 552 5-inch, three out of the four enemy guns were still firing back.[2] Fortunately the German batteries proved equally ineffective, often straddling the Allied warships but inflicting only two hits, both on HMS *Glasgow* and neither serious.

Minesweeping and port-clearance parties immediately moved into the docks at Cherbourg to begin their work according to the procedure laid down in Ramsay's 'Operation Neptune – Naval Orders'. The overall clearance operation was directed by Commodore W. A. Sullivan, USN, who the year before had cleared the port of Naples. The bulk of the minesweepers being British, responsibility for minesweeping was given to Commander J. R. G. Temple, RN. Sullivan and

Temple faced a colossal task, as Ramsay saw for himself when he visited Cherbourg on 6 July:

> The damage is unbelievable, the place lending itself readily to demolition owing to peculiar construction of the Keys [sic]. Dry dock basins undamaged but blocked by sunken ships & craft. It will take anything up to three months to clear these wrecks, but meantime temporary measures such as landing stores in Duck & L.C.T.s & barges can be started. Later on coasters & later M/T ships . . .[3]

By 16 July over a hundred mines had been swept for the loss of three minesweepers and seven other smaller craft. Not least of the hazards thoughtfully left behind by the Germans were all manner of underwater explosive devices. These were tackled by British 'P' parties – young volunteer divers practised in the art of finding such devices in muddy waters and disarming them by finger-tip feel. Over a six-week period they explored the entire bottom of the Cherbourg docks. It therefore stands greatly to the credit of the clearance and minesweeping parties that by the beginning of August 8,500 tons of stores were being discharged in Cherbourg every day. A month later that figure would have doubled.[4]

The capture of Cherbourg opened the way for Force Pluto to begin in mid-August laying the cross-Channel oil pipeline from the Isle of Wight ('Bambi'). However, the project encountered one technical or operational setback after another and as a result no oil was pumped through until 22 September. On 3 October both types of pipe, the HAMEL and the HAIS, failed. By the beginning of November 'Bambi' had been virtually abandoned, the Minister of Fuel and Power, Gwilym Lloyd George, reporting to the Prime Minister:

> Of the four pipe-lines eventually laid from the Isle of Wight to Cherbourg, two proved defective, and the other two broke when the pumping pressure was increased from 'reduced' to 'working'. A decision was consequently made to abandon this project at least for the time being.[5]

The 'Tombola' ship-to-shore system proved the more dependable, as the British Army had always believed it would, and the quiet village of Port en Bessin became a major oil terminal.

With the occupation of the Cotentin Peninsula the Allies possessed the depth of lodgement they needed in order to build up their armies for the breakout. All the while Montgomery proceeded remorselessly with his 1917-style attrition battle with the British 2nd Army and the 1st Canadian Army (formed on 23 July). His frontal offensives forced the enemy to commit his panzer divisions piecemeal to holding the line, whereupon they were crunched up by massed air and artillery bombardment.

The German Navy could do little to help its comrades in field-grey during this mincing process amid the hedgerows of the *bocage* – only nuisance attacks against the 'Trout Line' guarding the eastern flank of Allied shipping lying off the beaches. During July no fewer than ten night-time clashes took place between frigates and MTBs of the Royal Navy and enemy E-boats, which had been reinforced to a total of twenty. New but largely ineffective marvels of German technology took to the sea – the 'Marder' 2.5-knot electrically-propelled human torpedo with a range of 35 miles; the 'Linse' radio-controlled, explosive-packed motor boat; the 'Dackel' long-range circling torpedo.[6] The total bag of these devices in July and August amounted to the destroyer HMS *Quorn*, three minesweepers, two transports, one trawler and two landing craft sunk, and the Polish-manned cruiser *Dragon*, the old cruiser HMS *Frobisher*, the repair ship *Albatross* and a minesweeper damaged. Their own losses at the hands of the Royal Navy and Royal Air Force Coastal Command came to 96 '*Marders*' out of 147 despatched on sorties, and 30 out of 60 '*Linses*'.[7]

The U-boats fared no better in their own renewed attempts to interfere with Allied cross-Channel traffic, losing seven boats to the Royal Navy and two to Coastal Command in the Channel and the Bay of Biscay between 1 July and 4 August but sinking in return only two ships.[8]

Since neither the German Navy nor the Luftwaffe (reduced to hit-and-run raids and minelaying) could choke back the flow of Allied military power into Normandy, it continued to fall to the German 7th Army and 5th Panzer Army to hold it back in battle as best they could. But by the fourth week of July they had no more reserves in hand either to patch the front or mount counter-attacks. When this was reported to Hitler along with the warning that the front must soon collapse, Hitler gave his customary absurd order to stand fast rather than retire in good time. By now six panzer divisions were deployed along the 1st Canadian Army and the British 2nd Army front; only two facing the American 1st Army. The time had come for Montgomery to launch the breakout which he had so patiently and cunningly prepared. On 25 July the American 1st Army struck south in 'Operation Cobra' against an enemy defence demoralised or obliterated by over 4,700 tons of bombs dropped by nearly 1,900 aircraft, burst through during the next two days, and poured south-westwards and then westwards into Brittany.

This sweeping American advance now had an unfortunate by-product: it revived the Prime Minister's slumbering opportunism. Hitherto he had interfered little in the strategic and tactical design of 'Neptune'/'Overlord', except to favour the sailors with advice about the high efficacy of naval gunfire against shore targets. Rather as Chairman of the 'Overlord' Preparations Committee he had constructively put his energies to serving Eisenhower's needs. Now on 4 August he proposed to Roosevelt that 'Anvil' (now renamed 'Dragoon'), the landing on the Côte d'Azur scheduled for 15 August, should after all be abandoned; this time in order to free warships and assault shipping for improvised landings at St Nazaire and other ports along the southern coast of Brittany (the Prime Minister in his memoirs however gives Bordeaux as his chosen objective).[9] Here was the gambler of the Dardanelles and Norway, of Dakar and the Aegean Islands, come to life again to vex the Allied leadership in the very climax – ironically enough – of the most carefully, most thoroughly planned and prepared combined operation ever. On 5 August Churchill convened a meeting with Eisenhower, Cunningham, Ramsay (who was 'thoroughly aggrieved & annoyed' at being hauled back from a much-needed leave),[10] and Bedell Smith, Eisenhower's Chief of Staff. The Prime Minister employed all his relentless powers of persuasion and pressure, especially on the Supreme Allied Commander, to induce them to back his proposal. 'We argued for 2½ hours,' wrote Ramsay in his diary, 'with Ike holding firm & the P.M. doing all he could to move him. I supported Ike strongly which didn't please the P.M. C.N.S. [Cunningham] supported P.M. We left off with nothing done.'[11] To his wife Ramsay reported that night that he could well have remained at home in Scotland

> . . . had it not occurred to the P.M. to think of one of his hot schemes & wanted to discuss it. Well we've discussed it and I believe killed it & so now we are no further on. When this kind of thing happens I wish we had a P.M. who left the Forces to run the war. At other times I appreciate the value of the P.M. boosting things . . .[12]

On 9 August Churchill had finally to bow before the adamant refusals of Eisenhower, the US Joint Chiefs and even Roosevelt himself to abandon 'Dragoon'; evidence of how diminished was his sway as a war-lord compared with former years.[13]

The Americans had been continuing to race on. By 6 August they had completely cut off the Brittany peninsula. On the 10th Nantes on the Loire fell, and the German troops isolated in Brittany fell back into the fortress-ports like Brest. Eisenhower now ordered the American forces to swing eastwards and then northwards to meet the British and Canadians driving down southwards, so cutting off the German armies in Normandy altogether. Hitler played into his hands by ordering his troops to launch a counter-offensive towards the west coast of the Cotentin Peninsula, with the unrealistic objective of severing the American communications. This only thrust the German head deeper into the Allied trap. By 12 August the 7th Army and 5th Panzer Army were struggling to escape as the trap closed at Falaise; a marvellous target for the Allied air forces. On 22 August the Falaise pocket was squeezed flat. The Battle of Normandy was over; the wreckage of the German defenders was retreating pell-mell towards the Low Countries and the Fatherland.

Since the Royal and United States Navies put the Allied expeditionary force ashore on D-Day, the enemy had lost 400,000 men killed, wounded and missing; 1,300 tanks; 20,000 vehicles; 500 assault guns; and 1,500 field guns. The equivalent of five panzer divisions and twenty infantry divisions had been destroyed, and the equivalent of six other panzer divisions and twelve infantry divisions badly mauled.[14] This was complete victory; victory on a scale that dwarfed the Allied successes in the Mediterranean theatre; victory on the shortest route to the enemy heartland; the first victory won by Western democracies over a great German army since 1918; victory which abundantly, triumphantly, fulfilled the object of 'Operation Neptune' as defined back in April by Admiral Ramsay on page one of his 'Naval Orders' in the soberest of staff language: '. . . to carry out an operation from the United Kingdom to secure a lodgement on the Continent from which further offensive operations can be developed . . .'

And still the unsung service of the Royal and United States Navies and the Merchant Marine continued to make it all possible. By the end of August they had landed in France the stupendous totals of 2,052,000 men, 438,461 vehicles and 3,098,259 tons of stores.[15] Yet now that its main mission was accomplished, the 'Neptune' fleet had begun to disperse. The three American battleships and HMS *Ramillies*, together with the cruisers USS *Augusta*, *Quincy* and *Tuscaloosa* had sailed to the Mediterranean along with much assault shipping to take part in the 'Dragoon' landings in the South of France on 15 August. Mounted and launched according to the well-established patterns of Mediterranean long-distance amphibious operations, 'Dragoon' encountered only light opposition. On 28 August French troops occupied Marseille, while American troops pushed on up the Rhône valley to join (on 15 September) the eastern flank of Eisenhower's armies in Alsace. This same month, with the German E-boats in the Channel now a spent force, the Admiralty withdrew from Ramsay some fifty flotilla vessels for employment as escorts to the North Russian convoys (see above, pp. 747–8), or sent as reinforcements to the Eastern Fleet.

In any case the Allied armies by their advance along the Channel coast had repaid their debt to the navies by shifting the front line for skirmishing with E-boats and other small craft from the Bay of Biscay and the English Channel to the southern North Sea. On 16 August Dönitz ordered the U-boats based on the now isolated Biscay ports to make for Norway, so finally liquidating the priceless strategic asset of direct access to the Atlantic which he had exploited to the very verge of victory in 1940–43. The vast U-boat pens lay empty now under their indestructible carapaces of concrete, at one with Roman walls and Crusader castles; prodigies of military engineering to be marvelled at by future ages. The slinking away to Norway of the Biscay boats was successfully covered by a diversionary offensive in the Channel by eight U-boats, which sank six merchantmen, the Canadian corvette *Regina*, a minesweeper and a landing craft (infantry). Nonetheless the month of August 1944 signalled yet another massacre of U-boats at the hands of the Royal Navy and Coastal Command, twelve being destroyed in the Bay of Biscay and another four in the Channel.[16]

At the beginning of September it seemed for a heady moment as though the Allied armies' pursuit could roll straight on into the heart of Germany. Eisenhower wanted this pursuit to be conducted by both his army groups – Montgomery's 21st and General Omar Bradley's 12th. Montgomery argued instead for a single concentrated thrust north of the Ardennes by his own Army Group (augmented by American divisions) aimed at the Ruhr industrial area. But the acrimonious debate turned entirely on the question of logistics. The Allied lines of communication to their United Kingdom base still ran through the Normandy beaches and the British Mulberry harbour, although Cherbourg was beginning to be of some help. On 13 September 1944, after consulting Admiral Ramsay, Montgomery and Bradley, Eisenhower issued a directive for the next stage of the campaign in which he sombrely stated:

> Our port position is such that a stretch of a week or ten days of bad weather in the Channel – a condition that is growing increasingly probable as the summer recedes – would paralyse our activities and so make the

> maintenance of our forces exceedingly difficult, even in defensive roles . . . without improved communications speedy and prolonged advance by our forces, adequate in strength and depending on bulk oil, ammunition and transport, is not a feasible operation . . .[17]

In his judgment therefore '. . . the object we must now attain, one which has been foreseen as essential from the very inception of the OVERLORD plan, is the gaining of deep water ports to support major forces in an invasion of Germany'. And above all this meant ports north of the Seine, in order to shorten overstretched land communications. Thus final victory on the Western Front – the march of Anglo-American armies to meet the Red Army in the heart of the Reich – depended just as much as 'Overlord' on solving a basic problem of a Continental campaign reliant on sea-communications: that of adequate port capacity. Hitler and the German high command understood this perfectly. This was why the German garrisons now isolated in strongly fortified ports along the French Atlantic and Channel coasts had been ordered to hold out to the last; this was why, as the Allies had already discovered to their dismay in Cherbourg, ingeniously comprehensive schemes of sabotage and mining had been prepared against the day when resistance must cease.

The Channel ferry ports, Boulogne, Calais, Dunkirk and Ostend, had all been invested by Canadian troops between 6 and 8 September, but of them only Ostend fell without delay. Boulogne held out until 22 September; Calais until 1 October; Dunkirk until the end of the war. At Boulogne Royal Navy port-clearance parties found 26 sunken ships blocking the harbour entrance; it was not until mid-October that a channel had been opened and the wrecked cranes and cratered quays sufficiently cleared to permit five coasters to berth.[18] In Ostend the clearance parties found the basins and harbour entrance fouled by fourteen sunken ships, many of the quays totally demolished, and others partly so. It was a tribute to the efforts of the clearance parties that the first coasters crept their way in to Ostend on 25 September, and that by the end of the month 1,000 tons of stores were being unloaded each day. Yet it took until mid-November completely to clear and widen a channel into the harbour; until the end of November for daily discharges to rise to 5,000 tons.[19] No quick solution in the Channel ports, then, to Eisenhower's acute supply crisis at the beginning of September.

Of the three great deep-water ports along the Channel and North Sea coasts of France and Belgium, Le Havre was the first to fall, on 12 September, to the 50th and 51st British Infantry Divisions after the Royal Air Force had stunned and demoralised the defenders by dropping 9,500 tons of bombs in the previous seven days, and HMS *Warspite* (patched up again after being mined in July in the Thames) and the monitor HMS *Erebus* had helped things along with 15-inch shells. Royal Navy port-clearance parties immediately moved into the port to begin their work, but the enemy had carried out his blocking, booby-trapping and demolition with such thoroughness that Le Havre was not to be fully operational until mid-October.[20] On 19 September Brest, in the west of Brittany, surrendered after a bitterly fought siege of 40 days which cost the American 3rd Army more than 10,000 men killed and wounded.[21] Here a culminating bombardment by massed artillery supplemented by that ubiquitous and ever-useful old warrior, HMS *Warspite*, did the trick. In the original 'Overlord' planning high hopes had been entertained of Brest as a supply port, but in the event the prize went to the German demolition parties. So colossal was the problem presented by all the sunken blockships and the lavish sowing of oyster pressure mines that no attempt to clear Brest was made until 1945.[22]

In all the circumstances it was therefore extraordinarily fortunate that Antwerp fell to the British 11th Armoured Division on 4 September. Here was the ideal deep-water port, located conveniently close in the rear of Montgomery's 21st Army Group. There was however a snag. It lay 80 miles up the Scheldt from the North Sea, and the Germans held bridgeheads on the south bank of the river as well as the Dutch islands of South Beveland and Walcheren to the north. As Admiral Ramsay wrote in his diary, 'Antwerp is useless until the Scheldt Estuary is cleared of the enemy.'[23]

On the day before Antwerp fell Ramsay therefore signalled SHAEF 'For Action', with copies to 21st Army Group, the Admiralty and the C-in-C Nore, to warn:

> It is essential that if Antwerp and Rotterdam [the latter in fact not to fall until the end of the war] are to be opened quickly enemy must be prevented from
> (i) Carrying out demolitions and blocking in ports
> (ii) Mining and blocking Scheldt . . .
>
> 2. Both Antwerp and Rotterdam are highly vulnerable to mining and blocking. If enemy succeeds in these operations the time it will take to open ports cannot be estimated.
> 3. It will be necessary for coastal batteries to be captured before approach channels to the river routes can be established.[24]

Eisenhower himself immediately hauled in this warning. When next day he signalled Montgomery to turn down the Field-Marshal's strategy of concentrating on the Ruhr and insist instead on his own 'broad front' step-by-step offensive, he remarked: 'While we are advancing we will be opening the ports of Havre and Antwerp, which are essential to sustain a powerful thrust into Germany . . .'[25] Moreover the Supreme Commander was repeatedly to allude to the importance of opening Antwerp during the ensuing debate with Montgomery over future strategy.[26] In a key strategic directive of 13 September after conferences with Montgomery, Bradley and Admiral Ramsay, he specifically instructed that while the Allied armies advanced into Germany, 'Northern Group Armies [i.e., Montgomery] must secure the approaches to Antwerp or Rotterdam quickly . . .'[27] Montgomery's own orders next day, defining the Allied objective as the Ruhr, certainly did observe that 'on the way to it we want the ports of Antwerp and Rotterdam . . .', but they placed the clearance of Antwerp second to an offensive by the 2nd Army across the Maas and Lower Rhine.[28] The orders instructed the 1st Canadian Army first of all to capture Boulogne and Calais, and only then to direct 'its whole energies' towards 'operations designed to enable full use to be made of the port of Antwerp . . .'[29]

Neglecting therefore the overriding importance to the Allied campaign of first clearing the Scheldt, Montgomery chose instead to embark (with Eisenhower's acquiescence, be it said) on 'Operation Market Garden', the attempt to drive across the Maas and Lower Rhine at Arnhem by landing the American 82nd and British 1st Airborne Divisions to seize the bridges while powerful ground forces bludgeoned their way north to link up with them. Between 17 and 26 September this offensive failed of its purpose, the 1st Airborne Division being virtually destroyed, never to be reconstituted.

Meanwhile Antwerp remained closed; other captured ports were only slowly, if at all, becoming usable. The Allied supply position remained hideously precarious[30]– with a long winter campaign now in the offing. For by this time the professional competence and moral resilience of the German Army had punctured the Allies' post-Normandy victory euphoria. From the first week in September onwards Allied spearheads along the whole front from the North Sea to Alsace stumbled up against the familiar screen of battlegroups. Headlong chase gave way to slow, small and painful advances in the autumn rains and mud. It became depressingly plain that the Allies now faced a long slog into 1945 – a winter campaign huge in its demands for replacements of men, weapons and equipment, for ammunition, motor and aviation fuel and stores of every kind. Yet Allied communications by land and sea were already stretched humming taut, with all parts by no means bearing an even strain.

In this new and unwelcome situation, the Allies' entire continental strategy once more turned on ships and on ports where they could unload. In particular the clearing of the Scheldt had now acquired a desperate urgency. On 5 October Admiral Ramsay, who had been becoming more and more worried in the course of the previous month about the failure to tackle this, attended a meeting at Supreme Allied Headquarters (now at Versailles, with a forward command post at Rheims) held to discuss future policy. Present were Eisenhower, Sir Alan Brooke, Tedder, Leigh-Mallory, Montgomery, Bradley and General J. L. Devers (commanding the newly constituted US 6th Army Group). According to Ramsay's diary for that day

> Monty made the startling announcement that we could take the Ruhr without Antwerp. This afforded me the cue I needed to lambast him for not having made the capture of Antwerp the immediate objective at highest priority, & I let fly with all my guns at the faulty strategy we had allowed. Our large forces were now practically grounded for lack of supply, & had we now got Antwerp and not the [Arnhem] corridor we should be in a far better position for launching the knock-out blow . . . I got approving looks from Tedder & Bedell Smith, and both of these, together with CIGS, told me after the meeting that I had spoken their thoughts & that it was high time someone expressed them . . .[31]

Three days later came fresh trouble on the supply front: the Channel gales struck again at the Normandy beaches and the Mulberry harbour, and even caused damage to the harbour of Cherbourg. Ramsay was therefore the more relieved to understand that Montgomery's plan for 21st Army Group

> . . . has been modified to give greater priority to Canadian army at expense of 2nd army, so as to concentrate on capture of entrances to Antwerp & of confluences of Rotterdam & the Dutch Islands. I feel sure that this is due to my address at the recent C-in-Cs meeting & the intervention of C.I.G.S. who backed my remarks & told me he intended to speak to Monty. I regard this as a major achievement. The administrative position of the armies is undoubtedly bad & Ike & SHAEF are properly fussed – as they should be.[32]

Ramsay congratulated himself too soon: Montgomery's fresh orders next day still placed the clearing of the Scheldt third in priority among tasks for his Army Group.[33] An infuriated Eisenhower signalled

Montgomery that the reduction in the flow of supplies through the Mulberry and Cherbourg because of the gale 're-emphasises the supreme importance of Antwerp':

> . . . I must repeat that we are now squarely up against the situation which has been anticipated for months and our intake into the Continent will not repeat not support our battle. Unless we have Antwerp producing by the middle of November our entire operations will come to a standstill. I must emphasise that, of all our operations on our entire front from Switzerland to the Channel, I consider Antwerp of first importance . . .[34]

Despite this and a later broadside from the Supreme Commander it was not until 16 October that Montgomery at last unequivocally ordered:

> 1. The free use of the port of Antwerp is vital to the Allied cause, and we must be able to use the port soon.
> 2. Operations destined to open the port will therefore be given complete priority over all other offensive operations in 21 Army Group, without any qualification whatsoever . . .[35]

Thus did the commander of the 21st Army Group finally acknowledge the crucial importance of seaborne supply up the Scheldt and through Antwerp – six weeks late.[36]

Meanwhile, with the main offensive to clear the Scheldt still yet to begin, Eisenhower himself was more than ever glad that he had insisted on 'Operation Dragoon' against all pressure, and now enjoyed the use of Marseille and Toulon, by this time together handling some 13,000 tons of stores a day.[37]

The Dutch islands of South Beveland and Walcheren which commanded the Scheldt from the north were defended by the 70th ('stomach trouble') Infantry Division, all men with gastric disorders and requiring special rations – a mark of the German Army's dearth of manpower after three and a half years of gutting on the Russian Front.[38] Yet they were to fight with skill and determination. The coming campaign was to prove a tough struggle along muddy dykes and across wastes of water.

Admiral Ramsay and Lieutenant-General G. C. Simonds, commanding the 2nd Canadian Corps, jointly planned the campaign as a combination of frontal attacks overland along the dykes linking the islands to each other and to the mainland and landings from the Royal Navy's landing craft to turn the enemy's defences.[39] On 24–26 October 1944 a Canadian infantry brigade assaulted the South

Beveland isthmus, a hard fight. On the 26th the Royal Navy ferried units of the British 52nd Division across the eight-mile-wide estuary of the Scheldt in a little armada of amphibious craft to land on South Beveland's southern shore behind the defenders, opposite the Canadians. Nonetheless, it still took five days of water-logged combat to clear the enemy out of the island.

On 31 October was opened the attack on the neighbouring island of Walcheren; a place of ill-omen because a British expeditionary force had died there of malaria ('Walcheren fever') in 1807 during the Napoleonic Wars in a particularly futile exercise in maritime strategy. Once again Ramsay and Simonds coupled direct overland attack with a seaborne outflanking movement. Bomber Command having smashed breaches in the sea-dykes, Walcheren was now merely a rim of land flooded in the middle. On 31 October Canadian troops began fighting their way westwards along the narrow causeway from South Beveland to Walcheren; by 2 November they had secured a precarious bridgehead at the Walcheren end. The day before, and following heavy air and artillery attack on enemy batteries, the Royal Navy had landed an assault force at Flushing in the south of the island and another at Westkappelle in the extreme west. It took the Flushing assault force four days of battle, building by building, to clear the town and its docks.

Ramsay and Simonds had designed the Westkappelle landing as a miniature repetition of the assaults on D-Day. Firstly, a bombarding squadron consisting of HMS *Warspite* (in the last shoot of her distinguished service since Jutland) and the monitors *Erebus* and *Roberts* hammered the German coastal batteries with 15-inch salvoes; then massed artillery at Breskens on the south bank of the Scheldt joined in; and finally, as the assault waves headed for the shore, 27 landing craft armed with guns or rockets, together with rocket-firing Typhoon aircraft, smothered the enemy beach defences at close range with explosive. Despite the loss of twenty landing craft to enemy shells and the usual kind of snags and hold-ups on beaching under accurate artillery and machine-gun fire, the leading assault waves (Royal Marine and Inter-Allied Commandos) soon overran the shore batteries and secured beach-heads. Now began a step-by-step advance outwards from Westkappelle along the rim of dyke leading round the north and south of the island. But on 3 November Ramsay and the Royal Navy again exploited the mobility of seapower, this time by landing two British infantry brigades on the eastern shore of Walcheren in order to outflank the German defence penning the Canadians into their bridgehead at the end of the causeway from South Beveland. Five days later the commander of the 70th Division surrendered with his 2,000 remaining soldiers.

Both banks of the Scheldt were finally clear of German troops. But now came the formidable job of sweeping 80 miles of estuary and river. To accomplish it Ramsay deployed more than ten squadrons of minesweepers working from both ends under the command of Captain H. G. Hopper, RN (Captain Minesweeping, Sheerness). At the cost of one vessel sunk with all hands and after a total of 267 mines had been swept, Hopper's minesweepers completed their task on 26 October, a week under the estimate.[40] That day three coasters reached Antwerp. On 28 November the first convoy of nineteen Liberty ships came alongside the quays. Antwerp was at last open for business, no fewer than 60 days after Allied troops first captured it.[41]

By this time too Le Havre and the Channel ports had been cleared and opened, and the second Pluto pipeline ('Dumbo') successfully laid between Dungeness and Boulogne, pumping through 600 tons of petroleum a day by the beginning of December. By March 1945 (with eleven pipelines laid), a daily average of over 3,000 tons would be pumped through Dumbo.[42]

So the Allied Expeditionary Force's supply crisis passed. From November 1944 onwards through the winter and into the spring of 1945 seapower and sea-communications would feed the armies on the Western Front with all they needed, first to defeat the German counter-stroke in the Ardennes in December; then to chew their way forward to the Rhine in a new series of attrition battles; and finally to burst over the Rhine in April 1945 in the climactic offensive of the German war. In that month, 1,341,610 tons of stores were discharged through Antwerp (some two-thirds for the United States armies) and 288,809 tons of 'POL' (petrol, oil, lubricants); 91,505 tons of stores for 21st Army Group through Ostend, and 4,893 through Calais and Boulogne. Through Le Havre and Rouen for the American armies came 406,146 tons of stores and 144,721 tons of 'POL'; through Cherbourg and minor Normandy ports 228,585 tons of stores and 161,045 tons of 'POL'; and through Mediterranean French ports 484,631 tons of stores and 153,871 tons of 'POL'.[43] Such was the staggering arithmetic of the service rendered by seapower to victory in the decisive theatre of war.

Yet it is convincing proof of the cost-effectiveness in shipping of a Continental strategy based on short cross-Channel sea routes compared with long-distance 'blue water' strategy that the average deadweight tonnage of deep-sea cargo vessels required between the beginning of June and the end of December 1944 to support the

Western Front amounted to only about 17 per cent of that required in the summer of 1942 to supply the Middle East, Persian Gulf and India.[44] There is even more striking proof: whereas an average total of one million deadweight tons of shipping supported a maximum of 90 divisions on the Western Front, nearly *seven million* tons allotted to the Mediterranean theatre supported a maximum of only 27 divisions on the Italian front.[45]

Throughout the winter of 1944–45 and on into the spring the German Navy did its best to relieve the mounting pressure on the German Army on the Western Front by attacking the dense traffic of shipping from southern England to Antwerp and the Channel ports. From their Dutch bases the E-boats sneaked out on more than 350 sorties to lay mines or torpedo the unwary. 'Small Battle Units' – one- and two-man human torpedoes, 'Linse' remote-controlled explosive motor boats, the new 'Hecht' and 'Seehund' midget submarines – braved the hazards of the open sea and the watchful Allied patrols on the surface and in the air. But once again the E-boats and the 'Small Battle Units' proved no more than nuisance. From January 1945 to the end of the war they sank only 47 Allied ships totalling 108,213 tons, the bulk of these falling victim to E-boats.[46]

It was the U-boat that caused the Admiralty much greater concern, for new German technology and new patterns of deployment had largely mastered the Royal Navy's and Coastal Command's hitherto successful hunting devices and tactical methods.[47] Thanks to the 'Schnorchel' the U-boat had no longer to surface by day or night to recharge her batteries, so denying airborne 10cm radars a target. In any event U-boats were now fitted with metric band radar search receivers on their Schnorchel tubes which could give warning of 10cm radar signals if close enough. Because U-boat Command was now deploying its boats widely spread on individual missions, there was no need for the dense radio traffic necessary for controlling 'wolf-pack' operations, and in any case U-boats had little opportunity for radio-signalling now that they spent so much time submerged.

As a result of these developments neither Ultra nor HF/DF, key instruments of victory in the Battle of the Atlantic, were any longer of much use. And the U-boats' new favourite hunting ground lay in the inshore waters round the British Isles, rather than the high seas; here they could hide from sonar under the temperature layers created by tidal streams and river estuaries, or among the wrecks that strewed the bottom of these waters. The enemy had ushered in an entirely novel phase of submarine warfare, foreshadowing the techniques of the coming age of the nuclear submarine, and the Admiralty found itself baffled. As the First Sea Lord explained to the C-in-C, Mediterranean, on 1 September 1944:

> The submarines and the Oyster mines have been giving us considerable trouble. Curiously, we thought that if and when the submarines came into the Channel from the Atlantic, they would be easy to kill. Just the contrary was the case. Our escort groups had to learn a completely new technique as the submarines developed the habit of lying on the bottom and it was difficult to distinguish them from wrecks. However they have all cleared out now as they cannot work any longer from the Biscay ports . . . 44 essayed channel operations against the OVERLORD supply routes and of these 23, we think, have been sunk. They are now clustering round our coasts on the trade routes and will not be easy to deal with. They are so dispersed that it is actually taking a greater effort than when they went about in packs in the Atlantic.[48]

On 19 January 1945, when writing in much the same vein to the C-in-C, Home Fleet, the First Sea Lord gloomily added that the scientists 'have not yet caught up, and the air is 90 per cent out of the picture'[49] – meaning, that is, in terms of actual U-boat kills. In the meantime, and while new sonar techniques and hunting tactics were being evolved, the Royal Navy and Coastal Command could only attempt a blanket suppression of the U-boats by sheer numbers of ships and aircraft and density of patrolling, supplemented by extensive deep minefields in the Channel and Irish Sea. Western Approaches Command deployed 37 escort groups (fourteen of them from the Royal Canadian Navy), and the naval home commands a total of five destroyer flotillas, plus the Rosyth Escort Force – in all 426 destroyers, frigates, corvettes and sloops. By February 1945 no fewer than 528 aircraft out of Coastal Command's total strength of 793 were flying on anti-submarine duties.[50] This immense effort certainly succeeded in keeping shipping losses in British home waters down to fourteen merchantmen between September and December 1944, and in destroying in return 37 U-boats (including those sunk in the Arctic).[51] Yet this rate of destruction was lower in proportion to the total U-boat fleet than in 1940 and 1941.[52] At the beginning of 1945 the war of the U-boat therefore lay in stalemate, neither side being able to inflict decisive loss.

Yet Dönitz nonetheless cherished bright hopes of breaking this stalemate and unleashing a new and this time victorious U-boat offensive – not only in British home waters, but also in the Atlantic. Thanks to the resourcefulness of Albert Speer, Reichsminister for armaments, U-boat production had risen steeply through 1944 even in the face of Allied bombing. In January 1945 as many as thirty boats were commissioned; in March the U-boat arm reached its wartime peak of 459 boats.[53] Even worse from the British Admiralty's point of view, almost all the boats now being completed were the formidable new Type XXIs and Type XXIIIs, streamlined harbingers of the future. The 1,600-ton Type XXI could cruise as far as the Pacific without refuelling and reach a sprinting speed when deeply submerged of 16 to 17 knots on her electric motors; as fast as most Allied convoy escort vessels such as the British River class frigates or Castle class corvettes. Moreover, during a pursuit at this speed the noise caused by water rushing and bubbling along the pursuer's own hull would deafen his sonars. When dived to maximum depth under attack the Type XXI could cruise for nearly 300 miles at 6 knots on her electric motors, as against barely 100 miles and 2 knots by the VIIC U-boats of the Battle of the Atlantic. The anti-submarine forces' existing operational arithmetic of search and kill would thus be rendered null and void: whereas the area unit in searching for a traditional U-boat had been 31,400 square miles, it would be 282,000 square miles for the Type XXI.[54]

In sum, the Allied navies had no ready technical or operational answers to the Type XXI, about whose development and rate of production the Admiralty were kept depressingly well informed by Sigint and photo-reconnaissance.[55] On 18 December 1944 the Admiralty estimated that 95 Type XXIs were now under construction and 35 already completed.[56] A month later the First Sea Lord was warning the Chiefs of Staff that a new Battle of the Atlantic might be opened by the high-speed U-boats in February or March: '. . . the enemy may be able to maintain about 70, increasing to over 90, U-boats on patrol compared with about 60 during the height of the U-boat campaign in the Spring of 1943 . . .'[57] Given optimum morale in the U-boat crews and maximum numbers of U-boats on patrol, the First Sea Lord reckoned that 'merchant shipping losses of the order of 70 rising to 90 ships a month may possibly be expected compared with 60 a month during the spring of 1943 . . .' Such a scale of loss during the first half of 1945, he went on, 'may well prejudice the maintenance of our forces in Europe . . .'

From this second and potentially catastrophic Battle of the Atlantic, the Royal, Royal Canadian and United States Navies were in fact saved by the Allied armies on the Western Front and by the British and American heavy bomber forces – further repayment of their debt to seapower for making their own operations possible; a telling illustration of how sea, land and air operations can each promote the success of the others. For the advance of the Allied armies to the German frontier in the autumn of 1944 had served to push the German air-defence radars back from the Atlantic and the Channel coasts into the Reich itself, so giving the German fighters only very short warning of the approaching of bomber formations: a crippling handicap to an already enfeebled force. At the same time the ground stations for the bombers' navigational and target-finding devices such as H2S could be brought forward from southern England to the edge of German territory, so greatly extending the range at which accurate bombing was possible. The by-product of the Allied armies' conquests in 1944 was therefore a triumphant relaunching that autumn of the strategic air offensive against the German industrial machine; this time devastating in its accuracy against key targets such as petrol-from-coal plants, and only weakly resisted by the Luftwaffe.

Particularly effective was the so-called 'Transportation Plan', under which the Allied bomber forces progressively cut the German transport network – roads, rail, canals – to pieces, thus in the end paralysing industrial production. U-boat construction was especially vulnerable because it depended on shifting prefabricated hull sections up to 27 feet long and 25 feet high, weighing 150 tons, along the wide German canals to their points of assembly. In September 1944 Bomber Command blew the aqueduct on the Dortmund–Ems canal near Münster; in November it returned to blow it again after it had been painstakingly repaired. In November also the Command emptied the vital Mittelland canal, and emptied it again in January 1945. Neither canal carried any further traffic for the rest of the war. That month, Otto Merker, Speer's director of U-boat production, told him that ship-building had been 'especially hard hit by the various stoppages of canal navigation' and that they must switch to rail transportation;[58] an absurd suggestion in view of the current wrecking of the railways too. By March 1945 U-boat completions of all types had dropped to only ten.

As well as these industrial delays to production affecting the Type XXI and Type XXIII there were the inevitable technical teething troubles in newly completed U-boats to be overcome; crews to be trained in their operation. Dönitz sourly sums up the cumulative consequences for his hopes of a fresh Battle of the Atlantic: 'On account of the delays caused by the ever-increasing weight of the Allied air-raids on Germany, the first boats of the new Type XXIII were not commissioned until February, while the first Type XXI did not become operational until April 1945.'[59]

But by February Nazi Germany was already being fast squeezed to death between remorseless offensives by the Allied armies on the Western Front and the Red Army on the Eastern Front. By the end of the month the Anglo-Americans were nearing the Rhine along its entire length; the Russians were on the Oder barely sixty miles from Berlin. By April, when the first Type XXI U-boats became operational, the Western Allies were everywhere over the Rhine and racing forward against disintegrating resistance; on the 18th Field-Marshal Model and 325,000 soldiers cut off in the Ruhr surrendered. On the Eastern Front the Red Army smashed through the last German defence along the Oder and on the 25th completed the encirclement of Berlin. That same day American and Russian advanced guards linked up at Torgau on the Elbe, splitting what was left of the Reich into two. Thus did the armies in the most direct possible fashion put an end to Dönitz's hopes that his new U-boats might still win the war for Germany.

Yet his existing boats fought on. In April 1945 no fewer than 44 of them put to sea, including the first Type XXI (U-2511). The last weeks of the conflict saw as furious a struggle as ever between U-boats and Allied escorts and aircraft. The anti-submarine forces deployed their latest armoury – the British Squid mortar; the American aerial acoustic torpedo (codename 'Mark 24 Mine') which homed in on the sound of cavitation caused by a U-boat's propeller; the new 'retro-bomb' (a 36lb Hedgehog bomb fired *astern* by an aircraft over-flying at a height of 200 feet a submerged submarine located by the American 'Magnetic Anomaly Detector'); American 'Sono' buoys dropped into the water to transmit the sound of a U-boat by radio to patrolling aircraft. In the air, rocket-firing Typhoons of the 2nd Tactical Air Force based in Germany joined Coastal Command Mosquitoes and Beaufighters in attacking U-boats which rashly remained on the surface to fight it out with their anti-aircraft armament, and sank no fewer than 27 U-boats in the last five weeks of the war.[60] British and American heavy bombers accounted for another eighteen boats in their home bases.[61] Between 1 January and 8 May U-boat losses from all causes amounted to 151, of which 36 fell victim to the Royal Navy and/or the Fleet Air Arm, twelve to the United States Navy (mostly in the Atlantic or off the east coast of America), and three to the Royal Canadian Navy.[62] Yet in the same period this death-ride of the U-boats only achieved total sinkings of 46 merchant ships of 281,716 tons – an average of only 70,000 tons a month, barely a seventh of the 1942 average.[63]

On 30 April, while the surviving ships' companies of the German Navy were still steadfastly doing their duty, their Führer shot himself in his bunker next to the shattered Reichschancellery in a Berlin now virtually totally in the hands of the Red Army. In accordance with Hitler's political testament, Grand Admiral Dönitz now succeeded him as head of a Nazi state with just a week to run; an accolade from the Führer to the unwaveringly loyal commander who had so nearly won the war for him against the Western Allies.

At 1830 on 4 May a German delegation to Field-Marshal Montgomery's tactical headquarters sat at a trestle table in a tent pitched on Lüneburg Heath and signed an 'Instrument of Surrender', to take effect at 0800 on 5 May

> . . . of all German armed forces in Holland, in northwest Germany including the Friesian Islands and Heligoland and all the other islands, in Schleswig-Holstein, and in Denmark, to the C-in-C 21 Army Group. This to include all naval ships in these areas. These forces to lay down their arms and to surrender unconditionally.[64]

This was Britain's special moment of victory over Nazi Germany – a victory delivered in the end by armies, but armies which themselves had been delivered to the field of battle largely by the Royal Navy; a victory ultimately born of the Royal Navy's successful struggle to keep the sea-lanes to the British Isles open. Hence it was entirely apt that the German delegation should be led by the Commander-in-Chief of the German Navy, General-Admiral von Friedeburg; and that Montgomery should receive them beneath a Union Flag, also the flag flown at the main by an Admiral of the Fleet.

At 0241 on 7 May 1945 at Eisenhower's advanced headquarters in Rheims, General Alfred Jodl, Chief of Staff of the Armed Forces High Command (OKW), signed the unconditional surrender of all German forces by sea, land and air everywhere. At Russian insistence this surrender was formally ratified in Berlin next day, the German signatories this time being Field-Marshal Keitel, General Stumpf (C-in-C of the Luftwaffe), and once again General-Admiral von Friedeburg. Sadly, however, the British admiral who by his efficiency, common sense, tact and team spirit had done more than anyone except Eisenhower himself to enable 'Operation Neptune'/'Overlord' to succeed was not present at these ceremonies to witness the fulfilment of his endeavour. For Sir Bertram Ramsay had been tragically killed on 2 January 1945 when his aircraft crashed on take-off from a snow-covered airfield in France. He was replaced as ANCXF by Vice-Admiral Sir Edward Burrough.

At the end of this war there was no German fleet left to be conducted into a British base with studied drama by the Royal Navy. Of major surface ships, only the cruisers *Prinz Eugen* and *Nürnberg* surrendered intact, in Copenhagen. Bombing had destroyed the pocket battleships *Scheer* and *Lützow* in Kiel, the cruiser *Emden* in Swinemünde and *Köln* in Wilhelmshaven. The cruiser *Seydlitz* had been scuttled in Königsberg in East Prussia and the *Hipper* in Kiel. The Russians took over the wreck of the *Gneisenau* at Gotenhafen (Gdynia) and the uncompleted aircraft carrier *Graf Zeppelin* at Stettin. The badly damaged cruiser *Leipzig* fell into British hands in Denmark.

The humiliation of mass surrender was thus reserved for the U-boats, who were ordered by an Admiralty signal at noon on 8 May to surface, report their positions and sail to designated British ports. Two hundred and twenty-one boats chose to scuttle themselves in harbour or at sea rather than surrender, including 82 Type XXIs and twenty XXIIIs. This latter figure shows by what a narrow margin the final victory of the Allied armies had averted a major onslaught at sea to which British and American anti-submarine technology would have had no immediate answer. All four experimental Walter boats (hydrogen-peroxide fuelled) so far in commission were also scuttled.[65] In the course of the next month 150 U-boats, among them seventeen Type XXIIIs and one Type XXI, sailed under escort to British anchorages. Above their swastika flags blazed the White Ensign in token of the Royal Navy's victory in the hardest war of its four centuries of history.[66]

For the second time in 25 years and because of the follies of British policy in the 1920s and 1930s, the Royal Navy had had to fight the U-boat and a German fleet of formidable ships. It had had to do so while also contending – because of those same follies – with the Italian and Japanese Navies, and when irreparably weakened by pre-war disarmament. To wage war against such odds had cost the Navy in casualties nearly one tenth of its total wartime strength of some 800,000 men and women – 50,860 killed, 14,685 wounded and 7,401 taken prisoner.[67] The British Merchant Marine, staunch shipmate of the Royal Navy throughout the worst of the storm, the very sinew of Britain's survival and victory – it too had paid dearly, with 30,248 crewmen drowned or killed in action. Royal Air Force Coastal Command, the Royal Canadian Air Force and Allied maritime air forces had lost 1,515 aircraft by enemy action, and suffered 8,874 aircrew killed and another 2,601 wounded.[68]

So once more the Royal Navy (this time in partnership with the Royal Air Force) had 'kept England's wall that is the sea', and with it the cause of liberty. And for all the importance of technology and tactics, of staff work and strategy, the Royal Navy had prevailed because its officers and bluejackets, 'Hostilities Only' as much as RN, RNR and RNVR, were throughout animated by the spirit of Nelson's last order flying amid the gunsmoke of Trafalgar: 'Engage the enemy more closely.'

Now the German prong of the triple threat – the only one of the three that had directly menaced the independence of the United Kingdom – lay broken. But there still remained the third prong. Before a bankrupt Britain could concentrate on the enormous task of restoring her lost prosperity, there had to be finished off that other war, the war with Japan in defence of the British imperial legacy in the East.

28

To Restore an Empire

The strategic anatomy of the Japanese war stood in total contrast to that of the German war. Whereas Germany was a continental power which could only be decisively defeated on land, Japan was an island power much like Britain; and like Britain she depended on the sea communications to move and supply her far-off garrisons and expeditionary forces, to bring home raw materials and fuel on which her war industries depended. In this essentially maritime conflict, the *Schwerpunkt* or main thrustline of the Allied counter-offensive lay along the direct route westward across the Central Pacific from Pearl Harbor to the Philippines, and then north via the island of Okinawa to Japan itself. This thrustline, in which each stage was measured in thousands of miles of blue Pacific water, was the equivalent of the 'Neptune–Overlord' thrustline across the Channel to France and then overland into Germany. But unlike 'Neptune–Overlord', which were truly Allied operations under an integrated Anglo-American command, the Pacific was a purely American sphere, jealously guarded as such by Admiral Ernest King, COMINCH and Chief of Naval Operations, and waged by Admiral C. W. Nimitz's Pacific Fleet.

The American strategic counter-offensive began once Japan's own initial march of conquest had been halted by the United States Navy in the Battles of the Coral Sea on 4–8 May 1942 and Midway on 4–5 June. The Battle of the Coral Sea (south of the Solomon Islands) afforded the first example in naval history of a decisive naval action in which the main surface forces never sighted each other, and the outcome turned entirely on carrier strikes. Though both sides lost a carrier (the USS *Lexington* and the Japanese *Shoho*), the battle ended in a strategic defeat for the Japanese, for they abandoned their objective of landing an expedition on the south coast of New Guinea in order to consummate their occupation of the island.[1] The victory in the Coral Sea ended the direct threat to Australia and opened the way to the eventual clearing of New Guinea by Australian and American troops. It served as the necessary prelude to a ferocious struggle by land and sea for the Solomon Islands, in turn the first stage in General Douglas MacArthur's island-hopping campaign in the South-West Pacific during 1942–44 towards the Philippines.

Fought a month after the Coral Sea, the Battle of Midway in a single encounter swung the fortunes of the Pacific war against Japan, and so changed the course of history. Admiral Isoruku Yamamoto, the Commander-in-Chief of the Japanese Combined Fleet and the planner of the strike on Pearl Harbor, committed seven battleships, four fleet carriers (with over 300 aircraft), twelve heavy cruisers and many destroyers in support of a landing on the American island of Midway, 1,135 miles north-west of Pearl Harbor. By occupying Midway Yamamoto intended to entice the remaining ships of the US Pacific Fleet, and in particular the fleet carriers that had escaped him on 7 December 1941, into an ambush where they could be annihilated by overwhelming numbers. But the American Command was not taken by surprise as Yamamoto hoped, for they had been forewarned by decrypts of the Japanese JN25 naval cypher employing the equivalent of the Enigma machine. In good time to meet Yamamoto before the attack on Midway could take place Admiral Nimitz deployed his only three available fleet carriers (with some 230 aircraft) although, owing to the massacre in Pearl Harbor on 7 December 1941, entirely without battleship support. In a confused and ferocious three-day battle in which luck as well as skill favoured the Americans, Yamamoto lost four fleet carriers to Nimitz's one (USS *Yorktown*). Even though Yamamoto still enjoyed a superiority of seven battleships (including the 70,000-ton, 18-inch-gun *Yamato*) to none, he broke off the Midway operation and retired. Midway signalled the moment of the total eclipse of the battleship by the aircraft carrier after four centuries of dominance of naval warfare; an eclipse that had begun to cast its shadow in November 1941 with the Fleet Air Arm's strike on the Italian Fleet in Taranto.[2]

Her catastrophic defeat in the Battle of Midway forced Japan ineluctably on to the strategic defensive in the Pacific. From now on the Imperial Japanese Navy could only fight tenaciously against ever swelling American might in ships and maritime airpower while the task forces of the US Pacific Fleet and the landing forces of the US

Army and Marine Corps fought their way island by island, year by year, westwards across the central Pacific towards the Philippines and Japan.

During the years 1942–44 Britain and the Royal Navy played virtually no part in this Pacific war, although the carrier *Victorious* was lent to the US Navy in the south-west Pacific area for a time in 1942 when the Americans were so short of carriers, and ships of the Royal Australian and Royal New Zealand Navies served with distinction in the same area. The dominions of Australia and New Zealand, the source of so much anxiety to the pre-war Admiralty, no longer remained a direct British concern, for they passed in a strategic sense from the British Empire into the American when Britain haplessly reneged on her long-standing promise to send a great fleet to Singapore to protect them. Britain's sphere of responsibility in the war against Japan was restricted to the Indian Ocean and the Bay of Bengal. In May 1942 the Japanese had finally driven British forces out of Burma into the Indian state of Assam. Britain's immediate concern now lay, therefore, with the defence of India; no longer the 'jewel in the Crown' of Empire, but an economic and strategic burden which the British government wished to dump after the war if it could only reach a deal with Indian political leaders in negotiations already in progress.

In the meantime, and using India as a main base, the British hoped eventually to reconquer Burma and thereafter Malaya and Singapore. Yet even if and when these ultimate objectives had been attained, the Royal Navy and British Empire land forces would still be some 2,400 miles distant from the decisive theatre where the war against Japan must finally be won – the seas between the Philippines and the Japanese home islands. Thus the British effort in Burma and South-East Asia could never be more than peripheral in importance, leading to a strategic cul-de-sac; the equivalent of the Mediterranean campaign in the German war.

In the wake of the destruction of Force Z (HMS *Prince of Wales* and *Repulse*) on 8 December 1941 and the surrender of Singapore on 15 February 1942 the Admiralty had cobbled together a new Eastern Fleet based on Ceylon and commanded by Admiral Sir James Somerville, formerly Flag Officer, Force H, in the Mediterranean and no stranger to operations against great odds. Count the ships and Somerville's command looked – certainly to the Prime Minister – like a formidable enough fleet: five battleships, three aircraft carriers, seven cruisers and sixteen destroyers.[3] But judge the combat-worthiness of the ships

Above) 'At 1320 HMS *Prince of Wales,* flagship of Force and the Eastern Fleet, capsized and sank. . . .' The estruction of Force Z (*Prince of Wales* and battlecruiser *epulse*) on 10 December 1941 cost the Japanese only ght aircraft. (IWM) *(Right)* Admiral Sir T.S.V. Phillips with, left, his Chief of Staff, Captain Palliser) 'had ever personally experienced air attack on a task force t sea.' Phillips was appointed by the First Sea Lord to ommand the Eastern Fleet after three years at a desk s Vice Chief of Naval Staff. He went down with *Prince f Wales.* (IWM)

(Above) '. . . thanks to their armoured decks the destruction was mostly limited to parked aircraft.' The fleet aircraft carrier HMS *Formidable* hit by a Japanese kamikaze suicide bomber during 'Operation Iceberg' (the attack on Okinawa) in 1945. (IWM) *(Below, left)* 'For the Royal Navy he entertained the underdoggish and now quite anachronistic Anglophobia so prevalent in the US Navy in the early 1920s.' Admiral Ernest J. King, Chief of Naval Operations and C-in-C, United States Fleet (COMINCH). (Hulton) *(Below, right)* Admiral Sir Bruce Fraser, C-in-C, Home Fleet, 1942–44, Eastern Fleet, 1944, and the British Pacific Fleet, 1944–46. He sank the German battlecruiser *Scharnhorst* on 26 December 1943 in an action off Norway's North Cape. (IWM)

ove) 'The first refinery lost half its production; the nd was put totally out of action for six months.' The ish Pacific Fleet's carrier strike on oil refineries at mbang on Sumatra, January 1945. (IWM) *(Below,* Admiral C. W. Nimitz, C-in-C, US Pacific Fleet, er whose command the British Pacific Fleet served 945 as 'Task Force 57'. (Hulton) *(Below, right)* 'On larch 1945, Admiral Rawlings reported his fleet for duty to Admiral Nimitz. . . .' Vice-Admiral Sir Bernard Rawlings, Second-in-Command of the British Pacific Fleet, deputed by Sir Bruce Fraser, to command the fleet at sea. (IWM)

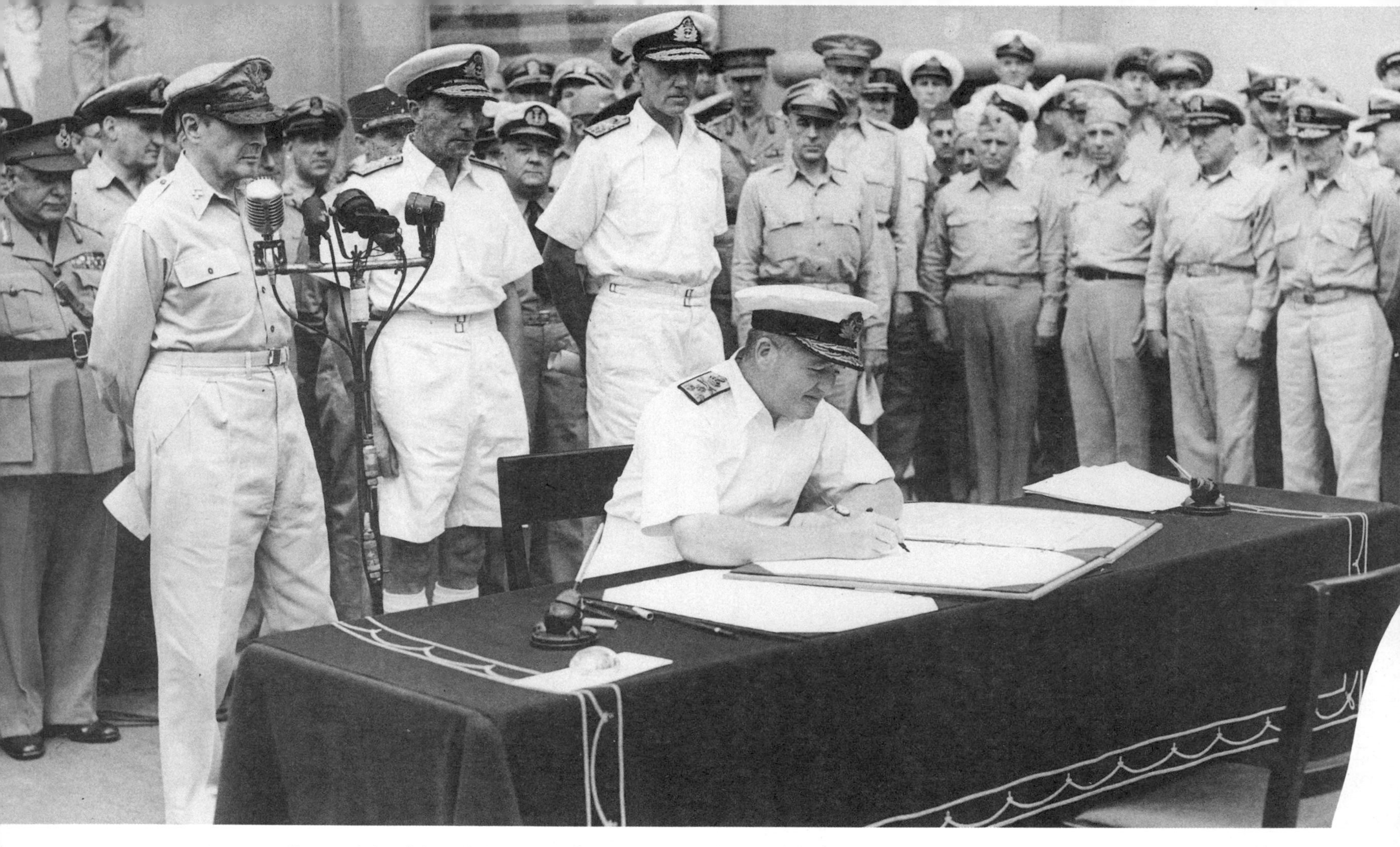

'In second place [after a Chinese general] signed Admiral Sir Bruce Fraser for the United Kingdom.' The ceremony

and aircraft, the state of training of the crews and their ability to work together as a fleet unit, and the picture became very different. Of Somerville's battleships four were the 'R' class: *Resolution*, *Ramillies*, *Revenge* and *Royal Sovereign*; floating museums of Great War naval technology preserved intact by inter-war economies in defence expenditure. His fifth battleship, *Warspite*, another Great War veteran but reconstructed in 1934–37, had just returned to service after having battle damage off Crete repaired in America. Somerville's two fleet carriers, *Indomitable* and *Formidable*, were certainly modern ships, but they and his light carrier *Hermes* only embarked a combined total of some 57 strike aircraft and 36 fighters, all of them inferior in performance to Japanese aircraft. Most of Somerville's cruisers were also out-of-date.

The state of his fleet depressed even Somerville, an admiral temperamentally robust enough. In February 1942, on his way out to Ceylon, he wrote privately: 'My old Battleboats are in various states of disrepair & I've not a ship at present that approaches what I should call a proper standard of fighting efficiency . . .'[4] He also found his Fleet Air Arm crews well below the standard of his old Mediterranean carrier *Ark Royal*. 'The fact is,' he wrote at the beginning of March, 'that until I get this odd collection of boats together & train them up they aren't worth much . . .'[5]

In April 1942, just after Somerville had arrived in Ceylon with this 'odd collection of boats' and a month before the Battle of the Coral Sea, Admiral Nagumo, with four of the fast carriers employed in the Pearl Harbor strike and four battleships, lashed out across the Indian Ocean with the aim of destroying, neutralising or cowing the new British Eastern Fleet. Somerville prudently kept his 'R' class battleships well out of Nagumo's way while trying – though unsuccessfully – to close the Japanese at night with his carriers in order to launch air strikes. Thanks to Somerville's evasive tactics Nagumo only succeeded in sinking the old carrier *Hermes* and the cruisers *Cornwall* and *Dorsetshire*, although much damage was done by Japanese aircraft to shore installations at Colombo and by Japanese warships to merchant traffic in the Bay of Bengal. Nonetheless Nagumo had achieved his strategic objects, for the Admiralty now ordered Somerville to pull his vulnerable fleet back some 3,000 miles to Kilindini on the East African coast, 'a small narrow winding harbour', Somerville described it to his wife, 'with thick green jungly stuff each side . . . It's a very snug harbour but too congested for my party . . .'[6]

For Somerville the two years that followed were a time of gnawing frustration because the state of his fleet prohibited bold offensive strokes. Of his carrier aircraft only the American Martlet fighter impressed him as 'undoubtedly good'.[7] The Fulmar was 'no match for the Japanese Zero fighter'; the Albacore and Swordfish were 'too slow for day strikes'.[8] All in all he judged his carrier striking force at present to be 'a very poor thing'.[9] Somerville was not only constrained by his fleet's lack of battle-worthiness but also by its short range. He bitterly recorded during Nagumo's April 1942 raid that the Japanese ships 'have tremendous endurance while my old battleboats & destroyers have none . . .'[10] For want of a fleet train to refuel and replenish his ships at sea (an American novelty which the Royal Navy had yet to develop) he had to resort to a secret shore base at Addu Atoll (in the south of the Maldive Islands) whenever he undertook distant sorties across the Indian Ocean. For the ships' companies Addu offered a landfall as starkly unpleasant as either Iceland or Kola; but at the opposite extreme: 'The heat is simply indescribable,' Somerville wrote to his wife, 'a burning, torturing sort of heat from which there is no escape . . .'[11]

Thus Somerville could only hope, in his own words, 'to create diversions and false scents, since I am now the poor fox'.[12] His main task now lay in guarding the vital sea route up the east coast of Africa to the Red Sea and Egypt, on which the campaign in the Western Desert in 1942 so completely depended. The one major British maritime offensive operation in eastern waters in 1942 was in fact mounted from the United Kingdom, and was directed not against the Japanese but the Vichy French. For the Vichy French island colony of Madagascar commanded the convoy routes from Britain to the Middle East and India via the Mozambique Channel (lying between Madagascar and the east coast of Africa). In London it was feared that Japan might well decide to include the island in her current wave of conquest. The decision was therefore taken in principle on 7 March to forestall her – and in particular, as the Prime Minister put it to the Prime Minister of South Africa, 'to storm and occupy Diego Suarez' – the port and naval base at the north-eastern point of the island.[13] Planning now began.

This time a joint expedition with General de Gaulle's Free French forces was ruled out; the memory of Dakar in 1940 still stung. The speed and efficiency with which the all-British venture ('Operation Ironclad') was planned and organised demonstrates how much had been learned from the fumblings and bumblings of Norway and indeed Dakar, not least thanks to the work of Combined Operations on the techniques and equipment needed for assault landings. On 14 March 1942 the Chiefs of Staff submitted their outline proposals; on

18 March the final decision was made to go ahead; on the 19th the Admiralty signalled to all concerned the make-up of the naval forces and announced the appointment of Rear-Admiral E. N. Syfret (Flag Officer, Force H) as Combined Commander-in-Chief. On 13 March (actually the day before the COS submitted their plan), and on 23 March the motor transport and stores ships sailed with convoys OS22 and OS23 for Durban. The landing force itself – five assault ships carrying a Royal Marine Commando and three infantry brigade groups under Major-General R. G. Sturges, Royal Marines – sailed with the regular Durban convoy WS17. Early on 1 April Syfret put to sea from Gibraltar with the battleship *Malaya*, the cruiser *Hermione* and five destroyers, plus corvettes and minesweepers.

The mounting of 'Ironclad' no less serves as a remarkable demonstration of the flexibility and long reach of seapower. The objective lay some 9,000 miles from the United Kingdom, while the naval task force had to be put together by major reshuffling of resources. In order that Syfret could take Force H with him, ships had to be sent from the Home Fleet to fill the gap at Gibraltar – and those ships in turn had to be replaced temporarily by the United States Navy.

On 22 April, with his strength now augmented by the carrier *Illustrious*, the cruiser *Devonshire* and four more destroyers, Syfret reached Durban, where he transferred his flag to HMS *Ramillies* (from the Eastern Fleet at Kilindini).

Now followed a week of final planning in conjunction with Somerville (who released the carrier *Indomitable* to Syfret in order to strengthen the close air support for the landings), General Sturges and the South African government. On 25 April the first (slow) of two convoys sailed from Durban for Madagascar; on the 28th the second (fast). But only on 1 May did the executive order arrive from London that 'Ironclad' was to be launched on 5 May, so making the last-minute tactical arrangements more of a scramble than was comfortable. At 1500 on the 4th, on the signal 'proceed in execution of previous orders',[14] the task forces had begun to head for their deployment positions. For Captain R. D. Oliver in the *Devonshire* the coming night proved a nerve-twanging experience, responsible as he was for shepherding no fewer than 34 ships, including several large liners, through reefs which the French judged too difficult to navigate at night. But the only casualty was the corvette *Auricula*, sunk by a mine. At 0330 on 5 May the landing forces anchored at the lowering positions for the three assault beaches. Barely seven weeks had elapsed since the COS submitted their first outline for the expedition.

The British tactical plan for taking Diego Suarez exemplified the principle of the 'indirect approach'. The town and the neighbouring naval base of Antsirane lay deep inside a landlocked bay of irregular shape, the only entrance from the open sea being a narrow gut (the Orija Pass) to the eastwards, commanded by coastal defence batteries. Near the port and the naval base were more such batteries. The British command therefore decided to kick down Diego Suarez's back door by landing on the western coast of the island, which was separated by the width of a narrow peninsula from the port and the naval base, and then advancing eastwards inland.

After the cruiser *Hermione* had distracted the defenders' attention in the opposite direction by a night-time display of pyrotechnics off the entrance to Diego Suarez Bay and carrier aircraft had struck at the airport and at shipping in the harbour, the landing forces went ashore at 0430 away to the west against little or no opposition from a weak and surprised defence. They pushed on inland to cover the ten or twelve miles to Diego Suarez and Antsirane while behind them the anchorage filled with ships and the beaches with stores. By 1700 No. 5 Royal Marine Commando, on the northerly of the two axes of advance, had occupied the peninsula jutting into Diego Suarez bay on which the town itself was situated: complete success.

To the south, however, the Army's brigade groups came up against French defences covering the rear of the naval base of Antsirane. At General Sturges's request the Royal Navy agreed to land a party behind the French position. The destroyer *Anthony* (Lieutenant-Commander J. M. Hodges) embarked 50 of the *Ramillies*'s Royal Marines under Captain M. Price, RM, and at around 2000 on 6 May steamed at high speed and in rough seas straight through the Orija Pass, trading salvoes with French batteries as she did so. Now came the problem of getting alongside the quay at Antsirane in the dark in a strange harbour and in the face of a strong wind blowing off the shore. Despite setbacks Commander Hodges finally managed to hold his ship's stern to the quay long enough for the Royal Marines to swarm ashore – another small victory for cool nerves and superb seamanship. To Captain Price's little party now quickly surrendered the commandant of the naval base as well as an *embarras de richesse* of other French personnel.

At 1040 on the 7th Admiral Syfret with the *Ramillies*, *Devonshire* and *Hermione* and four destroyers began shelling the shore batteries commanding the Orija Pass, but ceased fire after only ten minutes on learning that the French defence had collapsed. At 1630 the British task force steamed triumphantly along swept channels into the great bay of Diego Suarez. 'Ironclad' had turned out to be an exemplary

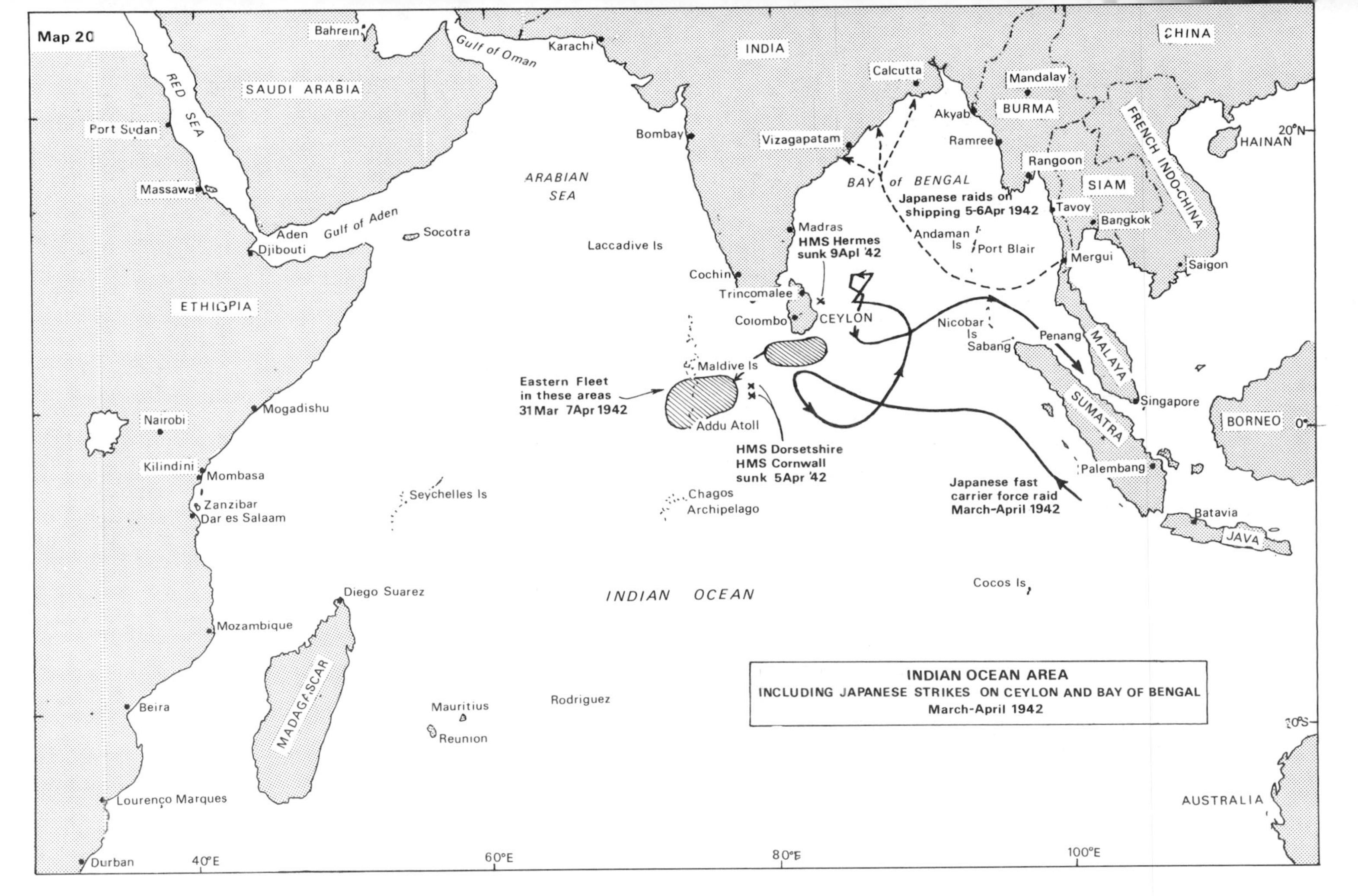

Map 20
INDIAN OCEAN AREA
INCLUDING JAPANESE STRIKES ON CEYLON AND BAY OF BENGAL
March-April 1942
Bahrein
Gulf of Oman
Karachi
INDIA
Calcutta
Mandalay
CHINA
RED SEA
SAUDI ARABIA
Akyab
BURMA
FRENCH INDO-CHINA
Port Sudan
Bombay
Vizagapatam
Ramree
20°N
HAINAN
Rangoon
ARABIAN SEA
BAY of BENGAL
SIAM
Massawa
Japanese raids on shipping 5-6Apr 1942
Tavoy
Bangkok
Madras
Aden
Gulf of Aden
Socotra
HMS Hermes sunk 9Apl '42
Andaman Is
Port Blair
Djibouti
Laccadive Is
Mergui
Saigon
Cochin
Trincomalee
ETHIOPIA
Colombo
CEYLON
Nicobar Is
Sabang
Penang
MALAYA
Maldive Is
Eastern Fleet in these areas 31Mar 7Apr 1942
Singapore
Mogadishu
SUMATRA
BORNEO
0°
Nairobi
Addu Atoll
HMS Dorsetshire
HMS Cornwall
sunk 5Apr '42
Kilindini
Mombasa
Palembang
Japanese fast carrier force raid March-April 1942
Seychelles Is
Chagos Archipelago
Zanzibar
Dar es Salaam
Batavia
JAVA
Cocos Is
Diego Suarez
INDIAN OCEAN
Mozambique
MADAGASCAR
Beira
Mauritius
Rodriguez
10°S
Reunion
Lourenço Marques
AUSTRALIA
Durban
40°E
60°E
80°E
100°E

combined operation, not least on account of the 'most cordial' co-operation between the services, as Syfret put it in his later report.[15]

The most serious casualties to the task force occurred three weeks later, when a Japanese midget submarine successfully attacked the *Ramillies* and a tanker in the bay, sinking the tanker and inflicting serious damage on the battleship, although she was able to steam to Durban after emergency repairs.

There still remained in Vichy French control the rest of the 900-mile coastline of Madagascar facing the Mozambique Channel and its dense convoy traffic. Since the Vichy French authorities were resolved to resist rather than surrender at discretion, a further campaign had to be mounted from September 1942 onwards to subdue the whole island. On 5 November the surrender of the Governor-General of the colony finally concluded a venture which Churchill justly described in his favourite eighteenth-century language as 'a model for amphibious descents'.[16]

In contrast, Admiral Sir James Somerville, C-in-C, Eastern Fleet, provoked the Prime Minister's keen displeasure because of his reluctance to take the offensive against the Japanese Navy. In July 1942 he minuted to the First Lord of the Admiralty and the First Sea Lord that Somerville had two 'first-class carriers' as well as the *Warspite*, and yet he 'has been doing nothing for several months, and we cannot really keep this fleet idle indefinitely'.[17] In the autumn the Admiralty cut the Eastern Fleet down to one carrier and two battleships, the remainder being needed in the Mediterranean to support 'Operation Torch'. In spring 1943 Somerville lost his sole remaining carrier and another battleship, so reducing his fleet to cruisers and destroyers and rendering the Indian Ocean a strategic backwater.

However, the Prime Minister was even more keenly and continuously dissatisfied with the performance of the British Empire land forces on the Assam–Burma front. An offensive by the 14th Army down the Arakan Peninsula of Burma in September 1942 (aided by the Royal Navy's light forces along the coast) ended ignominiously eight months later with the beaten British troops back on their startline. What Churchill angrily called 'the welter of inefficiency and lassitude which has characterised our operations on the Indian front'[18] cost Wavell his job as Commander-in-Chief in India. Instead Wavell was appointed Viceroy, with the even more thankless role of negotiating a deal with Indian politicians over post-war Indian independence. The new Commander-in-Chief in India, General Sir Claude Auchinleck, all too soon began to weary Churchill with his catalogues of shortages of every kind and the problems involved in constructing from scratch road and rail communications up from Bengal to the Burma front. Just as when Auchinleck was C-in-C, Middle East, in 1942, his military realism struck the Prime Minister as want of an offensive spirit.

In August 1943 the 'Quadrant' summit conference in Quebec approved Churchill's final answer to the problem of 'lassitude' in British operations in the East – the appointment of the young and dashing Lord Louis Mountbatten (in the rank of Acting Admiral) as Supreme Allied Commander of a new South-East Asia Command responsible for all operations by sea, land and air in India, Burma, Ceylon, Siam, Sumatra and Malaya. Although much senior to him in all but acting rank, Somerville now became Mountbatten's naval commander, the equivalent of Cunningham in 'Torch' and Ramsay in 'Husky', although he also remained responsible to the Admiralty as C-in-C, Eastern Fleet: an uneasy dual role.

At first Somerville welcomed Mountbatten's advent as bringing energy and leadership to the Indian scene of fusty imperial pomp and tropical torpor epitomised for Somerville himself by a brief stay with the Viceroy, then Lord Linlithgow, in Delhi: 'The Viceroy's house appeared to be three times the size of Buckingham Palace with an army of black bearers in scarlet and gold uniforms littering every passage . . . You could easily drown yourself in the baths, and the plumbing is late Victorian . . .'[19]

But all too soon Somerville's feelings towards Mountbatten soured into disillusionment. A protracted quarrel opened between them; one fomented by certain members of their staffs. For Mountbatten, a man rivalling Nelson in his hunger for admiration and surpassing him in appetite for personal aggrandisement, chose to run South-East Asia Command on authoritarian lines similar to MacArthur's style in the South-West Pacific. He and his eventually enormous war staff handed down operational plans for the land, sea and air Cs-in-C tamely to carry out; a sad contrast to Eisenhower's system whereby the Supreme Commander, with only a tiny staff of his own, acted as chairman of a committee of Cs-in-C, who with their own staffs remained responsible for planning. Moreover it was Mountbatten's mistaken belief – or contention – that the three British Chiefs of Staff in London had each orally granted him total authority over the land, air and sea Cs-in-C in South-East Asia, even to the sacking of them if he so decided. After the war this contention was specifically repudiated by Brooke and Portal, and pronounced by Cunningham (as Dudley Pound's successor as First Sea Lord) as being in Pound's case in the last degree unlikely.[20]

Mountbatten's assumption of dictatorial authority and his assertion of a right to almost royal courtesies when visiting ships of the Eastern Fleet clashed ever more sharply with Somerville's over touchy sense of his independence as a C-in-C responsible to the Admiralty. As 1943 turned to 1944 the First Sea Lord found himself the recipient of Somerville's copious complaints about the Supreme Commander's Caesar-like pretensions. The upper echelon of SEAC was not a happy ship; hardly a help to efficiency and morale.[21]

Despite Mountbatten's undoubted energy and eagerness to take the offensive, he could not for a long time prevail over the lack of resources which had bedevilled his predecessors. By land and sea the war in South-East Asia remained from 1943 far into 1944 in a true tropical doldrum. In April 1943 a long-debated project ('Anakim'), first mooted a year earlier by Wavell in a fit of over-optimism for an amphibious landing at Rangoon to take the Japanese in Burma in the rear, had to be postponed *sine die* because forthcoming Mediterranean operations would swallow up landing craft and naval forces. Churchill's own cherished project for 1944, a landing in Sumatra ('Operation Culverin'), likewise succumbed to lack of landing craft (needed for 'Neptune' as well as the Mediterranean), and to the opposition of the Chiefs of Staff and the Americans.[22] Meanwhile, the stalemate on the Burma front was broken only by the 14th Army's resounding defeat of a local Japanese offensive in the Arakan in February–March 1944, and by Major-General Orde Wingate's 'long range penetration' offensive behind the enemy front in northern Burma in the same period, which ended in the almost complete destruction of his four brigades of élite troops.[23]

At sea the only exception to the operational doldrums in the Indian Ocean and Bay of Bengal in early 1944 was provided by British and enemy submarines. In February and March German and Japanese U-boats mounted a fresh offensive against Allied merchant shipping along the route between Africa and India, compelling Somerville to restore convoy as best he could while starved of surface and air escorts. For want of air cover the troopship *Khedive Ismail* was torpedoed and sunk on 12 February off the Maldive Islands even though actually in a convoy. The packed vessel foundered in just two minutes with the loss of 1,300 lives, including Wrens, ATS (Auxiliary Territorial Service, the Army equivalent of the Wrens) and nursing sisters. It was scant consolation for so heavy a loss that the destroyers HMS *Petard* and *Paladin* promptly destroyed the attacker.

For British submarines the problem lay in a lack of worthwhile targets, for Japanese traffic in the waters off Burma, Malaya and the

Dutch East Indies was now largely restricted to junks. Nonetheless HMS *Tally Ho* (Lieutenant-Commander Bennington) put down the light cruiser *Kuma* (5,100 tons) off Penang on 11 January 1944; and on the 26th HMS *Templar* seriously damaged the light cruiser *Kitagami* in the same sea area. These were major wounds to the Imperial Japanese Navy in a region where its resources in surface ships had become slender because of the demands of the crisis in the Pacific.

By this time Somerville's Eastern Fleet was at last being rebuilt with ships released from European waters thanks to the Italian surrender, the crippling of the *Tirpitz* by X-Craft in September 1943 and the sinking of the *Scharnhorst* in December. On 23 January 1944 the battlecruiser *Renown* (flying the flag of Vice-Admiral Sir Arthur Power, Second-in-Command designate of the Eastern Fleet) arrived in Ceylon with the battleships *Queen Elizabeth* and *Valiant* and the fleet carrier *Illustrious*, together with cruisers, destroyers, escorts and submarines released from the Mediterranean. Power's squadron was the first instalment of the 146 ships which the Admiralty had decided to send to the Indian Ocean, including another fleet carrier, *Victorious* (she arrived in August), fourteen cruisers and 24 fleet destroyers.[24]

At long last Somerville was freed from the frustrations of enforced passivity. On 16 April 1944 he put to sea from Trincomalee with two carriers, three battleships, six cruisers and twelve destroyers, in accordance with Mountbatten's instruction to attack oil storage tanks, an airfield and the harbour installations at Sabang, an island off the north-east tip of Sumatra. It was the first time he had been able to take the offensive since hoisting his flag nearly two years before. Alongside the White Ensign in his battle-squadron flew the Stars-and-Stripes (the carrier USS *Saratoga*, on loan from the South-West Pacific area), the French tricolor (the fast battleship *Richelieu*), the Dutch tricolor (the cruiser HNLMS *Tromp* and a destroyer) and the stars of the Southern Cross of Australia and New Zealand (the cruiser HMNZS *Gambia* and four Australian destroyers). On the 19th the attack went in – aircraft from the carriers, the heavy guns of the battleships. Three out of four oil storage tanks were set on fire, 24 Japanese aircraft destroyed on the ground and another three in the air, and the port badly knocked about, all for the loss of one fighter from the *Saratoga*.[25] When the Fleet returned to Trincomalee, it had steamed 7,000 miles.

On the fleet's return to Ceylon for replenishment the *Saratoga* was due to sail to the United States for a refit. Admiral King, the COMINCH, therefore suggested that Somerville should accompany her as far as Java in order to launch a strike from her and the *Illustrious* on the port of Sourabaya. This was done. As the air groups returned to the carriers, huge billows of black smoke towering into a tropical sky signified the total destruction of the oil refinery at Wonokromo nearby. On 18 May the USS *Saratoga* and her escort parted company with the Eastern Fleet after what Somerville in a farewell signal called 'a profitable and very happy association'.[26]

Somerville put to sea yet again on 22 July 1944 to attack Sabang, his carriers this time being the *Illustrious* and *Victorious*. At dawn three days later the carriers opened the attack with strikes on Japanese airfields. Then the great guns of the battleships smashed at the harbour installations while the cruiser HNLMS *Tromp* and British destroyers under the command of that outstanding destroyer officer Captain R. G. Onslow, RN, bombarded targets from close inshore. Onslow then took his ships in a bold run across the harbour entrance, loosing torpedoes into the harbour as he raced past. Jubilantly Somerville wrote afterwards to the First Sea Lord, Admiral Sir Andrew Cunningham:

> The party did everyone a world of good and especially some of the big ships who had not had a chance to fire their main armaments in action previously in this war . . . I am sure you would have liked to have seen the Inshore Squadron going into the harbour led by Dick Onslow as it was a most inspiring sight; he used rather a broader line of bearing than I expected, and his tail seemed to be leaning up against some of the shell bursts on the targets under fire on the East side of the harbour . . .[27]

From March to October 1944 the Eastern Fleet carried out eight such air strikes, the ships joining in twice by bombarding shore targets. Yet although locally damaging to the Japanese and uplifting to British morale such raids were no substitute for a major British strategic offensive in the East – especially in view of the staggering advances and colossal victories of the United States Navy and American amphibious forces in the Pacific. The month of June 1944 saw the Americans land on the three Mariana islands of Guam, Tinian and Saipan, deep in the heart of the original Japanese defensive perimeter and 'only' (in Pacific terms) 1,200 miles from the Philippines. Admiral Raymond Spruance's 5th Fleet (seven battleships, fifteen carriers with 956 aircraft, 21 cruisers and 69 destroyers) massacred the Japanese battlefleet's attempt to interfere with the invasion in what became known as 'The Great Marianas Turkey Shoot'.[28] This Battle of the Philippine Sea cost the Japanese nearly 500 aircraft (and, more important, their irreplaceable pilots) and a fleet carrier.[29] By August the resistance by the Japanese in the last of the Mariana islands had sputtered out; the way lay open for the leap to the Philippines.

In the South-West Pacific area MacArthur's strategy of leapfrogging Japanese-held islands so that their garrisons were left isolated and impotent had by mid-summer 1944 carried him north-westwards through the Bismarck Archipelago and the Admiralty Islands. His troops had reached the western tip of New Guinea. For him too the way was now clear for an attack on the Philippines. The two American thrustlines across the Pacific had thus converged, enabling Nimitz's and MacArthur's forces mutually to support each other in the next grand phase of operations.

What form should take the British contribution (and in particular that of the Royal Navy) to the final defeat of Japan, especially after Germany had been beaten into surrender? This question provoked the bitterest of all the wartime battles between Winston Churchill and the Chiefs of Staff.

At the 'Sextant' summit conference in Cairo on 22–26 November 1943 Roosevelt and Churchill initialled a Combined Chiefs of Staff paper which stated as a 'General Concept' that 'the main effort against Japan should be made in the Pacific'.[30] According to the paper the British Eastern Fleet was therefore only to be built up to a strength sufficient to carry out operations or pose threats in South-East Asia. All other available Royal Navy ships were to be formed into a British Pacific Fleet with a main base in Australia, advanced bases in the Solomon and Bismarck Islands, and operating either with MacArthur's forces towards the Philippines or with Nimitz's fleet in the central Pacific.[31] This strategy of locating the principal British naval effort against Japan in the Pacific rather than the waters off South-East Asia was enthusiastically embraced by the British Chiefs of Staff, but not by the Prime Minister. In January 1944 he disavowed the Cairo Conference CCOS paper, opting instead for 'Culverin', his pet project for invading Sumatra. In any case he was deeply sceptical about the soundness of the proposal to create a British Pacific Fleet, minuting to the War Cabinet Defence Committee that it was not yet certain that the United States Fleet needed or desired heavy British support.[32]

On 3 February 1944 the COS condemned 'Culverin' as strategically irrelevant and also scouted proposals by Mountbatten for major offensive operations across the Bay of Bengal, on the score that these would be peripheral to the decisive attack on Japan in the Pacific and – like 'Culverin' – a wasteful diversion of resources. Here was the mirror image of Marshall's objections to Brooke's 'blue water' strategy in the Mediterranean. The Chiefs of Staff argued that all available merchant shipping and warships should be concentrated in the Pacific alongside the Americans. As Brooke explained to Field-Marshal Sir John Dill, head of the British military mission in Washington, a few weeks later:

> I am quite clear in my own mind that strategically it is right for us to use all our forces in close co-operation from Australia across the Pacific in the general direction of Formosa. By operating our forces alongside of MacArthur we can pool resources at sea and in the air for various closely connected steps. Whereas by retaining our forces in the Indian Ocean we operate independently, incapable of close cooperation, with the result that operations will be more protracted.[33]

But however technically correct these strategic arguments might be, they did not answer the Prime Minister's pertinent query as to whether the Americans would want to accept a British Pacific Fleet. They did not take into account the likelihood that a British Pacific Fleet would be operationally redundant in view of the great size (still increasing) of the United States Pacific Fleet. The truth is that the Chiefs of Staff (really Brooke again) were thinking politically as much as strategically – about renewing the British link with the dominions of Australia and New Zealand; about gaining through sharing in the victory some voice in United States policy in regard to the Pacific war and later the treatment of Japan. Brooke admitted after the war:

> The first of these alternatives [operations based on India] was the easiest to stage but limited itself to the recapture of British possessions without any direct participation with American and Australian forces in the defeat of Japan. I felt that at this stage of the war it was vital that British forces should participate in direct action against Japan in the Pacific. First of all from a Commonwealth point of view to prove to Australia our willingness to fight with them for the defence of Australia as soon as the defeat of Germany rendered such action possible. Secondly, I felt it was important that we should operate with all three services alongside of the Americans in the Pacific against Japan in the final stages of the war. I therefore considered that our strategy should aim at the liberation of Burma by South East Asia Command based on India, and the deployment of new sea, land and air forces to operate with bases in Australia alongside of forces in the Pacific.[34]

But for Churchill the very attractiveness of a South-East Asia strategy lay in that it would concentrate British resources on an almost entirely British theatre of war, and lead to the reconquest of British imperial possessions – in contrast to the Pacific where Britain must remain a very junior partner and one probably surplus to military requirements.

On 13 March 1944 President Roosevelt (prompted by Churchill) wrote to the Prime Minister to say that there 'will be no specific operation in the Pacific during 1944 that would be adversely affected by the absence of a British Fleet detachment . . .'[35] And certainly Admiral King had no wish for a British Pacific Fleet, in part because of his Anglophobe suspicion of the Royal Navy, in part because he believed it would be operationally unnecessary and logistically a burden on American resources.

For logistics supplied another important thread in the argument. A main base in Australia, advanced bases in the Pacific and a fleet train would all have to be created before a British Pacific Fleet could begin to operate – a heavy financial and material burden on a bankrupt Britain. Even then American logistical support during fleet operations would almost certainly be needed. In India, on the other hand, British naval and other bases already existed; more lay within reach of recapture in Burma and Malaya. Moreover the Minister of War Transport, Lord Leathers, estimated that to support a British effort in the Pacific, 6,000 miles further to the east than the Bay of Bengal, would take two and a half times the tanker tonnage at present envisaged for South-East Asia Command, as well as an extra half million tons of cargo shipping.[36] The Prime Minister seems to have taken far more note than Brooke and his fellow Chiefs of Staff of all these extra costs involved in starting up a British Pacific strategy from scratch.[37]

The battle between the Prime Minister and the Chiefs of Staff came to a climax in March 1944 with the delivery of a massive (in every sense) Churchillian memorandum in favour of 'Culverin' in particular and the South-East Asia theatre in general, and an equally massive attempt at its rebuttal, paragraph by paragraph, by the Chiefs of Staff, plus a fresh memorandum of their own.[38] Brooke now privately feared that the Prime Minister was trying to line up the War Cabinet against the Chiefs of Staff on the question of a Pacific strategy, writing in his diary that 'it looks very serious and may well lead to the resignation of the Chiefs of Staff Committee'.[39] It was indeed as serious as that. It remained so until April when a washy compromise was reached by which there was to be a British Empire campaign (British, Australian and New Zealand sea, land, and air forces) in the Pacific based on northern Australia, but with its own thrustline through Timor–Celebes–Borneo–Saigon instead of a mere furnishing of extra strength to American operations. This so-called 'Middle Strategy' gradually found its way to a high Whitehall shelf, not least because the Americans disliked it as doubling up MacArthur's line of advance further to the north, and because they were keen that the British should concentrate on clearing Burma in order to bring help to Chiang Kai Shek, whose corrupt and feeble Kuomintang régime American opinion persisted in regarding as a worthwhile ally.

Early in August Churchill held a three-day staff conference in London, attended by Mountbatten as well as Cabinet Ministers and the Chiefs of Staff, to try again to decide on a British strategy for the war with Japan. In regard to South-East Asia, it was agreed to launch a seaborne landing at Rangoon as soon as forces (including landing craft) could be released from the German war, with Churchill's old favourite, 'Culverin', as a fill-in during the meantime. But the conference – now Churchill too – also agreed that 'the greatest offer of naval assistance should be made at once to the US Joint Chiefs of Staff, it being impressed on them that it is our desire to share with them in the main operations against the mainland of Japan or Formosa'.[40]

By this time, of course, Nimitz had won the crushing victory of the Battle of the Philippine Sea, and the Mariana islands had all fallen into American hands. The United States had less need than ever of British assistance in the Pacific, especially naval assistance. Nevertheless at the 'Octagon' summit conference in Quebec that September the Prime Minister formally offered Roosevelt the 'British main fleet', including 'our best and most modern battleships, adequately supported by fleet aircraft carriers, escort carriers, cruisers, etc' to take part in major operations against Japan under American command.[41] Although Roosevelt accepted the offer in principle, Admiral King in a Combined Chiefs of Staff meeting next day still fought a dour rearguard action. According to the record, he stated that he was not

> prepared to accept a British fleet which he could not employ or support. In principle he wished to accept a British fleet in the Pacific but it would be entirely unacceptable for the British main fleet to be employed for political reasons in the Pacific and thus necessitate the withdrawal of some of the United States Fleet.[42]

He stressed the need for a British fleet to be self-supporting; he also sought to sidetrack the employment of such a fleet away from the central Pacific to MacArthur's subsidiary area of the South-West Pacific. Eventually, after the First Sea Lord and his fellow British

Chiefs of Staff had exerted the heaviest possible pressure, the Combined Chiefs of Staff

> (a) Agreed that the British fleet should participate in the main operations against Japan in the Pacific.
> (b) Took note of the assurance of the British Chiefs of Staff that this fleet would be balanced and self-supporting . . .[43]

So after all Brooke, Cunningham and Portal had their way, even though Churchill still insisted that Britain should make her separate amphibious thrusts in South-East Asia as well – first at Rangoon and later in Malaya.

In hindsight Churchill's earlier preference for concentrating the British effort in South-East Asia alone makes by far the better politico-strategic sense. It would have enabled Britain to win her own, if peripheral, victory against Japan in her own theatre; to play a middle-sized fish in a middle-sized pond. Logistically and economically too it would have made good sense. Brooke and his colleagues' solution, which meant playing the sprat in the largest pond in the world, could only expose Britain's shrunken relative stature as a power and above all as a naval power. Brooke's thinking in fact anticipates the British illusions of the post-war era (which he was fully to share and to foster as CIGS until 1946) – those of forging the Commonwealth into a political and strategic entity, with Britain as its leader and hence a 'world power'; and of this 'world power' securing 'a place at the top table' by means of expensive military pretensions.

In the autumn of 1944 it only remained for the Admiralty to complete a fleet base in Australia; arrange for an advanced base in the Pacific; assemble and equip a fleet train; form and equip the fleet itself, and despatch it.

To settle the command structure of the British Pacific Fleet proved simple enough, requiring as it did only typewriters and paper. By agreement between the First Lord of the Admiralty, A. V. Alexander, the First Sea Lord, Cunningham, and the Prime Minister, Admiral Sir Bruce Fraser was appointed Commander-in-Chief, British Pacific Fleet, hoisting his flag in Ceylon on 22 November 1944.[44] Since 23 August he had been commanding the Eastern Fleet in succession to Somerville, who had been posted to Washington as the only available British admiral with sufficient weight of personal broadside to engage the curmudgeonly Ernie King. 'I would much sooner have command of a trawler,' wrote Somerville to Fraser in May 1944 of this impending job.[45]

Because Fraser was to take the bulk of the Eastern Fleet's strength on with him in the guise of the new Pacific Fleet, the former fleet was abolished in favour of an 'East Indies Station' commanded by Vice-Admiral Sir Arthur Power (hitherto Second-in-Command of the Eastern Fleet). The East Indies 'Fleet' would only consist of two old battleships, twenty auxiliary carriers, six cruisers, 22 destroyers and some 120 escorts.[46]

The Admiralty appointed Vice-Admiral C. S. Daniel as 'Vice-Admiral, Administration' to the new Pacific Fleet. It fell to him in collaboration with the Australian government and Navy Board to arrange for the reception of a mass of stores and equipment, including nine floating docks, to be sent out from the United Kingdom, and for the construction of all the victualling and stores sheds, ammunition depots and base workshops needed for a main fleet base – a crucial and colossal task. He was also to act as the permanent representative in Australia of the C-in-C, British Pacific Fleet, until the latter arrived in person.

'The position of the British C-in-C was I think unique,' Admiral Fraser was to write after the war of his own place in the command structure. 'Responsible to the British Admiralty for the maintenance & welfare of the Fleet & for supplies coming from 12,000 miles away. Responsible to the Australian & New Zealand Govts [sic] for shore based activities. Responsible to the American Admiral Nimitz for operations.'[47] Because of such complicated relationships Fraser decided on arrival in Australia at the end of 1944 to fly his flag ashore in Sydney, deputing his Second-in-Command, Vice-Admiral Sir Bernard Rawlings, to command the Fleet at sea.

The finding of the merchant tonnage to support the Fleet operations and bring all its supplies 12,000 miles from the United Kingdom proved a rather less simple matter than making these flag appointments. In February 1944 the Admiralty was reckoning that 95 ships totalling about one million cargo tons would be required for the fleet train – and this at a time when Britain's annual import programme was down to 24 million tons, as against a pre-war average of some 60 million.[48] It had taken the Prime Minister himself to resolve a bitter argument between the Admiralty and the Ministry of War Transport over the release of shipping for the fleet train. On 9 April 1944 he minuted:

> The Fleet Train is limited by the need of getting an absolute irreducible minimum of 24 million tons of imports this year and next. All Naval and Military requirements must be subordinated to this decisive rule, without which the life and the war effort of Britain cannot be maintained. In working out your Fleet Train you must observe these requirements.
>
> 2. The priorities are as follows:
> (a) 24 million tons of imports this year and next
> (b) The Fleet Train permissible on this basis
> (c) The fighting Fleet that can be carried by the said Fleet Train . . .[49]

The tonnage of the brand-new ships allotted to the Admiralty for this purpose would be made good by the release to the Ministry of War Transport of an equivalent tonnage of merchant shipping currently in Admiralty control. But in any event the Admiralty was only going to receive 293,000 tons of shipping for its fleet train instead of its original bid for one million tons (or 1½ million if a proposed fleet train for the Indian Ocean is also included).[50]

'The fighting Fleet that can be carried by the said Fleet Train' therefore amounted in March 1945, when it first joined Nimitz's command, to two fast battleships (*King George V*, flying Rawlings's flag, and *Howe*), four fleet carriers (*Indomitable*, *Victorious*, *Indefatigable* and *Illustrious*), five cruisers (*Swiftsure*, *Black Prince*, *Argonaut*, *Euryalus* and HMNZS *Gambia*), and eleven destroyers (two of them Australian).[51] Designated 'Task Force 57' by Nimitz, the British Pacific Fleet was much less than half the size of its American opposite number, Task Force 58, which comprised ten fleet carriers, six light carriers, seven battleships, eighteen cruisers and fifty-eight destroyers.[52] However, the small size of the British Pacific Fleet reflected more than the limit imposed by the available fleet train. For on balance and with the exception of anti-submarine forces and escort carriers the entire Royal Navy in 1945 together constituted a weaker striking force than Task Force 58.

In 1945 Britain had in commission only six modern fleet carriers, four light fleet carriers, five modern battleships and 41 modern cruisers.[53] Except for the *Vanguard* (laid down in 1940, launched in 1944, but not completed until 1946) new battleship construction had been halted by Prime Ministerial decision in August 1940 (see above, pp. 380–1 and 437–8). Except for the *Eagle* (laid down in 1942 but also not completed until after the war) new fleet carrier building had likewise been halted. Not a single new cruiser was begun after 1941.[54] The consequence was that as a battlefleet the Royal Navy actually shrank during the war, with only five battleships in commission in 1945 as against twelve in 1939; 41 cruisers as against 52. Necessity had gone far to transform the Royal Navy into an anti-submarine force, with 39 escort carriers (though capable of fleet operations), and nearly 600 other escort ships of all kinds, as against only 101 in 1939.[55]

In contrast the United States Navy commissioned between 7 December 1941 and the end of the Second World War a total of eight new battleships, no fewer than seventeen fleet (or in American parlance 'fast') carriers, nine light carriers (one of which was sunk), 77 escort carriers (excluding those passed to the Royal Navy under Lend-Lease), thirteen heavy cruisers and 33 light cruisers.[56]

Yet even though British naval shipbuilding resources had been deliberately concentrated on anti-submarine escorts, the Royal Navy had still come to depend critically on American yards for such vessels – all 39 escort carriers; 99 frigates as against 86 from British yards; almost all landing ships (tank). Canadian shipbuilders too had helped out the Royal Navy, supplying it with some 200 vessels, including 27 corvettes, sixteen big landing craft (tank) and many minesweepers.[57]

A navy is no more than the armour and the weapons-system of seapower. The hull, providing essential buoyancy, is the national wealth. The propulsion is commercial and industrial success, which creates the national wealth. By the end of the Second German War in May 1945 British national wealth, once the greatest in the world, had given way to bankruptcy, with overseas debts exceeding reserves of gold and foreign currency by nearly fifteen times.[58] Whereas in 1870 Britain's foreign trade had nearly equalled that of France, Germany and the United States put together,[59] in 1945 her export trade had collapsed to less than one-third of the 1939 level, and her visible exports could finance no more than one-tenth of her overseas requirements.[60] Worse still, the British industrial machine, once the envied model for the rest of the world, had been revealed by the war to the government, though not to the British people at large, as out-of-date in equipment, methods and attitudes; crippled by poor management and obstructive workforces; and weak in advanced technologies. All this was especially true of shipbuilding.

Thus by 1945 the economic buoyancy which for two centuries had sustained the Royal Navy in its world mastery had been entirely lost. The technological dynamism which had once driven the expansion of British seapower had yielded to hobbling arthritis. And yet at this same time – it is a poignant paradox – the seamanship and fighting spirit of the officers and men of the Royal Navy itself had never been greater. Adversity had rescued the Navy from the arrogant complacency bequeathed by the Victorian era, and which had marred its performance in the Great War; had awoken it from the conservatism and torpor of the inter-war years; and had restored it to the bold, hardy, resourceful and highly professional service that it was in Nelson's time.

But now it was the United States Navy instead which enjoyed the buoyancy of swelling national wealth, and American seapower whose expansion was being driven by technological prowess coupled with dynamic industrial growth. However, there was another factor in this eclipsing of British world naval mastery by America – the sheer scale of America's continental economy, which would have dwarfed Britain's island economy even if Britain had managed to retain her early Victorian dynamism. For example, the British turned out 4,133 major and minor landing craft during the war; the United States 63,218.[61] In naval shipbuilding overall, Britain produced 2.4 million tons in the course of the war; the United States 8.2 million tons.[62] Add in merchant shipbuilding too and the dwarfing of the British industrial effort becomes even more apparent – 8.3 million tons of merchant vessel from British yards, but 50 million tons from American.[63]

So the era of Britain's twin commercial and maritime supremacies, each serving to promote the other, had come to an end some two centuries after it had first opened with Marlborough's victorious war against Louis XIV. Yet this was hardly evident to the British public in the splendid hour of Nazi Germany's downfall. Indeed, a full awareness of Britain's eclipse as a world power had still to sink into the minds of even her military leadership, which had just successfully promoted the creation of a British Pacific Fleet and wished thereby to resume the old burden of imperial defence with regard to Australia. In fact, the Pacific Fleet was the precursor and prototype of the post-war global navy built round the fleet carrier to which successive British governments and Boards of Admiralty were to cling until the mid 1960s, when cruel economic and political reality at last put an end to their nostalgic self-delusion, and the Royal Navy dwindled into an anti-submarine force largely deployed in the eastern Atlantic and home waters. It is no wonder, therefore, that in 1945 the people of Britain, to say nothing of their leaders, saw British seapower as still majestically riding the oceans, when in truth it was like a ship still on even keel, not yet perceptibly lower in the water, but with her bottom blown out.

On 15 March 1945 Admiral Rawlings reported his fleet for duty to Admiral Nimitz, C-in-C, US Pacific Fleet, from his 'intermediate' base at Manus in the Admiralty Islands. Constructed by the Americans out of nothing, Manus was generously allotted by them for use by the British Pacific Fleet. On its way from Ceylon the British Pacific Fleet had launched the biggest and most destructive British carrier air strike in South-East Asian waters when Rear-Admiral Sir Philip Vian – with the fleet carriers *Indomitable*, *Indefatigable*, *Victorious* and *Illustrious*, the battleship *King George V*, three cruisers and ten destroyers – attacked the oil refineries at Palembang on the Dutch island of Sumatra.[64] The first strike force – 43 American-built Avenger bombers escorted by some 80 fighters – took off at dawn on 24 January 1945, and delivered their bombs accurately on the Pladjoe refinery despite a determined Japanese fighter defence, barrage balloons and dense anti-aircraft fire. On 29 January Vian launched a second strike with 46 Avengers on the Soengei Gerong refinery. Once again funeral pyres of black smoke signalled the success of the attacks. The first refinery lost half its production; the second was put totally out of action for six months. Vian lost sixteen aircraft in action and 25 more from various other causes. He reached Fremantle in Australia on 4 February, ready for the final preparations of the British Pacific Fleet for service with the Americans.[64a]

On 19 March Sir Bernard Rawlings sailed with that fleet from Manus to Ulithi, in the Western Caroline Islands, there to join with the United States Fifth Fleet commanded by Admiral R. A. Spruance and replenish his ships again. On 23 March he put to sea on the British Pacific Fleet's first operational sortie as Task Force 57 in the Fifth Fleet.

Since the final decision had been taken at the 'Octagon' Conference in Quebec in September 1944 that a British fleet should be sent to the Pacific, Japan had suffered a further series of colossal defeats by sea and land. In Burma the British Empire 14th Army (British, Indian and West African troops) under Lieutenant-General Sir William Slim had been carrying out a sustained offensive ever since December 1944, aided by operations by ships of Vice-Admiral Sir Arthur Power's East Indies Fleet along the Burmese coast of the Bay of Bengal. This was a shore of a thousand jungly islands and swampy channels and inlets ('chaungs'); a true watery maze beneath the dense overhead cover of tropical vegetation.

> The mangrove swamps are filled with scorpions and mosquitoes and every kind of poisonous stinging insect. The silence of the perpetual twilight is

Map 21
THE PACIFIC THEATRE
1944-5
SAKHALIN
HOKKAIDO
JAPAN
SEA OF JAPAN
HONSHU
Kamaishi
Hitachi
Tokyo
Hiroshima
Nagasaki
SHIKOKU
KYUSHU
CHINA
Shanghai
Amami Gunto
Okinawa Gunto
Sakishima Gunto
Foochow
Amoy
Swatow
Hong Kong
FORMOSA
NANSEI SHOTO
NANPO SHOTO
Bonin Is
Iwojima
PACIFIC OCEAN
2,200 Nautical miles to Pearl Harbor
Wake I
(BRITISH TARGETS IN OPERATION ICEBERG March April 1945)
PHILIPPINES
LUZON
Manila
MINDORO
SAMAR
LEYTE
PALAWAN
MINDANAO
SOUTH CHINA SEA
BRITISH PACIFIC FLEET JOINS US 5th FLEET March 1945
Guam
Ulithi
Yap
Palau Is
CAROLINE Is
MARSHALL Is
4 days steaming
BRITISH PACIFIC FLEET INTERMEDIATE BASE
CELEBES SEA
BORNEO
HALMAHERA
Nauru
Manus
New Ireland
New Britain
NEW GUINEA
Bougainville
SOLOMON Is
Palembang
JAVA SEA
Batavia
CELEBES
CERAM
BANDA SEA
JAVA
BALI
LOMBOK
FLORES
SOEMBA
TIMOR
ARAFURA SEA
Darwin
11 days steaming Manus-Sydney
New Hebrides
New Caledonia
AUSTRALIA
Fremantle
Sydney
BRITISH PACIFIC FLEET MAIN BASE
NEW ZEALAND
45°N
30°N
15°N
0°
15°S
30°S
120°E
135°E
150°E
165°E

broken only by the creaking of mangrove roots and the splash of the most loathsome denizen of the place, the crocodiles . . .[65]

Just as along the Dalmatian coast of Yugoslavia (see above, p. 691) the Royal Navy's light forces – often commanded by RNVR officers – conducted an aggressive guerrilla war against enemy shipping. But the Navy also provided the 14th Army with its customary humdrum but supremely useful services by ferrying forward stores and reinforcements, and by putting troops ashore to cut off or hamper the Japanese retreat.

Not all such operations were small in scale. On 21 January 1945 a task force including the battleship *Queen Elizabeth*, the light cruiser *Phoebe*, the escort carrier *Ameer*, two destroyers and two sloops landed the 26th Indian Division on the big offshore island of Ramree in order to capture it as a base for further 'descents' to the southward. The landing itself successfully followed the well-established procedures, but it then took a month before the last of the Japanese garrison were killed or taken prisoner. On 26 January the Navy also successfully landed 500 Royal Marines on the neighbouring island of Cheduba. The last of all these ventures up the 'chaungs' in a climate like a steambath took place on 13 March 1945 when a brigade was lifted from Ramree to land at Letpan, halfway down the Burmese coast from the Indian border.[66]

Seven days later, away to the east in the great central plain of Burma, General Slim consummated the destruction of the defending Japanese Army in a brilliant battle of encirclement round Mandalay. The road to the capital, Rangoon, lay open; the campaign in Burma was over except for pursuit. The city was to fall on 2 May 1945 to a now redundant amphibious landing ('Dracula', successor to the aborted 'Anakim' of 1943).

In the central Pacific, the main theatre of war, during the months since the 'Octagon' Conference in Quebec, American forces had been relentlessly smashing their way nearer and nearer Japan. In October 1944 the US Pacific Fleet had won a crushing victory over the Japanese fleet in a complex, sprawling battle comprising four separate major engagements and collectively known as the Battle of Leyte Gulf. In this, the largest naval battle in history, involving no fewer than 282 ships and some 2,000 aircraft, the Japanese lost four carriers, three battleships (including the 70,000-ton *Musashi*), six heavy cruisers, three light cruisers and eight destroyers; the Americans only one light carrier, two escort carriers and three destroyers.[67] This victory, gutting Japanese naval power, opened the way to the successful invasion of the Philippines by assault forces from Nimitz's Central Pacific Command and MacArthur's South-West Pacific Command. By the beginning of March 1945 the main Philippine island, Luzon, was in American hands. By the end of March the Americans had also taken the island of Iwojima in the Bonin Islands after ferocious fighting, so giving them an airbase for attacking Japan itself.

Now it was the turn of Okinawa in the Ryukyus, last step before the Japanese home islands: 'Operation Iceberg'. The American Expeditionary Force itself numbered 1,205 vessels from battleships (ten of them) to landing craft. The covering force consisted of the two Fast Carrier Task Forces of Admiral Spruance's 5th Fleet – Admiral Marc Mitscher's Task Force 58 and Admiral Rawlings's British Pacific Fleet (Task Force 57). Mitscher's Task Force 58 was divided into four task groups each virtually as strong in carriers, battleships, cruisers and destroyers as Rawlings's entire fleet.[68] But in aircraft the disparity in strength was even greater, for Mitscher's carriers embarked 1,218 aircraft to Rawlings's 218.[69]

The disparity in average numbers of aircraft embarked per carrier does not tell the whole story of Task Force 57's inferiority in carrier aviation compared with Task Force 58. For whereas Mitscher's ships flew an operationally compatible range of reconnaissance, fighter, torpedo and dive-bomber aircraft, Rawlings's ships were equipped with a ragbag of British and American types. This in itself complicated flying operations, for the carriers were compelled to turn into the wind again and again in order to launch aircraft with different take-off requirements, and so lost speed of advance. The American-supplied aircraft – the Vought Corsair two-seater fighter (maximum speed 180 mph); the Grumman Hellcat single-seat fighter (maximum speed 380 mph); and the Grumman Avenger torpedo-bomber (maximum speed 251 mph) – were all specifically designed like Mitscher's for carrier work. So too was Rawlings's British-made Firefly fighter-reconnaissance aircraft (maximum speed 316 mph),[70] although this had at first proved another of the aircraft industry's turkeys, the prototype in 1942 being so unstable that it killed a test pilot.[71] The Firefly only reached the squadrons two years later. However, the Vickers Supermarine Seafire fighter, a fifth of Rawlings's total strength, was simply a naval version of the Spitfire, an aircraft originally designed for the short-range air defence of Great Britain operating from grass airfields. At sea in the Pacific the Seafire's lack of range restricted it to a defensive role near the carriers, while its undercarriage proved yet again unable to cope with the thudding impact of deck landings. During 'Operation Iceberg' the British Pacific Fleet lost 46 aircraft in deck landing crashes, of which 28 were Seafires – as against an estimated total of 84 Japanese aircraft destroyed in aerial combat or on the ground.[72]

The enforced reliance on the inadequate Seafire, and the fact that 167 out of the British Pacific Fleet's 218 aircraft were American (supplied under Lend-Lease), served as a further indictment of the incompetence of the British aircraft firms – Fairey and Blackburn – which had been charged since the 1920s with building for the Fleet Air Arm. But here is also reflected the continuing legacy of the Admiralty's loss of authority over maritime aviation and aircraft procurement in 1918, and of the belatedness of the restoration of its control over carrier flying operations in 1937; the legacy too of the Royal Air Force's continued management of the design and procurement of aircraft for the Fleet Air Arm even after 1937 (see above, pp. 24–6 and 38–9).

Yet the British Pacific Fleet exemplifies the backwardness of British naval technology and operational technique, the poverty of the industrial resources behind the Royal Navy, in more ways than just carrier aviation. Although all its ships – battleships, fleet carriers, cruisers, destroyers – had been designed during the late 1930s rearmament period, their boiler, engine room and propulsion technology remained of strictly Great War specification, so rendering them inefficient in performance and wasteful of fuel, and consequently slower to gain speed and of shorter endurance than American ships (see above, p. 481). Their anti-aircraft target-acquisition and fire-control systems were similarly out-of-date. According to one expert in 1978,

> It may seem strange now that after some twenty-five years of design and experiment by the acknowledged experts and designers of the day in this field, there did not exist any anti-aircraft system in the fleet by the end of the war that had really any chance of destroying an enemy aircraft.[73]

The failure stemmed from the pre-war Admiralty decision not to adopt a tachymetric fire control system as in the American and German Navies (see above, pp. 46–8) which could acquire and retain a target more quickly and accurately than the scientifically more primitive and operationally laborious British system. The same expert sums up the consequences:

> It is small wonder, then, that the Director Layer and Trainer were faced with an extremely difficult task in merely getting on to and keeping on target, while, for the guns to hit it, the task was virtually impossible, especially bearing in mind the very great inaccuracy of the fuzes in use.[74]

By 1945 the problem of inaccurate fuzes had certainly been solved, thanks to the supply by the Americans of radio-proximity fuzes, a radar device invented by British scientists but which Britain lacked the industrial capacity to manufacture. This did not however solve the problem of the clumsy and partly manually operated British fire-control system. The United States Navy had adopted a mechanised fire-control system, the Mark 63, for anti-aircraft fire, including a highly compact predictor. Unfortunately the Admiralty was unable to find a British firm capable of manufacturing it to the necessary close tolerances.[75] Moreover, in the American system the hydraulic machinery for training the turrets and laying the guns was remote-controlled, automatically following the predicted position of the enemy aircraft, whereas in British ships the guns were trained and elevated by operators at the mounting following pointers in receivers in front of them. The American system eliminated the potential errors inherent in such manual operation, which demanded much practice to achieve accuracy. No wonder the Superintending Scientist at the Admiralty Research Laboratory reported in July 1943 after a visit to the United States:

> I am convinced that by and large, the Americans have beaten us in the field of Remote Fire Control [i.e., including remote *power* control] . . . [They are] unquestionably well ahead of ourselves so far as Remote Fire Control for gun mountings is concerned, and their developments in hydraulics for this purpose are remarkable . . .[76]

This scientist contrasted the 'enthusiastic engineers' who ran the American precision-engineering industries with the 'mere dogsbodies' in British firms 'to be listened to only if it suits the convenience of those in authority'. A distinguished British engineer in the field of fire control remarked that the British attitude appeared to be: 'How can we best solve this problem on a short-term basis with our existing resources'; how on the other hand the American attitude appeared to be: 'What sort of resources and facilities shall we need as a starting point for the solution of this problem?'[77] This same engineer noted that the fire-control equipment in British ships was in any event 'without exception . . . dependent for its existence in one way or another on foreign made – and designed – precision machine tools! – either American or Continental, because the equivalent British type does not exist'.[78] The experts laid the blame for this British backwardness in fire control impartially on such poverty of enterprise and competence within British industry and on the purblind conservatism of the Naval Ordnance Department, which took until 1944 to accept that the Americans and Germans enjoyed better fire-control systems.[79]

However, in one major respect British ship design proved superior to American – the fleet carriers' 3-inch armour over the flight deck, which enabled them to brush off the impact of Japanese 'Kamikaze' ('Wind of Heaven') suicide attacks in the coming action off the Ryukyus. Nonetheless a penalty had to be paid for the extra weight of the armour in terms of the number of aircraft embarked, amounting to little more than half the number in an American carrier.

But it was in the replenishment of the fleet at sea during prolonged operations far from its advanced base and some 5,000 miles from its main base in Australia that the British Pacific Fleet most glaringly displayed the Royal Navy's technical backwardness.

During four years of war in the Pacific the Americans had perfected the concept of the fleet train, which was no less than a mobile advanced base complete with oil tankers, stores ships, ammunition ships, hospital ships, aircraft and ship repair vessels, floating dry-docks and tugs, all in lavish numbers; all of them purpose-built vessels crewed by the United States Navy.[80] The British Pacific Fleet's train by contrast more resembled a maritime version of the motley procession of hired carts, sutlers' waggons and camp-followers that trailed behind eighteenth-century armies.[81] Under the command of Rear-Admiral D. B. Fisher (Rear-Admiral, Fleet Train) were vessels wearing the White Ensign or the Blue Ensign of the Royal Fleet Auxiliaries, converted merchantmen wearing the Red Ensign (some of them with all-Chinese or all-Lascar crews), other merchantmen belonging to Britain's allies and wearing a colourful variety of national ensigns. The ships of the fleet train themselves varied greatly in speed, so further complicating Admiral Fisher's problem of operating his polyglot command; and in particular he lacked enough fast tankers able to keep station with the battlefleet. Moreover, the equipment in the ships was no less improvised and inadequate. It did not help that British operational techniques for replenishing at sea were not so rapid and efficient as American.

According to Rear-Admiral Sir Philip Vian (Flag Officer, 1st Aircraft Carrier Squadron, comprising all four British fleet carriers),

> The British method of fuelling big ships at sea, which was by means of buoyant hoses trailed astern of the tanker, was primarily at fault. It was an awkward, unseaman-like business compared with the American method, in which the two ships concerned steamed along abreast of one

> another a short space apart. For some reason we had failed to benefit from American experience to fit our tankers and warships with the necessary tackle to employ this method. We were to suffer for it until we did so.
>
> Furthermore, our tankers of the Fleet Train, hastily collected and hastily fitted out, were often inexperienced and ill-equipped. The fuelling gear would become entangled, or hoses would burst. On such occasions fuelling took up to six hours longer than it should have done; and only by steaming at full speed through the night could the flying-off position be reached in time for our first day's operations.[82]

All in all it was therefore fortunate that although the deal with Admiral King had called for the British Pacific Fleet to be self-sufficient the local American logistic authorities, in the words of a signal from Admiral Fraser to the Admiralty,

> have interpreted self-sufficiency in a very liberal sense . . . American authorities are most open handed in allowing the B.P.F. to draw from these [surplus] items, but this has been subject to the over-riding proviso that in doing so it has not been necessary to refer the matter to the next higher authority. Whenever it has been necessary so to refer such questions . . . the request has always met with refusal.[83]

As with other of the Royal Navy's wartime weaknesses, this failure to develop the ships, techniques and tackle for replenishing task forces at sea owed itself to past clinging to outmoded professional habits of mind coupled with pre-war lack of funds. Up to the middle of the Second World War the Royal Navy had remained loyal to the Victorian logistical concept of a chain of fixed naval bases or fuelling stations along the main imperial strategic axes, such as Gibraltar, Malta, Alexandria, Aden, Bombay, Trincomalee and Singapore. It was intended that squadrons would return to such bases, or to United Kingdom bases in regard to operations in home waters, in order to replenish after sorties *à la* Jutland.[84] Between 1936 and 1939 an Admiralty Supply Ships Committee had certainly studied the possible need for stores and ammunition ships, recommending that some 50 vessels should be taken up from trade and converted. This was far from the concept of a complete fleet train. Yet even in the case of operations in home waters, such as the chase of the *Bismarck*, or in the northern seas, as in the Norway campaign of 1940 and the later Russian convoys, British fleet commanders had been seriously hampered by their inability to refuel and re-ammunition their ships at sea, and the consequent need to return home after only a few days' operations. The same was true of convoy operations in the Mediterranean and the Atlantic. Even the German Navy, stationing tankers and supply vessels far from German ports for the benefit of its raiders, had something to teach the Royal Navy in this regard.

Only from the middle of the war onwards did it become more and more the custom for oilers to refuel British warships in mid-Atlantic or mid-Arctic or in the course of Mediterranean convoy runs. And only at this time did the Admiralty decide to convert some existing armed merchant cruisers into repair ships. But not until summer 1943 did it reach a decision to create fleet trains as such – one for the Indian Ocean and one for the Pacific; and not until September that year did it draw up its final staff requirement for the size and composition of the trains.

By this time, of course, Britain was suffering from a desperate shortage of ships of all kinds, while her shipyards and equipment industries were choked with existing work. The whole of 1944 was spent in a struggle to find and convert the necessary vessels. Cuts had to be made accordingly in the existing naval shipbuilding and merchant-ship repair programmes. The United States helped out by supplying some of its purpose-built fleet-train ships; Canada also helped by converting other vessels. That a fleet train was cobbled together in time to support the Pacific Fleet in spring 1945 may therefore be accounted a feat of typically resourceful British improvisation, but it nevertheless represents a sad falling-off from the standards of logistical professionalism achieved by the Royal Navy in its days of greatness in the eighteenth century;[85] it demonstrates afresh that as a seapower Britain was now only the poor relation clad in darns and patches, striving to put on a brave front.

The battle for Okinawa and neighbouring islands in the Ryukyus lasted from 18 March 1945, when Mitscher's Task Force 58 began a fortnight of preliminary air strikes against enemy airfields, till 21 June, when organised Japanese resistance on Okinawa ceased. For the American armed forces it proved the bloodiest of all the Pacific battles, costing the United States Navy over 4,900 sailors killed or missing and nearly 5,000 wounded, and the Army 7,613 killed or missing, 31,807 wounded and more than 26,000 non-battle casualties.[86] The American carrier forces (including auxiliary carriers) lost 763 aircraft. Thirty ships and craft were sunk, mostly by Kamikaze attack, and 368 others damaged, including the carriers *Wasp*, *Yorktown* and *Franklin*.[87] But for the Japanese the campaign brought complete defeat and catastrophic loss – 110,000 army casualties in the land battle, over 1,500 Kamikaze aircraft and their suicidal pilots, and the last remnant of the Japanese battlefleet, the 70,000-ton battleship

Yamato. She too had been despatched on a suicide mission, for Japan was now so short of oil that she could be fuelled for an outward voyage only. Caught by American carrier aircraft on 7 April, she sank after being struck by ten torpedoes and five bombs.[88]

The key role of covering the amphibious forces during the landings and the subsequent operations against the 2,000 Japanese aircraft based in the southernmost Japanese home island of Kyushu fell to Admiral Mitscher's Task Force 58. His ships kept the sea for two and a half months, a prodigious achievement even by American standards, and they did so despite massed air attacks pressed home with suicidal desperation (quite literally so in the case of the Kamikazes). The British Pacific Fleet (Task Force 57) was allotted the subsidiary task of suppressing the Japanese airfields on the Sakashima Gunto, a group of islands to the south of Okinawa, so that they could not be used as a staging point for air reinforcements from Formosa to Okinawa.[89] Task Force 57 launched its first air strikes on 26 March and kept them up until 20 April, when it had to return to Leyte in order to replenish, replace lost or damaged aircraft, take on fresh pilots and relieve fighter wings which had reached the end of their operational tour. So far Task Force 57 had largely escaped the savage air onslaughts delivered by the Japanese against Mitscher's Task Force 58, although the *Indefatigable* was hit by a Kamikaze at the base of her 'island' (inflicting little damage) and the destroyer HMS *Ulster* was put out of action by a near-miss from a bomb and had to be towed back to Leyte by HMNZS *Gambia*. During its fortnight's absence at Leyte the British Pacific Fleet's role in 'Iceberg' was taken over by American escort carriers of the Fifth Fleet's Carrier Support Group.[90]

Task Force 57 returned to its station on 4 May for a further three weeks of action against airfields in the Sakashima Gunto and also Formosa. But this time the British ships caught the edge of the storm of Japanese air attack. The carriers *Formidable*, *Indomitable* and *Victorious* were all hit, although thanks to their armoured decks the destruction was mostly limited to parked aircraft.

As it turned out, this was the last time in the Second World War that the ships' companies of a British battle squadron would experience that routine of life while closed up for action under heavy air attack which had become so familiar in the Mediterranean and the Arctic – the donning of clean underwear and of anti-flash hoods under tin hats; the 'action breakfast' of ham roll, tea, bread and butter and marmalade; 'action pie' at midday of meat, carrots, onions, potatoes and peas encased Cornish-pasty-style between two thick crusts of pastry, and brought back to each battle station by the 'mess cook', a traditional name dating from the Nelsonian era when each mess cooked its own food. For the last time too was heard under heavy air attack the staccato banging of the pom-poms, the deeper detonation of the high-angle guns; or from bridge and battery was seen a sky thickly blotched with puffs of smoke from exploding shells and alive with enemy aircraft. The novelty now lay in that those aircraft did not always pull out of a dive at the last moment like a Stuka, but instead kept on coming until the pilot's service to his Emperor terminated in a ball of flame and exploding metal. So for the last time too in the Second World War the sick-bay staffs in a British battlesquadron had to do what they could for sailors roasted or maimed and ripped.

On 25 May 1945 Admiral Rawlings set course for Manus with the British Pacific Fleet's role in 'Operation Iceberg' completed. The Fleet had destroyed an estimated 88 Japanese aircraft in the air (including four by ships' gunfire) or on the ground, plus eight Kamikazes, but had lost in return no fewer than 134 aircraft of its own. Of these, 30 had been destroyed in combat; 23 as a result of Kamikaze hits on the carriers; and 46 in deck-landing crashes. In addition 69 aircraft had been damaged to the point of needing replacement even though ultimately repairable. Of these, fifteen had suffered damage in deck-landings; nine in Kamikaze attacks, and no fewer than 28 in an accidental fire in the *Formidable*.[91]

At Manus the British Pacific Fleet dispersed to Sydney (eleven days' steaming away) and other bases in order to refit and train for the final operations against the Japanese home islands. It would be some six weeks before it rejoined the American fleet.

More than 2,000 miles away to the south-west Vice-Admiral Sir Arthur Power's East Indies Fleet was finding it difficult to locate targets in seas now virtually emptied of Japanese warships and shipping.[92] Nevertheless, on 10 May 1945 the submarines *Statesman* and *Subtle* patrolling in the Malacca Straits sighted a Japanese heavy cruiser escorted by a destroyer. Unable to get within attacking range, the submarines reported their find to the C-in-C, who ordered an air and surface search. On the 15th an aircraft from the escort carrier *Shah* spotted the cruiser – the 10,000-ton *Haguro* – whereupon Avengers bombed and damaged her. Now five destroyers of the 26th Flotilla, *Saumarez*, *Venus*, *Vigilant*, *Virago* and *Verulam* (all of wartime construction), steamed at 27 knots to close the 85 miles between them and the *Haguro*. After searching for her along a bearing calculated from her guessed 'farthest on' position, they picked her up on their radar screens shortly after midnight, and pounced on her simultaneously from different directions in a superbly timed and executed attack. Shattered by no fewer than eight torpedoes, the *Haguro* went down in a few minutes. It could be said that the 26th Flotilla (Captain M. L. Power) had avenged HMS *Exeter*, the cruiser sunk by the Japanese in March 1942 in the Battle of the Java Sea along with her escorting destroyers.

The Royal Navy's submarines in the waters off Malaya and the Dutch East Indies found themselves reduced to the role of sharks snapping up small fry, for Japanese merchant traffic had ceased except for coasters and junks. But now and again a submarine captain was excited to see through his periscope a worthier target. On 8 June 1945 Commander A. R. Hezlet in the *Trenchant* sighted the 10,000-ton heavy cruiser *Ashigawa* in the narrow waters of the Banka Strait off Sumatra, and promptly hit her with five torpedoes. The *Ashigawa* sank in half an hour. And British midget submarines or X-Craft towed to the target area by conventional submarines repeated in Far Eastern seas their 'Boy's Own Paper' feats of daring against the *Tirpitz*.

On 31 July 1945 the XE1 (Lieutenant J. E. Smart, RNVR), towed by HMS *Sparks* (Lieutenant D. G. Kent) and XE3 (Lieutenant I. E. Fraser, RNR), towed by HMS *Stygian* (Lieutenant G. S. C. Clarabut), carried out a sortie up the Johore Strait between Malaya and Singapore island with the task of sinking two Japanese cruisers lying off the former British naval base.[93] The XE1 proved unlucky, for encounters with enemy surface craft so delayed her approach to her own designated target, the cruiser *Myoko*, that she laid her mines instead alongside the XE3's victim, the 10,000-ton *Takao*, at an anchor in shallow water. The XE3 successfully crawled along the muddy bottom of the Strait to reach her attacking station beneath the *Takao*. But now came setback and hazard. There was not enough depth to open the hatch whence the diver must exit with the limpet mines to attach to the *Takao*'s bottom. Nevertheless the diver, Leading-Seaman J. J. Magennis, managed to squeeze his way out of the partially open hatch – only to find that a thick crust of barnacles made it impossible to fix the limpets. It took him an exhausting three-quarters of an hour to scrape a clear space and successfully complete his task. As the XE3 made her escape down the Strait the *Takao* was reduced by the limpet mines to a useless wreck sitting on the seabed. Both Fraser and Magennis were awarded the Victoria Cross for this remarkable exercise in engaging the enemy more closely.

On that same day far to the north, off Saigon in Indo-China, the XE4 (Lieutenant M. H. Shean, RANVR), towed by HMS *Spearhead* (Lieutenant-Commander R. E. Youngman, RNR), found and cut the Saigon–Hong Kong and Saigon–Singapore submarine telegraph cables. Further to the north still, off Hong Kong, the XE5 (Lieutenant H. P. Westmacott), towed by HMS *Selene* (Lieutenant-Commander H. R. B. Newton), succeeded after a three-day search in thick mud in putting the Hong Kong–Singapore cable out of action too. These were the same X-Craft commanders who in 1943 had destroyed a munitions ship and a floating dock in Bergen harbour.

It was not until 16 July that the British Pacific Fleet joined Admiral Halsey's 3rd Fleet off Japan, there to serve as an extra group in his Fast Carrier Force, launching air strikes against targets in Japan itself. By this time the enemy air forces had spent themselves, and the 3rd Fleet ranged up and down the Japanese coasts at will and virtually unscathed. Admiral Rawlings's own main anxiety lay in his ramshackle fleet train, which made it difficult to keep up with Halsey's ships, and even forced him to ask the Americans to refuel three of his cruisers. Back in Sydney Admiral Fraser, the Commander-in-Chief, British Pacific Fleet, reported to the Admiralty on how Halsey 'with easy grace' was 'striking here one day and there the next, replenishing at sea and returning to harbour as the situation demands. With dogged persistence the British Pacific Fleet is keeping up . . . but it is tied by a string to Australia, and much handicapped by its few small tankers.'[94] Nonetheless the American command deliberately left the British Pacific Fleet out of a major strike on 24 July against the remaining ships of the Japanese Navy lying immobilised in Kure naval base. Halsey accepted the advice of his chief of staff that the British ships should be so excluded in order, in Halsey's words, 'to forestall a possible post-war claim by Britain that she had delivered even a part of the final blow that demolished the Japanese fleet'.[95] So much for Sir Alan Brooke and his colleagues' naïve hopes that to contribute a British Pacific Fleet would earn a share in the victory and a voice in American counsels.

On 6 and 9 August 1945 the only two atomic bombs yet manufactured were exploded above the cities of Hiroshima and Nagasaki. On the 14th Japan announced her unconditional surrender. Yet whatever the motivation or merits or demerits of the American decision to drop the atomic bombs, whatever the effect on the Japanese leadership and especially the Emperor Hirohito, the truth is that Japan was already on the point of collapse as an industrial society – incapable of prosecuting the war further. It had not been the titanic battles and famous victories of the American surface fleets and amphibious forces that had brought her to this pass, but the American submarine, which had achieved against the island seapower of Japan the war-deciding victory which had eluded Dönitz against the island seapower of Great Britain.

For the Japanese war effort, like Britain's, had been utterly dependent on seaborne imports of food, fuel-oil and raw materials – in her case, from her newly conquered empire in Malaya, the Dutch East Indies and South-East Asia. On the very day of Pearl Harbor the United States Navy was authorised to carry out unrestricted submarine warfare against Japan, using its big 1,500-ton boats with their cruising range of 12,000 miles. This submarine 'Battle of the Pacific' was to follow a pattern exactly opposite to that of the Battle of the Atlantic. Here it was the submarines which possessed radar to help them in the search for victims; the Japanese warships that were blindfolded by lack of it until late 1943 onwards. Moreover, Japan learned nothing from parallel British experience in the Atlantic. She failed to organise a proper convoy system until 1944, and even then it existed more in name than in fact. She failed to mount anything like the immense British anti-submarine operational and research effort. Even the Imperial Japanese Navy's anti-submarine tactics lacked the skill and tenacity of the Royal Navy's, and American submariners fought a successful battle against enemy escorts, sinking 41 in 1944 for the loss of only six of their own number.

In 1943 Japan lost a million more tons of shipping than she built. Whereas she needed 3 million tons to keep civilian life going in the home islands, and another 3 million to support the war, she now possessed only 5 million tons in all. In 1944 American submarines sank 2½ million tons of shipping. By March 1945 Japan had lost 88 per cent of the merchant tonnage with which she had begun the war, and her oil imports finally ceased, available stocks amounting to only one-sixth of her requirements.[96] Lack of fuel now paralysed Japanese industry and what remained of the Japanese Navy and Air Force. With imports of rice, wheat and soya at a standstill, the Japanese people themselves faced starvation.

Perhaps, therefore, the two atomic bombs were dropped in order to impress Stalin's Soviet Union (which invaded Japanese-occupied Manchuria on 8 August 1945) as much as the leaders of Japan.

At 0856 on Sunday, 2 September, 1945 – scattered morning clouds in a sky that would soon clear to summer blue – the Japanese Foreign Minister, Mamoru Shigemitsu, in the top hat and morning coat of traditional diplomacy, and the Chief of the Army General Staff, General Yoshijiro Umezu, in baggy khaki and jackboots, came aboard the battleship USS *Missouri*, flagship of the 3rd Fleet, at her mooring in Tokyo Bay to sign the formal instrument of Japan's surrender.[97] When the Japanese delegation stepped on to the *Missouri*'s quarter deck they saw before them a green baize-covered table bearing the surrender documents; they saw behind a rope barrier a watching audience of senior Allied officers and civilian dignitaries; they saw above them American bluejackets and cameramen of all nations crowding every vantage point of the battleship's superstructure. Aloft flew the five-star flag of Fleet Admiral Nimitz, Commander-in-Chief, US Pacific Fleet, along with the personal flag of General Douglas MacArthur, now the Supreme Commander, Allied Powers, for the surrender and occupation of Japan.

For several minutes the Japanese stood immobile and alone before all these hostile eyes while the *Missouri*'s chaplain gave an address over the tannoy, followed by the American national anthem played on a record – the opening scene in an occasion as dramatically stage-managed as that other humiliation of a defeated enemy nearly 27 years earlier on board HMS *Queen Elizabeth* in the November fogs of the Firth of Forth.

Then General MacArthur, Admiral Nimitz and Admiral Halsey, C-in-C, 3rd Fleet – both admirals wearing open-necked American khaki drill rather than traditional white ducks – walked forward on to the quarter deck to begin the ceremony of surrender. Flanking MacArthur as he stood at the microphone behind the table were the skeletal figures of the American General Wainwright, who had surrendered the Philippines in 1942, and the British General Percival, who had surrendered Singapore. Both had been flown to Tokyo from a prison camp in Manchuria. Firstly MacArthur made a short but flowery speech expressing his 'earnest hope of all mankind that from this solemn occasion a better world shall emerge out of the blood and carnage of the past'.[98] Then he gestured to Shigemitsu to approach and seat himself on the opposite side of the table. At 0904 Shigemitsu signed the instrument of surrender, followed by General Umezu. MacArthur thereupon put his own signature on the document of acceptance of the surrender on behalf of all the Allied powers. Fleet Admiral Nimitz signed next. Then came the turn of the representatives of America's Allies, with a Chinese general in first place. In second place signed Admiral Sir Bruce Fraser for the United Kingdom; in third, a Soviet general; in fourth, General Sir Thomas Blamey for Australia; and thereafter the Canadian, French, Dutch and New Zealand representatives.

The signing done, MacArthur proclaimed: 'These proceedings are now closed.' The Second World War was formally over. The Japanese delegation left the *Missouri* to the twittering of the bosuns' pipes. At 0925, 450 carrier aircraft and hundreds of United States Army Air Force aircraft thundered over the flagship and the surrounding fleet of 258 Allied (overwhelmingly American) vessels from battleships to landing craft anchored in the bay.

Yet the British Pacific Fleet was not present in this mighty array – only a squadron composed of HMS *Duke of York* (flying the flag of Admiral Sir Bruce Fraser, who had steamed up from Australia for the occasion), HMS *King George V*, HMS *Indefatigable*, the cruisers HMS *Newfoundland* and HMNZS *Gambia*, and ten destroyers (two of them Australian). For when, on 14 August, the Japanese government had announced its acceptance of the Allied terms of unconditional surrender, the British Pacific Fleet had been about to return to Sydney at the end of its second tour of duty, and no extra tankers were available to keep it on station in Japanese waters. For want of just three fast fleet oilers Admiral Fraser had had no alternative but to order the main body of his Fleet south as already arranged. The warships themselves could easily have kept going – on VJ-Day the *King George V* had steamed for 52 days without once stopping her engines. To the bitter disappointment of the officers and men of the Fleet only a token force was left with Halsey to serve as a British presence.[99]

And even the victorious culmination of Churchill's preferred Indian Ocean and South-West Asia strategy, Britain's own war against Japan, had been relegated to anti-climax by order of MacArthur in his capacity as Supreme Commander, Allied Powers. For on 19 August, when the entire East Indies Fleet together with landing forces was steaming for Penang in Malaya and for Singapore, MacArthur instructed that no landings or formal surrenders of Japanese forces were to take place until after the completion of his own grand ceremony on board the *Missouri*.[100] A similar prohibition applied to a squadron detached by Admiral Fraser from the British Pacific Fleet to Hong Kong.[101]

In Tokyo Bay on that evening of 2 September 1945 Admiral Halsey went aboard HMS *Duke of York* at Admiral Fraser's invitation to witness the ceremony of 'Sunset' conducted with all the Royal Navy's traditional precision and pageantry. 'Massed bands of all the British ships played splendid martial music and a hymn,' wrote an American eyewitness to his wife. 'The flags of all the signatory Allies were flying from the signal yards, and all were slowly lowered in unison during the sunset hymn' – which was 'The Day Thou Gavest, Lord is Ended'.[102]

The 'Amen' fell away on the evening air. In His Majesty's ships, so few amidst that immense American fleet, the White Ensign was gathered in.

Sunset.

APPENDIXES

APPENDIX A

Abbreviations

AA = anti-aircraft
ABDA = American, British, Dutch, Australian
ABE Committee = Assessors on Bomb versus Battleship Experiments Committee
ACI = Atlantic Convoy Instructions
ACNS(H) = Assistant Chief of Naval Staff (Home)
AEAF = Allied Expeditionary Air Force
AEF = Allied Expeditionary Force
AFHQ = Allied Forces Headquarters
AI = Air Intelligence
ANCXF = Allied Naval Commander, Expeditionary Force
ASV = Air-to-Surface Vessel radar
ATS = Auxiliary Territorial Service

BEF = British Expeditionary Force
BLO = Bombardment Liaison Officer
BST = British Summer Time
BUCO = Build-up Control Organisation

CAM = Catapult Aircraft Merchant ship
CCOS = Combined Chiefs of Staff
CETF = Commander, Eastern Task Force
CIC = Combined Intelligence Committee
CID = Committee of Imperial Defence
CIGM = Chief Inspector of Gun Mountings
CIGS = Chief of the Imperial General Staff

CNO = Chief of Naval Operations
CNTF = Central Naval Task Force
COMINCH = Commander-in-Chief, United States Fleet
COPP = Combined Operations Pilotage Parties
COREP = Control Organisation for Repair
COS = Chief(s) of Staff
COSSAC = Chief of Staff to the Supreme Allied Commander
COTUG = Control Organisation for Tugs
CTC = Combined Training Centre
CVE = Escort Aircraft Carrier

DNI = Director of Naval Intelligence
DNO = Director of Naval Ordnance
DTM = Director of Torpedoes and Mines
DUKW = 'Duck' amphibious truck (D = 1942, year of origin, the fourth year of war; U = Utility; K = Front-wheel drive; W = Six-wheeled.)

E-boat = German fast torpedo boat
ENTF = Eastern Naval Task Force

FAT = Feder-Apparat Torpedo
FDC = Fighter Direction Centre
FDS = Fighter Direction Ship
FOB = Forward Observer, Bombardment
FOBAA = Flag Officer, British Assault Area
FOO = Forward Observation Officer
FS = French Ship

GC and CS = Government Code and Cypher School (Bletchley Park or 'Ultra')
GCI = Ground Coastal Interception
GHQ = General Headquarters
G/R = General Reconnaissance

HA = High Angle
HACS = High Angle Control System
HF/DF = High Frequency Direction Finding
HMAS = His Majesty's Australian Ship
HMCS = His Majesty's Canadian Ship
HMNZS = His Majesty's New Zealand Ship
HMS = His Majesty's Ship

HNLMS = Her Netherlands Majesty's Ship
HNorMS = His Norwegian Majesty's Ship
HON = 'Husky Naval Orders'

ISTDC = Inter-Service Training and Development Centre

JCS = Joint Chiefs of Staff
JIC = Joint Intelligence Committee

LCA = Landing Craft (Assault)
LCI = Landing Craft (Infantry)
LCM = Landing Craft (Mechanised)
LCS = Landing Craft (Support)
LCT = Landing Craft (Tank)
LSI = Landing Ships (Infantry)
LSI(L) = Landing Ships Infantry (Large)

MAC = Merchant Aircraft Carrier
ME = Middle East
MI = Military Intelligence
MTB = Motor Torpedo Boat

NCETF = Naval Commander, Eastern Task Force
NCWTF = Naval Commander, Western Task Force
NID = Naval Intelligence Department
NOIC = Naval Officer in Charge

OB = Ordnance Board
OIC = Operational Intelligence Centre
OKH = Oberkommando des Heeres (German Army High Command)
OKM = Oberkommando der Kriegsmarine (German Naval High Command)
OKW = Oberkommando der Wehrmacht (German Armed Forces High Command)
ON = 'Operation Neptune – Naval Orders'
ONAD = 'Operation Neptune – Administrative Orders'
ONCO = 'Operation Neptune – Communication Orders'

PLUTO = Pipe Line Under The Ocean
POL = Petrol, Oil, Lubricants
PP = German ship-to-ship signals

PR = Photographic Reconnaissance
PRU = Photographic Reconnaissance Unit

R and D = Research and Development
RASC = Royal Army Service Corps
R-boat = German motor minesweeper
RM = Royal Marines
RN = Royal Navy
RNorN = Royal Norwegian Navy
RNR = Royal Naval Reserve
RNVR = Royal Naval Volunteer Reserve

SCAEF = Supreme Commander, Allied Expeditionary Force
SHAEF = Supreme Headquarters, Allied Expeditionary Force
Sigint = Signals Intelligence
SIS = Secret Intelligence Service
SOFC = Senior Officer, Ferry Craft

TIS = Theatre Intelligence Section
TON = 'Torch Naval Orders'
TRE = Telecommunications Research Establishment
TURCO = Turn Round Control

U-boat = German submarine (*Unterseeboot*)
USN = United States Navy
USNR = United States Naval Reserve

VCNS = Vice Chief of Naval Staff
VHF = Very High Frequency
VLR = Very Long Range

WAAF = Women's Auxiliary Air Force
WRNS (Wrens) = Women's Royal Naval Service

Y Service = interception of radio signals

APPENDIX B

Notes to Text

Prologue – 1918: *'The German Ensign Will Be Hauled Down At Sunset'* (pages 1–16)

1. See Buist Papers, Churchill Archives Centre, BUIST 1/4.
2. Ibid; see also W. S. Chalmers, *The Life and Letters of David, Earl Beatty*, London, Hodder and Stoughton, 1951, p. 349. The account of the German internment is drawn from Chalmers, op cit, pp. 342–9; S. W. Roskill, *Admiral of the Fleet Earl Beatty; The Last Naval Hero: An Intimate Biography*, New York, Atheneum, 1981, pp. 276–80.
3. Ibid, p. 273.
4. Ibid.
5. Ibid, p. 275.
6. Arthur J. Marder, *From the Dreadnought to Scapa Flow; The Royal Navy in the Fisher Era, 1904–1919*, Vol II, *The War Years: To the Eve of Jutland*, London, Oxford University Press, 1965, p. 4.
7. Correlli Barnett, *The Swordbearers*, second edition, London, Hodder and Stoughton, 1987, p. 181.
8. Roskill, *Beatty*, op cit, p. 166.
9. Ibid, p. 160 and footnote.
10. See Marder, op cit, Vol III, *Jutland And After, May 1916–December 1916*, London, Oxford University Press, 1966, pp. 166–74; Roskill, *Beatty*, op cit, pp. 186–92, 254; see also Barnett, op cit, pp. 181–94.
11. Barnett, op cit, p. 187.
12. Roskill, *Beatty*, op cit, pp. 186–7.
13. Barnett, op cit, p. 188.
14. See Roskill, *Beatty*, op cit, p. 63; Dr J. T. Sumida (ed), *The Pollen Papers*, Publication of the Navy Records Society, Vol 124, London,

George Allen and Unwin for The Navy Records Society, 1984, especially Dr Sumida's General Introduction, pp. 1–7.

15. Sumida, op cit, pp. 194–236; Dreyer Papers, Churchill Archives Centre, Cambridge, DRYR 2/1, 2/2.
16. Roskill, *Beatty*, op cit, p. 185.
17. Ibid, pp. 152–4, 180–1; Marder, op cit, Vol III, pp. 41–3, 148–54.
18. See Papers of Admiral Sir Reginald Hall, Churchill Archives Centre, HALL; Denniston Papers, DENN 1/1–4, 2/1.
19. Quoted in Correlli Barnett, *The Great War*, London, Park Lane Press, 1979, p. 106.
20. See Marder, op cit, Vol IV, *1917: Year of Crisis*, pp. 134–5, 150–2.
21. Marder, op cit, Vol IV, Chapters V–VII, especially pp. 104–6, 108–9, 112–65.
22. See Roskill (ed), *The Naval Air Service*, Vol I, London, The Navy Records Society, 1969, *passim*, but especially pp. 484–6, 545, 639–41, 651, 658–63.
23. Ibid, Vol I, Appendix I, p. 747.
24. Marder, op cit, pp. 3–24; Roskill, *The Naval Air Service*, op cit, Vol I, pp. xi–xvii.
25. Marder, op cit, p. 11.
26. Roskill, *The Naval Air Service*, op cit, Vol I, pp. 740–4.
27. Report by Squadron-Commander C. L'E. Malone, Commanding HMS *Ben-My-Chree*, to the Director of the Air Department, 14 August 1915; AIR 1/665, reproduced in Roskill, *The Naval Air Service*, op cit, Vol I, pp. 221–3; see also Marder, op cit, pp. 19–21.
28. Letter No 3343/H.F.0022 of 11 September 1917 from Admiral Sir David Beatty, C-in-C, Grand Fleet, to the Admiralty, entitled 'Considerations of an Attack by Torpedo Planes on the High Seas Fleet', in Adm 1/8486, reproduced in Roskill, *The Naval Air Service*, op cit, Vol I, p. 541.
29. Second Report of the Committee on Air Organisation and Home Defence against Air Raids, 17 August 1917, CAB 24/22, reproduced in Roskill, *The Naval Air Service*, op cit, Vol I, p. 512.
30. Ibid.
31. Letter from Geddes to Lord Weir, Secretary of State for the Air Force, 22 May 1918, in ADM 116/1805, reproduced in Roskill, *The Naval Air Service*, op cit, Vol I, pp. 670–1.
32. Roskill, *Naval Policy Between the Wars*, Vol 1, *The Period of Anglo-American Antagonism 1919–1929*, London, Collins, 1968, p. 71.
33. CAB 32/3, Pt I, E-10, quoted in Correlli Barnett, *The Collapse of British Power*, London, Eyre Methuen, 1972, paperback edition, Alan Sutton, 1984, p. 252.
34. CAB 27/627, COS 928, 'The Situation in the Far East', 18 June 1939.
35. Ibid.

Part I: Britannia Lets the Trident Slip

1. *Dreams of Peace and the Shrinking Navy, 1918–1931* (pages 19–28)

1. Paul M. Kennedy, *The Rise and Fall of British Naval Mastery*, London, Allen Lane, 1976, p. 260.
2. Roskill, *Naval Policy Between the Wars*, op cit, Vol I, Appendix D, p. 586.
3. First Interim Report of the Committee on National Expenditure, Cmd 1581. See Roskill, *Naval Policy Between the Wars*, op cit, Vol I, pp. 230–3.
4. Ibid, p. 221.
5. CAB 32/46, Documents and Stenographic Notes of the Imperial Conference, 1926, E-9; For the course of the Washington Conference, see CAB 30/1A, 1B, 9–10, 11–13, 15–16, 26, 31; Roskill, *Naval Policy Between the Wars*, op cit, Vol 1, Chap VIII; and for a summary, Barnett, *The Collapse of British Power*, op cit, pp. 263–74.
6. See Barnett, *The Collapse of British Power*, op cit, pp. 20–68, 274–8, 282–98, on the nature and impact of romantic internationalism on British total strategy in the 1920s.
7. Cited in CAB 27/626, FP (36)2, Memorandum by Sir Maurice Hankey for the Cabinet Committee on Foreign Policy, dated 1 May 1936, summarising the history of deliberations on the proposal for a League of Nations, 1916–19. The Admiralty memorandum was dated 23 December 1918.
8. Barnett, *The Collapse of British Power*, op cit, p. 275.
9. CAB 27/407, CP 195 (29): for the history of the Singapore base, see Barnett, *The Collapse of British Power*, op cit, pp. 279–82, 288; Paul Haggie, *Britannia at Bay; The Defence of the British Empire against Japan 1931–1941*, Oxford, Clarendon Press, 1981, pp. 1–24; Roskill, *Naval Policy Between the Wars*, op cit, Vol I, passim.
10. CAB 29/117, LNC(29)5.
11. Oscar Parkes, *British Battleships: 'Warrior' 1860 to 'Vanguard' 1950; A History of Design, Construction and Armament*, London, Seeley Service, 1970, pp. 566, 612 and 614–15.
12. Cf S. W. Roskill, 'A Sailor's Ditty Box', unpublished personal memoir in the Churchill Archives Centre.
13. Bernard Ireland, *The Rise and Fall of the Aircraft Carrier*, London and New York, Marshall Cavendish, 1979, p. 23; Roskill, *Naval Policy Between the Wars*, op cit, Vol I, pp. 496–7, 528.
14. Ireland, op cit.
15. See Till, 'Airpower and the Battleship' in Bryan Ranft (ed), *Technical Change and British Naval Policy 1860–1939*, London, Hodder and Stoughton, 1977, pp. 110–20; Roskill, *Naval Policy Between the Wars*, op cit, Vol I, pp. 113–16.

16. Roskill, *Naval Policy Between the Wars*, op cit, Vol I, pp. 223–5.
17. The Balfour Enquiry, 1921; the Geddes Committee, 1921; the Balfour Committee, 1923; the Salisbury Committee, 1923; the Colwyn Committee, 1925.
18. See Roskill, *Naval Policy Between the Wars*, op cit, Vol I, Chapters VI, X and XV for detailed accounts of these transactions.
19. Sir William James, *Admiral Sir William Fisher*, London, Macmillan, 1943, p. 124.
20. S. W. Roskill, 'A Sailor's Ditty Box', op cit.
21. Ibid.
22. Report to the Committee of Imperial Defence Sub-Committee on Preparations for the League Disarmament Conference, CAB 27/476, CDC(31)2.
23. Ibid.
24. Ibid.

2. *The Triple Threat and Belated Rearmament, 1932–1939* (pages 29–56)

1. CAB 53/22, COS 295.
2. Ibid.
3. Ibid.
4. CAB 53/23, COS 310.
5. Ibid.
6. Ibid.
7. Ibid.
8. Roskill, *Naval Policy Between the Wars*, op cit, Vol II, p. 306.
9. See Roskill, ibid, pp. 306–9 for an account of the negotiations.
10. CAB 16/123, DRC 37.
11. CAB 53/25, COS 392.
12. Roskill, *Naval Policy Between the Wars*, op cit, Vol II, p. 261.
13. CAB 53/25, COS 392.
14. CAB 23/83 11(36).
15. CAB 27/606, MF(36)1.
16. CAB 53/30, COS 560.
17. See David Reynolds, *The Creation of the Anglo-American Alliance 1937–1941: A Study in Competitive Co-operation*, London, Europa Publications, 1981, Chapters 1 and 2; Christopher Thorne, *Allies of a Kind: The United States, Great Britain and the War Against Japan, 1941–1945*, London, Hamish Hamilton, 1978.
18. CAB 29/159, AFC1.
19. Barnett, *The Collapse of British Power*, op cit, pp. 217–18.
20. See ibid, Part IV, 'An Imperial Commonwealth', for a detailed account of these transactions between 1921 and 1937.
21. Ibid, p. 231; Roskill, *Naval Policy Between the Wars*, op cit, Vol. II, pp. 435–6.

22. CAB 16/209 SAC 2.
23. See Barnett, *The Collapse of British Power*, op cit, pp. 386–439 for an analysis of the reasons for the delay in commencing British rearmament, and especially the role of public opinion in 1933–35.
24. CAB 16/112, DPR(DR)9, 12 February 1936.
25. See Roskill, *Naval Policy Between the Wars*, op cit, Vol II, pp. 217 and 326–7; N. H. Gibbs, *Grand Strategy*, Vol I, *Rearmament Policy*, London, HMSO, 1976, pp. 332–55.
26. CAB 16/112 DRC 37; Gibbs, op cit, pp. 334–5.
27. Meeting of the DPRC, 21 October 1937, in CAB 16/137, DPR 44.
28. Nineteenth, 20th, 22nd and 25th Admiralty reports to the DPRC, January, February, May and December 1938, CAB 16/142, DPR 244 and 249; CAB 16/143, DPR 271 and 293.
29. Meetings of the DPRC, 18 March, 22 April and 29 April 1937, in CAB 16/137, DPR 36, 38 and 39.
30. Twelfth report by the Admiralty to the DPRC, April 1937, in CAB 16/141, DPR 194.
31. Sixteenth report by the Admiralty to the DPRC, October 1937, CAB 16/142, DPR 224.
32. Fifth report of the Admiralty to the DPRC, October 1936, in CAB 16/142, DPR 129.
33. See Barnett, *The Audit of War*, London, Macmillan, 1986, Chapter Seven, for a detailed account of aircraft production during the rearmament period 1936–39.
34. Eighteenth report by the Air Ministry to the DPRC, for November 1937, CAB 16/142, DPR 236.
35. M. M. Postan, D. Hay and J. D. Scott, *Design and Development of Weapons*, London, HMSO and Longmans, Green, 1964, p. 136: CAB 16/137, DPR 40, meeting of the DPRC on 24 June 1937.
36. Postan, Hay and Scott, op cit, p. 137.
37. Ibid, pp. 134–5.
38. See John Terraine, *The Right of the Line: The Royal Air Force in the European War 1939–1945*, London, Hodder and Stoughton, 1985, pp. 30–5.
39. See Roskill, *Naval Policy Between the Wars*, op cit, Vol II, Chapter XIII for an account of the whole matter.
40. CAB 24/270, CP 199(37), 21 July 1937.
41. See Roskill, *Naval Policy Between the Wars*, op cit, Vol II, pp. 408–11.
42. Ibid, Vol 1, p. 542.
43. Hideo Takubo, article 'To Fight a Losing Battle; Yamamoto Isoruku and the Pacific War', in *The East*, Vol VII, No 3, March 1971, p. 59.
44. Ireland, *The Rise and Fall of the Aircraft Carrier*, op cit, pp. 25–9; Admiral of the Fleet Lord Hill-Norton and John Dekker, *Sea Power*, London, Faber and Faber, 1982, p. 62; H. T. Lenton and J. J. Colledge, *Warships of World War II*, London, Ian Allan, 1964, pp. 61–3.

45. See Parkes, *British Battleships*, op cit, pp. 663–9; Roskill, *Naval Policy Between the Wars*, op cit, Vol II, pp. 279–80, 326–9, 671; Eric Grove, Christopher Chant, David Lyon, Hugh Lyon, *The Hardware of World War II*, Galley Press, London, 1984, pp. 186–7, 146–7.
46. Parkes, op cit, pp. 663–9.
47. Ibid, pp. 569–76, 614–17, 648–9.
48. Grove, Chant, Lyon and Lyon, op cit, pp. 188–95; Lenton and Colledge, op cit, pp. 39–48.
49. Edgar J. March, *British Destroyers 1892–1953*, London, Seeley Service, 1966, p. 287.
50. Ibid, pp. 322–8.
51. Ibid, p. 335.
52. David Henry, 'British Submarine Policy, 1918–1939', in Ranft, *Technical Change and British Naval Policy 1860–1939*, op cit, especially pp. 102–8.
53. 'Notes for the 1937 Naval Estimates', 26 February 1937, quoted by Henry, in Ranft, op cit; see also Willem Hackmann, *Seek and Strike; Sonar, Antisubmarine Warfare and the Royal Navy 1914–54*, London, HMSO, 1984, Chapter V, especially pp. 125–34.
54. Ranft, op cit, p. 100.
55. C. B. A. Behrens, *Merchant Shipping and the Demands of War*, London, HMSO and Longmans, Green, 1955, pp. 37–8.
56. Ranft, op cit, p. 102.
57. Roskill, 'A Sailor's Ditty Box', op cit.
58. ABE 63, in CAB 16/179, cited in Roskill, *Naval Policy Between the Wars*, op cit, Vol II, p. 420.
59. Ibid.
60. Postan, Hay and Scott, op cit, p. 435.
61. Ibid, p. 457.
62. Roskill, *Naval Policy Between the Wars*, op cit, Vol II, p. 333.
63. Roskill quotation from ibid, p. 334. For the incapability of the British armaments and engineering firms to manufacture the tachymetric system, and possible consequent pressure on the Admiralty, see letter from Rear-Admiral M. W. St. L. Searle, to Captain Roskill, 1 May 1979 in Roskill Papers, Churchill Archive Centre, ROSK 7/29; see also the present work, Chapter 28, pp. 886–8, below and relevant documentary source references.
64. Roskill, *Naval Policy Between the Wars*, op cit, Vol II, p. 333; see also Rear-Admiral M. W. St. L. Searle, unpublished paper, 'The Air Threat and the Home Fleet at the Outbreak of War, 3rd September, 1939' in ROSK 4/11.
65. Ibid.
66. Roskill, *Naval Policy Between the Wars*, op cit, Vol II, p. 453.
67. See A. Wells, 'Naval Intelligence in an era of technical change' in Ranft, op cit, pp. 136–7; Denniston Papers, Churchill Archives Centre,

DENN 1/4; F. H. Hinsley with E. E. Thomas, C. F. G. Ransom and R. C. Knight, *British Intelligence in the Second World War*, Vol I, London, HMSO, 1979, Chapter 2, especially pp. 50–3, 62–3.
68. Wells, in Ranft, op cit, pp. 133–41.
69. Terraine, op cit, pp. 70 and 223.
70. Lieutenant-Commander Sir Godfrey Style in a letter of 5 January 1979 to Captain S. W. Roskill, in ROSK 7/210.
71. Ibid.
72. Roskill, *Naval Policy Between the Wars*, op cit, Vol II, p. 462.
73. Admiral Sir John Kelly, in ROSK 5/125; see also Admiral J. H. Godfrey, 'Memoirs', pp. 299–300, Churchill Archives Centre, GDFY.
74. Letter from Captain S. W. Roskill to Admiral Crutchley, 23 July 1975, in ROSK 7/210.
75. Letter of July 1936, in the Chatfield MSS, CHT/4/6, copy in ROSK 7/210.
76. Admiral Sir Victor Crutchley in a letter to Captain S. W. Roskill, 29 July 1979, in ROSK 7/210.
77. Admiral Sir Angus Cunninghame-Graham to Captain S. W. Roskill, 16 December 1979, in ROSK 7/210.
78. Undated letter in ROSK 5/124.
79. Commander Robert Bower, in a letter to Captain S. W. Roskill, 8 March 1970, in ROSK 5/125.
80. See Barnett, *The Collapse of British Power*, op cit, pp. 550–2; R. P. Shay Jr, *British Rearmament in the 1930s: Politics and Profits*, Princeton, the Princeton University Press, 1977, Chapter VII; G. C. Peden, *British Rearmament and the Treasury 1932–1939*, Edinburgh, Scottish Academic Press, 1979, Chapters IV and V; see also CAB 27/648, Committee on Defence Programmes and Acceleration, appointed by the Cabinet on 26 October 1938, especially its Report, CP 247(38).
81. CAB 27/648, CP 247(38).
82. CP 234(38).
83. Roskill, *Naval Policy Between the Wars*, op cit, Vol II, pp. 458–9.
84. Ibid, p. 461.
85. Ibid, p. 431.
86. Roskill, *The War at Sea 1939–1945*, Vol I, *The Defensive*, London HMSO, 1954, p. 25.
87. Ibid, p. 2.
88. Roskill, *Naval Policy Between the Wars*, op cit, Vol II, p. 483.

3. *'Winston Is Back'* (pages 57–96)

1. Winston S. Churchill, *The Second World War*, Vol I, *The Gathering Storm*, London, Cassell, 1948, pp. 320–1.
2. Admiral of the Fleet Lord Fraser of North Cape, 'Churchill and the Navy', in Sir James Marchant (ed), *Winston Spencer Churchill;*

Servant of the Crown and Commonwealth, London, Cassell, 1954, pp. 78–9.

3. Churchill, op cit, Vol I, p. 321.
4. Admiral Sir Geoffrey Dickens, in undated letter to S. W. Roskill in ROSK 5/124.
5. Admiral of the Fleet Lord Cunningham of Hyndhope, *A Sailor's Odyssey*, London, Hutchinson, 1951, pp. 583–4.
6. ROSK 4/124, letter from Admiral Sir William Davis to Captain Roskill, 20 October 1961.
7. Ibid.
8. Captain G. R. G. Allen, quoted in Arthur Marder, 'Winston is Back: Churchill at the Admiralty 1939–40' in *The English Historical Review*, Supplement 5, London, Longman, 1972, p. 2.
9. Roskill, *War at Sea*, op cit, Vol I, p. 61.
10. Ibid, pp. 53–8; and Appendix G; Admiral K. Dönitz, *Memoirs: Ten Years and Twenty Days*, London, Weidenfeld and Nicolson, 1958, Chapter 5; Cajus Bekker, *Hitler's Naval War*, London, Macdonald, 1974, pp. 26–35.
11. Dönitz, op cit, p. 47.
12. Roskill, *The War at Sea*, op cit, Vol I, p. 60; Elke C. Weale, John A. Weale and Richard Barker, *Combat Aircraft of World War Two*, London, Bracken Books, 1985, p. 114.
13. Roskill, *The War at Sea*, op cit, Vol I, Appendix E, pp. 582–5.
14. Ibid.
15. Ibid, p. 51, Table 3.
16. Figures from ROSK4/73; Roskill, *The War at Sea*, op cit, Vol I, Appendix D and E, pp. 577–87.
17. All ROSK 4/73.
18. ROSK 4/7; Postan, Hay and Scott, *Design and Development of Weapons*, op cit, *passim*.
19. ROSK 4/7; Terraine, *The Right of the Line*, op cit, p. 70, Note 2.
20. Weale, Weale and Barker, op cit, p. 192.
21. Air Historical Branch Monograph II/117/1(B), p. 56, quoted in Terraine, op cit, p. 100; see Terraine, op cit, pp. 98–100 for an account of these operations.
22. Terraine, op cit, p. 100.
23. Ibid, pp. 95–100.
24. Churchill, op cit, Vol I, p. 331.
25. Roskill, *The War at Sea*, op cit, Vol I, pp. 103–4; Dönitz, op cit, pp. 54–9: Peter Padfield, *Dönitz: the Last Führer*, London, Victor Gollancz, 1984, pp. 190–207.
26. Roskill, *The War at Sea*, op cit, Vol I, pp. 92–4.
27. Ibid, p. 106. All statistics of merchant shipping losses in the present work are drawn from Roskill, *War at Sea*, op cit. The Naval Historical Branch are currently engaged in a complete re-examination of the data.

28. Ibid, Table 4, p. 67.
29. Ibid.
30. Cf British Strategic Memorandum to the Anglo-French Staff Conversations, April 1939, CAB 29/159, AFC 7; evidence of Sir Alan Barlow, Under-Secretary at the Treasury, to the Strategical Appreciation Committee, April 1939, CAB 16/209, SAC 4; C. Webster and N. Frankland, *The Strategic Air Offensive Against Germany 1939–1945*, Vol I, *Preparation*, London, HMSO, 1961, pp. 271–84.
31. ROSK 4/92, TSD/FDS/X.280/49, Memorandum to Captain Roskill; Roskill, *War at Sea*, op. cit Vol I, pp. 105–6; Dönitz, op cit, pp. 55–6; Bekker, op cit, p. 21.
32. Martin Gilbert, *Winston S. Churchill 1939–41*, Vol VI, *Finest Hour, 1939–41*, London, Book Club Associates, 1983, p. 37.
33. ROSK 4/49, Rear-Admiral T. V. Briggs, unpublished account entitled 'The First Air Attack on a Fleet at Sea: "Where is the Ark Royal?"' As a Lieutenant-Commander, Briggs was *Ark Royal*'s gunnery officer at the time.
34. Ibid.
35. Ibid.
36. See Roskill, *War at Sea*, op cit, Vol I, p. 179.
37. Ibid, pp. 73–6.
38. Cited in Gilbert, op cit, Vol VI, p. 62.
39. ROSK 4/49.
40. Roskill, *War at Sea*, op cit, Vol I, p. 80.
41. Ibid, pp. 80–1.
42. NID 24/X.11a/46 in ROSK 4/49. The following account of the action between *Rawalpindi* and the two German battleships is drawn from the Naval Intelligence Department's translation of *Scharnhorst*'s log in ibid.
43. HMS *Newcastle*'s log for November 1939 in ADM 53/109923.
44. Roskill, *War at Sea*, op cit, Vol I, p. 87.
45. Vice-Admiral F. Ruge, *Sea Warfare 1939–1945*, London, Cassell, 1957, pp. 38–9.
46. Roskill, *War at Sea*, op cit, Vol I, p. 114.
47. Churchill, op cit, Vol I, p. 405.
48. Ibid.
49. Ibid, p. 407.
50. Roskill, *War at Sea*, op cit, Vol I, pp. 113–17.
51. Despatch of Rear-Admiral Sir Henry Harwood, KCB, OBE, to the Lords Commissioners of the Admiralty, 30 December 1939; published in the Supplement to the London Gazette of Tuesday, 17 June 1947.
52. Ibid.
53. Ibid; Roskill, *War at Sea*, op cit, Vol I, p. 118.
54. Despatch of Sir Henry Harwood, op cit.

55. Ibid.
56. Ibid.
57. Report in ROSK 4/84.
58. Cf accounts by Commander Kurt Diggins, Lt-Cmdr Günter Schiebusch, Captain Jürgen Wattenberg, Commander F. W. Rasenack, cited in E. Millington-Drake (ed), *The Drama of Graf Spee and the Battle of the River Plate; a Documentary Anthology: 1914–1964*, London, Peter Davies, 1964, pp. 227–30. The account of the action of 13 December 1939 is drawn from ibid; Despatch of Sir Henry Harwood, op cit; Roskill, *War at Sea*, op cit, Vol I, pp. 118–20.
59. Admiral Sir Guy Grantham, memorandum of 19 August 1966, to Arthur Marder, cited in Marder, 'Winston is Back', op cit, p. 30.
60. Despatch of Sir Henry Harwood, op cit.
61. See Millington-Drake, op cit, Part VII for the events and decisions of the aftermath of the action.
62. Quoted in ibid, p. 368.
63. CAB 65/2, WM88(39)2 and WM90(39)8.
64. ROSK 4/43. The general account of the mining campaigns of 1939–40 is based on ADM 186/799, Naval Staff History, *Home Waters and the Atlantic*, Vol I, *September 1939–April 1940*, Chapter VIII; Roskill, *War at Sea*, op cit, Vol I, pp. 96–102, 123–8.
65. ROSK 4/43: Letter No. 704, 29 August 1953, from Commander M. G. Saunders, Foreign Documents Section, Cabinet Office Historical Section, to Captain S. W. Roskill.
66. Postan, Hay and Scott, *Design and Development of Weapons*, op cit, p. 443.
67. ROSK 4/43, letter from Saunders to Roskill, op cit.
68. See ADM 186/799 Naval Staff History, *Home Waters*, op cit, Chapter VIII.
69. ADM 199/299, comments by Churchill on a 'Most Secret' Memorandum from Pound of 3 December 1939.
70. Cited in Marder, 'Winston is Back', op cit, p. 31; see also Gilbert, op cit, pp. 26–7.
71. Pound to Forbes, 15 September 1939, copy in ROSK 4/49.
72. Ibid.
73. ROSK 4/49 photocopy of letter from Pound to Forbes, 20 January 1940.
74. ADM 205/4, Note marked 'Most Secret' and 'To be passed round only in a box' 'Notes on "C"'.
75. Ibid.
76. ADM 205/4, Note of 20 September 1939.
77. Marder, 'Winston is Back', op cit, p. 32.
78. Cited in ibid, p. 33.
79. Ibid, p. 36.
80. See Roskill, *Churchill and the Admirals*, London, Collins, 1977, p. 94, and Footnote 8.

4. *'A Very Hazardous Affair': Norway, 1939–1940* (pages 97–118)

1. ADM 205/3, 'Norway and Sweden'; Memorandum for the War Cabinet, 23 September 1939.
2. Cited in Marder, 'Winston is Back: Churchill at the Admiralty 1939–40', op cit, p. 39.
3. CAB 65/2, 116(39)4. See also ADM 205/2, First Lord's Personal Minute to First Sea Lord on Swedish iron-ore traffic and on mining the Leads, 27 November 1939.
4. CAB 66/4, WP(39)162, 'Norway – Iron-Ore Traffic', 16 December 1939.
5. Ibid.
6. CAB 65/2, 111(39)6.
7. J. R. M. Butler, *Grand Strategy*, Vol II, *September 1939–June 1941*, London, HMSO, 1957, p. 100.
8. Gilbert, *Winston S. Churchill*, op cit, Vol VI, pp. 108–9. See also Churchill's own notes of 22 December 1939 for use in Cabinet, in ADM 116/4471.
9. CAB 66/4, WP(39)179: Military Implications of a Policy aimed at stopping the export of Swedish iron ore to Germany.
10. CAB 66/4, WP(40)5; Scandinavia: Report of the Chiefs of Staff Committee.
11. CAB 65/11, 2(40)1; 3 January 1940, Confidential Annexe.
12. CAB 65/11, 1(40)1; 2 January 1940.
13. CAB 65/11, 10(40)1, Confidential Annexe.
14. CAB 80/7, COS 218.
15. Cf the CIGS, on 19 February, on how the land forces once ashore, 'would be quite capable of looking after themselves' against German air attack (CAB 79/3, COS No. 34, 19 February 1940); the Chief of Air Staff on the acceptability of the 'considerable risks' for the sake of the great advantages to be won (CAB 65/11, 45(40)1, Confidential Annexe).
16. See General Sir David Fraser, *And We Shall Shock Them: The British Army in the Second World War*, London, Hodder and Stoughton, 1983, pp. 31–2, 36–7, 41; J.L. Moulton, *The Norwegian Campaign: A Study of Warfare in Three Dimensions*, London, Eyre and Spottiswoode, 1966, pp. 49–50.
17. Chartwell Papers CHAR 19/3 Churchill Archives Centre, a Note on the War in 1940, 25 December 1939, sent to Pound, cited in Martin Gilbert, op cit, Vol VI, p. 112.
18. CAB 65/11, 46(40)9.
19. CAB 65/12, 66(40)2.
20. CAB 65/12, 68(40)4.
21. For the evolution of German plans, see Butler, op cit, pp. 104–5, 114–15, 124–5; Moulton, op cit, pp. 61–8.
22. Quoted in Moulton, op cit, p. 65.

23. Bekker, *Hitler's Naval War*, op cit, pp. 98–9.
24. F. H. Hinsley, *British Intelligence in the Second World War*, op cit, Vol I, p. 116. The account which follows of Allied Intelligence in regard to 'Weserübung' is drawn from this work, pp. 116–25.
25. The account of British Intelligence failures which follows is based on Hinsley, op cit, Vol I, pp. 116–25.
26. Ibid, p. 123.
27. Ibid.
28. Ibid, p. 125.
29. Gilbert, op cit, Vol VI, p. 199.
30. CAB 65/12, 77(40)2, Confidential Annexe.
31. CAB 79/85, COS meeting No. 60, 20 March 1940.
32. Roskill, *War at Sea*, op cit, Vol I, p. 157.
33. Ibid.
34. Transcript of Edwards's contemporary diary in ROSK 4/75.
35. Ibid.
36. Ibid.
37. Roskill, *War at Sea*, op cit, Vol I, p. 159.
38. Ibid.
39. ROSK 4/50, letter from Lieutenant-Commander Godfrey Style, who as Flag-Lieutenant handled Forbes's operational and cypher signals, to Captain Roskill, 10 March 1979.
40. Ibid.
41. The account of *Glowworm*'s action is based on Roskill, *War at Sea*, op cit, Vol I, pp. 158–60; Moulton, op cit, pp. 76–7; Bekker, op cit, p. 100.
42. Roskill, *War at Sea*, op cit, Vol I, p. 160.
43. ROSK 4/76, letter from Vice-Admiral W. J. Whitworth to Dr Denny of the Cabinet Office Historical Section, 5 June 1950.
44. Roskill, *War at Sea*, op cit, Vol I, p. 170.
45. Ibid, p. 171.
46. ROSK 4/76, letter to Captain Roskill, 19 June 1951.
47. ROSK 4/75, Edwards's diary.
48. Roskill, *War at Sea*, op cit, Vol I, p. 174.
49. This account of Warburton-Lee's attack is based on Roskill, *War at Sea*, op cit, Vol I, pp. 174–5; Moulton, op cit, pp. 110–13; Bekker, op cit, pp. 117–18.
50. Moulton, op cit, pp. 108–9; Bekker, op cit, pp. 115–17.
51. CAB 65/6, 85(40), 8.30 am, 9 April.
52. Ibid.

5. *A Churchillian Disaster: Norway, 1940* (pages 119–139)

1. Roskill, *War at Sea*, op cit, Vol I, p. 178.
2. Ibid.
3. Moulton, *The Norwegian Campaign*, op cit, p. 148.

4. CAB 83/3, MC(40)18, 10 April 1940.
5. CAB 65/12, 87(40)5, 88(40)5, 90(40)3, Confidential Annexes.
6. Ibid.
7. CAB 65/5, 92(40).
8. CAB 65/12, 91(40)3, Confidential Annexe.
9. CAB 65/12, 92(40)5, Confidential Annexe.
10. CAB 83/3, MC(40)23.
11. ROSK 4/75.
12. Letter of 15 April 1940 to King George V, Royal Archives, cited in Gilbert, *Winston S. Churchill*, op cit, Vol VI, p. 243.
13. *The Rise and Fall of the German Air Force (1939 to 1945)*, Air Ministry, London, 1948, p. 63.
14. ROSK 4/75.
15. Terraine, *The Right of the Line*, op cit, pp. 116–17; ROSK 4/75.
16. CHAR 19/2, Churchill Archives Centre, quoted in Gilbert, op cit, Vol VI, p. 251.
17. Ibid.
18. ADM 199/1929, 'Most Secret, Most Immediate', 1350, 17 April 1940.
19. Gilbert, op cit, Vol VI, p. 251.
20. ADM 199/1929.
21. CAB 65/6, 98(40).
22. ROSK 4/75, 'Notes on Allied Operations in the Narvik Area'.
23. Ibid.
24. Moulton, op cit, p. 168; Fraser, *And We Shall Shock Them*, op cit, pp. 38–40.
25. Letter from Colonel Beckwith to Major-General Moulton, Moulton, op cit, p. 174, Footnote 1.
26. Signal at 1157 on 14 April, cited in ROSK 4/75.
27. Signal cited in ibid.
28. Ibid.
29. CAB 83/3, MC40(27).
30. Roskill, *War at Sea*, op cit, Vol I, p. 186.
31. CAB 79/85, COS No. 87, Confidential Annexe.
32. Moulton, op cit, pp. 205–6.
33. ROSK 4/75.
34. CAB 82/3, MC(40)35; see also CAB 79/85, COS No. 98, 26 April 1940; CAB 65/12, 105(40)2, 27 April 1940.
35. Moulton, op cit, pp. 209–10.
36. Roskill, *War at Sea*, op cit, Vol I, p. 189.
37. A. Carton de Wiart, *Happy Odyssey*, London, Jonathan Cape, 1950, p. 174.
38. Admiral of the Fleet Sir Philip Vian, *Action This Day: War Memoirs of Admiral of the Fleet Sir Philip Vian*, London, Muller, 1960, p. 47.
39. Moulton, op cit, pp. 211–12; Roskill, *War at Sea*, op cit, Vol I, pp. 189–90.

40. ROSK 4/75. Even in the first month of the war Forbes was writing to Pound that he had 'a sort of bare feeling' every time he went to sea 'as I never seem to have any cruisers and very few destroyers to screen the big ships'. Signal of 27 September 1939 in ADM 205/2.
41. Moulton, op cit, pp. 224, 229.
42. ROSK 4/75.
43. Ibid.
44. ADM 199/1929, 'Most Secret'.
45. CAB 65/13, 135(40)9, Confidential Annexe.
46. Moulton, op cit, p. 249.
47. Roskill, *War at Sea*, Vol I, pp. 197–8.
48. See Hinsley, op cit, Vol I, pp. 141–2.
49. Ibid.
50. ROSK 4/77, letter from Rear-Admiral A. S. Bolt to Captain Roskill, 18 December 1979.
51. ROSK 4/76; Captain G. A. (Hank) Rotherham, *It's Really Quite Safe*, Belleville, Ontario, 1985, p. 147.
52. ADM 199/478, ERD/219.
53. Account of the sinking of the *Glorious* based on ROSK 4/76 and 77; ADM 199/478, account compiled by Commander J. E. Broome (captain of HMS *Veteran*, which picked up survivors) from evidence of survivors of the sunk ships; and report of 3 July 1940 to the First Sea Lord on the sinking of *Glorious*, including a summary of the Court of Enquiry. The Leading Signalman who read *Glorious*'s signal to *Ark Royal* was in *Diana*, commanded by Commander E. G. Le Geyt, who on 15 September 1968 wrote the account of the exchange of signals on the back of a note in ADM 199/478 to the VCNS, dated 20 June 1940, on a different topic altogether; Bekker, *Hitler's Naval War*, op cit, pp. 155–61.
54. Rotherham, op cit, pp. 142–6.
55. Moulton, op cit, p. 258.
56. Ibid, p. 260.
57. Roskill, *War at Sea*, op cit, Vol I, p. 198.

6. *'Operation Dynamo': the Dunkirk Evacuation* (pages 140–167)

1. Roskill, *War at Sea*, op cit, Vol I, pp. 210–11.
2. Churchill Archives Centre, Ramsay Papers RMSY 8/5: Report on 'Operation Dynamo', Dover Despatch A. 14/0/876/40 of 18 June 1940, by Flag Officer Commanding Dover. The account of 'Dynamo' which follows is based on this despatch and on David Divine's superb book *The Nine Days of Dunkirk*, London, Faber and Faber, 1959, except where otherwise cited.
3. RMSY 8/10.
4. Ibid.
5. Ibid.

6. RMSY 8/5.
7. Ibid.
8. RMSY 8/10.
9. Ibid.
10. Cited in Divine, op cit, pp. 150–1.
11. Ibid, pp. 154–5.
12. Ibid, p. 155.
13. Ibid, p. 172.
14. Ibid, p. 176.
15. RMSY 8/10.
16. Divine, op cit, p. 181.
17. Ibid, p. 184.
18. Ibid, p. 186.
19. RMSY 8/5.
20. Divine, op cit, p. 144.
21. Cited in ibid, p. 145.
22. RMSY 8/5.
23. Terraine, *The Right of the Line*, op cit, p. 157.
24. Ibid.
25. RMSY 8/5.
26. Divine, op cit, p. 204.
27. RMSY 8/5.
28. Ibid.
29. Ibid.
30. Ibid.
31. Ibid.
32. Ibid.
33. Ibid.
34. Ibid.
35. Cited in Divine, op cit, p. 221.
36. RMSY 8/5, List of ships which took part in 'Operation Dynamo', 25 October 1940.
37. RMSY 8/5.
38. RMSY 8/10.
39. Cited in Divine, op cit, p. 115.
40. Quoted in Gilbert, *Winston S. Churchill*, op cit, Vol VI, p. 464.
41. Ibid.
42. Roskill, *War at Sea*, op cit, Vol I, pp. 231–2.
43. Ibid, p. 239.
44. Ibid, Appendix H, pp. 593–7.
45. Behrens, *Merchant Shipping and the Demands of War*, op cit, p. 109.
46. Ibid, Footnote 3.
47. Ibid, Appendices XXXII, p. 242 and XLIX, p. 295.
48. CAB 66/11, WP40(40)324.

Part II: Storm Force

7. *The Wall of England* (pages 171–206)

1. Somerville Papers, Churchill Archives Centre, SMVL 7/19, Report of the proceedings of Force H, 28 June–4 July 1940.
2. ADM 205/6.
3. Signal cited in Gilbert, *Winston S. Churchill*, op cit, Vol VI, pp. 632–3.
4. ADM 205/4.
5. CAB 65/7, 176(40).
6. Ibid.
7. CAB 65/13, 179(40)3, Confidential Annexe.
8. Ibid.
9. Ibid.
10. Hinsley, *British Intelligence in the Second World War*, op cit, Vol I, pp. 150–3.
11. Roskill, *War at Sea*, op cit, Vol I, pp. 240–1.
12. CAB 65/13, 184(40)5.
13. ADM 205/6.
14. Cited in Roskill, *Churchill and the Admirals*, op cit, p. 151.
15. Ibid, p. 154.
16. Roskill, *War at Sea*, op cit, Vol I, p. 243; Gilbert, op cit, Vol VI, p. 629.
17. PREM 3/179/1.
18. SMVL 7/19.
19. Ibid.
20. Cited in Somerville's report on 'Catapult', SMVL 7/19.
21. CAB 65/14, 192(40); Roskill, *Churchill and the Admirals*, op cit, pp. 157–8.
22. In SMVL 7/19.
23. Cited in Gilbert, op cit, Vol VI, p. 634.
24. Ibid.
25. SMVL 7/19.
26. Ibid.
27. Hinsley, op cit, Vol I, p. 153.
28. Report of Operations by Commanding Officer, HMS *Hood*, to Vice-Admiral commanding Force H, No. 0130/T, 5 July in SMVL 7/19.
29. Report of Operations by Commanding Officer, HMS *Resolution* to Vice-Admiral commanding Force H, 4 July 1940 in ibid.
30. Quoted by Somerville in his own report, in ibid.
31. Ibid.
32. *Resolution*'s report in ibid.
33. Ibid.
34. Gilbert, op cit, Vol VI, p. 52.
35. See David Reynolds, *The Creation of the Anglo-American Alliance 1937–41; A Study in Competitive Co-operation*, op cit, Chapter 3.

36. Roskill, *War at Sea*, op cit, Vol I, p. 112.
37. CAB 66/7, WP(40)168.
38. Cited in Reynolds, op cit, p. 114.
39. See Reynolds, op cit, Chapters 4 and 5, especially pp. 121–31; also James R. Leutze, *Bargaining for Supremacy: Anglo-American Naval Relations 1937–1941*, Chapel Hill, North Carolina, 1977, Chapters 6–8.
40. ROSK 4/94, letter to Vice-Admiral Sir Geoffrey Blake, ACNS (Foreign), 28 October 1940.
41. Cited in Correlli Barnett, *Bonaparte*, London, Allen and Unwin, 1978, p. 98.
42. CAB 66/7, WP(40)168.
43. CAB 66/7, WP(40)169, 26 May 1940.
44. See Terraine, *The Right of the Line*, op cit, Chapters 16–25, for a magnificent and detailed account of the Battle of Britain.
45. Roskill, *War at Sea*, op cit, Vol I, p. 249 and Appendix Q, p. 614.
46. Dönitz, *Memoirs: Ten Years and Twenty Days*, op cit, p. 114.
47. Cited in Roskill, *War at Sea*, op cit, Vol I, pp. 248–9.
48. Ibid, pp. 250–1.
49. Ibid, p. 252.
50. Ibid, p. 258.
51. The summary of Intelligence during the invasion summer and autumn which follows is based on Hinsley, op cit, Vol I, pp. 161–3, 172–6, 183–9.
52. Ibid, p. 175.
53. Ibid, pp. 188–9.
54. Roskill, *War at Sea*, op cit, Vol I, p. 257.
55. Ibid, but see CAB 69/1, [Defence Committee (Operations)] 39(40).
56. Ibid.
57. Dönitz, op cit, pp. 111–12.
58. Ibid.
59. Ibid.
60. Ibid, pp. 91–7.
61. Ibid, p. 102.
62. Roskill, *War at Sea*, op cit, Vol I, pp. 349–50.
63. Ibid.
64. Dönitz, op cit, p. 105.
65. Roskill, *War at Sea*, op cit, Vol I, p. 350.
66. Cited in Dönitz, op cit, p. 108.
67. Roskill, *War at Sea*, op cit, Vol I, p. 351.
68. Ibid, pp. 351–2.
69. Ibid, pp. 277–80.
70. Ibid, p. 289.
71. AHB/II/117/3(A)i, p. 209.
72. Terraine, op cit, p. 242.
73. Ibid, pp. 232–3.

74. Ibid.
75. ABH/II/3(B) ii, p. 3.
76. Roskill, *War at Sea*, Vol I, Appendix R, Table I, p. 616.
77. Ibid, Table II, p. 617.
78. Gilbert, op cit, Vol VI, p. 936.
79. Butler, *Grand Strategy*, op cit, Vol II, p. 258.
80. Minute to Ismay, 5 June 1940, cited in Gilbert, op cit, Vol VI, pp. 472–3.
81. Arthur Marder, *Operation 'Menace': The Dakar Expedition and the Dudley North Affair*, London, OUP, 1976, p. 11. The following account of 'Menace' is based on Marder, op cit, John Williams, *The Guns of Dakar: September 1940*, London, Heinemann, 1976; Gilbert, op cit, Vol VI, *passim*, and Hinsley, op cit, Vol 1, pp. 149–58.
82. Marder, *Operation 'Menace'*, op cit, pp. 16–17.
83. Ibid, p. 21.
84. Letter from Commander T. C. Crease to Marder, 22 November 1973, cited in ibid, p. 57.
85. Ibid, p. 36.
86. Hinsley, op cit, Vol I, pp. 154–8.
87. Ibid, p. 155.
88. Marder, op cit, pp. 104–5.
89. Ibid, pp. 118–19.
90. Ibid, p. 128.
91. Ibid, p. 141.
92. Ibid, p. 148.
93. Ibid, p. 159.
94. James Leutze (ed), *The London Observer; The Journal of General Raymond E. Lee 1940–1941*, London, Hutchinson, 1972, p. 71.

8. *'Blue Water Strategy': The Mediterranean, 1940* (pages 207–250)

1. CAB 53/21, COS 560, Annual Review for 1937.
2. Ibid.
3. CAB 29/159, AFC 1, British Strategic Memorandum to Anglo-French Staff Talks.
4. CAB 27/625, FP(36)51, meeting of the Cabinet Foreign Policy Committee, 13 June 1939.
5. CAB 29/159, AFC 1.
6. Major I. S. O. Playfair with Commander G. M. S. Stitt, RN, Brigadier C. J. C. Molony, Air Vice-Marshal S. E. Toomer, *The Mediterranean and Middle East*, Vol I, *The Early Successes Against Italy (to May 1941)*, London, HMSO, 1954, p. 47.
7. Ibid, p. 84.
8. Signal 2330/16/6/40 to C-in-C, Mediterranean Fleet.
9. CAB 79/5, COS 40, 183rd meeting, Min 3.

10. Ibid.
11. ROSK 4/67.
12. CAB 80/13, COS (40) 469 (JP).
13. Ibid.
14. CAB 79/5, COS (40) 185th meeting, Min. 3.
15. Cunningham, *A Sailor's Odyssey*, op cit, pp. 241–2.
16. CAB 80/13, Annexe to COS (40) 521.
17. Cited in Winston S. Churchill, *The World Crisis: The Eastern Front*, Thornton Butterworth, London, 1931, p. 271.
18. Churchill, *The Second World War*, op cit, Vol II, p. 385, message of August 1940.
19. Letter of 13 July 1940, photocopy in ROSK 4/64. The account of this sortie to Malta is based on Cunningham's report to the Admiralty of 29 January 1941, Narrative, Fleet Operations – Period 7th to 13th July 1940, in ADM 199/1048, War History Case 7952, Naval Operations in the Mediterranean 1940.
20. Cunningham, *A Sailor's Odyssey*, op cit, p. 262.
21. Ibid.
22. ROSK 4/64, photocopy of letter from Cunningham to Pound, 3 August 1940.
23. Cunningham, op cit, p. 259.
24. Photocopy of letter of 13 July 1940, ROSK 4/64; account of action off Calabria is based on Cunningham's Despatch, supplement to the London Gazette No. 38273, 1948.
25. Photocopy of letter of 13 July 1940, ROSK 4/64.
26. Ibid.
27. Ibid.
28. Lenton and Colledge, *Warships of World War II*, op cit, p. 39.
29. Photocopy of letter of 13 July 1940, ROSK 4/64.
30. Ibid.
31. Roskill, *War at Sea*, op cit, Vol I, Appendix H, p. 293; Cunningham, *A Sailor's Odyssey*, op cit, p. 234.
32. Hinsley, *British Intelligence in the Second World War*, op cit, Vol I, p. 199.
33. Ibid, p. 209.
34. ROSK 4/64, Cunningham's letter to Pound, 13 July 1940; Hinsley, op cit, Vol I, p. 209.
35. ROSK 4/64.
36. Hinsley, op cit, Vol I, pp. 206–7, 210–11.
37. ADM 223/89 Section II, quoted in Hinsley, op cit, Vol I, p. 211.
38. Hinsley, op cit, Vol I, pp. 207–8.
39. Roskill, *War at Sea*, op cit, Vol I, p. 307.
40. Hinsley, op cit, Vol I, pp. 211–12.
41. ADM 186/800, p. 61, quoted in Hinsley, op cit, Vol I, p. 212.
42. Photocopy of letter from Cunningham to Pound, 3 August 1940 in ROSK 4/64.

43. ROSK 4/64, letter to Pound, 13 July 1940.
44. Cited in Oliver Warner, *Cunningham of Hyndhope: Admiral of the Fleet*, London, John Murray, 1967, p. 90.
45. Cunningham, op cit, p. 203.
46. Warner, op cit, p. 93.
47. Ibid, p. 75.
48. Quoted in ibid, p. 111.
49. Admiral Sir Geoffrey Oliver, quoted in ibid, p. 62.
50. Quoted in ibid, p. 110.
51. Cited in ibid, p. 107.
52. Ibid, p. 62.
53. Ibid, p. 24.
54. Commander G. N., later Admiral Sir Geoffrey, Oliver, quoted in Warner, op cit, p. 63.
55. Captain G. N. Brewer, quoted in Warner, op cit, p. 51.
56. Playfair, op cit, Vol I, pp. 119–21.
57. Ibid, pp. 154–5; SMVL 3/22.
58. 13 July 1940, SMVL 3/22.
59. Ibid.
60. Personal letter from Vice-Admiral Sir Geoffrey Blake to First Sea Lord, December 1940, ROSK 4/40.
61. SMVL 7/3. Report of Proceedings of Force H for the Period 30 August 1940 to 3 September 1940, p. 1.
62. Ibid.
63. Ibid.
64. Ibid.
65. The account of Cunningham's operations in 'Hats' is based on the orders, signals and reports, plus the C-in-C's own report dated 14 January 1941, contained in ADM 199/1049, War History Case 7953, Naval Operations September–December 1940, except where otherwise cited.
66. Cunningham, *A Sailor's Odyssey*, op cit, p. 273.
67. Midshipman Terence Lewin, unpublished journal.
68. ROSK 4/64, photocopy of letter to Pound of 19 August 1940.
69. Ibid.
70. Playfair, op cit, Vol I, p. 204.
71. Ibid.
72. Gilbert, *Winston S. Churchill*, op cit, Vol VI, p. 772.
73. Playfair, op cit, Vol I, p. 190, Footnote 1.
74. Ibid, p. 191.
75. CAB 69/11, DO(40), 25th meeting, 12 August 1940.
76. Playfair, op cit, Vol I, pp. 245–7.
77. Ibid, p. 248.
78. SMVL 7/4. Report of Proceedings of Force H for the Period 11th September 1940, to 14th September 1940.

79. Roskill, *Churchill and the Admirals*, op cit, p. 163, Footnote.
80. For full analyses, though with differing interpretations, of 'the Dudley North affair', see Roskill, *Churchill and the Admirals*, op cit, pp. 159–67; Marder, *Operation 'Menace'*, op cit, pp. 193–264; see also the Dudley North Papers in the Churchill Archives Centre, NRTH 1/4; see ADM 205/11 for the First Sea Lord's dockets on the affair.
81. Lenton and Colledge, op cit, p. 36.
82. Ibid, p. 44.
83. Except where otherwise cited, the account of Somerville's part in 'Collar' is based on his report, dated 18 December 1940, on 'The Action Between British and Italian Forces on 27 November 1940' in ADM 199/1049; and Battle Summary No. 9, 'Action off Cape Spartivento', 27th November 1940, in ADM 234/325.
84. Ibid.
85. See SMVL 3/22, letters from Somerville to his wife, 28 and 29 November 1940.
86. ADM 1/19177, Churchill to A. V. Alexander, the First Lord of the Admiralty, 20 July 1940.
87. SMVL 3/22, letter of 16 November to his wife.
88. See Record of Court of Enquiry into the loss of the Hurricanes in ADM 199/1048, Case 6183.
89. SMVL 3/22, letter of 18 November to his wife.
90. Ibid: quoted in letter from Somerville to his wife, 8 December 1940.
91. Cunningham, op cit, p. 293.
92. Ibid, p. 294.
93. Ibid, p. 273.
94. Lenton and Colledge, op cit, p. 61.
95. The account of the Taranto Operation is based on ADM 234/325, Battle Summary No. 10 – Mediterranean Operations, 4 to 14 November 1940, Air Attack on Taranto, 11 November 1940, dated 1943; ADM 199/1048 War History Case 7952; Playfair, op cit, Vol I, pp. 236–7; Roskill, *War at Sea*, op cit, Vol I, pp. 300–1; P. K. Kemp, *Fleet Air Arm*, London, Herbert Jenkins, 1954, pp. 124–7; J. Winton, *Air Power at Sea 1939–45*, London, Sidgwick and Jackson, 1976, pp. 24–6; D. Newton and A. Cecil Hampshire, *Taranto*, London, William Kimber, 1969, *passim*.
96. Cunningham, op cit, p. 285.
97. Quoted in Winton, op cit, p. 24.
98. Weale, Weale and Barker, *Combat Aircraft of World War Two*, op cit, p. 138.
99. Winton, op cit, p. 25.
100. Newton and Hampshire, op cit. pp. 140–1.
101. See ADM 199/1048, War History Case 7952, Naval Operations in the Mediterranean 1940, for technical details of British torpedoes and the damage to Italian ships.

102. Cunningham, op cit, p. 286.
103. For a succinct account of O'Connor's campaign, see Correlli Barnett, *The Desert Generals*, 2nd edition, London, Allen and Unwin, and Pan Books, 1983; John Baynes, *The Forgotten Victor: General Sir Richard O'Connor, KT, GCB, DSO, MC*, London, Brassey's Defence Publications, 1989.

9. *'Grey Water Strategy': The Atlantic, 1941* (pages 251–277)

1. The Battle of the Atlantic; Directive by the Minister of Defence, 6 March 1941. Printed in full as Appendix O in Roskill, *War at Sea*, op cit, Vol I, p. 609.
2. Grove, Chant, Lyon and Lyon, *The Hardware of World War II*, op cit, p. 149.
3. Roskill, *War at Sea*, op cit, Vol I, p. 462.
4. Dönitz, *Memoirs: Ten Years and Twenty Days*, op cit, pp. 131–40.
5. ADM 205/7, File No. 7.
6. Ibid.
7. Ibid.
8. ADM 234/578, Naval Staff History, Second World War, *Defeat of the Enemy Attack on Shipping 1939–1945: A Study of Policy and Operations*, Vol IA, Text and Appendices, p. 63.
9. Ibid.
10. Ibid, p. 64.
11. Ibid, pp. 18–19.
12. Ibid, p. 65.
13. Postan, Hay and Scott, *Design and Development of Weapons*, op cit, pp. 390–2; ADM 234/578, p. 68.
14. ADM 234/578, p. 67.
15. ADM 205/7, File No. 7.
16. ADM 234/578, p. 74.
17. Ibid; see Chapter 15 below, for a full account of the state of long-range aircraft in 1942.
18. ADM 234/578, p. 68.
19. Quoted in Terraine, *The Right of the Line*, op cit, p. 404.
20. ADM 234/578, p. 34; Roskill, *War at Sea*, op cit, Vol I, p. 361.
21. Padfield, *Dönitz; the Last Führer*, op cit, p. 230.
22. Roskill, *War at Sea*, op cit, Vol I, p. 362.
23. The account of 1941 operations in the Battle of the Atlantic is based on ADM 234/578; ADM 186/802, German Naval History, *The U-boat War in the Atlantic*, Vol I; and Roskill, *War at Sea*, op cit, Vol I, Chapter XXI.
24. Roskill, *War at Sea*, op cit, Vol I, p. 452.
25. Ibid.
26. ADM 234/578, p. 69.

27. ADM 205/7, File No. 7, letter of 16 April 1941.
28. Roskill, *War at Sea*, op cit, Vol I, p. 464, Table 14.
29. Cited in J. M. A. Gwyer, *Grand Strategy*, Vol III, Part I, p. 12, London, HMSO, 1964; cited previous statistics on shipping position from ibid, p. 9.
30. Cited in Correlli Barnett, *The Great War*, London, The Park Lane Press, 1979, p. 106.
31. The account that follows is based on Hinsley, *British Intelligence in the Second World War*, op cit, Vol I, pp. 336–9, and Vol II, pp. 163–74.
32. Dönitz, op cit, pp. 141–2.
33. Padfield, op cit, p. 229.
34. ADM 205/7, File No. 7, C-in-C, Western Approaches, Correspondence with First Sea Lord, December 1940 to November 1941.
35. Hinsley, op cit, Vol II, Appendix 9, p. 681.
36. Ibid, p. 682.
37. Ibid, p. 173.
38. Roskill, *War at Sea*, op cit, Vol I, p. 47.
39. ADM 234/578, p. 73.
40. See Reynolds, *The Creation of the Anglo-American Alliance, 1937–1941*, op cit, Chapter Eight, and Gilbert, *Winston S. Churchill*, op cit, Vol VI, *passim*, for accounts of the developing political and strategic relationship between the US and UK in 1940–41.
41. ADM 205/7, File No. 7, Memorandum from Commander Goodenough, Plans Division, Naval Staff, to VCNS and First Sea Lord, 8 April 1941.
42. Cited in Reynolds, op cit, p. 214.
43. Ibid, p. 215.
44. Ibid, p. 216.
45. ADM 234/578, pp. 80–1; Roskill, *War at Sea*, op cit, Vol I, p. 471.
46. Roskill, *War at Sea*, op cit, Vol I, p. 472.
47. Ibid, p. 473.
48. Lenton and Colledge, *Warships of World War II*, op cit, p. 255.
49. Weale, Weale and Barker, *Combat Aircraft of World War Two*, op cit, p. 200.
50. Dönitz, op cit, p. 181.
51. CAB 81/1.
52. Roskill, *War at Sea*, op cit, Vol I, p. 615, Appendix R.
53. Cf John Terraine's use of this traditional phrase in the title of his book on the Royal Air Force in the European War.
54. Dönitz, op cit, p. 182.

10. *'The* Bismarck *Must Be Sunk at All Costs'* (pages 278–316)

1. Bekker, *Hitler's Naval War*, op cit, p. 211.
2. Quoted in ibid, p. 216.
3. Quoted in Baron Burkhard von Müllenheim-Rechberg, *Battleship*

Bismarck, A Survivor's Story, translated by Jack Sweetman, London, The Bodley Head, 1980, p. 57.

4. Ibid.
5. Ibid.
6. Bekker, op cit, p. 218.
7. Ibid, p. 219.
8. See Ludovic Kennedy, *Pursuit: The Chase and Sinking of the Bismarck*, London, Collins, 1974, p. 30.
9. Müllenheim-Rechberg, op cit, p. 27.
10. Parkes, *British Battleships: 'Warrior' 1860 to 'Vanguard' 1950; A History of Design, Construction and Armament*, op cit, p. 671.
11. Technical description of *Bismarck* drawn from ibid, p. 671; Grove, Chant, Lyon and Lyon, *The Hardware of World War II*, op cit, pp. 146–7; Mullenheim-Rechberg, op cit, pp. 21–8. These authorities do not always agree on details of dimensions, thickness of armour, etc.
12. Quoted in Ludovic Kennedy, op cit. Except where otherwise cited the following account of the pursuit of the *Bismarck* is based on this excellent and highly readable book; on ADM 234/322 Battle Summary No. 5, 'The Chase and Sinking of the German battleship "Bismarck", May 23–27, 1941, according to information up to November 1948' (especially in regard to timings); Müllenheim-Rechberg, op cit; Roskill, *War at Sea*, op cit, Vol I, Chapter XIX.
13. Exchange cited in Müllenheim-Rechberg, op cit, p. 78.
14. Hinsley, *British Intelligence in the Second World War*, op cit, Vol I, pp. 339–41.
15. Ibid, p. 341.
16. Ludovic Kennedy, op cit, p. 41.
17. G. A. Rotherham, *It's Really Quite Safe*, op cit, p. 198.
18. Quoted in ADM 234/322.
19. Cunningham, *A Sailor's Odyssey*, op cit, p. 280.
20. Ludovic Kennedy, op cit, p. 38.
21. Quoted in Roskill, *Churchill and the Admirals*, op cit, p. 121.
22. ADM 234/322.
23. Ludovic Kennedy, op cit, p. 68.
24. Ibid, p. 71.
25. Admiral Sir Ralph Edwards to Captain S. W. Roskill, 3 May, no year given, in ROSK 4/17.
26. See Correlli Barnett, *The Swordbearers*, op cit, pp. 144–7; Marder, *From the Dreadnought to Scapa Flow*, op cit, Vol II, *Jutland and After*, London, Oxford University Press, 1966, pp. 57–60, and Chart No. 4.
27. See Roskill, *War at Sea*, op cit, Vol I, p. 402.
28. Admiral Sir Ralph Edwards to S. W. Roskill, 3 May, year undated, in ROSK 4/17.
29. ADM 234/322.
30. ROSK 4/17, letter to S. W. Roskill.

31. ROSK 4/17, copy of a letter from Captain Colin McMullen, RN, in 1941 as a *Prince of Wales*'s gunnery control officer, to Ludovic Kennedy, undated. See also letter to S. W. Roskill in same file from McMullen, 29 May 1979.
32. Naval Staff Battle Summary in ADM 234/322.
33. See letter from John W. Wilkinson, one-time Chief Designer at Vickers-Armstrong, to S. W. Roskill, dated 1965, in ROSK 4/17.
34. Ludovic Kennedy, op cit, pp. 99–100; Müllenheim-Rechberg, op cit, pp. 116–18.
35. Cited in Ludovic Kennedy, op cit, p. 102.
36. Ibid, p. 54.
37. ADM 234/322.
38. ADM 234/509, The sinking of the *Bismarck*, 27th May 1941 – Official Despatches.
39. Ibid.
40. Ibid.
41. Ibid.
42. Ludovic Kennedy, op cit, p. 108.
43. ROSK 4/17, letter from Admiral of the Fleet Lord Tovey to S. W. Roskill, 14 December 1961.
44. Ludovic Kennedy, op cit, p. 103.
45. ROSK 4/17; note by Admiral Sir William Davis.
46. Ibid.
47. ROSK 4/17, Tovey to S. W. Roskill, 1 January 1962.
48. ADM 234/322.
49. ADM 234/509.
50. Hinsley, op cit, Vol 1, p. 342.
51. ROSK 4/17, Note by Admiral Sir William Davis.
52. The account of 25 May is based on ADM 234/322; SMVL 7/9 No. 448/17; Hinsley, op cit, Vol I, pp. 342–5; Ludovic Kennedy, op cit, pp. 130–2; Roskill, *War at Sea*, op cit, Vol I, pp. 410–11.
53. SMVL 7/9, No. 448/17.
54. Ibid.
55. Ibid.
56. Quoted in Müllenheim-Rechberg, op cit, p. 147.
57. Ibid.
58. Ibid, p. 148.
59. Ibid, p. 149.
60. Ibid, p. 148.
61. SMVL 7/9, No. 448/17.
62. Ibid.
63. Ludovic Kennedy, op cit, pp. 151–2.
64. SMVL 7/9, No. 448/17.
65. Note by Admiral Sir William Davis in ROSK 4/17.
66. Ibid.

67. ADM 234/322.
68. SMVL 7/9 No. 448/17.
69. Ludovic Kennedy, op cit, p. 164.
70. SMVL 7/9, No. 448/17.
71. ADM 234/509.
72. Müllenheim-Rechberg, op cit, p. 186.
73. ADM 234/322.
74. SMVL 7/9, No. 448/17.
75. Cited in Ludovic Kennedy, op cit, p. 182.
76. Ibid, p. 200.
77. ADM 234/322.
78. Müllenheim-Rechberg, op cit, p. 196.
79. Quoted in ibid.
80. Ludovic Kennedy, op cit, p. 205.
81. Figures from Müllenheim-Rechberg, op cit, p. 243.
82. ADM 234/322.
83. SMVL 7/9, No. 448/170.
84. ADM 234/509.
85. ADM 234/322.
86. Ibid.
87. ROSK 4/17, First Sea Lord to C-in-C, Home Fleet, 1137B/27/5/41; text confirmed to Captain S. W. Roskill by the Cabinet Office Historical Section; authorship admitted by Churchill in *The Second World War*, Vol III, London, Cassell, 1964, p. 282.
88. ROSK 4/17, Tovey to Captain S. W. Roskill, 20 November 1954.
89. See ADM 234/324, 'Disguised Raiders 1940–1'.
90. Hinsley, op cit, Vol I, p. 345.
91. Raeder, *Struggle for the Sea*, London, William Kimber, 1959, p. 214.

11. *Greek Prelude: The Battle of Matapan* (pages 317–345)

1. See Correlli Barnett's *The Desert Generals*, op cit, pp. 44–64, for an account of the latter stages of O'Connor's campaign.
2. ROSK 4/64, photocopy.
3. The following account of British Intelligence in relation to German forward moves in the Balkans and Mediterranean, December 1940–January 1941 is based on Hinsley, *British Intelligence in the Second World War*, op cit, Vol I, Chapters 11 and 12.
4. Playfair, *The Mediterranean and the Middle East*, op cit, Vol I, p. 315.
5. Hinsley, op cit, Vol I, p. 385.
6. Lenton and Colledge, *Warships of World War II*, op cit, p. 46.
7. The account of the attack on *Illustrious* is based on ADM 186/801, Naval Staff Narrative, Mediterranean; November 1940–December 1941; CAB 106/346, Despatches re Mediterranean Convoy Operations January 1941–August 1942; Playfair, op cit, Vol I,

pp. 311–28; Cunningham, *A Sailor's Odyssey*, op cit, pp. 301–9: ROSK 4/64.
8. Cunningham, op cit, p. 303.
9. Ibid.
10. ROSK 4/64, photocopy of letter of 18 January 1941.
11. Cunningham, op cit, p. 303.
12. The following account of the bombardment of Genoa on 9 February 1941 is based on ADM 186/797, BS No. 7, 'The Bombardment of Genoa 9 February 1941'.
13. ADM 186/797.
14. Playfair op cit, Vol I, p. 325; Gilbert, *Winston S. Churchill*, op cit, Vol VI, p. 1001.
15. ROSK 4/64, photocopy of letter of 18 January 1941.
16. Gilbert, op cit, Vol VI, p. 987.
17. Ibid.
18. Ibid, p. 1001.
19. Ibid.
20. See Cunningham, op cit, p. 316; ROSK 4/64, photocopy of letter from Cunningham to First Sea Lord, 11 March 1941.
21. Terraine, *Right of the Line*, op cit, p. 331.
22. CAB 105/1, 0/34651m 10/1.
23. Ibid, 9972(M.O.5) 11/1.
24. Ibid. Wavell's signal says 'Benghazi' even though O'Connor's victory was at Beda Fomm.
25. CAB 69/2, DO(41)7th, 10 February 1941.
26. Ibid.
27. CAB 69/2, DO(41)8th, 11 February 1941.
28. CAB 80/25, COS (41)83.
29. CAB 69/2, DO(41)8th, 11 February 1941, Confidential Annexe.
30. CAB 105/2, Hist (B)2 (Final) No. 8. Telegram of 14 February 1941 from Cs-in-C to Chiefs of Staff (transmitted by HQ RAF Middle East to Air Ministry for onward distribution). The following quotation from the signal by Admiral Cunningham to the Admiralty on the same date is taken from ibid, No. 6.
31. Ibid.
32. CAB 69/2, DO(41)7.
33. Cited in Gilbert, op cit, Vol VI, p. 1013.
34. Ibid.
35. Eden.
36. Hinsley, op cit, Vol I, p. 361.
37. CAB 80/57 COS(41)43(0) (Revise) Policy in the Mediterranean and Middle East, 24 February 1941.
38. Ibid. General R. H. Haining, VCIGS, signed in Dill's place.
39. CAB 65/21 WM(41) 20th, Confidential Annexe.
40. Ibid.

41. CAB 65/21, WM(41) 21st Minute 2, Confidential Annexe.
42. Cunningham, op cit, p. 318.
43. CAB 79/9, COS (41) 82nd, 4 March 1941.
44. Ibid.
45. CAB 65/22, WM(41) 24th, Confidential Annexe.
46. CAB 79/9, COS(41) 90th, Annexe 1.
47. CAB 69/2, DO(41)9th, 5 March 1941, Confidential Annexe.
48. Ibid.
49. CAB 65/22, WM (41)26, Confidential Annexe.
50. ROSK 4/64, photocopy of letter of 11 March 1941.
51. Ibid.
52. See Hinsley, op cit, Vol I, pp. 403–5 for an account of Intelligence prior to the Battle of Matapan.
53. Cunningham, op cit, p. 326.
54. The following account of the Battle of Matapan is based on ADM 186/795, Naval Staff History: Battle Summary No. 44, The Battle of Cape Matapan, 28th March 1941; Cunningham, op cit, pp. 325–36; Playfair, op cit, Vol II, pp. 61–70; S. W. C. Pack, *The Battle of Matapan*, London Batsford, 1961. Unless otherwise stated, all courses and timings are from ADM 186/795.
55. Obituary of Rear-Admiral Fisher in the *Daily Telegraph*, 22 April 1988.
56. Vice-Admiral Sir Geoffrey Barnard, then fleet gunnery officer, quoted in Pack, op cit, p. 39.
57. Cunningham, op cit, p. 328.
58. Ibid, p. 327.
59. Ibid, p. 327.
60. Quoted in Pack, op cit, p. 93.
61. Weale, Weale and Barker, *Combat Aircraft of World War Two*, op cit, pp. 139–40.
62. ADM 186/795, Appendix G.
63. ADM 186/795.
64. Cunningham, op cit, p. 329.
65. Quoted in Pack, op cit, p. 111.
66. Ibid.
67. Ibid.
68. Quoted in Pack, op cit, p. 115.
69. ADM 186/795.
70. ADM 186/795, Appendix D.
71. Cunningham, op cit, p. 331.
72. Quoted in Pack, op cit, p. 132.
73. Ibid.
74. Ibid.
75. Cunningham, op cit, p. 331.
76. Ibid, p. 332.
77. ADM 186/795.

78. Cited in Pack, op cit, p. 118.
79. Cunningham, op cit, p. 332.
80. Ibid, p. 333.

12. *Catastrophe in the Mediterranean, 1941* (pages 346–377)

1. Playfair, *The Mediterranean and the Middle East*, op cit, Vol II, *The Germans Come to the Aid of their Ally (1941)*, p. 83.
2. The account of 'Demon' is based on Playfair, op cit, Vol II, pp. 93–106; Cunningham, *A Sailor's Odyssey*, op cit, pp. 352–9.
3. Cunningham, op cit. p. 354.
4. Ibid, p. 356.
5. Ibid, p. 357.
6. Playfair, op cit, Vol II, p. 104, Note.
7. Hinsley, *British Intelligence in the Second World War*, op cit, Vol I, p. 416.
8. Gilbert, *Winston S. Churchill*, op cit, Vol VI, p. 1072; CAB 65/22, WM(41)44, Minute 2, Confidential Annexe.
9. Quoted in Playfair, op cit, Vol II, p. 125.
10. Ibid.
11. Gilbert, op cit, Vol VI, p. 1076.
12. Playfair, op cit, Vol II, p. 129.
13. Hinsley, op cit, Vol I, p. 419.
14. ADM 234/320. Battle Summary No. 4, Naval Operations of the Battle of Crete, 20th May to 1st June 1941 (1952).
15. Gilbert, op cit, Vol VI, p. 1078.
16. Cunningham, op cit, p. 366.
17. The account of naval operations in the Crete Campaign is based on ADM 234/320, BS No. 4; Cunningham, op cit, Chapter XXIX; Playfair, op cit, Vol II, Chapter VII. All details of timings, positions and courses are drawn from ADM 234/320.
18. Cunningham, op cit, pp. 336–7.
19. Ibid, p. 370.
20. ADM 234/320.
21. Cunningham, op cit, p. 371.
22. ADM 234/320.
23. Cunningham, op cit, p. 372.
24. Ibid, p. 373.
25. ADM 234/320; Cunningham, op cit, p. 374.
26. Cunningham, op cit, p. 374.
27. Ibid, pp. 374–5.
28. ADM 234/320.
29. Ibid.
30. Cunningham, op cit, p. 375.
31. Ibid, pp. 375–6; ADM 234/320.
32. ADM 234/320.

33. For the land battle for Crete, see Playfair, op cit, Vol II, Chapter VII; I. McD. G. Stewart, *The Struggle for Crete 20 May–1 June 1941; A Story of Lost Opportunity*, London, OUP, 1966; John Hale Spencer, *Battle for Crete*, London, Heinemann, 1962.
34. ADM 234/320, p. 28.
35. ADM 234/320.
36. Ibid.
37. Ibid.
38. Ibid, p. 33.
39. Cunningham, op cit, p. 384.
40. ADM 234/320.
41. Ibid.
42. Cited in ibid, p. 33, Footnote 4.
43. ADM 234/320, Appendices A and D.
44. ROSK 4/65.
45. Cited in Gilbert, op cit, p. 1072.
46. ROSK 4/64, signal 0059/15/4/41.
47. Ibid.
48. Cunningham, op cit, p. 342.
49. Ibid.
50. Ibid, p. 343.
51. Ibid, p. 347.
52. ADM 186/797, BS No. 19, The Bombardment of Tripoli, 21 April 1941.
53. Ibid.
54. Cunningham, op cit, p. 348.
55. Ibid, p. 350.
56. Ibid, p. 351.
57. See CAB 106/346, Despatches on Mediterranean Convoy Operations January 1941–August 1942; Playfair, op cit, Vol II, p. 453; Cunningham, op cit, pp. 360–3.
58. Cunningham, op cit, p. 363.
59. Playfair, op cit, Vol II, pp. 269–70.
60. Ibid, p. 281.
61. Ibid.
62. ROSK 4/66.
63. Cunningham, op cit, p. 414.
64. Ibid.
65. Ibid, p. 412.
66. The following account of the loss of *Ark Royal* is based on ADM 234/508, BR 2055, Technical Report of Loss and Damage to H.M.S. ARK ROYAL (1942).
67. Ibid.
68. Ibid.
69. Ibid.

70. Ibid.
71. Ibid.
72. Ibid.
73. Ibid.
74. Cited in Cunningham, op cit, p. 423.
75. Ibid, p. 424.
76. Ibid.
77. Ibid.
78. Ibid, p. 433.
79. ROSK 4/63. Figures supplied to Captain Roskill by Historical Section, TSD, Admiralty, February 1952.

13. *The Sinking of HMS* Prince of Wales *and* Repulse (pages 378–426)

1. ROSK 4/79, brief prepared in Cabinet Office Historical Section for Captain Roskill as official naval historian on 'Political Decisions relating to the Sending of the *Prince of Wales* and the *Repulse* to the Far East'.
2. Ibid.
3. CAB 79/24, COS (41) 25th.
4. CAB 32/9, E-8 and E-9, cited by C. Barnett in *The Collapse of British Power*, op cit, p. 279.
5. ADM 205/7, File No. 4.
6. See Correlli Barnett, *The Audit of War*, op cit, Chapter Six, for an analysis based on wartime official investigations.
7. ADM 205/7, File No. 4.
8. ADM 205/5.
9. Ibid, memorandum from the First Sea Lord to the First Lord, January 1940; First Sea Lord to the Controller, 3 February 1940; Admiralty Memorandum to the War Cabinet, February 1940.
10. Ibid, notes by First Sea Lord and Director of Plans for a Board Meeting on 5 September 1940.
11. Postan, Hay and Scott, *Design and Development of Weapons*, op cit, p. 63.
12. Ibid, p. 61, Table 6.
13. ROSK 4/79.
14. CAB 32/128, E(PD)(37)5, cited in Barnett, *The Collapse of British Power*, op cit, p. 441.
15. For the mid-war economic balance sheet of Empire, see Hancock and Gowing, *British War Economy*, London, HMSO and Longmans, Green, 1949, *passim*; Behrens, *Merchant Shipping and the Demands of War*, op cit, Chapter IX, especially Appendix XXXIX, p. 248; S. Woodburn Kirby, *The War Against Japan*, Vol I, *The Loss of Singapore*, London, HMSO, 1957, p. 477, Appendix I; Barnett, *The Collapse of British Power*, op cit, p. 132.
16. The following account of Anglo-American diplomacy towards Japan

and strategic discussions in 1940–41 is based on Reynolds, *The Creation of the Anglo-American Alliance*, op cit, pp. 132–44, 204–5, and Chapter Nine; Paul Haggie, *Britannia at Bay: The Defence of the British Empire Against Japan*, op cit, pp. 171–208; Christopher Thorne, *Allies of a Kind; The United States, Great Britain and the War Against Japan 1941–1945*, op cit, Part One, Chapters Two and Three.

17. Cited in Barnett, *The Collapse of British Power*, op cit, p. 301.
18. CAB 66/10, WP(40)302, 31 July 1940.
19. Cited in Haggie, op cit, p. 189.
20. Cited in ibid, p. 191; see also Gilbert, *Winston S. Churchill*, op cit, Vol VI, pp. 1044–7.
21. Cited in Haggie, op cit, p. 193.
22. CAB 80/27, COS 230, 11 April 1941.
23. CAB 80/28, COS 365, 10 June 1941.
24. Reynolds, op cit, p. 238; there is a brief, too brief, mention in Gilbert, op cit, Vol VI, p. 1160.
25. Reynolds, op cit, p. 239.
26. Cited in Haggie, op cit, pp. 202–3.
27. Reynolds, op cit, p. 225.
28. See S. Woodburn Kirby, op cit, Vol I, Map 21, opposite p. 374.
29. CAB 53/21, COS Appreciation of the Far East Situation, 28 May 1937.
30. Ibid.
31. Ibid.
32. CAB 66/10, WP(40)302, 31 July 1940, The Situation in the Far East in the event of Japanese Intervention against us.
33. Churchill to Ismay, 10 September 1940, in Churchill *The Second World War*, op cit, Vol II, *Their Finest Hour*, pp. 591–2.
34. Churchill, *The Second World War*, op cit, Vol III, *The Grand Alliance*, p. 565.
35. Ibid, Vol IV, *The Hinge of Fate*, p. 43.
36. See Woodburn Kirby, op cit, Vol I, pp. 162–5.
37. The following account of the debates leading to the despatch of the *Prince of Wales* and *Repulse* to Singapore and their subsequent operations is based on ROSK 4/79, brief prepared for Captain Roskill as official historian on 'Political Decisions relating to the Sending of the *Prince of Wales* and the *Repulse* to the Far East', and M.0251/42, 'Loss of H.M. Ships *Prince of Wales* and *Repulse* on 10th December 1941; Narrative of Operations of Force Z', being a report by the Director of Plans and the D.D.D.(F) dated 20 January 1942; ADM 234/330, Naval Staff History, B.S. No. 14 (Revised), 'Loss of His Majesty's Ships *Prince of Wales* and *Repulse*, 10th December 1941' (1955).
38. ROSK 4/79, M.0251/42.
39. ADM 205/6, memorandum by First Sea Lord to First Lord, 1 August 1940, on 'Re-Distribution of the Fleet in the event of war with Japan'.

40. CAB 79/24, COS(41) 360th.
41. ADM 205/10, 25 August 1941.
42. Ibid.
43. Ibid, 26 August 1941.
44. Ibid, 28 August 1941.
45. Ibid, 29 August 1941.
46. Ibid.
47. Ibid.
48. Ibid.
49. CAB 69/2, DO(41) 65th.
50. Ibid.
51. Ibid.
52. Ibid.
53. Ibid.
54. ROSK 4/79, photocopy of letter of 17 October 1941.
55. CAB 69/2, DO(41) 65th.
56. Ibid.
57. ROSK 4/79, photocopy of letter of 17 October 1941.
58. CAB 79/24, COS(41) 360th, 20 October 1941.
59. Ibid.
60. ROSK 4/79, note by Captain Roskill.
61. Churchill Archives Centre, A. V. Alexander Papers, AVAR 5/6/16.
62. ROSK 4/79, copy of note to the First Sea Lord on 15 September 1941.
63. CAB 79/24, COS(51) 360th.
64. Ibid.
65. ROSK 4/79, note by Captain Roskill.
66. CAB 79/24, COS(41) 360th.
67. Ibid.
68. CAB 69/8, DO(41) 66th.
69. ROSK 4/79, copy by Captain Roskill of signal 2023/20/10/41.
70. See Roberta Wohlstetter, *Pearl Harbor: Warning and Decision*, Stanford, California, Stanford University Press, 1962, Chapter 3, especially pp. 170–86.
71. Ibid, passim, especially Chapter 5 and pp. 393–96.
72. Ibid, p. 211.
73. Cf Hinsley, *British Intelligence in the Second World War*, op cit, Vol II, pp. 75–7.
74. Reynolds, op cit, p. 240; Woodburn Kirby, op cit, pp. 89–90.
75. Woodburn Kirby, op cit, pp. 95–6.
76. See ROSK 4/79, Brief prepared for Captain Roskill on 'Political Decisions, etc'.
77. ROSK 4/79, copy of letter to Mrs Barker.
78. ROSK 4/79, photocopy of letter of 30 January 1943.
79. AVAR 5/6/16, undated handwritten letter from First Sea Lord to First Lord.

80. ADM 234/330, p. 2, Footnote 2: message 1648a, 21 October 1941.
81. See ADM 234/330, p. 2, on this point.
82. ADM 205/10.
83. ADM 234/330, Appendix D, p. 24.
84. Ibid.
85. Ibid.
86. Ibid.
87. Ibid.
88. Geoffrey Brooke, *Alarm Starboard: A remarkable true story of the war at sea*, Cambridge, Patrick Stephens, 1982, p. 90.
89. Ibid, p. 91.
90. ADM 234/330, Appendix D.
91. Ibid.
92. Ibid.
93. Brooke, op cit, p. 93.
94. Roskill, *War at Sea*, op cit, Vol I, p. 561.
95. Ibid, p. 562.
96. Reynolds, op cit, p. 246.
97. ROSK 4/79.
98. Richard Pool, *Course for Disaster: From Scapa Flow to the River Kwai*, London, Leo Cooper, 1987, p. 55.
99. Ibid.
100. Brooke, op cit, p. 94.
101. ADM 234/330, p. 7. The following narrative of the sortie of Force Z is based on this, and on ROSK 4/79, M.0251/42.
102. ADM 234/330, p. 8, Footnote 1.
103. ROSK 4/79, photocopy of letter to Mrs Barker, 25 February 1943.
104. ADM 234/330, p. 8.
105. Ibid, p. 10.
106. Ibid, p. 8.
107. Ibid.
108. Pool, op cit, p. 56.
109. Ibid.
110. Cited in Pool, op cit, p. 57 and Brooke, op cit, p. 97.
111. ADM 234/330, Appendix D(I), p. 31.
112. ADM 205/5, carbon copy of memorandum of 25 August 1940, unsigned and without initials, but almost certainly drafted by Phillips as VCNS, as the style of the advocacy indicates.
113. Somerville and Lord Cork both had no doubt about Phillips's role; see SMVL 3/22, letters from Somerville to his wife, 16 and 18 November 1940; Roskill, *Churchill and the Admirals*, op cit, p. 170.
114. ADM 234/330, Appendix D(I).
115. Pool, op cit, p. 58.
116. Weale, Weale and Barker, *Combat Aircraft of World War Two*, op cit, p. 169.

117. ADM 234/330, p. 11.
118. ROSK 4/79, photocopy of letter of 29 January 1942 in Cunningham papers.
119. ROSK 4/79, M.0251/42; Michael Goodenough, when 4th Sea Lord, to Captain Roskill, 8 May 1951.
120. ROSK 4/79.
121. Pool, op cit, p. 59.
122. The following account of the sinking of Force Z on 10 December 1941 is based on ADM 234/330.
123. Ibid, p. 18.
124. Lenton and Colledge, *Warships of World War II*, op cit, pp. 18 and 22.
125. Cited in ADM 234/330, p. 13.
126. ROSK 4/79, letter from Admiral Sir William Davis to Captain Roskill, 12 January 1979.
127. Ibid.
128. Pool, op cit, p. 64.
129. Ibid, p. 65.
130. Cited in ADM 234/330, p. 17, Footnote 1.
131. Pool, op cit, p. 66.
132. ADM 234/330, p. 17.
133. Ibid.
134. Ibid.
135. Brooke, op cit, p. 107.
136. Ibid, p. 108.
137. ROSK 4/79, M.0251/42.
138. ADM 234/330, Appendix F.
139. Roskill, *War at Sea*, op cit, Vol I, p. 417.
140. Pool, op cit, p. 67.
141. AVAR 5/7/8.
142. Gilbert, *Winston S. Churchill*, op cit, Vol VII, *Road to Victory*, London, Heinemann, 1986, pp. 5–6; Woodburn Kirby, op cit, Vol I, pp. 254–62.
143. AVAR 5/7/8.
144. For the Battle of the Java Sea, see Woodburn Kirby, op cit, Vol I, pp. 438–43; Roskill, *War at Sea*, op cit, Vol II, pp. 13–18.
145. CAB 16/209, SAC 1.
146. Cited in Gilbert, op cit, Vol VII, p. 1274.

Part III: The Long Voyage Home

14. *'If We Lose the War at Sea, We Lose the War'* (pages 429–457)

1. Roskill, *War at Sea*, op cit, Vol III, Part II, Appendix I, pp. 439–46.
2. See Terraine, *The Right of the Line*, op cit, pp. 70–115, 251–89, 459–81.
3. See Barnett, *The Audit of War*, op cit, Chapter Nine.

4. See Fraser, *And We Shall Shock Them: The British Army in the Second World War*, op cit, pp. 24–212.
5. Gwyer, *Grand Strategy*, op cit, Vol III, Part I, pp. 357–8.
6. Churchill, *The Second World War*, op cit, Vol IV, p. 176.
7. Gwyer, op cit, p. 359.
8. Ibid.
9. Ibid, pp. 364–5.
10. Ibid, p. 398.
11. Cmd 6332: *Agreements between the Prime Minister and the President of the United States of America*, cited in Behrens, *Merchant Shipping and the Demands of Wars*, op cit, pp. 287–8.
12. Roskill, *War at Sea*, op cit, Vol II, p. 115.
13. Cited in ibid, p. 43.
14. Cf Roskill 5/10, Paper for First Sea Lord by Admiral Sir Geoffrey Blake, 'Air Support for Naval Forces', 17 February 1942.
15. Roskill, *War at Sea*, op cit, Vol II, p. 92.
16. J. A. Turner, *Administration of the Navy Department in World War II*, U.S. Department of the Navy, Washington, 1959, p. 879.
17. Cited in Butler, *Grand Strategy*, op cit, Vol III, part II, p. 502.
18. Postan, Hay and Scott, *Design and Development of Weapons*, op cit, p. 289.
19. Ibid, pp. 269–90.
20. Ibid.
21. See Barnett, *The Audit of War*, op cit, Chapter Six.
22. Postan, Hay and Scott, op cit, pp. 294–5.
23. Roskill, *War at Sea*, op cit, Vol I, Appendix R, p. 618, Table 2.
24. Behrens, op cit, p. 252 and Footnote 1.
25. Ibid.
26. See analysis in Behrens, op cit, pp. 284–5.
27. Ibid, p. 284.
28. An average of 1.5 to 2 million deadweight tons over the twelve months: Behrens, op cit, p. 291.
29. Behrens, op cit, pp. 276–7.
30. CAB 69/4, DO(42)23, 5 March 1942.
31. Dönitz, *Memoirs: Ten Years and Twenty Days*, op cit, p. 182.
32. Ibid, p. 197.
33. Ibid.
34. Roskill, *War at Sea*, op cit, Vol II, p. 96.
35. Ibid.
36. ROSK 5/10.
37. ADM 205/18.
38. Cited in Roskill, *War at Sea*, op cit, Vol II, p. 97.
39. Churchill, *The Second World War*, op cit, Vol IV, p. 103.
40. Roskill, *War at Sea*, op cit, Vol II, p. 97.
41. Cited in ADM 234/578, Naval Staff History, Second World War: *The*

Defeat of the Enemy Attack on Shipping 1939–1945; A Study of Policy and Operations, Vol 1A (Text and Appendices), Historical Section, Admiralty, 1957, p. 86.

42. S. E. Morison, *History of United States Naval Operations in World War II*, Vol I, *The Battle of the Atlantic, September 1939–May 1943*, Boston, Little, Brown, 1947, p. 143.
43. Ibid.
44. Dönitz, op cit, p. 220.
45. Ibid, p. 221.
46. Ibid, pp. 221–2.
47. Hinsley, *British Intelligence in the Second World War*, op cit, Vol II, pp. 176–7.
48. The following account of the passage of *Scharnhorst* and *Gneisenau* is based on RMSY 8/16 in the Churchill Archives Centre, a dossier of relevant signals and of subsequent reports by the principal British participants, including Vice-Admiral Ramsay's own report as V-A, Dover, to the Admiralty, No. 145/211. F/42 of 16 February 1942; and ADM 186/803, BR 1736 (7) (48), BS No. 11, The Passage of the *Scharnhorst*, *Gneisenau* and *Prinz Eugen* Through the English Channel, 12 February 1942 (1948), and A.F.O.P. 228/49, containing additional material.
49. ADM 186/803.
50. Hinsley, op cit, Vol II, p. 179, Footnote.
51. Ibid, pp. 179–80.
52. RMSY 8/16, signal 1252/3/2/42 to all Cs-in-C.
53. Ibid.
54. ADM 186/803.
55. Ibid.
56. See RMSY 8/16, signal to the Admiralty, DF355, 11 February 1942. All the relevant signals are contained in this file.
57. RMSY 8/16, signal, 11 February 1942.
58. Hinsley, op cit, Vol II, pp. 182–3.
59. ADM 186/803, p. 5, Footnote 1 and p. 6, Footnote 2.
60. Ibid.
61. Ibid, p. 7.
62. RMSY 8/16.
63. RMSY 8/16. No. 145/211. F/42. See also sources cited in Footnote 64.
64. See RMSY 8/16, Report by Lieutenant-Commander E. N. Pumphrey, RN, Senior Officer, H.M.M.T.B.s, dated 13 February 1942; Enclosure No. 3 to Dover letter No. 145/211, F/42; Report by Lieutenant (T).D. J. Long, Senior Officer M.T.B.s 32, 71 and 18, 12 February 1942.
65. RMSY 8/14. Enclosure No. 2 to Dover letter of 16.2.42 No. 145/211. F/42, Report by Wing-Commander J. Constable-Roberts, Air Staff Officer to Flag Officer Commanding, Dover.

66. Dover No. 145/211, F/42, dated 16 February 1942.
67. Ibid; Reports by Wing-Commander T. P. Gleave, RAF, Commanding RAF Manston; by Sub-Lieutenant Lee, RN, Observer, Swordfish, W.5983. Report from Intelligence Officer, Manston, on interrogation of survivors from 825 Squadron.
68. Weale, Weale and Barker, *Combat Aircraft of World War Two*, op cit, pp. 138 and 169.
69. Rotherham, *It's Really Quite Safe*, op cit, pp. 205–6.
70. ADM 186/203, p. 14.
71. Bekker, *Hitler's Naval War*, op cit, p. 234.
72. Lenton and Colledge, *Warships of World War II*, op cit, pp. 81–8; Bekker, op cit, Appendix I, p. 370.
73. Ibid.
74. *The Times*: leading article of 14 February 1942.
75. Cmd 6775: 'Report of the Board of Enquiry appointed to enquire into the circumstances in which the German Battle Cruisers *Scharnhorst* and *Gneisenau* and Cruiser *Prinz Eugen* proceeded from Brest to Germany on February 12th 1942, and on the operations undertaken to prevent this movement.'
76. Ibid.
77. Roskill, *War at Sea*, op cit, Vol I, Appendix R, p. 618, Table II; Vol II, Appendix O, p. 486, Table II.
78. The following summary is based on Hinsley, op cit, Vol 2, pp. 176–9 and 228–33.
79. See ibid, Appendix 1, Part (i), p. 636.
80. Ibid, Appendix 9, p. 682.
81. Cited in ibid, Vol 2, p. 230.
82. Roskill, *War at Sea*, op cit, Vol II, p. 199.

15. *'The Battle of the Air', 1942* (pages 458–490)

1. Cited in Terraine, *The Right of the Line*, op cit, p. 413.
2. CAB 69/4, DO(42)14.
3. CAB 69/4, DO(42)15, 'Bombing Policy', 14 February 1942.
4. Cited in Terraine, op cit, p. 418.
5. Ibid.
6. Ibid, p. 419.
7. CAB 69/4, DO(42)23.
8. Ibid.
9. Ibid.
10. Ibid.
11. Ibid.
12. CAB 69/4, DO(42)24, 8 March 1942.
13. Ibid.
14. Ibid.

15. CAB 69/4, DO(42) 8th, Minute 1.
16. Ibid.
17. Ibid.
18. Ibid.
19. CAB 69/4, DO(42)34, 'Air forces: Cooperation with the Army and Navy'; the paper was in response to the First Sea Lord's memorandum DO(42)23 in CAB 69/4, and COS (42)164, of 10 March 1942 by the CIGS, entitled 'Army Air Requirements', in CAB 80/35.
20. CAB 69/4, DO(42)34.
21. Ibid.
22. Ibid.
23. Ibid.
24. See ADM 205/15, 19, 22A, and 25, 27, 28, *passim*.
25. CAB 66/30, WP(42)483.
26. Cited in C. Webster and N. Frankland, *The Strategic Air Offensive Against Germany 1939–1945*, op cit, Vol I, Parts 1, 2 and 3, pp. 330–3.
27. Ibid, p. 334.
28. CAB 69/4, DO(42)47, The Bombing of Germany. Report by Mr Justice Singleton, 20 May 1942.
29. Ibid.
30. Ibid.
31. Webster and Frankland, op cit, Vol I, p. 479, and Footnote 1, also Annexe V.
32. Roskill, *War at Sea*, op cit, Vol II, Appendix O, p. 386, Table II.
33. ADM 205/15, Part 4.
34. ADM 234/578, Appendix 11, p. 8.
35. Ibid.
36. Ibid.
37. Ibid.
38. CAB 79/20, COS(42), 180th Minute 12.
39. Ibid.
40. CAB 80/64, COS(42), 183(O), 23 June 1942.
41. Ibid.
42. Ibid.
43. Roskill, *War at Sea*, op cit, Vol II, Appendix O, p. 486, Table II.
44. CAB 79/21, COS(42), 188th, 24 June 1942.
45. CAB 80/37, COS (42)332, General Policy for the Employment of Air Forces.
46. Ibid.
47. CAB 80/37, COS (42)341, 14 July 1942, Provision of Long-Range Aircraft for Anti-Submarine Patrols, memorandum by CAS.
48. Ibid.
49. CAB 80/64, COS(42)204(O), 18 July 1942.
50. CAB 80/64, COS(42)172(O) 'Air Against the Sea'.

51. CAB 65/31, WM(42) 111th, Minute 2, Confidential Annexe.
52. Cited in Terraine, op cit, p. 425.
53. Ibid.
54. Ibid, p. 426.
55. CAB 66/26, WP(42)311, A Review of the War Position. Note by the Prime Minister.
56. Ibid.
57. Ibid.
58. Ibid.
59. CAB 66/28, WP(42)374 and WP(42)399.
60. CAB 66/30, WP(42)481.
61. ADM 205/24, The Anti-Submarine War.
62. Ibid.
63. CAB 70/5, DO(S)(42)88.
64. Ibid.
65. Ibid.
66. ADM 205/26.
67. Ibid.
68. CAB 66/30, WP(42)483, 24 October 1942.
69. CAB 80/65, COS(42)345(O)(Final).
70. CAB 80/65, COS(42)379(O), 'An Estimate of the Effects of an Anglo-American Bomber Offensive Against Germany'.
71. CAB 80/65, COS(42)393(O), 15 November 1942, Note by the First Sea Lord: 'Implications of the Policy on Estimating the Effects of an Anglo-American Bomber Offensive against Germany'.
72. Cf ADM 205/27, exchange of letters between the First Sea Lord and the Prime Minister, 10–19 December 1942.
73. CAB 86/2, AU(42) 3rd.
74. ADM 205/27, Notes for the Prime Minister's meeting by the First Sea Lord, 13 November 1942.
75. Ibid.
76. Ibid.
77. Ibid.
78. Ibid.
79. Ibid.
80. Ibid.
81. ADM 205/21, reviews dated 23 December 1942.
82. Roskill, *War at Sea*, op cit, Vol II, Appendix O, p. 486, Table II.
83. Ibid.
84. See CAB 86/2, AU(42) 3rd.
85. ROSK 5/12.
86. CAB 86/2, AU(42) 5th.
87. Roskill, *War at Sea*, op cit, Vol II, Appendix O, pp. 485–6, Tables I and II.
88. Behrens, *Merchant Shipping and the Demands of War*, op cit, p. 316.

89. ADM 234/578, p. 104, ADM 234/384, p. 103.
90. Terraine, op cit, pp. 404–6.
91. In AIR 41/47, Vol III, p. 83.
92. Ibid.
93. BT 28/377, Report on Vickers-Armstrong (Aircraft) Ltd, Weybridge; cited in Barnett, *The Audit of War*, op cit, p. 154.
94. AIR 41/47, Vol III, p. 83.
95. Ibid, p. 84.
96. ROSK 5/12, photocopy of paper by Joubert to the First Sea Lord, 27 September 1942, 'The Anti-Submarine War'.
97. Ibid.
98. Webster and Frankland, op cit, Vol I, p. 481; see also ADM 234/578.
99. Webster and Frankland, op cit.
100. Cited in Padfield, *Dönitz: the Last Führer*, op cit, pp. 249–50.
101. Ibid; ADM 234/578, p. 104, cites a similar note by Dönitz which it dates to 21 August.
102. ADM 234/578, p. 106.
103. Ibid.
104. See AVIA 10/104; Barnett, *The Audit of War*, op cit, Chapter 9; Postan, Hay and Scott, *Design and Development of Weapons*, op cit, pp. 378–9.
105. CAB 66/27, WP(42)352, August 1942.
106. ROSK 5/10, Notes by First Sea Lord, 13 November 1942.
107. ADM 205/15, Part 4, Memorandum to the First Sea Lord, 24 June 1942, annotated by him; see also ADM 234/578, p. 23.
108. ADM 234/578.
109. Ibid, pp. 18–19.
110. Ibid.
111. Ibid, p. 89.
112. Churchill Archives Centre, Maclean Papers, MCLN 2/1, Report by Captain I. G. Maclean, RN, entitled 'Trends in Naval Propulsion Machinery', 7 July 1946; MCLN 2/3 Report by Rear-Admiral I. G. Maclean, Deputy Engineer-in-Chief of the Fleet, 'Maritime Supremacy: the State of the British Marine Engineering Industry', April 1955; see also Grove, Chant, Lyon and Lyon, *The Hardware of World War II*, op cit, p. 196 and p. 215; Edgar J. March, *British Destroyers; A History of Development, 1892–1953*, op cit, pp. 322, 341, 354 and 500. The boiler pressures of British Second World destroyers, at 300 psi, represented only a small advance on the 250 psi reached at the end of the Great War.
113. ADM 234/578, p. 33.
114. Ibid, p. 25.
115. Ibid, p. 34.
116. Ibid, p. 105.
117. Ibid, p. 105.
118. ADM 205/23.

119. Lenton and Colledge, *Warships of World War II*, op cit, pp. 85–6, 104–5.
120. Ibid, p. 201.
121. The following account of Escort Unit B6's battle together with all quotations is drawn from ADM 234/370, BR 1736(45) BS No. 51, Naval Staff History, Second World War, *Convoy and Anti-Submarine Warfare Reports*. No. 4. *Passage of Convoy S.C.104 – October 1942*, Report of Proceedings on Convoy SC104 by Commanding Officer HMS FAME covering the period 9th–19th October 1942; including Report from Commanding Officer HMS VISCOUNT, reporting Attacks on Two U-boats and Movements of VISCOUNT when ordered to Proceed Independently; Report Received from the Commanding Officer, HNORMS POTENTILLA.
122. Roskill, *War at Sea*, op cit, Vol II, p. 213.
123. Ibid, Appendix O, p. 485, Table I.
124. Behrens, op cit, Appendix XLVI, p. 283.

16. *The Verdun of Maritime War: Malta, 1942* (pages 491–526)

1. Hinsley, *British Intelligence in the Second World War*, op cit, Vol II, p. 349.
2. ADM 205/14, minutes of 16 and 17 June 1942.
3. Cunningham, *A Sailor's Odyssey*, op cit, p. 442.
4. Ibid, p. 443.
5. ADM 234/353, Naval Staff History, B.S. No. 32, Malta Convoys (1945), based on war diaries and operational reports.
6. Quoted in Playfair, *The Mediterranean and the Middle East*, op cit, Vol III, Part II, p. 451.
7. Ibid.
8. See Nigel Hamilton, *Monty: The Making of a General 1887–1942*, London, Hamish Hamilton, 1981, pp. 745–6; Barnett, *The Desert Generals*, op cit, p. 272.
9. Cf Torres Vedras and Masséna's enforced retreat from Portugal, 1810–11.
10. Butler, *Grand Strategy*, op cit, Vol III, Part II, p. 445.
11. ROSK 5/95, photocopy of letter to Vice-Chief of the Naval Staff, 9 January 1942.
12. Ibid.
13. Ibid.
14. See Terraine, *The Right of the Line*, op cit, pp. 343–4.
15. ROSK 5/95, letter of 9 January 1942.
16. Cunningham, op cit, p. 442.
17. Ibid, pp. 442–3.
18. The following account of Operation MG1 is based on ADM 234/353, B.S. No. 32.
19. Ibid, p. 4.

20. Hinsley, op cit, Vol II, p. 347.
21. ADM 234/353, B.S. No. 32, p. 5.
22. Ibid.
23. Quoted in ibid, p. 9.
24. Ibid.
25. Cited in ibid, p. 7.
26. Ibid.
27. Cunningham, op cit, p. 452.
28. Vian, *Action This Day*, op cit, p. 90.
29. Cited in ADM 234/353, p. 13.
30. Minute reproduced as frontispiece in Vian's memoirs.
31. Vian, op cit, p. 92.
32. Cited in ADM 234/353, p. 12.
33. Cunningham, op cit, p. 457.
34. Ibid, p. 459.
35. Grove, Chant, Lyon and Lyon, *The Hardware of World War II*, op cit, p. 202.
36. Cited in Roskill, *War at Sea*, op cit, Vol II, p. 61.
37. The following account of 'Operation Harpoon' is based on ADM 234/353, unless otherwise stated.
38. Ibid, p. 18.
39. Ibid.
40. Staff Minute M.08465/42, cited in ibid, p. 20.
41. Ibid.
42. Ibid, p. 21.
43. See Roskill, *Churchill and the Admirals*, op cit, p. 189.
44. Ibid.
45. The following account of 'Operation Vigorous' is based on ADM 234/353, unless otherwise stated.
46. Ibid, p. 27.
47. ROSK 5/95, letter to S. W. Roskill, 28 November 1954.
48. Ibid.
49. Ibid.
50. ADM 234/353, p. 29.
51. Ibid, p. 28.
52. Ibid, p. 29.
53. Quoted in ibid, pp. 32–3.
54. Quoted in ibid, p. 33.
55. Lenton and Colledge, *Warships of World War II*, op cit, p. 41.
56. Quoted in ADM 234/353, p. 33.
57. Quoted in ibid, pp. 33–4.
58. Ibid.
59. Weale, Weale and Barker, *Combat Aircraft of World War Two*, op cit, p. 161.
60. ADM 234/353, p. 34.

61. ROSK 5/95, letter to S. W. Roskill, 28 November 1954.
62. Ibid: letters to S. W. Roskill of 6 and 16 November 1954.
63. ROSK 5/97, letter to S. W. Roskill, 22 November 1957.
64. Quoted in Barnett, *The Desert Generals*, op cit, p. 194.
65. Lampton Burn, *Down Ramps; Saga of the 8th Armada*, London, Carroll and Nicholson, 1948, p. 57.
66. ROSK 5/99, photocopy of letter of 18 November 1942.
67. See Hinsley, *British Intelligence in the Second World War*, op cit, Vol II, pp. 380, 392–3, 395–7, 403–5.
68. Playfair, *The Mediterranean and the Middle East*, op cit, Vol IV, *The Destruction of the Axis Forces in Africa*, pp. 9–10, Footnotes 1 and 2, p. 15.
69. Behrens, *Merchant Shipping and the Demands of War*, op cit, Appendix L, p. 296.
70. See ibid, Chapter XIII, for an analysis of the shipping and import problem in 1942.
71. The following account of 'Operation Pedestal' is based on ADM 234/353, unless otherwise stated.
72. Ibid, p. 39.
73. Weale, Weale and Barker, op cit, p. 159.
74. Ibid, p. 134.
75. ADM 234/353, p. 42.
76. Ibid, p. 45.
77. Ibid.
78. Cited in Roskill, *War at Sea*, op cit, Vol 2, p. 308.
79. See Martin van Crefeld, *Supplying War*,Cambridge, Cambridge University Press, 1977, Chapter 6.
80. Ibid.
81. Ibid.
82. Ibid, pp. 198–9.
83. Ibid.
84. Ibid, p. 199.

17. *Grand Strategy for a Maritime Alliance – I* (pages 527–536)

1. Michael Howard, *Grand Strategy*, Vol IV, London, HMSO, 1972, p. xv.
2. Ibid, p. xvi.
3. Ibid.
4. Ibid.
5. Ibid.
6. For a running historical analysis of the 'Continental' school of strategy versus the 'blue water' school since Elizabeth I, see C. Barnett, *Britain and Her Army 1509–1970*, London, Allen Lane, 1970.
7. Basil Liddell Hart, *The British Way in Warfare*, London, Faber, 1932.
8. CAB 69/4, DO(42) 10th on 14 April 1942.

9. Fraser, *And We Shall Shock Them: The British Army in the Second World War*, op cit, p. 249.
10. Howard, op cit, Vol IV, p. xvii.
11. Gilbert, *Winston S. Churchill*, op cit, Vol VII, pp. 100–1.
12. See Gwyer, *Grand Strategy*, op cit, Vol II, Part I, p. 327.
13. Ibid, pp. 364–5.
14. Fraser, op cit, p. 256.
15. Howard, op cit, Vol IV, pp. xvii–xix.
16. Cited in Gwyer, op cit, Vol II, Part II, p. 627.
17. Gilbert, op cit, Vol VII, p. 143.
18. Ibid, p. 144.
19. Gwyer, op cit, Vol II, Part II, pp. 632–3.
20. Howard, op cit, Vol IV, p. xx.
21. Ibid.
22. Fraser, op cit, p. 258.
23. Howard, op cit, Vol IV, p. xxi.
24. Ibid, p. xxii.
25. See ibid, p. xxiii for the text.
26. Ibid.
27. Ibid, pp. xxiv–xxv.
28. Ibid.

18. *'A Quite Desperate Undertaking': 'Operation Torch'* (pages 537–572)

1. Lenton and Colledge, *Warships of World War II*, op cit, p. 46.
2. ROSK 8/21, photocopy of a letter from Cunningham to Admiral Sir Bertram Ramsay, 3 November 1942.
3. Ibid.
4. Alfred D. Chandler (editor), *The Papers of Dwight David Eisenhower. The War Years: I*, Baltimore and London, the Johns Hopkins Press, 1970, p. 577.
5. Cited in Cunningham, *A Sailor's Odyssey*, op cit, p. 493.
6. Ibid, p. 577.
7. Ibid, p. 466.
8. Ibid.
9. Ibid, p. 469.
10. See RMSY 8/18.
11. The following account of the development of combined operations from the 1920s to 1942 is based on L. E. H. Maund, *Assault from the Sea*, London, Methuen, 1949, Chapters I–III, VI, VII; Bernard Fergusson, *The Watery Maze: The Story of Combined Operations*, London, Collins, 1961, Chapters I–VII.
12. N. Hamilton, *Monty: the Making of a General*, op cit, p. 286.
13. Maund, op cit, p. 8.
14. Ibid, p. 9.

15. Ibid, pp. 9–16.
16. Ibid, p. 68.
17. RMSY 8/22.
18. Philip Ziegler, *Mountbatten*, London, Collins, 1985, p. 175.
19. Ibid, p. 170.
20. Ibid.
21. Postan, Hay and Scott, *Design and Development of Weapons*, op cit, p. 285.
22. Maund, op cit, pp. 82–3.
23. Lenton and Colledge, op cit, p. 585.
24. Samuel Eliot Morison, *History of United States Naval Operations in World War II*, Vol II, *Operations in North African Waters, October 1942–June 1943*, Boston, Little, Brown, 1960, p. 24.
25. Ibid, p. 20.
26. Butler, *Grand Strategy*, op cit, Vol III, Part II, p. 641.
27. Ibid.
28. See Ziegler, op cit, pp. 192–6; and Hamilton's lame attempt to excuse Montgomery, partly by blackening Mountbatten, in Hamilton, op cit, Chapter 16.
29. See Maund, op cit, pp. 114–15; Fergusson, op cit, Chapter VII.
30. Chandler (ed), op cit, Vol I, p. 526.
31. Cited in Howard, *Grand Strategy*, Vol IV, Appendix II, pp. 600–1.
32. Ibid, p. 119.
33. Chandler (ed), op cit, Vol I, p. 461.
34. Cited in Howard, op cit, Vol IV, p. 126.
35. Ibid, p. 128.
36. Ibid.
37. Ibid, p. 130.
38. Ibid, p. 136.
39. Chandler (ed), op cit, Vol I, p. 464, Footnote 1.
40. Ibid, p. 556.
41. Eisenhower to Marshall, 12 September 1942, in ibid.
42. Roskill, *War at Sea*, op cit, Vol II, p. 319, Table 25; Morison, op cit, Vol II, pp. 36–40.
43. Eisenhower's directive to Hewitt, 13 October 1942, cited in full in Chandler (ed), op cit, Vol 1, pp. 611–12.
44. Playfair, *The Mediterranean and the Middle East*, op cit, Vol IV, p. 140.
45. ADM 234/359, BS No. 38, 'Operation Torch'; Invasion of North Africa, November 1942 to February 1943, (1948).
46. Lenton and Colledge, op cit, p. 68.
47. Ibid, p. 58.
48. Ibid, p. 282.
49. Ibid.
50. Ibid, p. 25.
51. RMSY 8/21, photocopy of letter of 12 November 1942 to Ramsay.

52. Behrens, *Merchant Shipping and the Demands of War*, op cit, p. 312.
53. Ibid, Chapter XIII, but especially p. 308.
54. The following account of 'Torch' is based on ADM 234/359 unless otherwise stated.
55. Roskill, *War at Sea*, op cit, Vol II, p. 318, and Map 32, facing p. 317.
56. Ibid, p. 317.
57. Ibid.
58. Dönitz, *Memoirs: Ten Years and Twenty Days*, op cit, p. 279.
59. RMSY 8/21, letter of 3 November 1942.
60. Dönitz, op cit, p. 279.
61. RMSY 8/21, letter of 3 November 1942.
62. Ibid.
63. Ibid.
64. Ibid.
65. Chandler (ed), op cit, Vol I, p. 651.
66. RMSY 8/21, letter of 3 November 1942.
67. ADM 234/359.
68. Ibid.
69. Morison, op cit, Vol II, p. 50.
70. Playfair, op cit, Vol IV, p. 116; ADM 234/359.
71. Hinsley, *British Intelligence in the Second World War*, op cit, Vol II, p. 487.
72. Ibid, p. 481.
73. Chandler (ed), op cit, Vol II, p. 667.
74. The following account of the Algiers landings is based on ADM 234/359; Playfair, op cit, Vol IV, pp. 138–46; Roskill, *War at Sea*, op cit, Vol II, pp. 324–5.
75. Playfair, op cit, Vol IV, Map 18, facing p. 141.
76. ADM 234/359.
77. Playfair, op cit, Vol IV, Map 18, facing p. 141.
78. Ibid.
79. Playfair, op cit, Vol IV, Map 19, facing p. 147. The following account of the Oran landings is based on ADM 234/359; Playfair, Vol IV, pp. 146–50; Roskill, *War at Sea*, op cit, Vol II, pp. 325–8.
80. ADM 234/359.
81. Ibid.
82. Playfair, op cit, Vol IV, Map 19, facing p. 147.
83. Weale, Weale and Barker, *Combat Aircraft of World War Two*, op cit, p. 91.
84. RMSY 8/21, letter of 12 November 1942.
85. See Morison, op cit, Vol I, Chapters II–VII.
86. Ibid, p. 90.
87. Playfair, op cit, Vol IV, p. 163.
88. RMSY 8/21, letter of 21 November 1942.
89. RMSY 8/21, letter of 12 November 1942.

90. Playfair, op cit, Vol IV, pp. 156–7.
91. Hinsley, op cit, Vol II, p. 493.
92. Chandler (ed), op cit, Vol I, letter to Marshall of 20 October 1942.
93. RMSY 8/21, letter to Ramsay, 12 November 1942.
94. RMSY 8/21, letter to Ramsay, 4 December 1942.
95. Behrens, op cit, p. 312.
96. Ibid and Appendix LII, p. 323.
97. Ibid.
98. ADM 234/359, Appendices D and D2, pp. 92–3.
99. Behrens, op cit, Appendix LII, p. 323.
100. Martin Blumenson, *Rommel's Last Victory*, London, Allen and Unwin, 1968, p. 54.
101. Roskill, *War at Sea*, op cit, Vol II, Appendix O, p. 486, Table 2.
102. See Behrens, op cit, Chapter XIV.

19. *'The Battle of the Atlantic Is Getting Harder'* (pages 573–613)

1. Roskill, *War at Sea*, op cit, Vol II, Appendix O, p. 486.
2. ADM 234/578, p. 90.
3. Roskill, *War at Sea*, op cit, Vol II, Appendix O, p. 486.
4. Ibid.
5. ADM 205/20.
6. Ibid, 1 October 1942.
7. Cited in ADM 234/578, p. 91.
8. ADM 205.
9. Ibid.
10. See C. Barnett, *The Audit of War*, op cit, Chapter 6, but especially pp. 116–19.
11. Postan, Hay and Scott, *Design and Development of Weapons*, op cit, p. 62; Roskill *War at Sea*, op cit, Vol II, Appendix O, p. 486.
12. Postan, Hay and Scott, op cit, pp. 62 and 300.
13. Behrens, *Merchant Shipping and the Demands of War*, op cit, pp. 366–7.
14. Dönitz, *Memoirs: Ten Years and Twenty Days*, op cit, p. 296.
15. ADM 234/578, p. 90.
16. Behrens, op cit, p. 363.
17. The following account of the balance of the Sigint struggle at the turn of 1942 and 1943 is based on Hinsley, *British Intelligence in the Second World War*, op cit, Vol 2, Chapter 26.
18. Ibid, p. 547.
19. Roskill, *War at Sea*, op cit, Vol II, p. 378.
20. Hinsley, op cit, Vol II, p. 548.
21. Ibid, Appendix 9, p. 682.
22. Ibid, p. 552.
23. Ibid, Appendix 9, p. 682.
24. Ibid, p. 552; Roskill, *War at Sea*, op cit, Vol II, p. 475.

25. Hinsley, op cit, Vol II, pp. 553–4.
26. Ibid, p. 551.
27. Roskill, op cit, Vol II, p. 364.
28. ROSK 5/132A, unpublished memoir by Admiral G. C. Cunninghame-Grahame, 'Random Recollections of Hitler's War'.
29. Ibid.
30. Bowen Papers, Churchill Archive Centre, EGBN 3/4, 'The Radar Battle of the Bay of Biscay', by A. C. B. Lovell, PhD, in the Telecommunications Research Establishment journal for July 1945, but written in 1944.
31. Ibid. See also EGBN 2/4, unpublished Technical Monographs in Wartime Research and Development in the Ministry of Aircraft Production: A.S.V. (The Detection of Surface Vessels by Airborne Radar); Chief Writer: R. A. Smith, TRE (Telecommunications Research Establishment).
32. See Barnett, *The Audit of War*, op cit, Chapter 9 for an account of radio and radar production based on Cabinet and departmental records; also ROSK 5/132A, EGBN 2/4 and 3/4; Postan, Hay and Scott, op cit, pp. 403–13, 428–30, 452–8.
33. See Barnett, *The Audit of War*, op cit, pp. 172–6.
34. ROSK 5/1, Captain S. W. Roskill, letter to Rear-Admiral W. J. M. McClure, 27 July 1979.
35. See Barnett, *Audit of War*, op cit, p. 169.
36. EGBN 3/4.
37. Ibid.
38. Ibid.
39. See Terraine, *The Right of the Line*, op cit, p. 437.
40. EGBN 3/4.
41. Ibid.
42. ADM 234/241, Anti-U-Boat Operations.
43. All ibid, p. 86.
44. Lenton and Colledge, *Warships of World War II*, op cit, p. 68.
45. Ibid.
46. ADM 234/241; ADM 205/30, Admiralty Review of Proceedings of the Anti-U-Boat Warfare Committee, 20 August 1943.
47. See Bernard Ireland, *The Rise and Fall of the Aircraft Carrier*, p. 60; ADM 234/241.
48. ROSK 5/24, Admiralty Review of Proceedings of the Anti-U-Boat Warfare Committee, 20 August 1943.
49. M. 054165/43 in ROSK 5/3.
50. Ibid.
51. ROSK 5/3, C.C.S. 335, 3 September 1943, 'Employment of CVEs in Offensive Action Against U-Boats'.
52. Ibid.
53. ADM 234/241, Appendix 4; ADM 205/30, Admiralty Review of

Proceedings of Cabinet Anti-U-Boat Warfare Committee, 20 August 1943.

54. ADM 205/30, Admiralty Review of Proceedings of Cabinet Anti-U-Boat Warfare Committee.
55. Postan, Hay and Scott, op cit, pp. 294–5.
56. ADM 234/241, p. 94.
57. Lenton and Colledge, op cit, pp. 172–4, 225–32.
58. Postan, Hay and Scott, op cit, p. 292.
59. Ibid, p. 292.
60. Dönitz, op cit, p. 95.
61. Ibid, p. 97.
62. Goodeve Papers, Churchill Archives Centre, GOEV 3/1, Most Secret Memorandum, Responsibility in Development Work; shallow-setting Depth-Charges, September 1942.
63. ROSK 5/25; GOEV 3/1.
64. ADM 205/30, Admiralty Review of Proceedings of Anti-U-Boat Warfare Committee; Terraine, op cit, pp. 430–3, 445.
65. Ibid.
66. The scientists included Edward (later Sir Edward) Bullard of HMS *Osprey* (the Anti-Submarine Warfare Establishment), Charles (later Sir Charles) Goodeve, FRS, then a Commander in the RNVR, serving in the new Admiralty Anti-Aircraft Weapons and Devices Department; Richard Keynes of the Admiralty Anti-Submarine Warfare Establishment (all future Fellows of the Royal Society). The service officers included Captain G. H. Oswald, RN (Department of Naval Ordnance); Captain G. O. C. Davies, RN of the Anti-Aircraft Weapons and Devices Department, Goodeve's superior; Major Jefferies of MD 1; Commander R. H. Stokes Rees of the Fort Halsted Experimental Establishment; and Colonel L. V. Blacker, inventor of the Spigot Mortar. For the development of the Hedgehog, see ROSK 4/14, Memorandum by Captain G. H. Oswald; GOEV 3/1, account by Sir Charles Goodeve.
67. ROSK 4/14.
68. GOEV 3/1.
69. Anthony Watts, *The U-Boat Hunters*, London, Macdonald and Jane, 1976, caption, p. 141.
70. Keynes Papers, Churchill Archives Centre, KEYN/1, letter from R. D. Keynes to the Director Scientific Research and Development Department, 26 August 1942, with reference to early 1940.
71. Ibid.
72. Captain Oswald in ROSK 4/14.
73. Ibid.
74. GOEV 3/1.
75. See Anthony Watts, op cit, pp. 139–43, for a technical description.
76. Ibid, p. 144.

77. Roskill, *War at Sea*, op cit, Vol I, p. 359; Watts, op cit, pp. 172–3.
78. ADM 205/30, Admiralty Review of Proceedings of Anti-U-Boat Warfare Committee; Watts, op cit, pp. 173–4.
79. Watts, op cit, pp. 174–5.
80. Ibid, pp. 175–6; ADM 205/30, Admiralty Review of Proceedings of Anti-U-Boat Warfare Committee.
81. ADM 205/30, Admiralty Review of Proceedings of Anti-U-Boat Warfare Committee.
82. ROSK 5/25, photocopy of letter from Rear-Admiral C. D. Howard-Johnston to J. D. Brown of the Naval Historical Branch, 23 February 1980.
83. Ibid.
84. ADM 234/578, p. 106.
85. Roskill, *War at Sea*, op cit, Vol II, p. 371.
86. Ibid; ADM 234/578.
87. Cited in Hinsley, op cit, Vol II, p. 557.
88. Ibid.
89. Dönitz, op cit, p. 317.
90. ADM 234/578; unless otherwise cited the following account in this chapter of the Battle of the Atlantic January–May 1943 is based on ADM 234/578.
91. Hinsley, op cit, Vol II, p. 558.
92. ADM 234/578.
93. Hinsley, op cit, Vol II, p. 559.
94. Ibid; ADM 234/578.
95. Dönitz, op cit, p. 322.
96. Cited in Roskill, *War at Sea*, op cit, Vol II, p. 357.
97. Hinsley, op cit, Vol II, pp. 560–1.
98. Roskill, *War at Sea*, op cit, Vol II, p. 357.
99. Dönitz, op cit, p. 325.
100. Hinsley, op cit, Vol II, p. 561.
101. Roskill, *War at Sea*, op cit, Vol II, p. 358.
102. ADM 234/578.
103. See Roskill, *War at Sea*, op cit, Vol II, p. 365.
104. Cited in Dönitz, op cit, p. 327.
105. Ibid.
106. Cited in Hinsley, op cit, Vol II, p. 563; see Roskill, *War at Sea*, op cit, Vol II, pp. 365–6, and Terraine, op cit, pp. 443–4.
107. CAB 86/3, AU(43)90.
108. CAB 65/37, 42(43), Confidential Annexe.
109. ADM 234/578.
110. ROSK 5/3, Report to Vice-Admiral, Aircraft Carriers, Home Fleet, 31 March 1943.
111. Roskill, *War at Sea*, op cit, Vol II, p. 372.
112. Ibid, Appendix K, p. 475.

113. Ibid; Grove, Chant, Lyon and Lyon, *The Hardware of World War II*, op cit, pp. 149–51.
114. Hinsley, op cit, Vol II, p. 568.
115. Ibid, p. 569.
116. Ibid.
117. Ibid.
118. Roskill, *War at Sea*, op cit, Vol II, p. 372.
119. Cited in ibid.
120. Ibid and Appendix J, p. 470, Table I.
121. Hinsley, op cit, Vol II, p. 569.
122. Ibid.
123. Cf Roskill, *War at Sea*, op cit, Vol II, Map 40.
124. ADM 234/358, p. 96.
125. Ibid.
126. Ibid.
127. Ibid.
128. ADM 234/578, p. 95.
129. Ibid, p. 107.
130. EGBN 3/4.
131. ADM 205/30; Terraine, op cit, p. 446.
132. Dönitz, op cit, p. 343.
133. Hinsley, op cit, Vol II, p. 570.
134. Lenton and Colledge, op cit, p. 115; Edgar J. March, *British Destroyers, A History of Development 1892–1953*, op cit, Chapter 15.
135. Lenton and Colledge, op cit, p. 100.
136. Ibid, p. 225.
137. Ibid, p. 170.
138. Cited in Roskill, *War at Sea*, op cit, Vol II, p. 374.
139. Lenton and Colledge, op cit, p. 86.
140. Hinsley, op cit, Vol II, p. 570.
141. Ibid.
142. Lenton and Colledge, op cit, p. 240.
143. Roskill, *War at Sea*, op cit, Vol II, pp. 375–6.
144. Hinsley, op cit, Vol II, p. 571.
145. ADM 234/578.
146. Hinsley, op cit, Vol II, p. 571.
147. ADM 234/578, pp. 94 and 96.
148. Cited in ADM 234/578, p. 93.
149. Dönitz, op cit, pp. 312–13.
150. Ibid, p. 269.
151. Ibid, p. 326.
152. Cited in ADM 234/578, p. 97.
153. Ibid.
154. ADM 234/578, p. 97.
155. See Behrens, op cit, p. 372, Chapter XVIII and XIX, especially pp. 411–12.

20. *Grand Strategy for a Maritime Alliance – II* (pages 614–626)

1. Churchill, *The Second World War*, op cit, Vol IV, *The Hinge of Fate*, London, Cassell, 1951, pp. 604–5.
2. Hinsley, *British Intelligence in the Second World War*, op cit, Vol II, pp. 454–60.
3. Roskill, *War at Sea*, op cit, Vol II, p. 341.
4. Cunningham, *A Sailor's Odyssey*, op cit, p. 517.
5. Howard, *Grand Strategy*, op cit, Vol IV, pp. xxiv–xxv.
6. CAB 66/30, WP(42)483, 24 October 1942.
7. CAB 80/65, COS(42)345(O)(Final), 30 October 1942; CAB 79/24, COS(42) 304th, 30 October 1942.
8. Howard, op cit, Vol IV, pp. 208–9.
9. Ibid.
10. CAB 80/66, COS(42)429(O), 3 December 1942.
11. CAB 80/66, COS(42)452(O), 13 December 1942.
12. CAB 80/66, JP(42) 1005, 12 December 1942.
13. CAB 80/66, COS(42)452(O), 12 December 1942.
14. Ibid.
15. CAB 79/58, COS(42) 198th(O), 16 December 1942.
16. Ibid.
17. Ibid.
18. CAB 80/66, COS(42)485(O), 29 December 1942.
19. CAB 80/66, COS(42)466(O)(Final); CAB 69/4, DO(42) 20th, 29 December 1942.
20. Behrens, *Merchant Shipping and the Demands of War*, op cit, p. 331; see also pp. 319–22.
21. Printed in full as Appendix III(B) in Howard, op cit, Vol IV, pp. 614–16.
22. Ibid.
23. Fraser, *And We Shall Shock Them: the British Army in the Second World War*, op cit, p. 321.
24. Howard, op cit, Vol IV, p. 252.
25. Gilbert, *Winston S. Churchill*, op cit, Vol VII, p. 253.
26. Howard, op cit, Vol IV, p. 254.
27. Ibid.
28. Ibid.
29. Ibid, p. 294.
30. Cited in full in Howard, op cit, Vol IV, Appendix III(D), pp. 621–2.
31. Cunningham, op cit, p. 520.
32. ROSK 5/102, photocopy of letter of 15 March 1943.
33. Cunningham, op cit, p. 529.

21. *The Invasion of Sicily: 'Operation Husky'* (pages 627–656)

1. See ROSK 5/102, photocopy of letter from Cunningham to First Sea Lord, 15 March 1943; ROSK 5/99, letter from Cunningham to Captain

S. W. Roskill, 12 November 1953; Roskill *War at Sea*, op cit, Vol II, pp. 435–7.

2. ROSK 5/99, letter of 12 November 1953 to Captain Roskill.
3. Cited in Carlo D'Este, *Bitter Victory, The Battle for Sicily July–August 1943*, London, Collins, 1988, p. 113.
4. Chandler (ed), *The Papers of Dwight D. Eisenhower*, op cit, Vol II, pp. 1046–7.
5. D'Este, op cit, p. 86.
6. Ibid, p. 87.
7. Cited in D'Este, op cit, p. 82.
8. Ibid, p. 112.
9. RMSY 8/23. The extracts from Ramsay's letters to his wife cited by Rear-Admiral W. S. Chalmers in his biography of Ramsay, *Full Cycle, The Biography of Admiral Sir Bertram Home Ramsay*, London, Hodder and Stoughton, 1959, cannot be relied upon, because Chalmers edited the extracts without indicating that he had sometimes omitted important material in their midst.
10. Ibid.
11. Ibid.
12. Ibid, letter of 14 April 1943.
13. Ibid.
14. Ibid.
15. Howard, *Grand Strategy*, op cit, Vol IV, p. 365.
16. RMSY 8/23, letter to his wife, 28 April 1943.
17. ROSK 5/98, photocopy of letter to the First Sea Lord, 28 April 1943.
18. ROSK 5/102, photocopy of No. 1 (Med)00358/R, 1 January 1944, covering reports on the invasion of Sicily.
19. ROSK 5/98, photocopy of letter.
20. Ibid.
21. RMSY 8/23, letter of 6 May 1943.
22. Letter to First Sea Lord, 8 May 1943, quoted in Cunningham, *A Sailor's Odyssey*, op cit, p. 538.
23. RMSY 8/23, letter to his wife, 10 May 1943.
24. Hinsley, *British Intelligence in the Second World War*, op cit, Vol III, Part 1, pp. 71–2.
25. ROSK 5/102, Royal Naval Staff College Course, Greenwich: Course No. 5, 1948. OPERATION HUSKY II – Execution. Phase IV, by Commander E. V. St J. Morgan, para 3.
26. ROSK 5/102, photocopy of covering letter to General Eisenhower by Admiral Sir Andrew Cunningham, enclosing reports on the invasion of Sicily, No. 1/Med/00358/R, 1 January 1944.
27. Ibid.
28. ROSK 5/105, photocopy of letter to First Sea Lord, 5 August 1943.
29. Ibid.
30. ROSK 5/102, OPERATION HUSKY I – Preparation. Phase III, by

Commander E. V. St J. Morgan, Royal Naval Staff College, Greenwich: Course No. 5, 1948, paras 12–13.
31. ROSK 5/102, photocopy of letter to Eisenhower, 1 January 1944.
32. Ibid.
33. ROSK 5/102, Morgan, op cit, I, PHASE III, para 27.
34. ADM 199/860, Husky Naval Orders.
35. Hinsley, op cit, Vol III, Part 1, pp. 78–9.
36. ADM 199/860, Husky Naval Orders.
37. Maund, *Assault from the Sea*, op cit, p. 256.
38. ROSK 5/102, letter of 1 January 1944.
39. Hinsley, op cit, Vol III, Part 1, p. 76.
40. See D'Este, op cit, pp. 213–16.
41. Terraine, *The Right of the Line*, op cit, p. 566.
42. RMSY 8/23, letter of 11 July 1943.
43. RMSY 8/23, letter to his wife of 28 May 1943.
44. RMSY 8/23, letter of 11 July 1943.
45. Morgan, op cit, I, paras 16–20; II, paras 26–7.
46. Hinsley, op cit, Vol III, Part 1, p. 75.
47. Ibid, p. 76.
48. Ibid, p. 83.
49. Howard, op cit, Vol IV, p. 361.
50. Hinsley, op cit, Vol III, Part 1, pp. 76–80.
51. Morgan, op cit, II, para 10.
52. Ibid, para 11.
53. ROSK 5/102, letter from Cunningham to Eisenhower, 1 January 1944.
54. See D'Este, op cit, Chapters 12 and 13.
55. ROSK 5/102, letter to Eisenhower, 1 January 1944; see also Hinsley, op cit, Vol 3, Part 1, p. 86, Footnote 1.
56. Hinsley, op cit, Vol III, Part 1, p. 86.
57. ROSK 5/102, letter of 1 January 1944.
58. Ibid.
59. RMSY 8/23, letter from Ramsay to his wife 11 July 1943.
60. Ibid.
61. Morgan, op cit, II, para 23.
62. Ibid; see also D'Este, op cit, Chapter 15.
63. Howard, op cit, Vol IV, p. 468.
64. Cunningham, op cit, p. 537.
65. Ibid, p. 553.
66. Roskill, *War at Sea*, op cit, Vol III, Part I, p. 139.
67. Ibid.
68. D'Este, op cit, pp. 301–5; Terraine, op cit, pp. 574–7, 578–9.
69. Terraine, op cit, pp. 574–5.
70. Cited in Roskill, *War at Sea*, op cit, Part I, p. 115.
71. ROSK 5/105, photocopy of letter to First Sea Lord, 5 August 1943.
72. See D'Este, op cit, p. 301.
73. ROSK 5/102, letter of 1 January 1944.

74. Ibid.
75. D'Este, op cit, p. 514.
76. Ibid.
77. Hinsley, op cit, Vol III, Part 1, pp. 95–9.
78. Roskill, *War at Sea*, op cit, Vol III, Part I, p. 149.
79. D'Este, op cit, p. 502.
80. Ibid; see also Roskill, *War at Sea*, op cit, Vol III, Part I, Map 11, facing p. 145.
81. Roskill, *War at Sea*, op cit, Vol III, Part I, p. 150.
82. See D'Este, op cit, Appendix I, p. 607.
83. Ibid, Appendix E, p. 597.
84. Ibid, Appendix I, p. 609.
85. Alexander Werth, *Russia at War, 1941–1945*, London, Barrie and Rockcliff, 1964, p. 683.
86. Howard, op cit, Vol IV, p. 419.
87. CAB 84/53, JP(43)99 (Final), 3 May 1943.
88. Howard, op cit, Vol IV, p. 417.
89. Ibid, pp. 417–18.
90. Ibid, p. 415.
91. Ibid.
92. Ibid.
93. Ibid, pp. 415–16.
94. Ibid, p. 419.
95. Ibid, p. 421.
96. Ibid, p. 422.
97. Ibid, p. 428.
98. Ibid, p. 431.
99. Ibid.
100. Printed in full in Howard, op cit, Vol IV, Appendix VI(C), pp. 660–7.
101. Ibid.
102. Ibid.
103. CAB 84/53, JP(43)99(Final), 3 May 1943.
104. Churchill, *The Second World War*, op cit, Vol IV, p. 630.
105. Howard, op cit, Vol IV, p. 498.
106. Ibid.
107. 13 July, cited in ibid, p. 502.
108. Ibid.
109. Ibid, p. 503.
110. Ibid.
111. Ibid, p. 564.

22. *'Some Underbelly; Some Softest Part': The Mediterranean, 1943–1945* (pages 657–692)

1. ADM 234/358, BR 1736(36) BS No. 37, The Invasion of Italy: Landing at Salerno ('Avalanche') (Naval Operations), 9th September 1943

(1946). The following account of the invasion of Italy is based on this Naval Staff History unless otherwise stated.

2. Ibid, p. 5.
3. Howard, *Grand Strategy*, op cit, Vol IV, p. 506.
4. Ibid.
5. Ibid.
6. Lenton and Colledge, *Warships of World War II*, op cit, p. 69.
7. ROSK 5/105, photocopy of letter of 5 August 1943.
8. ADM 234/358, p. 11.
9. Ibid, p. 13.
10. Ibid.
11. Cited in ibid, p. 14.
12. Hinsley, *British Intelligence in the Second World War*, op cit, Vol III, Part 1, p. 391 and Footnote 1.
13. ADM 234/358.
14. ROSK 5/105, note by Captain Roskill of fleet strength as of 1 October 1943.
15. Behrens, *Merchant Shipping and the Demands of War*, op cit, p. 391 and Footnote 1.
16. ADM 234/358.
17. See Howard, op cit, Vol IV, Chapter XXVII, for a lucid account of the Italian surrender negotiations.
18. ROSK 5/105, photocopy of letter of 5 August 1943.
19. ADM 234/358.
20. ADM 234/358, p. 17.
21. Ibid.
22. ROSK 5/105, photocopy of letter of 26 August 1943.
23. Ibid.
24. Ibid.
25. ADM 234/358, p. 18.
26. Ibid.
27. ADM 234/358; there is no mention in Hinsley, op cit, Vol 3, Part 1.
28. Cited in ADM 234/358, p. 17.
29. Lenton and Colledge, op cit, p. 64.
30. All ADM 234/358.
31. The following account of naval operations during 'Avalanche' is based on ADM 234/358, from which all otherwise unattributed quotations are drawn.
32. Hinsley, op cit, Vol III, Part 1, p. 110.
33. Roskill, *War at Sea*, op cit, Vol III, Part I, p. 168, Footnote 1; Robert Cecil (ed), *Hitler's War Machine*, London, Leisure Books, 1975, pp. 193, 209.
34. Hinsley, op cit, Vol III, Part 1, p. 111.
35. Roskill, *War at Sea*, op cit, Vol III, Part 1, p. 169.
36. Cunningham, *A Sailor's Odyssey*, op cit, p. 563.

37. Ibid.
38. Ibid, p. 565.
39. Roskill, *War at Sea*, op cit, Vol III, Part 1, Appendix H, pp. 382–5.
40. RMSY 8/22, lecture on Combined Operations, September 1943.
41. See Dominick Graham and Shelford Bidwell, *Tug of War; The Battle for Italy, 1943–1945*, London, Hodder and Stoughton, 1986, Chapters 3–6, for a first-class account of the Battle of Salerno.
42. Ibid, pp. 53–4.
43. Ibid.
44. Ibid, p. 43.
45. Ibid, p. 53.
46. Ibid.
47. Ibid, pp. 50–1.
48. ADM 234/358.
49. Lenton and Colledge, op cit, p. 24.
50. See Graham and Bidwell, op cit, pp. 61–7.
51. Weale, Weale and Barker, *Combat Aircraft of World War Two*, op cit, p. 149.
52. ROSK 5/105, Admiral Sir Geoffrey Oliver, 'Some Notes on the Project to Shorten the Front at Salerno, September, 1943', for Captain Roskill, dated 20 January 1953.
53. Graham and Bidwell, op cit, pp. 78–9.
54. ROSK 5/105, notes cited.
55. Ibid.
56. Ibid.
57. 'The Allied Navies at Salerno', article in the *US Naval Institute Proceedings*, Vol 79, No. 9, September 1953, p. 972.
58. Graham and Bidwell, op cit, p. 97.
59. Ibid, pp. 103–6.
60. See Graham and Bidwell, op cit, p. 106.
61. Cunningham, op cit, p. 575.
62. Gilbert, *Winston S. Churchill*, op cit, Vol VII, p. 502.
63. See Howard, op cit, Vol IV, pp. 61, 198, 213, 227, 232–3, 252, 377, 381–3.
64. Cited in ibid, p. 382.
65. Ibid, p. 489.
66. Ibid.
67. ROSK 5/106, No. 385 of 12 August 1943, photocopy of transcript of signal in brief prepared for Captain Roskill as official naval historian.
68. Cited in Gilbert, op cit, Vol VII, p. 497.
69. See ibid, p. 497 and pp. 502–5.
70. The following account of operations in the Aegean is based on ADM 234/364, 'Aegean Operations – 7th September to 28th November 1943: British occupation and German re-occupation of KOS and LEROS', unless otherwise cited.

71. ROSK 5/106, photocopy of transcript of exchanges of signals, September and October 1943; see also ADM 234/364, Appendix E.
72. Ibid, No. 9974 of 31 September 1943.
73. Ibid, CC 315 of 28 September 1943.
74. Ibid, NAF 438, to CCOS and COS.
75. Gilbert, op cit, Vol VII, p. 520.
76. Roskill, *War at Sea*, op cit, Vol III, Part I, p. 203.
77. See Gilbert, op cit, Vol VII, pp. 527–8, 532–3, 536, 546, 559–64.
78. David Fraser, *Alanbrooke*, London, Collins, 1982, p. 366.
79. Ibid.
80. Cf Churchill's memorandum to the COS on 19 July 1943 advocating a combination of Mediterranean/Balkan offensives and a landing in Northern Norway as a substitute for 'Overlord' in 1944, cited in Gilbert, op cit, Vol VI, pp. 444–5.
81. Fraser, *Alanbrooke*, op cit, p. 373.
82. Gilbert, op cit, Vol VII, pp. 547–8.
83. Ibid, pp. 541–2; Fraser, op cit, pp. 370–1.
84. Gilbert, op cit, Vol VII, p. 563, citing CAB 80/77, Minutes of Second Plenary meeting, 24 November 1943.
85. Gilbert, op cit, Vol VII, p. 571, citing CAB 80/77, first meeting, 28 November 1943.
86. Ibid.
87. Fraser, *Alanbrooke*, op cit, p. 391.
88. Gilbert, op cit, Vol VII, pp. 611–18.
89. Ibid, p. 628.
90. The following account of naval operations in 'Shingle' is based on ADM 234/873, 'Orders, Reports and Signals relating to Operation Shingle', unless otherwise cited.
91. Roskill, *War at Sea*, op cit, Vol III, Part I, p. 304, Table 19.
92. Ibid.
93. ADM 234/873; Roskill, *War at Sea*, op cit, Vol III, Part I, p. 307.
94. Ibid, p. 30; Cecil (ed), op cit, p. 207.
95. See Graham and Bidwell, op cit, Chapters 9–13; John Ellis, *Cassino; the Hollow Victory; The Battle for Rome January–June 1944*, London, André Deutsch, 1984, passim.
96. Graham and Bidwell, op cit, p. 401.
97. Ibid.
98. Hinsley, op cit, Vol III, Part 1, p. 29.
99. Behrens, op cit, Appendix LXX (ii)A, 9, p. 455; estimate of April 1944.
100. Graham and Bidwell, op cit, p. 399.
101. Fraser, op cit, p. 429.
102. Ibid.
103. Chandler (ed), *The Papers of Dwight D. Eisenhower*, op cit, Vol IV, letter from Eisenhower to Churchill, 11 August 1944; Gilbert, op cit, Vol VII, pp. 863–80.

104. See Graham and Bidwell, op cit, Chapters 23–4; Douglas Orgill, *The Gothic Line: The Autumn Campaign in Italy 1944*, London, Heinemann, 1967, passim.

23. *'Such Desolate and Dangerous Voyages': The Arctic Convoys, 1941–1945* (pages 693–749)

1. CAB 80/65, COS(42)345(O)/(Final), 30 October 1942.
2. All figures from ROSK 5/78, 'Answers to questions put by Lord Ismay'; undated paper.
3. ADM 234/369, p. 3, Footnote 2; BS No. 22, Arctic Convoys 1941–45 (1954). Unless otherwise cited, the following account of Arctic convoy operations, 1941–45, is based on this Naval Staff History.
4. Ibid, p. 6.
5. Ibid.
6. Ibid.
7. Ibid, p. 7.
8. This account of the passage of PQ12 and QP8 is based on ibid, pp. 7–20.
9. Ibid, p. 6.
10. Hinsley, *British Intelligence in the Second World War*, op cit, Vol II, pp. 200–1.
11. Cited in ibid, p. 8.
12. Cited in ibid, p. 8.
13. See Hinsley, op cit, Vol II, pp. 205–10.
14. Ibid, p. 210.
15. Ibid.
16. ADM 234/369.
17. Ibid, p. 21.
18. Roskill, *War at Sea*, op cit, Vol II, pp. 123–4.
19. Cited in ADM 234/369, p. 21.
20. Ibid.
21. Ibid, p. 21 and Footnote 4.
22. Lenton and Colledge, *Warships of World War II*, op cit, p. 48.
23. Ibid, p. 102.
24. ADM 234/369, p. 38.
25. Ibid, p. 33.
26. Ibid, p. 133.
27. Cited in ibid, p. 34.
28. Ibid.
29. CAB 69/4, DO 42(37).
30. Cited in Gilbert, *Winston S. Churchill*, op cit, Vol VII, p. 75.
31. Lenton and Colledge, op cit, p. 44.
32. ADM 234/369.
33. Ibid.

34. Cited in Gilbert, op cit, Vol VII, p. 98.
35. Ibid.
36. Ibid.
37. Ibid, pp. 98–9.
38. ADM 234/369, p. 39, Footnote 2.
39. Lenton and Colledge, op cit. p. 102.
40. Cited in ADM 234/369, p. 38.
41. Ibid, p. 39, Footnote 1.
42. Cited in ibid, p. 46.
43. ADM 205/19.
44. ADM 234/369, p. 47, Footnote 3.
45. Cited in ibid, p. 48, Footnote 3.
46. Report of proceedings, cited in ibid, p. 49.
47. Cited in ibid, p. 50.
48. Ibid.
49. Ibid.
50. Cited in ibid, p. 51.
51. Ibid.
52. ADM 234/369, p. 54 citing *London Gazette*, 17 October 1950, pp. 514–15.
53. Ibid.
54. ADM 234/369; the following operational account of the fate of PQ17 is based on this Naval Staff History, pp. 53–71, except where otherwise cited.
55. Ibid.
56. Signal 1145A/ 16 March 1942, cited in ibid, p. 23, and Footnote 3.
57. Ibid.
58. ROSK 5/72, notes made from First Sea Lord's papers, Vols 14, 21, 22.
59. Ibid, p. 55.
60. Lenton and Colledge, op cit, p. 86.
61. ROSK 5/72, letter to S. W. Roskill from Vice-Admiral Sir John Hayes, November 1981.
62. ADM 234/369, p. 59, Footnote 1.
63. Ibid, Footnote 2.
64. Ibid.
65. The account of Sigint during the PQ17 operation is based on Hinsley, op cit, Vol II, pp. 214–23 and ROSK 5/72, photocopy of unpublished memoir by Vice-Admiral Sir Norman (then Commander) Denning, the OIC officer responsible for evaluating the likely operations of the German surface fleet.
66. Hinsley, op cit, Vol II, p. 214.
67. Ibid, p. 215.
68. Ibid.
69. Ibid, p. 216.

70. ROSK 5/72, Denning's memoir.
71. Ibid.
72. Ibid.
73. Ibid.
74. Ibid.
75. Ibid.
76. Ibid.
77. Ibid.
78. Ibid.
79. Ibid.
80. Ibid.
81. Ibid.
82. Ibid.
83. Ibid.
84. All cited in ADM 234/69, p. 62.
85. Ibid, p. 60.
86. Ibid.
87. Ibid.
88. Cited in ibid, p. 67.
89. Cited in ibid.
90. Hamilton's report of proceedings, cited in ibid, p. 63.
91. Cited in ibid, p. 69.
92. Ibid, Footnote 1, p. 65.
93. Ibid.
94. See Morison, *History of United States Naval Operations in World War II*, op cit, Vol I, pp. 186–92.
95. Roskill, *War at Sea*, op cit, Vol II, p. 143.
96. CAB 65/31, WM(42)101.
97. Lenton and Colledge, op cit, p. 46.
98. Prime Minister, Personal Minutes, M.294/2, 'Secret', 'Action this Day', 15 July 1942, CHAR 20/67, cited Gilbert, op cit, Vol VII, p. 147.
99. Ibid.
100. CAB 79/22, COS (42) 205th.
101. Cited in ADM 234/369, p. 73.
102. Lenton and Colledge, op cit, p. 22.
103. Ibid, p. 68.
104. Ibid, p. 46.
105. Roskill, *War at Sea*, op cit, Vol II, pp. 278–9.
106. Hinsley, op cit, Vol II, p. 213.
107. Ibid, pp. 224–5.
108. Ibid, p. 226.
109. ADM 234/369.
110. Ibid, p. 77.
111. Cited in ibid, p. 78.

112. Hinsley, op cit, Vol II, pp. 194–5, 227.
113. ADM 234/369, p. 79.
114. Ibid, p. 85.
115. Ibid, p. 83.
116. All ibid.
117. Cited in ibid, p. 103.
118. Gilbert, op cit, Vol VII, p. 365.
119. ROSK 4/17, letter of 9 September 1961 to S. W. Roskill.
120. ROSK 5/77, photocopy of 'Hush' signal to First Sea Lord, 30 June 1943.
121. Ibid.
122. Gilbert, op cit, Vol VII, p. 499.
123. Ibid.
124. ROSK 5/125, letter to S. W. Roskill from Ludovic Kennedy (then in HMS *Tartar*, one of the destroyers concerned), 9 February 1975.
125. ROSK 5/125, letter from Admiral Sir Ralph Edwards to S. W. Roskill, 4 August 1954.
126. Admiral J. H. Godfrey, cited in ROSK 5/125.
127. ROSK 4/79, photocopy of letter of 7 March 1942.
128. ROSK 4/124, letter to S. W. Roskill from Admiral Sir Ralph Edwards, 28 July 1954.
129. Churchill, *The Second World War*, op cit, Vol V, p. 146.
130. Ibid, p. 145.
131. Lenton and Colledge, op cit, p. 155.
132. ADM 234/349–50, TIRPITZ: An account of the various attacks carried out by the British Armed Forces and their effect upon the German battleship. Vol I, Report and Appendices (1948). Vol II, Evidence for Detailed Accounts of Damage. The following account of 'Operation Source' is drawn from ADM 234/347, B.S. No. 29. Attack on the *Tirpitz* by Midget Submarines, 22 September 1943; C. E. T. Warren and J. Benson, *Above Us the Waves*, London, Harrap, 1953, Chapters XIV–XVII; Hinsley, op cit, Vol III, Part 1, pp. 258–62.
133. Hinsley, op cit, Vol III, Part 1, p. 258.
134. Hinsley, op cit, Vol III, Part 1, p. 261.
135. Ibid.
136. See AIR 41/48 for a full account of the *Lützow* episode. Also Hinsley, op cit, Vol III, Part 1, pp. 256–8.
137. See AIR 41/48.
138. Terraine, *The Right of the Line*, op cit, pp. 549–58; Max Hastings, *Bomber Command*, London, Michael Joseph 1979, pp. 237–69; Webster and Frankland, *The Strategic Air Offensive Against Germany 1939–1945*, op cit, Vol II, pp. 191–211, and 268.
139. ADM 234/369, p. 108 et seq.
140. ROSK 5/77, photocopy of brief prepared for Captain Roskill by Foreign Documents Section of the Cabinet Office Historical Section;

FDS 109/56: 'Background Information on the Circumstances Leading to *Scharnhorst*'s Last Operation – source: German Naval Archives.'
141. Ibid.
142. Ibid.
143. Ibid.
144. Bekker, *Hitler's Naval War*, op cit, p. 346.
145. Ibid.
146. Ibid, p. 349.
147. ROSK 5/77, FDS 109/56.
148. Ibid.
149. Grove, Chant, Lyon and Lyon, *The Hardware of World War II*, op cit, p. 145.
150. Parkes, *British Battleships; A History of Design, Construction and Armament*, op cit, p. 663.
151. Hinsley, op cit, Vol III, Part 1, pp. 267–8.
152. Ibid, p. 266.
153. Ibid.
154. The following operational account of the destruction of the *Scharnhorst* is based on ADM 234/343, BS No. 24, Sinking of the *Scharnhorst*.
155. ROSK 5/77, photocopy of letter from Captain A. G. F. Ditcham to John Winton, 10 November 1984.
156. Ibid.
157. Ibid.
158. Hinsley, op cit, Vol III, Part 1, p. 274.
159. The following account of Fleet Air Arm attacks on the *Tirpitz* is based on ADM 234/349–50, ADM 234/345, BS No. 27, Naval Attacks on *Tirpitz*.
160. Weale, Weale and Barker, *Combat Aircraft of World War Two*, op cit, p. 140.
161. Ibid, p. 200.
162. See ROSK 5/142, photocopy of translation of German reports on F.A.A. attacks on the *Tirpitz*, prepared by the Naval Intelligence Department, January 1946.
163. Ibid.
164. See ibid, translation of German damage report giving details of damage hit by hit.
165. See ADM 234/349–50, pp. 10–13.
166. ROSK 5/142, German reports.
167. See also ADM 234/349, pp. 11–13; ADM 234/350, pp. 85–92.
168. ADM 234/369, p. 133.
169. ADM 234/369, p. 124.
170. Lenton and Colledge, op cit, p. 73.
171. ADM 234/369, p. 124.
172. Despatch quoted ADM 234/369, p. 72, Footnote 5.
173. Ibid, p. 129.

Part IV: Victory

24. *'Neptune': Problems, Puzzles and Personalities* (pages 753–780)

1. Cited in Roskill, *Churchill and the Admirals*, op cit, p. 233.
2. Cf Max Hastings, *Overlord: D-Day and the Battle of Normandy 1944*, London, Michael Joseph, 1974; Carlo D'Este, *Decision in Normandy; the Unwritten Story of Montgomery and the Allied Campaign*, London, Collins, 1983.
3. The following account of Intelligence with regard to invasion preparations up to the end of 1943 is based on Hinsley, *British Intelligence in the Second World War*, op cit, Vol III, Part 2, pp. 10–19.
4. Cf Philip Ziegler, *Mountbatten; the Official Biography*, op cit, pp. 177–9.
5. Ibid, p. 213.
6. Ibid, pp. 213–15.
7. CP 216, cited in ROSK 5/121, brief prepared for Captain Roskill as official naval historian on 'The Artificial Harbours and Breakwaters up to D-Day'. The following account of the evolution of the artificial harbours is based on this brief unless otherwise cited.
8. Quoted in ROSK 5/121, brief cited.
9. Ibid.
10. Cf Ziegler, op cit, pp. 207–8; ROSK 5/121, brief cited.
11. COS(44)1st(O), quoted in ROSK 5/121, brief cited.
12. The following account of 'Pluto' is based on ROSK 5/121, 'A Brief Account of Operation Pluto', a brief prepared for Captain Roskill.
13. ROSK 5/122, summary of Cs-in-C's reports on 'Neptune' prepared for Captain Roskill by the Naval Historical Branch.
14. Report on 'Neptune', 2865 Ply 1486 of 4.8.1944, Enclosure 2, as summarised in ROSK 5/122.
15. Ibid.
16. RMSY 8/22. Lecture on Combined Operations, written in late summer 1943, but here as re-drafted for publication in 1948 in CB.04211, 'Fighting Experience'.
17. D'Este, *Decision in Normandy*, op cit, pp. 55–6, Footnotes 2 and 3, p. 56.
18. Montgomery of Alamein, *Memoirs*, London, Collins, 1958, pp. 205, 210–12.
19. RMSY 8/26, diary for 1944.
20. RMSY 8/27A, letter of 4 January 1944.
21. Ibid.
22. Cited in Chalmers, *Full Cycle*, op cit, p. 182.
23. Chandler (editor), *The Papers of Dwight D. Eisenhower*, op cit, Vol III, p. 880 and Footnote 1.
24. RMSY 8/27A, letter to his wife, 11 January 1944. It must be repeated that the quotations from Ramsay's diary and letters in Chalmers's

biography, *Full Cycle*, are unreliable, for Chalmers confuses extracts from each source and edits out material from quotations without indicating the omissions.

25. RMSY 8/27A, letter to wife, 6 January 1944.
26. Ibid.
27. RMSY 8/26, diary for 5 January 1944.
28. Ibid, diary for 6 January 1944.
29. Ibid.
30. John Ehrman, *Grand Strategy*, Vol V, London, HMSO, 1956, p. 233.
31. RMSY 8/26, diary for 6 January 1944.
32. Ehrman, op cit, Vol V, p. 234.
33. RMSY 8/26, 7 January 1944.
34. Ibid, 8 January 1944.
35. Ibid, 10 January 1944.
36. Ibid, 12 January 1944.
37. Ibid, diary for 15 January 1944.
38. Ibid, 17 January 1944.
39. Chandler (ed), op cit, Vol III, pp. 1673–4.
40. RMSY 8/26, diary for 26 January 1944.
41. Ibid, diary for 4 February 1944.
42. Ibid, diary for 14 February 1944.
43. Ibid, diary for 21 February 1944.
44. Ibid.
45. Ibid, 22 February.
46. Chandler (ed), op cit, Vol III, p. 1763.
47. Cf RMSY 8/26, Ramsay's diary for 6 March 1944.
48. Chandler (ed), op cit, Vol III, p. 1763.
49. Ibid.
50. Ibid, signal of 20 March 1944.
51. Ehrman, op cit, Vol V, p. 247.
52. RMSY 8/26, diary for 7 March 1944.
53. Ibid, diary for 26 January 1944; ROSK 5/118, photocopy from First Sea Lord's Papers, Vol 34, statement of Naval Forces to be made available for 'Neptune', memorandum from First Sea Lord to Prime Minister, 18 March 1944.
54. RMSY 8/26, 7 March 1944.
55. All ROSK 5/121; brief on 'Neptune' prepared for Captain Roskill, and based on First Sea Lord's Papers, Vol 32.
56. ROSK 5/121, document cited.
57. ROSK 5/32, xerox of Paper P.P.O. 01014/42 of 26 December 1942, 'Naval Shipbuilding: Policy for the Present War'.
58. Roskill, *War at Sea*, op cit, Vol III, Part II, Appendix S, pp. 436–7.
59. Chandler (ed), op cit, Vol III, pp. 1723–4; ROSK 5/121.
60. RMSY 6/26, diary for 17 February 1944.
61. RMSY 8/26, diary for 14 January 1944.

62. Ibid, diary for 6 May 1944.
63. Ibid, diary for 11 January 1944.
64. Ibid, diary for 3 March 1944.
65. Ibid, 11 January 1944.
66. Ibid, diary for 8 March 1944.
67. Ibid.
68. Hinsley, op cit, Vol III, Part 2, pp. 32–3; the following account of Intelligence during the preparation of 'Neptune' is drawn from this volume, pp. 17–100, unless otherwise cited.
69. Ibid, p. 35.
70. Ibid, pp. 76–7.
71. Ibid, p. 77.
72. Ibid, p. 38.
73. Ibid, p. 92.
74. RMSY 8/26, diary for 14 May 1944.
75. Hinsley, op cit, Vol III, Part 2, p. 50.
76. Ibid, p. 96.
77. RMSY 8/26, diary for 24 March 1944.
78. Hinsley, op cit, Vol III, Part 2, p. 88.
79. ROSK 5/120.
80. Ibid.
81. ANCXF's Report, Vol I, p. 5, cited in ADM 234/366, BS No. 39, Operation 'Neptune'; landings in Normandy, June, 1944 (1947), p. 13.
82. RMSY 8/27A, letter to his wife, 24 April 1944.
83. Ibid.
84. Ibid.
85. Ibid, letter of 1 May 1944.
86. Cited in Chalmers, op cit, p. 206.
87. Montgomery's speaking notes, cited in D'Este, *Decision in Normandy*, op cit, p. 74.
88. Ibid.
89. Ibid, p. 76.
90. RMSY 8/27A.
91. Ibid.
92. Ibid.

25. *'A Never Surpassed Masterpiece of Planning'* (pages 781–809)

1. The summary of 'Operation Neptune – Naval Orders' is drawn from the Orders themselves, as are all quotations unless otherwise cited. The copy consulted is held in the Naval Historical Branch.
2. Ibid.
3. See Hinsley, *British Intelligence in the Second World War*, op cit, Vol III, Part 2, pp. 47–9.
4. Ibid.

5. Report by ANCXF, Vol I, p. 94, quoted in ADM 234/366, p. 57, Footnote 2.
6. ADM 234/366, pp. 49–53.
7. ADM 234/366, p. 49, Footnote 1, citing ANCXF Report, Vol 3, p. 6.
8. Ibid, p. 51.
9. Ibid, p. 53.
10. ADM 234/366, p. 23.
11. ADM 234/366, p. 54, Footnote 1, citing ANCXF Report, Vol I, p. 28: see also RMSY 8/26, diary for 26–28 February 1944.
12. ADM 234/366, p. 54, Footnote 1.
13. 'Operation Neptune – Naval Orders', ON9.
14. Webster and Frankland, *Strategic Air Offensive Against Germany*, op cit, Vol II, pp. 22–31; Terraine, *The Right of the Line*, op cit, pp. 542–5.
15. Hastings, *Bomber Command*, op cit, pp. 261–9; Terraine, op cit, pp. 556–8.
16. See Terraine, op cit, pp. 619–20; Hastings, op cit, pp. 269–71.
17. Ehrman, *Grand Strategy*, op cit, Vol V, pp. 292–7.
18. ADM 234/366, p. 57.
19. ADM 234/366, p. 60.
20. RMSY 8/26, diary for 3 February 1944.
21. ADM 234/366, pp. 30–1.
22. ADM 234/366, p. 62, Footnote 3.
23. Ibid, p. 62, quoting ANCXF Report, Vol I, pp. 27–8.
24. ADM 234/366, p. 31, quoting ANCXF Report, Vol I, p. 28.
25. ADM 234/366, p. 64.
26. Ibid, p. 64.
27. RMSY 8/26, diary for 27 April 1944.
28. ADM 234/366, p. 65.
29. RMSY 8/26, 2 and 3 May 1944; see also ADM 234/366, p. 66.
30. ADM 234/366, p. 68.
31. Ibid, citing ANCXF Report, Vol I, pp. 6, 27.
32. Ibid, p. 68.
33. Hinsley, op cit, Vol III, Part 2, p. 89.
34. RMSY 8/26, diary for 1–2 May 1944.
35. ADM 234/366, p. 69.
36. RMSY 8/26, diary for 29 April 1944.
37. RMSY 8/27A, letter of 11 May 1944.
38. Ibid, letter to his wife 26 May 1944.
39. Ibid, letter of 29 May 1944.
40. ADM 234/366, p. 70.
41. Cited in ibid, p. 72.
42. Eisenhower, *Report by the Supreme Commander to the Combined Chiefs of Staff on the Operations in Europe of the Allied Expeditionary Force, 6 June 1944 to 8 May 1945*, London, HMSO, 1946, p. 11.
43. CAB 98/40 series: Overlord Preparations Committee and Sub-Committees.

44. See ADM 234/578, pp. 113–18; ROSK 5/24, 'U-boat AA Weapons', brief for Captain Roskill by Foreign Documents Section, Cabinet Office Historical Section, 12 May 1955.
45. ADM 234/578, p. 118.
46. Ibid.
47. Ibid, p. 121.
48. Dönitz, *Memoirs*, op cit, pp. 354, 424–5.
49. Ibid, pp. 265–6.
50. ROSK 5/19, brief for Captain Roskill on Walter U-boats by the Foreign Documents Section, Cabinet Office Historical Section, 12 May 1955.
51. Hinsley, op cit, Vol III, Part 2, p. 156.
52. Dönitz, op cit, pp. 356–7.
53. Ibid, p. 420.
54. Hinsley, op cit, Vol III, Part 2, p. 99.
55. RMSY 8/26, diary for 31 May 1944.
56. ROSK 5/121, citing ANCXF Report.
57. Hinsley, op cit, Vol III, Part 2, p. 94.
58. Ibid.
59. Ibid, Appendix 10, p. 830.
60. Ibid, p. 834.
61. Ibid, p. 81.
62. Ibid.
63. RMSY 8/26, diary for 26 May 1944.
64. ADM 234/366, p. 71, Footnote 4.
65. Ibid, p. 85.
66. ADM 234/366, p. 71, Footnote 2.
67. RMSY 8/26, diary for 30 May 1944.
68. Ibid.
69. ADM 234/366, p. 72.
70. RMSY 8/26, diary for 1 June 1944.
71. ADM 234/366, p. 72.
72. RMSY 8/26, diary for 2 June 1944.
73. RMSY 8/26, diary for 3 June 1944.
74. Ibid.
75. Ibid.
76. Ibid, 4 June 1944.
77. ADM 234/366, p. 75, citing ANCXF Report, Vol I, p. 10.
78. Montgomery, *Memoirs*, op cit, p. 248.
79. L. F. Ellis, *Victory in the West*, Vol I, London, HMSO, 1962, p. 143.
80. RMSY 8/26, diary for 4 June 1944.
81. Ibid.
82. Roskill, *War at Sea*, op cit, Vol III, Part II, pp. 39–40.
83. RMSY 8/26, diary for 5 June 1944.

26. *'This Great Enterprise': 'Operation Neptune'* (pages 810–838)

1. The following account of the landing of 'Operation Neptune' on 5–6 June is based on ADM 234/366, pp. 78–105; Ellis, *Victory in the West*, op cit, Vol I, pp. 160–222; Roskill, *War at Sea*, op cit, Vol III, Part II, pp. 41–59; Morison, *History of United States Naval Operations in World War II*, op cit, Vol XI, pp. 77–153.
2. Cited in Roskill, *War at Sea*, op cit, Vol III, Part II, p. 41, Footnote 2.
3. Ellis, op cit, Vol I, pp. 222–3.
4. ADM 234/366, p. 86, citing ANCXF Report, Vol I, p. 10.
5. ROSK 5/121, brief on 'Neptune' preparations for Captain Roskill by the Naval Historical Branch.
6. ADM 234/366, p. 87, citing ANCXF Report, Vol I, p. 58.
7. ROSK 5/121, brief for Captain Roskill on preparations for D-Day, Appendix.
8. For this reason and because of prior coverage in this book of 'Operation Neptune – Naval Orders', the account of D-Day which follows is not exhaustive.
9. ROSK 5/119, photocopy of Letter of Proceedings to Rear-Admiral Commanding Second Cruiser Squadron from the Commanding Officer of HMS *Warspite*, 16 June 1944.
10. ADM 234/366, p. 74, citing ANCXF Report, Vol I, p. 11.
11. The following summary of D-Day bombardments is based on ROSK 5/119, 'Naval Bombardment in Neptune', brief prepared for Captain Roskill by the Naval Historical Branch.
12. Morison, op cit, Vol XI, p. 124.
13. ROSK 5/119, 'Naval Bombardment in Neptune'.
14. ROSK 5/119, letter to Captain Roskill by Vice-Admiral M. H. A. Kelsey, 12 September 1955. Kelsey as Captain of the *Warspite* had witnessed American shooting from aboard a US cruiser when *Warspite* was ordered to support the Americans on 7 June because they were running low on ammunition, owing to such wasteful practices as ranging with eight-gun salvoes.
15. Ellis, op cit, Vol I, p. 187, citing official reports by Kirk and Hall.
16. ADM 234/366, pp. 91–3; Morison, op cit, Vol XI, p. 102.
17. ADM 234/366, pp. 93–7; Morison, op cit, Vol XI, pp. 130–51.
18. Cf Admiral Hall's subsequent report, cited in Ellis, op cit, Vol I, p. 191.
19. See Hastings, *Overlord: D-Day and the Battle of Normandy*, op cit, pp. 90–102.
20. Cited in ADM 234/366.
21. See ibid, pp. 97–9 for Force G's D-Day operations.
22. Cited in ibid, p. 51.
23. See ADM 234/366, pp. 99–102 for operations on 'Juno'.
24. Cited in Ellis, op cit, Vol I, p. 180.
25. ADM 234/366, pp. 102–5.

26. See D'Este, *Decision in Normandy*, op cit, p. 127.
27. See ibid, Chapter 8, for an account of 3rd Division's D-Day.
28. Cited in ROSK 5/119, 'Naval Bombardment in Neptune'.
29. Ibid, citing report of the Naval Commander, Force S.
30. Ellis, op cit, Vol I, p. 22; Roskill, *War at Sea*, op cit, Vol III, Part II, p. 51.
31. Ibid.
32. Chandler (ed), *The Papers of Dwight D. Eisenhower*, op cit, Vol II, p. 1908.
33. ADM 234/366.
34. RMSY 8/26, diary for 8 June 1944.
35. ROSK 5/120, brief for Captain Roskill by the Naval Historical Branch.
36. Ellis, op cit, Vol I, p. 217.
37. RMSY 8/26, diary for 7 June 1944.
38. Morison, op cit, Vol XI, pp. 164–5.
39. Cited in ibid, p. 165.
40. RMSY 8/27A, letter of 8 June 1944.
41. Ibid.
42. RMSY 8/26, diary for 7 June 1944.
43. RMSY 8/27A, letter of 8 June 1944.
44. ADM 234/366, pp. 119–20.
45. ADM 234/366, p. 119 citing ANCXF Report, Vol I, p. 95.
46. Eisenhower, *Supreme Commander's Report*, op cit, p. 32.
47. Ibid, p. 72.
48. Cited in Hinsley, *British Intelligence in the Second World War*, Vol III, Part 3, p. 165.
49. Ibid, p. 162.
50. Cited in ROSK 5/120, Summary of account by Captain Jones, RN, commanding 10th Destroyer Flotilla, covering the night action off French coast with four German destroyers on the night of 8/9 June 1944; eyewitness information from Admiral of the Fleet Lord Lewin, then serving in HMS *Ashanti*.
51. Ibid.
52. Ibid; ADM 234/366, p. 112.
53. Hinsley, op cit, Vol III, Part 3, pp. 154–61.
54. ADM 234/366, pp. 136–7.
55. Terraine, *Business in Great Waters*, London, Leo Cooper, 1989, p. 647.
56. Ibid; ADM 234/366.
57. Ellis, op cit, Vol I, map opposite p. 262.
58. Cited in ibid.
59. Roskill, *War at Sea*, op cit, Vol III, Part II, p. 62.
60. ADM 223/163, Admiralty Weekly Intelligence Report No. 226, 'Gale off Normandy'; see ADM 234/366, pp. 139–40 for account of the gale.
61. ADM 223/163, WIR No. 226.

62. Ellis, op cit, Vol I, p. 274.
63. RMSY 8/26, diary for 23 June 1944.
64. Ibid.
65. Cf Ellis, op cit, Vol I, pp. 274 and 301.
66. ADM 234/366, pp. 141–2.
67. ADM 234/363, BS No. 49, The Campaign in North-West Europe, June 1944–May 1945 (1952), p. 3.
68. RMSY 8/26, diary for 30 July 1944.

27. *Victory in Europe* (pages 839–859)

1. Morison, *History of United States Naval Operations in World War II*, op cit, Vol XI, pp. 198–205.
2. Ibid, pp. 205–10.
3. RMSY 8/26, diary for 6 July 1944.
4. Morison, op cit, Vol XI, p. 218.
5. Cited in ROSK 5/121, A Brief Account of Operation Pluto.
6. See Roskill, *War at Sea*, op cit, Vol III, Part II, Appendix W, p. 454 for details.
7. ADM 234/363, B.S. No. 49, pp. 5–11.
8. Roskill, *War at Sea*, op cit, Vol III, Part II, pp. 126–8.
9. Churchill, *The Second World War*, op cit, Vol VI, p. 61.
10. RMSY 8/27A, letter to his wife, 5 August 1944.
11. RMSY 8/26, diary for 5 August 1944.
12. RMSY 8/27A.
13. See Gilbert, *Winston S. Churchill*, op cit, Vol VII, pp. 875–81; Chandler (ed), *The Papers of Dwight D. Eisenhower*, op cit, Vol IV, pp. 2055–6.
14. Chandler (ed), op cit, Vol IV, p. 2103, letter from Eisenhower to Combined Chiefs of Staff, 30 August 1944.
15. Ellis, *Victory in the West*, op cit, Vol I, p. 478.
16. Roskill, *War at Sea*, op cit, Vol III, Part II, pp. 130–4.
17. Chandler (ed), op cit, Vol IV, p. 2136.
18. Ellis, op cit, Vol II, p. 132.
19. Ibid.
20. ADM 234/363, pp. 33–4.
21. Ibid, pp. 21–2.
22. Ibid.
23. RMSY 8/26, diary for 4 September 1944.
24. Cited in Ellis, op cit, Vol II, p. 5.
25. Chandler (ed), op cit, Vol IV, p. 2130.
26. See Ellis, op cit, Vol II, pp. 9–10, 16–19, 23, 25–7.
27. Ibid, p. 25.
28. Ibid, p. 27.
29. Ibid.
30. See ibid, pp. 133 and 135.
31. RMSY 8/26, diary for 5 October 1944.

32. Ibid, 8 October 1944.
33. Ellis, op cit, Vol II, p. 84.
34. Chandler (ed), op cit, Vol IV, p. 2215.
35. Ellis, op cit, Vol II, pp. 91–2.
36. See ibid, pp. 83–4.
37. Ibid.
38. Ibid, p. 113.
39. The following summary of the Walcheren campaign is drawn from ADM 234/363, pp. 46–53; Ellis, op cit, Vol II, pp. 113–23.
40. ADM 234/363, pp. 53–4.
41. Ellis, op cit, Vol II, p. 127.
42. Ibid, p. 135.
43. Ibid, Appendix VII, p. 408.
44. Behrens, *Merchant Shipping and the Demands of War*, op cit, p. 398 and Footnote 3.
45. Even the 'lock-up' element in the Mediterranean total came to nearly 1 million tons. Ibid, p. 391, Footnotes 1 and 2.
46. Roskill, *War at Sea*, op cit, Vol III, Part II, p. 279, Table 35.
47. See Dr Marc Milner, 'The Dawn of Modern Anti-Submarine Warfare; Allied Responses to the U-boats, 1944–5' in the *RUSI Journal*, Vol 134, No. 1, pp. 61–8, for an illuminating discussion of new technology and its effect on operations.
48. ROSK 5/118, citing First Sea Lord's papers.
49. ROSK 5/25; see also ibid, copy of letter from the First Sea Lord to the C-in-C, British Pacific Fleet, 19 January 1945.
50. Roskill, *War at Sea*, op cit, Vol III, Part II, p. 287, Table 37 and p. 289; see also ROSK 5/25, Tables I, II and III, and summary by the Cabinet Office Historical Section of escort forces as on 1 January 1945, prepared for Captain Roskill.
51. Roskill, *War at Sea*, op cit, Vol III, Part II, p. 185.
52. Dönitz, *Memoirs*, op cit, p. 425.
53. Roskill, *War at Sea*, op cit, Vol III, Part II, p. 285.
54. Milner, article cited.
55. Hinsley, *British Intelligence in the Second World War*, op cit, Vol III, Part 2, pp. 474–87.
56. Ibid, p. 481.
57. CAB 80/90, COS(45)14(O), A Forecast of the Results of the U-Boat Campaign during 1945. Memorandum by the First Sea Lord.
58. Terraine, *Business in Great Waters*, op cit, p. 655.
59. Dönitz, op cit, p. 428.
60. Roskill, *War at Sea*, op cit, Vol III, Part II, p. 301.
61. Ibid, Appendix Y, pp. 467–8.
62. Ibid.
63. Ibid, Appendix Z, pp. 477–8.
64. Ellis, op cit, Vol I, p. 339.

65. ROSK 5/19, 'Walter U-boats – Situation at the end of the War', brief prepared for Captain Roskill by Foreign Documents Section, 12 May 1955; Roskill, *War at Sea*, op cit, Vol III, Part II, pp. 302–3.
66. In 1939–45 the Royal Navy was more stretched and in danger of losing control altogether of vital sea areas, England herself in far worse peril of extinction, than even during the American War of Independence, 1778–1783.
67. Roskill, *War at Sea*, op cit, Vol III, Part II, p. 305, Footnote 2.
68. Ibid; air force figures supplied by the Air Historical Branch.

28. *To Restore an Empire* (pages 860–898)

1. See Morison, *History of United States Naval Operations in World War II*, op cit, Vol IV, pp. 3–65, for an account of the Battle of the Coral Sea.
2. See Morison, op cit, Vol IV, pp. 69–156, for an account of the Battle of Midway.
3. Roskill, *War at Sea*, op cit, Vol II, p. 23.
4. SMVL 3/27, letter to his wife, 22 February 1942.
5. Ibid, letter to his wife, 2 March 1942.
6. Ibid, letter of 13 March 1943.
7. SMVL 8/1, letter to the First Sea Lord, 11 March 1942.
8. Ibid.
9. Ibid, letter to First Sea Lord, 15 July 1942.
10. SMVL 3/27, letter to his wife, 6 April 1942.
11. Ibid.
12. Cited in Roskill, *War at Sea*, op cit, Vol II, p. 29.
13. Churchill, *The Second World War*, op cit, Vol IV, p. 202.
14. ADM 234/331, BS No. 16, Naval Operations at the Capture of Diego Suarez (Operation 'Ironclad'), May 1942 (1943). See also ROSK 5/91.
15. ADM 234/331.
16. Churchill, *The Second World War*, op cit, Vol IV, p. 202.
17. Cited in Gilbert, *Winston S. Churchill*, op cit, Vol VII, p. 146.
18. Roskill, *War at Sea*, op cit, Vol III, Part I, pp. 213–14.
19. SMVL 8/1, letter to First Sea Lord, 11 March 1943.
20. See ROSK 5/57, for Captain Roskill's postwar correspondence with Cunningham, Brooke, Portal and Mountbatten on the subject, as also for photocopies of correspondence between Somerville and Cunningham in 1943–4.
21. Ibid; but also see SMVL 8/2, letters from Somerville to First Sea Lord, 1943–4.
22. See Ehrman, *Grand Strategy*, op cit, Vol V, pp. 152–3.
23. See Shelford Bidwell, *The Chindit War: the Campaign in Burma 1944*, London, Hodder and Stoughton, 1979, *passim*.
24. ADM 234/377, Naval Staff History, Second World War: *War with*

Japan. Vol IV, The South-East Asia Operations and Central Pacific Advance (1959). See p. 203 for sinking of *Kuma* and *Kitagami*.

25. Ibid, pp. 209–11.
26. Ibid, p. 213.
27. SMVL 8/2, letter of 27 July 1944. For an account of the attack on Sabang, see ADM 234/377, pp. 215–16.
28. Morison, op cit, Vol VIII, pp. 213–319.
29. Ibid.
30. Ehrman, op cit, Vol V, p. 422.
31. Ibid, p. 424.
32. Ibid, p. 427.
33. Cited in Fraser, *Alanbrooke*, op cit, p. 412.
34. Cited in ibid, pp. 413–14.
35. Cited in Ehrman, op cit, Vol V, p. 451.
36. Ibid, p. 449.
37. Cf ibid, p. 438 and pp. 477–8.
38. Both are quoted in full in Ehrman, Vol V, pp. 441–9.
39. Cited in Fraser, op cit, p. 416.
40. See CAB 79/79, COS(44) 264th–269th (O), 8–9 August 1944. Quotation is from CAB 79/79, COS(44) 269th (O).
41. Cited in Gilbert, op cit, Vol VII, pp. 957–8.
42. The session is quoted in full in Ehrman, op cit, Vol V, pp. 520–3.
43. Ibid, p. 523.
44. See ROSK 5/129, photocopy of memorandum from First Lord to Prime Minister on 'Command and Redeployment of the Fleet in Far Eastern Waters', 25 October 1944, in First Sea Lord's papers Vol 34; and signal from Prime Minister to Prime Minister of Australia, 8 November 1944.
45. SMVL 8/A, letter of 6 May 1944.
46. ROSK 5/129, First Lord to Prime Minister: 'Command and Redeployment of the Fleet in Far Eastern Waters', 25 October 1944.
47. ROSK 5/129, Admiral of the Fleet Lord Fraser of the North Cape to Captain Roskill, 20 May 1959.
48. Ehrman, op cit, Vol V, pp. 477–8.
49. Cited in Ehrman, op cit, Vol V, pp. 477–8; see also Behrens, *Merchant Shipping and the Demands of War*, op cit, Chapter XIX.
50. Ehrman, op cit, Vol V, p. 477.
51. Roskill, *War at Sea*, op cit, Vol III, Part II, p. 343.
52. Morison, op cit, Vol XIV, Appendix 1, pp. 382–5.
53. Roskill, *War at Sea*, op cit, Vol III, Part II, Appendix S, pp. 436–7.
54. Ibid, Vol II, Appendix B, p. 449.
55. Cf ibid, Vol I, Appendix D, pp. 577–9 and Vol III, Part II, Appendix S, pp. 436–7.
56. Fleet Admiral Ernest J. King, *U.S. Navy at War 1941–45: Official Reports to the Secretary of the Navy*, Washington, United States Navy Department, 1946, Appendix B, pp. 252–7.

57. Lenton and Colledge, *Warships of World War II*, op cit, pp. 64–73; ROSK 5/25, brief prepared for Captain Roskill by the Admiralty Historical Section, 1956; H. Duncan Hall, *North American Supply*, London, HMSO and Longmans, Green, 1955, pp. 400–1.
58. Barnett, *The Audit of War*, op cit, p. 40.
59. R. C. K. Ensor, *England 1870–1914*, Oxford, Clarendon Press, 1966, p. 104.
60. Barnett, *The Audit of War*, op cit, p. 401; Hall, op cit, p. 445.
61. Hall, op cit, pp. 401 and 403.
62. Ibid, p. 424.
63. Ibid, p. 425.
64. ADM 234/377, Naval Staff History, Second World War; *War With Japan*, op cit, Vol IV, The South-East Asia Operations and Central Pacific Advance (1957), p. 19.
65. Ibid, pp. 21–2.
66. Ibid.
67. Morison, op cit, Vol XIV, Appendix I, pp. 382–5.
68. Ibid; ROSK 5/129, brief prepared for Captain Roskill on 'The Pacific April–June 1945'. See also ADM 234/379, Naval Staff History, *War with Japan*, op cit, Vol VI, Advance to Japan, when it is opened to the public in 1992.
69. Ibid.
70. Weale, Weale and Barker, *Combat Aircraft of World War Two*, op cit, pp. 141, 200, 210.
71. ADM 205/18, Memorandum by the Chief of Naval Air Services, 14 October 1942.
72. ROSK 5/129, Statistics of B.P.F. in Iceberg, taken from M. 07991/45 in W.H.S. 9251. See also ADM 199/555, The British Pacific Fleet in Iceberg, and ADM 234/368, BS No. 47: Naval operations in the assault and capture of Okinawa, March–June 1945, Operation 'Iceberg' (1958).
73. ROSK 7/29, the history of 'The Flyplane Electric Predictor System – A Brief Account of its History and Application', by Mr Humphrey Nelson, sent to Captain Roskill on 23 July 1978.
74. Ibid.
75. Ibid.
76. Clausen Papers, Churchill Archives Centre, CLSN 1/2, 'The American Position with Power Control for Gunnery Purposes: Report on a Visit to the US and on some matters arising', by J. M. Ford, Superintending Scientist, Admiralty Research Laboratory, July 1943.
77. Ibid; 'Impressions of a Visit to America, August and September 1944' by Hugh Clausen.
78. Ibid.
79. CLSN 1/2 and 1/3; see also letter from Captain Roskill, a radar and gunnery expert, to Rear-Admiral M. W. St L. Searle, 11 May 1978 in ROSK 7/29.

80. Cf Logistic Support Groups, Fifth Fleet, in Morison, op cit, Vol XIV, Appendix 1, pp. 386–8.
81. For a summary of the history of the British Fleet Train, see ROSK 5/129, 'The Fleet Train', a brief prepared for Captain Roskill by the Naval Historical Branch. The relevant contemporary detailed files are in ADM 199/1740–69.
82. Vian, *Action this Day*, op cit, p. 175.
83. ADM 234/118, 1319/BPF/1780/OPS, Despatch on Operations from 22 November 1944 to Middle of July 1945, dated 23 November 1945, p. 12.
84. ROSK 5/129.
85. Cf N. M. Rodger, *The Wooden World; An Anatomy of the Georgian Navy*, London, Fontana Press, 1986, *passim* but especially Chapter III.
86. Morison, op cit, Vol XIV, p. 282.
87. Ibid.
88. Ibid, chart on p. 207.
89. The following summary of 'Iceberg' is based on ROSK 5/129, 'The Pacific April–June 1945', prepared for Captain Roskill. See also ADM 234/368 and ADM 199/555.
90. Morison, op cit, Vol XIV, p. 250; Grove, Chant, Lyon and Lyon, *The Hardware of World War II*, op cit, p. 206.
91. ROSK 5/129, Note for Captain Roskill, 'Statistics of B.P.F. in Iceberg', taken from M.07991/45 in W.H.S. 9251; see also ibid, 'Statistics on B.P.F. in Iceberg', taken from C.B.3301 (draft), Chapter XV, pp. 343–4, which gives slightly different figures.
92. The summary of British surface and submarine operations in South-East Asian waters in summer 1945 is drawn from ADM 234/377, Naval Staff History, *War with Japan*, op cit, Vol IV, The South-East Asia Operations and Central Pacific Advance (1957), pp. 16–20.
93. The account of the exploits of the X-Craft at Singapore and off Saigon and Hong Kong is drawn from ADM 234/382, Naval Staff History, *Submarines*, Vol III, Operation in Far Eastern Waters, Including the Operations of Allied Submarines (1950), pp. 111–12.
94. Roskill, *War at Sea*, op cit, Vol III, Part II, p. 374.
95. Cited in ibid, p. 375.
96. ADM 234/378, Naval Staff History, *War with Japan*, op cit, Vol V, The Blockade of Japan, pp. 100, 102 and Tables 13, 13A, B and C; J. F. C. Fuller, *The Second World War 1939–45*, London, Eyre and Spottiswoode, 1962, pp. 386 and 390; B. H. Liddell Hart, *History of the Second World War*, London, Cassell, 1970, pp. 682–3.
97. The account of the surrender ceremony aboard USS *Missouri* is drawn from Morison, op cit, Vol XIV, pp. 363–70.
98. Cited in Morison, op cit, Vol XIV, p. 365.
99. Roskill, *War at Sea*, op cit, Vol III, Part II, p. 378; see also ROSK 6/58, notes from Admiral Rawlings to Captain Roskill on the draft of *War at Sea*, op cit, Vol III, Chapter VII.

100. Ibid, p. 382.
101. Ibid, p. 383.
102. Vice Admiral T. S. Wilkinson to his wife, 2 September 1945, cited in Morison, op cit, Vol XIV, p. 369. After being later widowed, she married Admiral Sir Harry Moore of the Royal Navy.

Bibliography

I UNPUBLISHED SOURCES

1. *Public Record Office*

a. Admiralty (ADM series)

ADM 1 Admiralty and Secretariat Records (selected files)
ADM 53 Ships' Logs
ADM 116 Admiralty and Secretariat Records (selected files)
ADM 186 series: Naval Staff History; Battle Summaries (BS):
ADM 186/795 BS No 44, 'The Battle of Cape Matapan, 28 March 1941'
ADM 186/797 BS No 7, 'The Bombardment of Genoa 9 February 1941'
ADM 186/797 BS No 19, 'The Bombardment of Tripoli 21 April 1941'
ADM 186/799 *Home Waters and the Atlantic*, Vol I, *September 1939–April 1940*
ADM 186/801 Naval Staff Narrative, *Mediterranean, November 1940–December 1941*
ADM 186/802 German Naval History, *The U-boat War in the Atlantic*
ADM 186/803 BS No. 11, 'The Passage of the *Scharnhorst*, *Gneisenau* and *Prinz Eugen* through the English Channel, 12th February 1942' (1948)
ADM 199 series War History Cases and Papers (selected files)
ADM 205 series First Sea Lord's Papers
ADM 234 series: Naval Staff History: Narratives and Battle Summaries:

ADM 234/118 Despatch on Operations [of the British Pacific Fleet] from 22 November 1944 to Middle of July, 1945, dated 23 November 1945

ADM 234/241 Anti-U-boat Operations

ADM 234/320 BS No 4, 'Naval Operations of the Battle of Crete, 20th May to 1st June 1941' (1952)

ADM 234/322 Battle Summary No 5, 'The Chase and Sinking of the German Battleship "Bismarck", May 23–27, 1941, according to information up to November 1948'

ADM 234/324 'Disguised Raiders 1940–1'

ADM 234/325 BS No 10, 'Mediterranean Operations, 4th to 14th November 1940. Air Attack on Taranto, 11th November 1940' (1943)

ADM 234/330 BS No 14 (Revised), 'Loss of His Majesty's Ships *Prince of Wales* and *Repulse*, 10th December 1941' (1955)

ADM 234/331 BS No 16, 'Naval Operations at the Capture of Diego Suarez (Operation "Ironclad"), May 1942' (1943)

ADM 234/345 BS No 27, 'Naval Attacks on *Tirpitz*'

ADM 234/349–50 TIRPITZ. An account of the various attacks carried out by the British Armed Forces and their effect upon the German battleship' (1948). Vol 1, Report and Appendices (1948)

ADM 234/353 BS No 32, 'Malta Convoys' (1945)

ADM 234/358 BS No 37, 'The Invasion of Italy: Landing at Salerno ("Avalanche") (Naval Operations), 9th September 1943' (1946)

ADM 234/359 BS No 38, '"Operation Torch"; Invasion of North Africa, November 1942 to February 1943'.

ADM 234/363 BS No 49, 'The Campaign in North-West Europe, June 1944–May 1945' (1952)

ADM 234/364 BS No 36, 'Aegean Operations – 7th September to 28th November 1943: British occupation and German re-occupation of KOS and LEROS'

ADM 234/366 BS No 39, 'Operation "Neptune"; Landings in Normandy, June 1944' (1947)

ADM 234/368 BS No 47, 'Naval operations in the assault and capture of Okinawa, March–June 1945, Operation "Iceberg"' (1958)

ADM 234/369 BS No 22, 'Arctic Convoys 1941–45' (1954)

ADM 234/370 BS No 51, *Convoy and Anti-Submarine Warfare Reports*, No. 4. *Passage of Convoy S.C.104 – October 1942*

ADM 234/377 Naval Staff History, Second World War: *War with Japan*. Vol IV, 'The South-East Asia Operations and Central Pacific Advance' (1959)

ADM 234/378 Naval Staff History, *War with Japan*, Vol V, 'The Blockade of Japan' (1957)

ADM 234/382 Naval Staff History, *Submarines*, Vol III, 'Operation in Far Eastern Waters, Including the Operations of Allied Submarines' (1950)

ADM 234/508 BR 2055, 'Technical Report of Loss and Damage to H.M.S. ARK ROYAL' (1942)

ADM 234/509 The sinking of the *Bismarck*, 27th May 1941: Official Despatches
ADM 234/578 *Defeat of the Enemy Attack on Shipping, 1939–1945: A Study of Policy and Operations*, Vol 1A (Text and Appendices 1957)
ADM 234/873 'Orders, Reports and Signals relating to Operation Shingle'

b. *Air Ministry (AIR series)* Air Historical Branch Narratives:
AIR 41/10 The Rise and Fall of the German Air Force
AIR 41/19 The Royal Air Force in the Maritime War, Vol VI, The Mediterranean and Red Sea
AIR 41/20 A Review of the Campaign in Norway
AIR 41/23 The Liberation of North-West Europe, Vol I
AIR 41/24 The Liberation of North-West Europe, Vol II
AIR 41/25 The Middle East Campaigns, Vol II
AIR 41/26 The Middle East Campaigns, Vol III
AIR 41/34 The Italian Campaign, Vol I
AIR 41/44 The Middle East Campaigns, Vol I
AIR 41/45 The Royal Air Force in the Maritime War, Vol I
AIR 41/46 The Royal Air Force in the Maritime War, Vol II
AIR 41/47 The Royal Air Force in the Maritime War, Vol III
AIR 41/48 The Royal Air Force in the Maritime War, Vol IV
AIR 41/52 The Sicilian Campaign, Vol I
AIR 41/58 The Italian Campaign, Vol II
AIR 41/59 The Sicilian Campaign, Vol I
AIR 41/66 The Liberation of North-West Europe, Vol III
AIR 41/67 The Liberation of North-West Europe, Vol IV
AIR 41/68 The Liberation of North-West Europe, Vol V

c. *Cabinet and Cabinet Committees (CAB series)*
CAB 16/109–12 Reports, Proceedings and Memoranda of the Defence Requirements Sub-Committee of the Committee of Imperial Defence 1933–5
CAB 16/123 Defence Policy Requirements Committee of the Cabinet 1936
CAB 16/136–144 Minutes of Meetings of the Defence Policy Requirements Committee of the Cabinet 1936–9
CAB 16/209 Strategic Appreciation Committee of the Committee of Imperial Defence 1939
CAB 23/52–100 Conclusions of the Cabinet Meetings 1926–39
CAB 24 series Cabinet Memoranda 1919–1939
CAB 27/407 Fighting Services Committee 1929–30
CAB 27/606 Mediterranean Fleet Cabinet Committee 1936
CAB 27/627 Minutes and Memoranda of the Cabinet Committee on Foreign Policy 1936–9
CAB 27/648 Defence Programmes and Their Acceleration Cabinet Committee 1938
CAB 29/117, 118 Naval Conference, London, 1930

CAB 29/159 Anglo-French Staff Conversations, London, 1939
CAB 32 series Imperial Conferences 1921–1939
CAB 53/1–11 Committee of Imperial Defence: Meetings of the Chiefs of Staff Committee 1929–39
CAB 53/12–54 Committee of Imperial Defence: Memoranda of the Chiefs of Staff Committee 1923–39
CAB 65 series Conclusions of the War Cabinet 1939–45
CAB 66 series War Cabinet Memoranda (CP and WP series)
CAB 69 series War Cabinet Defence Committee (Operations)
CAB 70 series War Cabinet Defence Committee: (Supply)
CAB 79 series Chiefs of Staff Committee: Minutes of Meetings 1939–45
CAB 80 series Chiefs of Staff Committee: Memoranda 1939–45
CAB 81 series Chiefs of Staff Committee: Sub-Committees 1939–45
CAB 82 series Deputy Chiefs of Staff Committee 1939–45
CAB 83/1–5 Ministerial Committee on Military Coordination 1939–40
CAB 84 series Joint Planning Committee
CAB 86/1 Battle of the Atlantic Committee 1941–2
CAB 86/2–7 Anti-U-Boat Warfare Committee 1942–45
CAB 98/40 'Overlord' Committee 1944
CAB 105 series War Cabinet: Telegrams

2. *Churchill Archives Centre, Churchill College, Cambridge*

ANCG: Admiral Sir Angus Cunninghame-Graham of Gartmore: Naval papers and memoirs
AVAR: Earl Alexander of Hillsborough: Political papers
BRME: Captain J. H. Broome: Papers on Convoy PQ17, 1942
BUIS: Commander Colin Buist, RN: Naval signals of surrender of German fleet, 1918
CLSN: Hugh Clausen, Naval armaments engineer: technical papers and lectures
CUNN: Admiral of the Fleet Viscount Cunningham of Hyndhope: Correspondence and material from various sources for the biography by Oliver Warner
DENM: Captain H. N. Denham: Memoirs, papers and correspondence concerning his time as Naval Attaché in Stockholm, 1940–45
DENN: A. G. Denniston: Papers on codebreaking in Room 40 during World War I and ID 25 in World War II
DRAX: Admiral Sir Reginald Plunkett-Ernle-Erle-Drax: Naval and political papers
DUPO: Admiral of the Fleet Sir Dudley Pound: Letters, cuttings and notes collected for a projected biography by Donald McLachlan
EGBN: Edward George Bowen, scientist: Papers on the development of radar
FWCT: Commander H. J. Fawcett: Anti-submarine warfare papers

GDFY: Admiral J. H. Godfrey: Memoirs
GOEV: Sir Charles Goodeve: Papers concerning weapons development
KEYN: Professor Richard Keynes: Anti-submarine Experimental Establishment correspondence and papers on naval radar development
MANP: Admiral Sir Manley Power: Autobiography
MCLN: Rear-Admiral Ian Maclean of Pennycross: Naval Papers
MLBE: Donald McLachlan and Patrick Beesly: Material for the *History of Naval Intelligence 1939–45*, and other works on naval intelligence
NRTH: Admiral Sir Dudley North: Papers concerning his dismissal from command, Gibraltar, 1940
OLVR: Admiral Sir Geoffrey Oliver: Naval and personal papers
RMSY: Admiral Sir Bertram Ramsay: Naval and personal papers; diaries
ROSK: Captain Stephen Roskill, RN: Historical and family papers including 'A Sailor's Ditty Box', a personal memoir
SMVL: Admiral Sir James Somerville: Naval and personal papers
WDVS: Admiral Sir William Davis: Autobiography
WLLS: Admiral of the Fleet Sir Algernon Willis: Naval papers

II PUBLISHED SOURCES

Barnett, Correlli, *The Audit of War*, Macmillan, London, 1986
Bonaparte, Allen and Unwin, London, 1978
Britain and Her Army, 1509–1920, Allen Lane, London, 1970
The Collapse of British Power, Eyre Methuen, London, 1972
The Desert Generals, Allen and Unwin, London, 1983
The Great War, Park Lane Press, London, 1979
The Swordbearers, Hodder and Stoughton, London, 1987
Baynes, John, *The Forgotten Victor; General Sir Richard O'Connor, KT, GCB, DSO, MC*, Brassey's Defence Publications, London, 1989
Beesly, Patrick, *Very Special Intelligence: The Story of the Admiralty's Operational Intelligence Centre 1939–1945*, Hamish Hamilton, London, 1977
Behrens, C. B. A., *Merchant Shipping and the Demands of War*, HMSO, and Longmans, Green, London, 1955
Bekker, Cajus, *Hitler's Naval War*, Macdonald, London, 1974
Bidwell, Shelford, *The Chindit War: the Campaign in Burma, 1944*, Hodder and Stoughton, London, 1979
Blumenson, Martin, *Rommel's Last Victory*, Allen and Unwin, London, 1968
Brooke, Geoffrey, *Alarm Starboard: A remarkable true story of the war at sea*, Patrick Stephens, Cambridge, 1982
Burn, Lampton, *Down Ramps: Saga of the 8th Armada*, Carroll and Nicholson, London, 1948
Butler, J. R. M., *Grand Strategy*, Vol II, *September 1939–June 1941*, HMSO, London, 1957; Vol III, Part II, June *1941–August 1942*, HMSO, London, 1961
Carton de Wiart, A., *Happy Odyssey*, Jonathan Cape, London, 1950

Cecil, Robert (ed), *Hitler's War Machine*, Leisure Books, London, 1975
Chalmers, Rear-Admiral W. S., *Full Cycle, The Biography of Admiral Sir Bertram Ramsay*, Hodder and Stoughton, London, 1959
The Life and Letters of David, Earl Beatty, Hodder and Stoughton, London, 1951
Max Horton and the Western Approaches, Hodder and Stoughton, London, 1954
Chandler, Alfred D. (ed), *The Papers of Dwight David Eisenhower, The War Years*, Vols I–IV, Johns Hopkins Press, 1970
Churchill, Winston S., *The Second World War*, Vol I, *The Gathering Storm*, Vol II, *Their Finest Hour*, Vol III, *The Grand Alliance*, Vol IV, *The Hinge of Fate*, Cassell, London, 1948–54
The World Crisis: The Eastern Front, Thornton Butterworth, London, 1931
Cunningham, Admiral of the Fleet Lord, *A Sailor's Odyssey*, Hutchinson, London, 1957
Cunninghame-Graham, Angus, *Random Naval Recollections, 1905–51.* Famedram Publishers, Gartochan, 1979.
D'Este, Carlo, *Bitter Victory, The Battle for Sicily, July–August 1943*, Collins, London, 1988
Decision in Normandy; the Unwritten Story of Montgomery and the Allied Campaign, Collins, London, 1983
Divine, David, *The Nine Days of Dunkirk*, Faber and Faber, London, 1959
Dönitz, Admiral Karl, *Memoirs: Ten Years and Twenty Days*, Weidenfeld and Nicolson, London, 1959
Ehrman, John, *Grand Strategy*, Vol V, *August 1943–September 1944*, HMSO, London, 1956
Eisenhower, Dwight D., *Crusade in Europe*, HMSO, London, 1945
Supreme Commander's Report, HMSO, London, 1946
Ellis, John, *Cassino: the Hollow Victory; the Battle for Rome, January–June 1944*, André Deutsch, London, 1948
Ellis, L. F., *Victory in the West*, HMSO, London, 1962
Ensor, R. C. K., *England 1870–1914*, Clarendon Press, Oxford, 1966
Fergusson, Bernard, *The Watery Maze: The Story of Combined Operations*, Collins, London, 1961
Fraser, David, *Alanbrooke*, Collins, London, 1982
And We Shall Shock Them: The British Army in the Second World War, Hodder and Stoughton, London, 1983
Fuller, J. F. C., *The Second World War, 1939–45*, Eyre and Spottiswoode, London, 1962
Gibbs, N. H., *Grand Strategy*, Vol I, *Rearmament Policy*, HMSO, London, 1976
Gilbert, Martin, *Winston S. Churchill*, Vol VI, *Finest Hour, 1939–41*, Book Club Associates, London, 1983; Vol VII, *Road to Victory 1941–45*, Heinemann, London, 1986
Graham, Dominick and Bidwell, Shelford, *Tug of War; The Battle for Italy, 1943–1945*, Hodder and Stoughton, London, 1986

Grove, Eric, Chant, Christopher, Lyon, David and Lyon, Hugh, *The Hardware of World War II*, Galley Press, London, 1984
Gwyer, J. M. A., *Grand Strategy*, Vol III, Part I, *June 1941–August 1942*, HMSO, London, 1964
Hackmann, Willem, *Seek and Strike; Sonar Antisubmarine Warfare and the Royal Navy, 1914–54*, HMSO, London, 1984
Haggie, Paul, *Britannia at Bay; The Defence of the British Empire against Japan, 1931–1941*, Clarendon Press, Oxford, 1981
Hall, H. Duncan, *North American Supply*, HMSO and Longmans, Green, London, 1955
Hamilton, Nigel, *Monty: the Making of a General, 1887–1942*, Hamish Hamilton, London, 1981; Monty: Master of the Battlefield, 1942–1944, Hamish Hamilton, London, 1983; Monty: The Field-Marshal, 1944–1976, Hamish Hamilton, London, 1986
Hancock, W. K. and Gowing, M. M., *British War Economy*, HMSO and Longmans, Green, London, 1949
Hardy, Hilbert, *The Minesweepers' Victory: A Silent Service of the Royal Navy*, Keydex, Weybridge, 1976.
Hastings, Max, *Bomber Command*, Michael Joseph, London, 1979
Overlord; D-Day and the Battle of Normandy, 1944, Michael Joseph, London, 1984
Hill-Norton, Admiral of the Fleet Lord, and Dekker, John, *Sea Power*, Faber and Faber, London, 1982
Hinsley, F. H., with Thomas, E. E., Ransom, C. F. G. and Knight, R. C., *British Intelligence in the Second World War. Its Influence on Strategy and Operations* (3 Vols) (Vol III Part Two by F. H. Hinsley with E. E. Thomas, C. A. G. Simkins and C. F. G. Ransom), HMSO, London, 1979–1984
Howard, Michael, *Grand Strategy*, Vol IV, *August 1942–September 1943*, HMSO, London, 1972
Ireland, Bernard, *The Rise and Fall of the Aircraft Carrier*, Marshall Cavendish, London, 1979
James, Sir William, *Admiral Sir William Fisher*, Macmillan, London, 1943
Kemp, P. K., *Fleet Air Arm*, Herbert Jenkins, London, 1954
Kennedy, Ludovic, *Pursuit: The Chase and Sinking of the Bismarck*, Collins, London, 1974
Kennedy, Paul M., *The Rise and Fall of British Naval Mastery*, Allen Lane, London, 1976
King, Fleet Admiral Ernest J., *U.S. Navy at War, 1941–45: Official Reports to the Secretary of the Navy*, United States Navy Department, 1946
Lenton, H. T., and College, J. J., *Warships of World War II*, Ian Allan, London, 1964
Leutze, James R., *Bargaining for Supremacy: Anglo-American Naval Relations, 1937–41*, Capel Hill, North Carolina, 1977
(ed), *The London Observer: The Journal of General Raymond E. Lee, 1940–41*, Hutchinson, London, 1972

Liddell Hart, B. H., *The British Way in Warfare*, Faber and Faber, London, 1932

History of the Second World War, Cassell, London, 1970

March, Edgar J., *British Destroyers: A History of Development, 1892–1953*, Seeley Service, London, 1966

Marchant, Sir James (ed), *Winston Spencer Churchill, Servant of the Crown and Commonwealth*, Cassell, London, 1954

Marder, Arthur J., *From the Dreadnought to Scapa Flow; The Royal Navy in the Fisher Era, 1904–1919*, Vol III, *The War Years: To the Eve of Jutland*, Vol IV, *Jutland and After*, Oxford University Press, 1965

Operation 'Menace': The Dakar Expedition and the Dudley North Affair, Oxford University Press, 1976

'Winston is Back: Churchill at the Admiralty, 1939–40' in *The English Historical Review*, Supplement 5, Longmans, London, 1972

Maund, L. E. H., *Assault from the Sea*, Methuen, London, 1949.

McLachlan, Donald, *Room 39: Naval Intelligence in Action 1939–45*, Weidenfeld and Nicolson, London, 1968

Millington-Drake, E. (ed), *The Drama of the Graf Spee and the Battle of the River Plate: a Documentary Anthology: 1914–1964*, Peter Davies, London, 1964

Milner, Marc, *North Atlantic Run: The Royal Canadian Navy and the Battle of the Convoys*, University of Toronto Press, Toronto, 1985

Montgomery of Alamein, *Memoirs*, Collins, London, 1958

Morison, Samuel Eliot, *History of United States Naval Operations in World War II*, Vol I, *The Battle of the Atlantic, September 1939–May 1943*, Vol II, *Operations in North African Waters, October 1942–June 1943*, Little, Brown, Boston, 1960, Vol XI, *The Invasion of France and Germany 1944–1945* (1957), Vol XIV, *Victory in the Pacific 1945* (1960)

Moulton, J. L., *The Norwegian Campaign: A Study of Warfare in Three Dimensions*, Eyre and Spottiswoode, London, 1966

Müllenheim-Rechberg, Baron Burkhard von, *Battleship Bismarck: A Survivor's Story*, transl. Jack Sweetman, The Bodley Head, London, 1980

Newton, Don, and Hampshire, A. Cecil, *Taranto*, William Kimber, London, 1969

Orgill, Douglas, *The Gothic Line: The Autumn Campaign in Italy, 1944*, Heinemann, London, 1967

Pack, S. W. C., *The Battle of Matapan*, Batsford, London, 1961

Padfield, Peter, *Dönitz: the Last Führer*, Victor Gollancz, London, 1984

Parkes, Oscar, *British Battleships: 'Warrior' 1860 to 'Vanguard' 1950; A History of Design, Construction and Armament*, Seeley Service, London, 1970

Peden, G. C., *British Rearmament and the Treasury, 1932–1939*, Scottish Academic Press, Edinburgh, 1979

Playfair, Major-General I. S. O., *The Mediterranean and the Middle East*, Vol I, with Commander G. M. S. Stitt, RN, Brigadier C. J. C. Molony and Air Vice-Marshal S. E. Toomer, *The Early Successes against Italy (to May 1941);* Vol II, with Captain F. C. Flynn, RN, Brigadier C. J. C. Molony and Air

Vice-Marshal S. E. Toomer, '*The Germans come to the aid of their Ally*' (1941), Vol III, with Captain F. C. Flynn, RN, Brigadier C. J. C. Malony and Group-Captain T. P. Gleave, *British Fortunes Reach Their Lowest Ebb, September 1941 to September 1942*; Vol IV, with Brigadier C. J. C. Molony, Captain F. C. Flynn, RN, and Group-Captain T. P. Gleave, *The Destruction of the Axis Forces in Africa*, HMSO, London, 1954.

Pool, Richard, *Course for Disaster: From Scapa Flow to the River Kwai*, Leo Cooper, London, 1987

Postan, M. M., Hay, D. and Scott, J. D., *Design and Development of Weapons*, HMSO and Longmans, Green, London, 1964

Pugh, Philip, *The Cost of Seapower; The Influence of Money on Naval Affairs from 1815 to the Present Day*, Conway Maritime Press, London, 1986

Raeder, Admiral, *Struggle for the Sea*, William Kimber, London, 1959

Ranft, Bryan (ed.), *Technical Change and British Naval Policy, 1860–1939*, Hodder and Stoughton, London, 1977

Reynolds, David, *The Creation of the Anglo-American Alliance, 1937–1941: A Study in Competitive Co-operation*, Europa Publications, London, 1981

Rodger, N. M., *The Wooden World; An Anatomy of the Georgian Navy*, Fontana, London, 1989

Rohwer, Jürgen, *The Critical Convoy Battles of March 1943*, Ian Allan, London, 1977

Roskill, S. W., *Admiral of the Fleet Earl Beatty; The Last Naval Hero: An Intimate Biography*, Athenaeum, New York, 1981

Churchill and the Admirals, Collins, London, 1977

Naval Policy Between the Wars, Vol I, *The Period of Anglo-American Antagonism, 1919–1929*, Collins, London, 1968, Vol II, *The Period of Reluctant Rearmament*, 1981

The War at Sea, 1939–1945, Vol I, *The Defensive*, HMSO, London, 1954; Vol II, *The Period of Balance*, HMSO, London, 1956; Vol III, *The Offensive*, Part I, *1st June 1943–31st May 1944*, HMSO, London, 1960; Part II, *1st June 1944–14th August 1945*, HMSO, London, 1961

(ed), *The Naval Air Service*, The Naval Records Society, London, 1969

Rotherham, G. A., *It's Really Quite Safe*, Belville, Ontario, 1985

Ruge, Vice-Admiral F., *Sea Warfare, 1939–1945*, Cassell, London, 1957

Shay, R. P., Jr, *British Rearmament in the 1930s. Politics and Profits*, Princeton University Press, 1977

Sumida, Dr J. T. (ed), *The Pollen Papers*, George Allen and Unwin for The Naval Records Society, London, 1984

Spencer, John Hale, *Battle for Crete*, Heinemann, London, 1962

Stewart, I. Mc. D. G., *The Struggle for Crete, 20 May–1 June 1941: A Story of Lost Opportunity*, Oxford University Press, 1966

Tedder, Marshal of the Royal Air Force, Lord, *With Prejudice*, Cassell, London, 1966

Terraine, John, *Business in Great Waters*, Leo Cooper, London, 1989

The Right of the Line: The Royal Air Force in the European War, 1939–1945, Hodder and Stoughton, London, 1985

Thorne, Christopher, *Allies of a Kind; The United States, Great Britain and the War Against Japan, 1941–1945*, Hamish Hamilton, London, 1978

Turner, J. A., *Administration of the Navy Department in World War II*, US Department of the Navy, 1959

Van Crefeld, Martin, *Supplying War*, Cambridge University Press, 1977

Vian, Admiral Sir Philip, *Action this Day: the War Memoirs of Sir Philip Vian*, Frederick Muller, London, 1960

Waddington, C. H. *Operational Research in World War II: Operational Research against the U-boat.* Elek Science, London, 1973.

Warner, Oliver, *Cunningham of Hyndhope: Admiral of the Fleet*, John Murray, London, 1967

Warren, C. E. T., and Benson, J., *Above Us the Waves*, Harrap, London, 1953

Watts, Anthony, *The U-Boat Hunters*, Macdonald and Jane's, London, 1976

Weale, Elke C., Weale, John A. and Barker, Richard, *Combat Aircraft of World War Two,* Bracken Books, London, 1985

Webster, C. and Frankland, N., *The Strategic Air Offensive Against Germany, 1939–1945*, Vol I, *Preparations*; Vol II, *Encounter*; Vol III, *Victory*; Vol IV, *Annexes and Appendices*, HMSO, London, 1961

Werth, Alexander, *Russia at War, 1941–1945*, Barrie and Rockliff, London, 1964

Williams, John, *The Guns of Dakar: September 1940*, Heinemann, London, 1976

Winton, J., *Air Power at Sea, 1939–45*, Sidgwick and Jackson, London, 1976

Wohlstetter, Roberta, *Pearl Harbor: Warning and Decision*, Stanford University Press, California, 1962

Woodburn Kirby, S., *The War against Japan*, Vol I, *The Loss of Singapore,* HMSO, London, 1957

Ziegler, Philip, *Mountbatten*, Collins, London, 1985

RUSI Journal, Vol 134, No 1, Marc Milner, 'The Dawn of Modern Anti-Submarine Warfare; Allied Responses to the U-boats, 1944–5'

Telecommunications Research Establishment Journal, July 1945, A. C. B. Lovell, 'The Radar Battle of the Bay of Biscay'

Index

INDEX

Index

INDEX